WORD 2000
PREMIUM EDITION

MASTERING™
WORD 2000
PREMIUM EDITION

Michael Miller

SYBEX®

San Francisco • Paris • Düsseldorf • Soest • London

Associate Publisher: Cheryl Applewood
Contracts and Licensing Manager: Kristine O'Callaghan
Acquisitions & Developmental Editor: Sherry Bonelli
Editors: Jeff Gammon, Malka Geffen, Ronn Jost
Technical Editor: Scott Warmbrand
Book Designers: Patrick Dintino, Catalin Dulfu,
Franz Baumhackl
Electronic Publishing Specialists: Cyndy Johnsen,
Bill Gibson, Kate Kaminski
Project Team Leader: Leslie Higbee
Proofreader: Jennifer Campbell
Indexer: Matthew Spence
CD Coordinator: Kara Schwartz
CD Technicians: Ginger Warner, Keith McNeil
Cover Designer: Design Site
Cover Illustrator/Photographer: Jack D. Myers,
Design Site

Library of Congress Card Number: 99-69762

ISBN: 0-7821-2662-6

Manufactured in the United States of America

10 9 8 7 6 5 4 3 2 1

*To all my former publishing colleagues
who have remained in publishing (and
haven't left for the maybe-greener
pastures of the dot-com world):
You know that there is no greater
satisfaction than a well-crafted
manuscript, no greater pleasure than
the feel of a newly printed book, and
no greater reward than a satisfied
reader—and all the stock options in
the world won't change that.
Keep the faith!*

ACKNOWLEDGMENTS

Thanks to everyone at Sybex who has shaped and shepherded this project, including but not limited to Brianne Agatep, Senoria Bilbo-Brown, Sherry Bonelli, Jennifer Campbell, Jeff Gammon, Malka Geffen, Leslie Higbee, Ronn Jost, Kara Schwartz, Scott Warmbrand, and my old friend Jordan Gold. Thanks also to Melanie Hauser for helping to assemble the software on the accompanying CD and to the individual developers and publishers of each of these programs. Finally, special thanks to all the developers at Microsoft who have created a word processing program so dense and complex that it requires a 1,000+ page book to master!

CONTENTS AT A GLANCE

Introduction . . . . *xxxv*

PART I	LEARNING NEW FEATURES AND CREATING NEW DOCUMENTS	1
1	Word 2000 Basics for New Users	3
2	Discovering the New Features of Word 2000	33
3	Customizing Word 2000	71
4	Creating, Editing, and Saving Simple Documents	119
5	Navigating Word	159
6	Correcting Your Spelling and Grammar	177
7	Printing, Faxing, and E-mailing Word Documents	209

PART II	CREATING TEXT-BASED DOCUMENTS	231
8	Formatting Text	233
9	Working with Paragraphs and Styles	251
10	Setting Up Pages and Sections	285

PART III	CREATING COMPLEX DOCUMENTS	311
11	Adding Annotations	313
12	Working with Fields	333
13	Incorporating Indexes and Tables of Contents	353

PART IV	CREATING VISUAL DOCUMENTS	375
14	Creating Tables	377
15	Creating Charts and Graphs	419
16	Adding Graphics and Drawings	457
17	Linking and Embedding Objects	493

PART V	CREATING LABELS AND MAILINGS	507
18	Creating and Printing Envelopes and Labels	509
19	Working with Databases and Mail Merge	523

PART VI **CREATING LARGE AND TEAM-EDITED DOCUMENTS** **555**

20 Organizing Documents with Outlines 557
21 Inserting Contents of Other Documents 573
22 Working with Master Documents 585
23 Collaborating on Team Documents 603

PART VII **CREATING WEB DOCUMENTS** **623**

24 Creating Web Pages with Word 625
25 Creating Interactive Web Pages 657
26 Publishing Word Documents on the Web 687

PART VIII **CREATING AUTOMATED DOCUMENTS** **697**

27 Creating Ready-to-Use Documents with Templates 699
28 Designing Forms 711
29 Automating Your Documents with Macros 739
30 Employing VBA for More Sophisticated Automation 759

PART IX **TIPS, TRICKS, AND TROUBLESHOOTING** **795**

31 Forty Things You Probably Didn't Know You Could Do in Word 797
32 Using Word with Office 2000 837
33 Using the Tools and Utilities on the CD 865
34 Finding Help 889
35 Common Word Problems and Solutions 905

MASTER'S REFERENCE

Master's Reference 973

APPENDIX

A Installing and Updating Word 1091

Index *1098*

TABLE OF CONTENTS

Introduction . . . .*xxxv*

PART I • LEARNING NEW FEATURES AND CREATING NEW DOCUMENTS   **1**

1   Word 2000 Basics for New Users   **3**

Understanding Word and Getting Started 4
  Launching Microsoft Word 5
  Creating and Opening Documents 6
Getting to Know the Word Workspace 8
  Viewing a Word Document 9
  Zooming through Different Display Sizes 13
  Viewing Different Parts of the Same Document Simultaneously 17
  Editing Multiple Documents in Multiple Windows 18
  Using Word's Status Bar 18
Commanding Word with Pull-Down Menus 20
  Choosing Between Full and Personalized Menus 20
  Word's Pop-Up Menus 21
Commanding Word with Toolbars 22
  Hiding, Displaying, and Moving Toolbars 22
Commanding Word with the Keyboard 22
  Using the Keyboard to Go Directly to Menu Commands 23
  Using Word's Function Keys 23
  Using Shortcut Keys to Automate Operations 24

2   Discovering the New Features of Word 2000   **33**

Introducing the New and Improved Features of Word 2000 34
  Working with Simplified Program Management Features 35
  Using Improved File Management Options 39
  Discovering Enhanced Personalization Settings 42
  Using Improved Editing Tools 45
  Working with Improved Proofing Tools 50
  Utilizing Enhanced Output Options 51
  Using New and Improved Web Editing Tools 53
  Understanding the New Web-Based Collaboration 58
  Using New International Support Features 59
Using Word 2000 with Previous Versions 60
  Saving to Previous Word Formats 60
  Identifying Known Compatibility Issues 64

Switching from WordPerfect to Word 66
    Helping WordPerfect Users 66
    Navigating WordPerfect within Word 67
    Configuring Word 2000's Compatibility Options 67
    Learning Shortcut Keys for WordPerfect Operations 68

3   **Customizing Word 2000**   **71**

Customizing Word 2000: Where to Begin 72
    Understanding the Customize Dialog Box 72
    Understanding the Options Dialog Box 75
Customizing Word's Appearance 84
    Configuring Your Personal Workspace 84
    Configuring Your Toolbars 92
    Configuring Your Menus 101
    Configuring Your Keyboard Shortcuts 103
Customizing How Word Works 104
    Configuring Your User Information 104
    Configuring Your Editing Options 104
    Configuring Your Proofing Options 107
    Configuring Your Internet Options 112
    Configuring Your Printing Options 114
    Configuring Your File Locations 116
    Configuring Your Compatibility Options 116

4   **Creating, Editing, and Saving Simple Documents**   **119**

Creating a New Document 120
    Creating a Blank Document—Fast 120
    Creating a Document from a Template 120
    Using a Wizard to Create a New Document 125
Opening an Existing Document 127
    Six Ways to Open a Word Document 128
    Using the Open Dialog Box 128
    Managing File Properties 138
Entering Text 139
    Entering Text with Click and Type 140
    Entering Text in a Text Box 141
    Entering Pre-Written Text with AutoText 144
Editing Text 145
    Selecting Text 146
    Deleting Text 148
    Copying Text 148
    Moving Text 149
    Using Collect and Paste 149
    Using the Paste Special Command 150
    Undoing and Redoing Your Editing 152

Saving Your Documents 152
    Saving a New Document 153
    Saving an Existing Document 154
    Saving a Document in a Different Format 155
    Saving and Backing Up Your Documents Automatically 155

5 Navigating Word   **159**

Moving Around in Your Documents 160
    Navigating with the Keyboard 160
    Moving with the Mouse 161
Finding Specific Places in Your Documents 163
    Using the Select Browse Object Tool 163
    Using the Go To Command 164
    Using Document Map 165
    Using Bookmarks 166
    Using Find and Replace 168

6 Correcting Your Spelling and Grammar   **177**

Proofing Your Spelling 178
    Configuring Word's Spell Checker 179
    Correcting Your Spelling on the Fly 180
    Running the Spell Checker on Your Entire Document 183
    Using Custom Dictionaries 185
Checking Your Grammar 188
    Configuring Word's Grammar Checker 189
    Correcting Your Grammar on the Fly 192
    Running the Grammar Checker on Your Entire Document 192
    Understanding Word's Readability Statistics 193
Proofing with Word's Other Language Tools 195
    Finding the Right Word with Thesaurus 195
    Working with Hyphens 196
Making Changes Automatically 199
    Correcting Typos with AutoCorrect 199
    Formatting Faster with AutoFormat 204

7 Printing, Faxing, and E-mailing Word Documents   **209**

Printing a Document 210
    Getting Ready: Before You Print 210
    Printing a Document—Fast! 214
    Printing with Options 214
Faxing a Document 220
    Sending a Document via Fax 220
    Determining whether You Have Fax Software on Your System 221
    Using Word 2000's Fax Wizard 222

E-mailing a Document 223
   Before You Send an E-mail 223
   E-mailing Your Document as a Stand-alone Message 227
   E-mailing Your Document as an Attachment 229

PART II • CREATING TEXT-BASED DOCUMENTS   231

8   Formatting Text   233

The Least You Need to Know About Text Formatting 234
   Understanding Fonts 234
   Viewing Installed Fonts and Character Attributes 235
   Setting Word's Default Font 236
Fundamental Font Formatting 236
   Format Fonts—Fast! 237
   Using the Font Dialog Box 238
   Changing Fonts, Styles, and Sizes 239
   Recoloring Your Text 240
   Underlining Your Text 240
   Selecting Other Font Attributes 241
   Using Animated Text 242
   Changing the Case of Your Text 242
   Highlighting Text 243
Scaling, Spacing, and Kerning 243
   Scaling Your Text 244
   Adjusting Character Spacing 244
   Kerning Character Pairs 245
   Adding Subscripts and Superscripts 246
Adding a Drop Cap 247
Inserting Special Characters 248

9   Working with Paragraphs and Styles   251

Formatting Paragraphs 252
   Formatting Fast from the Toolbar 252
   Understanding Paragraph Formatting in Detail 253
   Aligning Paragraphs 254
   Indenting Paragraphs 255
   Determining Line and Paragraph Spacing 257
   Controlling Widows, Orphans, and Page Breaks 258
   Setting Tabs 259
   Adding Borders and Shading 261
Creating Lists 263
   Working with Bulleted Lists 264
   Working with Numbered Lists 267
Formatting with Styles 271
   Understanding Styles 271

Viewing Styles 274
Applying Styles 276
Using Keyboard Shortcuts for Common Styles 276
Using Styles from a Different Template 276
Modifying Styles 279
Creating New Styles 281

10 Setting Up Pages and Sections | 285

Configuring Your Page 286
Understanding Word's Default Page Setup 287
Setting Paper Size and Orientation 287
Setting Page Margins 289
Configuring Vertical Text Alignment 291
Adding Background Colors and Page Borders 292
Understanding Document Sections 297
Starting a New Section 297
Viewing Section Breaks 298
Deleting Section Breaks 299
Copying Section Formatting 299
Working with Page Numbers 300
Adding Page Numbers to a Header or Footer 300
Adding Page Numbers Anywhere on the Page 301
Changing Page Numbering in Different Sections of Your Document 302
Using Headers and Footers 303
Viewing Headers and Footers 303
Editing Header and Footer Text 303
Adding Page Numbers, Dates, and Times to Your Header and Footer 304
Adding Prepared Text with AutoText 305
Creating a Unique Header or Footer for Your First Page 305
Managing Odd and Even Headers and Footers 306
Managing Multiple Columns 307
Creating a Multiple Column Layout 307
Adjusting Column Widths and Spacing 308
Adjusting Vertical Alignment 309

PART III • CREATING COMPLEX DOCUMENTS | 311

11 Adding Annotations | 313

Annotating Text with Footnotes and Endnotes 314
Inserting Footnotes and Endnotes 316
Changing the Appearance of Footnotes and Endnotes 320
Converting Footnotes to Endnotes, and Back Again 322
Labeling Elements with Captions 324
Appending Captions 325
Editing and Formatting Captions 326

Cross-Referencing within Your Document 328
    Inserting an Automatic Cross-Reference 328
    Cross-Referencing Text via Bookmarks 330

12 Working with Fields · 333

Understanding Fields 334
    Word's Field Categories 334
    Using Arguments 335
    Modifying Fields with Switches 335
Viewing Fields 336
    Showing and Hiding Field Codes 336
    Displaying Field Shading 337
    Printing Field Codes Instead of Results 338
Adding Fields to Your Document 338
    Using the Field Dialog Box 339
    Inserting Fields Manually 340
Managing Field Results 341
    Updating Field Results 341
    Not Updating Field Results 342
    Formatting Field Results 342
Word 2000 Field Instant Reference 343

13 Incorporating Indexes and Tables of Contents · 353

Indexing a Document 354
    Creating Index Entries 355
    Creating an Index 361
Creating a Table of Contents 366
    Preparing for a Table of Contents 366
    Building Your Table of Contents 366
    Formatting Your Table of Contents 370
    Updating Your Table of Contents 370
Creating a Table of Figures 371
    Building Your Table of Figures 372
    Formatting Your Table of Figures 372
    Updating Your Table of Figures 372
Creating a Table of Authorities 373
    Marking Citations 373
    Building Your Table of Authorities 374

PART IV · CREATING VISUAL DOCUMENTS · 375

14 Creating Tables · 377

Understanding Tables 378
    Reviewing the Parts of a Table 378
    Working with the Tables and Borders Toolbar 379

Navigating within a Table 379
Displaying or Hiding Table Gridlines 380
Creating Tables 380
Inserting a Blank Table 380
Creating Side-by-Side Tables 384
Nesting Tables 384
Converting Tables 385
Editing Tables 388
Entering Table Data 389
Selecting Table Contents 390
Inserting and Deleting Rows and Columns 391
Inserting and Deleting Individual Cells 392
Deleting and Clearing Your Entire Table 393
Moving and Copying within a Table 393
Merging and Splitting Cells 394
Splitting a Table 395
Resizing Table Elements 396
Resizing Manually 396
Resizing Automatically 399
Formatting Tables 400
Formatting the Entire Table 400
Formatting Individual Cells 406
Working with Cell Contents 410
Sorting Cells 410
Numbering Cells within Your Table 413
Working with Formulas and Functions 413
Creating Complex Equations 417

15 Creating Charts and Graphs   419

Understanding Microsoft Graph 2000 420
Working with the Graph 2000 Applet 420
Navigating the Graph 2000 Workspace 421
Adding a Graph to Your Document 422
Creating a Graph from Existing Data 422
Creating a Graph Linked to Data in Your Document 422
Creating a Graph from Scratch 423
Positioning and Configuring Graph Objects 424
Moving a Graph 425
Copying a Graph 425
Deleting a Graph 426
Resizing a Graph 426
Setting Text Wrapping 426
Adding a Border and Shadow 427
Editing Your Graph Data 427
Changing Numbers 427
Changing Data Orientation 428
Formatting Datasheet Numbers 431

Formatting Your Graph 432
   Changing Graph Types 432
   Adding Elements to Your Graph 434
   Formatting the Chart and Plot Areas 441
   Formatting Axes and Gridlines 443
   Formatting Graph Text 446
   Formatting Data Series and Data Points 446
   Formatting 3-D Charts 451

16 Adding Graphics and Drawings   457

Mastering the Drawing and Picture Toolbars—and the Format Object Dialog Box 458
   Understanding the Drawing Toolbar 458
   Understanding the Picture Toolbar 459
   Understanding the Format Object Dialog Box 459
Working with Different Types of Graphics 460
   Using Word Clip Art 460
   Importing Picture Files 467
   Adding Fancy Text with WordArt 472
   Drawing with AutoShapes 475
Formatting Graphic Objects 478
   Repositioning and Resizing 478
   Aligning Multiple Objects 481
   Layering Images 482
   Grouping and Ungrouping 483
   Rotating and Flipping 483
   Cropping Unwanted Elements 484
   Wrapping Text 486
   Working with Borders and Fills 488
   Adding Shadows and 3-D Effects 489

17 Linking and Embedding Objects   493

Understanding Object Linking and Embedding 494
   Understanding How Linking and Embedding Differs from Cutting and Pasting . . . 495
   Understanding How Linking Differs from Embedding and When to Use Which . . . 495
Inserting Linked Objects into Your Documents 496
   Using the Paste Special Command 497
   Using the Object Command 498
   Editing Linked Data 499
   Editing Links 499
   Updating Links Before Printing 501
Embedding Objects in Your Documents 502
   Embedding Existing Data 502
   Creating a New Embedded Object 502
   Editing Embedded Objects 503
   Converting an Embedded Object to Another File Format 504

PART V • CREATING LABELS AND MAILINGS   **507**

18 Creating and Printing Envelopes and Labels   **509**

Printing Envelopes 510
   Configuring Word for Envelope Printing 510
   Printing a Single Envelope 513
   Choosing Envelope Addressing Options 514
   Attaching an Envelope to a Document for Later Printing 515
Printing Labels 517
   Configuring Word for Specific Types of Labels 518
   Creating a New Label Type 518
   Printing a Label 519
   Printing an Entire Sheet of Labels 521

19 Working with Databases and Mail Merge   **523**

Planning for a Merged Mailing 524
Creating a Merged Mailing with the Mail Merge Helper 525
   Step 1: Creating Your Main Document 525
   Step 2: Opening or Creating a Data Source 526
   Step 3: Editing Your Document and Inserting Merge Fields 533
   Step 4: Merging Your Data and Outputting the Merged Mailing 537
Printing Envelopes and Labels for a Merged Mailing 542
   Printing Merged Labels 542
   Printing Merged Envelopes 545
   Creating Attached Merge Envelopes 549
Merging Database Data for Other Types of Documents 550
   Creating a Merged Catalog 550
   Querying a Database for Specific Information 552

PART VI • CREATING LARGE AND TEAM-EDITED DOCUMENTS   **555**

20 Organizing Documents with Outlines   **557**

Understanding Word 2000's Outline View 558
   Using the Outline Toolbar 559
   Changing the Outline Display 561
   Displaying *Both* Outline and Normal Views at the Same Time 562
Setting Up an Outline 564
   Assigning Outline Styles 564
   Promoting and Demoting Outline Levels 565
   Reorganizing Your Outline 565
   Numbering Your Outline 567
Creating a New Document from an Outline 569
Printing an Outline 571

21 Inserting Contents of Other Documents   573

Pasting Text from Other Documents 574
   Pasting Text as Normal 575
   Pasting Text as Special 576
   Pasting Text as a Link 577
Inserting Files into Your Word Document 578
   Inserting a Whole File 578
   Inserting Part of a File 579
   Inserting a Linked File 580
Inserting Database Data into Your Word Document 580
Inserting an Automatic Summary into Your Document 582

22 Working with Master Documents   585

Creating a Master Document 586
   Creating a New Master Document from Scratch 588
   Converting an Existing Document into a Master Document 590
   Assembling a Master Document from Existing Documents 591
Saving, Opening, and Printing Master Documents 591
   Saving a Master Document and Its Subdocuments 592
   Saving a Master Document as a Web Page 592
   Opening a Master Document 593
   Printing a Master Document 593
Working with Subdocuments 593
   Using Outline View with Your Master Document 594
   Converting a Subdocument into Part of the Master Document 596
   Deleting a Subdocument from the Master Document 596
   Adding a New Subdocument 597
   Splitting Subdocuments 597
   Combining Subdocuments 597
   Renaming Subdocuments 598
   Formatting Subdocuments 599
   Printing Subdocuments 599
Adding a Table of Contents, Index, and Cross-References 600
   Creating a Table of Contents 600
   Creating an Index 600
   Inserting Cross-References 601
Locking and Unlocking a Master Document 601

23 Collaborating on Team Documents   603

Password-Protecting Your Files 604
   Requiring a Password for Access 604
   Removing or Changing a Password 606
Tracking Changes and Comments in Your Documents 606
   Enabling Revision Tracking 607

Making Revisions 608
Merging Revisions from Multiple Reviewers 608
Reviewing Revisions 609
Inserting Comments While Editing 612
Saving Multiple Versions of a Document in a Single File 614
Saving the Current Version 615
Viewing a Previous Version 615
Sharing Documents Through Web-Based Discussions and Subscriptions 616
Understanding Discussions 616
Connecting to a Discussion Server 617
Viewing Discussions 617
Starting and Participating in Discussions 618
Subscribing to Workgroup Documents 620

PART VII · CREATING WEB DOCUMENTS   **623**

24 Creating Web Pages with Word   **625**

Understanding Web Pages and HTML 626
Understanding How HTML Works 626
Publishing Pages to Make a Site 628
Understanding How Word 2000 Works with Web Pages .628
Adding Web Functionality to Normal Word Documents 630
Inserting Hyperlinks from the Standard Toolbar 630
Using AutoFormat to Convert Typed Addresses to Real Links 633
Editing a Hyperlink 633
Viewing Web Documents in Word 635
Using Web Layout View 635
Using Web Page Preview 636
Creating Basic Web Documents 637
Saving Existing Word Documents in HTML Format 638
Using the Web Page Wizard 640
Starting from a Web Page Template 641
Enhancing Web Pages 642
Applying Web Themes 642
Formatting Web Page Text 645
Formatting Your Web Page Background 646
Adding Graphics to Your Web Page 646
Adding Horizontal Lines between Sections 648
Using Tables to Organize Your Page 650
Redesigning Your Pages with Frames 651

25 Creating Interactive Web Pages   **657**

Understanding the Web Tools Toolbar and Design Mode 658
Working with the Web Tools Toolbar 658
Working in Design Mode 659

Adding Multimedia Components to Your Web Page 660
  Adding Scrolling Text 660
  Adding a Movie Clip 663
  Adding a Background Sound Clip 665
Creating Web Forms 666
  Understanding How Forms Collect Data 667
  Adding a Form to a Web Page 668
  Setting the Properties of a Web Form Control 669
  Word 2000's Web Form Controls 670
Working with Web Scripts 678
  Working with Scripts in Your Documents 679
  Using Microsoft Script Editor 682

26 Publishing Word Documents on the Web   687

Determining Where to Publish Your Web Pages 688
  Finding Hosts for Personal Pages 689
  Finding Hosts for Business Pages 690
Publishing Your Web Pages 691
  Publishing Web Pages Using Web Folders 691
  Publishing Web Pages Using FTP 693
  Publishing Web Pages Using the Web Publishing Wizard 694
  Publishing Web Pages Using Host Services 695
  Publishing Web Pages over a Network 695

PART VIII • CREATING AUTOMATED DOCUMENTS   697

27 Creating Ready-to-Use Documents with Templates   699

Understanding Templates and Add-Ins 700
  Getting a Head Start on New Documents with Word's Templates 700
  Enhancing How Word Works with Add-Ins 701
Working with Word's Built-In Templates 701
  Loading a Template or Add-In 702
  Unloading a Template or Add-In 703
  Switching Templates in Your Current Document 704
Modifying Existing Templates 705
  Making Changes to an Existing Template 706
  Using the Organizer to Modify Templates 706
Making Your Own Templates 708
  Saving a New Template 708
  Creating a New Template Based on an Existing Template 709
  Creating a New Template Based on an Existing Document 710
  Loading Add-Ins and Templates Automatically 710

28 Designing Forms 711

Designing a Usable Form 712
    Using a Table for Form Layout 713
    Adding Text Boxes 714
    Adding Borders and Shading 714
    Adding Art and Graphics 715
    Adding Controls and Fields 716
Creating Printed Forms 717
Creating Automated Forms 718
    Creating a Form Template 718
    Designing Your Form 719
    Adding and Defining Form Fields 720
    Adding and Defining ActiveX Controls 727
    Automating Your Form with Macros 734
    Preparing a Form for Distribution 735
    Distributing the Form 735
    Completing an Automated Form and Collecting the Data 736

29 Automating Your Documents with Macros 739

Understanding Macros 740
    Understanding How Macros Are Created 740
    Examining Some Macro Examples 741
Creating Macros 742
    Using the Macro Recorder 743
    Recording a Macro 743
    Editing a Macro 746
Running Macros 748
    Running a Macro 748
    Assigning a Macro 749
Managing Macro Projects 750
    Copying a Macro Project to a Different Document or Template 751
    Deleting a Macro Project 752
    Renaming a Macro Project 752
Protecting Against Macro Viruses 752
    Enabling Word 2000's Macro Security 753
    Adding a Digital Signature to a Macro Project 755

30 Employing VBA for More Sophisticated Automation 759

Understanding Visual Basic for Applications 760
Using the Visual Basic Editor 761
    Understanding the VB Editor Workspace 762
    Understanding VB Editor Toolbars 769

Writing Programs with VBA 771
    Designing Forms 772
    Creating New Modules 772
    Writing Statements 773
    Creating Procedures 777
    Understanding Objects 779
    Debugging Your Program 780
Using VBA with Word Macros 781
    Editing Prerecorded Macros 781
    Adding Functionality and Creating New Macros 784
    Making Macros Run Automatically 786
Putting It All Together: Creating a Macro for Inserting Data 787
    Preparing the Macro 787
    Creating the Form 788
    Writing the Code 790
    Assigning the Macro to a Keyboard Shortcut 793

PART IX · TIPS, TRICKS, AND TROUBLESHOOTING   795

31   Forty Things You Probably Didn't Know You Could Do in Word   797

Customizing the Word Workspace 798
    Tip 1: Creating Your Own Personal Menu 798
    Tip 2: Calculating Totals Anywhere in Your Documents 799
    Tip 3: Viewing Your Styles while You Work 799
    Tip 4: Customizing Keyboard Shortcuts from the Keyboard 800
    Tip 5: Printing All Word Shortcut Key and Menu Assignments 801
    Tip 6: Showing Measurements in the Ruler 801
    Tip 7: Double-Clicking for Key Dialog Boxes 802
    Tip 8: Using Automatic Scrolling 803
Editing and Formatting Text 804
    Tip 9: Returning to Where You Left Off 804
    Tip 10: Editing in Print Preview 805
    Tip 11: Copying Character and Paragraph Formatting 805
    Tip 12: Copying Formatting Over and Over 806
    Tip 13: Removing Formatting Quickly 806
    Tip 14: Balancing Your Columns 806
    Tip 15: Sorting Non-table Text 807
    Tip 16: Creating Links within and between Your Word Documents 807
Working with Bullets and Special Characters 808
    Tip 17: Inserting Special Characters from the Keyboard with AutoCorrect 808
    Tip 18: Inserting Special Characters from the Keyboard with Character Codes 809
    Tip 19: Inserting International Characters from the Keyboard 811
    Tip 20: Inserting Different Bullets in Bulleted Lists Automatically 812
    Tip 21: Creating Your Own Graphical Bullets 813

Proofing Your Documents 814
  Tip 22: Correcting Your Spelling Dictionary 815
  Tip 23: Finding Synonyms Fast 815
Creating Fancy Documents 816
  Tip 24: Using Pictures in a Bar Chart 816
  Tip 25: Creating a Gradated Header or Footer Bar 818
  Tip 26: Adding a Watermark to Your Page's Background 819
  Tip 27: Printing Postage on Your Envelopes 821
  Tip 28: Laying Out Pages with Tables 821
Automating Word 823
  Tip 29: Shrinking a Long Document 824
  Tip 30: Changing Line Spacing—Fast! 824
  Tip 31: Typing Shortcuts to Long Words 824
  Tip 32: Creating Automated Click Here and Type Fields 825
  Tip 33: Creating a Document from Dialog Boxes 826
  Tip 34: Using the Letter Wizard to Reuse Existing Letters 829
  Tip 35: Generating a Table of Contents from Another Document 830
  Tip 36: Creating Windows Shortcuts for Word Templates and Documents 831
Making Word More Than a Word Processor 831
  Tip 37: Using Word for Presentations 832
  Tip 38: Using Word as a Spreadsheet 833
  Tip 39: Using Word as a Database 834
  Tip 40: Using Word as a Drawing Program 834

32 Using Word with Office 2000   **837**

Using Word with Microsoft Office Tools 838
  Using the Office Shortcut Bar 838
  Using Binders 841
  Using Office Small Business Tools 844
Using Word with Outlook 845
  E-mailing with Word and Outlook 845
  Creating Merged Mailings with Outlook Contacts 845
  Tracking Word Activity in the Outlook Journal 846
Using Word with Excel 848
  Using Word Data in Excel Worksheets 848
  Adding Excel Worksheets to Word Documents 849
  Adding Excel Charts to Word Documents 852
Using Word with PowerPoint 853
  Creating a PowerPoint Presentation from a Word Document 853
  Creating a Word Document from a PowerPoint Presentation 854
  Adding PowerPoint Slides to Your Word Documents 857
Using Word with Access 859
  Importing Access Data into Word Documents 860
  Publishing Access Data to a Word Table 861

Using Word with Publisher 862
 Editing Publisher Stories in Word 862
 Inserting Word Documents into Publisher Documents 863
Using Word with Photo Editor 864

33 Using the Tools and Utilities on the CD   865

Installing Programs from the CD 866
 Introducing the Tools and Utilities on the CD 866
 Installing the Programs You Want 868
Enhancing Word's Functionality 868
 PRIME for Word 2000 868
 SOS Office Helpers 871
 OfficeExpress 2000 872
 Symbol Selector 873
 Document Converter 874
Working with Names and Addresses 875
 GPDATA 876
 Aladdins ~ Word Documents 877
Producing Better Envelopes and Faxes 878
 KazStamp 878
 Mighty Fax 880
Protecting Your System from Viruses 881
 Virus ALERT for Word 2000 881
 ChekMate Lite 882
 ChekOf 883
Converting Word Documents to HTML and Help Files 884
 WordToWeb 884
 EasyHTML/Help 885
Extending Word with Specific Solutions 885
 BioSpel 886
 MedSpel 886
 ScreenPro 886

34 Finding Help   889

Using Word 2000's Built-In Help System 890
 Browsing the Table of Contents 890
 Asking the Answer Wizard 891
 Searching the Index 892
 Using the Office Assistant 894
 Learning about Specific Elements with What's This? 895
 Displaying Program Information 896
Going Online for More Help 897
 Using Microsoft Office Update 898
 Searching the Microsoft Knowledge Base 899
 Asking Questions on Microsoft's Newsgroups 901
 Finding Non-Microsoft Resources on the Web 902
Getting Help Over the Phone and Elsewhere 903

35 Common Word Problems and Solutions 905

Troubleshooting Error Messages 906
Understanding the Most Common Error Messages 906
Tracking Down Major Problems 908
Fixing Specific Problems 909
Repairing and Reinstalling Word 911
Troubleshooting General Word Problems 913
Word Won't Start 913
You Can't Find a Menu Command or Toolbar Button 915
You Have Problems Viewing Your Text Onscreen 915
Troubleshooting Files and Damaged Documents 916
You Accidentally Deleted a File 916
Your Document Is Damaged 916
Your Document Won't Open 918
You're Having Problems Recovering an AutoRecovered Document 919
You Can't Find a File You Want to Open 920
Your Document Opened with a Different Filename 920
You Receive an Error Message when Saving a File 920
Your Document Was Saved with an Unexpected Extension 922
Troubleshooting Editing 923
You Accidentally Deleted or Cut Some Text 923
When You Enter Text, Existing Text Is Deleted 923
Word Automatically Selects Text when You Click Your Mouse or Press a Key 923
Words Are Automatically Capitalized 923
Click and Type Doesn't Work 924
You Receive an Error Message when Undoing Editing Changes 924
Document Map Doesn't Display Your Document's Headings 925
Find and Replace Doesn't Return the Expected Results .925
Troubleshooting Formatting 926
A Font Isn't Displaying Properly 926
Justified Text Leaves Gaps between Words 926
Text That Used to Be 10-Point Is Now 12-Point 927
Bullet Characters Don't Display Properly 927
Tabs and Paragraph Indents Disappear when You Add or Remove Bullets
or Numbering 927
Paragraph Formatting Changes when You Delete Text .927
A New Paragraph Doesn't Have Expected Formatting 928
You Can't Underline a Blank Space or Line 928
Graphics or Text in a Line Appear Cut Off 928
Text Was Unexpectedly Formatted as a Hyperlink 929
Headings Aren't Numbered when Outline Numbering Is Enabled 929
Paragraph Borders Are Cut Off 929
Troubleshooting Styles and Templates 930
Not All Available Styles Appear in the Style List 930
A Style Has Changed Unexpectedly 930
Styles Look Different in Your Master Document and Subdocuments 931

Your Custom Toolbars Disappear when You Save a Document as a Template 931
Macros, AutoText Entries, and Other Settings Are Missing 931
You Can't Copy Items to a Template 931
You Can't Save a Document Template as a Word Document 931
Troubleshooting Columns 932
Columns Aren't Visible 932
Vertical Lines between Your Columns Aren't Visible 932
Text in Columns Is Much Narrower Than Expected 932
Columns Won't Balance 933
Text above Columns Suddenly Turns into Multiple Columns 933
Tables in Columns Have Disappeared 933
You Receive an Error Message when Changing Page Orientation or Paper Size ... 933
Columns Don't Work in Headers, Footers, Comments, or Text Boxes 934
Troubleshooting Sections and Pages 934
Your Document Background Doesn't Display or Print 934
Watermarks Don't Display Properly 934
Pages Don't Break Properly 935
Page Borders Don't Display Properly 935
Troubleshooting Master Documents 936
You Can't Open a Master Document or Subdocument 936
You Have Problems Saving a Master Document and Its Subdocuments 937
Page Numbers, Headers, or Footers Are Incorrect or Missing 937
Cross-References Are Replaced by Error Messages 938
Your Table of Contents or Index Contains Error Messages 938
Subdocuments Are Created Incorrectly 938
Troubleshooting Indexes and Tables of Contents 938
Page Numbers Are Incorrect 938
Unwanted Codes and Error Messages Are Displayed 939
Some Headings Don't Appear in the TOC 939
Your TOC Contains Nonheading Text 939
An Index Entry Has a Backslash (\) Instead of a Colon (:) 939
Troubleshooting Headers and Footers 940
Your Header or Footer Is Missing or Only Partially Printed 940
Codes Are Visible in Your Header or Footer 940
Date, Time, or Other Items Are Incorrect 940
You Can't View Page Numbers 940
You Can't Remove Page Numbers 941
Your Top or Bottom Margin Changed after Creating the Header or Footer 941
Changing One Section Header or Footer Changed Them All 942
Troubleshooting Footnotes, Endnotes, Captions, Cross-References, and Bookmarks . 942
You Deleted Footnote Text, but the Reference Still Appears in the Document 942
Some Footnotes or Endnotes Have Disappeared 942
Part of a Footnote Was Continued on the Following Page 943
Some Captions Aren't Numbered Correctly 943
Cross-References or Captions Aren't Updated Correctly 943
A Bookmark Error Message Is Displayed 943

Troubleshooting Tables and Sorting 944
  Part of the Text within a Cell Is Hidden or Cut Off 944
  Your Table Is Cut Off at the End of a Page 944
  Your Table Extends past the Edge of the Page 944
  Numbers That Contain Hyphens Are Sorted Incorrectly 945
Troubleshooting Graphics 945
  Graphics Aren't Displayed or Don't Print Properly 945
  Objects Don't Align, Distribute, or Position Properly 947
  You Encounter Problems while Editing Pictures 949
  You Encounter Border, 3-D, and Shadow Problems 950
  You Can't Control Freehand Drawing 950
  A Drawing Object Disappeared when You Ran the Letter Wizard 951
Troubleshooting Revisions 951
  Tracked Changes Don't Appear in Your Document 951
  You Can't Accept or Reject Changes 951
  Comparing Documents Doesn't Work 951
  Your Document Lost Its Versioning Information 951
Troubleshooting Linking and Embedding 952
  You Can't Edit a Linked or Embedded Object 952
  Large Linked or Embedded Objects Appear Cropped 953
  You Encounter Problems with Excel Objects in Word 953
Troubleshooting Mail Merges 953
  Merge Fields Are Printed Instead of Data 953
  Merged Document Contains Blank Lines 954
  An Error Message States the Data File Is a Main·Document 954
  A Mail Merge Field Changed when the Letter Wizard Was Launched 954
Troubleshooting Printing, Faxing, and E-mail 955
  Tracking Down Common Printer Problems 955
  Word Won't Print 959
  Graphics Don't Print Right or At All 959
  Complex Documents Don't Print Right or At All 960
  Your Document Looks Different on Paper than Onscreen .961
  Text Is Cut Off at the Edges 961
  An Extra Page Is Printed with Each Document 962
  You Receive an Error Message when Printing 962
  Troubleshooting Fax Problems 964
  Troubleshooting E-mail Problems 964
Troubleshooting Web Pages 965
  The Hyperlink Command Doesn't Appear on the Pop-Up Menu 965
  An Error Message Appears when You Click a Hyperlink 965
  Graphics Don't Display on Your Web Page 965
  Text and Graphics Aren't Positioned Properly 966
  Frames Are Missing or Displayed Incorrectly 966
  HTML Codes Change after You Save a Web Page 967
  Users Can't Access Your Web Page 967

Troubleshooting Forms 967
   Form Fields Don't Work 967
   Field Codes Are Displayed Instead of Form Fields 967
   The Tab Key Doesn't Move the Insertion Point to the Correct Form Field 968
   Check-Box Size Doesn't Change when Formatted 968
   Problems with Form Macros 968
Troubleshooting Macros and VBA 968
   You Made a Mistake while Recording a Macro 969
   Running a Macro Produces an Error Message 969
   You Copied a Toolbar, but Your Macros Weren't Copied 969
   A Macro Won't Run 969
   You Can't Change Word's Security Level 970
   A Macro Virus Warning Appears when There Are No Macros in a File 970
   A Word Document Is Infected with a Macro Virus 970
   You Encounter Problems Starting the Visual Basic Editor 971

MASTER'S REFERENCE   **973**

Master's Reference   **973**

APPENDIX   **1091**

A   Installing and Updating Word   **1091**
Understanding Word 2000's System Requirements 1092
Installing Word 2000 1092
   Examining a Typical Installation 1093
   Choosing Custom Installation Options 1094
   Using the Installation CD–*After* Word Is Installed 1095
Installing Additional Word 2000 Components 1095
Repairing a Damaged Installation 1096

Index. *1098*

INTRODUCTION

Microsoft Word is the most popular word processing program in the world, and Word 2000 is the latest and greatest version of that program. Most computer users use Word at least once a day—more than they use any other program. The more you know about using Word, the more productive you'll be—and the more sophisticated documents you'll create.

As you no doubt have discovered, Word is a very complex program. Word 2000 lets you create everything from simple letters to highly graphical Web pages to interactive forms and custom applications. In fact, Word 2000 includes a complete programming environment, which can be a little intimidating if all you're used to doing is popping out the occasional memo or report!

How can you take advantage of all this program power and create more efficient *and* more effective documents? It's simple; when you want to master all the capabilities of Word 2000, you need the comprehensive information and expert advice contained in *Mastering Word 2000 Premium Edition.*

Who This Book Is For

Mastering Word 2000 Premium Edition is written with the experienced Word user in mind. I assume that you know your way around Windows and that you aren't intimidated by the Word workspace. You may be new to Word 2000 (you're probably upgrading from an earlier version), but you're not new to word processing in general. You don't need a lot of hand holding, and you're confident enough to try some new things in your quest to improve both your productivity and your ability to create powerful and eye-catching documents.

If the above paragraph doesn't describe you at all—if you're a true beginner or easily intimated by computers—then I suggest you put this book down for a period and read instead one of Sybex's excellent beginner's guides to Word, such as *Word 2000: No Experience Required.* Once you've become comfortable with the program, then come on back and use this book to help you truly master the program.

What You Need to Get Started

To use this book, you need a computer and a copy of Microsoft Word 2000. (If you haven't yet installed your copy of Word, see Appendix A for instructions.)

To get the most out of Word, you probably should have the rest of Microsoft Office 2000 installed on your system, especially Outlook 2000, which is necessary for mail merges and sending Word documents via e-mail. It also helps to have a connection to the Internet, as well as a Web browser (such as Internet Explorer) installed on your PC, so you can get the most out of Word's Web-creation features. Finally, you might want to consider beefing up your copy of Word with the tools and utilities included on the CD accompanying this book, which are discussed later in this introduction.

What You'll Find in This Book

Unlike most other Word references, this book is organized not by program features but by the types of documents you'll create with Word. If you're like most users, you couldn't care less that Word has a feature called Mail Merge, but you do want to learn how to create a form letter you can send to multiple recipients. *Mastering Word 2000 Premium Edition* shows you how to create the documents you need and, in the process, shows you how to master the program features necessary to create those documents.

If you want even more hands-on instruction, you should turn to the eight Word Workshops included on the CD accompanying this book. These Workshops are hands-on exercises that lead you step by step through the creation of the type of document featured in the first eight sections of this book. For example, Part IV of the book focuses on visual documents, and the CD's Word Workshop 4 leads you through the creation of a newsletter, complete with multiple columns, pictures, and other graphics.

The sections in this book progress from simple documents to complex documents, as detailed in the following list of parts.

Part I: Learning New Features and Creating New Documents

This section presents an overview of how to use the standard features of Word as well as the new features of Word 2000 (which should be of interest for you upgraders in the audience). From there, you're taken through the skills you need to master in order to create, edit, save, and print simple documents.

Part II: Creating Text-Based Documents

This section focuses on the skills necessary to edit and format text-based documents, such as how to format text, paragraphs, styles, pages, and sections (including headers, footers, columns, and margins).

Part III: Creating Complex Documents

In this section, you move beyond simple, text-based documents into more sophisticated documents. You learn how to use footnotes, endnotes, cross-references, fields, indexes, and tables of contents to create long and complex documents.

Part IV: Creating Visual Documents

Once you've mastered text-based documents, it's time to tackle more visual documents. In this section, you learn how to incorporate tables, charts and graphs, pictures, drawings, and other graphics into your documents.

Part V: Creating Labels and Mailings

One of Word's many uses is its capability to facilitate mailings, large or small. This section shows you how to use Word to create envelopes, labels, and what Word calls merged mailings (importing names from an outside database or address book).

Part VI: Creating Large and Team-Edited Documents

Word can create short documents, and it can create long documents; this section deals with how to create and manage the latter. You'll learn how to use outlines to organize your documents, how to collaborate on documents in a group environment, how to create large documents from multiple smaller documents, and how to master Word's Master Documents feature.

Part VII: Creating Web Documents

Many of the new features in Word 2000 are designed to ease the creation of Web-based documents. This section helps you to master Word's Internet-related features, to create everything from simple Web pages to interactive Web forms, and then to publish your pages online.

Part VIII: Creating Automated Documents

Power users know that Word can be used as a "front end" for custom documents and applications. This section shows you how to create automated documents with Word, using templates, forms, macros, and Visual Basic for Applications.

Part IX: Tips, Tricks, and Troubleshooting

When you reach this section, you should know how to create just about every type of document imaginable, so Part IX looks back and examines some of the neat things you can do with Word and some of the not-so-neat things that Word can do to you. You'll learn 40 things you didn't know Word can do, how to use Word with other Office 2000 applications, how to find help when you need it, and how to troubleshoot Word's most common, and most vexing, problems. You'll also learn about the powerful tools and utilities included on the CD that accompanies this book. (Read ahead a few paragraphs to learn even more about this book's CD!)

Master's Reference

Don't want to read an entire 1,000+ page book to find out how to perform a single operation? Then turn to the Master's Reference, where all of Word's key operations are presented in their simplest form, alphabetically. When you need to do something fast, just look it up here and follow the step-by-step instructions. There's no faster way to get productive with Word!

What You'll Find on the CD

The CD accompanying this book is an incredible collection of powerful and useful tools and utilities you can use to enhance Microsoft Word and increase your individual productivity. The contents of this easy-to-install CD include:

Adobe Acrobat Reader The software necessary to read on your computer screen the electronic text of this book, *Office 2000 Complete*, and the Word workshops.

Aladdins ~ Word Documents A Microsoft Outlook add-in that allows you to quickly compose Word documents using Outlook contact data.

BioSpel A custom dictionary that includes more than 15,000 biological terms.

ChekMate Lite   An anti-virus program that checks for file, boot, and partition sector viruses on your system.

ChekOf   A utility that monitors Word's security level settings and warns you if they're lowered or disabled.

Document Converter   A freestanding program that converts documents between a number of popular formats.

EasyHTML/Help   A powerful development tool that enables you to create Windows Help files from Microsoft Word documents.

GPDATA   A simple, freestanding address book you can use to insert names and addresses into Word documents.

KazStamp   A program that works with Word to create great-looking, custom envelopes.

MedSpel   A custom dictionary that includes more than 20,000 medical terms.

Mastering Word 2000 Premium Edition   The complete text of this book. (Viewable with the Adobe Acrobat Reader.)

Mighty Fax   A fax program that installs as a Windows printer driver so you can fax directly from Word.

Office 2000 Complete   The complete text of Sybex's comprehensive guide to Microsoft Office 2000—a great way to learn about the *other* programs included in the Office suite! (Viewable with the Adobe Acrobat Reader.)

OfficeExpress 2000   A graphics tool that acquires images from scanners, digital cameras, and other sources and then enables you to touch up, enhance, and apply special effects to your images before you insert them into your Word documents.

PRIME for Word 2000   An extremely useful collection of tools and utilities that integrate within Word to provide enhanced functionality of most program operations.

ScreenPro   A Word template designed specifically for screenwriters.

SOS Office Helpers   Another collection of tools and utilities that integrate within Word to provide enhanced program functionality.

Symbol Selector   A utility that makes it easier to select and insert symbols and special characters into your documents.

Virus ALERT for Word 2000   An anti-virus program that detects macro viruses in Word templates and documents.

Word Workshops Eight separate "labs" that lead you step-by-step through the creation of different types of Word documents. The workshops correspond to the first eight sections of this book: Creating Business Letters, Creating a Company Report, Annotating and Indexing a Company Report, Creating a Newsletter, Setting Up a Mass Mailing, Creating a Multiple-Chapter Book, Creating a Personal Web Site, and Creating an Automated Form. Follow the steps in these workshops to create great-looking, fully featured documents. (Viewable with the Adobe Acrobat Reader.)

WordToWeb A powerful program that seamlessly converts existing Word documents to HTML format.

Book Conventions

To get the most out of this book, you should understand some of the conventions I used when writing and presenting the manuscript. You won't need a road map to use this book (any book that needs instructions isn't very reader-friendly, to be sure!), but if you know how I'm presenting certain types of information, it will help you get more productive faster.

Using the Menus

Most Word operations are activated from the pull-down menus. To indicate which command you should choose on a particular menu, I use the notation *menu name* ➤ *menu item*. For example, if you need to pull down the File menu and select Save, the text will tell you to select File ➤ Save.

Using the Keyboard

Many Word operations can also be accessed via keyboard *shortcuts*, which are activated when you press two or more keys together at the same time. I indicate these multiple-key operations by listing the keys with a + sign in between. As an example, to insert an index entry you press the Alt, Shift, and X keys simultaneously; I notate this as Alt+Shift+X.

In some cases, you need to press one key, release it, and then press another. In these instances, I'll put a comma between the two keystrokes, like this: Alt+F, P. In this example, you press Alt+F, release, and then press P. (This opens the Print dialog box, by the way.)

Tips, Notes, and Warnings

Throughout the book you'll find a variety of tips, notes, and warnings, separate from the main text. These elements point out things that are related to the point at hand but not always essential in executing the task at hand. These elements look like this:

 TIP A tip is used to provide advice on getting the job done either more effectively or more efficiently.

 NOTE A note is used to impart interesting, but not essential, information.

 WARNING A warning is used to alert you of potential problems or issues—things you probably ought to consider before you execute the task at hand.

More Information in Sidebars

When there is a lot of additional information to impart—information that is not directly related to the task at hand yet still of potential interest to many readers—I put that information outside the main text in a *sidebar*. You'll find three types of sidebars throughout this book, as follows:

MASTERING THE OPPORTUNITIES

Get More Productive with Opportunities Sidebars

Sidebars marked with the Mastering the Opportunities header present information that takes you beyond typical Word use. Some of the best advice in the book is contained in this type of sidebar.

MASTERING TROUBLESHOOTING

Fix Your Problems with Troubleshooting Sidebars

Sidebars marked with the Mastering Troubleshooting header present information designed to help you deal with potential problems related to the task at hand. (Note that this book also features a comprehensive troubleshooting section for all types of Word-related problems in Chapter 35.)

Read More About It in Generic Sidebars

Sidebars without a header, like this one, contain background information about the task at hand. They're interesting to read but not necessary to get the task done.

Get Ready to Master Word 2000!

If you're like me, you've read more than enough introductory material, and you're ready to get into the meat of this book. Now it's time for you to learn how to master Word 2000, so turn the page and start reading!

Author Biography

Michael Miller is a writer, speaker, consultant, and the president/founder of The Molehill Group, a strategic consulting and authoring firm based in Carmel, Indiana.

Mr. Miller has been an important force in the book publishing business since 1987, and served for more than a decade as senior executive at one of the world's largest publishing companies. As the author of more than 35 best-selling how-to books, Mr. Miller has written about topics ranging from computers to home theater systems to vocabulary improvement.

From his first book in 1989 to this, his latest title, Michael Miller has established a reputation for practical advice, technical accuracy, and an unerring empathy for the needs of his readers. Many regard Mr. Miller as the consummate reporter on new technology for an everyday audience.

More information about the author and The Molehill Group can be found at www.molehillgroup.com. You can e-mail the author directly at author@molehillgroup.com.

PART I

Learning New Features and Creating New Documents

- *Exploring new and essential features of Word 2000*

- *Customizing Word for your own preferences*

- *Creating and saving simple documents*

- *Printing, faxing, and e-mailing Word documents*

CHAPTER 1

Word 2000 Basics for New Users

Understanding how Word 2000 works   4

Getting to know Word's various views   9

Working with multiple panes and zoom views   13

Viewing multiple documents   18

Working with pull-down menus   20

Right-clicking for pop-up menus   21

Using Word's toolbars   22

Using Word's keyboard commands   22

If you're a new user of Microsoft Word, welcome to the program! Microsoft Word 2000 is the latest version of the world's most popular word processing program and a terrific tool for all your computer-based writing needs.

With Word 2000, you can create virtually any type of document, from simple memos and letters to complex multi-section reports and newsletters. You can even use Word to create personalized mass mailings and print address labels and envelopes. In fact, with its hundreds of powerful features and commands, there is little you *can't* do with Word 2000.

Of course, before you can use Word, you have to know how Word works. This chapter serves as a basic introduction to Word's features and interface; you'll not only learn *how* Word works, but you'll learn *where* to find all of its many features!

If you're a more experienced Word user, you may want to skip this chapter and go directly to Chapter 2, which focuses on the new and changed features of Word 2000 and the skills you need in order to adapt to the new version.

Understanding Word and Getting Started

Quite simply, Word is a word processing program. You use it to enter, edit, and format words in sentences, paragraphs, and pages.

Word 2000 works within the Microsoft Windows environment and shares the standard Windows interface and operability. If you already know how to use other Windows programs, you can probably find your way around Word without much trouble.

 NOTE If you're unfamiliar with the way Windows works, check out Sybex's *Mastering Windows 98 Premium Edition*, available wherever computer books are sold.

Like many other Windows applications, Word 2000 enables you to create new documents, open and edit existing documents, and save your work as either an existing or a new document. You can work on more than one document at a time, and copy and paste text and objects from one document to another—as well as within a single document.

Launching Microsoft Word

Before you can use Word to work with documents, you must have the program up and running on the Windows desktop. There are several ways to launch the Microsoft Word program:

- Click the Windows Start button and select Programs ➢ Microsoft Word.

- Select the Microsoft Word icon on the Windows desktop (if one was created during the Word installation).

- Open My Computer or Windows Explorer, navigate to the Program Files\ Microsoft Office\Office folder and select the Winword.exe file.

- Click the Windows Start button and select Run; when the Run dialog box appears, enter **C:\Program Files\Microsoft Office\Office\Winword.exe** in the Open box, then click OK.

- Click the Windows Start button and select New Office Document; when the New Office Document dialog box appears, select a tab that includes Word documents, select a type of Word document, then click OK. (This launches Microsoft Word and loads a blank document of the selected type.)

- From the Microsoft Office Shortcut Bar, click the New Office Document button; when the New Office Document dialog box appears, select a tab that includes Word documents, select a type of Word document, then click OK. (This launches Microsoft Word and loads a blank document of the selected type.)

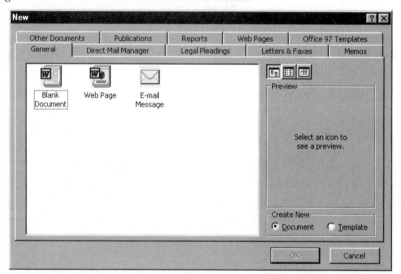

Creating and Opening Documents

Once Word is launched, you can either create a new document, or open and edit an existing one. (You can also have multiple documents open at one time, if you so wish.)

You create a new document by selecting File ➢ New, then selecting a document template from the New dialog box. You can also create a generic Word document by clicking the New button on Word's Standard toolbar.

 To open an existing document from within Word, select File ➢ Open or click the Open Document button on Word's Standard toolbar. When the Open dialog box appears, navigate to the desired file (one with a .DOC extension), select the file, and click Open.

You can now enter and edit text in the open document. The blinking cursor indicates your *insertion point* for new text. When you start typing, the new text is entered at the insertion point. You can reposition the insertion point with your mouse or with your keyboard's arrow keys.

Any text you enter can be deleted by using the Backspace key (deletes the previous character) or the Delete key (deletes the next character). Text you enter can be formatted via commands on the Format menu or the Formatting toolbar. Non-text elements (pictures, objects, and so on) can be inserted via the commands on the Insert menu.

When you're through editing the document, you must save it as a separate file. Files created by Microsoft Word are automatically assigned the .DOC extension; as an example, a file named FILE1 would be saved as FILE1.DOC. To save a new file, select File ➤ Save As; when the Save As dialog box appears, select a location for the file, assign it a name, and click Save.

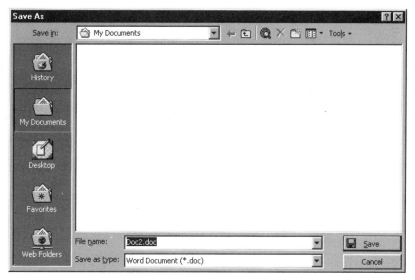

 To save changes made to an existing file, just select File ➤ Save (or click the Save button on Word's Standard toolbar). If you select File ➤ Save for a not-yet-saved document, Word will automatically display the Save As dialog box so you can specify a filename and location.

 NOTE To learn more about creating, opening, and saving Word documents, see Chapter 2.

Getting to Know the Word Workspace

Before you start to use Word, you should familiarize yourself with Word's interface so you know where to look when you want to perform specific operations.

The Word workspace is divided into seven main parts, from top to bottom:

Title Bar   This is where you find the filename of the current document, as well as buttons to minimize, maximize, and close the current Word window.

Menu Bar   Virtually all Word commands are accessible from these pull-down menus. When you use your mouse to click a menu item, the menu pulls down to display a full range of commands and options.

 TIP   You can also pull down a menu by typing the Alt key along with the key representing the underlined letter for the desired menu item. As an example, the File menu has the letter "F" underlined; when you type Alt+F, the File menu is pulled down for use. In addition, pressing F10 changes the program's focus to the menu bar, where you can use your keyboard's arrow keys to navigate through the menus.

Toolbars   Word contains sixteen different toolbars that you can display anywhere in the Word workspace. By default, the Standard and Formatting toolbars are docked at the top of the workspace, just underneath the menu bar. Click a button on any toolbar to initiate the operation associated with that button.

Ruler   This allows you to measure the width of a document and assign tabs and margins.

Document   This main space displays your current document in one of several views (discussed in the next section).

View Buttons and Scroll Bar   The View buttons let you switch between different views of a button; the scroll bar lets you scroll left and right through the current page. (The scroll bar along the side of the workspace lets you scroll through a document from top to bottom.)

Status Bar   This provides important information about your current document as well as instant access to several key functions.

Figure 1.1 shows the components of a typical Word workspace.

PART

I

Learning New Features and
Creating New Documents

FIGURE 1.1
The Word 2000
workspace

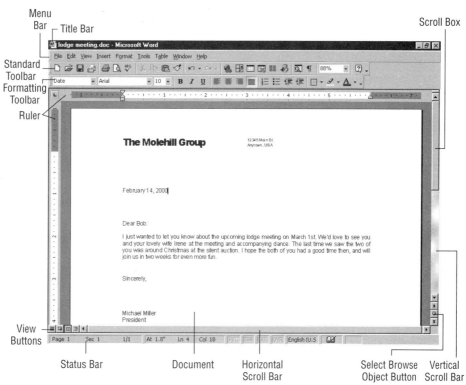

Viewing a Word Document

Word allows you to view a document in a fashion that best suits your own particular needs. All four views are "live," in that you can fully edit all text and graphics from any view. Just pick the view that works best for you—and don't hesitate to change views as necessary.

Normal View

Normal view (shown in Figure 1.2) displays your document with a simplified layout. You'll see all your text normally, but certain types of graphic objects, backgrounds, headers and footers, and pictures won't be displayed. Because of this simplified layout,

Normal view is a very fast way to work with the text in your documents, but is not ideal for full-page layout.

 TIP In Normal view, you can choose to display styles associated with each paragraph. Select Tools ➢ Options to display the Options dialog box, select the view tab, select a value greater than 0 for the Style Area Width option, then click OK.

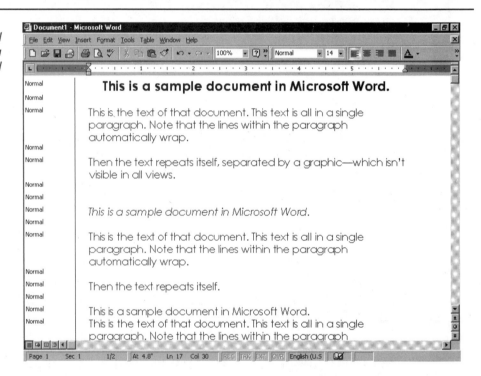

Web Layout View

 Web Layout view (shown in Figure 1.3) is used to work on documents that will be displayed on the Web. In this view, you can see all elements of your document (including graphics and backgrounds) as they would be displayed in a Web browser.

FIGURE 1.3
*Word 2000's Web
Layout view*

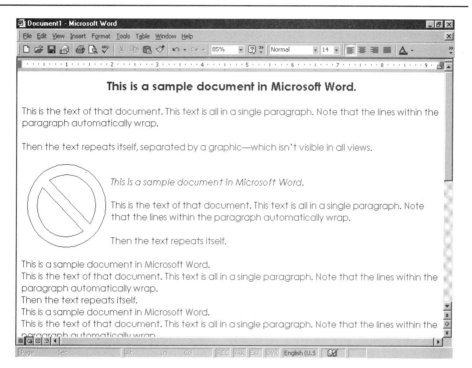

Print Layout View

Print Layout view (shown in Figure 1.4) displays all the elements on your page (including graphics, headers and footers, and backgrounds) as they appear when printed. This view, while slower than Normal view for text editing, is the preferred view for full-page layout.

FIGURE 1.4
*Word 2000's Print
Layout view*

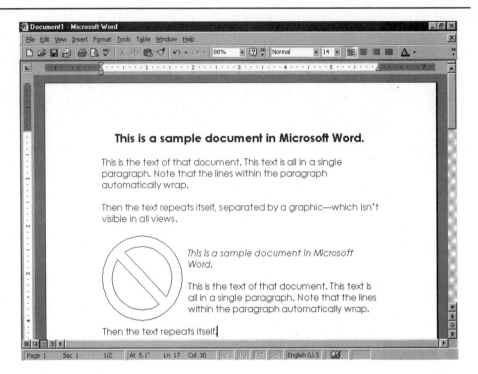

FIGURE 1.4
*Word 2000's Print
Layout view*

Outline View

Outline view (shown in Figure 1.5) displays your document as an outline. In this view, you can quickly see the structure of your document, and easily rearrange entire sections with a few mouse clicks. While headers and footers, graphics, and backgrounds do not appear in this view, you can collapse an outlined document to see only the main headings, or expand a document to show all (or selected) headings and body text. This view is also the preferred view for working with large master documents and is discussed in-depth in Chapter 20.

FIGURE 1.5
*Word 2000's
Outline view*

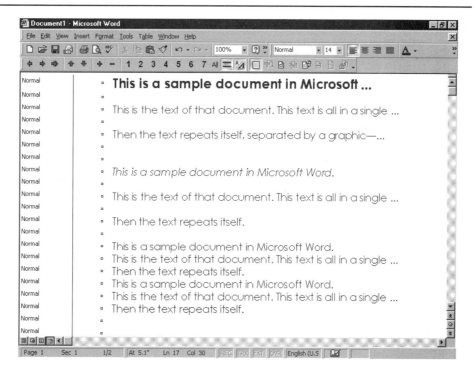

 NOTE In addition to the four editing Views, Word 2000 also includes two *preview* views, both accessible from the File menu. *Print Preview* displays your current document exactly as it will appear on the printed page; in this view you can choose to display the full page, a zoomed view of the page, or multiple pages on a single screen. *Web Page Preview* opens your Web browser and displays your current document as a Web page. While you can actually edit text in Print Preview (you can't do any editing in Web Page Preview), these preview views are typically used to see how your document looks in final form, and are not designed for your main document creation and editing.

Zooming through Different Display Sizes

With Word 2000, you're not limited to viewing your document at its preset size. There are several ways you can change the size that documents appear in your workspace window.

MASTERING THE OPPORTUNITIES

Which View Should You Use?

Word 2000's different views are each optimized for specific types of work. Which type of work you're doing should determine which view you use.

Outline View If you're in the formative stages of creation, think about using Outline view. In this view, it's easy to see your entire document at a glance and shift sections around as your structure solidifies. Outline view is also a good view to use when you're trying to get your hands around large or complex documents.

Document Map View Another view to think about when working with large documents is the Document Map view. This isn't a standard view (and doesn't have a View button assigned to it), but can be accessed by selecting View ➢ Document Map, or by clicking the Document Map button on the Standard toolbar. In Document Map view, an outline of your document appears in a separate left pane, while the document itself (in whatever standard view you select) is displayed in the right pane. You can't edit the outline in the Document Map pane (as you can in Outline view), but you can click a heading in the Document Map to jump directly to that part of your document in the right pane. In addition, the Document Map view helps you to better grasp the structure of more complex documents.

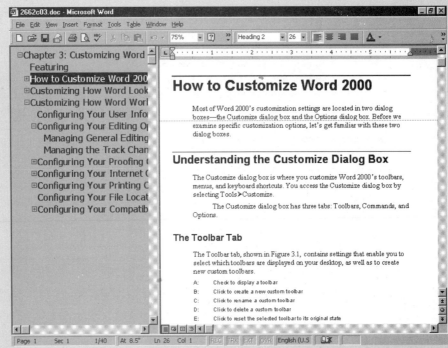

Continued ▶

Normal View If your document is primarily text with little fancy formatting, the fastest working mode is Word's Normal view. In this view, most graphics and non-text objects are hidden, making the screen display fast and efficient.

Print Layout View On the other hand, if you're working on a document that combines text with pictures and other objects, you probably want to use the Print Layout view. In this view you can drag and drop elements around the screen to your heart's content, effectively turning Word into a powerful desktop publishing program. What you see onscreen in Print Layout view should more or less mirror what you see in Print Preview, and on your printed page.

Web Layout View Finally, if you're using Word to create a Web page, you should be using the Web Layout view. None of Word's other views accurately represent the way your document will look on the Web; Web Layout view is the closest thing to editing within a Web browser.

The Standard toolbar includes a Zoom command in the form of a pull-down list. Pull down the list and select a pre-set zoom level (from 10% to 500%); 100% zoom displays your document at the size it will appear when printed. You can also choose to have your document automatically fill up the entire width of your screen by selecting the Page Width option.

TIP If you can't view an entire line of text on your screen—if the text extends past the edges of your screen—decrease your zoom level.

Another way to change the display size of your documents is to select View ➢ Zoom. This displays the Zoom dialog box (shown in Figure 1.6), where you can select from both preselected and custom zoom levels. This dialog box also previews the zoom level that you select.

FIGURE 1.6
Use the Zoom dialog box to increase or decrease the size of your document onscreen.

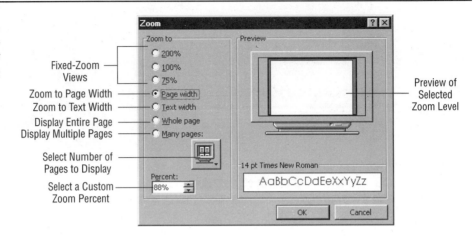

You'll find the following options in the Zoom dialog box:

200%, 100%, and 75%   Represent the fixed-zoom views.

Page Width   Zooms the document (including margins) to the full width of your screen.

Text Width   Zooms the document so that the text in your document fills the full width of your screen.

Whole Page   Displays your entire document on a single screen.

Many Pages   Displays multiple pages on a single screen; click the button next to this option to select how many pages you want to display per screen.

Zoom Control   Lets you select a custom zoom percent.

NOTE   The Page Width, Text Width, Whole Page, and Many Pages options are available only when you're using Word in Print Layout view.

Finally, you can choose to hide all of Word's menus and toolbars and display your document using your entire computer screen. When you select View ➢ Full Screen, your document fills up your entire screen; to return to normal viewing, click the Close Full Screen button in the floating toolbar.

Viewing Different Parts of the Same Document Simultaneously

Word lets you split a document in two parts and display both parts on your screen at the same time. This makes it easier to compare different parts of your document, or to cut and paste elements from one part of your document to another.

To split your document, position your cursor on top of the split bar at the top of the right-hand vertical scroll bar. When your cursor changes shape, drag the split box down the scroll bar to the desired position. Your document will now be split into two "live" panes, as shown in Figure 1.7.

 TIP You can also split a document by selecting Window ≻ Split.

FIGURE 1.7
A Word document split into two panes

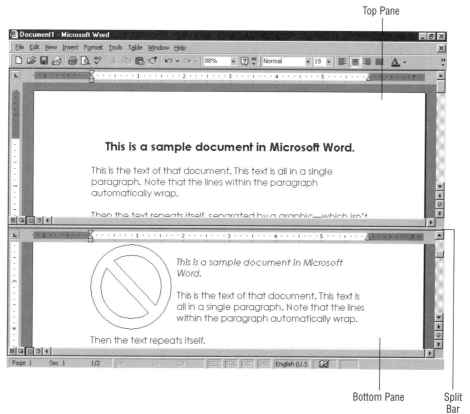

This is a sample document in Microsoft Word.

This is the text of that document. This text is all in a single paragraph. Note that the lines within the paragraph automatically wrap.

Then the text repeats itself, separated by a graphic—which isn't

This is a sample document in Microsoft Word.

This is the text of that document. This text is all in a single paragraph. Note that the lines within the paragraph automatically wrap.

Then the text repeats itself.

Top Pane

Bottom Pane   Split Bar

To return to a single pane, you can either double-click the split bar or drag the bar to the very top or bottom of your screen.

 TIP Another way to view multiple parts of a document at the same time is to open a duplicate window for the current document. To do this, select Window ➢ New Window.

Editing Multiple Documents in Multiple Windows

In Word 2000, multiple documents are displayed in separate Word windows. This contrasts with previous versions of Word, where multiple documents were displayed in their own sub-windows within a single Word window.

Since each Word document appears as a separate instance of Word, multiple documents appear as multiple buttons on the Windows Taskbar. This approach lets you quickly and easily switch between documents by clicking Taskbar buttons or pressing Alt+Tab.

If you want to arrange multiple documents on your screen, you can resize and rearrange them manually, or select Windows ➢ Arrange All. When you select this command, all open Word documents are stacked horizontally on the Windows desktop.

Using Word's Status Bar

At the bottom of the Word workspace is the Status bar, shown in Figure 1.8. This section of the screen not only displays key information about the current document, but also allows you instant access to specific Word features.

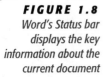
FIGURE 1.8
Word's Status bar displays the key information about the current document

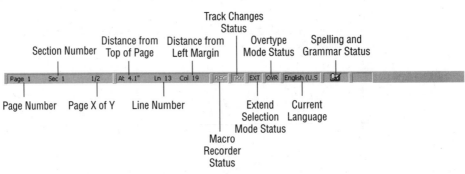

Table 1.1 details the parts of the Status bar, from left to right.

TABLE 1.1: WORD 2000'S STATUS BAR

Status Bar Item	Description
Page Number	Displays the page number of the current page.
Section Number	Displays the section number of the current page for those documents broken into discrete sections.
Page X of Y	Displays the current page number (X) and the total number of pages in the document (Y).
At	Displays the distance (in inches) from the top of the page to the insertion point.
Ln	Displays the line number (on the current page) of the insertion point.
Col	Displays the distance (in characters) from the left margin to the insertion point.
REC	Displays status of the Macro Recorder. (Dimmed is "off.") Double-click this section to turn the Macro Recorder on or off.
TRK	Displays status of the Track Changes feature. (Dimmed is "off.") Double-click this section to turn Track Changes on or off.
EXT	Displays status of the Extend Selection mode. (Dimmed is "off.") Double-click this section to turn the Extend Selection mode on or off.
OVR	Displays status of the Overtype mode. (Dimmed is "off.") Double-click this section to turn Overtype mode on or off.
Language	Displays current language.
Spelling and Grammar	Displays status of Word's spelling and grammar checkers. When spelling/grammar checking is in process, an animated pen appears over this icon; if an error is found, an "X" appears. Double-click the icon to resolve the found error.
Background Save	A disk icon appears when Word is saving your document.
Background Print	A printer icon appears when Word is printing your document. (You can double-click the printer icon to cancel the current print job.)

TIP If you double-click anywhere to the left of the REC section in the Status bar, Word displays the Find and Replace dialog box, which lets you find specific text, replace specific text, or go to a specific place in the current document.

Commanding Word with Pull-Down Menus

Virtually everything you want to do in Word 2000 can be found on one of Word's pull-down menus. Word's menus are organized by function, so if you know what kind of thing you want to do, pull down that menu and look for the specific command you need. (As an example, if you want to work with files, pull down the File menu to find commands such as New, Open, Save, and Print.)

To choose a menu item, move your cursor to the menu you want and click the name of the menu. This "pulls down" the menu; click a specific menu item to select it.

Some menu items lead to submenus. For example, when you pull down the View menu and select Toolbars, another menu appears (branching off the Toolbars item) showing all the available toolbars. Menu items with submenus typically have an arrow to the right of the item name.

Other menu items lead to dialog boxes. For example, when you pull down the View menu and select Zoom, you display the Zoom dialog box. Menu items that lead to dialog boxes usually have an ellipse (...) after the item name.

While you typically access Word's menus with your mouse, you can also access the menus with your keyboard. When you press the F10 key, Word's focus changes to the menu bar; you can then use the right and left arrow keys to move through the menus, the down arrow key to pull down any menu, and the Enter key to select any menu item.

Choosing Between Full and Personalized Menus

In previous versions of Word (and in most programs you're used to using), when you pull down a menu, you know what you're going to see. That is, all the commands on all menus are always visible.

Not so with Word 2000.

Realizing that its numerous features can sometimes be overwhelming to casual users, Word 2000 incorporates *personalized* menus that (by default) only show those items that you've recently used. These menus are sometimes called "short" menus, since they don't include all the commands found on the full "long" menus. So if you never use a particular menu item, you won't see it when you pull down that menu.

The only problem with this feature is that it's now somewhat difficult to find those menu items that you don't frequently use. Fortunately, you can easily display items otherwise "hidden" on a particular menu by clicking the down arrow at the bottom of the menu. This expands the menu to show all items, recently used and otherwise.

If you'd prefer to turn off the personalized menu feature (and display all the items on all menus—even those items you might never use), select Tools ➤ Customize to display the Customize dialog box. Click the Options tab and then uncheck the Menus Show Recently Used Commands First option. Click OK to continue.

 TIP   If you find yourself constantly hunting for commands not displayed on the "short" menus, save yourself some grief and turn off the personalized menu feature.

Word's Pop-Up Menus

In addition to Word's pull-down menus, Word 2000 also includes a number of context-sensitive pop-up menus. These menus contain commands specific to a particular task, object, or area of the program, and are displayed when you right-click your mouse.

It would be impossible to discuss every single pop-up menu that might appear as you use Word 2000, since these menus are generated based on what you're currently doing within the program. For example, if you right-click your mouse while you're entering text, you see the pop-up menu displayed below. If you right-click over a Word toolbar, you see a pop-up menu containing all the available toolbars. If you right-click within a table, you see a pop-up menu containing commands appropriate for table editing.

A good rule of thumb is if you need to perform a task, right-click your mouse. Chances are you'll see a pop-up menu that contains that one command you need to use.

 TIP   Pop-up menus are often the fastest way to find task-specific commands.

Commanding Word with Toolbars

Menus are text-based groupings of commands; toolbars are like menus, except they're button-based. That means that instead of pulling down a menu and navigating through a list of commands, all you have to do is click a button with your mouse. In most cases, clicking a button on a toolbar is the fastest way to accomplish a specific task within Word.

Hiding, Displaying, and Moving Toolbars

Word 2000 contains sixteen built-in toolbars, not all of which are displayed by default. When you first start Word, you'll see just two toolbars, both docked at the top of the screen—the Standard and the Formatting toolbars. Other toolbars can be displayed as needed, and you can move any toolbar to occupy any part of your screen. You can even create your own custom toolbars for your own specific Word needs.

The easiest way to determine which toolbars are displayed is to select View ➢ Toolbars, which displays a submenu listing all available toolbars. (You can also right-click any toolbar to display this same list as a pop-up menu.) Check those toolbars you want to display, and uncheck those you want to hide. Word remembers your toolbar configuration, and displays your selected toolbars in all new documents you open.

You can move any toolbar to any area of the screen by grabbing the thick handle on the far left of the toolbar with your mouse and dragging the toolbar to a new position. If you drag a toolbar to any side of the screen (top, bottom, left, or right) the toolbar automatically "docks" to the side. If you drop the toolbar in the middle of the screen, it remains there as a floating window.

At the far right of every toolbar is a down arrow. When you click this arrow, a submenu appears listing all buttons that can be added to or deleted from the current toolbar. Check those buttons you want to add, and uncheck those you want to hide.

If two toolbars docked side-by-side are longer than the available space, buttons at the end of one or both of the toolbars will not be displayed. Instead, a More Buttons arrow will appear; click this double-arrow to display a submenu of the extra buttons.

 NOTE To learn how to create your own custom toolbars, see Chapter 3.

Commanding Word with the Keyboard

Since Word is a Windows-based application, virtually all operations in Word are designed for access via a mouse or similar pointing device. Many Word users, however, are more comfortable using the keyboard to access essential operations—and experienced "keyboard jockeys" insist that they can perform most tasks faster with the keyboard than they can with the mouse.

While not all Word operations can be accessed via the keyboard (you can't use the keyboard to access toolbars, for example), most mouse-based operations have special keyboard equivalents. If you're one of those who prefer using the keys, pay close attention to the following sections, which detail how to use Word without a mouse.

Using the Keyboard to Go Directly to Menu Commands

All of Word's menus can be accessed via the keyboard. To access the menu bar, press F10; this positions the cursor over the menu bar and lets you navigate through the menus using the left and right arrow keys. Use the down arrow key to open a menu, then use the Enter key to select a specific menu item.

You can also go direct to any main menu by pressing the Alt key plus the underlined letter on that menu. For example, the "F" in the File menu is underlined, so pressing Alt+F opens the File menu. Once a menu is opened, you can press the underlined letter for any menu item to activate that command immediately.

Using Word's Function Keys

Some of Word's most popular operations have been mapped directly to the function keys at the top of your computer keyboard. Table 1.2 displays Word's function key assignments.

TABLE 1.2: WORD 2000 FUNCTION KEY ASSIGNMENTS

Function Key	Command
F1	Help
F2	Move Text
F3	Insert AutoText
F4	Repeat
F5	Go To
F6	Other Pane
F7	Spelling and Grammar
F8	Extend Selection
F9	Update Field
F10	Menu Mode (access menu bar)
F11	Next Field
F12	Save As

TIP To display a list of Word's function key assignments as a toolbar, select Tools ➢ Customize, and when the Customize dialog box appears, select the Toolbars tab. Check the Function Key Display option in the Toolbars list, then click Close.

Using Shortcut Keys to Automate Operations

Many other Word operations can be accessed directly via a series of key combinations. These *shortcut keys* let you press two or more keys together to initiate a specific operation. Most shortcut keys combine either the Alt or Ctrl keys with another key.

As an example, pressing Ctrl+B activates Word's boldface text command. Pressing Alt+Ctrl+F inserts a footnote in your text.

 TIP To print a list of all Word shortcut keys and menu commands, select Tools ➢ Macro ➢ Macros. When the Macros dialog box appears, pull down the Macros in the list and select Word Commands, pull down the Macro Name list and select ListCommands, then click Run. Word now generates a document listing all commands, which you can print for your personal use.

There are literally hundreds of different keyboard shortcuts available in Word 2000, most of which are unknown to many users. For your reference, all of Word 2000's major shortcut keys (as well as the function key assignments) are listed in Table 1.3:

TABLE 1.3: WORD 2000 SHORTCUT KEYS

Command	Shortcut Key
Access Pull-Down Menus	F10
All Caps	Ctrl+Shift+A
Annotation	Alt+Ctrl+M
Apply Heading 1	Alt+Ctrl+1
Apply Heading 2	Alt+Ctrl+2
Apply Heading 3	Alt+Ctrl+3
Apply List Bullet	Ctrl+Shift+L
AutoFormat	Alt+Ctrl+K
AutoText	Alt+Ctrl+V
Bold	Ctrl+B
Bookmark	Ctrl+Shift+F5

Continued ▶

TABLE 1.3: WORD 2000 SHORTCUT KEYS (CONTINUED)

Command	Shortcut Key
Browse Next	Ctrl+PgDn
Browse Previous	Ctrl+PgUp
Cancel	Esc
Center Paragraph	Ctrl+E
Change Case	Shift+F3
Change Font Size	Ctrl+Shift+P
Clear	Del
Close Document	Ctrl+W *or* Ctrl+F4
Close or Exit	Alt+F4
Close Pane	Alt+Shift+C
Copy	Ctrl+C *or* Ctrl+Insert
Copy Format	Ctrl+Shift+C
Copy Text	Shift+F2
Create AutoText	Alt+F3
Customize Add Menu Shortcut	Alt+Ctrl+=
Customize Keyboard Shortcut	Alt+Ctrl++ ("plus"sign on numeric keyboard only)
Customize Remove Menu Shortcut	Alt+Ctrl+-
Cut	Ctrl+X *or* Shift+Del
Decrease Font Size	Ctrl+Shift+,
Decrease Font Size One Point	Ctrl+[
Delete Previous Word	Ctrl+Backspace
Delete Word	Ctrl+Del
Display Browse Dialog Box	Alt+Ctrl+Home
Display Font Dialog Box	Ctrl+D
Display Help	F1
Double Underline	Ctrl+Shift+D
Extend Selection	F8
Find	Ctrl+F

Continued ▶

TABLE 1.3: WORD 2000 SHORTCUT KEYS (CONTINUED)

Command	Shortcut Key
Find Next	Shift+F4
Go Back	Shift+F5
Go To	Ctrl+G *or* F5
Hanging Indent	Ctrl+T
Hidden Text	Ctrl+Shift+H
Highlight Character to the Left	Shift+←
Highlight Character to the Right	Shift+→
Highlight Next Line	Shift+↓
Highlight Next Paragraph	Ctrl+Shift+↓
Highlight Next Word	Ctrl+Shift+→
Highlight Previous Line	Shift+↑
Highlight Previous Paragraph	Ctrl+Shift+↑
Highlight Previous Word	Ctrl+Shift+←
Highlight to End of Column	Ctrl+Shift+End
Highlight to End of Line	Shift+End
Highlight to End of Page	Shift+PgDn
Highlight to End of Window	Alt+Ctrl+Shift+PgDn
Highlight to Start of Column	Ctrl+Shift+Home
Highlight to Start of Line	Shift+Home
Highlight to Start of Window	Alt+Ctrl+Shift+PgUp
Highlight to Top of Page	Shift+PgUp
Increase Font Size	Ctrl+Shift+.
Increase Font Size One Point	Ctrl+]
Indent	Ctrl+M
Insert AutoText entry	F3
Insert Column Break	Ctrl+Shift+Enter
Insert Date Field	Alt+Shift+D

Continued ▶

TABLE 1.3: WORD 2000 SHORTCUT KEYS (CONTINUED)

Command	Shortcut Key
Insert Endnote	Alt+Ctrl+D
Insert Field Characters	Ctrl+F9
Insert Field Codes	Alt+F9
Insert Footnote	Alt+Ctrl+F
Insert Hyperlink	Ctrl+K
Insert List Number Field	Alt+Ctrl+L
Insert Non-Breaking Hyphen	Ctrl+-
Insert Non-Breaking Space	Ctrl+Shift+Spacebar
Insert Page Break	Ctrl+Enter
Insert Time field	Alt+Shift+T
Italic	Ctrl+I
Justify Paragraph	Ctrl+J
Left Align Paragraph	Ctrl+L
Link Header and Footer	Alt+Shift+R
Lock Fields	Ctrl+F11
Macro	Alt+F8
Mail Merge check	Alt+Shift+K
Mail Merge Edit Data Source	Alt+Shift+E
Mail Merge to Document	Alt+Shift+N
Mail Merge to Printer	Alt+Shift+M
Mark Citation	Alt+Shift+I
Mark Index Entry	Alt+Shift+X
Mark Table of Contents Entry	Alt+Shift+O
Maximize Application	Alt+F10
Maximize Document	Ctrl+F10
Merge Field	Alt+Shift+F
Microsoft Script Editor	Alt+Shift+F11

Continued ▷

TABLE 1.3: WORD 2000 SHORTCUT KEYS (CONTINUED)

Command	Shortcut Key
Microsoft System Info	Alt+Ctrl+F1
Move Cursor One Character to the Left	←
Move Cursor One Character to the Right	→
Move Document	Ctrl+F7
Move Down One Paragraph	Ctrl+↓
Move Left One Word	Ctrl+←
Move One Line Down	↓
Move One Line Up	↑
Move Right One Word	Ctrl+→
Move Text or Graphics	F2
Move to End of Column	Alt+PgDn
Move to End of Document	Ctrl+End
Move to End of Line	End
Move to End of Row	Alt+Shift+End
Move to End of Window	Alt+Ctrl+PgDn
Move to Start of Column	Alt+PgUp
Move to Start of Document	Ctrl+Home
Move to Start of Line	Home
Move to Start of Row	Alt+Home
Move to Start of Window	Alt+Ctrl+PgUp
Move Up One Paragraph	Ctrl+↑
New File	Ctrl+N
Next Cell	Tab
Next Field	F11
Next Misspelling	Alt+F7
Next Object	Alt+↓
Next Window	Ctrl+F6

Continued ▐▶

TABLE 1.3: WORD 2000 SHORTCUT KEYS (CONTINUED)

Command	Shortcut Key
Normal Style	Ctrl+Shift+N
Normal View	Alt+Ctrl+N
Object Properties	Shift+F1
Open Document	Ctrl+O
Other Pane	Shift+F6
Outline Collapse	Alt+Shift+-
Outline Demote	Alt+Shift+→
Outline Expand	Alt+Shift++ ("plus" key on numeric keypad only)
Outline Move Down	Alt+Shift+↓
Outline Move Up	Alt+Shift+↑
Outline Promote	Alt+Shift+←
Outline Show First Line Only	Alt+Shift+L
Outline View	Alt+Ctrl+O
Overtype	Insert
Page Field	Alt+Shift+P
Page View	Alt+Ctrl+P
Paste	Ctrl+V *or* Shift+Insert
Paste Format	Ctrl+Shift+V
Previous Cell	Shift+Tab
Previous Field	Shift+F11 *or* Alt+Shift+F1
Previous Object	Alt+↑
Previous Window	Ctrl+Shift+F6
Print	Ctrl+P
Print Preview	Ctrl+F2
Proofing	F7
Redo	Alt+Shift+Backspace
Repeat	F4 *or* Alt+Enter

Continued ▶

TABLE 1.3: WORD 2000 SHORTCUT KEYS (CONTINUED)

Command	Shortcut Key
Replace	Ctrl+H
Reset Character	Ctrl+Space
Reset Paragraph	Ctrl+Q
Resize Document	Ctrl+F8
Restore Application	Alt+F5
Restore Document	Ctrl+F5
Right Align Paragraph	Ctrl+R
Save	Ctrl+S
Save As	F12
Select All	Ctrl+A
Select Column	Ctrl+Shift+F8
Show All	Ctrl+Shift+8
Show All Headings	Alt+Shift+A
Show Heading 1	Alt+Shift+1
Show Heading 2	Alt+Shift+2
Show Heading 3	Alt+Shift+3
Show Heading 4	Alt+Shift+4
Show Heading 5	Alt+Shift+5
Show Heading 6	Alt+Shift+6
Show Heading 7	Alt+Shift+7
Show Heading 8	Alt+Shift+8
Show Heading 9	Alt+Shift+9
Shrink Selection	Shift+F8
Small Caps	Ctrl+Shift+K
Spike	Ctrl+F3
Split Document Window	Atl+Ctrl+S
Style	Ctrl+Shift+S

Continued ▶

PART

I

Learning New Features and
Creating New Documents

TABLE 1.3: WORD 2000 SHORTCUT KEYS (CONTINUED)

Command	Shortcut Key
Subscript	Ctrl+=
Superscript	Ctrl+Shift+=
Symbol Font	Ctrl+Shift+Q
Thesaurus	Shift+F7
Toggle Field Display	Shift+F9
Toggle Master Subdocuments	Ctrl+\
Toggle Revision Marks	Ctrl+Shift+E
Underline	Ctrl+U
Undo	Ctrl+Z
Unhang Indent	Ctrl+Shift+T
Unindent	Ctrl+Shift+M
Unlink Fields	Ctrl+6
Unlock Fields	Ctrl+4
Update AutoFormat	Alt+Ctrl+U
Update Fields	Alt+Shift+U
Update Source	Ctrl+Shift+F7
Visual Basic Code	Alt+F11
Web Go Back	Alt+←
Web Go Forward	Alt+→
Word Underline	Ctrl+Shift+W

NOTE   To learn how to create new keyboard shortcuts, see Chapter 3.

CHAPTER 2

Discovering the New Features of Word 2000

Working with simplified program management   35

Discovering enhanced personalization   42

Working with changed menu commands   43

Using improved editing tools   45

Using new and improved Web editing tools   53

Using Word 2000 with previous versions   60

Identifying known compatibility issues   64

Switching from WordPerfect to Word   66

I f you've used previous versions of Microsoft Word, you're familiar with how the program works and with its key features. You want to know what's different about this new version, and how Word 2000's new and changed features will affect the way you do what you do with the program.

Even if you're a new user, you're still probably interested in many of Word 2000's new features—such as the improved Web editing tools and new personalized menus. Think of this chapter, then, as presenting the newest features of Word 2000—for both new and experienced users!

Introducing the New and Improved Features of Word 2000

Word 2000, like every new version of Microsoft Word, attempts to improve the user experience by adding features and enhancing functionality. While the main interface and core operations remain the same as that of Word 97, Word 2000 adds a number of bells and whistles to the previous version of the program. It also changes a few things, so read on to find out what's new and different in Word 2000.

MASTERING THE OPPORTUNITIES

Basic Skills for Upgraders

Once you upgrade to Word 2000 and familiarize yourself with the new features (and where Microsoft moved your favorite old features), it's time to practice a few skills that might prove useful as you go forward.

First, if you haven't already, learn to use your right mouse button. (Not the left one that you click all the time—the right one that you seldom, if ever, use.) The context-sensitive menus that pop up when you click the right mouse button more often than not contain precisely the commands you need in any given situation. You can fumble around in the pull-down menus or try to remember what the icons on the toolbar buttons mean—or you can just right-click and select your command without even moving your cursor.

Continued ▶

Second, get used to trying to find "missing" commands on Word 2000's short menus—or turn off the personalized menus and go back to the full menus you've gotten used to over the years. There's no harm at all in opening the Customize dialog box, clicking the Options tab, and turning off the Menus Show Recently Used Commands First option.

Third, learn to love the Web. You're going to find more and more people incorporating hyperlinks into their Word documents, and even a few people using Word to create full-blown HTML Web pages. Soon, you'll open up a Word document and find lots of blue links to other documents and Web pages—so get on the bandwagon!

Finally, if you're sharing documents with Word users who haven't upgraded yet, learn to turn off some of Word 2000's new features—or your friends will start complaining about the strange-looking documents you keep sending them! As an example, I know from personal experience that Word 2000's new object positioning commands do not translate backward, resulting in documents with incorrectly placed graphics and pictures. Just because Word 2000 can do it doesn't mean Word 97 or Word 95 can read it! So when in doubt, go for the lowest common denominator—even if it means avoiding some of the neat new features of the program.

Working with Simplified Program Management Features

Word 2000 builds on several of Microsoft's initiatives to simplify the management of the program itself. This new version—as with all Office 2000 applications—completely revamps the installation procedure and adds a degree of "self-healing" in the event of program misconduct.

New Install on Demand Feature

Realizing that Word's program files had grown rather large and were taking up a massive amount of hard disk space—and also noting that not all users actually used all parts of the program—Microsoft has made an effort to "componentize" its key Office 2000 applications. What this means is that a typical installation doesn't install the entire Word 2000 program; some lesser-used components are left uninstalled, thus saving a few megabytes of disk space on your system.

Most users will never miss the components that aren't part of a typical install. If, however, you go to use one of these components and it isn't yet installed, Word 2000 will prompt you to insert your installation CD to install the component. This feature is called Install on Demand, and the inconvenience of installing a few files in the middle of your daily operation is balanced by the disk space saved by less comprehensive installation.

NOTE For a full list of program components that are installed (and left uninstalled) in a typical installation, see Appendix A, "Installing and Updating Word."

New Detect and Repair Feature

 Have you ever run into a problem that required you to reinstall an entire software program? With Word 2000, minor program problems can be found and fixed automatically, thanks to the new Detect and Repair feature.

Detect and Repair can fix a number of common program-related problems, including missing files and corrupted or missing registry settings. If you experience problems with Word 2000, all you have to do is run the Detect and Repair utility, then follow the on-screen instructions.

 WARNING Detect and Repair only fixes problems associated with Word program files, and does not repair problems in your personal document files.

To run Detect and Repair, follow these steps:

1. Select Help ➢ Detect and Repair.

2. When the initial Detect and Repair dialog box appears, check the Restore My Shortcuts While Repairing option, then click Start.

3. Word now launches the Installer program, which checks for missing or corrupted files. Follow the on-screen instructions to reinstall any bad or missing files.

Detect and Repair can fix most of Word 2000's simple program file-related problems. More serious problems, however, may require the reinstallation of the entire Word 2000 program.

 NOTE For more information on troubleshooting Word 2000 problems, see Chapter 35.

Easier Sharing of Program Settings

 Like all Office 2000 applications, Word 2000 makes it easier to share program settings from one computer to another. This is useful if you use Word on more than one computer, or if a corporation wishes to duplicate a specific configuration on multiple machines.

Word 2000 creates a *user profile* that includes custom templates, dictionaries, and AutoCorrect and AutoFormat lists, as well as the settings you specify in the Options and Customize dialog boxes. Windows loads this user profile every time you log onto your computer.

If you're using Word 2000 on a network, your user profile is actually stored on your network server. Your network administrator can configure the corporate version of Word 2000 so that your user profile travels with you to any computer on the network you log onto.

Enhanced Help System

The Help system in Word 2000 has been overhauled from the inside out. Help files are now HTML-based, which means you'll find links from within the Help system to other Help pages, wizards, and online resources. The Help system also includes a new Answer Wizard, which attempts to provide information based on your plain-English queries.

Another new feature in the Word 2000 Help system is Office on the Web (shown in Figure 2.1), which accesses a special Microsoft Office Update site. This feature expands the traditional Help system to include up-to-date information and solutions.

FIGURE 2.1
Expand Word 2000's built-in Help system with the Microsoft Office Update Web site.

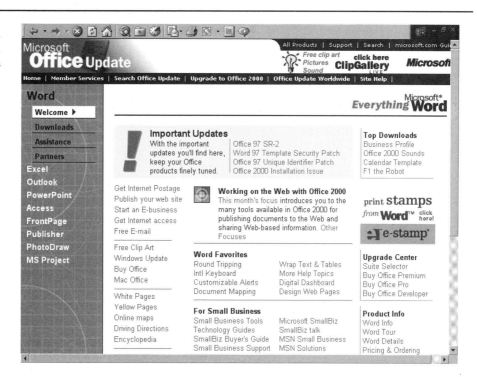

NOTE For more information on Word 2000's Help options, see Chapter 34.

Better Protection from Macro Viruses

 Microsoft recognized the growing problem of Word documents infected with computer viruses transmitted inside macros, and added a new level of macro virus protection to Word 2000. You can now indicate different security levels for Microsoft Word; the higher security levels require that any macro included in a document needs to be accompanied by a digitally signed certificate of authentication. If Word encounters a macro without the proper authentication, it warns you of a potential security problem.

To change the security level in Word 2000, follow these steps:

1. Select Tools ➤ Macro ➤ Security.

2. When the Security dialog box appears, select the Security Level tab.

3. Choose either High, Medium, or Low security, then click OK.

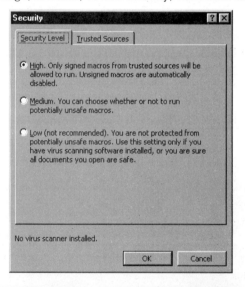

 WARNING Word 2000 does not actually scan your files to find and remove macro viruses. To best protect your system from all types of macro viruses, you should install a separate antivirus software program that does perform file scanning, such as Norton AntiVirus or McAfee VirusScan. The CD accompanying this book includes two macro-specific antivirus programs, Virus ALERT for Word 2000 and ChekMate Lite. See Chapter 33 for more information about these two programs.

Word 2000's security levels are described in Table 2.1:

TABLE 2.1: WORD 2000'S MACRO SECURITY LEVELS	
Security Level	**Description**
High	Runs only those macros that have been digitally signed and are confirmed as coming from a trusted source
Medium	Warns you when Word encounters a macro from a source not on your list of trusted sources
Low	Turns off all macro virus protection

NOTE For more information on protecting your system against Word macro viruses, see Chapter 29.

Using Improved File Management Options

Word 2000 includes several developments designed to make it easier for you to manage your Word document files. These enhancements are common across all Office 2000 applications.

New Open and Save As Dialog Boxes

Word 2000 incorporates new dialog boxes for the Open and Save As file operations. Both of these dialog boxes include a new Places bar so you can go directly to those folders and locations you use the most. As you can see in Figure 2.2, these dialog boxes also enable you to perform many different file operations from within these dialog boxes (such as copying, renaming, and deleting) that you formerly could only do from within My Computer or Windows Explorer.

Also new in these dialog boxes is the ability to access the Web when opening and saving files, as well being able to print a document from within the dialog box. Pull down the Tools menu to access additional file management tools.

FIGURE 2.2
Use the new features in the Open and Save As dialog boxes to manage your files from within Word.

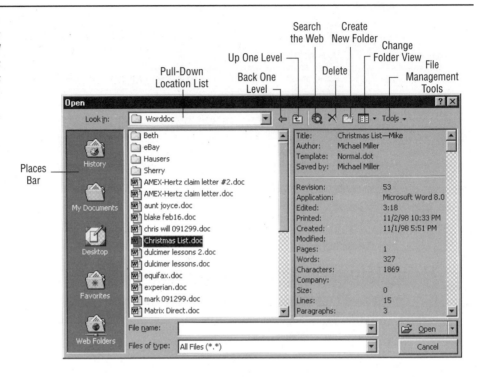

NOTE For more information on opening and saving Word files, see Chapter 4.

Where Are My Old Templates?

Word 2000 stores its Word template files in the new \Program Files\Microsoft Office\Templates\1033 folder. When you view the contents of this folder, you'll see all the template files but no template folders, as you did in previous versions of Word. In Word 97 (and previous versions), the template files were organized into template folders, which corresponded to the template tabs in the New dialog box. In Word 2000, the template folders are unnecessary because Word "knows" which tab each of these template files belong to.

Continued ▶

This folder only stores Word 2000's pre-made templates; any new templates you create are stored in a different location. Your Word 2000 custom templates are now stored in the \Windows\Application Data\Microsoft\Templates folder—unless you're on a network (using user profiles) or using Windows NT, in which case your custom templates are stored in the Profiles*username*\Application Data\Microsoft\Shared\Templates folder. If you want to add a new tab to the New dialog box for your custom templates, you have to create a new folder in the \Windows\Application Data\Microsoft\Templates folder, and store the template files for this tab in the new folder.

Which still begs the question—where are the templates you used in previous versions of Word? When you open the New dialog box, you see a tab titled Office 97 Templates. This is where you'll find all your old templates—both your custom templates and the original Word 97 (and previous) templates. These old template files are stored in the same directory where they've always been stored (typically \Microsoft Office\Template*customfolder*\, although this can differ from installation to installation), but are referenced via a shortcut in the \Windows\Application Data\Microsoft\Templates folder.

To make your old templates more accessible, you'll want to move them from their old directory to the \Windows\Application Data\Microsoft\Templates folder. If you had created a separate tab/folder for your old custom templates, just move that entire folder into the new folder, and a new tab for your old templates will automatically be created in the New dialog box.

New Single Document Interface

One of the most important and most controversial new features of Word 2000 is the new single document interface.

In previous versions of Word, multiple documents were displayed in sub-windows within the main Word program window. This changes in Word 2000, so that multiple documents are displayed in separate Word windows. Since each Word document appears as a separate instance of Word, multiple documents appear as multiple buttons on the Windows Taskbar. This approach lets you quickly and easily switch between documents by clicking Taskbar buttons or pressing Alt+Tab.

This change takes a little getting used to and clutters up the Windows Taskbar if you have too many documents open at the same time, but ultimately makes it easier to switch between open documents. Just don't be surprised when you start seeing more and more Word buttons on the Taskbar as you open additional documents!

Discovering Enhanced Personalization Settings

Most users like to create a comfortable environment in which to perform their word processing tasks. Word 2000 offers more personalization options than previous versions of the program—including one attempt at "intelligent" personalization, via the new personalized menus feature. This last new feature is an attempt to simplify Word's with shorter menus for most users—although some users may find it somewhat confusing.

New Personalized Menus

This new feature was undoubtedly well-intentioned, but has become one of the most disliked new features of Word 2000. The intent was to simplify an increasingly complex program, by hiding those menu items that users don't frequently access. With the personalized menus feature activated, you only see recently used items on Word's pulldown menus. Items you haven't recently used are not displayed.

The problem with this, of course, is when you need to access a less-frequently used command, you won't be able to find it! The short personalized menus do the intended job of simplifying Word 2000's menus, but create the new problem of confusing the user.

There are several ways around the personalized menu dilemma. First, if you click the down arrow at the bottom of any short menu, the menu will expand to show all available commands for that menu—effectively displaying the full, long menu.

Second, you can simply turn off the personalized menus feature. To do this, follow these steps:

1. Select Tools ➢ Customize.
2. When the Customize dialog box appears, select the Options tab.
3. Uncheck the Menus Show Recently Used Commands First option.
4. Click OK.

A third option is to go into the Options tab of the Customize dialog box, leave the Menus Show Recently Used commands First option checked, but also check the Show Full Menus After a Short Delay option. With this option selected, the short menu will expand into a long menu if you just hold the menu open for a few seconds. This is Word's equivalent of holding the refrigerator door open, hoping for something edible to appear; the program figures that if you stare at a menu long enough, you're looking for a command that wasn't automatically displayed.

TIP To reset the recently viewed commands on Word's personalized menus, go to the Options tab of the Customize dialog box and click the Reset My Usage Data button.

Changed Menu Commands

In addition to its new personalized menus, Word 2000 moves some existing menu commands to new positions within the menu system. The new menu organization was designed to be more logical and intuitive than the old menu structure, but if you were used to finding a command in a certain location, and it isn't there any more, then you need to know to where that command was moved.

Table 2.2 lists those menu commands that changed or moved in Word 2000.

TABLE 2.2: MENU COMMANDS CHANGED OR MOVED IN WORD 2000	
Old Command	**Moves Here:**
File ➢ Templates	Tools ➢ Templates and Add-Ins
File ➢ Send	File ➢ Send To ➢ Mail Recipient
File ➢ Add Routing Slip	File ➢ Send To ➢ Routing Recipient
File ➢ Find File	File ➢ Open ➢ Tools
File ➢ Summary Info	File ➢ Properties
Edit ➢ AutoText	Insert ➢ AutoText
Edit ➢ Bookmark	Insert ➢ Bookmark
View ➢ Page Layout	View ➢ Print Layout
View ➢ Master Document	Moved to the Outline toolbar
View ➢ Annotations	View ➢ Comments
Insert ➢ Annotation	Insert ➢ Comment
Insert ➢ Frame	Frames have been replaced by Text Boxes and Pictures
Insert ➢ Form Field	Moved to the Forms toolbar
Insert ➢ Database	Moved to the Database toolbar
Format ➢ Heading Numbering	Format ➢ Bullets and Numbering ➢ Outline Numbered
Format ➢ Style Gallery	Format ➢ Theme
Format ➢ Picture	Unavailable if no picture is selected

Continued ⫸

PART

I

Learning New Features and
Creating New Documents

TABLE 2.2: MENU COMMANDS CHANGED OR MOVED IN WORD 2000 (CONTINUED)

Old Command	Moves Here:
Tools ➢ Spelling	Tools ➢ Spelling and Grammar
Tools ➢ Grammar	Tools ➢ Spelling and Grammar
Tools ➢ Thesaurus	Tools ➢ Language ➢ Thesaurus
Tools ➢ Hyphenation	Tools ➢ Language ➢ Hyphenation
Tools ➢ Revisions	Tools ➢ Track Changes ➢ Highlight Changes
Tools ➢ Revisions ➢ Review	Tools ➢ Track Changes ➢ Accept or Reject Changes
Tools ➢ Revisions ➢ Compare Documents	Tools ➢ Track Changes ➢ Compare Documents
Tools ➢ Revisions ➢ Merge Documents	Tools ➢ Merge Documents
Table ➢ Insert Table	Table ➢ Insert ➢ Table
Table ➢ Delete cells	Table ➢ Delete ➢ Cells
Table ➢ Select row	Table ➢ Select ➢ Row
Table ➢ Select column	Table ➢ Select ➢ Column
Table ➢ Select table	Table ➢ Select ➢ Table
Table ➢ Convert text to table	Table ➢ Convert ➢ Text to table
Help ➢ Microsoft Word Help Topics	Help ➢ Microsoft Word Help
Help ➢ Answer Wizard	Help ➢ Microsoft Word Help ➢ Answer Wizard

Improved Toolbar Customization

Word has always enabled you to customize its toolbars. Unfortunately, that customization was a little clumsy. (In fact, you can still customize Word 2000's menus the old way, by selecting Tools ➢ Customize to display the Customize dialog box, then selecting the Commands tab and dragging a new button to any open toolbar.)

With Word 2000, however, you can now customize any toolbar without opening any additional dialog boxes. At the far right of every toolbar is a new More Buttons button. When you click this down arrow (and click the resultant Add or Remove Buttons command), a pull-down menu appears that displays related buttons you can add to the current toolbar. Check those buttons you wish to add to the toolbar, and uncheck any buttons you wish to remove—and the toolbar will be reorganized automatically.

If you want to add buttons that aren't displayed on the pull-down menu (for commands that aren't closely related to the current toolbar), select Customize from the pull-down menu. This displays the Customize dialog box, where you can add *any* command to any menu the old-fashioned way.

 TIP To return a menu to its original state, select Reset Menu from the More Buttons menu.

 NOTE For more information on personalizing Word's toolbars, see Chapter 3.

Using Improved Editing Tools

Word 2000 adds several new editing tools—and improves a few old ones—to help make your document creation and editing easier and more versatile than ever before.

New Click and Type Text Insertion Feature

In previous versions of Word, you inserted text in-line at the text insertion point, or you created a text box to add "floating" text. With Word 2000, you can add text (or any other element) anywhere in your document—just by clicking your mouse.

Word 2000's new Click and Type feature allows you to double-click in any blank space in a document and then start typing. Your new text will be positioned exactly where you placed it, and no other formatting is necessary.

To activate Click and Type, select Tools ➤ Options to display the Options dialog box. Select the Edit tab, check the Enable Click and Type option, then click OK.

WARNING Click and Type is active in only Print Layout and Web Layout views. You can't use Click and Type in Normal or Outline views.

To insert text or other items with Click and Type, follow these steps:

1. From within Print Layout or Web Layout view, position your cursor over a blank area of your document.

2. When the cursor changes shape (representing the current paragraph alignment of the Click and Type text), double-click.

3. To insert text, start typing. Your text will be automatically aligned according to its position on the page. (For example, Click and Type text inserted on the far right side of a page will be right aligned; text inserted in the middle of the page will be centered.)

NOTE There are actually six different Click and Type cursors. Each cursor represents the paragraph alignment that will be applied if text is inserted at that particular point in your document. So there's an Align Left Click and Type cursor, an Align Right cursor, a Center cursor, and so on.

4. To insert a table, graphic, or other item, pull down the Insert menu and select the item you want to insert. The item will be automatically inserted at the Click and Type insertion point.

Once you've inserted text or another element with Click and Type, you can format that text or element as you would normally, by selecting the text/element and applying normal Word formatting commands. You can also delete the inserted text or element, if necessary.

Click and Type does come with some limitations. First, you can only use it in Print Layout or Web Layout views. Second, you can only use it in blank areas of your document; you can't insert text on top of text or other existing objects. Third, you can't use Click and Type in any area of your document that contains multiple columns, bulleted and numbered lists, floating objects, pictures with top and bottom text wrapping, or indents.

These limitations aside, Click and Type adds some real desktop publishing power to Word 2000. It's a welcome addition.

 NOTE   For more information on inserting text into your documents, see Chapter 4.

Improved Object Placement Capability

 Just as Click and Type makes it easier to place an element on your page, Word 2000's improved object placement controls make it easier to specify how that object appears on the page. When you place an element (text box, graphic, etc.) on your page in Page Layout or Web Layout view, you can double-click the object to display the Format dialog box, shown in Figure 2.3.

FIGURE 2.3
*The Format dialog box
features several new
object placement
options.*

TIP You can also display the Format dialog box by right-clicking the element and selecting Format, or by selecting the object and then choosing Format ➢ Object (where Object is the type of object selected).

When the Format dialog box appears, select the Layout tab to view all of Word 2000's page layout options. The basic options provide five different ways to wrap text around your object, as well as three different horizontal alignments. (You can also horizontally position the object anywhere on your page by dragging it with your mouse.)

Word 2000 provides even more positioning options when you click the Advanced button. The Advanced Layout dialog box appears, and includes several methods to precisely position your object on the page, plus additional text wrapping options. Use these options if you want to create a truly professional desktop published document.

 NOTE For more information on positioning objects within a Word document, see Chapter 16.

New Collect and Paste Operation

 Word, like all Windows applications, has always allowed you to cut or copy text and other elements from one place to paste into another place, either within the same document or between documents. In the past, you've been limited to cutting/copying/pasting one item at a time; the last item you cut or copied was what got pasted when you used the Paste command.

In Office 2000 and Word 2000, however, the Cut/Copy/Paste function has been made more flexible by what Microsoft calls Collect and Paste. With Collect and Paste, you can store up to twelve different cut or copied items in the Clipboard, and then select which of the multiple items you want to paste into your document.

 TIP You can view the contents of any cut or copied text by hovering your cursor over that item's icon on the Clipboard toolbar. Word will then display a ScreenTip of the item's first fifty text characters.

To best use Collect and Paste, you should have the Clipboard toolbar displayed on your desktop. You start by cutting or copying the text or other element as normal, but when you're ready to paste, go to the Clipboard toolbar and click the specific item you want to paste. (If you have the Clipboard menu docked, you'll need to pull down the Items menu to display the Clipboard items.) The item you selected will then be pasted into your document.

 WARNING　If you use Word's standard Paste command when you have multiple text objects in the Clipboard, all Clipboard text will be pasted into your document.

 NOTE　For more information on cutting, copying, and pasting elements in your documents, see Chapter 4.

Enhanced Table Editing and Formatting Options

 Microsoft is constantly improving the table creation capabilities in Microsoft Word. The last version of the program, Word 97, added the ability to manually draw tables on your pages. Word 2000 adds several new options for creating ever-more sophisticated tables.

Among the new table editing and formatting features in Word 2000 are the following:

Enhanced Text Alignment　Now you can specify both the horizontal and vertical alignment of text within your tables.

Moving and Resizing　Word 2000 adds the power to manually move and resize your table using your mouse. You can also use your mouse to adjust the row height within a table.

Nested Tables　These are tables that reside within cells in other tables—so you can have a table within a table.

In addition, the options for wrapping text around a table have also been enhanced. Most of these new options are accessible when you select Table ≻ Table Properties to display the Table Properties dialog box.

 NOTE　For more information on working with tables in Word 2000, see Chapter 14.

Working with Improved Proofing Tools

Word is all about words—and Word 2000 makes it easier than ever to enter words in your documents and to make sure you have the right words in the right places.

 NOTE For more information on proofing your Word documents, see Chapter 6.

More Intelligent AutoCorrect Feature

 Microsoft introduced the AutoCorrect feature in Word 97 to help you detect and correct typos and misspellings on the fly. In Word 2000, AutoCorrect has been made more intelligent, with the following enhanced functionality:

- More powerful spelling correction, using Word's main dictionary (instead of a predefined list of spelling corrections, as was the case with Word 97).

- More personalized spelling correction, using a new user-created *exceptions list* to prevent unwanted changes to nonstandard words.

- International spelling correction, with separate lists of AutoCorrect entries for different languages.

In short, AutoCorrect in Word 2000 corrects more mistakes than it did in Word 97, making fewer annoying mistakes of its own.

Improved Spelling Dictionary, Thesaurus, and Grammar Checker

 All of Word 2000's proofing tools have been improved. The result is faster, more accurate, and more flexible document checking.

Among the major improvements are:

Spelling Dictionary Word 200 integrates the main dictionary into the Auto-Correct function, as well as the ability to check spelling in different languages. The main spelling dictionary has also been expanded to include a broader range of proper names, for people, places, and organizations.

Thesaurus Word 2000 includes a completely new thesaurus than the one used in previous versions of the program. This new thesaurus, developed by Bloomsbury

Publishing PLC, enables you view a list of synonyms by right-clicking any word and selecting Synonyms from the pop-up menu.

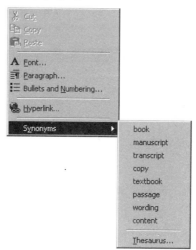

Grammar Checker   Grammar-checking technology continues to evolve, and Word 2000's state-of-the-art grammar checker flags more mistakes and offers easier-to-understand comments and suggestions than the grammar checker used in previous versions of the program.

Utilizing Enhanced Output Options

Just as editing and proofing have been improved in this latest version of Word, Word 2000 also offers several enhanced output options. In particular, the Print dialog box offers a few new options, and the ability to e-mail Word documents has been enhanced.

More Flexible Printing Function

Word 2000 adds a few enhancements to the basic Word printing function. In the basic Print dialog box (accessed when you select File ➢ Print), there is a new Zoom section. As shown in Figure 2.4, this section includes two new options:

- Pages per sheet, which enables you to print multiple pages from your document (at a reduced size, of course) on a single sheet of paper.

- Scale to paper size, which enables you to automatically rescale your document so that it can print on a different size of paper. (This is especially useful when switching from a U.S.-standard paper size to a non-U.S. size, such as the A4, A5, and A6 formats.)

FIGURE 2.4
Use the new Zoom options to quickly fit your document to different page sizes.

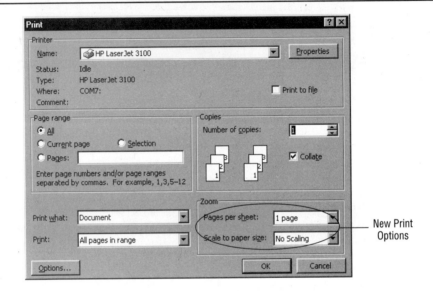

New Print Options

Word 2000 also supports more paper sizes than offered in previous versions, as well as more types of labels and envelopes.

New E-mail Options

Word 2000 has been fully integrated with the Internet so you can use Word as your e-mail editor, or choose to e-mail documents directly from Word (instead of through your standard e-mail program). Word 2000 enhances the e-mail features originally added to Word 97 with the capability to send any Word document as an HTML-format e-mail message. After you've created and saved your Word document, click the E-Mail button on Word's Standard toolbar (or select File ➤ Send To ➤ Mail Recipient). This adds an e-mail header to your document, which you use to address and send the document to anyone on the Internet.

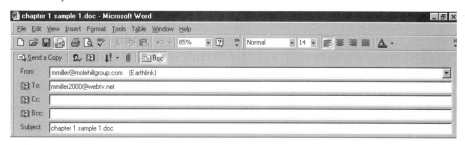

 WARNING Word's e-mail functionality is available only if you're using Microsoft Outlook as your e-mail program. This functionality is not available with other e-mail software.

 NOTE For more information on using Word for your e-mail-related tasks, see Chapter 7.

Using New and Improved Web Editing Tools

In addition to using Word for e-mail purposes, you can now use Word 2000 to create HTML-based Web pages. While not quite as powerful as a dedicated HTML editor program (such as Microsoft FrontPage 2000), using Word as your HTML editor has the benefit of using a familiar program for your Web page creation.

 NOTE For more information on creating simple Web pages, see Chapter 24.

New Web Page Preview

In addition to the Web Layout editing view, Word 2000 also includes a new Web Page Preview function. When you select File ➢ Web Page Preview, Word automatically launches your designated Web browser (such as Microsoft's Internet Explorer or Netscape Navigator) and uses it to display your current document, as shown in Figure 2.5.

FIGURE 2.5

View your Web documents in a Web browser when you open Word's Web Page Preview.

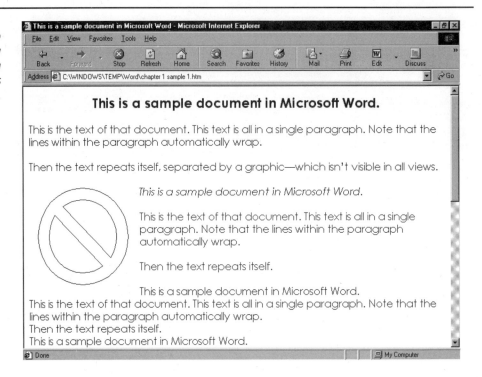

New Web Page Wizard

Word 97 added the capability to save Word documents in HTML format. Word 2000 expands on this capability by introducing the Web Page Wizard, which automates Web page creation with customized Web templates. You launch the Web Page Wizard (shown in Figure 2.6) by selecting File ➢ New to display the New dialog box. Select the Web Pages tab, then select Web Page Wizard and click OK. Follow the on-screen instructions to create your new pre-designed Web page.

FIGURE 2.6
*Use the Web Page
Wizard to simplify
Web page creation.*

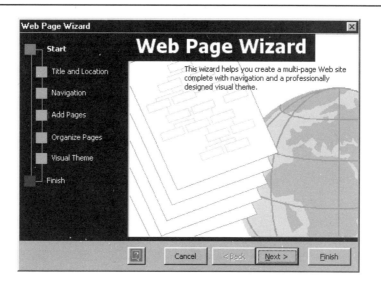

⚠ **TIP** You can also manually create a new Web page by selecting any of the Web page templates in the New dialog box—or save an existing Word document in HTML format by selecting File ➢ Save As Web Page.

New Web Themes

It's easy to design a bad-looking Web page—all you have to do is use the wrong combination of colors and formatting. Fortunately, Word 2000 provides a tool that makes it hard to design a bad-looking Web page.

A *theme* is a combination of fonts, text colors, and background colors used to format a Web document. Word 2000's themes can be applied to any document, but are particularly applicable to your Web-based documents.

To select a theme, select Format ➢ Theme to display the Themes dialog box, shown in Figure 2.7. You can now select a theme from the Choose a Theme list, and see how it works with your document in the preview window. Click OK to apply the theme.

FIGURE 2.7
Use Word 2000's
Themes to apply a
common design to
your Web pages.

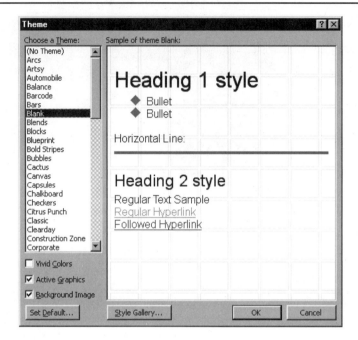

New Web Frame Creation Capability

Word 2000 enhances the program's HTML functionality by introducing the ability to create Web pages that include multiple frames. To add a frame to your Web page, display the Frames toolbar from within Web Layout view and select one of the five frame layout options (above, below, left, right, and a special "TOC in a frame" option).

Improved Hyperlinking

Word 2000 now includes an Insert Hyperlink button on its Standard toolbar, which lets you quickly and easily insert links to other Web pages in your documents. When you click the Insert Hyperlink button, you display the Insert Hyperlink dialog box. From here you can choose to insert a link to another Web page or document, to another location in your current document, to a new document, or to an e-mail address.

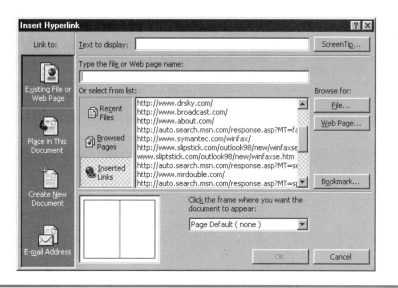

 TIP   Word 2000 can automatically create a hyperlink when you type a Web or e-mail address in your document. To activate this feature, select Tools ➢ AutoCorrect to display the AutoCorrect dialog box; select the AutoFormat As You Type tab, and check the Internet and Network Paths With Hyperlinks option.

New VBScript Web Scripting

 If you want to create really complex Web pages—complete with forms and buttons and controls—then you need to add behind-the-scene *scripts* to your pages. Word 2000 lets you use VBScript to program these features into your pages, via the new Microsoft Script Editor (shown in Figure 2.8). To add VBScript code and commands to a Web page, activate Web Layout view and select Tools ➢ Macro ➢ Microsoft Script Editor. From here you can add a variety of VBScript controls to your Web page, to create a truly interactive experience when users browse your page on the Web.

 NOTE   For more information on using the Microsoft Script Editor, see Chapter 25.

FIGURE 2.8
Use the Microsoft Script Editor to add interactive functionality to your Web pages.

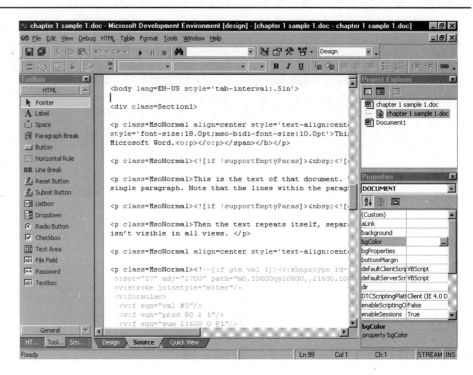

FIGURE 2.8
Use the Microsoft Script Editor to add interactive functionality to your Web pages.

Understanding the New Web-Based Collaboration

One of the major new features of Word 2000 is the enhanced capability for multiple users to work on a single document simultaneously. This *group collaboration* is facilitated via Web-based subscriptions and discussions.

WARNING Microsoft's Office Server Extensions must be installed on a Windows NT server for Web Discussions and Subscriptions to be available. Collaboration features are not available to individual users not connected to a discussion server.

Most of Word 2000's Web collaboration features are accessed via the special Discussions toolbar, which is displayed when your network or Web server is enabled with Microsoft's Office Server Extensions. This toolbar is not otherwise available to non-networked users.

NOTE For more information on Web-based collaboration, see Chapter 23.

New Web Subscriptions and Notifications

 Word 2000 users sharing the same Web server have the option to subscribe to particular documents, and then to be automatically notified via e-mail when those documents change. You can choose to be notified immediately, once a day, or weekly when a subscribed-to document is changed, created, or deleted—so you'll always know what's happening with your group-edited documents.

To subscribe to a document, click Subscribe on the Discussions toolbar. When the Document Subscription dialog box appears, check the File option to subscribe to a specific document, or the Folder option to subscribe to all documents in a folder. Pull down the When list to select when you wish to receive notification of changes and at what time you wish to be notified. Enter your e-mail address in the Address box, then click OK.

New Web Discussions

 Further enabling Web-based collaboration, Word 2000 provides the capability for users to hold discussions over the Web, using both Word 2000 documents and HTML files. Word 2000 discussions are really threads of individual comments made by users who have subscribed to a specific collaborative document.

Users can add their comments either in-line in the document or in a discussion pane at the bottom of the page. To initiate or participate in a discussion about a specific document, all you have to do is access that document on your discussion server.

 TIP You can also use Microsoft NetMeeting, included with Office 2000, to hold real-time online meetings with other members of your team.

Using New International Support Features

Microsoft Word is the word processing program of choice for tens of millions of users around the world. Given the prevalence of cross-location collaboration within multinational corporations and the need for individuals and companies to communicate and collaborate electronically with partners in other countries, Microsoft has greatly enhanced the international support features in Word 2000.

New Global Interface and Enhanced Multilingual Editing

In previous versions of Word, different language versions of the program were distributed as completely different pieces of software. In Word 2000, Microsoft developed a single global version of the program from which individual language interfaces are activated. In other words, all the features of all supported languages are built into the main program; you turn on those features associated with the language in which you choose to work. Features that are only used in specific languages are hidden until you need to use them.

To enable Word to work with different languages, click the Windows Start button, then select Programs ➤ Microsoft Office Tools ➤ Microsoft Office Language Settings. When the Microsoft Office Language Settings window opens, select the Enabled Languages tab and check those languages you wish to use. Follow the on-screen instructions to install these language components from your Office installation CD.

New Language AutoDetect

Further enhancing Word 2000's multilingual features, the program is designed to automatically detect the language being used and change the language settings accordingly. When you start typing in another language, Word's spelling, grammar, and other proofing tools automatically reset to the new language. Word even offers multiple-language AutoCorrect lists and automatically applies the correct list for the language you're using.

Another benefit of Word's Language AutoDetect feature is the ability to automatically display foreign-language documents with the correct foreign fonts loaded and displayed. For example, if you load a document with text in Japanese, that document is automatically displayed with the proper Japanese characters.

Using Word 2000 with Previous Versions

You've already upgraded to Word 2000, but chances are that not all of your colleagues or friends have made the jump to the new version. As with any software upgrade, the new version's new features may make it difficult to exchange files with users of previous versions of the program. The following sections detail some of the issues you may encounter when sharing Word 2000 documents with users who haven't yet upgraded.

Saving to Previous Word Formats

The file format used in Word 2000 is the same file format used in Word 97, and any documents you save in Word 2000 should be readable by users of Word 97. The only

problems you may encounter involve those new features of Word 2000 that don't necessarily translate well when viewed in Word 97; these compatibility problems are discussed in the next section.

The Word 2000/Word 97 file format is *not* fully compatible with Word 95 (6.0) or
previous versions of the program, even though they all share the .DOC file extension.
If you know your document is going to be used by users of these older versions of the
program, you need to save your document in the older file format. When you select
File ➤ Save As to display the Save As dialog box, pull down the Save As Type list and
select Word 6.0/95 (or the appropriate older version).

When you save a Word 2000 document as a Word 6.0/95 file, Word warns you that
some of the features in your document aren't supported by Word 6.0/95, and displays
a summary of those features and how they will appear when viewed in Word 95.
When you open the saved document in Word 95, you will find that some formatting
has been lost or changed, as Word warned you.

Fortunately, Word 2000 allows you to turn on and off various program settings to
make it easier for you to share documents with users of older versions of Word and
other word processing programs. Select Tools ➤ Options to display the Options dialog
box, then select the Compatibility tab (shown in Figure 2.9).

FIGURE 2.9
Configure Word 2000
for optimum
compatibility with
other programs.

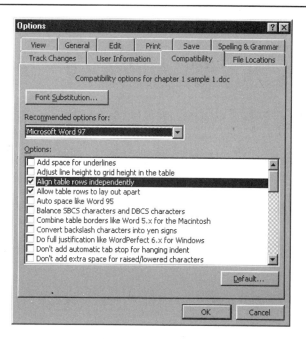

When you pull down the Recommended Options For list, you see a list of supported word processors. Selecting a word processor (or previous Word version) from this list automatically enables those options that facilitate cross-program or cross-version use. The easiest way to make sure your Word 2000 documents can be used with another program is to select the program in the Recommended Options For list and click OK.

You can also check and uncheck individual options manually—in effect, creating custom compatibility settings. If you find yourself experiencing the same compatibility problems over and over, revisit this Options list and enable those compatibility options that are affecting your work.

 MASTERING THE OPPORTUNITIES

Batch Converting Files from Other Formats

If your system or organization includes a lot of documents created in another file format, you may want to use Word 2000's Conversion Wizard to convert those files to the Word 2000 format all at one time. The Conversion Wizard lets you convert files from the following formats:

- HTML

- Lotus 1-2-3

- Microsoft Excel

- Microsoft Word 4.0–5.1 for Macintosh

- Microsoft Word 6.0/95 (Windows and Macintosh)

- Microsoft Works 4.0 for Windows

- MS-DOS Text with Layout

- Outlook Address Book

- Personal Address Book

- RTF (Rich Text Format)

- Schedule+ Contacts

Continued ▶

- Text

- Text with Layout

- Windows Write

- WordPerfect 5.x

- WordPerfect 6.x

The Conversion Wizard can also convert Word 2000 files back to many of these other file formats.

You use the Conversion Wizard to convert multiple files, one folder at a time. Follow these instructions to run the wizard:

1. Select File ➢ New to display the New dialog box.

2. From the New dialog box, select the Other Documents tab.

3. Select Batch Conversion Wizard and click OK.

4. When the Conversion Wizard appears, follow the on-screen instructions to select which format you wish to convert from (or to), which folder you wish to convert, and where you want to save the converted files.

When you click Finish, the Conversion Wizard will automatically convert all selected files to the new format. Make sure you watch over the conversion process, however, as any errors encountered during the operation will be reported and need to be dealt with.

Identifying Known Compatibility Issues

Not all features of Word 2000 translate well into older versions of Word. Table 2.3 lists some of the known compatibility issues you may encounter.

TABLE 2.3: KNOWN COMPATIBILITY ISSUES WITH WORD 2000

Word 2000 Feature	May Display Like This in Older Versions
24-bit colors	Displayed as the closest of Word's 16 core colors
Active hyperlink	Displayed as blue underlined text, but not active (Word 95 and previous)
Allow page breaks option in tables	Not supported
Animated text	Displayed as italic text
Automatic numbering in table cells	Converted to regular text
Background shape	Not displayed
Cell margins	Not displayed
Character shading and text highlighting	No character shading or text highlighting (Word 95 and previous)
Decorative border styles	Displayed as single line border
Decorative table border styles	Displayed as box border styles
Diagonal cell borders	Not displayed
Double strikethough text	Displayed as single strikethrough
Drawings	Simple drawings are displayed properly; more complex or overly formatted drawings may be displayed in a more simple format
Embedded fonts	Not supported; Word 95 assigns the closest font available
Embossed text	Displayed as gray text
Engraved text	Displayed as gray text
Gutter position on top	Displayed to the left
Horizontally scaled characters	Displayed as regular text
Microsoft ActiveX controls on Web forms	Converted to metafiles; no longer editable
Microsoft Visual Basic objects	Not supported (Word 95 and previous)
Nested tables	Nested table is removed; text from the nested table is displayed as a paragraph above the outer table cell

Continued ▶

TABLE 2.3: KNOWN COMPATIBILITY ISSUES WITH WORD 2000 (CONTINUED)

Word 2000 Feature	May Display Like This in Older Versions
Objects aligned horizontally right, center, inside, or outside	Shifted slightly
Objects middle or bottom aligned	Shifted to top alignment
Objects positioned relative to character	Shifted to be positioned relative to column; may also shift slightly
Objects positioned relative to line	Shifted to be positioned relative to paragraph; may also shift slightly
Objects with tight or through text wrapping	Displayed as square text wrapping
OLE objects with text wrapping	Converted to OLE objects in text boxes
Outline and heading numbered lists	Numbers are converted to regular text (Word 95 and previous)
Overlapping objects	Some objects may be obscured when overlapped
Page border	Not displayed
Password protection	May be lost
Pictures with text wrapping in tables	Pictures are moved to the paragraph above the table
Spacing between cells	Not displayed
Special underline text (heavy, dashed, dot, wavy, etc.)	Displayed as single underline text
Text border	Not displayed
Text with underline color different from text color	Underline color is displayed as same color as text
Text wrapping break	Displayed as a regular line break
Unicode characters	May be lost; foreign language characters are most likely to be affected
Versioning	Not supported
Vertical text direction in tables	Displayed as horizontal text
Vertically aligned table text	Aligned at the top of the cell
Vertically merged table cells	Split into separate cells
Web page frames	Not supported
WordArt	Converted to a Windows metafile, and cannot be edited (Word 95 and previous)

TIP If your Word 2000 documents display differently when viewed in other programs or versions, use the options on the Compatibility tab in the Options dialog box to turn off those new Word 2000 features that are not converting properly to other file formats.

Switching from WordPerfect to Word

Word 2000 makes it relatively easy for WordPerfect users to switch to Microsoft Word. There are several Word 2000 features you'll want to check out if you are a converting WordPerfect user, most of which are accessible via the Help for WordPerfect users dialog box (shown in Figure 2.10). Select Help ➢ WordPerfect Help to display this dialog box.

FIGURE 2.10
Word 2000 makes WordPerfect users feel at home with its WordPerfect Help options.

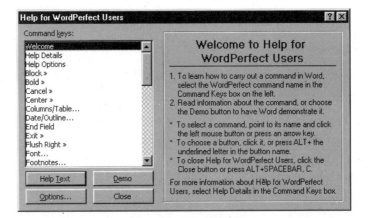

Helping WordPerfect Users

Word 2000 includes a special Help system for ex-WordPerfect users. With WordPerfect Help activated, you will receive instructions for Word-equivalent procedures when you press any WordPerfect shortcut keys.

To activate WordPerfect Help, select Help ➢ WordPerfect Help. When the Help for WordPerfect users dialog box appears, select a command from the Command Keys list to learn the Word equivalent. You can also view additional information about that command or operation (in a separate freestanding dialog box) by clicking the Help Text, or see a demo of how to perform that task by clicking the Demo button.

 TIP You can turn on WordPerfect Help full time by clicking the Options button in the Help for WordPerfect Users dialog box and then selecting the Help for WordPerfect Users option in the Help Options dialog box. You can also select whether you want to display Help Text or a Demo automatically, or provide Mouse Simulation or Demo Guidance.

Navigating WordPerfect within Word

With WordPerfect Navigation activated, the function of certain keys (PgUp, PgDn, Home, End, and Esc) in Word 2000 is changed to its WordPerfect 5.1 for DOS equivalent. To activate WordPerfect Navigation, select Help ➢ WordPerfect Help to display the Help for WordPerfect Users dialog box, then click the Options button. When the Help Options dialog box appears, check the Navigation Keys for WordPerfect Users option and click OK.

Configuring Word 2000's Compatibility Options

To better share Word 2000 documents with WordPerfect users, you should properly configure Word 2000's compatibility options. Select Tools ➢ Options to display Word 2000's Options dialog box, then select the Compatibility tab. Pull down the Recommended Options For list and select one of the two WordPerfect options (DOS or Windows). Word 2000 will now turn on and off the appropriate features to ensure your documents can be read and edited by WordPerfect users.

Learning Shortcut Keys for WordPerfect Operations

There are certain WordPerfect operations that you probably used quite frequently using specific WordPerfect keyboard shortcuts. Table 2.4 details the Word 2000 shortcut keys for these common WordPerfect commands.

TABLE 2.4: WORD 2000 SHORTCUT KEYS FOR WORDPERFECT COMMANDS

WordPerfect Command	Word 2000 Shortcut Key
Block	Shift+arrow key
Bold	Ctrl+B
Center text	Ctrl+E
Comment	Alt+Ctrl+M
Date code	Alt+Shift+D
Delete block	F8, then arrow key, then Del
Delete previous word	Ctrl+Backspace
Delete to end of line	Shift+End, then Del
Delete to end of page	Shift+↓, then Del
Delete word	Ctrl+Del
Double underline	Ctrl+Shift+D
Endnote	Alt+Ctrl+E
Exit	Alt+F4
Font	Ctrl+D
Footnote	Alt+Ctrl+F
Help	F1
Indent	Ctrl+M
Italic	Ctrl+I
Justify text	Ctrl+J
Left align text	Ctrl+L
Mark index entry	Alt+Shift+X
Mark table of authorities entry	Alt+Shift+I
Mark table of contents entry	Alt+Shift+O

Continued ▶

TABLE 2.4: WORD 2000 SHORTCUT KEYS FOR WORDPERFECT COMMANDS (CONTINUED)

WordPerfect Command	Word 2000 Shortcut Key
Print	Ctrl+P
Replace	Ctrl+H
Retrieve File	Ctrl+O
Reveal codes	Shift+F1, then click
Right align text	Ctrl+R
Save	Ctrl+S
Save As	F12
Search	Ctrl+F
Small Caps	Ctrl+Shift+K
Spell check	F7
Subscript	Ctrl+=
Superscript	Ctrl+Shift++
Thesaurus	Shift+F7
Underline	Ctrl+U
Undo	Ctrl+Z
View Document	Ctrl+F2

CHAPTER 3

Customizing Word 2000

Configuring your personal workspace   **72**

Customizing Word's toolbars   **92**

Rearranging Word's menus   **101**

Creating new keyboard shortcuts   **103**

Configuring your editing options   **104**

Customizing your proofing options   **107**

Configuring your Internet options   **112**

Setting your printing options   **114**

Assigning file locations   **116**

Configuring compatibility options   **116**

Everyone likes to personalize their workspace. Think about it: you probably arrange your desk *just so,* adjust your chair *just so,* and even program your telephone so that your favorite people are on speed dial. So why shouldn't you personalize the software program you use every day?

Word 2000 is easy to personalize. You can add elements to or take elements off your workspace; you can create custom toolbars and menus and keyboard shortcuts; you can even tell Word to turn on or off features that affect compatibility with other versions and programs. In short, you can make Word 2000 *your* Word 2000.

Customizing Word 2000: Where to Begin

Most of Word 2000's customization settings are located in two dialog boxes: the Customize dialog box and the Options dialog box. Before we examine specific customization options, let's get familiar with these two dialog boxes.

Understanding the Customize Dialog Box

Just as you may think, the Customize dialog box is where you customize Word 2000's toolbars, menus, and keyboard shortcuts. You access the Customize dialog box by selecting Tools ➤ Customize.

The Customize dialog box has three tabs: Toolbars, Commands, and Options.

The Toolbars Tab

The Toolbars tab, shown in Figure 3.1, contains settings that enable you to select which toolbars are displayed in the Word workspace, as well as to create new custom toolbars. (See the "Configuring Your Toolbars" section later in this chapter for detailed instructions.)

From this tab you can:

- Select which toolbars to display (check to display, uncheck to hide).
- Create new custom toolbars (click the New button).
- Rename custom toolbars (click the Rename button).
- Delete custom toolbars (click the Delete button).
- Reset toolbars to their default setting (click the Reset button).

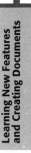

PART

I

Learning New Features
and Creating Documents

FIGURE 3.1
Use the Toolbars tab to display and create toolbars.

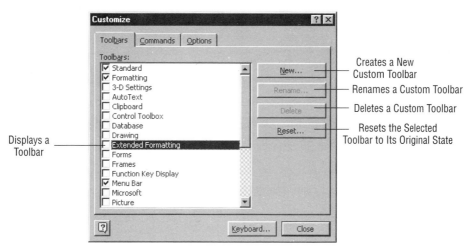

Creates a New
Custom Toolbar

Renames a Custom Toolbar

Deletes a Custom Toolbar

Resets the Selected
Toolbar to Its Original State

Displays a
Toolbar

The Commands Tab

The Commands tab, shown in Figure 3.2, enables you to add new buttons to your toolbars and to remove existing buttons. Every command available in Word is listed in this dialog box by category; select a category, select a command, and then drag that command onto any toolbar displayed on your Desktop.

FIGURE 3.2
Use the Commands tab to add new buttons to your toolbars.

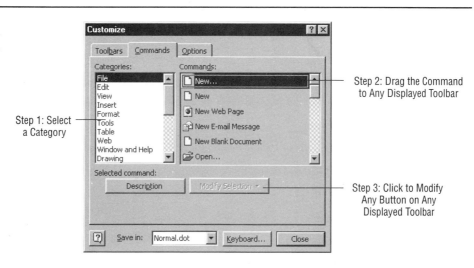

Step 2: Drag the Command
to Any Displayed Toolbar

Step 1: Select
a Category

Step 3: Click to Modify
Any Button on Any
Displayed Toolbar

The Modify button on this tab enables you to modify any button on any toolbar; you can choose to display either text only or an image plus text. You can even edit and create new graphics images for any of your toolbar buttons!

The Options Tab

The Options tab, shown in Figure 3.3, is where you find the options to turn on or off Word 2000's sometimes-unpopular personalized menus feature. This tab also contains a handful of settings that didn't fit anyplace else, including commands for menu animations, ScreenTips, and large icons. (See the "Configuring Your Menus" section later in this chapter for more information.)

 NOTE As explained in Chapter 2, personalized menus can be confusing to some users and are frequently turned off so users can see *all* the options on Word's menus.

FIGURE 3.3
Go to the Options tab to turn on or off Word 2000's personalized menus.

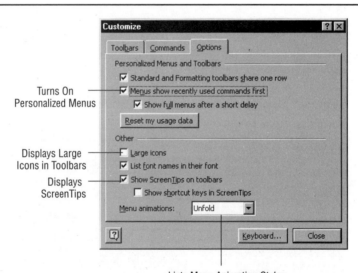

Turns On Personalized Menus

Displays Large Icons in Toolbars

Displays ScreenTips

Lists Menu Animation Styles

The Keyboard Button

At the bottom of every tab in the Customize dialog box is a Keyboard button. When you click this button, you display the Customize Keyboard dialog box, shown in Figure 3.4. You use the settings in this dialog box to create new keyboard shortcuts.

FIGURE 3.4
Create new keyboard shortcuts in the Customize Keyboard dialog box.

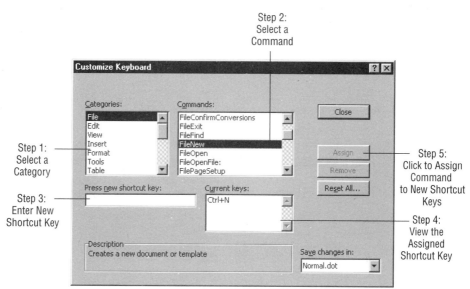

This dialog box works similarly to the Options tab in the Customize dialog box. All commands are listed by category; select a category, select a command, and then press the key(s) you wish to assign to this command. Click the Assign key to confirm the new shortcut key.

Understanding the Options Dialog Box

It's only logical that the Options dialog box is where you configure most of Word 2000's operating and display options. You access the Options dialog box by selecting Tools ➢ Options.

The Options dialog box has ten tabs: View, General, Edit, Print, Save, Spelling & Grammar, Track Changes, User Information, Compatibility, and File Locations.

The View Tab

The View tab, shown in Figure 3.5, enables you to select which elements are displayed in the Word workspace. This tab contains four major sections:

Show   Lets you to turn on and off a variety of general workspace elements.

Formatting Marks   Lets you turn on or off various text formatting marks.

Print and Web Layout Options   Lets you turn on or off elements for the Print Layout and Web Layout views.

Outline and Normal Options   Lets you turn on or off elements in the Outline and Normal views and also allows you to set the style area width (for Normal view).

FIGURE 3.5
Choose which elements appear onscreen via the View tab.

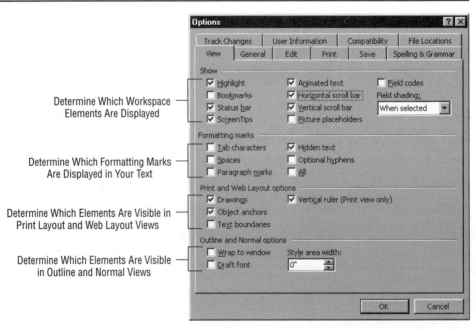

For more information on these options, see the "Configuring Your Personal Workspace" section later in this chapter.

The General Tab

The General tab, shown in Figure 3.6, contains options for various Word 2000 program operations. From this tab, you can turn on or off background repagination, blue background and white text display, feedback sounds, feedback animation, conversion confirmation, automatic link updates, mail as attachments, and help and navigation keys for WordPerfect users. You can also configure Word's recently used file list and measurement units, and click the Web Options or E-mail Options to configure Word's various Internet-related features.

FIGURE 3.6
*Configure various
program operations
from the General tab.*

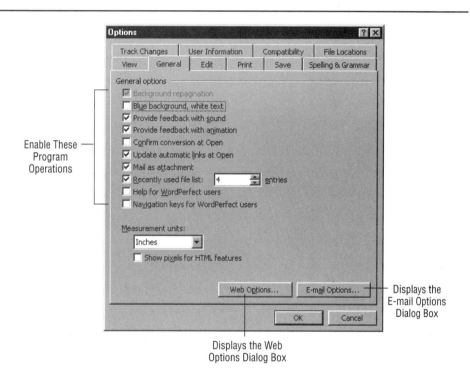

Enable These
Program
Operations

Displays the
E-mail Options
Dialog Box

Displays the Web
Options Dialog Box

The Edit Tab

The Edit tab, shown in Figure 3.7, lets you turn on or off various Word editing options, including Typing Replaces Selection, Drag-and-Drop Text Editing, Use the INS Key for

Paste, Overtype Mode, Use Smart Cut and Paste, Tabs and Backspace Set Left Indent, and Allow Accented Uppercase in French. You may choose automatic selection of entire words, and consider the new Click and Type feature. You can also select Word's default Picture Editor from this tab.

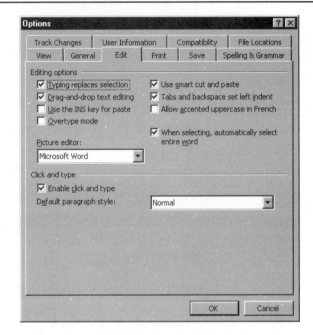

FIGURE 3.7
Check those editing options you want to enable.

The Print Tab

The Print tab, shown in Figure 3.8, is where you configure Word's various printing options. This tab allows you to turn on or off general printing options (Draft Output, Update Fields, Update Links, Allow A4/Letter Paper Resizing, Background Printing, Print PostScript Over Text, and Reverse Print Order), select what items are included with the printed document (Document Properties, Field Codes, Comments, Hidden Text, and Drawing Objects), choose to print data only for forms, and select your printer's default tray. (See the "Configuring Your Printing Options" section later in this chapter for more detailed information.)

FIGURE 3.8
*Configure Word's
printing options from
the Print tab.*

Enable or Disable
Printing Options

Determine Which Items
Are Printed with
Your Documents

Prints Data
Only in Forms

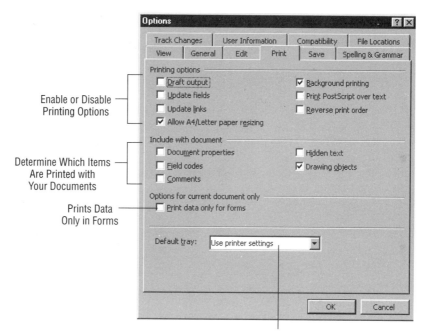

Configures Default Printing Tray

The Save Tab

The Save tab, shown in Figure 3.9, contains options that affect how and where Word saves your documents. You can turn on or off the following operations: Always Create Backup Copy, Allow Fast Saves, Prompt for Document Properties, Prompt to Save Normal Template, Embed TrueType Fonts, Save Data Only for Forms, Allow Background Saves, and Save AutoRecover Info at specific intervals. You can select the formats in which you wish to save your documents and elect to disable Word 2000 features not supported by Word 97. This tab also allows you to assign a password to the current file and to make it read-only.

FIGURE 3.9
Configure how Word saves your files from the Save tab.

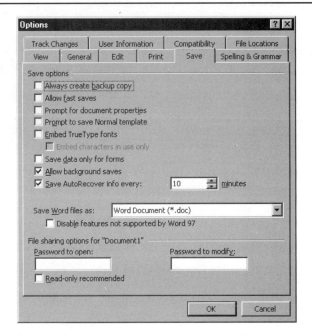

FIGURE 3.9
Configure how Word saves your files from the Save tab.

The Spelling & Grammar Tab

The Spelling & Grammar tab, shown in Figure 3.10, contains a variety of settings for Word 2000's proofing tools.

The Spelling section of this tab allows you to turn on or off features for checking spelling as you type, hiding spelling errors, always suggesting corrections, suggesting corrections from the main dictionary only, and ignoring uppercase words, words with numbers, and Internet and file addresses. You can also select a custom dictionary from the pull-down list, or click the Dictionaries button to display the Custom Dictionaries dialog box, where you can manage multiple custom dictionaries.

The Grammar section of this tab allows you to turn on or off features for checking grammar as you type, hiding grammatical errors, checking grammar at the same time as spelling, and showing readability statistics. You can also set the grammar checker to check for a specific writing style (from the Writing Style pull-down list), and click the Settings button to display the Grammar Settings dialog box, where you can turn on or off specific grammar rules.

FIGURE 3.10
Configure Word's proofing options from the Spelling & Grammar tab.

Configure — Spelling Options

Lists Available — Spelling Dictionaries

Configure — Grammar Options

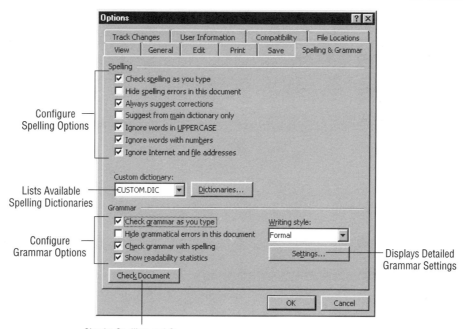

Displays Detailed — Grammar Settings

Checks Spelling and Grammar

 TIP To recheck your document using any new settings you've assigned, click the Check Document button.

The Track Changes Tab

The Track Changes tab, shown in Figure 3.11, enables you to configure Word's Track Changes feature. You can select which colors and marks you use for various types of editing, including inserted text, deleted text, and changed formatting. In addition, you can determine how you want to draw attention to editing changes via the Changed Lines element.

 NOTE Learn more about Word's change-tracking options in Chapter 23.

FIGURE 3.11
Set the colors and marks to track your editing changes.

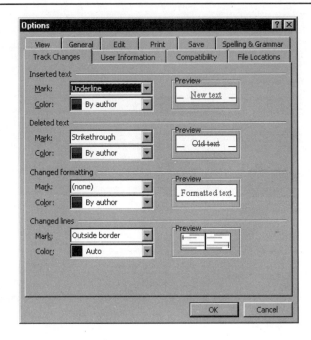

The User Information Tab

Use the User Information tab, shown in Figure 3.12, to enter or change the user information Word uses for various templates and automated documents. This includes your name, initials, and address.

FIGURE 3.12
Enter your name, initials, and address in the User Information tab.

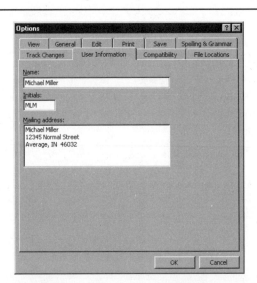

The Compatibility Tab

The Compatibility tab, shown in Figure 3.13, is where you configure Word 2000 to work with older versions and other word processing programs. You can select preset combinations of options for specific programs (from the Recommended Options For list), turn on or off specific program operations (from the Options list), and select which fonts should be used when specified fonts aren't available (by clicking the Font Substitution button).

FIGURE 3.13
Configure Word to work with other programs from the Compatibility tab.

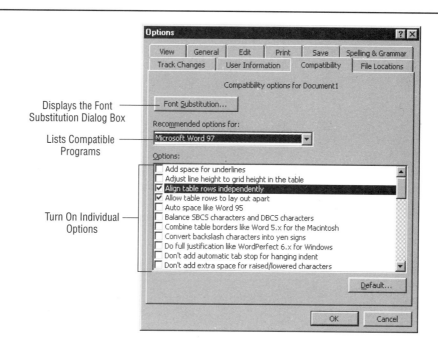

Displays the Font Substitution Dialog Box

Lists Compatible Programs

Turn On Individual Options

NOTE To learn more about configuring Word 2000's compatibility with other programs, see Chapter 2.

The File Locations Tab

The File Locations tab, shown in Figure 3.14, is used to instruct Word where to look for specific types of files. In particular, you can set default file locations for documents, clip-art pictures, user templates, workgroup templates, user options, AutoRecover files, tools, and Word's startup files.

FIGURE 3.14
*Specify default locations
for Word files from the
File Locations tab.*

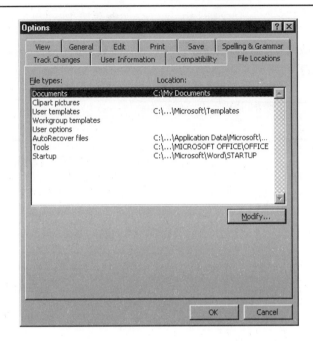

To change a file location, select the file type, and click the Modify button. When the Modify Location dialog box appears, select a new location, and click OK.

Customizing Word's Appearance

Just about any element you see in the Word 2000 workspace can be moved, modified, or deleted. Want your menu bar at the bottom of the screen? No problem. Want to float the Drawing toolbar off to the side? Piece of cake. Want to show every single format mark in your document—paragraph marks, line breaks, you name it? It's doable.

Read on to discover how to turn the default Word workspace into *your* personal workspace.

Configuring Your Personal Workspace

There are a number of changes you can make to the Word 2000 workspace. Most of these changes are made from either the Customize (select Tools ➤ Customize) or the Options (select Tools ➤ Options) dialog boxes.

MASTERING THE OPPORTUNITIES

Customizing on a Corporate Scale

Microsoft offers a variety of tools to help corporations customize their Word 2000 (and Office 2000) installations. Most of these tools are contained within the Microsoft Office 2000 Resource Kit, which is a collection of information, tools, and utilities for corporate deployment.

The following items of interest to Word 2000 users and system administrators are among the many tools and utilities in the Office 2000 Resource Kit:

- Custom Installation Wizard
- Language Version
- Profile Wizard
- Removal Wizard
- Answer Wizard Builder
- Microsoft Office Converter Pack
- MultiLanguage Pack Support Files

With these tools, corporate system administrators can manage and customize the installation of Word 2000 across the entire organization and set up custom user profiles so that similar Word features and components are available to all users.

You can find out more about the Office 2000 Resource Kit—and download the kit itself—at www.microsoft.com/office/ork/.

Displaying or Hiding Screen Elements

Word 2000 lets you display or hide a number of different screen elements, such as scroll bars and rulers. Here are some of the changes you can make:

Hide Horizontal and Vertical Scroll Bars By default, Word 2000 displays both a horizontal and a vertical scroll bar for on-screen scrolling in either direction. If you'd rather not display the scroll bars (you seldom need to scroll back and forth across a document), go the View tab in the Options dialog box, and uncheck the Horizontal Scroll Bar and/or the Vertical Scroll Bar options.

WARNING Since the horizontal scroll bar, at the bottom of the screen, also contains the four View buttons, you won't be able to change views with the click of a button if you turn off this toolbar.

Display a Vertical Ruler By default, Word 2000 displays a horizontal ruler for setting tabs and margins in documents. You can turn on a similar vertical ruler in Word's Print Layout view by accessing the View tab in the Options dialog box and then checking the Vertical Ruler option.

 TIP If you want to hide all rulers, pull down the View menu, and uncheck the Ruler option.

Hide the Status Bar If you never use the Status bar and want to free up some screen space, go to the View tab in the Options dialog box, and uncheck the Status Bar option.

Turn Off ScreenTips By default, Word 2000 displays a pop-up ScreenTip when you hover your cursor over any screen element. If you'd rather not see these informative-yet-sometimes-annoying tips, go to the View tab in the Options dialog box, and uncheck the ScreenTips option.

 TIP You can turn off the ScreenTips for Word's toolbars by opening the Customize dialog box, selecting the Options tab, and unchecking the Show ScreenTips on Toolbars option. Alternatively, the toolbar ScreenTips will display the corresponding shortcut keys if you check the Show Shortcut Keys in ScreenTips option.

Hide Animated Text Word 2000 enables you to create documents that, when viewed onscreen, contain text with animation effects. If you'd rather not be annoyed by these text effects, go to the View tab in the Options dialog box, and uncheck the Animated Text option.

Show Bookmarks If you want to view the location of bookmarks you've added to your documents, go to the View tab in the Options dialog box, and check the Bookmarks option.

Display Placeholders instead of Pictures If a document contains a lot of graphics, it may take a long time and lots of computer memory to display all these pictures onscreen. For a faster-loading document, you can hide the pictures and display placeholders (gray boxes) instead. To activate the placeholder option, go to the View tab in the Options dialog box, and check the Picture Placeholders option.

Show Text Highlighting   Highlighting text with a background color (as you would mark paper with a yellow text highlighter) is a good way to draw attention to specific passages in a document. If you end up with too much highlighting or just want to display a clean, unhighlighted document, however, go to the View tab in the Options dialog box, and uncheck the Highlight option.

Show All Field Codes   When you insert certain preformatted elements into your documents, such as page numbers or day and date information, what you're really inserting is a Word *field*. By default, you see the result of the field (the calculated page number, or today's date, for example), not the code within the field itself. If you want to see the underlying field codes, go to the View tab in the Options dialog box, and check the Field Codes option.

 NOTE   To learn more about Word field codes, refer to Chapter 12.

Configure Field Shading   If you prefer to see the results of your inserted fields but also want to identify where your field codes are located without actually displaying them, you can turn on *field shading*. This option shades all field results, which makes it easy to search for and find the fields within a document. To activate field shading, go to the View tab in the Options dialog box, pull down the Field Shading list, and select Always. (This shading only appears onscreen; your documents print without the shading.)

Displaying Formatting Marks

Underlying every Word document is a series of hidden codes that activate various formatting features. Word uses codes for tabs, spaces, paragraph marks, hidden text, and optional hyphens within words. Normally, you don't see these codes, and you probably don't want to see the codes in most instances. But if you're having trouble with the way a document is formatting—odd page breaks, weird spacing between characters, and so on—chances are your problems are caused by some extra formatting characters. To find these problem characters, you have to make them visible.

 NOTE   Formatting marks are only visible onscreen; they do not appear on your printed documents.

The Word document in Figure 3.15 is shown with all formatting marks displayed. As you can see, marks are displayed for every space on your screen—for the spaces between words and paragraphs. With all formatting marks visible, it's easy to find any extra spaces between words, or stray paragraph marks.

FIGURE 3.15
Use visible formatting marks to view all the spaces and breaks within a document.

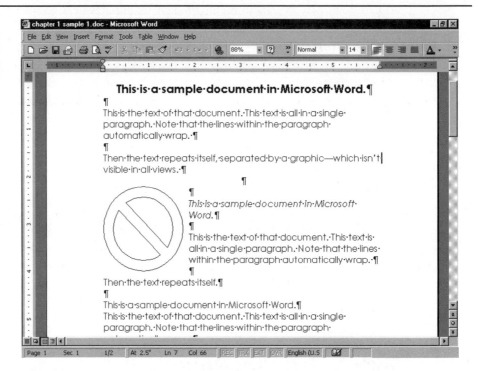

Turn on Word's formatting marks by accessing the View tab in the Options dialog box and then checking the marks you wish to display. If you want to see *all* formatting marks, check the All option. (And remember to turn off the formatting marks when you want to view your documents normally again!)

You can also turn on Word's formatting marks by clicking the Show/Hide button on Word's Standard toolbar. Clicking this button toggles on and off the display of paragraph and other formatting marks in the current document.

TIP If you're a longtime WordPerfect user, you're used to seeing character marks onscreen. To make the Word interface resemble your old WordPerfect interface more, you may want to turn on some or all of Word's formatting marks.

Displaying or Hiding Objects in Word's Layout Views

Word 2000 enables you to customize, to some degree, what you see onscreen in its Print Layout and Web Layout views. When you go to the View tab in the Options dialog box, you have the option of displaying or not displaying the following items in your documents:

Drawings   Check this option to display all objects created with Word's drawing tools; uncheck to hide all drawings. *Not* displaying drawings can speed up the display of your documents onscreen.

Object Anchors   Check this option to display the anchors within your text that indicate the placement of inserted objects.

Text Boundaries   Check this option to show all text boundaries onscreen, including margins and graphics boundaries, as shown in Figure 3.16.

Vertical Ruler   Check this option to display a vertical ruler (in Print Layout view only).

FIGURE 3.16
Display Word's text boundaries to better judge the layout of your text.

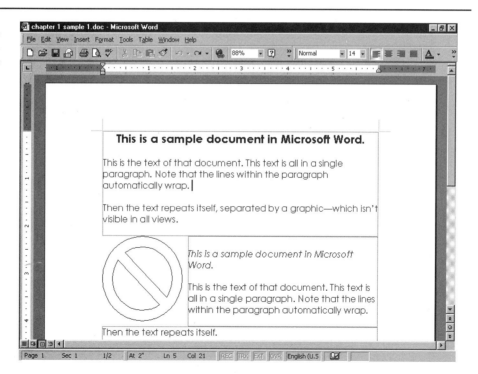

Configuring the Screen for Word's Non-Layout Views

You can also configure how Word looks when you're using either Normal or Outline view. When you access the View tab in the Options dialog box, you can configure your display in the following manner:

Let Your Text Fill the Screen Width   By default, text in the Normal and Outline views extends only as far as the normal page margin. Since you're probably not really desktop publishing in these views, however, there's no reason to limit the text to this width. When you check the Wrap to Window option, your text will extend to the right edge of your Word window, however wide the window is.

Use a Faster Font   By default, text in the Normal and Outline views displays using the font(s) chosen when you formatted the document. If you're only interested in what you typed and not how it looks, you can speed up the screen display by using the standard draft font (Courier) for all your on-screen text, as shown in Figure 3.17. Just check the Draft Font option.

FIGURE 3.17
Ugly but fast: Word's Normal view with the Draft Font and Wrap to Window options selected and the Style area displayed

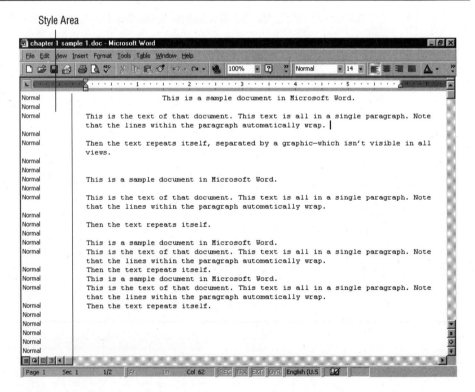

WARNING When you choose the Draft Font option, you can't view any text formatting, including boldface and italics.

Customize the Style Area   When you're in either Normal or Outline view, the selected style for each paragraph can be displayed in a Style area on the left side of the screen. To turn on or change the width of the Style area, select a setting from the Style Area Width list. (If the Style area is visible, you can also use your mouse to drag the area border to a different size.)

 TIP To hide the Style area, enter a width of 0 for Style Area Width.

Working with a Blue Screen

If you've been using word processing programs so long that you remember the DOS days when text was displayed as white type against a blue screen and you long for the look of those WordStar and WordPerfect screens, you're in luck. Word 2000 lets you switch from the standard black-on-white display to a white-on-blue display, just like you had in the old days. To switch to a blue screen display, go to the Options dialog box, select the General tab, and check Blue Background, White Text. With this option selected, your screen will look like the one in Figure 3.18, except yours will be in color, of course.

FIGURE 3.18
Word 2000 with a white-on-blue display for that old-timey word processor look

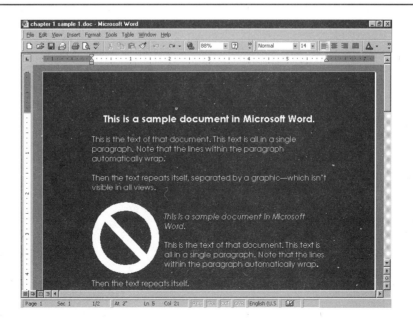

MASTERING THE OPPORTUNITIES

Make Word 2000 Look like Word 97

Every time a program updates to a new version, the look and feel is bound to change to some degree. It should be no surprise, then, that the Word 2000 interface differs slightly from the Word 97 interface.

If you want to get your Word 97 interface back, however, there are a few things you can do. Begin by selecting Tools ➤ Customize to display the Customize dialog box, and then click the Options tab. Uncheck the Standard and Formatting Toolbars Share One Row option, and uncheck the Menus Show Recently Used Commands First option.

Deselecting these options gives you a single row of toolbars underneath the menu bar and turns off the annoying personalized menu function, both of which help to make Word 2000 look a little more like Word 97.

Configuring Your Toolbars

Clicking a button on a toolbar is one of the fastest ways to get something done in Word. While the Standard and Formatting toolbars—the two default toolbars—contain some of the most-used Word commands, there are times when you want to have some of Word's other toolbars visible on your Desktop. And once you get three or more toolbars on your Desktop, you probably want to position them in a way that best suits your work. You might even start to wish for some toolbars of your own design— toolbars that contain just the right combination of commands for your own particular type of work.

Fortunately, Word lets you customize toolbars in just about every way imaginable. Read on to learn how to move, dock, customize, and create your own custom toolbars.

Hiding and Displaying Toolbars

Word 2000 includes 16 built-in toolbars, any or all of which can be displayed onscreen at the same time. There are two ways to select which toolbars are displayed or hidden on your Desktop:

- Select Tools ➤ Customize to display the Customize dialog box. Select the Toolbars tab, check those toolbars you wish to display, uncheck those you wish to hide, and then click Close.

- Right-click anywhere on any visible toolbar or menu bar; this displays a list of all available toolbars. Check the toolbars you wish to display, and uncheck those you wish to hide.

The toolbars you select to display will remain on your desktop until you select a different combination, even through multiple Word sessions.

Moving and Docking Toolbars

Any Word 2000 toolbar can be placed anywhere on your screen. Toolbars can float in windows above the Word workspace, or they can be "docked" to any of the four sides of the screen.

You move a toolbar by grabbing its title bar with your mouse and dragging it to a new location; release your mouse button to drop the toolbar into position.

If you drag a toolbar all the way to the edge of the screen, the toolbar automatically docks itself to the side. To undock or move a docked toolbar, grab the thick bar at the far left (if docked at the top or bottom) or the top (if docked on either side) of the toolbar and drag the toolbar to a new position.

Some toolbars take on slightly different appearances depending on where they're positioned or docked. For example, the Formatting toolbar looks like this when docked in its normal position at the top of the screen:

The same toolbar looks like this when docked at the side of the screen:

Note that the former pull-down lists for styles, fonts, font sizes, and zooming are now simple buttons that, when clicked, display Style, Font, Font Size, and Zoom dialog boxes.

If you grab the Formatting toolbar and drag it to the center of the screen, it appears as a floating window. In this configuration, the pull-down lists are pull-down lists again:

 TIP If a docked toolbar has more buttons than can be displayed in the available space, a "more" arrow appears on the More Buttons button at the end of the toolbar. Click the "more" arrow to display a list of the hidden buttons.

Adding and Removing Toolbar Buttons

You don't have to settle for Word's default toolbar configurations; you can add and remove buttons to and from any Word toolbar. This is so easy to do, and Word provides two ways to do it.

The toolbar editing method familiar to experienced Word users uses tabs in the Customize dialog box. To add and remove toolbar buttons from the Customize dialog box, follow these steps:

 NOTE To use the Customize dialog box method, you first must display the toolbar(s) you want to edit.

1. Select Tools ➢ Customize to display the Customize dialog box.

2. To remove a button from any visible toolbar, use your mouse to drag the button off the toolbar. (After you've dragged it off the toolbar, drop it anywhere—it automatically vanishes!)

   To add a button to any visible toolbar, select the Commands tab in the Customize dialog box, select a category from the Category list, select a command from the Commands list, and then use your mouse to drag the command from dialog box onto the toolbar.

3. Click Close when done.

 TIP To view a description of any command in the Customize dialog box, select the command, and click the Description button.

This method can also be used to rearrange toolbar buttons. While the Customize dialog box is displayed, use your mouse to drag a button from one location to another within the same toolbar. You can also drag buttons from one toolbar to another while the Customize dialog box is open.

 TIP To reset any toolbar to its original, unedited state, open the Customize dialog box, and select the Toolbars tab. Select the toolbar you want to restore, and then click the Reset button. Alternatively, you can click the More Buttons button on any toolbar, select the Add or Remove Buttons command, and then select Reset from the drop-down list.

 New to Word 2000 is the ability to add and remove toolbar buttons directly from the toolbar without first opening the Customize dialog box. To edit a toolbar in place, follow these steps:

1. Click the More Buttons button, found at the far-right side or the bottom of a docked toolbar or on the left of the title bar of a floating toolbar, to display the pop-up menu.

2. Select Add or Remove Buttons from the pop-up menu.

3. When the list of available buttons for this specific toolbar appears, check the buttons you wish to display, and uncheck those you wish to remove.

4. To add buttons not found on the drop-down list, select Customize to display the Customize dialog box, and add new buttons from the Commands tab.

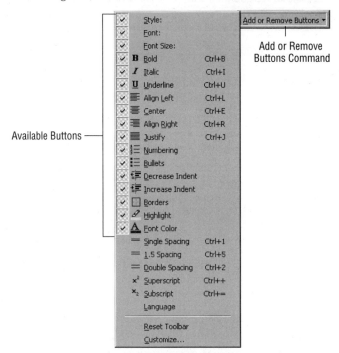

The main limitation to this in-place toolbar editing is that you can only select from those buttons listed, which, theoretically, are the most common commands for that particular toolbar operation. If you want to add buttons not found on the drop-down list, you need to use the preceding Customize dialog box editing method.

Adding Pull-Down Menus to Toolbars

Some of the commands you can add to a toolbar are actually pull-down menus. A pull-down menu command is indicated in the Command list by an arrow at the far right of the command label.

You add a menu to a toolbar as you would add any command. The difference is, after the menu has been added, that it appears as a pull-down menu (when the toolbar is docked) and behaves as any menu found on the menu bar. Remember, however, that when a toolbar is undocked (floating on the workspace), menus don't always pull down; sometimes they appear as regular buttons and display dialog boxes when clicked.

Grouping Buttons on a Toolbar

You can group the buttons on a toolbar by adding divider lines between selected buttons. Using divider lines is a good way to group like items together, which, especially on crowded toolbars, helps you identify particular types of commands.

To add a divider line and, thus, begin a new group on the toolbar, follow these steps:

1. Select Tools ➤ Customize to open the Customize dialog box.
2. Select the Commands tab.
3. Keeping the Customize dialog box open, move your cursor to the toolbar you want to edit, and click the button that will start your new group.
4. Return to the Customize dialog box, and click the Modify Selection button.
5. When the pop-up menu appears, select Begin a Group.

Word now inserts a divider line in front of the button you selected, creating a new button group on your toolbar.

Changing the Way Buttons Are Displayed

Once you place your buttons, you can modify the way they look in a number of ways. All modification is done from the Customize dialog box by following these steps:

1. Select Tools ➤ Customize to open the Customize dialog box.
2. Select the Commands tab.
3. Keeping the Customize dialog box open, move your cursor to the toolbar you want to edit, and click the button you want to modify.
4. Return to the Customize dialog box, and click the Modify Selection button.
5. When the pop-up menu appears, select the option you wish to apply.

 TIP Another way to display this menu is to open the Customize dialog box and right-click the button you want to modify.

From this menu, you can choose to display the button in one of several ways:

Default   As determined by Word 2000.

Text Only (Always)   Hides the button image and displays the button label only.

Text Only (Menus)   Hides the button image and displays only the label, but only when the toolbar is docked; the image is still displayed when the toolbar is floating.

Image and Text   Displays both the graphic image and the button label.

Changing and Editing Button Images

Don't like the image associated with a particular button? Then change it!

Word 2000 presents several options for changing button images, all of which are available from the Modify Selection button/menu on the Commands tab of the Customize dialog box:

Choose from a Preselected List of Images   Select the desired button, and then select Change Button Image from the menu to display a list of 42 button images. (This is the easiest way to assign an image to a button command that doesn't have an associated graphic image.)

Copy an Image from Another Button   Select the button image you want to copy, and then select Copy Button Image from the Modify Selection menu. Now select the button you want to change, and select Paste Button Image from the menu. This duplicates the first image onto the second button.

 TIP   To restore the original image to any button, select the button, and then select Reset Button Image from the Modify Selection menu.

Edit an Existing Image   This is the most involved option of the three listed here but is the one sure way to create a unique image for any toolbar button. Select the button whose image you want to change, and select Edit Button Image from the menu. This displays the Button Editor window, shown in Figure 3.19. Then edit or draw your new button in the Picture area, block by block, with your cursor. You can select different colors from the Color chooser and use the arrow keys to move your entire image within the button area. Your button-in-process is displayed in the Preview area. Click Clear to clear the image area, and click OK when you're done.

FIGURE 3.19
*Use the Button Editor to
create custom button
images.*

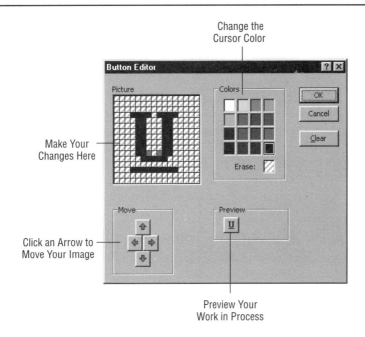

Change the
Cursor Color

Make Your
Changes Here

Click an Arrow to
Move Your Image

Preview Your
Work in Process

Assigning a Hyperlink to a Button

You can assign a Web page or e-mail address hyperlink to any button on any toolbar.
Just follow these steps:

1. Select Tools ➢ Customize to open the Customize dialog box.

2. Select the Commands tab.

3. Keeping the Customize dialog box open, move your cursor to the toolbar you
   want to edit, and click the button you want to modify.

4. Return to the Customize dialog box, and click the Modify Selection button.

5. When the pop-up menu appears, select Assign Hyperlink ➢ Open.

6. When the Assign Hyperlink: Open dialog box appears, enter the address of the hyperlink in the Type the File or Web Page Name box, and then click OK.

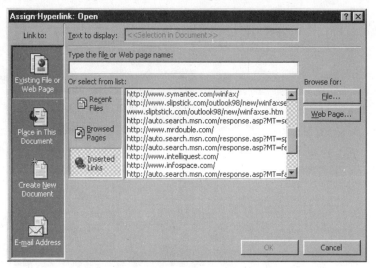

Once a hyperlink is assigned, the Assign Hyperlink command changes to the Edit Hyperlink command. To remove a hyperlink from a button, select Edit Hyperlink ➢ Remove Link.

Creating New Toolbars

Editing existing toolbars gets you only so far. For total control of your toolbar environment, you'll want to create your own custom toolbars. For example, you might want to create a toolbar that contains the styles used in a particular Word template, or one that includes special editing commands you use for a specific job.

To create a new toolbar, follow these steps:

1. Select Tools ➢ Customize to display the Customize dialog box.

2. Select the Toolbars tab.

3. Click the New button.

4. When the New Toolbar dialog box appears, enter the new toolbar's name in the Toolbar Name box.

5. Select which template(s) this toolbar is assigned to from the Make Toolbar Available To pull-down list.

6. Click OK.

Your new, empty toolbar now appears, floating on top of the Word workspace. Use the skills presented earlier in this chapter to add new buttons to this toolbar, and create something new and truly unique!

Configuring Your Menus

In Word 2000, pull-down menus are just one kind of element you can add to any toolbar. In fact, the menu bar is just another toolbar, capable of being hidden, displayed, or moved, as you would any other toolbar, which means you can use most of Word's toolbar customization options to modify your menus as well.

Moving the Menu Bar

You're probably used to Word's pull-down menus being located in the menu bar located at the very top of the Word workspace, above the Standard and the Formatting toolbars and below the Word title bar. In Word 2000, however, the menu bar is a type of toolbar and, thus, can be moved anywhere on your screen.

To move the menu bar, grab the thick bar at the far left (beside the File menu), and drag the entire menu bar to a new location. If you drag it to the bottom or either side of the Word workspace, the menu bar will dock with the edge of the workspace. If you drop the menu in the middle of the workspace, it will appear as a floating window on top of the workspace.

Grab Here to Move
the Menu Bar

 TIP To hide the menu bar, go to the Toolbars tab in the Customize dialog box, and uncheck the Menu Bar option. Repeat this procedure but check the Menu Bar option to redisplay the menu bar.

Adding Items to the Menu Bar

You can add new menus and commands to the menu bar as you would add items to any toolbar. Just follow these steps:

1. Select Tools ➢ Customize to display the Customize dialog box.

2. Select the Commands tab.

3. Select a category from the Category list, select a menu or command from the Command list, and then use your mouse to drag the selected item from the dialog box onto the menu bar.

4. Click Close when done.

To remove an item from the menu bar, open the Customize dialog box, and then drag the item off the menu bar.

Rearranging Items on a Pull-Down Menu

If you don't like the order in which commands appear on a pull-down menu, you can rearrange them. Just follow these steps:

1. Select Tools ➤ Customize to display the Customize menu.
2. Pull down the menu you wish to rearrange.
3. Grab the command you wish to move, and drag it to a new position.

While the Customize dialog box is open, you can also drag a command completely off a menu, which removes the command from the menu, or drag commands from one menu to another.

Managing Personalized Menus

By default, Word 2000's menus display only those commands you've recently used. This new feature, designed to simplify Word's admittedly complex menu system, is called *personalized menus*.

If you'd rather see all the commands all the time for all of Word's menus, you can turn off the personalized menus. To do this, follow these steps:

1. Select Tools ➤ Customize.
2. When the Customize dialog box appears, select the Options tab.
3. Uncheck the Menus Show Recently Used Commands First option.
4. Click OK.

If you want to use the personalized menus feature but occasionally want to view all the commands on a specific menu, you have two options:

- Click the down arrow at the bottom of any "short" menu; this causes the menu to expand to show *all* available commands for that menu.
- Open the Customize dialog box, select the Options tab, and check the Show Full Menus After a Short Delay option. With this option selected, any "short" menu will expand into a "long" menu when you hold the menu open for a few seconds.

 TIP To reset the recently viewed commands on Word's personalized menus, go to the Options tab of the Customize dialog box, and click the Reset My Usage Data button.

Configuring Your Keyboard Shortcuts

Word 2000 comes with more than 100 different commands and operations assigned to shortcut key combinations. By pressing the assigned key combination, you can activate the command or operation directly from the keyboard. This is extremely useful if you have a frequently used operation that's buried deep within Word's menu system or if you're just more comfortable pressing keys than you are clicking mouse buttons.

 TIP To print a list of all Word shortcut keys and menu commands, select Tools ➤ Macro ➤ Macros. When the Macros dialog box appears, pull down the Macros In list, select Word Commands, pull down the Macro Name list, select ListCommands, and then click Run. Word now generates a document listing all commands, which you can print for your personal use.

You can edit any of these shortcut key assignments, as well as assign other commands and operations to new shortcut keys. Just follow these steps:

1. Select Tools ➤ Customize to display the Customize dialog box.

2. From any tab, click the Keyboard button.

3. When the Customize Keyboard dialog box appears, select a category from the Category list, and then select a specific command or operation from the Command list.

 TIP If there is already a shortcut assigned to this command or operation, the key(s) for that shortcut will appear in the Current Keys box. You can assign more than one shortcut key combination to any single command or operation.

4. Move your cursor to the Press New Shortcut Key box, and press the key combination you wish to use for this shortcut.

5. Select a document or template from the Save Changes To list; this will be where the shortcut is stored.

6. Click the Assign key to assign this command/operation to the selected key(s).

 WARNING If you attempt to use a shortcut key combination that is already assigned to another command or operation, your new assignment will replace the previous assignment.

You can also assign styles, symbols, macros, fonts, and AutoText entries to shortcut keys. Just scroll down to the bottom of the Categories list to see which of these items are available for shortcut key assignment.

To remove shortcut keys from a command or operation, select the command, and click the Remove button. To reset all shortcut keys to their original assignments, click the Reset All button.

Customizing How Word Works

Not only can you customize how Word 2000 looks onscreen but you can also customize (to some degree) how Word 2000 actually works. In particular, you can configure certain editing, proofing, printing, and Internet-related options, as discussed in the next sections of this chapter. Most of these options are configured via tabs in the Options dialog box (accessible by selecting Tools ➢ Options).

Configuring Your User Information

When you first install Word 2000, you are prompted to enter a few bits of personal information: your name, initials, and address. (If you upgraded from a previous version of Word, this information was probably entered automatically during a previous install.) This information is used both to identify your documents and as default information for certain templates and Wizards.

You can change your user information by following these steps:

1. Select Tools ➢ Options to display the Options dialog box.

2. Select the User Information tab.

3. Edit or enter the appropriate information.

4. Click OK.

Configuring Your Editing Options

Certain of Word 2000's editing operations can be personalized for your own desired usage. All of these options are found on various tabs in the Options dialog box.

Managing General Editing Options

Word 2000 lets you configure a variety of general editing options. Here are some of the editing operations you can configure from the Edit tab in the Options dialog box:

Enter Text Anywhere Word 2000's new Click and Type feature lets you add freestanding text anywhere in your document just by double-clicking any empty space. To activate this feature, check the Enable Click and Type option. You can also select the default paragraph style to be used by all Click and Type text.

Type Over Existing Text   By default, anything new you type is added to your existing text. (This is called the Insert mode.) However, Word 2000 lets you toggle to Overtype mode (where what you type replaces any text already on your page) in one of three ways. First, you can check the Typing Replaces Selection option on the Edit tab in the Options dialog box. Second, you can double-click the OVR section on Word's Status bar. Third, you can press the Insert key on your keyboard. These last two methods let you quickly toggle between Insert and Overtype modes.

Paste Text with the Insert Key   Normally, your keyboard's Insert key is used to toggle between Insert and Overtype modes, as just described. However, you can configure Word to use this key as a shortcut key for pasting any cut or copied text. To enable pasting via the Insert key, check the Use the INS Key for Paste option.

Select Part of a Word, Select the Whole Word   For faster editing, you can configure Word to select the entire word (and its trailing space) when you drag your cursor over just part of the word. To activate this feature, choose the When Selecting, Automatically Select Entire Word option.

Move Text with Your Mouse   By default, Word lets you highlight a block of text with your mouse and then drag and drop it in a new location. This drag-and-drop editing can be turned off by unchecking the Drag-and-Drop Text Editing option.

Automatically Adjust Spacing while Cutting and Pasting   You can configure Word to intelligently adjust the spacing around any text you cut from or paste into your documents. To activate this feature, check the Use Smart Cut and Paste option.

Adjust Indents from the Keyboard   Normally, you'd set a document's left-paragraph indent from either the vertical ruler or from the Paragraph dialog box (accessible when you select Format ➤ Paragraph). If you prefer to set this indent from your keyboard, configure Word so that pressing Tab (when your cursor is positioned at the beginning of a paragraph) moves the indent in by half an inch and pressing Backspace moves the indent out by the same amount. To activate this feature, check the Tabs and Backspace Set Left Indent option.

Allow French Formatting   For Word to allow the proper accenting for French words and documents, check the Allow Accented Uppercase in French option.

Other general editing options are available from the General tab of the Options dialog box. Here are the operations you can manage from this location:

Prepare Documents When Opened   Word 2000 provides two settings that better prepare your documents when they are first opened. Check the Confirm

Conversion at Open option if you want to manually select the conversion tool when opening text in a non-Word format; uncheck this option to have Word automatically select the correct converter. Check the Update Automatic Links at Open option to have Word automatically update any links to other documents.

Repaginate Automatically   To automatically repaginate documents as you add and delete text, check the Background Repagination option.

 NOTE   When you work in Print Layout view, background repagination occurs automatically.

Provide Feedback for Program Events   Word provides feedback when certain program events occur, such as when initiating printing or opening a dialog box. To activate system sounds for these events, check the Provide Feedback with Sound option; to activate animated cursors during these events, check the Provide Feedback with Animation option.

Control the Number of Recently Used Files Listed   When you pull down Word's File menu, you see a list of the most-recently used files. You can control the size of this list (from zero to nine entries) by selecting a number from the Recently Used File List control.

Activate WordPerfect Help   If you're an ex-WordPerfect user, you can turn on two features that should help ease the transition to Word 2000. Check the Help for WordPerfect Users option to activate a special WordPerfect Help system, or check the Navigation for WordPerfect Users option to make certain Word keys perform like their WordPerfect equivalents.

 NOTE   To learn more about Word 2000's options for WordPerfect users, see Chapter 2.

Managing the Track Changes Feature

Word's Track Changes feature lets you keep track of all changes made to a document, especially when edited by multiple users. You manage the configuration for this feature from the Track Changes tab in the Options dialog box.

Every editor of a document can select how he or she wants their editing marks to appear in the document. Use this tab to configure the color and style used to mark the following types of revisions:

- Inserted text
- Deleted text

- Changed formatting
- Changed lines

Just pull down the appropriate lists to make your selection. Your choice of styles and colors are displayed in the Preview areas next to each type of mark.

 TIP You can also control some of Word's editing operations via the use of preformatted templates, add-in components, and automated macros. For example, you can configure a template to automatically display custom toolbars and menus that provide access to a selected or restricted set of operations and styles. To learn more about these powerful features, see Chapter 27 and Chapter 29.

Configuring Your Proofing Options

Word 2000 includes a host of proofing tools, from simple spell checking to on-the-fly proofing with AutoCorrect. The following sections detail these proofing options, including how to configure each one.

 NOTE To learn more about Word's proofing tools, see Chapter 6.

Managing Spell Checking

You manage Word's spell checking options from the Spelling & Grammar tab in the Options dialog box; from here, you can configure the following features:

Spell Check as You Go—or Not To have Word spell check words as you type, flagging misspelled words with a red squiggly underline, check the Check Spelling as You Type feature. If you're annoyed by this constant nagging and would rather spell check your document in one fell swoop, uncheck this option. If you want to spell check as you go but don't want to see the squiggly red lines (or don't want *others* to see them!), check the Hide Spelling Errors in This Document option.

Choose Which Words to Ignore Just because a word isn't in Word's dictionary doesn't mean it's misspelled. Many specialty words and proper nouns that aren't included in the dictionary will be flagged as misspelled unless you configure Word to ignore them while spell checking. To have Word ignore certain types of words while spell checking, take your pick of the following options: Ignore Words in UPPERCASE, Ignore Words with Numbers, and Ignore Internet and File Addresses.

Display Suggested Spellings   When you perform a batch spell check, Word displays by default a list of suggested spellings for each misspelling it finds. You can turn off this feature by unchecking the Always Suggest Corrections option. Also by default, Word gets its suggestions from a combination of the main Word dictionary and the custom dictionaries you create. If you only want to display suggestions from the main dictionary, check the Suggest From Main Dictionary Only option.

Choose Your Dictionary   Word enables you to create any number of custom spelling dictionaries. You can select which custom dictionaries you want to use from the Custom Dictionary list, or manage your custom dictionaries by clicking the Dictionaries button to display the Custom Dictionaries dialog box.

Managing Grammar Checking

Word 2000 includes an advanced grammar checking utility that parses and analyzes your sentences and suggests grammatical corrections and improvements. You can configure a number of settings for the grammar checker from the Spelling & Grammar tab in the Options dialog box, including:

Grammar Check as You Go—or Not   To have Word check the grammar in your document as you type, check the Check Grammar as You Type feature. If you'd rather have Word check your grammar when you're finished writing, uncheck this option. If you want to check your grammar as you go but don't want to display the squiggly green lines left by the grammar checker, check the Hide Grammatical Errors in This Document option. To check your grammar and spelling in a single operation, check the Check Grammar with Spelling option.

Hide the Readability Statistics   By default, Word displays a dialog box of readability statistics when it's done checking your grammar. To hide this dialog box, uncheck the Show Readability Statistics option.

Set Your Style   Word's grammar checker applies different grammar rules depending on the particular writing style you're using. For example, grammar is less strict in the Casual style than it is in the Formal or the Technical styles. To set your style, select an option from the Writing Style list. To fine-tune the rules in any selected style, click the Settings button to display the Grammar Settings dialog box.

 TIP   To recheck your document's spelling and grammar after you've changed any of these options, click the Check Document button on the Spelling & Grammar tab of the Options dialog box.

Managing Hyphenation

Word uses various rules to control how it hyphenates words that have to be split between two lines. Access these rules by selecting Tools ➤ Language ➤ Hyphenation to display the Hyphenation dialog box.

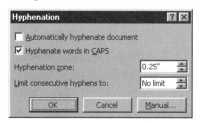

To activate Word's automatic hyphenation feature, check the Automatically Hyphenate Document option. If you don't use automatic hyphenation, no words will be hyphenated unless you manually do so.

To manually hyphenate a word, highlight the word, open the Hyphenation dialog box, and click the Manual button. When the Manual Hyphenation dialog box appears, the recommended hyphenation for that word is displayed with the breaking hyphen highlighted. You can change the breaking hyphen by selecting another hyphen within the word, or force the word *not* to be hyphenated by clicking the No button; click Yes when done.

 NOTE If you click the Manual button *without* first highlighting a word, you will be taken to the first word in the document that needs to be hyphenated, then the next, and so on through the entire document.

When you use automatic hyphenation, there are several settings you can configure:

Hyphenate Words in CAPS   Uncheck this option if you don't want words that are typed entirely in capital letters (typically proper nouns, product or company names, and acronyms) split between lines.

Hyphenation Zone   This setting determines how far in from the right margin you want to hyphenate your document. Select a wider zone to minimize the number of hyphenated words; select a narrower zone to decrease raggedness along the right margin.

Limit Consecutive Hyphens To...   This setting determines the number of consecutive lines that can contain hyphenated words.

Managing AutoCorrect

AutoCorrect is a Word feature that, when activated, corrects a variety of typing mistakes in real time; you make the mistake, and then Word automatically corrects it.

Turn on and off the types of mistakes you want corrected from the AutoCorrect tab in the AutoCorrect dialog box. (Select Tools ➤ AutoCorrect, and then select the Auto-Correct tab.)

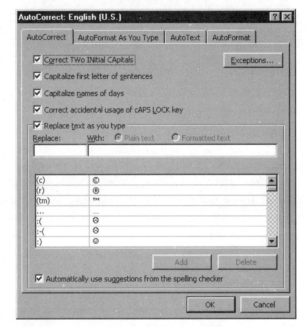

Here are some of the typos you can choose to AutoCorrect:

- Correct TWo INitial CApitals
- Capitalize first letter of sentences
- Capitalize names of days
- Correct accidental use of cAPS LOCK key

In addition, you can choose to have AutoCorrect automatically replace certain words or keystrokes with other words or symbols as you type. For example, with this option activated, any time you type **(c)**, Word will replace it with ©, the proper copyright symbol. You can also add to the list of replacement text, as desired.

Managing AutoFormat

Word 2000's AutoFormat feature automatically applies to your documents certain types of formatting, such as headings, bulleted lists, numbered lists, borders, symbols, and so on. You can choose to run AutoFormat as you type or after your writing is finished.

To configure AutoFormat to run as you type, select Tools ➤ AutoCorrect, and then select the AutoFormat As You Type tab. To configure AutoFormat to run after a document is finished, select the AutoFormat tab.

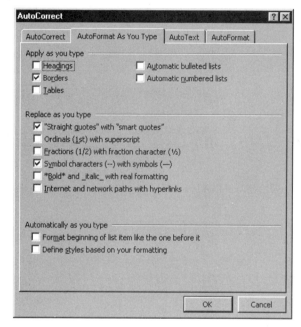

Both of these tabs let you turn on or off similar AutoFormat options, such as:

- Applying headings, borders, tables, and lists
- Replacing straight quotes with smart quotes, fractions with fraction characters, ordinals with superscripts, symbol characters with symbols, and Internet and network paths with hyperlinks
- Automatically formatting lists and defining styles based on formatting
- Preserving styles

To automatically format a document in a single pass, select Format ➤ AutoFormat. When the AutoFormat dialog box appears, select whether you want to AutoFormat

Now (without any user prompts) or AutoFormat and Review Each Change. You can also select a document type to better target the automatic formatting process.

Managing AutoText

The only Word 2000 proofing tool that we have left to discuss is called AutoText. AutoText lets you enter and store snippets of pre-written text, which you can then quickly insert into your documents by selecting Insert ➤ AutoText or by selecting an item from the All Entries button on the AutoText toolbar.

To configure AutoText, select Tools ➤ AutoCorrect to display the AutoCorrect dialog box, and then select the AutoText tab; from here, you can enter new or delete old AutoText text, as well as choose to display or not to display AutoComplete tips when you enter text or dates in your documents.

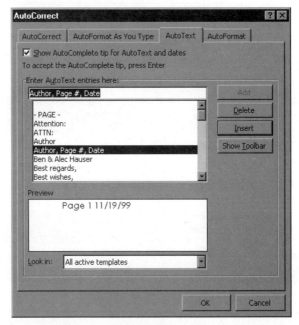

Configuring Your Internet Options

Since Word 2000 adds a variety of Internet-related features, it also adds a number of Internet-related configuration options. In particular, you can configure Word 2000's Web and e-mail settings.

Managing Web Settings

You manage Word 2000's Web-related settings from the Web Options dialog box, accessible by selecting Tools ➢ Options, selecting the General tab, and clicking the Web Options button. This dialog box has five tabs for the following options:

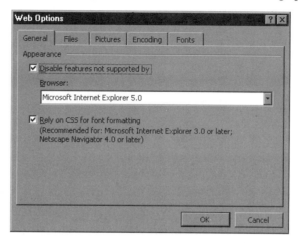

General   Where you can choose to disable features not supported by specific browsers and to use cascading style sheets (CSS) for font formatting.

Files   Where you can choose to organize supporting files in a folder, use long filenames whenever possible, update links when saving files, and check to see if Word and Office are your default Web page editors.

Pictures   Where you can choose to rely on VML to display graphics, allow .PNG as an output format, and set the size of your target monitor when inserting graphics.

Encoding   Where you can set encoding formats for reloading and saving documents.

Fonts   Where you can set your default character set, proportional font, and fixed-width fonts.

 TIP   Most users shouldn't have to change any of Word 2000's Web or e-mail settings, as the default configuration works well on most systems.

Managing E-mail Settings

You manage Word 2000's e-mail–related settings from the E-mail Options dialog box, accessible when you select Tools ➤ Options, select the General tab, and click the E-mail Options button. This dialog box has the two following tabs:

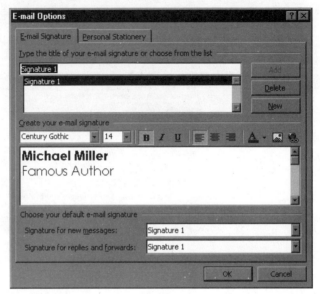

E-mail Signature   Where you create, edit, and format the signature to include with your Word-based e-mail messages.

Personal Stationery   Where you select the themes, stationery, and fonts for new, reply, and forwarded e-mail messages.

Configuring Your Printing Options

Basic options that control how and what Word prints are found on the Print tab of the Options dialog box (select Tools ➤ Options).

Managing General Printing Options

You can control a number of printing operations from the Option dialog box's Print tab, including:

Update Your Documents *before* You Print   You can choose to have Word update all fields and links to other documents before you initiate printing; this way, you can be sure that what you're printing is as up-to-date as possible. Check the Update Fields and Update Links options for optimum freshness.

Print Faster   By default, Word prints all documents with full format. To speed up printing, however, you can choose to have Word print without graphics or all selected fonts; check the Draft Output option to activate. In addition, you can turn off the Word setting that allows documents in the background while other Windows applications run in the foreground, which actually slows down the printing process. To force Word to use all available resources for printing, uncheck the Background Printing option. Finally, another way to speed up printing is to hide all the graphics when you're printing forms; check the Print Data Only for Forms option to speed up forms printing (for your current document only).

Print in Order   By default, Word prints pages in numerical order (1, 2, 3, and so on). If you want to *reverse* the order in which Word prints your document, check the Reverse Print Order option.

Print to the Right Size   Word 2000 includes the capability to automatically resize your document to print on a different size of paper than what you originally specified. To enable this feature, check the Allow A4/Letter Paper Resizing option.

Allow PostScript Effects   If you're using a PostScript printer, you can configure it so that graphics can be printed over text in your documents; check the Print Post-Script Over Text option.

Finally, you can select which default tray to use on your printer by selecting an option from the Default Tray list. When in doubt, select the Use Printer Settings option.

Controlling What Prints with Your Documents

By default, when you print a document, that's all you print—just the document as displayed onscreen. If you choose, however, Word allows you to print some formatting commands that are normally hidden during the printing process. Here are the normally hidden items you can choose to print:

Document Properties   Prints the statistics and summary information for the current document on a separate page at the end of the document.

 TIP   You can display the summary information for your document by selecting File ➢ Properties.

Field Codes   Prints the actual codes, rather than the results, for any fields contained in your document.

Comments   Prints all comments contained in your document on a separate page at the end of the document.

Hidden Text   Prints all normally hidden text in your document.

Drawing Objects   When this option is checked, which it is by default, all drawing objects in your document print as normal. *Uncheck* this option to display gray boxes instead of drawings, thus speeding up the printing process.

 TIP   Additional printer configuration settings can be found in the Print (select File ➢ Print) and Page Setup (select File ➢ Page Setup) dialog boxes and are discussed in Chapter 7.

Configuring Your File Locations

Word looks for specific types of files in specific folders on your computer's hard drive. The following is a list of file types that Word keeps track of:

- Documents
- Clip-art pictures
- User templates
- Workgroup templates
- User options
- AutoRecover files
- Tools
- Startup files

To change the default location for any of these file types, follow these steps:

1. Select Tools ➢ Options to display the Options dialog box.
2. Select the File Locations tab.
3. Select the file type location you want to change.
4. Click the Modify button.
5. When the Modify Location dialog box appears, select a new folder for the selected file type, and then click OK.

Configuring Your Compatibility Options

Word 2000 allows you to turn on or off selected features that affect compatibility with previous versions of Word and with other word processing programs. These compatibility options are found on the Compatibility tab of the Options dialog box (select Tools ➢ Options).

NOTE To learn more about making Word 2000 compatible with other versions and programs, refer to Chapter 2.

Managing Compatibility with a Specific Program

The easiest way to ensure that the documents you create with Word 2000 are fully compatible with other programs is to let Word turn off specific features not found in the other program. To do this, follow these steps:

1. Select Tools ➢ Options to display the Options dialog box.
2. Select the Compatibility tab.
3. Pull down the Recommended Options For list, and select a specific program or previous version of Word; this automatically selects the proper items from the following Options list.
4. Click OK.

Word 2000 has preselected document compatibility settings for the following programs:

- Microsoft Word 6/Word 95
- Microsoft Word 97
- Microsoft Word for MS-DOS
- Microsoft Word for the Macintosh 5.*x*
- Microsoft Word for Windows 1
- Microsoft Word for Windows 2
- WordPerfect 5.*x*
- WordPerfect 6 for DOS
- WordPerfect 6.*x* for Windows

When you select one of these compatibility settings, Word 2000 turns off the features that are not supported by the selected program.

TIP If a specific word processor is not listed in the Recommended Compatibility Options For list, or if you just want to deactivate selected features, you can check individual compatibility options in the Options list.

Managing Font Substitution

You'll sometimes load a document on your machine that was created by someone else, and that document will be formatted with fonts that the other user had installed but that you don't have installed on your machine. When this happens, you need to substitute fonts you have installed for those referenced-but-absent fonts or else the document won't display or print properly.

To manage the font substitution process, follow these steps:

1. Select Tools ➢ Options to display the Options dialog box.

2. Select the Compatibility tab.

3. Click the Font Substitution button.

4. When the Font Substitution dialog box appears, any missing fonts are displayed in the Font Substitutions list. Select the font you need to replace, and then pull down the Substituted Font list to select a replacement. Repeat this step for all missing fonts.

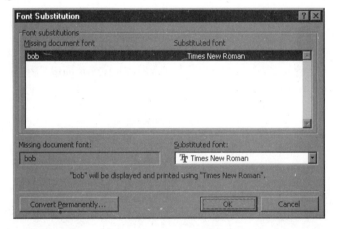

5. To retain the original document formatting and substitute these fonts on your PC only, click OK.

6. To permanently replace all the missing fonts in the document with the substitute fonts, click the Change Permanently button, and then click OK.

 WARNING If you click the Change Permanently button, any other user accessing your copy of the document will see the substituted fonts, not the originals.

CHAPTER 4

Creating, Editing, and Saving Simple Documents

Creating a new document   120

Opening an existing document   127

Entering text with Click and Type   140

Entering text in a text box   141

Entering pre-written text with AutoText   144

Using Collect and Paste   149

Using the Paste Special command   150

Undoing and redoing your editing   152

Saving your documents   152

Saving and backing up your documents automatically   155

Now that you've learned the new features of Word 2000 and learned how to customize the program to your own personal preferences, it's time to start creating your first documents. This chapter presents the essential skills necessary to create, edit, and save simple Word documents—those skills you'll use every time you use the program.

Creating a New Document

There are several ways to create a new document in Word—some are as simple as clicking a button; others require you to enter specific information in a step-by-step wizard.

 WARNING Creating a document is not the same as saving it—and unless your document is saved, it won't be available for future use. To learn how to save your documents to disk, see the "Saving Your Documents" section later in this chapter.

Creating a Blank Document—Fast

When you first launch Microsoft Word, the program appears on your desktop with a blank document already loaded. This initial document, which uses Word's Normal template, is the simplest type of document you can create with Word. It doesn't offer a lot of fancy styles or formatting options, just some basic styles and the opportunity for you to start typing on essentially a blank slate.

 Once Word is launched, you can create a similar new document by clicking the New Blank Document button on Word's Standard toolbar. This loads a blank document, based on the Normal template, into the Word workspace. While you can use this initial blank document to create any type of document you wish, you'll probably find it more efficient to start with a more specific *template* for your new document.

Creating a Document from a Template

Any new Word document you create is based on what Word calls a *template*. A template is a specific combination of styles and settings, including page layout settings, fonts, keyboard shortcuts, menus, AutoText entries, macros, and other special formatting.

Understanding Word Templates

Word uses two types of templates—*global* templates and *document* templates. Global templates, such as the Normal template used when Word loads its initial blank document, contain settings that are used by all documents. Document templates, on the other hand, contain settings that are available only to documents based on that template. This combination of template types means that any document you create can share settings from both a specific document template and from any global template.

When you create a new document, you select (from the New dialog box) the document template on which you wish to base your new document.

 NOTE To learn how to create your own templates, see Chapter 27.

Using Templates to Create a New Document

To create a new Word document based on a specific document template, follow these steps:

1. Select File ➢ New to display the New dialog box (shown in Figure 4.1).

FIGURE 4.1
Use the New dialog box to create a new document based on an existing template.

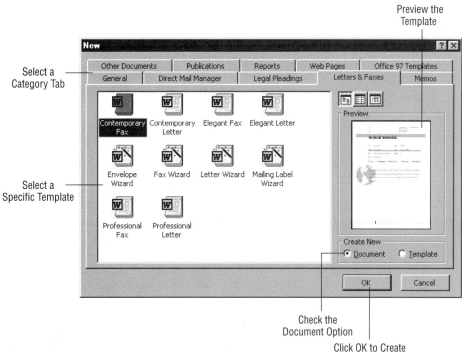

Select a Category Tab

Select a Specific Template

Preview the Template

Check the Document Option

Click OK to Create the New Document

TIP You can also create a new document by clicking the Start menu and selecting New Office Document, or by clicking the New Office Document button on the Microsoft Office Shortcut Bar.

2. Select the tab that contains the type of document you want to create.

3. Select the document template you wish to use; a sample document is previewed to the right of the template list.

4. Make sure the Document option is checked in the Create New section.

5. Click OK; your new blank document—based on your selected template—is now displayed in the Word workspace.

Understanding Word Document Types

You can actually create four different types of documents with Microsoft Word:

Document   All Word documents have a .DOC extension. The Word 2000 .DOC format is file-compatible with Word 97, but (in spite of the identical extension) not file-compatible with versions of Word prior to Word 97.

Template   Word templates are stored in a different file format than Word document. All Word templates have a .DOT extension.

Web Page   When you use Word to create a Web page, the file is stored in HTML format with an .HTM extension.

E-mail Messages   When you use Word (in conjunction with Outlook 2000 or Outlook Express) to create an e-mail message, that message is typically not saved on your hard disk. (It's sent, not saved.) If you do choose to save the message, it is saved in a standard Word .DOC format file.

Word 2000's Pre-Made Templates

Word 2000 includes 40 different pre-made templates and wizards, as detailed in Table 4.1:

TABLE 4.1: WORD 2000 TEMPLATES

Tab	Templates
General	Blank Document Web Page E-mail Message
Direct Mail Manager (available when you install Office 2000's Direct Mail Manager utility, discussed in Chapter 19)	Simple Form Letter Flyer Wizard Letter Wizard Postcard Wizard
Legal Pleadings	Pleading Wizard
Letters & Faxes	Contemporary Letter Elegant Letter Professional Letter Contemporary Fax Elegant Fax Professional Fax Letter Wizard Fax Wizard Envelope Wizard Mailing Label Wizard
Memos	Contemporary Memo Elegant Memo Professional Memo Memo Wizard
Other Documents	Agenda Wizard Batch Conversion Wizard Calendar Wizard Contemporary Resume Elegant Resume Professional Resume Resume Wizard
Publications	Brochure Directory Manual Thesis

Continued ▐▶

TABLE 4.1: WORD 2000 TEMPLATES (CONTINUED)	
Tab	**Templates**
Reports	Contemporary Report
	Elegant Report
	Professional Report
Web Pages	Column with Contents
	Frequently Asked Questions
	Left-aligned Column
	Personal Web Page
	Right-aligned Column
	Simple Layout
	Table of Contents
	Web Page Wizard

In addition, all templates from previous versions of Word—including any custom templates you previously created—are located in a tab labeled Office 97 Templates.

Adding and Attaching New Templates

After a new document is created, you can add other global templates to the open document. The document will then be able to share any of the settings and styles present in the new global template.

To add a new global template to an existing document, follow these steps:

1. Select Tools ➤ Templates and Add-Ins to display the Templates and Add-Ins dialog box, shown in Figure 4.2.

FIGURE 4.2

Use the Templates and Add-Ins dialog box to add and attach templates to your documents.

Select from This List to Add a New Global Template

Click to Attach a Different Document Template

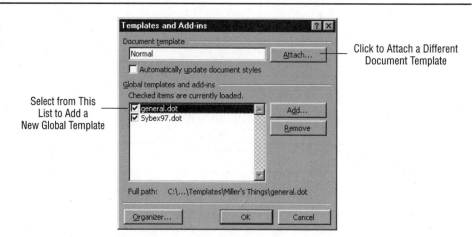

2. To load any template listed in the Global Templates and Add-Ins list, check that template.

3. If the template you want does not appear in the Global Templates and Add-Ins list, click the Add button to display the Add Template dialog box, select the template you want, then click OK.

4. Click OK when done.

Word also lets you change which document template is attached to any specific document. To attach a different document template to your document, follow these steps:

1. Select Tools ➤ Templates and Add-Ins to display the Templates and Add-Ins dialog box.

2. Click the Attach button.

3. When the Attach Template dialog box appears, select the template you want, then click OK.

4. If you want to update all the styles in your document to reflect the styles in the new document template, check the Automatically Update Document Styles option.

5. Click OK when done.

 WARNING When you attach a new document template to a document, it replaces the original document template—which is no longer attached.

Using a Wizard to Create a New Document

Word 2000 provides several *wizards* that help you create specific types of pre-designed documents. Each wizard leads you step-by-step through the document creation. Follow each step (and enter the appropriate information) to create a completed document.

All of Word's template wizards are listed (along with normal document templates) in the New dialog box (select File ➤ New). As an example, let's look at the Letter Wizard, located on the Letters & Faxes tab.

When you select the Letter Wizard and click OK, you're asked if you want to create a single letter or to send a batch of letters to a mailing list. Answer appropriately, then click OK.

You now see the first screen of the Letter Wizard, as shown in Figure 4.3. Each screen of the wizard asks for specific types of information: screen one deals with the Letter Format, screen two with Recipient Info, screen three with Other Elements, and screen four with Sender Info. Fill in each screen appropriately, and click the Next button when you're done with each screen. When you're finished entering your information on the final screen, click the Finish button—and Word displays your finished letter. Make any final changes to the letter as necessary, then save and print it.

FIGURE 4.3
Creating a predesigned letter with Word's Letter Wizard

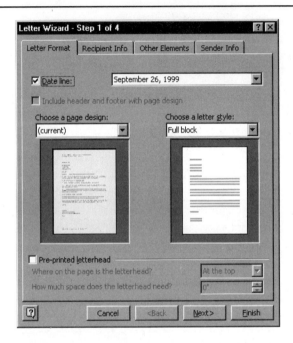

TIP   You can also use the Letter Wizard to modify an existing letter. To run the wizard on an existing document, open the document and select Tools ➤ Letter Wizard.

Word 2000 includes the following document-creation wizards:
- Agenda Wizard (Other Documents tab)
- Batch Conversion Wizard (Other Documents tab)
- Calendar Wizard (Other Documents tab)
- Envelope Wizard (Letters & Faxes tab)

- Fax Wizard (Letters & Faxes tab)
- Flyer Wizard (Direct Mail Manager tab—not available on all installations)
- Letter Wizard (Letters & Faxes tab)
- Mailing Label Wizard (Letters & Faxes tab)
- Memo Wizard (Memos tab)
- Pleading Wizard (Legal Pleadings tab)
- Postcard Wizard (Direct Mail Manager tab—not available on all installations)
- Resume Wizard (Other Documents tab)
- Web Page Wizard (Web Pages tab)

MASTERING THE OPPORTUNITIES

Creating a New Document from a Copy of Another Document

Another way to create a new document is to base it on an existing document—by creating a copy of the existing document. To do this, follow these steps:

1. Select File ➢ Open (or click the Open Document button on Word's Standard toolbar) to display the Open dialog box.

2. Select the document you want to make a copy of.

3. Click the arrow next to the Open button, then select the Open as Copy option.

This opens a copy of the selected document; you can then edit this copy (without affecting the original document) and save the new document under a different filename.

Opening an Existing Document

Once you've created and saved a document, it's easy to reopen that document for further editing. Word 2000 even lets you open documents created in other programs.

Learning New Features and Creating New Documents

Six Ways to Open a Word Document

Word 2000 lets you open an existing document using any one of six different methods:

- Select File ➢ Open; when the Open dialog box appears, select the file to open, then click Open.

- Click the Open Document button on Word's Standard toolbar; when the Open dialog box appears, select the file to open, then click Open.

TIP   You can bypass using the Open button by double-clicking the file(s) you wish to open. You can also open multiple files at one time by holding down the Ctrl key while selecting the files.

- Click the Windows Start button and select Open Office Document; when the Open Office Document dialog box appears, navigate to any Word document (.DOC extension), select the document, and click Open. (If Word is not running, this launches the program and loads the selected document.)

- From the Microsoft Office Shortcut Bar, click the Open Office Document button; when the Open Office Document dialog box appears, navigate to any Word document (.DOC extension), select the document, and click Open. (If Word is not running, this launches the program and loads the selected document.)

- Use My Computer or Windows Explorer to navigate to any Word document (.DOC extension) and double-click the document. (If Word is not running, this launches the program and loads the selected document.)

- Click the Windows Start button and select Run; when the Run dialog box appears, enter the complete path of a Word document (.DOC extension) in the Open box, then click OK. (If Word is not running, this launches the program and loads the selected document.)

Using the Open Dialog Box

The Open dialog box, shown in Figure 4.4, has been upgraded in Word 2000 to include new file management capabilities. (Similar capabilities exist in the Save As dialog box.)

FIGURE 4.4
Use the Open dialog box to open existing documents and manage your files.

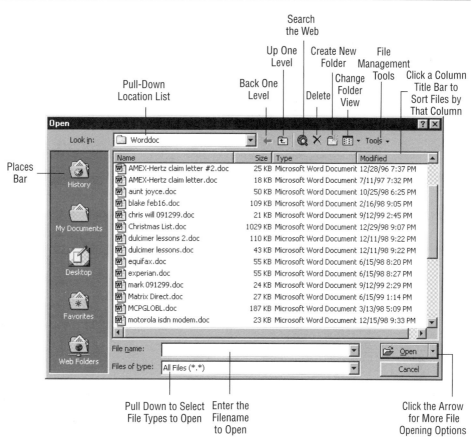

Navigating Through Your Files

New in Word 2000 are several navigation features, most noticeable of which is the Places bar at the left of the Open dialog box. This bar includes buttons that, when clicked, display files stored in five popular folders:

History   This folder includes your most recently used documents.

My Documents   Microsoft created this folder for default storage of all important Office documents.

Desktop   Not a folder per se, but rather a list of all items residing on the Windows desktop; click this button to access My Computer.

Favorites   This folder, primarily associated with the Internet Explorer Web browser, is where you store your favorite Web pages and files.

Web Folders   This folder contains any Web pages you've created.
Click any button on the Places bar to display the contents of the selected folder.

You can also navigate through the files on your system by using the pull-down Location list (which functions as a "tree" display for all the drives on your system) or the Back and Up buttons on the toolbar. The Back button moves you back one step, while the Up button moves you up one level in your folder list.

Displaying Files

For the current folder, you can display files of a certain type by pulling down the Files of Type list and selecting one of the listed file types. You can also enter part of a file-name and a *wildcard* into the File Name box, then press Enter, to display all matching filenames. As an example, if you enter **a***, Word will display all files that start with the letter *a*.

NOTE   A wildcard is a character that stands in for one or more other characters. The most common wildcard is *****, which can represent any character or characters from that point to the end of the filename. Entering **abc.*** searches for all documents named *abc* with any file extension; entering ***.*** searches for all documents, period.

With Word 2000, you can select from several different *folder views* in the Open dialog box. You toggle through the available views by clicking the Views button, or select from a pull-down menu of views by clicking the down arrow next to the Views button. The available folder views include:

List   This view lists all files in the current folder, arranged in columns. No file details are displayed in this view.

Details   This view displays a list of files complete with the size of the file, the type of file, and when the file was last modified. In this view, you can sort the files by any column by clicking a specific column title bar; click again to sort the column in the opposite direction. You can also drag the right edge of any column title bar to resize that particular column.

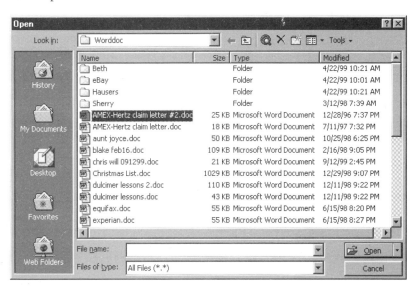

Properties This view displays two panes in the dialog box. The left pane lists the files in the current folder, while the right pane lists details about the selected file.

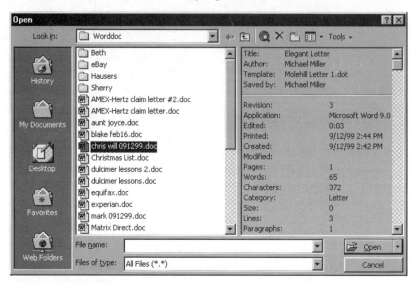

Preview This view also displays two panes. The left pane lists the files, while the right pane previews the selected document.

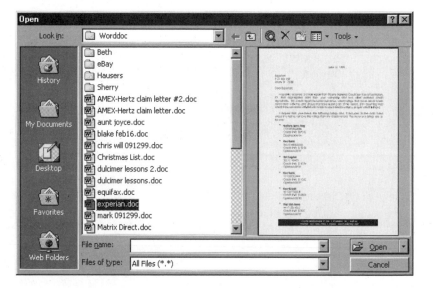

WARNING Only documents with the preview option enabled are displayed in the preview pane.

Opening Files

From within the Open dialog box, Word gives you two ways to open a file:

- Select the file, then click the Open button.
- Double-click the file.

 TIP Word lets you open more than one file at a time. To open multiple contiguous files (several in a row), hold down the Shift key when selecting the files. To open multiple non-contiguous files (separated by other files), hold down the Ctrl key when selecting the files.

Word also provides several options when opening a file. These options are available when you click the down arrow on the Open button:

Open   Opens the file normally.

Open Read-Only   Opens the file as a read-only document—which means you can look at it, but you can't edit it.

Open as Copy   Opens a copy of the selected document, which you can edit and save under a different filename.

Open in Browser   For Web documents, opens the document in your Web browser instead of in Word.

Finding Word Documents

If you can't manually find a particular document, you can have Word search for the document. The Open dialog box contains a special Find tool that lets you search for documents according to a wide variety of criteria.

 NOTE Don't confuse this Find tool with Word's Find command (select Edit ➢ Find). This tool finds files to open; the Find command finds text within an opened file. For more information on the Find command, see Chapter 5.

Follow these steps to find a file with the Find tool:

1. Select File ➢ Open to display the Open dialog box.

2. Select Tools ➤ Find to display the Find dialog box, shown in Figure 4.5.

FIGURE 4.5
*Use Word 2000's Find
tool to search for files
on your system.*

Current
Search
Criteria

Enter New
Search Criteria
(Filename,
Contents,
Keywords, etc.)

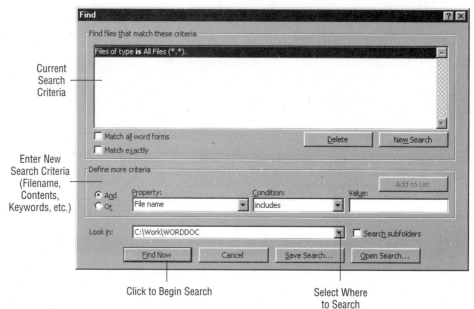

Click to Begin Search

Select Where
to Search

3. Pull down the Property list and select a property you wish to search for.

4. Select an option for the selected property from the Condition list.

5. If you're searching for a property that contains a value, enter that value in the Value box. (For example, if you're searching for a filename, enter all or part of the filename in the Value box.)

6. Pull down the Look In list and select the drive or folder you want to search. (If you want to search all subfolders beneath the current drive or folder, check the Search Subfolders option.)

7. Click the Add to List button to add this particular criteria to the Find Files list.

8. When you're done adding criteria to your search, click Find Now to begin the search.

 TIP You can repeat a saved search by selecting it from the Find Files list and clicking Find Now.

After Word completes its search, all files matching your search criteria will be listed in the Open dialog box. Use the standard procedure to open the specific file(s) you were looking for.

Here are some tips for fine-tuning your search for Word files:

Specify Where to Look   You *can* have Find search your entire hard disk (or all the hard disks on your system), but it's more efficient to specify a particular folder from the Look In list. Microsoft suggests that you store all your documents either in the My Documents folder, or in subfolders within this folder. If you do this, you can specify to search in \My Documents—and check the Search Subfolders option to search all subfolders contained in the selected folder.

Search for Specific Properties   With the Find tool, you're not limited to searching by filename. You can also search by a variety of document properties, including most of the properties listed in the document's Properties dialog box—author, category, comments, keywords, date of last modification, file size, and number of characters, lines, paragraphs, or pages. It's easy to configure a search for files that were authored by a specific person, containing specific keywords, or that were modified within the past week.

Set a Condition   Each property you select has its own selectable conditions for searching. For example, if you select to search by the Last Modified property, you can select from a list of conditions that include Today, Yesterday, Last Week, This Week, and so on. Some conditions allow you to enter a *value*. As an example, if you select to search by the File Name property using the Includes condition, you would enter the words or characters you want the filename to include into the Value box.

Search by Multiple Criteria   All criteria you configure and add to your Find Files list combine to create your final search. You can add as many criteria to your Find Files list as necessary; your final search looks for files that match *all* the criteria listed.

Go Boolean   One option most users miss is the ability to specify And or Not before creating a new criteria. By default, And is selected, so that *both* criteria *must* be matched for a successful search: Find files that match Criteria 1 AND Criteria 2. If you check the Or option when creating a criteria, then the search looks for files that match *either* criteria: Find files that match Criteria 1 OR Criteria 2. It's a subtle difference, but an important one.

Save and Reuse Your Searches   If you've created a search that you think you will use again in the future, click the Save Search button to save all the criteria you've selected. When you want to reuse a search, click the Open Search button to choose from all searches you've previously saved.

Find Files Faster with Find Fast

Microsoft Office 2000 includes a special utility to speed up the searches you execute with Word 2000's Find tool. *Find Fast* automatically creates an index of the files on each of your hard disks; the Find tool can then search this index for the files you specify, rather than searching your entire hard disk. As you can imagine, it's faster to search an index file (that has already searched the hard disk) than it is to search the hard disk itself.

Find Fast creates an index file for each local drive on your computer. It indexes all Office documents, and logs all document properties. Each index file is automatically updated, and in most cases you don't have to do anything manually for Find Fast to do its job.

If you want to modify Find Fast's operation—or create an index for a network drive or folder *not* located on your local PC—open the Windows Control Panel and select the Find Fast icon. Information about each index file is displayed, and you can pull down the Index menu to perform any of the following operations:

- Create index

- Update index

- Delete index

- Update interval (time in between automatic indexes)

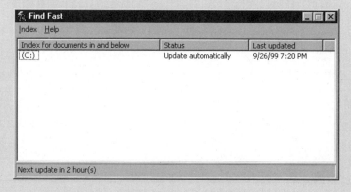

You can also choose to run Find Fast when you log onto your computer, show a log of your indexes, or pause any in-process indexing.

Opening a Document Created with a Different Program

Word 2000 provides a number of file converters that you can use to automatically open files created with programs other than Word 2000. Some of these converters are installed by default during a typical installation; others may need to be installed manually.

To open a document of a different file type, pull down the Files of Type list in the Open dialog box, then select the file type you wish to open. The selected file(s) will be opened and temporarily converted to Word 2000 format. To permanently convert and save the file to Word 2000 format, select File ➤ Save As and select Word Document (.*doc) from the Save As Type list. To save the document in its native file type, select File ➤ Save (or click the Save button on Word's Standard toolbar).

Other File Operations

What other file operations can you perform in the Open dialog box? Here are some of the available options:

Add to Favorites   Adds the selected file to your Favorites folder.

Copy   Copies the selected file to the Clipboard.

Create Shortcut   Creates a shortcut to the selected file in the current folder.

Cut   Cuts the selected file from the current folder and places a copy of the file in the Clipboard.

Delete   Deletes the selected file from the current folder; no copy is placed in the Clipboard.

Paste   This command is not available on any menu, but you can press Shift+Ins to paste any cut or copied file into the file listing section of the dialog box.

Print   Prints the selected file without opening the file.

Properties   Displays the Properties dialog box for the selected file.

Quick View   Uses the Windows Quick View utility to display a simplified version of the selected document without loading the document into Word.

Rename   Enables you to enter a new filename for the selected file.

Send To   Allows you to "send" the file to any location listed on the Send To menu.

Some of these operations are available when you select a file and pull down the Tools menu; other options are available by right-clicking a file and selecting from the pop-up menu.

Managing File Properties

All Word documents can be described via a set of file properties and statistics. Some of these properties are automatically generated by Word; others can be entered and edited by you.

You display the file properties for the current document by selecting File ➤ Properties. This displays the File Properties dialog box, shown in Figure 4.6.

FIGURE 4.6
Display and edit information about your document from the File Properties dialog box.

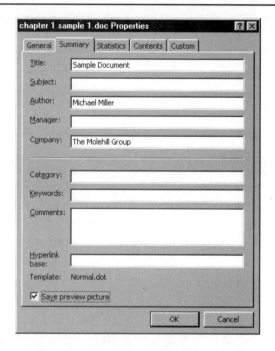

 TIP Make a printout of a document's properties by selecting File ➤ Print to display the Print dialog box. Pull down the Print What list and select Document Properties, then click OK.

Each tab displays a different category of information, as detailed in Table 4.2:

TABLE 4.2: WORD 2000 FILE PROPERTIES

Tab	Description
General	Automatically-generated statistics, including file type, location, and size, plus when the file was created, last modified, and last accessed.
Summary	A combination of automatically-generated and user-entered information, including title, subject, author, category, keywords, comments, and assigned template.
Statistics	More automatically-generated statistics, including total number of pages, paragraphs, lines, words, and characters.
Contents	Automatically-generated list of the document's headings. (NOTE: For this feature to work, you have to check the Save Preview Picture option on the Summary tab.)
Custom	A variety of user-selected properties.

When the properties for a document have been properly entered, you can search for documents that meet specific criteria (size, keyword, date modified, and so on) using the Property list in the Find tool on the Open dialog box.

 TIP To display a preview of your document when the file is selected in My Computer or Windows Explorer, select the Summary tab in the Properties dialog box and check the Save Preview Picture option.

Entering Text

The blinking cursor in a Word document indicates your *insertion point*. The insertion point is where new text is entered into your document—and entering text is as simple as pressing keys on your keyboard.

You move the insertion point with your mouse by clicking a new position in your text. You move the insertion point with your keyboard by using one of the keys or key combinations listed in Table 4.3:

TABLE 4.3: KEYBOARD SHORTCUTS FOR MOVING THE INSERTION POINT

Move Insertion Point	Key(s)
One character to the left	←
One character to the right	→
One line down	↓
One line up	↑
One paragraph down	Ctrl+↓
One paragraph up	Ctrl+↑
One word to the left	Ctrl+←
One word to the right	Ctrl+→
To end of column	Alt+PgDn
To end of document	Ctrl+End
To end of line	End
To end of row	Alt+Shift+End
To end of window	Alt+Ctrl+PgDn
To start of column	Alt+PgUp
To start of document	Ctrl+Home
To start of line	Home
To start of row	Alt+Home
To start of window	Alt+Ctrl+PgUp

Entering Text with Click and Type

When you're operating in either Print Layout or Web Layout views, you have access to a new feature of Word 2000 that enables you to double-click in any blank space in a document and then start typing. This new feature, called *Click and Type,* positions your new text exactly where you placed it, without the need to create a separate text box.

 NOTE Before you can use Click and Type, you need to make sure that the feature has been enabled in your copy of Word. To do this, select Tools ➤ Options to display the Options dialog box. Select the Edit tab, check the Enable Click and Type option, then click OK.

To insert text using Click and Type, follow these steps:

1. From within Print Layout or Web Layout view, position your cursor over a blank area of your document.

2. When the cursor changes shape, double-click.

3. When the insertion point starts blinking, start typing.

The text you enter with Click and Type will be automatically aligned according to its position on the page—which is indicated by the shape of the Click and Type cursor. For example, Click and Type text inserted on the far right side of a page will be right aligned; text inserted in the middle of the page will be centered.

 WARNING You can only use Click and Type in Print Layout or Web Layout views, and in blank areas of your document. You can't use Click and Type in any area of your document that contains multiple columns, bulleted and numbered lists, floating objects, pictures with top and bottom text wrapping, or indents.

Entering Text in a Text Box

Before Word 2000, to enter text in blank areas of your document you had to use *text boxes.* While Click and Type lets you add text anywhere without a text box, you still might want to incorporate text boxes within your documents. Text boxes provide a variety of formatting options that aren't available with Click and Type text.

Creating a New Text Box

To add a text box to your document, follow these steps:

1. Select Insert ➤ Text Box (or click the Text Box button on the Drawing toolbar).

2. Your cursor changes to a crosshair shape; position the cursor in your document and draw the text box with your mouse.

Figure 4.7 shows how a text box looks within a typical document.

FIGURE 4.7

Use text boxes to insert freestanding text that needs to be highly formatted.

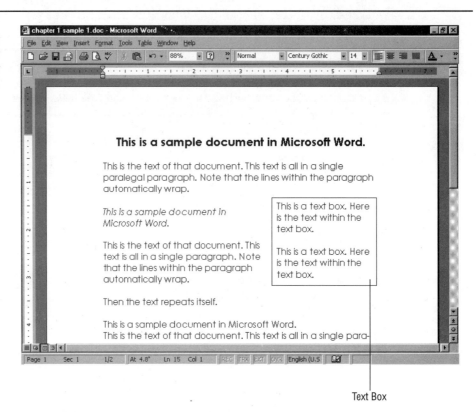

Text Box

You can resize the text box by clicking anywhere on its border, then grabbing one of the sizing handles along the box's border and dragging it to resize the box. To move a text box, grab the box anywhere along the border *except* at a sizing handle, and drag the box to a new position.

To add text to a text box, simply position your cursor inside the text box; this should activate the insertion point. Once the insertion point starts blinking, you can start typing.

Formatting a Text Box

Text boxes can utilize the following types of formatting:

- Text wrapping
- Shadow
- 3-D effects

- Border styles and colors
- Fill colors and effects

To format a text box, double-click the text box border to display the Format Text Box dialog box. You can then select the tab that contains the formatting options you want to change.

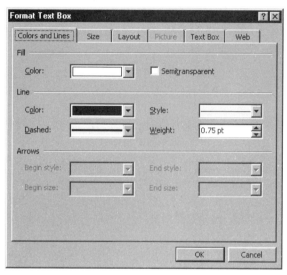

 NOTE Formatting a text box is identical to formatting any other graphic object within Word. To learn more about working with graphic objects, see Chapter 16.

You format and align the text within a text box as you would any other type of text. You can also change the direction of the text within a text box by selecting the entire text box and then selecting Format ➢ Text Direction. When the Text Direction dialog box appears, select a new orientation and click OK.

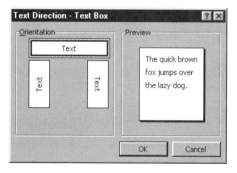

Entering Pre-Written Text with AutoText

While most of the text you enter into your documents will come from good old-fashioned typing, Word 2000 offers a way to automate the entering of various types of "boilerplate" text. The AutoText feature lets you create pre-written snippets of text, and then enter them into your documents with a few clicks of your mouse.

Inserting AutoText

Word 2000 comes with several dozen pre-written AutoText entries. There are two ways to insert an AutoText entry into your text:

- Select Insert ➢ AutoText, then select a category and entry from the resulting submenu.
- Display the AutoText toolbar, then click the All Entries button and select a category and entry from the resulting list.

When you select an AutoText entry, the AutoText text is inserted into your document at the current insertion point.

 TIP Some AutoText entries include fields that are automatically updated or calculated by Word. For example, selecting Header/Footer ➢ Create By inserts the text Created By *yourname*, where *yourname* is replaced by the name you entered as part of Word's user information.

You can also enter AutoText via Word's AutoComplete feature. To activate Auto-Complete, select Tools ➢ AutoCorrect to display the AutoCorrect dialog box, then select the AutoText tab and check the Show AutoComplete Tip option. When Auto-Complete is activated, typing the first few characters of an AutoText entry will display a ScreenTip containing the complete AutoText entry. To accept the ScreenTip and insert the complete AutoText entry, press Enter. To ignore the suggestion, just continue typing.

Creating New AutoText Entries

You can quickly and easily create your own AutoText entries for text that you find yourself entering on a frequent basis. Just follow these steps:

1. Enter the text for your AutoText entry somewhere in your current document, then select the text.

 TIP To store paragraph formatting with the entry, include the paragraph mark (typically the space *after* the entry) when you select the text. To view paragraph marks, click the Show/ Hide button on Word's Standard toolbar.

2. Click the New button on the AutoText toolbar. (Alternately, you can select Insert ➢ AutoText ➢ New, or press F3.)

3. When the Create AutoText dialog box appears, enter a name for the new entry (or accept the suggested name), then click OK.

4. Word now stores your entry in the AutoText list.

To delete an AutoText entry, select Insert ➢ AutoText ➢ AutoText (or click the Auto-Text button on the AutoText toolbar). When the AutoCorrect dialog box appears (with the AutoText tab selected), select the name of the AutoText entry you want to delete, then click Delete.

Print All Your AutoText Entries

To keep track of all the AutoText entries available in Word, you may want to make a printout of the entries. To do this, follow these steps:

1. Select File ➢ Print to display the Print dialog box.

2. Pull down the Print What list and select AutoText Entries.

3. Click OK to begin printing.

Editing Text

Once you've entered your text, you'll want to edit it. (Unless you're perfect, you're bound to have made some mistakes—or simply want to rearrange your words a bit.) This means you need to learn the skills and commands necessary to edit text in your Word documents.

Selecting Text

The first step to editing text is selecting text. Any text you select will appear as white text against a black highlight, as shown in Figure 4.8. Once you've selected a block of text, you can then edit it in a number of ways—including cutting, copying, deleting, and moving.

FIGURE 4.8
A block of text selected
in a document

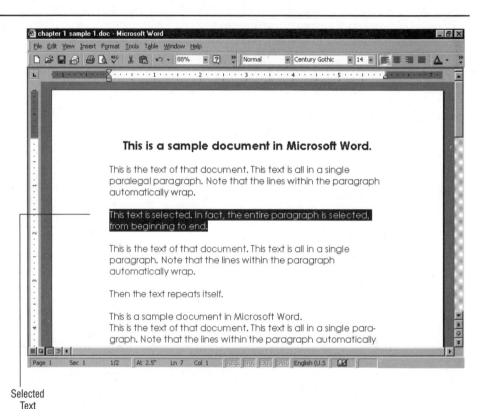

Selected
Text

Selecting Text with a Mouse

The easiest way to select text is with your mouse. There are several ways to use your mouse to select blocks of text, including:

- Position the cursor at the start of the text you want to select. Hold down the left mouse button and highlight the entire range of text; release the button when the range is completely highlighted.

- Position the cursor at the start of the text you want to select and click the mouse once to anchor the insertion point. Hold down the Shift key and then move the cursor to the end of the range of text, and click the mouse once again to anchor the end of the selection.

- Double-click a word to select the entire word.
- Triple-click anywhere in a paragraph to select the entire paragraph.
- Move your cursor to the left of a line of text and click the mouse to highlight the entire line.
- Move your cursor to the left of a paragraph and double-click the mouse to highlight the entire paragraph.

Selecting Text with the Keyboard

You can also select text using your keyboard. In general, you use the Shift key—in combination with other keys—to highlight blocks of text. Table 4.4 lists the key combinations you use for selecting text:

TABLE 4.4: KEYBOARD SHORTCUTS FOR SELECTING BLOCKS OF TEXT

Select This Text	Key(s)
Select character to the left	Shift+←
Select character to the right	Shift+→
Select next line	Shift+↓
Select next paragraph	Shift+Ctrl+↓
Select next word	Shift+Ctrl+→
Select previous line	Shift+↑
Select previous paragraph	Shift+Ctrl+↑
Select previous word	Shift+Ctrl+←
Select to end of column	Shift+Ctrl+End
Select to end of line	Shift+End
Select to end of page	Shift+PgDn
Select to end of window	Shift+Alt+Ctrl+PgDn
Select to start of column	Shift+Ctrl+Home
Select to start of line	Shift+Home
Select to start of window	Shift+Alt+Ctrl+PgUp
Select to top of page	Shift+PgUp

Deleting Text

There are four ways to delete a block of selected text:

- Press the Del key
- Press the Backspace key
- Right-click the selection and select Delete from the pop-up menu
- Select Edit ➤ Clear

You can also delete text one character at a time. Press Del to delete the next character in your document, or press Backspace to delete the previous letter. To delete the next word in your document, press Ctrl+Del; to delete the previous word, press Ctrl+Backspace.

 TIP Whether you want to delete, cut, copy, or paste, you can find the appropriate command on a context-sensitive pop-up menu. Just select your text (or anchor your insertion point) and right-click; the resulting pop-up menu will contain the command for the operation you want to perform.

Copying Text

There are two ways to copy text from one location to another: using the Copy command, and using Windows' Drag and Drop operation.

Using the Copy Command

To copy a block of text—which leaves the original text in place—follow these steps:

1. Select the text you want to copy.
2. Select Edit ➤ Copy. (Alternately, you can press either Ctrl+C or Ctrl+Ins, or click the Copy button on Word's Standard toolbar.)
3. Reposition the insertion point where you want to paste the text.
4. Select Edit ➤ Paste. (Alternately, you can press either Shift+V or Shift+Ins, or click the Paste button on Word's Standard toolbar.)

Copying via Drag and Drop

You can also use Windows' Drag and Drop operation to copy text using your mouse. Just follow these steps:

1. Use your mouse to select the text you want to copy.

2. Hold down the Ctrl key.

3. Place the cursor on the selected text, then click the mouse button and drag the text to the new location.

4. Release both the mouse button and the Ctrl key.

 TIP If you use the right mouse button for the drag and drop operation, Word will display a pop-up menu when you drop your selection in place. Select from any operation on this menu (move, copy, link, or create hyperlink) to apply the operation to the drag-and-dropped text.

Moving Text

There are two methods for moving text from one location to another within your document: the Cut and Paste method and the Drag and Drop method.

Moving via Cut and Paste

To use Word's Cut and Paste commands to move a block of text, follow these steps:

1. Select the text you want to move.

2. Select Edit ➤ Cut. (Alternately, you can press either Ctrl+X or Shift+Del, or click the Cut button on Word's Standard toolbar.)

3. Reposition the insertion point where you want to paste the text.

4. Select Edit ➤ Paste. (Alternately, you can press either Shift+V or Shift+Ins, or click the Paste button on Word's Standard toolbar.)

Moving via Drag and Drop

To use Windows' Drag and Drop function to move text with your mouse, follow these steps:

1. Use your mouse to select the text you want to move.

2. Place the cursor on the selected text, then click the mouse button and drag the text to the new location.

3. Release the mouse button.

Using Collect and Paste

 Word 2000 enhances the standard Cut/Copy/Paste function with the new Collect and Paste feature. With Collect and Paste, you can store up to twelve different cut or copied items in the Clipboard (a location in your system's memory where Windows stores cut and copied data), and then select which of the multiple items you want to paste into your document.

 TIP You can view the contents of any cut or copied text by hovering your cursor over that item's icon on the Clipboard toolbar. Word will then display a ScreenTip of the item's first fifty text characters.

To best use Collect and Paste, you should have the Clipboard toolbar displayed on your desktop (select Tools ➤ Customize, select the Toolbars tab, and check the Clipboard option), then follow these steps:

1. Cut or copy the text you want to paste.

2. Reposition the insertion point where you want to paste the text.

3. Go to the Clipboard toolbar and click the button for the item you want to paste. (If you have the Clipboard menu docked, you'll need to pull down the Items menu to display the Clipboard items.) The item you selected will then be pasted into your document.

 WARNING If you use Word's standard Paste command when you have multiple text objects in the Clipboard, *all* Clipboard text will be pasted into your document.

Using the Paste Special Command

You can cut or copy text from *any* Windows program and paste it into a Word document. However, if you use the standard Paste command, the text will be inserted in its native format, with its original formatting. While this may be acceptable, you may prefer to paste text into your document in a different format.

To change the way Word pastes text into your document, use the Paste Special command. You access this function by selecting Edit ➢ Paste Special when you're ready to paste a selection. This displays the Paste Special dialog box.

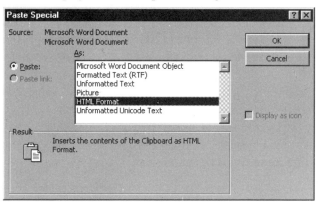

From the Paste Special dialog box, you'll see the following Paste As options:

Microsoft Word Formatted Object   Inserts the text as an editable document. (This option is more commonly used for pasting pictures and other embedded objects.)

Formatted Text (RTF Format)   Retains most of the formatting of the original text.

Unformatted Text   Inserts the text with the formatting of the paragraph where the insertion point is located.

 TIP   Use the Unformatted Text option to ensure that the text you paste shares the formatting of the surrounding text.

Picture   Inserts the text as a bitmapped picture. (This option more commonly used for pasting pictures and other graphics.)

HTML Format   Inserts the text in HTML format, for Web-based documents.

Unformatted Unicode Text   Inserts the text without any formatting.

 WARNING   Not all cut or copied text can be pasted in all possible formats.

As you can see, several of the options in this dialog box are more commonly used for pasting non-text objects. Still, the options presented here provide some useful alternatives when pasting text that comes from other sources—or even from differently formatted sections of the same document.

Undoing and Redoing Your Editing

What if you perform an operation—delete a block of text, copy a word, or even type a few characters—that you didn't mean to do? Is there any way to "take back" mistakes you make while using Word?

 Fortunately, Word 2000 has a powerful Undo command. When you click the Undo button on Word's Standard toolbar (or select Edit ➢ Undo), your last action will be reversed. If you click Undo again, the action before that will be reversed. In fact, virtually all your actions during an editing session are capable of being reversed, if you click Undo enough times.

You can see a list of all actions available for undoing by clicking the down arrow on the Undo button. This displays a list of all reversible actions; select any number of actions from this list to undo them.

 To *redo* any action you've undone, click the Redo button (next to the Undo button on Word's Standard toolbar). Like the Undo button, you can click the button to redo one action at a time, or click the down arrow on the button to display a list of all actions that can be redone.

 TIP The Edit menu contains a Repeat command (select Edit ➢ Repeat) that functions similarly to the Redo command but with some important differences. When you've undone an action, the Repeat command works to redo it. However, if no action has been undone, the Repeat command simply repeats your last action. Use the Repeat command when you have to enter multiple instances of identical text.

Saving Your Documents

In order to store a document for further use, it must be saved as a file on a disk. You can save a Word document to a folder on your hard disk, to a removable disk, or even to a recordable or rewritable CD.

Saving a New Document

The first time you save a document, you need to give it a name and select a location for the saved file. You do so by following these steps:

1. Select File ➢ Save As to display the Save As dialog box (as shown in Figure 4.9).

FIGURE 4.9
Use the Save As dialog box to select a name and location for new documents.

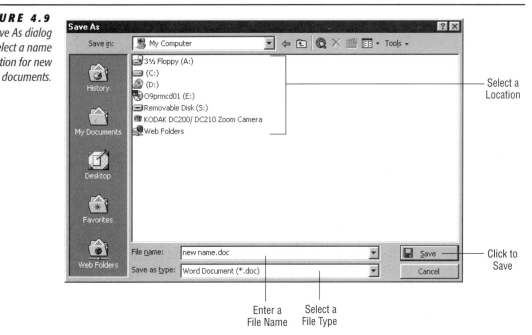

Select a Location

Click to Save

Enter a File Name   Select a File Type

2. Navigate to the folder where you want to save the document.

3. Enter a name for the document in the File Name box.

4. Make sure that Word Document (*.doc) is selected in the Save as Type list.

5. Click the Save button.

NOTE The Save As dialog box functions almost identically to the Open dialog box. See "Using the Open Dialog Box" earlier in this chapter for more information.

Naming Your Files

If you've been using computers for more than five years, you remember the days when all files had to be saved using what was called the "8.3" convention. In those days, the MS-DOS operating system required that files have no more than an eight-character name followed by a three-character extension—thus the "eight dot three" convention.

With Windows 95, however (and carried over to Windows 98 and beyond), such file naming restrictions have been eliminated. You can now assign filenames up to 256 characters long, with no restrictions on the length of (or number of) extensions. These filenames can even include spaces and special characters, so if you want to name your file MY BRAND NEW WORD FILE.DOC, you can.

Note, however, that there are still a few special characters that cannot be used when naming files. The forbidden characters include the following: **\ / : * ? " < > |**

Saving an Existing Document

If you've saved a document once, it already has a name and a location, and you don't have to use the Save As command when it's time to save your next round of changes—although you can, if you want to. Instead, use the simpler Save command, which saves your changed document without displaying any dialog boxes or prompting you for any input.

TIP To speed up your standard saves, make sure Word is configured to save in the background; this way you can continue to work on your document (or in another Windows application) while your documents are saving. To enable background saves, select Tools ➤ Options to display the Options dialog box, then select the Save tab and check the Allow Background Saves option.

There are three ways to save a document with the Save command:

- Select File ➤ Save
- Click the Save button on Word's Standard toolbar
- Press Ctrl+S

TIP If you select the Save instead of the Save As command for a previously unsaved document, Word will automatically open the Save As dialog box instead.

Saving a Document in a Different Format

If you want to save your document in a format other than the default Word 2000 format, you have to use the Save As dialog box and select a different file type from the Save as Type list. Follow these steps:

1. Select File ➤ Save As to display the Save As dialog box.
2. Navigate to the folder where you want to save the document.
3. Enter a name for the document in the File Name box.
4. Pull down the Save as Type list and select a different file type.
5. Click the Save button.

Word allows you to save documents in a variety of file formats, including multiple versions of Microsoft Word (for Windows, DOS, and Macintosh), HTML, MS-DOS Text, RTF, Windows Write, WordPerfect, and Microsoft Works. Word automatically assigns the correct extension for the file type you select.

Saving and Backing Up Your Documents Automatically

As a matter of habit, you should train yourself to save your documents frequently—every five minutes or perhaps even more frequently with important files. Since it's easy to forget, it's not uncommon for a lot of changes to be made in between file saves. This is bad, however, because every change you make that *isn't* saved can be lost if your system crashes or your power goes out.

To provide a bit more protection for your data in between manual saves, Word 2000 offers two functions that automatically save or back up your files in the background. These functions don't replace your need to use the File ➤ Save command, but they do create a kind of safety net so you don't lose all your changes when the worst happens.

Using AutoRecover

AutoRecover is a special utility that runs in the background and—at preset intervals—saves changes you make to your documents in a separate recovery file. If you have to restart Word or reboot your PC without having saved any open documents, when Word restarts, it automatically opens the recovery file. While your very latest changes might not have made it into the recovery file, chances are Word saved more (in the background) than you did (via manual save).

WARNING AutoRecover is *not* a replacement for regularly saving your documents. If you don't save an opened recovery file, it will be deleted—and all your unsaved changes lost.

To turn on and configure AutoRecover, follow these steps:

1. Select Tools ➢ Options to display the Options dialog box.

2. Select the Save tab.

3. Check the Save AutoRecover Info Every option.

4. Select an interval from the Minutes list.

5. Click OK.

The longer interval you set, the less frequently Word saves your changes. The shorter interval you set, the safer you'll be.

Creating Automatic Backups

You can also configure Word to automatically save a spare copy of every document you save. Creating a duplicate of each file might sound like a "belt and suspenders" approach to word processing, but it ensures that you always have a copy of your document that isn't too far out of date.

To enable the backup copy function, follow these steps:

1. Select Tools ➢ Options to display the Options dialog box.

2. Select the Save tab.

3. Check the Always Create Backup Copy option.

4. Click OK.

With this feature activated, each time you save a document, a backup copy is created and replaces the previous backup copy.

Recovering an Unsaved or Damaged Document

If your system crashes when you're working on a document, three things can happen:

- Nothing; your document may not be damaged.
- Your document may be undamaged, but you may lose any editing you've not yet saved.
- The contents of your document may be corrupted.

If you're able to restart Word and reload the document without any loss of data, you're in good shape.

If, on the other hand, you've done a lot of editing and haven't saved your changes, there is a possibility you can recover some of the changes you made since your last save—*if* you've enabled Word's AutoRecover feature. When you restart Word after a system crash or power failure, all documents that were open at the time will appear in the Word workspace, restored to their condition as of the last automatic save. You will need to resave an AutoRecovered document to retain the post-save changes.

 TIP When Word launches with the recovery file open, you should immediately use the Save As command to save the recovery file with a proper filename.

If the system crash has physically corrupted a document, you may still be able to recover some or all of the document's contents. Select File ➤ Open to display the Open dialog box, then pull down the Files of Type list and select Recover Text from Any File. (This option is only available if you've checked the Confirm Conversion at Open option on the General tab of the Options dialog box, and if you've installed this particular file converter.) Select the file you want to recover, then click Open. Word will attempt to recover the file; the resulting document may lack some of the formatting of your original, but most of if not all of the text should be recoverable.

If none of these actions can recover your file, then you can restore your file from the automatically created backup file. (This assumes you've enabled the automatic backup function, of course.) To open a backup file, follow these steps:

1. Select File ➤ Open (or click the Open button on Word's Standard toolbar) to display the Open dialog box.

2. Select All Files from the Files of Type list.

3. Click the Views button and select the Details view.

4. Look for the backup file. The filename should begin with "Backup of" and the file type should be listed as "Microsoft Word Backup Document."

5. Select the backup file and click Open.

Once the backup file is loaded, make sure you use the Save As command to save it under an appropriate filename.

 WARNING The backup file will not contain any changes you've made since the last backup was created.

CHAPTER <u>5</u>

Navigating Word

Navigating with the keyboard   160

Moving with the mouse   161

Using the Select Browse Object tool   163

Using the Go To command   164

Using Document Map   165

Using bookmarks   166

Using Find and Replace   168

Going places and finding things. That's kind of what life is about, isn't it? While it may be difficult to think of word processing as life in miniature, a large part of what you do in Word involves going places and finding things—within your documents.

Navigation skills are key to your efficient operation of Word 2000. Read this chapter to learn the many ways to navigate within Word, as well as how to find (and replace) specific places and elements within your documents.

Moving Around in Your Documents

There are many ways to navigate both within a Word document and between documents. Since you'll probably be using the keyboard a lot for entering text, you should familiarize yourself with Word's keyboard navigation commands. In addition, since you are using Word within the Windows environment, it's also important that you know how to navigate Word with your mouse.

Navigating with the Keyboard

The arrow keys on the keyboard will probably be your most-used Word navigation keys, by themselves and in conjunction with other key combinations. As you might expect, pressing an arrow key moves the cursor or the insertion point in your document in the direction of the arrow. The right arrow moves the cursor one character to the right, the left arrow moves it one character to the left, the up arrow moves it up one line, and the down arrow moves the cursor down one line.

Pressing the Ctrl key in conjunction with any arrow key effectively increases the distance moved in the specified direction by a factor of one. Ctrl+→ moves the cursor one whole word to the right; Ctrl+← moves it one word to the left. Ctrl+↑ moves the cursor up one paragraph, while Ctrl+↓ moves it down one paragraph.

 TIP When you press the Shift key in conjunction with any navigation key (or key combination), you *highlight*, or select, the text as you go. So, for example, pressing Shift+← highlights one character to the left, and pressing Shift+Ctrl+← highlights one word to the left.

The other navigation keys you'll frequently use are the PgUp, PgDn, Home, and End keys. Pressing PgUp or PgDn moves the document up or down one screen, respectively. The Home key takes you to the beginning of the current line, while the End key takes you to the end of the line. When you press Ctrl+Home, you go to the very begin-ning of the document, and pressing Ctrl+End takes you to the very end of the docu-ment. Table 5.1 details the operation of these key navigation keys:

TABLE 5.1: WORD 2000 NAVIGATION KEYS

Cursor Movement	Key/Key Combination
Moves left one character	$\leftarrow$
Moves right one character	$\rightarrow$
Moves down one paragraph	Ctrl+$\downarrow$
Moves left one word	Ctrl+$\leftarrow$
Moves down one line	$\downarrow$
Moves up one line	$\uparrow$
Moves right one word	Ctrl+$\rightarrow$
Moves to end of column	Alt+PgDn
Moves to end of document	Ctrl+End
Moves to end of line	End
Moves to end of row	Alt+Shift+End
Moves to end of window	Alt+Ctrl+PgDn
Moves to start of column	Alt+PgUp
Moves to start of document	Ctrl+Home
Moves to start of line	Home
Moves to start of row	Alt+Home
Moves to start of window	Alt+Ctrl+PgUp
Moves up one paragraph	Ctrl+$\uparrow$
Moves down one screen	PgDn
Moves up one screen	PgUp

Moving with the Mouse

The main mouse-based means of navigation is via the vertical scroll bar at the right of the Word workspace, shown in Figure 5.1. Clicking the up or down arrows scrolls your document either up or down, one line at a time. (Note that continuously depressing the up or down arrows scrolls the screen in the specified direction until you release the mouse button.) Clicking on the open scroll bar above or below the scroll box moves your document one screen up or down.

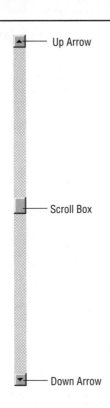

FIGURE 5.1
Use the vertical scrollbar to navigate back and forth through your document.

Up Arrow

Scroll Box

Down Arrow

A faster way to move through your document is to drag the scroll box up or down on the scroll bar. When you grab the scroll box with your mouse, a ScreenTip displays the page number of the current page. As you drag the scroll box to a new position, the page number of the new position is displayed, making it easy for you to go to a specific page in your document.

TIP If you have a mouse with an added scroll wheel (such as the Microsoft IntelliMouse), you can use this miniature wheel to scroll through your document without ever touching a scroll bar.

Finding Specific Places in Your Documents

Navigating through your document is one thing; finding a specific place in your document is another. Word 2000 offers several tools to help you find things in your documents, including the Go To, Find, and Replace commands, and the powerful but relatively obscure Select Browse Object tool. In addition, you can use bookmarks to jump directly to a specified point in your document, or switch to the Document Map view to view an outline of your document and then jump to specific sections.

 TIP Word automatically remembers the last three locations within the current document where you edited or entered text. To return to your previous location, press Shift+F5. Keep pressing Shift+F5 to proceed backward through your preceding locations.

Using the Select Browse Object Tool

The vertical scroll bar also contains the little-known Select Browse Object tool. This tool—actually three buttons at the bottom of the vertical scroll bar—lets you jump quickly between different types of document elements.

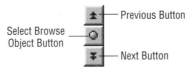

You select what document element you wish to browse by clicking the Select Browse Object button; this displays a pop-up menu of two search commands (Go To and Find) and ten different element types you can browse for:

- Field
- Endnote
- Footnote
- Comment
- Section
- Page
- Edits
- Heading
- Graphic
- Table

Select which type of element you want to browse, and then click the Previous or the Next button to jump to the next instance of that element within your document.

 TIP The Select Browse Object pop-up menu also includes a Go To option that displays the Find and Replace dialog box with the Go To tab selected, and a Find option that displays the Find and Replace dialog box with the Find tab selected.

Using the Go To Command

The fastest way to go to a specific point in your document is by using Word's Go To command, which is located on the Go To tab in the Find and Replace dialog box. You can display the Find and Replace dialog box, shown in Figure 5.2, in one of four ways:

- Select Edit ➢ Go To.
- Press F5.
- Press Ctrl+G.
- Double-click anywhere on the left half of Word's status bar.

FIGURE 5.2
Use the Go To command to go directly to a specific element in your document.

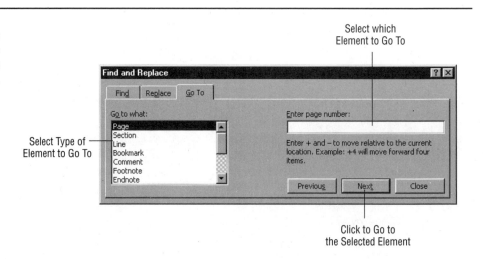

Select which Element to Go To

Select Type of Element to Go To

Click to Go to the Selected Element

Within the Find and Replace dialog box, you select what kind of element you want to go to: a specific page, section, line, bookmark, comment, footnote, endnote, field, table, graphic, equation, object, or heading. Just follow these steps to go to a specific place in your document:

1. Select Edit ➢ Go To to display the Find and Replace dialog box; make sure the Go To tab is selected.

2. From the Go to What list, select the type of element you want to go to.

3. Enter the specific element you want to go into the Enter box. (This box varies depending on the type of element selected.)

4. Click the Go To button to go to the selected location.

If you don't enter a specific element to go to, the Go To button changes to a Next button and a Previous button is enabled. This allows you to go to the next or previous instance of a particular element (for certain types of elements only) instead of to a specific location within your document.

TIP If you want to move to a relative point in your document (for example, five pages beyond the current page), enter the point preceded by a + (forward, relative to) or – (backward, relative to). To go forward five pages, for example, enter **+5** and press Next.

Using Document Map

In addition to the standard Normal, Outline, Print Layout, and Web Layout views, Word 2000 includes a special Document Map view. When you display your document in Document Map view, you display a new pane at the left of the Word workspace.

The Document Map pane, shown in Figure 5.3, displays an outline of your document's headings. While Document Map is similar to Word's Outline view, you can't edit from within the Document Map; you can only use it to view major headings and jump to corresponding sections. You activate Document Map view by selecting View ➢ Document Map or by clicking the Document Map button on Word's Standard toolbar.

TIP When Document View is enabled, you can still select one of Word's four standard views for the main document display.

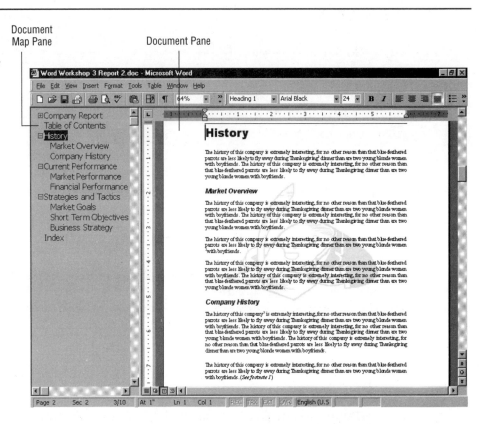

Word's Document Map not only provides a quick overview of your document's structure but also serves as a navigational tool. To jump to a particular section in your document, all you have to do is click that heading in the Document Map.

Using Bookmarks

One efficient way to find a specific location in your document is to bookmark that location for future reference. Once a location is bookmarked, you can quickly and easily jump directly to that bookmark.

NOTE Don't confuse Word bookmarks (which identify particular points in documents) with bookmarks used in Web browsers (which store favorite Web sites).

Adding a Bookmark

To add a bookmark to your document, follow these steps:

1. Position the insertion point where you want to add the bookmark.

2. Select Insert ➤ Bookmark.

3. When the Bookmark dialog box appears, enter a name in the Bookmark Name box.

4. Click the Add button.

 NOTE Bookmark names must begin with a letter and can't contain spaces, but they can contain numbers and the underscore character.

To delete a bookmark, select Insert ➤ Bookmark to open the Bookmark dialog box, select the bookmark, and click the Delete button.

Viewing Your Bookmarks

By default, bookmarks are hidden when you're viewing your document. If you'd rather see your bookmarks (if you want to find and delete a bookmark, for example), you can configure Word to display all bookmarks. Just select Tools ➤ Options to display the Options dialog box, select the View tab, and check the Bookmarks option.

 TIP Some bookmarks, such as cross-references, remain hidden, even when the View Bookmarks option is selected. To display these hidden bookmarks, select Insert ➤ Bookmark to display the Bookmark dialog box, and then check the Hidden Bookmarks option.

Jumping to a Bookmark

To jump to a specific bookmark, follow these steps:

1. Select Insert ➤ Bookmark to display the Bookmark dialog box.

2. Select a bookmark.

3. Click the Go To button.

You can also jump to a bookmark with the Go To command or from the Select Browse Object tool.

Using Find and Replace

Find and Replace are versatile commands that let you specify detailed criteria for finding places and things within your documents and then, if you choose, replacing what you find with something different. With the Find command, you can search for specific text, formatting (including styles), and special characters; the Replace command, as it sounds, enables you to replace your search items quickly and easily.

 NOTE Don't confuse the Find command with the Find tool found on the Tools menu in Word's Open dialog box (select File ➤ Open). The Find *command* finds text within the current document; the Find *tool* finds files to open. For more information on the Find tool, see Chapter 4.

Using the Find Command

The general operation of the Find command is as follows:

1. Select Edit ➤ Find or press Ctrl+F to display the Find tab of the Find and Replace dialog box, shown in Figure 5.4.

2. To display all search options, click the More button.

3. Enter the text you're searching for in the Find What box. (If you're searching for formatting or special elements, as described in steps 5 and 6, you don't have to enter any text here.)

4. Under Search Options, select any additional options for your search, if any. Also, use the pull-down list to select which direction to search.

5. If you want to find specific formatting in your document, click the Format button, choose a format from the list, and then enter or select the appropriate information as determined by the format you are searching.

FIGURE 5.4
*Search for specific text,
formatting, or other
elements from the
Find tab.*

Enter What You
Want to Find

Click to Begin
Search

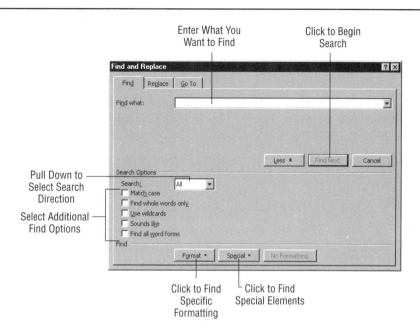

Pull Down to
Select Search
Direction

Select Additional
Find Options

Click to Find
Specific
Formatting

Click to Find
Special Elements

6. If you want to find special elements in your document, click the Special button,
   and choose an element from the list.

7. Click the Find Next button to jump to the next instance of what you're searching for.

Once you've entered your search criteria, you can press Shift+F4 to find the next
instance of the item without displaying the Find and Replace dialog box. When Word
reaches the end of the document, it asks if you want to continue your search at the
beginning; click Yes if you want to continue to search from the top.

In most instances you'll probably be searching for plain text; to do so, just enter the
text you want to find in the Find What box, and click Find Next. When you click the
More button, however, you display additional options you can use to expand your
search, including:

WARNING Selected certain of these options disable certain other conflicting options.
For example, selecting the Use Wildcards option disables the Find Whole Words Only option.

Search Direction Pull down this unlabeled list to determine the direction of
your search: All (which starts at the top of your document and searches down),

Down (which searches from the current location to the end of your document), or Up (which searches from the current location backward to the top of your document).

Match Case   When you check this option, Find will look for text that matches exactly the case of the text you enter. (Normally, Find is case insensitive.) For example, with Match Case selected, searching for *SoftWare* will find only *Soft-Ware*; with this option turned off, Find will locate *SoftWare, Software, software,* and *SOFTWARE,* if they all exist in your document, of course.

Find Whole Words Only   When you check this option, Find will search for instances where the text you specify appears as a separate and distinct word, *not* as part of a larger word. For example, with this option selected, searching for *how* will only find *how*; with this option turned off, Find will find words such as *how, show, however,* and so on.

Use Wildcards   Check this option if you want to use wildcards (such as the * character) to search for partial words. (More information on wildcards is presented in the "Searching with Wildcards" section at the end of this chapter.)

 TIP   You must turn on the Use Wildcards option if you want to search for special characters from within the Find What box.

Sounds Like   When you check this option, Find looks for words that sound the same as the text you entered, even if they're spelled differently. For example, with this option checked, searching for *doe* will locate both *doe* and *dough*.

Find All Word Forms   With this option enabled, Find looks for all forms of the words you're looking for. For example, with this option checked, searching for *run* will find *run, ran,* and *running*.

 TIP   The Find All Word Forms option is valuable when using the Replace command. For example, with this option enabled, choosing to replace *walk* with *run* will also replace *walking* with *running* and *walked* with *ran*.

In addition to these Find options, you can click the Format button to search for specific formatting within your document or click the Special button to search for special elements in your text. The Format and Special options are discussed later in this section.

Using the Replace Command

Word's Replace command works similarly to the Find command, except you have the added option of replacing the item you found with something different. You can use Replace to replace text, formatting, styles, and other special elements.

To use the Replace command, follow these steps:

1. Select Edit ➤ Replace or press Ctrl+H to display the Replace tab of the Find and Replace dialog box, shown in Figure 5.5.

FIGURE 5.5
Search for and replace
selected text,
formatting, or other
elements from the
Replace tab.

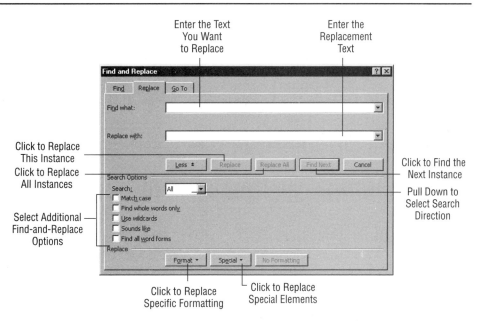

Enter the Text
You Want
to Replace

Enter the
Replacement
Text

Click to Replace
This Instance

Click to Replace
All Instances

Select Additional
Find-and-Replace
Options

Click to Find the
Next Instance

Pull Down to
Select Search
Direction

Click to Replace
Specific Formatting

Click to Replace
Special Elements

2. To display all options for finding and replacing, click the More button.

3. Enter the text you want to replace in the Find What box. (If you're searching for formatting or special elements, as described in steps 6 and 7, you don't have to enter any text here.)

4. Enter the replacement text, if any, in the Replace With box.

5. Under Search Options, select any additional options for the operation, if any. Also, use the pull-down list to select which direction to search.

6. If you want to replace specific formatting in your document, click the Format button, choose a format from the list, and then enter or select the appropriate information as determined by the format you are searching.

7. If you want to replace special elements in your document, click the Special button, and choose an element from the list.

8. Click the Replace button to replace just the currently selected item, or click the Replace All button to find and replace all instances in your document at once.

9. Click the Find Next button to find the next instance.

As step 8 notes, you can choose to replace the currently highlighted instance of the designated text or item or to search your document and automatically replace all instances that match your search criteria. If you choose to replace one instance at a time, which lets you confirm or cancel each potential replacement, you can either click the Find Next button or press Shift+F4 to find the next instance of the item.

In most instances, you'll probably be replacing plain text; to do so, just enter the text you want to find in the Find What box, and click Find Next.

 NOTE The search options on the Replace tab are identical to the options on the Find tab.

Finding and Replacing Formatting

In addition to finding and replacing plain text, you can also find and replace only that text that contains a specific type of formatting, or you can find and replace specific formatting applied to *any* text in your document.

Word enables you to find and replace the following types of document formatting:

Font You can search by font, font style (bold, italic, etc.), size, color, spacing, and other properties. As an example, you can use this option to replace all 12-point, bold, Garamond text with 10-point, italic Times New Roman.

Paragraph You can search for paragraphs with specific alignment, indentation, and spacing. As an example, you can use this option to change all centered paragraphs to be left-aligned.

Tabs You can search for tab stops by alignment or by leader character. As an example, you can replace all dotted leader tabs with dashed leaders.

Language   You can search for blocks of text tagged with specific languages or replace one language tag with another. (This option does *not* translate text from one language to another!)

Frame   You can search for frames with specific text wrapping, position, or size. As an example, you can change all left-aligned frames to have right alignment.

Style   You can search for paragraphs tagged with specific styles. As an example, you can change all of your Heading 1 paragraphs to be styled as Heading 2s.

Highlight   You can search for all highlighted text and then replace highlighted text with non-highlighted text, or vice versa.

To find and/or replace text with a specific format, follow these steps:

1. Select either the Find or the Replace tab in the Find and Replace dialog box.

2. Enter the text you're looking for in the Find What box.

3. Click the Format button, and select a specific format from the list; this displays a dialog box specific to the formatting you selected to find. From this new dialog box, select the criteria for your search.

4. If you're replacing text, enter the new text in the Replace With box. If you're keeping the text but changing the formatting, enter the same text in the Replace With box that you entered into the Find What box. (If you're only using the Find command, ignore this step.)

5. Click the Format button again, select a new format from the list, and then select new options from the resulting dialog box. (If you're only using the Find command, ignore this step also.)

6. Click Find to find text with the selected formatting; click Replace to replace the selected text/formatting with new text and/or formatting.

You can also search for specific formatting independent of the associated text. To do this, repeat the preceding steps but leave the Find What and Replace With boxes blank.

 TIP   To clear the formatting search criteria, click the No Formatting button in the Find and Replace dialog box.

Finding and Replacing Special Elements

You can also search for special elements within your documents. When you click the Special button on either the Find or Replace tabs, you can choose from a list of elements that includes:

- Paragraph mark
- Tab character
- Comment mark
- Any character
- Any digit
- Any letter
- Caret character
- Column break
- Em dash
- En dash
- Endnote mark
- Field
- Footnote mark
- Graphic
- Manual line break
- Manual page break
- Nonbreaking hyphen
- Nonbreaking space
- Optional hypen
- Section break
- White space

To find and/or replace these special characters, follow these steps:

1. Select either the Find or Replace tab in the Find and Replace dialog box.

2. Position your cursor in the Find What box.

3. Click the Special button to display the special characters list. Select the character you want to find; that character is automatically inserted into the Find What box.

4. If you want to select a replacement character, position your cursor in the Replace With box, and then click the Special button. Select a replacement character from the special characters list; that character is automatically inserted into the Replace With box.

5. Click Find to find the next instance of the special character; when the character is located, click Replace to replace the first character with the second character, and repeat as necessary.

 TIP If you know the keyboard combination or special code for a character, you can enter it directly in either the Find What box or the Replace With box, bypassing the Special button.

You can use the Replace command to "batch edit" special characters throughout your document. For example, if you've entered (c) for the copyright symbol throughout your document, you can choose to replace (c) with © throughout.

Searching with Wildcards

Wildcards are special characters that let you search for multiple characters in a query. As an example, the * wildcard searches for any combination of characters from its insertion point onward; so when you enter *dead**, you search for any word that starts with *dead,* including *deadline, deadly,* and *deaden.*

Table 5.2 lists some of the more popular wildcard characters you can use when searching in Word.

TABLE 5.2: COMMON WILDCARD CHARACTERS

Wildcard	Finds This	Example
*	Any characters following the existing text	*Mon** finds *Monty, money,* and *monster.*
?	Any single character	*B?b* finds *Bob, bib,* and *Bab.*
[xyz]	Any of the characters specified within the brackets	*B[oi]b* finds *Bob* and *bib.*
[x-y]	Any range of characters (from x to y)	*[B-D]ob* finds *Bob, cob,* and *DOB.*
[!x]	Any single character *except* the single character within the brackets	*B[!o]b* finds *bib* and *Bab* but not *Bob.*
[!x-y]	Any single character *except* the range of characters within the brackets	*[!B-D]ob* finds *fob, gob,* and *sob,* but not *Bob, cob,* and *DOB.*

Continued ▐▶

TABLE 5.2: COMMON WILDCARD CHARACTERS (CONTINUED)

Wildcard	Finds This	Example
<(xy)	Specified character(s) at the beginning of a word	<(UN) finds *undo, uncouth,* and *UNCLE.*
(xy)>	Specified character(s) at the end of a word	(ED)> finds *busted, changed,* and *seed.*
{n}	Exactly *n* occurrences of the preceding character	10{2} finds *100* (two occurrences of the character *0*).
{n,}	At least *n* occurrences of the preceding character	10{3,} finds *1000, 10000, 100000,* and so on (at least three occurrences of the character *0*).
{n,m}	From *n* to *m* occurrences of the preceding character	10{2,4} finds *100, 1000,* and *10000* (from two to four occurrences of the character *0*).
@	One or more occurrences of the preceding character	10@ finds *10, 100, 1000, 10000,* and so on.

Remember, though, to use wildcards with the Find or the Replace command, you have to check the Use Wildcards option.

CHAPTER **6**

Correcting Your Spelling and Grammar

Proofing your spelling   178

Using custom dictionaries   185

Checking your grammar   188

Understanding Word's readability statistics   193

Finding the right word with Word's thesaurus   195

Working with hyphens   196

Correcting typos with AutoCorrect   199

Formatting faster with AutoFormat   204

After you've created your document and entered and edited your text, it's time to proof your document for errors. While you could employ a human proofreader (and pay dearly for the privilege!), it's easy to use Word 2000's proofing tools to find and fix errors in your document automatically.

Word includes several different proofing tools—including a spell checker, grammar checker, and thesaurus—that make proofing your document quick, easy, and effective. You can even choose to have these tools work in real time, as you type your document. Read on to learn more about Word's proofing tools—and how best to use them!

Proofing Your Spelling

All versions of Word have included a spell checker, and each new version of the program has, in some way, enhanced the capabilities of this useful tool. The main improvement in Word 2000 is an expansion of the main spelling dictionary, adding a broader range of proper names for people, places, and organizations. In addition, Word's main spelling dictionary has been integrated into the AutoCorrect function, so that spelling mistakes can literally be corrected as you type.

There are actually three ways to check your spelling with Word 2000:

Automatic Spell Checking   Flags potential misspellings as you type—but doesn't automatically correct them.

AutoCorrect Spell Checking   Uses Word 2000's AutoCorrect function to automatically change any misspelled words as you type.

Batch Spell Checking   Checks your entire document for misspellings in one operation.

Understanding Spell Checking

Word's spell checker isn't a very smart program. Essentially, all it does is try to make matches—between words in your document and words in the program's main spelling dictionary.

The spelling dictionary is, for want of a better description, a large database file. It contains hundreds of thousands of words, just as a regular dictionary does. When you run Word's spell checker, it goes through your document, word for word, searching for each word in the spelling dictionary database. If it finds the word in the database, it assumes that it's spelled correctly, and moves on to the next word.

Continued ▸

When the spell checker encounters a word *not* in the dictionary's database, it assumes the word is misspelled, and alerts you to that fact. (It even suggests potential respellings, based on words in the dictionary that are spelled similar to the word you misspelled.)

There are a number of reasons why the spell checker isn't very smart. First, any word *not* in the dictionary—even if it's spelled correctly—is assumed to be misspelled. (And, as most users soon realize, there are a *lot* of real words not in the main spelling dictionary!) Second, the spell checker can't tell if you used the wrong word—so if you typed *threw* when you should have typed *through*, the spell checker says the word is spelled correctly, when it really isn't, kind of. Third, the spell checker can only offer respelling suggestions from its own limited dictionary—and even then, it sometimes suggests words that have no relation to the misspelled word, other than a similarity in spelling.

So, if you believe everything the spell checker tells you, you won't catch all the misspellings in your document—and you'll change some words that weren't misspelled. The best advice is to take the spell checker's messages as suggestions, and make the final call on each word yourself.

Configuring Word's Spell Checker

Before you use Word's spell checker, there are a few configuration options you might want to check or change. You access Word's spelling options by selecting Tools ➢ Options to display the Options dialog box, and then selecting the Spelling & Grammar tab.

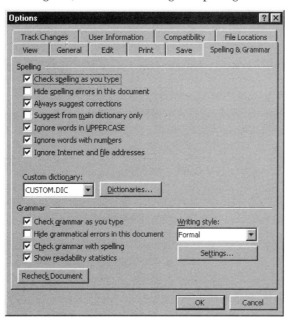

Here are some of the options you can set:

Suggest Corrections By default, Word always suggests corrections when it finds a potentially misspelled word. If you find these suggestions annoying, you can turn them off by unchecking the Always Suggest Corrections option. If you want Word to limit its suggestions to the main spelling dictionary (instead of incorporating words from the custom dictionaries, as it does by default), check the Suggest From Main Dictionary Only option.

Hide Your Mistakes from Others If other users will be reading your document onscreen, you may want to hide any spelling errors flagged by the spelling checker. To hide these wavy red lines, check the Hide Spelling Errors in This Document option.

Ignore Problem Words Certain types of words tend to get flagged as misspelled, when in fact they're spelled correctly. These words—typically proper nouns—include words in all uppercase (often used for organizations or products), words with numbers (often used for products, especially in the computer industry!), and Internet and network addresses. To have the spell checker skip over these types of words when proofing your document, check the Ignore Words in UPPERCASE, Ignore Words with Numbers, and Ignore Internet and File Addresses options.

Correcting Your Spelling on the Fly

For the past several versions of Microsoft Word, spell checking has been totally integrated into the editing process. In older versions of Word, however, you had to run spell checking as a one-pass operation because Word didn't have on-the-fly checking. With Word 2000, Automatic Spell Checking has been augmented with AutoCorrect Spell Checking, so that Word can check—and automatically correct—your spelling just as fast as you can type words into your document.

Flagging Misspellings as You Type

By default, Word 2000 is set with Automatic Spell Checking enabled. With Automatic Spell Checking, Word checks the spelling of each word as you type it into your document. Any word not found in the spelling dictionary is assumed to be misspelled, and flagged with a wavy red underline, as shown in Figure 6.1.

 NOTE The red wavy underline applied to potentially misspelled words only appears on–screen; these proofing marks do *not* appear in your printed documents.

 TIP You can turn off Automatic Spell Checking by selecting Tools ➢ Options to display the Options dialog box, then selecting the Spelling & Grammar tab and *unchecking* the Check Spelling as You Type option.

FIGURE 6.1
*Potentially misspelled
words are flagged with
a wavy red underline.*

Misspelled Words

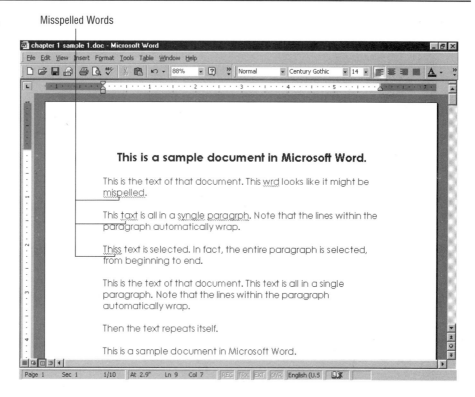

At any time in the editing process, you can examine the spelling any of the flagged words. When you right-click a potentially misspelled word, Word displays a pop-up menu with the following options, as shown in Figure 6.2:

FIGURE 6.2
*Right-click a misspelled
word to access spelling
options.*

Suggested Words   The spell checker will typically suggest one or more words that it thinks could represent the correct spelling of the flagged word. (If the phrase "no spelling suggestions" is displayed, that means the spell checker had no idea what you were trying to type!) Click to accept a word; Word then replaces the flagged word with the correction you selected.

Ignore All   When you select this option, the spell checker ignores all instances of the flagged word—and leaves the word spelled as is—throughout your entire document. Select Ignore All when you don't want to change the word, but also don't want to permanently add it to Word's dictionary. (Selecting this option does *not* add the flagged word to the spell dictionary.)

Add   When you select this option, the flagged word is added to Word's custom dictionary. Select this option when you use a new word that you expect to use often in the future.

AutoCorrect   Select this option to display a second list of suggested corrections. When you select a word from the AutoCorrect list, you replace the flagged word with the corrected word *and* add the spelling error and its correction to the Auto-Correct list—so, in the future, Word will correct this mistake automatically as you type. Select this option if you use AutoCorrect Spell Checking.

Language   When you select this option, you can change from English spell checking to another language. If no other languages are displayed, select the Set Language option to display the Language dialog box and choose a new language.

Spelling   Select this option to display the Spelling dialog box (shown in Figure 6.3), which contains additional spelling options (discussed in the "Running the Spell Checker on Your Entire Document" section of this chapter).

NOTE   The options displayed may differ, depending on how badly the flagged word is misspelled.

In most cases you'll right-click a misspelled word, select a respelling from the pop-up menu, and be done with it. While you can select Ignore All to ignore this and all other instances of this particular word, most users don't bother—and live with the red wavy underlines for correctly spelled words that Word doesn't recognize.

Spell Checking with AutoCorrect

You can also use Word 2000's AutoCorrect feature to automatically *correct* misspellings as you type. (Remember, Automatic Spell Checking only *flags* potentially misspellings—it doesn't correct them for you.)

To turn on AutoCorrect Spell Checking, select Tools ➢ AutoCorrect to display the AutoCorrect dialog box. Select the AutoCorrect tab, then check the Automatically Use Suggestions from the Spelling Checker option.

 WARNING For AutoCorrect Spell Checking to function, the Check Spelling as You Type option must also be selected on the Spelling & Grammar tab of the Options dialog box.

When AutoCorrect Spell Checking is enabled, AutoCorrect will automatically correct most—but not all—misspellings as you type.

AutoCorrect *will* correct:

- Common misspellings with only one suggested correction
- Words listed in AutoCorrect's Replace Text as You Type list
- Previously misspelled words you've added to the AutoCorrect list

AutoCorrect will *not* correct:

- Misspellings with more than one suggested correction
- Misspellings with no suggested corrections
- Words listed in AutoCorrect's exception list

As an example, AutoCorrect *will* automatically replace "teh" with "the." However, it will *not* attempt to correct "teeh," which has several suggested corrections. Any potentially misspelled words *not* corrected by AutoCorrect are flagged with the usual red wavy line for you to examine manually.

If AutoCorrect corrects something it shouldn't have corrected, click Undo on the Standard toolbar (or select Edit ➢ Undo) to remove the correction, then retype the original word. AutoCorrect will automatically add the correction to its exceptions list, so it won't make that (incorrect) correction again.

 NOTE To learn more about AutoCorrect, see the "Correcting Typos with AutoCorrect" section later in this chapter.

Running the Spell Checker on Your Entire Document

Many users prefer to check the spelling of their documents in a single operation. When you choose to run the spell checker as a separate operation, it proceeds through your document from top to bottom, checking each word in order.

You can initiate Batch Spell Checking in one of several ways:

- Select Tools ➢ Spelling and Grammar

- Click the Spelling and Grammar button on Word's Standard toolbar
- Press F7

When Word's spell checker finds a potentially misspelled word, it displays the Spelling dialog box, shown in Figure 6.3. The potentially misspelled word is listed in the Not in Dictionary box, and suggested respellings are listed in the Suggestions list.

FIGURE 6.3
Use the Spelling dialog box to fix spelling errors found by Word's spell checker.

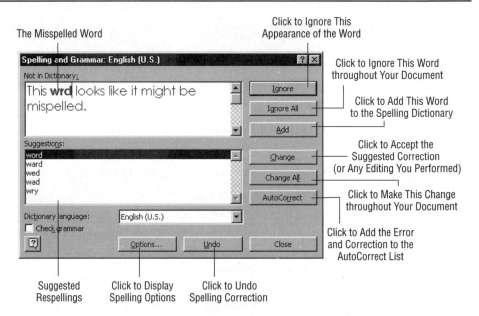

The Misspelled Word

Click to Ignore This Appearance of the Word

Click to Ignore This Word throughout Your Document

Click to Add This Word to the Spelling Dictionary

Click to Accept the Suggested Correction (or Any Editing You Performed)

Click to Make This Change throughout Your Document

Click to Add the Error and Correction to the AutoCorrect List

Suggested Respellings

Click to Display Spelling Options

Click to Undo Spelling Correction

From here you have the following options:

Ignore the Word   If you want to accept the current spelling (but *not* add the word to Word's spelling dictionary), click Ignore. If you want to accept all appearances of this word throughout your document, click Ignore All.

Add the Word to the Spelling Dictionary   If you've entered a correctly spelled word that isn't yet contained within the spelling dictionary, click the Add button to accept the current spelling and add the word to the dictionary.

Accept a Suggested Correction   If the spell checker has listed the correct spelling of the word, select the correction from the Suggestions list and click the Change button. If you want to replace all appearances in your document of the misspelled word with this correction, click the Change All button.

Edit the Word   You have the option of correcting the misspelling yourself. Position your cursor in the Not in Dictionary box and edit the misspelled word, then click Change (to change this appearance of the word) or Change All (to change all appearances of the word throughout your document).

Add the Correction to the AutoCorrect List   After you've either accepted a correction or edited the word (but *before* you click Change or Change All), you can add the misspelling/correction combination to Word's AutoCorrect list. Just click the AutoCorrect button, then click the Change or Change All buttons to execute the correction.

After you change or ignore a misspelling, Word's spell checker moves to the next potentially misspelled word in your document. When the spell checker reaches the end of your document, it displays a dialog box informing you that the spell checking is complete.

 TIP To have Word skip parts of your document when performing a spell or grammar check, select the text you don't want to check, then select Tools ➢ Language ➢ Set Language to display the Language dialog box. Check the Do Not Check Spelling or Grammar option, then click OK and initiate your spell or grammar check.

Using Custom Dictionaries

A standard spelling check is performed using Word's main spelling dictionary. However, you can also add one or more *custom dictionaries* to your system, and incorporate them into your spell checks.

You use custom dictionaries to add words that aren't included in Word's main dictionary. By default, Word creates its own custom dictionary (filename CUSTOM.DIC), in which it stores all the words you add (by clicking the Add button) during your spell checks, and checks against both the main and the CUSTOM.DIC dictionary during spell checks.

You can also add other custom dictionaries to your system—either dictionaries you create, or specialty dictionaries you obtain from third parties. For example, you might create a custom dictionary that includes technical terms and product names specific to a particular company or industry, or add a specialty dictionary with terms specific to a given profession.

PART

I

Learning New Features and
Creating New Documents

NOTE The CD accompanying this book includes two custom dictionaries: *BioSpel* (containing biological terms) and *MedSpel* (containing medical terms). See Chapter 33 for more information.

Adding a Custom Dictionary to Your System

If you've obtained a custom dictionary file from a third party, follow these steps to add the dictionary to your system:

1. Copy the custom dictionary file to a folder on your hard disk. (If you copy the file to the `\Windows\Application Data\Microsoft\Proof` folder, you can now skip to step 7 and activate the dictionary; otherwise, proceed to step 2.)

2. Select Tools ➢ Options to display the Options dialog box.

3. Select the Spelling & Grammar tab.

4. Click the Dictionaries button to display the Custom Dictionaries dialog box.

5. Click the Add button to display the Add Custom Dictionary dialog box.

6. Navigate to the folder that contains the new custom dictionary file, select the file, and click OK.

7. To activate the new dictionary, return to the Custom Dictionaries dialog box and check the box next to the dictionary's name.

8. Click OK when done.

To delete any custom dictionary from your system, click the Remove button. To deactivate a dictionary without removing it from your system, uncheck the box next to the dictionary's name.

Creating a New Custom Dictionary

To create a new custom dictionary, follow these steps:

1. Select Tools ➢ Options to display the Options dialog box.
2. Select the Spelling & Grammar tab.
3. Click the Dictionaries button to display the Custom Dictionaries dialog box.
4. Click the New button to display the Create Custom Dictionary dialog box.
5. Enter a name for your new dictionary in the File Name box.
6. Click the Save button to return to the Custom Dictionaries dialog box.

 TIP If you want to use a custom dictionary only to check text in a specific language, select the dictionary and then select a language from the Language list.

7. To activate the new dictionary, make sure the box next to the dictionary's name is checked.
8. Click OK when done.

Once you've created a new custom dictionary, you can start to add words to its dictionary list.

Adding Words to a Custom Dictionary

There are two ways to add words to a custom dictionary—during a spell check, and as a separate operation.

To add a word to a custom dictionary during a spell check, just click the Add button (or select Add from the pop-up menu) when the spell checker identifies a potential misspelling. The word will be added to the currently selected custom dictionary. (To change the selected dictionary, click the Options button or select Tools ➢ Options to open the Options dialog box; select the Spelling & Grammar tab and select a new dictionary from the Custom Dictionary list.)

To add, edit, or delete words directly in a custom dictionary file, follow these steps:

1. Select Tools ➢ Options to display the Options dialog box.
2. Select the Spelling & Grammar tab.
3. Click the Dictionaries button to display the Custom Dictionary dialog box.
4. Select the dictionary you want to edit, then click the Edit button.

5. The custom dictionary file will now be loaded into Microsoft Word. Add words by typing them (one per line) into the file. Delete words by deleting them (making sure to delete the entire line). Edit words as you would normally.

6. When you're finished editing, save and then close the file as you would normally.

 TIP If you accidentally add an incorrectly spelled word to your custom dictionary, you can edit the dictionary file to either respell or delete the word.

Checking Your Grammar

Not only can you proof the spelling of individual words within Word documents, but you can also proof the way in which those words are put together. Word 2000 includes a state-of-the-art grammar checker that analyzes your documents for grammatical correctness, and offers suggestions on how to improve your writing.

Grammar Checking—Pros and Cons

Grammar checking is more involved than spell checking. Where a spell checker only has to compare one word against the records in a database, a grammar checker has to "read" your document—in phrases, sentences, and paragraphs—and then *parse* what you've written into its component parts of grammar. With your writing thus dissected, the grammar checker tries to analyze the meaning of what you've written, and compares it to accepted rules of grammar for a specific style of writing. The grammar checker then flags parts of your document that may be grammatically incorrect, and offers suggestions on how to improve the passages in question.

Frankly, grammar checking is a feature that is either greatly loved or greatly hated by Word users. Since it is the most subjective and imprecise of all of Word's tools, many users find themselves frequently disagreeing with the grammar checker's suggestions—or not quite understanding how to actually implement the suggestions. Other users, who may be less confident of their writing skills, appreciate the major changes in readability possible by following the grammar checker's simplest recommendations.

If you're one of those that hates grammar checking, learn how to turn it off. Otherwise, you'll find yourself doing a *lot* of manual rewriting.

Continued ▸

You see, since grammar and writing style can't be automatically corrected by a simple software program, you have to rewrite the offending phrases yourself. At the end of the day, Word is a great word processing tool, but it can't do your writing for you. You have to make your own grammatical and stylistic choices—both of which are part of your own personal writing "voice." Make your choices, find your voice, and don't let anyone—or any software tool—dictate your writing style!

Configuring Word's Grammar Checker

Word 2000's grammar checker includes a master list filled with specific grammatical rules. According to the style of writing selected, certain rules are turned on or off. This way you can configure the grammar checker to be more or less "strict," depending on whether you've selected a more or less formal writing style.

You configure the grammar checker by selecting Tools ➢ Options to display the Options dialog box, and then selecting the Spelling & Grammar tab. From here you can:

- Turn on Automatic Grammar Checking (check the Check Grammar as You Type option)
- Hide the wavy green lines the grammar checker uses to flag potential grammatical problems (check the Hide Grammatical Errors in This Document option)
- Check your documents for grammar at the same time you check for spelling errors (check the Check Grammar with Spelling option)
- Display a grammatical analysis of all checked documents (check the Show Readability Statistics option)

Selecting a Writing Style

You can select how formal or casual you want your documents to read; Word's grammar checker will change accordingly the individual rules it uses to check your documents.

You select a grammatical style from the Writing Style list on the Spelling & Grammar tab of the Options dialog box. You can choose from five pre-selected writing styles:

Standard   The default style, which is good for all-around writing

Casual   The style with the fewest number of rules, which is good for personal correspondence and informal communication

Formal   The style with the most rules, and the preferred style for contracts and other serious correspondence

Technical   A combination of rules particularly suited for technical writing

Custom   A style that lets you make your own rules

You can select different writing styles for different documents; select the style that best matches the kind of writing you're about to do.

Configuring Individual Grammatical Rules

You can customize any of the preset writing styles—in addition to the Custom style—by turning on or off specific grammatical rules. Follow these steps to select individual rules:

1. Select Tools ➢ Options to display the Options dialog box.
2. Select the Spelling & Grammar tab.
3. Click the Settings button to display the Grammar Settings dialog box.

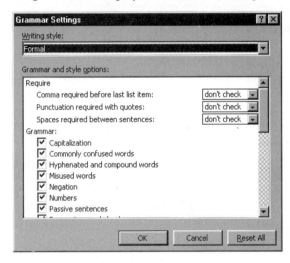

4. Select a style from the Writing Style list.
5. Check those rules you wish to employ, and uncheck those you wish to ignore.
6. Click OK.

The different types of rules available are described in Table 6.1:

TABLE 6.1: WORD 2000'S WRITING RULES

Type of Rule	Description
Capitalization	Makes sure that proper nouns (and titles preceding proper nouns) are capitalized, and also checks that you're not capitalizing words that shouldn't be capitalized
Commonly Confused Words	Looks for homophones and other commonly misused words, such as its/it's, principal/principle, your/you're, and so on
Hyphenated and Compound Words	Looks for words that shouldn't be hyphenated but are, and vice versa; also looks for closed compound words that should be open, and vice versa
Misused Words	Looks for incorrect usage of adjectives and adverbs, as well as comparatives and superlatives

Continued ▐▶

TABLE 6.1: WORD 2000'S WRITING RULES (CONTINUED)

Type of Rule	Description
Negation	Looks for instances of multiple negation ("can't not")
Numbers	Suggests when numbers should be spelled out ("twelve") or entered as numerals ("12")
Passive Sentences	Searches out the passive voice and suggests how to rewrite
Possessives and Plurals	Looks for instances of possessives used in place of a plurals (and vice versa), and corresponding apostrophe problems
Punctuation	Looks for all sorts of incorrect punctuation, including commas, colons, quotations, semicolons, and so on
Relative Clauses	Looks for incorrect use of relative pronouns and associated punctuation (when to use "who" vs. "which," for example)
Sentence Structure	Checks for sentence fragments, run-on sentences, overuse of conjunctions, and so on
Subject-Verb Agreement	Searches for disagreements between subjects and verbs
Verb and Noun Phrases	Looks for incorrect noun and verb phrases, incorrect verb tenses, and so on ("a" vs. "an," for example)
Clichés	Checks for the use of overused words and phrases
Colloquialisms	Searches for colloquial words and phrases
Contractions	Suggests when contractions should be spelled out in more formal writing
Gender-Specific Words	Advises against gender-specific language and suggests gender-neutral replacements (replacing "postman" with "postal worker," for example)
Jargon	Warns against excessive use of technical or industry-specific words and phrases
Sentence Length	Warns against sentences that include more than 60 words
Sentences Beginning with "And," "But," and "Hopefully"	Advises against starting sentences with these adverbs
Successive Nouns	Warns against use of more than three nouns in a row
Successful Prepositional Phrases	Warns against use of three prepositional phrases in a row
Unclear Phrasing	Advises when phrasing is ambiguous
Use of First Person	Suggests when "I," "me," and "my" shouldn't be used in technical writing
Wordiness	Looks for long or vague clauses or modifiers
Words in Split Infinitives	Looks for two or more words between "to" and any infinitive verb

Check a rule to activate it; uncheck a rule to remove it from the grammar checker's list. You can also select optional application of the following stylistic rules:

- Comma required before last list item (always, never, don't check)
- Punctuation required with quotes (inside, outside, don't check)
- Spaces required between sentences (1, 2, don't check)

In general, the more rules applied, the more formal the writing; the fewer the rules, the more conversational the writing. If you prefer a "looser" style (and don't want to be annoyed with a lot of grammar-related queries), try turning off some of the more restrictive individual rules.

Correcting Your Grammar on the Fly

When Automatic Grammar Checking is enabled, Word checks your document as it is being typed. Any grammatically questionable phrases are flagged with a wavy green underline.

To examine (and possibly fix) a flagged phrase, right-click anywhere within the phrase. Word displays a pop-up menu that contains a brief explanation of why the phrase was flagged. From here, you can select to Ignore the advice, or you can go back into your document to edit the phrase to be more grammatically correct. (Some simple suggestions—such as adding or changing a punctuation mark—are "live" so they can be selected to replace the original offending text.)

 TIP If you want to display the more full-featured Grammar dialog box, select the Grammar command on the pop-up menu.

Running the Grammar Checker on Your Entire Document

 Many users prefer to turn off Automatic Grammar Checking but then batch-check a document's grammar after they've completed their first-draft writing. To run Word's grammar checker at the same time you run Word's spell checker, go to the Spelling & Grammar tab in the Options dialog box and check the Check Grammar with Spelling option. With this option selected, you run the grammar checker (and the spell checker) when you select Tools ➤ Spelling and Grammar, click the Spelling and Grammar button on Word's Standard toolbar, or press F7.

When you run the grammar checker in this fashion, Word displays the Spelling and Grammar dialog box (shown in Figure 6.4) when it encounters a grammatical problem.

PART

I

Learning New Features and
Creating New Documents

FIGURE 6.4
*Use the Spelling and
Grammar dialog box to
fix grammatical
problems in your
documents.*

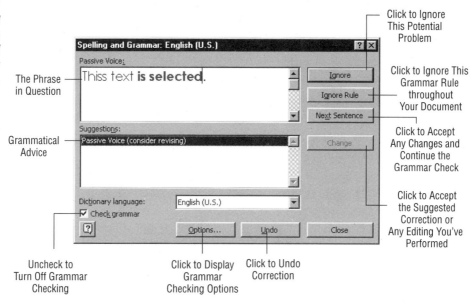

From here you have the following options:

Fix the Phrase   You can edit the phrase as it appears in the top text box or return to your document and edit the text there. Click Change to accept the change, and then click Next Sentence to resume grammar checking.

Ignore the Problem   If you want to keep your text as is, click Ignore.

Ignore the Rule   If you want to ignore the rule that flagged this particular phrase (for example, if you're tired of being hounded about passive voice), click Ignore Rule. The grammar checker will then turn off this grammar rule for the balance of the current document.

Turn Off the Grammar Checker   To turn off the grammar checker (and continue spell checking the current document), uncheck the Check Grammar option.

Remember, even though the grammar checker identifies potential grammatical problems, you'll have to fix most of the problems yourself.

Understanding Word's Readability Statistics

You can also elect to display a grammatical "report card" for the current document when Word finishes running the grammar checker. The Readability Statistics dialog box, shown in Figure 6.5, contains the following information about your current document:

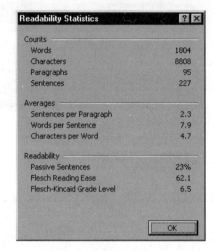

- Word, character, paragraph, and sentence counts
- Average number of sentences per paragraph, words per sentence, and characters per word

 TIP   If all you want is a count of your document's characters, words, lines, paragraphs, or pages (without the other readability statistics), select Tools ➢ Word Count to display the Word Count dialog box.

- The percent of total sentences that use passive voice; lower is generally better
- The Flesch Reading Ease score; the higher the score, the more readable the document (for most documents, aim for a score in the 60-70 range)
- The Flesch-Kincaid Grade Level, which indicates the approximate reading level of your document (a score of 6.0 indicates that a sixth grader can understand your document, for example)

Examine this report card (in particular, the Flesch Reading Ease and Flesch-Kincaid Grade Level scores) to determine if your document is easy enough to be read by your target audience.

 NOTE   To display readability statistics, you must check the Show Readability Statistics option on the Spelling & Grammar tab of the Options dialog box.

Proofing with Word's Other Language Tools

In addition to the spell checker and grammar checker, Word 2000 also includes two
other language tools—a real-time thesaurus, and an automatic hyphenation function.

Finding the Right Word with Thesaurus

Word 2000 includes a completely new thesaurus with easier operation. With Word 2000's
thesaurus, you're just a few clicks away from finding a better word than the one you originally typed.

Using the Full Thesaurus

To use Word's thesaurus, follow these steps:

1. Position the insertion point anywhere in the word you wish to look up, or simply
    highlight the word.

2. Select Tools ➢ Language ➢ Thesaurus (or press Shift+F7) to display the Thesau-
    rus dialog box, shown in Figure 6.6.

FIGURE 6.6
*Use the Thesaurus
dialog box to look for
similar words.*

The Original Word
Selected in Your Text

Definitions of the
Selected Word

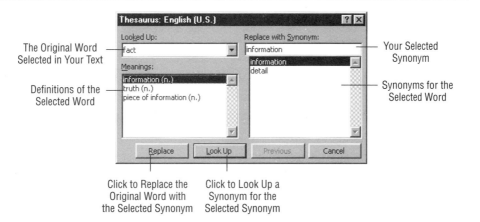

Your Selected
Synonym

Synonyms for the
Selected Word

Click to Replace the
Original Word with
the Selected Synonym

Click to Look Up a
Synonym for the
Selected Synonym

 WARNING If the selected word is not found in Word's thesaurus, the dialog box will
display a "not found" message and a list of words with similar spellings in case the selected
word happened to be spelled incorrectly.

3. If the selected word has more than one definition, select the proper meaning from the Meanings list.

4. Select a word from the Replace with Synonym list.

5. To look up synonyms of the selected synonym, click Look Up; click Previous to return to the original word.

6. To replace the selected word with the selected synonym, click Insert.

 TIP   In some cases, the Word 2000 thesaurus will also display antonyms for the selected word.

Looking Up Synonyms Quickly

 Word 2000 also offers the option of displaying a short list of synonyms directly from a pop-up menu. Just right-click any word and select Synonyms from the pop-up menu. You can then select any of the listed synonyms, or select Thesaurus to display the more full-featured Thesaurus dialog box.

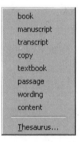

Note, however, that when you use the pop-up synonym feature, Word only displays synonyms for the first meaning of multiple-meaning words. If you want access to all the meanings and synonyms in Word's thesaurus, press F7 or select Tools ➢ Language ➢ Thesaurus to display the full Thesaurus dialog box.

 WARNING   You can't right-click to find a synonym for any word that has been flagged by the spell checker or grammar checker.

Working with Hyphens

By default, none of the words in your document are hyphenated. That means that if you type a long word at the end of a line, the word *won't* be broken in two; instead, the word is shifted to the start of the next line.

Without hyphenation, your documents can include huge gaps of white space on individual lines—especially if the text in the host paragraph is justified. Instead, you might want to consider hyphenating words that appear at the end of long lines of text. Hyphenation—whether manual or automatic—can make your documents look more professional.

Using Automatic Hyphenation

Word 2000 includes the capability to automatically hyphenate your document as you type. With automatic hyphenation enabled, Word will automatically insert hyphens as needed to ensure smooth line breaks throughout your document.

NOTE If you later edit the document and change line breaks, then Word rehyphenates the document.

To turn on automatic hyphenation, follow these steps:

1. Select Tools ➤ Language ➤ Hyphenation to display the Hyphenation dialog box.

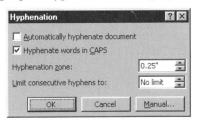

2. Check the Automatically Hyphenate Document option.

3. Use the Hyphenation Zone control to select the amount of space you want to leave between the end of a line, between the end of the last word in a line, and the right margin. (The wider the zone, the fewer number of hyphens used; the narrower the zone, the neater the right margin.)

4. Use the Limit Consecutive Hyphens To control to select the number of consecutive lines that can be hyphenated.

5. If you don't want to hyphenate words in all uppercase (which are often proper nouns), uncheck the Hyphenate Words in Caps option.

6. Click OK to activate the automatic hyphenation.

When you activate automatic hyphenation, any existing text in your document will be automatically hyphenated. To *unhyphenate* a document, follow the above steps and *uncheck* the Automatically Hyphenate Document option.

Hyphenating Words—Manually

If you'd rather choose when and where to apply hyphenation in your document, you should disable automatic hyphenation and use Word's manual hyphenation feature. When you manually hyphenate your document, you'll be asked to confirm all proposed word breaks in your document.

To use manual hyphenation, follow these steps:

1. Select Tools ➢ Language ➢ Hyphenation to display the Hyphenation dialog box.

2. Click the Manual button.

3. Word now proceeds through your document checking for necessary hyphenation. When it finds a long word at the end of a line (or at the beginning of the following line), it displays the Manual Hyphenation dialog box, with the selected word displayed. Dictionary-proper hyphens are inserted between each of the word's syllables, and the recommended breaking hyphen is selected and blinking.

4. To accept the recommended breaking hyphen, click Yes. To choose *not* to hyphenate this word, click No. To select a different breaking hyphen, click a new hyphen and click Yes.

You can end the manual hyphenation process at any time by clicking the Cancel button.

 WARNING There is no way to automatically remove hyphens inserted via the manual hyphenation process. If you want to remove manually inserted hyphens, you'll have to delete each hyphen manually, one at a time.

Controlling Hyphenation

To better control potential hyphenation, you can manually insert either *nonbreaking hyphen* or *optional hyphen* characters within specific words in your text.

A non-breaking hyphen tells Word to *not* hyphenate the word at that point. For example, if you don't want to ever hyphenate the word "killer," you'd insert a non-breaking hyphen between the two *l*s.

An optional hyphen tells Word that if the word has to be hyphenated, this is where you want to hyphenate it. For example, inserting an optional hyphen between the *o* and the *m* in the word "automatic" tells Word to hyphenate the word at that point ("auto-matic").

You insert a non-breaking hyphen by pressing Ctrl+Shift+-. You insert a breaking hyphen by pressing Ctrl+-. None of these marks appear in your printed documents *unless* the word is actually hyphenated.

Making Changes Automatically

Word 2000 includes two powerful tools that can fix your mistakes on the fly—Auto-Correct and AutoFormat. While these two tools work in a similar fashion (in real time, while you're entering your text), there are some fundamental differences between them. Read on to learn more.

Correcting Typos with AutoCorrect

AutoCorrect is a powerful feature of Word 2000 that can automatically detect and correct all manner of common typing mistakes—misspelled words, bad grammar, incorrect capitalization, and plain old typos. It works automatically *while you type*, so that your mistakes are corrected almost instantaneously.

If you've checked the spelling and grammar of your document while you type—inserting the little wavy lines under misspelled or ungrammatical text—you've already been using AutoCorrect. But interactive spelling and grammar checking is only a small part of what AutoCorrect can do. You can use AutoCorrect to automatically fix typos as they occur, and to quickly replace selected text with special replacement text—for example, when you type **(c)**, AutoCorrect can instantly replace it with the © character.

Word 2000's version of AutoCorrect is the second iteration of the feature. (Auto-Correct made its first appearance in Word 97.) Among the new and upgraded features of AutoCorrect in Word 2000 are the integration of Word's main spelling dictionary, a new user-created *exceptions list* to prevent unwanted changes to nonstandard words, and global spelling correction with separate lists of AutoCorrect entries for different languages.

Configuring AutoCorrect

Before you use AutoCorrect to correct typos and replace selected text, you need to configure it for these special uses. To activate and configure these features of AutoCorrect, follow these steps:

1. Select Tools ➤ AutoCorrect to display the Options dialog box.
2. Select the AutoCorrect tab, shown in Figure 6.7.

FIGURE 6.7
Access the AutoCorrect dialog box to activate and configure the AutoCorrect feature.

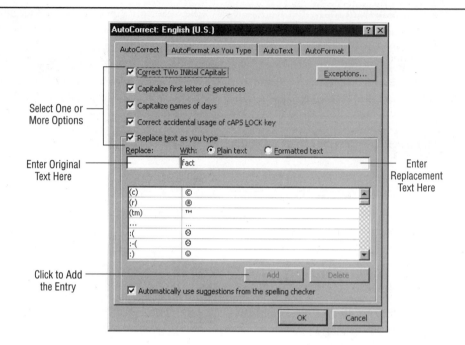

Select One or More Options

Enter Original Text Here

Enter Replacement Text Here

Click to Add the Entry

3. Check the AutoCorrect options you wish to activate, as described in Table 6.2.

4. Click OK to activate.

Table 6.2 describes the various typos and items you can have AutoCorrect automatically correct or change:

TABLE 6.2: AUTOCORRECT OPTIONS

Option	Description	Example
Correct TWo INitial Capitals	If you accidentally type two uppercase letters at the start of a word, changes the second letter to lowercase	Changes *INdiana* to *Indiana*
Capitalize the first letter of sentences	If you forget to capitalize the first letter of a sentence, automatically changes the first letter to uppercase	Changes *this is a new sentence* to *This is a new sentence*
Capitalize names of days	If you forget to capitalize the names of the days of the week, automatically changes the first letter to uppercase	Changes *wednesday* to *Wednesday*

Continued ▶

TABLE 6.2: AUTOCORRECT OPTIONS (CONTINUED)		
Option	Description	Example
Correct accidental usage of cAPS lOCK key	If you accidentally hit the Caps Lock key on your keyboard, you'll reverse the use of uppercase and lowercase letters; this option senses the mistake, switches the reversed uppercase/lowercase letters, and resets the Caps Lock key to the "off" position	Changes *tHIS IS A NEW SENTENCE* to *This is a new sentence*
Replace text as you type	Automatically replaces text from the first column of the list with replacement text from the second column	Replaces *(c)* with ©
Automatically use suggestions from spelling checker	Automatically replaces common misspelled words with correct spellings, as listed in Word's main spelling dictionary	Replaces *teh* with *the*

NOTE The Automatically Use Suggestions from Spelling Checker option can be enabled only if the Replace Text as You Type option is also enabled.

You can configure AutoCorrect with any combination (or all) of these options enabled.

Using AutoCorrect on the Fly

Once AutoCorrect is activated, it starts working the very next time you enter text into a document. When you make a mistake, misspell a word, or enter any text found in the AutoCorrect list, AutoCorrect will change or replace the text you just typed, automatically. There's nothing you need to do except keep typing!

Adding Entries to the AutoCorrect List

The AutoCorrect list contains almost a thousand different words and replacements. As you use AutoCorrect, however, you are sure to find other words that you either misspell frequently or want to replace with other text.

For example, if you continually misspell "Microsoft" as "Microsft," you might want to enter the **Microsft/Microsoft** pair in the AutoCorrect list. As another example, if you frequently use a long, hard-to-type word (such as "pennyfarthing"), you can configure AutoCorrect so when you type a short "dummy" word (such as "abc"), it automatically gets replaced by the longer word (in this instance, you create the **abc/ pennyfarthing** pair).

To add a new listing to the AutoCorrect list, follow these steps:

1. Select Tools ➤ AutoCorrect to display the AutoCorrect dialog box.

2. Select the AutoCorrect tab.

3. Enter the word or phrase you want to replace in the Replace box.

4. Enter the correct word or phrase in the With box.

5. Click the Add button.

You can also add an AutoCorrect entry directly from your text. When you use this method, you can include formatting with your replacement text—or select a graphic object to use as your replacement.

 NOTE To add an AutoCorrect entry directly from your text, you must have the Replace Text as You Type option selected in the AutoCorrect dialog box.

1. In your document, select the text or graphic that you want to store as the Auto-Correct entry. (If you want to include formatting with a text entry, make sure you include the paragraph mark as part of your selection.)

2. Select Tools ➤ AutoCorrect to display the AutoCorrect dialog box; the AutoCorrect tab will already be selected, and the text or graphics you selected in your document will already be pasted into the With box.

3. Enter the text you want to replace in the Replace box. (It's often easier if you enter a memorable name for this shortcut here.)

4. If you want to save the replacement text *without* its original formatting, check the Plain Text option; if you want to save the replacement text *with* its original formatting, check the Formatted Text option.

5. Click the Add button.

 TIP To quickly store symbol characters as AutoCorrect entries, select Insert ➤ Symbol to display the Symbol dialog box, select the symbol you wish to add, then click the AutoCorrect button. When the AutoCorrect dialog box appears, enter the original text (or a name for the symbol) in the Replace box, then click Add.

To delete an entry from the AutoCorrect list, go to the AutoCorrect dialog box, select the entry you want to remove, then click Delete.

Managing AutoCorrect's Exception List

New to Word 2000 is the AutoCorrect *exception list*. This feature lets you specify corrections you *don't* want AutoCorrect to make. For example, you can instruct AutoCorrect *not* to change "eBay" to "Ebay" when it comes at the start of a sentence.

The AutoCorrect exceptions list can include three different kinds of exceptions:

- *Don't* capitalize a word after a specific abbreviation
- *Don't* "correct" a word that has mixed uppercase and lowercase letters (such as "CareerPath")
- *Don't* correct a specific misspelling

To add items to AutoCorrect's exception list, follow these steps:

1. Select Tools ➢ AutoCorrect to display the AutoCorrect dialog box.

2. Select the AutoCorrect tab.

3. Click the Exceptions button to display the AutoCorrect Exceptions dialog box.

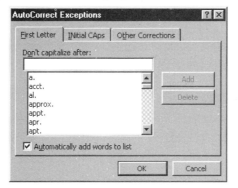

4. To keep AutoCorrect from capitalizing a word after a specific abbreviation, select the First Letter tab, then enter the abbreviation (including the period) in the Don't Capitalize After box.

5. To keep AutoCorrect from "fixing" a word with mixed uppercase and lowercase letters, select the INitial CAps tab, and then enter the word (with its *correct* capitalization) in the Don't Correct box.

6. To keep AutoCorrect from correcting specific misspellings, select the Other Corrections tab, and then enter the word in the Don't Correct box.

7. Click Add to add your entry to the exceptions list and return to the AutoCorrect dialog box.

 WARNING   Any "replace/with" pairs in the AutoCorrect list will take precedence over entries in the exceptions list.

You can also configure the AutoCorrect exceptions list to automatically include any AutoCorrect changes that you undo while editing. Just check the Automatically Add Words to List option in the AutoCorrect Exceptions dialog box. With this option enabled, any time you *undo* an AutoCorrect correction, that correction will be added to the exceptions list—so that AutoCorrect won't repeat the same mistake twice.

Formatting Faster with AutoFormat

AutoFormat is similar to AutoCorrect in that it can automatically replace certain characters with symbols as you type, as well as automatically apply headings, bullets, numbered lists, and borders to your text. (AutoFormat also happens to share some tabs in the AutoCorrect dialog box.) You can use AutoFormat either as you type, or in a separate document-wide operation.

Configuring AutoFormat

You configure the two different types of AutoFormat on separate tabs in the AutoCorrect dialog box. Both tabs share many of the same options, although some options are specific to just one of the operations.

To configure either type of AutoFormat, follow these instructions:

1. Select Tools ➢ AutoCorrect to display the AutoCorrect dialog box.

2. To configure the real-time version of AutoFormat, select the AutoFormat as You Type tab (shown in Figure 6.8); to configure the single-operation "batch" Auto-Format, select the AutoFormat tab.

3. Check those options that you want to apply to your documents, as described in Table 6.3.

4. Click OK.

FIGURE 6.8
*Use one of the two
AutoFormat operations
to automatically format
elements of your
documents.*

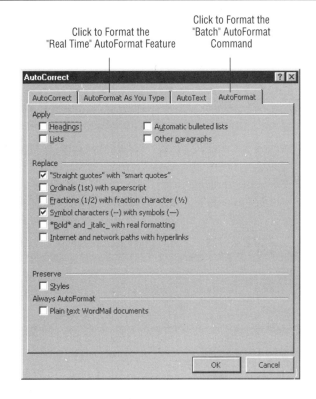

Click to Format the
"Real Time" AutoFormat Feature

Click to Format the
"Batch" AutoFormat
Command

Table 6.3 details the options you can choose to apply when using AutoFormat;
those options specific to one of the two versions are so indicated.

TABLE 6.3: AUTOFORMAT OPTIONS	
Option	**Description**
Apply headings	Automatically applies Heading 1 through Heading 9 styles to headings
Apply borders *(As You Type only)*	Automatically applies character and paragraph border styles when you type three or more hyphens, underscore characters, or equal signs
Apply tables *(As You Type only)*	Automatically creates a table when you type a series of hyphens and plus signs (+----+----+), with one column for each pair of plus signs

Continued ▶

TABLE 6.3: AUTOFORMAT OPTIONS (CONTINUED)

Option	Description
Apply automatic bulleted lists	Automatically applies bulleted-list formatting if you type *, >, or – (followed by a space or tab) at the beginning of a paragraph
Apply automatic numbered lists *(As You Type only)*	Automatically applies numbered-list formatting to any paragraph you start with a number (or letter) followed by a period and a space or tab
Apply lists *(AutoFormat only)*	Automatically applies list styles and bullet styles to numbered, bulleted, and other lists
Apply other formats *(AutoFormat only)*	Automatically applies a variety of paragraph styles, including Body Text, Salutation, and so on
Replace "straight quotes" with "smart quotes"	Automatically replaces characters as you type
Replace ordinals (1st) with superscript	Automatically replaces characters as you type
Replace fractions (1/2) with fraction character (∫)	Automatically replaces characters as you type
Replace symbol characters (--) with symbols (—)	Automatically replaces characters as you type
Replace *bold* and _italic_ with real formatting	Automatically replaces characters as you type
Replace Internet and network paths with hyperlinks	Automatically adds hyperlinks to any Internet addresses you type
Automatically format beginning of list item like the one before it *(As You Type only)*	Automatically formats all items in a list like the first item in the list
Automatically define styles based on your formatting *(As You Type only)*	Automatically creates a new paragraph style based on any manual formatting you apply to a paragraph
Preserve styles *(AutoFormat only)*	When you run the AutoFormat command, doesn't change any paragraph styles you've already applied to your document
Always AutoFormat plain text Word-Mail documents *(AutoFormat only)*	Automatically formats plain-text e-mail messages when you open them in Word

You can select any, all, or none of these options for automatically formatting your documents.

Using AutoFormat on the Fly

As soon as you enable options on the AutoFormat as You Type tab, Word will begin automatically formatting any new text you enter into your document. So, as an example, if you type **www.molehillgroup.com**, AutoFormat will convert this text into a live hyperlink to www.molehillgroup.com.

Assuming you have the appropriate options enabled, here are some of the neater things you can do with the real-time version of AutoFormat:

Start a Bulleted List   You can start a bulleted list by typing – **Item one** and pressing Enter. This turns the dash into a bullet, and sets up the next text you enter to be the second bulleted item.

Start a Numbered List   You can start a numbered list by typing **1. Item one** and pressing Enter. This sets up the next text you enter to be the second numbered item—and automatically inserts the "2." for you!

Create a Border   You can create a full-width border over your next block of text by typing --- and pressing Enter. The next text you enter will now be bordered by a solid line.

Create a Table   You can create a three-column table by typing +---+---+---+ and then pressing Enter. The table that is created can then be expanded and formatted as you would any normal table.

And don't forget the AutoCorrect-like real-time replacements that AutoFormat can do, such as replacing 1/2 with $^1/_2$, or -- with —, or 1st with 1st. If you're like most Word users, you'll find that you want to enable all of these AutoFormat replacement options!

Running AutoFormat on Your Document

You can also run AutoFormat in a separate operation on your entire document. Typically, you want to run the AutoFormat command after you've completed writing your document, so that all the designated formatting can be changed in a single pass.

To execute the AutoFormat operation, follow these steps:

1. Select Format ➢ AutoFormat to display the AutoFormat dialog box.

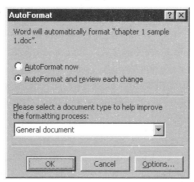

2. To run AutoFormat completely automatically (with no interaction on your part) check the AutoFormat Now option. To confirm or reject each suggested Auto-Format change, check the AutoFormat and Review Each Change option.

3. Select one of the following document types from the pull-down list: General Document, Letter, or Email.

 TIP To enable or disable any of the AutoFormat options, click the Options button to display the AutoFormat tab in the AutoCorrect dialog box.

4. Click Go to begin formatting.

If you selected the AutoFormat Now option, all the formatting changes are made automatically. If you selected the AutoFormat and Review Each Change option, you'll see a new AutoFormat dialog box.

 TIP After you've run AutoFormat, you can use Word's Style Gallery to apply a professional-looking design to your entire document. When the second AutoFormat dialog box appears, click the Style Gallery button to select a new style for your document. If you want to change your document's style at a later time, select Format ➢ Theme to display the Theme dialog box, then click the Style Gallery button to open the Style Gallery.

If you want to accept all of AutoFormat's changes without reviewing them individually, click the Accept All button. If you want to reject all of AutoFormat's changes without reviewing them, click the Reject All button. If you want to review AutoFormat's changes one at a time, click the Review Changes button; this displays the Review Auto-Format Changes dialog box.

Click the Find buttons to move back and forth through the formatting changes. To accept a change, you don't have to do anything—just move on to the next change. To reject a change, click the Reject button. To change your mind and accept a change you previously rejected, click the Undo button.

 TIP If you don't like AutoFormat's results, select Edit ➢ Undo to immediately undo the entire formatting operation.

CHAPTER **7**

Printing, Faxing, and E-mailing Word Documents

Configuring Word for printing   210

Previewing your printout   212

Changing printers   215

Printing part of a document   216

Resizing to a different paper size   217

Printing a draft   218

Printing to a file   218

Faxing a document   220

E-mailing your document as a stand-alone message and as an attachment   227

Now that your document is created, edited, proofed, and saved, you have one last task ahead of you: It's time to print!

Word 2000 offers a variety of printing options, and not just for regular documents. You can print letters, memos, reports, and newsletters, plus envelopes and labels, either one at a time or as part of a mass mailing. You can even output your Word documents in ways other than printing: via fax or e-mail.

In short, Word lets you output your documents in just about any way imaginable. Before you start printing, however, read on to learn how to master Word's many printing features.

Printing a Document

Printing a document in Word can be as simple as clicking the Print button on the Standard toolbar or as complex as configuring a host of not-always-easy-to-grasp printing options for unusual print jobs.

Getting Ready: Before You Print

Before you actually print your document, you can elect to customize Word's printer settings and to preview your printout onscreen.

Configuring Word for Printing

There are several configuration options you can set within Word that will affect how your documents are printed. All of these options are accessible in the following manner:

1. Select Tools ➢ Options to display the Options dialog box.
2. Select the Print tab.

3. Check the options you want to enable; uncheck those you want to disable.
4. Click OK.

PART

I

Learning New Features and
Creating New Documents

These printing options are discussed in detail in the "Configuring Your Printing Options" section of Chapter 3.

 TIP Make sure that all the fields and links are updated in your document before you print by checking the Update Fields and Update Links options in the Options dialog box.

Other print options are available on the Print dialog box, which is displayed when you select File ➢ Print or press Ctrl+P. From the Print dialog box, you can select which printer you wish to use for this print job, which part(s) of your document you want to print, and how many copies you want to print, as well as several other specialized print options. These options are discussed in the "Printing with Options" section later in this chapter.

If you click the Properties button in the Print dialog box, you display a short version of the Properties dialog box for the selected printer. While the details in this dialog box differ from printer to printer, you typically can select paper size, paper source, orientation, and various device options for this printer.

 MASTERING THE OPPORTUNITIES

Configuring Printer Options in Windows

Since your printer services *all* the programs on your PC, most printer settings are configured from within the Windows operating system. You access most of these settings by clicking the Windows Start button and selecting Settings ➢ Printers. This displays the Printers window, where all of the printers that are installed on your system are listed.

Continued ▶

To configure an existing printer, right-click that printer's icon, and select Properties from the pop-up menu. Since all printers have different feature sets, the Properties dialog box for each of your printers is different as well. Most Properties dialog boxes contain multiple tabs. As an example, the Properties dialog box for the HP LaserJet 3100 printer contains General, Details, Color Management, Sharing, Paper, and Print Quality tabs. Select the tab that contains the settings you wish to configure, make your choices, and then click OK.

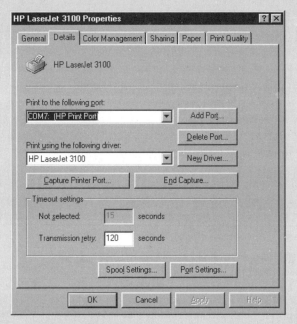

There are several ways to install a new printer in Windows; the easiest is to use the Add Printer Wizard. When you select the Add Printer icon in the Printers window, you launch the Wizard, which leads you step by step through the addition of a new printer to your system.

After you've installed a printer, you can choose to make that printer your default printer. (The default printer is the one that gets printed to automatically when you click Word's Print button.) To make a printer your default, right-click that printer's icon in the Printers window, and select Set as Default from the pop-up menu; the default printer is always indicated by a check mark in the Printers window.

Previewing Your Printout

Unless you own stock in a paper company, it's a good idea to preview your documents onscreen before you print them so you can minimize the wasted paper caused by unexpected print format glitches. (Our trees and landfills will also benefit from this simple practice, and you'll save some bucks on paper costs, besides.) Word 2000 includes a special Print Preview view, which you open by selecting File ➤ Print Pre-view, by clicking the Print Preview button on Word's Standard toolbar, or by pressing Ctrl+F2.

As you can see in Figure 7.1, the Print Preview screen displays your document exactly as it will appear when output by your printer.

FIGURE 7.1

Preview your documents before you print with Word's Print Preview view.

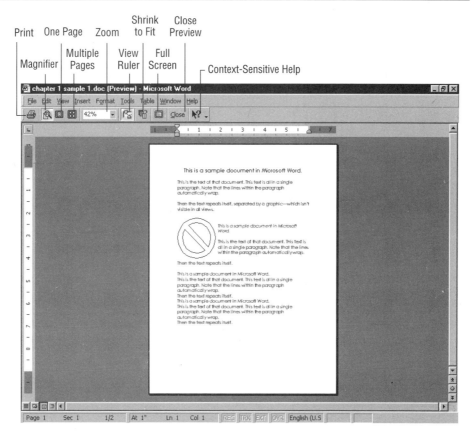

When using Print Preview, you have several options available:

Navigate from Page to Page   Click above or below the scroll box on the verti-cal scroll bar to move to the previous or next page in your document. Use the scroll bar as normal to move to specific locations within your document.

View More than One Page at a Time   By default, Print Preview shows you one page (the current page in your document) onscreen. To display multiple pages in the Print Preview window, click the Multiple Pages button, and select how many pages you wish to view at one time. Return to single-page view by clicking the One Page button.

Zoom Your View   To zoom in on the current page, click the Magnifier button on the Print Preview toolbar. This changes your cursor to a magnifying glass, which you then position anywhere in the document you want to zoom in on, and click your mouse button. To zoom back out, click your mouse button again. Alternately, you can pull down the Zoom control and select a specific-percentage zoom. Finally, if you want to get rid of Word's menus and Status bar, you can click the Full Screen button to display Print Preview in full-screen mode; click the Full Screen button again to return to normal Print Preview.

Shrink to Fit   If your document spills over (by a few lines) to an unwanted final page, click the Shrink to Fit button to downsize all your fonts and shrink the entire document enough to fit on fewer pages.

Print or Quit   If you like what you see in Print Preview, you can initiate printing by clicking the Print button. If you want to return to your document for some more editing, click the Close Preview button to close Print Preview and return to regular editing mode.

 TIP   You can actually perform some editing functions from within Print Preview. When the Magnifier control is turned off, your cursor changes to its normal shape, and you can perform normal, keyboard-based editing operations within your document.

Printing a Document—Fast!

The fastest way to print a document is with Word's fast-print option. When you initiate a fast-print of your document, you send your document directly to your default printer, bypassing the Print dialog box and all other configuration options.

 You can fast-print a document by clicking the Print button on Word's Standard toolbar.

 TIP   To cancel an in-progress print job, double-click the printer icon on Word's status bar to open the print window. To pause the print job, select Document ➢ Pause Printing; to completely cancel the print job, select Document ➢ Cancel Printing.

Printing with Options

Of course, there are times when fast printing isn't an option (if you need to tweak the way your document prints, for example, or if you want to print to a different, or non-default, printer). For these instances, you need to use Word's Print dialog box to initiate printing.

Open the Print dialog box, shown in Figure 7.2, by selecting File ➤ Print or by pressing Ctrl+P.

FIGURE 7.2

Use the Print dialog box to determine what and how you print.

Lists Available Printers

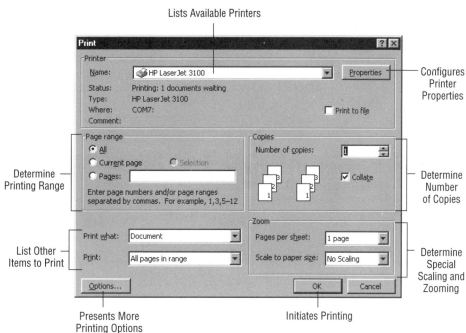

Configures Printer Properties

Determine Printing Range

Determine Number of Copies

List Other Items to Print

Determine Special Scaling and Zooming

Presents More Printing Options

Initiates Printing

Once you have the Print dialog box displayed, you can configure any one of a number of options specific to your particular print job. Once you've made your choices, click the OK button to start printing.

Changing Printers

If you make no changes, your document will print to the Windows default printer. To select a different printer for this particular print job, pull down the Printer Name list, and select a different printer.

Printing Part of a Document

By default, Word will print your entire document, from the first page to the last. To print just part of a longer document, select the appropriate option in the Page Range section of the Print dialog box:

All   The default option, which prints all the pages in your document.

Current Page   Prints only the page where the insertion point is currently anchored.

Selection   Prints only text currently selected in your document.

Pages   Prints a range of pages.

Table 7.1 lists the commands used to control the page ranges printed via the Pages option. These commands are useful when you don't want to print a long document in its entirety; instead, you can choose to print only selected pages.

TABLE 7.1: PAGE RANGE COMMANDS

Print Range	What You Enter	Example
Noncontiguous pages	Individual page numbers, separated by commas	1, 2, 4, 7
Contiguous pages	The starting and the ending page, separated by a dash	1-5
Multiple page ranges	Each range, separated by commas	1-5, 9-12
Pages across multiple sections	Type **p#s#-p#s#** (where p = page and s = section)	p1s1-p10s3
Entire section	Type **s**, followed by section number	s2
Multiple, noncontiguous sections	Sections (as above), separated by commas	s2, s4

You can also combine these commands into multiple-command strings. For example, if you wanted to print page 1, pages 4 through 9, and then page 20, you'd enter **1, 4-9, 20**.

The easiest way to print a small section of your document is to highlight the section, select File ➢ Print to display the Print dialog box, check the Selection option, and click OK to print; the text and graphics you selected—and only that selection—will be printed.

If you just want to print the odd or even pages in your document, pull down the Print list at the very bottom of the Print dialog box, and select either Odd Pages or Even Pages.

TIP Some printers let you use different papers for different parts of your document, which, for example, enables you to use one paper stock for the cover page and another paper stock for the body of the document. To use this feature, select File ➤ Page Setup to display the Page Setup dialog box, and then select the Paper Source tab. Select one paper tray (containing one type of paper) from the First Page list and a second paper tray (containing a different type of paper) from the Other Pages list.

Printing Multiple Copies

It's easy to print multiple copies of your document. Just use the Number of Copies control to select the number of copies you want to print (the default is 1).

If you want your multiple copies collated (so your printer prints pages 1, 2, 3; 1, 2, 3; 1, 2, 3; and so on), make sure the Collate option is checked. If you prefer for all copies of each individual page to print together (so your printer prints pages 1, 1, 1; 2, 2, 2; 3, 3, 3; and so on), uncheck the Collate option.

Printing Information about Your Document

You can use the Print What list to select other items—other than the document itself—to print. You can elect to print any or all of the following items:

Document Prints the entire document, as normal.

Document Properties Prints assorted properties and statistics for your current document.

Styles Prints a list of styles used in the current document.

AutoText Entries Prints a list of all your AutoText entries.

Key Assignments Prints a list of all your keyboard shortcuts.

 TIP When you select printing options and items in the Print dialog box, you're only selecting them for that specific document during that particular print run. If you want to configure printing options to encompass all your print jobs, select Tools ➤ Options to display the Options dialog box, and select the Print tab; check any or all of the Document Properties, Field Codes, Comments, or Hidden Text options to include these items with every document you print.

Resizing and Shrinking Document Pages

 Word 2000 adds new capabilities for automatically resizing your document to fit different-sized paper and for shrinking your document to fit multiple pages per sheet.

To resize your document for a different paper type, select File ➤ Print to open the Print dialog box, pull down the Scale to Paper Size list, and select a new paper type. This is particularly useful if you created your document for standard U.S. letter–size paper but need to print on a European A4 or A5 format printer.

To fit more than one page of your document on a single sheet of paper, open the Print dialog box, pull down the Pages Per Sheet list, and select how many pages you want to print per sheet. You can choose to print from 1 to 16 pages per sheet.

 TIP If your document runs over to an extra page by just a line or two, Word 2000 enables you to shrink your document to eliminate the last-page runover. To do this, open Word's Print Preview, and click the Shrink to Fit button. Word will automatically decrease the font size of all the text in your document, effectively shrinking what's fit to print. (Shrink to Fit works best on shorter documents.)

Printing a Draft

By default, Word prints your entire document, including all graphics and fonts, as laid out onscreen. If you want to speed up your printing mid-process, you can choose to print a draft of your document without all the graphics and with the default system font.

To enable draft printing, click the Options button from the Print dialog box. When the Options dialog box appears, make sure the Print tab is selected, and then check the Draft Printing option. As long as this option is enabled, everything you print will be in draft mode; uncheck this option to return to normal printing.

 TIP Another way to speed up document printing is to hide any graphics used to create form pages. To do this, go to the Print tab on the Options dialog box, and check the Print Data Only for Forms option.

Printing to a File

If you want to print your document from another PC (for example, if you want to avail yourself of the high-quality printers at a local copy center), you have two options.

What seems like the simplest option is to copy your document file to the other PC, open it with that PC's copy of Word, and then print. While this option seems simple, it can get messy if your document file is extremely large (and thus difficult to transport) or if the other PC doesn't have the same version of Word installed as you do on your computer.

WARNING Different versions of Word sometimes display or print the same document differently. To learn more about Word compatibility issues, see Chapter 2.

A second option is to create a *print file* for your document and then print the print file on another computer. The advantage to this option is that any computer using the same print language (such as PostScript) will print the file exactly as it was saved, with no arbitrary changes. You can also create higher resolution output with this method if the target printer has a higher resolution than your normal printer.

To create a print file for your document, you first have to make sure that the driver for the target printer is installed in Windows. Once the driver is installed, follow these steps:

1. Select File ➢ Print to display the Print dialog box.

2. Pull down the Printer Name list, and select the target printer you'll be using.

WARNING Do not select *your* printer in the Printer Name list; you must select the *target* printer to create a print file specifically for that printer. (If you don't know what printers are available at your local copy center, call ahead to find out.)

3. Check the Print to File option.

4. Click OK.

5. When the Print to File dialog box appears, enter a name and a location for the print file, and then click OK.

You can now take the print file to the other computer and print it there, assuming the computer is hooked up to a compatible printer, of course. You don't even have to have Word installed to print the print file.

To print a print file, you have to enter the computer's MS-DOS mode. (If the computer is running Windows 95 or Windows 98, click the Start menu, and select Programs ➢ MS-DOS Prompt.) From the MS-DOS command prompt, enter the following command:

```
COPY \PATH\FILENAME.PRN LPT1 /B
```

Enter the actual path and filename in the command, of course, and then press Enter.

The print file will now be copied to the computer's printer port (LPT1) in binary format (/B), which results in the printer printing the contents of the file.

NOTE To learn how to print envelopes and mailing labels, turn to Chapter 18.

 MASTERING THE OPPORTUNITIES

Printing without Word

You don't have to launch Word 2000 to print Word documents. You can print Word documents—or any documents, actually—from within Windows.

To do this, open My Computer or Windows Explorer, and navigate to the file(s) you want to print. (That's right, with this method, you can print multiple files at the same time!) Select the file(s), and then right-click your mouse to display the pop-up menu. Select Print, and one copy of the selected file(s) will be printed on your default printer.

You can also use this trick to print files from Word's Open or Save As dialog boxes.

Faxing a Document

If you have fax software installed on your system, you can send a Word document via fax pretty much the same way you would print the same document. That is, the fax software appears in your printer list, and you choose to "print" the document to the fax software, which then does its thing and faxes the document (at very high quality) to its intended recipient(s).

Sending a Document via Fax

It's quite easy to send any Word document as a fax message, using your PC's modem and your regular phone line. The pages in your document print out on the recipient's fax machine just as if you'd actually printed them out and then scanned them into a fax machine on your end of the line. The advantages to sending a Word document as a fax are that you don't have to print it out and that the output quality on the other end is extremely high.

To send a document as a fax from within Word, follow these steps:

1. Select File ➢ Print to display the Print dialog box.

2. Pull down the Printer Name list, and select your fax program from the list of printers.

3. Select any other desired options from within the Print dialog box.

4. Click OK to start printing.

At this point, Word will send your document—in electronic format—to your fax software. In most cases, your fax software will now launch, providing you with additional options (such as attaching a cover sheet) before it actually sends the fax.

Determining whether You Have Fax Software on Your System

You may already have fax software installed on your PC. Even if you don't, there are several low-cost options available to you.

Using Windows 95's Microsoft Fax

Do you already have fax software installed? You do if you're running Windows 95 as your operating system. Windows 95 came complete with the Microsoft Fax utility, which is part of that operating system's Windows Messaging System. You configure Microsoft Fax for your system by opening the Windows Control Panel and selecting the Mail and Fax icon. You "print" to Microsoft Fax by selecting Microsoft Fax from the Printer Name list in Word's Print dialog box.

Unfortunately, Windows 98 removed Microsoft Fax from its complement of utilities. So if your PC came fresh from the factory with Windows 98 preinstalled, you don't have Microsoft Fax on your system.

However, if you upgraded to Windows 98 from Windows 95, chances are that Microsoft Fax is still installed on your system. (Upgrading to Windows 98 doesn't automatically delete the Microsoft Fax utility.) If you see Microsoft Fax in your list of printers, then the program is still installed, and you're all set.

Using Office 2000's Symantec WinFax Starter Edition

If you have all of Microsoft Office 2000 (not just Word 2000) installed on your system *and* you installed Outlook 2000 in Internet Mail Only mode, you also have Symantec WinFax Starter Edition installed on your PC.

WARNING Symantec WinFax Starter Edition was *not* installed if you installed Outlook 2000 in Corporate or Workgroup modes.

PART

I

Learning New Features and
Creating New Documents

Access WinFax SE from within Outlook. To configure the utility, select Tools ➢ Options ➢ Fax. You can "print" to WinFax from within Word by selecting Symantec WinFax Starter Edition from the Printer Name list in Word's Print dialog box.

 TIP To learn more about upgrading from WinFax Starter Edition to Symantec's full-featured WinFax Pro, see their Web page: www.symantec.com/winfax/starter/compare.html.

Working with Other Fax Programs

If you don't have either Microsoft Fax or Symantec WinFax SE installed on your system, you'll need to seek out a different fax program for your PC. Many modems and some printers come with their own fax programs, so you should look for those options in Windows's list of printers. You can also purchase and install one of a number of third-party fax programs, such as WinFax Pro, available wherever software is sold.

 TIP The CD-ROM included with this book includes MightyFax, a fax program that installs as a printer driver within Windows and is thus available as a printer option in Word's Print dialog box. For more information on using MightyFax, see Chapter 33.

Using Word 2000's Fax Wizard

You can also use Word 2000's Fax Wizard to prepare and send any Word document as a fax, complete with customized cover sheet. To use the Fax Wizard with your fax software, follow these steps:

1. From within your document, select File ➢ Send To ➢ Fax Recipient to run the Fax Wizard.

 TIP You can also run the Fax Wizard by selecting File ➢ New to display the New dialog box, selecting the Letters & Faxes tab and then selecting the Fax Wizard template.

2. From the Start page, click Next.
3. From the Document to Fax page, select which document you want to fax, and check whether you want to send it with or without a cover sheet. (At this page, you can also select to create and send just a cover sheet.) Click Next.

4. From the Fax Software page, select which fax program you want to use to send the fax. (At this page, you can also choose to simply print the document so you can send it from a separate fax machine.) Click Next.

5. From the Recipients page, enter the name(s) and fax number(s) of your intended recipient(s). Click Next.

6. From the Cover Sheet page, select one of the three styles (Professional, Contemporary, or Elegant) for your fax's cover sheet. Click Next.

7. From the Sender page, confirm or complete your sender information; this information will be added to your cover sheet. Click Next.

8. When the Finish screen appears, click Finish.

Word now displays your fax cover sheet onscreen, where you can edit it as necessary. (Now is a good time to add some comments to the cover sheet, for instance.) A Send Fax Now button is also displayed onscreen; click this button to send the fax and cover sheet to your intended recipients.

E-mailing a Document

 In addition to printing and faxing, Word 2000 also enables you to output your documents via e-mail. In fact, if your system is configured properly, you can choose to send any Word document either as an e-mail message or as an attachment to another e-mail message.

Before You Send an E-mail

Before you send your first e-mail message, you should make sure your system can actually use Word to send e-mail messages, and then configure the way Word creates your messages.

Word E-mail System Requirements

Word 2000's e-mail features only work on properly configured systems. Here's what you need in order to send Word documents via e-mail:

- To send a Word document as an e-mail message, you must have either Outlook 2000 or Outlook Express 5 installed on your PC and configured as your default e-mail editor.

- To send a Word document as an attachment to an e-mail message, you need any 32-bit e-mail program compatible with the Messaging Application Programming Interface (MAPI) installed on your machine. Naturally, both Microsoft

Outlook (any version) and Outlook Express (any version) both fit the bill. The attachment feature also works with Lotus cc:Mail or any other 16-bit e-mail program compatible with Vendor Independent Messaging (VIM).

- To send *any* e-mail messages, your PC must have a connection to the Internet, either via modem and Internet Service Provider or via a network gateway.

MASTERING TROUBLESHOOTING

HTML E-mail—or Not

When you use Word as your e-mail editor and send Word documents as e-mail messages, you're sending e-mail messages in HTML format. HTML is a rich format, enabling you to incorporate color, fonts, borders, and graphics in your messages. However, not all e-mail programs can receive and display HTML messages.

You're okay if you're sending messages to anyone using an HTML-compatible e-mail program; they'll be able to read your messages exactly as formatted. Compatible programs include Microsoft Outlook, Outlook Express, Netscape Communicator, Eudora, and later versions of cc:Mail.

Unfortunately, other e-mail programs, including earlier versions of cc:Mail still used by many corporations, cannot read HTML e-mail messages. These programs can only read plain-text messages, and when they attempt to open an HTML e-mail, the results can vary. In some instances, the text of the HTML message will come through but you'll lose the formatting; in other instances, the message gets completely garbled or even kicked back by the recipient's e-mail server.

One big system that can't send or receive full HTML e-mail is America Online. When you send an HTML e-mail to an AOL user, the text of the message will likely get through, but the formatting gets extremely garbled.

So what do you do if you want to send a message to an AOL user or anyone else without HTML-compatible e-mail software? The answer is simple: don't send them HTML e-mail! If you must send a Word document to a non-HTML e-mail user, send the document as an attachment. Most e-mail recipients, except those using WebTV or Juno, should be able to receive, save, and open Word documents sent as e-mail attachments.

Because so many users cannot yet receive HTML e-mail, it's difficult to recommend using Word as your e-mail editor. In fact, whatever e-mail program you use (Outlook, Communicator, Eudora, et al.), I recommend you turn off the option to send messages in HTML format and default to sending all your e-mail messages in plain-text format instead.

Creating a Signature

A *signature* is a personalized block of text added to the end of outgoing e-mail messages that identifies you and communicates a small amount of personal information. You don't have to use a signature in your messages, although it is an accepted form of vanity on the Internet.

You create your signature from the E-mail Options dialog box. Display this dialog box by selecting Tools ➢ Options to display the Options dialog box, selecting the General tab, and then clicking the E-mail Options button.

 WARNING If you create a personal signature, keep it short—no more than three lines, tops. Other users don't want their valuable bandwidth and screen space wasted on overly intrusive signatures.

When you open the E-mail Options dialog box, select the E-mail Signature tab, as shown in Figure 7.3. From this tab, you can create and configure one or more e-mail signatures, following these steps:

FIGURE 7.3
Create a signature for your messages from the E-mail Options dialog box.

1. Enter a title for your signature in the Type the Title box.
2. Enter the text for your signature in the large text box.

3. Use the formatting tools to apply different fonts, styles, alignment, and colors to your signature; you can even add hyperlinks and pictures.

4. When your signature is complete, click the Add button.

5. To create another signature at this time, click the New button, and repeat steps 1–4.

6. To determine which signature is used for all new messages you create, make a selection from the Signature for New Messages list.

7. If you want to use a signature when you reply or forward messages (and most users don't), make a selection from the Signature for Replies and Forwards list.

8. Click OK.

Selecting Stationery and Fonts

Word calls its preformatted e-mail message templates *stationery;* you design your stationery using specially selected *themes*. You can use themes and stationery to create very colorful and visually interesting e-mail messages.

You select your default stationery theme and select other formatting options from the Personal Stationery tab of the E-mail Options dialog box. Display this dialog box by selecting Tools ➤ Options to display the Options dialog box, selecting the General tab, and then clicking the E-mail Options button.

The Personal Stationery tab of the E-mail Options dialog box contains the following options:

Theme or Stationery for New E-mail Message   To pick a theme for your stationery, click the Theme button to display the Theme or Stationery dialog box, where you can choose from one of dozens of preselected themes.

 WARNING   E-mail messages incorporating stationery will only be fully viewable by users with HTML-compatible e-mail programs. Note that many Internet users frown on e-mail messages that incorporate stationery and other visual elements, as they create larger files that take longer to download over the Internet.

Font for New Mail Messages   To choose which font you want to use when sending new e-mail messages via Word, click the Font button, and make a selection from the Font dialog box.

Font for Replying or Forwarding Messages   To choose which font you want to use when replying to or forwarding e-mail messages via Word, click the Font button, and make a selection from the Font dialog box.

Mark My Comments With If you want to mark your comments in replies or forwarded messages, check the Mark My Comments With option, and enter your name (or other message) in the associated text box.

You don't have to make any selections on either tab of the E-mail Options dialog box. If you don't create a signature, don't pick a theme or stationery, and don't select any special fonts (for new messages, forwarded messages, or replies), your e-mail messages will be created using a single font with no fancy special effects, which is the way most e-mail messages are sent on the Internet.

E-mailing Your Document as a Stand-alone Message

Word 2000 allows you to create a document as usual and then send that document as a stand-alone e-mail message. When you utilize this feature, you're essentially using Word as an e-mail editor while still using Outlook or Outlook Express as your e-mail engine.

WARNING You can only send Word documents as standalone messages if you're using either Microsoft Outlook 2000 or Outlook Express 5 as your e-mail program.

To send a Word document as an e-mail message, follow these steps:

1. Select File ➢ Send To ➢ Mail Recipient, or click the E-mail button on Word's Standard toolbar. Word now adds an e-mail header to your document, as shown in Figure 7.4.

2. Enter the e-mail address of the intended recipient in the To: box. To enter multiple recipients, either press Enter after each recipient or insert a semi-colon between each recipient.

3. If you want to send a carbon copy of this message to other recipients, enter their e-mail addresses in the Cc: box.

4. If you want to send a blind carbon copy of this message to other recipients, click the Bcc: button to display the Bcc: box, and then enter the e-mail address(es) in the Bcc: box.

TIP The names/addresses of blind-carbon-copy recipients are not displayed in messages sent to regular and carbon copy recipients.

FIGURE 7.4

Use an e-mail header to address and send a Word document as an e-mail message.

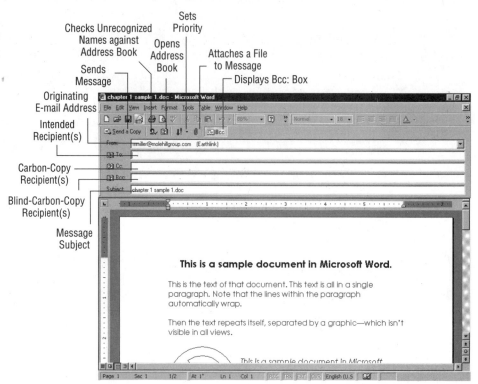

5. Enter a title for this message in the Subject: box.

6. If you want to assign a priority level to this message so that recipients receive the message flagged as High, Medium, or Low priority, click the down arrow on the Priority button, and select a priority.

NOTE If you have Outlook 2000 installed in Corporate or Workgroup mode, the e-mail header includes two other options: Message Flag (which enables you to follow up on the status of your message) and Options (which allows you to set specific sensitivity, delivery, and tracking options).

7. To attach another file to this message, click the Attach File button to display the Insert Attachment dialog box. Locate and select the file(s) you want to attach, and then click the Attach button. You can attach multiple files of any type to any e-mail message; files you select to attach are displayed in an Attach box under the Subject box.

8. When all the forms are filled in and all the options selected, click the Send a Copy button to send this message.

When you click the Send a Copy button, Word activates the Outlook (or Outlook Express) engine, connects to the Internet (as configured within Windows), and sends your message on its way.

NOTE If you're using Outlook or Outlook Express as your e-mail program, you can select (within those programs, not from within Word) to use Word as your default e-mail editor. To do this from within Outlook/Outlook Express, select Tools ➤ Options to display the Options menu, and then select the Mail Format tab. Check the Use Microsoft Word to Edit E-mail Messages option, select a message format from the Send in This Message Format list, and then click OK.

E-mailing Your Document as an Attachment

You can also choose to send any Word document as an attachment to an e-mail message created with another program. This option is preferred if your recipients are incapable of receiving HTML e-mail.

To send a Word document as an attachment to an e-mail message, follow these steps:

1. Select File ➤ Send To ➤ Mail Recipient (as Attachment).

2. Your e-mail program will now create a new e-mail message, with your Word document loaded as an attachment.

3. Complete the addressing information, enter the text of your message as is normal for your e-mail program, and then send the message.

After the message is sent, your recipients will receive your new message with your Word file (in standard .DOC format) attached. They can then open the document directly or save the document to their hard disk to open and edit later.

NOTE Word 2000 also enables you to route documents to multiple editors via e-mail. To learn more about this and other forms of document collaboration, see Chapter 23.

PART II

Creating Text-Based Documents

- *Formatting text and fonts*

- *Working with paragraphs and styles*

- *Applying borders and shading*

- *Setting up pages and sections*

- *Designing multiple-column documents*

CHAPTER **8**

Formatting Text

Setting Word's default font 236

Changing fonts, styles, and sizes 239

Highlighting text 243

Scaling your text and adjusting character spacing 244

Adding subscripts and superscripts 246

Inserting special characters 248

Word lets you format, to some degree, virtually every element in a document. This chapter covers the formatting you do to the individual text characters in Word; the next two chapters deal with paragraph and page/document-wide formatting, respectively.

The Least You Need to Know About Text Formatting

Text formatting in Word is essentially font formatting. For any given character in your document, you can change its typeface, size (in points), style (bold, italic, etc.), color, spacing, kerning, and other attributes. The more you know about fonts, the better you'll be able to format the fonts in your documents.

Understanding Fonts

In Word, a font is a *typeface,* such as Arial or Helvetica or Times New Roman. Each font can be displayed and printed in different sizes, specified in *points*. (The larger the point size, the bigger the character.) Each font can also be displayed in one of four basic *styles*: Regular, Bold, Italic, or Bold Italic.

Each font has its own unique characteristics. Some fonts are better for displaying small text; some are better for larger text and headlines. Some fonts convey a "fun" image; others radiate tradition and conservatism. You should pick fonts for your documents that match the image and message that you're trying to convey.

 TIP Don't use too many fonts in a single document—it makes the page less readable, plus it takes more time to print!

Fonts that give every character the same width—such as Courier—are called *monospace* fonts. Fonts with characters of different widths—where the *m* is wider than the *i*—are called *proportional* fonts. Most fonts are proportional; some designers use monospace fonts to display programming code or instructions, or to replicate a typewritten look.

Fonts with "tails" at the ends of their letters are called *serif* fonts; fonts without tails are called *sans serif* fonts. Times New Roman is an example of a serif font; Arial is an example of a sans serif font.

 TIP Different fonts have different types of impact in your printed documents. Typically, you want to use serif fonts for body text (they're more readable in small sizes and large blocks) and sans serif fonts for headlines (they have more impact when big and bold).

MASTERING THE OPPORTUNITIES

Managing Fonts in Windows

The Windows operating system uses TrueType font technology. TrueType makes it easy to add and remove fonts from any Windows-based PC—and TrueType fonts reproduce faithfully, independent of the attached output device.

To manage your fonts within Windows, select Start ➤ Settings ➤ Control Panel to open the Control Panel, then select the Fonts icon. The resulting Fonts window displays all fonts currently installed on your system.

To add a new font, select File ➤ Install New Font from the Fonts window. When the Add Fonts dialog box appears, navigate to the location of the font file for the new font, select the file, then click OK. Windows will now go through the font installation procedure, which copies the new fonts to your hard disk and registers them with Windows. When you next access Word, your new fonts will show up in the Font list along with all your previously installed fonts.

Viewing Installed Fonts and Character Attributes

All fonts that are available for your current document are displayed in the Fonts list on Word's Formatting toolbar. When you pull down this list (which you can do with your mouse, or by pressing Ctrl+Shift+F), all fonts are listed—using their native font. (This means that the listing for Tahoma appears in this list in the Tahoma font; the listing for Arial Black appears in Arial Black.)

PART
II

Creating Text-Based
Documents

Your most recently used fonts are positioned at the top of the Fonts list; all other fonts are listed alphabetically beneath the recent fonts.

To view the formatting applied to any character in your text, select Help ➢ What's This (or press Shift+F1) and click a single character. Word now displays the character formatting and paragraph formatting for the selected character. (Press Esc to turn off the What's This feature.)

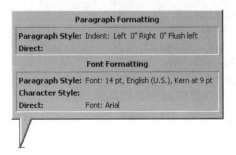

Setting Word's Default Font

When you open a new document, Word applies a *default font* to your text. In Word 2000 the default font is 12 point Times New Roman; in previous versions of Word, the default was 10 point Times New Roman. (I have no doubt that Microsoft increased the default font size as a courtesy to its aging and increasingly vision-impaired user base.)

If you want to change Word's default font, follow these steps:

1. Within an open document, format a block of text as you want your default font to appear, then select that text.

2. Select Format ➢ Font.

3. When the Font dialog box appears, the properties of your selected text will be preloaded. Make any additional changes, as necessary.

4. Click the Default button.

5. When the confirmation dialog box appears, click Yes.

Any new document you create will use these new default font settings.

Fundamental Font Formatting

There are many ways to access Word's formatting commands: from the Formatting toolbar, from the selected text's pop-up menu, or from the Fonts dialog box.

MASTERING TROUBLESHOOTING

Substituting Fonts

If you open a Word document created by another user that contains fonts not installed on your computer, Word will attempt to display text formatted with the missing font with the closest available font. You can specify a specific replacement font for any document by selecting Tools ➢ Options to display the Options dialog box, then selecting the Compatibility tab. From this tab, click the Font Substitution button to display the Font Substitution dialog box.

In this dialog box, all current substitutions are shown in the Font Substitutions list. To change a substitution, select the original (missing) font from the Missing Document Font list, then select a new font from the Substituted Font list. These changes will only apply when the document is opened on your system; to save the font changes to the document itself, click the Convert Permanently button.

If you want to use a font in your document that you think probably won't be installed on another user's computer, you can forestall any problems by *embedding* that font within your document. Embedding fonts ensures that all users will see exact fonts you use; documents with embedded fonts, however, create much larger files than would be created otherwise.

To embed fonts, select Tools ➢ Options to display the Options dialog box, then select the Save tab. Check the Embed TrueType Fonts option and click OK. This embeds the entire character set for a given font; to embed only specific characters—only recommended if other users won't be editing and adding text to the document—also check the Embed Characters in Use Only.

Creating Text-Based Documents

Format Fonts—Fast!

To format fonts—fast—use the buttons on Word's Formatting toolbar. This toolbar includes the most common formatting commands you'll use on your text.

 TIP Common formatting commands can also be found on the context-sensitive pop-up menu that appears when you right-click selected text.

To format a block of text, highlight the text and then click the desired format button. You can also turn on formatting for all text at the insertion point by clicking the format button and then typing at the insertion point.

Table 8.1 shows the text formatting you can apply from the Formatting toolbar.

TABLE 8.1: FONT FORMATTING COMMANDS ON THE FORMATTING TOOLBAR

Operation	Format Button	Keyboard Shortcut
Bold	Bold	Ctrl+B
Italicize	Italic	Ctrl+I
Underline	Underline	Ctrl+U
Change font	Font	Ctrl+Shift+F
Change font size	Font Size	Ctrl+Shift+P
Change font color	Font Color	*None*
Highlight text	Highlight	*None*

 TIP If you have a block of text that is perfectly formatted and you want to apply the same formatting to a different selection, use Word's Format Painter tool, found on the Standard Toolbar. Begin by selecting the preformatted text, then click the Format Painter button. When the cursor changes shape, "paint" (select) the text to which you want to apply that formatting. All the new text you select will be automatically formatted in the style of the originally selected text.

Using the Font Dialog Box

A more extensive selection of text and font formatting options is found in the Font dialog box, shown in Figure 8.1. To display the Font dialog box, select Format ➢ Font. From here you can select one of the following three tabs:

Font On this tab you'll find basic character formatting options, including font, font style, size, color, and other effects.

Character Spacing This tab presents options that let you control character scale, spacing, and positioning.

Font Effects This tab lets you apply various on-screen animation effects for your text.

FIGURE 8.1
Use the Font dialog box
to apply an extensive
selection of font
formatting.

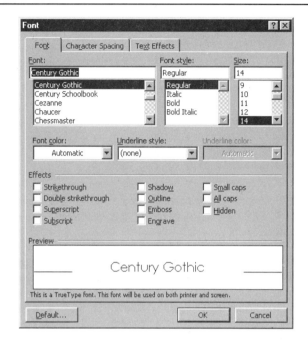

Changing Fonts, Styles, and Sizes

To change the basic font (typestyle), style, and size of any selected text, follow these steps:

1. Select the text to change.
2. Select Format ➤ Font to display the Font dialog box.
3. Select the Font tab.
4. Select a new font from the Font list.
5. Select a new style (Regular, Italic, Bold, or Bold Italic) from the Font Style list.
6. Select a new font size from the Size list.
7. Click OK to apply the new formatting.

 TIP You can also change font and size—as well as apply Bold and Italic formatting—from the Formatting toolbar.

Recoloring Your Text

By default, Word's "automatic" text color displays black type against a light background and light (normally white) text against a darker background. To change the color of selected text, follow these steps:

1. Select the text to recolor.
2. Select Format ➢ Font to display the Font dialog box.
3. Select the Font tab.
4. Pull down the Font Color list and select a new color.
5. Click OK to apply the new formatting.

 TIP You can also change Font Color from the Formatting toolbar.

To apply a color not listed in the Font Color list, select the More Colors option at the bottom of the pull-down list. This displays the Colors dialog box. Click the Standard tab to select from palette of 124 colors; to see even more colors, select the Custom tab and drag your cursor to a new color, or use the Hue, Saturation, Luminance, Red, Green, and Blue controls to custom "mix" a specific color.

Underlining Your Text

Word 2000 offers a number of different underlining options for your text—much more than were present in previous versions of the program. When you click the Underline button on the Formatting toolbar, you apply a simple single underline to the selected text. When you use the underlining options in the Font dialog box, however, you can choose from more than a dozen different underlining styles—in a variety of colors!

To apply fancy underlining to your text, follow these steps:

1. Select the text to underline.
2. Select Format ➢ Font to display the Font dialog box.
3. Select the Font tab.
4. Pull down the Underline Style list and select a specific style.

 TIP If you want to underline only words—not spaces—select the Words Only option from the Underline Style list.

5. Pull down the Underline Color list and select a color for your underline; the underline can be a different color from your text.

6. Click OK when done.

Selecting Other Font Attributes

Word 2000 makes available eleven additional font attributes, ten of which are shown in Figure 8.2. You enable these effects by checking a particular option on the Font tab of the Font dialog box.

FIGURE 8.2

Most of Word 2000's special font attributes, presented together on a single page

Regular
Italic
Bold
Bold Italic
<u>Underline</u>
~~Strikethrough~~
~~Double strikethrough~~
Super script
Sub script
Shadow
Outline
Emboss
Engrave
Small Caps
ALL CAPS

 WARNING Be careful when applying these text effects in documents you'll be sharing with users of older versions of Word. Not all of these effects translate well to Word 97, Word 95, or previous versions.

The one font attribute not shown in Figure 8.2 is *hidden text*. When you select this option, the selected text is made invisible in your document and won't appear on any printouts. To "unhide" hidden text onscreen, select Tools ➤ Options to display the Options dialog box, select the View tab, then check the Hidden Text option. Some users like to use hidden text to leave notes to themselves within their documents.

> **WARNING** It is impossible to use some of these text effects together at the same time. For example, you can't apply both a shadow and embossing to the same text, just as text can't be both small caps *and* large caps.

Using Animated Text

Word 2000 adds the dubious capability to "animate" text onscreen. (Obviously, you can't animate text on a printed page!) You can choose from the following animation effects:

- Blinking background
- Las Vegas lights
- Marching black ants
- Marching red ants
- Shimmer
- Sparkle text

You apply animation effects by following these steps:

1. Select the text to animate.
2. Select Format ➢ Font to display the Font dialog box.
3. Select the Text Effects tab.
4. Select an animation effect from the Animations list; you can check out any animation in the Preview box.
5. Click OK.

Be aware that many users find these animation effects to be *really* annoying—so use them sparingly!

Changing the Case of Your Text

If you need to change uppercase text to lowercase (or vice versa), you *could* just retype the text in question—or you could use Word's Change Case command. Follow these steps:

1. Select the text to change.
2. Select Format ➢ Change Case to display the Change Case dialog box.

3. Select one of the following options: Sentence case., lowercase, UPPERCASE, Title Case, or tOGGLE cASE.

4. Click OK to apply the new case.

Highlighting Text

To apply a colored highlight to selected text—much as you would with a colored marker to printed text—follow these steps:

1. Select the text to highlight.

2. Click the Highlight button on Word's Formatting toolbar.

You can change the color of the highlight by clicking the down-arrow on the Highlight button, and selecting a new color from the drop-down menu.

Scaling, Spacing, and Kerning

For most users, Word's fonts as normally applied (with appropriate formatting) are "good enough" for their day-to-day use. However, if you want to produce a truly professional-looking document, Word makes available some typographic controls that improve the appearance of your output in some subtle ways.

These typographic controls are available on the Character Spacing tab of the Font dialog box. Display these controls by selecting Format ➤ Font, then selecting the Character Spacing tab.

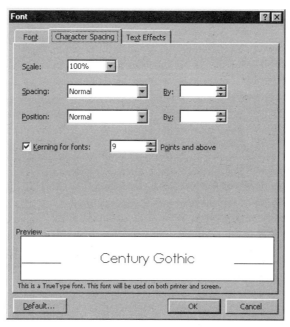

PART
II

Creating Text-Based Documents

Scaling Your Text

Text *scaling* is simply the horizontal stretching or narrowing of selected characters. You use this control when your text goes a little too wide (you scale it back a tad), or isn't quite wide enough to fit a designated space (you stretch it to fit). Figure 8.3 shows text that has been stretched and condensed.

FIGURE 8.3

Text scaling in
Word 2000

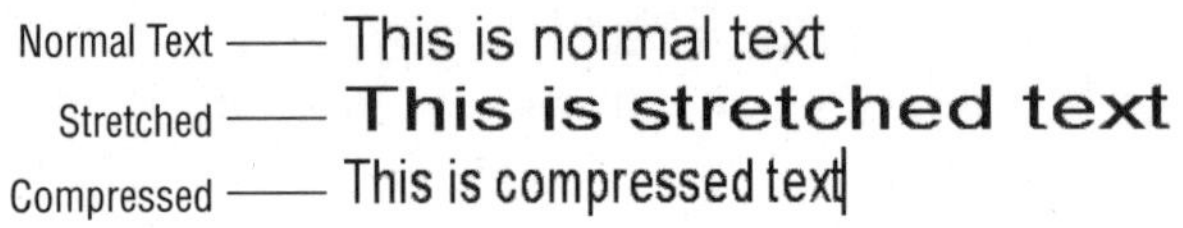

Normal Text —— This is normal text
Stretched —— This is stretched text
Compressed —— This is compressed text

To apply text scaling, follow these steps:

1. Select the characters you want to scale.

2. Select Format ≻ Font to display the Font dialog box.

3. Select the Character Spacing tab.

4. Pull down the Scale list and select a value (in terms of percent of the original). Select a value greater than 100 percent to stretch the text; select a value less than 100 percent to compress the text.

5. Click OK to apply the scaling.

 TIP View the effects of your scaling, spacing, or positioning *before* they're applied via the Preview box on the Character Spacing tab.

Adjusting Character Spacing

Character spacing involves the adjustment of the space between characters. You expand your character spacing to "open up" your text; you condense the character spacing to "tighten" text.

As you can see in Figure 8.4, changing the character spacing can create some interesting typographical effects. Expanded spacing often adds a degree of impact or openness, especially at larger type sizes. Condensed spacing can help you fit more text in a given space and, in some cases, help your text "read" faster.

FIGURE 8.4

Expanding or condensing character spacing can have subtle effects on your text.

Normal Text ——— This is a sample paragraph in Microsoft Word. I really enjoy typing these paragraphs, since it gives me a chance to practice my typing skills. Of course, it's fairly easy to just type a few sentences, and then cut and paste them repeatedly to create a phony document. Kind of like this.

Expanded ——— This is a sample paragraph in Microsoft Word. I really enjoy typing these paragraphs, since it gives me a chance to practice my typing skills. Of course, it's fairly easy to just type a few sentences, and then cut and paste them repeatedly to create a phony document. Kind of like this.

Condensed ——— This is a sample paragraph in Microsoft Word. I really enjoy typing these paragraphs, since it gives me a chance to practice my typing skills. Of course, it's fairly easy to just type a few sentences, and then cut and paste them repeatedly to create a phony document. Kind of like this.

To adjust character spacing, follow these steps:

1. Select the text you want to adjust.
2. Select Format ➤ Font to display the Font dialog box.
3. Select the Character Spacing tab.
4. To increase character spacing, pull down the Spacing list and select Expanded; to decrease character spacing, select Condensed.
5. Pull down the By list and select a value for expanding or condensing your text.
6. Click OK.

 WARNING Don't overdo it when changing your character spacing. Too much condensing or expanding can make for totally unreadable text.

Kerning Character Pairs

While character spacing changes the spacing between all characters equally, kerning adjusts the spacing only between certain *pairs* of letters. For example, a character with a wide top (such as V) can be spaced closer to a character with a wide bottom (A, for example). Figure 8.5 shows an example of text kerning.

PART

II

Creating Text-Based Documents

Normal Text —— **VACATION WATER**

Kerned —— **VACATION WATER**

Kerning is perhaps the easiest way to add a subtle professionalism to your documents. Professional typographers will typically apply kerning for text at larger sizes in their documents. Kerning also has great impact in titles and headlines.

To activate kerning in your documents, follow these steps:

1. Select the text you want to kern.

2. Select Format ➢ Font to display the Font dialog box.

3. Select the Character Spacing tab.

4. Check the Kerning for Fonts option.

5. Select a point size from the Points and Above list; all text this size or larger will be kerned, while smaller text will remain as is.

6. Click OK.

 WARNING Turning on kerning can slow down the display of text on your computer screen.

Adding Subscripts and Superscripts

Word enables you to format selected text as subscripts (positioned below the normal text baseline) and superscripts (positioned above the baseline). Subscripts and superscripts are used frequently in formulas and equations.

To apply subscript or superscript formatting, follow these steps:

1. Select the text you want to format.

2. Select Format ➢ Font to display the Font dialog box.

3. Select the Character Spacing tab.

4. To create a subscript, select Lowered from the Position list. To create a superscript, select Raised.

5. Select a point value from the By list.

6. Click OK.

TIP For a slightly different effect, decrease the point size of any superscript or subscript text.

Adding a Drop Cap

One of the more popular text effects is a drop cap letter. As you can see in Figure 8.6, a drop cap enlarges the first character of the paragraph.

FIGURE 8.6
Add a drop cap to your opening paragraph.

T his is a sample paragraph in Microsoft Word. I really enjoy typing these paragraphs, since it gives me a chance to practice my typing skills. Of course, it's fairly easy to just type a few sentences, and then cut and paste them repeatedly to create a phony document. Kind of like this. This is a sample paragraph in Microsoft Word. I really enjoy typing these paragraphs, since it gives me a chance to practice my typing skills. Of course, it's fairly easy to just type a few sentences, and then cut and paste them repeatedly to create a phony document. Kind of like this.

Word lets you create two types of drop caps. *Dropped*, which is the standard drop cap, places the letter down inside your document's left margin; an *In Margin* drop cap places the letter outside the left margin. For either type of drop cap, Word lets you adjust the number of lines the character drops, as well as the font used for the drop cap.

To create a drop cap, follow these steps:

1. Place the insertion point anywhere within the paragraph that will contain the drop cap.

2. Select Format ➢ Drop Cap to display the Drop Cap dialog box.

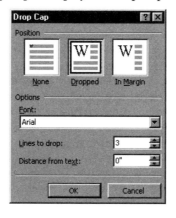

3. From the Position section, select the type of drop cap you want to apply (None, Dropped, or In Margin).

4. Select a new font for the drop cap from the Font list, or leave the drop cap as is for it to remain in the same font as the rest of the paragraph.

5. Pull down the Lines to Drop list to select how big you want the drop cap to be.

6. Pull down the Distance from Text list to determine the spacing between the drop cap and the rest of the paragraph.

7. Click OK.

To remove a drop cap, repeat steps 1–3, and select None for the Position.

Inserting Special Characters

Word provides full access to all symbols and special characters that are part of the font families installed on your system. Symbols are typically graphical characters (such as ➢ and ☺), while special characters are typically typographic characters (such as — and ©).

To insert symbols and special characters into your text, follow these steps:

1. Position the insertion point where you want to insert the symbol or special character.

2. Select Insert ➢ Symbol to display the Symbol dialog box.

3. Select the Symbol tab to display all symbol characters from all installed font families; select the Special Character tab to display all special characters in the current font family.

4. On the Symbol tab, select the Font family that contains the symbol you want, then either scroll through all characters or jump to a subset of characters by selecting an option from the Subset list.

5. Click the symbol or special character you want to insert.

6. Click the Insert button.

This procedure adds the symbol or special character at the insertion point, and keeps the Symbol dialog box open for additional use. To close the Symbol dialog box, click Cancel.

MASTERING THE OPPORTUNITIES

Insert a Symbol from the Keyboard

Word enables you to configure shortcut keys to insert any symbol or special character directly into your document. Just follow these steps:

1. Select Insert ≻ Symbol to display the Symbol dialog box.

2. Select either the Symbol or Special Character tab and select a symbol.

3. Click the Shortcut Key button to display the Customize Keyboard dialog box.

4. Move the cursor to the Press New Shortcut Key box and type your preferred key combination.

5. Click Assign.

Now you can insert the assigned symbol at the insertion point by pressing the shortcut key combination.

PART

II

Creating Text-Based
Documents

CHAPTER <u>9</u>

Working with Paragraphs and Styles

Aligning and indenting paragraphs　254

Applying line and paragraph spacing　257

Controlling widows, orphans, and page breaks　258

Setting tabs　259

Adding borders and shading　261

Working with bulleted and numbered lists　264

Applying styles　276

Modifying styles　279

Creating new styles　281

Word's paragraph formatting options let you format one paragraph at a time or assign a document-wide style to format multiple paragraphs simultaneously. You can alter just about every property of a paragraph: fonts, alignment, indentation, tabs, line spacing, line breaks, and more. You can even format paragraphs as bulleted or numbered lists and pick your own personalized bullets!

Read on to master Word's paragraph formatting features and learn a powerful way to create better-looking documents!

Formatting Paragraphs

Text (or font) formatting, discussed in Chapter 8, lets you format one character at a time; paragraph formatting affects how an entire paragraph looks. There are several ways to access Word's paragraph formatting options, including:

- Click a paragraph-formatting button on the Formatting toolbar.
- Right-click within a paragraph, and select Paragraph from the pop-up menu.
- Select Format ➤ Paragraph to display the Paragraph dialog box.

When you're ready to format a paragraph, you don't have to select the entire paragraph; just position the insertion point anywhere within the paragraph, and the entire paragraph will be formatted.

 WARNING If you select a block of text within a paragraph, only that block of text will receive the paragraph formatting you select; the rest of the paragraph will not change formatting.

Formatting Fast from the Toolbar

The most popular paragraph formatting options—alignment, indentation, lists, and borders—can be applied with a click of the mouse. All you have to do is access Word's Formatting toolbar, which contains nine different paragraph formatting buttons.

Table 9.1 details the fast paragraph formatting you can apply from the Formatting toolbar.

TABLE 9.1: PARAGRAPH FORMAT COMMANDS ON THE FORMATTING TOOLBAR		
Operation	**Format Button**	**Keyboard Shortcut**
Create a numbered list	Numbering	None
Create a bulleted list	Bullets	None
Left-align paragraph	Align Left	Ctrl+L

Continued ▶

TABLE 9.1: PARAGRAPH FORMAT COMMANDS ON THE FORMATTING TOOLBAR (CONTINUED)		
Operation	**Format Button**	**Keyboard Shortcut**
Right-align paragraph	Align Right	Ctrl+R
Center paragraph	Center	Ctrl+E
Justify paragraph	Justify	Ctrl+J
Increase paragraph indentation	Increase Indent	Tab
Decrease paragraph indentation	Decrease Indent	Backspace
Add border to paragraph	Border	None

Understanding Paragraph Formatting in Detail

For a more comprehensive assortment of paragraph formatting commands, select Format ➤ Paragraph to display the Paragraph dialog box. This dialog box includes two tabs:

Indents and Spacing   Enables you to configure paragraph alignment, indentation, and line spacing.

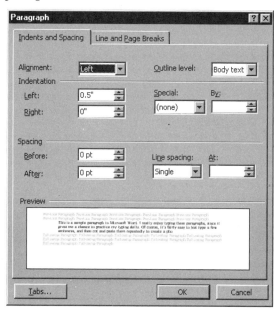

Line and Page Breaks   Enables you to configure various pagination options, including widow and orphan control.

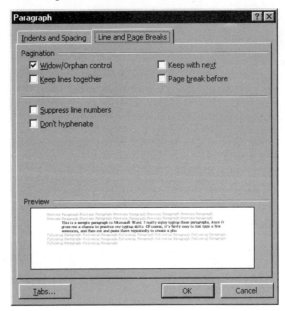

Other paragraph formatting can be executed from the Tabs (select Format ➢ Tabs), Bullets and Numbering (select Format ➢ Bullets and Numbering), and Borders and Shading (select Format ➢ Borders and Shading) dialog boxes. In addition, you can set tabs and indentation from Word's horizontal ruler, and use buttons on the Formatting toolbar to apply alignment and to turn on and off bullets and numbering.

Aligning Paragraphs

Word provides four options for aligning the text within your paragraph:

Left-Aligned   Creates a ragged right edge.

Right-Aligned   Creates a ragged left edge.

Justified   Creates even left and right edges.

Centered   Centers the text and leaves both left and right edges ragged.

Figure 9.1 shows each type of paragraph alignment.

You can set alignment for the current paragraph by clicking the appropriate alignment button on Word's Formatting toolbar or by following these steps:

1. Select Format ➢ Paragraph to display the Paragraph dialog box.

2. Select the Indents and Spacing tab.

3. Pull down the Alignment list, and make a selection.

4. Click OK.

PART

II

Creating Text-Based Documents

FIGURE 9.1

Word lets you align your paragraphs four different ways.

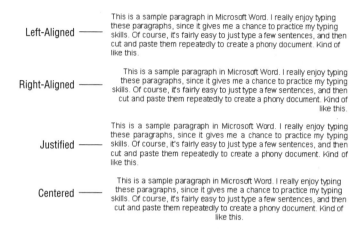

Left-Aligned —— This is a sample paragraph in Microsoft Word. I really enjoy typing these paragraphs, since it gives me a chance to practice my typing skills. Of course, it's fairly easy to just type a few sentences, and then cut and paste them repeatedly to create a phony document. Kind of like this.

Right-Aligned —— This is a sample paragraph in Microsoft Word. I really enjoy typing these paragraphs, since it gives me a chance to practice my typing skills. Of course, it's fairly easy to just type a few sentences, and then cut and paste them repeatedly to create a phony document. Kind of like this.

Justified —— This is a sample paragraph in Microsoft Word. I really enjoy typing these paragraphs, since it gives me a chance to practice my typing skills. Of course, it's fairly easy to just type a few sentences, and then cut and paste them repeatedly to create a phony document. Kind of like this.

Centered —— This is a sample paragraph in Microsoft Word. I really enjoy typing these paragraphs, since it gives me a chance to practice my typing skills. Of course, it's fairly easy to just type a few sentences, and then cut and paste them repeatedly to create a phony document. Kind of like this.

Indenting Paragraphs

Word lets you determine how far in from the left and right margins the current paragraph is indented. You might choose to indent a paragraph to draw attention to it; for example, indenting a quoted paragraph in a newsletter by half an inch from both the left and the right draws attention to the quote and distinguishes it from the normal text. (See Figure 9.2 for an example of indented text.)

FIGURE 9.2

Indent a paragraph to set it apart from the rest of your text.

This is a sample paragraph in Microsoft Word. I really enjoy typing these paragraphs, since it gives me a chance to practice my typing skills. Of course, it's fairly easy to just type a few sentences, and then cut and paste them repeatedly to create a phony document. Kind of like this.

Normal

This is a sample paragraph in Microsoft Word. I really enjoy typing these paragraphs, since it gives me a chance to practice my typing skills. Of course, it's fairly easy to just type a few sentences, and then cut and paste them repeatedly to create a phony document. Kind of like this. —— Indented

This is a sample paragraph in Microsoft Word. I really enjoy typing these paragraphs, since it gives me a chance to practice my typing skills. Of course, it's fairly easy to just type a few sentences, and then cut and paste them repeatedly to create a phony document. Kind of like this.

To indent a paragraph using the Paragraph dialog box, follow these steps:

1. Select Format ➢ Paragraph to display the Paragraph dialog box.

2. Select the Indents and Spacing tab.

3. In the Indentation section, choose both Left and Right values, in inches.

4. Click OK.

You can also change indentation using Word's horizontal ruler. All you have to do is click and drag the left- and right-indent markers to new positions.

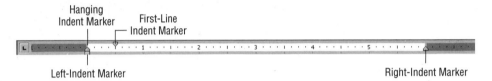

Word also lets you indent just the first line of a paragraph. You can choose to have the first line either indented or outdented as a hanging indent. (With a hanging indent, the first line is positioned at the left margin, and all following lines are indented a specified distance.) Both types of first-line indents are shown in Figure 9.3.

FIGURE 9.3

Word offers two types of first-line indents: First Line and Hanging.

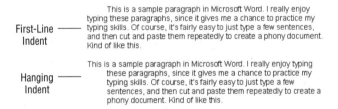

To set first-line indenting, follow these steps:

1. Select Format ➢ Paragraph to display the Paragraph dialog box.

2. Select the Indents and Spacing tab.

3. In the Indentation section, pull down the Special list, and select First Line, Hanging, or (none).

4. Select a value for the indent from the By: list.

5. Click OK.

TIP You can also set first-line indents from the horizontal ruler. To set a traditional first-line indent, reposition the first line indent marker; to set a hanging indent, reposition the hanging indent marker. (When you use your mouse to move these markers, make sure you don't grab the left indent marker by mistake!)

Determining Line and Paragraph Spacing

Before the advent of today's versatile word processing programs, typists became accustomed to entering a blank line between paragraphs for separation. While you may still choose to insert blank lines between paragraphs in Word, it's easier and more appealing to apply automatic spacing before and after paragraphs.

 TIP The actual spacing between paragraphs is the sum of the "after" spacing of the top paragraph and the "before" spacing of the bottom paragraph. Remember to figure *both* spacing specifications when calculating the real distance between your paragraphs.

To apply paragraph spacing to a selected paragraph, follow these steps:

1. Select Format ➢ Paragraph to display the Paragraph dialog box.
2. Select the Indents and Spacing tab.
3. In the Spacing section, select both the Before value for the space above the current paragraph and the After value for the space below the paragraph.
4. Click OK.

While the Spacing controls affect the space before and after the given paragraph, you can also control the line spacing within your paragraph. Using the Line Spacing control on the Indents and Spacing tab, you can select from the following options:

Single   Inserts no extra space between lines.

1.5 lines   Inserts half a line between lines.

Double   Formats traditional double spacing, with a full line between lines.

At Least   Inserts a value you select from the At list as the minimum space between lines; larger fonts may exceed this line-spacing value.

Exactly   Inserts a value you select from the At list as the specific space between lines, regardless of the font size.

Multiple   Sets line spacing at a selected number of lines.

Creating Text-Based Documents

PART II

WARNING If you select the Exactly option, make sure that the value (in points) is not smaller than the font size, or you'll get overlapping lines.

Figure 9.4 shows examples of the Single, 1.5 Lines, and Double spacing options.

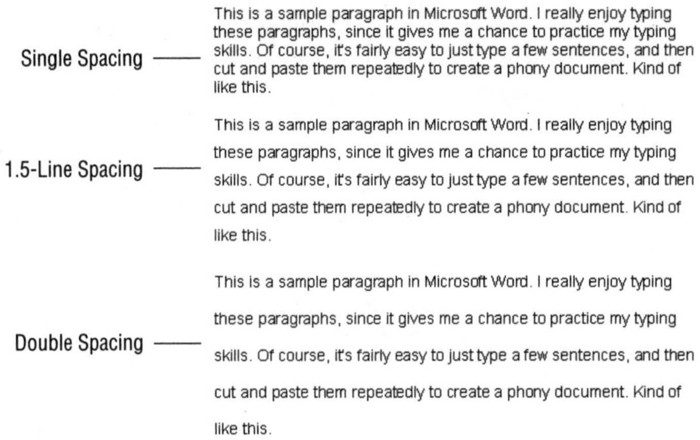

FIGURE 9.4
Different line-spacing options

Single Spacing ———

This is a sample paragraph in Microsoft Word. I really enjoy typing these paragraphs, since it gives me a chance to practice my typing skills. Of course, it's fairly easy to just type a few sentences, and then cut and paste them repeatedly to create a phony document. Kind of like this.

1.5-Line Spacing ———

This is a sample paragraph in Microsoft Word. I really enjoy typing these paragraphs, since it gives me a chance to practice my typing skills. Of course, it's fairly easy to just type a few sentences, and then cut and paste them repeatedly to create a phony document. Kind of like this.

Double Spacing ———

This is a sample paragraph in Microsoft Word. I really enjoy typing these paragraphs, since it gives me a chance to practice my typing skills. Of course, it's fairly easy to just type a few sentences, and then cut and paste them repeatedly to create a phony document. Kind of like this.

Controlling Widows, Orphans, and Page Breaks

There's nothing much more annoying (at least for some of us) than when the last sentence of a paragraph straggles onto the next page, sitting by itself as a lonely reminder of the page before, unless, of course, it's when a paragraph breaks to the next page in *precisely* the wrong place. That's why Word 2000 offers a variety of pagination options you can employ to control when and where your paragraphs break across multiple pages.

You access Word's pagination options in the following manner:

1. Select Format ➢ Paragraph to display the Paragraph dialog box.

2. Select the Line and Page Breaks tab.

3. Check the desired option in the Pagination section.

4. Click OK.

Table 9.2 describes each of Word's pagination options.

TABLE 9.2: WORD'S PAGINATION OPTIONS	
Option	**Description**
Widow/Orphan Control	Prevents the last line or word of a paragraph from printing by itself at the top of the next page (known as a *widow*), and prevents the first line of a paragraph from printing by itself at the bottom of a page (known as an *orphan*)
Keep Lines Together	Keeps an entire paragraph together without line breaks
Keep with Next	Keeps the current paragraph and the following paragraph on the same page (no page breaks allowed in between)
Page Break Before	Forces a page break before the current paragraph; forces the current paragraph to start at the top of a page

Setting Tabs

You can use tabs in your text to align blocks of text and to indent individual lines. Word allows you to use multiple tabs on a line, so you can create multi-column lists without inserting a formal table in your text.

Types of Tabs

You can set five different types of tab stops, each aligning the text at the tab in a different fashion. Table 9.3 describes the different tab stops.

TABLE 9.3: TAB STOP ALIGNMENTS	
Type	**Description**
Left	Text aligns flush left (and extends to the right) at the tab stop.
Center	Text is centered at the tab stop.
Right	Text aligns flush right (and extends back to the left) at the tab stop.
Decimal	The decimal point in a number aligns at the tab stop; similar to a right-tab stop, except numbers to the right of the decimal point extend right of the tab stop.
Bar	Inserts a vertical line at the tab stop.

PART

II

Creating Text-Based
Documents

Setting Tabs with the Ruler

While you can set precise tab-stop values in the Tabs dialog box, the easiest way to insert tab stops is via the horizontal ruler. Follow these steps:

Left Tab   Center Tab   Right Tab   Decimal Tab   Bar Tab

1. Click the Tab button (at the far left of the horizontal ruler) until it changes to the type of tab you want to insert.

2. Click on the horizontal ruler where you want to insert a tab stop.

You can move any tab on the ruler by grabbing it with your mouse and dragging it to a new position. To remove a tab, simply drag it off the ruler.

Setting Tabs with the Tabs Dialog Box

If you want to set more precise tab stops, or if you want to use *leader characters* between tabs, you need to use the Tabs dialog box. Follow these steps:

1. Select Format ➢ Tabs to display the Tabs dialog box.

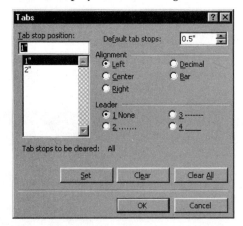

2. Enter the position for the tab stop (in inches from the left margin) in the Tab Stop Position box.

3. Choose an alignment for the tab stop.

4. Choose a leader character for the tab.

NOTE Leader characters are characters inserted between the end of the normal text and the beginning of the tab text, like this: Text............Tab. Leaders are often used when creating lists or directory listings.

5. Click the Set button to set this tab.

You can set multiple tab stops for any given paragraph. You can also delete all tab stops in the current paragraph by clicking the Clear button.

 TIP If you only set one tab stop, or if you set zero tab stops, Word assumes a series of tabs spaced half an inch apart, starting half an inch from either the left margin or the first set tab. To change this default tab spacing, go to the Tabs dialog box, and change the Default Tab Stops value.

Adding Borders and Shading

Word 2000 enables you to add a border around any selected paragraph, to add shading behind the paragraph text, or to add both borders *and* shading! You access these options from the Borders and Shading dialog box (select Format ➤ Borders and Shading).

Adding a Border to Your Paragraph

You can add borders to the top, bottom, left, or right of your paragraph. Word lets you apply several preselected border types, or you can choose your own border style, width, and color.

To add a border around the current paragraph, follow these steps:

1. Select Format ➤ Borders and Shading to display the Borders and Shading dialog box.

2. Select the Borders tab.

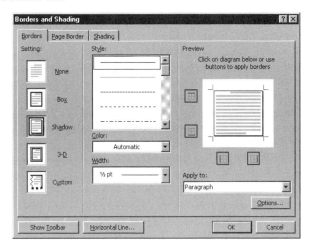

PART

II

Creating Text-Based Documents

3. Select the type of border you want to apply from the Setting section: None, Box, Shadow, 3-D, or Custom.

TIP When you select the Custom setting, you can select different line styles, colors, and widths for each side of your paragraph.

4. If you want to change the style of the border, make a selection from the Style list.

5. If you want to change the color of the border, make a selection from the Color list.

6. If you want to change the width of the border, make a selection from the Width list.

7. If you want to turn off or on the border for any specific side of your paragraph, click the Top, Bottom, Left, or Right buttons in the Preview section.

TIP A border on the Top of the current paragraph (what appears to be a horizontal line) can serve as an effective divider between major sections of your document.

8. Make sure that Paragraph is selected in the Apply To list.

9. Click OK.

To set the spacing between the border and the paragraph text, click the Options button on the Borders tab to display the Border and Shading Options dialog box. From here, you can select the distance (in points) between the border and the text on all four sides of the paragraph.

Adding Paragraph Shading

You can add color shading behind selected paragraphs, whether or not the paragraph is bordered. To add paragraph shading, follow these steps:

1. Select Format ➤ Borders and Shading to display the Borders and Shading dialog box.

2. Select the Shading tab.

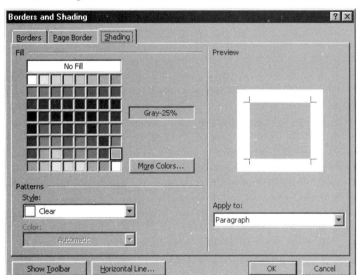

3. Select a shading color from the Fill section; click the More Colors button to choose from an expanded palette of colors.

4. Select a shading percent from the Style list. (A lower percent creates a lighter shading, while a higher percent is a darker shading; 100% applies the solid color selected.)

5. Make sure that Paragraph is selected in the Apply To list.

6. Click OK.

 TIP Choose your shading colors carefully; too dark a shading can make regular black text hard to read. If you choose a dark shading, you may want to change the text color to something lighter, like white.

Creating Lists

You can format any group of paragraphs as either a bulleted or a numbered list. Word even lets you determine what type of bullets or numbers are used in the list!

PART

II

Creating Text-Based
Documents

MASTERING THE OPPORTUNITIES

Creating Lists with AutoFormat

If you have the automatic lists functions enabled within the AutoFormat As You Type feature, you can create bulleted and numbered lists without clicking a single button or pulling down a single menu.

- First, you need to enable the automatic lists functions. Select Tools ➢ AutoCorrect to open the AutoCorrect dialog box, and then select the AutoFormat As You Type tab. Check both the Automatic Bulleted Lists and Automatic Numbered Lists options, and then click OK.

Now you can create automatic lists as you type. To create a bulleted list, start a paragraph with the >, *, or – characters, followed by either a space or a tab, and then enter your text as usual. When you press Enter at the end of the paragraph, the initial character will be converted to a bullet, and a new bulleted paragraph will be formatted and ready at the insertion point.

To create a numbered list, start a paragraph with either a number or a letter, followed by a period, and then followed by either a space or a tab. When you press Enter at the end of the paragraph, the paragraph will be formatted as the first item in a numbered list, and the paragraph that follows it will continue both the formatting and the numbering.

Working with Bulleted Lists

Bulleted lists are great ways to set off item listings within your documents. Instead of creating great long paragraphs containing lots of things separated by lots of commas, you can break out each item into its own short bulleted paragraph (as short as a single word!), which makes it easier for your reader to browse quickly through the item listings.

Creating a Bulleted List

The fastest way to create a bulleted list is to highlight the paragraphs in your list and then click the Bullets button on Word's Formatting toolbar. This indents the selected paragraphs and applies the default button character at the start of each paragraph.

TIP If you click the Bullets button while you're entering text, both your current paragraph and all paragraphs you create thereafter will be bulleted. To stop entering items in the bulleted list, click the Bullets button again (toggling off the bullets feature) or press Enter after a blank paragraph.

You can also insert a bulleted list from the Bullets and Numbering dialog box, which is discussed in the next section.

Changing Bullet Characters

If you don't like Word's default bullet character, you can select a new character (and apply additional bullet formatting) from the Bullets and Numbering dialog box. Follow these steps:

1. Select the bulleted text you want to reformat.
2. Select Format ➢ Bullets and Numbering to display the Bullets and Numbering dialog box.
3. Select the Bulleted tab.

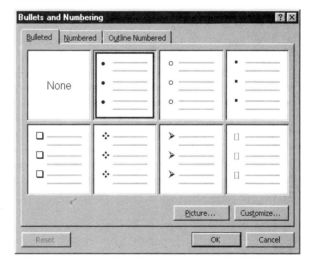

4. Select a new bullet type.
5. Click OK.

If you don't like any of the bullet types presented, you can choose to use any character from any installed font family as your default list bullet. Just click the Customize button on the Bulleted tab; this displays the Customize Bulleted List dialog box.

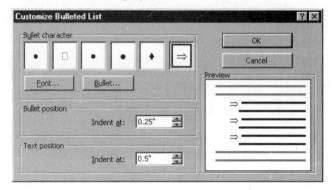

In this dialog box, you can do the following:

Choose a New Font for Your Bullet   Click the Font button to display the Font dialog box, and then select a new font family.

 TIP   The following relatively common font families are good sources for bullet characters: Symbol, Webdings, Wingdings, Wingdings 2, and Wingdings 3.

Choose a New Bullet Character   Click the Bullet button to display the Symbol dialog box, and then select a character to use as your bullet.

Change the Indentation of Your Bullet   From the Bullet Position section, choose a new value from the Indent At list.

Change the Indentation of the Text *after* Your Bullet   From the Text Position section, choose a new value from the Indent At list.

In each of the preceding scenarios, view how your bulleted text looks in the Preview section, and then click OK to apply your new bullet formatting.

Creating a Picture Bullet

 If you go through all of your available fonts and still can't find a bullet you like, you can choose to make your own with Word 2000's new picture bullet feature. This feature lets you use any graphics file as a bullet character.

To create a picture bullet, follow these steps:

1. Select Format ➤ Bullets and Numbering to display the Bullets and Numbering dialog box.

2. Select the Bulleted tab.

3. Click the Picture button to display the Picture Bullet dialog box.

4. Select the Pictures tab.

5. Click on a bullet, and select Insert Clip from the pop-up menu.

6. Click OK.

To add your own images to Word's bullet gallery, click the Import Clips button on the Picture Bullet toolbar to display the Add Clip to Clip Gallery dialog box. Navigate to the graphics file you want to include, select the file, and then click the Import button.

TIP You can import graphics from a special Clip Gallery Web site by clicking the Clips Online button.

Working with Numbered Lists

Numbered lists work pretty much the same way as bulleted lists but with some unique formatting options.

Creating a Numbered List

The fastest way to create a numbered list is to highlight the paragraphs in your list and then click the Numbering button on Word's Formatting toolbar. This indents the selected paragraphs and applies the default numbering style.

TIP If you click the Numbering button while you're entering text, both your current paragraph and all paragraphs you create thereafter will become part of the numbered list. To stop entering items in the numbered list, click the Numbering button again (toggling off the numbering feature) or press Enter after a blank paragraph.

Changing Number Formats

To change the style of your numbered list (from 1., 2., 3. to I, II, III or A, B, C, for instance), follow these steps:

1. Select the numbered text you want to reformat.

2. Select Format ➤ Bullets and Numbering to display the Bullets and Numbering dialog box.

3. Select the Numbered tab.

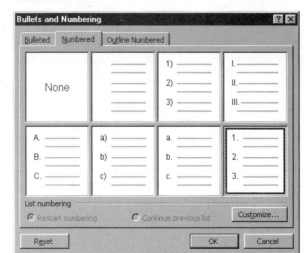

4. Select a new number type.

5. Click OK.

If you don't like any of the numbered lists presented, you can create a custom list style by clicking the Customize button on the Numbered tab; this displays the Customize Numbered List dialog box.

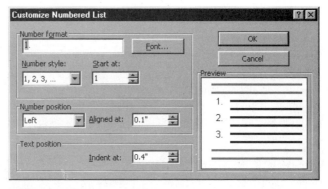

In this dialog box, you can do the following:

Choose a New Font for Your Numbers   Click the Font button to display the Font dialog box, and then select a new font family.

Choose a New Style for Your List   Pull down the Number Style list, and select a new numbering style.

Change the Starting Number for Your List Select a starting number from the Start At list.

Change the Alignment and Indentation of Your Numbers From the Number Position section, select an alignment (Left, Center, or Right), and then choose a new value from the Indent At list.

Change the Indentation of the Text *after* Your Numbers From the Text Position section, choose a new value from the Indent At list.

In each of the preceding scenarios, view how your numbered list looks in the Preview section, and then click OK to apply your new list formatting.

Continuing Numbering in Other Lists

Imagine that you're working in a new document. You've created one numbered list and then reverted back to normal text. Now you create a *second* numbered list; should it start with the number *1,* or should it continue the numbering from your previous list?

To select whether or not to continue numbering in a new list, follow these steps:

1. Position your cursor in the first numbered item in the second list.

2. Select Format ➤ Bullets and Numbering to display the Bullets and Numbering dialog box.

3. Select the Numbered tab.

4. To start the numbering of this new list at the number *1* (or at *A, I,* or whatever the first item is in your selected list style), check the Restart Numbering option.

5. To continue the numbering from the previous numbered list, check the Continue Previous List option.

6. Click OK.

Using Outline Numbering

If you're working with an outline, you can apply special *outline numbering* to your document. Outline numbering includes numbering for *subsections,* such as 1.1 or A.1, for documents with a hierarchical structure.

To apply outline numbering, follow these steps:

1. Select Format ➤ Bullets and Numbering to display the Bullets and Numbering dialog box.

PART

II

Creating Text-Based
Documents

2. Select the Outline Numbered tab.

3. Select an outline number type.

4. Click OK.

TIP Outline numbering functions similarly to the numbered list feature in that you can click the Customize button to customize your outline style.

MASTERING THE OPPORTUNITIES

Adding Line Numbers

Line numbers aren't numbered lists; they're simply numbers displayed for each line of your printed document. By numbering each line, it's easy to go to a specific phrase or item. (As you might imagine, line numbers are particularly useful in legal papers and contracts.)

To turn on line numbering for a document, select File ➢ Page Setup, and then select the Layout tab. Click the Line Numbers button to display the Line Numbers dialog box, and then check the Add Line Numbering option. Select any other options that apply, and then click OK.

Formatting with Styles

While it takes a little effort to set up, Word's styles feature is, in the end, the most efficient way to format larger documents. When you learn to create and apply styles, you're truly mastering Word 2000!

Understanding Styles

If you have a preferred paragraph format that you use over and over, you don't have to format each paragraph individually; you can assign all your formatting to a paragraph style and then apply that style to multiple paragraphs across your entire document.

Why Use Styles?

While you can work with Word for years without concerning yourself with the styles feature—using text and regular paragraph formatting for all your formatting needs—there are several reasons to use styles in your documents, beyond the obvious efficiency reasons. Here are a few practical reasons to learn how to use styles:

- Word uses styles to determine how to format your documents with the Auto-Format command.
- Word uses styles to assign outline levels when you're viewing your documents in Outline view.
- Word uses styles to create tables of contents.
- Word uses styles to help summarize your document with the AutoSummarize command.
- Word uses styles when converting your documents to HTML for Web publishing.
- Other programs—especially desktop publishing programs, such as PageMaker and QuarkXPress—rely on Word's styles when converting from the Word format to their proprietary formats.

If you don't use Word's styles—and use them properly—many of these features and functions will be unavailable to you.

Paragraph Styles versus Character Styles

This is a little confusing, but there are actually two different types of styles. *Paragraph styles*—the most common type of style—include formatting options for all paragraph and character/font attributes. *Character styles* include formatting options for character/font attributes only. In a way, character styles are a subset of paragraph styles.

When you create a new style, you can specify whether you're creating a paragraph or a character style. Character styles take precedence over paragraph styles, so text formatted with a character style inserted into a paragraph formatted with a paragraph style will retain its character style formatting.

About the only time you'll use character styles is if you have a word or phrase (such as a company or product name) that you always want to appear in a certain way. As an example, let's say that the XYZ.com company insists that its name always be presented in blue, 14-point Century Gothic type. You can create a character style with these attributes and apply it to each occurrence of XYZ.com in your text; no matter what the style of the surrounding paragraph, XYZ.com will always appear in blue, 14-point Century Gothic type.

Given the rather limited applications of character styles, the balance of this chapter will deal primarily with paragraph styles, unless noted otherwise.

Styles and Templates

Most Word templates come with a selection of predesigned styles specific to that type of document. For example, the Contemporary Letter template includes over 100 different styles (although only about three dozen are actively used), including Attention Line, Caption, CC List, Mailing Instructions, Return Address, and Title. You merely need to apply the appropriate styles to the appropriate paragraphs.

For any of Word's hundreds of built-in styles, you can choose to use them as is, to modify any of their attributes, or to use them as building blocks to create your own custom styles. Most all style configuration options are accessible via the Style dialog box (select Format ➢ Style).

 NOTE Any manual formatting that you apply directly to text or to paragraphs overrides the global formatting of the paragraph's style. For example, if a style dictates 12-point text, you can manually select text within a paragraph and change the font size of just the selected text; the manual formatting takes precedence over the style formatting.

Style Attributes

Styles include formatting for the following elements:

Font   Configures any attribute in Word's Font dialog box, including options for font choice, style, size, color, effects, character spacing, and text effect.

Paragraph   Configures any attribute in Word's Paragraph dialog box, including options for alignment, indentation, outline level, before and after spacing, line spacing, pagination, and widow/orphan control.

Tabs   Configures any attribute in Word's Tabs dialog box, including tab stop position, alignment, and leader characters.

Border Configures any attribute on the Borders and Shading tabs in Word's Borders and Shading dialog box, including border style, color, width, and shading color and style.

Language Determines the language assigned to the style, as determined in the Language dialog box.

Frame Configures any attribute in Word's Frame dialog box, including text wrapping, width, size, and horizontal and vertical positioning.

Numbering Configures almost all the attributes in Word's Bullets and Numbering dialog box, including bullet style, numbering style, outline numbering, and customized list styles.

When you apply a style to a paragraph, all of these formatting options are applied. As an example, you might have a style you use for section headings. This style would include formatting for the heading text (font, style, size, and color), the paragraph options (line spacing, paragraph spacing, and margins), and perhaps a border or section number. When you apply the new style to the paragraph, the paragraph is automatically reformatted with all the properties of the style, which is both quicker and easier than applying each of those individual formatting options individually.

Working with the Normal Style

Every predesigned Word template includes a style named Normal. If you don't specify a style for a paragraph, Word automatically applies the Normal style to your text as a default.

The Normal style is also the base style for other styles in your template. When you modify the Normal style (discussed in the "Modifying Styles" section, later in this chapter), all styles based on the Normal style are also changed.

Table 9.4 describes the major attributes of the Normal style.

TABLE 9.4: ATTRIBUTES OF WORD'S NORMAL STYLE

Element	Setting
Font	Times New Roman
Size and style	12-point Normal
Language	English
Alignment	Left
Line spacing	Single
Paragraph spacing	0 points before and after
Pagination	Widow/Orphan Control enabled
Border	None
Numbering	None

PART

II

Creating Text-Based
Documents

Viewing Styles

There are a number of ways to view the styles available in a Word document.

The style assigned to the current paragraph is always displayed (and easily viewed) in the Style box on the Formatting toolbar. Just position the insertion point within a paragraph, and look at the toolbar; the name of the assigned style is always present.

If you want to be able to view all paragraph/style associations within your document as you scroll through it, use Word's Normal view (click the Normal View button), and activate the Style Area (select Tools ➤ Options to display the Options dialog box, select the View tab, and select at least a 1" value for Style Area Width). As you can see in Figure 9.5, the style for each paragraph is listed beside each paragraph in the Style Area.

FIGURE 9.5
Use the Style Area in Normal view to see which styles are assigned to which paragraphs.

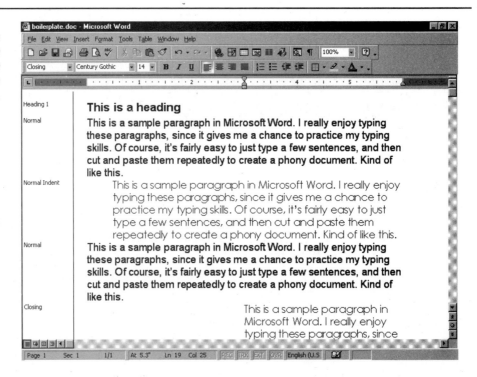

To view the specific text and paragraph properties of the style assigned to a particular paragraph, enable Word's What's This? feature by pressing Shift+F1 or selecting Help ➤ What's This? When the cursor changes to a question mark, click on any character within the paragraph and Word displays a pop-up box listing the properties of the assigned paragraph style. (Remember to turn off What's This? by pressing Esc.)

The most frequently used styles in your current document are listed on the Style list in Word's Formatting toolbar. Just pull down this list (or press Ctrl+Shift+S) to view all available styles.

You can view all styles available in the current document or template from the Style dialog box, shown in Figure 9.6. Select Format ➢ Style to display this dialog box. You can then pull down the List list to select what styles you want to list—just those Styles In Use, All Styles, or User-Defined Styles. The styles are listed in the Styles list.

FIGURE 9.6
View, modify, and
create styles in the
Style dialog box.

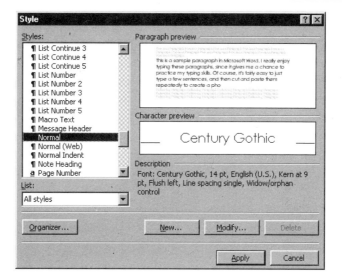

PART

II

Creating Text-Based
Documents

NOTE All the styles available in all your templates and documents are listed in Word's Organizer. See the "Managing Styles with the Organizer" section later in this chapter for more details.

Applying Styles

Applying a style to a paragraph is easy; just follow these steps:

1. Position the insertion point anywhere in the paragraph.
2. Pull down the Style list on Word's Formatting toolbar, or press Ctrl+Shift+S.
3. Select a style.

The current paragraph is now reformatted according to the options in the selected style.

Using Keyboard Shortcuts for Common Styles

Word includes several common styles across all global templates. These styles have been preassigned to specific shortcut keys so that you can apply these styles directly from your keyboard.

Table 9.5 presents Word's preassigned style shortcut keys.

TABLE 9.5: STYLE SHORTCUT KEYS

Style	Keyboard Shortcut
Normal	Ctrl+Shift+N
List Bullet	Ctrl+Shift+L
Heading 1	Alt+Ctrl+1
Heading 2	Alt+Ctrl+2
Heading 3	Alt+Ctrl+3
Heading 4	Alt+Ctrl+4

To apply a style with a shortcut key, position the insertion point anywhere in the paragraph, and then press the key combination.

Using Styles from a Different Template

When you select a template to use for a specific document, you use the styles that are included in that template. You're not limited to that template's styles; however, you can import styles from other templates to use in any given document.

Copying Styles via the Style Gallery

The easiest way to preview and use styles from other templates is with Word's Style Gallery. Follow these steps:

1. Select Format ➤ Theme to open the Theme window.

2. Click the Style Gallery button to open the Style Gallery window, shown in Figure 9.7.

FIGURE 9.7

Use the Style Gallery to preview and copy styles from another template.

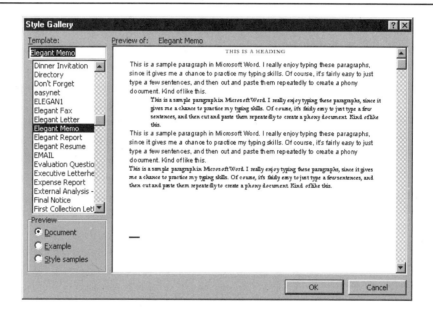

3. Select a template from the Template list.

4. Check the Document option to preview how your document would look using styles from the selected template.

5. Click OK to copy the styles from the selected template into your current document.

Copying Styles via the Organizer

Word's Organizer lets you copy styles, AutoText entries, toolbars, and macro project items from one document or template to another. Follow these steps to copy styles:

1. Select Format ➤ Style to display the Style dialog box.

2. Click the Organizer button to display the Organizer dialog box, shown in Figure 9.8.

FIGURE 9.8
Copy, delete, or rename styles with Word's Organizer.

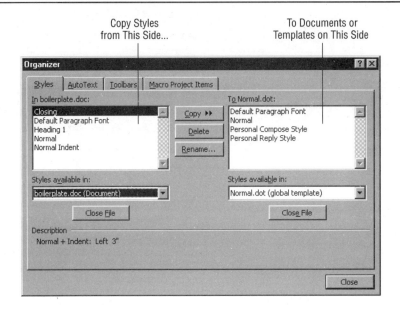

3. Select the Styles tab.

4. Close all open documents and templates by clicking both Close File buttons.

5. Click the Open button on the left side of the dialog box, and select the document or template you want to copy from.

6. Click the Open button on the right side of the dialog box, and select the document or template you want to copy to.

7. On the left side of the dialog box, select where you want to copy from (via the Styles Available In list) and what styles you want to copy.

8. On the right side of the dialog box, select where you want to copy the styles to (via the Styles Available In list).

9. Click the Copy button.

 TIP You can also use the Organizer to delete or rename styles within a specific document or template.

Modifying Styles

Word's predesigned styles might be perfect for your needs, or you may want to modify a style to better suit the specific demands of any given document. Word offers two ways to modify styles: an easy way, and a harder (but more precise) way.

Modifying by Example

You can configure Word so that any time you manually change the formatting for a paragraph the style for that paragraph is automatically updated to reflected the new formatting. This option is enabled separately for each style in your document.

To turn on this option for a specific style, follow these steps:

1. Select Format ➢ Style to open the Style dialog box.

2. Select the style you wish to enable.

3. Click the Modify button to display the Modify Style dialog box, shown in Figure 9.9.

PART

II

Creating Text-Based Documents

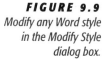

FIGURE 9.9
Modify any Word style in the Modify Style dialog box.

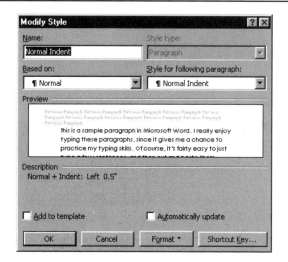

4. Check the Automatically Update option.

5. Click OK.

 WARNING The Automatically Update option can be dangerous; every formatting change you make to the selected style is automatically reflected in every other paragraph in your document using that style, so you can't make one-time-only changes without global ramifications!

With the Automatically Update option enabled, all you have to do to globally modify a style is change any formatting in any paragraph using the selected style. All other paragraphs using the same style will then be updated to reflect your changes.

Modifying Manually

You can manually modify any or all properties of any style from the Modify Style dialog box.

To modify a style, follow these steps:

1. Select Format ➢ Style to display the Style dialog box.

2. Select the style you want to edit.

3. Click the Modify button to display the Modify Style dialog box.

4. Click the Format button to display a list of properties to format.

5. Select the style property you want to edit.

6. When the selected property dialog box appears, make your changes, and click OK to return to the Modify dialog box.

7. To change the style that automatically follows this style in your document, select a new style from the Style For the Following Paragraph list.

 TIP You can automate your documents to some degree by selecting which style should follow the currently selected style, using the Style For the Following Paragraph list. When you press Enter at the end of one paragraph, the next paragraph will be automatically formatted in the style previously selected. As an example, you might configure Word so that a Normal paragraph automatically follows a Heading paragraph.

8. To make your changes apply to all future documents using this template, check the Add to Template option. To have your changes affect only the current document, leave this option unchecked.

9. Click Apply to apply this style to the current paragraph and close the dialog box, or click Cancel to close the dialog box without applying the style.

 WARNING When you click Cancel in the Style dialog box after modifying a style, you don't cancel the modifications made to the selected style; those modifications were saved when you clicked OK in the Modify dialog box. (If you really wanted to cancel your modifications, you should have clicked Cancel back in the Modify dialog box.)

This is the preferred method for modifying styles, as you can easily see the current settings and go directly to the property you want to change.

Assigning a Shortcut Key to Your Style

Word enables you to assign your own shortcut key to any style, which makes it easier to apply your most frequently used styles.

To assign a shortcut key, follow these steps:

1. Select Format ➤ Style to display the Style dialog box.

2. Select a style.

3. Click the Modify button to display the Modify Style dialog box.

4. Click the Shortcut Key button to display the Customize Keyboard dialog box.

5. Enter the shortcut key in the Press New Shortcut Key box.

6. Click Assign to assign the key(s) to the selected style.

PART
II

Creating Text-Based
Documents

Creating New Styles

When modifying a style isn't enough, you can create new styles to use in this or any Word template or document. You create a new style based on an existing style, so you're never really starting from scratch.

New Styles by Example

The easiest way to create a new style is by formatting a paragraph as you'd like the style to appear and then using that paragraph as the basis for the new style. Follow these steps:

1. Format a paragraph exactly as you want your style to appear.

2. Select the entire paragraph.

3. Click inside the Style box on Word's Formatting toolbar, and type over the existing style with a name for your new style.

4. Press Enter.

You have now created a new style based on the formatting in the selected paragraph.

New Styles in Detail

The other, more detailed method of creating a new style involves selecting an existing style, modifying it, and saving the new style under a new name. This method allows more precise formatting of more options than does the simpler "by example" method just discussed.

 NOTE When you base a new style on an existing style, any changes to the base style are reflected in the "based on" styles. For example, if you based a new style on the Normal style and then changed the Normal style's font size from 12 points to 14 points, the new style based on the Normal style will also see its font size change from 12 points to 14 points.

To create a new style using the detailed method, follow these steps:

1. Select Format ➤ Style to display the Style dialog box.

2. Click the New button to display the New Style dialog box.

3. Enter a name for your new style in the Name box.

 TIP You can create a short *alias* for any long style name; it's often easier to enter a few letters when selecting a style than an entire descriptive style name. You can apply the alias when creating a new style or by renaming an existing style using the Organizer. Just enter a comma after the full style name, and then type a short alias, like this: **Style Name, SN**, where SN is your short alias.

4. Pull down the Based On list, and select the existing style on which you're basing the new style.

5. Pull down the Style for the Following Paragraph list, and select which style should follow this style in your document.

6. To change a specific property, click the Format button, and select the style property you want to edit; when the selected property dialog box appears, make your changes, and click OK to return to the New Style dialog box.

7. To add your new style to all documents based on this template, check the Add to Template option; to add this style only to the current document, leave this option unchecked.

8. To assign your new style to a shortcut key, click the Shortcut Key button to display the Customize Keyboard dialog box; enter the shortcut key in the Press New Shortcut Key box, and then click Assign.

9. Click OK.

Your new style will now appear in the Style list on the Formatting toolbar and is available for use in the current document.

 NOTE Another way to format the paragraphs and text in your document is to use Word 2000's new themes feature. While themes are primarily intended for use when creating Web pages, you can also use themes for normal, non-Web Word documents. To learn more about themes, see Chapter 24.

PART

II

Creating Text-Based Documents

CHAPTER 10

Setting Up Pages and Sections

Setting paper size and orientation   287

Setting page margins   289

Adding background colors and page borders   292

Understanding document sections   297

Working with page numbers   300

Viewing and editing headers and footers 303

Creating a multiple column layout   307

Adjusting column widths and spacing   308

In Chapter 8 you learned how to format text and fonts; in Chapter 9 you learned how to format paragraphs and styles. Now it's time to format something bigger—the entire page!

Word 2000 offers a variety of page-formatting features and options. You can:

- change the size of your page and its orientation
- add a border or background graphic to your page
- number your pages and add vital information to their headers and footers
- format your pages for multiple columns, and arrange them in separate sections throughout your documents

The page and section formatting you apply does not interfere with the paragraph styles and direct text formatting you mastered in the previous chapters. Think of your page as an empty box that you fill with all your other elements—your characters and paragraphs, your pictures and other objects. This chapter shows you how to reshape and resize that box to create the most appropriate and best-looking container for your text and graphics.

So read on and learn how to master Word 2000's page and section formatting!

Configuring Your Page

Page formatting options in Microsoft Word are found in a number of places. Basic sizing, layout, and margin settings are found in the Page Setup dialog box (select File ➤ Page Setup). Page borders are found in the Borders and Shading dialog box (select Format ➤ Borders and Shading), and page backgrounds are found in the Background submenu (select Format ➤ Background). Keep these locations in mind as you learn how to execute specific formatting operations.

 TIP Page formatting information can be stored in a Word template. To learn more about creating templates, see Chapter 27.

Understanding Word's Default Page Setup

When Word creates a new document, it applies certain default page settings to your document (unless otherwise specified by a specific template). The more important of these default settings are listed in Table 10.1.

TABLE 10.1: WORD'S DEFAULT PAGE SETTINGS

Option	Setting
Top margin	1"
Bottom margin	1"
Left margin	1.25"
Right margin	1.25"
Gutter	0"
Gutter position	Left
Paper size	Letter
Orientation	Portrait
Vertical alignment	Top

If you can live with these settings—great. If not, you can change every one of these settings—and more—using the information presented throughout this chapter.

You can also change Word's default page setup. Just use the options in the Page Setup dialog box to configure a new page setup, and then click the Default button (on any tab).

Setting Paper Size and Orientation

If you live in the U.S., you're probably used to using 8.5" x 11" as your default paper size. But other countries commonly use different size paper—and certain types of documents are often printed in nonstandard formats.

Using a Different Paper Size

To change the size of your document, follow these steps:

1. Select File ➢ Page Setup to display the Page Setup dialog box.
2. Select the Paper Size tab, shown in Figure 10.1.

FIGURE 10.1
*Use the Paper Size tab
of the Page Setup
dialog box to configure
size and orientation.*

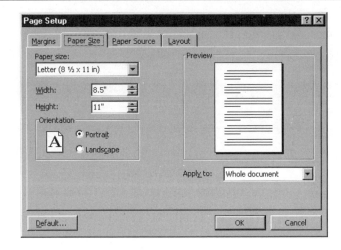

3. Pull down the Paper Size list and select a preconfigured paper type, *or...*

   Adjust the Width and Height controls to create a custom paper size.

4. To apply this new size to your entire document, pull down the Apply To list and select Whole Document; to apply this new size from this point forward in your document (leaving previous pages at their original size), select This Point Forward.

5. Click OK.

TIP When you change the paper size of a document that already contains text and other elements, the text will be automatically rearranged to flow into the new document size. You may want to check the position of inserted pictures and objects, as well as page breaks, and reposition those elements that didn't make a perfect transition to the new paper size.

Switching from Portrait to Landscape

You can also change the *orientation* of your document. Normal orientation (taller than wide) is called *portrait* orientation. Turning the paper on its side (wider than tall) creates a *landscape* orientation.

To change from portrait to landscape mode (or vice versa), follow these steps:

1. Select File ➢ Page Setup to display the Page Setup dialog box.

2. Select the Paper Size tab.

3. Check the Portrait option if you have a tall document; check the Landscape option if you have a wide document.

4. Click OK.

Setting Page Margins

If your paper is 8.5" wide, you don't actually print across the entire 8.5" of the paper. You have to leave *margins* on either side (and the top and bottom) of the page, both for readability and for practical reasons.

In terms of readability, it's tough to read text that goes all the way to the edge of the paper; you need some white space there to provide some "padding" for the eyes. In terms of practicality, many printers don't print all the way to the edges of a piece of paper; there is at least a 0.25" space that can't be used for printing, regardless.

For these reasons, you need to design your documents to include an appropriate margin on all sides.

 WARNING If you try to print outside the printable area of your printer, Word will display the following warning:

One or more margins are set outside the printable area of the page.

If you see this warning box, click the Fix button to have Word increase the margin width to fit the capabilities of your printer. Not fixing this problem will result in the edges of your document not printing correctly (or at all).

Setting Margins from the Ruler

In Print Layout view only, you can control your document's margins from Word's rulers. As shown in Figure 10.2, the dark areas on either end of the ruler are your document's current margins; use your mouse to drag the *inside* end of a margin and resize it. If both horizontal and vertical rulers are displayed, you can adjust all four margins in your current document.

FIGURE 10.2
Adjusting margins from the horizontal ruler

Margin

Margin

Drag This End to Resize

Drag This End to Resize

NOTE To set margins from the rulers, you first must have the rulers displayed in the Word workspace. To display Word's rulers, select View ➤ Ruler and make sure that the Ruler option is selected. If you don't see a vertical ruler in Print Layout view, select Tools ➤ Options to display the Options dialog box, select the View tab, and then check the Vertical Ruler option.

Setting Margins in Detail

You can more precisely set the margins for a document from the Page Setup dialog box. Follow these steps:

1. Select File ➤ Page Setup to display the Page Setup dialog box.

2. Select the Margins tab, shown in Figure 10.3.

FIGURE 10.3
Use the Margins tab to set precise margin measurements—and turn on gutters and mirror margins.

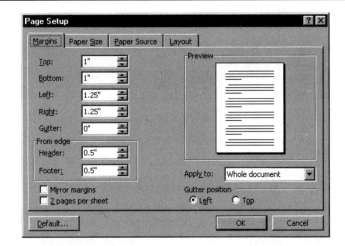

3. Select values (in inches) for the Top, Bottom, Left, and Right margins.

4. Click OK.

 TIP If you're not sure what size margin to set, go with 1" all the way around. This works most of the time, unless you have some document-specific need for a larger or smaller margin.

Working with the Gutter

You can configure Word to add extra space in the document's margin to allow for binding. This is particularly useful for large documents that require comb, wire, or perfect binding.

To configure a gutter appropriate for your document, follow these steps:

1. Select File ➢ Page Setup to display the Page Setup dialog box.

2. Select the Margins tab.

3. Select a size for your gutter using the Gutter control. Typical gutters range from 0.5" to 1".

4. Check the appropriate gutter position (Left or Top; Left is more typical).

5. Click OK.

 TIP To print two left and right pages side-by-side on a landscape paper, check the 2 Pages Per Sheet option on the Margins tab.

Enabling Mirror Margins

If you're printing on both sides of a page—so that your document has distinct left and right pages—you may want to *mirror* the margins on the opposing pages. With mirrored margins, if you set a 0.5" left margin on the outside of the left hand page, Word would automatically apply a 0.5" *right* margin on the outside of the *right* hand page. Mirror margins also apply gutter configurations properly for both left and right pages.

To set mirror margins, follow these steps:

1. Select File ➢ Page Setup to display the Page Setup dialog box.

2. Select the Margins tab.

3. Check the Mirror Margins option.

4. Click OK.

 TIP If you're preparing a document to be bound, you'll want to print on both sides of the page, select an appropriate gutter space, and turn on mirror margins.

Configuring Vertical Text Alignment

In Chapter 9, you learned how to set the *horizontal* alignment of your paragraphs— right, left, centered, or justified. Word also enables you to set the *vertical* alignment of all text on your page. With this control, if your text doesn't fill up an entire page, you can have it all drop to the bottom of the page, or center itself in the middle of the page, or stay at the top (the traditional top alignment).

To configure your document's vertical text alignment, follow these steps:

1. Select File ➢ Page Setup to display the Page Setup dialog box.

PART

II

Creating Text-Based Documents

2. Select the Layout tab.

3. Pull down the Vertical Alignment list and select one of the following options: Top, Center, Justified, or Bottom.

4. To apply this alignment to your entire document, pull down the Apply To list and select Whole Document; to apply this new size from this point forward in your document (leaving previous pages at their original size), select This Point Forward.

5. Click OK.

Adding Background Colors and Page Borders

Black text on white paper is fine, but there will come a time when you need something slightly less conventional. When you want to make your document stand out from the crowd, use Word 2000 to add backgrounds and borders to your pages—with just a few clicks of the mouse!

Incorporating Background Colors

To change from a white page to a color background, follow these steps:

1. Select Format ➢ Background.

2. Select a format from the color submenu, *or*

   Select More Colors to display the More Colors dialog box and select from a larger palette of colors, *or*

   Select Fill Effects to display the Fill Effects dialog box, and then select a new fill effect or texture for your background.

3. Click OK.

 TIP If you're changing to a dark background, check to see if your normal black text is still readable. If not, consider changing your font color to white throughout.

You can create some really neat backgrounds using Word's Fill Effects dialog box. Here is some of what you can do:

Create a Blend To make one color blend into another, select the Gradient tab. Here you can choose from three types of gradients (one-color, two-color, or one of

Word's preselected gradients); then choose the shading style (horizontal, vertical, diagonal, etc.) and the direction of the blend.

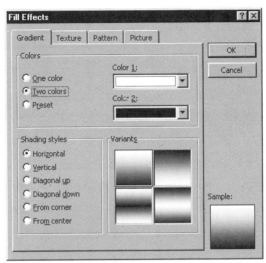

Add a Texture   Select the Texture tab to choose from one of Word's preselected textures, or click the Other Texture button to pick a graphic to tile in the background of your document.

Pick a Pattern   Select the Pattern tab to choose from one of many two-color patterns, and then select both colors for the pattern.

Put a Picture in the Background   For your Web-based documents (and viewable in Web Layout view only), select the Picture tab to select a picture to layer in the background of your Web page.

 WARNING   Word 2000 doesn't allow you add background graphics to traditional print documents. If you're designing a Web document, however, you can incorporate background graphics. To learn more about Word's Web-creation features, see Chapter 24.

Creating a Watermark

While you can't use a picture in the background of your printed documents, Word does let you insert a *watermark* to appear behind your text. Watermarks are actually linked to headers and footers (discussed in the "Using Headers and Footers" section of this chapter), but can be positioned anywhere on your page. Watermarks appear on all pages that include the linked-to header or footer.

PART

II

Creating Text-Based
Documents

One popular use of a watermark is to create a watermark of your company logo. When you insert the logo as a watermark, it appears screened back behind your text on every page of your document, as shown in Figure 10.4.

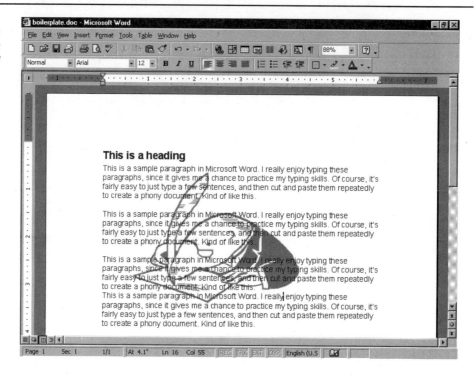

To create a watermark, follow these steps:

1. Select View ➤ Header and Footer.

2. Position the insertion point in either the header or footer, and then select Insert ➤ Picture ➤ *item*, where *item* is the type of object (picture, clip art, Word Art, etc.) you want to insert.

3. Double-click the picture to display the Format Picture dialog box, select the Layout tab, select Behind Text, and then click OK.

4. Click the Close button on the Header and Footer toolbar.

5. Use your mouse to reposition and resize the object as appropriate.

To view your watermark, switch to Print Layout view (or activate Word's Print Preview).

TIP If your watermark is printing too dark, you can edit it to make it lighter. Select View ➢ Header and Footer, and then double-click the watermark graphic to display the Format Picture dialog box. Select the Picture tab, and then pull down the Color list and select Watermark. Adjust the Brightness and Contrast controls to more appropriate levels and click OK.

Working with Page Borders

Word 2000 enables you to apply a "framing" effect to your page by adding a border around the page edges. You can choose from a variety of border weights and styles, and even choose a color border.

There are several instances when you might want to use page borders in your documents. For example, if you're using Word to create a certificate or award, a border—especially one created with graphic elements—adds a nice effect. As another example, using a border on the *title page* of a report helps to set off this initial page from the body of the report. Figure 10.5 shows how a title page looks with a typical border applied.

PART
II

Creating Text-Based
Documents

FIGURE 10.5
*Add a page border to
your document's title
page for a unique
"framing" effect.*

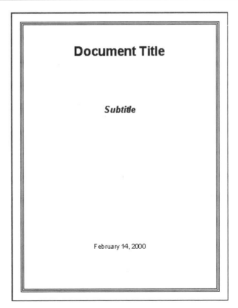

To add a border to the pages in your document, follow these steps:

1. Select Format ➢ Borders and Shading to display the Borders and Shading dialog box.

2. Select the Page Border tab.

3. Select the type of border you want to apply from the Setting section: None, Box, Shadow, 3-D, or Custom.

 TIP When you select the Custom setting, you can select different line styles, colors, and widths for each side of your paragraph.

4. If you want to change the style of the border, make a selection from the Style list.

5. If you want to change the color of the border, make a selection from the Color list.

6. If you want to change the width of the border, make a selection from the Width list.

7. If you want to turn off (or on) the border for any specific side of your page, click the Top, Bottom, Left, or Right buttons in the Preview section.

8. Pull down the Apply To list and select what part(s) of your document you want to border: Whole Document, This Section, This Section—First Page Only, This Section—All Except First Page.

9. Click OK.

To set the spacing between the border and the text on your page, click the Options button to display the Border and Shading Options dialog box. From here you can select the margin for your border, as well as whether the border appears in front of or behind your text.

Creating a Graphical Page Border

 Word 2000 enables you to use repeating graphic elements as a page border. As you can see in Figure 10.6, graphical borders consist of a single graphic image repeated over and over to surround your page.

To create a border made of repeating graphic elements, pull down the Art list on the Page Borders tab and select one of the many preselected graphic-based borders. Configure the other page border options as usual and click OK.

 NOTE If you want to create a border from your own graphic images, you first have to add those images to Word's Clipart Gallery, as described in Chapter 16.

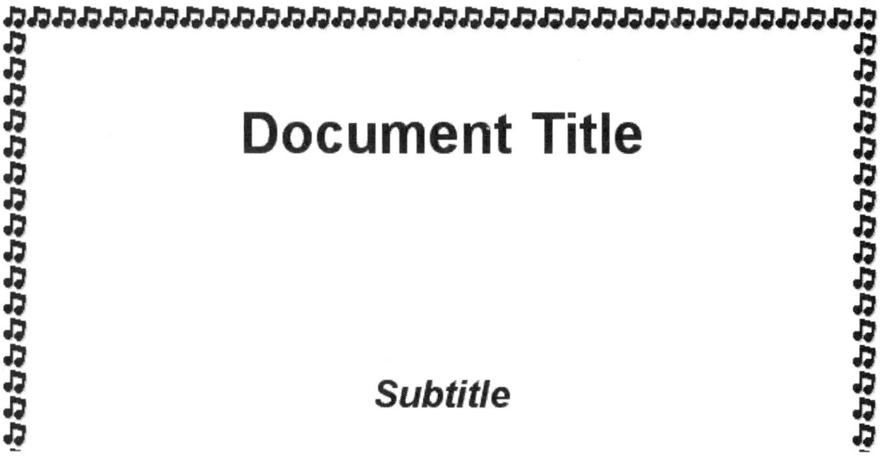

FIGURE 10.6
Create a page border made up of repeating graphics.

Document Title

Subtitle

Understanding Document Sections

If your document is short, you may be able to use the same page formatting throughout the entire document. But if your document is long, you might have a need to vary certain formatting or layout options—you might need one part of your single-column document to utilize a two-column layout, or you might want to number different sections of your document differently.

When you need to make major layout changes to parts of your documents, you will use Word's *sections* feature. Word lets you break documents up into multiple sections, with each section having its own formatting and layout.

Starting a New Section

When you need to start a new section in your document, follow these steps:

1. Position your cursor where you want to start a new section.
2. Select Insert ➢ Break to display the Break dialog box.
3. Select one of the four Section Break Types.
4. Click OK.

Table 10.2 details the types of section breaks you can insert into your documents:

TABLE 10.2: WORD'S SECTION BREAKS	
Section Break Type	**Description**
Next Page	Starts the new section at the top of the next page
Continuous	Starts the new section at the insertion point
Even Page	Starts the new section at the top of the next even page
Odd Page	Starts the new section at the top of the next odd page

Note that the new section maintains all the formatting of the previous section—until you change it. At that point, any layout or page formatting changes you make apply only to the current section, not to other sections (either earlier or later) in your document.

 NOTE Any time you choose a "from this point on" formatting option, Word automatically inserts a section break at that point—thus creating a new section from that point on.

Viewing Section Breaks

If you're working in Normal view, you'll see a section break marker (as shown in Figure 10.7) wherever a section break occurs. The section break marker will also indicate which type of section break (Next Page, Continuous, Even Page, or Odd Page) it represents.

 TIP In Normal view, markers for all types of breaks are visible, including page breaks, column breaks, and text wrapping breaks.

If you're using Print Layout or Outline views, section breaks are not automatically displayed—and are thus hard to locate. To toggle on section break visibility in these two modes, click the Show/Hide button on Word's Standard tool bar. When toggled on, this command not only displays paragraph marks, but also section, page, column, and text wrapping breaks.

FIGURE 10.7
Viewing a section break in Word's Normal view

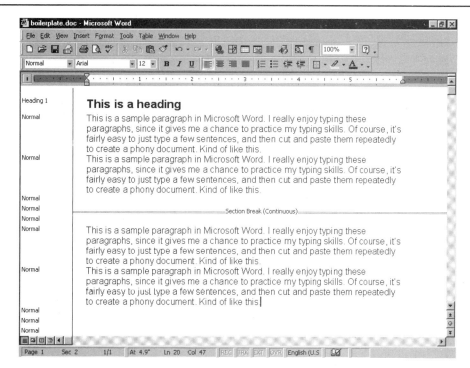

Deleting Section Breaks

To delete a section break—and thus "merge" the first section with the second section—simply delete the section break marker. Note that when you merge two sections together, the second section assumes the formatting (including header/footer contents and formatting) of the first section.

Copying Section Formatting

All the formatting information for a given section—page layout, margins, page borders, shading, column layout, and so on—are contained within the section break marker. To copy formatting from one section to another, all you have to do is copy the section break marker and paste it where you want the new, identically-formatted section to begin.

Working with Page Numbers

If your document is more than a few pages long, you probably want to include page numbers for the reader's convenience. Word 2000 automatically calculates the current page number even if you're working with a multiple-section document, and you can include that page number anywhere on your page.

Adding Page Numbers to a Header or Footer

Page numbers are often included as part of a header or footer. To add automatic page numbering to your document's header or footer, follow these steps:

1. Select Insert ➤ Page Numbers to display the Page Numbers dialog box.

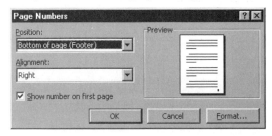

2. Pull down the Position list and select either Top of Page (Header) or Bottom of Page (Footer).

3. Pull down the Alignment list and select a horizontal alignment for the page number: Left, Right, Center, Inside, or Outside. (Inside and Outside are relative to the inside and outside edges of bound pages.)

4. To configure the number format of the page number, click the Format button to display the Page Number Format dialog box. Pull down the Number Format list to select a number format (1, 2, 3 or A, B, C or some similar format), configure any other appropriate settings and click OK.

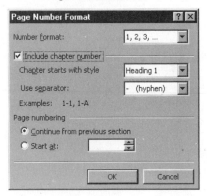

TIP To include the chapter number (of a multiple-chapter document) along with the page number, check the Include Chapter Number option in the Page Number Format dialog box. You'll need to select the paragraph style assigned to the chapter heads from the Chapter Starts with Style list, and you can choose to include a separator between the chapter number and page number by making a selection from the Use Separator list.

5. If you don't want to show the page number on the first page of your document (if you have a separate title page, for example), *uncheck* the Show Number on First Page option.

6. Click OK.

Adding Page Numbers Anywhere on the Page

When you add page numbers to your header or footer using the above method, you can actually move that page number frame anywhere on your page—just as you can move a watermark linked to a header or footer.

All you have to do is use your mouse to grab the page number frame from the header or footer and drag it anyplace else on your page. It will remain linked to your header or footer (requiring you to open the header/footer to edit or delete the page number), but will be displayed on your page where you positioned it.

 MASTERING THE OPPORTUNITIES

Inserting Page Numbers into Your Text

To add a page number in-line with your text, you can use one of two methods.

Method one uses Word's AutoText feature, and proceeds as follows:

1. Position your insertion point where you want to insert the page number.

2. Select Insert ➤ AutoText ➤ AutoText to display the AutoText dialog box.

3. From the list of AutoText entries, select - PAGE - .

4. Click the Insert button to insert the PAGE field into your text.

Continued ▶

PART

II

Creating Text-Based Documents

You can also insert a page field into your text manually, as follows:

1. Position your insertion point where you want to insert the page number.

2. Select Insert ➤ Field to display the Insert Field dialog box.

3. From the Categories list, select Numbering.

4. From the Field Names list, select Page.

5. Make sure that the Preserve Formatting During Updates option is checked.

6. Click OK.

While using a page field to insert a page number doesn't offer as many numbering options as does the header/footer method, it does allow you to have a reference to an automatically updated page number within the text of your document.

 NOTE To learn more about Word's automatic fields, see Chapter 12.

Changing Page Numbering in Different Sections of Your Document

The Page Number Format dialog box provides options that allow you to change your page numbering for different sections of your document. This is useful if you want to start each new section or chapter from the number "1."

To change the page numbering in different sections, follow these steps:

1. If you haven't yet done so, insert a section break to start a new section in your document.

2. Click the first page of the new section.

3. Select Insert ➤ Page Numbers to display the Page Numbers dialog box.

4. Click the Format button to display the Page Number Format dialog box.

5. To change the starting page number of this section, check the Start At option and select a page number from the Start At list. For example, to restart the page numbering at 1, select 1 from the list.

TIP If you want the new section to pick up the page numbering from the previous section, check the Continue from Previous Section option.

6. Click OK.

Using Headers and Footers

Headers and footers are repeating sections at the top (header) or bottom (footer) of your document. You can use headers and footers to display information about your document, such as title, subject, author, date, chapter number, or page number.

Viewing Headers and Footers

Headers and footers do not appear as part of your normal document text—in fact, they aren't visible at all unless you're in the Print Layout mode. You can't even use the arrows on your keyboard to move the insertion point to a header or a footer.

To work within a header or footer, you have to select View ➤ Header and Footer. This switches Word to Print Layout view (if you weren't in that view already), "opens" the header for editing, and displays the Header and Footer toolbar. You use the commands on this toolbar to edit and format your header and footer.

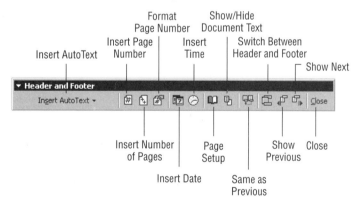

Editing Header and Footer Text

To add text to a header or footer, follow these steps:

1. Select View ➤ Headers and Footers to open the header editing area.

2. Enter text as usual within the header.

3. Click the Switch Between Header and Footer button on the toolbar to switch to the footer editing area.

4. Enter text as usual within the footer.

5. Click Close to close the header/footer editing areas.

TIP You can format text within a header or footer as you'd format any normal text elsewhere in your document. You can apply individual text/font formatting, or select Format ➢ Paragraph to format the header or footer "paragraph" attributes. You can even select Format ➢ Style to edit either the Header or Footer styles (individually). And don't forget to use Word's ruler to reposition the tabs within the header or footer, if necessary.

Adding Page Numbers, Dates, and Times to Your Header and Footer

Certain automated fields can be added to your header or footer directly from the Header and Footer toolbar. When you add these fields, they're kept automatically updated by Word as your document changes over time.

Figure 10.8 shows a header with all of these automated fields added.

FIGURE 10.8
Use your header to display page number, number of pages, and the current date and time.

Header -Section 1-

Page 1 of 2   10/3/99   7:17 PM

Inserting a Page Number

To add an automated page number to your header or footer, click the Insert Page Number button. You can format the style of the page number by clicking the Format Page Number button to display the Page Number Format dialog box, discussed earlier in this chapter.

WARNING When you add a page number to your header/footer in this fashion, you can't drag it elsewhere on the page as you can when you use the Insert ➢ Page Numbers method, discussed earlier.

Calculating the Total Number of Pages

To add an "*X* of *Y* pages" line, insert the page number, type **of**, and then click the Insert Number of Pages button. This field contains the calculated total number of pages in your document.

Inserting the Date and Time

To add today's date to your header/footer, click the Insert Date button. To add the current time, click the Insert Time button.

Adding Prepared Text with AutoText

If you want to make creating a header or footer really easy, use one of the prewritten header/footer entries in Word 2000's AutoText list. When you click the Insert Auto-Text button on the Header and Footer toolbar, you can choose from a list of ten popular header/footers.

Just select an entry from the list to insert it into your document at the insertion point.

All of these entries use automated fields to generate the complete header/footer text. For example, selecting the Filename entry inserts the actual filename of your document; the Created By entry inserts the text "Created by" followed by your username.

You can't go wrong by using one of these AutoText entries to create your header or footer.

TIP If you want to get more creative with your header/footer text, you can use any of Word's field codes to insert a variety of automated fields into your header or footer. To learn more about field codes, see Chapter 12.

Creating a Unique Header or Footer for Your First Page

If your document has a separate title page, you may want to create a header or footer for that page that is different from the running header/footer throughout the rest of your document. (You may even want to eliminate the header and footer completely from the title page.) Follow these steps:

1. Position your cursor on the first page of your document.
2. Select View ➤ Header and Footer to display the header/footer editing area (and the Header and Footer toolbar).

PART

II

Creating Text-Based
Documents

3. Click the Page Setup button on the Header and Footer toolbar to display the Page Setup dialog box.

4. Select the Layout tab.

5. Check the Different First Page option.

6. Click OK.

7. Edit the first page's header and footer as desired; if you don't want a header or footer on the first page, simply delete all text and other elements from the header/footer areas.

8. To edit the header/footer for the following pages, navigate to the next page and begin editing.

9. Click the Close button to return to normal editing.

Managing Odd and Even Headers and Footers

If you're producing a bound document with printing on both sides of the paper (so that you have opposing pages), you may want to create slightly different headers or footers for the left and right pages. If so, follow these steps:

1. Select View ➢ Header and Footer to display the header/footer editing area (and the Header and Footer toolbar).

2. Click the Page Setup button on the Header and Footer toolbar to display the Page Setup dialog box.

3. Select the Layout tab.

4. Check the Different Odd and Even option.

5. Click OK.

6. Move to an even-numbered page (typically a left-hand page) and edit the header/footer.

7. Move to an odd-numbered page (typically a right-hand page) and edit the header/footer.

8. Click the Close button to return to normal editing.

TIP   By default, Word allows you to create different headers/footers for each section of your document; just edit each section's header/footer separately. To use the *same* header/footer across two sections, position your cursor on the first page of the new section, select View ➢ Header and Footer, and then click the Same as Previous button.

Managing Multiple Columns

Certain types of documents—newsletters, especially—lend themselves to multiple column layouts. Word 2000 lets you quickly and easily apply multiple-column formatting to your entire document, or just to selected sections. The result—such as the document shown in Figure 10.9—is a very professional look, when done right.

FIGURE 10.9
It's easy to create a three-column newsletter within Word.

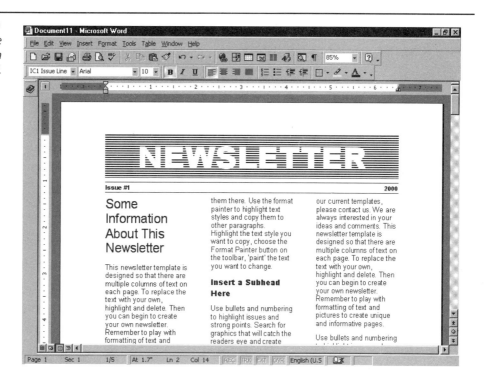

Creating a Multiple Column Layout

To change the layout of the current section of your document (or, if your document isn't divided into sections, your entire document) to a multiple-column layout, follow these steps:

1. Position your cursor where you want the multiple-column layout to begin.

2. Select Format ➤ Columns to display the Columns dialog box.

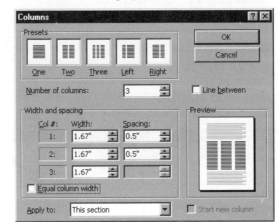

3. Select one of the preset column styles: One column, Two column, Three column, Left (two columns with smaller left column), or Right (two columns with smaller right column).

4. If you want a line between your columns, check the Line Between option.

5. Pull down the Apply To list and select whether you want to apply this column layout to your Whole Document, or just This Point Forward to the end of your document.

6. Click OK.

If you want to return to a single (or other) column layout later in your document, just repeat these steps and select a different layout at that point.

Adjusting Column Widths and Spacing

If you don't like any of Word's preset column layouts, you can create your own by specifying custom column widths and spacing. Follow these steps:

1. Position your cursor where you want the new column layout to begin.

2. Select Format ➤ Columns to display the Columns dialog box.

3. Select how many columns you want from the Number of Columns list.

4. If you want your columns to be of equal width, check the Equal Column Width option; if you want columns of different width, *uncheck* this option.

5. If you selected unequal column widths, select the width and spacing for each column in the Width and Spacing area. (Don't worry—Word won't let your total width exceed the total available width.)

6. If you want a line between your columns, check the Line Between option.

7. Pull down the Apply To list and select whether you want to apply this column layout to your Whole Document, or just This Point Forward to the end of your document.

8. Click OK.

 TIP Don't go overboard with too many columns on a page. Columns that are too narrow display text in extremely short lines, which become very hard to read.

Adjusting Vertical Alignment

By default, Word aligns all your column text to the top of the column. This results in ragged column bottoms. If you prefer even column bottoms, you can set Word's vertical alignment to justify your text vertically. Here's how you do that:

1. Position your cursor where you want the new vertical alignment to begin—typically the same place you started the multiple-column layout.

2. Select File ➢ Page Setup to display the Page Setup dialog box.

3. Select the Layout tab.

4. Pull down the Vertical Alignment list and select Justified.

5. Pull down the Apply To list and select This Point Forward.

6. Click OK.

Creating Text-Based Documents

 MASTERING THE OPPORTUNITIES

Inserting Page, Column, and Section Breaks

Whether you're working with columns, pages, or sections, you sometimes need to insert manual *breaks*. For example, if you want to ensure that a certain story starts at the top of a new column, you need to insert a manual column break before the first word of the story. Likewise, if you want a certain element to appear at the top of a new page (or *not* appear at the bottom of a page), you insert a page break before that element.

Continued ▸

To insert any manual break within Word, position the insertion point where you want the break to occur, and then select Insert ≻ Break to display the Break dialog box. From here you can select the type of break you wish to apply; then click OK to insert the break.

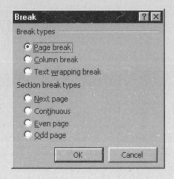

Here are the options you find in the Break dialog box:

Page Break Forces the text after the break to appear at the top of the next page. (Press Ctrl+Enter to insert a page break directly from your keyboard.)

Column Break Forces the text after the break to appear at the top of the next column. (Press Ctrl+Shift+Enter to insert a column break directly from your keyboard.)

Text Wrapping Break Forces the text after the break to continue below the next picture, table, or other object.

Section Break: Next Page Starts a new section at the top of the next page.

Section Break: Continuous Starts a new section *at the break*, without forcing a page break of any kind.

Section Break: Even Page Starts a new section at the top of the next even-numbered page.

Section Break: Odd Page Starts a new section at the top of the next odd-numbered page.

You can get rid of any break by simply deleting the break marker. You can see all break markers when you're using Word's Normal view. If you're using Print Layout or Outline view, you need to click the Show/Hide button on Word's Standard toolbar to make all breaks visible within your document.

PART III

Creating Complex Documents

- *Adding footnotes, endnotes, and other annotations*

- *Working with automated fields*

- *Inserting the current time, date, and page number*

- *Building indexes and tables of contents*

CHAPTER 11

Adding Annotations

Adding a footnote or endnote   **316**

Copying, moving, and deleting footnotes and endnotes   **319**

Changing the appearance of footnotes and endnotes   **320**

Converting footnotes to endnotes, and back again   **322**

Appending captions   **325**

Editing and formatting captions   **326**

Inserting an automatic cross-reference   **328**

Cross-referencing text via bookmarks   **329**

Sometimes the text you write isn't enough. When you need to comment on something within your main text, provide additional information, or reference something elsewhere in your document, you'll likely benefit from mastering Word's annotation features. This chapter will help you to learn all about those elements that aren't part of your document's main text: footnotes, endnotes, captions, and cross-references.

Annotating Text with Footnotes and Endnotes

When you have something more to say about an item but don't want to interrupt the flow of your main text, use a footnote or an endnote to place your comment outside the body of your document. Footnotes and endnotes function similarly, differing only in where they appear in your document; footnotes appear on the bottom of the referencing page, and endnotes are grouped at the very end of your document.

Refer to Figure 11.1 to see how footnotes appear on a page. A *note reference mark* is placed in superscript at the end of the text that references a footnote; the *note text* appears at the bottom of the page.

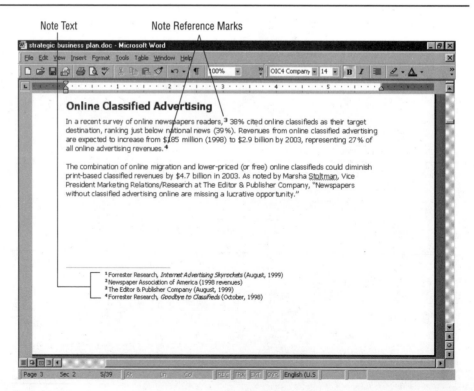

FIGURE 11.1
Use footnotes to add information to your document without adding to your main text.

Refer to Figure 11.2 to see how endnotes appear in a document. The note text here references corresponding note reference marks placed within the main text of your document.

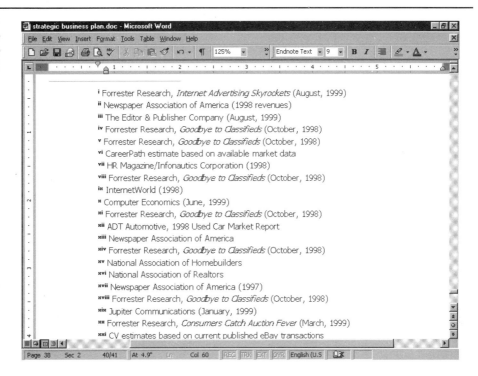

 TIP If you work with a lot with footnotes and endnotes, you should probably stick to Print Layout view, where it's easier to view and edit your note text than in Normal or Outline view.

Footnotes and endnotes appear in their actual position onscreen when you're using Word's Print Layout view. If you're using Normal or Outline views, however, you don't see the corresponding note text; you only see the note reference marks. To view or edit footnotes in Normal or Outline views, double-click a note mark or select View ➤ Footnotes to display Word's Notes pane, shown in Figure 11.3. Edit your note text appropriately, and then click the Close button to close the pane.

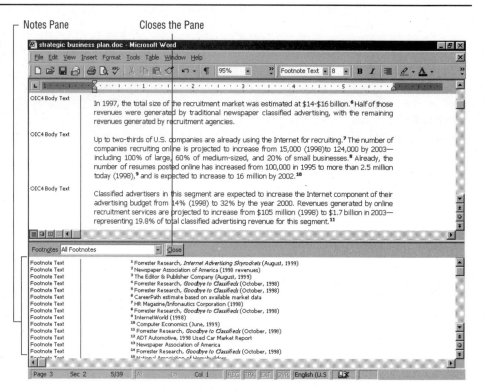

FIGURE 11.3
Use the Notes pane to edit your footnotes and endnotes in Normal or Outline view.

NOTE If you select View ➤ Footnotes to open the Notes pane, you'll first be prompted by the View Footnotes dialog box. Select either View Footnote Area (to view your footnotes) or View Endnote Area (to view your endnotes), and click OK to open the Notes pane. Within the Notes pane, the Footnotes (or Endnotes) list contains several selections. Pull down the list, and select All Footnotes (or All Endnotes) to view all the footnotes or endnotes in your document. Use the other options on this list to edit other note elements, such as separators and continuation notices.

Inserting Footnotes and Endnotes

Inserting footnotes and endnotes involves identifying the text you want to reference, inserting a note reference marker, and then entering the accompanying note text. Unless specified otherwise, all footnotes and endnotes are automatically numbered by

Word; when you insert a footnote or endnote before an existing note, all notes afterward are automatically renumbered accordingly.

 NOTE If you save your document as a Web page, Word automatically changes your footnotes and endnotes to hyperlinks and moves the corresponding note text to the end of the page.

Adding a Standard Footnote or Endnote

To insert a footnote or endnote in your text, follow these steps:

1. Position the insertion point at the end of the word or phrase where you want the note reference mark.

2. Select Insert ➤ Footnote to display the Footnote and Endnote dialog box.

 TIP You can use your keyboard to insert a footnote by pressing Alt+Ctrl+F, and to insert an endnote by pressing Alt+Ctrl+D.

3. Select whether you want to insert a Footnote or an Endnote.

4. To use standard note numbering, make sure the Autonumber option is checked.

5. Click OK.

6. Word inserts a note reference mark in your text and the reference number in the note text, and it moves the insertion point to the beginning of the note text. If you're in Print Layout view, your insertion point will be positioned either at the bottom of your page (for a footnote) or at the end of your document (for an endnote). If you're in Normal or Outline view, Word opens the Notes pane to display your note text.

7. Enter the note text, and then return to writing or editing the rest of your document. (If you were editing in the Notes pane, click Close to close the panel and return to your main text.)

PART

III

Creating Complex
Documents

TIP You can view note text without scrolling to the footnote or endnote section of your document. Just hover your cursor over the note reference number, and Word displays a ScreenTip containing the referenced note text.

You can return to edit your note text at any time. If you're in Print Layout view, just navigate to the appropriate footnote or endnote; if you're in Normal or Print Layout view, double-click a specific note reference mark to display the Notes pane for editing.

Referring to Existing Note Text

In many cases, you use footnotes and endnotes to reference supporting documents or publications (for example, the publication where you obtained a specific quote or fact). If you use information from the same source multiple times throughout your document, you don't have to enter that source every time you reference it; you can have Word insert a cross-reference to note text from a previous footnote or endnote.

Here's how it works:

1. Position the insertion point at the end of the word or phrase where you want the note reference mark.

2. Enter the text *see footnote* (or *see endnote*), in italics.

3. Select Insert ➢ Cross-Reference to display the Cross-Reference dialog box.

4. Pull down the Reference Type list, and select either Footnote or Endnote.

5. Pull down the Insert Reference To list, and select either Footnote Number or Endnote Number.

6. Select which footnote or endnote you want to reference from the For Which list.

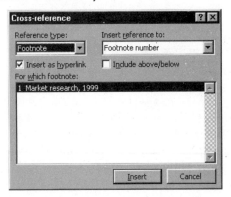

7. Click the Insert button to insert the cross-reference.

8. Click Close to close the dialog box.

NOTE Cross-references are discussed in depth in the "Cross-Referencing within Your Document" section, later in this chapter.

Word now inserts a cross-reference into your text that references the note mark of the selected footnote or endnote. If that note mark gets renumbered at a later time, the cross-reference will automatically update to display the new number.

Continuing Long Footnotes

You should try to keep your note text relatively short; if the information is important enough to warrant a huge amount of text, you should find a way to work it into the body of your document in the first place.

However, if you find a long footnote to be necessary, sometimes the combination of a longish footnote and a particular page design will force a footnote to continue from the bottom of one page to the bottom of the next. By default, Word simply flows the footnote to the next page, with no notice of continuation. Fortunately, you can add a continuation notice to your flowing footnotes by following these steps:

1. Switch to Word's Normal view.

 NOTE You can only add and edit continuation notices in Word's Normal view.

2. Select View ➤ Footnotes to display the View Footnotes dialog box.
3. Check the View Footnote area, and click OK to open the Notes pane.
4. Pull down the Footnotes list, and select Footnote Continuation Notice.
5. Enter the text for your continuation notice. (Something like "Continued on next page" works fine.)
6. Click Close to close the Notes pane.

Word automatically inserts your continuation notice where necessary. To view your continuation notice within your document, you'll need to switch to Print Layout view.

Copying, Moving, and Deleting Footnotes and Endnotes

When you want to copy or move a footnote or endnote, you don't copy or move the note text itself; all you move is the note reference mark. When you move the mark, the note text automatically moves with it.

Here's how you copy or move a footnote or endnote:

1. Select the note reference mark you want to copy or move.

2. Select Edit ➢ Cut or Edit ➢ Copy, as appropriate.

3. Reposition the insertion point where you want to insert the footnote or endnote.

4. Select Edit ➢ Paste.

Word now pastes the note reference mark into your text and repositions the corresponding note text in its proper place in your document.

 TIP You can cut, copy, and paste text directly to and from your note text. Just select the given note text, and edit as necessary.

Deleting a footnote or endnote is as simple as deleting the note reference mark. You don't have to manually delete the note text; it goes away when the note reference mark is deleted.

Changing the Appearance of Footnotes and Endnotes

Word's standard footnote and endnote styles are adequate for most needs. However, if you want to use a different kind of note reference mark or to change the footnote or endnote font, you'll want to access Word's footnote and endnote settings, most of which are found in the Note Options dialog box, as follows:

1. Select Insert ➢ Footnote to display the Footnote and Endnote dialog box.

2. Click the Options button to display the Note Options dialog box.

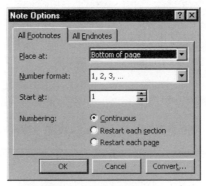

3. Select either the All Footnotes tab or the All Endnotes tab.

4. Change the settings as appropriate, and then click OK.

Choosing Different Note Reference Marks

By default, Word uses 1, 2, 3 numbering for footnotes and i, ii, iii numbering for endnotes. You can change the note reference marks Word applies by choosing a different scheme from the Number Format list in the Note Options dialog box. The numbering formats available include:

- 1, 2, 3
- a, b, c
- A, B, C
- i, ii, iii
- I, II, III
- *, †, ‡

You can also select a custom symbol for any specific note reference mark. To do this, from within the Footnote and Endnote dialog box, check the Custom Mark option, and either enter a character in the Custom Mark box or click the Symbol button to select a symbol character to use.

Changing Note Numbering

By default, Word applies continuous numbering to footnotes and endnotes (separately) throughout your document. You can, however, select the following optional numbering schemes:

Restart Each Section   Restarts all footnote and endnote numbering at 1 at the start of each new section in your document.

Restart Each Page   Restarts, for footnotes only, all numbering at 1 with each new page.

You reset these numbering options in the Note Options dialog box.

You can also change the start number for your footnote/endnote numbering. This is useful if you want to continue numbering from an existing document to a new document. Just change the number in the Start At list of the Note Options dialog box.

Putting Note Text in a Different Place

By default, footnotes appear at the bottom of the referenced page and endnotes appear at the end of your document. You can, however, opt to place your footnotes underneath the last text on your page (which is not necessarily at the bottom of your page, if your text actually ends mid-page) and select to group your endnotes at the end of each *section* of your document. You can change both of these settings in the Notes Options dialog box.

Formatting Note Text and Separators

While some users want to minimize the intrusion of note reference marks in their text, others feel that Word's default marks are wimpy and difficult to notice when scanning the text. You may also find that the font used for note text doesn't fit with your specific page design or template. Fortunately, it's easy to change the font, font style, and size of text used for both note reference marks and note text.

Word applies separate styles to note reference marks and to note text. The easiest way to change the appearance of either of these elements is by modifying their styles.

 NOTE To learn more about Word's styles, see Chapter 9.

To change the style of either element, select one of the elements, and then select Format ➤ Style to display the Style dialog box. Select the desired style from the Styles list, and then click the Modify button to display the Modify Style dialog box. Click the Format button to select which aspect of the style to modify, and then make your modification.

Word's note reference marks are automatically assigned either the Footnote Reference or Endnote Reference style, which, by default, is nothing more than the default paragraph font superscripted. You may want to add boldface to this style or even choose a different font style. (If you really want to make your note reference marks stand out, use the Arial Black style.) You should, however, retain the superscript formatting.

Word's note text is automatically assigned either the Footnote Text or Endnote Text style, which is based on the Normal style. Many users prefer to assign this style a smaller font size (8 points is a good option) and a sans serif font (such as Arial) to make the footnotes and endnotes less obtrusive in their documents. You can also change the amount of space above the note text paragraph and the indentation of the text after the reference mark in the note text.

Converting Footnotes to Endnotes, and Back Again

What if you inserted a bunch of footnotes in your document but later decided that they'd look better at the end of your text as endnotes? Word lets you change all your footnotes to endnotes en masse, and vice versa. Here's how you convert from one to the other:

1. Select Insert ➢ Footnote to display the Footnote and Endnote dialog box.

2. Click the Options button to display the Note Options dialog box.

3. Click the Convert button to display the Convert Notes dialog box.

4. Select one of the following options: Convert All Footnotes to Endnotes, Convert All Endnotes to Footnotes, or Swap Footnotes and Endnotes.

5. Click OK to begin the conversion.

 TIP Your list of endnotes is the last element in your document and prints on the last page, but not necessarily on a *separate* page. If you want to separate your endnotes from the rest of your document, force a page break (press Ctrl+Enter) at the start of the endnotes section.

 MASTERING THE OPPORTUNITIES

Navigating Footnotes and Endnotes

While you can scroll through your document looking for annotations, it is sometimes more convenient to jump directly to the next footnote or endnote in your document.

The easiest way to jump to any annotation is to use the Select Browse Object control at the bottom of Word's vertical scrollbar. Click the Select Browse Object button to display the menu of browsable objects, and then select either Browse by Endnote or Browse by Footnote. When you click the Next or the Previous arrows, you'll jump directly to the next or previous endnote or footnote.

Labeling Elements with Captions

Footnotes and endnotes are traditional ways to annotate the main text of your document. If you want to annotate figures, tables, equations, and other similar elements, you use *captions*. Word automatically numbers your captions and assigns them a label corresponding to their object type (table, equation, or figure).

Refer to Figure 11.4 for a typical Word caption.

FIGURE 11.4
Use captions to label figures, tables, and equations in your documents.

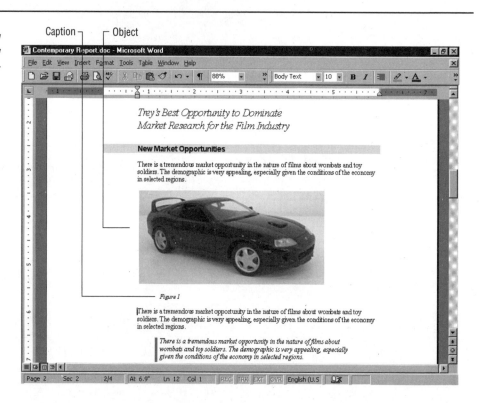

 TIP Word's captioning feature is somewhat limiting as to the text you can use to accompany pictures and other items. If you want a more descriptive custom caption, consider using a table to insert your picture and accompanying text. See Chapter 14 for more information.

Appending Captions

You can add captions to objects in your document manually, or you can configure Word to automatically create captions for specified elements.

Adding Captions Manually

To add a caption to an existing element, follow these steps:

1. Select the object you want to caption.

2. Select Insert ➤ Caption to display the Caption dialog box.

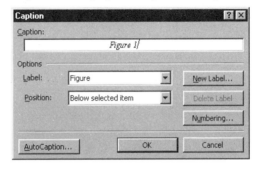

3. Pull down the Label list, and select the type of label: Figure, Table, or Equation. (If you want to create a new label not on the list, see the "Changing Caption Labels" section later in this chapter.)

4. Pull down the Position list, and select where you want to place the caption (either Above Selected Item or Below Selected Item).

5. In the Caption box, either accept the default text or enter your own text.

6. Click OK to insert the caption.

Word automatically inserts the caption, in the position you specified, in the format *Figure 1*, *Table 4*, or something similar.

Adding Captions Automatically

Since caption labeling is somewhat automatic, why not have Word automatically add captions to every figure, table, or equation you create? It's easy to do when you follow these steps:

1. Select the object you want to caption.

2. Select Insert ➤ Caption to display the Caption dialog box.

PART

III

Creating Complex
Documents

3. Click the AutoCaption button to display the AutoCaption dialog box.

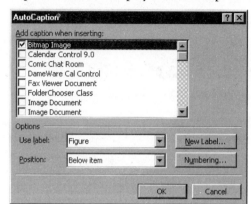

4. In the Add Caption When Inserting list, check those items you want to automatically caption.

5. Pull down the Label list, and select the type of label (Figure, Table, or Equation) you want to apply to the selected item. (If you want to create a new label not on the list, click the New Label button.)

6. Pull down the Position list, and select where you want to place the caption (either Above Selected Item or Below Selected Item).

7. Click OK to enable the automatic captioning.

With automatic captioning enabled, whenever you insert one of the selected objects, Word automatically inserts the appropriate caption.

Editing and Formatting Captions

There's not much about Word's captions that you can change, save for the caption's label and number format.

Adding New Caption Labels

If the labels *Figure, Table,* and *Equation* are too limiting, you can create your own custom labels for your captions. Follow these steps:

1. From the Caption dialog box, click the New Label button to display the New Label dialog box.

2. Enter the text for your new label in the Label box, and then click OK.

3. Your new label now appears in the Label list in the Caption dialog box; select the new label, and continue with your caption configuration.

Changing the Number Format

By default, Word numbers your captions in the 1, 2, 3 format. If you want to use another number format for your captions, follow these steps:

1. From the Caption dialog box, click the Numbering button to display the Caption Numbering dialog box.

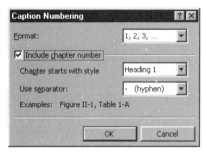

2. Pull down the Format list, and select a different number format.

3. Click OK.

You can choose from any of these number formats:

- 1, 2, 3
- a, b, c
- A, B, C
- i, ii, iii
- I, II, III

Adding Chapter Numbers to Your Captions

If you're working within a long document—one that includes separate chapters—you can choose to include the chapter number in your captions. Follow these steps to enable this feature:

1. From the Caption dialog box, click the Numbering button to display the Caption Numbering dialog box.

2. Check the Include Chapter Number option.

3. Pull down the Chapter Starts with Style list, and select the heading style assigned to the chapter headings in your document.

PART

III

Creating Complex
Documents

4. You need to select a separator character to fit between the chapter number and the caption number. Pull down the Use Separator list and select from the hyphen (-), period (.), colon (:), em dash (—), or en dash (–).

5. Click OK.

Depending on the options you selected, your captions will look similar to *Chapter 1: Figure 1* or *Chapter 2—Figure A*.

Cross-Referencing within Your Document

A cross-reference is a mention of one part of your document in another part of your document. For example, if you talk in-depth about mallard ducks on page 5 of your text and then briefly mention ducks again on page 10, you can insert a cross-reference on page 10 to the additional coverage on page 5.

There are two ways to insert cross-references with Word 2000: using Word's Cross-Reference command and using field codes.

Inserting an Automatic Cross-Reference

The easiest way to insert a cross-reference is with Word's Cross-Reference command. Just follow these steps:

1. Within your document, type the lead-in text to the reference. (For example, you might type *For more information, see.*)

2. Select Insert ➢ Cross-Reference to display the Cross-Reference dialog box.

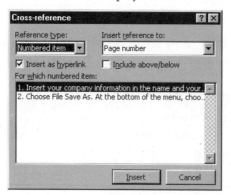

3. Pull down the Reference Type list, and select what kind of element you want to reference (Numbered Item, Heading, Bookmark, Footnote, Endnote, Equation, Figure, or Table).

4. Pull down the Insert Reference To list, and select how you want to reference the selected item. (This list changes depending on the reference type selected.)

5. If you want your references (regardless of the option selected in step 4) to include an "above" or "below" pointer, check the Include Above/Below option (not available for all options).

6. Select the specific item you want to reference from the For Which list.

7. Click Insert to insert the automatic cross-reference.

In the preceding steps, steps 3 and 6 determine *what* you reference, and steps 4 and 5 determine *how* the reference appears in your text. For example, if you choose to reference a bookmark, you can choose to refer to the referenced item in the following ways:

Bookmark Text   Inserts the full text of the bookmark, as in *For more information, see About the Mallard Duck.*

Page Number   Inserts the page number of the bookmark, as in *For more information, see page 5.*

Paragraph Number   Inserts the relative number of the bookmarked paragraph, as in *For more information, see paragraph (a)(ii).* (Used primarily in legal or outlined documents.)

Paragraph Number (No Context)   Inserts the specific paragraph number (with no hierarchical reference) of the bookmarked paragraph, as in *For more information, see paragraph (ii).* (A specific variation for legal or outlined documents.)

Paragraph Number (Full Context)   Inserts the line number with the hierarchical reference of the bookmarked paragraph, as in *For more information, see paragraph 1.(a)(ii).* (Another variation for legal or outlined documents.)

Above/Below   Inserts a reference to where the bookmark appears relative to the current text, as in *For more information, see above.*

To edit any cross-reference, select the entire cross-reference text, and then select Insert ➤ Cross-Reference. When the Cross-Reference dialog box appears, make any appropriate changes (up to and including changing the referenced item), and click OK. Your cross-reference text will automatically reflect your changes.

PART

III

Creating Complex
Documents

TIP Word can automatically turn any cross-reference into a live hyperlink that, when clicked, jumps you to the cross-referenced element. Just check the Insert as Hyperlink option in the Cross-Reference dialog box.

Cross-Referencing Text via Bookmarks

If you want to reference a particular block of text, you first need to "name" that text with a bookmark. The best way to do this is to bookmark the nearest heading to the text that will be referenced and not the text itself. (If you insert the text of the bookmark into your cross-reference, you want to include as little text as possible, so *About the Mallard Duck* is preferable to a long paragraph of duck-related text.)

Here is the step-by-step procedure for adding and then cross-referencing a bookmark in your text:

1. Select the text you want to bookmark, typically a relevant heading or passage.

2. Select Insert ➤ Bookmark to display the Bookmark dialog box.

3. Enter a name for the bookmark in the Bookmark Name box.

4. Click the Add button.

5. Move your insertion point to where you want to add the cross-reference.

6. Type the lead-in text to the reference, typically something along the lines of *For more information, see.*

7. Select Insert ➤ Cross-Reference to display the Cross-Reference dialog box.

8. Pull down the Reference Type list, and select Bookmark.

9. Pull down the Insert Reference To list, and select how you want to reference the bookmark, typically with either Bookmark Text or Page Number.

10. Select the specific bookmark you want to reference from the For Which Bookmark list.

11. Click Insert to insert the automatic cross-reference.

 NOTE For more information on managing bookmarks, see Chapter 5.

MASTERING THE OPPORTUNITIES

Smart Cross-References with Fields

Cross-references are actually fields inserted into your document via an automated procedure. (To verify this, turn on the View Field Codes option in the Options dialog box.) Fields are special codes that act as placeholders for data that might change within your document. You can manually insert fields within your text when you want to refer to specific elements within your text (for example, to insert any text formatted with a specific style).

Let's say you want to insert a cross-reference to the current chapter heading. Just follow these steps:

1. Position the insertion point where you want to insert the reference, and type the initial reference text (*For more information, see*).

2. Select Insert ➢ Field to display the Field dialog box.

3. From the Categories list, select Links and References.

4. From the Field Names list, select StyleRef.

5. Click the Options button to display the Field Options dialog box, and then select the Styles tab. From the Name list, select the style assigned to the heading level you want referenced (a heading used only for chapter titles in this case), and then click Add to Field. Click OK to return to the Field dialog box.

6. Click OK.

Word then automatically adds the title of the current chapter to your cross-reference text.

To learn more about fields, see Chapter 12.

PART

III

Creating Complex
Documents

CHAPTER 12

Working with Fields

Word's field categories   334

Using arguments   335

Modifying fields with switches   335

Adding fields with the Field dialog box   339

Inserting fields manually   340

Updating field results   341

Not updating field results   342

Formatting field results   342

Word 2000 field instant reference   343

Within your text you sometimes insert certain types of data that are changeable. Maybe it's a page number, or a date, or a reference to a heading or a bookmark. The data you insert is actually variable, and you don't want to have to retype the data every time the variable changes.

What you need is a kind of placeholder for the variable data. You want to insert a placeholder for today's date, for example, that would ultimately be replaced by the actual date when you print your document. Or you want a placeholder for the current page that would ultimately be replaced by the actual page number—wherever that placeholder text happened to end up in your final document.

When you want a placeholder for a variable piece of data, you want to use Word's *fields* feature. A field is a placeholder for data that might change within your document. Fields take their places in your text, and are updated with the actual current value of the data they reference.

Using fields makes Word extremely versatile and powerful. When you master Word's fields, you attain a level of control over your documents that simply isn't possible otherwise.

Understanding Fields

Fields are inserted into your text through a field *code*. Each field code represents a certain type of data or action to be inserted in your text. For example, the PAGE code inserts the number of the current page and the DATE code inserts the current date. You insert field codes in your text surrounded by curly brackets, like this: { PAGE }.

Word's Field Categories

Word 2000 includes about a hundred different field codes; see Table 12.2, at the end of this chapter, for a complete list of these codes. Microsoft groups these codes into nine main categories:

- Date and Time
- Document Automation
- Document Information
- Equations and Formulas
- Index and Tables
- Links and References

- Mail Merge
- Numbering
- User Information

Using Arguments

Many fields incorporate *arguments* after the field code. Think of an argument as additional instructions for the field command. For example, the SYMBOL code inserts a symbol character into your text—but by itself (without an accompanying argument) you don't know *which* symbol it inserts! So when you use the SYMBOL field, you need to follow the code with the *charnumber* argument—where *charnumber* represents the character number of the symbol you want to insert. In this example, the final field code looks something like this: { SYMBOL 132 }

Arguments are also used when you construct *formulas* within Word—and, in fact, a formula is actually a specific Word field. In a formula, the argument can represent numbers and operators, or cells (or ranges of cells) within a table.

 NOTE Learn more about table formulas in Chapter 14.

Modifying Fields with Switches

Many Word fields also incorporate either mandatory or optional *switches*. A switch alters the behavior or formatting of a field, in a specified fashion, and is signified by a *backslash* character (\) followed by a letter—sometimes followed by an argument for that particular switch.

For example, the INDEX code by itself inserts an index into your text; adding the \c switch (to create this field code: { INDEX \c }) makes it a multiple-column index.

Multiple switches can be applied to a single code. When you apply more than one switch, you apply them sequentially. Back to the INDEX example, another optional switch (\h " ") inserts a blank line between index groupings. To apply this option *and* create a multiple column index, you create this field code: { INDEX \c \h " "}

Word uses two types of switches—*general* and *field-specific*. General switches can be used on almost any field and typically specify formatting options. Field-specific switches are specific to a particular field code, and specify options that modify that particular code.

PART

III

Creating Complex
Documents

Table 12.1 shows the general switches you can use with most field codes.

TABLE 12.1: WORD'S GENERAL FIELD SWITCHES		
Switch	**Name**	**Description**
*	Format	Specifies number formats, capitalization, and character formatting
\#	Numeric Picture	Specifies how a numeric result is displayed, including decimal places and currency symbols
\@	Date-Time Picture	Specifies date or time format
\!	Lock Result	Locks the field and prevents the updating of field results

 WARNING The general switches in Table 12.1 cannot be used with the following field codes: AUTONUM, AUTONUMLGL, AUTONUMOUT, EMBED, EQ, FORMTEXT, FORMCHECKBOX, FORMDROP-DOWN, GOTOBUTTON, LISTNUM, MACROBUTTON, RD, TA, TC, or XE.

Viewing Fields

Word offers several ways to view the field codes in your documents. In fact, you can even choose to *print* the field codes—instead of the field's results!

Showing and Hiding Field Codes

You can toggle between the code and the result for any specific field by highlighting the field and pressing Shift+F9. You can toggle between showing and hiding the field codes for your entire document by pressing Alt+F9.

To configure Word to always display field codes instead of results, follow these steps:

1. Select Tools ➢ Options to display the Options dialog box.
2. Select the View tab.
3. Check the Field Codes option; uncheck this option to display results instead of codes.
4. Click OK.

Figure 12.1 shows what a field code looks like when displayed in a document.

FIGURE 12.1
Viewing a field code in your document

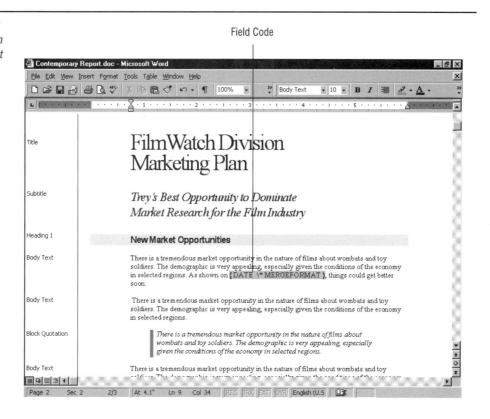

Displaying Field Shading

You can also choose to highlight all the field results in your document (by shading the field/result). Just follow these steps:

1. Select Tools ➤ Options to display the Options dialog box.

2. Select the View tab.

3. To display shading at all times, pull down the Field Shading list and select Always. To display shading only when a field is selected, pull down the Field Shading list and select When Selected. To never display shading, pull down the Field Shading list and select Never.

4. Click OK.

PART

III

Creating Complex Documents

Printing Field Codes Instead of Results

Normally, when you print a document containing fields, you print the results of the fields, not the fields themselves—even if you chose to display or shade your field codes onscreen. You can choose to print field codes instead of results, however, by following these steps:

1. Select Tools ➢ Options to display the Options dialog box.
2. Select the Print tab.
3. Check the Field Codes option.
4. Click OK.

MASTERING THE OPPORTUNITIES

Navigating Fields

Instead of scrolling through your document looking for shaded fields, it's more convenient to jump directly from field to field.

You can use the keyboard to jump to the next field in your document by pressing F11. Pressing Shift+F11 jumps to the previous field.

You can also use the Select Browse Object control to jump from field to field. Click the Select Browse Object button (at the bottom of Word's vertical scrollbar) to display the menu of browsable objects, then select Browse by Field. When you click the Next or the Previous arrows, you'll jump directly to the next or previous field in your document.

Adding Fields to Your Document

There are several ways you can insert fields into your documents. You can insert them manually (entering all the codes and switches and arguments by hand) or use Word's Field dialog box to automate the insertion process.

You can add field codes anywhere in your document. You can use fields in your standard body text, in table cells, in text boxes, and even in headers and footers. Wherever you can anchor your insertion point, you can add a field!

Using the Field Dialog Box

The easiest way to add a field to your document is via the Field dialog box. When you use this method, you're presented with all the arguments and switches and formatting options for the field you choose—so you don't have to remember all the details, and insert them manually!

To insert a field using the Field dialog box, follow these steps:

1. Position the insertion point where you want to insert the field code.
2. Select Insert ➢ Field to open the Field dialog box, shown in Figure 12.2.

FIGURE 12.2
Use the Field dialog box to automate the creation of field codes.

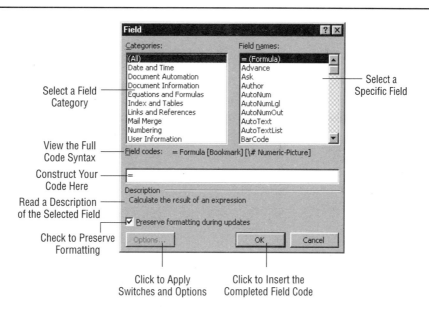

Select a Field Category

View the Full Code Syntax

Construct Your Code Here

Read a Description of the Selected Field

Check to Preserve Formatting

Select a Specific Field

Click to Apply Switches and Options

Click to Insert the Completed Field Code

3. Select a field category from the Categories list.
4. Select a specific field from the Field Names list.
5. If you want to apply switches, formatting, or other options to your code, click the Options button to display the Field Options dialog box. Select the appropriate switches/options/formatting and click OK.
6. If you want to preserve the field formatting when you update your field codes (and you probably do), check the Preserve Formatting During Upgrades option.
7. Review the code you've constructed in the code box.
8. Click OK to insert the code.

PART

III

Creating Complex Documents

The advantage of inserting codes with the Field dialog box is that all syntax, switches, options, and formatting are presented automatically. You don't have to guess about the correct syntax, or try to remember all possible switches—they're all presented onscreen, ready for the choosing.

Inserting Fields Manually

Some users prefer to do things by hand. If this suits your style, it is possible to enter field codes into your text manually.

At first glance, you might think that adding a field code is as easy as typing two curly brackets ({}) and entering the code between them. This thinking, however, is wrong!

The curly brackets used by field codes are not the standard curly brackets! Just typing this info into your normal text will only insert something that looks like a code—but it won't be a real code, and won't return any results.

To insert a code manually, you have to tell Word you're entering a field. You do this by pressing Ctrl+F9, and *then* typing your code.

Follow these steps to enter a field code manually:

1. Position the insertion point where you want to insert the field code.

2. Press Ctrl+F9.

3. Word inserts a set of field code brackets ({ }) at the insertion point, as shown in Figure 12.3.

4. Type your field code—and all appropriate switches—between the brackets. Make sure you leave a space between the beginning/end of your code and the curly bracket on either side.

To view the results of your newly inserted field code, highlight the code and press F9.

 TIP Certain frequently used field codes can be inserted directly via keyboard shortcuts. To insert the DATE field, press Alt+Shift+D. To insert the PAGE field, press Alt+Shift+P. To insert the TIME field, press Alt+Shift+T.

FIGURE 12.3
Inserting a field code manually

Insert the Code between
the Curly Brackets

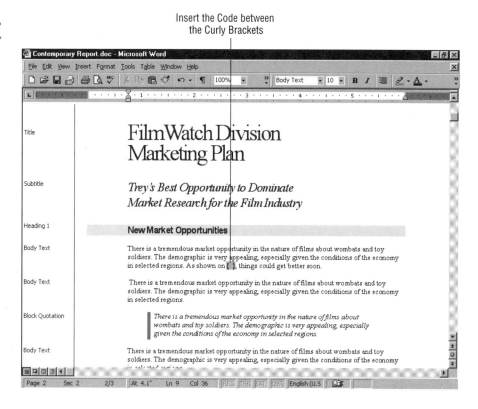

Managing Field Results

Once you've inserted a field code, you're not necessarily done with it. To ensure that the data displayed is always current and that it displays the way you want, you need to master some simple field management operations.

Updating Field Results

When your document changes, your fields change. For example, a PAGE field that shifts from page to page during the editing process will yield different results; a DATE field displays different results on different days.

PART

III

Creating Complex
Documents

By default, the field results that appear in your document display their original values—until you update them. There are several ways to update the field results in your document:

- To update a single field, select the field/results and press F9.
- To update all the fields in your document, select your entire document (select Edit ➤ Select All) and then press F9.
- To update the all the fields in your document before you print the document, select Tools ➤ Options to display the Options menu, then select the Print tab and check the Update Fields option in the Printing Options section.

Not Updating Field Results

Sometimes you *don't* want to update the results of your fields. For example, if you want the DATE field to represent the date you created the document, not the date of the last edit, you want this field *not* to be updated. Word 2000 offers several ways to keep your fields from updating—and thus present their original results for all time.

Locking and Unlocking Fields

If you want to *temporarily* keep a field from updating, you can *lock* the field. Then, when you want to display updated results, you can *unlock* the field.

To lock a selected field, press Ctrl+F11. To unlock a field, press Shift+Ctrl+F11.

Unlinking Fields

If you want to *permanently* keep a field from updating, you *unlink* the field—and turn the current results into standard text.

 WARNING You can't relink an unlinked field; unlinking is a permanent operation.

To unlink a field, select the entire field/results, then press Ctrl+Shift+F9. If you want to display an updated result, you have to delete the unlinked text and insert a new field in this location.

Formatting Field Results

Whether your fields return text or numbers, you can format the way the results appear in your document. You use three of Word's four general formatting switches (*, \#, and \@) to format your field results. These switches all have multiple arguments or variations, which you use to apply specific types of formats.

Word 2000 Field Instant Reference

If you're serious about using fields to automate your Word documents, use Table 12.2 as an instant reference to all the fields (and associated switches) available in Word 2000.

TABLE 12.2: WORD FIELD CODES

Field	Usage	Description	Switches
=(FORMULA)	= formula [book-mark] [\# Numeric-Picture]	Calculates the result of a formula	
ADVANCE	ADVANCE [switches]	Offsets following text within a line	\d (down) \l (left) \r (right) \u (up) \x (moves text horizontally relative to column or frame) \y (moves text vertically relative to page)
ASK	ASK bookmark "Prompt" [switches]	Prompts user for text to assign to a bookmark	\d (inserts default bookmark text) \o (prompts at the beginning of merge for bookmark text)
AUTHOR	AUTHOR "NewName"	Inserts document's author's name (from Summary Info)	
AUTONUM	AUTONUM	Inserts an automatic number	
AUTONUMLGL	AUTONUMLGL	Inserts an automatic number in legal format	
AUTONUMOUT	AUTONUMOUT	Inserts an automatic number in outline format	
AUTOTEXT	AUTOTEXT Auto-TextEntry	Inserts an AutoText entry	

Continued ▸

Creating Complex Documents

TABLE 12.2: WORD FIELD CODES (CONTINUED)

Field	Usage	Description	Switches
AUTOTEXTLIST	AUTOTEXTLIST "Literal Text" \s "Style-name" \t "Tip text"	Inserts text based on style	
BARCODE	BARCODE \u "Literal Text" *or* bookmark \b [switches]	Inserts delivery point barcode	\b (inserts POSTNET barcode from address specified by bookmark) \f (inserts Facing Identification Mark) \u (inserts POSTNET barcode as U.S. postal address)
COMMENTS	COMMENTS ["NewComments"]	Inserts comments from Summary Info	
COMPARE	COMPARE Expression1 Operator Expression2	Compares two values and returns "1" if true or "0" if false	
CREATEDATE	CREATEDATE [\@ "Date-Time Picture"] [switches]	Inserts the date the document was created	\h (uses Hijri/Lunar calendar) \l (uses last format chosen using the Date and Time command)
DATABASE	DATABASE [switches]	Inserts data from an external database	\b (specifies which attributes of the \l switch apply to the table) \c (specifies instructions used by ODBC to connect to the database) \d (path and filename of the database) \f (specifies starting record for data insertion) \h (insets field names into the first row of the table) \l (applies selected Table Auto-Format to the query results) \o (inserts data at the beginning of a merge) \s (specifies SQL instructions to query the database) \t (specifies ending record for data insertion)
DATE	DATE [\@ "Date-Time Picture"] [switches]	Inserts today's date	\h (uses Hijri/Lunar calendar) \l (uses last format chosen using the Date and Time command)
DOCPROPERTY	DOCPROPERTY "Name"	Inserts value of the property chosen in Options	

Continued ▶

TABLE 12.2: WORD FIELD CODES (CONTINUED)

Field	Usage	Description	Switches
DOCVARIABLE	DOCVARIABLE "Name"	Inserts value of the NAME document variable	
EDITTIME	EDITTIME	Inserts total editing time of the document	
EQ	EQ Instructions	Creates a scientific equation	
FILENAME	FILENAME [switches]	Inserts the document's name and location	\p (adds path to the filename)
FILESIZE	FILESIZE [switches]	Inserts the size of the document	\k (displays size in kilobytes) \m (displays size in megabytes)
FILLIN	FILLIN ["Prompt"] [switches]	Prompts the user for text to insert in the document	\d (inserts default bookmark text) \o (prompts at the beginning of merge for bookmark text)
GOTOBUTTON	GOTOBUTTON Destination DisplayText	Moves the insertion point to a new location	
HYPERLINK	HYPERLINK "Filename" [switches]	Opens and jumps to the specified file	\l (specifies location in document to jump to) \m (specifies link is an HTML 2.0 image map) \n (causes hyperlink to open a new window) \o (specifies screen tip text for the hyperlink) \t (specifies frame target)
IF	IF Express1 Operator Expression2 TrueText FalseText	Evaluates two arguments	
INCLUDE-PICTURE	INCLUDEPICTURE "FileName" [switches]	Inserts a picture from a file	\c (identifies filter for the graphic format) \d (forces graphic data *not* to be stored with document)
INCLUDETEXT	INCLUDETEXT "FileName" [bookmark] [switches]	Inserts text from a file	\! (prevents fields in inserted file from being updated) \c (identifies text converter)

Continued ▐▶

Creating Complex
Documents

TABLE 12.2: WORD FIELD CODES (CONTINUED)

Field	Usage	Description	Switches
INDEX	INDEX [switches]	Creates an index	\b (uses bookmark to specify area to be index) \c (creates multiple-column index) \d (defines separator characters between sequence and page numbers) \e (defines separator characters between index entries and page numbers) \f (create index using only specified entry type) \g (defines separator characters used in a page range) \h " " (inserts blank line between groups in index) \h "A" (inserts heading letter between groups in index) \l (defines separator characters between page numbers for multiple-page references) \p (limits index to specified letters) \r (runs subentries onto same line as main entry) \s (includes referenced sequence number with page number) \y (enables use of yomi (far eastern) text for index entries) \z "####" (defines ID word for language used to generate index)
INFO	[INFO] InfoType ["NewValue"]	Inserts data from Summary Info	
KEYWORDS	KEYWORDS ["NewKeywords"]	Inserts keywords from Summary Info	
LASTSAVEDBY	LASTSAVEDBY	Inserts name of user who last saved document	

Continued ▐▶

TABLE 12.2: WORD FIELD CODES (CONTINUED)

Field	Usage	Description	Switches
LINK	LINK ClassName "FileName" [PlaceReference] [switches]	Inserts part of a file, using OLE	\a (turns on automatic updating) \b (inserts linked object as a bitmap) \d (forces graphic data *not* to be stored with document) \h (inserts linked object as HTML format text) \p (inserts linked object as a picture) \r (inserts linked object as RTF text) \t (inserts linked object as text)
LISTNUM	LISTNUM ["Name"] [switches]	Inserts an element in a list	\l (specifies level in the list) \s (specifies start-at value)
MACROBUTTON	MACROBUTTON MacroName DisplayText	Runs a macro	
MERGEFIELD	MERGEFIELD Field-Name	Inserts a mail merge field	
MERGEREC	MERGEREC	Inserts the number of the current merge record	
MERGESEQ	MERGESEQ	Inserts the merge record sequence number	
NEXT	NEXT	Goes to the next record in a mail merge	
NEXTIF	NEXTIF Expression1 Operator Expression2	Goes to the next record in a mail merge if the condition is met	
NOTEREF	NOTEREF book-mark [switches]	Inserts the number of a footnote or endnote	\f (keeps original formatting for reference mark) \h (creates hyperlink to marked footnote) \p (inserts relative position of footnote or endnote)
NUMCHARS	NUMCHARS	Inserts the document's character count	
NUMPAGES	NUMPAGES	Inserts the document's page count	
NUMWORDS	NUMWORDS	Inserts the document's word count	

PART

III

Creating Complex Documents

Continued ▶

TABLE 12.2: WORD FIELD CODES (CONTINUED)

Field	Usage	Description	Switches
PAGE	PAGE	Inserts the number of the current page	
PAGEREF	PAGEREF bookmark	Inserts the number of the page containing the specified bookmark	
PRINT	PRINT "Printer-Instructions"	Downloads commands to a printer	\p cell (current table cell) \p page (current page) \p para (current paragraph) \p pic (next picture in current paragraph) \p row (current table row)
PRINTDATE	PRINTDATE [\@ "Date-Time Picture"]	Inserts the date the document was last printed	
PRIVATE	PRIVATE	Stores data for documents converted from other file formats	
QUOTE	QUOTE "LiteralText"	Inserts literal text (text entered within quotes)	
RD	RD "FileName" [switch]	Creates an index, table of contents, table of figures, and/or table of authorities by using multiple documents	\f (specifies paths are relative to current document)
REF	REF bookmark [switches]	Inserts bookmark text	\f (includes and increments footnote, endnote, or comment numbers) \h (creates hyperlink to marked paragraph) \n (inserts paragraph number) \p (inserts relative position of marked paragraph) \r (inserts paragraph number in relative context) \t (suppresses all non-delimiter characters) \w (inserts paragraph number in full context)
REVNUM	REVNUM	Inserts the number of times the document has been saved	

Continued ▶

TABLE 12.2: WORD FIELD CODES (CONTINUED)

Field	Usage	Description	Switches
SAVEDATE	SAVEDATE [\@ "Date-Time Picture"]	Inserts the date the document was last saved	
SECTION	SECTION	Inserts the current section number	
SECTIONPAGES	SECTIONPAGES	Inserts the total number of pages in current section	
SEQ	SEQ identifier [bookmark] [switches]	Inserts an automatic sequence number	\c (inserts previous sequence number) \h (hides the field result) \n (inserts the next sequence number) \r (rests sequence number to the number following the switch) \s (resets sequence number at the specified heading level)
SET	SET bookmark "Text"	Assigns new text to a bookmark	
SKIPIF	SKIPIF Expression1 Operator Expression2	Skips a record in a mail merge if the condition is met	
STYLEREF	STYLEREF Style-Identifier [switches]	Inserts text from nearest paragraph formatted with specified style	\l (searches from bottom of page) \n (inserts paragraph number) \p (inserts relative position of paragraph) \r (inserts paragraph number in relative context) \t (suppresses all non-delimiter characters) \w (inserts paragraph number in full context)
SUBJECT	SUBJECT ["New-Subject"]	Inserts document subject from Summary Info	
SYMBOL	SYMBOL CharNum [switches]	Inserts specified symbol character	\a (uses ANSI characters) \f (specifies font for symbol) \h (inserts symbol without changing line spacing) \j (uses Shift-JIS characters) \s (specifies font size for symbol) \u (uses Unicode characters)

Continued ▮▶

PART

III

Creating Complex
Documents

TABLE 12.2: WORD FIELD CODES (CONTINUED)

Field	Usage	Description	Switches
TA	TA [switches]	Marks an entry for a table of authorities	\b (boldfaces page number) \c (defines category number) \i (italicizes page number) \l (defines long citation) \r (includes range of pages in page number) \s (defines short citation)
TC	TC "Text" [switches]	Marks an entry for a table of contents	\f (identifies entry for use in documents with multiple tables) \l (identifies outline level) \n (suppresses page number)
TEMPLATE	TEMPLATE [switches]	Inserts the name of the current template	\p (adds path to filename)
TIME	TIME [\@ "Date-Time Picture"]	Inserts the current time	
TITLE	TITLE ["NewTitle"]	Inserts the document's title from Summary Info	
TOA	TOA [switches]	Creates a table of authorities	\b (creates a TOA from area specified by bookmark) \c (creates a TOA for entries with specified category number) \d (defines separator between sequence and page numbers) \e (defines separator characters between table entries and page numbers) \f (removes formatting of entries) \g (defines characters used in a page range) \h (includes category headings) \l (defines separators between page numbers for multiple-page references) \p (replace two or more references to same authority with "passim") \s (includes sequence number with page number)

Continued ▶

TABLE 12.2: WORD FIELD CODES (CONTINUED)

Field	Usage	Description	Switches
TOC	TOC [switches]	Creates a table of contents or table of figures	\a (builds table of figures without including caption labels and numbers) \b (builds TOC from area specified by bookmark) \c (builds a table of figures of the given label) \d (defines separator between sequence and page numbers) \f (builds a TOC from TC entries instead of outline levels) \h (hyperlinks entries and page numbers within TOC) \l (defines TC entries' field level used to build TOC) \n (builds TOC without page numbers) \o (builds TOC by using outline levels instead of TC entries) \p (defines separator between table entries and page numbers) \s (builds TOC by using a sequence type) \t (builds TOC by using style names other than standard outline styles) \w (preserves tab characters within table entries) \x (preserves newline characters within table entries) \z (hides page numbers when shown in Web Layout view)
USERADDRESS	USERADDRESS ["NewAddress"]	Inserts address from User Information	
USERINITIALS	USERINTIALS ["NewInitials"]	Inserts user initials from User Information	

Continued ▶

PART

III

Creating Complex Documents

TABLE 12.2: WORD FIELD CODES (CONTINUED)

Field	Usage	Description	Switches
USERNAME	USERNAME ["NewName"]	Inserts user name from User Information	
XE	XE "Text" [switches]	Marks an index entry	\b (boldfaces page number) \f (defines index entry type) \i (italicizes page number) \r (includes bookmark's page range in page number) \t (inserts specified text in place of page number) \y (enables use of yomi, or far eastern, text for index entries)

CHAPTER **13**

Incorporating Indexes and Tables of Contents

Marking index entries   *355*

Building an index   *361*

Formatting your index   *364*

Building your table of contents   *366*

Formatting your table of contents   *370*

Creating a table of figures   *371*

Building a table of authorities   *374*

f you're creating a long document, it's important for readers to have multiple points of entry into your text. Not all readers will read the entire document; some readers will want to reference specific parts of the document or look up particular information.

For readers who want to reference limited information within a longer document, *indexes* and *tables of contents* are key. An index is a listing of key words or concepts and is typically found at the end of a document, with references to where those words or ideas appear in your text. A table of contents (TOC) is like a master outline to your document, either by section or chapter or heading (or sometimes a combination of these), complete with page numbers indicating where each referenced item starts.

You need only look at this very book to see the value of indexes and tables of contents. When you first bought this book, chances are you turned either to the index (to look up a particular topic) or to the table of contents (to determine what topics were covered in the book). Few readers will read this entire book cover-to-cover; almost all will reference the index or the table of contents—or both.

Indexing a Document

Indexing is a long and tedious process. There is no way around that fact. To create an index, you first have to mark all the words or terms you want to appear in the index, which is the tedious part. Once the index terms are marked, Word makes it easy to actually assemble the index. But there's no way around it: each index term has to be marked manually.

When you create the index itself, you can build a list of main index entries and then insert *subentries* below the main entries. For example, if your document had several references to music by the Beatles, you might specify *Beatles* as a main entry and individual Beatles albums (*Abbey Road, Sgt. Pepper's Lonely Hearts Club Band,* and so on) as subentries under the main Beatles entry. Word even lets you specify third-level entries, below subentries; in our Beatles example, you might index the songs on each album as third-level entries beneath the album subentries, like this:

```
Beatles, The, 24, 47, 87
    Abbey Road, 24
        "Octopus's Garden," 24
        "Something," 24
    Sgt. Pepper's Lonely Hearts Club Band, 47
        "A Day in the Life," 47
        "She's Leaving Home," 47
```

You specify the level of indexing when you mark an index entry.

Creating Index Entries

As was just explained in the preceding section, an index is built from words you mark in your document. You can choose to mark each occurrence of a word separately or to mark all occurrences of a word automatically. You can even choose to create a separate list of words you want indexed—called an AutoMark file—and index those words automatically.

MASTERING THE·OPPORTUNITIES

Marking Your Index Later

Most users find it easiest to mark index entries *after* they've created their document. This way, all the spelling has been corrected and all the editing completed, so you can confidently mark all occurrences of a word without worrying about corrections or edits changing the words in your document. It's also easier, many think, to mark all the index entries in one pass rather than trying to incorporate index marking while you're entering the original text.

Another approach is to use an AutoMark file (discussed later in this chapter) to create a master list of index entries and then use Word's AutoMark features to automatically mark all occurrences of these entries in your document. Then, after this "heavy lifting" has been done, you can go back through your document and mark any additional entries you want to add.

Whatever approach you employ, make sure you review your completed index after it's built. Chances are, you'll find something missing and will need to go back and mark just a few more entries and then rebuild your index!

Marking Index Entries

Marking a word or phrase as an index entry is easy. Just follow these steps:

1. Select the word or phrase you want to index.

2. Press Alt+Shift+X to display the Mark Index Entry dialog box.

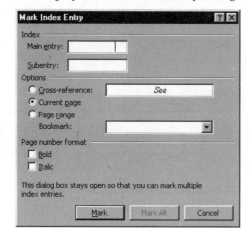

3. If you want the selected word or phrase to be a main index entry, make sure the selection appears in the Main Entry box. If you want the selection to be a subentry, copy the selection from the Main Entry to the Subentry box, and enter the name of the main entry in the Main Entry box. If you want the selection to be a third-level entry, enter a main entry and a subentry, enter a colon (:) after the subentry, and type the selection after the colon, leaving no space in between. (The result looks like this: *subentry:third-level entry*.) Word actually supports up to seven levels of index entries.

4. Make any other selections within the dialog box.

TIP While you're marking index entries, you can tell Word how you want the entries formatted within the final index—in particular, whether you want the page numbers bold or italic. Check the Bold option to boldface the page number in the index, check the Italic option to italicize the page number, or check both to both boldface and italicize the page number. You can also use standard character formatting (bold, italic, underline, and so on) directly on the text *within* the Main Entry and Subentry boxes.

5. Click Mark to mark this entry.

NOTE The Mark Index Entry dialog box doesn't close after you mark the entry; it stays open so you can mark additional entries in your document. You'll need to click the Cancel button after you've marked your final entry to close this dialog box.

When you mark an index entry, Word inserts the XE field code at that point in your document. For example, let's say you want to mark the word *Bob* as an index entry. When you mark the entry via the Mark Index Entry dialog box, Word inserts the following code after the word: { XE "Bob" }. This code is added as hidden text, which is only visible if you toggle on the Show/Hide button on Word's Standard toolbar; it doesn't automatically appear when you press Alt+F9 to display your other field codes.

 NOTE To learn more about Word's field codes, see Chapter 12.

Marking All Occurrences of a Word

You can mark all occurrences of a word manually, or—after you've marked the first occurrence—you can have Word mark the rest automatically. Follow these steps:

1. Select the word or phrase you want to index.

2. Press Alt+Shift+X to display the Mark Index Entry dialog box.

3. Indicate whether the selection is to be a main entry, subentry, or third-level entry.

4. Click the Mark All button to mark all instances of this selection throughout your document.

Using the preceding Bob example, clicking the Mark All button would automatically index all the *Bob*s in your document.

MASTERING THE OPPORTUNITIES

Marking Entries Other Than Words

In addition to marking words and phrases, you can also mark symbol characters, with a slight additional effort. In either the Main Entry or Subentry boxes, enter the following *immediately after* the symbol character you want to mark: **;#** (semi-colon and number sign). So, for example, if you wanted to index the at symbol (@), the entry (after your editing) should look like this:

    @;#

You can also mark pictures as index entries, even though there is no existing text to mark. Just select the picture or graphic, press Alt+Shift+X to open the Mark Index Entry dialog box, and then manually type the index entry into either the Main Entry or Subentry boxes. Word won't insert the picture in your index but will insert the index entry text you type.

PART

III

Creating Complex
Documents

Marking Index Entries with Different Text

Just because you select a word or a phrase when marking entries doesn't mean that's how the selection has to appear in your index. Let's say you want to mark the word *Bob* as it appears in your text but want it to actually be referenced under the more formal *Robert* in your index. Here's what you do:

1. Position the insertion point directly after the word or phrase you want to index.

2. Press Alt+Shift+X to display the Mark Index Entry dialog box.

3. Enter the word(s) and/or phrase(s) you want to appear in the index into either the Main Entry or Subentry boxes.

4. Click either Mark or Mark All.

Using our Bob example, you'd position the insertion point after the word *Bob* and then enter **Robert** in the Main Entry box. When you create your index, the word *Robert* will appear in the index, referencing the page where you marked the word *Bob*.

When might you want to replace the actual text with different text for your index? Here are some situations where you might want to consider doing this:

When You're Indexing a Person's Full Name   If the name appears as *Richard Beemis* in the text, you may want the index entry to appear as *Beemis, Richard*.

When You're Indexing a Title That Starts with *A* or *The*   If the title of the movie is *The Maltese Falcon*, you might want the index entry to appear as *Maltese Falcon, The*.

When You're Indexing an Abbreviation   Your text might call it *SAT*, but you might want the index entry to read *Scholastic Aptitude Test (SAT)*.

When You're Indexing a Plural or a Past Tense   If the word in the text is *cats*, you may want the index entry to appear as *cat*. Likewise with *defenestrated*; you may want the index entry to be the present tense *defenestrate*.

TIP   Word alphabetizes your index using the entry text that appears in the Make Index Entry dialog box or XE field, *not* by the actual text in the body of your document.

Marking Index Cross-References

Sometimes you want an index entry to point to another index entry. This is typically an option if you have an item or idea that can go by several different names. For example, this book is about Microsoft Word 2000, but you can also refer to the product as Microsoft Word, Word 2000, or just plain Word. You might want to reference all these variations to a single index listing (to *Microsoft Word 2000,* for example) so that the index listing for *Word* would include, instead of the page number, the reference "see *Microsoft Word 2000.*"

Here's how you cross-reference other index entries:

1. Select the word or phrase you want to index.
2. Press Alt+Shift+X to display the Mark Index Entry dialog box.
3. Indicate whether the selection is to be a main entry, subentry, or third-level entry.
4. Check the Cross-Reference option.
5. Enter the text you want to use for the cross-reference into the Cross-Reference box. (*See* is good, as is *See also.*)
6. Click either the Mark or the Mark All button.

Marking a Range of Pages

If a concept is covered over a range of pages in your document (even though the indexed word only appears on one of the pages), you may want to reference the entire page range in your index. To do this, you first have to bookmark the page range, and then mark the bookmark as an index entry.

Follow these steps:

1. Select the entire range of text you want to index.
2. Select Insert ➤ Bookmark to display the Bookmark dialog box.
3. Enter a name for the bookmark in the Bookmark Name box, and then click Add.
4. With the insertion point anywhere within the bookmarked text, press Alt+ Shift+X to display the Mark Index Entry dialog box.
5. Check the Page Range option, pull down the Bookmark list, and select the bookmark you want to index.
6. Click the Mark button.

Editing and Deleting Index Entries

To edit an index entry, you have to edit the inserted field code. Click the Show/Hide button on Word's Standard toolbar to display all hidden codes, and then go to the index entry you want to edit. Position the insertion point within the code, and then edit appropriately.

To delete an index entry, highlight the entire field code (including the curly brackets), and press Delete.

PART

III

Creating Complex Documents

Automatic Indexing from an AutoMark File

Some users prefer to make a list of the words they want included in the index separate from the main document itself and then to build the index from this separate word list. This way, you can view your index holistically, with more control over the shape of your entire index and the words indexed.

Using this method, the separate word list is actually created in a separate concordance file (which Word calls an AutoMark file) using a two-column table. The first column holds the words you want to mark as index entries; the second column holds the text for the corresponding index entry. (See the preceding Bob/Robert example.) You use a separate row in the table for each word you want to index. After you create the concordance file, you use Word's AutoMark feature to search your document for the words in your concordance file and automatically mark them as index entries.

Follow these steps to create an AutoMark file, and then use it to mark entries in your text:

1. Click the New button on Word's Standard toolbar to create a new blank document.

2. Select Table ➤ Insert ➤ Table to display the Insert Table dialog box.

3. Select 2 for number of columns and 1 for number of rows, and then click OK to insert the table in the new document.

4. In the first column of the first row of your table, enter the word(s) or phrase(s) you want Word to search for and mark as an index entry.

 TIP To have your index include all forms of a given word, create separate rows for each word form. For example, if you want to index the word *run,* you should also create entries for the words *ran* and *running.*

5. In the second column, enter the text for this index entry as you want it to appear in the index listing.

 TIP If you want this entry to be a subentry, you should enter the following in the second column: ***mainentry:subentry****,* where *mainentry* is your main index entry and *subentry* is the specific entry.

6. Press Tab to create a new row in your table for your next entry.

7. Repeat steps 4–6 for each index entry you want to mark.

8. When you're done entering index entries, select File ≻ Save As to save the file with a name of your choosing.

9. Open or switch to the document you want to index.

10. Select Insert ≻ Index and Tables to display the Index and Tables dialog box.

11. Select the Index tab.

12. Click the AutoMark button to display the Open Index AutoMark File dialog box.

13. Find and select your AutoMark file, and then click Open.

Word now searches through your main document for each occurrence of the text in the first column of the table in your AutoMark file and then marks each occurrence as an index entry.

 TIP If you use an AutoMark file to mark a batch of index entries in your document, you can still mark additional index entries manually.

Creating an Index

Once all the index entries in your document have been marked, you can build the actual index listing, which Word does automatically, based on your formatting preferences.

Building Your Index

Most indexes are placed at the end of a document. While Word lets you insert an index anywhere in your document, most readers will be confused if they don't find it where they expect it to be—at the end.

To create an index for your document, follow these steps:

1. Anchor your insertion point where you want to insert the index—typically at the end of your document, starting on a blank page.

 TIP To force a page break to start your index on a new page, press Ctrl+Enter.

2. Make sure that all field codes and hidden text are not visible in your document. (You may need to toggle off the Show/Hide button on Word's Standard toolbar.)

PART

III

Creating Complex
Documents

WARNING If field codes and hidden text are displayed in your document, it can throw off the pagination of your real text.

3. Select Insert ➢ Index and Tables to display the Index and Tables dialog box.

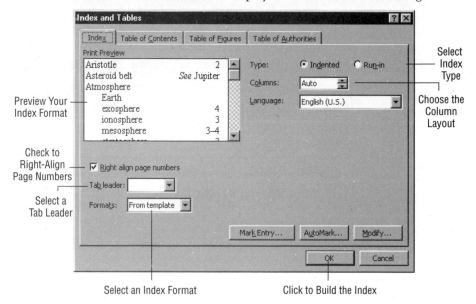

Preview Your Index Format

Check to Right-Align Page Numbers

Select a Tab Leader

Select Index Type

Choose the Column Layout

Select an Index Format

Click to Build the Index

4. Select the Index tab.

5. If you want subentries to appear indented and below their main entries, check the Indented option; if you want subentries to appear on the same line as the main entry, check the Run-In option.

6. Select the number of columns for your index from the Columns list. (Two or three columns are common for most indexes.)

7. If you want page numbers to line up at the right margin, check the Right Align Page Numbers option, and then select a tab leader (for the space between the entry and the page number) from the Tab Leader list. If you want page numbers to appear next to the entries, uncheck this option.

8. Select a format for the index from the Formats list, or click Modify to create your own format.

TIP The index format you select is previewed in the Print Preview box.

9. When all options are selected, click OK to create the index.

Word now scans your document for all index entries (actually, for XE field codes) and builds the index based on these entries and according to the options you selected. Your final index should look something like the one shown in Figure 13.1.

FIGURE 13.1
A completed index for a Word document

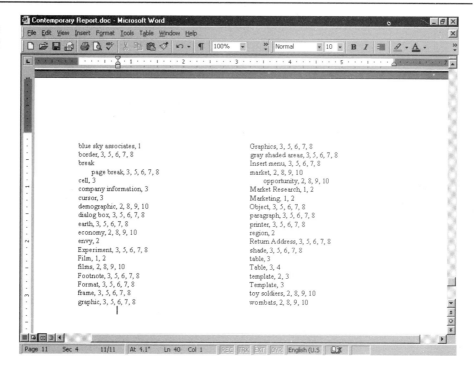

 TIP When Word builds an index, it doesn't automatically title the index. You'll have to insert your own *Index* heading at the top of the index page, before the index field itself.

Formatting Your Index

Word 2000 includes six predesigned index formats, plus the capability for you to design your own format.

The six predesigned formats include:

Classic Groups entries by letter, with a centered letter heading.

Fancy Uses a centered letter heading and a multiple-line horizontal rule between groupings.

Modern Left-aligns the letter heading and uses a single-line horizontal rule between groupings.

Bulleted Left-aligns the letter heading, with no horizontal rules.

Formal Left-aligns the letter heading, uses no horizontal rules, but right-aligns the page numbers with a tab leader.

Simple Does not group entries by letter, and entries thus have no letter separators.

There are several ways you can modify the format of your index. You can choose to right-align your page numbers (although most indexes do not use this option) and insert tab leaders between the index entries and corresponding page numbers. You can also choose to display subentries either underneath and indented from the main entries or on the same line as the main entries.

For more significant modifications, you have to modify the styles of the different index-level listings. To do this, select From Template from the Format list, and then click the Modify button. When the Style dialog box appears, you can modify the styles used for each level of entries in your index. When you use this option, you can select different font styles and sizes for each index level, as well as have some levels use tab leaders and other levels not use them.

 NOTE To learn more about modifying Word styles, see Chapter 9.

You can also manually apply character formatting (bold, italic, and so on) to any word or character in your index. Note, however, that you're applying formatting to the result of a Word field; if you update the field, the field results are recreated from scratch and all manual character formatting is lost.

TIP You can create an index that incorporates multiple documents by using Word's master document feature. Add all the documents to your master document, expand all the subdocuments, and then build your index. See Chapter 22 for more information.

Updating Your Index

If you edit your document after you create an index, you may move the position of existing index entries or add new entries to (or delete existing ones from) your document. After you make changes to your document, you should always update your index by selecting the entire index (actually, you're selecting the field code used to create the index) and pressing F9.

 WARNING Any manual formatting you've applied to your index results will be lost when you update the index.

Indexing Only Part of Your Document

If you only want to index part of your document (one section of a multiple-section document, for example), you have to create your index using bookmarks and the INDEX field. (The standard Index and Tables dialog box doesn't offer this option.) Follow these steps:

1. Select the entire section of your document you want to index.
2. Select Insert ➢ Bookmark to display the Bookmark dialog box.
3. Enter a name for the bookmark in the Bookmark Name box, and then click Add.
4. Move your insertion point to where you want to add the index.
5. Press Ctrl+F9 to insert a field.
6. Inside the curly brackets, type **INDEX \b bookmark**, where *bookmark* is actually the name of the bookmark.
7. Select the field you just entered, and press F9.

Word will now insert an index that covers only the section of your text that was bookmarked.

PART

III

Creating Complex Documents

Creating a Table of Contents

The index is the last part of your document that readers see; the table of contents (TOC) is one of the first things they see. A detailed table of contents is necessary to guide readers through a long or complex document; by viewing your document's sections, chapters, or major headings, they see in a glance what is essentially an outline to your document's contents.

Preparing for a Table of Contents

To build a logical table of contents, your document needs to be constructed in a logical manner. The most important thing to remember is that you have to assign specific styles to different levels of headings within your document. You also have to be *consistent* when you assign these styles; don't assign Heading 1 to one chapter title or heading and Heading 2 to another, for example.

Word creates a table of contents based on your selected heading styles. When you create a TOC, Word looks for every paragraph formatted with a specific style and then uses those paragraphs as TOC entries. So if Heading 1 is assigned as the first-level listing in your TOC, all paragraphs formatted as Heading 1 are listed as first-level entries in your TOC.

When you construct your document, think logically, and think, more or less, in hierarchical outline form. Big chunks of your document should be prefaced by major headings (Heading 1 style, perhaps), while smaller bits within the larger chunks should be prefaced by minor headings (Heading 2 style, perhaps), and so on, to whatever level of granularity best suits a particular document.

When in doubt, use Word's default styles, and assign Heading 1 to your first-level headings, Heading 2 to your second level headings, and so on.

Building Your Table of Contents

It's easier to create a table of contents than it is to create an index because you don't have to mark your TOC entries as you do your index entries. As the preceding section discussed, Word builds the TOC from selected heading styles in your document; specific styles are assigned to specific levels in your TOC, and Word does the rest automatically.

Follow these steps to insert a table of contents into your document:

1. Anchor the insertion point where you want to insert the table of contents, typically after the title page but before the first page of your main text.

2. Select Insert ➢ Index and Tables to display the Index and Tables dialog box.

3. Select the Table of Contents tab.

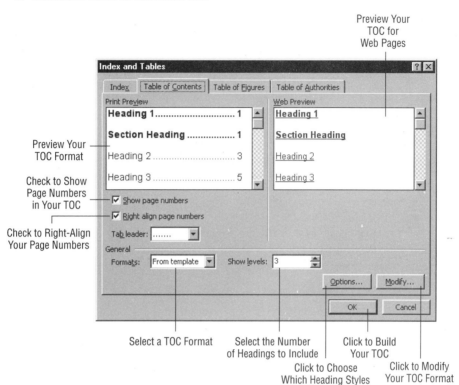

Preview Your
TOC for
Web Pages

Preview Your
TOC Format

Check to Show
Page Numbers
in Your TOC

Check to Right-Align
Your Page Numbers

Select a TOC Format

Select the Number
of Headings to Include

Click to Build
Your TOC

Click to Choose
Which Heading Styles
to Assign to TOC Levels

Click to Modify
Your TOC Format

4. If you want to show page numbers in your TOC (and you probably do), check the Show Page Numbers option. If you check this option, you can also select to right-align your page numbers (which is common) by checking the Right Align Page Numbers option.

5. Select a design for your TOC from the Formats list; if you want to customize your TOC design, click the Modify button to modify the styles used in your TOC.

6. Select how many levels you want to display in your TOC from the Show Levels list.

7. To assign different heading styles to specific TOC levels, click the Options button to display the Table of Contents Options dialog box. Check the Styles option and then a number in the TOC Level box next to each Available Style you want to include in your TOC. (For example, if you want the Heading 1 style

PART

III

Creating Complex
Documents

to be the first level in your index, enter **1** in the Heading 1 TOC Level box. Click OK when done to return to the Index and Tables dialog box.)

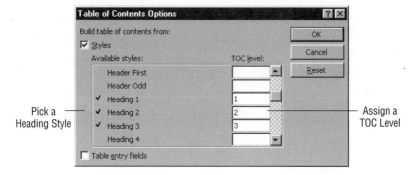

Pick a Heading Style

Assign a TOC Level

 WARNING If you don't want a specific style, such as one of Word's default Heading styles, listed in your TOC, be sure to delete any number appearing in the corresponding TOC Level box.

8. When all options are selected, click OK to build the table of contents.

Word now creates a table of contents like the one shown in Figure 13.2.

FIGURE 13.2
A typical Word table of contents

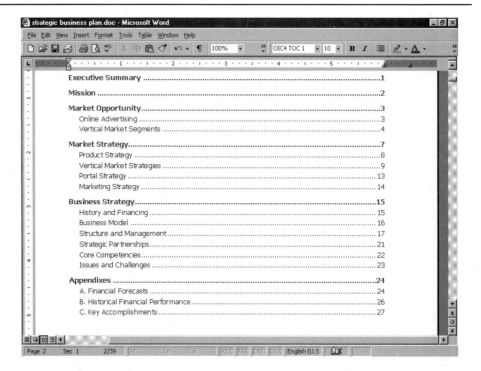

TIP When Word builds a table of contents, it doesn't automatically title the TOC. You'll have to insert your own *Table of Contents* heading at the top of the page, before the TOC field itself.

 MASTERING THE OPPORTUNITIES

Tips for Terrific TOCs

Here are some tips to keep in mind when building a TOC:

- Make sure you have all your TOC levels assigned, and don't have too many levels assigned. Look to see whether multiple styles are assigned to the same TOC level and that you're not missing any level assignments. It also doesn't hurt to be sure you're assigning TOC levels to the styles that you actually used in your document!

- Make sure you've hidden all field codes and hidden text before you create the TOC; displaying these elements onscreen can mess up the page numbering of your document's real text.

- By default, each entry in your TOC is also formatted as a hyperlink to the corresponding section within your document. Click on a TOC entry to jump directly to that section in your document.

- When Word creates a table of contents, it inserts the TOC field code next to each heading that is included in the TOC. If you want to manually edit or delete individual TOC entries, display your document's fields (press Alt+F9), and either edit or delete the TOC code next to the heading in question.

- You can have more than one table of contents in your document. For example, you may want one TOC to be fairly detailed and a second "contents at a glance," such as the one at the beginning of this book, to include only one or two TOC heading levels. Just insert each TOC separately, and when you insert the second TOC, answer No when Word asks if you want to replace your existing table of contents.

Continued ▶

PART

III

Creating Complex Documents

- You can create a TOC that incorporates headings from multiple documents by using Word's master document feature. Add all the documents to your master document, expand all the subdocuments, and then build your TOC. (See Chapter 22 for more information on master documents.)

- If you want to create a TOC for only *part* of your document (one section of a multiple-section document, for example), you have to create the TOC index using bookmarks and the TOC field. Just select the entire section you want in your TOC, assign it a bookmark name, move your insertion point to where you want to add the index, and press Ctrl+F9 to insert a field. Inside the curly brackets, type: **TOC \b *bookmark***, where *bookmark* is actually the name of the bookmark; select the field you just entered, and press F9 to update the field.

- To quickly create a TOC on a Web page, based on Word's standard heading styles, select Format ➤ Frames ➤ Table of Contents in Frame. This adds a scrollable frame to your Web page and builds the TOC in that frame. Users can then click a hyperlinked entry in the TOC frame to jump to that point in your document in the main frame. (To learn more about using Word to create Web-based documents, see Chapter 24.)

Formatting Your Table of Contents

As with indexes, there are several ways to format your tables of contents, including:

Show and Right-Align Page Numbers   Check the Show Page Numbers option to display page numbers for your TOC listings, and check the Right Align Page Numbers option to line up these page numbers against the right margin.

Pick a Predesigned Format from the Formats List   Word includes six predesigned formats that match the formats available for indexes, which were described earlier in this chapter.

Modify TOC Listing Styles   You can modify the styles assigned to each level of listing in your TOC. Just click the Modify button to display the Style dialog box, and then modify any aspect of any TOC style as appropriate.

Format Character Attributes Manually   You can manually format (make bold, italic, and so on) individual words and characters in your newly created TOC, although this formatting will be lost whenever you update the TOC.

Updating Your Table of Contents

Whenever you modify your document, you'll need to update your TOC. To do this, select the entire TOC, and then press F9.

NOTE You can also update your TOC by right-clicking anywhere in the TOC and selecting Update Field from the pop-up menu. When the Update Table of Contents dialog box appears, select either Update Page Numbers Only or Update Entire Table.

MASTERING THE OPPORTUNITIES

Creating a Table of Contents Manually

In addition to creating a table of contents from heading styles in your document, you can also mark specific sections of your text to appear in your table of contents. When you build your TOC, the entries you've selected manually (which are tagged with the TC field code) are inserted into the TOC, along with any style-generated entries.

To mark any bit of text as a TOC entry, follow these steps:

1. Select the text you want to appear as the TOC entry.

2. Press Alt+Shift+O to display the Mark Table of Contents Entry dialog box.

3. If necessary, edit the text in the Entry box to reflect how you want the TOC entry to appear.

4. Make sure that C (for table of contents) is selected in the Table Identifier list.

5. Pull down the Level list, and select the TOC level you want to apply to this entry.

6. Click OK.

You can also use this method to mark entries for tables of authorities and tables of figures by selecting either A or F from the Table Identifier list.

Creating a Table of Figures

If your document includes a lot of figures, tables, or equations (all identified with captions), you might want to create a *table of figures*, listing all the figures used in your document. You create a table of figures (TOF) similar to the way you create a table of contents, and you can create separate tables for figures, tables, and equations.

PART

III

Creating Complex
Documents

Building Your Table of Figures

To insert a table of figures into your document, follow these steps:

1. Anchor the insertion point where you want to insert the table of figures, typically either after the table of contents or before the index.

2. Select Insert ➢ Index and Tables to display the Index and Tables dialog box.

3. Select the Table of Figures tab.

4. If you want to show page numbers in your TOC (and you probably do), check the Show Page Numbers option. If you check this option, you can also select to right-align your page numbers (which is common) by checking the Right Align Page Numbers option, and then select a specific tab leader from the Tab Leader list.

5. Select a design for your TOF from the Formats list; if you want to customize your TOF design, click the Modify button to modify the styles used in your TOF.

6. Pull down the Caption Label list to select what kind of table you want to build: Figure, Table, or Equation.

   If you want to base your TOF on a style other than Caption, Table, or Equation, click the Options dialog box to display the Table of Figures Options dialog box. Select an alternate style or table identifier, and then click OK to return to the Index and Tables dialog box.

7. When all the options are selected, click OK to build your table of figures.

Formatting Your Table of Figures

You format your TOF as you would a TOC. You can check the Show Page Numbers option to display page numbers; check the Right Align Page Numbers option to line up page numbers against the right margin; pick a predesigned format from the Formats list; modify existing TOF styles by clicking the Modify button and using the Style dialog box; and manually format character attributes for individual words within your TOF.

Updating Your Table of Figures

You update a TOF as you would a TOC. Select the entire table, and then press F9. You can also right-click anywhere within the TOF and select Update Field from the pop-up menu; when the Update Table of Figures dialog box appears, select either Update Page Numbers Only or Update Entire Table.

Creating a Table of Authorities

Citations are used in many legal documents to cite cases, rulings, statutes, and other items of relevance to the current document. You mark citations in your document similar to the way you mark index entries, and then you create a master list of citations, called a *table of authorities* (TOA), at the end of your document.

Marking Citations

Follow these steps to mark citations in your document:

1. Select the first occurrence of a citation in your document.

2. Press Alt+Shift+I to open the Mark Citation dialog box.

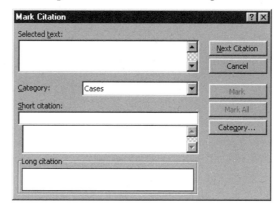

3. The selected citation appears in the Select Text Box. Edit this text as you want it displayed in the table of authorities.

4. Pull down the Category list, and select the category (Cases, Statutes, and so on) for this citation.

 TIP To edit citation categories, click the Category button to display the Edit Categories dialog box. Select a category from the list, and enter the new name in the Replace With box.

5. Edit the text in the Short Citation box as appropriate (typically only the case reference).

6. Click Mark to mark this selection or Mark All to mark all occurrences of this citation.

PART

III

Creating Complex
Documents

Building Your Table of Authorities

Once you have all the citations marked in your document, you can build your table of authorities. Building a TOA is very similar to building an index or a TOC; follow these steps:

1. Anchor the insertion point where you want to insert the table of authorities.

2. Select Insert ➢ Index and Tables to display the Index and Tables dialog box.

3. Select the Table of Authorities tab.

4. Select what type of authority to include in your TOA from the Category list. By default, Word includes all citation types in your TOA; you can choose to create different TOAs for different categories of citations.

5. If you want to replace any instance of five or more references to the same authority with the word *Passim,* check the Use Passim option.

6. To retain the original character formatting for long citations, check the Keep Original Formatting option.

7. Select a tab leader (for the space between the citation and the page number) from the Tab Leader list.

8. Select a predesigned TOA format from the Formats list, or click the Modify button to modify individual TOA styles.

9. When all the options are selected, click OK to build the table of authorities.

You can create one TOA that includes all the different authorities in your document, or make different TOAs for each specific type of authority.

 TIP Remember to update your TOA when your document changes by selecting the TOA and pressing F9.

PART IV

Creating Visual Documents

- *Creating and formatting tables*

- *Creating charts and graphs*

- *Adding graphics and drawings*

- *Linking and embedding objects*

CHAPTER **14**

Creating Tables

Inserting a blank table 380

Entering table data 389

Inserting and deleting rows and columns 391

Merging and splitting cells 394

Resizing table elements 396

Formatting tables 400

Sorting cells 410

Working with formulas and functions 413

Creating complex equations 417

A table is a great way to organize information, using a structured series of rows and columns. Looking somewhat like a spreadsheet (and containing similar basic math functions), a table in Word can span multiple pages, and its cells can contain both text and graphics. There are probably more uses for Word tables than you're aware of—and more editing and formatting options, as well.

Understanding Tables

Even though a table can be internally complex, with myriad rows and columns, to Word 2000 it's nothing more than an object inserted into a document. You should approach a table as a separate object, editing it and formatting it separately from the rest of your document.

Reviewing the Parts of a Table

Figure 14.1 details the parts of a typical table.

FIGURE 14.1
A typical table in Word 2000

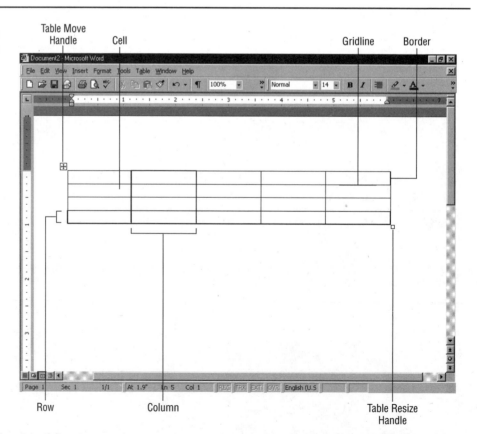

You can move the entire table by dragging the table move handle and resize the entire table by dragging the table resize handle. Individual row, column, and cell editing operations are discussed in the "Editing Tables" section later in this chapter.

The line around the outside of the table is called the *border,* while the internal lines between cells are called *gridlines.* Columns run up and down, while rows run side to side—and a cell is an intersection of a specific row and column. You can format the table as a whole, or you can format individual cells.

Working with the Tables and Borders Toolbar

 All table-related commands and operations can be found on Word's Table menu. You can also choose to display the Tables and Borders toolbar, shown in Figure 14.2, which contains most common table-related commands. You display the Tools and Borders toolbar by clicking the Tables and Borders button on Word's Standard toolbar.

FIGURE 14.2
Use the Tables and Borders toolbar to edit your tables.

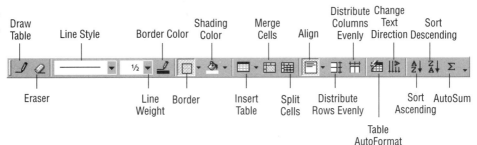

Navigating within a Table

You use relatively standard Word navigation commands to move around inside a table. Table 14.1 details Word's table navigation commands.

TABLE 14.1: TABLE NAVIGATION COMMANDS

To Move Here:	Press This:
Next cell	Tab
Previous cell	Shift+Tab
Next row	↓

Continued ▶

TABLE 14.1: TABLE NAVIGATION COMMANDS (CONTINUED)

To Move Here:	Press This:
Previous row	↑
First cell in the row	Alt+Home
Last cell in the row	Alt+End
First cell in the column	Alt+PgUp
Last cell in the column	Alt+PgDn

Displaying or Hiding Table Gridlines

When you're working with a table, you can choose how to view that table in the Word workspace. If you want to view the table as it will ultimately be printed out, you can hide the on-screen gridlines Word uses to separate the table cells. If you'd rather see just where the cells are (and aren't), you can choose to display the non-printable gridlines.

To hide or display gridlines for a table, pull down the Table menu and toggle the Hide Gridlines/Show Gridlines command on or off. Remember that these gridlines are for your editing convenience only—they won't show up when you print your document.

Creating Tables

Word provides numerous ways to add a table to your document. In all cases, the table is added at the insertion point.

Inserting a Blank Table

More often than not you'll start with a blank table, into which you insert text and to which you apply formatting. Word 2000 offers four different ways to insert a blank table into your documents.

Using the Insert Table Dialog Box

The most precise way to insert a table is to use the Insert Table dialog box, shown below.

To insert a table using the Insert Table dialog box, follow these steps:

1. Select Table ➢ Insert ➢ Table to display the Insert Table dialog box.

2. In the Table Size section, select the Number of Columns and the Number of Rows.

3. In the AutoFit Behavior section, select whether you want your columns to have a Fixed Column Width (and if so, whether you want the width to be determined automatically or selected manually); whether you want your columns to be automatically sized to the width of their contents (AutoFit to Contents); or whether you want your table and its columns to be automatically sized to the width of a Web browser (AutoFit to Window).

4. If you want to apply a predesigned format to your table, click the AutoFormat button to display the Table AutoFormat dialog box; select a format and click OK.

5. If you want the options you selected to apply to all new tables you create, check the Set as Default for New Tables option.

6. Click OK to create the table at your document's insertion point.

Using the Insert Table Grid

Another way to insert a table is to visually select the number of rows and columns it should contain. This method is available when you click the Insert Table button on Word's Standard toolbar, as described below.

1. Click the Insert Table button on Word's Standard toolbar to display the pull-down grid.

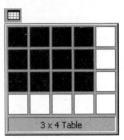

2. Using your mouse—and starting from the top-left corner—drag your cursor over the number of rows and columns you want your table to contain.

 TIP On first appearance, the Insert Table grid displays five columns and four rows. To make a table with more rows and/or columns, press the Shift key while you push the cursor past the edges of the grid to extend the number of rows and columns available.

3. When you have the correct number of rows and columns selected, click your mouse button; a table drawn to your specifications is added at your document's insertion point.

Drawing a Table

When you click the Tables and Borders button on Word's Standard toolbar, you display the Tools and Borders toolbar. On this toolbar you'll find the Draw Table command, which lets you draw borders and gridlines on your page to define your column graphically.

1. Click the Tables and Border button on Word's Standard toolbar to display the Tables and Borders toolbar.

 2. From the Tables and Borders toolbar, click the Draw Table button.

3. The cursor changes to a pencil shape. Move the cursor to where you want to place the top-left corner of your table, then click your mouse button and drag the cursor down and to the right; release the mouse button when you've reached the bottom-right corner of your table.

4. Use the pencil-shaped cursor to draw lines within the table border you just created. Draw a horizontal line to represent a gridline separating two rows; draw a vertical line to represent a gridline separating two columns.

5. If you want to erase a gridline you've drawn, click the Eraser button on the Tables and Borders toolbar and use your mouse to erase the line in question.

As you can see in Figure 14.3, the rows and columns you draw don't have to be of equal size or symmetrical. This is the recommended method if you need to create a table with an unusual row-and-column arrangement.

FIGURE 14.3
Drawing a table with the Draw Table command

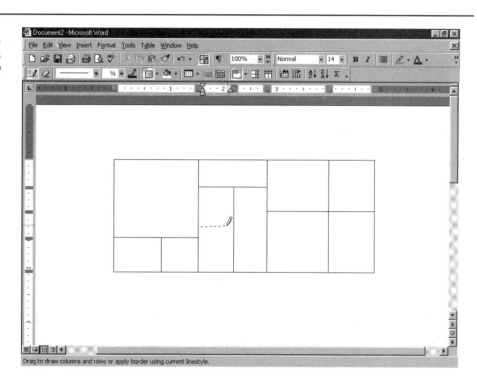

Using AutoFormat to Create a Table from the Keyboard

If you have the Apply Tables as You Type option selected in Word's AutoFormat feature, you can type a series of characters with your keyboard—Word will automatically convert those characters into a table.

NOTE Turn on the Apply Tables as You Type feature by selecting Tools ➢ AutoCorrect to open the AutoCorrect dialog box; select the AutoFormat as You Type tab, go to the Apply as You Type section, and check the Tables option.

With this option enabled, you type a plus sign (+) followed by a series of hyphens (-), followed by another plus sign, and so on. Each plus sign you type signifies a column border; the hyphens represent the intercolumn spacing. For example, if you type +-----+-----+------+ Word replaces your typing with a three-column table.

 NOTE If you use the AutoFormat method to insert a table, Word has no way of knowing how many rows to create, so the table is created with just the first row.

Creating Side-by-Side Tables

 Thanks to Word 2000's Click and Type feature, you can now insert a new table side-by-side with an existing table. Assuming your existing table doesn't fill the entire page width, all you have to do is double-click your cursor where you want to insert the new table (next to the existing table), then click the Draw Table button and draw your new table.

 WARNING If you draw your new table too wide, it won't fit in the remaining page width—and will automatically position itself *under* your existing table.

Nesting Tables

 Also new in Word 2000 is the capability to insert a new table inside the cell of an existing table—creating, in effect, a *nested* table. All you have to do is position the insertion point inside a table cell, then use any of the previously discussed methods to insert a new table. As you can see in Figure 14.4, the new table is inserted at the insertion point *inside* the selected cell.

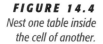

FIGURE 14.4
*Nest one table inside
the cell of another.*

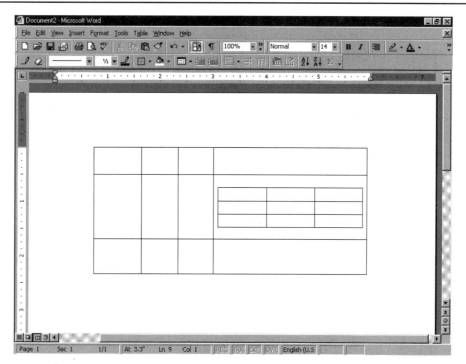

This technique is useful if you have really complex information to present.

Converting Tables

Another way to create a table is to convert *existing* data—either text or data from another source—into a table.

Converting from Text to Table

You can take any existing text in your document and turn it into a table. This works best if the text you want to convert is table-like, with tabs inserted to separate elements within lines.

To convert text to a table, follow these steps:

1. Select the text you want to convert.

2. Select Table ➢ Convert ➢ Text to Table to display the Convert Text to Table dialog box.

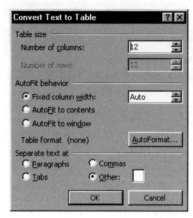

3. Word figures out the best way to create a table from your selected text and enters what it thinks are the proper settings in this dialog box. Confirm or change the settings as appropriate, then click OK.

The most important part of this dialog box is the Separate Text At section. This section details how the text is to be separated into columns, as follows:

- If the column break is to come at a tab stop, check the Tabs option.
- If a column break is to come at each new paragraph, check the Paragraphs option. (If you select Paragraphs, you'll have to manually select the number of rows and columns at the top of the dialog box.)
- If you want the column break to come at each comma in your text, check the Commas option.
- If you want to use some other character to delineate your column breaks, check the Other option and enter the character in the box.

As an example, if you have four paragraphs that you want to turn into a two-column, two-row table, you'll check the Paragraphs option, and set both the Number of Rows and the Number of Columns to 2. The first two paragraphs will be converted into the first row of the new table; the last two paragraphs will make up the second row.

Converting from Table to Text

You can also take an existing Word table and turn it into standard text—with no rows or columns. To do this, follow these steps:

1. Select the entire table—or that part of the table you want to convert.

2. Select Table ➤ Convert ➤ Table to Text to display the Convert Table to Text dialog box.

3. Select how you want the column breaks to be converted—into paragraphs, tabs, commas, or some other character.

4. Click OK to convert the table.

TIP If the table you're converting contains a nested table, you can choose to also convert the nested table into text (by checking the Convert Nested Tables option) or to insert the nested table as a nonnested table within your newly converted text (by *unchecking* the Convert Nested Tables option).

Word takes your table and turns it into standard text. As an example, if you choose to convert column breaks into paragraphs, each cell in your table becomes a separate paragraph. If you choose to convert column breaks into tabs, each row of your table becomes a separate paragraph, and each cell within a row gets separated with a tab stop.

Converting from Another Data Source

If you have a database created in another program (such as Microsoft Access), you can import that data into Word and display it in a newly created table.

NOTE Importing database data uses Microsoft's object linking and embedding (OLE) technology, so that when data is changed in the source file, it is automatically updated in your Word document. To learn more about OLE, see Chapter 17.

Before you start, know that this is a fairly complex procedure, probably not suited for inexperienced or casual users.

1. In Word, display the Database toolbar and click the Insert Database button to display the Database dialog box.

2. Click the Get Data button to display the Get Data Source dialog box.

3. Make sure you're displaying all file types (not just Word documents), then select the file you want to import and click Open.

4. If you're presented with a Header Record Delimiters dialog box, select which characters separate columns (from the Field Delimiters list) and which characters separate rows (from the Record Delimiters list). Click OK to proceed.

NOTE When converting a database to a table, the database records become table rows, and the database fields become table columns.

5. When you're returned to the Database dialog box, click the Table AutoFormat button if you want Word to automatically format the table. If you want to format the table manually (or use AutoFormat at a later time), proceed to the next step.

6. From the Database dialog box, click Insert Data to display the Insert Data dialog box.

7. Select which records (rows) you want to insert (All or a selected range).

8. If you want the inserted data to be automatically updated when the source file changes, check the Insert Data as Field option.

9. Click OK.

Word imports the data from the selected file and uses it to create a Word table. All the fields in the database become columns in your table, and the individual records become individual rows.

Editing Tables

Creating your table is just the beginning; now you have to fill it with text or graphics, and edit its contents appropriate to the task at hand.

Entering Table Data

You enter *anything*—text or graphics—into a table one cell at a time. Use your keyboard or mouse to position the insertion point inside the cell you want to fill, and then insert whatever you want to insert.

Entering Text

Entering text is as easy as typing at the insertion point—as long as the insertion point is anchored inside a table cell. Think of each cell as a mini-document; pressing Enter while typing in a cell inserts a line break *inside that cell*.

 NOTE Any text you enter into a table cell is assigned the Normal style by default.

When typing inside a cell, the Tab key functions differently from how it functions when typing in regular body text. When you press Tab inside a table, you move the insertion point to the next cell—either the next cell to the right or (if you're at the end of a row) the first cell in the next row. (Pressing Shift+Tab moves the insertion point *back* one cell.) If the insertion point is in the very last cell in your table (bottom right), pressing Tab inserts a new row at the end of your table—and moves the insertion point to the first cell in the new row.

Obviously, if you want to insert a tab stop inside a table cell, you *cannot* use the Tab key. Instead, to add a tab stop inside a cell, press Ctrl+Tab.

Inserting Graphics

You can also insert graphics into individual cells of your table. As you can see in Figure 14.5, this is a great way to organize pictures on a page; by using the constrained layout of a table's rows and columns, you can easily control how pictures are blocked out on your page.

You insert a graphic into a table as you would insert a graphic anywhere in your document. Just position your insertion point in the cell where you want to put the picture, then select Insert ➢ Picture and choose what kind of picture you want to insert.

If you've configured your table to AutoFit the column width to the cell contents, your table will be resized to accommodate the full width of your picture. If yours is a fixed-width table, you'll need to manually resize your picture to fit within the constraints of the cell.

FIGURE 14.5
Use a table to lay out pictures on your page.

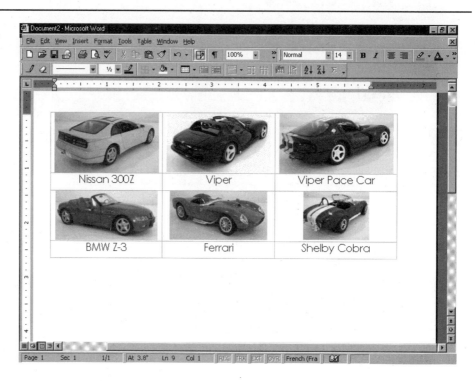

Selecting Table Contents

Within your table, you can choose to select your entire table; individual rows or columns within your table; individual table cells; or selected text within a cell. Table 14.2 details how to select elements when working with tables.

TABLE 14.2: SELECTING ELEMENTS OF A TABLE

To Select This:	Do This:
Entire table	Click the table move handle
Row	Click to the left of the row
Multiple rows	Click to the left of the first row, then drag across adjacent rows
Column	Click at the top of the column

Continued ▶

TABLE 14.2: SELECTING ELEMENTS OF A TABLE (CONTINUED)

To Select This:	Do This:
Multiple columns	Click at the top of the first column, then drag across adjacent columns
Cell	Click the left edge of the cell
Multiple cells	Drag across adjacent cells
Text within a cell	Click and then drag within a cell

Inserting and Deleting Rows and Columns

There are several ways to insert rows or columns. For example, you can right-click after selecting a row or column, or go to the Tables and Buttons toolbar and click the arrow on the Insert button to display the drop-down Insert menu. The most versatile method, however, is to use commands found on the Table menu.

When you select Table ➢ Insert or Table ➢ Delete, you are presented with a number of options. For example, you can choose to insert a new row *above* the current row or a new row *below* the current row. (In Word 97 you had only a single Insert option—which inserted new elements in front of the current element.)

To insert or delete a row or column, you first need to select a row or column within your table, and then you can select the appropriate command to execute. Table 14.3 details the insert/delete commands available.

TABLE 14.3: INSERTING AND DELETING ROWS AND COLUMNS

To Do This:	Use This Command:
Insert before current column	Table ➢ Insert ➢ Columns to the Left
Insert after current column	Table ➢ Insert ➢ Columns to the Right
Insert before current row	Table ➢ Insert ➢ Rows Above
Insert after current row	Table ➢ Insert ➢ Rows Below
Delete selected column(s)	Table ➢ Delete ➢ Columns
Delete selected row(s)	Table ➢ Delete ➢ Rows

MASTERING THE OPPORTUNITIES

Adding a New Row while Entering Data

When you're at the end of your table and you still have more data to enter, you *could* use the Table ➤ Insert ➤ Rows Below command to add a blank row after the current last row—but there's a simpler way to do this. When you've finished entering text in the very last cell in your table (far bottom right), just press Enter, as if you were going to move to the next (currently nonexistent) cell. Word will automatically insert a new blank row after the previous last row and move your insertion point to the first cell in that row.

Inserting and Deleting Individual Cells

Inserting and deleting individual cells within a table are slightly more complex operations than inserting or deleting entire rows and columns, because removing one cell from a row or column leaves the row or column one cell short—and what do you do with that space?

When you delete a cell from your table, the cells *after* the deleted cell have to be moved. You have a choice—you can move the other cells below the deleted cell *up* to fill in the now-empty space, or you can move the other cells to the right of the deleted cell *over* to fill in the space. Here's how it works:

1. Select the cell(s) you want to delete.

2. Select Table ➤ Delete ➤ Cells.

3. When the Delete Cells dialog box appears, select either Shift Cells Up (to fill in the space from below) or Shift Cells Left (to fill in the space from the right).

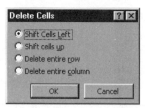

4. Click OK to delete the cell(s) and move the adjoining cells.

If you want to delete the entire row or column—and not just an individual cell— select either Delete Entire Row or Delete Entire Column in the Delete Cells dialog box.

WARNING When you delete a cell and shift the adjoining cells to fill the space, you potentially affect either the row or the column integrity of your table.

Deleting and Clearing Your Entire Table

To get rid of your entire table, all you have to do is position the insertion point anywhere within the table, then select Table ➤ Delete ➤ Table. This deletes everything in your table—all the rows, columns, cells, borders, and gridlines.

If you want to leave the skeleton of your table intact but delete all the data within the cells, select your entire table and press Delete. This clears all the cells, but leaves the row/column layout (and corresponding borders and gridlines) intact.

Moving and Copying within a Table

Moving or copying elements within a table requires a bit of finesse; the operations aren't quite as obvious as one would hope.

Moving Rows and Columns

To move a row or column from one location to another within your table, follow these steps:

1. Select the row(s) or column(s) to move.

2. Use your mouse to drag the selected element to a new location within the table.

Copying Rows and Columns

To copy a row or column to an additional location within your table (leaving the original row/column in place), follow these steps:

1. Select the row(s) or column(s) to copy.

2. Hold down the Ctrl key and drag the selected element to another location within the table.

Moving or Copying Text to Insert in an Existing Cell

To move or copy a block of text from one cell to insert within another cell—without deleting any existing text in the second cell—follow these steps:

1. Select the text to move or copy, but *don't* select the end-of-cell mark.

2. Select either Edit ➤ Cut (to move) or Edit ➤ Copy (to copy).

3. Position the insertion mark within the text in the destination cell.

4. Select Edit ➤ Paste.

Moving or Copying Text to Replace Text in Another Cell

To move or copy a block of one text to another cell—and replace that cell's contents and formatting with the cut/copied text and formatting—follow these steps:

1. Select the text to move or copy, making sure you also select the end-of-cell mark. (You may need to turn on paragraph marks to perform this task.)

2. Select either Edit ➢ Cut (to move) or Edit ➢ Copy (to copy).

3. Highlight the destination cell.

4. Select Edit ➢ Paste.

Merging and Splitting Cells

If you want the contents of one cell to spread across several rows or columns—if the selected cell contains a table title or header, for example—you can *merge* that cell with other cells to create a single large cell. (Illustrating this example, Figure 14.6 shows several cells within a row merged to create a title row.)

FIGURE 14.6
Merging cells within a row to create a large title row

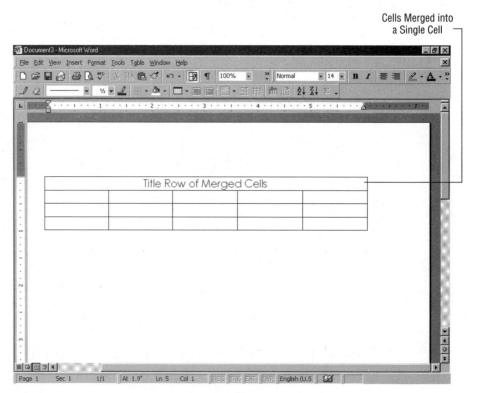

Cells Merged into a Single Cell

Title Row of Merged Cells

To merge cells, follow these steps:

1. Select the cells you want to merge.
2. Select Table ➤ Merge Cells.

 TIP If you have the Tables and Borders toolbar displayed, you can use the Eraser tool to erase the gridline between cells and merge them together.

If you later want to split cells you've merged, follow these steps:

1. Select the merged cell.
2. Select Table ➤ Split Cells.
3. When the Split Cells dialog box appears, select how many rows and columns you want to split the cell into, then click OK.

 WARNING The Split Cells command doesn't split the contents of the selected cell; all the contents remain in the first cell, while the split cells are created empty.

You can use the Split Cells command to split *any* cell, not just merged cells. Just remember that if you split a cell within a row or column, you run the risk of throwing off the existing row/column alignment.

 TIP You can also split cells using the Draw Table command on the Tables and Borders toolbar. When you draw a new gridline within an existing cell, you split the cell at that point—and split the cell contents accordingly.

Splitting a Table

Not only can you split cells, you can also split entire tables. To split one table into two, follow these steps:

1. Select the row that you want to be the first row of the new table.
2. Select Table ➤ Split Table.

Word creates a second table with a paragraph of normal text between the two tables.

MASTERING THE OPPORTUNITIES

Breaking Across Pages

If you have a long table and want it to flow across multiple pages, you don't have to split the table—you only have to insert a page break. Position the insertion point anywhere in the first cell of the row you want to send to the top of the next page, then press Ctrl+Enter. (If you don't insert a manual page break, the table will break at a natural point—which may be within a cell!)

If your table flows to another page, you probably want to repeat the table's heading row across each page of the table—otherwise, readers won't be able to tell what's in each column if they look at any page but the first. To repeat a heading, select the row (or rows), then select Table ➢ Heading Rows Repeat; this will repeat the selected row at the top of each new page occupied by your table.

If your table is extra wide, it may break within a row *between columns*. If you don't want your table to break across pages width-wise, select Table ➢ Table Properties to display the Table Properties dialog box, then select the Row tab and *uncheck* the Allow Row to Break Across Pages option.

Resizing Table Elements

Word's default table layout might be perfect for you—or it might not. If you don't like the way your columns or rows line up, you can easily resize them to fit your particular data or design needs.

Resizing Manually

You can resize rows, columns, or individual cells either within your table—using the column and row markers on Word's rulers—or by setting precise measurements in the Table Properties dialog box.

TIP   You can resize your entire table—and have your rows and columns automatically adjust to fit the new size—by grabbing the table resize handle (bottom-right corner of your table) and dragging it to a new position.

Resizing Columns

To resize a column in your table, follow one of these three procedures:

- Within the table, position your cursor on the gridline on the right side of any cell within the column you want to resize. Hold down your mouse button and drag the column boundary to a new position.

 WARNING If you drag a column boundary or marker while a row or individual cell is selected, you will adjust the column size for only that particular row.

- Move your cursor to the horizontal ruler at the top of the workspace, position the cursor on the column marker you want to move, and drag it to a new position.

Move the Column Marker to Resize

 TIP To view precise measurements when resizing a column or row, hold down the Alt key while moving the column or row marker on the ruler.

- With the insertion point somewhere in the column you want to resize, select Table ➤ Table Properties to display the Table Properties dialog box. Select the Column tab, then check the Preferred Width option and set a new width; if necessary, change the units of measurement with the Measure In control. If you want to resize other columns, use the Previous Column and Next Column buttons to move back and forth between columns. Click OK when done.

TIP The most precise sizing is achieved when you use the Table Properties dialog box.

Resizing Rows

To resize a row in your table, follow one of these three procedures:

- Within the table, position your cursor on the gridline below any cell within the column you want to resize. Hold down your mouse button and drag the row boundary to a new position.

 WARNING You can't resize a row to be smaller than necessary to hold the text it contains (you *can* resize a row to be larger).

- Move your cursor to the vertical ruler at the left side of the workspace, position the cursor on the row marker you want to move, and drag it to a new position.

Move the Row
Marker to Resize

- With the insertion point somewhere in the row you want to resize, select Table ➤ Table Properties to display the Table Properties dialog box. Select the Row tab, then check the Specify Height option and set a new height. You can also specify that the row needs to be At Least or Exactly the height specified; if you select At Least, the row can grow larger to accommodate additional text or a larger graphic. If you want to resize other rows, use the Previous Row and Next Row buttons to move back and forth between columns. Click OK when done.

Resizing Individual Cells

There are two ways to resize the width of an individual cell:

- Select the entire cell (not just the text within the cell) and move the column boundaries or row boundaries within the table (*not* the column or row markers on the rulers).

- With the insertion point anywhere within the cell, select Table ➤ Table Properties to display the Table Properties dialog box. Select the Cell tab and change the Preferred Width setting, then click OK.

WARNING You can't resize the height of an individual cell; if you try to change the height of a cell, you change the height of the entire row.

Resizing Automatically

Word 2000 includes several features that help you size your rows and columns automatically—without manual mouse intervention.

Resizing to Fit with AutoFit

 Word 2000's new AutoFit command automatically resizes your table's columns to fit the width of their contents. To use AutoFit, position your insertion point anywhere in your table, then select Table ➢ AutoFit ➢ AutoFit to Contents. This will resize your columns so that the columns with the longest contents are sized wider than columns with shorter contents.

 NOTE AutoFit adjusts only column width, not row height.

Once you activate AutoFit, your table's columns will resize themselves automatically as you enter new text into each cell. For example, if you enter a very long word into a cell in the first column, that column will grow wider (and the others will grow narrower). To turn *off* this interactive AutoFit feature, select Table ➢ AutoFit ➢ Fixed Column Width.

 TIP AutoFit also includes an option that is useful if you're inserting a table in a Web document. When you select Table ➢ AutoFit ➢ AutoFit to Window, Word configures your document's HTML code so that your tables are automatically resized when users resize the width of their Web browser window.

Distributing Rows and Columns Evenly

If you'd rather have all your columns (or selected columns) be the same width, select the columns you want to resize, then select Table ➢ AutoFit ➢ Distribute Columns Equally. This divides your table into columns of equal width. (For example, if your table is six inches wide and you have three columns—and you selected all three—this command resizes each column to an identical two-inch width.)

A similar command exists for equally sizing rows in your table. Select the rows you want to resize, then select Table ➢ AutoFit ➢ Distribute Rows Equally.

Formatting Tables

When Word first creates a table, it assigns the Normal style to all the table text and applies a black, 0.5-point border and gridlines to the entire table. Although that look might be appealing in some instances, chances are that different formatting will not only make your table more attractive, but also make it more effective in communicating the message of its contents.

Word allows you to apply different types of formatting to your entire table and to individual cells within your table. Read on to learn how to turn boring tables into interesting presentations of data.

Formatting the Entire Table

Many of Word's formatting options—including borders and shading—can be applied to an entire table. In addition, as with any object, you can configure how your table aligns on your page.

Moving or Copying a Table within Your Document

Prior to Word 2000, if you wanted to move your table, you had to cut and paste it into a new location. With Word 2000, however, you can use the new table move handle (located at the top-left corner of the table) to move your table with your mouse.

All you have to do is grab the table move handle and drag your table to a new position. Your entire table moves as a single object as you drag it from one location to another within your document.

If you click the table move handle, you highlight the table as a whole, and can then easily cut or copy the table using standard Word commands. To cut or copy your table in this fashion, follow these steps:

1. Click the table move handle to select the entire table.
2. Right-click your mouse to display the pop-up menu.
3. Select either Cut or Copy from the pop-up menu.
4. Reposition the insertion point where you want to reinsert the table.
5. Right-click your mouse button again and select Paste from the pop-up menu.

Aligning a Table and Wrapping Text

Once you have your table positioned where you want it, you can select how you want it *aligned* on that page—and how you want surrounding text to flow around it.

Word 2000 adds the capability to left-align, right-align, or center your table at its current position. You also gain the capability of wrapping text around the side(s) of your table. (Previous to Word 2000, there was no text wrapping around tables.)

To configure your table's alignment and text wrapping, follow these steps:

1. With the insertion point anywhere inside the table, select Table ➢ Table Properties to display the Table Properties dialog box.

2. Select the Table tab.

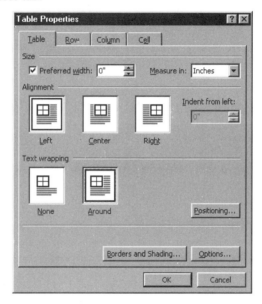

3. In the Alignment section, select either Left, Center, or Right alignment.

TIP If you select Left alignment, you can also select the amount of space you want to indent the table from the left margin.

4. In the Text Wrapping section, select None if you want no text to wrap around the side(s) of your table; select Around if you want text to wrap around your table's side(s).

5. Click OK.

If you enable text wrapping for your table, you have the option of setting more precise wrapping settings. From within the Table Properties dialog box, click the Option button (active only if Text Wrapping is selected) to display the Table Positioning dialog box. From here you can select:

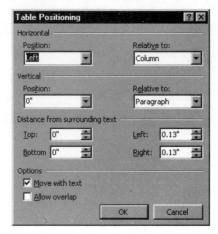

Horizontal Position   You can select how you want your table positioned horizontally on the page, choosing from the following positions: Left, Right, Center, Inside, or Outside relative to the current Page, Margin, or Column.

Vertical Position   You can select how you want your table positioned vertically on the page, choosing from the following positions: Top, Bottom, Center, Inside, or Outside relative to the current Page, Margin, or Paragraph.

Distance from Surrounding Text   You can set precise measurements for the buffer zone between your table and the wrapping text, on all four sides.

Other Options   You can choose to have the table Move with Text (so that when your text changes, the table moves with it) and to Allow Overlap between your table and other text and pictures when viewed in a Web browser.

Make your selections, then click OK to apply the settings and close the dialog box.

Setting Cell Margins

Each cell in your table has its own internal margins—which you can see from the horizontal ruler when your cursor is located inside a table. You can change these settings globally (for the entire table) or adjust the settings manually for each individual cell.

To set the table's global margins and spacing, follow these steps:

1. With the insertion point anywhere inside the table, select Table ➢ Table Properties to display the Table Properties dialog box.

2. Select the Table tab and click the Options button to display the Table Options dialog box.

3. In the Default Cell Margins section, set the Top, Bottom, Left, and Right margins that Word will apply to each cell in your table. (This effectively pads how close the text appears to any surrounding gridline.)

4. If you want to insert spacing *between* cells (in addition to the normal internal cell margins), check the Allow Spacing between Cells option and choose a setting.

5. If you want to turn on the AutoFit to Contents feature (discussed earlier) for your entire table, check the Automatically Resize to Fit Contents option.

6. Click OK to close the dialog box and apply the new settings.

Applying Borders and Gridlines

Some of the more effective formatting you can apply to your table is through the application of border and gridline colors and styles—which can be accomplished via the Borders and Shading dialog box.

Word enables you to add different types of borders to the top, bottom, left, or right border of your table—and to vertical and horizontal gridlines inside the table. Word lets you apply several preselected border types—or you can choose your own border style, width, and color.

To add or modify the borders and gridlines in your table, follow these steps:

1. With the insertion point anywhere in your table, select Format ➢ Borders and Shading to display the Borders and Shading dialog box.

2. Select the Borders tab.

3. Select the type of border you want to apply from the Setting section: None, Box, All, Grid, or Custom.

TIP When you select the Custom setting, you can select different line styles, colors, and widths for each side of your paragraph.

4. If you want to change the style of the border, make a selection from the Style list.

5. If you want to change the color of the border, make a selection from the Color list.

6. If you want to change the width of the border, make a selection from the Width list.

7. To apply the border style, color, and width to any side border or inside gridline of your table, click the appropriate line segment in the preview diagram.

8. Make sure that Table is selected in the Apply To list.

9. Click OK.

Remember that you can select different border styles and colors for the outside border and the inside gridlines of your table. Whatever selections are made in the Style/Color/Width sections apply when you click a line segment in the preview diagram.

Applying Table Shading

You can add color shading to your entire table (or to selected cells—see the "Applying Cell Borders and Shading" section later in this chapter) by following these steps:

1. With the insertion point anywhere in your table, select Format ➤ Borders and Shading to display the Borders and Shading dialog box.

2. Select the Shading tab.

3. Select a shading color from the Fill section; click the More Colors button to choose from an expanded palette of colors.

4. Select a shading percentage from the Style list. (A lower percentage creates a lighter shading, while a higher percentage creates a darker shading; 100 percent applies the solid color selected.)

5. Make sure that Table is selected in the Apply To list.

6. Click OK.

TIP Choose your shading colors carefully; a shading that is too dark can make regular black text hard to read. If you choose a dark shading, you may want to change the text color in your table to something lighter—such as white.

Formatting the Easy Way—with AutoFormat

The easiest way to apply formatting to your entire table is to use Word's AutoFormat command. With this command you can choose from dozens of predesigned table formats (affecting borders, gridlines, shading, and fonts) and apply them to your table with a click of your mouse.

To apply an AutoFormat to your table, follow these steps:

1. With your insertion point anywhere in your table, select Table ➢ Table AutoFormat to display the Table AutoFormat dialog box.

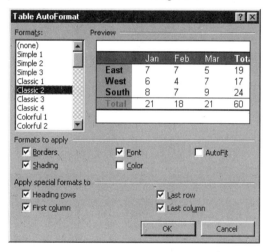

2. From the Formats to Apply section, select those elements to which you want to apply formatting: Borders, Shading, Font Color, and AutoFit.

 TIP You can see the effect of applying formats to specific elements by checking and unchecking the elements and watching the changes in the Preview section.

3. Select whether you want to apply special formats to your table's Heading Rows, First Column, Last Row, or Last Column.

TIP The special formats that are part of some—but not all—formats create *total* and *heading* rows and columns in your table.

4. Select the table format you want from the Formats list; you can preview each format (with your specific options applied) in the Preview section of the dialog box.

5. Click OK to AutoFormat your table.

If you don't like the AutoFormat results, *immediately* select Edit ➤ Undo AutoFormat to put things back the way they were—before you make any additional changes.

 TIP If you're printing in black and white, avoid the colorful table formats—and be wary of the 3-D effects formats, as well. You should test print your table after applying an AutoFormat, just to be sure that what looks good onscreen looks as good on paper.

Formatting Individual Cells

You're not limited to formatting your table as a whole. You can also select specific cells and apply individual formatting to those cells.

Aligning Text within Cells

Word 2000 lets you align text within a cell both horizontally (left, right, center) and vertically (top, bottom, middle). To align your text horizontally and vertically at the same time, make sure you have the Tables and Borders toolbar displayed, then follow these steps:

1. Position the insertion point anywhere in the cell you want to align.

 2. Click the arrow next to the Align button on the Tables and Borders toolbar.

3. When the pull-down menu appears, select one of the nine combinations of horizontal and vertical alignment.

TIP You can set horizontal alignment separately by clicking one of the four alignment buttons on Word's Formatting toolbar. You can set vertical alignment separately by selecting Table ➤ Table Properties to display the Table Properties dialog box, then selecting the Cell tab and choosing one of the three Vertical Alignment options.

Pay particular attention to your text's vertical alignment. If some cells in a row have a lot of text and some have little, determine whether you want the short-text cells to have the text sitting on top of the cell with lots of white space below, sitting on the bottom of the cell with lots of white space above, or centered in the middle of the cell with equal amounts of white space above and below. Typically, you'll want to use Bottom alignment for cells in your header row, and either Top or Center alignment for cells in the main part of your table—although this can vary by design and personal preference.

Changing Text Orientation

 If you're using the far-left column of your table for row labels—and the cells within the table itself are deep with text—you may want to make the column labels narrower by rotating the label text 90 degrees. As you can see in Figure 14.7, this creates a much more efficient table—and a nice-looking effect.

FIGURE 14.7
Rotate row labels 90 degrees for a more efficient table.

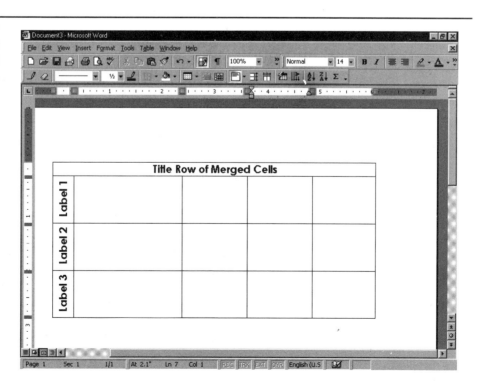

To change the orientation of text within a cell, follow these steps:

1. Position the insertion point anywhere within the cell with the text you want to rotate.

2. Select Format ≻ Text Direction to display the Text Direction dialog box.

3. Select one of the two vertical directions for your text.

4. Click OK.

TIP If you change the orientation of your text 90 degrees, you'll probably also want to change the vertical alignment to Middle—so that the text is centered vertically.

Setting Cell Margins

As you learned earlier in this chapter, you can configure all the cells in your table with global margin settings. You can also change the margins for any individual cell within your table.

To change the margins for any specific cell, follow these steps:

1. Position the insertion point anywhere in the cell you want to configure, then select Table ≻ Table Properties to display the Table Properties dialog box.

2. Select the Cell tab and click the Options button to display the Cell Options dialog box.

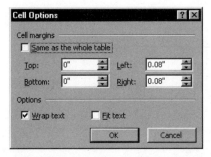

3. To configure this cell's margins differently from the table's global margins, *uncheck* the Same as the Whole Table option.

4. Set the Top, Bottom, Left, and Right margins separately.

5. Click OK.

The Cell Options dialog box includes two other extremely useful options:

Wrap Text   Check this option to make sure that if you enter too much text into your cell, it automatically wraps to a new line (and expands the cell height to accommodate the extra line). This option is enabled by default.

Fit Text   This option is the opposite of the Wrap Text option. When Fit Text is enabled, the font size of the text in a cell is reduced until all the text fits within the current cell width.

 TIP   Most users prefer to turn Wrap Text on and Fit Text off to maintain a consistent look within their tables.

Applying Cell Borders and Shading

Just as you can apply border styles and shading to your entire table, you can also apply *different* border styles and shading to specific cells. Just follow these steps:

1. Select the entire cell you want to format, then select Format ➢ Borders and Shading to display the Borders and Shading dialog box.

2. Click the Borders tab to change the top, left, right, or left border of the selected cell; make sure Cell is selected in the Apply To list.

3. Click the Shading tab to change the shading for the selected cell; make sure Cell is selected in the Apply To list.

4. Click OK to apply the formatting.

Figure 14.8 shows a table with different border and shading formatting applied to cells within the table.

FIGURE 14.8
A well-formatted table—complete with individual cell borders and shading

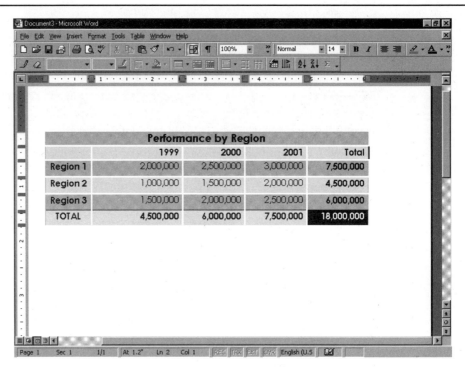

Working with Cell Contents

A pretty table is nice, but a table that actually works for you can be even better. Although most users tend to use Word tables just for text, you can also have Word sort the text in a table, number the cells within a table, and turn your table into a mini-spreadsheet—complete with mathematical calculations.

Sorting Cells

Once you've entered text or numbers into a table, you might want to reorder the way this data appears. Word 2000 offers the option of sorting the cells within your table by any column—and subsorting the results by a second and third column.

To sort your table, follow these steps:

1. Select all the rows and columns in your table that you want to sort—including the header row.

2. Select Table ➢ Sort to display the Sort dialog box.

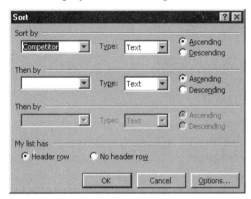

 TIP For quick, uncomplicated, single-column sorting, select your rows and columns and click either the Ascending Sort or the Descending Sort buttons on the Tables and Borders toolbar.

3. If your table has a header row, check the Header Row option; if not, check No Header Row.

4. Pull down the Sort By list and select which column you want to sort by.

5. Pull down the Type list and select what type of data is in the selected column (text, number, or date).

6. Check whether you want to sort in Ascending (1, 2, 3 or a, b, c) or Descending (3, 2, 1 or c, b, a) order.

 TIP If you want your sorting to be case-sensitive (so that *a* sorts before *A*), click the Options button in the Sort dialog box; when the Sort Options dialog box appears, check the Case Sensitive option and click OK.

7. If you want to subsort by a second column, select a column in the Then By list, select the Type of data, and choose an Ascending or Descending sort.

8. If you want to subsort by a *third* column, fill in the information in the last Then By section.

9. Click OK to sort your table.

WARNING If you don't select all the cells in your table, your data will appear out of alignment—you'll have columns associated with the wrong rows at some point. If this happens to you, select Edit ➢ Undo Sort to undo your sort, then reselect the cells in your table and start over again.

Word sorts your table, sorting by the first column first, then sorting those results by the second column (if selected), then sorting *those* results by the third column (if selected).

MASTERING THE OPPORTUNITIES

Sorting Text *Anywhere* in Your Document

Although Word's Sort command is located on the Table menu (and, in limited form, as buttons on the Tables and Borders toolbar), you can use the Sort command to sort data *anywhere* in your document—within a table or not.

When you use the Sort command outside of a table, it sorts any selected text by *paragraph*. So if you select four paragraphs and initiate a sort, the paragraphs will be sorted in alphabetical order—with a paragraph starting with the word *ABBA* placed in front of a paragraph starting with the word *Zorro*.

Nontable sorting is particularly useful if you have long bulleted lists. You can enter the list text in any order, then use the Sort command to re-sort the bullets in alphabetical order.

To sort nontable text, follow these steps:

1. Select the text you want to sort—typically, multiple paragraphs or multiple list items.

2. Select Table ➢ Sort to display the Sort dialog box.

3. Make sure that Paragraphs is selected in the Sort By list.

4. Pull down the Type list and select either text, number, or date.

5. Check whether you're sorting in Ascending or Descending order.

6. Click OK.

Numbering Cells within Your Table

Just as you can have Word automatically number the lines in your document (see Chapter 9), you can also have Word automatically number the cells within your table. Just follow these steps:

1. Select the cells you want to number.

2. Click the Numbering button on Word's Formatting toolbar.

 TIP   If you want to number only the rows in your table, select just the first column of cells.

Working with Formulas and Functions

If you're entering numbers into your table, chances are you want to *do something* with those numbers. You may want to insert a *total* line at the bottom of a column of numbers or multiply the contents of two columns together to use as a third column. These tasks are easily done in a spreadsheet program (such as Microsoft Excel), but most users are unaware that you can perform simple calculations from within a Word table—essentially turning your table into a mini-spreadsheet.

Quick Totals

The most common calculation is totaling a column or row of numbers. Since this function is so popular, Word put an AutoSum button on the Tables and Borders toolbar so that you can perform this calculation with a single button click.

Here's how it works:

1. Position the insertion point in a blank cell at the bottom of a column of numbers or in a blank cell at the end of a row of numbers.

2. Click the AutoSum button on the Tables and Borders toolbar.

AutoSum automatically totals all the numbers in the previous cells and inserts the total in the current cell.

 WARNING   Unlike similar functions in spreadsheets, an AutoSum total does *not* automatically update if numbers in the preceding cells are changed. If you change the data in your table, select the summed cell and press F9 to update the field.

Note that AutoSum totals only those cells that contain numbers; it stops its calculation with the first nonnumeric cell. Also note that an empty cell is *not* counted as a zero, but as a nonnumeric cell, and will stop the AutoSum calculation.

Simple Formulas

You can create simple formulas within any Word table cell, using common algebraic operators such as + and – to add and subtract. In addition to the algebraic operators, Word formulas can also contain numbers, references to cells within your table, and *functions*.

You insert formulas into your cells via the Formula dialog box. Just position the insertion point in the cell that will contain the formula, and then choose Table ➢ Formula to display the Formula dialog box. You enter your formula into the Formula box (at the top of the Formula dialog box), starting with an equal sign (=), and then enter the rest of your formula *after* the equal sign.

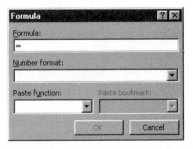

 NOTE When you select Table ➢ Formula, Word guesses which formula or function you want to use and inserts its guess in the Formula box in the Formula dialog box. If this is the correct formula, accept it as is; if Word guessed wrong, delete this formula and enter your own.

For example, if you want to add one plus two, enter this formula into the Formula box: **=1+2**. When you click OK, the result (or *value*) of the formula is displayed in the selected cell.

Table 14.4 lists the operations (and associated operators) you can use in a Word formula.

TABLE 14.4: WORD FORMULA OPERATIONS AND OPERATORS	
Operation	**Operator**
Add	+
Subtract	–
Multiply	*
Divide	/
Percentage	%
Powers and roots	^
Equal to	=
Less than	<
Less than or equal to	<=
Greater than	>
Greater than or equal to	>=
Not equal to	<>

 NOTE A Word table formula is actually one of Word's calculated *fields*. To learn more about Word fields, see Chapter 12.

Referencing Table Cells

You're not limited to adding straight numbers in your formulas. You can also reference other cells within your table.

Although not formally labeled as such, every cell in your table has a specific name. A cell's name is a combination of its column and row locations. The first column in your table is column A, the second column is B, the third is C, and so on. The first row in your table is row 1, the second row is 2, the third is 3, and so on. So the cell in the top-left corner of your table—residing in both column A and row 1—is dubbed A1. The cell to the right of it is B1; the cell just below B1 is B2.

You can use these cell names—called *references*—within your formulas. For example, if you want to add the first two cells in the first column, enter this formula: **=A1+A2**.

You can also reference a *range* of cells. In naming a *range reference*, you use the names of the first and the last cells in the range, separated by a colon (:). So, for example, if you want to name the range that starts with cell A1 and ends with cell A10, name the range A1:A10. Since ranges can span multiple rows and columns, it's not uncommon to see a range name like A1:C10 (which includes cells from ten different rows and three different columns).

TIP You can name a cell or range of cells using Word's bookmark function, and then include the name of the bookmark within the table formula. For example, if you bookmark a cell and name it YEARLYSALES, you can calculate the average monthly sales with the formula =YEARLYSALES/12.

Using Functions

In addition to the basic algebraic operators, Word includes a variety of *functions* that replace the complex steps present in many complex formulas. For example, if you want to total all the cells in column A, you can enter the formula **=A1+A2+A3+A4**—or you can use the SUM function, which lets you sum a column or row of numbers without having to type every cell into the formula. In short, a function is a type of prebuilt formula.

You enter a function in the following format: *=function(argument)*, where *function* is the name of the function and *argument* is the range of cells or other data you want to calculate. In the example presented in the previous paragraph, to sum cells A1 through A4, you'd use the following function-based formula: **=SUM(A1:A4)**.

You can easily add a function to your formula from within the Formula dialog box. Just follow these steps:

1. Position the insertion point within the Formula box where you want to add the function.

2. Pull down the Paste Function list and select the function you want to insert.

3. The function is now inserted in the Formula box, with the insertion point positioned between the parentheses; enter the argument for this function.

4. Click OK to insert the completed formula into the current cell in your table.

As an example, if you want to average the numbers contained in cells A1 through B10, enter the formula **=AVE(A1:B10)**. You can also create more complex formulas, such as =AVE(A1:B10)+AVE(C1:D10) or =SUM(A1:A4)/10.

TIP Using Word to perform complex calculations can be an exercise in frustration—Word is a word processor, after all, not a spreadsheet program. If you need to perform anything beyond a simple calculation, consider using Microsoft Excel to do the calculating, and then importing the Excel worksheet into your Word document. (See Chapter 32 for more information on using Word and Excel together.)

Creating Complex Equations

In addition to using the formulas that perform actual calculations, Word can create complex scientific and mathematical equations. These equations don't actually equate (you have to use Word's formulas for that), but they are essential if you're creating scientific or technical documents.

Word creates equations using the Equation Editor applet. You launch Equation Editor and create an equation in the following way:

1. Anchor the insertion point where you want to add the equation.

2. Select Insert ➤ Object to open the Object dialog box.

3. Select the Create New tab.

4. Select Microsoft Equation 3.0 from the Object Type list and click OK.

5. Word inserts an equation object in your document and displays the Equation toolbar. The top row of the toolbar contains mathematical symbols, while the bottom row contains templates or frameworks with additional symbols. Click each button to display a menu with additional symbols and options.

Top Row Contains More
Than 150 Mathematical Symbols

Bottom Row Contains
Templates and Frameworks

6. Build the equation by selecting symbols from the Equation toolbar and typing variables and numbers from the keyboard.

When you're done editing your equation, click anywhere else in your Word document to close the Equation Editor and return to the Word workspace. Figure 14.9 shows the kind of equation you can create with Equation Editor.

FIGURE 14.9
*Use the Equation Editor
to build complex
scientific and
mathematical
equations.*

$$\sum_{i-1}^{n} x_i^2$$

CHAPTER **15**

Creating Charts and Graphs

Understanding Microsoft Graph 2000   420

Creating a graph from existing data   422

Creating a linked graph   422

Positioning and configuring graph objects   424

Adding a border and shadow   427

Editing your graph data   427

Changing graph types   432

Adding elements to your graph   434

Formatting 3-D charts   451

In Chapter 14, you learned how to display numeric data in tables. Some readers like to have their data presented this way; they think in terms of rows and columns and discrete data points, and they are probably capable of performing complex calculations in their heads.

Other readers, however, prefer to view data in a more visual fashion. Instead of looking at each individual number, they like to see *trends*, with the big picture presented in living color. These readers don't like tables; they like *graphs*.

Graphs can provide immediate impact for the data in your document. A pie chart with one dominant slice immediately conveys the most important data point; if presented in tabular fashion, the big number would still be just one of many numbers within the table. A line or bar chart rising unstoppably from left to right immediately conveys growth; again, those same numbers presented in a table are just numbers.

Read this chapter to master Word's powerful graphing features and add visual power to the data in your documents!

 NOTE For the purposes of this chapter, the terms *graph* and *chart* are used interchangeably. Even Microsoft confuses these two words; for instance, the command to create a graph or a chart is Insert Microsoft *Graph* 2000 *Chart*.

Understanding Microsoft Graph 2000

Word 2000 uses a separate applet to create graphs in your documents. Microsoft Graph 2000 is an extremely versatile graphing tool, functioning almost identically to the graphing functions in the Microsoft Excel 2000 spreadsheet program. When you choose to insert a graph in a Word document, Word automatically launches the Graph 2000 applet, which you then use until you finish your graph and return to Word.

Working with the Graph 2000 Applet

While Graph 2000 is open—that is, while your chart is editable—you're operating from within the Graph 2000 applet and do not have access to the rest of your document. When you move your cursor back into your document (and click to anchor the insertion point), you automatically close the Graph 2000 applet and return to Word.

While you're working in Word, the graph you created isn't "live"; it's just another object inserted into your Word document. To make it live for editing, you have to double-click it, which opens the Graph 2000 applet and makes the graph editable.

With Graph 2000 open, you have access to two parts of your graph object: the *datasheet* (a mini-spreadsheet) and the graph itself. The graph is created from data in the datasheet; you can enter data into the datasheet manually or have Word insert the data

automatically when you create a graph from existing Word data. Any time you change
the data in the datasheet, the graph is automatically updated to reflect the new data.

 NOTE Graphs created in Graph 2000 are linked to your Word documents via Microsoft's
Object Linking and Embedding (OLE) technology. To learn more about OLE, turn to Chapter 17.

Navigating the Graph 2000 Workspace

Since Graph 2000 is a separate application, it has its own workspace, menus, and toolbars. When you launch Graph 2000 from within Word, however, Graph 2000 shares the
Word workspace, but it substitutes its own toolbars and menus for the standard Word
elements. When you double-click a chart in your document, you open Graph 2000 and
switch to its interface; when you close Graph 2000, you return to the Word interface.

Refer to Figure 15.1 for an example of the Graph 2000 interface.

FIGURE 15.1
*Graph 2000 uses the
Word workspace but
substitutes its own
menus and toolbars.*

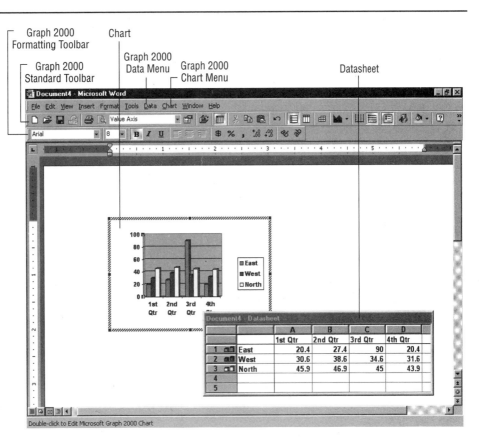

Adding a Graph to Your Document

When you're using Graph 2000, you have two ways to create a graph: from existing data in your document (from a table, for example) or from a template of dummy data that you use to create a graph from scratch. If you choose to create a graph from existing data, you can also create a "live" link to that data so that your graph changes when the data is updated.

 NOTE You can also paste graphs from Microsoft Excel into your Word documents. See Chapter 32 for more information.

Creating a Graph from Existing Data

You may already have data in a particular document. If you used Word's table commands to create a table full of data, you can use Graph 2000 to automatically display that data in a graph. And your data doesn't have to be in a table; you can take *any* data from your document, as long as it can be easily visualized in rows and columns. (For example, if you've created a table-like listing using tab stops, you can select this section of your document to graph.)

 NOTE To learn more about Word tables, see Chapter 14.

To create a graph from data in your current document, follow these steps:

1. Select the table or data listing that you want to use.
2. Select Insert ➢ Picture ➢ Chart.

Word launches Graph 2000 and creates a column chart directly underneath the data you selected.

Creating a Graph Linked to Data in Your Document

The graph you create from Word data isn't linked to the original data, which means that if you change the data in your document the Graph 2000 graph does *not* automatically update. So if you change the data, you have to open your graph and edit the datasheet manually to reflect the new data. Unless, of course, you know how to link the data from your document to your graph.

To create a graph that is linked to the data in your document (so that when your data changes, your graph is automatically updated), follow these steps:

1. Select the table or data listing that you want to use.

2. Select Edit ➢ Copy.

3. Position the insertion point where you want to add the graph to your document.

4. Select Insert ➢ Picture ➢Chart.

5. When Graph 2000 launches and creates its dummy chart, position your cursor within the datasheet, and press Ctrl+A to select the entire datasheet.

6. Press Delete to delete the dummy data from the datasheet.

7. Position the insertion point in cell A1 (top-left corner) of the datasheet, and then select Edit ➢ Paste Link.

8. When asked if you want to replace existing data, answer Yes.

Graph 2000 now pastes your selected data into the datasheet and creates the corresponding chart. Because you used the Paste Link command (instead of the standard Paste command), the graph you created is linked to the original data; so, when you change the data, the chart is updated automatically.

 TIP You can also use the above technique to have Graph 2000 graph data from other programs. Just copy the data from the other program, select Insert ➢ Picture ➢ Chart to open Graph 2000, and then select Edit ➢ Paste Link to insert the external data into Graph 2000's datasheet.

Creating a Graph from Scratch

You don't have to have data in your Word document in order to create a Graph 2000 graph. You can create graphs from scratch and then enter data directly into the Graph 2000 datasheet.

To create a graph from scratch, follow these steps:

1. Position the insertion point where you want to insert the graph.

2. Select Insert ➢ Picture ➢ Chart.

3. When the Graph 2000 workspace appears, delete the dummy data from the datasheet, and enter your new data.

Graph 2000 automatically updates the default chart with the new data you enter into the datasheet.

Positioning and Configuring Graph Objects

A Graph 2000 graph is like any other object in your Word document. You can move it, you can copy it, you can delete it, you can resize it, and you can configure how it looks and acts within your document.

As you can see in Figure 15.2, when you select your graph object (by single-clicking, *not* double-clicking), you display eight *selection handles*. When these handles are displayed, you can grab them to resize the graph object, or simply position your cursor over the graph to drag the entire object to a new position.

FIGURE 15.2
Use the selection handles to move and resize your graph.

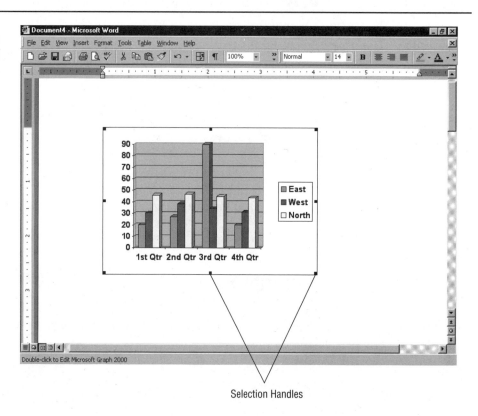

Selection Handles

 WARNING Selecting a graph is different from opening the graph. You select the graph object with a single-click and then can move or configure it as you would any other Word object. You open the graph with a double-click, and Word then switches to the Graph 2000 workspace so you can edit the graph itself.

Moving a Graph

To move your graph to another position within your document, follow these steps:

1. Click the graph to select the entire object.

2. Use your mouse to drag the graph to a new position in your document.

Alternatively, you can cut the graph from its current position and paste it into a new position, as follows:

1. Click the graph to select the entire object.

2. Select Edit ➢ Cut.

3. Move the insertion point to where you want to reposition the graph.

4. Select Edit ➢ Paste.

 TIP You can also press Shift+Del to cut and Shift+Ins to paste the graph.

Copying a Graph

To make a copy of your graph elsewhere in your document, follow these steps:

1. Click the graph to select the entire object.

2. Select Edit ➢ Copy.

3. Move the insertion point to where you want to add the copy of the graph.

4. Select Edit ➢ Paste.

When you make a copy of a graph, you copy everything about the graph, including the graph's data. Once you copy the graph, you probably want to open the copy to enter new data into the datasheet so that the new graph is truly a new graph. (If you copy a linked graph, the copy doesn't retain the links to the original data.)

 TIP When you want to replicate a particular graph format throughout your document, start each new graph by copying the original graph (to make sure you have identical formatting), and then edit the data for the new graph.

Deleting a Graph

To delete a graph from your document, follow these steps:

1. Click the graph to select the entire object.
2. Press Delete.

When you delete a graph, you also delete the corresponding datasheet.

Resizing a Graph

To resize a graph on your page, follow these steps:

1. Click the graph to select the entire object.
2. Grab one of the selection handles on the outside of the object.
3. Use your mouse to drag the handle to a new position, thus resizing the graph.

 TIP Be aware that resizing a graph object can distort the contents of the graph itself. (This is because the graph was created to fill a particular size space; when you resize the space without resizing the graph contents, Graph 2000 and Word have to stretch or squish the graph contents to match.) A better way to resize a graph is to open the graph first and then resize the graph object from within Graph 2000, which then automatically resizes the graph contents at the same time. When you return to Word, the object is resized and the graph contents are adjusted accordingly.

Setting Text Wrapping

As with any object in a Word document, you can configure how you want text to wrap around the object on your page. To adjust text wrapping for your graph object, follow these steps:

1. Click the graph to select the entire object.
2. Select Format ➢ Object to display the Format Object dialog box.
3. Select the Layout tab.
4. Select a Wrapping Style (In Line with Text, Square, Tight, Behind Text, or In Front of Text).
5. Click OK to apply the text-wrapping format.

TIP For more precise positioning and text-wrapping options, click the Advanced button on the Layout tab. See Chapter 16 for more information on formatting objects on a page.

Adding a Border and Shadow

You can also add a border around your graph object and add a drop shadow to that border. Just follow these steps:

1. Click the graph to select the entire object.
2. Select Format ➢ Borders and Shading to display the Borders dialog box.
3. Select the Borders tab.
4. Select a border style from the Setting list.
5. If you want to create a custom border, use the Style, Color, and Width controls to apply specific borders to particular sides (or all sides) of the graph.
6. Make sure Picture is selected in the Apply To list.
7. Click OK to apply the border.

To apply a border with a drop shadow, select the Shadow setting.

Editing Your Graph Data

Any time you need to change the data on which your graph is based, you have to open the chart and make changes within the graph's datasheet (unless, of course, you created a linked graph, as described previously). Just double-click the graph in your document, and the Word workspace should change to the Graph 2000 workspace, with the datasheet displayed and ready for editing.

 If the datasheet is not visible in the Graph 2000 workspace, click the View Datasheet button to toggle on the datasheet display. Click the button a second time to hide the datasheet window.

Changing Numbers

You edit the contents of a Graph 2000 datasheet as you'd edit the contents of a Word table or Excel spreadsheet. Use the mouse or the keyboard arrow keys to move from cell to cell; use the Delete and Backspace keys to delete cell contents; and use the keyboard to type new data into any selected cell.

In addition, you might find a dozen or so other operations useful when adding data to and deleting data from a large datasheet. Table 15.1 details these editing commands.

TABLE 15.1: GRAPH 2000 DATASHEET COMMANDS

Operation	Keyboard Shortcut
Enter the current time	Ctrl+Shift+;
Enter today's date	Shift+;
Move to beginning of row	Home
Move to cell A1	Ctrl+Home
Move to end of row	End
Move to last cell in datasheet	Ctrl+End
Move to the next cell	Tab
Move to the previous cell	Shift+Tab
Open a non-empty cell for editing	F2
Select entire column	Ctrl+Spacebar
Select entire datasheet	Ctrl+A
Select entire row	Shift+Spacebar

Changing Data Orientation

In a typical two-dimensional chart, you have two axes: the *category axis* (also called the *x-axis*) and the *value axis* (also called the *y-axis*). Typically, the category axis is non-numeric, while the value axis plots numeric values. For example, in the graph in Figure 15.3, the category axis runs along the bottom of the chart and the value axis runs along the left side.

 TIP If you're looking at a bar chart, the direction the bars "grow" represents the value axis.

When Graph 2000 looks at the data in your datasheet, it needs to know what is what—whether the row heading or the column heading should represent the categories in your graph. To switch between row headings and column headings for your graph's category axis, use the By Row and By Column buttons on Graph 2000's Standard toolbar.

FIGURE 15.3
*Figuring out a
graph's categories
and data values*

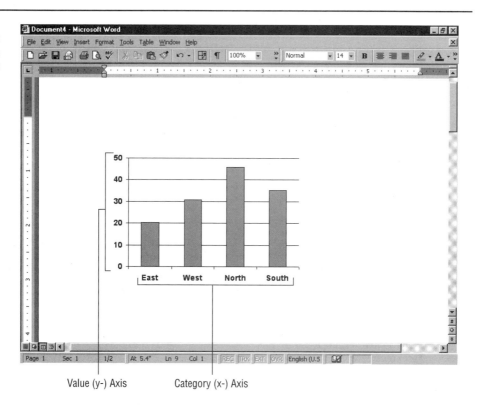

Value (y-) Axis   Category (x-) Axis

Creating Visual
Documents

 TIP If you select the row heading for the category axis, then the column heading represents additional *series* of data, and vice versa. Additional series are displayed side-by-side on the category axis in 2-D charts, or on a separate *z-axis* in 3-D charts. If you're creating a pie chart, only the first series is plotted.

As an example, let's consider the datasheet represented in Figure 15.4.

 When you click the By Row button, Graph 2000 arranges things by row and uses the datasheet's column headings as the graph's category axis, as shown in Figure 15.5.

FIGURE 15.4
Determine whether the row headings or the column headings represent the graph's categories.

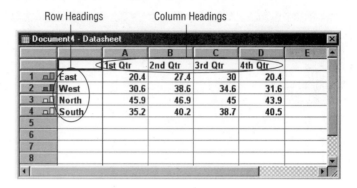

FIGURE 15.5
A chart with column headings used for the category axis

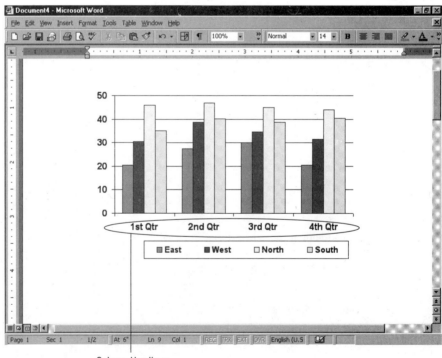

Column Headings

When you click the By Heading button, Graph 2000 arranges things by heading and uses the datasheet's row headings as the graph's category axis, as shown in Figure 15.6. This is essentially a 90-degree flip of the graph in Figure 15.5.

FIGURE 15.6
*A chart with row
headings used for the
category axis*

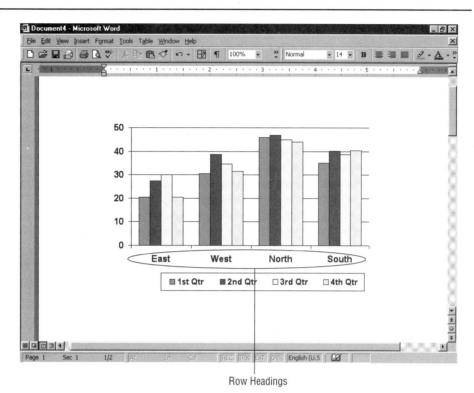

Row Headings

This is more than a little confusing, so if you're not sure how your data should graph, click back and forth between the By Row and By Heading buttons until your data displays as you want it.

Formatting Datasheet Numbers

When you apply number formats to your datasheet, this formatting is also applied to the corresponding data in your Graph 2000 graph. Here's how to apply number formats to your datasheet data:

1. Select the cells to format.

2. Click one of the number format buttons on the Graph 2000 Formatting toolbar, *or*

   Select Format ➢ Number to display the Format Number dialog box, select a format from the Category list, and select a desired configuration for this number format. Click OK to apply the format.

You don't have to apply number formatting within your datasheet, because you can format the numbers separately within the graph itself.

TIP While you can use character formatting (bold, italic, and so on) to format your data in the datasheet, this formatting is not carried over to the corresponding chart. For this reason, you probably shouldn't waste the time prettying up your datasheets; in this instance, bare functionality is the most efficient course of action.

Formatting Your Graph

Once your graph is created, you now have a plethora of formatting options available. You can change the chart type, the chart color, and the chart background and gridlines; in short, you can totally customize the way you display data visually within your document!

To edit your graph, you first have to reopen Graph 2000. As you probably remember, you do this by double-clicking on the graph in your document; this should make the graph "live" and change the Word workspace to the Graph 2000 workspace. To return to Word, just move your cursor off the graph, back onto your document, and then click your mouse.

Changing Graph Types

Graph 2000 includes a variety of built-in graph types. You should pick the chart type that best reflects the type of data you're presenting, realizing, of course, that you will have plenty of opportunities to reformat the standard charts to your personal tastes.

There are two ways to change graph types: the quick way and the powerful way.

Changing Your Graph from the Toolbar

A total of 18 graph types are available from a pull-down menu on Graph 2000's Standard toolbar. If you want to use one of these graph types, follow these steps:

 1. From within Graph 2000, click the arrow next to the Chart Type button on the Standard toolbar to display the pull-down menu.

2. Click a specific graph type.

Graph 2000 now applies the chosen graph type to the open graph.

Changing Your Graph—with Options

If you want to choose from a greater variety of graph types and gain the capability of choosing from additional sub-types and custom types, then you need to use the Chart Type dialog box. Follow these steps:

1. From within Graph 2000, select Chart ➤ Chart Type to display the Chart Type dialog box.

2. Select the Standard Types tab.

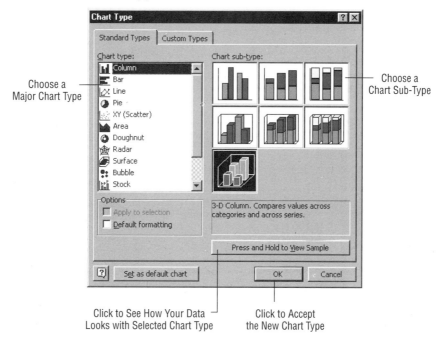

Choose a
Major Chart Type

Choose a
Chart Sub-Type

Click to See How Your Data
Looks with Selected Chart Type

Click to Accept
the New Chart Type

3. Select one of the major chart types from the Chart Type list.

4. Select a variation on the chart type from the Chart Sub-Type list.

5. To view how your data will look in the selected chart type, click the Press and Hold to View Sample button.

6. Click OK to apply the new chart type to your data.

 TIP If you want to apply the default chart formatting (for fonts, colors, and so on) and lose any formatting you've applied to your existing chart, check the Default Formatting option.

Once you've changed the chart type, you can then reformat the chart in a number of ways, including adding additional elements to the graph.

MASTERING THE OPPORTUNITIES

Using and Creating Custom Charts

If you select the Custom Types tab in the Chart Type dialog box, you see a list of 20 additional chart types. These chart types are all custom-designed to demonstrate some of Graph 2000's most interesting formatting features. While most of these chart types are more interesting than they are useful, you can select and use any of these types just as you would the built-in chart types on the Standard Types tab.

What *is* useful about the Custom Types tab is that you can use it to store chart types that you create. Once you've applied all the custom formatting you want to your chart (read the rest of this chapter for more information about that), select Chart ≻ Chart Type to open the Chart Type dialog box, and then select the Custom Types tab. Check the User-Defined option, and then click the Add button to display the Add Custom Chart Type dialog box. Enter a name for your new chart type in the Name box and a short description in the Description box; when you click OK, Graph 2000 adds your newly created chart type to the custom types list. When you want to reapply your custom formatting to future charts, all you have to do is access the Custom Types tab, check the User-Defined option, and choose your personal chart type from the Chart Type list.

TIP By default, Graph 2000 opens every new graph as a clustered column chart. If you'd rather have your new graphs created as a different type by default, select the chart type on either the Standard Types tab or the Custom Types tab, and click the Set as Default Chart option. The next time you insert a new graph, it will be created using the chart type you just selected.

Adding Elements to Your Graph

By default, every new graph has a legend, x- and y-axis labels, a gray background, and horizontal gridlines. You can delete or change any of the graph elements shown in Figure 15.7 or add additional elements to better define your graph.

FIGURE 15.7

*Elements of the
default graph*

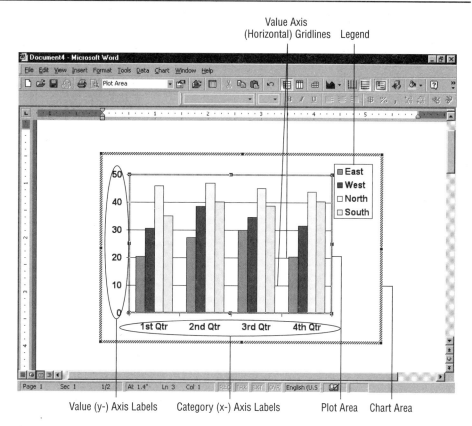

Value Axis
(Horizontal) Gridlines   Legend

Value (y-) Axis Labels   Category (x-) Axis Labels   Plot Area   Chart Area

Adding a Title

One of the first things you may want to add to your graph is a title. To add a graph
title, follow these steps:

1. From within Graph 2000, select Chart ➢ Chart Options to display the Chart
Options dialog box.

2. Select the Titles tab.

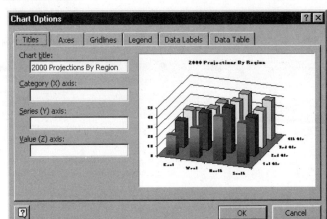

3. Enter a title into the Chart Title box.

4. Click OK.

Once you've added a title, you can format the font, size, style, and color of the title text by double-clicking the title text box in the graph and choosing specific settings from the Format Chart Title dialog box.

TIP You can also use the Titles tab to create titles for the category and value axes. If you add titles to these axes, the titles appear either below or to the side of the axes labels.

Adding Data Labels

Sometimes readers might have a difficult time ascertaining specific values for the bars, columns, lines, or slices in your graphs. When you want your audience to have easy access to precise values, add those values directly to the data points in your graph.

Depending on the chart type selected, Graph 2000 lets you add some combination of the following labels to any point, bar, chart, or slice in your graph:

- Value (for most chart types)
- Percent (for pie charts)
- Label (for most chart types)
- Label and percent (for pie charts)
- Bubble sizes (for bubble charts)

To add labels to all the data points within a data series (to all the related columns in a column chart, for example), follow these steps:

1. Double-click a point/bar/column/slice within the data series. (The entire series should be selected.)
2. When the Format Data Series dialog box appears, select the Data Labels tab.
3. Select the type of data label to add to this series.
4. Click OK.

 TIP If you have multiple series in your chart, you have to add data labels separately to each series.

You can also add a label to a single data point within the series. Just follow these steps:

1. *Single-click* the point/bar/column/slice to select the entire series.
2. Single-click again to select just that single point/bar/column/slice.
3. Double-click the point/bar/column/slice to open the Format Data Point dialog box.
4. Select the type of data label to add to this data point.
5. Click OK.

Adding Trendlines

Even though the points and columns may go up and down over the years, there is always a trend behind any set of data. To plot that trend as a *trendline* on top of your existing graph, follow these steps:

1. Within your graph, select the data series you want to track.
2. Select Chart ➢ Add Trendline to display the Add Trendline dialog box.
3. Select the Type tab.
4. Select the Trend/Regression type. (For most purposes, Linear is the current selection.)
5. Make sure that the correct data series is selected in the Based On Series list.
6. Click OK to add the trendline to your chart.

Creating Visual Documents

Adding Gridlines and Borders

To add or delete gridlines for any axis on your chart, follow these steps:

1. Select your chart's plot area.

2. Select Chart ➢ Chart Options to display the Chart Options dialog box.

3. Select the Gridlines tab.

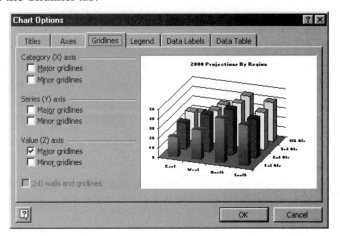

4. To display standard gridlines for a specific axis, check the Major Gridlines option for that axis.

5. To display minor gridlines for a specific axis, check the Minor Gridlines option for that axis.

6. Uncheck the option for any gridline you don't want to display.

7. Preview your chart with and without gridlines in the preview panel.

8. Click OK to apply the current gridline selection.

 TIP In most cases, adding minor gridlines creates too much visual clutter in your chart, so stick to major gridlines whenever possible.

Adding a Legend

You use a legend in your chart to distinguish between different data series. Let's say that you were tracking sales in four different regions (east, west, north, and south) over four different years. If you create a column chart, you probably want to display the years on the category axis (along the bottom of the chart); the sales level obviously becomes the value axis (along the left side of the chart). Within each year, then, columns (in different colors) are displayed for each of your four regions. How does the reader know that the red columns represent the east region, and the blue columns represent the west? Via the legend, of course.

Legends appear in little boxes that can be displayed anywhere on your chart. By default, Graph 2000 places the legend in the upper-right corner of the graph, but you can move and resize it so that it stretches across the bottom, floats in the upper left, or appears anywhere you place it.

You can also format your legend in a number of ways. In addition to changing its shape (using the selection handles), you can change the shading, border, and font type, style, size, and color, and you can even add a drop shadow behind the border. For a different effect, eliminate the shading and border completely so that the legend text and series references appear to be floating over your chart.

Follow these steps to add and format a legend:

1. From within your graph, click the Legend button on the Standard toolbar. This adds a legend to the top-right corner of your chart.

2. To format the legend, double-click the legend box to display the Format Legend dialog box.

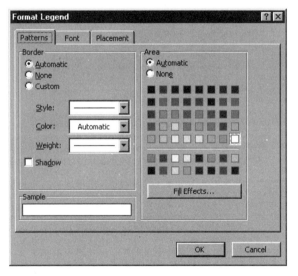

3. To change the border and shading of the legend box, select the Patterns tab, and make the appropriate selections.

4. To add a drop shadow behind the legend box, check the Shadow option on the Patterns tab.

5. To change the text within the legend box, select the Font tab, and make the appropriate selections.

6. To choose from one of five preset positions for your legend (Bottom, Corner, Top, Right, and Left), select the Placement tab, and make a selection.

7. Click OK to close the Format Legend dialog box.

8. To manually reposition your legend, grab the box with your mouse, and drag it into a new position.

 TIP When you choose an automatic legend position, Graph 2000 automatically resizes and repositions your graph accordingly. If you manually move your legend, you may need to resize or reposition your graph's plot area to prevent the legend from overlapping the presentation of critical data.

9. To resize or reshape your legend, grab one of the selection handles with your mouse, and drag it to create a new legend shape. Note that when you stretch or condense your legend, the legend text and series references automatically reposition themselves accordingly.

To delete a legend, simply select it and press Delete, or click the Legend button on the Standard toolbar to toggle off the legend display.

Adding Callouts

Once you have your graph sized, positioned, and formatted exactly where you want it, you can add *callouts* to point out specific items of interest. For example, you might want to call out an unusual data point or a data series with extraordinary importance.

You have to add a callout manually, using a text box and an arrow. Here's what you do:

 1. From within your graph, click the Drawing button on the Standard toolbar to display the Drawing toolbar.

 2. Click the Text Box button on the drawing toolbar.

3. Use the mouse to draw a text box on your graph where you want to insert the callout text.

4. Click within the text box, and type the text for your callout.

5. To change the formatting of the callout text, select all the text within the text box, and then use the text formatting commands (bold, italic, and so on) on the Formatting toolbar. Alternatively, you can select Format ➢ Font to display the Format Text Box dialog box, select the Font tab, and make the appropriate selections there.

6. You probably want the text to appear to float over your graph, with no border or shading to the text box. To format the text box, double-click the text box (*not*

the text inside) to display the Format Text Box dialog box, and then make the appropriate selections from the Colors and Lines tab.

7. Once the textbox is added and formatted, click the Arrow button on the Drawing toolbar.

8. Use your mouse to draw a line from the textbox to the data point you want to point to.

 WARNING If you draw the line from the data point to the text box, the arrowhead will be pointing in the wrong direction!

9. To format the line you just drew, double-click the line to display the Format AutoShape dialog box.

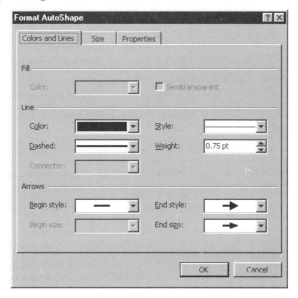

10. Select the Colors and Lines tab to adjust the line's color, style, weight, and end (arrow) style. Click OK when done.

You can move the callout within your chart by grabbing the textbox with your mouse and dragging it to a new position. Note, however, that if you move the textbox you'll also have to reposition the end of the callout's line.

Formatting the Chart and Plot Areas

Your chart has two different interior areas that can be formatted separately. As shown back in Figure 15.7, the entire interior of the chart is called the *chart area*; the area bordered by the *x*- and *y*- axes is called the *plot area*. The formatting you apply to the chart area affects the entire background of the chart; any formatting you apply to the plot area takes precedence (for the plot area *only*) over your chart area formatting.

 TIP Sometimes it's difficult to select either the chart area or plot area within your graph. To make sure you have the correct area selected for formatting, pull down the Chart Objects list on the Standard toolbar, select either Chart Area or Plot Area, and *then* begin your formatting.

Formatting the Chart Area

To format the chart area, follow these steps:

1. Select your graph's chart area.

2. Select Format ➢ Selected Chart Area to display the Format Chart Area dialog box.

3. Select the Patterns tab.

4. By default, the chart area is not bordered. To apply an automatic border, check the Automatic option in the Border section. To apply a custom border, check the Custom option, and then select a specific Style, Color, and Weight for the border.

5. To apply a drop shadow to the chart area, check the Shadow option.

6. By default, the chart area does not have a shaded background, so the chart in your document automatically picks up your document's background color. To add a color background to the chart area, select a color from the Area section, or click the Fill Effects button to display the Fill Effects dialog box. (See the "Fancy Fills" sidebar later in this chapter for more information on the options in this dialog box.)

7. To change the default text for your entire chart, click the Font tab, and make the appropriate selections. If you want the fonts to automatically rescale if you resize your graph, check the Auto Scale option.

8. Click OK to apply your changes.

Changing the Plot Area

To format the plot area, which only affects the area inside the *x*- and *y*-axes, follow these steps:

1. Select your graph's plot area.

2. Select Format ➢ Selected Plot Area to display the Format Plot Area dialog box.

3. To change the border around the plot area, check the Custom option in the Border section, and then select a specific Style, Color, and Weight for the border.

4. To change background fill in the plot area, select a color from the Area section, or click the Fill Effects button to display the Fill Effects dialog box. (Once again, see the "Fancy Fills" sidebar later in this chapter for more information on the options in this dialog box.)

5. Click OK to apply your changes.

 TIP Sometimes Graph 2000 resizes the plot area in ways that minimize the size of your graph. You can select the plot area and use your mouse to move it around the total chart area, or resize it to shrink or increase the size of the graph.

Formatting Axes and Gridlines

Graph 2000 enables you to format the scale, tick marks, and fonts used for each axis individually. You can also format the gridlines displayed for any axis.

Configuring Axis Settings

To format an axis, you must first select the axis. You should be able to do this by clicking anywhere on the axis border or text; if you find it difficult to select the axis itself (and not the entire plot area), just pull down the Chart Objects list on the Standard toolbar, and select either Category Axis or Value Axis.

You have to format each axis separately, following this procedure:

1. Select the axis to format.

2. Select Format ➤ Selected Axis to display the Format Axis dialog box.

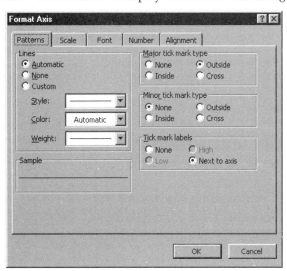

3. To format the axis border and tick marks (the little lines corresponding to the axis text), select the Patterns tab. To format the border, choose a line Style,

Color, and Weight from the Lines section. To format the tick marks for the major value or category labels, choose one of the four options (Inside, Outside, Cross, or None) from the Major Tick Mark Type section. If you want to display minor tick marks (and you typically won't), make a similar selection from the Minor Tick Mark Type section. To change where the tick mark labels appear (Next to Axis, High, Low, or None), make a selection from the Tick Mark Labels section.

4. To format the *scale* of the selected axis (typically represented by the gridline on your chart) select the Scale tab. To accept Graph 2000's default scale, make sure that all the boxes in the Auto column are checked. To change the scale displayed (if you think there are too many gridlines, or not enough, for example), change either the Minimum value, the Maximum value, the Major Unit value (typically corresponding to the gridlines on your chart), or the Minor Unit value.

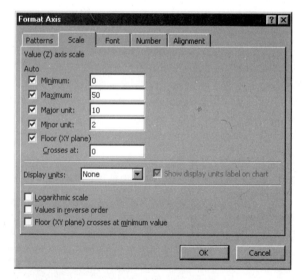

5. To format the font used for the axis text, select the Font tab, and make the appropriate selections.

6. To change the number format of the axis text, select the Number tab, and select a format from the Category list. If there are additional subformats available, choose one from the Type list.

7. To change the way your axis text is displayed, select the Alignment tab. You can accept Graph 2000's Automatic alignment, or you can change the angle of the text

with the Degrees control or by dragging the "clock hand" in the box on the right. If you want your text to be stacked vertically, click the vertical box on the left.

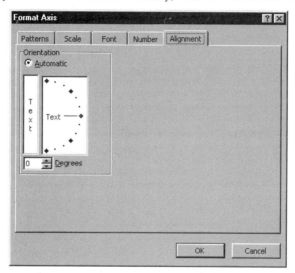

8. Click OK to apply your axis formatting.

Configuring Your Gridlines

You can change the style and color of any gridline in your chart. Just follow these steps:

1. Select the gridlines you want to change.

 TIP When you select one gridline, you select all gridlines of that type (major or minor) for the selected axis.

2. Select Format ≻ Selected Gridlines to display the Format Gridlines dialog box.
3. Select the Patterns tab.
4. You can accept the Automatic gridline format, or check the Custom option and choose a new Style, Color, and Weight.
5. Click OK to apply the new formatting.

 TIP To display gridlines for a particular axis, click either the Category Axis Gridlines or the Value Axis Gridlines button on the Standard toolbar.

Formatting Graph Text

You can format all the text in your graph at one time (using the Font tab in the Format Chart Area dialog box) or with all other text of the same type (all the text on an axis, for example). When you select the Font tab in any of the appropriate Format dialog boxes, here are the options to which you have access:

Font   You can choose a different font type (Arial, Times New Roman, etc.) from this list.

 TIP   While this isn't a hard-and-fast rule, using a sans serif font, such as Arial, is a good choice for small text within a chart, such as axis or legend text.

Font Style   From this list, you can choose to display your text as either Regular, Italic, Bold, or Bold Italic.

Size   You can choose a font size from this list.

Underline   If you want to underline your text, pull down this list, and choose from Single or Double underlines.

Color   To change the color of your text, pull down this list, and choose from one of the preselected colors.

Background   To change the background behind your text, pull down this list, and choose from Transparent or Opaque.

Effects   If desired, check either the Strikethrough, Superscript, or Subscript options.

Auto Scale   This is a confusing option, which is enabled by default. When Auto Scale is checked, the font sizes you choose can change (either larger or smaller) if you resize your graph or select parts of your graph. If you want to fix the size of your text, be sure to *uncheck* the Auto Scale box.

Remember, you can set different font attributes for different types of text within your chart; just select the text in question, and then select Format ➢ Font.

Formatting Data Series and Data Points

You can format the color and border of the columns, bars, points, and slices within most types of charts. You can change the attributes for all elements within the same data series, or you can format specific data points separately.

To format an entire data series, follow these steps:

1. Click once on any point within the series to select the entire series.

2. Select Format ➢ Selected Data Series to display the Format Data Series dialog box.

3. To change the series border, select the Patterns tab. You can accept the Automatic border, eliminate the border (by checking the None option), or format a Custom border with the Style, Color, and Weight controls. You can also select the Shadow option to display a drop shadow; this can be applied even if you choose not to use a border.

4. To change the series fill color, select the Patterns tab. You can select the Automatic color, select a new color from the Area color list, or click the Fill Effects button to display the Fill Effects dialog box, which is discussed in the "Fancy Fills" sidebar later in this chapter. If you want negative values to be displayed in a contrasting color, check the Invert if Negative option.

5. If you're formatting a line chart, you'll see a Marker section on the Patterns tab. You can accept Graph 2000's Automatic marker, choose None, or choose a new Style, Foreground color, Background color, and Size for these markers. You can also elect to add a Shadow to the marker and, from the Line section, to display the line between markers as a Smoothed Line.

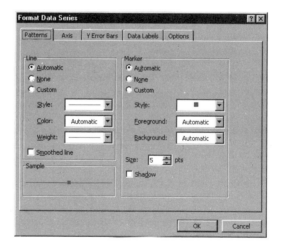

6. To add labels to the points in this data series, select the Labels tab. Depending on the chart type, you can select from the following types of labels: Value (for most chart types), Percent (for pie charts), Label (for most chart types), Label and Percent (for pie charts), and Bubble Sizes (for bubble charts).

 TIP To format a separate data point, you have to select that data point separate from the series. The easiest way to do this is to click once on the point to select the series and then to click a second time to select that specific bar/column/slice/point. (This is *not* the same as double-clicking; this is clicking once, waiting a second, and then clicking again.) Once that particular data point is selected, you can then select Format ➢ Selected Data Point to format that data point in the same manner you'd format the entire series.

The other tabs in the Format Data Series dialog box are even more specific to the type of chart you're formatting. For example, the Options tab for a column or bar chart contains settings to adjust the Overlap between columns or bars and the Gap Width (essentially the width of the individual columns or bars); it also includes an option to display each column or bar within the series in a different color (check the Vary Colors by Point option). The Options tab for a Pie chart lets you rotate the pie by adjusting the Angle of First Slice, and to Vary Colors by Slice. Whatever kind of chart you're creating, make sure you select the Options tab to see what additional settings you can adjust.

 TIP You can "explode" a pie chart by using your mouse to drag a specific slice away from the center of the pie.

 MASTERING THE OPPORTUNITIES

Fancy Fills

Most users are happy with solid color fills for their columns/bars/slices, but some powerful effects can be created when you use Graph 2000's Fill Effects dialog box (accessed from the Fill Effects button on the Patterns tab of most graph Format dialog boxes).

The Fill Effects dialog box lets you add four different types of fills to the selected data point or chart/plot background:

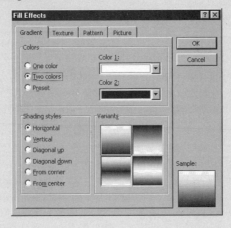

Continued ▶

Gradient   Select the Gradient tab to add a color fade to the selected element. You can choose from 24 preselected gradients (check the Preset option) or from One-Color (fading into either white or black) or Two-Color gradients. Once you select your gradient colors, you can choose the direction of the fade from the Shading Styles list. The following is an example of gradation; note how the columns appear to fade up from the *x*-axis (the bottom gradient color is set to the same color as the chart area background).

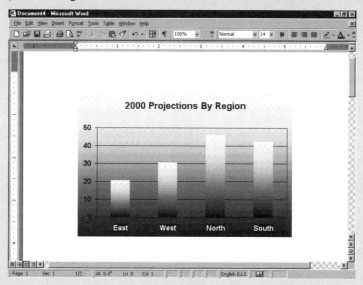

Texture   Select the Texture tab to apply a preset textured background to the selected element. Click the Other Texture button to import a graphics file to use as a background texture. The following is an example of textures.

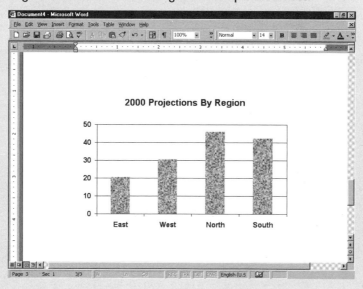

Continued ▷

Pattern Select the Pattern tab to display a one- or two-color pattern to the selected element. This option is useful if you're printing in black-and-white and need to distinguish different series in a bar, column, area, or pie chart. The following is an example of patterns.

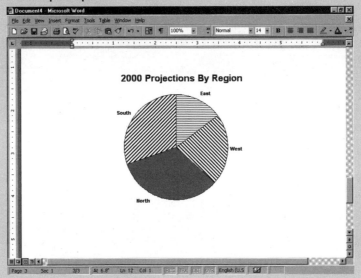

Picture Select the Picture tab to insert a picture into the selected element. While you can use this option to spruce up the chart or plot area of your graph, even more interesting effects can come when you use pictures for the bars and columns in your chart. You can opt to stretch a picture (so a single picture is used in all bars or columns, no matter what the value) or, even better, to stack multiple pictures to show larger values. The following is an example of a stacked-picture column chart.

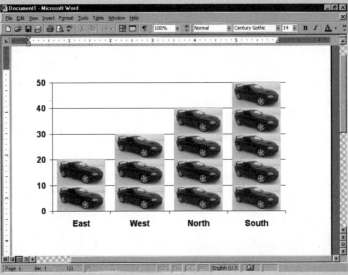

Continued ▶

For even more effective charts, you can combine different types of formatting for different elements. Don't limit yourself to Graph 2000's default fill colors and patterns; use your imagination and the Fill Effects dialog box to create truly unique graphs.

Formatting 3-D Charts

If you've created a 3-D chart of any type, you also have the option of configuring various elevation, rotation, and perspective settings. When you select Chart ➤ 3-D View, you display the 3-D View dialog box.

 NOTE The 3-D View dialog box varies somewhat, depending on whether you have a 3-D column, bar, line, area, surface, or pie chart.

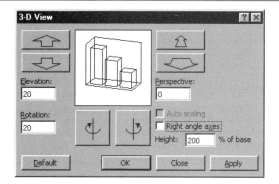

Depending on your specific chart type, the 3-D View dialog box offers the following settings:

Elevation Determines the height the chart is viewed from. A full 90-degree elevation looks down on the chart from directly above. Figure 15.8 shows two charts, one with a low elevation and one with a high elevation.

FIGURE 15.8
Changing the elevation of a 3-D chart changes the height it's viewed from.

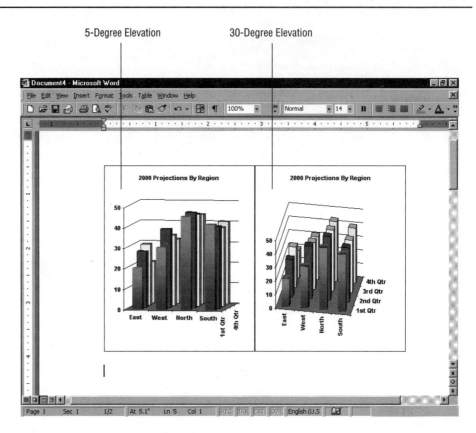

Rotation   Rotates the chart a full 360 degrees around the z-axis. Figure 15.9 shows two charts at different degrees of rotation.

TIP For many chart types, you can also manually rotate the chart by grabbing and moving the chart's selection handles with your mouse.

FIGURE 15.9
Changing the rotation
of a 3-D chart provides
different views of
complex data.

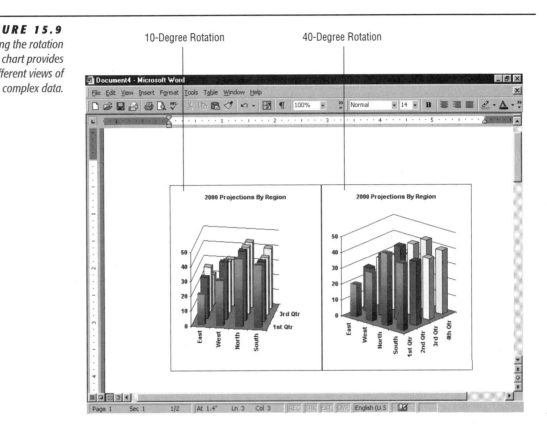

Perspective   Controls the depth of the chart. A greater perspective makes the front of the chart wider than the rear. Figure 15.10 shows how a change in perspective affects the display of your data.

 WARNING The Perspective option is unavailable for 3-D bar charts or when the Right Angle Axes option is checked.

FIGURE 15.10

Changing a 3-D chart's perspective changes the way some data is perceived.

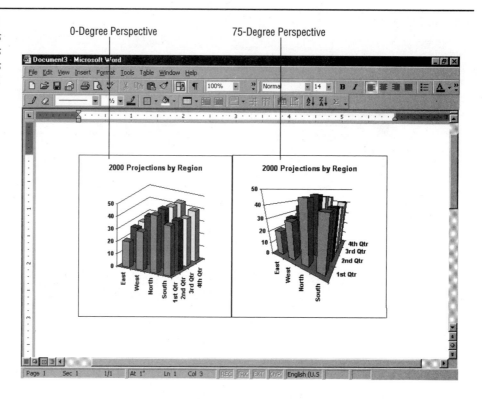

Height   Lets you adjust the percentage ratio between the height of the chart and the width of the base. A higher percentage creates a tall and narrow chart; a lower percentage creates a short and wide chart. See Figure 15.11 for some examples.

Right Angle Axes   Removes all perspective from the chart (sets the axes at right angles to each other and the height to 100 percent of the base).

Auto Scaling   Available only when Right Angle Axes is checked, automatically resizes a 3-D chart to be closer in size to its 2-D version.

TIP   Use a 3-D chart instead of a 2-D chart when you have multiple series to graph or when you want to add some depth to your bars/columns/pies/lines.

FIGURE 15.11
*Use the Height control
to create tall and
narrow or short and
wide 3-D charts.*

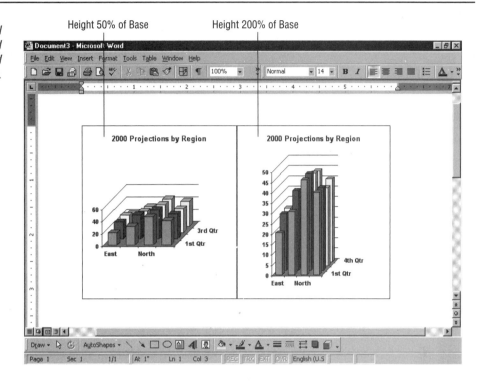

CHAPTER **16**

Adding Graphics and Drawings

Using Word clip art   460

Importing picture files   467

Adding fancy text with WordArt   472

Drawing with AutoShapes   475

Cropping unwanted elements   484

Wrapping text around objects   486

Working with borders and fills   488

Adding shadows and 3-D effects   489

In Chapter 15 you learned about *one* type of graphic object you can insert into your Word documents. Word 2000 offers several other types of graphic objects—all of which add visual interest and impact to otherwise plain-text documents.

In this chapter you'll learn how to master clip art, picture files, WordArt, and AutoShapes—how to add them to your documents and format them for maximum impact. Just remember, all text and no graphics make for a dull document!

Mastering the Drawing and Picture Toolbars—and the Format Object Dialog Box

Most of Word's graphics editing commands can be found on either the Drawing toolbar or the Picture toolbar. If you work a lot with graphics, get to know these toolbars—you'll use them often.

To display either or both of these toolbars, follow these steps:

1. Right-click any visible toolbar to display the full list of available toolbars.

2. Check which of the toolbars you want to display.

 TIP To hide a toolbar, repeat this procedure—but *uncheck* the toolbars you don't want to display.

Although these toolbars are full-featured, additional formatting options are available from the Format Object dialog box—which you can display by double-clicking the object you want to format, clicking the Format Object button on the Picture toolbar, or selecting Format ≻ Object.

Understanding the Drawing Toolbar

The Drawing toolbar is used to format practically every nontext object you insert in your documents—from text boxes to clip art, and more. This toolbar also contains the commands necessary to add AutoShapes to your document.

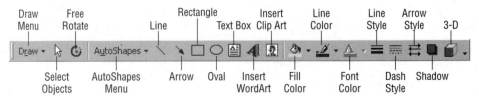

Understanding the Picture Toolbar

The Picture toolbar contains commands necessary to edit and format pictures and other graphic objects. On this toolbar you'll find the Crop and Text Wrapping commands, useful in a variety of situations.

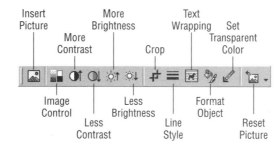

Understanding the Format Object Dialog Box

To see all your object formatting commands in one place—with additional options not available from either the Drawing toolbar or the Picture toolbar—use the Format Object dialog box. This dialog box has six different tabs filled with commands and options, as detailed in Table 16.1.

TABLE 16.1: FORMAT OBJECT DIALOG BOX COMMANDS

Tab	Description
Colors and Lines	This tab contains commands for fill color, line style and color, and arrow style.
Size	This tab contains commands for sizing, scaling, and rotating.
Layout	This tab contains commands for text wrapping and precise object placement.
Pictures	This tab is enabled only if you're formatting a picture, and contains commands for cropping and image control.
Text Box	This tab is enabled only if you're formatting a text box, and contains commands for internal margins.
Web	This tab lets you enter alternate text when your picture is displayed in a Web document.

PART
IV

Creating Visual
Documents

NOTE The Format Object dialog box never appears with the words *Format Object* in its title bar; the word *Object* always reflects the type of object you're formatting. So if you're formatting a picture, the dialog box is called the Format Picture dialog box; if you're formatting an AutoShape, it's called the Format AutoShape dialog box. Likewise, the command on the Format menu reflects the type of object you're formatting; depending on the type of object, you may select Format ➤ Picture, Format ➤ AutoShape, or Format ➤ Text Box.

Working with Different Types of Graphics

Microsoft Word 2000 lets you add a number of different types of graphics to your document—from clip art to imported pictures to freehand drawings. All are added via similar methods (from the Insert menu) and have similar general formatting (discussed in the "Formatting Graphic Objects" section later in this chapter). However, all have unique characteristics and options, so we'll look at each graphic type separately.

Using Word Clip Art

Word 2000 comes with thousands of clip-art images, stored in the Clip Gallery. Clip art consists of prepared images—typically line art, not bitmapped images—that can be incorporated in any document you create. Most of the clip-art images in the Clip Gallery are stored in the Windows metafile (.WMF) format, and can be edited and ungrouped into their separate lines and components.

The Clip Gallery includes images of everything from scenic backgrounds to pictures of people.

 NOTE A line-art image is typically a purely black and white image—with no color or gray tones—composed of a series of lines. Bitmapped images are composed of individual bits of color (or gray) that combine to create the complete image. The drawings you make with Word's AutoShape commands are line art; a .JPG or .GIF picture is a bitmap.

 TIP In addition to clip-art images, the Clip Gallery includes sounds and video clips.

Inserting Clip Art from the Gallery

Word 2000 makes it easy to insert clip-art images from the Clip Gallery. Just follow these steps:

1. Anchor the insertion point where you want to insert the image.

2. On the Drawing toolbar, click the Insert Clip Art button (or select Insert ➢ Picture ➢ Clip Art from Word's menu bar) to display the Insert ClipArt window, shown in Figure 16.1.

PART
IV

Creating Visual
Documents

FIGURE 16.1
Use the Clip Gallery to find and insert clip-art images for your documents.

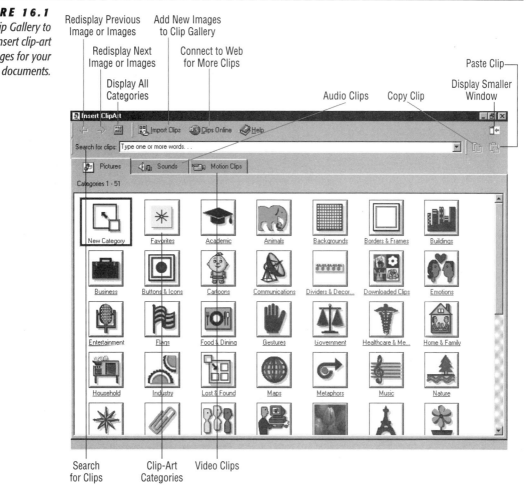

3. Select the Pictures tab.

4. To search for a specific image, enter your query in the Search for Clips box and press Enter. To display images within a major category, click the category icon.

5. To insert a specific image into your document, click the image to display the pop-up menu shown in Figure 16.2, then click the Insert Clip button.

FIGURE 16.2

Click an image to display the pop-up menu, then select Insert Clip.

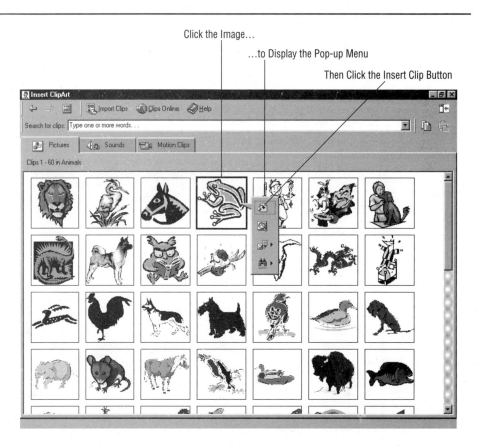

Click the Image...

...to Display the Pop-up Menu

Then Click the Insert Clip Button

 TIP You can also use your mouse to drag any image from the Clip Gallery window into your document.

Word inserts the selected clip-art image into your document at the insertion point.

NOTE The Insert ClipArt window stays open, in case you want to insert more images; close the window by clicking the window's Close button (the *X* in the top-right corner of the window).

Modifying Clip Art

If a Clip Gallery image is in the Windows metafile format (.WMF), you can convert it to a group of drawing objects—which can then be *ungrouped* and modified using tools on Word's Drawing toolbar.

 WARNING Images in non-.WMF formats—such as .BMP, .JPG, .GIF, or .PNG—cannot be converted into drawing objects and modified.

To convert and modify a .WMF image, follow these steps:

1. Select the image in your document.

2. Select Format ➢ Picture to display the Format Picture dialog box.

3. Select the Layout tab.

4. Select any wrapping style *except* In Line with Text.

5. Click OK to close the dialog box.

6. With the image still selected, move to the Drawing toolbar and select Draw ➢ Ungroup.

The single image is ungrouped into many smaller images, as shown in Figure 16.3.

Use the tools on the Drawing toolbar to modify the picture as appropriate, then *regroup* the images back into a single picture by following these steps:

1. On the Drawing toolbar, click the Select Object button.

2. Use your mouse to draw a boundary around all the images you want to regroup.

3. From the Drawing toolbar, select Draw ➢ Group.

You can now move and resize the image as a single image—which you *cannot* do while it's ungrouped into its component images.

FIGURE 16.3
*Ungrouping an image
into dozens of
component images—
each image has its own
selection handles*

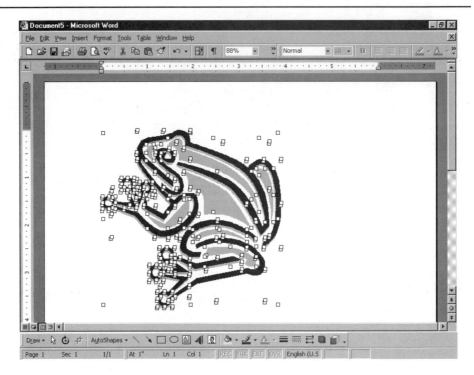

Managing the Clip Gallery

Using the Clip Gallery is an easy way to manage all the images on your hard disk. You're not limited to the initial images in the Gallery; Word also lets you add your own images and create your own categories.

Follow these steps to add your own images to the Clip Gallery:

1. From the Drawing toolbar, click the Insert Clip Art button to display the Insert ClipArt window.

2. Click the Pictures tab.

3. Select the category where you want to add the new image.

4. Click the Import Clips button to display the Add Clip to Clip Gallery dialog box.

5. Navigate to the image you want to add, then select that file.

6. To place a copy of this file in the Clip Gallery, select the Copy into Clip Gallery option. To cut this file from its current location and paste it into the Clip Gallery, select the Move into Clip Gallery option. To keep the file in its current location—and have the Clip Gallery access it there—select Let Clip Gallery Find This Clip in Its Current Folder or Volume.

7. Click the Import button to display the Clip Properties dialog box.

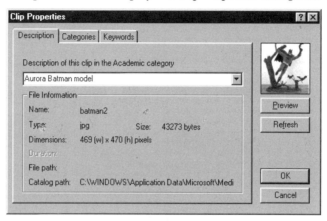

8. Click the Description tab and enter a description of this image.

9. Click the Categories tab and confirm the category (or categories) to which you want to add this image.

10. To assign a keyword to this image, click the Keywords tab, click the New Keyword button, enter a new keyword in the New Keyword dialog box, then click OK.

11. Click OK to add the image to the Clip Gallery.

 TIP To add a new category to the Clip Gallery, open the Insert ClipArt dialog box, select the Pictures tab, then click the New Category category to display the New Category dialog box. Enter a name for the new category, then click OK.

MASTERING THE OPPORTUNITIES

Other Sources of Clip Art

You're not limited to the clip-art images in Word's Clip Gallery. Many more images are available on the Internet, at a variety of Web sites.

A good place to start is Microsoft's Clip Gallery Live. When you click the Clips Online button in the Insert ClipArt dialog box, Word launches your Web browser, establishes an Internet connection, and jumps to the Clip Gallery Live Web site, where you can preview and download additional picture, sound, and movie clips.

Numerous Web sites specialize in clip-art images and other artwork, including the following:

- Art Today (www.arttoday.com)
- Barry's Clip Art Server (www.barrysclipart.com)
- ClipArtConnection (www.clipartconnection.com)
- ClipArtNow (www.clipartnow.com)
- Corbis (www.corbis.com)
- Icon Bank (www.iconbank.com)
- Mediabuilder (www.mediabuilder.com)
- Smithsonian Photo Archive (photo2.si.edu)

There are also several Web search engines and directories that let you scour the Internet for the images you need, including the following:

- About.com Web Clip Art Links (webclipart.about.com)
- Alta Vista Photo and Media Finder (image.altavista.com)
- Amazing Picture Machine (www.ncrtec.org/picture.htm)
- Arthur (www.ahip.getty.edu/arthur/)
- Clip Art Review (www.webplaces.com/html/clipart.htm)
- Clipart Directory (www.clipart.com)

Continued ▶

- Lycos Image Gallery (www.lycos.com/picturethis/)

- NCrtec Good Photograph and Image Sites (www.ncrtec.org/tools/picture/goodsite.htm)

- WebSEEk (www.ctr.columbia.edu/webseek/)

- Yahoo! Image Surfer (ipix.yahoo.com)

In addition to these Web sites, a large number of Usenet newsgroups specialize in posting images of various types. Although many of these newsgroups are erotic in nature, a large number of general-interest picture newsgroups are also available. Look in the alt.binaries.pictures.* hierarchy for the groups that focus on pictures.

Importing Picture Files

Beyond the images in Word's Clip Gallery, you can import virtually any graphics file into a Word document. Table 16.2 describes the major graphics formats with which Word can work.

TABLE 16.2: WORD-COMPATIBLE GRAPHICS FORMATS

File Format	Description
.BMP (also .RLE and .DIB)	A simple graphics format (standing for *bitmap*) that is the default format for Windows Desktop backgrounds.
.CGM	A vector graphics format, standing for *computer graphics metafile*.
.CDR	The graphics format used by CorelDRAW.
.EMF	Enhanced metafile, an enhanced version of the standard Windows metafile (.WMF) format.
.EPS	Encapsulated PostScript, a vector graphics format for high-resolution graphics.
.FPX	FlashPix format.
.GIF	A popular Web-based graphics format (pronounced "jif") .GIF files can include transparent backgrounds (so a Web-page background can show through) and multiple images for a simple animated effect.
.JPG	Another popular Web-based graphics format (pronounced "jay-peg") .JPG files are often slightly smaller than comparable GIF files.

Continued ▐▶

File Format	Description
TABLE 16.2: WORD-COMPATIBLE GRAPHICS FORMATS (CONTINUED)	
.JSH, .JAH, and .JBH	Hanako graphics formats (used in Japan).
.PCD	Kodak PhotoCD format for storing digital photographs.
.PCT	Macintosh PICT format.
.PCX	An older bitmapped graphics format (pronounced "pee-see-ex").
.PNG	Portable network graphics, a newer format not yet widely used.
.TIF	Tagged image file format (pronounced "tif")—a high-quality graphics format popular with professional desktop publishers.
.WMF	A file format used for graphics in Windows applications; stands for *Windows metafile format.*
.WPG	The graphics format used by WordPerfect applications.

Inserting a Picture File

To insert a graphics file into your document, follow these steps:

1. Position the insertion point where you want to add the picture.

2. Select Insert ➤ Picture ➤ From File to display the Insert Picture dialog box.

3. Navigate to the file you want to insert, select the file, and click the Insert button.

Word inserts the picture into your document. You can now reposition, resize, and reformat the picture as appropriate.

 TIP By default, Word *embeds* pictures in your documents—which increases the size of your Word file accordingly. You can reduce the size of your Word file by *linking* the picture instead of embedding it. You do this in the Insert Picture dialog box, by clicking the arrow to the right of the Insert button to display a drop-down menu. Select Link to File from this menu to establish a link to the selected picture. (Note that linked pictures cannot be edited—although they print just like an embedded picture.) To learn more about linking to files (picture or otherwise), see Chapter 17.

Working with Digital Photographs

Word 2000 lets you import digital photographs directly from a TWAIN-compatible scanner or digital camera.

NOTE You don't have to use the following procedure to incorporate digital photographs in your Word documents. Virtually all scanners and digital cameras enable simple uploading of pictures to your hard disk. Any photograph saved in a standard graphics format (.JPG, .GIF, .TIF, etc.) can be imported normally into Word via the Insert ➢ Picture ➢ From File command.

Follow these steps to scan or upload a photograph directly into your Word document:

1. Select Insert ➢ Picture ➢ From Scanner or Camera to display the Insert Picture from Scanner or Camera dialog box.

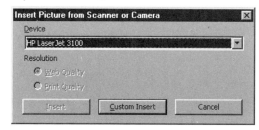

2. Pull down the Device list and select the device (scanner or camera) you're using.

3. If you're using this picture in a Web-based document, check the Web Quality option. If you'll be printing this picture in a normal document, check the Print Quality option.

TIP When you're scanning images, try to keep your scanned files as small as possible. Large files not only use up valuable disk space, but also can slow down your screen display. One way to reduce file size when scanning is to reduce the dots per inch (DPI) in your scanned image. Scanning at a DPI higher than what your printer can print is a waste of detail; in fact, scans often look better if they're 50 to 100 DPI less than your printer's maximum DPI.

4. If you're scanning an image and using predefined scanner settings, click Insert. If you're scanning an image and want to change image settings—or if you're uploading the image from a digital camera—click Custom Insert to open the software that came with your scanner or camera; make the appropriate adjustments, then initiate the scan or upload. (If the Insert button is grayed out, it's probably because your scanner software doesn't support automatic scanning; if this is the case, use the Custom Insert button instead.)

Word inserts the scanned/uploaded photograph into your document, where you can reposition, resize, or reformat it as appropriate.

NOTE Many third-party software programs let you gain more functionality from your scanned images. One such program, OfficeExpress 2000, adds optical character recognition (OCR) capabilities and various photo-editing features, and is available on the CD that accompanies this book. For more information on OfficeExpress 2000, see Chapter 33.

Formatting Pictures

Once a picture is inserted into your document, you can use the commands on the Picture toolbar to make minor formatting changes to the picture. Here are some of the editing/formatting options possible from the Picture toolbar:

 Add a Border to the Picture Click the Line Style button and select a border line style.

 Change how Text Wraps around the Picture Click the Text Wrapping button and select a text wrapping style.

 Change the Picture to a Screened-back Watermark Click the Image Control button, then select Watermark.

 Change the Picture to Black and White Click the Image Control button, then select Black and White.

 Crop the Edges of the Picture Click the Crop button to change the cursor to a cropping tool; using the cropping tool, drag the picture's selection handles to crop the picture's edges.

 Decrease Picture Brightness Click the Less Brightness button.

Decrease Picture Contrast Click the Less Contrast button.

 Display the Picture in Grayscale Tones Click the Image Control button, then select Grayscale.

 Increase Picture Brightness Click the More Brightness button.

 Increase Picture Contrast Click the More Contrast button.

 Make Part of Your Picture Transparent (so Your Page Background Shows Through) Click the Set Transparent Color button to change the cursor to a transparent color tool, then click the tool on the color in your picture that you want to make transparent.

 If you want to undo all picture formatting (and return the picture to its original state), click the Reset Picture button on the Picture toolbar.

Preparing Pictures for the Web

If the picture you've added is intended for viewing on the Web, you can specify *alternative text* to display either while the picture loads or if the picture *doesn't* load. Follow these steps:

1. Select Format ➢ Picture to display the Format Picture dialog box.

2. Select the Web tab.

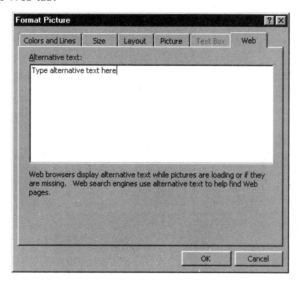

3. Enter the alternative text into the large text box.

4. Click OK.

Other Picture-Editing Software

If you've ever tried to use Word 2000 to do any major picture editing, you've no doubt come to the conclusion that although Word is a great word processor, it's a lousy picture editor. It's no secret that Word 2000 has limited picture-editing capabilities; if you need to do some big-time picture editing, you need to augment Word with a more serious, dedicated graphics program.

Continued ▶

One such graphics program is included with Microsoft Office 2000. The Microsoft Photo Editor, although not installed in most normal Office installations, can be installed separately from your Office installation CD. When it's installed, you can launch it by selecting Start ➤ Programs ➤ Microsoft Office Tools ➤ Microsoft Photo Editor.

Photo Editor provides a number of image-editing tools, and lets you crop, resize, sharpen, soften, despeckle, posterize, and emboss your images. The program also enables you to apply a variety of special effects, including chalk and charcoal, negative, notepaper, watercolor, stained glass, and stamp.

Certain versions of Microsoft Office 2000 also include Microsoft PhotoDraw, a more fully featured graphics-editing program. This program lets you apply 3-D effects, use artistic and photo brush strokes, enhance pictures with designer effects (including transparencies, fades, and distortions), modify AutoShapes, and create professional-quality designs. This program is very sophisticated and worth checking out if it came with your version of Office.

In addition, OfficeExpress 2000 (included on the CD accompanying this book) provides a wealth of picture-editing functions—much more than you'll find built into Word or contained with Microsoft Photo Editor. To learn more about OfficeExpress 2000, see Chapter 33.

Adding Fancy Text with WordArt

When normal text isn't fancy enough—even with all of Word's formatting options applied—turn to the text-as-graphics created by Microsoft's WordArt applet. With WordArt you can create shadowed, skewed, rotated, and stretched text, as well as text scrunched into a variety of shapes.

Remember that WordArt text isn't really text, it's a graphic. WordArt inserts text as a drawing object, which means you can use any of Word's drawing tools to add additional formatting to the WordArt text.

 TIP WordArt is best used for larger text items, such as headlines, titles, and headings. It is less effective in long blocks of text or at small type sizes.

Inserting WordArt

To insert WordArt text, follow these steps:

1. Position the insertion point where you want to place the WordArt text.

2. From the Drawing toolbar, click the Insert WordArt button to display the Word-Art Gallery window.

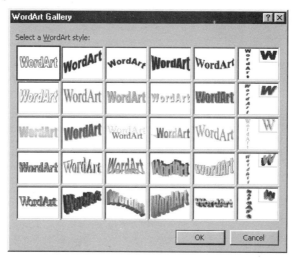

3. Select a WordArt style, then click OK to display the Edit WordArt Text dialog box.

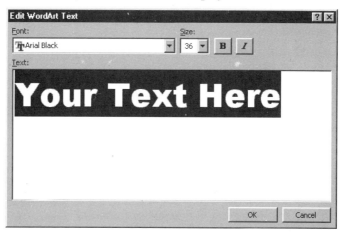

4. Select a font from the Font list and a font size from the Size list.

5. If you want to boldface or italicize your WordArt text, click the Bold or Italic buttons.

6. Enter the text for your WordArt in the Text box.

7. Click OK to insert the WordArt object into your document.

With the WordArt object inserted in your document, as shown in Figure 16.4, you can use the commands on the WordArt toolbar to edit the object, or you can use commands on the Drawing toolbar to apply standard object formatting.

FIGURE 16.4
Use WordArt to create fancy text effects.

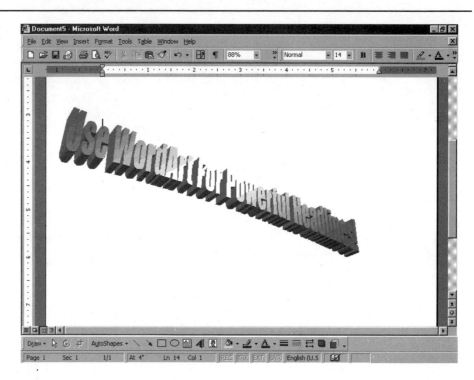

Editing WordArt

When you select a WordArt object, Word automatically displays the WordArt toolbar. From this toolbar you can perform the following operations on the selected WordArt:

Edit WordArt Text   To edit the text in your WordArt object, click the Edit Text button to display the Edit WordArt Text dialog box. Enter, edit, and delete text in the Text box, then click OK.

Switch to a Different WordArt Style   Click the WordArt Gallery button to display the WordArt Gallery, and choose from one of the preselected styles of WordArt.

Change Color and Outline Style   You can change the color of your WordArt text and add or change the outline around the text. Click the Format WordArt button to display the Format WordArt dialog box, then select the Colors and Lines tab. Select a fill color, as well as a line color and weight, then click OK to apply.

 Apply a Different Shape   WordArt can stretch and squish to fill any one of a number of predefined shapes. To change the shape container for your Word-Art, click the WordArt Shape button and choose from one of the forty different shapes.

 Rotate Your Text   To rotate your WordArt object clockwise or counterclock-wise, click the Free Rotate button to display the green rotation handles on the WordArt object. Grab one of the handles with your cursor and drag the object around to a new position.

 Determine Text Wrapping   To determine how text wraps around your WordArt object, click the Text Wrapping button and select one of the options from the pull-down menu.

 Change the Height of Your Letters   To make all the letters in your Word-Art text the same height (even the lowercase ones), click the Same Letter Heights button. (Click the button again to toggle back to normal height.)

 Stack Text Vertically   To make your WordArt text flow top-to-bottom instead of left-to-right, click the Vertical Text button.

 Align Text Horizontally   To left-align, center, right-align, or justify your WordArt text, click the Alignment button and select from the pull-down menu.

 Stretch the Text   To stretch the letters in your text to fill the full width of the WordArt object, click the Alignment button and select Stretch Justify. To add extra spacing between letters to fill the full width, click the Alignment button and select Letter Justify.

 Adjust Letter Spacing   To tighten or loosen the spacing between characters in your WordArt text, click the Character Spacing button and select from the pull-down menu.

Drawing with AutoShapes

When you want to *draw* a picture in your document, you use Word's AutoShapes to create a drawing object. A *drawing object* is composed of lines and shapes you add via the AutoShape commands, and can then be formatted with different styles and colors.

The AutoShapes menu on the Drawing toolbar includes several different types of shapes:

Lines, including straight lines, curves, arrows, and squiggly lines (through the Scribble tool)

Basic Shapes, including rectangles, ovals, triangles, diamonds, boxes, cylinders, and hearts

Block Arrows, including big, bold arrows pointing in various directions

Flowchart, including various shapes for use in procedural or programming flowcharts

Stars and Banners, including starbursts, stars, and various banners

Callouts, including various comic book–style word and thought balloons

In addition, if you click the More AutoShapes option, you display the More AutoShapes dialog box, where you can choose from additional shapes located in Word's Clip Gallery.

Inserting an AutoShape

To create a drawing in your document, start with an AutoShape, as follows:

1. From the Drawing toolbar, click the AutoShapes button and select the type of AutoShape you want to draw.

2. Use your mouse to position the cursor where you want to start the AutoShape in your document.

3. Press and hold the mouse button while you drag the cursor across the area where you want the AutoShape.

4. When you're done drawing the AutoShape, release the mouse button.

Changing AutoShapes

Once you've added an AutoShape to your document, you're not necessarily stuck with it. Word allows you to change from one AutoShape to another, without deleting and redrawing. Follow these steps:

1. Select the AutoShape you want to change.

2. From the Drawing toolbar, select Draw ➢ Change AutoShape, then select a new AutoShape.

Word changes the original AutoShape to the new shape you selected.

Creating a Free-Form Drawing

All of the above procedures work fine when you're adding a discrete AutoShape object. When you want to *draw* an object, however, you have to use one of the AutoShape line tools.

Word includes six different AutoShape line tools; three draw straight lines or arrows, and three draw curved lines. You'll use the curved line tools to make a free-hand drawing.

PART
IV

Creating Visual
Documents

TIP You can also insert a free-form drawing within a separate drawing object by selecting Insert ➤ Picture ➤ New Drawing. This inserts a rectangular object in your document and opens the AutoShapes toolbar; you can then create your drawing within this object, and format the borders, shading, and text wrapping of the object separately from the drawing contained within.

The Curve tool enables you to draw a curved line. After you click the Curve button, position your cursor where you want the line to start, then click (but don't hold!) the mouse button to anchor the starting point. Next, move the cursor to where you want the midpoint (or hump) of the curve to appear and click the mouse button again. Finally, move the cursor to the end of the curve and *double-click* the mouse button to anchor the end of the curved line.

TIP You don't have to stop with a single curve. If you single-click at the third point and continue on to a fourth, fifth, and more points, you create a line containing several curves. The line doesn't end until you double-click your mouse.

The Freeform tool works just like the Curve tool, except the Freeform tool draws a sharp corner at each click of your mouse, not a smooth curve. You click at each point you want your line to change direction, and double-click to end the line.

To truly *draw* onscreen, use the Scribble tool. When you click the Scribble button, your cursor changes to a pencil. You click and hold your mouse button to draw with the cursor; when you release the mouse button, you stop drawing. You can draw anything you're capable of—straight lines, curves, scribbles, you name it.

Figure 16.5 shows an example of what results when you use the Curve, Freeform, and Scribble tools in your document.

TIP You can change the shape of a free-form drawing by moving the points used to create the line. Right-click the drawing and select Edit Points from the pop-up menu; when the individual points are displayed, drag them with your mouse to reshape your line.

FIGURE 16.5
Drawing with AutoShape line tools

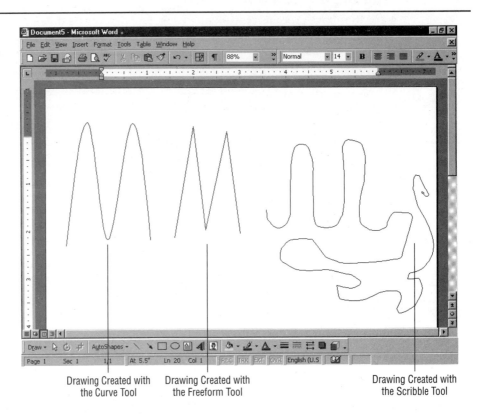

Drawing Created with the Curve Tool

Drawing Created with the Freeform Tool

Drawing Created with the Scribble Tool

Formatting Graphic Objects

Most graphic objects in your Word documents can be formatted with similar effects. The following sections discuss the most common formatting options available—and how to apply those formats.

 TIP A text box is also a type of graphic object, and can be formatted with the commands discussed in the following sections. To learn more about Word text boxes, see Chapter 4.

Repositioning and Resizing

The easiest things to do with your graphic are moving it or resizing it.

Moving a Graphic

To move a graphic object, simply select it and then—after your cursor changes to a four-pointed arrow—drag it to a new position.

 TIP You can more accurately position your objects by applying a grid to your page and snapping the objects to the grid. To apply a grid, go to the Drawing toolbar and select Draw ➢ Grid to display the Drawing Grid dialog box; select the appropriate grid settings, then check the Snap Objects to Grid option. To nudge objects one grid point at a time (or one pixel at a time if you're not using a grid), select Draw ➢ Nudge ➢ Up (or Down, Left, or Right)—or simply press the appropriate arrow key once per nudge.

This procedure *roughly* positions your object. To more *precisely* position the object on your page, follow these steps:

1. Select the object.

2. Select Format ➢ Object to display the Format Object dialog box.

3. Select the Layout tab and click the Advanced button to display the Advanced Layout dialog box.

4. Select the Picture Position tab.

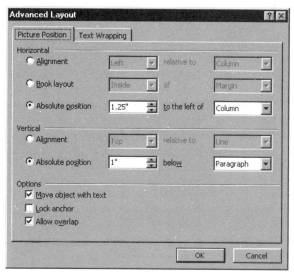

5. In the Horizontal section, check the Absolute Position option. Pull down the To the Left Of list and select which element you want to position this graphic next to; most often you'll select Page or Margin. Use the Absolute Position list to select how far from this element you want to position your object horizontally.

6. In the Vertical section, check the Absolute Position option. Pull down the Below list and select which element you want to position this graphic below; most

often you'll select Page or Margin. Use the Absolute Position list to select how far below this element you want to position your object vertically.

 TIP You can also select the Alignment options and align your object relative to another page element.

7. If you want your object to move as you add or delete text, check the Move Object with Text option; if you want your object to lock into its current position, uncheck this option and check the Lock Anchor option.

8. If multiple objects on the same page share the same text wrapping style, you can allow them to overlap by checking the Allow Overlap option; unchecking this option forces the objects to reposition themselves to avoid overlap.

9. Click OK when done.

Resizing a Graphic

To resize a graphic, simply grab one of its selection handles and drag it to a new position. If you want the graphic to retain its original vertical/horizontal ratio, hold down the Shift key while you resize the object.

You can also precisely resize or scale any object by using the Format Object dialog box. Just follow these steps:

1. Select the object.

2. Select Format ≻ Object to display the Format Object dialog box.

3. Select the Size tab.

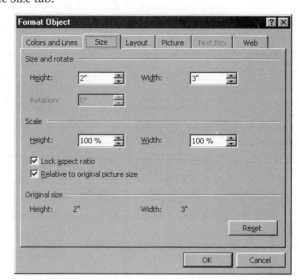

4. Use the Height and Width controls in the Size and Rotate section to adjust the object's dimensions separately. Use the Height and Width controls in the Scale section to select dimensions as a percentage of the picture's original size. (Check the Relative to Original Picture Size option to maintain the percentages as they relate to the original, unedited picture.)

 TIP To maintain the object's height/width ratio, check the Lock Aspect Ratio option. With this option enabled, when you adjust either the Height or the Width control, the other control is automatically adjusted to maintain the original aspects of the object.

5. Click OK when done.

 NOTE The Size tab in the Format Picture dialog box also features a Rotation control that lets you precisely rotate your object by degree.

Aligning Multiple Objects

If you have more than one object on a page—for example, if you've created several boxes to make an organization chart or flowchart—you can *try* to line them up by eye-balling them, or you can *precisely* align them using Word's alignment commands. Using these commands, you can align objects vertically (by the top, middle, or bottom of the objects) or horizontally (by the left edge, right edge, or center of the objects). You can also equally space multiple objects on the page by *distributing* them horizontally or vertically.

To align multiple objects, follow these steps:

1. Select the objects you want to align, by either selecting each object individually (while holding the Shift key) or using the Select Objects tool to draw a boundary around all the objects.

2. From the Drawing menu, select Draw ➤ Align or Distribute, then select one of the alignment options.

To space objects equally across your page, select the objects, then select either Draw ➤ Align or Distribute ➤ Distribute Horizontally, or Draw ➤ Align or Distribute ➤ Distribute Vertically.

Layering Images

If you have multiple images on your page, you can make them overlap—thus creating interesting layering effects. An object on top of (or what Word calls *in front of*) another object obscures the object below (or *behind*); you can stack multiple objects in multiple layers.

Figure 16.6 shows objects layered on a page.

FIGURE 16.6
Layering objects on your page

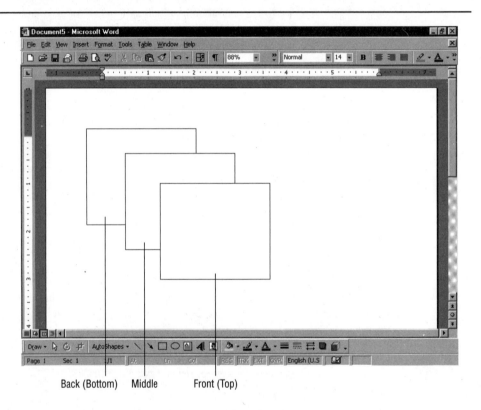

Back (Bottom)   Middle   Front (Top)

 TIP Layering is a great way to display text on top of a graphic. Just layer the text above (or in front of) the graphic—and make sure the text has a transparent background so that the graphic shows through.

To send an object up or down through the layers, follow these steps:

1. Select the object to move.
2. From the Drawing toolbar, select Draw ➤ Order, and then select one of these layering options:
   - Bring to Front sends the selected object to the top of the stack
   - Send to Back sends the selected object to the bottom of the stack
   - Bring Forward moves the selected object up or forward one layer
   - Send Backward moves the selected object down or backward one layer
   - Bring in Front of Text moves the selected object on top of the text on your page—thus obscuring the text beneath
   - Send Behind Text moves the selected object below the text on your page—thus making the object a background image

Grouping and Ungrouping

Complex objects are composed of multiple objects grouped together. When smaller objects are grouped together into a single, large object, you can move and resize all the objects together as one; when a larger object is ungrouped, you can edit each component object individually.

To group multiple objects, follow these steps:

1. On the Drawing toolbar, click the Select Object button.
2. Use your mouse to draw a boundary around all the images you want to regroup.
3. From the Drawing toolbar, select Draw ➤ Group.

 TIP You can also select what to group by selecting each component object individually (while pressing the Shift key).

To ungroup a complex object, follow these steps:

1. Select the object to ungroup.
2. From the Drawing toolbar, select Draw ➤ Ungroup.

You can also regroup a recently ungrouped object by selecting Draw ➤ Regroup.

Rotating and Flipping

Most graphics on your page can also be rotated—by degree—or flipped from side-to-side or top-to-bottom.

Rotating an Object

Many—but not all—objects can be turned clockwise or counterclockwise on your page. Word includes a Free Rotate tool and the capability to automatically rotate an object in 90-degree increments.

To freely rotate an object, follow these steps:

1. Select the object.

2. Click the Free Rotate button on the Drawing toolbar; green rotation handles appear around the object, and your cursor changes shape to match the Free Rotate icon.

3. Grab any one of the rotation handles and drag the object around either clockwise or counterclockwise.

To rotate an object in 90-degree increments, simply go to the Drawing toolbar and select either Draw ➢ Rotate or Flip ➢ Rotate Left (to rotate counterclockwise), or Draw ➢ Rotate or Flip ➢ Rotate Right (to rotate clockwise).

Flipping an Object

To create a mirror image of an object left-to-right, select the object, move to the Drawing toolbar, then select Draw ➢ Rotate or Flip ➢ Flip Horizontal. To create a mirror image of an object top-to-bottom, select Draw ➢ Rotate or Flip ➢ Flip Vertical.

Cropping Unwanted Elements

If your picture contains extraneous elements that you'd rather not display—or if you simply want to focus on one element within your picture—you can crop the edges of the picture to focus on an interior element.

WARNING Word lets you crop only picture files—you can't crop drawing objects.

You can manually crop your picture with the cropping tool on the Picture toolbar—or more precisely crop your picture with controls in the Format Picture dialog box.

To manually crop a picture, follow these steps:

1. From the Picture toolbar, click the Crop button; the cursor changes to a cropping tool.

2. Grab a selection handle and drag it *in* to trim that edge of the picture, as shown in Figure 16.7.

FIGURE 16.7
Use the crop tool to trim the edges of a picture.

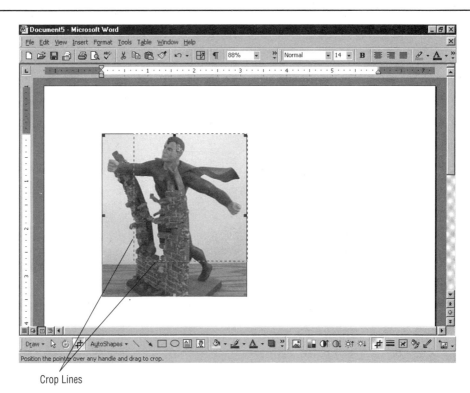

Crop Lines

To *precisely* crop a picture from the Format Picture dialog box, follow these steps:

1. Select the picture you want to crop.

2. Select Format ➤ Picture to display the Format Picture dialog box.

3. Select the Picture tab.

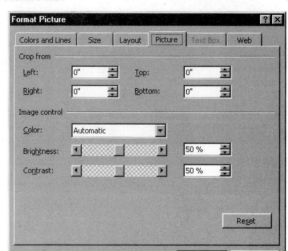

4. In the Crop From section, select how much you want to crop from the Left, Right, Top, and Bottom.

5. Click OK.

You can also use this dialog box to undo any cropping you've done to this picture. Just click the Reset button to return the picture to its uncropped state.

TIP You can also use the Picture tab in the Format Picture dialog box to precisely adjust the brightness and contrast of your picture.

Wrapping Text

When an object is sitting on your page, how does it interact with your text? You can choose to have the object appear behind your text (as a background image) or in front of your text (obscuring the text behind it), or you can choose to have the text *wrap* around the object.

When you decide to wrap text around an object, you can choose from several different wrapping styles:

In Line with Text   The object is treated as a character of text. The object is placed at the insertion point, and the text resumes on the other side of the object.

Square   Wraps text around all sides of a square surrounding the object.

Tight   Wraps text tightly around the edges of the actual image—*not* around the object's borders.

Through   Wraps text tightly around the edges of the actual image—and allows text to display inside any parts of the object that are open.

Top and Bottom   Wraps text around the top and bottom of the object only—no text will display around the sides of the object.

 WARNING   Several of these text-wrapping styles are new to Word 2000 and do not convert well to older versions of the software; if you open a Word 2000 text-wrapped object in Word 97, expect the object to be somehow mispositioned on your page.

Although some of these text wrapping options are available when you click the Text Wrapping button on the Picture toolbar, the best way to format an object's text wrapping is through the Format Object dialog box. Follow these steps:

1. Select the object.
2. Select Format ➤ Object to display the Format Object dialog box.
3. Select the Layout tab.
4. If the wrapping style you want is on this tab, select it and click OK. However, more options are available when you click the Advanced button to display the Advanced Layout dialog box.

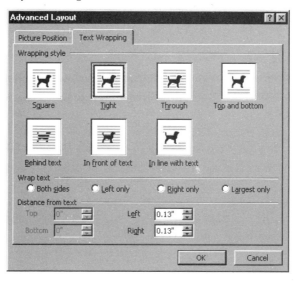

5. Select the Text Wrapping tab.

6. Select a wrapping style.

7. For the Square, Tight, and Through styles, select whether you want to wrap the text on Both Sides, Left Only, Right Only, or Largest (side) Only.

8. For the Square, Tight, Through, and Top and Bottom styles, move to the Distance from Text section and select how large a buffer you want to place between the object and the surrounding text.

9. Click OK when done.

 TIP Word also calls Behind Text and In Front of Text *wrapping styles,* even though, technically, the text doesn't wrap if either of these options are selected.

Working with Borders and Fills

Most objects on your page can be assigned a border. Some objects (not pictures and not all drawing objects) can be filled with a color or pattern. Here's how you do it:

 WARNING If you can't border or fill an object, these options won't be available on the Drawing toolbar when you select that object.

1. Select the object.

 2. From the Drawing toolbar, click the arrow next to the Line Color button and select a new color for the border.

 3. Click the Line Style button and select a new width for the border.

 4. If you want your border to consist of dashed lines, click the Dash Style button and select a specific type of dash.

 5. To fill the object, click the arrow next to the Fill Color button and select a new color. To see additional colors, select More Fill Colors to display the Colors dialog box. To add gradients, textures, patterns, or pictures to the object's background, select Fill Effects to display the Fill Effects dialog box.

 NOTE To learn more about applying various fill effects, see the "Fancy Fills" sidebar in Chapter 15.

Adding Shadows and 3-D Effects

You can also add drop shadows and 3-D effects to many objects. Figure 16.8 shows two objects with different shadow and 3-D effects applied.

FIGURE 16.8
Use shadows and 3-D effects to add depth to your objects.

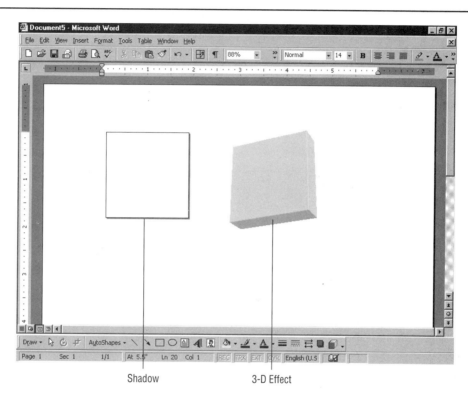

Shadow   3-D Effect

Adding Depth with a Shadow

To add a shadow to an object, follow these steps:

1. Select the object.
2. Click the Shadow button on the Drawing toolbar.
3. Select a shadow style from the pop-up menu.

WARNING   Not all shadow styles are available for all objects. Unavailable styles will be grayed out.

If you want to remove a shadow from an object, click the Shadow button and select No Shadow. If you want to change the size or color of the shadow, select Shadow Settings to display the Shadow Settings toolbar. From here you can move a shadow up, down, left, or right, or click the Shadow Color button and choose a different color for the shadow.

Adding "Pop" with a 3-D Effect

Word lets you add a variety of 3-D effects to your objects. Some of these effects work as advertised, making your object look as if it were popping off the page; other effects just look cheesy. You be the judge.

 WARNING Not all objects can accept 3-D effects. If some or all effects are grayed out when you select an object, those effects are unavailable.

To add a 3-D effect to an object, follow these steps:

1. Select the object.
2. Click the 3-D button on the Drawing toolbar.
3. Select a 3-D style from the pop-up menu.

If you want to remove a 3-D effect from an object, click the 3-D button and select No 3-D.

Word's 3-D effects come with numerous formatting options, all available when you click the 3-D button and select 3-D Settings to display the 3-D Settings toolbar. Here are the settings you can adjust:

 Tilt You can tilt—or rotate—the 3-D object up, down, left, or right.

 Depth You can increase or decrease the depth of the 3-D effect.

Direction   You can change the direction of the 3-D effect—as well as the perspective of the effect.

  Lighting   You can change the angle and the intensity of the effect's lighting.

  Surface   You can change the texture of the object/effect's surface; selections include Wire Frame, Matte, Plastic, or Metal.

Color   You can change the color of the 3-D effect.

The best way to choose a 3-D effect is to play with the various settings until you find an effect that works best in your document.

PART

IV

Creating Visual
Documents

CHAPTER 17

Linking and Embedding Objects

Understanding how linking and embedding differs from cutting and pasting   495

Understanding how linking differs from embedding and when to use which   495

Inserting linked objects into documents   496

Editing linked data   499

Updating links before printing   501

Embedding existing data   502

Creating a new embedded object   502

Editing embedded objects   503

To this point, you've worked with various elements in your Word documents, from plain text to fancy graphics objects. With the exception of charts created by Microsoft Graph 2000 (discussed in Chapter 15) and text created by Microsoft Word-Art (discussed in Chapter 16), all of the objects you've worked with in this book have been native to the Word 2000 program.

As you may remember, when you create a chart with Graph 2000, you actually leave the Word program, however briefly, and enter the Graph 2000 workspace. Whenever you double-click a Graph 2000 chart, you reopen Graph 2000, enabling you to edit the selected object. (A similar process is involved when you insert and edit WordArt objects.)

This embedding of another program in your document is part and parcel of Microsoft's Object Linking and Embedding (OLE) technology. With OLE, you can easily share data between different programs while working essentially within a single program environment. Any software program supporting OLE technology can create objects that can be linked to or embedded in other OLE-compatible programs. All of Microsoft's Office 2000 applications support OLE, as do many programs from companies other than Microsoft.

When you use OLE technology, you easily create a Word document containing data that is created and updated in other programs. For example, you can create an Excel worksheet to store financial data, and then link or embed that data in your Word document; whenever you update the spreadsheet, your Word document will automatically reflect the changes. Likewise, you can link or embed Excel charts, Access databases, and even PowerPoint presentations to your Word documents. Mastering OLE provides an efficient way to share data and information while adding even more power to your Word 2000 documents!

Understanding Object Linking and Embedding

Object Linking and Embedding makes Word more than just Word. The capabilities of virtually any OLE-compatible program can be added to Word, turning Word into a word processor-plus-spreadsheet or database or graphics editor or Acrobat viewer or... well, you get the picture.

You can use a linked or embedded object to insert all or part of a non-Word file into a Word document. You can create new embedded objects, or you can link to or embed already-existing files. All you need is Microsoft Word 2000 and any other OLE-compatible software program.

TIP Almost all Windows applications support OLE, letting you link or embed text or other data directly into your Word document. You can also link or embed text from other Word documents into your current Word document; objects linked/embedded from a Word document behave as do any other linked/embedded objects.

Understanding How Linking and Embedding Differs from Cutting and Pasting

Any data or item you cut from another document or program and paste into Word is nothing more than a "snapshot" from that other program. If you copy a chart from Excel and paste it into Word, you're pasting a picture of that chart. If you later change the chart (or its underlying data) in Excel, the chart you pasted into Word does *not* change; like a snapshot, it captures the chart as it looked at one moment in time and does not reflect any subsequent changes.

When you link or embed an object, however, it's sort of like you're establishing a live video feed back to the host program. If cutting/pasting takes a still picture, linking/embedding creates a series of moving pictures. The linked or embedded object, like a picture from a video camera, is constantly updated as the "scene" changes.

When should you choose cutting and pasting over linking and embedding? If you really want to insert a snapshot of data into your document, cutting and pasting does so quite efficiently, without a lot of hassles. Also, a pasted object is more portable than a linked or embedded object; you don't have to have the host application or original source file installed on your PC to view a pasted object, as you do with linking and embedding. So if you intend to share your document with others, pasting is a safer course of action than either linking or embedding.

However, if you want to minimize the size of your Word documents, choose linking over pasting. You should also choose linking over pasting if you want to share "live" data from another document; you should choose embedding over pasting if you want to insert data that can be edited at a later time.

Understanding How Linking Differs from Embedding and When to Use Which

As you might recall, linking and embedding both use OLE technology to share data with other programs, although they differ in where the source data is stored and how it is updated after you place it in your Word document.

When you link an object to your Word document, the source data is stored in its original program, and it's updated only when you open the original program and edit the original file. Linking is the more-efficient way to add data to your Word documents, since you only insert a link to the actual data, not the entire data file, which results in smaller file sizes for your Word documents. However, linked documents are not terribly portable; if you move the Word file to another PC without moving the source file and program as well, you break the links and possibly corrupt your Word document.

When you embed an object in your Word document, you embed the entire data file instead of linking to a separate file. Embedded objects become part of your Word file (thus increasing file size). You modify embedded data from within Word by opening an instance of the data's native program within the Word workspace.

You should use OLE linking when you truly want to share data between applications on a single PC or network; you keep the original source file as a parent file that links to child documents. You should use OLE embedding when you intend to move the Word document among different PCs or when you don't want to share the source data between applications or users.

MASTERING THE OPPORTUNITIES

Understanding How to Tell a Linked Object from an Embedded Object

Since linked and embedded objects both utilize the same OLE technology, it's sometimes difficult to tell which is which within your document. Here are some tips for distinguishing between the two different types of OLE objects:

- When you double-click a linked object, the source program always opens in a separate window. When you double-click an embedded object, you stay within the Word workspace, but Word's menus and toolbars are replaced with the menus and toolbars from the embedded application.

- When you select a linked object, Word's Edit menu adds a Linked Object command. When you select an embedded object, Word's Edit menu adds an Object command.

- You can also toggle the form fields to see if there is a link to an external file.

In both cases, you double-click the object, whether linked or embedded, to edit it. In neither case do you have to open the source application manually.

Inserting Linked Objects into Your Documents

When you link objects to your Word documents, you insert information (the *object*) created from another file (the *source* file) into your Word file (the *destination* file) and maintain a *connection* between the two files. The linked object does not become part of the destination file.

There are two ways to link objects to a Word document: You can use the Paste Special command or the Object command.

 TIP Since picture files (discussed in Chapter 16) typically are large files, pasting them into your Word documents can dramatically increase the size of your Word files. To minimize the size of your Word files, insert links to your picture files instead.

Using the Paste Special Command

The easiest way to insert an OLE object from another application into a Word document is to copy that object and then use the Paste Special command to paste a link into your document. Follow these steps:

1. In the source file, select the text, data, image, or object you want to link.

2. Select Edit ➤ Copy to copy the source object.

3. Move to your Word document, and position the insertion point where you want to insert the linked object.

4. Select Edit ➤ Paste Special to display the Paste Special dialog box, shown in Figure 17.1.

FIGURE 17.1
Use the Paste Special dialog box to paste linked data into your Word document.

View the Source File and Type

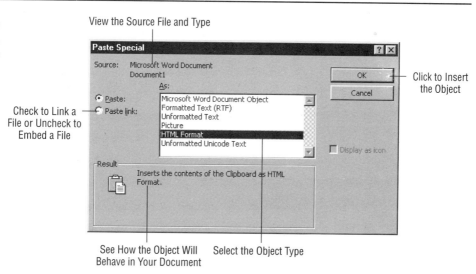

Check to Link a File or Uncheck to Embed a File

Click to Insert the Object

See How the Object Will Behave in Your Document

Select the Object Type

5. Select the object's native format from the As list.

6. Check the Paste Link option.

7. Click OK.

Using the Object Command

The second way to insert a linked object into your document is with the Object command. Follow these steps:

1. Anchor the insertion point where you want to insert the object in your document.

2. Select Insert ➢ Object to display the Object dialog box.

3. Select the Create from File tab, illustrated in Figure 17.2.

FIGURE 17.2
Use the Create from File tab in the Object dialog box to create a linked object from an existing file.

Enter the Source File's Name

Click to Browse for the Source File

Check the Link to File Option

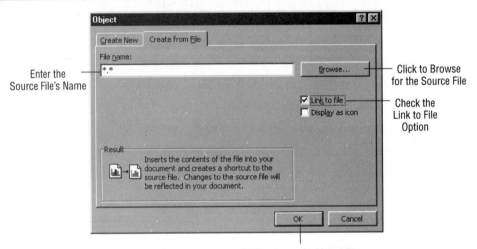

Click to Insert the Linked File

4. Enter the name of the source file, or click the Browse button to navigate to the source file.

5. Check the Link to File option.

6. Click OK.

TIP If you want to insert a picture as an OLE link, a third method is available to you. Select Insert ➢ Picture ➢ From File to display the Insert Picture dialog box, and then click the arrow to the right of the Insert button to display the drop-down menu. Select Link to File from this menu to establish a link to the selected picture.

Editing Linked Data

To edit the data in a linked object, you have to open the source file and application and then edit the data there. You cannot edit the source data from within Word.

There are several ways to open the source data, including:

- From the Windows Start menu, open the source application, and load the source file manually.

- Double-click the linked object.

 WARNING Double-clicking a linked object opens the source file for every application *except* PowerPoint. When you double-click a linked PowerPoint object, you launch a Power-Point slideshow.

- Select the linked object, and then select Edit ➢ Linked Object ➢ Edit Link.

- Right-click the linked object, and select Linked Object ➢ Edit Link from the pop-up menu.

After opening the source application and file, you then edit the data in the source file, save the edited source file, and close the source application. When you return to your Word document, the linked object will be updated automatically.

Editing Links

Word lets you change the way links are updated, switch to an alternate source file, or break the links to a specific file. All of these link-editing operations are accomplished when you select Edit ➢ Links to display the Links dialog box, shown in Figure 17.3.

FIGURE 17.3
Use the Links dialog box to edit various link properties.

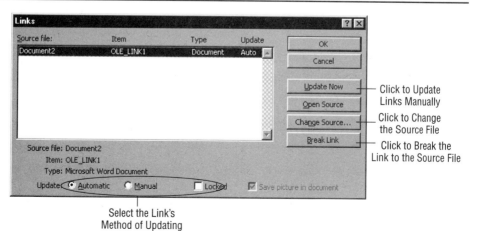

Click to Update Links Manually

Click to Change the Source File

Click to Break the Link to the Source File

Select the Link's Method of Updating

Part IV — Creating Visual Documents

Changing how a Link is Updated

To change the method of updating for any specific link, follow these steps:

1. Select the linked object.

2. Select Edit ➢ Links to display the Links dialog box, shown in Figure 17.3.

3. By default, links are configured for automatic updating. To freeze the link until you update it manually, check the Manual option. To prevent a linked item from being updated, check the Locked option.

4. Click OK.

If you choose manual updating, the object won't be updated until you return to the Links dialog box and click the Update Now button. If you choose the Locked option, the linked object won't be updated until you return to the Links dialog box, and uncheck this option.

Changing the Source File for a Link

Sometimes a source file is moved or deleted. In either of these two circumstances, you may want to specify a different source file for your linked object. To do this, follow these steps:

1. Select the linked object.

2. Select Edit ➢ Links to display the Links dialog box, shown in Figure 17.3.

3. Click the Change Source button to display the Change Source dialog box.

4. Select a new source file, and then click Open.

When you select a new source file, your original linked object is replaced by a new linked object from the new source file.

Breaking a Link to a Source File

If you want to permanently freeze the data in your linked object, you want to break the link so that no further updating occurs. You can *temporarily* freeze your data by using the Locked option, which was discussed in the preceding section, but for permanence, you have to sever the link completely.

To break a link to a source file, follow these steps:

1. Select the linked object.

2. Select Edit ➢ Links to display the Links dialog box, shown in Figure 17.3.

3. Click the Break Link button.

4. When asked if you really want to break the link, answer Yes.

WARNING Once you break a link, you can't reestablish it. (You *can* undo the break if you select Edit ➤ Undo immediately after the operation, however.) To establish a new link, you have to delete the inserted object and insert a new linked object.

MASTERING THE OPPORTUNITIES

Changing How Objects Are Displayed

There are three ways to display a linked or embedded object in your Word document. You can display the linked or embedded object exactly as it appears in the source program (complete with original formatting); you can display the object as an icon representing the source program; or you can display only the name of the object.

By default, Word displays the entire object. To switch to the icon display, select the object, and then select Edit ➤ Linked Object ➤ Convert to display the Convert dialog box. Check the Display As Icon option, and then click OK. (If you want to change the icon used to represent this object, click the Change Icon button to display the Change Icon dialog box, and then select from the list of icons or Browse for other icons in other files.)

To switch to the name-only display, you have to configure Word to hide all objects in your document. Do this by selecting Tools ➤ Options to display the Options dialog box, select the View tab, and check the Field Codes option in the Show section. This hides all objects, displaying only the field codes used to insert the objects.

Choose the full-object display when you'll be including the object in a printed document. Choose the icon or name display when you need to minimize the screen space occupied by the object or if you'll only be viewing your document onscreen.

Updating Links Before Printing

To make sure that all your linked objects are updated before you print your document, follow these steps:

1. Select Tools ➤ Options to display the Options dialog box.
2. Select the Print tab.
3. Check the Update Links option.
4. Click OK.

With the Update Links option enabled, Word will automatically update all the links in your documents before any documents are printed.

Embedding Objects in Your Documents

When you embed objects in your Word documents, you insert information (the *object*) into your Word file (the *destination* file); that information becomes a permanent part of your Word file. When you double-click an embedded object, the source program opens *within the Word workspace,* replacing Word's menus and toolbars with its own source elements.

There are two ways to embed an object in a Word document: by embedding existing data or by creating a new object from scratch.

Embedding Existing Data

You use the Paste Special command to insert existing data from another application as an embedded object, as follows:

1. In the source file, select the text, data, image, or object you want to embed.
2. Select Edit ➢ Copy to copy the source object.
3. Move to your Word document, and position the insertion point where you want to insert the linked object.
4. Select Edit ➢ Paste Special to display the Paste Special dialog box, shown back in Figure 17.1.
5. Select the object's native format from the As list.
6. Select the Paste option—*not* the Paste Link option!
7. Click OK.

Creating a New Embedded Object

When you choose to embed an object, you don't have to start with an existing object; you can launch the object's source application *within Word* to create a brand-new object.

Follow these steps:

1. Anchor the insertion point where you want to insert the object in your document.
2. Select Insert ➢ Object to display the Object dialog box.

FIGURE 17.4
*Select the Create New
tab to create a
completely new
embedded object.*

Select the Type of
Object to Embed

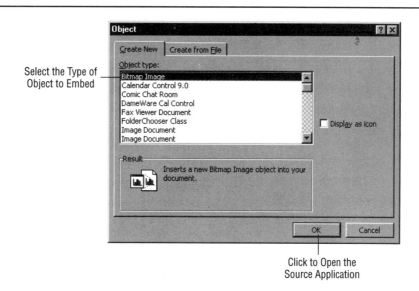

Click to Open the
Source Application

3. Select the Create New tab, shown in Figure 17.4.

4. The Object Type list lists all the different documents you can create from the OLE-compatible applications installed on your hard disk. Select an object from this list.

5. Click OK to open the source application.

6. When the source application window opens, create your new object.

7. Close the source application window to permanently embed the object in your Word document.

Editing Embedded Objects

Since the source file for your object is now embedded in your Word file, you have to open the source file and application from within Word. There are several ways to do this, including:

- Double-click the embedded object.

WARNING Double-clicking an embedded object opens the source data for every application *except* PowerPoint. When you double-click an embedded PowerPoint object, you launch a PowerPoint slideshow.

- Select the embedded object, and then select Edit ➤ Object ➤ Edit.
- Right-click the linked object, and select Object ➤ Edit from the pop-up menu.

When you execute any of these operations, Word opens the source application within the Word workspace, as shown in Figure 17.5, with the source data loaded. Make the appropriate changes to the source data, and then click within your Word document to close the source application and see your changes.

FIGURE 17.5
While editing an embedded Excel file within the Word workspace, Word's normal menus and toolbars are replaced by Excel elements.

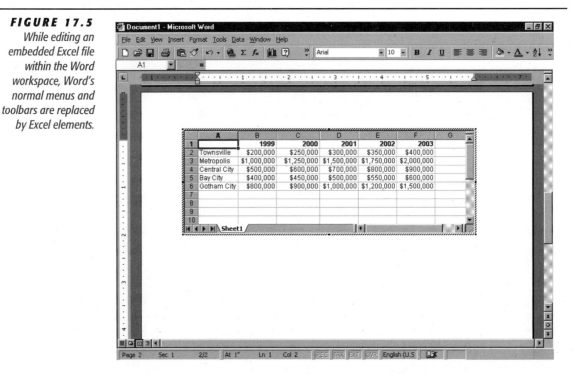

Converting an Embedded Object to Another File Format

A document with an embedded object is more portable than a document with a linked object since the document carries the source data along with it (instead of linking to a source file stored elsewhere). Still, in order for other users to edit embedded documents on their computers, they have to have the source application installed on their systems. If you want users to be able to edit a document but you're not sure whether they all have the source application installed on their PCs, you may want to convert the embedded object to a more common file format that can be edited on other PCs.

To convert an object's file format, follow these steps:

1. Select the object.

2. Select Edit ➢ Object ➢ Convert to display the Convert dialog box.

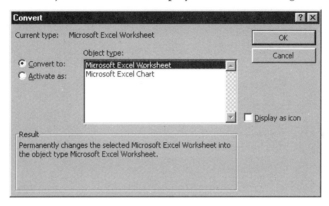

3. Select a new file type from the Object Type list.

4. Check the Convert To option.

5. Click OK

Not all objects can be converted to all file types. Only those applicable file types for the selected object are displayed in the Object Type list.

PART V

Creating Labels and Mailings

- *Creating and printing envelopes and labels*

- *Working with databases and mail merge*

- *Setting up a mass mailing*

CHAPTER 18

Creating and Printing Envelopes and Labels

Configuring Word for envelope printing   **510**

Printing a single envelope   **513**

Choosing envelope addressing options   **514**

Attaching an envelope to a document for later printing   **515**

Configuring Word for specific types of labels   **518**

Creating a new label type   **518**

Printing a label   **519**

Printing an entire sheet of labels   **521**

Almost all users use Word to create and print letters, but far fewer users know that they can use Word to print envelopes and mailing labels to accompany their letters. Word 2000 includes an easy-to-use Envelopes and Labels tool that lets you print virtually any kind of envelope or mailing label on your own computer printer.

Printing Envelopes

You use the Envelopes and Labels dialog box—displayed when you select Tools ➢ Envelopes and Labels—to print envelopes one at a time from your printer. This tool also lets you attach envelopes to Word documents for printing at a later time.

NOTE This section discusses printing *single* envelopes and labels from within Word. To learn how to print *multiple* envelopes and labels for a merged mailing, see Chapter 19.

Configuring Word for Envelope Printing

Before you print your first envelope, you need to tell Word what kind of envelope you're using. To do this, follow these steps:

1. Select Tools ➢ Envelopes and Labels to display the Envelopes and Labels dialog box.

WARNING The Envelopes and Labels dialog box is not accessible unless a document (blank or otherwise) is loaded in the Word workspace.

2. Select the Envelopes tab.
3. Click the Options button to display the Envelope Options dialog box.
4. Select the Envelope Options tab to set the options detailed in the following sections.

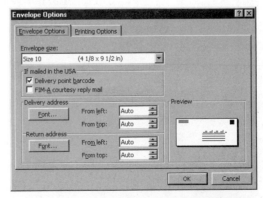

5. Select the Printing Options tab to configure the envelope feed method and direction for your printer. Select the Feed Method that best represents how envelopes feed into your printer, then select whether your envelopes feed in face up or face down, and from what tray you're feeding. (For most printers, AutoSelect Tray is the selected option.)

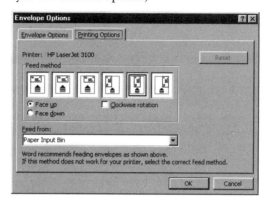

6. Click OK.

Most of the envelope configuration options you need to set are on the Envelope Options tab. The following sections detail these envelope options.

Envelope Size

Pull down the Envelope Size list to select from over a dozen standard envelope sizes. If your envelope doesn't appear on this list, select Custom Size from the list to display the Envelope Size dialog box, then enter the specific dimensions of the envelopes you're using.

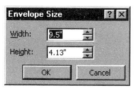

Delivery Point Barcode

When you check the Delivery Point Barcode option, Word prints a POSTNET barcode above the mailing address on your envelope, as shown in Figure 18.1. This barcode is a machine-readable representation of the zip code in your delivery address; printing this barcode on your envelopes can actually speed up the delivery of your mail.

Creating Labels and Mailings

FIGURE 18.1
Print a POSTNET
barcode above your
address to speed
up your mail's
delivery time.

Michael Miller
1234 Main St.
Indianapolis, IN 46224

║ı|ıl₁|ıl₁|ıl₁|ılıl₁ı₁ıllıll
Andy Taylor
55 Blue Mountain Dr.
Mayberry, NC 55469

 TIP To create more accurate POSTNET barcodes, use nine-digit zip codes whenever possible.

FIM-A Courtesy Reply Mail

This option prints a Facing Identification Mark (FIM-A) on courtesy reply mail to identify the front of the envelope during re-sorting. The FIM-A is necessary only if you're printing a courtesy reply mail envelope.

Delivery Address Font and Placement

In the Delivery Address section of the Envelope Options dialog box, click the Font button to display the Font dialog box. From here you can select a font, font size, and style for the delivery address.

If you're having trouble with the placement of the delivery address on your envelope, you can use the From Left and From Top controls to fine-tune the address positioning. The Auto selection works in most cases, but if the address prints a little off, you can specify precise placement from the left and the top of the envelope.

 TIP You can also change fonts directly in the Delivery Address and Return Address sections of the Envelopes and Labels dialog box. Just highlight the text you want to format, right-click, and select Font from the pop-up menu to display the Font dialog box.

Return Address Font and Placement

The Font, From Left, and From Top controls in the Return Address section work identically to the same controls in the Delivery Address section. Click the Font button to display the

Font dialog box and change the font for your return address; use the From Left and From Top controls to fine-tune the positioning of the return address on the envelope.

 TIP You can specify different fonts for your envelope's return and delivery addresses. For example, you may want to choose a smaller font size for the less important return address.

Printing a Single Envelope

To create and print a single envelope, follow these steps:

1. Select Tools ➤ Envelopes and Labels to display the Envelopes and Labels dialog box.
2. Select the Envelopes tab, shown in Figure 18.2.

FIGURE 18.2
*Use the Envelopes and
Labels dialog box to
print one-off envelopes.*

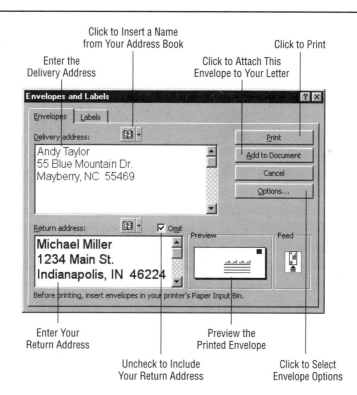

Click to Insert a Name
from Your Address Book

Enter the
Delivery Address

Click to Print

Click to Attach This
Envelope to Your Letter

Enter Your
Return Address

Uncheck to Include
Your Return Address

Preview the
Printed Envelope

Click to Select
Envelope Options

TIP You can also get to the Envelopes and Labels dialog box by opening either the Envelope Wizard or the Mailing Label Wizard from the Letters & Faxes tab of Word's New dialog box.

3. Enter the name and address of the recipient in the Delivery Address box.

4. If *your* name and address do not appear automatically, enter them in the Return Address blank.

5. If you *don't* want to print your return address on the envelope—if you're using a preprinted envelope that already includes a return address, for example—check the Omit option.

6. Insert an envelope in your printer as displayed in the Preview section of the dialog box.

7. Click Print to print the envelope.

 NOTE Many third-party software programs are available that help facilitate envelope printing from Word. One of these, KazStamp, is available on the CD included with this book. For more information about KazStamp, see Chapter 33.

Choosing Envelope Addressing Options

Although printing envelopes seems pretty simple, you should be aware of several options of this operation—all involving how you address your envelopes.

Adding Your Return Address Automatically

By default, Word will insert in the Return Address box the name and address you previously entered as part of your Word user information. You can accept this mailing address, you can edit it, or you can delete it and enter a different return address.

 TIP To change the mailing address in your user information, select Tools ➢ Options to display the Options dialog box, then select the User Information tab and edit appropriately.

Using Names from Your Address Book

Although you can manually type the recipient's name and address in the Delivery Address box, you can also choose from any names listed in your Windows Address Book. Follow these steps:

1. From within the Envelopes and Labels dialog box, click the Address Book button in the Delivery Address section to display the Select Name dialog box.

2. Select a name from your Address Book.

3. Click OK to insert the selected name (and address) into the Delivery Address box.

 NOTE The first time you access your Address Book from within Word, you'll see the Inbox Setup Wizard. Follow the on-screen instructions to tell Word about your Internet connection and e-mail account, and to choose the correct location for your Address Book.

If you've previously used the Envelopes and Labels dialog box to create envelopes or labels, you can click the arrow to the right of the Address Book button to choose from a list of recently used addresses. Select a specific address to insert it into the Delivery Address box.

Automatically Inserting the Name and Address from an Existing Letter

If you're writing a letter in the Word workspace—and you've added the recipient's address to the top of the letter—the Envelopes and Labels tool can automatically insert that address into the Delivery Address box. Just follow these steps:

1. From within your letter, select the recipient's name and address.

2. Select Tools ➤ Envelopes and Labels to display the Envelopes and Labels dialog box.

3. Select the Envelopes tab. The address you selected in your letter should be automatically inserted into the Delivery Address box.

4. Configure the rest of the envelope information as normal.

Attaching an Envelope to a Document for Later Printing

Once you've created an envelope, you don't have to print it right away. Word 2000 provides the option of *attaching* the envelope to your open document, for later printing. When you attach an envelope to your letter, it becomes part of your original Word document, as shown in Figure 18.3.

PART

V

Creating Labels and
Mailings

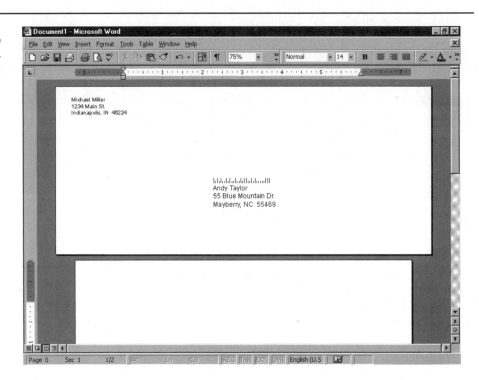

To attach an envelope to your document, follow these steps:

1. Select Tools ➢ Envelopes and Labels to display the Envelopes and Labels dialog box.

2. Select the Envelopes tab, and enter the appropriate information to create the envelope.

3. Click the Add to Document button.

Printing an Attached Envelope

To print an attached envelope, make sure the insertion point is somewhere in the envelope part of your document, then select File ➢ Print. You can now print the envelope (and *only* the envelope—you have to print the letter separately) as normal.

 TIP You don't have to attach an envelope to an existing document—you can attach any envelope to a *blank* document to take advantage of the other envelope attachment features.

Applying Fancy Formatting—and Graphics—to Your Envelope

If an envelope can be displayed in Word's Print Layout view—it can if you've attached it to a Word document—you can then edit it as you would any other Word document. The most important ramification of this option is the capability of adding graphics to your envelopes.

When you display an attached envelope in Print Layout view, use Word's standard graphics commands to insert clip art or picture files into your envelope. In particular, consider adding a graphic to your return address, perhaps in the form of a company logo. Whatever you do, *don't* let a graphic obscure the delivery address—or the post office won't be able to deliver your mail.

 NOTE For more information on inserting and formatting graphics files, see Chapter 16.

Saving Your Envelope Format as a Template

If you go to a lot of effort to create the perfect envelope design, you want to be able to reuse it when you need to print more envelopes in the future. If you've attached your envelope to a letter, change the letter text to make it somewhat generic, then save the entire document (letter and envelope) as a template, as follows:

1. Select File ➢ Save As to display the Save As dialog box.
2. Pull down the Save As Type list and select Document Template (.DOC).
3. Assign this template a new filename.
4. Click the Save button.

When you want to create a new letter/envelope based on this template, select File ➢ New to display the New dialog box, then open the saved template. A new document will be opened, based on the previous letter/envelope design.

Printing Labels

Creating a mailing label is similar to addressing an envelope—with some unique options for label configuration. Word lets you use just about any type of blank labels; you can find labels in all different sizes, typically with several labels per sheet.

Configuring Word for Specific Types of Labels

Before you print your first label, you need to tell Word what specific type of label you'll be using. Follow these steps:

1. Select Tools ➤ Envelopes and Labels to display the Envelopes and Labels dialog box.

2. Select the Labels tab.

3. Click the Options button to display the Label Options dialog box.

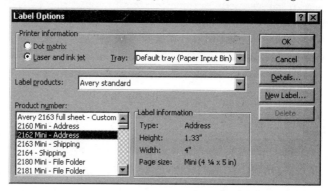

4. Select either the Dot Matrix or the Laser and Ink Jet option; if you're using a laser or inkjet printer, also select which tray of your printer you'll be using to print your labels.

5. Pull down the Label Products list and select the brand of label you're using.

6. Select the specific label type from the Product Number list.

7. If you want to confirm the information about the label you selected—or if your printer isn't printing a specific label properly—click the Details button to display the Label Information dialog box. Change any measurements, if necessary, then click OK to return to the Label Options dialog box.

8. Click OK.

Creating a New Label Type

If the label you're using isn't listed in the Label Options dialog box, you can create a new label template for your label. Follow these steps:

1. Select Tools ➤ Envelopes and Labels to display the Envelopes and Labels dialog box.

2. Select the Labels tab.

3. Click the Options button to display the Label Options dialog box.

4. Click the New Label button to display the New Custom dialog box.

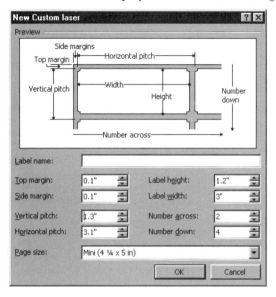

5. Enter the measurements of your label, and assign it a name.

6. Click OK.

Printing a Label

To print a single label from the Envelopes and Labels dialog box, follow these steps:

1. Select Tools ➢ Envelopes and Labels to display the Envelopes and Labels dialog box.

2. Select the Labels tab, shown in Figure 18.4.

3. Type the recipient's name and address in the Address box. As an alternative, you can click the Address Book button to display the Select Name dialog box, then select a name from your Address Book; when you click OK, the name you selected will be inserted into the Delivery Address box. Also, if you've previously used the Envelopes and Labels dialog box to create envelopes or labels, you can click the arrow to the right of the Address Book button to choose from a list of recently used addresses; select an address to insert it into the Delivery Address box.

 TIP If you want to print a label for your return address—*not* a normal delivery address label—check the Use Return Address option to automatically insert your return address in the Delivery Address box.

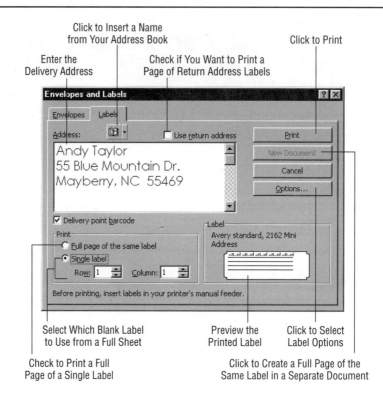

4. If you want to print a POSTNET barcode on your label, check the Delivery Point Barcode option.

 WARNING The Delivery Point Barcode option isn't available if you're printing a very small label or using a dot-matrix printer.

5. To set the font used on your label, highlight the entire address and then right-click. When the pop-up menu appears, select Font. When the Font dialog box appears, select a font, style, and font size, then click OK.

6. If you want to print a full page of this label, check the Full Page of the Same Label option. If you want to print a single label, check the Single Label option, then select which row and column on your label sheet you want to print (you can use a single sheet of labels to print multiple labels over time).

7. Confirm that everything is configured properly, insert the sheet of labels into your printer's feed tray, then click Print to print the label(s).

Your printer should now print a perfectly aligned label, ready to be applied to the envelope or package of choice.

Printing an Entire Sheet of Labels

You can use the Envelopes and Labels dialog box to print a single label with a single address, or to print an entire page of identical labels. There are several ways to create a page of labels, including:

Printing a Page of Normal Delivery Labels To print an entire page of the same label, fill in the rest of the Envelopes and Labels dialog box as normal, but check the Full Page of the Same Label option.

Printing a Page of Return Address Labels To print an entire page of return address labels (it's always nice to have preaddressed return labels for all the letters you send—and the bills you pay!), check the Use Return Address option *and* the Full Page of the Same Label option.

Creating a Document of Labels If you want to create a new document consisting of a full page of identical labels, click the New Document button. This creates a regular Word document that you can edit in the normal ways—including adding graphics to the labels in Print Layout view. Once you have your custom labels fully designed, save them as a separate document—which you can open and print again when you need more labels in the future.

 NOTE To print multiple labels with different addresses for a merge mailing, see Chapter 19.

CHAPTER <u>**19**</u>

Working with Databases and Mail Merge

Creating your main document   525

Opening or creating a data source   526

Editing your document and inserting
merge fields   533

Merging your data and outputting the
merged mailing   537

Printing merged labels and envelopes   542

Creating a merged catalog   550

Querying a database for specific
information   552

One of the more powerful features of Word 2000 is its capability to create form letters and merged mailings, using names and data from any number of external sources. You create a single "boilerplate" letter and envelope or label, identify the source of the names, addresses, and other information, and Word seamlessly merges the data into personalized letters, envelopes, and labels.

Word accomplishes this task via the Mail Merge Helper tool. This tool makes it easy to import data from external databases into Word documents.

In addition, certain versions of Microsoft Office 2000 include Direct Mail Manager, a powerful utility you can use to ease the creation of very large mass mailings. This utility is much more powerful and versatile than Word's Mail Merge Helper and should be your tool of choice if you have to prepare a very large mailing.

Planning for a Merged Mailing

Although you can create merged documents manually, using Word's fields feature (discussed in Chapter 12), it is much easier to have Word automate the process with the Mail Merge Helper.

You use the Mail Merge Helper to create form letters, mailing labels, envelopes, and other documents that merge data from external sources. The Mail Merge Helper guides you through organizing and gathering the data, merging it into a generic document, and then printing the personalized results.

Here are the general steps you'll go through when creating a merged mailing with the Mail Merge Helper:

1. **Create your *main document***, which should contain the generic text you want to repeat in each form letter, envelope, or mailing label.

2. **Open or create a *data source***, which should contain the individual data to be merged into the main document. (For example, for a merged envelope, the data source should contain the names and addresses of all the intended recipients.) Word can work with various types of data sources, including Excel spreadsheets, Access databases, or tables in other Word documents.

3. **Insert *merge fields* into your main document**. Merge fields are placeholders for the data that will be inserted from your data source.

4. **Merge the data, and output the merged documents**. Whether you're merging from a database, spreadsheet, or Word table, each row or record in the data source will produce an individual form letter, envelope, or label, which can then be sent directly to your printer for printing or distributed via e-mail or fax. You can also collect all the merged documents into a single new document, which can be edited and printed at a later time.

Creating a Merged Mailing with the Mail Merge Helper

Word's Mail Merge Helper, shown in Figure 19.1, completely automates the process of merging data from a data source into a Word document. When you select Tools ➢ Mail Merge and follow the step-by-step instructions in the Mail Merge Helper, you'll create a perfectly merged mailing with a minimal amount of work.

FIGURE 19.1
Use the Mail Merge Helper to automate merged mailings.

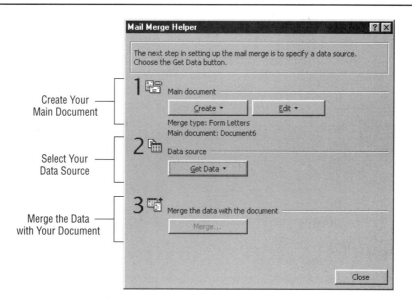

Create Your Main Document

Select Your Data Source

Merge the Data with Your Document

Step 1: Creating Your Main Document

The first step in creating a merged mailing is to create your main document. This form letter holds the boilerplate text that will be sent to all recipients; later, you'll insert special fields into this document as placeholders for the merged data from the data source.

To create a new form letter, follow these steps:

1. Create a new, blank document by clicking the New Blank Document button on Word's Standard toolbar, or open an existing document by clicking the Open Document button.

2. Select Tools ➢ Mail Merge to display the Mail Merge Helper.

3. In the Main Document section, click the Create button, and select Form Letters.

The current document now becomes your main document for the merged mailing. Leave the document as is for now; you can enter text into the document when you insert the fields for the merged data.

TIP If, at any time in this process, the Mail Merge Helper disappears from the screen, select Tools ➢ Mail Merge to redisplay it.

Step 2: Opening or Creating a Data Source

The individual data—not the boilerplate text—for your form letters and mailings isn't stored in your Word document; it has to come from a separate data source. Typically, you can store this data (names and addresses for a mailing, other data for other types of merges) in a database, a worksheet, an address book, or even a properly constructed table from another Word document. Word takes the data from this data source one name at a time and merges it into the proper places in your form letter.

If you look at your data as a table or a worksheet composed of rows and columns, as shown in Figure 19.2, each *column* represents a certain category of information (also called a *data field*—or just a *field*), like a first name, a last name, or a street address. The name of each data field is displayed in the first row of cells (also called the *header row*); each row below the header row represents a different individual (in the case of a form letter) and is called a *data record*.

When you're preparing a merged mailing, you can use already existing data, or you can use the Mail Merge Helper to help you set up a Word table as your data source. (Word tables are good for smaller mailing lists—with 63 or fewer columns—while Access databases or Excel spreadsheets are better for larger lists.)

As you plan a new data source, the key thing to keep in mind is what specific pieces of data you'll be using in your form letters and envelopes or labels. Generally, the more discrete the data bits, the better; so, for example, it's better to have separate first-name and last-name fields than a combined name field. (In fact, you might even want to stick in a middle name or nickname field, either of which you can leave blank if it doesn't apply to a particular individual.)

You should also take into account that you'll probably want to sort the data and perhaps extract data records that meet a certain criteria. For example, you may want to send a mailing only to people who live in Iowa, so you'll need to sort and separate by state, which you can't do if the state is just part of a larger address field; but you *can* do this if you have a separate state field. Again, more fields are better.

In any case, the best advice is to think through all the possible uses of your data and create enough fields in your data source to provide maximum versatility, no matter how you might use the data.

FIGURE 19.2

An Excel worksheet can serve as a data source for merged mailings.

The First Row Is the Header Row

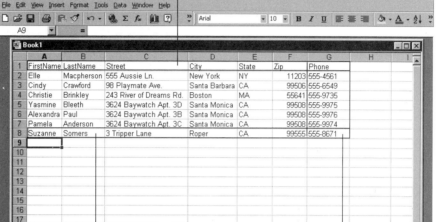

Each Row Is a Data Record   Each Column Is a Data Field

Setting Up a Word Table as a Data Source

If you haven't yet set up a data source, it's easy to create a Word table in a separate document to do the job for you. (Remember, though, you can only have a total of 63 fields, or columns, in the Word table.)

Follow these steps to create a data source in a Word table:

1. From the Mail Merge Helper, click the Get Data button, and then select Create Data Source to display the Create Data Source dialog box, shown in Figure 19.3.

PART

V

Creating Labels and
Mailings

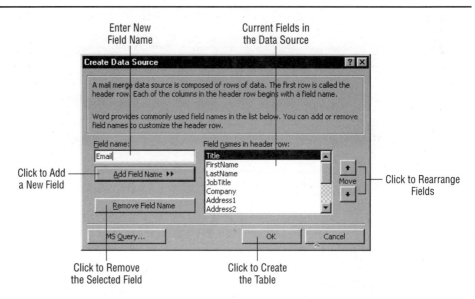

FIGURE 19.3
Use the Create Data Source dialog box to create a Word table for your data source.

Enter New Field Name

Current Fields in the Data Source

Click to Add a New Field

Click to Rearrange Fields

Click to Remove the Selected Field

Click to Create the Table

2. The Field Names in Header Row list contains a preselected collection of common fields. Scroll through this list, select any fields you don't want to include in your data source, and then click the Remove Field Name button to remove those fields.

3. To add new fields to your data source, enter the name for the field in the Field Name box, and then click the Add Field Name button.

4. To rearrange the order of a field, select a field in the Field Names in Header Row list, and then click either the up or the down arrow to move the field up or down in the list.

5. When all the fields are set up to your liking, click OK to display the Save As dialog box.

6. Specify a filename and location for your data source file, and then click Save.

7. Word now notifies you that your newly created data source contains no records. To add data to your data source table, click the Edit Data Source button.

8. Word now displays a Data Form dialog box, as shown in Figure 19.4. This data form includes all the fields in your data source.

FIGURE 19.4
The data you enter into the data form is added to the data source table.

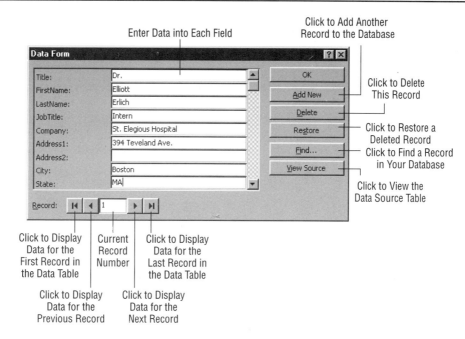

Enter Data into Each Field

Click to Add Another Record to the Database

Click to Delete This Record

Click to Restore a Deleted Record

Click to Find a Record in Your Database

Click to View the Data Source Table

Click to Display Data for the First Record in the Data Table

Current Record Number

Click to Display Data for the Last Record in the Data Table

Click to Display Data for the Previous Record

Click to Display Data for the Next Record

9. Enter data into all the fields in the data form; press the Tab key to advance to the next field.

10. Once you've completed the data form, press the Add New button to display a new record, and then repeat step 9.

11. When you're done adding records and entering data, close the Data Form dialog box by clicking OK.

At any time in the process, you can view the Word table in the data source document by clicking the View Source button. As shown in Figure 19.5, the data source table looks like any other Word table; you can edit the table's data, delete records (rows), add new records (rows), and sort the data by any field (column).

To ease the entry of information into the table, Word automatically displays the Database toolbar. Click the Data Form button to redisplay the Data Form dialog box, or click the Mail Merge Main Document button to switch to your mail merge document.

TIP You can also create a data source table without using the Mail Merge Helper, by inserting a new table within a blank Word document. If you do so, you'll have to open it via the Open Data Source option in the Mail Merge Helper, as discussed in the "Using an External Data Source" section that follows.

FIGURE 19.5

*New data source table,
ready for data entry*

Database Toolbar —

Header Row —

First Data Record —

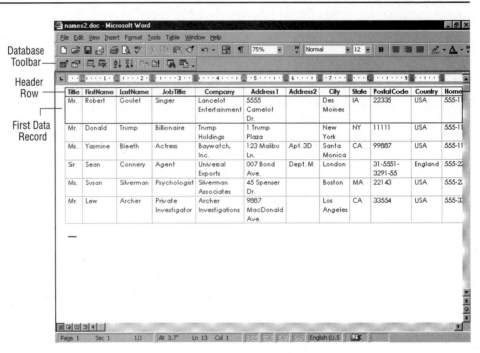

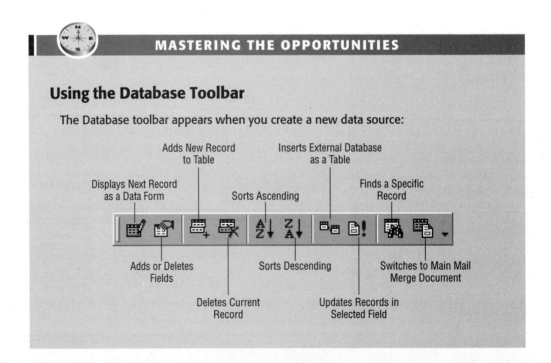

MASTERING THE OPPORTUNITIES

Using the Database Toolbar

The Database toolbar appears when you create a new data source:

Adds New Record to Table

Inserts External Database as a Table

Displays Next Record as a Data Form

Sorts Ascending

Finds a Specific Record

Adds or Deletes Fields

Sorts Descending

Switches to Main Mail Merge Document

Deletes Current Record

Updates Records in Selected Field

Using an External Data Source

If you already have a data source (from an Excel spreadsheet, let's say, or an Access database), you can merge data from that external file into your form letter. Word 2000 can use the following types of files as data sources for merged mailings:

- ASCII text files
- Electronic address books of the following types: Microsoft Outlook Address Book, Microsoft Outlook Contact List, Schedule+ 7.0 Contact List, Microsoft Exchange Server Personal Address Book, and any address lists created with a MAPI-compatible messaging system
- Files from any flat-file database program for which you have installed an open database connectivity (ODBC) driver
- Lotus 1-2-3 spreadsheets (versions 2.x–4.x)
- Microsoft Access databases
- Microsoft Excel workbooks
- Microsoft Word documents that contain properly formatted tables
- WordPerfect documents (versions 5.x–6.x for MS-DOS and 5.x–6.x for Windows)

Follow these steps to open an external file as your data source:

1. From the Mail Merge Helper, click the Get Data button, and then select Open Data Source to display the Open Data Source dialog box.

2. Navigate to the document you want to use as your data source, and then click the Open button.

After you click the Open field, Word displays a dialog box specific to the source application you've chosen. This dialog box, which is different for each application, lets you select which data from the source document you want to include in your merge. For example, if you're importing from an Excel spreadsheet, you see the Microsoft Excel dialog box, from which you can select the cells or range to use as your data source.

If you're merging with an Access database, the Microsoft Access dialog box appears. From here, you select the Tables tab, select a specific database table, select the Queries tab, and then select or modify a database query.

If the data source is an ASCII format file or a file format that Word doesn't automatically recognize, you see the Header Record Delimiters dialog box. A *delimiter* is a character used to separate things in the file; the data source file will have both field delimiters (the character used to separate fields) and record delimiters (the character used to separate records). In most instances, the field delimiter will be the Tab character and the Record delimiter will be the Enter character.

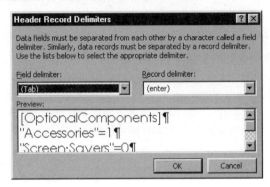

Using Names from Your Address Book

To use your Windows Personal Address Book, Outlook Address Book, or Microsoft Schedule+ Contacts as your data source, follow these steps:

1. From the Mail Merge Helper, click the Get Data button, and then select Address Book to display the Use Address Book dialog box.

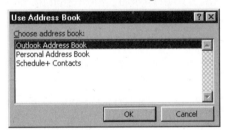

2. Select which address book to use as your data source, and then click OK.

If you use an address book as a data source, you'll be able to choose which names you merge in the upcoming fourth step of this process.

 NOTE There are several third-party programs that ease the merging of data between Outlook and other address books into Word documents. Two of those programs, Aladdins ~ Word Documents and GPData, are included on the CD that accompanies this book. See Chapter 33 for more information.

Step 3: Editing Your Document and Inserting Merge Fields

Once you've selected your data source, it's time to edit your form letter document and insert the fields to hold the merged data.

If the main document is not displayed onscreen, go to the Main Document section in the Mail Merge Helper, click the Edit button, and select your form letter document. Word now switches to your main document and displays the Mail Merge toolbar. You use this toolbar to facilitate the insertion of merge fields into your document.

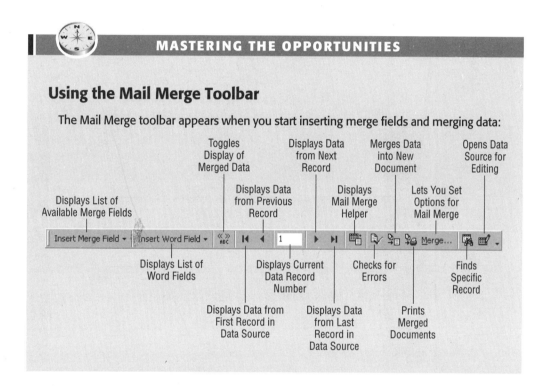

MASTERING THE OPPORTUNITIES

Using the Mail Merge Toolbar

The Mail Merge toolbar appears when you start inserting merge fields and merging data:

Inserting Merge Fields

You create your form letter as you would any Word document, but insert merge fields as placeholders where you want to merge data.

For example, if you want to personalize the form letter, you may want to replace the standard *Dear Sir* with *Dear Bob* or *Dear Jane* for each of your intended recipients. To do this, you would type **Dear** as normal, but follow that with a firstname field.

To insert a field in your document, follow these steps:

1. Position the insertion point where you want to add the merge field.

2. Click the Insert Merge Field button on the Mail Merge toolbar to display the list of available fields from your chosen data source.

3. Click the field you want to insert.

Word now inserts your selected field at the insertion point, as shown in Figure 19.6. Remember, the text you type will appear in every letter; the data added via merge fields will be personalized for each individual letter.

FIGURE 19.6

A merge field added to your document

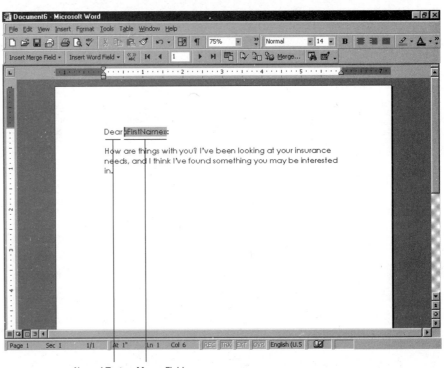

Normal Text   Merge Field

TIP You can copy or move the field within your document; just remember to select the entire field before you perform any editing operations.

Automating Your Merge with Word Fields

In addition to the merge fields that serve as placeholders for data from your data source file, you can also insert other Word fields into your document, including some field codes that help automate your mail merge.

 NOTE For more information on Word fields, see Chapter 12.

Here are the most important types of fields you can add to a mail merge document:

- Ask and Fill-In fields prompt you during the merge process for additional information, which is then added to the merged output.
- If fields add data to a merge only if a specific condition is met.
- Set fields allow you to assign text to a bookmark, which can then be used multiple times in the resulting merged documents.

Although you could insert these fields manually, using Word's Insert Field dialog box (select Insert ➤ Field), it's easier to insert the proper field as a complete process using the Insert Word Field menu on the Mail Merge toolbar.

Follow these steps:

1. Position the insertion point where you want to insert the field code.
2. Click the Insert Word Field button on the Mail Merge toolbar to display the list of available field operations.
3. Click the field operation you want to insert.
4. Word now displays an Insert Word Field dialog box specific to the field operation. Fill in the necessary data, or select the appropriate options, and then click OK to insert the complete field code for the selected operation.

Table 19.1 details the Word field code operations accessible via the Insert Word Field menu.

TABLE 19.1: WORD MAIL MERGE FIELD CODE OPERATIONS

Field Code Operation	Description
Ask	Prompts user to select a message to be inserted in the document
Fill-In	Prompts user for text to be inserted in the document

Continued ▐▶

PART

V

Creating Labels and
Mailings

TABLE 19.1: WORD MAIL MERGE FIELD CODE OPERATIONS (CONTINUED)

Field Code Operation	Description
If...Then...Else	Inserts one of two different text strings, depending on the contents of a specific field
Merge Record #	Inserts the record number of the current merge record into the merged document
Merge Sequence #	Inserts the sequence number of the current merge record into the merged document (will differ from Merge Record # field if data has been sorted or if you're using a subset of the total data source)
Next Record	Inserts data from the next record into the merged document
Next Record If	Inserts data from the next record into the merged document only if specified conditions are met
Set Bookmark	Inserts bookmarked text into every merged document
Skip Record If	Omits records from the merge if specified conditions are met

As an example, let's say you want to be prompted to add a personalized message to every letter in the merge mailing. While you're editing the main document, position the insertion point where you want to add the personalized message, then go to the Mail Merge toolbar, and select Insert Word Field ➤ Fill-In to display the Insert Word Field: Fill-In dialog box.

Enter the text you want to be prompted with into the Prompt box, move to the Default Fill-In Text box, and enter a block of default text to use if you *don't* enter a personalized message. Click OK to enter this Word field into your document.

When you initiate the merge, before each new form letter prints, you'll see a dialog box like the following, prompting you for a personalized message. When you enter text in the dialog box and click OK, your personalized message is added to that particular merged letter. When the next letter is ready to print, the dialog box is displayed again, and you enter a different personalized message.

NOTE If you *don't* enter a personalized message in the dialog box, any default text you entered into your document will be printed instead.

The Ask field operates similarly, giving you a list of messages to choose from for each recipient; the selected message is inserted into the current merge letter.

Step 4: Merging Your Data and Outputting the Merged Mailing

When your main document is completed, all merge fields inserted, and you've added the appropriate data to your data source, it's time to initiate the merge and create some form of output. Word lets you output the results of your merge mailing as printed documents, as e-mail messages, as fax messages, and as a separate file (for future editing and printing).

Checking for Errors

Before you merge, you probably want to confirm that the merge works, that the fields in your main document match up with the fields in your data source. To check your merge for errors, follow these steps:

1. From within your main merge document, click the Check for Errors button on the Mail Merge toolbar to display the Checking and Reporting Errors dialog box.

2. To check for errors prior to a merge, check the Simulate the Merge and Report Errors in a Separate Document option. (If you'd rather proceed with the merge

and be notified if any errors are found during the process, check the Complete the Merge, Pausing to Report Each Error As It Occurs option.)

3. Click OK to begin a simulated merge.

Word performs a merge without any output and notifies you of any errors found. (If no errors appear, you're notified of that as well.) If Word finds errors, return to either your data source or your main merge document to fix the conditions that caused the errors.

Previewing a Merged Document

If you want to see what your document looks like when data is merged into it, click the View Merged Data button on the Mail Merge toolbar. When this button is toggled on, data from the current record is inserted into the merge fields of your on-screen document, so you can view a simulation of the final output.

To view data from other records, use the arrow buttons on the Mail Merge toolbar, or enter a specific record number in the Go to Record box and press Enter. Click the View Merged Data button again to toggle back to a display of the field codes.

Printing Your Merged Document

When everything has been entered, inserted, checked, and previewed, it's time to initiate merging and printing of your merged documents. To start the merge and send the output to your printer, follow these steps:

1. Click the Merge button on the Mail Merge toolbar to display the Merge dialog box.

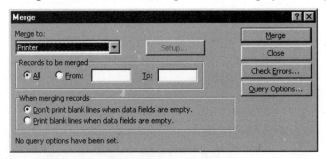

2. Pull down the Merge To list, and select Printer.

3. To check for errors before you merge, click the Check Errors button.

4. To merge all records from the data source, select the All option. To merge a range of records, check the From option, and enter a range in the From and To boxes.

5. To select only certain records to merge, click the Query Options button to display the Query Options dialog box; select the Filter Records tab, and then select which field you want to filter from the Field list. Select a comparison for that filter, and then enter specific text or a value in the Compare To box. (You can enter additional filters below the first filter, if desired.) As an example, you might want to limit your output to people living in New York; you'd select State from the Field list, select Equal To from the Comparison list, and enter NY in the Compare To box. Click OK when you're done filtering.

6. To sort your output in a different order, click the Query Options button to display the Query Options dialog box, and then select the Sort Records tab. Select a field from the Sort By list, and then select Ascending or Descending sort. If you want to subsort by additional fields, enter those options in the Then By boxes. Click OK when you're done selecting Sort options.

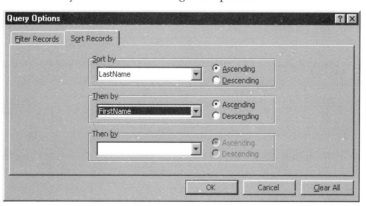

TIP You can also change the order in which your merged documents print by switching to your data source document and sorting those records in the desired order.

7. When all options have been selected, click the Merge button to begin the merge and to initiate printing.

Word will now begin the merge process. If you inserted any Word fields that require real-time input on your part, you'll see the appropriate prompt boxes onscreen during the merge; answer the prompts as appropriate to continue merging that particular record.

As each record in the data source is merged into your main merge document, that completed document is automatically sent to your printer. The merged documents will be printed in the order of the records in your data source or in the sort order you selected in the Query Options dialog box.

E-mailing or Faxing Your Merged Document

You don't have to print your merged documents; you can e-mail or fax them instead. To do this, however, the e-mail address or fax number for each recipient must be included as a field in your data source and inserted as a merge field somewhere in your merge document. The Mail Merge Helper can then extract that address information and use it to address and send the e-mail or fax version of your document.

To initiate e-mailing or faxing of your merged documents, follow these steps:

1. Click the Merge button on the Mail Merge toolbar to display the Merge dialog box.

2. Pull down the Merge To list, and select Electronic Mail.

3. Click the Setup button to display the Merge to Setup dialog box.

4. Pull down the Data Field with Mail/Fax Address list, and select which field contains either the e-mail address or the fax number.

5. If you're sending the merged documents as e-mail messages, enter a subject for this e-mail message into the Mail Message Subject Line box.

6. If you're sending the merged documents as *attachments* to e-mail messages (recommended if recipients cannot receive HTML e-mail), check the Send Document as an Attachment option.

7. Click OK to return to the Merge dialog box.

8. Select all other merge options, then click Merge to initiate the merge and send the messages.

 WARNING For merge faxing to work properly, you must have a fax program installed on your computer system. See Chapter 7 for more information.

Merging to a New Document

What do you do if you want to tweak each of your merged documents for individual recipients and don't want to bother with inserting Ask or Fill-In fields? The answer is to save the results of your merge in a separate document that you can then edit *before* you print.

When you choose to merge to a document, all the merged documents are saved in a single, large document. For example, if your main merge document is a one-page form letter and you have ten records in your data source, the new merged document will be a single file with ten separate pages—each page containing the results of one merged record.

This newly created file has already been merged, so you can edit it in any way you want (adding individualized text to specific messages, changing names and addresses, you name it). When you're done editing, just print the document, which prints all the individual form letters contained within.

To save a merge as a separate document, follow these steps:

1. Click the Merge button on the Mail Merge toolbar to display the Merge dialog box.

2. Pull down the Merge To list, and select New Document.

3. Select all other merge options, and then click Merge to initiate the merge.

Word now creates a new document, with each merged document located in a separate section of the document. Select File ➢ Save As to save this file; perform any necessary editing, and print at your convenience.

PART

V

Creating Labels and
Mailings

Printing Envelopes and Labels for a Merged Mailing

Creating envelopes or labels for a merged mailing is very similar to creating the merged form letter. You have the option of using the Mail Merge Helper to initiate the merged printing or, in the case of envelopes, to attach a matching envelope as part of the form letter itself.

As with the form letter, the names you use for your labels can come from a variety of data sources, including Word tables, Excel worksheets, Access databases, and your Windows or Outlook Address Book.

Printing Merged Labels

To print mailing labels for your merged mailing, follow these steps:

1. Create a new, blank document by clicking the New Blank Document button on Word's Standard toolbar.

2. Select Tools ➤ Mail Merge to display the Mail Merge Helper.

3. In the Main Document section, click the Create button, and select Mailing Labels.

4. In the Data Source section, click the Get Data button, and select Open Data Source to display the Open Data Source dialog box. Select the file that contains the data source (you're probably using the same file opened or created when you created your form letter), and click Open.

TIP If you're inserting names from an electronic address book, click the Get Data button, and select Use Address Book to display the Use Address Book dialog box; select which address book to use as your data source, and then click OK.

5. Word now informs you that you need to set up your main document; click the Set Up Main Document to display the Label Options dialog box.

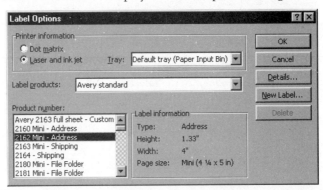

TIP If you don't automatically see the Label Options dialog box, return to the Mail Merge Helper, go to the Main Document section, and click the Setup button.

6. Select either the Dot Matrix or the Laser and Ink Jet option; if you're using a laser or ink-jet printer, also select which tray of your printer you'll be using to print your labels.

7. Pull down the Label Products list, and select the brand of label you're using.

8. Select the specific label type from the Product Number list.

9. If you want to confirm the information about the label you selected, or if your printer isn't printing a specific label properly, click the Details button to display the Label Information dialog box. Change any measurements, if necessary, and then click OK to return to the Label Options dialog box.

 NOTE For more information on setting up Word for specific types of labels, see Chapter 18.

10. Click OK to display the Create Labels dialog box, shown in Figure 19.7.

FIGURE 19.7
Using merge fields, create your labels in the Create Labels dialog box.

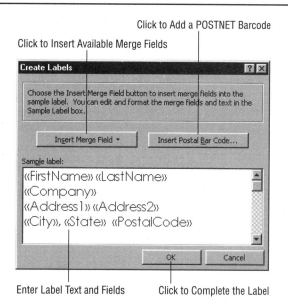

Click to Add a POSTNET Barcode

Click to Insert Available Merge Fields

Enter Label Text and Fields   Click to Complete the Label

PART

V

Creating Labels and Mailings

11. If you want to display a POSTNET barcode on your label, which helps the post office process your letter, it needs to appear on the *first* line of your label. Position the insertion point at the top of the Sample Label box, and click the Insert Postal Bar Code button to display the Insert Postal Bar Code dialog box. Pull down the Merge Field with Zip Code list, and select which field contains the Zip code information. Then pull down the Merge Field with Street Address list, and select which field contains the street address information. Click OK to return to the Create Labels dialog box.

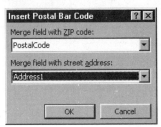

12. Now you can insert the fields you want to print on your label. (In most cases, these fields will be firstname, lastname, address, city, state, and postalcode.) To insert a field, click the Insert Merge Field button to display a list of available fields, and then click the field you want to insert. Each field is inserted at the insertion point; remember to put the appropriate fields on the appropriate lines and to leave spaces between certain fields, such as between the firstname and lastname fields.

13. Click OK when you're done creating the boilerplate label.

When you're ready to print the labels, you have two options:

Send the Labels Directly to Your Printer   To merge and print your labels directly, click the Merge to Printer button on the Mail Merge toolbar.

Save the Labels in a New Document   To save all the merged labels in a single new document that you can edit separately and print at a later time, click the Merge to New Document button on the Mail Merge menu. When the new document is created, as shown in Figure 19.8, select File ➤ Save As to save the document under a new name; edit the labels as necessary, and then print whenever you're ready.

FIGURE 19.8
Your merged labels can be saved to a file, where they can be edited before you print them.

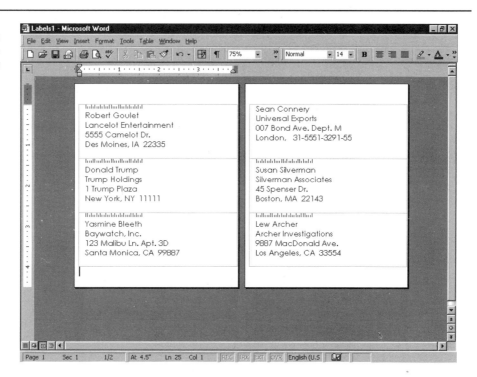

Printing Merged Envelopes

To create and print envelopes for your merged mailing, which is similar to creating and printing labels, follow these steps:

1. Create a new, blank document by clicking the New Blank Document button on Word's Standard toolbar.

2. Select Tools ➤ Mail Merge to display the Mail Merge Helper.

3. In the Main Document section, click the Create button, and select Envelopes.

4. In the Data Source section, click the Get Data button, and select Open Data Source to display the Open Data Source dialog box. Select the file that contains the data source (you're probably using the same file opened or created when you created your form letter), and click Open.

TIP If you're inserting names from an electronic address book, click the Get Data button, and select Use Address Book to display the Use Address Book dialog box; select which Address Book to use as your data source, and then click OK.

5. Word now informs you that you need to set up your main document; click the Set Up Main Document button to display the Envelope Options dialog box.

 TIP If you don't automatically see the Envelope Options dialog box, return to the Mail Merge Helper, go to the Main Document section, and click the Setup button.

6. Select the Envelope Options tab to set envelope size, inclusion of a Delivery Point (POSTNET) Barcode, and the font and placement for the delivery and return addresses.

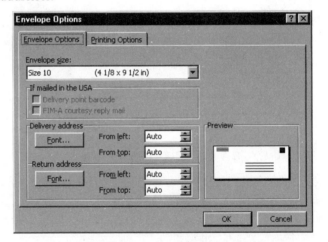

7. Select the Printing Options tab to configure the envelope feed method and direction for your printer. Select the feed method that best represents how envelopes feed into your printer, and then select whether your envelopes feed in face up or face down and what tray you're feeding from. (For most printers, Auto-Select Tray is the selected option.)

 NOTE For more information on setting up Word for envelope printing, see Chapter 18.

8. Click OK to display the Envelope Address dialog box, shown in Figure 19.9.

FIGURE 19.9
Using merge fields,
address your envelopes
in the Envelope Address
dialog box.

Click to Add a POSTNET Barcode

Click to Insert Available Merge Fields

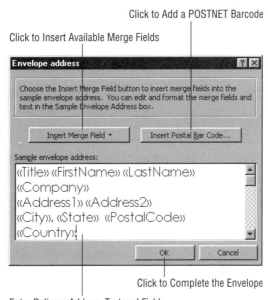

Click to Complete the Envelope

Enter Delivery Address Text and Fields

PART
V

Creating Labels and
Mailings

9. If you want to display a POSTNET barcode for your delivery address, which helps the post office process your letter, it needs to appear on the *first* line of the address. Position the insertion point at the top of the Sample Envelope Address box, and click the Insert Postal Bar Code button to display the Insert Postal Bar Code dialog box. Pull down the Merge Field with Zip Code list, and select which field contains the Zip code information. Then pull down the Merge Field with Street Address list, and select which field contains the street address information. Click OK to return to the Envelope Address dialog box.

10. Now you can insert the fields you want to include in the delivery address. (In most cases, these fields will be firstname, lastname, address, city, state, and postalcode.) To insert a field, click the Insert Merge Field button to display a list of available fields, and then click the field you want to insert. Each field is inserted at the insertion point; remember to put the appropriate fields on the appropriate lines and to leave spaces between certain fields, such as between the firstname and lastname fields).

11. When you're done entering delivery address information, click OK to return to the Mail Merge Helper.

12. Move to the Main Document section, and click the Edit button to switch to the main envelope document, shown in Figure 19.10.

FIGURE 19.10

Enter your return address in the main envelope document.

Enter Return Address

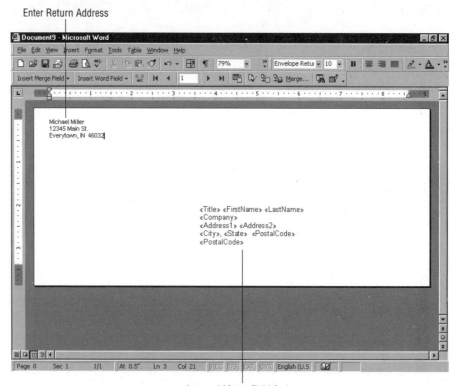

Inserted Merge Field Codes

13. Position the insertion point in the top-left corner of the envelope, and enter your return address. (If your envelopes have a preprinted return address, leave this area blank.) Enter any other text or graphics you want to appear on all the merged envelopes.

When you're ready to print the envelopes, you have two options:

 Send the Envelopes Directly to Your Printer To merge and print your envelopes directly, click the Merge to Printer button on the Mail Merge toolbar.

 Save the Envelopes in a New Document To save all the merged envelopes in a single new document that you can edit separately and print at a later time, click the Merge to New Document button on the Mail Merge menu. When the new document is created, select File ➤ Save As to save the document under a new name; edit the envelopes as necessary, and then print whenever you're ready.

Creating Attached Merge Envelopes

Another way to create envelopes for a merge mailing is to *attach* the envelopes to your main merge document. This method has the advantage of keeping the envelopes with the associated letters, both of which are linked to the exact same data source.

To create an attached merge envelope, follow these steps:

1. From within your completed merge document, select the fields for the recipient's name and delivery address.

2. Select Tools ➤ Envelopes and Labels to display the Envelopes and Labels dialog box.

3. Select the Envelopes tab; the delivery address for the current recipient should appear in the Delivery Address box.

4. If it isn't there already, enter your return address in the Return Address box, or check the Omit option if you're using envelopes with preprinted return addresses.

5. If you need to select an envelope type, click the Options button, and make your selections from the Envelope Options dialog box; click OK to return to the Envelopes and Labels dialog box.

6. Back in the Envelopes and Labels dialog box, make any additional configuration changes that are necessary, and then click the Add to Document button.

Word now attaches an envelope to your document; the delivery address on the envelope is keyed to the merge fields in your form letter. To print your merged envelopes, place your cursor anywhere in the attached envelope, and then click the Merge to Printer button on the Mail Merge toolbar.

Using the Direct Mail Manager for Bulk Mailings

If you have the Small Business, Professional, or Premium version of Microsoft Office 2000, you have access to a tool that can facilitate the creation of very large mailings through the U.S. Postal Service. Direct Mail Manager is a Wizard-like utility that can create form letters, mailing labels, and envelopes for bulk mailings, while taking advantage of all available bulk mail discounts.

Continued ▶

PART

V

Creating Labels and Mailings

The version of Direct Mail Manager included with Microsoft Office 2000 can handle mailings up to 3,500 pieces. If you have a larger mailing, you should contact Microsoft to purchase an enhanced version of the program.

Direct Mail Manager is not installed as part of the default Office 2000 installation; you'll need to insert the installation CD that contains Microsoft Small Business Tools and install Direct Mail Manager as a separate component.

Merging Database Data for Other Types of Documents

You can use Word's Merge Mailing feature to insert any type of data from external databases into any type of Word document. You're not limited to creating only form letters; you can also create catalogs, lists, schedules, directories, and other documents based on large volumes of data.

Creating a Merged Catalog

The key to merging multiple records into a single document (as opposed to multiple documents, as you did with form letters) is to create what Word calls a merged *catalog*. When you select Catalog from the Create list, the Mail Merge Helper knows to insert records from your data source one after another in your main merge document, creating a list of data from your data records.

As an example of the other types of documents you can create based on database information, let's take a look at a simple catalog or directory. For the purposes of this example, we'll assume you have the catalog data already stored in an Access database.

Follow these general steps to create a single-column catalog or directory:

1. Create a blank document by clicking the New Blank Document button on Word's Standard toolbar.

2. Select Tools ➢ Mail Merge to display the Mail Merge Helper.

3. In the Main Document section, click the Create button, and select Catalog.

4. In the Data Source section, click the Get Data button, and then select Open Data Source to display the Open Data Source dialog box.

5. Navigate to the document you want to use as your data source, and then click the Open button.

6. If you selected an Access database file as your data source, you'll see a Microsoft Access dialog box. Select the Tables tab, choose a specific database table, select the Queries tab, select or modify a database query, and then click OK.

7. From the Main Document section of the Mail Merge Helper, click the Edit Document button to display your main merge document.

8. Use the Insert Merge Fields menu to insert the fields necessary for your repeating data. If you're creating a telephone directory, for example, you may want to insert lastname, firstname, address, and phonenumber fields. Remember to press Enter at the end of the last field so that each record will start on a new line.

9. Align and format these fields on your page; you may want to consider inserting the fields within a single-row (but multiple-column) table to guarantee a fixed page layout. At this stage, you should also add any text you want to appear on all pages, including headers and footers.

10. Click the Merge button on the Mail Merge toolbar to display the Merge dialog box.

11. Pull down the Merge To list, and select New Document.

12. Select all other merge options, and then click Merge to initiate the merge.

After the merged document is created (see Figure 19.11), you can check it for accuracy, clean up the layout, and add any additional text necessary to create a good-looking catalog or directory. Remember to save the new document, and then print whenever you're ready.

PART V

Creating Labels and Mailings

FIGURE 19.11
Use the Mail Merge Helper's Catalog feature to create catalogs and directories based on database data.

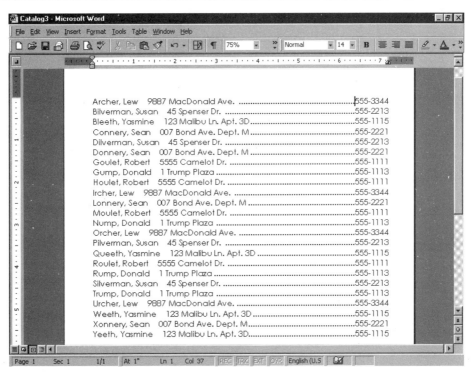

Querying a Database for Specific Information

You can also add information from a database directly into a Word document without using the mail merge feature. Word can import data from any application that supports Microsoft's Dynamic Document Exchange (DDE) technology and has access to an Open Database Connectivity (ODBC) driver installed on your system; such applications include Microsoft Access, Microsoft Excel, Microsoft Visual FoxPro, and dBASE.

Word enables you to use *queries* to filter, sort, and select specific fields from database files and then insert the resulting data directly into any Word document. You can even choose to insert the data as a linked object so that the data in your document is automatically updated when the data in the source database changes.

 NOTE See Chapter 17 to learn more about object linking and embedding.

To use the Microsoft Query tool to insert specific database data directly into a Word document, follow these steps:

1. Within your Word document, right-click any visible toolbar, and check the Database option to display the Database toolbar.

2. Position the insertion point where you want to insert the database data.

3. Click the Insert Database button on the Database toolbar to display the Database dialog box.

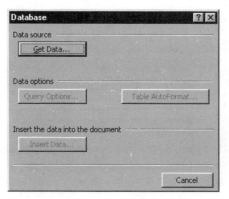

4. Click the Get Data button to display the Open Data Source dialog box.

5. Without selecting a file, click the MS Query button to display the Choose Data Source dialog box.

6. Select the type of data file you want to query, check the Use the Query Wizard to Create/Edit Queries option, and then click OK.

Word now launches the Query Wizard, which leads you step by step through the selection of a database file and its subsequent querying. Follow the on-screen instructions to extract specific data from the database and insert it into your document.

 WARNING Microsoft Query may not be included with all Office installations. If you try to execute a query and Query isn't installed, you'll be prompted to insert your Office installation CD to install the program.

PART VI

Creating Large and Team-Edited Documents

- *Organizing documents with outlines*

- *Inserting contents of other documents*

- *Working with master documents*

- *Collaborating with team documents*

CHAPTER 20

Organizing Documents with Outlines

Displaying outline levels   **561**

Expanding and collapsing a single section   **561**

Displaying the first line of text only   **562**

Displaying—or hiding—text formatting   **562**

Assigning outline styles   **564**

Promoting and demoting outline levels   **565**

Reorganizing your outline   **565**

Numbering your outline   **567**

Creating a new document from an outline   **569**

You probably remember outlining from your days in Mrs. Ricketts' English class back in high school or junior high. Before you could write a single word, you first had to outline your paper—or perhaps you were forced to outline some other work.

Boring.

In the real world, however, outlining can serve a very important purpose—especially if you're creating a long or complex document. Outlining, quite simply, helps you organize your thoughts. It forces a structure—a *hierarchical* structure—on your document. And, believe it or not, a structured document is easier to read—and easier to comprehend—than an unstructured, free-form document.

Understanding Word 2000's Outline View

One of Word 2000's views is the Outline view, shown in Figure 20.1. You enable Outline view for *any* document—even if you haven't consciously created an outline—by clicking the Outline View button next to the horizontal scroll bar.

In Outline view, higher-level headings appear to the left of lower-level headings, and all nonheading text appears as a single body-text level, regardless of what nonheading style is assigned to the text. The highest-level heading in your outline is designated *outline level one;* the next-highest level is outline level two, and so on. Word 2000 allows nine levels of headings plus the generic body-text level.

While you're operating in Outline view, you can quickly and easily restructure your document—without the normal cutting and pasting operations. You can rearrange headings and text by moving them up or down the outline (either with your mouse or with the Move Up or Move Down buttons on the Outline toolbar); you can also promote or demote items horizontally within the outline (again, using either the mouse or buttons on the toolbar).

NOTE Word's Outline view shows the structure of your document—*not* the formatting. The indentations and symbols you see in Outline view do not affect the way your document looks in Normal view and do not appear in your final printout.

FIGURE 20.1

Use Outline view to see the big-picture organization of your document.

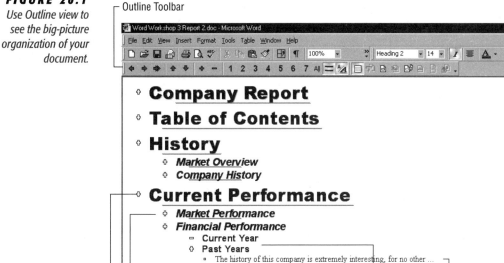

Outline Toolbar

Outline Level Two

Outline Level One

Plus Sign (+) Indicates This Section Contains Text—Click to Expand or Collapse

Minus Sign (–) Indicates This Section Does Not Contain Text

Outline Level Three

Body Text

Using the Outline Toolbar

When Outline view is enabled, Word displays the Outline toolbar, shown in Figure 20.2. Table 20.1 details the operation of each Outline toolbar button and the button's keyboard shortcut equivalent.

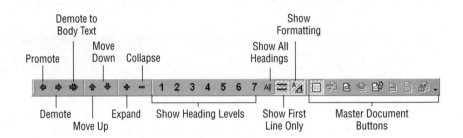

FIGURE 20.2
Use the Outline toolbar to manage the headings in your outline.

Button	Keyboard Shortcut	Description
Promote	Alt+Shift+←	Promotes paragraph to the next higher-level heading
Demote	Alt+Shift+→	Demotes paragraph to the next lower-level heading
Demote to Body Text	NA	Assigns selected paragraph to the body-text level
Move Up	Alt+Shift+↑	Moves paragraph up through the outline
Move Down	Alt+Shift+↓	Moves paragraph down through the outline
Expand	Alt+Shift++	Displays collapsed subheadings and body text under the selected heading
Collapse	Alt+Shift+–	Hides subheadings and body text under the selected heading
Show Heading 1	Alt+Shift+1	Shows only level-one headings
Show Heading 2	Alt+Shift+2	Shows level-one and level-two headings only
Show Heading 3	Alt+Shift+3	Shows heading levels one through three
Show Heading 4	Alt+Shift+4	Shows heading levels one through four
Show Heading 5	Alt+Shift+5	Shows heading levels one through five
Show Heading 6	Alt+Shift+6	Shows heading levels one through six
Show Heading 7	Alt+Shift+7	Shows heading levels one through seven
Show Heading 8	Alt+Shift+8	Shows heading levels one through eight
Show Heading 9	Alt+Shift+9	Shows heading levels one through nine

Continued ▶

TABLE 20.1: OUTLINE TOOLBAR (CONTINUED)		
Button	**Keyboard Shortcut**	**Description**
Show All Headings	Alt+Shift+A	Shows all headings and body text
Show First Line Only	Alt+Shift+L	Displays first line only of each level
Show Formatting	NA	Toggles on or off to show or hide character and paragraph (style) formatting within your outline

NOTE The Outline toolbar also includes eight buttons (at the right of the toolbar) that are used when working with master documents, but *not* used with normal outlines. See Chapter 22 for more information about working with master documents.

Changing the Outline Display

You can display the contents of your outline in several ways. Essentially, you can display as much or as little of your outline as you want.

Displaying Specific Levels Only

Word can display up to nine levels of headings (plus the body-text level) within your outline. If you want to view only the major sections of your document, however, you may not want to see all of the outline levels onscreen. To display only selected outline levels, click one of the Show Heading Level buttons on the Outline toolbar.

For example, if you want to see only the first level of your outline, click the Show Heading 1 button; only first-level headings will be displayed. If you want to see the first three levels of your outline, click the Show Heading 3 button; headings one, two, and three will be displayed.

Displaying All Levels

To quickly show *all* levels of your outline—including the body-text level—click the Show All Headings button. This button is actually a toggle, so clicking the button a second time will *hide* all levels of your outline.

Expanding and Collapsing a Single Section

If you want to see all the text and subheadings within a certain section of your document—but *not* within all sections—you can *expand* that section of your outline.

To expand a section of your outline, double-click the plus sign (+) next to that heading. You can also collapse the text and headings underneath an expanded heading by double-clicking the plus sign again. You can expand or collapse sections at any heading level; you could, for example, expand a level-one heading but then collapse a level-two heading underneath the expanded heading.

TIP To expand or collapse a section, you can also use the Expand and Collapse buttons on the Outline toolbar. In addition, if you have a Microsoft IntelliMouse mouse, you can collapse or display text by pointing to a heading, holding down the Shift key, and then rotating the IntelliMouse wheel forward or back.

Displaying the First Line of Text Only

If you want to view just an overview of your document, you don't want to read all the text in all your paragraphs. When you click the Show First Line Only button, Word displays *only* the first line of all headings and body text in your outline.

Although a single-line display is a great way to look at your outline, it can be a horrible way to *edit* your outline—since any text you type that extends past a single line will suddenly disappear. To redisplay the full text and headings, click the Show First Line Only button again—it's essentially an on/off toggle for this operation.

Displaying—or Hiding—Text Formatting

If you want to display the text in your outline with all its formatting intact—including both character formatting and paragraph (style) formatting—toggle the Show Formatting button on. If you prefer to see your outline as plain text—using Word's Normal style—toggle this button *off*.

Displaying *Both* Outline and Normal Views at the Same Time

By splitting your document screen, you can display two views of your document— using one pane to view your big-picture outline and another pane to view the detailed text, as shown in Figure 20.3.

FIGURE 20.3

Split your document into two panes so that you can use Outline view and Normal (or Print Layout) view at the same time.

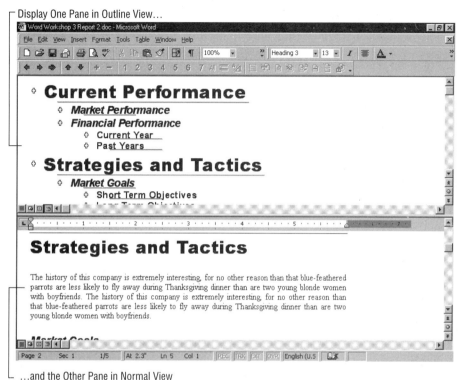

Display One Pane in Outline View…

…and the Other Pane in Normal View

To split your document into two views, follow these steps:

1. Position your cursor on top of the split box at the top of the right-hand vertical scroll bar; when your cursor changes shape, drag the split box down the scroll bar to the desired position, creating two individual panes.

2. Click one of the two panes, then click the Outline View button.

3. Click the second pane, then click either the Normal View or the Print Layout View button.

With your document thus split and displayed, you can make major changes in the Outline pane, and edit and format paragraph-level text in the Normal pane.

Setting Up an Outline

If you use Word's standard heading styles (Heading 1, Heading 2, and so on), you've already started setting up your outline. Word automatically assigns the built-in headings to corresponding outline levels—Heading 1 is assigned to outline level one, Heading 2 is assigned to outline level two, and so on.

If you've created your own styles, however—or if you want another style to appear as a heading in your outline—you need to change the outline style assignments within your document.

Assigning Outline Styles

By default, Word's built-in heading styles (Heading 1, Heading 2, and so on) are assigned corresponding outline levels. Any *nonheading* styles—including heading styles you've created from scratch—are assigned to the body-text level within your outline.

 WARNING If you switch to Outline view, select to show only a specified level of heading, and *don't see any text onscreen*, it's because you've used heading styles that have not been assigned to higher-level outline levels. Even if you think a heading is a higher level, Word by default recognizes only the built-in Heading X styles as legitimate outline heading levels; you'll need to manually assign outline levels to your nonstandard heading styles.

You can assign a new outline level to any style within your document by editing that style's properties. Follow these steps:

1. Position the insertion point anywhere within a paragraph formatted with the style you want to reassign.

2. Select Format ➢ Style to display the Style dialog box.

3. Click the Modify button to display the Modify Style dialog box.

4. Click the Format button and select Paragraph to display the Paragraph dialog box.

5. Select the Indents and Spacing tab.

6. Pull down the Outline Level list and select a different outline level.

7. Click OK to return to the Modify Style dialog box; click OK to return to the Style dialog box; click Cancel to close the Style dialog box.

Any style can be assigned to any outline level, and multiple styles can be assigned to the same outline level. (For example, you *could* assign both Heading 1 and Title to outline level one.)

Promoting and Demoting Outline Levels

To change the outline level of a specific paragraph, you *promote* or *demote* that paragraph within your outline. Promoting a paragraph assigns the next-highest heading style to that paragraph; demoting a paragraph assigns the next-lowest heading style to that paragraph.

Promoting or demoting a heading does *not* promote or demote the subheadings or text underneath that heading—unless those headings and text are fully collapsed. (That is, if you can see the heading, it doesn't change; if you *can't* see it, it does change.)

For example, if you demote a Heading 1 paragraph to Heading 3, the visible Heading 2 headings underneath the former Heading 1 paragraph remain formatted as Heading 2. (If those Heading 2 headings were *collapsed*—and therefore not visible—they *would* be demoted, to Heading 4.)

 TIP If you want to promote or demote all headings, subheadings, and text within a section, you must select all those elements (or collapse them underneath the superior heading) and *then* use the Promote or Demote buttons. All selected or collapsed text will be promoted or demoted accordingly; text *not* selected or collapsed—even if under a hierarchically superior heading—is not changed.

 To promote a paragraph within your outline, select the paragraph, then click the Promote button on the Outline toolbar (or press Shift+Tab). The selected heading will be promoted to the next higher level heading.

 To demote a paragraph within your outline, select the paragraph, then click the Demote button on the Outline toolbar (or press the Tab key). The selected heading will be demoted one level—down to, but no further than, outline level nine.

 Using the Demote button, you can demote headings only to level nine—*not* all the way to body text. If you want to demote a paragraph to the body-text level, click the Demote to Body Text button.

 TIP Since using the Tab key in Outline view demotes a paragraph, you have to use a different method if you want to enter an actual tab character in your outline text. To insert a tab character in Outline view, press Ctrl+Tab.

Reorganizing Your Outline

When you view your document from a bird's-eye level, you can easily see how it flows, and determine whether and how you need to reorganize it. In Normal or Print Layout views, moving one section to another location within your document would involve massive cutting and pasting; in Outline view, moving sections is a simple drag-and-drop operation.

Moving Sections with Your Mouse

The easiest way to move an entire section is to use your mouse to grab the plus sign (+) next to the section's heading. This will automatically select the entire section (including all subheadings and body text—and all collapsed elements); you can then drag the selected section up or down your outline to a new location.

 TIP It may be easier—at least *visually*—to collapse a section before moving it.

Moving Sections with the Toolbar Buttons

 You can also use the Move Up and Move Down buttons on the Outline toolbar to move a selected section up or down. Note, however, that these buttons will move only *selected* elements; if you select only a heading, the Move Up and Move Down buttons will move only the heading, *not* any uncollapsed subheadings or body text underneath the heading. For that reason, it's probably safer to use the drag-and-drop method for moving sections within your outline; when you grab the plus sign (+) next to a heading, all other elements within that section are automatically selected.

 WARNING When you rearrange a document in Outline view, any manual numbering you applied to your text will *not* be renumbered. (Any automatic numbering—for endnotes, footnotes, or captions, for example—*will* be automatically renumbered.) You'll want to switch to Normal or Print Layout view and proof your text to edit any affected numbering or references.

Sorting Sections within Your Outline

When you collapse an outline to show only selected heading levels, you can use Word's Sort command to alphabetize those headings—and have the collapsed body text and subheadings underneath those headings move as the headings move. (If you try to sort headings in any other view, Word tries to sort *every paragraph* within the selection; when you sort in Outline view, you sort only what's visible onscreen.)

To sort your headings within Outline view, follow these steps:

1. From within Outline view, display only those levels of headings you want to sort.

2. Select the section of your document you want to sort.

3. Select Table ➢ Sort to display the Sort Text dialog box.

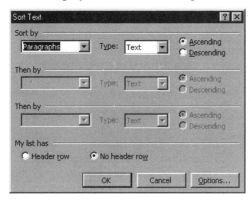

4. Make sure Paragraph is selected in the Sort By list, and Text is selected in the Type list.

5. Check either the Ascending or the Descending option.

6. Click OK to sort the headings.

Numbering Your Outline

By default, Word does not display your outline with numbered headings. If you want to apply outline numbering to your outline, follow these steps:

1. From within Outline view, select Format ➢ Bullets and Numbering to display the Bullets and Numbering dialog box.

2. Select the Outline Numbered tab.

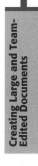

3. Select one of the Heading 1 numbering styles.

4. Click OK.

The result should look similar to Figure 20.4.

FIGURE 20.4
*A numbered outline–
thanks to Word's
outline-numbering
function*

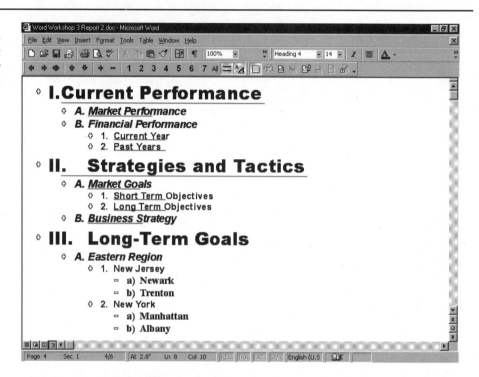

NOTE For more information on outline numbering, see the "Using Outline Numbering" section in Chapter 9.

 MASTERING THE OPPORTUNITIES

Using Outline View to Rearrange a Table

Word's tables are also visible—and editable—in Outline view. Since each row of a table is displayed as a separate body-text paragraph, when you choose to display all levels of your outline (by clicking the Show All Headings button on the Outline toolbar), your table will also be displayed.

Continued ▷

Once the rows of your table are displayed in Outline view, it's a simple matter to use your mouse (or the Move Up and Move Down buttons) to rearrange rows within your table. This is simpler and easier than the cutting and pasting (or sorting) you have to do to reorganize your table in Normal or Print Layout views.

Creating a New Document from an Outline

Up to this point, we've examined how you can use Word's Outline view to help organize an existing document. It's also possible—and quite useful—to *start* a new document from an outline and then fill in the blanks to flesh out the bare-bones document.

When you create a document from an outline, you are forced to think in a structured fashion. You must determine the major sections of your document *up front* and then plot out your entire document structure. After the structure is determined, you can then—and *only* then—start writing your main text, effectively filling in the space between section headings.

To create an outline for a new document, follow these steps:

1. From within a blank document, click the Outline View button to switch to Outline view.

2. As you can see in Figure 20.5, the insertion point—your first paragraph—will be automatically assigned the Heading 1 style. Enter the text for your first level-one heading.

3. When you press Enter to start a new line, that line will also be assigned the Heading 1 style. Continue entering level-one headings.

TIP In Outline view, all new paragraphs automatically retain the same style as the preceding paragraph, until edited otherwise. (This is different from editing in Normal or Print Layout views, where the next paragraph after a Heading 1 paragraph would revert to the Normal style.) This makes it easier to enter all your level-one headings at a single time.

4. When you're ready to enter a Heading 2 heading, press Tab within that heading line, as shown in Figure 20.6. Press Tab again to shift to the next lower level; press Shift+Tab to shift to a higher heading level.

PART

VI

Creating Large and Team-Edited Documents

FIGURE 20.5
Starting a new document in Outline view—enter all your Heading 1 headings first

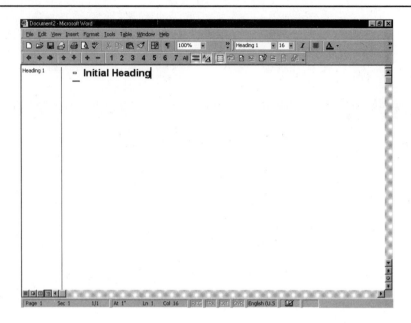

FIGURE 20.6
Press Tab to change from the Heading 1 to the Heading 2 style.

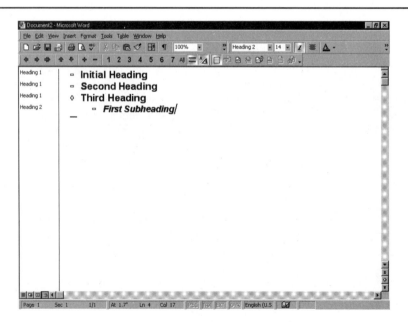

5. At any time, you can reorganize your headings by moving them up or down through your outline.

6. When your heading-level outline is complete, shift to Normal or Print Layout view to enter paragraph-level body text, graphics, and other elements.

TIP Often you'll want to use the outline of a Word document as the starting point for a PowerPoint presentation. You can send your Word outline directly to PowerPoint by switching to Outline view, then selecting File ➤ Send To ➤ Microsoft PowerPoint; PowerPoint will now launch with the Heading 1 headings in your outline transformed into individual PowerPoint slides. For more details on using Word with PowerPoint, see Chapter 32.

Printing an Outline

Printing works differently than usual when you're in Outline view—Word prints only what is displayed onscreen. If you collapse your outline to the highest-level headings, only those headings will print; if you expand your outline to display the first line of all outline levels—including body text—all those levels will print.

Here's how you print your outline:

1. From Outline view, display those outline levels you want to print.

2. Click the Print button on Word's Standard toolbar.

WARNING Word will insert any existing manual page breaks into your printed outline. If you want to print the outline straight through—without manual page breaks (which may make sense in the full document, but *not* in the outline)—you'll have to remove those page breaks before you print the outline.

CHAPTER 21

Inserting Contents of Other Documents

Pasting text as normal   575

Pasting text as special   576

Pasting text as a link   577

Inserting a whole file   578

Inserting part of a file   579

Inserting a linked file   580

Inserting database data   580

Inserting an automatic summary   582

One of the most common ways to create a large document is from bits and pieces of smaller documents. While Word 2000 includes a fancy (and difficult-to-use) feature called master documents (discussed in Chapter 22) just for this purpose, in reality most users piece together several smaller documents via less-sophisticated methods.

This chapter, then, is for the user who doesn't want to bother with the complexity of master documents but still wants to incorporate other files in a large Word document. The techniques discussed here are variations of general techniques discussed elsewhere in this book but are applied specifically to the task of creating large documents.

Pasting Text from Other Documents

The most used method of incorporating text from other documents is *pasting*. It's relatively easy to copy text from one document and paste it into another, even if the two documents are in different file formats. The challenge is to take advantage of Word's various options to simplify the pasting process and to make sure your new document is as up-to-date as possible.

MASTERING THE OPPORTUNITIES

Reusing Other Documents: Which Method Is for You?

In spite of all the sophisticated methods Word offers for combining documents and parts of documents (including master documents, OLE, and so on), most users rely on simple copying and pasting. The reason is simple: copying and pasting is the easiest way to insert text from one document into another, and it doesn't require any complicated or confusing techniques. Just copy and paste, and you're done!

Compare that to master documents (discussed in the next chapter), which is a very complicated procedure that is sometimes prone to error (both on your part and on Word's part). You could spend half an hour setting up a master document, which may or may not work correctly the first time out, or you could spend a few minutes copying and pasting. For most users, that's not a hard decision.

Continued ▶

If you're going to copy and paste, however, at least consider using some of the advanced paste options—in particular, using the Paste Special command and *linking* the pasted text back to the original document. Neither of these options are that complicated, nor do they add more than a few mouse clicks to your task.

With Paste Special, you can ensure that the text you paste picks up the formatting of your new document, which does not necessarily happen if you just use standard Paste. By picking up your current formatting, you actually save time that would otherwise be spent on reformatting the pasted text. Just select Edit ➤ Paste Special to display the Paste Special dialog box, and then select the Unformatted Text option.

While you're in the Paste Special dialog box, you should also check the Paste As Link option. This establishes a link between your pasted text and the document it came from, which means that if the original document changes, the linked text will also change automatically. A normal paste only pastes a "snapshot" of the original text into your document; a linked paste ensures that the information you pasted will always be kept up-to-date.

Pasting Text as Normal

Copying text from one document and pasting it into another is one of the basic skills you should have learned back in Chapter 4. The basic copy-and-paste technique works with any Windows application, so you can copy from an Excel spreadsheet, a Word-Perfect document, or even a plain-text document, for example, and then paste that text directly into your Word document.

To copy a block of text from one document to another, follow these steps:

1. Within the first document, select the text you want to copy.

TIP To select large blocks of text, position your insertion point at the start of the block, press and hold the Shift key, scroll to the end of the block, and click your mouse to reposition your insertion point at the end of the intended selection; as long as you continue to hold down your Shift key, everything between the two insertion points will be selected.

2. Still within the first document, select Edit ➤ Copy.

3. Move to your second (Word) document, and position the insertion point where you want to paste the text.

4. From within your second document, select Edit ➤ Paste.

The only problem in using this method is that the text is inserted in your new document using the formatting it contained in the old document. Chances are, you want this text to look like the rest of your new document, which you achieve either by reformatting the pasted text (which can be time-consuming) or by using Word's Paste Special command.

Pasting Text as Special

When you use the Paste Special command (instead of the standard Paste command), you can choose the formatting applied to your pasted text. With Paste Special, you have the option of pasting your text with the following options:

Microsoft Word Document Object   Inserts the text as an editable document. (This option is more commonly used for pasting pictures and other embedded objects.)

Formatted Text (RTF Format)   Retains most of the formatting of the original text.

Unformatted Text   Inserts the text with the formatting of the paragraph where the insertion point is located. (This is the best option if you want your pasted text to be formatted like the rest of your new document.)

Picture   Inserts the text as an uneditable, bitmapped picture into your document.

HTML Format   Inserts the text in HTML format, for Web-based documents.

Unformatted Unicode Text   Inserts the text without any formatting.

To use Paste Special, follow these steps:

1. Within the first document, select the text you want to copy.
2. Still within the first document, select Edit ➢ Copy.
3. Move to your second (Word) document, and position the insertion point where you want to paste the text.
4. From within your second document, select Edit ➢ Paste Special to display the Paste Special dialog box, shown in Figure 21.1.
5. Select one of the available formats. (Not all formats are available in all situations.)
6. Click OK.

FIGURE 21.1
Use the Paste Special dialog box to select different formatting options and to paste text as a link.

Check to Link Pasted Text to the Original Document

Select Desired Paste Format

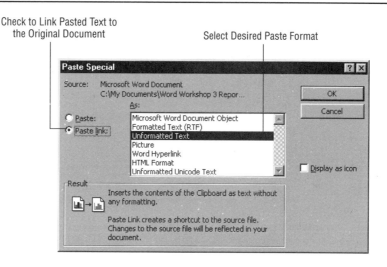

 TIP Use the Unformatted Text option (*not* Unformatted Unicode Text) to ensure that the text you paste shares the formatting of your new document.

Pasting Text as a Link

When you use the standard Paste command, you paste a "snapshot" of the original text into your new document. But what if the original document is a "live" document, containing information that is likely to change? If you pasted a snapshot of that text into your new document, that text is frozen for your purposes; if the original document changes, you'll never know, and your new document will quickly become outdated.

There is a way, however, to ensure that your new document is automatically updated whenever the original document is changed. All you have to do is to paste the text as a *link* to the original document. The pasted text will then be connected to the original document, so if the original text changes, the pasted version in your new document will also change automatically.

Pasting text as a link is a very simple procedure and builds on the Paste Special command. Just follow these steps:

1. Within the first document, select the text you want to copy.

PART
VI

Creating Large and Team-
Edited Documents

2. Still within the first document, select Edit ➢ Copy.

3. Move to your second (Word) document, and position the insertion point where you want to paste the text.

4. From within your second document, select Edit ➢ Paste Special, to display the Paste Special dialog box, shown previously in Figure 21.1.

5. Select one of the available formats.

6. Check the Paste As Link option.

7. Click OK.

 NOTE For more information about Word's linking and embedding features, see Chapter 17.

To update linked text (and objects) in your document, select Edit ➢ Links to display the Links dialog box, select the link to update, and then click the Update Now button. You can also ensure that all links are automatically updated before you print by selecting Tools ➢ Options to display the Options dialog box, selecting the Print tab, and then checking the Update Links option.

Inserting Files into Your Word Document

If you need to insert an entire file (rather than just a block of text) into your document, you can use Word's Insert File command. This command places the contents of an entire file into your new Word document, at the insertion point.

 TIP In some cases, you may need to convert the other document to Word format before it's inserted. To learn more about converting files and using Word's Batch Conversion Wizard, see Chapter 2.

Inserting a Whole File

Word lets you insert the contents of almost any type of file into your new document. Obviously, you can insert the contents of another Word file, but you can also insert the contents of plain-text files, Excel spreadsheets, and other file types.

To insert the contents of a file into your document, follow these steps:

1. Position the insertion point where you want to insert the file.

2. Select Insert ➤ File to display the Insert File dialog box.

3. Select the file to insert.

4. Click the Insert button.

The contents of the selected file will now be inserted into your document at the insertion point.

Inserting Part of a File

You can also use the Insert File command to insert only part of a document. In particular, you can insert a bookmarked section from a Word document or a range of cells from an Excel spreadsheet. To do so, follow these steps:

1. Position the insertion point where you want to insert the file.

2. Select Insert ➤ File to display the Insert File dialog box.

3. Select the file to insert.

4. Click the Range button to display the Set Range dialog box.

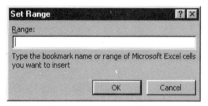

5. Enter the name of the bookmark or the range of cells you want to insert.

6. Click OK to return to the Insert File dialog box.

7. Click the Insert button.

 TIP If you want to insert a bookmarked section, you first have to define the bookmark in the document to be inserted.

Inserting a Linked File

When you use the Insert File command, you also have the option of linking the inserted contents back to the original file so they will be automatically updated if the original file is changed. To insert a linked file, follow these steps:

1. Position the insertion point where you want to insert the file.
2. Select Insert ➢ File to display the Insert File dialog box.
3. Select the file to insert.
4. Click the arrow next to the Insert button to display the pull-down menu.
5. Select Insert File.

Inserting Database Data into Your Word Document

If you want to insert database data into your Word document, you can just copy and paste the desired data, but a better option is to *query* the database to insert just the data that you want to use. When you query the database, you can filter, sort, and select specific fields to get exactly the information you want from the database. You can also establish a link to the database file so that whenever the data is changed in the source file it is automatically updated in your Word document.

To import database data to your Word document, follow these steps:

1. Position the insertion point where you want to insert the data.
2. Right-click any toolbar, and select Database to display the Database toolbar.
3. From the Database toolbar, click the Insert Database button.
4. When the Database dialog box (shown in Figure 21.2) appears, click the Get Data button.

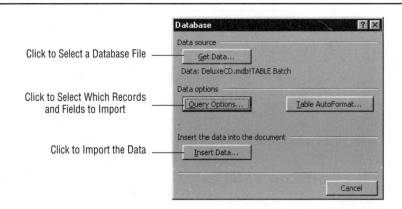

FIGURE 21.2
Use the Database dialog box to select which data to import.

5. When the Open Data Source dialog box appears, select the file you want to import, and then click the Open button.

 NOTE At this point, you can also choose to click the MS Query button and use Microsoft Query to create a sophisticated query of your database data. This procedure is recommended for advanced database users only; most users should ignore the MS Query button and follow the instructions given here.

---

6. If you're importing data from a Microsoft Access database, Word displays the Microsoft Access dialog box. Select the Tables tab to select a specific table to import, or select the Queries tab to select a query to import, and then click OK to return to the Database dialog box.

7. Click the Query Options button to display the Query Options dialog box.

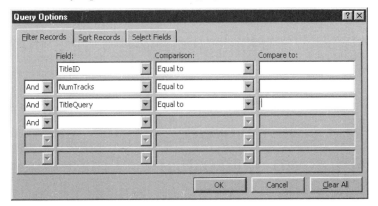

8. Select the Filter Records tab to select which records you want to import.

9. Select the Sort Records tab to select how you want the imported records sorted.

10. Select the Select Fields tab to select which fields you want to import.

11. Click OK to return to the Database dialog box.

12. Click the Insert Data button to display the Insert Data dialog box.

13. To import all records from the database, check the All option. To import only selected records, check the From option, and enter a range.

14. If you want the inserted data to be linked to the original data source and to be automatically updated when the original data source changes, check the Insert Data as Field option.

15. Click OK to insert the data.

When importing database data, it's best to link the data back to the source file by checking the Insert Data as Field option in the Insert Data dialog box. This actually inserts the data into your document as a DATABASE field, which can be updated either manually or automatically.

 NOTE For more information on using databases in Microsoft Word, see Chapter 19.

Inserting an Automatic Summary into Your Document

Another type of document you can insert into your document is a summary, which Word can generate for you automatically. Word 2000's AutoSummarize feature determines the key points of your document by analyzing your text and assigning a score to each sentence; sentences that contain frequently used words are assigned a higher score. You choose what percentage of the highest-scoring sentences to display in the summary, and then Word automatically generates text you can use as an executive summary for your document.

> **TIP** AutoSummarize works best on well-structured documents, such as reports, articles, and scientific papers.

To create an automatic summary of your document, follow these steps:

1. From within the document you want to summarize, select Tools ≻ AutoSummarize to display the AutoSummarize dialog box.

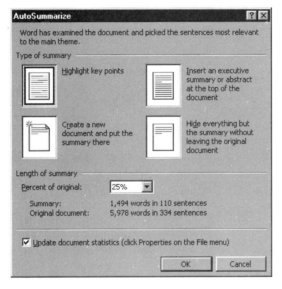

2. To insert an executive summary at the beginning of your document, select Insert an Executive Summary or Abstract at the Top of the Document. To create a new document containing your summary, select Create a New Document and Put the Summary There. To simply highlight the key points within your document (without creating a separate summary), select Highlight Key Points. To display only those highlighted points (while hiding the rest of the document onscreen), select Hide Everything but the Summary without Leaving the Original Document.

3. Using the Percent of Original box, select the level of detail you want to display; the bigger the number, the longer the summary.

4. To have AutoSummarize replace existing keywords and comments in your document's Properties dialog box, check the Update Document Statistics option; to maintain the existing keywords and comments, uncheck this option.

5. Click OK to create the summary.

PART

VI

Creating Large and Team-Edited Documents

Word now creates the type of summary you selected. If you chose to view your summary from within your document (by highlighting key points, as shown in Figure 21.3, or by hiding everything except the summary), Word displays the AutoSummarize toolbar. You can use this toolbar to fine-tune the number of comments highlighted; just drag the slider (or click the arrows) to change the Percentage of the Original document that is highlighted. You can also click the Highlight/Show Only Summary button to toggle between displaying your entire document (with key points highlighted) and displaying only the highlighted points.

FIGURE 21.3

The key points of your document highlighted with AutoSummarize

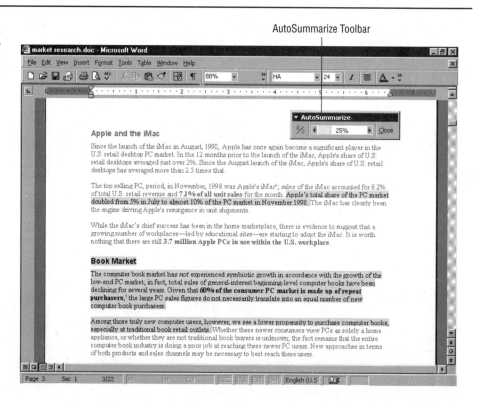

As you'll quickly discover, the summary that AutoSummarize creates is, more often than not, far from perfect. It's a good idea to think of the AutoSummarize summary as a starting point for a true executive summary; start with the AutoSummarize summary, and then edit it as appropriate.

CHAPTER **22**

Working with Master Documents

Creating, saving, opening, and printing master documents   586

Converting a subdocument into part of the master document   596

Deleting a subdocument from the master document   596

Adding a new subdocument   597

Splitting and combining subdocuments   597

Formatting subdocuments   599

Creating a table of contents and index   600

When you're creating very long documents in Word, it sometimes helps to deal with each section of the document separately—as if each section were a separate document—for editing purposes, but deal with the overall document for formatting, page numbering, indexing, and the like. How do you break a large document into smaller parts while maintaining the larger document?

In Word, you do this by creating a master document. A *master document* is a framework that contains multiple smaller documents; each *subdocument* can be edited as a separate document, but is combined with all the other subdocuments into the master document for indexing and printing.

Think of this book as a master document. This book (the master document) is composed of about three dozen subdocuments (chapters and appendixes), but for purposes of page numbering, formatting, indexing, and table of contents, it is treated as one very large document. It is more convenient to edit one chapter (subdocument) at a time; trying to edit the entire book as a single file would be unmanageable. However, the chapters do have to be combined to generate accurate page numbers, an index, and a table of contents; each chapter also must share the same formatting as all other chapters.

Any master document you create in Word functions in the same manner.

Creating a Master Document

You create a master document by breaking a large document into smaller—but related—subdocuments, or by combining multiple smaller documents into a single master document. You can open and edit each subdocument within the master document as a separate file, or you can use Word's Outline view to view and arrange the individual subdocuments within the master document. When you're ready to print, you only have to open the master document—not each subdocument—to print the entire document from the first page of the first subdocument to the last page of the final file.

All of the commands you use to create and work with master documents are located on the right side of the Outline toolbar (shown in Figure 22.1 and automatically displayed when you're in Outline view). (These commands are *not* available from Word's normal pull-down menus.)

FIGURE 22.1

Use the master-document buttons on the Outline toolbar to manage your master documents.

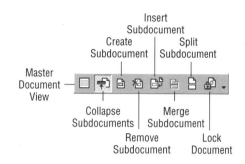

Master Document View

Create Subdocument

Insert Subdocument

Split Subdocument

Collapse Subdocuments

Remove Subdocument

Merge Subdocument

Lock Document

NOTE In addition to containing multiple subdocuments, a master document can also contain its own text and graphics separately from any subdocument.

MASTERING THE OPPORTUNITIES

Should *You* Use Word's Master-Documents Feature?

To be perfectly frank, Word's master-documents feature is difficult to use and very temperamental—you have to do everything *just right* to make things work properly, and there's very little margin for error. Given the level of difficulty, is this a feature you should be using?

The real advantage of using master documents is that you—or others in your workgroup—can work on individual sections of a large document separately. If you have ever worked with a very large document (100-plus pages), you know how unwieldy they are. It really is easier to work in smaller chunks, and then combine them at a later stage of development. This is the true strength of the master-documents feature.

Continued ▷

If you don't mind working with really large documents, there is little advantage to using master documents. You get the same document-organization benefits by inserting smaller documents into a large document, with the added benefit of being able to create live links from the original files to the combined document. If you're like most users, you're more comfortable working with pasted text or inserted documents than you are with the less-well-known master-documents feature.

To compare the different ways of working with large documents, make sure you read Chapter 21. Don't feel as if you have to use Word's master-documents feature—the older, less-sophisticated ways of dealing with large documents might be just right for you.

Creating a New Master Document from Scratch

If you have the forethought to consider your document as a master document from the start, you use Word's Outline view to create the structure of your document. When you designate major headings in your outline as subdocuments, Word automatically breaks up your document into its component parts, assigning names to each subdocument based on the text in the outline headings.

To create a master document from scratch, follow these steps:

1. Open a new blank document and switch to Outline view.

2. In Outline view, create an outline of your master document. Wherever you want to start a new subdocument (section), use outline level one (Heading 1); use different levels/headings for all headings and text within a section/subdocument.

3. Select all text you wish to turn into subdocuments. This should include multiple level-one headings.

 NOTE The heading style applied to the first heading in the selection will determine where each new subdocument starts. For example, if the first heading is formatted as Heading 1, each new occurrence of a Heading 1 will start a new subdocument. You don't have to start with Heading 1; if the first heading selected is Heading 3, each new Heading 3 will start a new subdocument in the selected text.

4. From the Outline toolbar, click the Create Subdocument button.

As you can see in Figure 22.2, Word creates multiple subdocuments within your master document. Each subdocument is designated by a border around its section in the outline.

FIGURE 22.2

Each section has been turned into a separate subdocument.

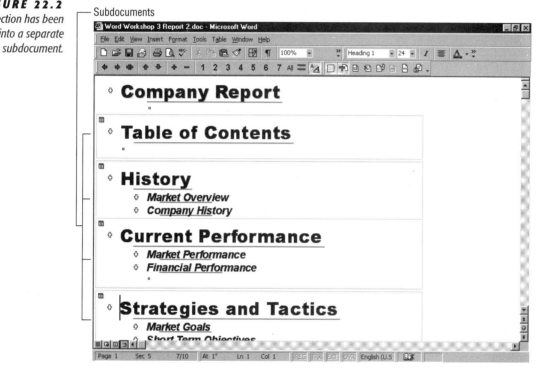

Each subdocument is assigned to a separate section within the master document. You can see how this works by switching to Normal view and observing the section breaks between the subdocuments (shown in Figure 22.3).

PART

VI

Creating Large and Team-
Edited Documents

FIGURE 22.3

Switch to Normal view to see each subdocument as a separate section within the master document.

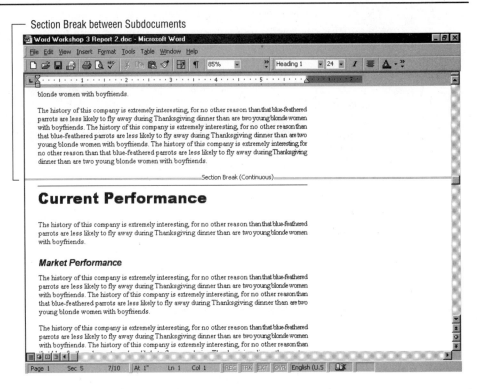

Section Break between Subdocuments

You can continue adding new sections within Outline view. You'll need to convert each new section into a subdocument manually, however, by selecting the section and then clicking the Create Subdocument button.

Converting an Existing Document into a Master Document

If you've already created a long document and wish to turn it into a master document (by breaking it into subdocuments), you follow a similar procedure to that of starting from scratch. Follow these steps:

1. Open the document you want to convert into a master document.

2. Switch to Outline view.

3. Select the text or sections you want to turn into subdocuments; make sure that the selection starts with a heading and that the heading level is consistent for each location where you want to start a new subdocument.

4. From the Outline toolbar, click the Create Subdocument button.

Word breaks your existing document into subdocuments, based on the text and headings selected. Remember that a new subdocument will start each time Word encounters the heading level used for the first heading in your selected text.

Assembling a Master Document from Existing Documents

Word also lets you combine documents you've already created into a single master document. In an ideal world, these documents should share a common heading system (that is, the use of Heading 1, Heading 2, and so on should be consistent between the documents), although this isn't absolutely necessary. Word will automatically assign styles from the master document to all subdocuments (which will change the way the subdocuments look and print), although you can choose to print subdocuments separately from the main document—and thus preserve the original document's formatting.

To create a new master document from existing Word files, follow these steps:

1. Create a new blank document and switch to Outline view.

2. Click the Insert Subdocument button to display the Insert Document dialog box.

3. Select a document to insert, then click OK.

4. Repeat steps 2 and 3 for each new document you wish to insert into your master document.

Each document you insert into your new master document becomes a separate subdocument. You can insert as many subdocuments as you wish; note that the original documents remain as is (under their original filenames) and are not linked to the new master document. (That is, when you edit the original documents, the text inserted as a subdocument does not change; you must edit the subdocuments separately.)

Saving, Opening, and Printing Master Documents

One advantage to using a master document is that you can save and print the entire document as a single document—instead of as multiple, smaller documents.

Saving a Master Document and Its Subdocuments

When you save a master document, Word saves not only the master document, but also all the subdocuments—in separate files. The saving of the subdocuments happens in the background; you only have to save and name the master-document file.

When Word saves each subdocument, it automatically assigns a filename to each subdocument, based on the first characters in the subdocument's heading. For example, a subdocument with an initial heading of "Sales Forecasts" might be named Sales Forecasts.doc.

To save a master document—and its corresponding subdocuments—follow these steps:

1. Display your master document in Outline view.

2. Select File ➢ Save As to display the Save As dialog box.

3. Assign the master document a filename and location, then click the Save button.

After the master document has been named and saved, you can save the document by clicking the Save button on Word's Standard toolbar.

 WARNING If your master document is too big, Word might not be able to save it. If you encounter difficulty saving a large master document, consider splitting it into several smaller documents as a short-term solution, then consider adding more memory to your computer system as a long-term solution.

Saving a Master Document as a Web Page

When you save your master document as an HTML file, each subdocument becomes a separate Web page. Follow these steps:

1. Display your master document in Outline view.

2. Select File ➢ Save As Web Page.

3. When the Save As dialog box appears, select a filename and location for the file, then click Save.

In this scenario the master file becomes the home page of a mini–Web site, containing links to all the subdocuments (subpages) contained within.

NOTE To learn more about how Word creates HTML Web pages, see Chapter 24.

Opening a Master Document

When you open a master document, you only have to open one document—*not* each subdocument individually. Just select File ➤ Open to display the standard Open dialog box, then select the master-document file. Word opens the master document *and* its component subdocuments.

Printing a Master Document

You print a master document as a combination of all its subdocuments—which means you have to expand all the subdocuments, change to Normal view, and *then* initiate printing. Just follow these steps:

1. From Outline view, expand all the subdocuments in the master document. (Select all the subdocuments, then click the Expand Subdocuments button on the Outline toolbar.)
2. Switch to Normal view.
3. Select File ➤ Print to display the Print dialog box.
4. Select the appropriate print options, then click Print.

In essence, once you expand all the subdocuments and switch to Normal view, you're looking at a single, big document—which you then print as you would any single document. The document has multiple sections (the subdocuments), but it's still a single document and prints as such.

 NOTE To learn how to print a subdocument within your master document, see the "Printing Subdocuments" section later in this chapter.

Working with Subdocuments

Once you've created your master document, you can easily change the structure of the document by adding, removing, combining, splitting, renaming, and rearranging subdocuments. You use Outline view to work with a master document, and move subdocuments up and down the outline as you would move any element in a normal outline. By default, all subdocuments are hidden when you open a master document, but you can expand or collapse subdocuments and switch in or out of Normal view to show or hide detail.

 NOTE To learn more about working with Word's Outline view, see Chapter 20.

Word gives you the option of opening subdocuments from within the master document, or of opening each subdocument as a separate file. One advantage to opening a subdocument on its own is that you can easily distribute the individual subdocuments to different users; the next time you open the master document, the edits to each individual subdocument are incorporated into the master document. In addition, it's less memory-intensive to open a smaller document than it is to open a larger one—and a smaller document is easier to scroll through.

When you're working from within a subdocument, you can edit it as you would any Word document. To ensure a consistent design across the entire document, however, the master document's template applies to all the subdocuments.

Using Outline View with Your Master Document

 You do all of your top-level work with your master document from Word's Outline view. (You access Outline view by clicking the Outline View button next to Word's horizontal scroll bar.)

From within this view, you can do the following:

 Collapse All Subdocuments To simplify the outline of your master document, you can collapse all your subdocuments by clicking the Collapse Subdocuments button. When you collapse your subdocuments, each subdocument appears as a hyperlink, as shown in Figure 22.4. When you click the hyperlink, the subdocument opens in a separate window for editing. (Your subdocuments continue to appear as hyperlinks, even in Normal and Print Layout views, until you expand them again.)

 NOTE The first time you collapse your subdocuments, a prompt will inform you that your documents are being saved. This is because Word must save and name your subdocuments before it displays them as hyperlinks within your master-document outline.

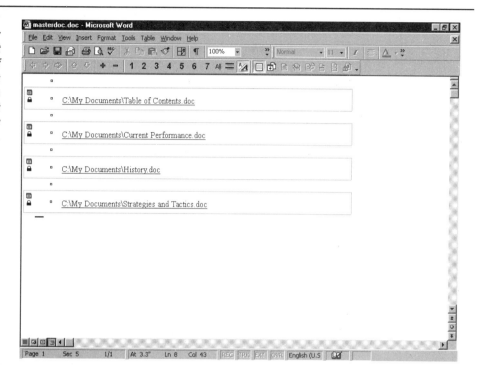

FIGURE 22.4
Collapse your subdocuments to get the big-picture view of your major document; click a hyperlink to open the subdocument in a separate window for editing.

Expand All Subdocuments To view the contents of your subdocuments (in Outline mode), click the Expand Subdocuments button. You'll need to expand your subdocuments to print your master document.

Rearrange Subdocuments within Your Master Document You treat subdocuments as you would any element in an outline. Thus you can rearrange subdocuments within the outline by moving them up or down with your mouse.

 TIP You may find it easier to move subdocuments if you've first collapsed subdocuments within the master-document outline.

Edit the Outline of Individual Subdocuments Once you've expanded your subdocuments, Word displays the contents of each subdocument as an outline, which you can then rearrange and edit as you would any outline. You can even move outlined elements from one subdocument to another.

Open a Subdocument for Editing in a Separate Window   To open a subdocument as a separate document for editing, double-click the Subdocument icon (if subdocuments are expanded) or the subdocument hyperlink (if subdocuments are collapsed). Any changes you make to the individual subdocument are reflected in the master document.

Converting a Subdocument into Part of the Master Document

Remember that the master document can contain its own text and graphics separately from any subdocument. If you want a subdocument to revert back into part of the master document (and thus *not* be available for separate editing), follow these steps:

1. Display your master document in Outline view.

2. Click the Expand Subdocuments button to expand all subdocuments.

3. Select the subdocument you want to convert.

4. Click the Remove Subdocument button.

Word removes the section breaks for the selected subdocument, making it part of the master document.

Deleting a Subdocument from the Master Document

If you want to completely delete a subdocument from your master document, follow these steps:

1. Display your master document in Outline view.

2. Click the Collapse Subdocuments button to collapse all subdocuments.

3. Select the subdocument you want to delete by clicking the Subdocument icon next to the subdocument hyperlink.

4. Press Delete.

This procedure deletes the subdocument from your master document, although the subdocument itself will continue to reside on your hard disk until you delete it separately.

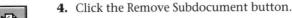

WARNING   Do *not* delete a subdocument file from your hard disk while it is still part of your master document. Likewise, do not use My Computer or Windows Explorer to change the location of an active subdocument file.

Adding a New Subdocument

To add a new subdocument to your master document, follow these steps:

1. Display your master document in Outline view.

2. Click the Expand Subdocuments button to expand all subdocuments.

3. Position the insertion point where you want to add the new subdocument.

4. Click the Insert Subdocument button to display the Insert Document dialog box.

5. Select a document to insert, then click OK.

Splitting Subdocuments

You might find, after working on your master document for awhile, that one or more of your subdocuments is actually too large and unwieldy, and would be better split into two separate subdocuments. To turn a single subdocument into two subdocuments, follow these steps:

1. Display your master document in Outline view.

2. Click the Expand Subdocuments button to expand all subdocuments.

3. Position the insertion point within the subdocument where you want the new subdocument to begin.

4. If necessary, add a heading to the second part of the subdocument; make sure the heading is formatted with the same style as the first heading in the subdocument.

5. With the insertion point positioned at the break point, click the Split Subdocument button.

Word splits the subdocument into two subdocuments, with the new subdocument beginning where you positioned the insertion point.

Combining Subdocuments

Just as you can split a large subdocument into two smaller subdocuments, you can also combine two (or more) smaller subdocuments into one larger subdocument. When

PART

VI

Creating Large and Team-
Edited Documents

you do this, the new subdocument will retain the filename of the first subdocument in the selection.

Follow these steps:

1. Display your master document in Outline view.

2. Click the Expand Subdocuments button to expand all subdocuments.

3. Select the subdocuments you want to combine. (Remember to hold down the Shift key while you select multiple subdocuments.)

4. Click the Merge Subdocuments button.

Word eliminates the section breaks between these subdocuments, converting them into one single section/subdocument.

NOTE After you combine multiple subdocuments, the original, uncombined subdocuments remain on your hard disk (but not in your master document). You can use My Computer or Windows Explorer to delete these now-unused files.

Renaming Subdocuments

If you don't like the names Word automatically assigned to your subdocuments, you can change them. Just follow these steps:

1. Display your master document in Outline view.

2. Click the Collapse Subdocuments button to collapse all subdocuments.

3. Select the subdocument you want to rename by clicking the Subdocument icon next to the subdocument hyperlink.

4. Select File ≻ Save As to display the Save As dialog box.

5. Select a new filename and/or location, then click the Save button.

WARNING Do *not* rename your subdocuments with My Computer or Windows Explorer; if you do, you'll break the links between your master document and the subdocuments.

When you rename a subdocument, you actually save the file under a new name—leaving the original subdocument, with its original filename, on your hard disk. To clean up your hard disk, use My Computer or Windows Explorer to delete the original, now-unused file.

Formatting Subdocuments

To ensure consistent formatting, the template used by your master document controls the styles used when you view and print the entire document, including all subdocuments—unless you view and print the subdocuments as separate documents. When the subdocuments are included with the master document, they share the master document's formatting, but when they're opened, viewed, and printed as individual documents, they retain their original formatting (if that formatting is different from the master document's formatting).

To format your master document in light of this fact, do as follows:

1. Display your master document in Outline view.

2. Click the Expand Subdocuments button to expand all subdocuments.

3. Switch to either Normal or Print Layout view.

4. Apply documentwide formatting by modifying styles and so on.

Since subdocuments are contained within their own sections of the master document, you can change any section-level formatting within each individual section as you would in any normal multiple-section document. This means you can set up section-specific page numbering, borders, headers, margins, or column layouts.

NOTE   For more information about formatting document sections, see Chapter 10.

Printing Subdocuments

Since a subdocument exists both as part of the master document and as a separate document, it's easy to print any subdocument separately from the master document. Just follow these steps:

1. Display your master document in Outline view.

2. Double-click the Subdocument icon for the subdocument you want to print (if subdocuments are expanded), or click the subdocument hyperlink (if subdocuments are collapsed).

3. When the subdocument opens in its own window, select File ≻ Print to display the Print dialog box.

4. Select the appropriate printing options, then click the Print button.

Word prints the selected subdocument, using the styles and formatting of the original document.

Adding a Table of Contents, Index, and Cross-References

One of the advantages of using a master document instead of multiple, smaller documents is that you can create a single table of contents and index for the entire document, across all subdocuments. Since the master document is nothing more than a combination of all the subdocuments, this is as simple as viewing the master document as a single document, then indexing or creating a table of contents for the combined document.

NOTE For more information on indexes and tables of contents, see Chapter 13.

Creating a Table of Contents

To create a table of contents for your master document, follow these steps:

1. Display your master document in Outline view.

2. Click the Expand Subdocuments button to expand all subdocuments.

3. Position the insertion point where you want to add the table of contents.

4. Select Insert ➢ Index and Tables to display the Index and Tables dialog box.

5. Select the Table of Contents tab.

6. Make the appropriate selections within this dialog box, then click OK to build the table of contents.

Word creates a table of contents for your entire master document, including all subdocuments.

Creating an Index

As you learned back in Chapter 13, there are two parts to the task of creating an index. First, you have to mark individual words and phrases as index entries; second, you have to build the index itself.

Marking index entries within a master document is no different than marking index entries within any document. As you work on the master document and on each subdocument separately, press Alt+Shift+X to display the Mark Index Entries dialog box, and complete the actions described in Chapter 13. You can add index entries for your master document from any view.

Once you've marked your index entries, you can build the index for your entire master document. Just follow these steps:

1. Display your master document in Outline view.
2. Click the Expand Subdocuments button to expand all subdocuments.
3. Position the insertion point where you want to add the index.
4. Select Insert ➢ Index and Tables to display the Index and Tables dialog box.
5. Select the Index tab.
6. Make the appropriate selections within this dialog box, then click OK to build the index.

Word indexes your entire master document as a single document, inserting the correct page numbers for each of the marked indexed entries.

Inserting Cross-References

Cross-references typically apply only within a single document. For this reason, you can't cross-reference one subdocument from within another subdocument—unless the subdocuments have been combined into a single master document.

To create a cross-reference within a master document, follow these steps:

1. Display your master document in Outline view.
2. Click the Expand Subdocuments button to expand all subdocuments.
3. Switch to Normal view.
4. Position the insertion point where you want to insert the cross-reference.
5. Select Insert ➢ Cross-Reference to display the Cross-Reference dialog box.
6. Make the appropriate selections within this dialog box, then click Insert.

NOTE To learn more about cross-references, see Chapter 11.

Locking and Unlocking a Master Document

Since a master document contains multiple subdocuments, it is relatively easy to distribute the subdocuments separately to members of a workgroup for simultaneous editing. When the subdocuments have been edited and saved—individually—you can reopen the master document to see all the changes automatically incorporated.

PART

VI

Creating Large and Team-
Edited Documents

NOTE If you're distributing subdocuments over a network, you need to be aware of several security features that Word 2000 includes. These features are designed to keep unauthorized users from accessing your documents, and are discussed in Chapter 23.

If someone is currently working on a subdocument, the document is locked to anyone else trying to access the folder at the same time. This means that others can view the subdocument, but they can't edit it while it is being edited by the first user; this prevents two or more users from trying to make changes to the subdocument simultaneously, which could be disastrous. The subdocument becomes unlocked when the first user closes the subdocument file.

You can tell that a subdocument is locked by the presence of a lock icon next to the subdocument in the master-document outline. (Note, however, that when subdocuments are collapsed in the master-document outline, all subdocuments appear locked.) In addition, if you try to open a locked subdocument separately, the words *Read-Only* appear in the subdocument's title bar.

You can also lock a subdocument manually, to keep others from editing the document. To lock a subdocument from within the master document, follow these steps:

1. Display your master document in Outline view.

2. Click the Expand Subdocuments button to expand all subdocuments.

3. Select the subdocument to lock.

4. Click the Lock Document button on the Outline toolbar.

You unlock a subdocument by repeating these steps and toggling the Lock/Unlock button to the Unlock position.

In addition to being able to manually lock subdocuments within your master document, you can restrict access to your master document or any subdocument to those users with a password. You can use passwords to keep unauthorized users from making changes to a document or from even viewing the document. See Chapter 23 for more information on using passwords to protect your documents.

CHAPTER 23

Collaborating on Team Documents

Password-protecting your files   **604**

Enabling revision tracking   **607**

Merging revisions from multiple reviewers   **608**

Reviewing revisions   **609**

Inserting comments while editing   **612**

Saving multiple versions of a document   **614**

Understanding and participating in discussions   **616**

Subscribing to workgroup documents   **620**

One of the benefits of Microsoft Word is the capability of having multiple users work on a single document and then being able to track (and accept or reject) the editing changes made by each user. Word 2000 offers several ways for users to collaborate on these team documents, including a new Web collaboration feature. Read on to learn how to master Word in a team-editing environment.

Password-Protecting Your Files

There are many ways you can share files with other users. You can e-mail files back and forth or hand the files back and forth on diskette. If you're in a corporate environment, the easiest way to share files is over the corporate network. However, whichever method you use, you should consider protecting it with a password so unauthorized users can't edit your work.

Requiring a Password for Access

Word 2000 lets you restrict access to your documents to those users with a password. You can use passwords to keep unauthorized users from making changes to a document or from even viewing the document.

 WARNING Remember to write down any password you assign, because even you won't be able to access a password-protected document if you lose the password!

To password-protect a document, follow these steps:

1. Open the document you want to protect.
2. Select File ➤ Save As to display the Save As dialog box.
3. Click the Tools button on the toolbar to display the pull-down menu.

4. Select General Options to display the Save dialog box.

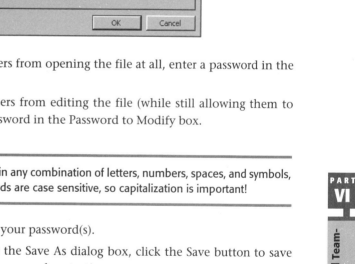

5. To keep unauthorized users from opening the file at all, enter a password in the Password to Open box.

6. To keep unauthorized users from editing the file (while still allowing them to view the file), enter a password in the Password to Modify box.

 NOTE A password can contain any combination of letters, numbers, spaces, and symbols, up to fifteen characters. Passwords are case sensitive, so capitalization is important!

---

7. When prompted, reenter your password(s).

8. When you're returned to the Save As dialog box, click the Save button to save the file with the selected password protection.

Once a file is password-protected, anyone trying to open the file is prompted for a password. When the correct password is entered, the file opens normally. If an incorrect password (or no password) is entered, Word generates an error message without opening the file.

Removing or Changing a Password

Passwords are great for keeping others out of your files but are annoying when they get in *your* way. Fortunately, Word lets you remove or change any password you've assigned, by following these steps:

1. Open the document you want to change.
2. Select File ➤ Save As to display the Save As dialog box.
3. Click the Tools button on the toolbar to display the pull-down menu.
4. Select General Options to display the Save dialog box.
5. To remove a password, select the asterisks in either the Password to Open or the Password to Modify boxes, and then press Delete.
6. To change a password, enter a new password in either the Password to Open or the Password to Modify boxes.
7. If you changed your password(s), reenter the new password(s) when prompted.
8. When you're returned to the Save As dialog box, click the Save button to save the file with the selected password protection.

Tracking Changes and Comments in Your Documents

Word offers the capability for multiple users to edit a document and for each user's comments and changes to be tracked individually. The author of the original document can then review the editing changes and choose to accept or reject any change made to the document.

 MASTERING THE OPPORTUNITIES

Setting the Rules

Before you share your Word files with other users, you should set some ground rules for the other users. Let them know what can and can't be changed.

Continued ▶

For example, it may be okay to edit the document's text, but you might not want them modifying your preset styles. You may also want to specify which parts of the document they should be editing so you can focus their work (and your subsequent attention).

Above all, make it clear to the other users what level of editing you're expecting. If you want someone to perform a simple grammatical edit and they respond with a full-blown stylistic and content edit, you're both going to be quite annoyed.

Remember, it's *your* document that you're sharing; you're the boss and can use Word's *track changes* feature to accept or reject any changes made by any other user.

Enabling Revision Tracking

When you want a document to be edited by other users in your workgroup and you want to track the changes they make, you need to enable Word's revision tracking function (also called the track changes feature). When revision tracking is enabled, Word inserts revision marks to highlight all changes to the original document. Later, when you review the changes, you can easily see what has been changed and by whom, since each reviewer's changes are marked with a different color.

To turn on revision tracking, follow these steps:

1. Open the document to be edited.

2. Select Tools ➢ Track Changes ➢ Highlight Changes to display the Highlight Changes dialog box.

3. Check the Track Changes while Editing option.

4. Click OK.

PART

VI

Creating Large and Team-Edited Documents

MASTERING THE OPPORTUNITIES

Using the Reviewing Toolbar

The easiest way to track and accept or reject changes is to use Word's Reviewing toolbar. You display this toolbar by right-clicking on any visible toolbar and then selecting Reviewing.

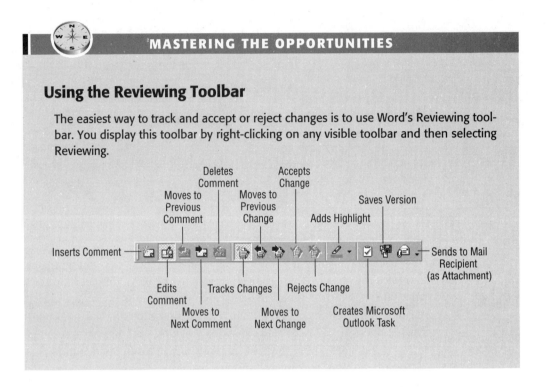

Making Revisions

A reviewer makes revisions to a workgroup document just as he or she would edit the document normally. The only, and very important, difference is that Word's track changes feature must be enabled for the reviewer's changes to be tracked. Otherwise, any changes made are entered *permanently* into the document, without any indication that they were inserted by the reviewer.

Merging Revisions from Multiple Reviewers

You may have distributed individual copies of your document for review by several reviewers. If this is the case, you're faced with reviewing comments in multiple versions of the document.

If you're in this situation, Word lets you *merge* all the changes from all the different versions of the document into a single document, which you can then review in a single pass. To merge revised documents, follow these steps:

1. Open the original document.

2. Select Tools ➢ Merge Documents to display the Select File to Merge Into Current Document dialog box.

3. Select one of the files to merge, and then click OK.

4. Repeat steps 2 and 3 to merge multiple documents.

Your original document now displays all the changes and comments made by each of the reviewers, with each reviewer tracked in a different color. You can now accept or reject changes as discussed in the next section.

 TIP   If, for some reason, a reviewer does not enable Word's track changes feature, you can still identify that reviewer's changes by using Word's Compare Documents command. This operation compares two documents and marks any changes made to the old document. To use this command, open the *newer* version of the document first, select Tools ➢ Track Changes ➢ Compare Documents, and open the older document. You can then accept or reject changes as you would using the standard track changes feature.

Reviewing Revisions

Once all the editing has been completed, it's time to review the changes that were made.

When you open the edited document (and you have the track changes feature enabled), you'll see that Word has marked each change with a *change mark* in the left margin, as shown in Figure 23.1. You can simply scroll to each marked change, or use the Next Change and Previous Change buttons on the Reviewing toolbar to jump from change to change.

All changed text is also displayed in color, with each reviewer's changes appearing in a different color. Newly inserted text is marked as underlined; deleted text is marked as strikethrough. Changed formatting is not noted within the text but only by the presence of the change mark in the margin.

PART

VI

Creating Large and Team-
Edited Documents

FIGURE 23.1
Review all the changes made to your original document, and then accept or reject the changes.

Deleted Text
Change Mark
Inserted Text

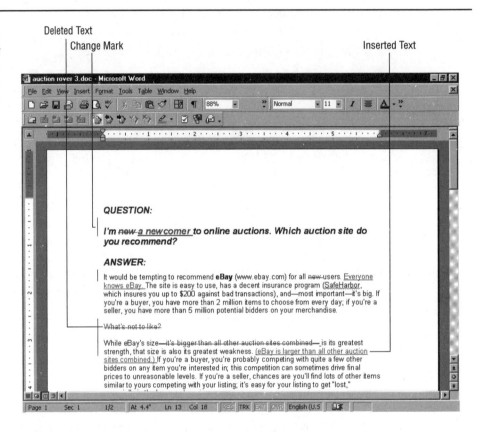

Accepting a Change

When you accept a change into your document, you permanently add that change to your text and remove all revision marks. From that point on, the changed text will appear as a normal part of your document.

To accept a change, follow these steps:

1. Position the insertion point somewhere within the changed text (or use the Next Change or Previous Change buttons to jump to and automatically select a change).

2. Click the Accept Change button on the Reviewing toolbar.

You can also choose to accept all the changes in the document with a single command. To do this, select Tools ➤ Track Changes ➤ Accept or Reject Changes to display the Accept or Reject Changes dialog box, and then click the Accept All button.

 WARNING Globally accepting or rejecting all changes in a document is a dangerous thing to do; it's too easy to miss an important change or accept an incorrect edit if you don't look at each edit separately.

Rejecting a Change

When you reject a change to your document, you permanently delete that change from your text and remove all revision marks. Rejecting a change is similar to accepting a change, as you can see from the following steps:

1. Position the insertion point somewhere within the changed text (or use the Next Change or Previous Change buttons to jump to and automatically select a change).

2. Click the Reject Change button on the Reviewing toolbar.

You can also choose to reject all the changes in your document with a single command. To do this, select Tools ➤ Track Changes ➤ Accept or Reject Changes to display the Accept or Reject Changes dialog box, and then click the Reject All button.

Changing How Revisions Are Displayed

If you don't like the way revisions are displayed in your document, Word enables you to change both the color and revision marks used. To do this, just select Tools ➤ Track Changes ➤ Highlight Changes to display the Highlight Changes dialog box, and then click the Options button to display the Track Changes dialog box. From here, you can make the following changes:

Change Revision Colors By default, Word automatically assigns a different color to each reviewer who made changes. If you'd prefer to assign a specific color for each type of revision (Inserted Text, Deleted Text, and Changed Formatting as well as for the Changed Lines used to indicate changes in the text), pull down the Color list next to each type of change, and select a specific color. To return to the default setting, select By Author from the Color list.

Change Revision Marks You can also change the revision marks used by Word to indicate different types of changes. To do this, pull down the Mark list next to each type of change, and select a new option.

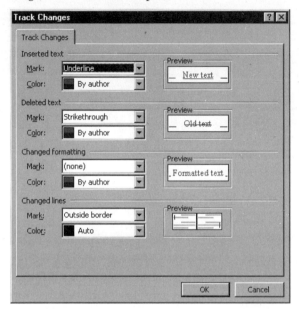

Inserting Comments While Editing

In addition to making changes to the text, a reviewer (or the document's original author) can also insert non-printing *comments* into the document. Inserting a comment is a good way to send a message to another reviewer or to the document's author without disturbing the text of the document.

When a comment is added, Word assigns it a number and enters it in a separate comment pane beneath the main document. Word then inserts a *comment reference mark* in the document and applies a yellow highlight to the text commented on. As with revision marks, Word tracks each reviewer's comments in a different color.

Inserting a Written Comment

To insert a comment, follow these steps:

1. Select the text you want to comment on.

2. Click the Insert Comment button on the Reviewing toolbar.

3. When the comment pane appears, as shown in Figure 23.2, enter your comment.

4. Click the Close button to close the comment pane.

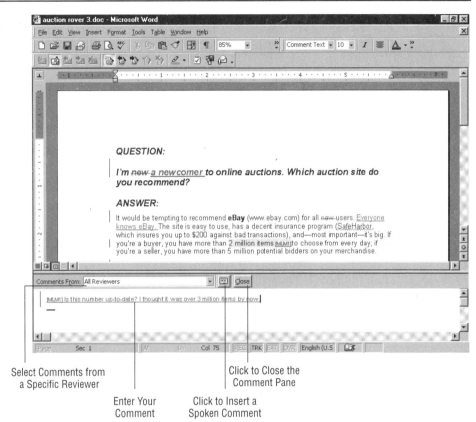

Select Comments from a Specific Reviewer

Click to Close the Comment Pane

Enter Your Comment

Click to Insert a Spoken Comment

Inserting a Spoken Comment

You can also record a spoken comment by clicking the Insert Sound Object button (in the comment pane); this displays the Sound Object dialog box. Click the Record button, and speak into your PC's microphone; click the Stop button when you are finished speaking, and close the Sound Object dialog box.

When you insert a spoken comment, Word inserts a sound object icon in your document following the text commented on. Double-click the icon to play back the spoken comment.

Reading Comments

When it comes to reading comments inserted into your document, you have two choices:

- Hover your cursor over the comment in your document to display a ScreenTip containing the text of the comment.

- Double-click the comment to display the comment pane, and read the comment there.

You can find the next comment within a document by clicking the Next Comment button on the Reviewing toolbar; click the Previous Comment button to jump back to the preceding comment. In addition, you can open the comment pane and edit any comments by clicking the Edit Comment button, and delete a comment completely by clicking the Delete Comment button.

 TIP If you want to draw attention to a specific section of text, you don't have to leave a comment; you can simply highlight that text. Click the Highlight button on the Reviewing toolbar to turn on the text highlighter, then drag your cursor over the text to be highlighted. (Make sure you click the Highlight button when done to turn off the highlighter.) To change the highlighter color, click the arrow next to the Highlight button, and select a new color.

Saving Multiple Versions of a Document in a Single File

In many environments, documenting every stage of a project is important. That means saving a copy of your document in each stage of development.

The simplest way to do this is to use Word's Save As command to save each version of your file under different filenames. This can become unwieldy, however, and take up a lot of disk space.

A better procedure would be to have Word save the different versions for you in a single file. When you enable Word's Versions feature, Word will save the current version of your document within the current file; you can then choose to view from within your main document file any version saved since enabling the Versions feature. (By default, Word displays only the current version.)

Saving the Current Version

To manually save the current version of the file within the current document, follow these steps:

1. From within your document, select File ➤ Versions to display the Versions dialog box.

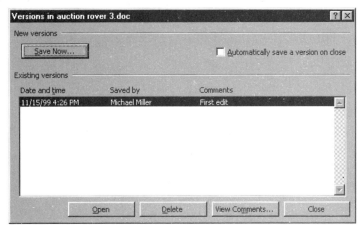

 TIP To have Word automatically save the current version whenever you close the file, check the Automatically Save a Version on Close option in the Versions dialog box.

2. Click the Save Now button to display the Save Version dialog box.

3. Enter any comments about this version of your document, and then click OK.

Viewing a Previous Version

Each time you save a version, Word records the date and time the version was saved and the name of the person (you!) who made the changes. You can choose to view any of these saved versions, in a separate window, at any time.

To view a saved version, follow these steps:

1. From within your document, select File ➤ Versions to display the Versions dialog box.

2. Select a version from the Existing Versions list.

3. Click the Open button.

Once a previous version is open, you can choose to save that version as a separate file (by using the Save As command) or to print that version. You can also delete a previous version by selecting it from the Existing Versions list and clicking the Delete button.

PART

VI

Creating Large and Team-Edited Documents

Sharing Documents Through Web-Based Discussions and Subscriptions

Word 2000 includes a new collaboration feature, called *Discussions,* which is available to users on a Windows NT network where a dedicated *discussion server* has been set up and configured with the Microsoft Office Server Extensions. This has not been a widely used feature, so it will not be covered in much depth here. Still, if you're one of the few who have a discussion server setup on your corporate network, you might want to consider this alternate method of sharing and editing workgroup files over your network.

 NOTE If you want to use Word 2000's Discussions feature, contact your network system administrator about installing the Microsoft Server Extensions on your corporate network.

Understanding Discussions

 Discussions are similar to comments (discussed earlier in this chapter) in that they also allow reviewers to insert their non-printable comments into a document. There are some important differences, however, including these:

Discussions Are "Live" Discussions take place in real time and can be accessed by multiple users simultaneously. As soon as a discussion remark is added, it can be read by any other users currently accessing the discussion.

Discussions Are *Threaded* Replies to a specific discussion comment are nested immediately after that remark, similar to the way articles are threaded on Usenet newsgroups.

Discussions Are Stored Separate from the Document Discussions are not part of a document; they are stored in a separate database.

Discussions Are Independent of Write Privileges Since discussions are separate from the original documents, reviewers can add discussion remarks to any document, including those they don't have access to edit directly.

Discussions Are Accessible from Your Web Browser Essentially, discussions take place on a mini-Web and can be accessed either from within Word 2000 or with any Web browser.

WARNING Word 2000's Discussions feature cannot be used on individual PCs running Windows 98, Windows 95, or Windows 3.x; it can only be used on a network running Windows NT, with the Microsoft Server Extensions installed.

Connecting to a Discussion Server

Before you can participate in a discussion, you first have to connect to a specific discussion server on your network. To do so, follow these steps:

1. Open the document you want to discuss.

2. If the Discussions toolbar is not displayed, select Tools ➤ Online Collaboration➤ Web Discussions.

3. From the Discussions toolbar, select Discussions ➤ Discussion Options to display the Discussion Options dialog box.

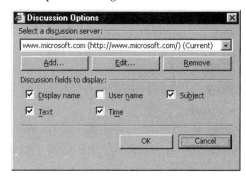

4. Pull down the Select a Discussion Server list, and choose your discussion server.

5. If your discussion server is not listed, click the Add button to display the Add or Edit Discussion Servers dialog box; enter the type and name of your discussion server, and then click OK to return to the Discussion Options dialog box.

6. Click OK to access the selected server.

Viewing Discussions

Whether you're accessing a Web discussion with Word 2000 or with your Web browser, you view all existing and ongoing discussions from the discussion pane, which is displayed underneath the main document. You also use the discussion pane to reply to, edit, and delete specific discussions.

PART

VI

Creating Large and Team-Edited Documents

NOTE You can only edit and delete those discussion remarks that *you* added, not those from other users.

To display the discussion pane (shown in Figure 23.3), click the Show/Hide Discussion Pane button on the Discussions toolbar. Click the button again to hide the discussion pane; the button is a toggle.

FIGURE 23.3
View Web discussions from Word or from your Web browser.

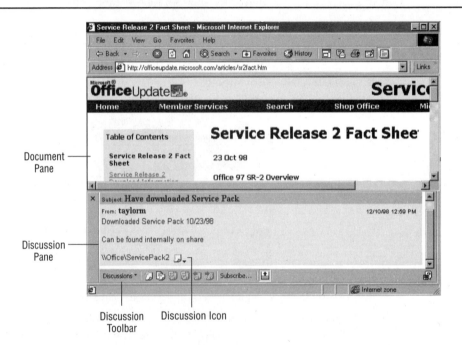

Document Pane

Discussion Pane

Discussion Toolbar

Discussion Icon

Starting and Participating in Discussions

Once you're connected to your discussion server, Word 2000 lets you initiate two different types of discussions. *Inline discussions* are inserted relative to a specific section of text; *general discussions* relate to the entire document, not to any specific section.

Starting an Inline Discussion

To start an inline discussion, follow these steps:

1. From within the document, select the text or graphic you want to comment on.
2. Click the Insert Discussion in the Document button on the Discussions toolbar.
3. When the Insert Discussion dialog box appears, enter a name for the discussion in the Discussion Subject box.
4. Enter your comments in the Discussion Text box.
5. Click OK to register your remarks.

When the discussion pane appears, a Discussion icon also appears at the end of the section you were discussing.

Starting a General Discussion

Starting a general discussion is similar to starting an inline discussion, except you don't have to select any specific text or graphic. Follow these steps:

1. From within the document, click the Insert Discussion About the Document button on the Discussions toolbar.
2. When the Insert Discussion dialog box appears, enter a name for the discussion in the Discussion Subject box.
3. Enter your comments in the Discussion Text box.
4. Click OK to register your remarks.

Replying to an Inline Discussion

To reply to an existing inline discussion, follow these steps:

1. Open the document containing the discussion to which you want to reply.
2. Click the Discussion icon next to the section you want to reply to.
3. Click the Show a Menu of Actions icon in the Discussions pane.
4. Select Reply to display the Reply dialog box.
5. Enter your reply in the Discussion Text box.
6. Click OK.

Replying to a General Discussion

Replying to a general discussion is similar to replying to an inline discussion; follow these steps:

1. Open the document containing the discussion to which you want to reply.

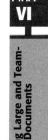

PART

VI

Creating Large and Team-Edited Documents

2. Click the Show General Discussions button on the Discussions toolbar.

3. Click the Show a Menu of Actions icon next to the discussion you want to reply to.

4. Select Reply to display the Reply dialog box.

5. Enter your reply in the Discussion Text box.

6. Click OK.

Subscribing to Workgroup Documents

Another feature available only to users of a network with the Microsoft Office Server Extensions installed is the ability to *subscribe* to a workgroup document or folder. When you've subscribed to a document or a folder stored on the server, you will be notified via e-mail of any selected changes made either to the specific document you selected or to all documents stored in the specific folder you selected.

You can select to be notified under any of the following conditions:

- Document is edited
- Document is deleted
- Document is moved
- New file is created in a folder
- Discussion remark is added to or deleted from a document

To subscribe to a document or a folder, follow these steps:

1. Open the document or folder you want to be notified about.

2. Click the Subscribe button on the Discussions toolbar to display the Document Subscription dialog box.

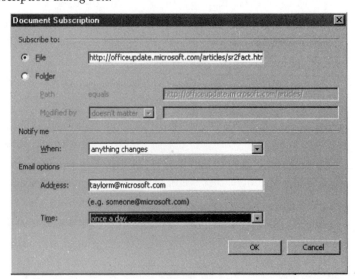

3. If you're subscribing to a specific document, check the File option. If you're subscribing to all the files within a folder, check the Folder option, and select an option from the Modified By list.

4. Pull down the When list, and select the specific conditions for when you want to be notified.

5. Enter your e-mail address in the Address box.

6. Pull down the Time list, and select when or how often you want to be notified of changes.

7. Click OK.

To cancel your subscription to a document or a folder, click the Cancel this Subscription hyperlink in any notification e-mail message you receive about that document or folder.

 WARNING Word 2000's subscription feature *cannot* be used on individual PCs running Windows 98, Windows 95, or Windows 3.*x*; it can only be used on a network running Windows NT, with the Microsoft Server Extensions installed.

PART VII

Creating Web Documents

- *Creating Web pages with Word*

- *Creating interactive Web pages and forms*

- *Publishing Word documents on the Web*

CHAPTER 24

Creating Web Pages with Word

Inserting hyperlinks   **630**

Saving existing Word documents in HTML format   **638**

Using the Web Page Wizard   **640**

Applying Web themes   **642**

Adding graphics to your Web page   **646**

Using tables to organize your page   **650**

Redesigning your pages with frames   **651**

Word isn't just for word processing anymore. With Word 2000, you can create sophisticated HTML Web pages—using many of the same tools and techniques you use to create normal Word documents.

Word 2000 enables you to take practically any Word document you create onscreen and turn it into an HTML Web page. Word can automatically convert any element in your documents into its Web page equivalent, producing instant Web pages from your existing documents—or providing you the power to create sophisticated Web pages from scratch, using Word's normal editing tools.

If you've never created a Web page before, this chapter provides both an overview of HTML Web pages and detailed instructions on how to use Word's basic Web features. Word 2000's more advanced Web features—including Web forms and scripts—are discussed in Chapter 25, and the techniques necessary to upload and publish your Web pages are discussed in Chapter 26. Taken together, these three chapters will help you master Word's Web page–creation features—and create great-looking Web pages.

Understanding Web Pages and HTML

A Web page is similar to a normal Word document in that they're both files, albeit in different formats. Like a .DOC format Word document, an .HTM or .HTML format Web page can contain both text and graphics, and can be as simple or complex as the needs and imagination of its creator.

Unlike normal Word documents, Web pages are created using a set of embedded *codes*. The overall coding system used to create a Web page document is called *HTML*, which stands for HyperText Markup Language. The codes in HTML work in the background to define what you see when you view a Web page in a Web browser.

Anyone can create a simple Web page, and there are enough sophisticated codes in HTML to enable professional Web page developers to create pages of incredible complexity. The most sophisticated Web pages move beyond static text and graphics to incorporate moving pictures and sounds, with varying degrees of interactivity.

One key feature of even the simplest Web pages is the *hyperlink*. A hyperlink is a piece of text or a graphic that is linked directly to another Web page—either on the current site or on any other computer on the Internet. Clicking a hyperlink makes the user jump to the linked page, wherever that page may be.

Understanding How HTML Works

HTML is nothing more than a series of codes. These codes tell any Web browser how to display different types of text and graphics. The codes are embedded in a document, so you can't see them; instead, you see the results of the codes as a finished Web page.

NOTE There are many sites on the Web where you can learn more about HTML and Web page development, including Web Diner (www.webdiner.com) and Webmonkey (www.webmonkey.com). In addition, you should check out any of the first-class HTML books from Sybex, including *Mastering HTML 4.0* and *Effective Web Design: Master the Essentials*.

If you were to examine the behind-the-scenes HTML code—such as the example shown in Figure 24.1—you'd see that it looks to be nothing more than normal text surrounded by instructions, enclosed within angle brackets. Each code turns on or off a particular attribute, such as boldface or italic text. Most codes are in sets of on/off pairs; you turn on the code before the text you want to affect, and then turn off the code after the text.

FIGURE 24.1

The behind-the-scenes HTML code used to create a typical Web page

```
 products[1] - Notepad
File  Edit  Search  Help
<html>

<head>
<title>Writing</title>

<meta name="Microsoft Theme" content="checkers 010">
<meta name="Microsoft Border" content="tlb, default">
</head>

<body bgcolor="#FFFFFF" text="#000000" link="#0000FF" vlink="#006699"
alink="#000000"><!--msnavigation--><table border="0" cellpadding="0" cellspacing="0"
width="100%"><tr><td><!--mstheme--><font face="Arial, Helvetica">
<p align="center"><img border="0" src="_borders/mrmoletop.jpg" width="640"
height="180"><!--mstheme--></font></td></tr><!--msnavigation--></table><!--msnavigation--><table
border="0" cellpadding="0" cellspacing="0" width="100%"><tr><td valign="top"
width="1%"><!--mstheme--><font face="Arial, Helvetica">

<div align="center">
  <center><!--mstheme--></font><table border="1" cellspacing="1" width="75%" bgcolor="#33CCCC"
bordercolordark="#999999" bordercolorlight="#CCCCCC">
    <tr>
      <td width="100%" bgcolor="#33CCCC"><!--mstheme--><font face="Arial, Helvetica">
        <dl>
          <div align="center">
            <dt><font size="2"><b>&quot;What impressed me the most... was how
              savvy the author is, and how he communicates those skills to his
              readers.&quot;</b></font></dt>
          </div>
          <div align="center">
            <center>
            <dt> </dt>
            </center>
          </div>
          <div align="center">
            <dt><i><font size="2"><b>John Nemerovski<br>
              <a href="http://www.mymac.com">Book Bytes</a></b></font></i></dt>
          </div>
```

For example, the code <b> is used to boldface the subsequent text; the code </b> turns off the boldfacing. Note that an off code is merely the on code with a slash before it, `</like this>`.

Other codes are used to insert items into a page, and therefore don't have corresponding off codes. For example, the code <hr> inserts a horizontal line into the page. You can create an HTML document by entering the appropriate codes manually in any text editor, or by using a program that works in the background to translate what you see onscreen into the appropriate HTML codes. These programs are called Web page editors (or HTML editors), and they enable you to bypass the tedious coding process and focus on designing the appearance of your Web page.

Publishing Pages to Make a Site

For a Web page to be viewed by other users, that page must reside on a *Web server,* a computer continuously connected to the Internet. When a Web page is *hosted* by a server, that page receives its own specific address (*URL* or *Uniform Resource Locator*); any user entering that address can view the corresponding page.

To move a Web page from your computer to a Web server, you must *publish* that page—a process that involves uploading the page and all accompanying graphics and files to the server, and then assigning the page a URL. When you have more than one page together on a server, you have a *Web site.* Again, anyone can create a Web site—although the more complex commercial sites require teams of developers to build and maintain the mountains of pages and links.

Understanding How Word 2000 Works with Web Pages

Although Word 97 enabled you to perform basic editing functions on Web pages, Word 2000 is the first version of Word to be a relatively full-featured Web page editor. With Word 2000 you can easily save any Word document in HTML format, and you can work with the Web Page Wizard and Web templates to create sophisticated Web pages from scratch. Word 2000 also enables you to add forms, scripts, and other interactive elements to your Web pages.

 NOTE To learn more about using Word's advanced Web page features, turn to Chapter 25.

If you choose to use Word as your Web page editor, you can use most of Word's standard editing functions—just as if you were creating a normal Word document. When you save your document in HTML format, Word automatically inserts the proper HTML codes so that the page can be read by any Web browser. You don't have to enter the HTML codes yourself; Word does all this work, in the background.

You work on your Web pages in Word 2000's new Web Layout view and preview your pages via Word's Web Page Preview (which automatically previews your in-process document in your Web browser). After you've saved your Web page (or multiple pages in a Web site), you use Word 2000's Web publishing tools to upload your pages to a Web server, so they're accessible to anyone on the Internet.

 NOTE To learn more about creating a Web site and publishing it on the Internet, see Chapter 26.

Of course, you don't have to turn your document into a Web page to place it on the Web. If your Word document is better viewed as a Word document, simply upload your document (in its native .DOC format) to your Web site and create a link to the document from one of your other Web pages. Users can then view the document as a Word file in their Web browser (if they're using a recent version of Internet Explorer) or *download* the document and view and edit it from within their copy of Microsoft Word.

 NOTE If you want to easily convert existing Word documents into HTML Web pages, check out *WordToWeb.* This versatile program can convert hundreds of documents at a time, break long documents into linked HTML pages, create an HTML table of contents and index, generate thumbnails for embedded graphics, and handle navigation links, cross-references, footnotes, and other details automatically. A trial version of WordToWeb is included on the CD accompanying this book; see Chapter 33 for more information.

MASTERING THE OPPORTUNITIES

Should You Use Word as Your Web Page Editor?

Word 2000 incorporates a number of new features that enable you to create HTML Web pages from within the word processing environment. Still, Word remains a word processor, *not* a Web page editor. Why would you want to—or *not* want to—use Word to create your Web pages?

Continued ▷

In Word's favor, it's easy to use—especially if you already use Word as your word processor. If you want to put a relatively simple text-based document on the Web, the quick and easy solution is to use Word to save that document in HTML format.

For more sophisticated Web pages, however, Word simply doesn't cut the mustard. It's difficult to lay out graphics-heavy pages in Word, and the way Word manipulates advanced HTML code is idiosyncratic at best. Word's translation of documents from .DOC to .HTML format is effective, but the basic .DOC format isn't as versatile as pure HTML.

To paraphrase a political candidate from a few years back: I know Web page editors—and Word is no Web page editor.

Serious Web page creators do not use word processing programs to design their Web pages—they use dedicated Web page or HTML editors. These programs—such as Microsoft FrontPage 2000, included with some versions of Office 2000—are purpose-specific, offering a combination of WYSIWIG editing and direct HTML code management, plus all the latest HTML, XML, and Java bells and whistles. These programs have significantly fewer limitations than Word and enable the creation of much more sophisticated Web pages.

In short, if you're serious about your Web pages, you'll skip most of this chapter and the next, and fire up FrontPage 2000 or a similar program. You'll find it easier to create just about any type of Web page—from simple pages to complex multilayered sites—using a tool designed specifically for that purpose.

Adding Web Functionality to Normal Word Documents

You don't have to create fancy Web pages to utilize Word 2000's new Web functionality. You can easily add hyperlinks to your Word document; when you click a hyperlink embedded in a Word document, Word automatically connects to the Internet and opens the linked page in your Web browser.

Inserting Hyperlinks from the Standard Toolbar

Word 2000 includes an Insert Hyperlink button on the Standard toolbar, which lets you quickly and easily insert hyperlinks within your documents. Follow these steps to insert a link to another Web page:

1. Within your document, select the text to which you want to apply the hyperlink.

2. Click the Insert Hyperlink button on Word's Standard toolbar to display the Insert Hyperlink dialog box.

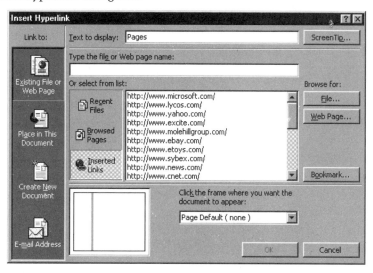

3. Click the Existing File or Web Page button at the left of the dialog box.

4. If no text appears in the Text to Display box, enter the text for the hyperlink. (If you selected text before you clicked the Insert Hyperlink button, that text should appear here; if you clicked the button without first selecting text, this box will be empty.)

5. Enter the URL for the hyperlink in the Type the File or Web Page Name box, *or*

Click the Web Page button to connect to the Internet, launch your Web browser, and navigate to the page to which you want to link, *or*

Select from the list of links displayed in the dialog box; you can choose to list Recent Files, Browsed Pages, or Inserted Links, *or*

If you want to display a ScreenTip when a cursor hovers over the link, click the ScreenTip button to display the Set Hyperlink ScreenTip dialog box; enter the text in the ScreenTip Text box, then click OK.

6. Click OK.

As you can see, there are a number of ways to choose the page to which you're linking. The easiest way is to enter the page's URL directly. If you've recently visited this page, you can choose it from the list of recently visited pages; if you don't know the page's URL, you can click the Web Page button to connect to the Internet and surf to the page manually.

Linking within Your Document

You don't have to link to another Web page—you can link to another location within your current Web page. To link within your document, follow these steps:

1. From within the Insert Hyperlink dialog box, click the Place in This Document button.

2. The dialog box lists the bookmarks and major headings within your current document. Click the plus sign (+) next to any element to expand the listings in that section.

3. Select the element to which you wish to link.

4. Click OK.

When a user clicks an intradocument link (also known as a *bookmark*—but a different kind of bookmark than that used in a normal Word document), they jump directly to the selected section of the page.

Linking to a New Document

Just in case your cart is getting ahead of your horse, Word enables you to create links to documents that don't exist yet. To link to a new document, follow these steps:

1. From within the Insert Hyperlink dialog box, click the Create New Document button.

2. Enter the name of the document you want to create into the Name of New Document box.

3. If the path displayed in the Full Path section isn't where the new document will reside, click the Change button to display the Create New Document dialog box, and select a new path.

4. If you want to proceed to edit the new document, check the Edit the New Document Now option; if you want to postpone editing, check the Edit the New Document Later option.

5. Click OK.

Word inserts the hyperlink *and* creates the new document; you can return to the document anytime to edit it properly.

Creating an E-mail Link

Some links in Web pages don't jump to another Web page; instead, these links (called *mailto links*) open your e-mail program to create and send an e-mail message. To insert a mailto link into your document, follow these steps:

1. From within the Insert Hyperlink dialog box, click the E-mail Address button.

2. Enter the e-mail address to which you want messages addressed into the E-mail Address box. (Alternatively, you can select an address from the list of recently used e-mail addresses.)

3. Enter a subject for these messages into the Subject box.

4. Click OK.

When you click your new mailto link, your e-mail program will launch and open a new message window; the selected e-mail address will be preloaded into the To: box, and the selected subject will be preloaded into the Subject: box.

Using AutoFormat to Convert Typed Addresses to Real Links

The Insert Hyperlink dialog box provides lots of options for the hyperlinks you add to your documents—but it can be somewhat time consuming to use this procedure. A simpler way to add a hyperlink is to use Word's AutoFormat feature to automatically convert all Web addresses you type into your document into real hyperlinks.

To use this feature, you first have to activate it, as follows:

1. Select Tools ➢ AutoCorrect to display the AutoCorrect dialog box.

2. Select the AutoFormat as You Type tab.

3. Check the Internet and Network Paths with Hyperlinks option.

4. Click OK.

With this option enabled, any Web address you type is automatically converted to a hyperlink to that address. For example, if you type **www.sybex.com** into your document, that text will be converted to a hyperlink to the www.sybex.com Web site.

TIP After you've added a hyperlink in this fashion, you can edit the link by right-clicking the link to display the pop-up menu, then selecting Hyperlink ➢ Edit Hyperlink to display the Edit Hyperlink dialog box (which is identical to the Insert Hyperlink dialog box).

Editing a Hyperlink

You can edit any hyperlink you've added to a document as you would any other Word object.

Selecting a Link

It is sometimes difficult to select all or part of hyperlinked text, since clicking your cursor within the linked text actually activates the hyperlink—making you jump elsewhere when you really wanted to stay where you where and do some editing. For that reason, examine these alternative methods of selecting any links you've added within your document:

Select the Entire Link   *Right-click* the link to display the pop-up menu, then select Hyperlink ➤ Select Hyperlink. Alternatively, you can use your keyboard to position the insertion point at the start of the text, then hold down the Shift key while you use the arrow keys to select the text.

Position the Insertion Point *within* the Linked Text   Use your keyboard's arrow keys to move the insertion point—do *not* attempt to click within the linked text.

Changing a Link

To change the URL (or document or e-mail address) to which the hyperlink is linked, follow these steps:

1. Right-click the link to display the pop-up menu.

2. Select Hyperlink ➤ Edit Hyperlink to display the Edit Hyperlink dialog box (which is identical to the Insert Hyperlink dialog box).

3. Make the appropriate changes, then click OK.

Copying and Pasting a Link

To copy a link to another location in your document, follow these steps:

1. Right-click the link to display the pop-up menu.

2. Select Hyperlink ➤ Copy Hyperlink.

3. Move the insertion point to where you want to paste the copy.

4. Select Edit ➤ Paste.

If you want to paste only the text *without* the hyperlink information, select Edit ➤ Paste Special (instead of Edit ➤ Paste) to display the Paste Special dialog box, select Formatted Text (RTF), then click OK.

Deleting a Link

To delete both the link and the link's text, select the entire hyperlink and then press Delete (or select Edit ➢ Clear). To retain the text but remove the hyperlink, follow these steps:

1. Right-click the link to display the pop-up menu.
2. Select Hyperlink ➢ Remove Hyperlink.

This removes all hyperlink information from the selected text—but leaves the text itself within your document.

Formatting a Link

By default, hyperlinks appear within your document as blue, underlined text. To change the way an individual hyperlink looks in your document, follow these steps:

1. Right-click the link to display the pop-up menu.
2. Select Font to display the Font dialog box.
3. Make the appropriate changes, then click OK.

If you want to change the appearance of all hyperlinks within your document, you need to modify two separate styles in your template—Hyperlink (for unclicked links) and Followed Hyperlink (for links that have been clicked—which typically turn purple).

Viewing Web Documents in Word

If you're creating documents that will be displayed on the Web, you want to view those documents as they'll appear online. Word 2000 offers two ways to view your Web documents—Web Layout view and Web Page Preview.

Using Web Layout View

Word 2000 includes a new Web Layout view that mirrors what your pages will look like when displayed in a Web browser. As you can see in Figure 24.2, Web Layout view essentially turns the Word workspace into a Web browser, where page elements look and behave as they would if viewed with Internet Explorer or Netscape Navigator. The one big difference between using Web Layout view and viewing the document with your browser (discussed in the following section) is that Web Layout view allows full editing functionality.

FIGURE 24.2
Use Web Layout view to edit your Web documents.

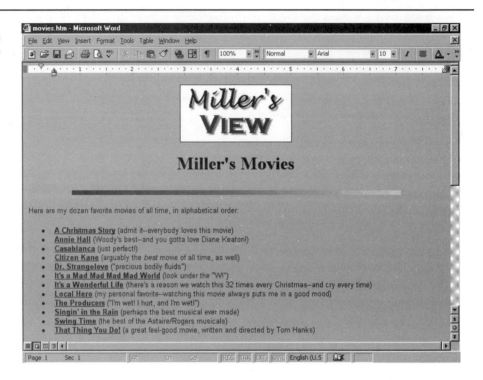

You activate Web Layout view by clicking the Web Layout View button (next to Word's horizontal scroll bar). Use Web Layout view when you know your document will be published as a page on the Web.

Using Web Page Preview

In addition to the Web Layout editing view, Word 2000 includes a new Web Page Preview function. When you activate Web Page Preview, Word automatically launches your default Web browser (either Internet Explorer or Netscape Navigator) and uses it to display your current document.

You activate Web Page Preview by selecting File ➢ Web Page Preview. Remember, though, that Web Page Preview is *not* an editing mode—when you're viewing a document in your browser, you can look, but you can't touch.

MASTERING THE OPPORTUNITIES

Using Word—as a Web Browser?

Believe it or not, Microsoft Word can actually be used as a Web browser. You can use Word to go onto the Internet, jump directly to any Web page address, and browse through Web pages, just as you would with Internet Explorer or Netscape Navigator.

Once you've established an Internet connection, launch Word and display the Web toolbar. This toolbar resembles the main toolbar in Internet Explorer, complete with an Address box, Back and Forward buttons, and a Favorites list.

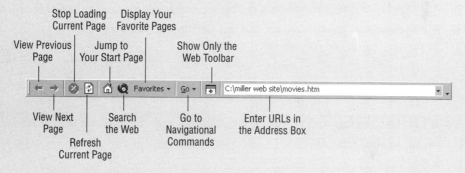

Although you *can* use Word as a Web browser, that doesn't mean you *should*. Most users would agree that Word is a *lousy* Web browser—lacking many navigational commands and the latest browser technology. In fact, depending on your system setup, you may not be *able* to use Word as a browser—on some systems, entering a URL into Word's Address box actually opens the Web page in Internet Explorer.

The bottom line is that although Word is OK to use for browsing Web pages on your hard disk (while you're working on them), for real Web browsing, use a real Web browser—such as Internet Explorer or Netscape Navigator.

Creating Basic Web Documents

There are three ways to create a Web page with Word 2000: You can simply save an existing document in HTML format; you can walk through the step-by-step instructions of the Web Page Wizard; or you can start a Web page from scratch by using one of Word 2000's built-in Web page templates.

Saving Existing Word Documents in HTML Format

Any Word document can be saved as a Web page by following these steps:

1. From within the document, select File ≻ Save As Web Page to display the Save As dialog box.

2. Make sure Web Page is selected from the Save As Type list.

3. Assign a name and location for your page.

4. Click the Save button.

 When you save a Word document as a Web page, the elements of your document are automatically coded so that they appear (in most cases) in a similar fashion when viewed with a Web browser. Unlike in previous versions of Word, the translation from .DOC to .HTML is very effective; most elements carry over to the new format. In fact, you can convert documents from .DOC to .HTML and then *back* to .DOC format, losing virtually nothing in the translation.

Table 24.1 details the changes that occur when you convert a normal Word document to HTML format.

TABLE 24.1: DIFFERENCES BETWEEN WORD AND HTML FORMATS

Word Format (.DOC)	HTML Format
Animated text	Displays as italics
Broken or dashed underlines	Display as normal underlines
Character borders	Do not display
Color underlines	Display as black underlines
Decorative border styles	Display as single-line borders
Double strikethrough	Displays as single strikethrough
Drop caps	Do not display
Emboss	Displays as gray text
Engrave	Displays as gray text
Footnotes	Moved to end of Web page
Graphics with text wrapping	Display as left aligned
Headers and footers	Do not display
Horizontally scaled characters	Display as normal text

Continued ▯

PART
VII

Creating Web Documents

TABLE 24.1: DIFFERENCES BETWEEN WORD AND HTML FORMATS (CONTINUED)

Word Format (.DOC)	HTML Format
Kerned text	Displays as normal (nonkerned) text
Line height set to *at least*	Displays as exact line height
Multiple column layouts	Display as single column
Outline text	Displays as normal text
Page borders	Do not display
Page margins (any setting)	Display as 0 margins
Page numbers	Do not display
Paragraph with negative left indent	Displays with left indent set to 0
Password protection	Inactive
Patterned or shaded text background	Displays as solid color background
Shadow text	Displays as normal text
Small caps	Display as all caps
Table absolute row height	Displays as *at least* row height
Table decorative borders	Display as single-line border
Table diagonal cell borders	Do not display
Table vertical text	Displays as regular horizontal text
Table with text wrapping	Displays as left aligned
Tabs	May not align properly
Text box with text wrapping	Displays as left aligned
Versioning	Inactive

 TIP Even though not all elements are displayed exactly the same when converted to HTML, they will return to normal if you reconvert your document from HTML back to .DOC format.

In addition, all graphics and objects in your document—including pictures, AutoShapes, WordArt, text boxes, Graph 2000 charts, and so on—are saved in either

.GIF, .JPEG, or .PNG format when you convert your document to HTML format. If you resave your document back to .DOC format, all these objects are returned to their original formats and can be edited normally.

Use Web Layout view to examine how any specific document changes when saved as an HTML Web page.

MASTERING TROUBLESHOOTING

Turning *Off* Word Features That Web Browsers Can't Use

Although most Word features have an HTML equivalent, not all do. In actuality, the Web *browser* has the limitations; not all browsers support all HTML or extended HTML features and functions.

To turn *off* those Word features not supported by Internet Explorer and Netscape Navigator, follow these steps:

1. Select Tools ➢ Options to display the Options dialog box.

2. Select the General tab.

3. Click the Web Options button to display the Web Options dialog box.

4. Select the General tab.

5. Check the Disable Features Not Supported By option, then pull down the Browser list and select a browser or set of browsers.

6. To ensure compatibility with older browsers, *uncheck* the Rely on CSS for Font Formatting option. (CSS stands for *cascading style sheets*, a feature supported only by newer Web browsers.)

7. Click OK.

Using the Web Page Wizard

Perhaps the easiest way to create a *new* Web page or site is to use Word 2000's new Web Page Wizard. This Wizard automates Web page creation with customized Web templates and leads you step by step through the process; all you have to do is follow the on-screen instructions.

The Web Page Wizard is particularly useful when you're creating multiple pages for a full-scale Web site. The Wizard lets you determine how many pages will comprise your site, how you'll navigate from page to page, and the look and feel of the entire site.

To create a Web page or site with the Web Page Wizard, follow these steps:

1. Select File ➤ New to display the New dialog box.

2. Select the Web Pages tab.

3. Select Web Page Wizard.

4. Click OK to display the Web Page Wizard.

The Web Page Wizard leads you through the following operations:

Title and Layout   This is where you create a directory for your site and assign the site a name.

Navigation   This step lets you select the layout for the links that navigate to the pages on your site. You can choose a Vertical Frame (links displayed along the left of each page), a Horizontal Frame (links displayed along the top of each page), or to have your links displayed on a Separate Page (for those browsers that don't support the frames feature).

Add Pages   Use this page of the Wizard to add and remove individual pages from your site.

Organize Pages   This step lets you move pages up or down in order on your site.

Visual Theme   From this page, click the Browse Themes button to display the Themes dialog box, and choose a coordinated look and feel for your site. (See the "Applying Web Themes" section, later in this chapter, for more details.)

When you complete the Web Page Wizard, Word automatically creates the pages you specified, according to the parameters you chose. The results are impressive.

Starting from a Web Page Template

You can also manually create a new Web page based on any of Word 2000's seven new Web page templates. These templates work similarly to how traditional Word templates work, but are optimized for frame-based Web pages.

NOTE   Word also offers a generic, blank Web page template, located on the General tab of the New dialog box.

To create a Web page based on one of these templates, follow these steps:

1. Select File ➢ New to display the New dialog box.

2. Select the Web Pages tab.

3. Select the template you want to use.

4. Click OK to create a new page based on the selected template.

Once you've created your new Web page, you can edit the dummy text and graphics, and use Word 2000's Web themes (discussed in the next section) to change the look and feel of your page.

Enhancing Web Pages

There are as many ways to personalize a Web page as there are to personalize a normal Word document. You can format any or all of the text; add hyperlinks to other Web pages; add pictures, graphical elements, and other objects; change the color or texture of the page background; and change the page layout by adding horizontal or vertical frames.

Applying Web Themes

It's easy to design a bad-looking Web page—all you have to do is use the wrong combination of colors and text styles. If you want to avoid design disasters—and create great-looking Web pages with a minimal effort—use Word 2000's new Web themes feature.

A *theme* is a combination of fonts, text colors, and background colors applied to a Web page or group of Web pages. You pick a theme, and then Word applies the selected formatting throughout your entire Web document.

To apply a theme, follow these steps:

1. From within your Web document, select Format ➢ Theme to display the Theme dialog box, shown in Figure 24.3.

2. Select a theme from the Choose a Theme list; the preview window shows how a sample page looks with this theme applied.

WARNING Not all themes are automatically installed in a standard Word installation. If you choose a theme that has not yet been installed, you'll be prompted to insert your Word 2000 installation CD and install the theme.

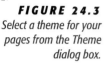

FIGURE 24.3
Select a theme for your pages from the Theme dialog box.

Select a Theme from This List

Preview Your Theme Here

Check to Display Brighter Colors

Check to Display Animated Graphics

Check to Display a Background Graphic Instead of a Background Color

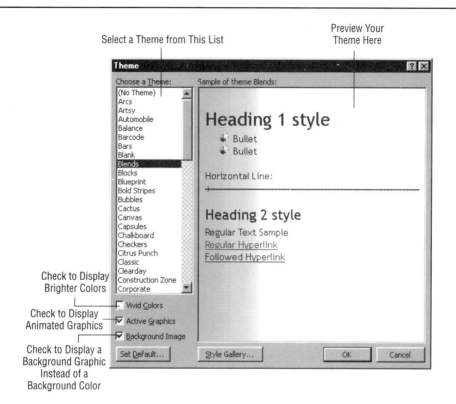

3. To display the theme with a brighter color scheme, check the Vivid Colors option.

4. To display the theme with animated elements (such as buttons or bullets that change color or shape when selected), check the Active Graphics option.

5. To display a background graphic instead of a background color, check the Background Image option; to display a background color, leave this option unchecked.

6. Click OK to apply the theme.

You can change themes at any time by repeating the above procedure. Word will automatically reformat your Web page based on any new theme you select.

The theme you select greatly affects not only the look but also the feel of your Web page. Figures 24.4 and 24.5 show the same document formatted with two completely different themes; the difference is dramatic.

FIGURE 24.4
The Artsy theme has a completely different feel from…

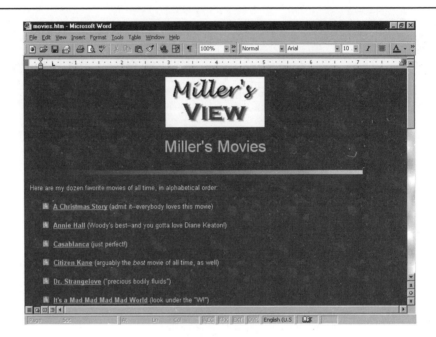

FIGURE 24.5
…the Straight-Edge theme.

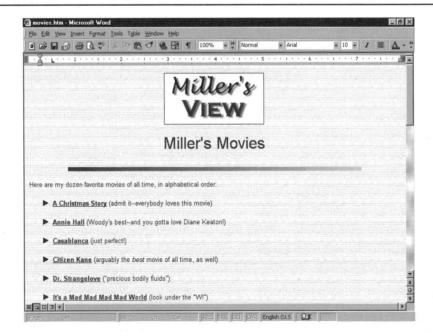

Once you've assigned a theme, you can still edit the individual elements of your page separately. Read on to learn more about other formatting options for your Web pages.

Formatting Web Page Text

You format text in a Web document the same way you format text normally, using the commands on Word's Formatting toolbar and Format menu. Know, however, that not all text formatting can be seen by all visitors to your Web page—in particular, be careful of the fonts you use in your document.

 NOTE For more information about Word's text formatting features, see Chapter 8.

The fonts you designate for your document do not travel with your document. When a person on another computer views your document onscreen (through his or her Web browser), the document is displayed using fonts installed on that *other* user's computer system. So if you designate a font that is *not* installed on another user's system, that person's Web browser will substitute a similar font (typically a generic serif or sans-serif font) for your desired font—with unpredictable results.

Because a page on the Web can be viewed by millions of users using myriad different computer systems, it is unlikely that all potential users will have all the fonts you designate installed on their systems—unless you use some very common fonts. Most users have some variation of Arial (sans-serif) and Times New Roman (serif) fonts installed on their systems; for maximum compatibility, limit yourself to these fonts in your Web documents.

 TIP The safest course of action is to use Word's built-in Normal style for all your body text and the built-in heading styles (Heading 1, Heading 2, and so on) for your document's headings. These styles will almost always reproduce well across all Web browsers.

In addition, be cautious about applying various text effects to your Web page text. As you saw in Table 24.1, some advanced effects (shadowing, embossing, and so on) simply do not have HTML equivalents. Boldface and italics are OK to use—and it's OK to vary your point size and text color—but beyond that, you're on shaky ground.

One last text-related tip—avoid using *underlining* in your Web pages. Since hyperlinks are typically underlined on a Web page, users tend to view *any* underlined text as a hyperlink. Since you don't want users click-click-clicking text that *isn't* a hyperlink (they'll get very annoyed very quickly), leave the underlining to the links.

Formatting Your Web Page Background

A Web page can have a plain, white background (or the default background assigned by any user's Web browser), or you can designate a color or a graphic to be used for the background of your Web page.

To add a color background to your Web page, select Format ≻ Background and select a color. To add a graphic to the background, follow these steps:

1. Select Format ≻ Background ≻ Fill Effects to display the Fill Effects dialog box.

2. Select the Picture tab.

3. Click the Select Picture button to display the Select Picture dialog box.

4. Select the graphics file you want to use.

5. Click Insert.

 NOTE For more information about Word's background formatting features, see Chapter 10.

Note that any file used as a background for a Web page *repeats* throughout the page. That is, if the picture is only half as tall as the page, the picture will be displayed *twice*—one on top of another. A picture that is less wide than the Web page will be repeated side to side.

Although this repeating effect can be annoying if you don't plan for it, it also offers some benefits. Perhaps the best use of this effect is to select a very small graphic and plan for it to repeat to create a *pattern* on your page. You can also use a short but wide graphic to fill the page in with an attractive background.

Adding Graphics to Your Web Page

A Web page, just like any Word document, benefits from the use of graphics. Web pages typically are graphics heavy; many Internet users tend to value pictures more than text when surfing the Web.

Inserting a Picture

Adding a picture to a Web page is just like adding a picture to a normal Word document. Follow these steps:

1. Position the insertion point where you want to add the graphic.

2. Select Insert ➢ Picture ➢ From File to display the Insert Picture dialog box.

3. Select the file you want to insert.

4. Click the Insert button.

 NOTE For more information about using picture files with Word 2000, see Chapter 16.

A great source of pictures designed specially for Web pages is Word's ClipArt Gallery. To insert a picture from the Gallery, follow these steps:

1. Position the insertion point where you want to add the graphic.

2. Select Insert ➢ Picture ➢ Clip Art to display the Insert ClipArt window.

3. Select the Pictures tab.

4. Click a category icon to display pictures within that category.

5. Click the image you want to insert; this displays a pop-up menu.

6. Click the Insert Clip button.

 Although you can use images from any ClipArt category, the images designed specifically for Web use are found in the Web Backgrounds, Web Banners, Web Bullets & Buttons, Web Dividers, and Web Elements categories.

 TIP When adding graphics to your Web page, always opt for a smaller file size whenever possible—smaller files take less time to download over a standard Internet connection. Use your graphics editing program to reduce not only the physical size of your picture, but also the number of colors used—both of which will reduce the size of the file itself.

Designating Alternative Text

 After you've inserted a picture in your document, you can specify *alternate text* for the image. This text is displayed as the picture is being loaded into the user's Web browser or if (for some reason) the picture can't be displayed. In addition, some Internet search engines use alternate text when they create their Web indexes and directories.

To add alternate text to any graphic, follow these steps:

1. Within your document, double-click the picture to display the Format Picture dialog box.

2. Select the Web tab.

3. Enter the text you want displayed if the picture can't be viewed.

4. Click OK.

Adding Horizontal Lines between Sections

You use horizontal lines to break up various sections of your Web page. You can insert plain lines or fancy lines; Word uses graphics to create the horizontal lines in your Web page.

Inserting a Horizontal Line

If you look for a *horizontal line* option on Word's Insert menu, you'll be disappointed. Word hides this feature in the Borders and Shading dialog box, for some unknown reason.

To insert a horizontal line, follow these steps:

1. Position the insertion point where you want to add the horizontal line.

2. Select Format ➤ Borders and Shading to display the Borders and Shading dialog box.

3. Click the Horizontal Line button to display the Horizontal Line dialog box.

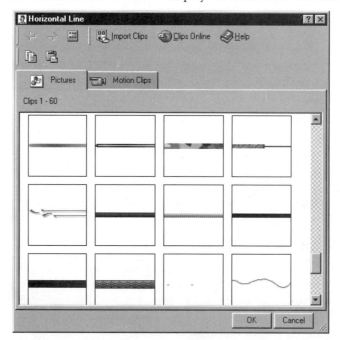

NOTE Word 2000's horizontal line feature is actually a subsection of the ClipArt Gallery—which means you could just use the ClipArt Gallery to insert a line, if you wanted.

4. Make sure the Pictures tab is selected.

5. Click the line you want to insert; this displays a pop-up menu.

6. Click the Insert Clip button.

Formatting a Horizontal Line

Once you've inserted a horizontal line into your document, you can format it in a number of ways. You can move it to another location, of course; you can also grab a selection handle and resize as necessary.

NOTE For more information about resizing and formatting lines and other objects, see Chapter 16.

Word 2000 also allows direct formatting of any horizontal line—including width, height, alignment, and image control. Just follow these steps:

1. Double-click the line to display the Format Horizontal Line dialog box.

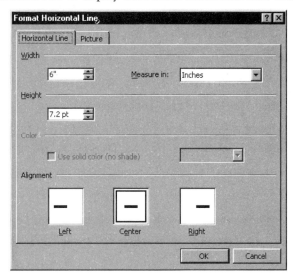

2. Select the Horizontal Line tab and adjust the Width, Height, and Alignment as necessary.

3. Select the Picture tab to adjust cropping, color, brightness, and contrast, as necessary.

4. Click OK.

Using Tables to Organize Your Page

One powerful but often overlooked design tool for Web pages is the *table*. You can use Word's table feature to block out your Web page in a grid, and precisely position text and objects on your page.

 NOTE For more information about using tables in Word, see Chapter 14.

One common approach is to use a simple two-column, single-row table to create the effect of a two-column Web page. You can size one column smaller than the other to make it look more like a sidebar; Figures 24.6 and 24.7 show an example of a table-designed Web page.

FIGURE 24.6
Use a simple two-column, one-row table...

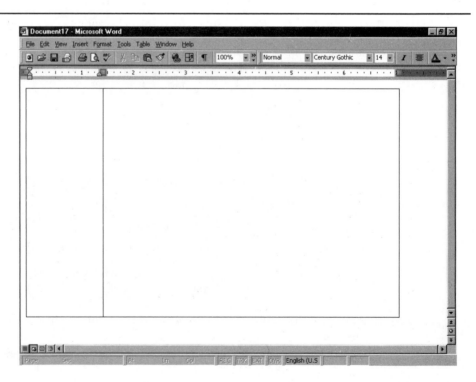

PART
VII

Creating Web Documents

FIGURE 24.7
...to create a sophisticated two-column Web page.

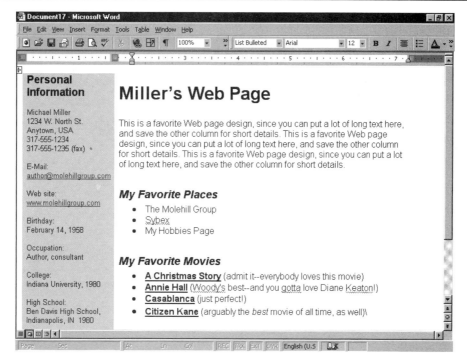

When you use tables in this fashion, it's often best to *not* apply any borders or gridlines. You can, however, apply shading to the individual cells; use different colors to set off one column from another.

 WARNING As detailed back in Table 24.1, many of Word's fancy table effects (such as decorative borders and vertical text) do not have HTML equivalents and thus should not be used when you're creating Web documents.

Redesigning Your Pages with Frames

 Web page *frames* enable you to display multiple pieces of information on a single page, much like you can by using tables—but with much greater versatility. Each frame contains its own separate Web page, which can be viewed separately; the page containing the frames is called a *frames page*. Figure 24.8 shows how frames can be used to create a sophisticated Web page layout.

FIGURE 24.8
Use frames to position complex information on a Web page.

Heading Frame

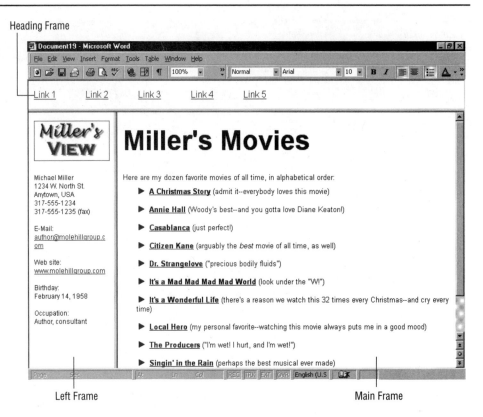

Left Frame   Main Frame

Using the Frames Toolbar

You add frames to your Web page by using the commands on the Frames toolbar. You display the Frames toolbar (shown in Figure 24.9) by right-clicking any visible toolbar, then selecting Frames.

FIGURE 24.9
Use the Frames toolbar to add frames to your pages.

Table of Contents in Frame

New Frame Right

New Frame Below   Frame Properties

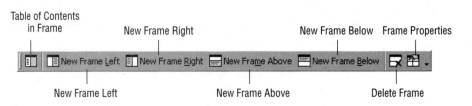

New Frame Left   New Frame Above   Delete Frame

Adding a Frame

To add a frame to your current Web page, make sure you're in Web Layout view, then follow these steps:

1. Position your cursor on the page or in an existing frame adjacent to where you want to add the new frame.

2. To add a frame to the left of your page, click the New Frame Left button on the Frames toolbar. To add a frame to the right of your page, click the New Frame Right button. To add a frame at the top of your page, click the New Frame Above button.

Adding a Navigation Frame

One of the more common uses for a frame is to use the frame for navigational purposes. When the frame contains links to the major parts of your Web page or site, users can simply click a link to jump directly to a specific section.

To create a table of contents in a navigational frame, follow these steps:

1. Anchor the insertion point in the main frame on your Web page.

2. Click the Table of Contents in Frame button on the Frames toolbar.

 WARNING The Table of Contents in Frame command works only if you've used Word's built-in heading styles (Heading 1, Heading 2, and so on) to organize your document.

Deleting a Frame

To delete a frame—and its contents—from your Web page, follow these steps:

1. Position the insertion point within the frame you want to delete.

2. Click the Delete Frame button on the Frames toolbar.

 WARNING When you delete a frame, you also delete all the frame's contents—text, graphics, and anything else contained in the frame.

Formatting a Frame

Word enables you to format your frame in various ways—from resizing the frame and adding a frame border to showing or hiding scroll bars within the frame.

Most frame formatting is done from the Frame Properties dialog box. You display this dialog box by clicking the Frame Properties button on the Frames toolbar.

Here are the most important frame formatting options:

Resize the Frame   The simplest way to resize a frame (within Web Layout view) is to use your mouse to drag the frame border to a new location. If you want more precise positioning, select the Frame tab within the Frame Properties dialog box, then select new Height or Width measurements. You can also choose whether your selected size refers to a *percent of the total Web page,* a *fixed measurement* (in inches), or a *relative multiple of other frames on the page.*

Add a Frame Border   To add a border to a frame, select the Borders tab in the Frame Properties dialog box and check the Show All Frame Borders option. You can then select a width and color for your border. To turn off frame borders, check the No Borders option.

Show or Hide Scroll Bars   If you have a lot of information in a small frame, you probably want users to be able to scroll through the frame (separately from the entire Web page). To display a scroll bar in a frame, select the Borders tab in the Frame Properties dialog box, pull down the Show Scrollbars in Browser list, and select If Needed. If you want the scroll bar to *always* be visible (even when not necessary), select Always from the list; if you never want to display the scroll bar, select Never.

Allow Users to Resize the Frame—or Do Not   If you want to preserve the integrity of your Web page design, you don't want users to be able to resize the frame from within their Web browsers. On the other hand, you may want users to have this freedom, so they can enlarge a frame to read its contents more easily. In either case, select the Borders tab in the Frame Properties dialog box, and either check the Frame Is Resizable in Browser option (to allow users to resize their own frames) or uncheck the option (to dictate fixed frame placement).

Change the Page Displayed within the Frame   Word automatically assigns the proper URL for each page displayed in a frame. If you want to manually change which page appears in which frame, select the Frame tab in the Frame Properties dialog box, then enter a new URL in the Initial Page box. You can also rename the current frame by entering a new name in the Name box. If you choose to link to another page from within the frame, you can select to automatically update the contents of the frame when the original page changes; just check the Link to File option.

MASTERING THE OPPORTUNITIES

Editing in HTML

For more precise control of your Web pages, Word enables you to view and edit the HTML code directly. Just follow these steps:

1. While viewing an HTML document, select View ➢ HTML Source to display the Microsoft Script Editor, with the current document loaded. (See Chapter 25 to learn more about the Microsoft Script Editor.)

2. Make any changes to the HTML code.

3. Select File ➢ Exit to save the changes and close the Script Editor.

If you choose to edit your HTML code manually, make sure you're well versed in HTML; nothing can screw up a Web page faster than an incorrect HTML code somewhere in your document.

CHAPTER 25

Creating Interactive Web Pages

Working with the Web Tools toolbar   **658**

Working in Design mode   **659**

Adding scrolling text   **660**

Adding a movie clip and background sound   **663**

Adding a form to a Web page   **668**

Setting the properties of a form control   **669**

Working with scripts in your documents   **679**

Using Microsoft Script Editor   **682**

In the previous chapter, you learned how to use Word 2000 to create basic Web pages, with text graphics, tables, and frames. It's possible, however, to create more complex Web pages with Word—pages that play music, display moving pictures, and accept input from users. To create these high-energy, interactive Web pages, you need to master Word's Design mode and to learn to use Web form controls.

In addition, if you're a really advanced Web page developer, you know you can create your own Web *scripts* to customize your advanced Web page effects. Word 2000 lets you add your scripts—created in either VBScript or JavaScript—directly to your pages, using the Microsoft Script Editor.

Read on to learn how to master these advanced techniques and to create truly interactive Web pages!

Understanding the Web Tools Toolbar and Design Mode

Most of Word's advanced Web page creation takes place in a special mode called *Design mode.* When Design mode is activated, you can draw *forms* on your page and insert *controls* into your forms and pages.

Word lets you create many different kinds of forms for many different kinds of documents; when you're designing Web pages, you want to create a Web form. Web forms let you interact with visitors to your site and let them interact with you.

A control is any element, such as a check box, an option button, or even a multimedia clip, that offers an option to users. You can insert controls into forms or, in some cases, directly into otherwise-normal Web pages.

You design forms and add controls in Word's Design mode, and you activate Design mode from the Web Tools toolbar.

 NOTE Forms, controls, and Design mode are all part of Visual Basic for Applications (VBA), which Word uses to automate various advanced tasks. Learn more about Visual Basic for Applications in Chapter 30.

Working with the Web Tools Toolbar

 The Web Tools toolbar includes commands that activate Design mode, create forms, and insert controls. You display the Web Tools toolbar, shown in Figure 25.1, by right-clicking any visible toolbar and then selecting Web Tools.

FIGURE 25.1
Use the Web Tools toolbar to create form pages for the Web.

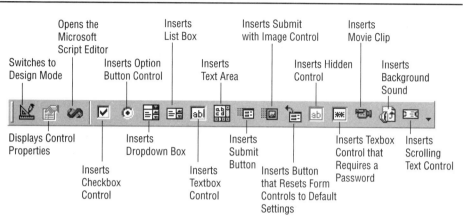

Opens the Microsoft Script Editor

Inserts List Box

Inserts Submit with Image Control

Inserts Movie Clip

Switches to Design Mode

Inserts Option Button Control

Inserts Text Area

Inserts Hidden Control

Inserts Background Sound

Displays Control Properties

Inserts Dropdown Box

Inserts Submit Button

Inserts Texbox Control that Requires a Password

Inserts Scrolling Text Control

Inserts Checkbox Control

Inserts Textbox Control

Inserts Button that Resets Form Controls to Default Settings

To insert most, but not all, controls, you first have to click the Design Mode button to switch to Design mode. However, the Movie, Sound, and Scrolling Text controls can be added directly to your page without switching to Design mode first.

Working in Design Mode

To switch to Design mode, click the Design Mode button on the Web Tools toolbar. As you can see in Figure 25.2, when you're in Design mode the Word workspace looks just like normal except for the Exit Design Mode button floating on top of the workspace. You click the Exit Design Mode button to exit Design mode and return to Word's normal *Run mode.*

Run mode is the opposite of Design mode. While you're in Design mode, nothing automated in your documents can be run—no macros, no forms, no controls. Essentially, your controls are all turned off. When you exit Design mode, you can run all your automated elements as normal, hence the name *Run mode.*

You switch to Design mode when you want to design your forms and insert your controls; when you switch back to Run mode, you can interact with the inserted forms and controls as a regular user.

FIGURE 25.2
*Use Design mode to
design forms and add
interactive controls to
your Web pages.*

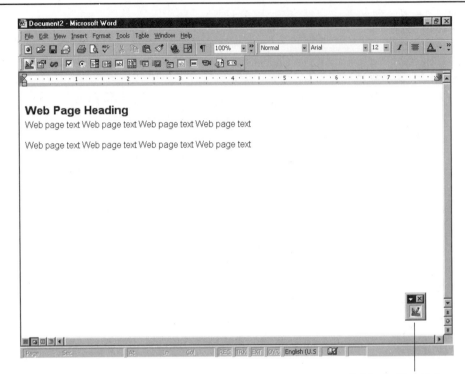

Exit Design Mode Button

Adding Multimedia Components to Your Web Page

The simplest controls you can add to your Web page are the Scrolling Text, Movie, and Sound controls. As you might recall, you don't have to switch to Design mode to add these controls.

Adding Scrolling Text

A scrolling text message (also known as a *marquee*) acts like a news ticker, drawing attention to a particular piece of text or section of your Web page. While it's difficult to demonstrate scrolling text on a static book page, Figure 25.3 provides a snapshot of scrolling text on a sample page.

FIGURE 25.3
Use a scrolling text message to give a news-ticker effect to your Web page.

Scrolling Text

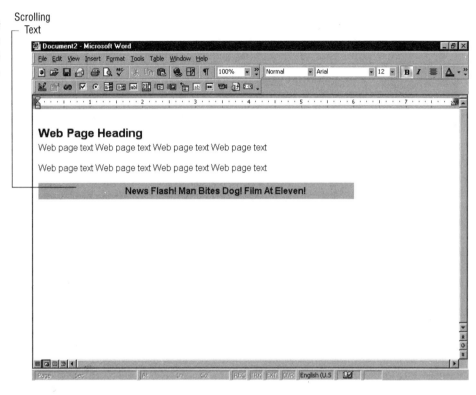

You add a marquee to your Web page via the Scrolling Text control. To do so, follow these steps:

1. From within your document (in Web Layout view), click the Scrolling Text button on the Web Tools toolbar to display the Scrolling Text dialog box.

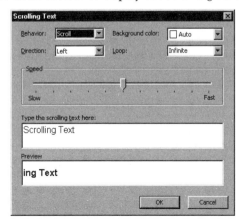

2. Enter your message in the Type the Scrolling Text Here box.

3. Pull down the Behavior list, and select whether you want the text to Scroll, Slide, or Alternate between the two behaviors.

4. To change the background color of the marquee, pull down the Background Color list, and select a new color.

5. Pull down the Direction list, and select whether you want the text to scroll to the Left or to the Right.

6. If you want to limit the number of times your message scrolls, pull down the Loop list, and select a value; if you want the message to scroll continuously, select Infinite.

7. Adjust the scrolling speed with the Speed slider.

8. Click OK when done.

 WARNING In Web browsers that don't support scrolling text, the text within the marquee will appear centered in the object but won't scroll.

Once your marquee has been created, you can format it in any of the following ways:

Move the Marquee   The Scrolling Text control is now just another object on your Web page. You can use your mouse to move it to a new position anywhere on your page.

Resize the Marquee   Just as you can move the object, you can also resize the object with your mouse. You can stretch it to make it wider or taller, or shrink it to make it narrower or shorter.

Format the Text   To change the font, size, or color of the text in the marquee, select the object, and select Format ➤ Font to display the Font dialog box. Make the appropriate changes, and then click OK. (You can also use any of Word's font-formatting commands, such as Bold or Italic, on the Formatting toolbar.)

Reformat the Scrolling Text Behavior   Double-click the Scrolling Text control to redisplay the Scrolling Text dialog box and make additional configuration changes.

 TIP   To temporarily stop the text from scrolling, right-click the object, and select Stop from the pop-up menu. To restart the scrolling, right-click the object, and select Play.

Adding a Movie Clip

Adding a video clip to your Web page is very similar to adding scrolling text: You insert a special Movie control. The control links to a movie file, which can reside on your Web page or be linked from another page on the Web.

The example in Figure 25.4 shows a snapshot of what a movie clip may look like in your document. (Typically, the first frame of the clip is displayed if the clip isn't running.) You can insert movie files in any of the following formats:

FIGURE 25.4
Add a movie clip to your Web page and you're ready for show time!

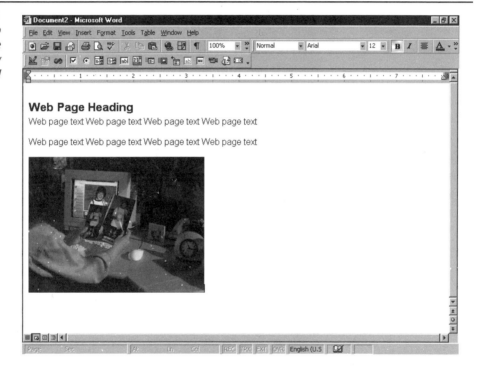

- .AVI
- .MOV
- .MOVIE
- .MPG
- .MPEG
- .QT (QuickTime)

To add a movie clip to your Web page, follow these steps:

1. From within your document (in Web Layout view), click the Movie button on the Web Tools toolbar to display the Movie Clip dialog box.

2. Enter into the Movie box the path and filename (or Web address) of the movie file you want to insert, or click the Browse button to navigate to the file.

3. Since not all browsers can support movie playback, you should indicate a graphics file that can substitute, when necessary, for the movie file. Enter into the Alternate Image box the path and filename (or Web address) of the substitute file, or click the Browse button to navigate to the file.

4. Enter into the Alternate Text box the text you want to display in case neither the movie file nor the alternate image can display.

5. To automatically play the movie when a user accesses the Web page, pull down the Start list, and select Open. To play the movie when the user moves the mouse over the movie image, pull down the Start list, and select Mouse-Over. To use *both* modes of activation, pull down the Start list, and select Both.

TIP Typically, movie files are large files, and users usually dislike downloading large files and especially loathe being *forced* to download large files. For this reason, you should avoid having a large movie clip play automatically when the page is accessed; instead, give the user the choice to play or not to play the clip.

6. Pull down the Loop list, and select the number of times you want the movie to repeat; if you want the movie to play continuously, select Infinite.

7. Click OK.

Once the movie clip has been added to your page, you can format it in any of the following ways:

Move the Clip Object   Use your mouse to move the Movie control to a new position anywhere on your page.

Resize the Clip Object   Stretch the clip object on your page to make it wider or taller, or shrink it to make it narrower or shorter.

TIP   Be careful not to change the dimensions of the clip object when resizing or your video clip will be out of proportion. (To maintain proportion while resizing, hold down the Shift key.) Also be careful not to over-enlarge the clip object; movie clips on a PC play more smoothly and look more crisp at a smaller size.

Reformat the Clip Object   Double-click the movie clip object to redisplay the Movie Clip dialog box and make additional configuration changes.

TIP   To play the movie while you're editing, right-click the object, and select Play from the pop-up menu; select Stop to cease playing.

Adding a Background Sound Clip

Have you ever visited a Web page and been greeted by a sound or a song? Word 2000 enables you to take advantage of this same effect—adding background audio to your Web page—by inserting a Sound control linked to an audio file.

You can insert or link to sound files in the following formats:

- .AIF
- .AIFF
- .AU
- .MID
- .MIDI
- .RMI
- .SND
- .WAV

You typically find shorter sounds in the .SND and .WAV formats and longer music clips in the .MID or .MIDI formats.

To add a background sound to your page, follow these steps:

1. From within your document (in Web Layout view), click the Sound button on the Web Tools toolbar to display the Background Sound dialog box.

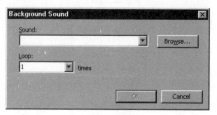

2. Enter into the Sound box the path and filename (or Web address) of the sound file you want to insert, or click the Browse button to navigate to the file.

3. If you want the sound to play just once, select 1 from the Loop list. If you want a song to play continuously, select Infinite from the Loop list.

 TIP Keep in mind that some MIDI files can be rather large and take a long time to download, and your Web page won't be completely displayed until this file is downloaded and the music starts. Also note that some users may become annoyed by background music in an infinite loop that they can't shut off.

4. Click OK.

To change the settings for your background sound, just click the Sound button on the Web Tools toolbar. This redisplays the Background Sound dialog box, ready to be reconfigured.

 NOTE If you selected Infinite looping and you're *not* in Design mode, you'll be subjected to the background sound continuously whenever your document is open for editing. The only way to turn off a background sound while editing is to switch to Design mode.

Creating Web Forms

If you surf the Internet with any regularity, you've encountered Web forms. The purpose of a Web form is to collect data from Web users and then to initiate some kind of action. For example, the Search box on any search site (such as Yahoo! or AltaVista) is a Web form; it collects data (in the form of your query) and then acts on it (by providing a list of matching Web pages). Another example of a Web form is the check-out page at Amazon.com or most any other e-tailer site; the form collects your data (name, address, credit card number, and so on) and then acts on it (by submitting your order for processing).

Understanding How Forms Collect Data

You use Word 2000's Design mode to create Web forms on your Web pages. Your form can be a complete page unto itself (like the e-tailer check-out pages) or just part of an existing page (like Yahoo!'s Search box). You add interaction to your forms with Web controls, which range from check boxes to list boxes to text boxes. (Refer to the "Word 2000's Web Form Controls" section, later in this chapter, for detailed information about available Web controls.)

Typically, whatever controls you incorporate in your form will be accompanied by a Submit (or Submit with Image) control. When users click the Submit button, all the information they've entered and/or selected (the data you want to collect) is then sent to your Web server for processing.

What happens to the data after it is submitted is controlled by a *script*. The script tells your Web server what to do with the submitted data. For example, submitted data can be added to a database or e-mailed directly to a specified e-mail address. You create your scripts using one of a number of scripting protocols. The following are the most common types of scripts are:

CGI (Common Gateway Interface)   CGI scripts are typically used on Unix or Linux servers and are written in either the Perl or Tcl/Tk scripting languages.

ASP (Active Server Pages)   ASP scripts are typically used on Windows NT or Windows 2000 servers and are written in either the VBScript or JavaScript scripting languages.

ISAPI (Internet Service Application Programming Interface)   ISAPI scripts are typically used on Windows NT or Windows 2000 servers and are written using complex, Windows-specific calls.

 NOTE   The scripting behind Web forms is beyond the scope of this book. For more information on creating Web scripts, check out the Web Developer's Virtual Library (www.wdvl.com), the Web Learning Center (www.weblearningcenter.com), or other similar Web sites.

Adding a Form to a Web Page

You can add a form to any Web page or create a page that is nothing but a form. When you create a form, Word inserts a Top of Form boundary at the top of the form and a Bottom of Form boundary below the form. As you can see in Figure 25.5, the controls you add to your form are inserted between these two boundaries, which are visible in Design mode but hidden when your page is viewed in a Web browser.

FIGURE 25.5

A form being created in Design mode

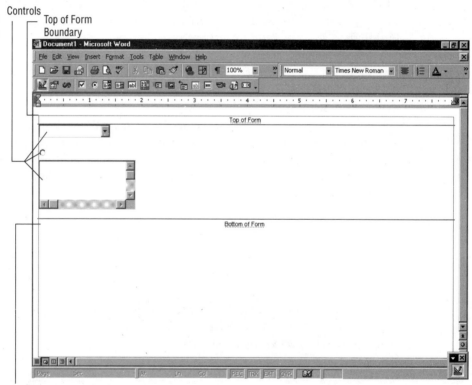

Controls — Top of Form Boundary

Bottom of Form Boundary

NOTE All the controls within a single form appear between the Top of Form and the Bottom of Form boundaries. You can have multiple forms on a single page; each form will have its own Top of Form and Bottom of Form boundaries.

PART

VII

Creating Web Documents

To create a form, you start by inserting a control into your document (while in Design mode), and then you add to your form with other controls. Just follow these steps:

1. From within Design mode, position the insertion point where you want to begin the form.

2. Click the control you want to insert from the Web Tools toolbar.

3. The control is now inserted between the Top of Form and the Bottom of Form boundaries, as shown previously in Figure 25.5.

4. If you want to resize the control, use your mouse to grab a selection handle on the control and resize it.

Continue adding controls (and rearranging them on your page, within the Top of Form and the Bottom of Form boundaries) until your form is completed. Once you've added controls, you need to set their properties, as described in the following section.

Setting the Properties of a Web Form Control

After you have added a control to you Web page, you have to set the properties for that control. The properties of a form control determine how data is communicated to a Web server and, for some controls, how the control appears on your Web page.

To set a control's properties, follow these steps:

1. From within Design mode, select the control.

2. Click the Properties button on the Web Tools toolbar to display the Properties dialog box for that control.

3. Select the Alphabetic tab to view the properties alphabetically; select the Categorized tab to view the properties by category.

4. Set the appropriate properties.

5. Close the Properties dialog box.

When you are finished setting the properties for each of your controls, click the Exit Design Mode button to return to Run mode.

Word 2000's Web Form Controls

 Word 2000 includes 11 form controls on the Web Tools toolbar. The following sections detail each of these controls and their key settings.

 NOTE The 11 form controls presented on the Web Tools toolbar are standard HTML controls that are widely used on the World Wide Web. You can also add any form controls found on Word's Control Toolbox toolbar to your Web pages, with some caution. The Control Toolbox controls are ActiveX-based, not HTML-based, but not all Web browsers support ActiveX controls. In addition, if you want to use these ActiveX controls, you'll need some knowledge of Visual Basic for Applications to customize the behavior of the controls. For most users, it is more practical to limit their controls to those found on the Web Tools toolbar.

The Checkbox Control

 You use a Checkbox control to enable users to select or deselect a specific item in your form. You can also insert Checkbox controls next to each item in a group of choices that are not mutually exclusive so that users can select more than one check box at a time. Figure 25.6 shows a typical grouping of Checkbox controls on a Web form.

FIGURE 25.6
Use a Checkbox control to register a user selection.

The key properties of a Checkbox control are as follows:

Checked   Determines whether the check box is selected by default.

HTMLName   Determines the name you assign to the control.

Value   Determines the text sent to a Web server if the box is selected.

The Option Button Control

You use an Option Button control to force a single selection between two or more choices. Since only one option can be selected at a time, selecting one option deselects the other options. Figure 25.7 shows how a set of option buttons appears on a Web page.

FIGURE 25.7
Use an Option Button control to force a choice from among several options.

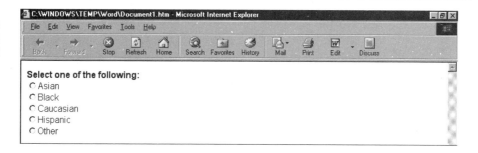

The key properties of an Option Button control are as follows:

Checked   Determines whether the option button is selected by default.

HTMLName   Determines the name you assign to the control. Use the same name for other option buttons in the same group; multiple groups are permitted on the same form.

Value   Determines the text sent to a Web server if the option button is selected.

NOTE   To place text beside an option button, type it directly on the form beside the button; the Option Button control doesn't have a caption property for this purpose.

The Dropdown Box Control

You use a Dropdown Box control to display a drop-down list of choices; the user can then select only one option from the list. (The items that appear in the list are entered via the DisplayValues property.) Figure 25.8 shows a typical Dropdown Box control on a Web page.

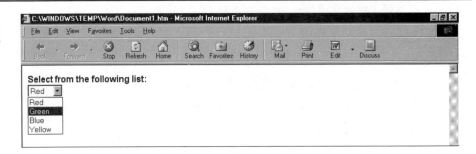

The key properties of a Dropdown Box control are as follows:

DisplayValues   Determines the items to display in the list. Enter all the items for the list, with each item separated by a semicolon (but no trailing spaces), as follows: *Item1;Item2;Item3.*

HTMLName   Determines the name you assign to the control.

MultiSelect   Determines whether the user can select more than one item from the list; the default value is False.

NOTE   If you change the MultiSelect property setting to True, the control becomes a List Box control.

Selected   Determines whether the first item appears in the box and whether the first item is selected by default; the default value is True.

Size   Determines the size of the font used for the list (defaults to 1).

Value   Determines the text sent to a Web server for each item appearing in the list. In most cases, the Value is the same as the DisplayValue, but it doesn't have to be, as long as the number of Values is equal to the number of DisplayValues. Values are separated with a semicolon, with no trailing spaces, as follows: *Value1;Value2;Value3.*

The List Box Control

You use a List Box control to display available choices in a scrolling list; users can select multiple choices from the list. Figure 25.9 shows a list box as used on a typical Web page.

FIGURE 25.9
Use a List Box control to display a scrolling list of choices.

The key properties of a List Box control are as follows:

DisplayValues   Determines the items to display in the list. Enter all the items for the list, with each item separated by a semicolon (but no trailing spaces), as follows: *Item1;Item2;Item3.*

HTMLName   Determines the name you assign to the control.

MultiSelect   Determines whether the user can select more than one item from the list; the default value is True.

Selected   Determines whether the first item appears in the box and whether the first item is selected by default.

Size   Determines how many lines appear in the list at one time; the default value is 3, unless the MultiSelect property is set to True (when it defaults to 1).

Value   Determines the text sent to a Web server for each item appearing in the list. In most cases the Value is the same as the DisplayValue, but it doesn't have to be, as long as the number of Values is at least equal to the number of DisplayValues. Values are separated with a semicolon, with no trailing spaces, as follows: *Value1;Value2;Value3.*

The Textbox Control

You use a Textbox control to accept one line of text input from a user. For example, the Search box on any search Web site is a Textbox control; Figure 25.10 shows another example.

FIGURE 25.10
Use a Textbox control to accept text input from users.

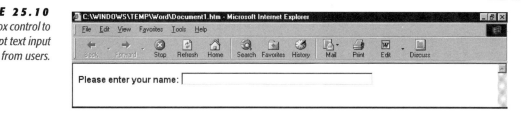

The key properties of a Textbox Box control are as follows:

HTMLName   Determines the name you assign to the control.

MaxLength   Determines the maximum number of characters the user can enter; the default is 0, which lets users enter an unlimited number of characters.

Value   Determines the default text to display in the text box. This is an optional property; most text boxes do not come with predisplayed text.

The Password Control

The Password control creates a text box that displays an asterisk (*) for each character entered by a user (instead of displaying the typed character itself) and is typically used for the input of passwords and other sensitive data. Figure 25.11 shows a password control in use.

FIGURE 25.11
Enable users to enter data in privacy via a Password control.

The key properties of a Password control are as follows:

HTMLName   Determines the name you assign to the control.

MaxLength   Determines the maximum number of characters the user can enter; the default is 0, which lets users enter an unlimited number of characters.

Value   Determines the default text, displayed as asterisks, for this field. This is an optional property; most password boxes do not come with predisplayed text.

The Text Area Control

A Text Area control is similar to a text box except that it's larger so users can enter multiple lines of text. Figure 25.12 shows a typical Text Area control used on a Web page.

FIGURE 25.12

Use a Text Area control to accept longer text input from users.

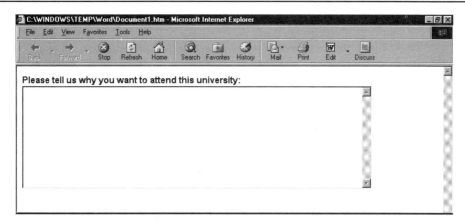

The key properties of a Text Area control are as follows:

Columns   Determines the width of the text area, expressed in number of columns.

HTMLName   Determines the name you assign to the control.

Rows   Determines the height of the text area, expressed in number of rows.

Value   Determines the default text to display in the text area. This is an optional property; most text areas do not come with predisplayed text.

WordWrap   Determines particulars about word wrapping. Set to Virtual or Physical to have text wrap within the box; set to Off to turn off text wrapping.

 NOTE   Not all Web browsers support the WordWrap property.

The Submit Control

 You use the Submit control (which appears as a button on your Web page) to enable users to submit the data they've entered and/or selected elsewhere on your form. Every form should have either a Submit or a Submit with Image control so users can submit the form page. Figure 25.13 shows a typical Submit control, in the form of an Enter button.

FIGURE 25.13
*Users click the Submit
control (in the form of
an Enter button) to
submit the data they've
entered or selected.*

The key properties of a Submit control are as follows:

Action Determines the URL of the script file that opens when the user clicks the Submit control button. You can also enter **mailto:*address*** to mail the contents of the form to the designated address.

Caption Determines the text that appears on the button; the default text is *Submit*.

Encoding Stores the MIME type used to encode the submitted form; the default type is application/x-www-form-urlencoded.

HTMLName Determines the name you assign to the control.

Method Determines the method to be used for submitting the form (either POST or GET).

The Submit with Image Control

The Submit with Image control can be substituted for the Submit control on your Web form. Where the Submit control creates a button, the Submit with Image control displays an image on your form that, when clicked, submits the data entered and/or selected by the user. Figure 25.14 shows how a Submit with Image control might look on a typical Web page.

NOTE When you publish your Web page to a Web server, make sure you also copy the file used for the button image.

FIGURE 25.14
If you don't like buttons, let users click an image to submit their Web form data or to perform an action.

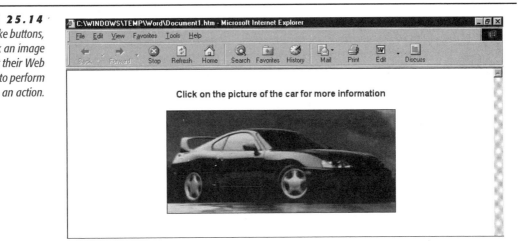

When you click the Submit with Image button on the Web Tools toolbar, Word first displays the Insert Picture dialog box. Select the image you want to use for this control, and then click the Insert button.

The key properties of a Submit with Image control are as follows:

Action   Determines the URL of the script file that opens when the user clicks the image. You can also enter **mailto:*address*** to mail the contents of the form to the designated address.

Encoding   Determines the MIME type used to encode the submitted form; the default type is application/x-www-form-urlencoded.

HTMLName   Determines the name you assign to the control.

Method   Determines the method to be used for submitting the form (either POST or GET).

Source   Determines the name of the graphics file.

The Reset Control

The Reset control creates a Reset button that allows users to reset the form to its original state, removing any data entered or selected. Figure 25.15 shows a typical Reset button.

FIGURE 25.15

A Reset control lets users delete their data without submitting it.

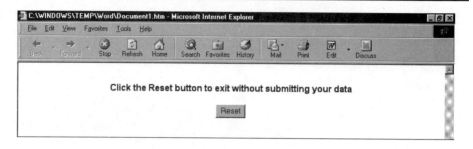

FIGURE 25.15

A Reset control lets users delete their data without submitting it.

The key properties of a Reset control are as follows:

HTMLName   Determines the name you assign to the control.

Caption   Determines the text that appears on the button; the default text is *Reset*.

The Hidden Control

The Hidden control is used to pass information to a Web server without the need for user interaction and is not visible to the user. As an example, you might use a Hidden control to pass on information about a user's operating environment when the entire Web form is submitted.

The key properties of a hidden control are as follows:

HTMLName   Determines the name you assign to the control.

Value   Determines the default text that is sent to a Web server from this control.

Working with Web Scripts

Web scripts are used to create custom, Web-based solutions. You use scripts to do the things that standard HTML code and forms can't do. One example of a very common script is a counter that displays the number of visitors to a Web site.

A script is a type of computer code—actually a simpler variation of a full-blown programming language—that developers use to add dynamic elements and operations to their Web pages. To create a script, you need to have some knowledge of computer programming.

Word 2000 lets you insert scripts written in either VBScript or JavaScript, using the Insert Script and the Microsoft Script Editor commands. VBScript is a variation of Microsoft's Visual Basic programming language, so if you're familiar with VB, you'll find VBScript very similar.

NOTE All the ins and outs of VBScript are beyond the scope of this book. To learn more about VBScript, check out Sybex's *Mastering Visual Basic 6* and *Expert Guide to Visual Basic 6*, available wherever computer books are sold or by accessing www.sybex.com.

MASTERING THE OPPORTUNITIES

Understanding how VBScript Works

If you use the Microsoft Script Editor to display scripts in a document, you'll see that VBScript code is inserted into the HTML code within paired <SCRIPT> tags, like this:

```
<SCRIPT LANGUAGE="VBScript">
<!--
    Function CanDeliver(Dt)
        CanDeliver = (CDate(Dt) - Now()) > 2
    End Function
-->
</SCRIPT>
```

As you can see in the preceding example, beginning and ending <SCRIPT> tags surround the script itself. The LANGUAGE attribute indicates which scripting language is used (in this case, VBScript).

Scripts (contained within what are called *SCRIPT blocks*) can be inserted anywhere in an HTML page. If a script is non-position-specific (and many are), they are most easily inserted in the HEAD section of your document.

Working with Scripts in Your Documents

 While this book does not purport to teach you VBScript programming, it is helpful to know how scripts are displayed and edited within your advanced Web-based documents.

Before you work with scripts in Word, you should add a handful of script-related commands to Word's Tools menu. Follow these steps to add these commands:

1. Select Tools ➢ Customize to display the Customize dialog box.

2. Select the Commands tab.

3. Select Tools from the Categories list.

4. From the Commands list, drag the Insert Script command and drop it on Word's Tools menu, in the Macro submenu.

5. From the Commands list, drag the Show All Scripts command and drop it on Word's Tools menu, in the Macro submenu.

6. From the Commands list, drag the Remove All Scripts command and drop it on Word's Tools menu, in the Macro submenu.

7. Click the Close button.

Displaying Script Anchors

Word can display a *script anchor* to indicate the presence of a script, as shown in Figure 25.16. This script anchor does not display when your Web page is viewed in a Web browser.

FIGURE 25.16

A script anchor indicates the presence of a script in your Web document.

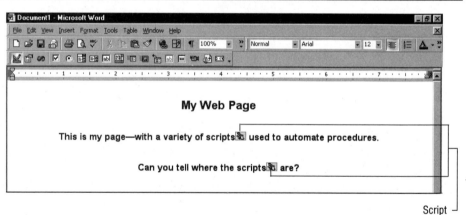

Script Anchors

To display all script anchors within your document, follow these steps:

1. Open the Web document you want to work with.

2. Select Tools ➤ Macro ➤ Show All Scripts.

TIP When you hover your cursor over a script anchor, a ScreenTip displays the first 50 characters of the script.

Adding a Script to Your Web Page

To insert a script in your Web page, follow these steps:

1. Open the Web document you want to edit, and position the insertion point where you want to add the script.

2. Select Tools ➢ Macro ➢ Insert Script.

3. Word now launches the Microsoft Script Editor.

4. Write your script in the Script Editor, and then return to Word when finished.

5. Word now displays the Refresh toolbar; click the Refresh button to update your Web page with the new script.

Editing a Script

To edit a script in your Web document, follow these steps:

1. From within your document, double-click the script anchor for the script you want to edit.

2. Word now opens the Microsoft Script Editor.

3. Make appropriate changes to the script, and then return to Word.

4. Click the Refresh button on the Refresh toolbar to update your Web page.

Moving or Copying a Script

Relocating a script within your document is easy; all you have to do is move or copy the script anchor, as follows:

Move a Script   Use your mouse to drag the script anchor to a new location.

Copy a Script   Hold down the Ctrl key while you use your mouse to drag the script anchor to a different location; a copy of the script anchor (and the underlying script) is placed in the new location.

 WARNING   Since some scripts are dependent on the structure of the Web page, when you move or copy a script from one Web page to another—or from one location on a Web page to another—the script might not run correctly or might return errors when it is run.

MASTERING THE OPPORTUNITIES

Working with Java Applets

A Java applet is a small software program, written in the Java programming language, that resides on a Web page and runs in a Web browser. Word handles Java applets much the same as it handles embedded scripts, even though the Java applet is a separate file referenced by your HTML document.

When you use Word to edit a Web page that contains a Java applet, an icon representing the applet appears on the page. (The icon does not appear when you view the page in a Web browser.) You can move or copy your Java Applet the same way you move or copy a script anchor. To modify the Java code, double-click the applet icon to open the Microsoft Script Editor, and modify the HTML code associated with the <APPLET> code.

Using Microsoft Script Editor

Word 2000 includes a special editor for the codes and scripts in your Web documents. The Microsoft Script Editor can be used to view and edit HTML code and create scripts using VBScript.

You launch Script Editor from within a Word document by selecting Tools ➤ Macro ➤ Microsoft Script Editor or by clicking the Microsoft Script Editor button on the Web Tools toolbar. When the Script Editor launches, your current document will be displayed.

WARNING Use Microsoft Script Editor to edit only HTML or Active Server Pages (.ASP) files. If you try to edit normal Word .DOC files in the Script Editor, various aspects of the file may be corrupted.

WARNING Microsoft Script Editor is a full-fledged programming environment and should only be used by experienced developers.

Switching between Views

Microsoft Script Editor can display your Web documents in three different views:

Source View This view, shown in Figure 25.17, displays the HTML source code and scripts for your document. Use Source View to add and edit VBScript code to your Web documents as well as to edit HTML code. When you're in Source View, lines of code and text are colored according to their function. For example, HTML tags are displayed in brown, code attributes in red, and attribute values in blue.

FIGURE 25.17
Use Script Editor's Source View to edit HTML code and add VBScript scripts to your Web pages.

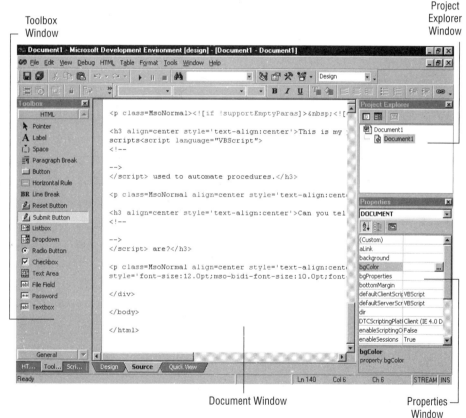

Toolbox Window

Project Explorer Window

Document Window

Properties Window

Quick View This view, shown in Figure 25.18, displays your document similar to how it would look in a Web browser but is a display-only view, so you can't use it to edit your documents.

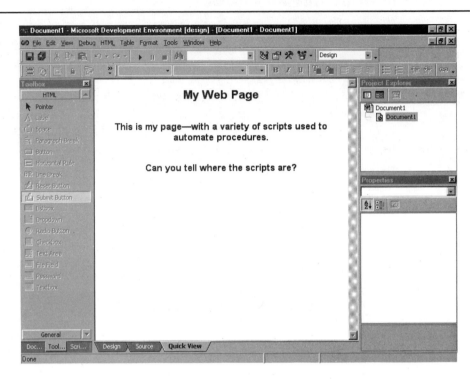

Design View This view, which is similar to Word 2000's Web Layout view, is not available if you started Script Editor from within Word. If you launch Script Editor as a freestanding program and *then* open up an HTML document, you can access this WYSIWYG view to design the elements on your Web page.

You switch views by clicking the appropriate tabs at the bottom of the Script Editor workspace.

Changing the Default Scripting Language

Microsoft Script Editor can use either VBScript or JavaScript as its scripting language. To change from one language to another, follow these steps:

1. From within Microsoft Script Editor, click the Source tab.

2. In the Properties window, select DOCUMENT from the pull-down list.

3. Enter either VBScript or JavaScript as the value of the defaultClientScript property.

Creating Scripts in the Script Editor

You create scripts in the Document window, while in Source View.

One way to create a script is to start in the Script Outline window. (To display this window, select the Script Outline tab at the bottom of the workspace.) The Script Outline window shows you all scriptable elements in your page. You select an element from the Script Outline window and then write the corresponding script in the Document window.

You can also insert a stand-alone SCRIPT block within the Document window. Anchor your insertion point where you want to add the script, and then select either HTML ➢ Script Block ➢ Client or HTML ➢ Script Block ➢ Server. The Editor inserts a SCRIPT block within the HTML code; you can then write the script within the <SCRIPT> and </SCRIPT> codes.

NOTE To learn more about Microsoft Script Editor and all its functions, select Help ➢ Contents (while within the Script Editor) to display the comprehensive Help system.

CHAPTER **26**

Publishing Word Documents on the Web

Finding hosts for personal and business pages   **689**

Publishing Web pages using Web folders **691**

Publishing Web pages using FTP   **693**

Publishing Web pages using the Web Publishing Wizard   **694**

Publishing Web pages using host services   **695**

Publishing Web pages over a network **695**

Your Web page is just another document on your hard disk—until you publish it on the Web. Publishing a Web page involves finding a host for the page and then uploading the page to that host's Web server. Once the page is on the host server, it will be assigned a Web address (URL)—and is then available for viewing by anyone surfing the Internet.

Several methods are available for publishing your pages on the Web. You can use Word 2000's new Web Folders feature; you can use the Internet's FTP protocol to upload pages directly; if you have FrontPage 2000 or FrontPage Express installed on your system, you can use Microsoft's Web Publishing Wizard to automate the publishing process; you can use the services or software provided by your Web hosting service; or you can (in some instances) simply copy your files over a network to a corporate or school Web server. Which method you use depends on what kind of Web hosting you're using and how comfortable you are with the various Web publishing techniques.

 NOTE For the purposes of this chapter, the terms *publishing, uploading,* and *saving* (with regard to Web pages) are interchangeable.

Determining Where to Publish Your Web Pages

For others to view your Web pages, the pages must be hosted on a Web server. If you want anyone on the Internet to view your pages, you have to find a public hosting service. If your pages are for internal corporate consumption, your hosting service is your company's intranet.

There are many different types of hosting services available. Which you choose depends on your particular needs—what kind of pages you're publishing, how many pages you're publishing, and what kind of traffic you hope to attract.

No matter which type of host you choose, you'll need to obtain some information from the hosting service before you publish your pages. You'll want to know the address of the hosting server and the URLs that will be assigned to your pages; what technologies the host server supports (scripts, extensions, forms, image maps, and so on); how much storage space you're allocated for your pages; and how your Web pages, graphics files, and other support files should be structured on the server (whether you need to create separate folders for bullets and pictures, for example).

Finding Hosts for Personal Pages

If your Web presence consists of a handful of personal pages—family photos, hobbies, and the like—you have a plethora of choices available for a host. Most of these hosting services are available at no charge for personal use (although some will charge if you publish a business-related page).

Among the options available to you are the following:

Your Internet Service Provider (ISP)   Most ISPs provide server space for their subscribers. This is especially true of the larger ISPs (such as Earthlink, Mind-Spring, and the like) and commercial online services (America Online, Prodigy, and so on). Check with your ISP to learn whether they offer free Web-page hosting and, if so, what limitations they impose.

NOTE   Some ISPs limit the amount of server space provided for Web pages. Others limit the amount of visitors to your pages. Check to learn what limits your ISP might impose—and whether they're reasonable limits, given your needs.

Your Company   Many corporations have public Web sites and allocate part of that Web site for employees' personal pages. Check with your employer to learn whether they'll let you post your pages on their site—and, if so, what limitations on size or content they might impose.

Your School   Most colleges and universities have large (and sometimes multiple) Web sites, and provide space for student and faculty Web pages. Some high schools, middle schools, and grade schools also offer limited Web space to students and teachers. Check with your school to learn whether you can use their space for free.

Home-Page Community Sites   Several sites on the Web specialize in hosting Web pages—and, in fact, build *home-page communities* around the millions of pages published by their users. The most popular home-page communities include AngelFire (www.angelfire.com), The Globe (www.theglobe.com), Tripod (www.tripod.com), and Yahoo! GeoCities (geocities.yahoo.com).

The home-page community sites are probably the most popular hosting choices for many users. All of these communities offer similar services (free Web pages for all—in exchange for placing ads in and around your pages) and work similarly. All give you the options of uploading pages you create on your own PC; creating pages by entering raw HTML code on their site; or using their Web-based Wizards or templates to create Web pages without coding.

TIP If you just want to create a simple, personal Web page, consider bypassing Word's Web-development features completely and using instead the step-by-step Wizards on GeoCities and other home-page community sites.

Finding Hosts for Business Pages

If you want to do business on the Web, don't expect a hosting service to provide their server space and services for free. If you're creating a business-oriented Web site, you'll need to find a *commercial* hosting service for your pages.

Commercial hosting services provide added value for your money. Typically, you'll get more server space, access to more technology (scripts, extensions, and so on), no restrictions on traffic, the capability to conduct e-commerce (taking orders, accepting credit cards, and so on), and the option to use your own unique domain name.

If you're running your business on the Web, you don't want your site's URL to be in a subdirectory of a subdirectory on someone else's site. (For example, if you publish a site on GeoCities, you'll be automatically assigned—no choice in the matter—a URL that looks something like www.geocities.com/neighborhood/1234/mydomain/.) If you want your customers to remember your URL, it's better to obtain your own unique domain name, in the form of www.mydomain.com.

 NOTE Internet domain names are available on a first come, first served basis. All the administration for assigning domain names is handled by a company called Network Solutions; although many third parties offer domain-name registration—and handle all the dirty work for you—they still go to Network Solutions to get the name assigned.

Obtaining a unique domain name takes a bit of time (you have some forms to fill in) and costs a bit of money (typically around $100). Many commercial hosting services can handle the paperwork for you, or you can go directly to a domain-name registration site (such as www.netnamesusa.com) or the official Network Solutions site at www.networksolutions.com.

You can search for a commercial hosting service at any of the following sites:

- C|NET's Ultimate Web Host List (webhostlist.internetlist.com)
- FINDaHOST.com (www.findahost.com)
- Host Investigator (www.hostinvestigator.com)
- HostFinders.com (www.hostfinders.com)
- HostSearch (www.hostsearch.com)
- TopHosts.com (www.tophosts.com)

As you evaluate commercial hosting services, carefully compare prices and services. There are significant differences between services, so make sure you get the best price/ service combination for your needs.

Publishing Your Web Pages

To publish a Web page, you upload it to a Web server. There are a number of ways to get your pages from here to there; you should choose the method that best suits your particular situation.

No matter how you upload your pages, you need to have the following before you click a single button:

- A connection to the Internet
- Permission to publish your pages on the designated host server
- The URL for the Web server where you'll be uploading your files
- The name of the folder on the server where you'll publish your files

If you do not have this information, contact your hosting service.

Publishing Web Pages Using Web Folders

Word 2000 offers a new Web Folders feature that eases the storage and publishing of Web pages. A Web folder is essentially a shortcut to a Web server; to use this feature, your host server must support the Web Folders feature.

NOTE Before you choose to use Web folders, check with your Web hosting service to learn whether they support Word's Web folders.

Creating a Web Folder

The easiest way to create a Web folder is to use Microsoft's Web Folder Wizard. Follow these steps:

1. Open My Computer.
2. Select the Web Folders icon to open the Web Folders window.
3. Click the Add Web Folder icon to launch the Web Folder Wizard.
4. Enter the location of your Web folder. This is typically the URL of your Web site; you can click the Browse button to launch your Web browser and navigate to the appropriate URL.
5. The Wizard validates the URL you provided, then creates the designated folder.

NOTE You can also launch the Web Folder Wizard from within Microsoft Word by opening either the Open or the Save As dialog boxes, clicking the Web Folders icon, and then clicking the Create New Folder button.

Saving a Document to a Web Folder Using Word

Once you've created a Web folder, you can save your Web documents to the Web folder. Follow these steps:

1. From within your document, select File ➤ Save As Web Page to display the Save As dialog box.

2. Click the Web Folders icon.

3. From the list of Web-folder sites, double-click the appropriate folder, then double-click the location where you want to save the page.

4. Enter the name of your page in the File Name box.

5. Click Save.

Word will connect to the Internet and save your file to the Web server hosting your pages.

 NOTE When you save a Web page to a Web folder, all supporting files (bullets, graphics, and so on) are by default organized in a supporting folder, which is also uploaded to your Web server.

Managing the Contents of a Web Folder

When you're using Web folders, you use My Computer or Windows Explorer to manage the contents of your Web site. From within My Computer or Windows Explorer, you can move, copy, rename, and delete files within your Web folder just as you would the contents of a normal folder.

From within My Computer or Windows Explorer, open the Web Folders window, then open the Web folder you want to manage. Windows will connect to the Internet and access your Web server, from which you can manage your Web pages.

Publishing Web Pages Using FTP

File Transfer Protocol (FTP) is one of the oldest Internet technologies. FTP existed long before the World Wide Web, and is used to upload and download files directly to Internet servers—no Web browser is needed.

To use this procedure, your hosting service must support FTP. Most commercial hosting services and home-page communities support FTP uploads to their servers.

Adding an FTP Site

Before you can save a document to an FTP site, you must add your host's FTP site to Word's list of Internet sites.

NOTE Before you add an FTP site, you'll need to obtain your host's FTP address and authorization procedure—which typically includes a login password.

Follow these steps:

1. Click the Open button on Word's Standard toolbar to display the Open dialog box.

2. Pull down the Look In list and select Add/Modify FTP Locations to display the Add/Modify FTP Locations dialog box.

3. Enter the address of the FTP site in the Name of FTP Site box.

4. If you log in to the FTP server anonymously, check the Anonymous option.

5. If you log in to the FTP server with a password, check the User option and enter your username and password.

6. Click the Add button.

Uploading Your Pages to an FTP Site

Once you've added the FTP site to your list, it's a simple procedure to upload your pages to the site. Follow these steps:

1. From within your document, select File ➤ Save As to display the Save As dialog box.

2. Pull down the Save In list and select FTP Locations.

3. From the list of FTP sites, double-click the site you'll be uploading to, then double-click the location at the site where your files will be stored.

4. Enter the name of your page in the File Name box.

5. Click Save.

Word connects to the Internet and uses its built-in FTP capabilities to upload your page to your FTP server.

Publishing Web Pages Using the Web Publishing Wizard

If Microsoft FrontPage Express or FrontPage 2000 is installed on your system, you have an advanced Web-publishing tool at your disposal. Microsoft's Web Publishing Wizard provides powerful site-publishing and management capabilities—much beyond those offered by Word's Web Folders feature.

To launch the Web Publishing Wizard, click the Windows Start button and then select Programs ➤ Internet Explorer ➤ Web Publishing Wizard.

Using the Web Publishing Wizard is a six-step process:

1. **Select a File or Folder.** This initial screen is used to select the file or folder (containing multiple files) that you want to publish to your Web server. To publish a file, click the Browse Files button and navigate to and select the desired file. To publish a folder and all its contents, click the Browse Folders button, then navigate to and select the desired folder; check the Include Subfolders option if you want to include subfolders within the selected folder. After you've selected the file or folder, click the Open button.

2. **Select a Web Server.** This screen is used to identify the Web server to which you'll be publishing. If you've already published to a server, its name will appear in the Web Server list; select the server to proceed. If you're publishing to a new server, click the New button to configure the Wizard for a specific server.

3. **Name the Web Server.** On this screen you provide a friendly name for your Web server; on subsequent uses, you can select the server by this name instead of its formal name/address.

4. **Select Your Connection Method.** Use this screen to specify how you connect to your Web server. If you know your connection method, pull down the Connection Method list and make a selection. If you *don't* know your connection method, click the Automatically Select Connection Method button and follow the on-screen instructions.

5. **Specify the URL and Local Directory.** This screen is where you enter the URL for your site on your Web server, as well as the location of your Web pages on your hard disk. Enter the location of your pages on the Web (including your personal folder) into the URL or Internet Address box; enter the path and folder of the pages on your hard disk into the Local Directory box.

6. **Publish Your Files.** If you've entered all the right information, click the Finish button to have the Web Publishing Wizard upload your files.

 NOTE If you don't have the Web Publishing Wizard on your system, you'll need to install either FrontPage Express or FrontPage 2000.

Publishing Web Pages Using Host Services

Many Web hosting services provide software or Web-based operations for uploading files to their servers. For example, GeoCities uses their File Manager page to upload existing files from their users and manage the files stored on their servers; other sites offer similar services.

Consult your Web hosting service for specific instructions on how to upload your files to their servers.

Publishing Web Pages over a Network

If you are connected to a corporate or educational network, you may be able to copy your Web pages over the network, directly to your corporate or educational Web server. Consult with your system administrator for specific instructions on how to publish your pages over the network.

NOTE If your company or school uses a Web server enabled for Word's Web folders, you can use this feature to publish your pages on the server.

Managing Supporting Files

When you save your Word files to a Web server, all supporting files (including graphics, bullets, lines, and so on) are by default stored in a supporting folder. If, at a later date, you move or copy your Web page to another location, you must also move the supporting folder to maintain the links and integrity of your main page.

For example, if you have a page named MYPAGE.HTM, all your supporting files will be stored in a folder named MYPAGE_FILES, and links to these files from within your main page will point to this folder. If you move the MYPAGE.HTM file, you'll also need to move the MYPAGE_FILES folder—or the links will point to a nonexisting location.

PART VIII

Creating Automated Documents

- *Creating ready-to-use documents with templates*

- *Designing printable and interactive forms*

- *Automating your documents with macros*

- *Employing VBA for more sophisticated automation*

CHAPTER **27**

Creating Ready-to-Use Documents with Templates

Using Word's templates   **700**

Enhancing Word with add-ins   **701**

**Loading and unloading templates
and add-ins**   **702**

**Switching templates in your current
document**   **704**

Making changes to existing templates   **706**

Using the Organizer to modify templates   **706**

Creating new templates   **709**

Face it, there are some things you use Word for that are just plain tedious. Entering the same text over and over, setting up the look and feel of a document; these tasks are more like chores. Wouldn't it be nice if you didn't have to perform these tedious tasks every time you open a document?

Word 2000 offers many ways to automate the most monotonous word processing jobs. The most sophisticated users can use Visual Basic for Applications to create macros, controls, and self-running applications within their Word documents. (See Chapters 29 and 30 for more information on these advanced features.) You don't have to be an experienced developer, however, to automate more basic tasks; all you have to do is to learn how to use Word's templates and add-ins.

Read on to discover how to master Word's templates and to create your own ready-to-use documents!

Understanding Templates and Add-Ins

Every Word document you've ever seen has been based on a *template*. A template is essentially the skeleton of your document, which you flesh out with your own specific content. You create new documents by opening a template and then adding your own content; you can create any number of new documents from a single template.

Getting a Head Start on New Documents with Word's Templates

A Word template provides the base settings for the most-used elements of your document, including:

- Fonts
- Styles
- Page layout
- Special formatting
- Key assignments
- Macros
- Menus
- AutoText entries

Word uses two different types of templates. A *global* template (such as the Normal template) is available to all documents. A *document* template is available only to specific documents based on that template. Any individual document can incorporate settings from both a document template and a global template.

Word provides a variety of both document and global templates and enables you to modify the built-in templates and create your own document templates. You can use the document templates you create to automate the construction of new documents based on those templates.

 NOTE For more information on using templates to create new documents, see Chapter 4.

Enhancing How Word Works with Add-Ins

An add-in is a supplemental program that adds custom commands or features to the Word program itself. Many of the programs found on the CD accompanying this book, for example, are add-in programs; you add them into Word to augment the program's basic functionality.

 NOTE For more information on the add-ins and utility programs included on the accompanying CD, see Chapter 33.

You can obtain add-ins from independent software vendors, or you can write your own add-in programs using Microsoft's Visual Basic Editor. You manage add-in programs similar to the way you manage templates, using Word 2000's Organizer (discussed in the "Using the Organizer" section later in this chapter).

Working with Word's Built-In Templates

Word includes a variety of built-in templates, all of which are discussed in Chapter 4. Some of these templates were installed when you installed Word 2000 on your computer; others are loaded the first time you use them.

Additional templates are available on your Word 2000 installation CD that are not installed as part of a standard installation. To install these extra templates, run the Setup program again, choose the Custom option, and select More Templates and Macros. This will install the new group of templates (and Wizards) to your hard disk.

TIP There are even more templates available on the Internet. Select Help ➢ Office on the Web to access a special Microsoft Web page with links to additional templates, Wizards, and macros.

Can I Use Templates from Earlier Versions of Word?

If you've been using Word for a few years, you probably got used to using the templates available with Word 97 and previous versions. You may have even created some of your own templates with previous versions of the program. Now that you've upgraded to Word 2000, however, you may find that these old templates have disappeared!

Fortunately, none of your old templates have been deleted; they've just been relocated. When you installed Word 2000, an Old Office Templates folder was created on your hard disk, and all your old templates were moved to that single folder. Word 2000 is fully compatible with these older templates, so you shouldn't hesitate to use any of these templates, if you so desire.

To use an older template, select the Office 97 Templates tab in the New dialog box. You can also use Word's Organizer to copy specific elements from your old templates to new templates; see the upcoming "Using the Organizer to Modify Templates" section for more information.

Loading a Template or Add-In

Aside from any templates and add-ins that load automatically (such as the Normal template and the document template you used to create the current document), you have to manually load any additional templates and add-ins you want to use. When you load a template or add-in, it remains loaded for the current Word session only. If you quit and then restart Word, the template or add-in is not automatically reloaded.

 TIP To have a template or add-in available whenever you start Word, store the add-in or template in your Word Startup folder. (Find the location of your Startup folder by selecting Tools ➢ Options to display the Options dialog box, and then selecting the File Locations tab.)

To load a template or add-in into your current document, follow these steps:

1. Select Tools ➤ Templates and Add-Ins to display the Templates and Add-Ins dialog box.

2. If the template or add-in you want to load is listed in the Global Templates and Add-Ins list, check the box next to that item.

   If the template or add-in you want is *not* displayed, click the Add button to display the Add Template dialog box. Navigate to and select the template or add-in you want to use, and then click OK to return to the Templates and Add-Ins dialog box. The template or add-in should now be listed, so return to and execute the first part of this step.

3. Click OK when finished.

Unloading a Template or Add-In

If you're not using the features of a specific template or add-in, you can *unload* it from your document, which also unloads it from your system's memory and speeds up Word's performance. To unload a document or template, follow these steps:

 NOTE Unloading a template or add-in unloads it for *this session only.*

1. Select Tools ➤ Templates and Add-Ins to display the Templates and Add-Ins dialog box.

2. To unload a template or add-in, uncheck the box next to the item's name.

3. Click OK.

PART

XIII

Creating Automated
Documents

Note that the Remove button actually doesn't remove anything from your hard disk; it only removes items from the list in this dialog box (and then only if the template or add-in isn't located in Word's Startup folder). In essence, you use the Remove button only to clean up the list; you still have to uncheck an item to unload it from the current document.

Switching Templates in Your Current Document

To change the template used by the current document, which is different from simply using the features of a template by temporarily loading it into your document, you have to *attach* a new template to the document, which then replaces the template previously attached. Follow these steps:

1. Select Tools ➢ Templates and Add-Ins to display the Templates and Add-Ins dialog box.

2. Click the Attach button.

3. When the Attach Template dialog box appears, select the template you want, and then click OK.

4. If you want to update all the styles in your document to reflect the styles in the new document template, check the Automatically Update Document Styles option.

5. Click OK when done.

 MASTERING THE OPPORTUNITIES

Previewing Templates from the Style Gallery

While you get a mini-preview of how a new document based on a selected template looks when you select File ➢ New to open the New dialog box, you can use the Style Gallery to display a larger preview of how your *current* document would look if a different template were attached. To use the Style Gallery for a template preview, follow these steps:

1. From within your current document, select Format ➢ Theme to display the Theme dialog box.

Continued ▸

2. Click the Style Gallery button to display the Style Gallery.

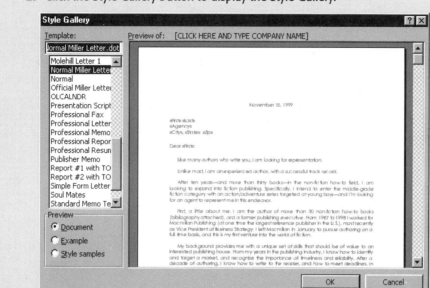

3. Check the Document option from the Preview section.

4. Select a different template from the Template list; Word displays your document formatted with this template in the Preview Of window.

If you like what you see and want to apply the styles from the new template directly to your document, click the OK button. Otherwise, click Cancel to return to your (unchanged) document.

Modifying Existing Templates

You can customize any of Word's existing templates, changing any of the template's elements—styles, fonts, page settings, and so on. When you save your modifications to a template, the next document you create based on that template will reflect those changes. Any existing documents based on the template will not be affected.

Making Changes to an Existing Template

To change an existing template, follow these steps:

1. Select File ➤ Open to display the Open dialog box.

2. Pull down the Files of Type list, and select Document Template.

3. Navigate to the folder containing the template you want to modify.

 NOTE Word's Normal template is located in the \Windows\Application Data\Microsoft\Templates\ folder. All other templates are located in the \Program Files\Microsoft Office\Templates\1033\ folder.

4. Select the folder to modify, and then click the Open button.

5. Make your changes to the template.

6. When you're done modifying the template, select File ➤ Save (or click the Save button on Word's Standard toolbar).

 TIP If you want all documents based on a template to retroactively reflect changes you make to the template, select Tools ➤ Templates and Add-Ins to open the Templates and Add-Ins dialog box, check the Automatically Update Document Styles Option, and then click OK.

Using the Organizer to Modify Templates

You can also modify the contents of a template via Word's Organizer utility, which enables you to copy elements and settings from one template or file to another.

As you can see in Figure 27.1, the Organizer includes four different tabs: Style, Auto-Text, Toolbars, and Macro Project Items. You select the source and the destination templates, and then choose whether to copy, rename, or delete selected elements.

FIGURE 27.1
Use the Organizer to
copy elements from
one template to
another.

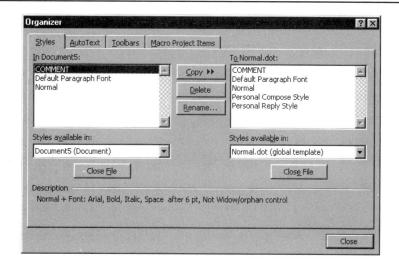

To use the Organizer, follow these steps:

1. Select Tools ➤ Templates and Add-Ins to display the Templates and Add-Ins dialog box.

2. Click the Organizer button to display the Organizer, shown in Figure 27.1.

3. To change either the source or the destination template or file, click the appropriate Close File button, click the Open File button, and select a different template or file.

4. Select the tab containing the element you want to copy, rename, or edit.

5. To copy an element, select the element from the source template list, and then click the Copy button to copy it to the destination template.

WARNING If you copy a toolbar that contains a custom macro, you must also copy that macro to the other template.

6. To rename an element in one of the templates, select the element, click the Rename button to display the Rename dialog box, enter the new name in the New Name box, and then click OK.

7. To delete an element from one of the templates, select the element, and then click the Delete button.

8. Click OK when done.

PART
XIII

Creating Automated
Documents

WARNING If you copy an element to a template that already contains an element by that name, you'll overwrite the existing element.

Making Your Own Templates

You can tap into some of Word's true power by creating your own templates. Remember, a template can include any combination of styles, fonts, page settings, and macros, including prewritten text. You could, for example, create a template containing blocks of "boilerplate" text, which you can personalize (without retyping the entire document!) whenever you create a new document based on that template.

Word offers two ways to create new templates. You can modify an existing template, or you can save an existing document as a template. Remember, also, that you can use the Organizer to modify the contents of any new template you create.

Saving a New Template

Templates are stored as .DOT (*not* .DOC) format files. You can save templates so that they appear on any of the tabs in the New dialog box, or you can create new tabs for the dialog box.

Saving to an Existing Tab

When you save a new template, Word automatically stores it in the \Windows\ Application Data\Microsoft\Templates\ folder and adds it to the General tab in the New dialog box. To move the template from the General tab to another tab, follow these steps:

1. Open My Computer or Windows Explorer, and navigate to the \Windows\ Application Data\Microsoft\Templates\ folder.

2. Switch to Microsoft Word, and select File ➢ Open to display the New dialog box.

3. Select the tab where you want to store the template.

 4. Drag the template file from My Computer or Windows Explorer and drop it into Word's New dialog box.

Creating a New Tab

You may want to create new tabs in the New dialog box for your new templates. To create a new tab, follow these steps:

1. Open My Computer or Windows Explorer and navigate to the `\Windows\ Application Data\Microsoft\Templates\` folder.

2. Select New ➤ Folder to create a new subfolder within the Templates folder.

3. Right-click the new folder icon, select Rename from the pop-up menu, and enter a name for the new folder.

The next time you open the New dialog box, your new tab will be displayed.

Saving to a New Tab

While you can't automatically save a new template to any existing tab except General, you *can* save a new template to a new tab you've created. Follow these steps:

1. When you're ready to save your new template, select File ➤ Save As to display the Save As dialog box.

2. Enter the name for the template in the File Name box.

3. Pull down the Save As Type list, and select Document Template.

4. Use the Save In list to navigate to and select the new folder you created within the `\Windows\Application Data\Microsoft\Templates\` folder.

5. Click the Save button.

The template will now be saved to your new folder and will appear on the new tab the next time you open the New dialog box.

Creating a New Template Based on an Existing Template

The easiest way to create a new template is to base it on an existing template and then make the appropriate modifications. Just follow these steps:

1. Select File ➤ New to open the New dialog box.

2. Select the tab that contains the template on which you want to base your new template.

3. Select the template on which you want to base your new template.

4. Check the Template option in the Create New section.

5. Click OK to open the template.

6. Make whatever changes you want to the template. (Remember, you can use the Organizer to easily copy and delete elements to and from this template.)

7. When you're done creating the template, select File ➢ Save As to display the Save As dialog box.

8. Enter the name for your new template in the File Name box.

9. Pull down the Save As Type list, and select Document Template.

10. Use the Save In list to navigate to and select the folder where you want to save the template. (By default, Word will save the template in the `\Windows\Application Data\Microsoft\Templates\` folder and place it on the General tab in the New dialog box.)

11. Click the Save button.

Creating a New Template Based on an Existing Document

You can turn any *document*—including the document's text and graphics—into a template. This is a great way to create a template for form letters or for documents with a lot of boilerplate text. Just follow these steps:

1. From within the document you want to save as a template, select File ➢ Save As to display the Save As dialog box.

2. Enter the name for your new template in the File Name box.

3. Pull down the Save As Type list, and select Document Template.

4. Use the Save In list to navigate to and select the folder where you want to save the template. (By default, Word will save the template in the `\Windows\Application Data\Microsoft\Templates\` folder and place it on the General tab in the New dialog box.)

5. Click the Save button.

When you create a new document based on this new template, Word will display the document exactly as you saved it, ready for editing.

Loading Add-Ins and Templates Automatically

To automatically load an add-in program or a template whenever you launch Word, copy the appropriate file to Word's Startup folder. Any file residing in this folder will be automatically launched and loaded into Word whenever you launch the program.

To specify the location of Word's Startup folder, follow these steps:

1. Select Tools ➢ Options to display the Options dialog box.

2. Select the File Locations tab.

3. Select Startup, and click the Modify button to display the Modify Locations dialog box.

4. Navigate to a new location, and then click OK.

CHAPTER 28

Designing Forms

Creating a form template   **718**

Designing your form   **719**

Adding and defining form fields   **720**

Adding and defining ActiveX controls   **727**

Automating your form with macros   **734**

Preparing a form for distribution   **735**

Distributing the form   **735**

Completing an automated form and collecting the data   **736**

Forms are a necessary evil in our lives, an efficient (though sometimes annoying) method of data collection. Filling in a form is the real-world equivalent of taking a test that combines fill-in-the-blank and multiple-choice questions; a form provides more structure for answers (data) than would a series of essay questions.

With a form, you direct the user to fill in just the information you need—in the format you need it. You can then take the data from a completed form and use it in any number of ways, although the most common use is to feed a database that can later be queried for specific uses.

Word is an ideal program for creating forms. You can use Word's design tools to create a great-looking form—and, if you want to enable electronic entry, use form fields and ActiveX controls to automate the form itself.

With Word 2000 you can create three different types of forms:

Paper Forms   These are normal Word documents that contain boxes users can select and fill in manually, using a pen or pencil.

Web-Based Forms   These are forms accessed via the Internet, using a Web browser. (See Chapter 25 for more information on Web-based forms.)

Forms You View and Complete within Microsoft Word   These are automated forms that accept user input onscreen, then direct that input to another document or database.

This chapter helps you master the design and construction of paper and Word-based forms—including adding interactivity to your forms with ActiveX controls.

Designing a Usable Form

Designing a form is no different from designing any other document—except that you need to think one page at a time.

It is important to carefully design a form page. You need to think about what information you need from the user and in what form you need it. Should a particular piece of information be entered as text (in which case you'll receive a variety of responses), or should you limit the responses to a select list? Think about how you'll use the data, how you'll sort it and filter it, then decide how you want to accept user input.

Consider the flow of the form, from top to bottom (and left to right along each horizontal line). Group similar items together; order items in a manner that is intuitive to the user. Consider how much explanatory text you'll need in the form.

Before you fire up Word, try sketching your form's layout on a piece of paper. Will your form flow like a text-based document, or should it be laid out in a grid? How many rows and columns should you include—and how symmetrical should the form appear? Do you need any other elements on the form—your company's logo, for example—and, if so, where should they go?

Once your form is sketched out, it's time to transfer that sketch to the Word workspace, using Word's standard editing features.

Using a Table for Form Layout

 If your form is based on a grid—whether simple or complex—consider using a table to lay out the form onscreen. You can use Word's standard table-creation commands, or (if you have a particularly complicated form) you can *draw* the table one line at a time by clicking the Draw Table button on either the Tables and Borders or the Forms toolbar.

Figure 28.1 shows a simple form created using a Word table.

PART
XIII

Creating Automated
Documents

FIGURE 28.1
Use a table to create the basic grid behind a form.

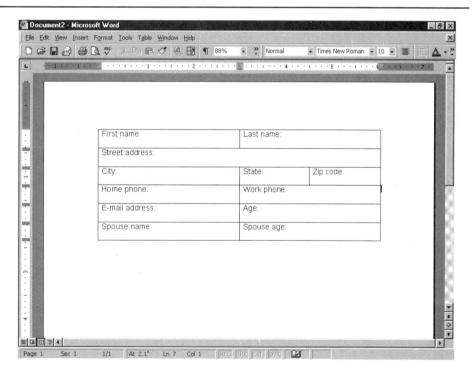

 NOTE For more information on using tables, see Chapter 14.

Adding Text Boxes

If you need to set off a section of your form, consider adding a text box. You can use a text box to set off noninput sections of your form; use Word's formatting options to apply a special border or background to the text box.

Figure 28.2 shows how a text box can be used to set off specific information in a form.

FIGURE 28.2
Use a text box to set off information in your form.

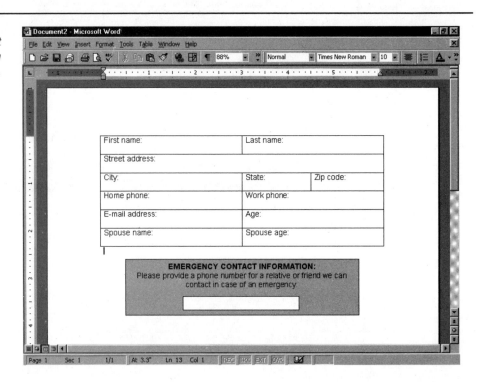

 NOTE For more information on using text boxes, see Chapter 4.

Adding Borders and Shading

You can use borders and shading to visually separate areas of your form. Heavier borders can be used as dividers; shading can be used to draw attention to specific areas or (when a darker color is used) to indicate boxes that don't need to be filled out.

Figure 28.3 shows a form formatted with various borders and shading.

FIGURE 28.3
*Use borders and
shading to visually
divide your form into
separate sections.*

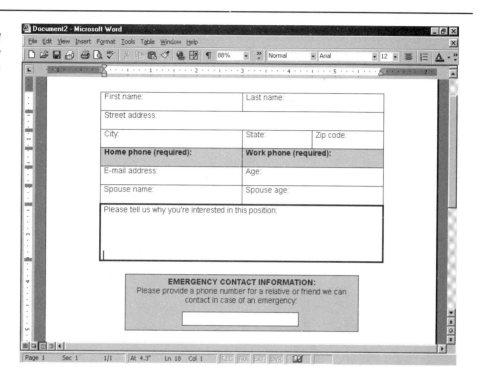

 NOTE For more information on using borders and shading, see Chapter 9.

Adding Art and Graphics

Most forms are boring combinations of lines and text—but it doesn't *have* to be that
way. You can create visually interesting forms by adding artwork, graphics, and pictures, as long as they don't get in the way of the user entering the data you need. Consider using a background graphic or watermark, or adding your company's logo
somewhere on the form.

Figure 28.4 shows how graphics can enhance the appearance of a form.

FIGURE 28.4
*Visually enhance your
form with artwork and
graphics.*

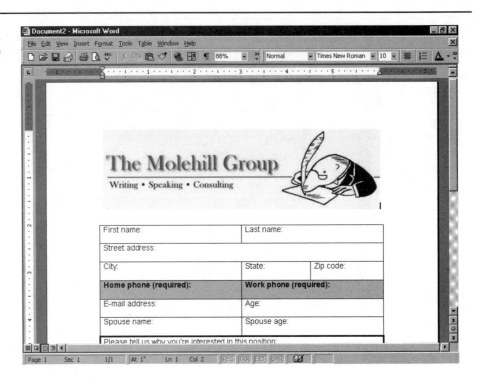

 NOTE   For more information on adding and formatting graphics, see Chapter 16.

Adding Controls and Fields

If you're designing an interactive form, you add the interactivity via *form fields* and *controls*. These objects—from check boxes and list boxes to text boxes—provide information to and accept data from the person filling out the form. You can use form fields to more easily create easy-to-use paper forms, and you *must* use both form fields and controls when creating forms to be completed within Word.

 NOTE   To learn how to use form fields and controls, see the "Creating Automated Forms" section, later in this chapter.

Creating Printed Forms

The simplest type of form you can create is a printed form. You don't have to worry about complicated controls or behind-the-scenes programming; all you have to do is lay out a form that's relatively easy to fill out.

 TIP You'll find many of the commands you need to create a form—including Draw Tables and Check Box Form Field—on the Forms toolbar. Display this toolbar by right-clicking any visible Word toolbar, then selecting Forms.

To create a printed form, follow these steps:

1. Select File ➢ New to open the New dialog box and create a new document.

2. To draw a grid for your form, select Table ➢ Draw Table (or click the Draw Table button on the Forms toolbar) and draw the appropriate gridlines.

3. To add borders to selected cells within your table, select Format ➢ Borders and Shading to display the Borders and Shading dialog box. Select the Borders tab, then make the appropriate selections.

4. To add shading to selected cells within your table, select Format ➢ Borders and Shading to display the Borders and Shading dialog box. Select the Shading tab, then make the appropriate selections.

 TIP You can use Word's form fields to simplify adding text fields and check boxes to your printed form. For more information, see the "Adding and Defining Form Fields" section, later in this chapter.

5. To add a check box to your form, click the Check Box Form Field button on the Forms toolbar.

 6. To insert a text box where users can write their responses, click the Text Form Field button on the Forms toolbar.

 7. Enter text for your form into the appropriate cells.

Once you've finished creating your form, save and print your document as normal.

Creating Automated Forms

An automated form is one that the user completes onscreen, from within Word. The user opens Word, creates a new document based on the form template, follows the onscreen instructions and fills out the appropriate information (onscreen, of course), then saves the document under a designated filename. The form file is then collected and the data within is compiled, usually in an Access database or Excel worksheet. The process is completely interactive; no forms are printed, and no pencils or pens are used.

Creating an automated form is much more complicated than creating a printed form. For a form to be viewed and completed onscreen, you have to add form fields and controls that enable the presentation and collection of data—and then figure out how to collect that data and what to do with it after you collect it.

 WARNING Building an automated form is, essentially, a mini–programming job; you have to program the behavior of each control you add, using Microsoft's Visual Basic for Applications programming language. For this reason, you shouldn't attempt to construct an interactive form unless you have some familiarity with computer programming.

The job of constructing an interactive form is a combination of several different tasks. In order, follow these steps:

1. Create a template.
2. Design and lay out a form.
3. Add and define form fields and controls.
4. Automate the form.
5. Prepare the form for distribution.
6. Distribute the form, electronically.
7. Collect the information.

The following sections walk you through these steps.

Creating a Form Template

Since the person filling out the form has to create a new document based on a template, your form has to be saved in Word template (.DOT) format. Word 2000 does not come with any built-in forms templates, so you have to start from scratch, creating a brand-new template for your form.

To create a new template for your form, follow these steps:

1. Select File ➢ New to open the New dialog box.

2. Select the General tab.

3. Select the Blank Document template.

 NOTE You can select any existing template on which to base your form template; the Blank Document template (which is essentially the Normal template) is recommended because it is less task specific than Word's other document templates.

---

4. Check the Template option in the Create New section.

5. Click OK to open the template.

6. Select File ➢ Save As to display the Save As dialog box.

7. Enter the name for your new template in the File Name box. (Make sure you give the template a descriptive name that will be understandable to those filling out your form.)

8. Pull down the Save As Type list and select Document Template.

9. Use the Save In list to navigate to and select the folder where you want to save the template. By default, Word will save the template in the \Windows\Application Data\Microsoft\Templates\ folder and place it on the General tab in the New dialog box.

10. Click the Save button.

Once you've created your new (currently blank) template, you can proceed to create your form. Make sure you save all your changes to the .DOT file (and not to a .DOC file, accidentally) so that you continue to create a *template,* not a document.

Designing Your Form

Next you get to lay out your form onscreen. Follow the suggestions presented in the "Designing a Usable Form" section, earlier in this chapter. Keep in mind that most users will be viewing the form on monitors with no more than 800×600 resolution, so don't make the form so wide users will need to scroll back and forth. In addition, realize that most users don't like to scroll through long pages, so try to keep your form as short as possible.

Adding and Defining Form Fields

With your basic form layout created, you can add *form fields* to collect data from the user. Form fields are three special Word fields designed to accept user input.

These three fields (FORMCHECKBOX, FORMDROPDOWN, and FORMTEXT) cannot be inserted into your document as you would insert a normal field. You have to use the Check Box Form Field, Drop-Down Form Field, and Text Form Field buttons on the Forms toolbar to insert these fields into your form.

 NOTE To learn more about Word fields, see Chapter 12.

Using Word's form fields is the easiest way to create an automated form. The other alternative—using ActiveX controls, discussed later in this chapter—involves a degree of programming expertise, using the Visual Basic for Applications language. Form fields, on the other hand, work like any other Word field; you set a few options via a dialog box, and no programming is required. If you're a beginning forms designer, stick with form fields for your data input, at least until you've gained some programming experience.

 MASTERING THE OPPORTUNITIES

Using the Forms Toolbar

The Forms toolbar includes commands to insert and edit Word's form fields—as well as commands used to insert or draw tables in your form. You display the Forms toolbar by right-clicking any visible Word toolbar, then selecting Forms.

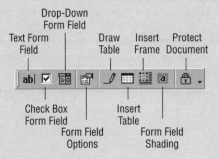

Adding a Form Field

To add a form field to your document, follow these instructions:

1. Position the insertion point where you want to add the form field.

2. Click the Text Form Field, Check Box Form Field, or Drop-Down Form Field button on the Forms toolbar.

Word inserts the selected field at the insertion point.

In the document, click where you want to insert the form field. After you've added a form field, you'll need to edit the options for that field; see the "Changing Form Field Options" section, later in this chapter, for detailed instructions.

The following sections provide more information about each of Word's three types of form fields.

Text Form Field

You use a text field to accept text input from a user. A text field can accept *any* type of text input, so you can use this form field for just about any type of data in your form—from free-form text to names and addresses to dates and numbers.

As you can see in Figure 28.5, a text field displays in-line with the regular text in your document; if you'd rather display a *box* for text entry, you have to use the ActiveX text-box control instead.

FIGURE 28.5
Accept any type of text input with a text form field.

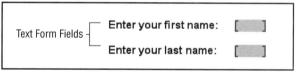

There are six types of text form fields you can add to your forms. You access these variations in the Text Form Field Options dialog box, which you display by selecting the field and then clicking the Form Field Options button on the Forms toolbar. Table 28.1 describes the different field types.

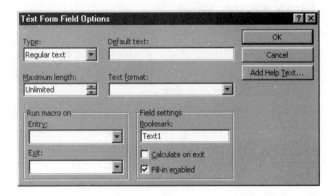

TABLE 28.1: TEXT FORM FIELD TYPES

Option	Characteristics
Regular Text	Accepts any type of input: text, numbers, symbols, or spaces
Number	Accepts numerical input only
Date	Accepts input in the form of a date only
Current Date	Displays current date generated by your system (does not accept any user input)
Current Time	Displays current time generated by your system (does not accept any user input)
Calculation	Automatically calculates numbers using Word's =(FORMULA) field (does not accept any user input)

For most user input, you'll want to choose the Regular Text, Number, or Date types. To display generated text, use one of the other three options.

NOTE You can specify a default entry in the text form field, so that the user has to type only responses different from the default response.

Check Box Form Field

You use a check box to enable a user to choose from among a group of options. You can also insert check boxes next to each item in a group of choices that are not mutually exclusive—so the user can select more than one item from a list.

Figure 28.6 shows a check box used in an interactive form.

FIGURE 28.6

Let users choose from one or more items via check boxes.

Where did you hear about us? (check as many as apply)

☒ Newspaper

☒ Magazine

☒ Television

☐ Radio

☐ Web site

☒ Friend/family

Drop-Down Form Field

You use this field to display a drop-down list of choices; the user then selects one option from the list. Figure 28.7 shows a drop-down list in action.

FIGURE 28.7

Present a list of options via a drop-down list.

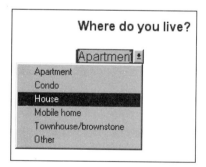

Where do you live?

Apartment ±
Apartment
Condo
House
Mobile home
Townhouse/brownstone
Other

Once you've added the drop-down form field to your form, you need to specify which items are included in the list. To add or remove items from the list, follow these steps:

1. Select the drop-down form field in your form.

2. Click the Form Field Options button on the Forms toolbar to display the Drop-Down Form Field Options dialog box.

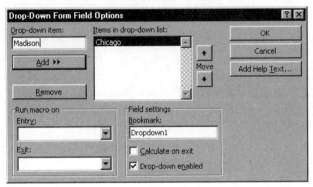

3. Add an item to the list by entering it into the Drop-Down Item box, then click the Add button.

4. Remove an item from the list by selecting it from the Items in Drop-Down List list, then click the Remove button.

5. To change the order of items in the drop-down list, select an item from the Items in Drop-Down List list and use the up or down arrows to move the item up or down through the list.

6. Click OK.

NOTE The first item in the Items in Drop-Down List list is the one that appears by default in the drop-down list.

Changing Form Field Options

Once you've added a form field to your form, you need to configure the field for your particular use. To set a field's properties, follow these steps:

1. Select the field you want to configure.

2. Click the Form Field Options button on the Forms toolbar to display the Options dialog box for that field.

3. Enter the necessary information and select the desired settings.

4. Click OK.

NOTE If you've protected a form, you'll need to remove the protection before changing field properties. To remove protection, click the Protect Form button on the Forms toolbar; remember to reprotect the form when done by clicking the Protect Form button again.

In addition, each form field incorporates the following generic options, which must be set:

Run Macro on Entry   Enter the name of a macro to run when the insertion point reaches this field.

Run Macro on Exit   Enter the name of a macro to run when the insertion point *leaves* this field.

 NOTE For more information on running macros in your forms, see the "Automating Your Form with Macros" section, later in this chapter.

Bookmark   The name of the bookmark assigned to this field.

Calculate on Exit   Check this option to have Word update and recalculate all the fields in your form when the insertion point leaves this field.

Fill-In Enabled   Check this option to allow users to input data into this field; uncheck to prevent users from using this field.

Disabling a Field

Not every field in your form has to be live. If you want users *not* to enter data in a particular form field, follow these steps:

1. Select the field you want to disable.
2. Click the Form Field Options button on the Forms toolbar to display the Options dialog box for that field.
3. Uncheck the Fill-In Enabled option.
4. Click OK.

Adding Help Text

It doesn't hurt to provide a little help for anyone using your form—just in case they can't figure out what to enter in any given field. Fortunately, Word allows you to create unique Help messages for each form field you include in your form, such as the Help message shown in Figure 28.8.

PART

XIII

Creating Automated Documents

FIGURE 28.8
*Create your own Help
messages for each of
the fields in your form.*

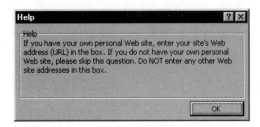

To create Help text for a specific form field, follow these steps:

1. Select the field to which you want to add a Help message.

2. Click the Form Field Options button on the Forms toolbar to display the Options dialog box for that field.

3. Click the Add Help Text button to display the Form Field Help Text dialog box.

4. To create a message that will be displayed in Word's status bar when the insertion point enters the form field, select the Status Bar tab. To display an AutoText entry in the status bar, check the AutoText Entry option and select an entry from the list. To display your own custom message, check the Type Your Own option and enter your message in the large text box.

5. To create a message that will be displayed in a message box (such as the one shown in Figure 28.8) when the user presses F1, select the Help Key (F1) tab. To display an AutoText entry in the message box, check the AutoText Entry option and select an entry from the list. To display your own custom message, check the Type Your Own option and enter your message in the large text box.

6. Click OK.

Remember that you need to create a separate Help message for each form field in your form.

Formatting Form Field Results

You may want users' input to appear in a different typeface or color than the surrounding text in the form. To change the font used to display these form field results, follow these steps:

1. Select the form field you want to format.

2. Select Format ➢ Font to display the Font dialog box.

3. Change the font type, size, or color, as appropriate.

4. Click OK to apply the new font formatting.

Adding or Removing Form Field Shading

You can select to have Word automatically shade all form fields used for input in your form—or to *not* display this shading. To set this option, click the Form Field Shading button on the Forms toolbar. This button is a toggle—clicking it on turns on form field shading; clicking it off turns off the shading.

Adding and Defining ActiveX Controls

Using form fields is the easiest way to add interactivity to a Word form; using ActiveX controls is more difficult, but also more versatile, because a *control* is a piece of programming code that behaves in a specific manner, as programmed.

Adding an ActiveX control to your form is a three-step process:

1. **Insert the control into your form,** by clicking the appropriate control button on the Control Toolbox toolbar.

2. **Set the properties for the control,** by clicking the Properties button on the Control Toolbox toolbar, then entering new values in the Properties dialog box. This determines how the control looks onscreen and what are (for some controls) the default values registered when the control is selected.

3. **Program the control,** by clicking the View Code button on the Control Toolbox toolbar, then writing your own custom VBA code in the Visual Basic Editor. This determines the behavior of the control when selected—as well as how and where the data generated by the control is handled.

WARNING Using controls in your forms requires at least a passing knowledge of Visual Basic programming, and thus is not for the casual user.

The following sections will walk you through each of these three steps—as well as show you how to switch to Word's *Design mode,* which you use for all your ActiveX control work.

MASTERING THE OPPORTUNITIES

Using the Control Toolbox Toolbar

You use the Control Toolbox toolbar to insert ActiveX controls into your forms. This toolbar contains commands to insert and edit form-related controls; you display this toolbar by right-clicking any visible Word toolbar, then selecting Control Toolbox.

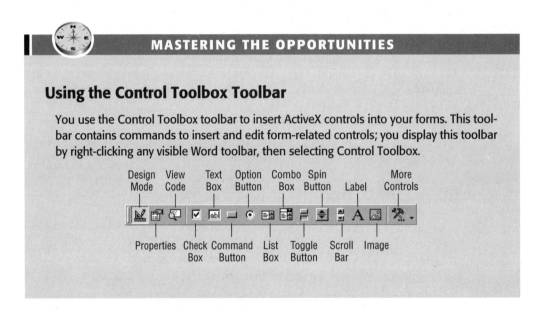

Switching to Design Mode

 To insert controls into your automated forms, you have to work in Word's Design mode. To switch to Design mode, click the Design Mode button on the Control Toolbox toolbar. When you're in Design mode, the Word workspace looks just like normal, except for the Exit Design Mode button floating on top of the workspace. You click the Exit Design Mode button to exit Design mode and return to Word's normal Run mode.

Run mode is the opposite of Design mode. While you're in Design mode, nothing automated in your documents can be run—no macros, no forms, no controls (essentially, your controls are all turned off). When you exit Design mode, you can run all your automated elements as you normally do—hence the name *Run mode.*

You switch to Design mode when you want to design your forms and insert your controls; when you switch back to Run mode, you can interact with these controls as would a regular user.

Adding an ActiveX Control

To add an ActiveX control to your form, follow these steps:

1. From within your form, click the Design Mode button on the Control Toolbox toolbar to switch to Design mode.

2. Position the insertion point where you want to add the control.

3. From the Control Toolbox toolbar, click the button for the control you want to add.

4. Use your mouse to position the control on your form.

While in Design mode, Word inserts a control as a floating object—which is why you can easily drag it to a new position. To insert a control in-line with your text (at the insertion point), hold down the Shift key while you click the control button on the Control Toolbox toolbar.

Visual Basic for Applications includes hundreds of different controls that can be used in any VBA-enabled application. Word has selected 11 of these controls as being especially useful for form designers; these controls, located on the Control Toolbox toolbar, are discussed in the following sections.

Check Box

You use a check box to allow a user to select or deselect a specific item in your form. You can also insert check boxes next to each item in a group of choices that are not mutually exclusive—so that users can select more than one check box at a time.

Text Box

Text boxes accept text input—words, numbers, dates, and so on—from users. You can make your text box as small or as large (multiple lines) as you want.

Command Button

A command-button control creates a button on your page. Users click the button to perform an action; you can specify any number of actions that the button activates. For example, you can program a *next* button to jump to another point in the form or a *save* button to save the form document.

Option Button

An option button has more in common with a check box than a command button, since an option button isn't a button, per se. You use an option button to force a user to choose from two or more selections; since only one item can be selected at a time, choosing one option unchooses the others. (In other words, an option button offers a mutually exclusive choice, where a check box can offer multiple choices.)

PART

XIII

Creating Automated
Documents

List Box

You use a list box to display available choices in a list; users can select multiple choices from the list.

NOTE The entries in a list-box control must be entered via the *object.*List property statement in a Visual Basic Editor Code window. See Chapter 30 to learn more about Visual Basic for Applications and the VB Editor.

Combo Box

A combo box is a combination of a list box and a text box. Users can either select an entry from the list or type their own entry in the box.

Toggle Button

A toggle button is a button that has both an on and an off position. You use toggle buttons to switch between states or modes. For example, you could use a toggle button to toggle between simple and detailed displays.

Spin Button

A spin button—often called a *spin control*—lets users click up and down arrows to select higher and lower values. You use a spin control in conjunction with another control, such as a text box.

Scroll Bar

You insert a scroll-bar control next to other controls—for example, next to a text box—so users can scroll through any list longer than the displayed control.

Label

The label control inserts a text label onto your form. Use labels anytime you need to describe or label items on your form.

Image

The image control inserts a picture or graphic onto your form.

Finding More ActiveX Controls and Registering Them

The 11 controls displayed on the Control Toolbox toolbar are only some of the hundreds of ActiveX controls available. When you click the More Controls button on the Control Toolbox toolbar, Word displays a list of additional controls you can add to your form. Click the name of a control to insert it in your form. (Note, however, that most of these additional controls have little relevance to form creation.)

Continued ▶

The controls listed when you click the More Controls button aren't all the ActiveX controls available, however. Only *registered* controls appear on this list. Other controls are available at a variety of programming Web sites and can be downloaded or copied to your hard disk.

When you copy an ActiveX control (a file with an .OCX or .DLL extension) to your hard disk, you have to register it from within Word. Follow these steps to register a new control:

1. Click the More Controls button on the Control Toolbox toolbar to display the list of ActiveX controls.

2. Scroll to the end of the list and click Register Custom Control to display the Register Custom Control dialog box.

3. Navigate to and select the control you want to register.

4. Click the Open button.

The new control will now appear in the More Controls list.

Two good sites for new ActiveX controls are Active-X.com (`www.active-x.com`) and the ActiveX section of CNET's Download.com (`www.activex.com`).

Setting ActiveX Control Properties

Once you've added an ActiveX control, you need to set its properties. Although properties differ by type of control, you typically can set the control's name, appearance, caption, and contents (in the case of list controls). All properties are accessible from the Properties dialog box; within the dialog box, you can display properties either alphabetically (on the Alphabetic tab) or by category (on the Categorized tab).

To set the properties of an ActiveX control, follow these steps:

1. Click the Design Mode button to switch to Word's Design mode.

2. Select the control you want to configure.

3. Click the Properties button on the Control Toolbox toolbar to display the Properties dialog box, shown in Figure 28.9.

FIGURE 28.9
Use the Properties
dialog box to determine
how a control looks and
acts; different controls
have different
properties.

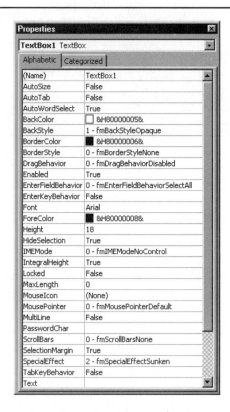

4. To view the properties alphabetically, select the Alphabetic tab; to view the properties by category, select the Categorized tab.

5. Change the desired properties.

6. Close the Properties dialog box by clicking the X button in the top-right corner.

 WARNING Do *not* double-click a control, thinking that it will open the Properties dialog box. Double-clicking a control opens the Visual Basic Editor for programming.

Programming an ActiveX Control

The Properties dialog box sets the look and feel of a control; to determine what a control actually *does,* you have to *program* the control, using the Visual Basic for Applications programming language.

All VBA programming is done in the Visual Basic Editor, shown in Figure 28.10. You display the editor—and write the code for a specific control—by following these steps:

1. Click the Design Mode button to switch to Word's Design mode.

2. Select the control you want to program.

3. Click the View Code button on the Control Toolbox toolbar (or just double-click the control) to open the Visual Basic Editor, shown in Figure 28.10.

4. Write the appropriate VBA code, then close the Visual Basic Editor and return to your form.

FIGURE 28.10
Use the Visual Basic Editor to write the VBA code that determines the behavior of your controls.

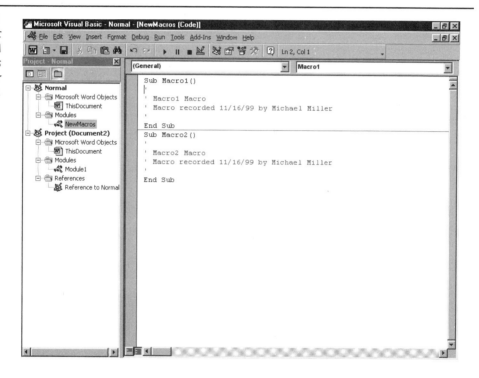

PART
XIII

Creating Automated Documents

NOTE For more information about programming in Visual Basic for Applications, see Chapter 30.

Automating Your Form with Macros

Even if you don't use ActiveX controls in your form, you can still automate your form by using *macros* assigned to form fields. Any macro saved in your form template file can be configured to run automatically when the user's insertion point enters or exits a form field.

For example, you could create a macro that activates other fields or jumps to another part of your form when a certain field is selected. Or you could use a macro to automatically fill in selected fields when a specific field is selected.

 NOTE For more information about creating macros, see Chapter 29.

To assign a macro to a form field, follow these steps:

1. From within your form, create the macro you want to use and store it in your template file.

 TIP You can also use macros from other files by copying them into your form template file.

2. Select the form field to which you want the macro assigned.

3. Click the Form Field Options button on the Forms toolbar to display the Form Field Options dialog box.

4. To run a macro when the insertion point *enters* the form field, pull down the Entry list and select the macro.

5. To run a macro when the insertion point *leaves* the form field, pull down the Exit list and select the macro.

6. Click OK.

 WARNING You *must* store the macros in your form template file. If you use a macro stored in the Normal template, that macro will not be available to others to whom you've distributed your form.

Preparing a Form for Distribution

Before you distribute a form to others, you must protect it so that other users can't edit the form itself, only enter data in the designated areas. To protect your form in this fashion, follow these steps:

1. Select Tools ➤ Protect Document to display the Protect Document dialog box.

 NOTE You must save your form template before you can protect it; remember to save the form as a Word template (.DOT) file.

2. Check the Forms option.

3. To assign a password to the form, enter a password in the Password box. (Anyone with the password can edit your actual form; anyone without a password can still enter information into your form.)

4. Click OK.

 TIP When you are creating or editing a form, you can quickly protect or unprotect the form by clicking the Protect Form button on the Forms toolbar.

Distributing the Form

Your form has been created, saved, and protected. Now you need to distribute it so others can use it.

There are many ways to distribute an electronic form. You can choose from any of the following:

Distribute by Diskette Copy your form file to diskette, then distribute the diskette to your potential respondents. Instruct them to fill out the form and then return the diskette (containing the completed form) to you or to a central point.

PART

XIII

Creating Automated
Documents

Distribute by E-mail   Use Word 2000's e-mail feature to send the form file directly to your list of respondents via e-mail attachment.

NOTE   See Chapter 7 for more information on sending documents via e-mail.

Distribute from an Internet/Intranet Site   Post a copy of the form file on a central Web site (either publicly on the Internet or privately on your company's intranet site) and instruct users how to download the file to their computers. You'll have to arrange a method for the users to return the completed form to you—either by e-mailing the completed file or by uploading it back to the central Web site.

TIP   If you want users to fill out the form online, you should create a Web-based form, as discussed in Chapter 25.

However you distribute your form, make sure you include detailed instructions as to what you want respondents to do and how you want them to do it.

Completing an Automated Form and Collecting the Data

Once your form has been distributed, your respondents have to complete the form. After they return the completed file, you have to do something with the data they've entered.

Filling in the Form

Filling in a form is simple. Make sure your respondents have a copy of Word 97 or Word 2000. Then they should follow these steps:

1. Copy the form file template to their hard disk, into their templates folder.

NOTE   In Word 2000, the template file should be copied to the `\Program Files\Microsoft Office\Templates\1033\` folder. In Word 97, the folder used to hold templates varies according to installation, but is most often the `\Program Files\Microsoft Office\Templates` folder.

2. From within their copy of Word, select File ➢ New to open the New dialog box.

3. Select the form template (should be in the General tab).

4. In the Create New section, check the Document option.

5. Click OK to create a new document based on your form template.

6. Fill in the form by entering information in each field or making selections from the check boxes, option buttons, and so on. Move to the next field by pressing the Tab key; return to the previous field by pressing Shift+Tab.

7. When the form is completed, select File ≻ Save As to display the Save As dialog box.

8. Enter a name for the completed form in the File Name box.

9. Make sure Word Document (*not* Word Template) is selected in the Save As Type box.

10. Click the Save button.

Once you have a completed form document, you can choose to print the data from that form or send the data to a database.

Printing Form Data

To print just the data from a form (and not the form itself), follow these steps:

1. Open the document that contains the completed form.

2. Select Tools ≻ Options to display the Options dialog box.

3. Select the Print tab.

4. Check the Print Data Only for Forms option.

5. Click OK to close the Options dialog box.

6. Click the Print button on Word's Standard toolbar.

Word prints only the data entered in the form.

NOTE If you based the design of the form on a preprinted form (such as a company invoice or a standard 1040 tax form) and the form fields appear in the same locations, you can insert the blank, preprinted forms in a printer and use the above procedure to fill out the preprinted forms.

Sending Form Data to a Database

To send the data from a completed form to a central database (or spreadsheet), you have to save the form data as a comma-delimited text file. You can then import the text file into your database or spreadsheet.

To save your form data as a text file, follow these steps:

1. Open the document that contains the completed form.

2. Select Tools ➢ Options to display the Options dialog box.

3. Select the Save tab.

4. Check the Save Data Only for Forms option.

5. Click OK to close the Options dialog box.

6. Select File ➢ Save As to display the Save As dialog box.

7. Enter a name for your output file in the File Name box.

8. Pull down the Save As Type list and select Text Only.

9. Click the Save button.

Word saves the data only from your form (and not the form itself) in a comma-delimited text file. Switch to whatever database or spreadsheet program you're using and open or import this text file into your database or spreadsheet.

 NOTE For information on using Word with Microsoft Access and Microsoft Excel, see Chapter 32.

CHAPTER 29

Automating Your Documents with Macros

Recording a macro   **743**

Editing a macro   **746**

Running a macro   **748**

Assigning a macro   **749**

Copying a macro project to a different document or template   **751**

Deleting and renaming macro projects   **752**

Protecting against macro viruses   **752**

Adding a digital signature to a macro project   **755**

When you have to do something over and over in Word, you need a macro. When you need to simplify a complex operation, you need a macro. When you want to add a nonstandard operation to a toolbar or menu, you need a macro.

Macros are like little robot helpers that operate in the background, doing the tasks you don't particularly like to do. Just as you'd program a robot to perform a specific task, you program a macro to carry out a specific operation step by step. When you run the macro—either automatically when you load a document or manually when you press a button or a shortcut key—the macro goes about its work, robotically stepping through each instruction until the specified operation is completed. It's better than doing the work yourself, which is the true benefit of using macros.

Understanding Macros

A macro is a set of instructions that automates a repeated or repetitive operation. You can use macros to automate the insertion of boilerplate text, to simplify complex formatting, or to control the operation of fields in a form. You can even create intricate macros that automate how a document behaves onscreen.

Word 2000 creates macros using the Visual Basic for Applications (VBA) programming language, which is a subset of the more robust Visual Basic language. Each macro consists of multiple lines of programming code, each line containing a specific instruction. When the macro is run, each line of code executes one after another, essentially completing the programmed operation step by step.

Understanding How Macros Are Created

You can create a macro in one of two ways. The hard way is to write the VBA code by hand, using Microsoft's Visual Basic Editor. (This method is discussed in the next chapter.) The easy way is to *record* your actions as you perform the operation and then have Word's Macro Recorder translate your actions into the appropriate VBA code automatically.

Once you've recorded a macro, you can edit it to clean up any mistake you made in recording or just to make it do something slightly different. When you edit a macro, you're editing the VBA code, using the Visual Basic Editor.

Macros you've created can be saved to a specific template or document and made to run automatically every time that template or document is opened. By default, Word stores macros in the Normal template, which makes them available for use with every Word document. If you want to use a macro in a single document or template only, you merely need to store it in that document or template.

All the new macros you create in a document or template are stored in *macro projects* that can be copied from one document to another, using Word's Organizer. You can assign macros to Word's menus, toolbars, or shortcut keys so you can literally run a macro with the push of a button or with the click of a mouse.

Examining Some Macro Examples

You can create macros to automate just about anything you might do within Word. When you use the Macro Recorder, your actions are recorded verbatim, so you can reproduce in a macro anything you enter onscreen.

For example, you might use a macro to insert boilerplate text. You would start the Macro Recorder, type the text onscreen, and then stop the recorder. When you play back that macro, Word retypes that text at the insertion point. Ideally, you'd assign that boilerplate text macro to a keyboard shortcut; whenever you need to insert the boilerplate text, press the shortcut key(s), and Word enters the text automatically.

You can also use a macro to insert text *fields*. Let's say you frequently insert the author name and the current date and time into your documents. You can turn on the Macro Recorder, insert the appropriate field codes for these generated fields, and then stop the recorder. When you run the macro, the field codes are automatically inserted, and the proper information is automatically generated.

It's also possible to create a macro that formats your text. If you often apply a consistent-yet-complex formatting (either to a word or to a paragraph), you can create a macro that selects your text and then applies the formatting. Just start the recorder, use the keyboard shortcut to select either a word (Ctrl+Shift+→) or a paragraph (Ctrl+Shift+↓), press Alt+O, F to open the Font dialog box, select the formatting you want (font, style, size, color, etc.), press Enter, and then stop recording. To use the macro, position the insertion point at the start of the desired word or paragraph, press the macro shortcut key(s), and watch as the word or paragraph is automatically formatted.

 WARNING You have to use the keyboard to select text when recording a macro; the Macro Recorder will not record mouse movements used to select text.

Consider also how you could use a macro to add a complex element to your document, such as a table, complete with sophisticated formatting (borders, shading, and the like). Just record your actions as you create and format the table, and then assign the macro to a toolbar button or shortcut key. When you click the button, Word will automatically insert a perfectly formatted table at the insertion point.

PART

XIII

Creating Automated
Documents

These are just some of the simpler operations for which you can create macros. Again, practically anything you can do within the Word workspace can be automated; think of the most time-intensive tasks you perform, and then create macros to turn them into one-step operations!

Creating Macros

With Word 2000, you can create a macro in one of two ways: by recording an operation with the Macro Recorder and by writing VBA code in the Visual Basic Editor.

The Macro Recorder is the easiest way to create a macro. Essentially, as the preceding section demonstrated, you use the Macro Recorder to record your actions as you perform an operation; those actions are automatically translated into the appropriate VBA code, with no intervention on your part necessary. When Word runs the macro, it plays back your actions by running the VBA code, thus executing the recorded operation.

Unfortunately, there are some limitations to the Macro Recorder method. Most limiting is the fact that the Macro Recorder doesn't record mouse movements— scrolling, moving the insertion point, selecting text or objects, and so on. (You *can* use the mouse to click menu items and toolbar buttons, but that's about it.) In addition, some possible actions are not easily recorded, such as those that involve drilling down through multiple dialog boxes.

If you want to directly execute an indirect operation, or if you want to automate a mouse-driven operation that Macro Recorder won't record, you need to create the macro using the Visual Basic Editor. When you write your own VBA code, you can create some very powerful and flexible macros, unlike any you can record with the Macro Recorder. To use the Visual Basic Editor, however, you need to know your way around the Visual Basic programming language, which means VBA macro creation is recommended for experienced developers only.

NOTE This chapter covers the use of the Macro Recorder to create simple macros. To learn more about using VBA to create complex macros, see Chapter 30.

MASTERING TROUBLESHOOTING

Using Older Macros

Word 2000 is fully compatible with macros stored in Word 97 documents or templates. You should also be able to run Word 2000 macros on Word 97 installations, unless the macros include commands new to Word 2000.

Prior to Word 97, Word used a different macro language called WordBasic. This older macro language is not compatible with VBA, and macros created in WordBasic must be converted to run on Word 2000 installations.

The first time you open a Word 6.x or Word 95 template (or create a new document based on an old template), Word 2000 automatically converts the WordBasic macros to VBA. You should see a message in Word's status bar while the macros are being converted; you'll need to save the template to save the converted macros.

This macro conversion process is permanent. Once you've saved a converted WordBasic macro in Word 2000, you won't be able run it again in Word 6.x or Word 95, even if you convert the template it is stored in back to the old format.

Using the Macro Recorder

Think of the Macro Recorder as you would a traditional tape recorder. You start recording a macro by pressing the Record button; you end recording with the Stop button.

What the Macro Recorder records is your *actions*. It records text being typed, menu items being selected, toolbar buttons being clicked, dialog boxes being opened, and just about any key on your keyboard being pressed. (It *doesn't* record most mouse movements, however, so you need to use the keyboard for most of your actions.) If you make a mistake recording an operation, you can stop and start over; you can also edit the code generated by the Macro Recorder to clean up any glitches you happened to record.

Recording a Macro

To record a macro, follow these steps:

1. Select Tools ➤ Macro ➤ Record New Macro to display the Record Macro dialog box, shown in Figure 29.1.

PART

XIII

Creating Automated
Documents

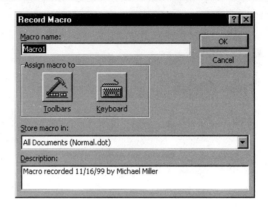

2. Enter a name for the macro in the Macro Name box.

WARNING If you give a new macro the same name as an existing macro, the new macro replaces the existing one. For this reason, avoid naming new macros with the same names as Word's built-in macros. (To view a list of Word's built-in macros, select Tools ➢ Macro ➢ Macros to display the Macros dialog box, and select Word Commands from the Macros In list.)

3. Pull down the Store Macro In list, and select where you want to store the macro—in the current document, in the current template (so the macro can be used in new documents), or in all documents (by using the Normal template).

4. If you want to enter a description for the macro, do so in the Description box.

5. To assign the macro to a toolbar or menu, click the Toolbars button to display the Customize dialog box, select the Commands tab, select the macro you're recording, and then drag it to a toolbar or menu. Click the Close button to proceed to step 6 and start recording.

To assign the macro to a shortcut key, click the Keyboard button to display the Customize Keyboard dialog box. Select the macro you're recording, enter the desired key or keys into the Press New Shortcut Key box, and then click Assign. Click the Close button to proceed to step 6 and start recording.

6. If you don't want to assign the macro to a menu, toolbar, or shortcut key, or after you've already done so, click the OK button to start recording.

7. Word now closes the Record Macro dialog box and displays the Macro Recording toolbar with recording activated, which is shown in Figure 29.2. Every action you perform from this point will be recorded as part of your macro.

FIGURE 29.2
The Macro Recording toolbar is displayed while you're recording a macro; click Stop Recording when done.

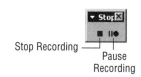

Stop Recording —— ⌐— Pause
Recording

8. Perform the actions you want to include in your macro.

NOTE While you can use your mouse to click menu commands, toolbar buttons, and options within dialog boxes, the Macro Recorder cannot record any other mouse movements. This means you have to use your keyboard to move the insertion point, select text, and the like.

9. When you're done recording your macro, click the Stop Recording button.

As soon as you click the Stop Recording button, your macro is complete. You may want to run the macro (see the "Running Macros" section later in this chapter) to make sure it works as intended. If your macro isn't perfect, you can edit it (see the "Editing a Macro" section later in this chapter), or just record it again.

When you rerecord a macro, make sure that you assign the same name as the macro you want to replace. Your new recording will replace the existing macro with the same name.

MASTERING THE OPPORTUNITIES

Macro Recording Tips

Here are some tips to keep in mind when creating macros with the Macro Recorder:

- Practice before you record. Plan out the actions necessary to complete the operation you're recording, and run through the operation at least once before you start recording.

Continued ▮▸

- Take your time. The Macro Recorder is not a real-time recorder; it executes actions at a fixed pace independent of how long it took you to record them. So don't feel like you have to rush through the operation you're recording; take the time to do it right.

- You can suspend your recording mid-macro in case you need to do some non-macro-related work. Just click the Pause Recording button, perform any actions you don't want to record, and then click the Resume Recorder button to start recording again. (The Pause button turns into a Resume button while you're paused.)

- Plan your actions to avoid any Word message boxes. For example, if your macro includes a command to close the current document, include a step to save the document first in order to avoid Word's message asking if you want to save your changes.

- To automate complex operations, you can call other macros from within a macro. If you choose to nest macros in this way, make sure the nested macro is saved into the same document or template as the macro you're currently recording.

Editing a Macro

If you make mistakes while recording, you can either edit the macro by hand or rerecord the entire operation. Editing is preferable if you've recorded a long and complex macro; it's easier to edit a line of code than it is to repeat all the actions that comprise the macro.

Using the Visual Basic Editor

You edit macros in the Visual Basic Editor, shown in Figure 29.3. Scroll through the code until you find the line you need to change, and then enter the appropriate edits. If you recorded some superfluous actions during the course of your macro recording, use this opportunity to delete those lines from the macro code as well.

 NOTE For more detailed information on using the Visual Basic Editor, see Chapter 30.

To edit an existing macro, follow these steps:

1. Select Tools ➢ Macro ➢ Macros to display the Macros dialog box.

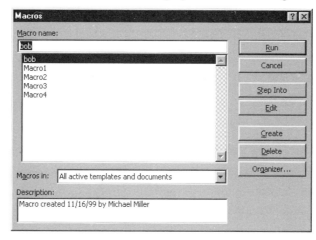

2. Select the name of the macro you want to edit from the Macro Name list.

3. Click the Edit button to open the Visual Basic Editor, shown in Figure 29.3.

FIGURE 29.3
Use the Visual Basic Editor to edit any mistakes you made while recording your macro.

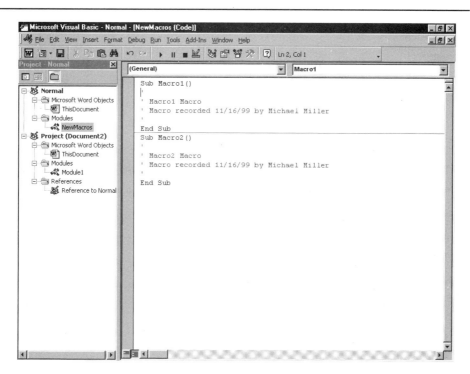

PART
XIII

Creating Automated Documents

4. Make the appropriate changes to your macro code, close the Visual Basic Editor, and return to your Word document.

Troubleshooting Your Macro, Step by Step

If you know there is a mistake in your macro but you don't know where the mistake is, you can run your macro step by step, using the Visual Basic Editor to examine your code as it executes one line at a time.

To step through a macro, follow these steps:

1. Select Tools ➢ Macro ➢ Macros to display the Macros dialog box.

2. Select the name of the macro you want to run from the Macro Name list.

3. Click the Step Into button to open the Visual Basic Editor with the first line of macro code highlighted.

4. To execute the next line of code, click the Run button on the Visual Basic Editor toolbar, or press F5.

5. When you come to a line that doesn't execute properly, edit the code.

6. When you're done troubleshooting, close the Visual Basic Editor, and return to your Word document.

Running Macros

There are many ways you can run a macro after you assign it to a menu, toolbar, or shortcut key. If you don't want to assign a macro to one of these elements, you can always run the macro from the Macros dialog box.

Running a Macro

To run a macro from the Macros dialog box, follow these steps:

1. Select Tools ➢ Macro ➢ Macros to display the Macros dialog box.

2. Select the macro you want to run from the Macro Name list.

3. Click the Run button.

Word now executes the selected macro.

TIP You can program a macro to run automatically when you launch Word or open a specific document or template. Learn more about these AutoExec, AutoOpen, and AutoNew macros in Chapter 30.

Assigning a Macro

If you use a macro frequently, it's easier to run the macro from a menu, toolbar, or keyboard shortcut than it is to drill all the way down the Macros dialog box. In order to run a macro without accessing the Macros dialog box, you first have to assign it to the desired screen element.

 NOTE To learn more about personalizing Word's menus, toolbars, and keyboard shortcuts, see Chapter 3.

Assigning to a Menu

To create a new menu item for your macro, follow these steps:

1. Select Tools ➤ Customize to display the Customize dialog box.
2. Select the Commands tab.
3. Select Macros from the Category list.
4. Select the macro you want to add from the Commands list, and then use your mouse to drag the macro from the dialog box onto the appropriate menu bar.
5. Click Close when done.

Once you've added the macro to your menu, you can reposition it within the pull-down menu by dragging it with your mouse to a new position. (You can only do this while the Customize dialog box is open.)

Assigning to a Toolbar

To create a new button on any toolbar for your macro, follow these steps:

1. Display the toolbar to which you want to add the new macro button.
2. Select Tools ➤ Customize to display the Customize dialog box.
3. Select the Commands tab.
4. Select Macros from the Category list.
5. Select the macro you want to add from the Commands list, and then use your mouse to drag the command from the dialog box onto the chosen toolbar.
6. Click Close when done.

Once you've added the macro button to the toolbar, you can add an image to the button. (Otherwise, the button will display the macro's name only.) To add an image to your button, see the "Changing and Editing Button Images" section in Chapter 3.

PART XIII

Creating Automated Documents

Assigning to a Keyboard Shortcut

To assign your macro to a keyboard key or keys, follow these steps:

1. Select Tools ➢ Customize to display the Customize dialog box.

2. From any tab, click the Keyboard button to display the Customize Keyboard dialog box.

3. Select Macros from the Category list.

4. Select the macro you want to assign from the Commands list.

5. Move your cursor to the Press New Shortcut Key box, and then press the key combination you wish to use for this shortcut.

6. Select a document or template from the Save Changes To list; this will be where the shortcut is stored.

7. Click the Assign button to assign this macro to the selected key(s).

Managing Macro Projects

All the new macros you create within a document or template are collected and stored in what Word calls a *macro project*. By using macro projects, you can manage all your macros within a document or template in one fell swoop. (By default, Word assigns the name NewMacros to the macro project within each document.)

 NOTE When you're viewing your Word documents from the Visual Basic Editor, a macro project is called a *program module*. You can copy macro code from one module to another from within the Visual Basic Editor workspace.

You manage your macro projects using Word's Organizer. Within Organizer, you can copy macro projects from one document or template to another, delete macro projects, and rename macro projects.

While you can't copy or rename individual macros from within Word (although there are rather convoluted procedures to perform these tasks from within the Visual Basic Editor, which is discussed in the next chapter), you *can* delete individual macros from a macro project.

Copying a Macro Project to a Different Document or Template

To copy a macro project from one document or template to another, follow these steps:

1. Select Tools ➢ Macro ➢ Macros to display the Macros dialog box.

2. Click the Organizer button to display the Organizer, as shown in Figure 29.4.

FIGURE 29.4
Use the Organizer to copy, delete, and rename macro projects.

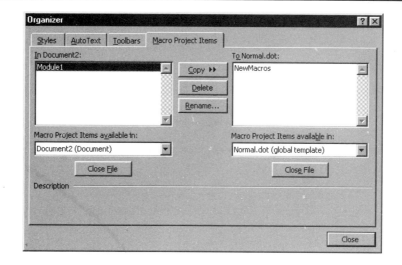

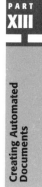

3. Select the Macro Project Items tab. The macro projects in the active document are displayed in the left-hand list; the macro projects in the Normal template are displayed in the right-hand list.

4. To change where you want to copy the macro project to or from, click the appropriate Close File button, click the Open File button, and select a new document or template.

5. From the appropriate list, select the macro project you want to copy.

6. Click the Copy button.

Close the Organizer when you're done copying elements.

WARNING You can't copy a macro project to a document or template that has a macro project of the same name. This is problematic because Word assigns the name New-Macros to the macro project in every document you create. To get around this glitch, rename the macro project (something other than NewMacros) before you copy it.

Deleting a Macro Project

To delete a macro project from a document or template, follow these steps:

1. Select Tools ➢ Macro ➢ Macros to display the Macros dialog box.

2. Click the Organizer button to display the Organizer, as shown in Figure 29.4.

3. Select the Macro Project Items tab. The macro projects in the active document are displayed in the left-hand list; the macro projects in the Normal template are displayed in the right-hand list.

4. Select the macro project you want to delete (from either list).

5. Click the Delete button.

 TIP Word also lets you delete individual macros from within a macro project. To delete an individual macro, select Tools ➢ Macro ➢ Macros to display the Macros dialog box, select the name of the macro you want to run from the Macro Name list, and then click the Delete key.

Renaming a Macro Project

To rename a macro project (which you may need to do before you copy a project to another document or template), follow these steps:

1. Select Tools ➢ Macro ➢ Macros to display the Macros dialog box.

2. Click the Organizer button to display the Organizer, as shown in Figure 29.4.

3. Select the Macro Project Items tab. The macro projects in the active document are displayed in the left-hand list; the macro projects in the Normal template are displayed in the right-hand list.

4. Select the macro project you want to rename (from either list).

5. Click the Rename button to display the Rename dialog box.

6. Enter a new name for the macro project in the New Name box, and then click OK.

Protecting Against Macro Viruses

A computer virus is similar to a biological virus. Just as a biological virus invades your body's system and replicates itself, a computer virus invades your computer's system and also replicates itself or inflicts damage on your system. Computer viruses can be destructive or simply annoying; in all cases, they are unwanted invaders of your computer system.

One of the newest and, unfortunately, fastest-growing types of computer viruses is the *macro virus*. These viruses are stored in the macro code contained in a document, template, or add-in, and thus can be transmitted within a Word document or template file. When you open the document or template, you run the macro and inadvertently activate the virus.

Some of these macro viruses are particularly nasty in that they replicate themselves into Word's Normal template, thus infecting every document you open from within Word. If other users open your infected documents, the macro virus is automatically transmitted to their computers as well.

The best defense against macro viruses is to not open any Word documents given to you by other users. Since this is impractical, the next-best defense is to use an anti-virus program to scan your files for viruses and then to clean any viruses it finds from your files. Most all-purpose anti-virus programs, such as Norton AntiVirus and McAfee VirusScan, will scan for and remove macro viruses. In addition, there are several dedicated utilities designed specifically to find and destroy macro viruses in your Word and Office documents.

 NOTE The CD accompanying this book includes Virus ALERT for Word 2000, an easy-to-use utility that scans for viruses within your Word files. For more information on this and other utilities included on the CD, see Chapter 33.

Enabling Word 2000's Macro Security

 While Word 2000 does not include virus scanning capabilities, it does include a way to help you reduce the likelihood of accepting virus-infected documents into your system. You can now indicate different *security levels* for Microsoft Word. The higher security levels, for instance, require that any macros included in documents be accompanied by digitally signed certificates of authentication; if Word encounters a macro without the proper authentication, it warns you of a potential security problem.

 NOTE Word's security level feature is enabled only if you have Internet Explorer 4 or higher installed on your system.

Word 2000's security levels are described in Table 29.1.

PART
XIII

Creating Automated
Documents

TABLE 29.1: WORD 2000'S MACRO SECURITY LEVELS

Security Level	Description
High	Runs only those macros that have been digitally signed and are confirmed as coming from a trusted source.
Medium	Warns you when Word encounters a macro from a source not on your list of trusted sources.
Low	Turns off all macro virus protection; all macros are enabled.

WARNING Word doesn't actually scan your documents to find and remove macro viruses. If you want this kind of protection, you need to purchase and install specialized anti-virus software.

Changing Security Levels

To change Word's security level, follow these steps:

1. Select Tools ➤ Macro ➤ Security to display the Security dialog box.

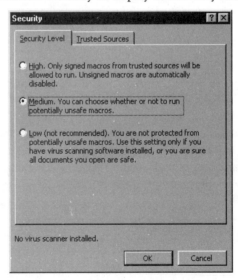

2. Select the Security Level tab.

3. Choose either High, Medium, or Low security.

4. Click OK.

NOTE You can monitor the status of Word's security settings with *ChekOf*, a utility included on the CD that accompanies this book. For more information on ChekOf, see Chapter 33.

Adding or Removing a Trusted Source

To add a macro developer to your list of trusted sources, follow these steps:

1. Either open the document or load the add-in that contains macros from the developer you want to add.

2. When the Security Warning box appears, check the Always Trust Macros from This Source Option.

 WARNING If the Security Warning box does not display the Always Trust Macros from This Source option, the macros in the document or add-in are not digitally signed. Word does not allow you to add a macro developer to the list of trusted sources without a digital signature.

To remove a developer from your list of trusted sources, select Tools ➤ Macro ➤ Security to display the Security dialog box, select the Trusted Sources tab, select the source you want to remove, and then click the Remove button.

Adding a Digital Signature to a Macro Project

To ensure others that the macros you create are virus-free, you can add a *digital signature* to any and all macros you create. A digital signature confirms that the macro came directly from you (the macro developer) and has not been tampered with. If another user has activated Medium or High security levels, you'll need to have your macros digitally signed to avoid setting off Word's security alarms when they attempt to open a file you have sent them.

You assign digital signatures to your macros from within the Visual Basic Editor. You'll need to create your own digital certificate (or obtain one from an authorized source), install the certificate in your macro project, and then sign the macro project.

Creating and Installing a Digital Certificate

To create your own digital certificate, you use a utility program (included with Office 2000) called Digital Signature for VBA Projects (SelfCert.exe). This program may not have been installed as part of your normal Office installation; if not, use the Office Setup program to selectively install this program now.

PART

XIII

Creating Automated
Documents

To create a new digital certificate, follow these steps:

1. Click the Windows Start button, and select Run to open the Run dialog box.

2. Click the Browse button to display the Browse dialog box.

3. Navigate to the `\Program Files\Microsoft Office\Office\` folder, and select the `SelfCert.exe` file; click the Open button to return to the Run dialog box.

4. Click OK to run the program.

5. When the Create Digital Certificate dialog box appears, enter your name into the Your Name box.

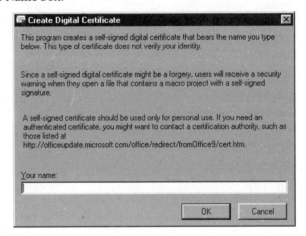

6. Click OK to create and install the digital signature within the Visual Basic Editor.

If you're part of a larger organization, you may want to use your company's digital certificate; you can also obtain digital certificates from commercial certification authorities, such as VeriSign, Inc.

NOTE To learn more about commercial certification authorities, visit the Microsoft Security Advisor Web site (`www.microsoft.com/security/`).

Digitally Signing a Macro Project

Once your digital certificate has been installed, follow these steps to digitally sign a macro project:

1. From within the document or template that contains the macro project you want to sign, select Tools ➢ Macro ➢ Visual Basic Editor to open the Visual Basic Editor.

2. From the Project Explorer, select the project you want to sign.

3. Select Tools ➢ Digital Signature to display the Digital Signature dialog box.

4. Click the Choose button to display the Select Certificate dialog box. To view a digital certificate, click the View Certificate button to display the Certificate window.

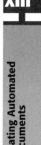

5. From the Select Certificate dialog box, select a digital signature from the list, and then click OK to return to the Digital Signature dialog box.

6. Confirm your selection, and then click OK.

CHAPTER 30

Employing VBA for More Sophisticated Automation

Using the Visual Basic Editor   **761**

Designing forms   **772**

Creating new modules   **772**

Writing statements   **773**

Creating procedures   **777**

Understanding objects   **779**

Debugging your program   **780**

Editing prerecorded macros   **781**

Adding functionality and creating new macros   **784**

To add sophisticated automation to your Word documents, you have to move beyond simple macro recording. Word 2000 includes a true programming language—Visual Basic for Applications—that you can use to add power to your macros and create fully functional add-ins and applications.

Although it's impossible to learn how to program in a single chapter, this chapter will help you understand how Visual Basic for Applications works, and how you can employ it within your Word documents.

Understanding Visual Basic for Applications

Visual Basic for Applications (VBA) is a variant of Microsoft's Visual Basic programming language. VBA 6, the version included with Word 2000, is a full-featured programming language, optimized for working within Microsoft applications. If you're familiar with Visual Basic, you'll be very comfortable programming in VBA.

Note that VBA isn't exclusive to Microsoft Word; it's also included with other Microsoft Office 2000 programs, including Microsoft Excel and Microsoft PowerPoint. You can use VBA to create programs that work within and between all of the Office applications.

Like any programming language, VBA is used to create *programs* (called *projects* by VBA). Each Word document or template is a separate project.

A VBA project consists of multiple elements—objects, modules, forms, and references to other documents or templates. Each element contains multiple lines of programming *code,* in the form of *statements* and *procedures.* Each statement is a specific instruction that is executed when the entire program is run.

The "Visual" part of Visual Basic for Applications indicates that VBA is a *visual* programming language, meaning that you don't have to type each line of code. Instead, you can use buttons from a control Toolbox to draw visual elements (such as buttons and lists) on a form; the VBA engine automatically generates the code that creates these objects. In many ways, writing a VBA program—or at least the *framework* for a program—is as easy as drawing objects in the workspace and then adding code that defines each object's behavior.

To create a VBA program, you use the *Visual Basic Editor* (VB Editor). The VB Editor is a program separate from Word that includes the menus, toolbars, and commands necessary to create a full-featured VBA program.

 NOTE This chapter provides only a brief overview of Visual Basic for Applications. For more in-depth information, check out Sybex's *Mastering Visual Basic 6,* available wherever computer books are sold. You should also consult the VB Editor's Help system (select Help ➢ Microsoft Visual Basic Help) for both conceptual and how-to help—including a comprehensive Visual Basic Language Reference.

Using the Visual Basic Editor

The VB Editor is a programming environment where you can create and edit VBA programs. Within the VB Editor workspace (shown in Figure 30.1), there are various windows, each with a different function. For example, you use the Code window to enter the VBA code; you use the Project Explorer to navigate between and display various projects and project components.

PART
XIII

Creating Automated
Documents

FIGURE 30.1
Use the Visual Basic Editor to edit Word macros and write full-fledged VBA programs.

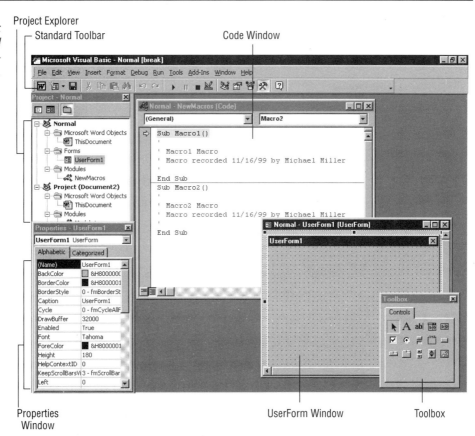

Project Explorer
Standard Toolbar
Code Window
Properties Window
UserForm Window
Toolbox

You launch the VB Editor from within Word by following these steps:

1. Open the document that contains the macros you want to edit.

2. Select Tools ➢ Macro ➢ Visual Basic Editor.

Understanding the VB Editor Workspace

Each separate window in the VB Editor has its own distinct function. The following sections show and describe the VB Editor windows.

Code Window

As shown in Figure 30.2, a Code window is used to write, display, and edit Visual Basic code. Each *module* in your program has its own Code window; you can display multiple Code windows on your Desktop simultaneously.

FIGURE 30.2
Use Code windows to write and edit code for your VBA modules.

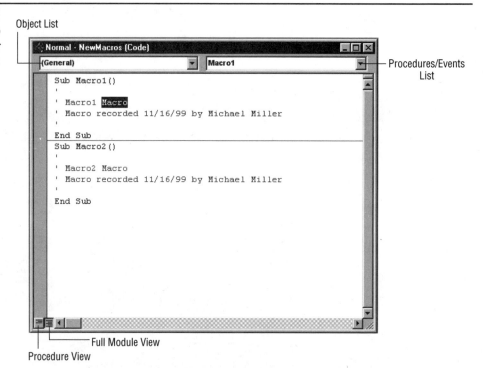

You open a Code window by using either of the following methods:

- Select a form or module in the Project window, then click the View Code button.
- Double-click a control or form in a UserForm window.

Within a Code window, you enter new lines of code (using your keyboard) or edit existing code. You can also insert prewritten lines of code by selecting objects from the Object list or events from the Procedures/Events list.

TIP To view the code for only the selected procedure, click the Procedure View button. To view all the code in the module, click the Full Module View button.

Project Explorer

The Project Explorer displays all the projects (programs or documents) currently open, and all the items contained within and referenced by each project. Figure 30.3 shows the contents of a typical Project Explorer, with multiple projects open.

PART
XIII

Creating Automated
Documents

FIGURE 30.3
View all your projects–
and their contents–
from the Project
Explorer.

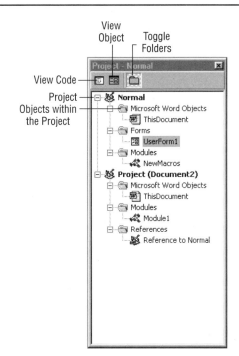

The contents of the Project Explorer are displayed in a hierarchical tree. You can choose to display the contents of each project alphabetically or organized by type of object by clicking the Toggle Folders button on or off.

To display the Code window for an object, select the object and then click the View Code button in the Project Explorer.

To display the object itself—which could be a dialog box, a message box, or even a complete document—select the object and then click the View Object button.

Object Browser

The Object Browser, shown in Figure 30.4, displays all the *available* objects in your project—even those not currently in use. You display the browser by first selecting a module within a project, then clicking the Object Browser button on the VB Editor's Standard toolbar. (You can also display the Object Browser by pressing F2.)

FIGURE 30.4
Use the Object Browser to view the properties, methods, and events in your project.

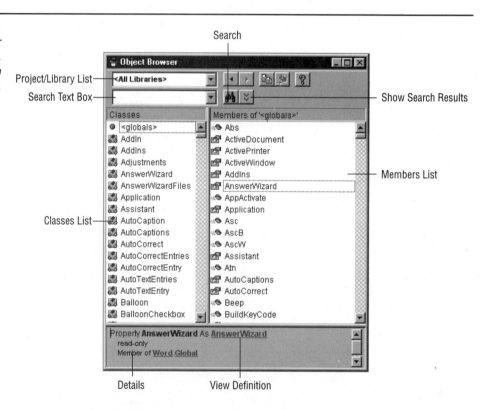

Once the Object Browser is displayed, select the name of the object class library you want to view from the Project/Library list; select <All Libraries> to view all available libraries. All the object classes within the project are displayed in the Classes list; if the selected object class is being used in an open project, that class appears in bold.

When you select an object class, the available functions for that class are displayed in the Members list. Functions that are being used in an open project appear in bold; information for a selected function is displayed in the Details section, at the bottom of the browser.

To view *where* the selected function is used in a project, select the item in the Members list and click the View Definition button. The VB Editor will display the Code window for the module or form that includes the selected object and function, with the cursor positioned at the start of the applicable code.

You can search for a particular object class or function by entering a string in the Search Text box, then clicking the Search button. The results of your search are shown in a separate Search Results pane; click the Show Search Results/Hide Search Results button to show or hide this pane.

Toolbox

The Toolbox, shown in Figure 30.5, displays the standard Visual Basic controls, plus any ActiveX controls and objects that have been added to the current project. You use the Toolbox to insert controls and objects into your project.

PART

XIII

Creating Automated Documents

FIGURE 30.5
Use the Toolbox to insert controls into your project.

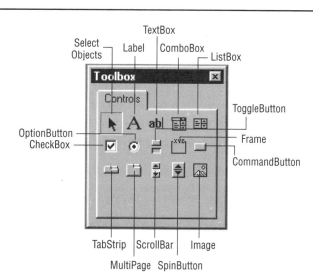

You can customize the Toolbox by adding additional controls and objects. To customize the Toolbox, follow these steps:

1. Select Tools ➢ Additional Controls to display the Additional Controls dialog box.

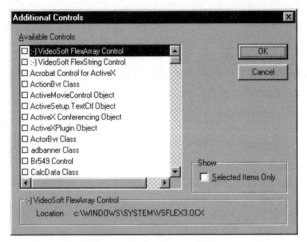

2. Check the controls you want to add to the Toolbox.

3. Click OK.

The standard controls available in the Toolbox include:

Select Objects   This button isn't a control per se; you click this button to select controls already drawn on a form.

Label   Places nonactionable text on a form.

TextBox   Inserts a box for user text input.

ComboBox   Inserts a combination list and text box.

ListBox   Inserts a list of selectable items.

CheckBox   Inserts a box that users can check to indicate a selection; users can select more than one check box in a group, because check boxes are *not* mutually exclusive.

OptionButton   Inserts a selectable button (it looks like a round check box) that forces a single user selection from a group of choices; unlike check boxes, Option-Buttons *are* mutually exclusive.

ToggleButton   Inserts a button that toggles on and off between states or options.

Frame   Inserts a frame that enables you to group controls within your form; to group controls, draw the frame first and then draw controls inside the frame.

CommandButton   Inserts a button that users click to execute a command.

TabStrip   Creates tabs within a dialog box.

MultiPage   Creates multiple *pages* within a dialog box.

ScrollBar   Inserts a scroll bar within a long list or large text box.

SpinButton   Inserts the up and down arrows necessary for users to click their way up and down a range of values.

Image   Inserts a graphical image from a picture file.

Properties Window

The Properties window, shown in Figure 30.6, lists the properties and their current settings for the selected object. Properties are listed either alphabetically (on the Alphabetic tab) or by category (on the Categorized tab). You display the Properties window by selecting an object, then clicking the Properties Window button on the Standard toolbar.

FIGURE 30.6
Change an object's properties in the Properties window.

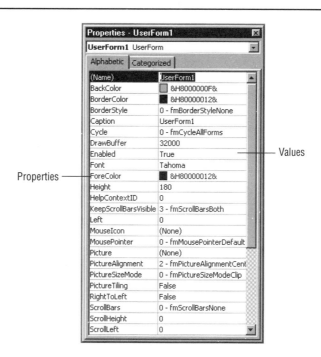

Properties

Values

To change the value for a specific property, select that property in the left column, then enter the value in the right column.

UserForm Window

A UserForm window displays visually the forms or dialog boxes within your project. Display the UserForm window for an object by selecting the object in the Project Explorer, then clicking the View Object button.

You also use UserForm windows to draw new forms and boxes; click buttons on the Toolbox to add controls to a form. Use the background grid to align objects and controls on the form.

Figure 30.7 shows a dialog box displayed in a UserForm window.

FIGURE 30.7

Use a UserForm window to draw new forms and dialog boxes.

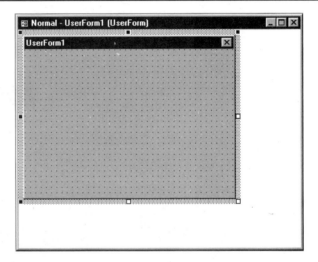

Immediate Window

You use the Immediate window to test lines of code without running an entire program. You type or paste code into the Immediate window, then the VB Editor executes the code.

To display the Immediate window, select View ➢ Immediate Window (or press Ctrl+G). To execute code in the Immediate window, enter a line of code, then press Enter.

NOTE The Immediate window also displays debugging output while a program is running.

Locals Window

The Locals window displays all the declared variables in the current procedure, along with their values. You display the Locals window by selecting View ➢ Locals Window.

Within the window, the Expression column lists the names of the variables; the Value column lists the value of the variables; and the Type column lists the type of the variables. Click the Call Stack button to display the Call Stack dialog box, which lists the procedures in the call stack.

Watch Window

The Watch window is displayed automatically when watch expressions are defined within your project. The Expression column lists the watch expressions; the Value column lists the value of the expression; the Type column lists the type of expression; and the Context column lists the context of the watch expression. You might see this window when you're debugging your programs within the VB Editor.

 NOTE Both the Locals and the Watch windows are less frequently used parts of the VB Editor workspace.

Understanding VB Editor Toolbars

Within the VB Editor workspace, several toolbars contain the most frequently used commands. All of the commands on the toolbars are also available from the pull-down menus.

Standard Toolbar

The Standard toolbar, which is always displayed at the top of the VB Editor workspace, contains buttons for the most frequently used menu items. The Standard toolbar is shown in Figure 30.8.

FIGURE 30.8
Use the Standard toolbar to execute most common procedures.

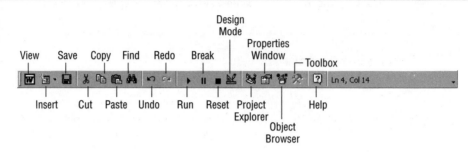

Edit Toolbar

The Edit toolbar is used when you're editing code in a Code window. You display the toolbar, shown in Figure 30.9, by selecting View ➤ Toolbars ➤ Edit.

FIGURE 30.9
Use the Edit toolbar when you're editing code.

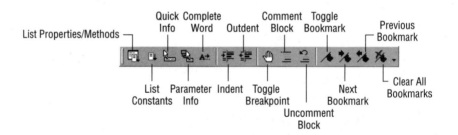

UserForm Toolbar

The UserForm toolbar, shown in Figure 30.10, is used when you're designing a form in a UserForm window. To display the UserForm toolbar, select View ➤ Toolbars ➤ UserForm.

FIGURE 30.10
Use the UserForm toolbar when you're editing or designing a new form or dialog box.

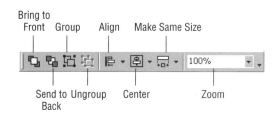

Debug Toolbar

The Debug toolbar is used when you're debugging your VBA code. You display this toolbar, shown in Figure 30.11, by selecting View ➢ Toolbars ➢ Debug.

FIGURE 30.11
Use the Debug toolbar when it's time to debug your code.

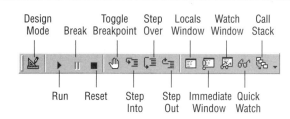

Writing Programs with VBA

Now that you know your way around the VB Editor workspace, it's time to learn the basics of Visual Basic programming.

In VBA, a complete program is called a *project,* and contains *forms* and *modules.* Both forms and modules contain their own programming code. An individual line of code is called a *statement;* a group of statements, executed together, is called a *procedure.*

When you run a program, the statements and procedures within the modules are executed, in order, and appropriate forms (representing dialog boxes and the like) are displayed as they're called from within the modules.

You can start a new project by creating a form and then programming modules around the form, or by creating a module and then adding forms and other modules to that module. All the modules and forms for a project are listed in the Project Editor and have their own individual Code windows. Within the Code windows, you'll find the statements and procedures that comprise the code for that module or form (or control).

PART
XIII

Creating Automated
Documents

Designing Forms

In VBA, anything you see onscreen—windows, dialog boxes, message boxes, and the like—is a form. Forms are displayed in UserForm windows and programmed via corresponding Code windows.

Creating a New Form

You create a new form by following these steps:

1. From within your project, select Insert ➤ UserForm.
2. When the new UserForm window appears, resize the form as necessary.
3. Double-click the form to display the form's Code window; enter the appropriate code for the form.

Adding Controls to Your Form

Forms contain *controls,* such as buttons, lists, and check boxes. Each control on a form is programmed via its own Code window.

To add controls to your form, follow these steps:

1. Display the form you want to edit in the UserForm window; the Toolbox should also be visible.
2. Click the button on the Toolbox for the control you want to add.
3. Use your mouse to draw and position the control on your form.
4. Use the commands on the UserForm toolbar to align the controls on your form.
5. Double-click a control to display that control's Code window, where you enter the code for that control.

Creating New Modules

A *module* is a set of declarations, followed by procedures. The declaration sets the stage for what follows (by defining objects, elements, and variables), while the procedure is the instruction set for what happens when the code is executed.

Types of Modules

VBA includes two different types of modules:

Standard Module   This module contains procedure, type, and data declarations and definitions.

Class Module   A class module contains the definition of a *class,* including its property and method definitions.

NOTE A *class* defines the properties of an object and the methods used to control the object's behavior.

Inserting a Module in Your Project

To create a new module, follow these steps:

1. From within your project, select either Insert ➤ Module (to create a standard module) or Insert ➤ Class Module (to insert a class module).

2. The VB Editor displays a Code window for your new module. Enter the module's code (in the form of statements and procedures) in this window.

Writing Statements

The core of a program is the programming *code*. In VBA, each line of code is called a *statement*. A statement is a complete instruction and can indicate an action, define a variable, or declare a new object.

 NOTE A statement is typically entered on a single line, although you can use a colon (:) to include more than one statement on a line. You can also use a *line-continuation character* (_) to continue a long statement on a second line.

Statements can contain keywords, operators, variables, constants, and expressions. You enter statements in Code windows, either by typing the code manually or by inserting pieces of code from the Objects or Procedures/Events lists. When a program is executed, the code is executed sequentially, one statement at a time.

 WARNING If you press Enter after entering a line of code and the line is displayed in *red*, there is an error somewhere in your statement.

In VBA, statements fall into one of three categories:

Declaration Statements These statements introduce variables, constants, or procedures into your project (called *naming* an item), or specify data types.

Assignment Statements These statements assign a value or expression to a variable or constant.

Executable Statements These statements initiate actions—such as executing a method or function. They can loop or branch through blocks of code and often contain mathematical or conditional operators.

Each type of statement is described in more detail in the following sections.

 TIP You can also enter *comments* into your code, so others examining your code can understand what you were trying to accomplish. A comment is essentially a statement that doesn't execute; Visual Basic ignores comment lines when executing the program's code. Comment lines begin with an apostrophe (') or with the word Rem (followed by a space). By default, comments are displayed in a Code window as green text.

MASTERING THE OPPORTUNITIES

All the Words in Code: Keywords, Variables, Constants, Operators, and Expressions

All VBA statements are comprised of some combination of *keywords, variables, constants,* and *expressions.*

A *keyword* is a word that is reserved for use because it has a special meaning within VBA. Keywords can be commands or parameters and include words such as For, Date, Else, False, and Next. You can't use a keyword as the name of a variable or constant.

A *variable* is actually a *location*—think of it as an empty shoebox—within your program that can contain any type of data. What goes into the shoebox is defined during the execution of your program and can change over the course of the program, based on executed events. Each variable is identified by a unique name.

A *constant* is an item that retains a constant value throughout the execution of a program. A constant can be a *string* (a combination of alphanumeric characters), a number, another constant, or any combination that includes arithmetic or logical operators. A constant is named and defined on first use within a program.

An *operator* is a word or symbol that represents a specific action or evaluation of numbers and text. For example, the + operator signifies addition; the Not operator is used to perform logical negation.

An *expression* is a combination of variables, constants, keywords, and operators that yields a string, number, or object. Expressions are used to perform calculations, manipulate characters, or test data within your program.

Declaration Statements

Declaration statements are used to name and define procedures, variables, constants, and arrays. When you declare an item, you also define its scope.

 NOTE An array is a series of objects, all of which are the same size and type—in other words, the elements of a list.

The following statement declares the variable Bob to be an integer:

```
Dim Bob As Integer
```

The following keywords can be used to declare items in VBA statements:

- Const
- Dim
- Private
- Public
- ReDim
- Static

Assignment Statements

Assignment statements assign a value or expression to a variable or constant. Assignment statements always include an equal sign (=).

The following statement assigns the value *32* to the variable Joe:

```
Joe = 32
```

Although you can use the Let and Set keywords within an assignment statement (as in Let Joe = 32), more often than not the keywords are omitted.

Executable Statements

An executable statement initiates action and often executes a method or function.

In the following statement, the MsgBox statement is executed (with the message "Operation Completed" displayed):

```
MsgBox "Operation Completed"
```

PART

XIII

Creating Automated
Documents

Decision Statements

A decision statement is a specific subcategory of executable statements. Decision statements contain conditional operators, such as If, Then, and Else, and execute actions if certain conditions are met.

The most common form of decision statement is the If...Then...Else statement. You create a series of statements—actually, a complete *procedure* (see the next section)—that executes a series of actions *if* the first statement is true. If the first statement *isn't* true, the actionable statements are skipped, and Visual Basic skips to the next statement or procedure.

Here is an example of a procedure utilizing an If...Then...Else statement:

```
Sub MakeLabel(value as Long)
    If value = 0 Then
        LabelOne.Font.Bold = True
        LabelOne.Font.Italic = True
    End If
End Sub
```

In this procedure, the font settings are set to bold and italics only if the value is equal to zero; if the value is any other number, the two embedded statements are skipped, and the program proceeds to the next block of code.

Other decision statements include Do...Loop, For Each...Next, and For...Next.

MASTERING THE OPPORTUNITIES

Understanding Syntax

Each type of statement within VBA—and there are over 70 documented statements—has its own *syntax* that must be followed precisely. Think of syntax as the grammar of a statement, the exact wording that controls how Visual Basic interprets the statement.

For example, the Dim statement (which declares a variable) uses the following syntax:

```
Dim [WithEvents]varname[([subscripts])] [As [New] type] [,
[WithEvents]varname[([subscripts])] [As [New]type]] . . .
```

Continued ▶

In this syntax, everything within a set of brackets ([]) is optional, making the only required elements the keyword `Dim` and the name of the variable (*varname*). So it would be proper syntax to write the statement:

```
Dim Mike
```

In this statement, the variable `Mike` is named—and that's it. However, you can also use the optional syntax for the `Dim` statement to specify how the variable responds to events triggered by an ActiveX object (`WithEvent`); to name dimensions within an array (*subscript*); to define `New` objects; and to define the *type* of variable. Whichever part of the statement you use, you have to follow the precise syntax—or Visual Basic won't know what you're talking about.

The syntax for each statement is listed in the Visual Basic Language Reference, which is part of the VB Editor's Help system. Select Help ➤ Microsoft Visual Basic Help to display the Help window, select the Contents tab, select the Visual Basic Language Reference, then open the Statements section to display an A-to-Z listing of all VBA statements.

VBA also includes a syntax-checking feature that checks each statement—as you enter it—for syntax errors and alerts you of any error. To enable VBA's syntax checking, select Tools ➤ Options to display the Options dialog box, select the Editor tab, and then check the Auto Syntax Check option.

Creating Procedures

A *procedure* is a group of statements that are executed as a unit. Procedures are called by name; a procedure name is always defined at the module level.

 WARNING All executable code for a procedure must be contained within the procedure; procedures can't be nested within other procedures.

A procedure is contained within on and off statements. For example, you start a Sub procedure with a Sub statement and end it with an End Sub statement, as follows:

```
Sub subname()
    statement
    statement
    statement
End Sub
```

PART

XIII

Creating Automated
Documents

Types of Procedures

The three types of procedures are as follows:

Sub   Performs a specific task, but doesn't return a value (like a macro)

Function   Performs a specific task and *does* return a value (like a formula)

Property   Creates and manipulates custom properties for forms and modules

Coding a Procedure by Hand

To manually create a procedure within a Code window, follow these steps:

1. Display the Code window for the module that will contain the procedure.

2. Type **Sub**, **Function**, or **Property**.

 TIP   To display the syntax for a given procedure, press F1.

3. Type the code for the procedure, using as many different statements as necessary.

4. The VB Editor will automatically conclude the procedure with the appropriate End Sub, End Function, or End Property statement.

Creating a Procedure with the Add Procedure Dialog Box

You can also use the Add Procedure dialog box to create a procedure:

1. Display the Code window for the module that will contain the procedure.

2. Select Insert ➤ Procedure to display the Add Procedure dialog box.

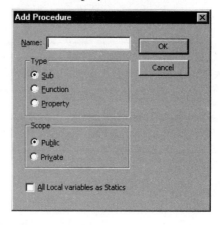

3. Enter the name of the procedure in the Name box.

4. Select what type of procedure you're adding (Sub, Function, or Property).

5. Select whether this is a Public or Private procedure.

6. Click OK.

Understanding Objects

An *object* is an element within an application, such as a bookmark, a footnote, or a style within Word. All the available objects in the current project are displayed in the Object Browser.

 NOTE An *object library* is a file (with an .OLB extension) that provides information to Visual Basic about available objects. You can use the Object Browser to examine the contents of an object library to get information about the objects provided.

Object Collections

All like objects within a project are called a *collection;* for example, the Styles object contains all styles used in a Word document. You can identify items in a collection by name or by number, such as *Styles(2)* to refer to the second style in a document.

Object Classes

The formal definition of an object is called a *class*. The class defines the properties of the object and the methods used to control the object's behavior.

Object Properties

All objects have specific *properties*. A property defines one of the object's characteristics (size, color, location, and so on) or behaviors (whether it is enabled, visible, etc.). To change the way an object looks or acts, you change the value of the appropriate property.

To set the value of a property, follow the reference to an object with a period, the property name, an equal sign (=), and the new property value. For example, the following statement changes the caption of the Tom object by setting the Caption property:

```
Tom.Caption = "I'm Tom!"
```

Object Events

An *event* is an action recognized by an object, such as clicking the mouse. Events can occur as a result of a user action or a specific procedure.

Object Methods

A *method* is an action that the object itself can perform. For example, the ComboBox object can perform the Add method, which adds a new entry to a ComboBox.

Debugging Your Program

Once your program or macro is written, it's time to determine whether it works as planned. The best way to do this is to run the program.

Running Your Program or Macro

You can run both freestanding programs and macros from within the VB Editor. To run a macro, select Run ➢ Run Macro. If, instead, you want to run a UserForm, select the UserForm window and choose Run ➢ Run Sub/UserForm. If you want to run the code within a Code window, place the cursor in a procedure and select Run ➢ Sub/UserForm; the current procedure will be executed.

Stepping through Your Code

If something doesn't run right, you need to *debug* the code you've written. The easiest way to do this is to *step* through the code, line by line. You perform this and other debugging operations from the Debug toolbar (select View ➢ Toolbars ➢ Debug).

To step through your code, follow these steps:

1. Select the macro or program code you want to debug.
2. Click the Step Into button on the Debug toolbar (or press F8).
3. The VB Editor executes the first line of code. If this line runs properly, click the Step Into button (or press F8) again to run the next line.
4. Repeat step 3 until you encounter the line that *doesn't* run; edit the line to fix the error.

You can also choose to run entire procedures rather than individual statements; press the Step Over button to run the next full procedure in the Code window.

Using VBA with Word Macros

Your most likely use of VBA will be to edit macros you've recorded from within Word. You can use the VB Editor to fix any errors introduced when you recorded a macro, clean up the sometimes sloppy code generated by the Macro Recorder, and add enhanced functionality to your macros. You can also use the VB Editor to create macros from scratch—such as creating a macro to display a message box or dialog box for a Word form.

Editing Prerecorded Macros

The Macro Recorder can record just about any action you can perform from within Word. But what do you do when you don't record a perfect performance? You *could* rerecord the macro from scratch, but it may be easier to open the VB Editor and make a few small edits to the underlying macro code.

Fixing Macro Errors

When you record a macro with the Macro Recorder, Word automatically generates the underlying code associated with your actions. It's very easy to find any errors in this code and then edit or delete the offending statements.

To edit prerecorded macro code, follow these steps:

1. From within Word, open the document or template that contains the macro you want to edit.

2. Select Tools ➢ Macro ➢ Macros to display the Macros dialog box.

3. Select the macro you want to edit from the Macro Name list.

4. Click the Edit button.

5. Word launches the Visual Basic Editor, with the Code window for the selected macro open in the workspace.

6. Locate the statement you want to edit and make the appropriate changes.

 TIP If you're not sure which statement is incorrect, display the Debug toolbar and click the Step Into button to run the macro one line at a time.

An error in a statement may be something that you did incorrectly when you recorded the macro; that is, the statement may be syntactically correct, but it performs an undesired action. This can happen when you press the wrong key or select the wrong option when recording a macro.

You may also find that you performed unnecessary actions when recording the macro. If this is the case, you can delete those statements corresponding to the unnecessary actions.

Removing Unnecessary Properties

If you record a macro that involves selecting an option in a dialog box, the macro recorder records the settings of *all* the options in the dialog box—even if you changed only *some* of the options. This introduces a lot of unnecessary code to your macro, because you need only those statements relating to *changed* options.

You can use the VB Editor to delete these unnecessary statements.

 TIP In some cases, changing options in text already formatted with nondefault settings will result in the recorded macro reapplying the *default* settings to the selected text. The only way to fix this is to delete those statements that reset options back to their default settings.

The following example includes a number of statements reflecting option settings in the Paragraph dialog box:

```
Sub Macro1()
With Selection.ParagraphFormat
    .LeftIndent = InchesToPoints(0)
    .RightIndent = InchesToPoints(0)
    .SpaceBefore = 6
    .SpaceAfter = 6
    .LineSpacingRule = 0
    .Alignment = wdAlignParagraphLeft
    .WidowControl = True
    .KeepWithNext = False
    .KeepTogether = False
    .PageBreakBefore = False
    .NoLineNumber = False
    .Hyphenation = True
    .FirstLineIndent = InchesToPoints(0)
    .OutlineLevel = 10
End With
End Sub
```

If all you did was change the left and right indent settings, you can delete all the other statements, resulting in the following more compact code:

```
Sub MyMacro()
With Selection.ParagraphFormat
    .LeftIndent = InchesToPoints(0)
    .RightIndent = InchesToPoints(0)
End With
End Sub
```

The shorter macro runs faster, because Word doesn't have to go through and "set" all those settings that don't actually change.

Removing Unnecessary Arguments

Word's Macro Recorder also records all the arguments included with a method, even if those arguments aren't actually used. You can use the VB Editor to delete those unnecessary statements that recorded unused arguments.

Take, for example, the Open method—the actions undertaken when you open a document. In this example, the macro recorded the opening of the document Test.doc, resulting in this code:

```
Sub Macro1()
Documents.Open FileName:="C:\My Documents\Test.doc", _
    ConfirmConversions:= False, ReadOnly:=False, _
    AddToRecentFiles:=False, PasswordDocument:="", _
    PasswordTemplate:="", Revert:=False, _
    WritePasswordDocument:="", _
    WritePasswordTemplate:="", Format:=wdOpenFormatAuto
End Sub
```

Examining this code, you'll see that any argument set to an empty string (" ") was *not* used when the document was opened. (In this example, none of the password-related arguments were used.) You can delete any statement containing an empty string, resulting in this more compact code:

```
Sub MyMacro()
Documents.Open FileName:="C:\My Documents\Test.doc", _
    ConfirmConversions:= False, _
    ReadOnly:=False, AddToRecentFiles:=False, _
    Revert:=False, Format:=wdOpenFormatAuto
End Sub
```

This revised macro will open a document more quickly than the previous macro did.

Adding Functionality and Creating New Macros

There are some operations you simply can't record with the Macro Recorder. Say, for example, you want to add a message box to a Word form that is displayed when the user completes the form—just how do you do that with the Macro Recorder?

The answer is, of course, that you can't. But you *can* create this type of macro from within the VB Editor and then incorporate the macro code into your document or template.

Adding a Message Box

One of the easiest nonrecordable objects you can add to your documents is a message box. In its simplest form, a message box pops up into the Word workspace and displays a prewritten message; you can also create message boxes that include buttons that initiate other operations.

A message box is added with the MsgBox function. The syntax for this function is as follows:

```
MsgBox(prompt[, buttons] [, title] [, helpfile, context])
```

Remember that anything in square brackets ([]) is optional.

The simplest procedure for adding a message box ignores all the optional elements, as in the following example:

```
Sub Nurse()
    MsgBox ("Hello, Nurse!")
End Sub
```

This creates a macro named Nurse and displays the simple message box shown in Figure 30.12; the OK button is added automatically, so that the user has some way of closing the dialog box.

FIGURE 30.12
Use the MsgBox function to create a simple message box.

Of course, you can also create message boxes that are more complex. The following example uses a number of variables and keywords to create a dialog box with Yes and No buttons that perform discrete actions:

```
Sub ExampleOne()
    Dim Msg, Style, Title, File, Response, MyString
    Msg = "Do you want to continue?"
    Style = vbYesNo + vbDefaultButton2
    Title = "Make a Choice"
    File = "NEW.DOC"
    Response = MsgBox(Msg, Style, Title, File, Ctxt)
    If Response = vbYes Then
        MyString = "Yes"
    Else
        MyString = "No"
    End If
End Sub
```

The resultant message box, shown in Figure 30.13, gives the user the option of continuing (by pressing Yes) or not (by pressing No). When the Yes button is pressed, the file NEW.DOC is opened. Note that the vbYesNo and vbDefaultButton2 options in the Style statement define the type of buttons displayed in the message box, and that the variable Msg is used to represent the message displayed in the box.

FIGURE 30.13

A message box with a Yes/No option

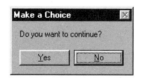

Adding a Dialog Box

Although message boxes can accept simple push-button input, if you want text input or other selections from your users, you have to create a custom dialog box.

Creating a dialog box is a more complex procedure than creating a message box. In general, here's what you have to do:

1. Select Insert ➢ UserForm to create a new UserForm.

2. Use the commands in the Toolbox to add controls to your new UserForm.

3. From the Properties window, set the properties for each control in the form.

4. From the UserForm's Code window, initialize each control.

5. Still in the Code window, write event procedures for each control to specify what actions are initiated when certain events (such as clicking a button) occur.

6. Display and test your code.

 NOTE Depending on the type of dialog box you want to create, there may already be a VBA function that creates it automatically. For example, the InputBox function creates a dialog box with a text-box control for user input—with a single line of code.

Making Macros Run Automatically

So far we've discussed macros that run when initiated by some sort of user action—when a user deliberately presses a button or shortcut key, or in response to a user action on a form or in a document. There are five types of macros, however, that run automatically, regardless of user action, when you open or close Word or Word documents.

Running an Automatic Macro—Automatically

Word recognizes five automatic macros, as follows:

AutoExec   Runs when you start Word or load a global template

AutoExit   Runs when you quit Word or unload a global template

AutoNew   Runs each time you create a new document

AutoOpen   Runs each time you open an existing document

AutoClose   Runs each time you close a document

When you assign one of these names to a macro, the macro will run automatically under its specified conditions. It's best to store these automatic macros in the Normal template, although all but AutoExec will run if stored in the active template or document.

Stopping an Automatic Macro from Running

You can prevent an automatic macro from running by pressing the Shift key when performing an operation that might trigger the automatic macro. For example, to prevent the AutoNew macro from running, press the Shift key when you click the OK button in the New dialog box—and don't release the button until the new document is fully displayed.

To prevent the AutoExec macro from running when you first start Word, open the Properties dialog box for the shortcut you use to start Word (typically located on the Programs menu) and add the /m switch to the end of the target command.

To prevent triggering an automatic macro from within another macro, add the following statement to your code:

```
WordBasic.DisableAutoMacro
```

Putting It All Together: Creating a Macro for Inserting Data

To demonstrate some of VBA's basic features and principles, we'll end this chapter with a step-by-step example of coding a VBA macro that:

- Displays a dialog box

- Asks for user input

- Inserts data in your document based on that user input

Preparing the Macro

Before you write this macro, let's define what we want it to do:

- Ask the user which of two different preexisting e-mail addresses he or she wants to use in a letter.

- Ask the user if he or she wants to insert a different e-mail address in the letter.

- Based on the user response, insert the appropriate e-mail address or addresses in the new document.

In general, what we need to do is this:

1. Open the template to which we'll attach the macro.
2. Open the VB Editor.
3. Create a macro named EmailAddresses.
4. Define the two different e-mail addresses we want to insert.
5. Create a dialog box containing check boxes for each of the predefined e-mail addresses, as well as a text box for a third, user-entered e-mail address.
6. Write a procedure (using If...Then statements) to insert the chosen (or entered) e-mail addresses into the current document.

You can start this operation by selecting Tools ➤ Macro ➤ Visual Basic Editor to open the Visual Basic Editor.

Creating the Form

From within the Visual Basic Editor, select the Normal project in the Project Explorer. Next you'll want to create the dialog box that you'll use in this macro, so select Insert ➤ UserForm. This opens a blank UserForm window on your Desktop and displays the Toolbox.

Before you add controls to this form, you need to set two of the form's properties. Select the form, then click the Properties Window button on the Standard toolbar to display the Properties dialog box, as shown in Figure 30.14. Change the (Name) property to **EmailBox** and the Caption property to **Choose an E-Mail Address.**

FIGURE 30.14

Use the Properties window to set the name and caption for your dialog box.

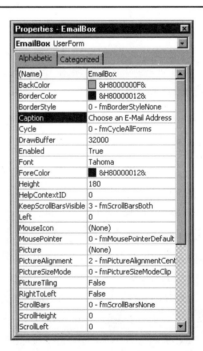

You want this dialog box to contain two check boxes, a text box, and a button (for entering the data). You also need to add a label above the text box to tell the user what to enter. Use the buttons in the Toolbox to draw these controls on your form, as shown in Figure 30.15.

FIGURE 30.15

Add check-box, text-box, and command-button controls to your dialog box.

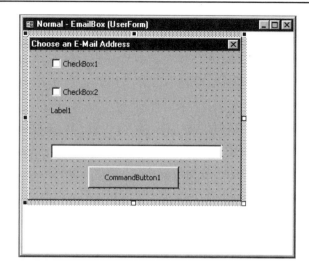

Next you have to set the Name and Caption properties for each of these controls. Select the Properties window for each of the controls and change the properties as shown in Table 30.1.

TABLE 30.1: PROPERTIES FOR EMAILBOX CONTROLS

Control	(Name)	Caption
CheckBox1	EmailAddress1	Insert Home E-Mail Address
CheckBox2	EmailAddress2	Insert Work E-Mail Address
Label1	EmailLabel	Enter Other E-Mail Address to Insert:
TextBox1	EmailAddress3	*N/A*
CommandButton1	EmailEnter	Insert Now

You can now rearrange the controls on the form, as necessary, as well as resize the entire dialog box to accommodate all the controls with as little wasted space as possible. You should now have a UserForm window that looks something like the one shown in Figure 30.16.

FIGURE 30.16
Your dialog box with renamed and recaptioned controls

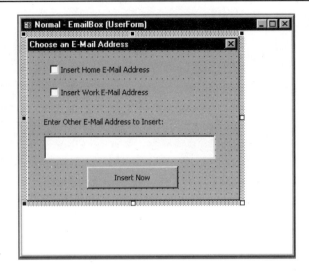

Writing the Code

Now that the form is created, you have to write the code that makes the form work when the macro is run.

Showing the Dialog Box

Begin by selecting the ThisDocument object for the Normal project (in the Project Explorer), then clicking the View Code button to display an empty Code window. We have to create a Sub procedure for this macro, which we want to name AutoOpen, so enter the following code in the window:

```
Sub EmailAddresses()


End Sub
```

Leave a blank line between the two lines of code.

To display the dialog box we just created, we enter the following statement into the code window, between the Sub and End Sub statements:

```
EmailBox.Show
```

Your completed code for this Code window looks like this:

```
Sub EmailAddresses()
    EmailBox.Show
End Sub
```

Making the Dialog Box Work

The bulk of your code will be associated with the dialog box UserForm itself. Double-click the Command button in the UserForm window to display the Code window for this UserForm. When this Code window opens, two lines of code are already entered:

```
Private Sub EmailEnter_Click()


End Sub
```

These statements create a procedure that executes all code entered between the statements when the button (named EmailEnter) in the dialog box is clicked.

Before we make anything happen within this procedure, we need to create and define variables for the three possible e-mail addresses. (It's easier to deal with short variable names in statements than it is to enter long strings of text.) We'll call the three variables Address1, Address2, and Address3, and define them with the following `Dim` statements:

```
Dim Address1 As String
Dim Address2 As String
Dim Address3 As String
```

Next, we'll assign values to the first two addresses; enter your own home and work addresses as appropriate:

```
Address1 = "mmiller@molehillgroup.com"
Address2 = "author@molehillgroup.com"
```

Now we're ready for the meat of the code. Your code needs to insert into your document the text associated with the variable when either of the check boxes is selected. You do this by creating an `If...Then` statement for each of the check boxes, using the TypeText method. Enter this code for the first check box:

```
If EmailAddress1 Then
    Selection.TypeText Text:=Address1
    Selection.TypeParagraph
End If
```

PART

XIII

Creating Automated
Documents

NOTE The TypeParagraph method inserts a line break after the inserted text; if you don't do this, all the text you insert will appear on the same line.

Enter the following code for the second check box:

```
If EmailAddress2 Then
    Selection.TypeText Text:=Address2
    Selection.TypeParagraph
End If
```

What do you do if the user enters a third e-mail address in the text box? You start by assigning any text entered into the EmailAddress3 text box to the Address2 variable, as follows:

```
Address3 = EmailAddress3.Text
```

Then you use the TypeText method to insert that variable text into your document:

```
Selection.TypeText Text:=Address3
Selection.TypeParagraph
```

 TIP This code inserts text at the insertion point in your Word document, using whatever text formatting is in place at the insertion point. You could use other Selection properties to format the text you're inserting; for example, Selection.Font.Bold = True turns on boldfacing for the subsequent text.

This completes the coding for your UserForm. The complete code should look like this:

```
Private Sub EmailEnter_Click()
    Dim Address1 As String
    Dim Address2 As String
    Dim Address3 As String
    Address1 = "mmiller@molehillgroup.com"
    Address2 = "author@molehillgroup.com"
    If EmailAddress1 Then
        Selection.TypeText Text:=Address1
        Selection.TypeParagraph
    End If
```

```
        If EmailAddress2 Then
            Selection.TypeText Text:=Address2
            Selection.TypeParagraph
        End If
        Address3 = EmailAddress3.Text
        Selection.TypeText Text:=Address3
        Selection.TypeParagraph
    End Sub
```

Assigning the Macro to a Keyboard Shortcut

With your code complete, you can return to Word and assign this macro to a keyboard shortcut. Follow these steps:

1. Select Tools ➤ Customize to display the Customize dialog box.

2. Click Keyboard to display the Customize Keyboard dialog box.

3. Select Macros from the Categories list, then select EmailAddresses.

4. Enter the desired keyboard shortcut keys in the Press New Shortcut Key box.

5. Click the Assign button.

6. Click the Close button.

Whenever you press the shortcut key combination, you'll display the dialog box shown in Figure 30.17; make your selections—your e-mail addresses will be entered into your current document automatically.

PART

XIII

Creating Automated
Documents

FIGURE 30.17

The result of your macro—a fully functional dialog box that inserts your e-mail addresses into the current document

Tips, Tricks, and Troubleshooting

- *Doing things you didn't know you could do*

- *Using Word with Office 2000*

- *Using the CD tools and utilities*

- *Finding help*

CHAPTER 31

Forty Things You Probably Didn't Know You Could Do in Word

Customizing the Word workspace   798

Editing and formatting text   804

Working with bullets and special characters   808

Proofing your documents   814

Creating fancy documents   816

Automating Word   823

Making Word more than a word processor   831

In the previous 30 chapters, you learned just about all there is to know about using Microsoft Word 2000. Now it's time to discover some little-known tips and tricks that will make you more productive, and will let you create neater-looking documents, than you would otherwise.

Customizing the Word Workspace

These tips help you personalize the way Word works, from creating your own personal menu to assigning new keyboard shortcuts.

Tip 1: Creating Your Own Personal Menu

You're used to the standard Word 2000 menus, but why limit yourself to these universal options? You can create your own personal pull-down menu, complete with your own selected operations and commands.

To create your own personal menu, follow these steps:

1. Select Tools ➤ Customize to display the Customize dialog box.

2. Select the Commands tab.

3. Select New Menu from the Categories list.

4. From the Commands list, drag the New Menu item to a position on Word's menu bar.

5. With the Customize dialog box still open (and the New Menu menu selected), click the Modify button to display the pop-up menu.

6. From the pop-up menu, enter a new Name for your menu.

7. With the Customize dialog box still open, select those commands you want on your new menu, and drag them to the menu label on the menu bar.

If you've created custom macros or have certain operations you perform over and over, add them to your custom menu for easier access. You can also create separate menus for each person using your PC; you can have a menu for yourself, one for your spouse, and one for each of your kids.

 NOTE To learn more about customizing Word's menus and toolbars, see Chapter 3.

Tip 2: Calculating Totals Anywhere in Your Documents

If you do a lot of number or table work in Word, you might long for a faster way to calculate a list of numbers than using the =(FORMULA) field, or a more versatile way than using the AutoSum command found on the Tables and Buttons toolbar. Fortunately, Word includes a hidden ToolsCalculate command that you can add to any toolbar and works anywhere within a document.

While the AutoSum button only works within a table, the ToolsCalculate command works in any text selection. All you have to do is select a series of numbers (separated by line breaks or by commas) and then activate the command; the sum of the selected numbers is displayed in the status bar and copied to the clipboard. You can then paste the total anywhere in your document by pressing Shift+Insert.

To add the ToolsCalculate command (as a button) to a toolbar, follow these steps:

1. Select Tools ➢ Customize to display the Customize dialog box.

2. Select the Commands tab.

3. Select All Commands from the Categories list.

4. From the Commands list, select the ToolsCalculate item, and drag it to the desired toolbar.

Once you've added this button to a toolbar, you can select any list of numbers and then click the ToolsCalculate button to calculate their total.

Tip 3: Viewing Your Styles while You Work

Throughout this document, you've seen screen shots of documents in Normal view (such as the one in Figure 31.1), each with a list of styles assigned to each paragraph. This list of styles is called the *style area*, and it's a great way for you to see at a glance the paragraph formatting within your document.

By default, Word does not display the style area. You can turn on the style area, however, by following these steps:

1. Select Tools ➢ Options to display the Options dialog box.

2. Select the View tab.

3. From the Style Area Width control, select a value greater than 0.

Once the style area is displayed, you can change its size by using your mouse to drag the divider line between the style area and your document text to a new position.

PART

IX

Tips, Tricks, and
Troubleshooting

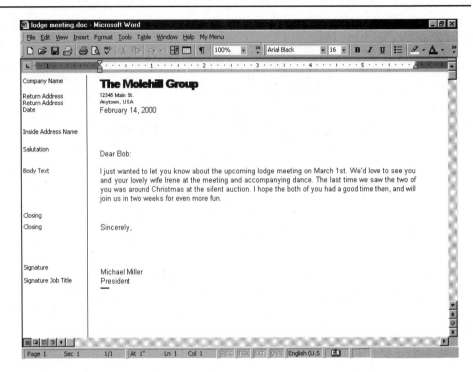

Tip 4: Customizing Keyboard Shortcuts from the Keyboard

As you learned in Chapter 3, you can create new keyboard shortcuts by opening the Customize dialog box, clicking the Keyboard button, and working within the Customize Keyboard dialog box. There's a faster way to assign shortcut keys, however, directly from your keyboard. Just follow these steps:

1. Press Ctrl+Alt++.

WARNING You have to press the "+" key on your numeric keypad; the + above the = won't work.

2. When the pointer changes to a four-leaf clover, click on the toolbar button or menu command that you want to assign to a shortcut key.

3. Word now opens the Customize Keyboard dialog box; enter the new shortcut keys in the Press New Shortcut Key box, click Assign, and then click Close.

 NOTE To learn more about Word's keyboard shortcuts, see Chapter 3.

Tip 5: Printing All Word Shortcut Key and Menu Assignments

To generate a list of all the commands in the current document, with corresponding shortcut key and menu assignments, follow these steps:

1. Select Tools ➤ Macro ➤ Macros to display the Macros dialog box.

2. Enter **ListCommands** in the Macro Name box.

3. When the List Commands dialog box appears, check either the Current Menu and Keyboard Settings option (to display only those commands assigned to menus or keyboard shortcuts) or the All Word Commands option (to display all commands).

4. Click Run.

Word now generates a document listing all your commands. To create a hard copy listing of these commands, print this document.

Tip 6: Showing Measurements in the Ruler

Although you can use your mouse to drag elements in either the horizontal or the vertical ruler (margins, indents, and tab stops), you're pretty much left to guess the precise measurements involved, unless, of course, you know this little Word secret.

When you drag any item in any ruler, hold down *both* mouse buttons and Word replaces the standard distance marks with measurements of the item being moved. As you can see in Figure 31.2, this is a much better way to ensure precise placement of margins, tabs, and paragraph indents.

PART

IX

Tips, Tricks, and Troubleshooting

FIGURE 31.2
Hold down both mouse buttons for precise ruler measurements.

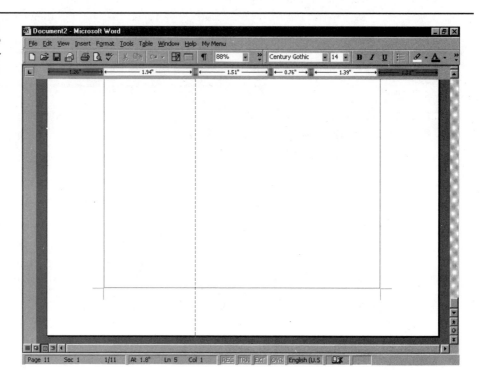

 NOTE To learn more about using Word's rulers, see Chapter 10.

Tip 7: Double-Clicking for Key Dialog Boxes

By now you're probably used to right-clicking your mouse on elements within your documents to display a pop-up menu of context-sensitive commands. You probably don't know, however, that you can double-click on areas of the Word workspace to display relevant dialog boxes.

For example, if you double-click in the empty margin areas on the left or right of the horizontal toolbar, you display the Page Setup dialog box. If you double-click on any tab on the ruler, you display the Tabs dialog box. If, in Normal view with the style area displayed, you double-click on any style name, you display the Style dialog box.

There are many more of these double-clicking "hot spots" hidden within Word; try to find more on your own!

Tip 8: Using Automatic Scrolling

You're probably used to using the up and down scroll bars to scroll back and forward through your document. If you do a lot of scrolling, however, you may want to automate your scrolling.

If you use a mouse with a thumbwheel, such as the Microsoft IntelliMouse, you can make your document scroll automatically by clicking the thumbwheel and then moving your mouse up (to scroll back) or down (to scroll forward). The more you move the mouse, the faster the document scrolls. You turn off the scrolling by clicking the left mouse button.

If you don't have a thumbwheel-equipped mouse, you can still automatically scroll through your documents, thanks to Word's built-in AutoScroll macro. Follow these steps to activate and use the AutoScroll macro:

1. Select Tools ➢ Macro ➢ Macros to display the Macros dialog box.

2. Select Word Commands from the Macros In list.

3. Select AutoScroll from the Macro Name list.

4. Click the Run button.

5. The vertical scrollbar will now change to look like the scrollbar in Figure 31.3, and your document will start scrolling. To select the direction of the scrolling, position the cursor either in the top half (to scroll up) or in the bottom half (to scroll down) of the vertical scrollbar. The farther you position the cursor from the middle of the scrollbar, the faster your document will scroll.

6. Stop scrolling by clicking the left mouse button.

 TIP If you find yourself using AutoScroll often, you should add this macro to one of Word's toolbars or menus, as described in Chapter 3.

FIGURE 31.3
Use the AutoScroll macro to automatically scroll through your document.

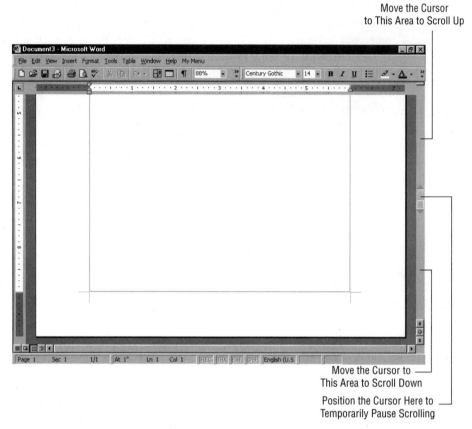

Move the Cursor
to This Area to Scroll Up

Move the Cursor to
This Area to Scroll Down

Position the Cursor Here to
Temporarily Pause Scrolling

Editing and Formatting Text

The tips in this section give you more power when you're editing and formatting the text in your Word documents.

Tip 9: Returning to Where You Left Off

When you reopen an existing document, Word automatically positions the insertion point at the beginning of the document. If you'd rather start where you stopped—your last editing point in your last session—press Shift+F5 after you reopen the document. The insertion point will then jump to where you left off the last time you edited the document.

Tip 10: Editing in Print Preview

 Most users use Word's Print Preview for a detailed look at how their document will look when printed. Fewer users know that Print Preview is an active editing view, which means you can actually edit your documents while you're viewing them in Print Preview!

 While you can edit at any time in Print Preview, you can't move the insertion point with your mouse until you turn off the Magnifier by toggling off the Magnifier button. With the Magnifier turned off, Print Preview acts exactly like any other Word view, and you can edit to your heart's content.

 NOTE To learn more about Word's Print Preview, see Chapter 7.

Tip 11: Copying Character and Paragraph Formatting

If you have a block of text formatted just right, with font type, size, color, and any other settings, you don't have to start from scratch when you want to apply the same formatting to another text block. You can use Word's Format Painter tool to "paint" the formatting from one text block to another.

Copying Character Formatting

Follow these steps to copy character formatting:

1. Select the text that contains the desired formatting.
2. Click the Format Painter button on Word's Standard toolbar.
3. Select the text that you want to format.

Copying Paragraph Formatting

Although you might know you can use Format Painter to copy character formatting, few users know you can use Format Painter to copy paragraph formatting. To copy the formatting of a paragraph (spacing, tabs, indents, alignment, and the like), *don't* select a block of text. Instead, just position the insertion point anywhere within the first paragraph, and then click the Format Painter button. Now use your mouse anywhere within the second paragraph, and click the mouse button.

 NOTE To learn more about character formatting, see Chapter 8; to learn more about paragraph formatting, see Chapter 9.

PART

IX

Tips, Tricks, and
Troubleshooting

Tip 12: Copying Formatting Over and Over

 Normally when you use the Format Painter tool, you can only copy a format once. To copy formatting multiple times, double-click the Format Painter button (instead of single-clicking it). You can now copy the formatting as many times as you want; click the Format Painter button again to turn off the operation.

Tip 13: Removing Formatting Quickly

To quickly remove character formatting from a section of text and return the text to that style's default attributes, follow these steps:

1. Select the text you want to unformat.

2. Press Ctrl+Spacebar.

To undo any changes to a paragraph's default format (including tabs, indents, spacing, and so on), position the insertion point anywhere within the paragraph, and then press Ctrl+Q.

Tip 14: Balancing Your Columns

When you're working with a multiple-column layout, Word completely fills one column with text before it wraps to the top of the next column. If you end up with a column only partially filled, your columns are unbalanced.

 NOTE You have to be in Print Layout view to properly view and edit columns in your documents.

To balance your columns—to align the bottoms of all columns on a page—you have to format that page as an individual section. To do this, follow these steps:

1. Position the insertion point at the end of the text in the last column.

2. Select Insert ➢ Break to display the Break dialog box.

3. Check the Continuous option in the Section Breaks section.

4. Click OK.

When Word inserts the section break, it also redistributes the columns within the first section so that they're all of equal length.

NOTE To learn more about working with multiple columns, see Chapter 10.

Tip 15: Sorting Non-table Text

You know that you can sort rows within a table by selecting Table ➤ Sort. But do you know that you can use this same command to sort other text within your document?

When you use the Sort command outside of a table, it sorts any selected text by paragraph. This means you can sort any number of contiguous paragraphs, including bulleted lists. To sort paragraphs within your document, follow these steps:

1. Select the paragraphs you want to sort.

2. Select Table ➤ Sort to display the Sort dialog box.

3. Make sure that Paragraphs is selected in the Sort By list.

4. Pull down the Type list, and select either Text, Number, or Date.

5. Check whether you're sorting in Ascending or Descending order.

6. Click OK.

 NOTE To learn more about working with tables, see Chapter 14.

Tip 16: Creating Links within and between Your Word Documents

As you learned in Chapter 24, you can use the Insert Hyperlink command to add Web page hyperlinks to your Word documents. It's also possible to use this command to add links to other Word documents on your computer or to other sections within your current Word document.

To insert a hyperlink to another Word document, follow these steps:

1. Select the text that will be linked.

 2. Click the Insert Hyperlink button on Word's Standard toolbar to display the Insert Hyperlink dialog box.

3. From the Places bar, select the Existing File or Web Page button.

4. Enter the location and name of the file you're linking to in the Link to File or Web Page Name box, or click the Recent Files button and select a file from the list, or click the File button to browse for the file.

5. Click OK.

Tips, Tricks, and
Troubleshooting

To insert a hyperlink to another section within your current document, follow these steps:

1. Select the text that will be linked.

2. Click the Insert Hyperlink button on Word's Standard toolbar to display the Insert Hyperlink dialog box.

3. From the Places bar, select the Place in This Document button.

4. From the Select a Place in This Document list, select the heading or bookmark you want to link to.

5. Click OK.

When users click one of these non-Web links, they jump to the document or to the selected heading or bookmark within the current document.

NOTE To learn more about inserting hyperlinks in Word documents, see Chapter 24.

Working with Bullets and Special Characters

All text doesn't have to be plain; sometimes you need to insert a special character or use a fancy bullet. Use the tips in this section to insert characters and symbols that are anything but plain!

Tip 17: Inserting Special Characters from the Keyboard with AutoCorrect

Typically, you insert special characters, such as the dollar sign, into your document by selecting Insert Symbol to display the Symbol dialog box and working from there. Certain frequently used characters, however, can be inserted directly from the keyboard *if* you have AutoCorrect configured properly.

To turn on this feature of AutoCorrect, follow these steps:

1. Select Tools ≻ AutoCorrect to display the AutoCorrect dialog box.

2. Select the AutoCorrect tab.

3. Check the Replace Text As You Type option.

4. Click OK.

Table 31.1 lists the AutoCorrect keyboard shortcuts for some of the more popular special characters.

TABLE 31.1: AUTOCORRECT KEYBOARD SHORTCUTS FOR SPECIAL CHARACTERS

Character	Type This
©	(c)
®	(r)
™	(tm)
… (ellipsis)	...
→	-->
←	<--
➔	==>
←	<==
⇔	<=>
☺	:)
☺	:|
☹	:(

Tip 18: Inserting Special Characters from the Keyboard with Character Codes

In addition to the AutoCorrect method of inserting special characters, there's another way to insert even more special characters and symbols directly from the keyboard. All you have to know is the character's *character code*. This is a four-digit number (starting with 0) that you enter by using the numeric keypad. When you press Alt in conjunction with the character code, the symbol or character is automatically inserted into your document.

For example, pressing Alt+0163 inserts the pound sign. Table 31.2 lists some of the more popular character codes you can use in your Word documents.

PART

IX

Tips, Tricks, and
Troubleshooting

TABLE 31.2: CHARACTER CODES FOR SPECIAL CHARACTERS AND SYMBOL

Character/Symbol	Type this
ƒ	Alt+0131
… (ellipsis)	Alt+0133
†	Alt+0134
‡	Alt+0135
ˆ	Alt+0136
‰	Alt+0137
Š	Alt+0138
‹	Alt+0139
Œ	Alt+0140
•	Alt+0149
– (en dash)	Alt+0150
— (em dash)	Alt+0151
˜	Alt+0152
™	Alt+0153
š	Alt+0154
›	Alt+0155
œ	Alt+0156
Ÿ	Alt+0159
¡	Alt+0161
¢	Alt+0162
£	Alt+0163
¤	Alt+0164
¥	Alt+0165
¦	Alt+0166
§	Alt+0167
©	Alt+0169
ª	Alt+0170

TABLE 31.2: CHARACTER CODES FOR SPECIAL CHARACTERS AND SYMBOL (CONTINUED)

Character/Symbol	Type this
«	Alt+0171
®	Alt+0174
°	Alt+0176
±	Alt+0177
²	Alt+0178
³	Alt+0179
´	Alt+0180
µ	Alt+0181
¶	Alt+0182
¹	Alt+0185
»	Alt+0187
1/4	Alt+0188
1/2	Alt+0189
3/4	Alt+0190
¿	Alt+0191
×	Alt+0215
÷	Alt+0247

TIP To select from a wide range of symbols and special characters, and to view their corresponding character codes, use the Windows Character Map utility. To launch Character Map, click the Windows Start button, and select Programs ➢ Accessories ➢ System Tools ➢ Character Map.

Tip 19: Inserting International Characters from the Keyboard

Certain international characters, such as accents, carets, and tildes, can be quickly inserted into your document by pressing the right combination of keys. Table 31.3 lists some of the more common international characters and their corresponding keyboard shortcuts.

PART

IX

Tips, Tricks, and
Troubleshooting

TABLE 31.3: KEYBOARD SHORTCUTS FOR INTERNATIONAL CHARACTERS

Character	Type This
à, è, ì, ò, ù, À, È, Ì, Ò, Ù	Ctrl+`, *letter*
á, é, í, ó, ú, ∆, Á, É, Í, Ó, Ú, ≈	Ctrl+', *letter*
â, ê, î, ô, û, Â, Ê, Î, Ô, Û	Ctrl+^, *letter*
ã, ñ, õ, Ã, Ñ, Õ	Ctrl+~, *letter*
ä, ë, ï, ö, ü, ÿ, Ä, Ë, Ï, Ö, Ü, Ÿ	Ctrl+:, *letter*
å, Å	Ctrl+@, a or A
æ, Æ	Ctrl+&, a or A
œ, Œ	Ctrl+&, o or O
ç, Ç	Ctrl+,, c or C
≤, √	Ctrl+', d or D
ø, Ø	Ctrl+', o or O
¿	Alt+Ctrl+Shift+?
¡	Alt+Ctrl+Shift+!
ß	Ctrl+Shift+&, S

Tip 20: Inserting Different Bullets in Bulleted Lists Automatically

When you have Automatic Bulleted Lists activated (on the AutoFormat As You Type tab of the AutoCorrect dialog box), you can start a bulleted list by typing a character (such as "-"), a space, the first item, and then pressing Enter. What you probably don't know is that the bullet character used in the resulting list is determined by the character that you type. Table 31.4 shows the characters to type to create specific bullet characters.

TABLE 31.4: BULLET CHARACTERS FOR AUTOMATIC BULLETED LISTS

Bullet	Type This
—	-
•	*
•	--
➢	>

TABLE 31.4: BULLET CHARACTERS FOR AUTOMATIC BULLETED LISTS (CONTINUED)	
Bullet	**Type This**
→	->
⇨	=>

Tip 21: Creating Your Own Graphical Bullets

Word offers a small selection of standard bullet characters you can employ in your bulleted lists. For truly unique lists, however, you can create a bullet from any graphic image. Read on to learn two ways to personalize your bullets in this fashion.

 NOTE To learn more about creating bulleted lists in your Word documents, see Chapter 9.

Method One: Using Word Clip Art

To use Word clip art for bullet characters, follow these steps:

1. Position the insertion point where you want to add your first bulleted item.
2. Select Format ➤ Bullets and Numbering to display the Bullets and Numbering dialog box.
3. Select the Bulleted tab.
4. Click the Picture button to display the Picture Bullet dialog box.
5. Click the bullet image you want to display from the pop-up menu.
6. Select Insert Clip from the pop-up menu.

Method Two: Using Imported Graphics

To use any imported graphic image as a bullet, as shown in Figure 31.4, follow these steps:

1. Position the insertion point where you want to add your first bulleted item.
2. Select Insert ➤ Picture ➤ From File to display the Insert Picture dialog box.
3. Navigate to and select the picture you want to use as a bullet.
4. Click the Insert button to insert the picture into your document.
5. Use your mouse to resize the picture to be the same height as a line of text.

 WARNING This method will not work if the graphic is sized larger than a line of text.

6. With the insertion point positioned immediately after the picture, press the space-bar and start typing your bulleted text.

7. When you press Enter at the end of the first item, a second item is created, also using your imported graphic as the bullet character.

FIGURE 31.4
Create bullets from any picture.

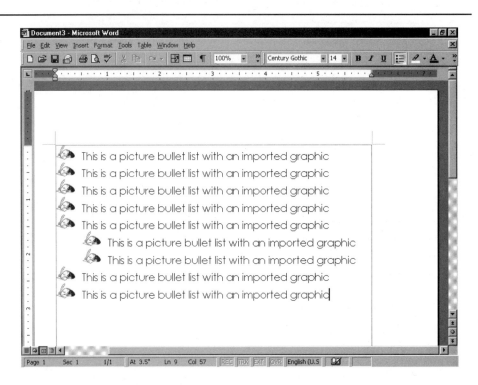

 NOTE For this method to work properly, you must have the Automatic Bulleted Lists option selected on the AutoFormat As You Type tab in the AutoCorrect dialog box.

Proofing Your Documents

The next two tips help you get the most from Word's proofing tools—in particular, the spell checker and the thesaurus.

Tip 22: Correcting Your Spelling Dictionary

If you've been using Word for any length of time, you've probably added a few words to your custom spelling dictionary that you shouldn't have. (It's easy to click the Add button by mistake and add yet another misspelled word to the dictionary!) All user-added words are stored in the CUSTOM.DIC file, and it's easy to edit that file to remove or fix any misspelled words. Follow these steps:

1. Select Tools ➤ Options to display the Options dialog box.

2. Select the Spelling & Grammar tab.

3. Click the Dictionaries button to display the Custom Dictionaries dialog box.

4. Select CUSTOM.DIC from the Custom Dictionaries list.

5. Click the Edit button.

6. Word now opens CUSTOM.DIC as a plain text document. Edit or delete the words in this document as necessary.

7. When you're done editing, select File ➤ Save to save the file.

8. Select File ➤ Close to close the custom dictionary document.

 NOTE To learn more about Word's spell check feature, see Chapter 6.

Tip 23: Finding Synonyms Fast

You're probably used to using Word's thesaurus by selecting a word and then pressing Shift+F7 (or selecting Tools ➤ Language ➤ Thesaurus). In Word 2000, however, there's a faster way to find synonyms. Follow these steps:

1. Position the insertion point anywhere within the word you want to check.

2. Right-click your mouse to display the pop-up menu.

3. Select Synonyms from the pop-up menu to display a list of synonyms for this word.

4. To replace the word with a synonym, select a synonym from the list.

To display the full Thesaurus dialog box (which presents even more options), select Thesaurus on the pop-up menu below the list of synonyms.

PART

IX

Tips, Tricks, and
Troubleshooting

NOTE To learn more about using Word's thesaurus, see Chapter 6.

Creating Fancy Documents

Most users don't spend the time to create truly great-looking documents, settling instead for boring, plain-text documents based on Word's rather generic templates. It doesn't take that much time to spice up your documents with pictures and other graphical elements; use the tips in this section to help you create documents that truly stand out from the crowd.

Tip 24: Using Pictures in a Bar Chart

Most users are used to seeing standard bar or column charts, either in 2-D or 3-D versions. For a fun change of pace, you can make a really eye-popping chart by using pictures in place of your bars or columns.

Figure 31.5 shows a column chart with a stacked graphic representing the normal column values. You can also opt to *stretch* a single graphic, as shown in the bar chart in Figure 31.6.

FIGURE 31.5
Use stacked graphics in place of a standard column chart.

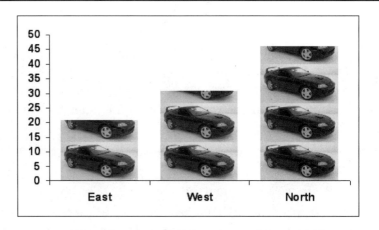

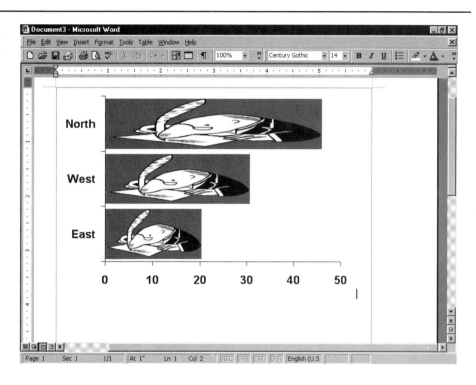

To create one of these unique charts, follow these steps:

1. From within your chart, click once on any column or bar to select all the columns or bars.

2. Select Format ➤ Selected Data Series to display the Format Data Series dialog box.

3. Select the Patterns tab.

4. Click the Fill Effects button to display the Fill Effects dialog box.

5. Select the Picture tab to display the Select Picture dialog box.

6. Navigate to and select the graphic file you want to use, and then click Insert to return to the Fill Effects dialog box.

7. To create a bar or column from a single graphic, check the Stretch option. To create a bar or column from a repeated graphic, check the Stack option. To set the scale for a stacked graphic, select the Stack and Scale option, and enter a value in the Units/Picture box.

8. Click OK to format the graph.

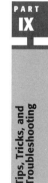

PART

IX

Tips, Tricks, and
Troubleshooting

NOTE To learn more about creating charts and graphs in Word, see Chapter 15.

Tip 25: Creating a Gradated Header or Footer Bar

Normal headers and footers are just plain text against the page background. Chances are, if you get fancy at all, adding a line above or below the header or footer is the extent of your customization.

Applying fancy formatting to your headers and footers, however, is one of the easiest ways to create a unique look for your document. After all, you only have to format the header or footer once, and what you do there doesn't effect any of the other text or graphics in your document. In short, by paying attention to your header and footer formatting, you get a lot of bang for your design buck.

One of my favorite header or footer designs is the gradated design shown in Figure 31.7. If you're printing a color document, you should coordinate the color of the header or footer bar and text with your document's main color scheme; if you're printing in black and white, the bar and text can be black.

FIGURE 31.7

Use fancy headers and footers to make your document stand out from the pack.

MY DOCUMENT   CHAPTER 24

You create this header or footer by adding a gradated rectangle object behind your header or footer text and then changing the color of the left-most text to white (to stand out against the dark part of the box). Here are the general steps you can use to create this effect:

1. Select View ➢ Header and Footer.

2. Configure the header or footer tabs for a single, right-aligned tab at the right margin.

3. Position your cursor at the left margin of the header or footer, and enter the left-side text.

4. Press Tab to tab to the right margin, and then enter the right-side text.

5. Select the left-side text, and configure it as white text.

6. Display the Drawing toolbar.

7. Draw a rectangle on top of the header or footer text.

8. Right-click the rectangle to display the Format AutoShape dialog box.

9. Select the Colors and Lines tab.

10. In the Lines section, pull down the Color list, and select No Line.

11. In the Fill section, pull down the Color list, and select Fill Effects to display the Fill Effects dialog box.

12. Select the Gradient tab.

13. Select a two-color gradient, with the first color white and the second color something dark.

14. Select a Vertical gradient, with the dark color on the left and white on the right.

15. Click OK to close the Fill Effects dialog box and return to the Format AutoShape dialog box.

16. Select the Format tab.

17. Select the Behind Text option.

18. Click OK.

Once the rectangle is positioned behind the text, you can resize and reposition it as necessary.

 NOTE To learn more about headers and footers, see Chapter 10.

Tip 26: Adding a Watermark to Your Page's Background

As shown in Figure 31.8, a screened-back graphic in the background of your page, also called a *watermark*, is a nice effect for many printed documents. The trick to creating a watermark is that it has to be added to your header or footer, *not* to the main body of your document. (Unless, of course, you're creating a Web page, as discussed in Chapter 24.)

To create a watermark, follow these steps:

1. Select View ➤ Header and Footer.

2. Position the insertion point in either the header or footer, and then select Insert ➤ Picture ➤ From File to display the Insert Picture dialog box.

3. Navigate to and select the picture you want to use as your watermark.

4. Click the Insert button to insert the picture into your document.

Tips, Tricks, and Troubleshooting

5. Double-click the picture to display the Format Picture dialog box.

6. Select the Layout tab.

7. Select Behind Text.

8. Select the Picture tab.

9. Pull down the Color list, and select Watermark.

10. Click OK to close the dialog box.

11. Use your mouse to reposition and resize the picture as necessary.

12. Click the Close button on the Header and Footer toolbar.

To view your watermark, switch to Print Layout view.

FIGURE 31.8
*Add a watermark in the
background of your
document pages.*

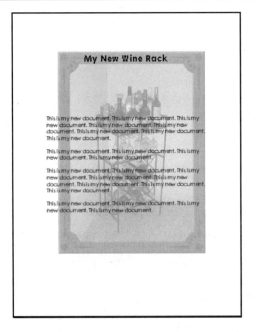

 NOTE To learn more about importing pictures into Word documents, see Chapter 16.

Tip 27: Printing Postage on Your Envelopes

The days of licking stamps are over.

Microsoft, in conjunction with E-Stamp, now offers the capability of printing "digital stamps" on your envelopes, using your own computer and printer. A digital stamp is a bar code adhering to the U.S. Postal Service's PC Postage standard.

The E-Stamp Internet Postage system enables you to download digital postage from the Internet and then print digital stamps on your envelopes via Microsoft Word. The general steps involved are as follows:

1. **Buy the postage.** Connect to the e-stamp.com Internet site, and then purchase and download as much postage as you need.

2. **Create the envelopes, with the digital stamps.** Use Word's envelope and labels feature to add digital stamps to your envelopes, along with recipient names and addresses.

3. **Print the envelopes.** When you click the Print button, E-Stamp automatically verifies the address, adds the ZIP+4 code, and then prints the envelope.

4. **Mail the envelopes.** The digital postage works just as a regular stamp would.

To learn more about digital stamps, visit Microsoft's E-Stamp Internet Postage Web site at officeupdate.microsoft.com/services/estampcohome.htm.

NOTE   To learn more about printing envelopes in Word, see Chapter 18.

Tip 28: Laying Out Pages with Tables

Many documents work just fine with text flowing from one column to another and from one page to the next. However, some documents (newsletters, brochures, and other relatively short, relatively *visual* documents) scream for more precise control over the placement of elements on a page. One of the easiest ways to control object placement is to lay out your page with a table.

 As you know, tables don't have to be symmetrical combinations of rows and columns; you can use the Draw Table tool (found on the Tables and Borders toolbar) to draw tables one cell at a time, for very complex configurations. This is the tool to use when creating a table to serve as the pattern for your underlying page.

 Let's say, for example, that you want to create a three-column page. You start by using the Draw Table tool to add a table to the page and to draw two vertical lines (thus creating three columns). If you want a headline at the top of the page, you use the Draw Table tool to draw a horizontal line across the top quarter of the page and then use the Eraser tool to erase the vertical lines above the horizontal line. You can also use the Draw Table tool to draw additional horizontal lines to separate stories, pictures, or other elements; use the Eraser tool to erase vertical lines within elements that span more than one column.

When you're done creating the table, you might have something that looks like Figure 31.9. After you fill in the cells with text and pictures, and reformat the table to eliminate gridlines and borders, you have a completed document similar to the one in Figure 31.10.

FIGURE 31.9

Use the Draw Table and Eraser tools to draw a pattern for your underlying page.

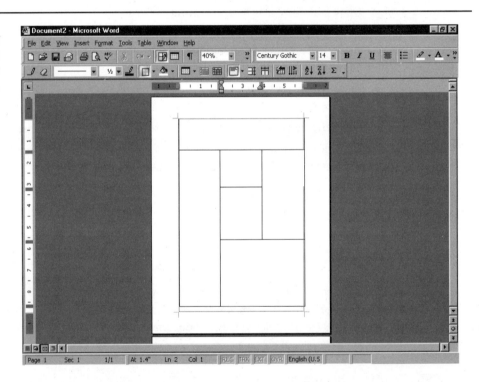

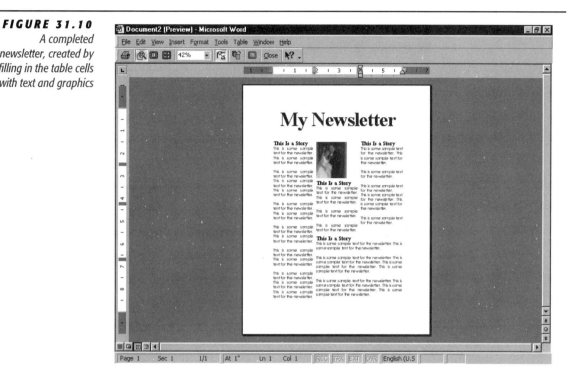

 NOTE To learn more about the Draw Table and Eraser tools, see Chapter 14.

Automating Word

Much of the power of Word comes from those commands and operations that you can somehow automate. After all, it's easier to click a button or press a key than it is to manually perform the multiple steps inherent in most complex tasks. Use the tips in this section, then, to help you use Word more efficiently by automating common and complex operations.

PART

IX

Tips, Tricks, and Troubleshooting

Tip 29: Shrinking a Long Document

If you have a document that runs a little long and spills a few lines onto an extra page, you can easily shrink that document to eliminate the spillover. Follow these steps:

1. Click the Print Preview button on Word's Standard toolbar to open the Print Preview window.

2. Click the Shrink to Fit button on the Print Preview toolbar.

3. Click the Close button to leave Print Preview.

The Shrink to Fit option downsizes all the fonts in your document to fit more content onto every page.

> **NOTE**   To learn more about Print Preview, see Chapter 7.

Tip 30: Changing Line Spacing—Fast!

The typical method to adjust line spacing for a paragraph is to select Format ➤ Paragraph and work within the Paragraph dialog box. A faster way is to use one of these keyboard shortcuts:

- Single space: Ctrl+1
- 1.5 lines: Ctrl+5
- Double space: Ctrl+2

Just position your insertion point anywhere within a paragraph, and then press the appropriate shortcut key combination.

> **NOTE**   To learn more about line spacing, see Chapter 9.

Tip 31: Typing Shortcuts to Long Words

Do you ever get tired of typing long words? I guarantee you do if you live in Indianapolis or Minneapolis or if your name is Kazmierczak or Bartholomew. No matter how fast and accurate your typing is, you're bound to get tired of typing these long words every day and stand a good chance of getting your fingers tangled trying to speed through even the most frequently used of these combinations.

A good solution to this problem is to use Word's AutoCorrect feature to create shortcuts, or abbreviations, that you can type in place of difficult words. When you type the shortcut, AutoCorrect will automatically replace your shortcut with the word itself.

For example, you could add the word *indy* to the AutoCorrect list to represent the word *Indianapolis*. Every time you type *indy,* Word automatically replaces it with the word *Indianapolis*.

To add shortcut words to the AutoCorrect list, follow these steps:

1. Select Tools ➢ AutoCorrect to display the AutoCorrect dialog box.

2. Select the AutoCorrect tab.

3. Enter into the Replace box the word or phrase you want to use as the shortcut.

4. Enter the corresponding word or phrase in the With box.

5. Click the Add button.

For this shortcut-to-long-words feature to function, you must have AutoCorrect activated. To do this, select Tools ➢ AutoCorrect to display the AutoCorrect dialog box, select the AutoCorrect tab, check the Replace Text As You Type option, and then click OK.

 NOTE To learn more about AutoCorrect, see Chapter 6.

Tip 32: Creating Automated Click Here and Type Fields

If you've ever used Word's Letter Wizard, you've seen automated fields labeled along the lines of Click Here and Type. When you click on one of these fields and enter your own text, your text replaces the Click Here and Type text.

You can add your own Click Here and Type fields to any document or template, which is a great way to create a semi-automated document. To add one of these fields, follow these steps:

1. Position the insertion point where you want to insert the field.

2. Press Ctrl+F9 to insert a blank field at the insertion point.

3. Inside the curly brackets, enter **Macrobutton NoMacro Click Here and Type**.

To view the new field, position your cursor inside the field code and press F9.

 NOTE To learn more about automating your document with field codes, see Chapter 12.

PART

IX

Tips, Tricks, and
Troubleshooting

Tip 33: Creating a Document from Dialog Boxes

Some Wizards and automated documents use Click Here and Type fields to solicit user input. Another method is to display a dialog box asking for input and then to insert the contents of that dialog box into the document.

You use the Visual Basic editor to create a macro that creates such a dialog box and then inserts the user input directly into the underlying document. Follow these steps to create this AddressBoxWizard macro:

 WARNING This tip should only be attempted by users who are well-versed in Visual Basic for Applications programming.

1. Open the document or template that you want to host the macro, and then select Tools ➤ Macro ➤ Visual Basic Editor to launch the VB Editor.

2. From the VB Editor's Project Explorer, select the document or template you want to work with.

3. Select Insert ➤ UserForm to open a new UserForm window. Change the (Name) property of this UserForm to *WizBox*; change the Caption property to *Enter Recipient Information*.

4. Use the buttons in the Toolbox to add five text boxes, five corresponding labels, and one button to the form, as shown in Figure 31.11.

FIGURE 31.11
Draw these controls on your new UserForm.

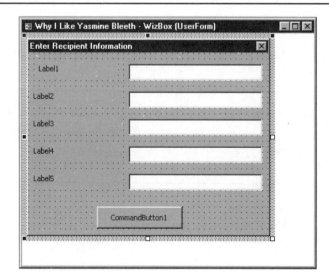

5. Configure the new controls as shown in Table 31.5 later in this section. Figure 31.12 shows how the WizBox dialog box looks after configuring control properties and rearranging the controls slightly.

FIGURE 31.12
The WizBox dialog box, with renamed and reconfigured controls

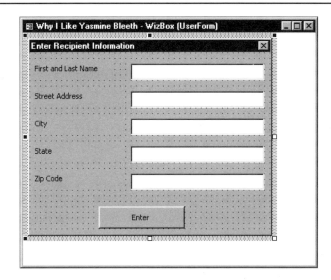

6. Return to the Project Explorer, select the ThisDocument object for the selected project, and then click the View Code button to display an empty Code window.

7. Within the new Code window, enter this code:

```
Sub AddressBoxWizard()
   WizBox.Show
End Sub
```

8. Move to the WizBox UserForm, and double-click the command button to display the Code window for this UserForm.

9. Enter the following code into the UserForm Code window:

```
Private Sub WizButtonEnter_Click()
   Dim EnterName As String
   Dim EnterAddress As String
   Dim EnterCity As String
   Dim EnterState As String
   Dim EnterZip As String
   EnterName = WizBoxName.Text
   EnterAddress = WizBoxAddress.Text
   EnterCity = WizBoxCity.Text
```

PART

IX

Tips, Tricks, and Troubleshooting

```
        EnterState = WizBoxState.Text
        EnterZip = WizBoxZip.Text
        Selection.TypeText Text:=EnterName
        Selection.TypeParagraph
        Selection.TypeText Text:=EnterAddress
        Selection.TypeParagraph
        Selection.TypeText Text:=EnterCity
        Selection.TypeText Text:=", "
        Selection.TypeText Text:=EnterState
        Selection.TypeText Text:=" "
        Selection.TypeText Text:=EnterZip
        Selection.TypeParagraph
    End Sub
```

▌ **TABLE 31.5: PROPERTIES FOR WIZBOX CONTROLS**

Control	(Name)	Caption
TextBox1	WizBoxName	*NA*
TextBox2	WizBoxAddress	*NA*
TextBox3	WizBoxCity	*NA*
TextBox4	WizBoxState	*NA*
TextBox5	WizBoxZip	*NA*
Label1	WizLabelName	First and Last Name
Label2	WizLabelAddress	Street Address
Label3	WizLabelCity	City
Label4	WizLabelState	State
Label5	WizLabelZip	Zip Code
CommandButton1	WizButtonEnter	Enter

With your code complete, you can return to Word and assign this macro to a keyboard shortcut, a menu item, or a toolbar button. When you run the AddressBoxWizard macro, Word displays the dialog box you created; when the user fills in the blanks and presses the Enter button, the text they entered is inserted into the current document, as shown in Figure 31.13.

FIGURE 31.13
The completed dialog box, and the resulting text inserted into a document

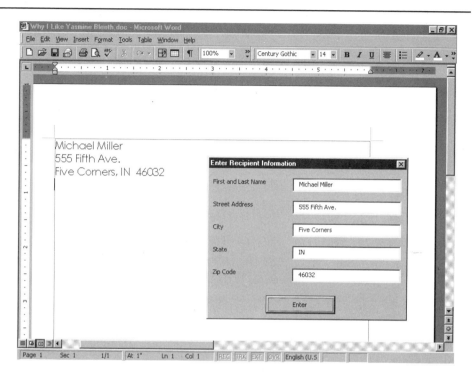

 NOTE To learn more about programming in VBA, see Chapter 30.

Tip 34: Using the Letter Wizard to Reuse Existing Letters

If you don't want to go to all the trouble of creating your own version of a letter Wizard, you can use Word's built-in Letter Wizard to reuse the formatting and content of any existing letter, while changing those elements necessary to create a new letter.

To run the Letter Wizard from within a document, follow these steps:

1. Open the letter you want to work with.

2. Select Tools ➤ Letter Wizard to display the Letter Wizard dialog box.

When you launch the Letter Wizard from within an existing document, the Wizard doesn't run step by step but instead displays a tabbed dialog box. Because the Wizard reads the content of the document, it only presents options to add or change selected elements; it keeps the important parts of what you already entered.

NOTE To learn more about Word's Letter Wizard, see Chapter 4.

Tip 35: Generating a Table of Contents from Another Document

In most instances, you'll want to insert a table of contents within the same document referenced by the TOC. There are some circumstances, however, where you'll want to use the TOC from one document in a separate document.

To insert the TOC from another document into your current document, follow these steps:

1. From within the document that you want to contain the TOC, position your insertion point where you want to insert the TOC.

2. Press Ctrl+F9 to insert a blank field at the insertion point.

3. Within the curly brackets, enter **RD** *"x:\\path\filename.doc"* where *x:\\path\filename.doc* is the drive, the path, and the filename of the document from which you want to generate the TOC.

 WARNING You must insert the path and the filename within quotation marks and use double backslashes after the drive letter, or the field code won't work.

4. Press Enter to move to the next line.

5. Select Insert ➢ Index and Tables to display the Index and Tables dialog box.

6. Select the Table of Contents tab.

7. Make whatever formatting selections you want, and then click OK.

Word now generates a table of contents based on the referenced document (that's the RD field code).

 NOTE To learn more about generating tables of contents, see Chapter 13.

Tip 36: Creating Windows Shortcuts for Word Templates and Documents

If you use a certain Word template or document over and over again, you may want to launch Word with that template (and a corresponding new document based on that template) or document pre-loaded. The easiest way to do this is to create a shortcut on the Windows Desktop to the selected template or document.

You create a Desktop shortcut by following these steps:

1. From within Windows, right-click on an empty area of the Desktop to display a pop-up menu.

2. From the pop-up menu, select New ➢ Shortcut.

3. When the Create Shortcut Wizard appears, click the Browse button to display the Browse dialog box.

4. Pull down the Files of Type list, and select All Files.

5. Navigate to and select the file you want to open, and then click the Open button to return to the Create Shortcut Wizard.

 NOTE Most Word templates can be found in the `\Windows\Application Data\Microsoft\Templates\` or `\Program Files\Microsoft Office\Templates\1033\` folders.

6. From the Wizard, click the Next button to display the select a Title for the Program box.

7. Enter a name for this shortcut in the Select a Name for the Shortcut box.

8. Click OK.

Windows now adds the shortcut you selected to the Windows Desktop. Click this shortcut to launch Word with that document (or a new document based on that template) preloaded.

Making Word More Than a Word Processor

Word 2000 is a great word processor. But do you know that you can also use Word as a presentation graphics, spreadsheet, database, and drawing program? If not, then these last four tips will be quite interesting to you!

PART

IX

Tips, Tricks, and
Troubleshooting

Tip 37: Using Word for Presentations

If you use Word for word processing, you probably use PowerPoint for your presentations, even though you don't have to. As you can see from the example in Figure 31.14, Word 2000 can actually be used as a serviceable presentation graphics program, though without the fancy screen transitions found in PowerPoint and similar applications.

FIGURE 31.14
Use Word, in Full Screen mode, to display landscape presentations.

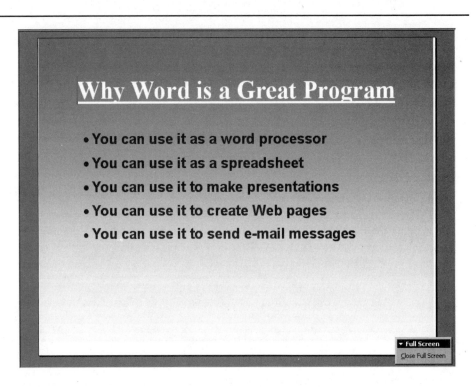

Here are the keys to using Word for on-screen or projected presentations:

- Set up your presentation to be displayed in landscape orientation. You do this by selecting File ➤ Page Setup to display the Page Setup dialog box; select the Paper Size tab, check the Landscape option, and then click OK.

- Apply a background graphic to your presentation using the watermark method discussed in Tip 26. Alternatively, use the same method to insert an AutoShape rectangle, filling up the entire screen, for a background color or gradient.

- Apply a border to your presentation by selecting Format ➤ Borders and Shading to display the Borders and Shading dialog box. Select the Page Border tab, select your border, and then click OK.

- Simplify your document by using larger type sizes and simple bulleted lists. (Use pictures for your bullets as discussed in Tip 23.)

- View your presentation from Word's Full Screen mode. (Activate Full Screen mode by selecting View ➤ Full Screen.) Press PgDn to move to the next page; press PgUp to move to the previous page.

Obviously, PowerPoint is a much better presentation program than is Word, even if you incorporate all these little tricks. Still, if you ever find yourself in a large room with a strange computer that doesn't have PowerPoint installed, you can use this tip to fashion a last-minute presentation using Microsoft Word.

Tip 38: Using Word as a Spreadsheet

Just as Word can be used as a presentation graphics program, it can also be used as a makeshift spreadsheet program. The key is to use Word's tables and =(FORMULA) field. As you can see in Figure 31.15, the result looks amazingly like an Excel worksheet.

FIGURE 31.15
Use Word's tables and =(FORMULA) features to create a fully functioning spreadsheet.

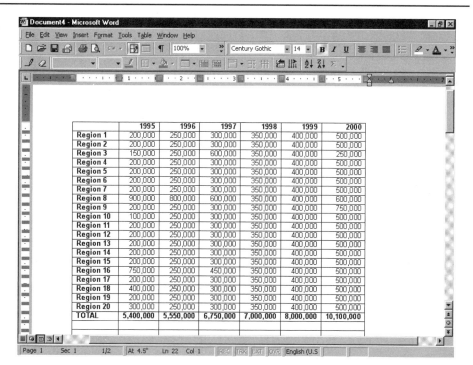

Here are the keys to using Word to create calculating spreadsheets:

- Insert a large table into your Word document. Make the table big enough to fill the entire page, if necessary—at least 8 columns wide by 50 rows deep, in portrait orientation.
- Format the table so that all cells that contain numbers are right-aligned.
- Use the Borders and Shading dialog box to display all gridlines.
- Use the =(FORMULA) field to perform numeric calculations. The easiest way to do this is to select Table ➢ Formula to display the Formula dialog box and then add functions and operators to create your own formulas.

Once you've entered data into your spreadsheet, you can graph the data within your table. Just select the desired cells, and then select Insert ➢ Picture ➢ Chart to display a new Microsoft Graph chart with the selected data preloaded.

 NOTE To learn more about Word's advanced table features, see Chapter 14; to learn about creating charts and graphs from Word tables, see Chapter 15.

Tip 39: Using Word as a Database

Let's be honest: Word isn't much of a database. But you can use Word to store simple collections of data, such as names and addresses, a home inventory, and the contents of your CD or videotape collection. You do this by creating a table to hold the data, with rows representing database records and each column representing a database field. The result looks a little like what you'd find in a very simple Access database.

 Once you've created your data table, you can use Word's Data Form command (found on the Database toolbar) to add data via a form rather than just inserting more data into the table.

 NOTE Learn more about Word's database features in Chapter 19.

Tip 40: Using Word as a Drawing Program

The final tip in this chapter is that you can use Word as a simple drawing program, similar to Microsoft Paint (included with Microsoft Windows). Although you can use the tools in the Drawing toolbar to draw directly on a Word page, the better approach—if you're serious about drawing—is to insert a separate drawing object into your document.

When you select Insert ➤ Picture ➤ New Drawing, Word opens a new drawing object. You can use the Drawing and AutoShapes toolbars to do your drawing; all that you create is inserted into your document as a single drawing object. You can then edit the drawing as a whole, which is easier than dealing with multiple disconnected objects sitting on top of your document.

 NOTE Learn more about Word's drawing features in Chapter 16.

CHAPTER **32**

Using Word with Office 2000

Using Word with Microsoft Office Tools   **838**

Using Word with Outlook   **845**

Using Word with Excel   **848**

Using Word with PowerPoint   **853**

Using Word with Access   **859**

Using Word with Publisher   **862**

Using Word with Photo Editor   **864**

Most users obtain their copy of Microsoft Word 2000 as part of the Microsoft Office 2000 suite of applications. Microsoft designed the Office applications to share a relatively common interface and many common operations, so that they would integrate and work well together. This chapter will show you the many ways Word 2000 can work with other Office 2000 applications, and help you master the Office integration.

 NOTE Word 2000 is available as a stand-alone program, as part of Microsoft Office 2000, and as part of Microsoft Works Suite 2000. Works Suite includes its own suite of applications—including spreadsheet and database programs—in place of Excel, Access, and other Office programs. If you obtained Word as part of Works Suite 2000, you have a full-blown version of Word, with a few additions—some extra templates, and a few changed menu commands (for better compatibility with other Works Suite applications).

Using Word with Microsoft Office Tools

In addition to the applications in the suite—Word, Excel, Access, and so on—Office 2000 also comes with some inter-application tools and utilities. Most of these tools help you use multiple Office applications together—such as the Office Shortcut Bar, which brings together common application operations, or binders, which enable you to create projects comprised of documents from several different applications.

Using the Office Shortcut Bar

The Office Shortcut Bar is a toolbar that sits on the Windows desktop and provides one-click access to many common Office operations. You can use the Shortcut Bar to open or create new Office applications, directly access e-mail and other Outlook operations, and launch Word and other office applications. You can even customize the Shortcut bar for the way that you personally use Microsoft Office.

Display the Shortcut Bar

To display the Office Shortcut Bar, click the Windows Start button and select Microsoft Office Tools ➤ Microsoft Office Shortcut Bar. By default, the Shortcut Bar docks itself on the right side of the Windows desktop (as shown in Figure 32.1)—and stays visible, even when applications are displayed full screen.

FIGURE 32.1
Use the Office Shortcut Bar to directly access common Office operations.

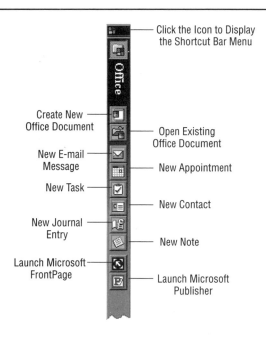

Click the Icon to Display the Shortcut Bar Menu

Create New Office Document

Open Existing Office Document

New E-mail Message

New Appointment

New Task

New Contact

New Journal Entry

New Note

Launch Microsoft FrontPage

Launch Microsoft Publisher

To hide the Shortcut Bar, click the Shortcut Bar icon to display the Shortcut Bar menu, then select Auto Hide. This causes the Shortcut Bar to disappear until you move your cursor to that edge of the screen, at which point it automatically reappears.

You can move the Shortcut Bar to any edge of your screen, or have it float over the Windows desktop. Just use your mouse to grab any open area of the bar, then drag it to a new location.

To close the Shortcut Bar, click the Shortcut Bar icon to display the Shortcut Bar menu, then select Exit.

PART

IX

Tips, Tricks, and
Troubleshooting

TIP To display the Shortcut Bar—in compacted format—on the toolbar of any active application window, click the Shortcut Bar icon to display the Shortcut Bar menu, select Customize to display the Customize dialog box, select the View tab, check the Auto Fit into Title Bar Area option, then click OK.

Use the Shortcut Bar to Open and Create Files

The most frequent use of the Shortcut Bar is to open and create files for any Office application. To open an existing file—for any Office application—follow these steps:

1. Click the Open Office Document button to display the Open Office Document dialog box.
2. Navigate to and select the file you want to open.
3. Click the Open button.

To create a new file—in any Office format you select—follow these steps:

1. Click the New Office Document button to display the New Office Document dialog box.
2. Click the tab that contains the type of document you want to create.
3. Select a document template.
4. Click the OK button.

Display Different Toolbars on the Shortcut Bar

Office enables you to use the Shortcut Bar to display other toolbars. When you activate multiple toolbars for the Shortcut Bar, buttons for each toolbar appear at either end of the Shortcut Bar; clicking a toolbar button switches the Shortcut Bar to that toolbar.

To add a toolbar to the Shortcut Bar, right-click any open area of the Shortcut Bar to display the pop-up menu; check toolbars you want to display, and uncheck those you don't want to see.

Add Buttons to the Shortcut Bar

To add buttons for other Office operations and applications—including Word—follow these steps:

1. Click the Shortcut Bar icon to display the Shortcut Bar menu.
2. Select Customize to display the Customize dialog box.
3. Select the Buttons tab.

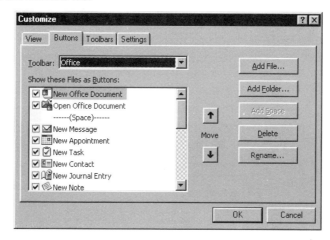

4. Check those buttons you want to display, and uncheck those you don't.
5. To add a button for a specific file, click the Add File button to display the Add File dialog box, navigate to and select the file you want to add, then click the Add button.
6. To change the order of buttons on the toolbar, select a button item, then use the Move up or down buttons to reposition the item in the list.
7. Click OK when done.

Using Binders

When your project includes files created in different Office applications—a report in Word, a spreadsheet in Excel, and an accompanying presentation in PowerPoint, for example—you can "bind" these different files together with Microsoft Office Binder. Think of a binder as an electronic binder clip, used to keep all related documents together in one place.

You can work on the different documents placed in a binder much as you would a Word Master Document. You can apply a consistent style; insert cross-document headers, footers, and page numbers; check spelling and grammar in a single operation; and then print the entire binder in one fell swoop.

PART

IX

Tips, Tricks, and Troubleshooting

To launch Microsoft Office Binder, click the Windows Start button, then select Microsoft Office Tools ➢ Microsoft Binder.

Create a Binder

You can create a binder from any combination of existing or new files from any Office application. As you can see in Figure 32.2, binder files are shown in the left pane of the Binder window; the contents of a selected file are shown in the right pane. When you select a particular file, the binder window changes to display the corresponding application's menus, toolbars, and workspace.

FIGURE 32.2

Use Microsoft Office Binder to bind files together from different Office applications.

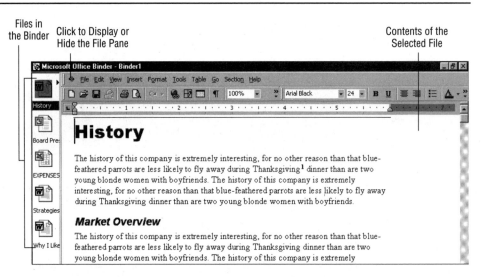

To add an existing file to the binder, follow these steps:

1. Select Section ➢ Add From File to display the Add From File dialog box.

2. Navigate to and select the file you want to add.

3. Click the Add button.

To add a *new* file to the binder, follow these steps:

1. Select Section ➢ Add to display the Add Section dialog box.

2. Select the tab that contains the type of document you want to add.

3. Select a document template.

4. Click the OK button.

Once a file has been added to a binder, you can change its position *within* the binder by dragging the file's icon to a new location in the File pane. Files within a binder are called *sections*.

Edit Binder Files

Once you've added files to your binder, you can edit any individual file (section) by selecting the file icon in the File pane. The Binder window then changes to resemble the window of that file's host applications—for example, if you select a Word file, the Binder window adds Word menus and toolbars to duplicate the Word workspace. You can then work on the file in its native environment while staying within the Binder window.

Add a Header and Footer

To add a single header or footer to all (or selected) documents within your binder, follow these steps:

1. Select File ➤ Binder Page Setup to display the Binder Page Setup dialog box.
2. Select the Header/Footer tab.
3. To select which sections will include this header or footer, go to the Apply Binder Header/Footer To section and check either the All Supported Sections option (to print the header and footer in all sections) or check those specific sections you want to print with the header/footer.
4. Pull down the Header or Footer list to select a prepared header or footer, *or*

   Click one of the Custom buttons to display the Custom Header or Custom Footer dialog box, enter and format your header/footer text, then click OK.
5. Click OK when done.

Save Your Binder

To save a binder you've created, follow these steps:

1. Select File ➤ Save Binder As to display the Save Binder As dialog box.
2. Select a location and name for your binder.
3. Click the Save button.

Print Your Binder

To print your binder, follow these steps:

1. Select File ➤ Print Binder to display the Print Binder dialog box.

PART

IX

Tips, Tricks, and
Troubleshooting

2. To print all sections in your binder, check the All Visible Sections option; to print only selected sections, check the Section Selected in Left Pane option.

3. To use consecutive numbering throughout your binder, check the Consecutive option; to have each section (document) numbered individually, check the Restart Each Section option.

4. Click OK.

 TIP You can preview your binder onscreen before your print it by selecting File ➢ Binder Print Preview.

To *not* print specific sections of your binder, you have to *hide* those sections. To hide a section, select the file's icon in the File pane, then select Section ➢ Hide.

Using Office Small Business Tools

Office 2000 includes several other business-related utility programs that either work directly with Word 2000, or might be of interest to Word users. The tools available to you differ depending on the version of Office you have (Standard, Professional, Premium, and so on) and your specific installation. Available programs are not all automatically installed onto your system; to install a new tool, rerun the Office setup program.

Among the small business tools available in various versions of Office 2000 are these:

Microsoft Business Planner   Templates, examples, and other resources to create business and marketing plans.

Microsoft Direct Mail Manager   A wizard-like application that automates large mass mailings.

Microsoft Small Business Customer Manager   Combines custom contact data from Microsoft Outlook with financial data from popular accounting programs to track customer profiles and purchasing.

Microsoft Small Business Financial Manager   Uses Microsoft Excel to analyze business data and create easy-to-read financial reports.

These tools—if they're installed on your system—are available when you click the Windows Start menu and select Microsoft Office Small Business Tools.

Using Word with Outlook

Microsoft Outlook 2000 is Office's combination e-mail, scheduling, and contact management program. You can use Outlook with Word to e-mail your Word documents and to create merged mailings—as well as track your work in Word via the Outlook Journal.

E-mailing with Word and Outlook

Any time you choose to e-mail a Word document—either as an HTML e-mail message or as an attachment to a regular e-mail message—you're using Outlook to handle the e-mail part of the operation. The Outlook e-mail engine is used to send your message/document through your Internet service provider over the Internet, and you can also use the Outlook Address Book to add your recipients' e-mail addresses to your message.

To send a Word document as an e-mail message, select File ➢ Send To ➢ Mail Recipient (or click the E-mail button on Word's Standard toolbar). This adds an e-mail header to your document; when you click the Send a Copy button, the Outlook e-mail engine is engaged to connect to your ISP and transmit the message.

To send a Word document as an attachment to another e-mail message, you can either use the Attachment feature in Outlook, or—from within Word—select File ➢ Send To ➢ Mail Recipient (as Attachment) to create a new Outlook message, with your Word document loaded as an attachment.

 NOTE   To learn more about e-mailing with Word, see Chapter 7.

Creating Merged Mailings with Outlook Contacts

A merged mailing is a large mailing—typically using a form letter, accompanied by personalized labels or envelopes—that merges names from an external data source into a Word document. When you create a merged mailing in Word, you can choose from many different data sources for your recipient list—Excel worksheets, Access databases, Word tables, or your Outlook Address Book. Using your Outlook Address Book as your data source enables you to send personalized mailings to all or selected names from your Outlook contact list.

PART

IX

Tips, Tricks, and
Troubleshooting

NOTE To learn more about creating merged mailings from the names in your Address Book, see Chapter 19.

Tracking Word Activity in the Outlook Journal

Outlook 2000 includes a utility called the *Journal*. You use the Journal to track the amount of time you spend working on any Office document. When you activate the Journal, it will record when and how long you've had any Word document open for editing.

Activate the Journal to Track Your Word Documents

To have the Outlook Journal track the time you spend working on Word documents, follow these steps:

1. From within Outlook, select Tools ≻ Options to display the Options dialog box.

2. Select the Preferences tab.

3. Click the Journal Options button to display the Journal Options dialog box.

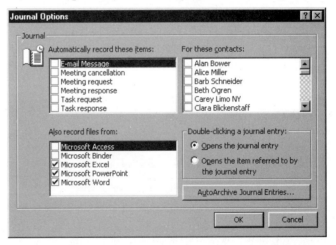

4. In the Also Record Files From list, check the Microsoft Word option.

5. Click OK.

Outlook will now track the time you spend editing any Word document on this computer.

Journal

Tracking Your Document Editing

Once you've activated Word tracking, all your Word editing sessions will appear in Outlook's Journal folder. You display the Journal by clicking the Journal button in the Outlook bar.

When the Journal is displayed (as shown in Figure 32.3), you see a list of all files you've opened, organized by date and time. You can choose to list files by day, week, or month; if you choose to display by day, the duration of each open project is indicated by a horizontal bar above each file name.

FIGURE 32.3
se the Outlook Journal to track how long you work on each Word document.

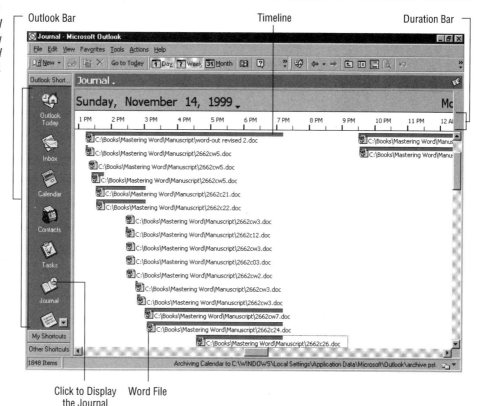

Outlook Bar — Timeline — Duration Bar

Click to Display the Journal — Word File

Viewing a Journal Entry

To display detailed information about a particular document's editing session, right-click the file icon and select Open Journal Entry from the pop-up menu. When the Journal entry appears, as shown in Figure 32.4, you can view the precise time the file was opened and the duration of the editing session. You can also assign this file to a contact by clicking the Contacts button and selecting a name from your Outlook contact list. Close the Journal entry by clicking the Save and Close button.

FIGURE 32.4

View the details of an editing session by opening that file's Journal entry.

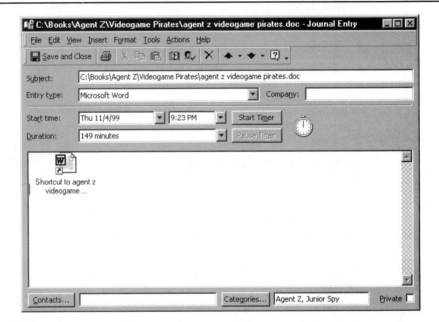

Using Word with Excel

Many Word users use it in conjunction with Excel every day. These two applications integrate well when you need to create documents with a mix of text (Word's forte) and numbers (Excel's specialty).

Using Word Data in Excel Worksheets

There are some instances where you want to use data from a Word document in an Excel worksheet. You might have a table or list that started simple and grew bigger and more complex, for example, and thus would be more easily managed in a dedicated spreadsheet program.

When you want to move data from Word to Excel, make sure that your data is contained either in a table or in a list, then follow these steps:

1. From within Word, select the numbers or cells you want to send to Excel.

2. Select Edit ➢ Cut (to move the data) or Edit ➢ Copy (to copy the data).

3. Switch to your Excel worksheet and select the cell where you want to insert the first (top-left) data point.

4. Select Edit ➢ Paste.

When you paste a Word table into an Excel worksheet, the cells from the table become cells in the worksheet. If you send a list to Excel, every tab signals the start of a new column; each new line starts a new row.

Take, for example, the following list, with each "column" defined by a tab mark:

333→999→000
000→999→888
123→999→887

 WARNING If you cut or copy a table or list that contains a calculated result—using the Word =(FORMULA) field—only the *results* of the field will be pasted into Excel, not the field code or formula itself.

Adding Excel Worksheets to Word Documents

It's very common to use Excel to do the "heavy lifting," number crunching–wise, and then import the worksheet into Word, where it can be formatted to match the rest of your document or report. There are two ways to add Excel data to Word documents—you can paste them, or you can embed them.

Paste an Excel Worksheet into a Word Table

When you paste an Excel worksheet into a Word document, you essentially paste the data from the worksheet into a Word table. You can then format the table as necessary or appropriate.

To paste Excel data into Word, follow these steps:

1. From within Excel, select the cells you want to send to Word.

2. Select Edit ➤ Cut (to move the data) or Edit ➤ Copy (to copy the data).

3. Switch to your Word document and position the insertion point where you want to add the new table.

4. Select Edit ➤ Paste.

Word now creates a table, with each cell in the table representing a cell from the Worksheet.

WARNING If you cut or copy a worksheet cell that contains a formula, only the *results* of the formula will be pasted into Word, not the formula itself.

Pasting vs. Embedding

If you want to move an entire worksheet into Word—not just the data within the worksheet—then you need to *embed* the worksheet as an Excel Worksheet Object. You can embed complete worksheets, selected cells from a worksheet, or even create a new object into which you can enter your own data. You can also choose to link the inserted object back to its original document—so if the original worksheet changes, the object in your Word document will automatically update itself to reflect those changes.

After the object has been inserted into your document, you have to edit it from within the embedded Excel environment; you cannot edit or format it using standard Word editing and formatting functions. When you double-click the object, it appears as it would within Excel, and the Word workspace switches to the Excel workspace—toolbars, menus, and all, as shown in Figure 32.5. You can now use Excel's editing functions to edit and format the data. Select anywhere outside the object to return to the Word workspace.

NOTE To learn more about object linking and embedding, see Chapter 17.

FIGURE 32.5

Embed an Excel worksheet object to retain all the editing features of Excel from within the Word environment.

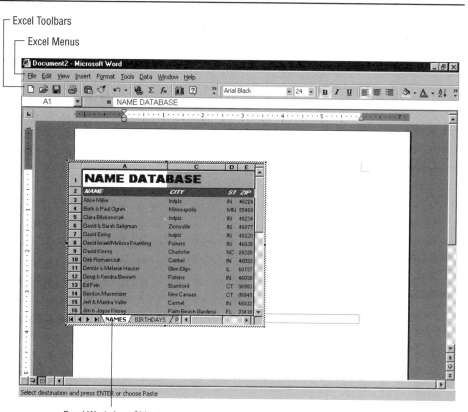

Excel Toolbars

Excel Menus

Excel Worksheet Object

Embed Individual Cells

To embed selected worksheet data into a Word document, follow these steps:

1. From within Excel, select the cells you want to send to Word.

2. Select Edit ➢ Cut (to move the data) or Edit ➢ Copy (to copy the data).

3. Switch to your Word document and position the insertion point where you want to add the new table.

4. Select Edit ➢ Paste Special to display the Paste Special dialog box.

5. If you want to create a link between the embedded object and the original worksheet, check the Paste Link option. If not, check the Paste option.

6. Select Microsoft Excel Worksheet Object from the As list.

7. Click OK.

Embed an Entire Worksheet

To embed an entire worksheet into a Word document, follow these steps:

1. From within Word, select Insert ➢ Object to display the Insert Object dialog box.

2. Check the Create From File tab.

3. Enter the location and name of the Excel worksheet file in the File Name box, or click the Browse button to locate the file.

4. Click OK.

Create a New Worksheet Object

To create a new Excel worksheet object from within Word, follow these steps:

1. From within Word, select Insert ➢ Object to display the Insert Object dialog box.

2. Check the Create New tab.

3. From the Object Type list, select Microsoft Excel Worksheet.

4. Click OK.

Adding Excel Charts to Word Documents

You can also embed Excel charts into your Word documents. You may want to use Excel to create your graphs and charts, since it has more sophisticated charting features than does Microsoft Graph, which is used within Word.

Embed an Excel Chart

You can't simply paste an Excel chart into Word; even if you use the standard Paste command, Word automatically uses the Paste Special command to embed the chart as a Microsoft Excel Chart object.

To copy an Excel chart into a Word document, then, follow these steps:

1. From within Excel, select the chart you want to send to Word.

2. Select Edit ➢ Copy.

3. Switch to your Word document and position the insertion point where you want to add the chart.

4. Select Edit ➢ Paste.

To edit or format the chart, double-click it. This switches the Word workspace into Excel editing mode from which you can use Excel chart editing and formatting commands.

Create a New Chart Object

You can also create a new Excel chart object from within Word by following these steps:

1. From within Word, select Insert ➤ Object to display the Insert Object dialog box.

2. Check the Create New tab.

3. From the Object Type list, select Microsoft Excel Chart.

4. Click OK.

You now have a great-looking chart embedded in your document—but based on what data? To edit the chart's source data, you need to double-click the chart to enter Excel editing mode, then select Chart ➤ Source Data to display and edit the Excel spreadsheet on which the new chart is based.

Using Word with PowerPoint

PowerPoint and Word are two applications that work extremely well together. Many people use PowerPoint for the "big picture" presentation, and Word for the "fine print" documentation and handouts. Recognizing this synergy, Microsoft has introduced special commands into both programs that make it easy to transfer information back and forth between the two applications.

Creating a PowerPoint Presentation from a Word Document

Often you'll want to use the outline of a Word document as the starting point for a PowerPoint presentation. You can do this by exporting your Word document to Power-Point, which then converts it into individual slides, based on Word's automatic heading styles.

Send a Word Outline to PowerPoint

You send a Word document directly to PowerPoint by selecting File ➤ Send To ➤ Microsoft PowerPoint. When you do this, PowerPoint launches with your Word document imported.

PowerPoint converts every Heading 1 paragraph that it encounters into start a new slide. This results in one slide for each major section of your document. The only problem is, *all* the text under each Heading 1 heading is crammed onto a single slide! To make a Word document fit into a presentation format, you'll have to do a lot of deleting within PowerPoint—or export the Word document while it's still a rough outline, without all the text added beneath each heading.

Exporting a Word outline, then, is probably the best way to make a PowerPoint presentation out of a Word document. When you start with your outline—with no body text yet written—you can send the outline directly to PowerPoint, and each Heading 1 paragraph will become a slide title, Heading 2 paragraphs will become the first-level bullets, Heading 3 paragraphs will become second-level bullets, and so on. You can then finish writing your Word document, content that the skeleton of your PowerPoint presentation is already in the bag.

Streamline the Process with PresentIt

You can ease the process of sending a Word document to PowerPoint by adding the undocumented PresentIt command to any Word toolbar.

To add Word's PresentIt command to a toolbar, follow these steps:

1. From within Word, select Tools ➢ Customize to display the Customize dialog box.

2. Select the Commands tab.

3. From the Categories list, select All Commands.

4. Select the PresentIt item and drag it to the selected toolbar.

5. Click the Close button to close the dialog box.

 When you click the PresentIt button, your current Word document is sent to PowerPoint and used to generate a new presentation, just as you would with the more involved File ➢ Send To ➢ Microsoft PowerPoint operation.

Creating a Word Document from a PowerPoint Presentation

PowerPoint offers several ways to send a presentation back to Word for documentation. You can use Word to create notes or pages to hand out with your presentation, or you can export your PowerPoint file into Word as an outline—which you can then elaborate on as a new Word document.

Create Presentation Handouts

To use Word to create handouts or notes based on your PowerPoint presentation, follow these steps:

1. From within PowerPoint, select File ➢ Send To ➢ Microsoft Word to display the Write-Up dialog box, shown in Figure 32.6.

FIGURE 32.6
Use PowerPoint's Write-Up dialog box to send a presentation to Word.

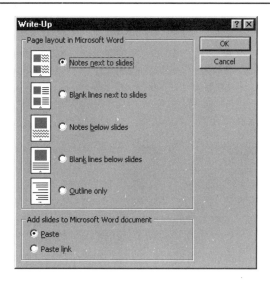

2. Select one of the first four options—Notes Next to Slides, Blank Lines Next to Slides, Notes Below Slides, or Blank Lines Below Slides.

3. To paste copies of the PowerPoint slides in your Word document, check the Paste option; to paste the slides as links back to the PowerPoint document, check the Paste Link option.

4. Click OK.

If you choose to let Word handle your presentation handouts, you can use all of Word's formatting functions to create some really great-looking handouts—much better than the handout pages you can generate from within PowerPoint.

PART
IX

Tips, Tricks, and Troubleshooting

Create a New Document Based on Your Presentation

You can also use Word to flesh out the contents in your PowerPoint presentation into a more complete document. To do this, you want to import your PowerPoint presentation into Word as an outline. Follow these steps:

1. From within PowerPoint, select File ➢ Send To ➢ Microsoft Word to display the Write-Up dialog box.

2. Check the Outline Only option.

3. Click OK.

Word now creates an outline based on your PowerPoint presentation. Slide titles become Heading 1 headings; first-level bullets on each slide become Heading 2 headings; second-level bullets become Heading 3 headings; and so on. You can then use this outline to create a new document, filling in the body text between all the automatically generated headings.

Print Meeting Minutes and Action Items

PowerPoint lets users take notes or schedule action items during presentations, using the Meeting Minder feature. Once these notes or items have been recorded, they can then be exported to Word for editing, formatting, and printing.

To send Meeting Minder notes and items to Word, follow these steps:

1. From within PowerPoint, select Tools ➢ Meeting Minder to display the Meeting Minder dialog box.

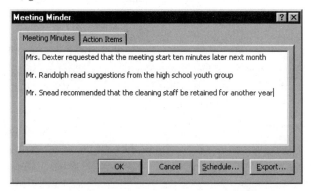

2. To display notes, select the Meeting Minutes tab; to display action items, select the Action Items tab.

3. From either tab, click the Export button to display the Meeting Minder Export dialog box.

4. Check the Send Meeting Minutes and Action Items to Microsoft Word option.

5. Click the Export Now button.

Word now creates a document that contains both the meeting minutes and the action items from your PowerPoint presentation.

Adding PowerPoint Slides to Your Word Documents

There are occasions where you'll want to include not only the text from a PowerPoint slide or presentation, but also the formatting of the presentation, in a Word document. Given the extensive formatting options available in PowerPoint, it's a great way to add some visual interest to your Word document—and call attention to the slide or presentation's key points.

Insert a PowerPoint Slide

Word lets you insert blank PowerPoint slides into your documents. Once a blank slide has been inserted, you can add text to the slide and format the slide, just as you would from within PowerPoint, resulting in a graphic that looks something like the one in Figure 32.7.

Follow these steps to add a single PowerPoint slide to your document:

1. From within Word, select Insert ➢ Object to display the Insert Object dialog box.

2. Check the Create New tab.

3. From the Object Type list, select Microsoft PowerPoint Slide.

4. Click OK.

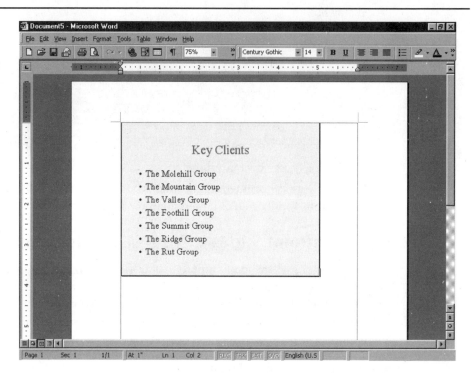

Once the slide has been added, double-click the slide to activate the PowerPoint editing mode. You can then click anywhere within the text areas of the slide to add text, or format the slide by right-clicking the slide and selecting any of the following options from the pop-up menu:

Slide Layout   Select this option to display the Slide Layout dialog box and choose from a variety of slide types—title slides, bulleted lists, charts, and so on.

Slide Color Scheme   Select this option to display the Color Scheme dialog box and either choose a preselected color scheme or create a custom color scheme for this slide.

Background   Select this option to display the Background dialog box and either add a color fill or graphic to the background of this slide.

Apply Design Template   Select this option to display the Apply Design Template dialog box and apply the design (including colors, fonts, graphics, and layout) from a PowerPoint template to this slide.

Within Word, this slide acts as any other graphic object, meaning you can resize it, reposition it, and select different text wrapping effects as you would any Word object.

Embed an Entire PowerPoint Presentation

For the ultimate in integration, you can embed an entire PowerPoint presentation in your Word document. When you do this, only the first slide of the presentation appears on your page; when you double-click this slide, you actually run the presentation onscreen.

To embed a presentation, follow these steps:

1. From within Word, select Insert ➤ Object to display the Insert Object dialog box.

2. Check the Create From File tab.

3. Enter the location and name of the PowerPoint presentation file in the File Name box, or click the Browse button to locate the file.

4. Click OK.

The first slide of the PowerPoint presentation now appears onscreen; you can reposition and format it as you would any Word object. You can also edit individual slides within the presentation by right-clicking the slide and selecting Edit from the pop-up menu; this activates the PowerPoint editing mode, where you can advance from slide-to-slide by using the PgDn and PgUp keys.

To run the presentation, double-click the slide. The presentation now launches in full-screen mode; use the PgDn key to advance to the next slide, and the PgUp key to back up to the previous slide. Press Esc to close the presentation and return to your Word document.

 TIP Additional PowerPoint commands are available from the pop-up menu when you right-click the screen during a presentation.

Using Word with Access

Microsoft Access 2000 is the high-powered database application included with many versions of Office 2000. You use Access as a data source for merged mailings or any other Word document that requires controlled insertion of large blocks of data.

When you use the commands on Word's Database toolbar you can control which database file you use, as well as what records and fields are inserted into your document. You use Word field codes to determine which Access data is inserted where.

 NOTE One of the most common uses of Access within Word is to create a merged mailing. You use the Access database as the *data source* where you store the names and addresses for your mailing; you import this data into your Word form letters, envelopes, and labels by using the Mail Merge Helper. For detailed instructions on creating a merged mailing, see Chapter 19.

Importing Access Data into Word Documents

You use the Insert Database command on Word's Database toolbar to insert data from an Access query or table directly into your Word document. Follow these steps:

1. From within Word, position the insertion point where you want to insert the contents of the database.

 2. From the Database toolbar, click the Insert Database button to display the Database dialog box.

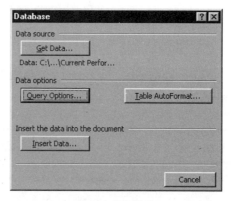

3. Click the Get Data button to display the Open Data Source dialog box.

4. Navigate to and select the Access database you want to use.

5. Click the Open button to display the Microsoft Access dialog box.

6. To import a table, select the Tables tab; to import a query, select the Queries tab.

7. Select the table or query you want to import.

8. Click OK to return to the Database dialog box.

9. To filter or sort records and fields from your database, click the Query Options button to display the Query Options dialog box.

Query Options			? X
Filter Records	So_rt Records	Sele_ct Fields	
	Field:	Comparison:	Compare to:
	TitleID ▼	Equal to ▼	12345
And ▼	NumTracks ▼	Greater than ▼	5
And ▼	▼	▼	
▼	▼	▼	
▼	▼	▼	
▼	▼	▼	
		OK	Cancel	C_lear All

10. To filter which records are imported, select the Filter Records tab; to sort the records in the database, select the Sort Records tab; to import only selected fields from the database, select the Select Fields tab.

11. Make the appropriate selections, then click OK to return to the Database dialog box.

12. Click the Insert Data button to display the Insert Data dialog box.

13. To insert all records from your database, check the All option; to insert only selected records, check the From option and enter a range of records.

14. To automatically update your Word document when the data source changes, check the Insert Data as a Field option.

15. Click the OK button.

Word now creates a table (as a DATABASE field), into which the selected data is inserted. To update the field, click anywhere within the table and press F9.

 NOTE To learn more about inserting data from Access databases—and using Microsoft's query tools—see Chapter 21.

Publishing Access Data to a Word Table

In Chapters 19 and 21 you learned how to import Access data by using Word commands and tools. You can also *export* Access data to Word by using commands found within the Access program. When you do this, the Access data is inserted into a new Word table, which you can then edit and format as you would any Word table.

Follow these steps to send data from Access to Word as a table:

1. From within Access, select or display the item you want to send to Word.

2. Select Tools ➤ Office Links ➤ Publish It with MS Word.

3. Access sends the selected data to a table in a new Word file.

 NOTE This new file is in RTF format, not standard Word format.

4. You can now save this new document as a Word file, or copy the table into an existing Word file.

Using Word with Publisher

Microsoft Publisher is included with many versions of Microsoft Office, and is used to create simple desktop published documents, such as newsletters, brochures, and so on. While you can enter and edit text directly into your Publisher documents, you can also use Word to do the "heavy lifting" necessary when you need to enter large quantities of text.

Editing Publisher Stories in Word

To edit Publisher text within Word, follow these steps:

1. From within Publisher, select the story or text frame you want to edit, as shown in Figure 32.8.

2. Right-click your mouse to display the pop-up menu.

3. From the pop-up menu, select Change Text ➤ Edit Story in Microsoft Word.

4. Word now launches with the Publisher story or text loaded. Enter or edit text from within Word, as you would a normal document.

5. When you're done editing the story or text in Word, select File ➤ Close & Return to Publication.

Word now closes, and your edited text is automatically inserted into your Publisher document.

FIGURE 32.8
Select a story in Publisher, then edit it in Word.

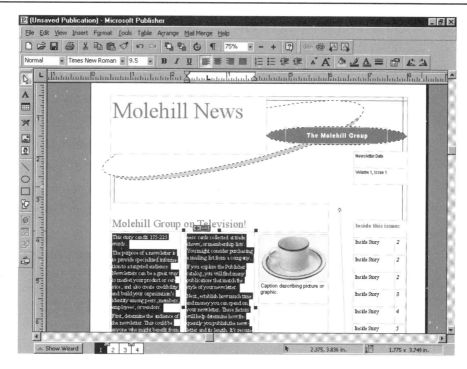

Inserting Word Documents into Publisher Documents

You can also insert Word documents directly into Publisher stories or text frames. Just follow these steps:

1. From within Publisher, select the story or text frame where you want to insert the Word document.

2. Select Insert ➤ Text File to display the Insert Text File dialog box.

3. Navigate to and select the Word file you want to import.

4. Click OK.

The Word file is now inserted into the selected frame.

PART

IX

Tips, Tricks, and
Troubleshooting

Using Word with Photo Editor

Microsoft Photo Editor is a program used to edit and retouch photographs and other graphics. If you want to insert a picture into a Word document, it's a good idea to touch it up in Photo Editor first, to remove red eye, remove scratches, and so on. Once a picture has been edited with Photo Editor, you can import it normally via Word's Insert ➢ Picture ➢ From File command.

If you prefer working with Microsoft Photo Editor to Word's built-in picture editing tools, you can configure Word to use Photo Editor as its default picture editor. Just follow these steps:

1. From within Word, select Tools ➢ Options to display the Options dialog box.

2. Select the Edit tab.

3. Pull down the Picture Editor list and select Microsoft Photo Editor.

4. Click OK.

The next time you select a picture within Word and select Edit ➢ Picture Object ➢ Open, Photo Editor will launch, with the selected picture open for editing. When you're done editing and you close Photo Editor, the edited picture will be automatically updated within your Word document.

CHAPTER **33**

Using the Tools and Utilities on the CD

Installing programs from the CD   **867**

Enhancing Word's functionality   **868**

Working with names and addresses   **876**

Producing better envelopes and faxes   **879**

Protecting your system from viruses   **882**

Converting Word documents to HTML and Help files   **885**

Extending Word with specific solutions   **886**

like to think that this book, by itself, is a pretty good value. We've added to that value by including a free CD containing all sorts of tools and utilities designed to make Word both easier to use and more powerful. The CD also includes the complete text—in electronic format—of Sybex's *Office 2000 Complete*, a comprehensive guide to the *other* applications in Microsoft Office 2000.

While complete instructions are included with each of the individual programs available on the CD (and don't forget to take a look at the readme file on the CD for additional instructions), this chapter provides you with a brief overview of all the programs so you can start using them to get more productive with Word *today!*

 NOTE All of the programs on the accompanying CD are copyrighted by their respective developers. While some of the programs are free for unlimited use, others are demo versions, limited-time trials, or shareware. If you decide to keep a particular program, you should contact the program's developer to purchase the full version of the program.

Installing Programs from the CD

Before we examine each of the programs on the CD, take a few minutes to determine which of the programs you want to install and how to install them.

Introducing the Tools and Utilities on the CD

The CD accompanying this book includes 17 individual programs. In addition, you'll find the complete text of this book, the complete text of Sybex's *Office 2000 Complete*, and eight special Word workshops that lead you step by step through creating different types of Word documents. All these texts are in Adobe Acrobat (.PDF) format; the Adobe Acrobat Reader is also included on the CD.

The contents of the CD include:

Adobe Acrobat Reader   The software necessary to read the text of this book, *Office 2000 Complete*, and the Word workshops that are on the accompanying CD.

Aladdins ~ Word Documents   A Microsoft Outlook add-in that allows you to quickly compose Word documents using Outlook contact data.

BioSpel   A custom dictionary that includes more than 15,000 biological terms.

ChekMate Lite   An anti-virus program that checks for file, boot, and partition sector viruses on your system.

ChekOf   A utility that monitors Word's security level settings and warns you if they're lowered or disabled.

Document Converter   A freestanding program that converts documents between a number of popular formats.

EasyHTML/Help   A powerful development tool that enables you to create Windows Help files from Microsoft Word documents.

GPDATA   A simple, freestanding address book you can use to insert names and addresses into Word documents.

KazStamp   A program that works with Word to create great-looking custom envelopes.

Mastering Word 2000 Premium Edition   The complete text of this book, in Adobe Acrobat format.

MedSpel   A custom dictionary that includes more than 20,000 medical terms.

Mighty Fax   A fax program that installs as a Windows printer driver so you can fax directly from Word.

Office 2000 Complete   The complete text of Sybex's comprehensive guide to Microsoft Office 2000—a great way to learn about the *other* programs included in the Office suite! (Viewable with the Adobe Acrobat Reader.)

OfficeExpress 2000   A graphics tool that acquires images from scanners, digital cameras, and other sources and then enables you to touch up, enhance, and apply special effects to your images before you insert them into your Word documents.

PRIME for Word 2000   An extremely useful collection of tools and utilities that integrate within Word to provide enhanced functionality of most program operations.

ScreenPro   A Word template designed specifically for screenwriters.

SOS Office Helpers   Another collection of tools and utilities that integrate within Word to provide enhanced program functionality.

Symbol Selector   A utility that makes it easier to select and insert symbols and special characters into your documents.

Virus ALERT for Word 2000   An anti-virus program that detects macro viruses in Word templates and documents.

Word Workshops   Eight separate labs that lead you step-by-step through the creation of different types of Word documents. The workshops correspond to the first eight sections of this book: Creating Business Letters, Creating a Company Report, Annotating and Indexing a Company Report, Creating a Newsletter, Setting

PART

IX

Tips, Tricks, and
Troubleshooting

Up a Mass Mailing, Creating a Multiple-Chapter Book, Creating a Personal Web Site, and Creating an Automated Form. Follow the steps in these workshops to create great-looking, fully featured documents. (Viewable with the Adobe Acrobat Reader.)

WordToWeb A powerful program that seamlessly converts existing Word documents to HTML format.

Detailed information about each program follows later in this chapter.

Installing the Programs You Want

You can install any or all of the programs on the accompanying CD, directly from the CD's main menu. All you have to do is click the name of the software program on the CD's menu, and then follow the on-screen instructions to install the software to your computer's hard drive.

 NOTE Neither Sybex nor the author of this book provide technical support for the programs included on the accompanying CD. You should contact a program's developer if you need assistance installing or running any of these tools and utilities.

Enhancing Word's Functionality

The majority of tools and utilities included on the CD are designed to enhance the functionality of the Word 2000 program. These programs range from simple, template-based add-ins to the powerful and sophisticated tools included with PRIME for Word 2000.

PRIME for Word 2000

PRIME for Word 2000 is a collection of tools and utilities that integrate directly with the Word environment. PRIME's tools install on Word's pull-down menus and provide one-click access to functions you probably didn't know you couldn't live without.

You can also choose to display two separate PRIME toolbars. The main PRIME toolbar includes PRIME's major tools, while the PRIME Quick Clicks toolbar provides single-click access to many useful mini-utilities.

PRIME's tools and utilities include:

PRIME Bookmark Manager Found on Word's Insert menu, the Bookmark Manager lets you view, modify, catalog, go to, rename, and delete bookmarks and their contents—as well as display bookmark statistics.

PRIME Bookmark Popup   Found on Word's Insert menu, the Bookmark Popup displays a sorted list of all bookmarks in your current document; select a bookmark to jump to that point in your document.

PRIME Command Bar Manager   Found on Word's Tools menu, the Command Bar Manager enables you to find, analyze, and modify the buttons on any Word toolbar, menu bar, or pop-up menu, even those sometimes hidden by Word.

PRIME Document Variable Manager   Found on Word's View menu, this utility enables you to add, view, modify, delete, and catalog document variables and their contents.

PRIME File Delete   Found on Word's File menu, File Delete enables you to delete the current document as well as to explore or empty the Windows Recycle Bin.

PRIME FileNew   Found on Word's File menu, this utility replaces Word's regular New command with a dialog box containing option buttons for frequently used templates, as shown in Figure 33.1.

FIGURE 33.1
PRIME's FileNew dialog box replaces Word's standard New dialog box and provides easier access to frequently used templates.

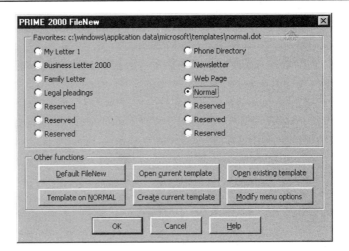

PRIME Find My Dot   Found on Word's File menu, Find My Dot displays the current document's parent template in a dialog box and then allows you to open the template or to create a new file based on the template.

PRIME Folder Now   Found on Word's File menu, Folder Now displays the other contents of the folder that holds the current Word document.

PART

IX

Tips, Tricks, and
Troubleshooting

PRIME Make a Mark   Found on Word's Insert menu, this utility takes currently selected text and creates a bookmark comprised of the first 15 characters of the selected text.

PRIME Proof Controller   Found on Word's Tools menu, Proof Controller lets you quickly toggle between proofing and "no proofing" for a selected section of your document.

PRIME Quick Clicks   These are mini-utilities found on the PRIME Quick Clicks toolbar, which is displayed when you select Tools ➤ PRIME Quick Clicks. The mini-utilities include PRIME Explore Documents Folder (displays your documents folder using Windows Explorer), PRIME File Properties (displays Word's Document Properties dialog box), PRIME Lock Fields (protects all fields in the current document), PRIME Organizer (displays Word's Organizer tool), PRIME Print Selection (prints the selected text), PRIME Reverser (reverses the two currently selected characters), PRIME Toggle Field Codes (toggles on and off the display of Word's field codes), PRIME Toggle Picture Placeholders (toggles on and off the display of picture placeholders), PRIME Toggle Tabs (toggles on and off the display of tab characters), PRIME Visual Basic Editor (launches the VB Editor), PRIME Unlock Fields (unprotects all fields), and PRIME Window Arrange All (arranges all documents in the Word workspace).

PRIME Recently Used Files   Found on Word's File menu, this utility clears the recently used file list, on Word's file menu and in various other Word dialog boxes.

PRIME Shortcut Now   Found on Word's File menu, this creates a shortcut for the current document, either on your Desktop or in any selected folder.

PRIME Window Manager   Found on Word's Window menu, this enables you to close, split, and arrange selected Word windows.

PRIME WorkBar   Installs as a separate pull-down menu on Word's main menu bar and is used to organize your working files. When you add files to the WorkBar, you can then reopen them from the WorkBar in a predetermined view and zoom level. You can store any type of Office file on the WorkBar and sort them by file name.

PRIME Zoomer   Found on Word's View menu, Zoomer presents more precise zoom controls than found with Word's standard zoom.

Personally, I find PRIME for Word 2000 to be an indispensable set of tools and utilities—things that Microsoft should have included with Word 2000 but didn't!

NOTE The version of PRIME for Word 2000 included on the CD is a 30-day trial version, © PRIME Consulting Group, Inc. To learn more about or to purchase the full version of PRIME for Word 2000 ($24.95), go to the PRIME Consulting Web site (www.primeconsulting.com), call 1-800-565-7069, or send e-mail to orders@primeconsulting.com.

SOS Office Helpers

Think of SOS Office Helpers as a mini version of the PRIME utilities. SOS Office Helpers installs as a new pull-down menu on Word's menu bar and includes the following utilities:

SOS Font Chooser   Displays a dialog box containing all available fonts as well as the bold and italic attributes. You select a font from this dialog box to apply to text in your document.

SOS Auto Text Chooser   Displays a dialog box containing all available AutoText entries. You select an entry from this list to add the AutoText to your document.

SOS Quick Art   Displays the SOS Quick Graphic Cataloguer dialog box, which enables you to quickly find, display, and insert graphics files from your hard disk.

SOS Office Helpers also include similar utilities for Excel and PowerPoint.

PART

IX

Tips, Tricks, and
Troubleshooting

NOTE The version of SOS Office Helpers included on the CD is a 30-day trial version, © Specialized Office Solutions. To learn more about or to purchase the full version of SOS Office Helpers ($14.95), go to the SOS Web site (www.compusmart.ab.ca/merkel/), or send e-mail to sos@compusmart.ab.ca.

OfficeExpress 2000

OfficeExpress 2000 is the picture editor that should have been built into Word 2000. This powerful program enables you to acquire scanned and digital camera images, touch up favorite photos, and apply optical character recognition (OCR) to scanned documents, all from within Microsoft Word.

The program installs a new pull-down menu on Word's menu bar. From the Express menu, you have the following options:

Get Photo   Acquires images from a file, scanner, digital camera, or other device.

Scan Image to OCR   Scans a document directly into the OfficeExpress optical character recognition function.

Open File to OCR   Opens a previously scanned document into the OfficeExpress OCR function.

Image Touchup   Accesses the OfficeExpress picture editing tools.

Options   Sets up OfficeExpress for your system.

OfficeExpress 2000 provides a variety of image editing tools, all accessible from the Image Touchup menu. These tools go far beyond Word's built-in picture editor and let you manipulate your images in a number of useful and creative ways.

When you select Express ➢ Image Touchup ➢ Enhancement and Effects, you display the Presto! TouchUp utility, shown in Figure 33.2. From here, you can choose to apply various camera, enhancement, color, and other effects—including swirls, ripples, wipes, and mosaics—as well as adjust color and tint and crop the picture.

When you select Express ➢ Image Touchup ➢ Frame and Shadow, you display the Frame and Shadow utility. From here, you can apply various frame, shadow, and button effects to your images.

FIGURE 33.2
se OfficeExpress 2000
s your primary picture
ditor, and apply some
neat special effects!

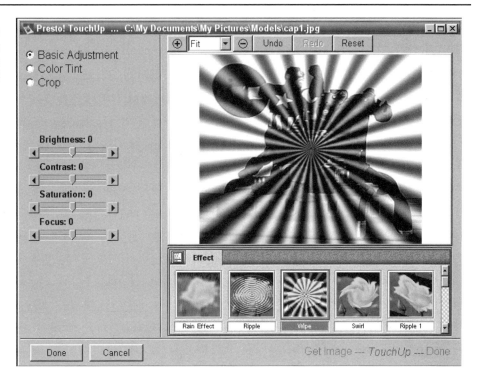

 NOTE The version of OfficeExpress 2000 included on the CD is a 15-day trial version, © New-Soft America, Inc. To learn more about or to purchase the full version of OfficeExpress 2000 ($49.95), go to the NewSoft Web site (www.newsoftinc.com), phone 510-445-8600, or send e-mail to sales@newsoftinc.com.

Symbol Selector

Normally, you insert symbols and characters into your Word documents via the Insert ➢ Symbol command. Word's Symbol dialog box, however, is a little hard to use, and the symbols are displayed quite small.

An easier way to insert symbols is with the Symbol Selector included on this book's CD. When this utility is installed, you can use it with any Windows application to view, insert, and print characters in any font—in any type of document.

As you can see in Figure 33.3, the Symbol Selector window displays characters in large, 14-point type, and you can even select larger point sizes, if you want. You can copy a font either as text or as a .WMF graphic and then paste it into any document. To print a complete character set, all you have to do is select File ➤ Print Symbol Set.

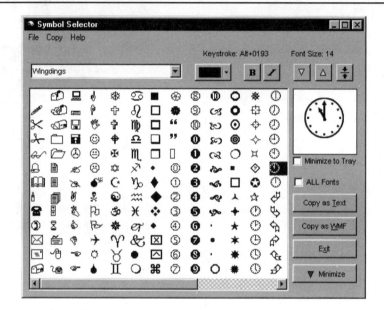

FIGURE 33.3

Use the Symbol Selector to copy and paste symbols and special characters into any document.

 NOTE The version of Symbol Selector included on the CD is a 30-day trial version, © Golightly, Inc. To learn more about or to purchase the full version of Symbol Set ($19.95), go to the RKS Software Store (www.rkssoftware.com), fax 703-534-4358, or send e-mail to sales@rkssoftware.com.

Document Converter

Document Converter is a freestanding program that converts batches of documents to and from a variety of popular file formats, including all of Word's historical formats.

Figure 33.4 shows the demo version of Document Converter included on the CD; you drag files or folders from the top-left window, drop them into the conversion list at the bottom of the screen, select a conversion format, and click the Convert button.

PART

IX

Tips, Tricks, and
Troubleshooting

FIGURE 33.4
Document Converter
lets you convert files
from one format to
another with drag-and-
drop convenience.

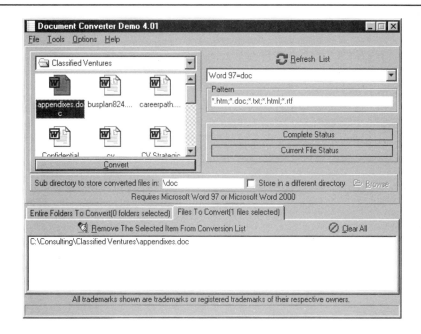

 NOTE The version of Document Converter included on the CD is a demonstration version, © KH Software Development, limited to converting three files at a time. To learn more about or to purchase the full version of Document Converter ($34.95), go to the KH Software Development Web site (www.khsd.com/dc.htm).

Working with Names and Addresses

One of the big headaches associated with creating a merged mailing in Word is the management of the data source—all the names and addresses to use in the mailing. Do you keep your names in a Word table, in an Excel worksheet, or in your Outlook Address book? How do you keep these names up-to-date on an ongoing basis and ensure a smooth merge when you want to create a form letter or a batch of envelopes or labels?

We've included two programs on this book's CD that should help take some of the pain out of making a merged mailing. GPDATA is a very simple address book you can use to store your names and send them, one at a time, to Word documents, and Aladdins ~ Word Documents is an add-in for Microsoft Outlook that makes it easier to choose and export names from Outlook's contact list.

GPDATA

GPDATA is a very simple address book designed specifically for storing and exporting names and addresses to Microsoft Word. There's nothing fancy here—no personal information manager or scheduler or anything like that—just names and addresses and a big button to press when you want to send a name and address to a Word document.

The main address book window, as you can see in Figure 33.5, is very simple. All the names in your database are listed in the middle window; you can also search for a specific name from the box at the top of the window.

FIGURE 33.5

Use GPDATA when you don't want to go through all the hassle of a big merged mailing.

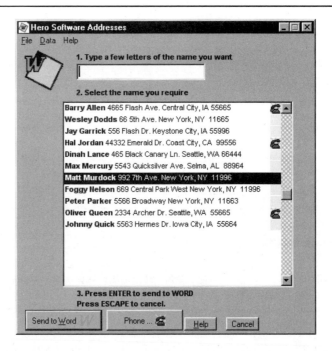

To add names to your GPDATA database, select Data ➤ Add New Record to Database to display the Add New Address dialog box. What's interesting about GPDATA is that you have a lot of flexibility over what you enter; you're not limited to very precise *first*

name, middle initial, last name type fields. In addition to the `Name`, `Address`, and `Telephone` fields, you also see a `Sort Code` field, where you enter whatever part of the name you want this record to be sorted by. (For example, if the person's name is Dr. Martin Q. Smith Jr., you might enter *SMITH* in the `Sort Code` field so it will be sorted by last name.)

To insert a name and address into a Word document, all you have to do is select the name and then click the Send to Word button. GPDATA will then insert the selected name and address into your current Word document, at the insertion point.

While you really can't use GPDATA for merged mailings, it's a very convenient program if you only need to insert a few names and addresses into your documents from time to time.

 NOTE GPDATA is shareware, © Richard Marks. If you use the software, you should register it ($15). To learn more about or to register your version of GPDATA, go to the Hero Software Web site (`www.6ga.co.uk`), or e-mail `richard@6ga.co.uk`.

Aladdins ~ Word Documents

Aladdins ~ Word Documents isn't an add-in to Microsoft Word; it's an add-in to Microsoft Outlook. With Aladdins installed, you can easily compose Word documents (letters, envelopes, and labels, including merged mailings) using Outlook contact data.

Aladdins gives you the choice of sending a single document to a single contact or of selecting multiple contacts for a mail merge. To send a Word letter to a single contact, switch to Outlook's Contacts view, select a contact, and then select Actions ➤ Aladdins New Word Document ➤ Word Document 1. This brings up the Compose Word Documents dialog box. Now you enter as much of your letter as you'd like, and then click the Compose Documents button. This inserts your contact information and the text you've entered directly into a new Word document.

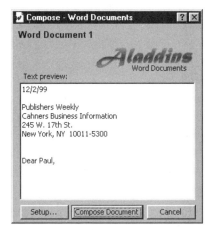

NOTE The first time you use Aladdins, you'll want to click the Setup button to configure the address, the date, and the salutation styles you want to use, as well as the Word template you want the letter to be based on. (You can actually create up to 10 different preset document types, each of which will be listed on the Aladdins New Word Document menu item.)

To create a mail merge with Aladdins, select Actions ➢ Aladdins New Word Document ➢ Custom Merge. When the Custom Merge dialog box appears, check whether you want to include all contacts or only selected contacts, as well as the Document Type you want to create (Form Letters, Mailing Labels, Envelopes, or Catalogs). Click the Fields button to display the Outlook Fields dialog box, and then check which Outlook fields you want to send to your Word document. When you click OK, Aladdins creates a data source file from the selected data and opens either a new or an existing (your choice) Word document with the Database toolbar selected. From here, you can insert merge fields and complete the merged mailing as described back in Chapter 19, with your data source already created and selected by Aladdins.

NOTE The version of Aladdins ~ Word Documents included on the CD is a 30-day trial version, © Manawatu Software Solutions. To learn more about or to purchase the full version of Aladdins (NZ$50, or approximately US$26), go to the Manawatu Software Solutions Web site (www.software-solutions.co.nz/aladdins_wd/alwdabout.htm), or send e-mail to technical@software-solutions.co.nz.

Producing Better Envelopes and Faxes

Word has a fairly robust printing capability, but there's still room for improvement, as you'll find with these two useful utilities.

KazStamp

Don't like to send letters in plain envelopes? Then use KazStamp to create your own personalized envelopes to use with Microsoft Word.

As you can see in Figure 33.6, you can create envelopes of virtually any shape or size in the main KazStamp window. You add the recipient's address and print an envelope manually from within the KazStamp program, or you can integrate KazStamp with

Word to print envelopes using address information in a Word letter. You can even have KazStamp access the Internet and look up the ZIP+4 information for any given address.

FIGURE 33.6
*e KazStamp to create
and print envelopes.*

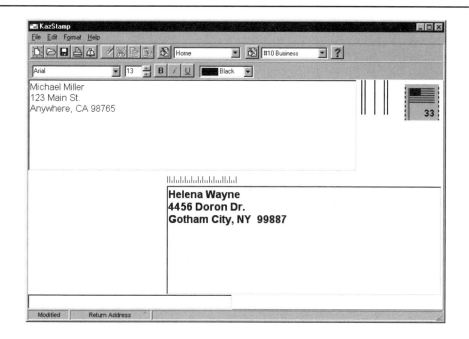

To integrate KazStamp with Word, you'll need to place a copy of the KazStamp.dot file in Word's startup directory. When you do this, Word will display a KazStamp toolbar. To print a KazStamp envelope from Word, select the recipient's address, and then press the Load button on the KazStamp toolbar. KazStamp will now launch with the recipient information loaded; you can make any additional changes within KazStamp, and then click the Print button to print the envelope.

NOTE   The version of KazStamp included on the CD is a limited-use version, © Kaczynski Software, that runs for only one hour at a time. To learn more about or to purchase the full version of KazStamp ($6), go to the Kaczynski Software Web site (www.execpc.com/~kazsoft/), or send e-mail to kazsoft@execpc.com.

PART

IX

Tips, Tricks, and
Troubleshooting

Mighty Fax

As discussed in Chapter 7, neither Word nor Windows 98 come with built-in fax programs. (Older versions of Windows came with fax software, but Microsoft took it out of Windows 98.) If you need a fax program for your system, look no further: Mighty Fax is here!

Mighty Fax is a fax program that also installs as a printer driver within Windows. That means when you want to send a fax from within Word (or any Windows application, actually), all you have to do is select File ➢ Print to display the Print dialog box, pull down the Name list, select Mighty Fax Printer Driver, and then press the Print button.

At this point, Mighty Fax starts up and displays a dialog box asking for the Fax Number, the Recipient, and the Subject for your fax. After you've entered this information, a second dialog box notifies you that the fax has been created and asks if you would like to switch to Mighty Fax.

Answer Yes and the Mighty Fax program launches. As you can see in Figure 33.7, you can now use Mighty Fax to send your fax (along with an optional cover sheet) through your computer's modem and over your phone lines. You can also use Mighty Fax as a stand-alone program to create new faxes (without using Word) and to receive and print faxes.

 NOTE The first time you use Mighty Fax, you'll see a Quick Setup Form dialog box; fill in the appropriate information for Mighty Fax to use for all your subsequent faxes.

 NOTE The version of Mighty Fax included on the CD is a 30-day trial version, © Golightly, Inc. To learn more about or to purchase the full version of Mighty Fax ($19.95), go to the RKS Software Store (www.rkssoftware.com), fax 703-534-4358, or send e-mail to sales@rkssoftware.com.

FIGURE 33.7
se Mighty Fax to send
our Word documents
as faxes.

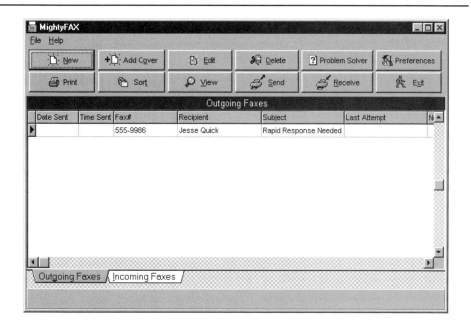

Protecting Your System from Viruses

Computer viruses are nasty things, and viruses transmitted via Word macros are becoming ever more prevalent. Unfortunately, save for its security level settings, Word 2000 has no active anti-virus capability. If you're worried about macro viruses infecting your system—and you should be—check out these programs on the accompanying CD.

Virus ALERT for Word 2000

Since Word 2000 doesn't have its own built-in virus-scanning capability, you need to install a third-party anti-virus program. Virus ALERT for Word 2000 is an anti-virus program designed just for Word 2000. It installs as a Word add-in, so it appears on Word's Standard toolbar and as a new pull-down menu on Word's menu bar.

To scan your system for viruses, select VA-Macro ➢ Scan for Viruses (or click the VAScan button on Word's Standard toolbar). When the Scan for Viruses dialog box

PART
IX

Tips, Tricks, and
Troubleshooting

(shown in Figure 33.8) appears, select the drives, directories, file types (documents and/or templates), and specific files you want to scan, and then click the Scan button. Virus ALERT now scans the selected files, directories, and/or drives for infected files.

FIGURE 33.8

Use Virus ALERT for Word 2000 to scan your system for macro viruses.

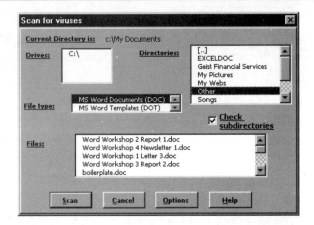

You can configure Virus ALERT to create a log of any infected files (but not to clean the files), to automatically clean any infected files, or to prompt you before cleaning any infected files. These options are set when you select VA-Macro ➤ Virus ALERT Options to display the Options dialog box and then select the Scan tab.

You can also use Virus ALERT to manually examine all the macros in your current document. When you select VA-Macro ➤ Macros, the Virus ALERT Macros dialog box is displayed. Select a template, and click the View Code for All button to display a dialog box containing the macro code.

NOTE The version of Virus ALERT for Word 2000 included on the CD is a 30-day trial version, © eVirus Corporation. To learn more about or to purchase the full version of Virus ALERT ($29.95), go to the eVirus Corporation Web site (www.evirus.com), phone 613-736-5040, or send e-mail to sales@evirus.com (for purchase information) or to support@evirus.com (for technical support).

ChekMate Lite

Where Virus ALERT scans your Word files for macro viruses, ChekMate Lite works in the background to alert you if your key system files become infected.

ChekMate Lite is a simple DOS-based program that is designed to detect new and known file, boot, and partition sector viruses. While it's not a substitute for virus-scanning software, such as Virus ALERT, it does provide an extra layer of protection against the most destructive types of computer viruses.

ChekMate Lite works by comparing the precise sizes of key system files with the file sizes it registers when you first install the program. If a file size changes, that indicates the presence of a virus in that file. When you run ChekMate Lite, a DOS window appears onscreen as the program checks each of the files and alerts you if any file sizes have changed.

 NOTE ChekMate Lite is free for your personal use, © Martin Overton (ChekWARE). To learn more about ChekMate Lite or to upgrade to the more fully featured ChekMate software ($45), go to the ChekWARE Web site (www.chekware.simplenet.com/cmindex.htm), or e-mail ChekWARE@Cavalry.com.

ChekOf

From the developer of ChekMate Lite comes this neat little utility to make sure that no one changes Word's security settings without you knowing it. ChekOf (pronounced like the name of the guy who sat beside Sulu on *Star Trek*) runs in the background and warns you if the security settings in Word are lowered from their initial settings. The program also displays an error message if Word's security level is set to Low, which is not recommended.

When you install ChekOf, make sure that a shortcut to the program is copied into the Windows Startup folder so the program will launch whenever you turn on your computer. When you click the ChekOf icon in the Windows taskbar, ChekOf displays a dialog box listing the security settings for all Office applications.

 NOTE ChekOf is shareware, © Martin Overton (ChekWARE). If you use the program, you should register it ($15). To learn more about ChekOf, or to register your copy, go to the ChekWARE Web site (www.chekware.simplenet.com/cmindex.htm), or e-mail ChekWARE@Cavalry.com.

PART

IX

Tips, Tricks, and Troubleshooting

Converting Word Documents to HTML and Help Files

While Word 2000 offers improved HTML editing capabilities, it's still not the most friendly environment available for creating files for the Web. In fact, converting a Word .DOC file to HTML format is still an iffy proposition with Word; the results, as they say, are variable.

A much better solution is to use a program specifically designed for converting documents to HTML format. The CD included with this book includes one such program (WordToWeb), plus another program (EasyHTML/Help) that lets you create your own Word and Windows help files.

WordToWeb

WordToWeb is designed to do one thing and one thing well: convert Word documents to HTML format. It offers much more flexibility and functionality than Word's built-in HTML conversion, and it can help you eliminate time you would otherwise spend hand-tweaking your documents within Word's Web Layout environment.

Why use WordToWeb? Put simply, it converts Word documents to Web pages better, and more automatically, than does Word itself. Plus, it's extremely easy to use.

When you launch WordToWeb, you're actually launching the WordToWeb Wizard. This Wizard walks you step-by-step through the entire document conversion process, asking for input on items such as:

- Which source document to convert
- What type of publication to create
- Whether or not to include a TOC or an index
- How to format the page background and other document properties
- Which page layout you want
- How to format tables
- How to format headings
- How to handle cross-references and automatic linking
- How to convert graphics from your documents

You can also run the WordToWeb Batch Converter, which converts multiple Word documents at one time. If you have a whole batch of old Word documents you need to put on the Internet, this is a great tool to use.

NOTE The version of WordToWeb included on the CD is a 30-day trial version, © Solutionsoft. To learn more about or to purchase the full version of WordToWeb ($299), go to the Solutionsoft Web site (www.solutionsoft.com/w2w.htm), phone 888-765-6738, or send e-mail to sales@solutionsoft.com.

EasyHTML/Help

EasyHTML/Help can also be used to create HTML documents, but its real claim to fame is its ability to create Windows Help files. With Windows 98, Help documents were moved to the HTML-like .CHM format. EasyHTML/Help (also known as EasyHH) lets you write your Help files in Word and then convert them to .CHM for inclusion with any custom applications you may be developing.

EasyHH works within Word as an add-in. You launch the program initially by opening the EX01.DOC file, which loads the EasyHH template, complete with a new EasyHTML/Help toolbar. Converting a document is pretty much as easy as clicking the Topic To button (to mark individual Web pages), clicking the Link button (to create links to your marked pages and other URLs), clicking the Process button (to create the HTML pages themselves), clicking the Results button (to look at your work in a browser), and then clicking the Build button (to convert the HTML into the .CHM Windows HTML Help format).

Of course, it's really a bit more complicated than this (considering that you have to properly construct the organization of your Windows Help files), but you get the gist. Make sure you fully read the instructions in the EX01.DOC file before you jump head-first into this complicated operation.

 NOTE The version of EasyHTML/Help included on the CD is a 30-day trial version, © Eon Solutions Ltd. To learn more about or to purchase the full version of EasyHTML/Help ($199), go to the EasyHTML/Help Web site (www.easyhtmlhelp.com), or send e-mail to sales@easyhtmlhelp.com (to purchase) or to support@easyhtmlhelp (for technical support).

Extending Word with Specific Solutions

The final products on this book's CD might not be for everyone. But if you're looking for a specific solution to a specific "vertical" problem, take a look and see if there's something for you!

PART

IX

Tips, Tricks, and
Troubleshooting

BioSpel

BioSpel is a custom spelling dictionary (in five separate files) that contains over 15,000 biological terms, from abdominis to zymogen. You install BioSpel as you would any custom dictionary, using the steps outlined in Chapter 6.

 NOTE BioSpel is shareware © R. Robinson. If you use the dictionary, you should register it ($10). To learn more about BioSpel, e-mail `third_wave@usa.net`; to register your copy, send a check or money order for $10 to R. Robinson, 9 Sundowner Ln., Springfield, IL 62707.

MedSpel

MedSpel is custom spelling dictionary (in five separate files) that contains over 20,000 medical terms, including:

- More than 1500 drug names (both trade and generic)
- Anatomical terms
- Dermatological terms
- Internal medicine terms
- Surgical terms
- DSM-IV terms
- ICD-9 terms
- And more

You install MedSpel as you would any custom dictionary, using the steps outlined in Chapter 6.

 NOTE MedSpel is shareware © R. Robinson. If you use the dictionary, you should register it ($7.50). To learn more about MedSpel, e-mail `third_wave@usa.net`; to register your copy, send a check or money order for $7.50 to R. Robinson, 9 Sundowner Ln., Springfield, IL 62707.

ScreenPro

ScreenPro is a custom Word template designed specifically for writing screenplays. When you create a new document based on the SCRNPR97.DOT template, the template automatically selects the Courier New font (the font of choice in Hollywood since it looks most like typewritten text) and then switches styles as needed as you progress through your script, adjusting line spacing, indentation, capitalization, and so on. It also displays the Screenplay toolbar, with buttons for title page, slug lines, and other essential script elements.

If you do any script writing at all, you'll appreciate the way ScreenPro helps to automate the screenwriting process.

NOTE ScreenPro is shareware, © Jack Passarella. If you use the template, you should register it ($10). To learn more about ScreenPro, e-mail jpassarella@lehigh-press.com; to register your copy, send a check or money order for $10 to Jack Passarella, P.O. Box 381, Swedesboro, NJ 08085.

CHAPTER 34

Finding Help

Using Word 2000's built-in Help system   **890**

Using the Office Assistant   **894**

Going online with Microsoft Office Update   **898**

Searching the Microsoft Knowledge Base 899

Asking questions on Microsoft's newsgroups   **901**

Getting help over the phone—and elsewhere   **903**

When you need help with Word 2000, where do you turn—other than this book, that is?

One of the first places you should turn is Word's built-in Help system—which isn't near as bad as it used to be. That might sound like damning with faint praise, but the truth is most users avoid built-in Help systems, remembering how poor such systems were in the not-so-long-ago computing past. The reality is, Word 2000's Help system is much improved over past systems, and can be used to answer many common questions.

If you can't find your answers in the built-in Help system, you can always go online for more help. Word 2000 offers a link to the Microsoft Office Update Web site, directly from Word's Help menu. This Web site is a good place to search for up-to-date news and information, as well as search for specific technical support and download Word updates and utilities.

Using Word 2000's Built-In Help System

When you need help with Word, all you have to do is press a key. When you press F1 (or select Help ➤ Microsoft Word Help) you open Word's built-in Help system. From here you can browse through the system's table of contents, ask specific questions from the Answer Wizard, or look up key words in the system's index.

Browsing the Table of Contents

When you click the Contents tab in the Help dialog box (shown in Figure 34.1), you see a list of major Help topics in the left pane. Click the + next to each major topic to display a list of subtopics topics within the major topic; click a specific topic (notated with a question mark icon) to display that topic in the right pane.

Within individual topics, you'll often find hyperlinks to related topics, indicated by underlined text. Click a link to display the related Help topic.

You can navigate back and forth through topics you've displayed by using the Back and Forward buttons in the Help toolbar. You can also choose to print the current topic by clicking the Print button, or copy Help text to a Word document by selecting the text and pressing Ctrl+Ins (then Shift+Ins to paste the text into the document).

FIGURE 34.1

Browse selected Help topics from the Contents tab.

Major Topic

Hide the Left Pane

Next Topic

Previous Topic

Print This Topic

Display Other Help Options

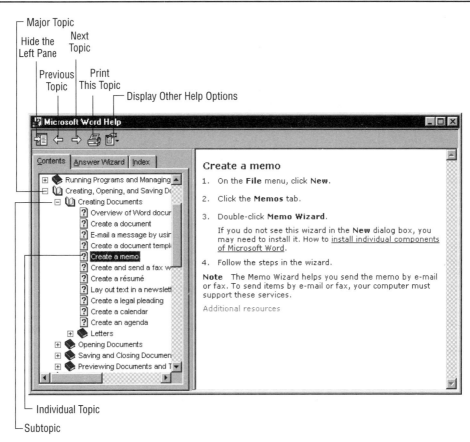

Individual Topic

Subtopic

Create a memo

1. On the **File** menu, click **New**.

2. Click the **Memos** tab.

3. Double-click **Memo Wizard**.

   If you do not see this wizard in the **New** dialog box, you may need to install it. How to install individual components of Microsoft Word.

4. Follow the steps in the wizard.

Note The Memo Wizard helps you send the memo by e-mail or fax. To send items by e-mail or fax, your computer must support these services.

Additional resources

 TIP To make the individual articles easier to read, you can hide the left pane by clicking the Hide button on the Help toolbar. Click the Show button to toggle back to the dual-pane view.

Asking the Answer Wizard

If you can't easily find the Help topic you want, you can ask a question of the Help system, which then generates a list of articles that should be of assistance. When you

PART

IX

Tips, Tricks, and Troubleshooting

select the Answer Wizard tab (shown in Figure 34.2), enter your query in the What Would You Like to Do? box, then click the Search button. A list of articles matching your query now appears in the Select Topic to Display list; select a topic from this list to display the contents of the topic in the right-pane.

FIGURE 34.2
Ask a question of the Answer Wizard.

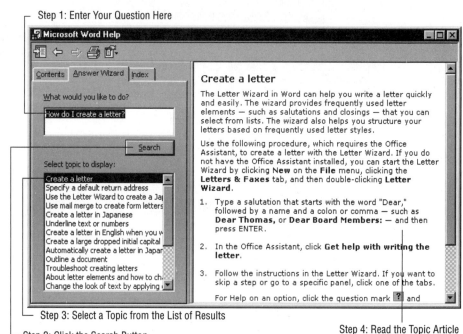

Step 1: Enter Your Question Here

Step 3: Select a Topic from the List of Results

Step 2: Click the Search Button

Step 4: Read the Topic Article

Searching the Index

All the key words in Word's Help system are included in a massive index. You can browse through the words in the index, or search for topics that contain a specific keyword.

When you select the Index tab, the dialog box changes to that shown in Figure 34.3. To search for keywords, enter the word in the Type Keywords box and click Search; topics containing that keyword are then listed in the Choose a Topic list. You display a specific topic by selecting it from the list.

PART

IX

Tips, Tricks, and
Troubleshooting

FIGURE 34.3

Search for keywords on the Index tab.

Enter a Keyword Search   Click to Search

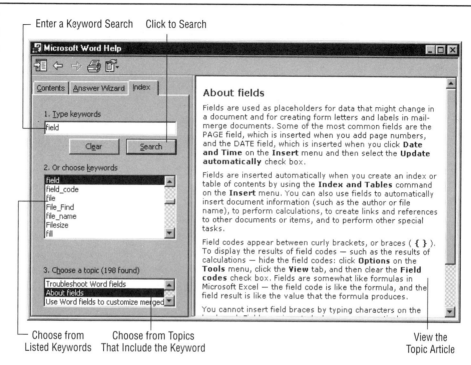

Choose from
Listed Keywords

Choose from Topics
That Include the Keyword

View the
Topic Article

You can browse through keywords by selecting a word from the Or Choose Keywords list. (If you enter a keyword in the Type Keywords box *without* clicking Search, that word will be highlighted in the Choose Keywords list.) After you select a word, click the Search button (or double-click the keyword) to display a list of topics that contain that keyword in the Choose a Topic list.

NOTE If you develop your own applications with Word and VBA, you can create your own Word Help files using a special HTML-like development language. You need a special program to develop Help files, such as EasyHTML/Help, which is included on the CD that accompanies this book. For more information on EasyHTML/Help, see Chapter 33.

Using the Office Assistant

One of the so-called features of Office 2000 is the Office Assistant. This is an animated character (and you can select from several available characters) that pops up onscreen to walk you through Help system, or just to offer advice when it thinks you need help.

As you can see in Figure 34.4, when you press the F1 key with the Office Assistant activated, it tries to figure out what you need help with, and asks you a series of questions designed to figure out the proper Help topic. If it can't figure out where you're stuck, it will display only the Type Your Question Here box; entering a question in the box and clicking Search is the equivalent of using the Answer Wizard in the standard Help system.

FIGURE 34.4
One of Word's somewhat annoying Office Assistants, trying to figure out what kind of help you need

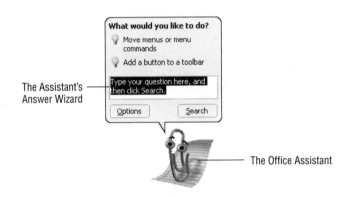

The Assistant's Answer Wizard

The Office Assistant

Turn Off the Office Assistant

Many users find the Office Assistant annoying, especially as it tends to pop up at the most unusual moments. For example, if you have the Office Assistant activated, if you open a new document, type "Dear *Name*," then press the Enter key, the Office Assistant butts in with the message "It looks like you're writing a letter. Would you like help?" Since it's unlikely you'll need help with every letter you write, this can get old very fast.

Fortunately, it's easy to turn off the Office Assistant. To temporarily hide the Office Assistant, select Help ≻ Hide the Office Assistant. To turn it off completely, follow these steps:

1. Click the Office Assistant to display the pop-up word balloon.

2. Click the Options button to display the Office Assistant dialog box.

3. Select the Options tab.

4. *Uncheck* the Use the Office Assistant option.

5. Click OK.

To turn the Assistant back on at any time, select Help ➢ Show the Office Assistant.

Change Office Assistant Characters

Office 2000 offers several characters you can use as your own personalized Office Assistant. To change Office Assistant characters, follow these steps:

1. Click the Office Assistant to display the pop-up word balloon.

2. Click the Options button to display the Office Assistant dialog box.

3. Select the Gallery tab.

4. Use the Forward and Back buttons to cycle through available characters.

5. When you find the character you want, click OK.

Additional characters can be found on your Office 2000 installation CD, and on the Microsoft Office Web site (www.microsoft.com/office/).

Learning about Specific Elements with What's This?

Have you ever wondered what a particular button or menu item was? You don't need to access the entire Help system if you just need to know about a specific screen element—you can use Word's What's This feature.

When you select Help ➢ What's This (or press Shift+F1), your cursor changes into a question mark. You can then click any screen element (toolbar button, menu item, or any element in a dialog box), and Word displays a ScreenTip describing that element, as shown in Figure 34.5. If you turn on What's This and click a character in your document, Word displays a pop-up box detailing the paragraph and character formatting of the selection, as shown in Figure 34.6.

FIGURE 34.5
Use What's This to display ScreenTips about Word screen elements.

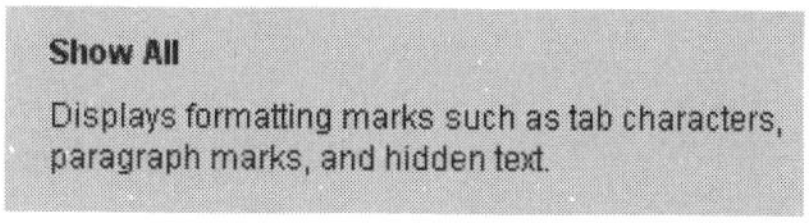

Show All

Displays formatting marks such as tab characters, paragraph marks, and hidden text.

FIGURE 34.6
*What's This can also
display paragraph and
character formatting
information about
selected text.*

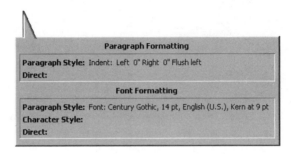

Displaying Program Information

If you ever contact technical support, you'll be asked what version of Word you have. The easiest way to obtain this information is to select Help ➢ About Microsoft Word, which displays the About Microsoft Word dialog box, shown in Figure 34.7.

FIGURE 34.7
*Display information
about your installation
in the About Microsoft
Word dialog box.*

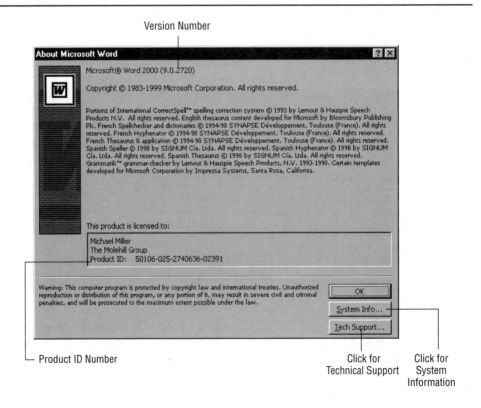

This dialog box not only displays the version number of the copy of Word installed on your system, it also provides access to more detailed system information. When you click the System Information button, you display Windows' Microsoft System Information utility, which contains much more detailed technical information about your entire computer system. Technical support staff may need to access this information to help you solve specific problems with your system.

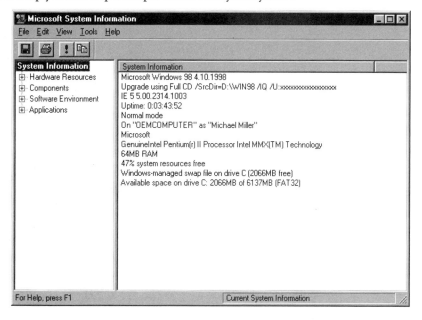

 TIP You can also display a list of Microsoft technical support options by clicking the Tech Support button in the About Microsoft Word dialog box.

Going Online for More Help

If you can't find the help you need within Word, you can go outside Word—all the way to the Internet—for more detailed and up-to-date support options. Microsoft uses its large Web site to provide a variety of support resources for all of its software customers—including fellow users of Word 2000.

Using Microsoft Office Update

Most Word support resources are housed in the Microsoft Office Update Web site. You can access this site from within Word by selecting Help ➢ Office on the Web; when you select this option, Word launches your Web browser, connects to the Internet (via your ISP), and goes directly to the Word section of the Microsoft Office Update Web site, shown in Figure 34.8.

FIGURE 34.8
Use the Microsoft Office Update site to obtain up-to-date information, support, and downloads.

 NOTE You can go directly to the Microsoft Office Update site by directing your Web browser to officeupdate.microsoft.com; from there, you can click the Word link to go to the Word section of the site.

Navigate the Site

The Word section of the Office Update site includes a variety of different Word-related resources, as well as quick links to related sites for other Office applications. If you're having trouble with Word, the main sections of interest are accessed from the menu bar at the left of the page. Click the Downloads link if you want to download program updates, patches, and utilities; click the Assistance link to access Microsoft's many technical support resources.

Get Online Help

When you click the Assistance link on the site's Welcome page, you jump to the Word Assistance page. Among the resources accessible from this page are the following:

- Articles for Microsoft Word 2000
- Microsoft Technical Support for Word
- Tips and Tricks for Word 2000
- Word Newsgroups
- Office Resource Kit
- Third Party Word Links

Click any link to jump to the specific resource. For example, when you click the Microsoft Technical Support for Word link, you are taken to the Word Support Page, which includes links to the following:

Knowledge Base Articles About Word   This displays a comprehensive list of Word-related articles from the Microsoft Knowledge Base (discussed in the next section).

Support Highlights for Word   This displays the hottest, most up-to-date support issues for Word.

Frequently Asked Questions About Word   This displays a list of the most common questions about Word usage and problems.

Troubleshooter for Word   This displays a handful of online Troubleshooters designed to walk you step-by-step through solving common Word problems. Click a link to go directly to that resource.

Searching the Microsoft Knowledge Base

The Microsoft Knowledge Base is a vast depository of articles detailing Microsoft's technical responses to a variety of user problems and questions. You can access the Knowledge Base through the Microsoft Office Update site, or go directly to support .microsoft.com/search/.

PART

IX

Tips, Tricks, and
Troubleshooting

As you can see from Figure 34.9, it's easy to query the Knowledge Base about your specific problem. Just follow these steps:

1. Pull down the My Search Is About list and select your specific program (Word 2000).

2. From section 2, select how you want to search; typically, you'll want to search by Keywords.

3. Enter your question in the My Question Is box.

 TIP If you've used the Knowledge Base before, it remembers your previous queries and lists them in the My Last 10 Searches list; to repeat a query, just select it from this list.

4. Check the Full Text option to search entire articles (recommended).

5. Check the Titles With Excerpts option to display a brief excerpt from each article in the results list (recommended).

6. Click Go to initiate the search.

FIGURE 34.9
Search the Knowledge Base for technical answers to specific questions

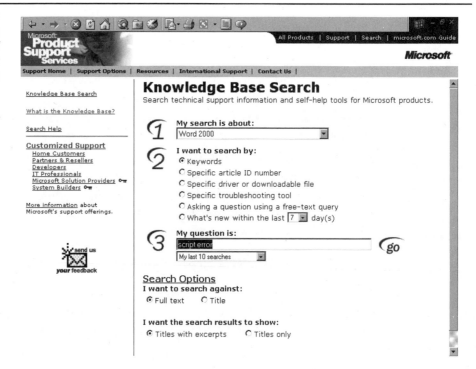

The Knowledge Base now displays a list of articles that match the keywords in your query. Click any article title to read the entire article.

The articles in the Knowledge Base range from generally informative to specifically technical. Since these articles log the responses of Microsoft's technical support and development staffs, it's likely that you'll find at least one article related to your query. Follow the advice in the articles to the best of your ability (some of the articles are quite technical), or continue searching if you can't find any relevant information.

 TIP Since Word 2000 and Word 97 are very similar in operation, try searching for Word 97 articles if you can't find a Word 2000 article that answers your question.

Asking Questions on Microsoft's Newsgroups

In addition to Microsoft's various Web-based resources, you can also find lots of helpful advice and information in Microsoft's Word-related Usenet newsgroups. Newsgroups are topic-related electronic message boards that you access on a Usenet *news server*. You can use either Microsoft Outlook or Outlook Express as a newsreader to read and post messages (called *articles*) on these newsgroups.

Each newsgroup is focused on a specific topic, and features lively discussions among users. You can browse the messages in a newsgroup to look for advice on a specific issue, or post your own messages asking questions of other users.

Table 34.1 lists those newsgroups related to Microsoft Word issues:

TABLE 34.1: WORD-RELATED NEWSGROUPS

Focus	Newsgroup
Application errors	microsoft.public.word.applicationerrors
Document management	microsoft.public.word.docmanagement
File conversion	microsoft.public.word.conversions
Fonts and printing	microsoft.public.word.printingfonts
Formatting long documents	microsoft.public.word.formatting.longdocs
General issues	microsoft.public.word.general
Graphics and drawing	microsoft.public.word.drawing-graphics
Mail merge	microsoft.public.word.mailmergefields
Networking setup	microsoft.public.word.setupnetworking

Continued ▐▶

PART

IX

Tips, Tricks, and
Troubleshooting

TABLE 34.1: WORD-RELATED NEWSGROUPS (CONTINUED)

Focus	Newsgroup
Numbering and lists	`microsoft.public.word.numbering`
Object linking and embedding interoperability	`microsoft.public.word.OLEinterop`
Page layout and design	`microsoft.public.word.pagelayout`
Programming and application development	`microsoft.public.word.programming`
Spelling and grammar	`microsoft.public.word.spelling-grammar`
Tables	`microsoft.public.word.tables`
VBA	`microsoft.public.word.vba`

Finding Non-Microsoft Resources on the Web

Microsoft isn't the only source of Word 2000 information on the Internet. There are numerous third-party sites that contain news, information, utilities, and other resources pertaining to Microsoft Word. Table 34.2 details the best of these recommended Web sites:

TABLE 34.2: THIRD-PARTY WORD-RELATED WEB SITES

Site	URL	Description
Baarns Consulting Microsoft Office Resource Center	`archive.baarns.com`	Consulting group specializing in Microsoft Office; site contains software, tips, and other resources
CNET Help.com	`www.help.com/cat/2/69/141/143/index.html`	Large collection of resources, downloads, tips, and message boards for Word users of every level—recommended
Computertips: Word Tips	`www.computertips.com/Microsoftoffice/MsWord/submenu.htm`	A variety of tips for Word users
Document Depot: MS Word Tips and Tricks	`www.uwtc.washington.edu/DocDepot/Documents/word/Default.htm`	Word tips and how-tos from the University of Washington

Continued ▶

TABLE 34.2: THIRD-PARTY WORD-RELATED WEB SITES (CONTINUED)		
Site	**URL**	**Description**
Microsoft Word Tips, Tricks, and Other Goodies	`www.cooper.edu/classes/eng/EID111/younes/word_tip.htm`	A nice collection of useful Word tips
MyHelpdesk.com	`www.myhelpdesk.com/Tabs/DirectoryTab.asp?ProductID=6`	Good collection of Word resources, including links to FAQs, training, tutorials, error messages, drivers, documentation, and downloads
OfficeCert.com	`www.officecert.com`	Resources for users preparing for Microsoft Office User Specialist (MOUS) certification
PC Magazine: Microsoft Word Tips	`205.181.113.18/pcmag/pctech/content/solutions/packs/msword.html`	From one of the most popular computer magazines, a collection of Word-related tips and techniques
Word Info	`www.wordinfo.com`	One of the best collections of Word-related news, information, resources, and links on the Web
WordTips	`www.vitalnews.com/WordTips/`	Subscribe to weekly newsletter full of tips and tricks for Word users
ZDNet Help & How-To: Microsoft Word	`www.zdnet.com/zdhelp/filters/subfilter/0,7212,6003255,00.html`	From one of the premiere computer sites on the Internet, a collection of news, information, tutorials, resources, and software downloads

Getting Help Over the Phone and Elsewhere

If you prefer to ask for help from a real person, you can choose to telephone Microsoft for real-time technical support. Microsoft's U.S. number for no-charge technical support is 425-462-9673; in Canada, you can call 905-568-2294.

In addition to this telephone-based technical support, Microsoft offers several other support options:

TTY/TDD Support   Available Monday through Friday only, at 425-635-4948 (U.S.) or 905-568-9641 (Canada).

FastTips Fax-Back Support   Provides Knowledge Base articles and answers to common questions, at 800-936-4100.

Support for Businesses   Microsoft offers several different support packages for businesses of different sizes. For more information, call 800-936-3500 (small and medium-sized businesses) or 800-936-3200 (large businesses), or go to www.microsoft.com/support/.

Specialized Support   Onsite and proprietary product support is available through Microsoft's network of Microsoft Certified Solution Providers (MCSPs) and Authorized Support Centers (ASCs); for more information about these options, call 800-765-7768 or go to www.microsoft.com/mcsp/.

Common Word Problems and Solutions

Troubleshooting error messages   **906**

Troubleshooting files and damaged
documents   **916**

Troubleshooting formatting   **926**

Troubleshooting tables and sorting   **944**

Troubleshooting graphics   **945**

Troubleshooting printing, faxing,
and e-mail   **955**

Troubleshooting macros and VBA   **968**

Word 2000 is a great program—when it works right. But when something goes wrong, it can be a very frustrating application with which to work.

This chapter is designed to help you troubleshoot most of the common problems encountered by Word users. Obviously, not all possible problems can be covered in a single chapter—or in a single book—but most of the big ones are here, as is plentiful advice on how to both avoid and track down the causes of most Word-related problems.

Most Word problems are actually Word *user* problems. That is, Word only did what you told it to do—and you told it to do something wrong. It's the old *garbage in, garbage out* scenario: If you enter something incorrectly or select the wrong command, Word will execute your mistake, often with unpredictable results. The solution to most Word problems, then, is to click the Undo button—and try again.

If your troubles persist, however, you probably do have a real problem. Use the advice in this chapter—and the skills you've learned throughout the rest of this book—to help you troubleshoot your problems, or go online to the Microsoft Knowledge Base (`support.microsoft.com/search/`) to search for specific technical solutions to your Word problems.

 NOTE Learn more about the Microsoft Knowledge Base and other sources of online help in Chapter 34.

Troubleshooting Error Messages

When something really major goes wrong with Word, it will generate an error message. The error message is accompanied either with instructions on what to do next or with a prompt to click a button to close down the program. The latter type of error message is the most disconcerting, naturally.

When you receive an error message, it's important to note the details generated and to follow the message's instructions on how to proceed. The details of the error message provide important clues as to what caused the problem; if the problem persists, you can use these clues to track down the cause of the recurring problem.

Understanding the Most Common Error Messages

There are three general types of *crash the program* error messages:

- Fatal exception errors
- Illegal operation errors
- Kernel errors

All three types of error messages are discussed in the following sections.

Fatal Exception Errors

An exception error is generated when something unexpected has happened within *Windows*—that is, this is really a Windows error message, not a Word error message. Still, it is an error that affects the Word program, typically when something goes wrong with memory access. For example, Word might try to read or write to a memory location that is technically off limits, potentially overwriting and corrupting other program code in that area of memory.

When you see a fatal exception error message, it will look something like this:

```
A fatal exception <XY> has occurred at xxxx:xxxxxxxx
```

In most cases the exception is nonrecoverable, meaning that Word will be forcibly shut down. In the most serious cases, you'll need to reboot your system before you can restart Windows.

Illegal Operation Errors

In Microsoft Word 2000, the most common error message accompanying a program crash is an illegal operation error. The error message will look similar to the following:

```
This program has performed an illegal operation and will be shut down
```

When you receive this type of error message, you should have the option of clicking a Details button to learn more about the problem. In most cases, when you click Details, you see the following message:

```
WINWORD caused an invalid page fault in module module name at address.
```

After you click OK, Word is shut down.

In this instance, the illegal operation was an *invalid page fault*. As with the fatal exception error, this happens typically when Word improperly attempts to use an area of random access memory.

Kernel Errors

A kernel error is a particular type of illegal operation error. This type of error is an invalid page fault that occurs between Word and Windows, and generates the typical illegal operation error message. When you click the Details button, however, you'll see a message like the following:

```
WINWORD caused an invalid page fault in module Kernel32.dll at address.
```

After you click OK, Word is shut down.

PART

IX

Tips, Tricks, and
Troubleshooting

Tracking Down Major Problems

If you receive an error message only once, it's probably not worth worrying about. If, however, Word keeps producing the same error message over and over, it's an indication that you have a major problem somewhere on your system. To find and fix the cause of any recurring error messages, you need to decipher the error messages themselves, then work backward to the particular scenario from which they're generated.

Deciphering the Message

Always—*always!*—click the Details button when you receive an error message. The details provide important clues as to the cause of this particular error.

In most cases, a module name will be listed in the details. The module name may be a printer driver file, a video driver file, or some other non-Word component. The module listed is probably at the root of the current problem.

 TIP If the module name listed is `Winword.exe`, you haven't learned much—all this means is that Word crashed, and you already know that.

If you know a particular driver is causing recurring problems, chances are the driver file is either missing, damaged, or out of date. You should attempt to remove and reinstall the driver file, making sure to obtain the latest version of the file from either Microsoft or the device's vendor. (For example, if a printer driver is causing problems, check with your printer manufacturer to get the most current version of the file.)

If removing and reinstalling the driver mentioned in the details doesn't correct your problem, you should search the Microsoft Knowledge Base (`support.microsoft.com/search/`) for articles about the problematic module.

Examining the Timing

Noting *when* an error occurs can help track down the cause of the problem. What were you doing when the error message was generated? If you constantly receive error messages when performing a specific operation, it's a good bet that *something* about that operation is causing the problem.

Determining the Scope

You should also try to determine the scope of the problem. Answer these questions:

Is the Problem Reproducible, or Does It Occur at Random? If you can't reproduce the problem, it may just be a random event and is probably not capable of being found. If the problem *can* be reproduced at will, you have a real issue that you should be able to identify.

Does the Problem Occur Only in Word, or Does It Also Occur in Other Applications? If your problem also occurs in Excel, Internet Explorer, or other Windows programs, the cause probably lies somewhere within the Windows operating system or with your system configuration.

Are There Known Issues about Word That Could Be Causing Your Problem? Don't reinvent the wheel; check the Microsoft Knowledge Base (support .microsoft.com/search/) to learn whether Microsoft has identified this problem as a built-in program bug—and to learn whether there is a workaround for the bug.

Does the Problem Happen with Only a Particular Document? If a particular document continually generates error messages, you may have a damaged document. Damaged documents often exhibit unusual behavior, such as incorrect pagination, faulty layout and formatting, unreadable characters, error messages, and program crashes. Try loading this document on another machine; if that PC also experiences problems, you have a bad document.

Fixing Specific Problems

Certain types of problems are unfortunately quite common in the Word environment. These problems typically involve printer drivers, video drivers, damaged files, and damaged fonts.

Printer Driver Problems

Most users don't realize that Word queries the printer driver even when you're not printing. Since Word needs information from the printer driver to properly format your document, a damaged printer driver can cause an error message anytime you're working on a document.

If you suspect that a bad printer driver is causing your problem, follow these steps to uninstall and then reinstall your printer driver:

1. Quit all Windows applications, but keep Windows itself open.
2. Click the Windows Start button, then select Settings ➤ Printers to display the Printers window.
3. Right-click the printer that is causing problems to display the pop-up menu.
4. From the pop-up menu, select Delete.
5. When asked to confirm the deletion, click Yes.
6. Still within the Printers window, select the Add Printer Wizard.
7. Follow the instructions in the Wizard to reinstall the printer you just deleted.

PART

IX

Tips, Tricks, and
Troubleshooting

Video Driver Problems

Just as Word constantly queries the printer driver while you're editing a document, it also queries your system's video driver for formatting information. If the video driver is damaged, it can generate error messages at any stage of the editing process.

You can find out whether a bad video driver is causing problems by installing a different video driver. (Windows' Standard Display Adapter—the VGA adapter—is a driver that should work on all systems, for troubleshooting purposes.) If your problems do not occur with the standard VGA adapter installed, you have some sort of problem with your original video driver. You should reinstall the video driver, making sure to use the latest version provided by your video card's manufacturer.

Custom Dictionary Problems

Whenever you enter a space or press the Enter key, Word's background spelling goes to work and attempts to check the previous word. If it doesn't find the word in the main dictionary, it checks your custom dictionary; if, for some reason, the custom dictionary is damaged, it can cause an error when accessed in this fashion.

If you have a damaged custom dictionary, you'll need to delete it and let Word go about creating a new custom dictionary the next time you initiate an editing session. Even better, you can simply rename your old CUSTOM.DIC file, let Word create a new CUSTOM.DIC file, and then manually copy the entries from the old file to the new one. This way you won't lose the entries you've added over time to the custom dictionary.

AutoCorrect Problems

Just as Word constantly accesses the custom dictionary, it also constantly accesses the AutoCorrect list. If you think your problem is in the AutoCorrect list file, you can delete the problem files from your hard disk.

AutoCorrect list files have the .ACL extension—and there are probably multiple files. Three of these files—Mso1033.acl, Mso2057.acl, and Mso3081.acl—should *not* be deleted; Word needs these files to run properly. All other .ACL files can be deleted or renamed to fix potential problems.

Font Problems

A damaged font file can cause error messages if you use that font in a particular document. To troubleshoot this problem, change the fonts in a troublesome document, one by one; if the problem goes away when you eliminate a particular font, you may have a damaged font file.

To delete a font file, open the Windows Control Panel and select the Fonts icon. From the Fonts window, drag the suspected font out of the window; this deletes the file from your system. You'll need to reinstall the font file if you wish to continue using that font in your documents.

Repairing and Reinstalling Word

If you're convinced that the problem is somewhere within Word—and *not* a general Windows problem or a problem caused by a damaged document—you have two choices:

- Troubleshoot the Word application, step by step
- Reinstall Word

At this point, I could give you detailed instructions on how to troubleshoot Word to determine just *where* the error is being generated. This would involve editing the Windows Registry, renaming the Normal template, and clearing the Startup folder. However, all this troubleshooting inevitably leads to reinstalling the Word application.

So, instead, I'll just jump ahead to the inevitable.

If you have a major Word-related problem, you might as well just reinstall the program—in steps. The first step is to repair any damaged or missing files.

Repairing Word

To repair any bad files in your Word program, follow these steps:

1. Close all Windows applications.
2. Click the Windows Start button, then select Settings ➤ Control Panel to open the Windows Control Panel.
3. Select the Add/Remove Programs icon to open the Add/Remove Programs dialog box.
4. Navigate to and select the Microsoft Word 2000 program.
5. Click the Add/Remove button to enter the Word (or Office) setup program.
6. From the Word or Office setup program, click the Repair Word (or Repair Office) button.

The setup program checks Word's installed files and replaces or reinstalls any files that appear to be damaged, corrupted, or missing. When the repair operation is complete, start Word and try to replicate your problem. If the problem no longer occurs, the repair procedure fixed whatever was wrong. If the problem continues, however, you need to remove and reinstall the complete Word program.

Uninstalling Word

Before you can reinstall Word, you need to uninstall it. Follow these steps:

PART

IX

Tips, Tricks, and
Troubleshooting

 WARNING Uninstalling Word can also delete any templates you've modified or created; you should back up these template files before you proceed with the uninstallation procedure.

1. Close all Windows applications.

2. Click the Windows Start button, then select Settings ➢ Control Panel to open the Windows Control Panel.

3. Select the Add/Remove Programs icon to open the Add/Remove Programs dialog box.

4. Navigate to and select the Microsoft Word 2000 program.

5. Click the Add/Remove button to enter the Word (or Office) setup program.

6. From the Word or Office setup program, click the Remove All button.

After the uninstallation procedure finishes, restart Windows and get ready to reinstall the program.

Reinstalling Word

To reinstall Word on your system, follow these steps:

1. Close all Windows applications.

2. Click the Windows Start button, then select Settings ➢ Control Panel to open the Windows Control Panel.

3. Select the Add/Remove Programs icon to open the Add/Remove Programs dialog box.

4. Navigate to and select the Microsoft Word 2000 program.

5. Click the Add/Remove button to enter the Word (or Office) setup program.

6. From the Word or Office setup program, choose to install the Word program, employing whichever options you desire.

When you reinstall Word, any customization you did previously will be lost. You'll have to go back through the program and set the Options, Customize, and interface settings back to your personal preferences.

If the Problem Persists...

If your problem *still* persists, it isn't a Word problem—the cause lies elsewhere in your system, perhaps in your Windows files. You can now try to troubleshoot Windows to track down the problem or call in a computer technician to perform professional troubleshooting.

Troubleshooting General Word Problems

What do you do if Word doesn't even start—or it starts and parts of the interface appear to be missing? Read this section to troubleshoot these and other general Word problems.

Word Won't Start

The causes of this problem range from incorrect command line settings to damaged program files.

Word Won't Start from the Shortcut

Every shortcut—whether on the Desktop or on the Programs menu—has a set of *properties* that allow it to find and start the program it represents. Among these properties is a simple listing of directory path and program name, otherwise known as the *target*. If the target is incorrect, your shortcut won't start Word.

To check and change the target information, right-click the Word shortcut to open the Properties dialog box. Select the Shortcut tab and examine the Target box. Make sure that the target path is the actual path to the `WINWORD.EXE` file. (Use My Computer or Windows Explorer to navigate to the target folder and see whether `WINWORD.EXE` is actually there.) If `WINWORD.EXE` is in a different location, change the Target information to reflect the proper location.

Word Won't Start when You Open a Document File

Anytime you select a document file in either My Computer or Windows Explorer, the associated program should automatically launch and then load the selected file. So if you select a Word document file, Word itself should automatically launch.

If this doesn't happen, Word has somehow become disassociated from the .DOC file format. To fix the problem, follow these steps:

1. Click the Windows Start button, then select Settings ➢ Folder Options to display the Folder Options dialog box.

2. Select the File Types tab.

3. Scroll through the Registered File Types list to see whether Microsoft Word Document is listed.

4. If Microsoft Word Document is listed, select it and click the Edit button to display the Edit File Type dialog box. In the Actions list, select Open and click the Edit button. In the Application Used to Perform Action box, make sure that the correct path is listed for the `WINWORD.EXE` file. Click OK when you've fixed any errors.

PART

IX

Tips, Tricks, and
Troubleshooting

5. If the Microsoft Word Document file type is *not* listed, click the New Type button to display the Add New File Type dialog box. Enter **.DOC** in the Associated Extension box, enter a name for this file type (Microsoft Word Document) in the Description of Type box, then click the New button under the Actions box. When the New Action dialog box appears, enter **Open** in the Action box, then enter the path to the `WINWORD.EXE` file in the Application Used to Perform Action dialog box. Click OK to close the New Action dialog box, then click OK to close the Add New File Type dialog box

6. Click OK to close the Folder Options dialog box

Word Tries to Start, Then Quits or Freezes

First, if your system freezes during Word's startup, you need to unfreeze the Word application. Do this by pressing Ctrl+Alt+Delete to display the Close Program dialog box. Select Microsoft Word from the list and click the End Task button. If this *doesn't* unfreeze your system, press Ctrl+Alt+Delete again (and perhaps again) to reboot your entire system.

Now try starting Word again. If the same problem occurs, turn your system off, restart it, then try again. If you still can't start Word, read on.

If Word won't start, you may not have enough free memory on your system. Try closing other Windows applications (to free up some memory) before restarting Word. If the problem persists, consider adding more memory to your PC.

Also, you may not have enough free disk space to run Word. Since Windows employs free disk space as extra memory on some systems, running out of disk space can cause your programs not to run. You may need to delete some unused files from your hard disk before you try restarting Word.

 TIP If Word—or any other Windows program—is closed unexpectedly, it leaves a number of .TMP files in the `\Windows\Temp\` folder. You should periodically visit this folder and delete these space-consuming files.

The last possibility is that, for some reason, one or more of your Word program files have been corrupted or erased from your hard drive. Although this is an unlikely occurrence, it sometimes can happen if you have to reboot your computer while in the middle of certain operations. The only fix to this is to use the Repair Word procedure available from the Add/Remove Programs utility (discussed in the "Repairing and Reinstalling Word" section earlier in this chapter)—or, in a worst-case scenario, you must uninstall and then reinstall the entire Word program.

You Can't Find a Menu Command or Toolbar Button

If you can't find a Word interface element, it's probably hidden. Try these solutions:

- If you can't find a menu item, try to expand the menu. If arrows appear at the bottom of the pull-down menu, click the arrows to show all menu options.

 TIP The display of shortened menus is a feature of Word 2000 called *personalized menus.* You can turn off this feature—and always display all menu items—by selecting Tools ➤ Customize to display the Customize dialog box, then selecting the Options tab and *unchecking* the Menus Show Recently Used Commands First option.

- If you can't find a toolbar button on a docked toolbar, the toolbar may not be large enough to display all buttons. Click the More Buttons button to display additional buttons for this toolbar—or undock the toolbar to make it float on your Desktop, where you can see all available buttons.

It's also possible that the menu item or toolbar button has been removed from the particular menu or toolbar. Use the Tools ➤ Customize command to add items to menus and toolbars, if necessary.

You Have Problems Viewing Your Text Onscreen

Another common Word problem is not being able to see your text onscreen—or having your text look garbled. This can be either a minor or a very major problem.

You Can't See Your Text

As you enter text onscreen, nothing appears—the insertion point moves, but the text appears to be invisible. What is going on here?

If you experience this situation, you probably have a color problem—in particular, you're typing white text on a white background. You'll need to change your font color back to black (or anything other than white) to see your text.

Naturally, you have the same problem with other color combinations. If you're typing black text into a text box with a black background, you'll also get invisible text. Remember to change the font color when you change backgrounds.

Your Text Appears Garbled

When you open a document that appeared fine before, but now looks like a random assortment of characters, you have a file problem. In particular, your file has somehow

PART

IX

Tips, Tricks, and
Troubleshooting

become damaged. Read the next section ("Troubleshooting Files and Damaged Documents") for more advice.

If you see boxes on your page where normal text characters should be, you might not have enabled editing for a particular language, or you might not have installed the right font for that language. Some fonts (Arial, Times New Roman, and a few others) support all European languages; most others don't.

Troubleshooting Files and Damaged Documents

File problems range from "lost" files and accidentally deleted files to totally trashed files.

You Accidentally Deleted a File

If you accidentally delete a Word file, you can probably undelete it. When you delete a file in a Windows application, that file is not actually deleted—it's just moved to the Windows Recycle Bin. This is a special folder that stores deleted files for an indeterminate amount of time—until it gets so full it truly has to delete them. After a file has been sent to the Recycle Bin, you can't open it or even find it in its normal location; you can, however, restore it to its original location.

To undelete a file, follow these steps:

1. On the Windows Desktop, select the Recycle Bin to open the Recycle Bin window.

2. Select the file you want to undelete and right-click it to display the pop-up menu.

3. Select Restore.

Window restores the file to its original location.

 WARNING If a file is not listed in the Recycle Bin window, it has already been deleted from the Recycle Bin and cannot be restored.

Your Document Is Damaged

Damaged document files can cause Word to exhibit unusual behavior. When you have a damaged file, you can try to recover the information contained within, or you can simply delete the file (if it's not important to you).

Identifying a Damaged Document

A damaged document can be identified in one of the following ways:

- The document cannot be opened within Word.
- The document opens but is corrupted, displaying garbage characters and incorrect formatting onscreen.
- The document causes Word to behave erratically or to crash.

Obviously, other problems can also cause any of these behaviors. You can normally determine whether you have a damaged document by seeing whether other documents behave similarly (if so, it's probably not that one document causing the problem) or whether the same document causes problems on another computer (if not, the document's probably OK).

Recovering a Damaged Document

If you have a damaged document, you can try several things to recover the document's contents.

First, you can try saving the file to another format and then converting it back into Word. The best format to try is .RTF (Rich Text Format), as this format preserves much of your original document formatting. After you save the document in .RTF format, close it, reopen it, and then save it back in standard Word .DOC format.

Second—and if the damaged document is mostly readable—you can copy the text of the damaged document to a new document. If you do this, you'll want to copy everything *except* the last paragraph mark, because Word associates a wide variety of formatting with this final paragraph mark. If you copy everything except the last paragraph mark to a new document, the corruption may be left behind in the original document's formatting.

 WARNING If your document contains section breaks, copy only the text between the section breaks; copying the section breaks could transfer any file corruption to a new document.

Third, you can use Word's Recover Text from Any File converter to extract the raw text from the damaged file. You will, however, lose any formatting that still remains in the document when you use this converter. To use this converter, select File ➤ Open to display Word's Open dialog box; from the Files of Type list, select Recover Text from Any File. When you click the Open button, Word opens and recovers the text from within your damaged document.

Tips, Tricks, and
Troubleshooting

If none of these techniques works, you can try opening the damaged document in WordPad (the simple word processor included with Microsoft Windows), as a plain text file. When the file opens, it will still probably have most of the garbage characters, but—if you're lucky—most of your text will be there as well. Delete the garbage and save the file—or copy the good parts to a new file.

Your Document Won't Open

If Word won't let you open a document, there could be any number of causes, including the following:

The Document May Be Damaged You can try to recover the text from the damaged document, using the methods just discussed.

The Filename or the Path Name May Exceed 223 Characters Shorten the filename or move the file to another folder that is closer to the top of the folder hierarchy, and then try to open the file again.

Your Disk May Be Full Try deleting some unnecessary files to make more space available.

The File May Be Password Protected If so, enter the correct password to open the file.

You can try several things if you're having trouble opening a document, including the following:

Open the Document as Plain as Possible Before you open the document, open the Options dialog box, select the View tab, and check the Draft Font and Picture Placeholders options. Next, switch to Normal view and try opening the document; if it opens, it will be as a very plain text document.

Insert the Document as a File in a New Document Open a new blank document, then select Insert ➢ File to display the Insert File dialog box. When you insert a document in this fashion, the final paragraph mark—which contains formatting information and possible file errors—is *not* inserted.

Try the Recover Text from Any File Converter As discussed in the previous section, select Recover Text from Any File in the Files of Type list in the Open dialog box; this may open files not otherwise openable.

Retry Your Password If you're having trouble opening a password-protected document, remember that passwords are case sensitive. Check to see whether your Caps Lock key is on, then try the password again.

You're Having Problems Recovering an AutoRecovered Document

If you have Word's AutoRecover feature activated (from the Save tab in the Options dialog box), Word automatically saves a copy of any open document at a regular interval. If Word crashes, AutoRecover should load the latest version of any otherwise-unsaved file the next time you launch Word.

If AutoRecover *doesn't* automatically load the recovered file, you can open the file manually. Just follow these steps:

1. From within Microsoft Word, select File ➢ Open to display the Open dialog box.

2. Locate the folder that contains your recovery files (usually the Windows\
   Application Data\Microsoft\Word folder).

3. Pull down the Files of Type list and select All Files.

4. Select the recovery file you want to open; each recovery file is named
   AutoRecovery Save of *Filename* and has the extension .ASD.

5. Click the Open button.

If you can't locate an AutoRecover file, any one of the following may have happened:

Word Didn't Have Time to Create the AutoRecover File   If the file was brand new, Word waits (by default) 15 minutes before it creates the first AutoRecover file.

You Already Opened the AutoRecover File—and Closed It without Saving It   When you close an AutoRecover file without saving it, the file is deleted. There is no way to recover unsaved changes after the AutoRecover file has been closed.

You Accidentally Deleted the Recovery File   If you deleted a file with an .ASD extension, you deleted an AutoRecover file.

The Document Was to Be a Master Document   Word doesn't create AutoRecover files for master documents.

You Were Using the Visual Basic Editor   If you were using the VB Editor to edit or create a macro, any changes made in the VB Editor were not yet reflected in your document and thus not saved in an AutoRecover file.

If you find the AutoRecover file doesn't contain your most recent changes, that's because AutoRecover (by default) is set to save files only every 10 minutes. If you want to set a different AutoRecover interval, select Tools ➢ Options to display the Options dialog box, select the Save tab, and select a new value from the Save AutoRecover Info Every control.

PART

IX

Tips, Tricks, and
Troubleshooting

You Can't Find a File You Want to Open

If you can't easily find a file in the Open dialog box, try these solutions:

Change the File Type   It's possible the file you're looking for doesn't match the file type selected. Pull down the Files as Type list and select All Files (*.*). This will display all files in the selected folder, not just .DOC files.

Change Folders   It's also possible your file isn't where you think it is. Try looking in a different folder—or even on a different disk.

Use the Find Command   From the Open dialog box, click the Tools button and then select Find. When the Find dialog box appears, make sure Search Subfolders is checked and that you have the right file type selected, then click Find Now. Also, don't be afraid to use wildcards in your search and to display all possible file types.

If you use the Find command and are dissatisfied with your search results, you could have a problem with Office 2000's Find Fast feature. In particular, if you try to search while Find Fast is in the middle of indexing your hard disk, it may return incomplete results. In addition, if Find Fast hasn't run in a while, the index may not be current, and you won't be able to locate newer files. You may want to turn off Find Fast to have Word search the disk manually; even though this will result in longer searches, the searches may be more accurate.

Your Document Opened with a Different Filename

If your document opens with a different filename, you may have Word configured to open documents as copies rather than as the original files. To reset this option, follow these steps:

1. Click the Windows Start button and then select Settings ➤ Folder Options to display the Folder Options dialog box.

2. Select the File Types tab.

3. In the Registered File Types list, select Microsoft Word Document.

4. Click the Edit button to display the Edit File Type dialog box.

5. In the Actions list, select Open, and then click Set Default.

You Receive an Error Message when Saving a File

Word can display many different error messages when it has problems saving a file. Here are some of the more common.

"There has been a network or file permission error. The network connection may be lost. *Filename.doc*"

This error message is often generated when you are working on a network and try to save a document that happens to be open on two or more computers running different operating platforms (Windows 98 and Windows NT, for example). If this is the case, try saving to your local hard drive and then transferring the local file to the network drive at a later time.

This message can also be generated when the Always Create Backup Copy option is enabled and you're on a server or operating system that doesn't support long filenames. If this is the case, turn off the Always Create Backup Copy option (on the Save tab in the Options dialog box).

Another cause of this message is when you're saving to a MAPROOT-type network drive connection on a NetWare server and spaces exist in the file- or folder name. In this instance, the solution is to shorten your file's name and remove any spaces from the name—in essence, to return to the old *8.3* convention.

It's also possible that there is an antivirus program running on the network that is scanning for macro viruses in shared network folders. If this is the case, the immediate solution is to turn off the antivirus program and then update the antivirus software to the latest version.

If you're on a Novell network, this error message can be generated when the AutoRecover files path is either blank or set to a network drive. If this is the case, open the Options dialog box, select the File Locations tab, and change the AutoRecover Files location to your local disk drive.

"The disk is full trying to write to *drive*..."

This message is generated under any of the following conditions:

The Disk You Are Trying to Save to Has Insufficient Free Disk Space Try deleting some files from your disk and then saving again.

The Office Folder Is in a Location to Which You Cannot Write Move the Office folder or change the folder's characteristics from Read-Only to Read/Write.

Your Temporary File Folder Contains a Large Number of Stray Temporary Files Use My Computer or Windows Explorer to remove .TMP files from the \Windows\Temp\ folder.

"The disk is full or too many files are open"

In addition to the possible causes listed under the previous error message, this message can be caused by corrupt or invalid links in your document. Try updating the fields in your document (select the entire document and then press F9); if an error occurs at this point, you may need to either unlink or delete the offending fields or objects.

"The file is too large"

Yes, documents can actually be too large to save. If this is your problem, you can divide the document into smaller parts by cutting and pasting part of the document into a new document, then saving each part individually. You can also convert the document into a master document and save its components as individual subdocuments.

"This document is read-only"

You can't make changes to a read-only document. Instead, you should use the File ➢ Save As command to save the document under a new name.

"Check drive"

This error message is generated when you try saving a file to a network server that contains characters not recognized by Windows. The solution is to remove these characters from your filename.

 WARNING Some common extended characters that can cause problems when you save a document include à, á, ò, ï, ñ, and ÿ.

Your Document Was Saved with an Unexpected Extension

If you tried to save a file with an extension other than the default extension for that file type (for example, naming a Word document DOCUMENT.BOB), you'll end up with two extensions (DOCUMENT.BOB.DOC). This is because Word automatically adds the default extension to your document, no matter what. You can rename the file from My Computer or Windows Explorer to get rid of the extraneous extension.

 TIP To save a Word document with an extension other than .DOC, you must enclose the entire filename in quotation marks ("DOCUMENT.BOB").

If your file ended up with two periods (for example, DOCUMENT..DOC), it's because you added a period after the filename (DOCUMENT.) and then Word added another period and the extension (.DOC). The bottom line is that you don't have to add the period after the filename; Word does this automatically.

Troubleshooting Editing

You can encounter a number of problems when editing your documents—everything from accidentally deleting a block of text to Find and Replace returning unexpected results. The most common editing problems are covered in this section.

You Accidentally Deleted or Cut Some Text

If you accidentally deleted a block of text, click the Undo button on Word's Standard toolbar to undo your mistake. If you accidentally *cut* text from your document, you could undo the operation, or you could select Edit ➢ Paste to paste back the text you just cut.

When You Enter Text, Existing Text Is Deleted

This problem is caused when you accidentally enable the Overtype mode. (You can tell you're in the Overtype mode when you see *OVR* on Word's status bar.) You can switch from Overtype to Insert mode (which *doesn't* replace characters as you type) by pressing your keyboard's Insert key.

If you find that Word defaults to the Overtype mode, you can change the default by selecting Tools ➢ Options to display the Options dialog box, then selecting the General tab. If the Overtype Mode option is checked, uncheck it.

Word Automatically Selects Text when You Click Your Mouse or Press a Key

If you can't keep from selecting text, you may have turned on Word's Extend Selection mode, which allows you to select text by clicking the mouse or pressing navigation keys. (When this mode is active, *EXT* is displayed on Word's status bar.) To cancel Extend Selection mode, press Esc, and then click anywhere in your document.

Words Are Automatically Capitalized

By default, AutoCorrect capitalizes the first letter in each sentence. If a word happens to follow a period—even if that period is used for an abbreviation, not to end a sentence—the word will automatically be capitalized. AutoCorrect will also capitalize words that should be in lowercase (as many new Internet names appear to be).

If you don't want AutoCorrect to capitalize a word, you have the following options:

- Turn off the Capitalize First Letter of Sentences option in the AutoCorrect dialog box.
- Undo the capitalization manually, by clicking the Undo button.

PART

IX

Tips, Tricks, and
Troubleshooting

If you manually undo a specific capitalization, AutoCorrect will add this word to its exceptions list so AutoCorrect won't make the same mistake twice.

Click and Type Doesn't Work

If you find that Word 2000's new Click and Type feature isn't always clicking and typing correctly, try any of the following:

Turn On Click and Type   It's possible you haven't yet enabled the Click and Type feature. Select Tools ➢ Options to display the Options dialog box, select the Edit tab, check the Enable Click and Type option, and then click OK.

Switch Views   Click and Type is available only in Print Preview and Web Layout views—*not* in Normal or Outline views.

Make Sure to Double-Click   Click and Type activates only when you double-click, *not* when you single-click.

Click a Blank Area   Click and Type will activate only in blank areas of your document. It will *not* activate in multiple columns, in bulleted lists, in numbered lists, next to floating objects, to the left or right of pictures with top and bottom text wrapping, or to the left or right of indents.

Exit Macro Recording Mode   Click and Type isn't available when you're recording a macro.

You Receive an Error Message when Undoing Editing Changes

Here's a documented bug in Word 2000: After you insert a text box, a picture, or a drawing object and then click Undo to remove any of these items, when you click Redo, the following error message may appear:

```
This program has performed an illegal operation and will be shut down.
```

When you click Details, the following error message appears:

```
WINWORD caused an invalid page fault in module MSO9.DLL at 015f:address.
```

 NOTE This problem occurs only when there is a text box in your document.

To decrease the chances of generating this error, make sure that no objects are selected before you insert the text box or drawing object.

Document Map Doesn't Display Your Document's Headings

Sometimes Word has trouble identifying nonstandard headings in your document. You shouldn't have any problems if you stick to the built-in heading styles (Heading 1, Heading 2, and so on) and outline-level paragraph formats (Level 1, Level 2, and so on), but if you create your own heading styles, you do so at your own risk.

If Word can't find any headings formatted with these heading styles or outline levels, it automatically searches the document for paragraphs that *look like* headings—short lines with larger font sizes, for example. Then Word applies an outline level to these headings and displays them in the Document Map. If Word can't find any such headings, the Document Map is blank.

As you can expect, the results from all this guessing on Word's part are variable. If you experience problems with Document Map displaying the wrong text as headings, you might want to think about returning to Word's built-in heading styles for this document.

Word will also have problems if you have heading text in tables or text boxes. Document Map will not display these headings.

Find and Replace Doesn't Return the Expected Results

If Find and Replace doesn't find the text you're looking for, make sure you've entered the query correctly, then follow these tips:

- Don't select text before starting the search—Word will search only the selected text.
- Select the No Formatting option.
- Select All from the Search Options list.
- Uncheck the Match Case option.
- Uncheck the Find Whole Words Only option.
- Uncheck the Use Wildcards option.
- Check the Sounds Like option.
- Check the Find All Word Forms option.

If you're having trouble finding or replacing some graphics or objects, know that Word can't find or replace floating objects, WordArt text, or drawing objects. Find and Replace can locate inline objects, however.

If you run Find and Replace while the Track Changes feature is enabled, you'll be surprised to find that Word will find deleted text that is still displayed onscreen. The only way around this little bug is to turn off revision marks (or accept changes) before you use Find and Replace.

PART

IX

Tips, Tricks, and Troubleshooting

Troubleshooting Formatting

You can run into all kinds of problems when formatting text and objects in Word. Read on to discover some of the more common formatting problems.

A Font Isn't Displaying Properly

If a certain font isn't displaying or printing properly, chances are that font isn't installed on your system. (This happens often when you open a document created on a different computer—one that has that font installed.) You can fix this problem in one of two ways.

First, you can simply install the missing font onto your system.

Second, you can use Word 2000's font substitution feature. Select Tools ➢ Options to display the Options dialog box, select the Compatibility tab, then click the Font Substitution button to display the Font Substitution dialog box. Select the missing font, and then pull down the Substituted Font list and select a replacement font.

You can also run into occasional problems with fonts that are installed on both systems (yours and the one on which the document was created). This problem is harder to track down, but some identical fonts don't display or print identically on some PCs. You'll typically notice this as a very slight difference in character spacing, ultimately leading to words being bumped to the next line and lines being bumped to the next page—eventually affecting your entire document layout. If this happens to you, you should first make sure that the fonts really are identical—and not just an automatic substitution by Word. If the fonts are the same and the problem continues, you'll have to either adjust your page layout manually to compensate or change to a different font. (This problem typically does *not* occur with the standard Arial or Times New Roman fonts.)

Justified Text Leaves Gaps between Words

When you justify text on a page, Word adds space between words so that all the lines will have equal length. In some circumstances, the interword spacing turns into huge, unappealing gaps, especially if:

- The line width is relatively narrow (as with multiple-column documents)
- The line contains extra-long words
- The font size is large
- The font type is nonproportional (such as Courier)

There are two solutions to this problem. First, you can change from justified alignment to left alignment. This leaves a ragged right edge, but still looks OK in most instances.

Second, you can turn on Word's automatic hyphenation. Select Tools ➢ Language ➢ Hyphenation to display the Hyphenation dialog box, check the Automatic Hyphenation option, then click OK. When you choose this option, Word will at least hyphenate any extra-long words, thus helping to fix some of the spacing problems inherent with justified alignment.

Text That Used to Be 10-Point Is Now 12-Point

In previous (pre-2000) versions of Word, the default font setting in the Normal template was 10-point Times New Roman. In Word 2000, however, the default font has been changed to 12 points. So when you create a new document, the Normal text will be larger than what you were used to.

Bullet Characters Don't Display Properly

Unless you've selected a different font for your bullets, Word uses characters from the Symbol font. If, for some reason, the Symbol font is damaged or missing, Word substitutes the Wingdings font. The problem is that not all characters are interchangeable between the two fonts. For example, the standard bullet character in Symbol translates into a clock face in Wingdings. If this happens to you, either reinstall the Symbol font or manually change your bullet (using the Bullets and Numbering dialog box) to something different.

Tabs and Paragraph Indents Disappear when You Add or Remove Bullets or Numbering

This is a major bug in Word. Whenever you add or remove bullets or numbering from a line (when creating a bulleted or numbered list—or changing the last item in a list back to normal), Word removes both tab characters and paragraph indents. If this happens to you—and it probably will—you'll need to manually reinsert the tab characters and reformat the paragraph indents for the affected line(s).

Paragraph Formatting Changes when You Delete Text

The lowly paragraph mark contains a large amount of important formatting information. The last paragraph mark in your document contains information for your entire

PART

IX

Tips, Tricks, and
Troubleshooting

document; the last paragraph mark in a section contains section formatting; and any normal paragraph mark contains formatting for that paragraph.

If you delete a paragraph mark, the following paragraph merges with the previous paragraph—and assumes the previous paragraph's style and formatting. This can sometimes lead to unexpected formatting changes—in the paragraph that *wasn't* deleted. If you delete a paragraph and/or its paragraph mark and end up reformatting the following paragraph by mistake, click the Undo button to return things to their previous conditions, and then do a more careful deletion.

 NOTE To view paragraph marks in your document, click the Show/Hide ¶ button on Word's Standard toolbar.

A New Paragraph Doesn't Have Expected Formatting

Many Word users have been surprised at the results when they try to insert a new paragraph between two paragraphs with different formatting. If you put the insertion point in the wrong location, you'll end up with the wrong paragraph formatting.

If you want the new paragraph to take on the characteristics of the *following* paragraph, position the insertion point at the start of the following paragraph and press the Enter key. (You'll need to press the up-arrow key to move the insertion point up one line to start typing the new paragraph.)

If you want the new paragraph to have the same attributes as the *preceding* paragraph, position the insertion point at the end of the preceding paragraph, press the Enter key, and then start typing.

You Can't Underline a Blank Space or Line

This is another bug in Word—you can't underline a blank space or line by using the Underline button on the Formatting toolbar.

There are, however, two ways to obtain the look you want:

- Type nonbreaking spaces (Ctrl+Shift+Spacebar) in place of a normal space, select the nonbreaking spaces, then click the Underline button.
- Type the underscore character (Shift+-) in place of a normal space.

Graphics or Text in a Line Appear Cut Off

If a line contains a character or graphic that is larger than the surrounding text, Word normally increases the spacing for that line to match the largest character or object.

However, if you have specified an exact line spacing on the Indents and Spacing tab of the Paragraph dialog box, Word is forced to apply *exact* spacing to that line—which could cut off the tops of any items larger than the exact spacing.

To format the line to properly display larger characters, open the Paragraph dialog box, select the Indents and Spacing Tab, and then select either a larger exact value for the Line Spacing setting or an option other than Exactly.

Text Was Unexpectedly Formatted as a Hyperlink

Word 2000 has an annoying habit of turning every piece of text that looks like a Web address or e-mail address into a hyperlink. This is especially troublesome if the text you type includes the @ character; almost universally, Word will interpret the surrounding text as an e-mail address and create a Mailto: hyperlink.

The only way to fix this annoying habit is to turn off Word's automatic hyperlinking. You do this by selecting Tools ≻ AutoCorrect to display the AutoCorrect dialog box, selecting the AutoFormat as You Type tab, and then unchecking the Internet and Network Paths with Hyperlinks option.

Headings Aren't Numbered when Outline Numbering Is Enabled

If you turn on outline numbering but your headings aren't numbered, you probably formatted your headings with custom heading styles. Outline numbering works automatically with Word's built-in heading styles (Heading 1, Heading 2, and so on); if you create custom styles, you have to modify the style to assign an outline numbering level. (See Chapter 9 to learn how to modify Word's styles.)

Paragraph Borders Are Cut Off

If you put a border around a paragraph and the paragraph falls across a page break, a bottom border *won't* appear at the bottom of the first page—nor will a top border appear at the top of the next page. The paragraph border splits just as the paragraph splits, and no two halves of a split paragraph are fully bordered.

If this bothers you, you should insert a page break before the bordered paragraph, so that the paragraph stays together on an single page.

PART

IX

Tips, Tricks, and
Troubleshooting

Troubleshooting Styles and Templates

Word's styles and templates are at best confusing, and at worst they are difficult to use and problematic. Read on to learn how to troubleshoot some of the more common problems users experience with these two important Word elements.

Not All Available Styles Appear in the Style List

By default, the Style list on Word's Formatting toolbar includes only a handful of default styles (Normal, Heading 1, and so on) and those styles you've actually used in the current document. Many more styles are typically available in any given template.

To view all available styles in the Style list, hold down the Shift key as you click the down arrow for the Style list.

A Style Has Changed Unexpectedly

If you find that a style you're using has suddenly changed properties, there are four possible causes:

Automatic Updating May Be Enabled   When automatic updating is enabled, any manual formatting changes you make to a paragraph based on this style automatically update the style itself and all other paragraphs formatted with the style. To turn off this feature, select Format ➢ Style to display the Styles dialog box, click the Modify button to display the Modify Style dialog box, then uncheck the Automatically Update option.

The Style May Be Based on Another Style That Has Changed   Many styles are based on other styles; when one of the base styles changes, all styles based on that style are also updated. To disconnect a based-on style from the base style, go to the Modify Styles dialog box, pull down the Based On list, and select No Style.

Your Document May Be Based on a Template That Has Changed   If you change the styles in a template and then reopen a document based on that template, styles in that document may be updated, based on changes to the template. If you don't want styles in documents based on a template to be updated in this fashion, select Tools ➢ Templates and Add-Ins to display the Templates and Add-Ins dialog box, then uncheck the Automatically Update Document Styles option.

The Current Template May Be Missing or Damaged   If a template becomes damaged or deleted, styles in that template will revert to the formatting in the Normal template. So if you accidentally delete a template (.DOT) file, documents based on that template could become reformatted.

Styles Look Different in Your Master Document and Subdocuments

When subdocuments are viewed as part of the master document, they share the template and styles of the master document. But when they're opened separately, subdocuments can (but don't necessarily have to) use their own individual templates and styles. So if you open a subdocument separately from the master document, it's quite possible that the document will look different from when it's opened as part of the master document.

Your Custom Toolbars Disappear when You Save a Document as a Template

When you save a document as a template, Word does not save any custom toolbars you may have created for that template. You'll need to use the Organizer to copy any toolbars from the template to the new document.

Macros, AutoText Entries, and Other Settings Are Missing

If you open a document and find that macros, AutoText entries, custom toolbars and menus, and shortcut keys are missing, it's likely that you moved or copied the document from one computer to another—and now Word can't find the template that contained the missing items. When you move or copy a document from one location to another, you have to copy the associated elements separately, using Word's Organizer. Alternately, you can copy the elements to the attached template, and then copy the template to the other computer.

You Can't Copy Items to a Template

If Word won't let you copy styles, macros, or other custom items to a template, it's because the template is protected in some manner. It's possible that the template is protected for revision tracking, comments, or forms—any of which can prevent items from being copied to the template. Turn off the template's protection and then copy the elements to the template, using Word's Organizer.

You Can't Save a Document Template as a Word Document

Word doesn't let you save an open template as a Word file—although you can save a Word file as a template. (Go figure!) If you have a .DOT file open, you have to save it as a .DOT file, no exceptions. To create a Word file based on this template, you first have

PART

IX

Tips, Tricks, and Troubleshooting

to save the template, and then click File ➢ New to display the New dialog box. You can then select your recently saved template and click OK—Word will create a new document based on the template, which you can save as a normal .DOC file.

If you're trying to save a document file and Word tries to force you to save it as a template, your system could be infected with a macro virus called the Concept Virus. This virus prevents you from saving a file as any type other than .DOT. If this is the case, install an antivirus program to clean the virus from your system.

Troubleshooting Columns

Creating multiple-column layouts is a little tricky and can lead to a number of problems. Read on to find out what causes some of the more common issues with Word's columns.

Columns Aren't Visible

First, make sure you're in Print Layout view, since Word doesn't display columns in Normal, Outline, or Web Layout views. Second, try typing more text—it's possible you've filled only the first column and thus don't have any text in the other columns. Third, consider making your column boundaries visible onscreen by selecting Tools ➢ Options to display the Options dialog box, selecting the View tab, and then checking the Text Boundaries option.

Vertical Lines between Your Columns Aren't Visible

As with columns themselves, lines between columns are visible only in Print Layout view. In addition, lines only appear between columns that are filled with text—so if your first two columns have text, a line will appear between them, but if the third column is empty, no line will appear between the second and third columns.

Word will not, however, display or print a line between columns if your document is divided into sections and the section containing multiple columns is followed immediately by a section with a landscape orientation. This is a known bug, and the only workaround is to manually draw lines between the columns, using Word's line-drawing tool.

Text in Columns Is Much Narrower Than Expected

When you use a multiple-column layout, by nature you're working with narrow lines of text. If you also have a hanging indent applied to your paragraphs, your text lines get even narrower. If you find your text is too narrow within a column, consider formatting your paragraphs without any indents.

Columns Won't Balance

This is a very common problem for Word users. You've set up a multiple-column layout, then find that the text at the bottom of your columns doesn't line up properly.

The key to creating balanced columns is to insert a continuous section break at the end of your columnar section. When you do this, Word automatically balances your columns, for a nice, clean look.

You might encounter some real problems when trying to get your columns to balance. For example, your paragraph formatting may be interfering with your column balancing. To ensure proper balancing, you want to turn off the following options: Widow/Orphan Control, Keep Lines Together, Keep with Next, and Page Break Before.

It's also possible that you're working with a document that was converted from another file format and you need to reset one of Word's compatibility options. Open the Options dialog box and select the Compatibility tab, then uncheck the Don't Balance Columns option.

Text above Columns Suddenly Turns into Multiple Columns

This problem is caused when you delete the section break leading into the multiple-column section of your document. When you do this, the first section takes on the formatting of the section breaks—hence the switch to multiple columns. If this just occurred, you may be able to reinsert the deleted section break by using Word's Undo command. If you're already past the undo stage, you'll need to insert a new section break and reformat the first section without multiple columns.

Tables in Columns Have Disappeared

If you've placed a table inside a single column in a multiple-column page, the table is visible only as long as it fits within the column. If you resize the table and make it too wide, it simply disappears.

The solution, of course, is to resize the table to fit within the column—or resize the column to hold the wider table.

You Receive an Error Message when Changing Page Orientation or Paper Size

This problem is indicated by the following error message:

```
Settings you chose for the left and right margins, column spacing, or
paragraph indents are too large for the page width in some sections.
```

PART

IX

Tips, Tricks, and
Troubleshooting

This message is sometimes generated when you're working with a multiple-column document and you change your document's page orientation from landscape to portrait, or when you change the paper size of your document. The problem is caused when you haven't selected the Equal Column Width option, which forces Word to apply the same column sizes to your new page setup, and the old sizes don't work. The solution is to select Format ➢ Columns to display the Columns dialog box, then check the Equal Column Width option.

Columns Don't Work in Headers, Footers, Comments, or Text Boxes

Although this may be a problem to you, it's not an official problem in Word, since you can't use multiple columns in any of these areas of your document. If you want to create the *appearance* of columns in these areas, insert a table with a single row and multiple columns.

Troubleshooting Sections and Pages

When you work with sections and pages, you have to do everything just right, or you'll end up with unexpected results. Read on to discover some of the more problematic areas of page and section formatting.

Your Document Background Doesn't Display or Print

This is a frustrating problem. Word lets you add a background color or graphic to your document—but then doesn't display it. That's because page backgrounds are for Web documents only—if you're using Print Layout, Normal, or Outline views, you won't see the background, nor can you print the background. You can see the background only in Web Layout view or when your document is posted to the Web.

You *can* add a background to a non-Web document, but not through the Borders and Shading dialog box. You have to add a watermark to your page, through either a header or a footer. See Chapter 31 for details—and read the next section to learn how to solve problems with watermarks.

Watermarks Don't Display Properly

Using a watermark to provide a background for your document can be a little tricky. You have to get the formatting just right so it doesn't overshadow the text of your document—and you must know how to work with headers and footers to get the watermark positioned properly.

If you find your watermark is appearing too dark on your page, you can lighten it by double-clicking the graphic to display the Format Picture dialog box, selecting the Picture tab, then pulling down the Color list and selecting Watermark. If the picture is still too prominent, use the Brightness and Contrast controls to lighten it even further.

If you find that your watermark isn't appearing on all pages of your document, you attached it to a header or footer that doesn't display on every page. For example, you may have set the header/footer to display only on odd or even pages, or in specific sections of your document. The solution to this problem is to copy your bookmark from its existing header/footer to all other headers/footers in your document, so that no matter what header or footer is displayed, your watermark will also display.

Pages Don't Break Properly

If you find an unwanted page break in your document, you may have accidentally inserted a manual page break. To search for all forced page breaks, switch to Normal view; you can remove any page break by selecting it and pressing the Delete key.

It's also possible that you inserted a section break that is forcing a new page. When you select the Next Page, Even Page, or Odd Page options when inserting a section break, Word automatically starts the new section on a new page. If you would rather have the new section flow without a page break, change the section break to a Continuous break.

Unwanted page breaks can also occur because of certain paragraph formatting. If you select the Keep Lines Together, Keep with Next, or Page Break Before pagination options, you can end up with paragraphs that don't break in the middle—making for awkward page breaks. To change the pagination affecting a page break, select the paragraph *after* the page break, then select Format ➢ Paragraph to display the Paragraph dialog box and uncheck the relevant pagination options.

If, on the other hand, Word didn't start a new page even though you inserted a manual page break, it's likely that you formatted the page break as hidden text and then specified that hidden text not be printed. To fix this problem, switch to Normal view and show all hidden text (by clicking the Show/Hide button on the Standard toolbar). Next, select the page break, select Format ➢ Font to display the Font dialog box, then uncheck the Hidden option.

Page Borders Don't Display Properly

If you find that your page borders aren't appearing on every page, that's probably because your document is divided into sections—and Word typically applies page borders to a single section only. To apply your page border to your entire document, select Format ➢ Borders and Shading to display the Borders and Shading dialog box, select the Page Border tab, then pull down the Apply To list and select Whole Document.

PART

IX

Tips, Tricks, and
Troubleshooting

If you can't see your page border at all, make sure you're using Word's Print Layout view. Page borders do not display in Normal, Outline, or Web Layout views.

If part of your page border isn't printing, check your border margins; the border may be positioned too close to the edge of the page. For most printers, you need at least one-half inch of nonprinting space on an 8.5-inch by 11-inch sheet of paper. To adjust your page-border margin, go to the Page Border tab in the Borders and Shading dialog box and click the Options button to display the Border and Shading Options dialog box. Pull down the Measure From list, select Edge of Page, then specify the appropriate larger margins.

It's also possible that there is too much distance between your page border and your text—which would also shove the border outside the printable page margin. Adjust this distance in the Border and Shading Options dialog box; pull down the Measure From list, select Text, and then adjust the margin settings.

Finally, your page margins for this document may be set too close to the edge of the page. Select File ➢ Page Setup to display the Page Setup dialog box, then adjust the margins appropriately.

If your page border doesn't move when you change your page margins, you need to change how the page border is measured. Return to the Border and Shading Options dialog box, pull down the Measure From list, and select Text. This positions the page border in relation to your text rather than to your page, which should solve your problem.

Troubleshooting Master Documents

Word's master document feature is one of the most troublesome features in all of Word. In fact, many Word experts (this author included!) recommend that most users avoid using master documents. However, if you insist on using this feature and you run into problems, read on to figure out what is going wrong.

Know that most master document problems relate to opening and working with subdocuments *outside* the master document. For the master document feature to work, you have to treat all the subdocuments as part of the master document and work on them only from within the master document. Anything you do to a subdocument outside the master document environment will not be reflected in the rest of the master document.

You Can't Open a Master Document or Subdocument

If you're on a network and sharing the master document (and its subdocuments) with other users in a group project, you won't be able to open a master document or subdocument that is currently being edited by another user. In some instances you may be able to open the document as read only, but you won't be able to edit or save it.

Remember, also, that subdocuments can be locked—and that you can't open a locked document. If you didn't do the locking, you'll have to talk to the person in charge of the master document to obtain editing privileges.

You Have Problems Saving a Master Document and Its Subdocuments

If your master document includes a very large number of subdocuments, Word won't be able to save your documents. Word places a limit on the number of subdocuments allowed in a master document, based on the number of files you have open, the size of those files, the number of other programs you're currently running, the amount of memory installed on your PC, the operating system you're using, and other system configurations. If you reach this limit when you try to save your large master document, Word won't be able to save *anything*.

If this happens to you, you should cancel the save operation and try one or more of the following:

- Close any other open programs.
- Convert some of the subdocuments into master document text.
- Remove the subdocuments from the master document and save them as separate documents.

Another common problem occurs when you save your master document to a different folder—and realize that your subdocuments were not saved to the new folder. This is because when you use the Save As command with your master document, you have to save each subdocument separately to the new location. You'll need to open your master document in Outline view, open and select each subdocument separately, then (for each subdocument) select File ➤ Save As and save each subdocument to the new folder. After each subdocument has been saved to the new location, you can then save the master document itself to that location.

Page Numbers, Headers, or Footers Are Incorrect or Missing

For page numbers, headers, and footers to work properly in a master document, you have to apply and configure these elements in the master document—*not* in a subdocument. You can then reformat these elements within individual subdocuments, but they have to be added to the master document itself.

If Word displays a header or footer only in part of your master document, that means you added the header or footer to an individual subdocument, rather than to the master document. Again, you have to work with headers and footers in the master document for them to be applied throughout the entire document.

PART

IX

Tips, Tricks, and
Troubleshooting

Cross-References Are Replaced by Error Messages

This happens when you update a cross-reference while working on an open subdocument instead of while within the master document. For cross-references to be updated properly, you must be working on a subdocument within the master document and then press F9 to update the cross-references.

Your Table of Contents or Index Contains Error Messages

If your TOC or index isn't working properly, you probably made the TOC or index into a separate subdocument—and opened it separately. Although you can use TOCs and indexes as separate subdocuments, you must open those subdocuments from within the master document, not as separate documents. Even better, your TOC or index should just be part of the master document text; this decreases the opportunity for problems to occur.

Subdocuments Are Created Incorrectly

This is another major problem and results from Word incorrectly assessing where your subdocuments should start and end. The best way to ensure that the subdocument breaks are properly inserted is to do all of the following:

- Select *all* the text you want to divide into subdocuments.
- Assign the proper (and the same) heading style to the heading at the beginning of each subdocument section.

If Word creates a subdocument incorrectly, undo the operation and check the heading style you're using to specify subdocuments.

Troubleshooting Indexes and Tables of Contents

Indexes and tables of contents are sometimes tricky to use properly and can cause some nettlesome problems. Read on to learn about Word's most common index and TOC problems.

Page Numbers Are Incorrect

Anytime you make a change to a previously indexed or TOC'ed document, you run the risk of changing the index and TOC references. In particular, any change that moves a page break will probably force you to update your index and TOC—otherwise, some of the page number references will be outdated.

Before you update your index or TOC, make sure you've hidden all fields and hidden text. If these elements are displayed onscreen, they will affect the page references in your index and TOC—and make those references incorrect when your document is printed *without* the hidden fields and hidden text.

Unwanted Codes and Error Messages Are Displayed

Indexes and TOCs are actually fields within your document. If you see the { INDEX } or { TOC } codes *instead* of the full index or TOC, that means you've configured Word to display field codes instead of field results. To toggle back to the field results display, right-click the field code to display the pop-up menu, then select Toggle Field Codes.

If your index or TOC is displayed but shows Error! Bookmark not defined instead of a page number, you need to update your index or TOC. Click to the left of the index or TOC, press F9, and then select Update Entire Table.

Some Headings Don't Appear in the TOC

When Word builds a table of contents, it looks for headings or TC fields within the text of your document—*not* within drawings, text boxes, or callouts. Any headings not in the main text simply won't appear in your TOC.

Your TOC Contains Nonheading Text

If your TOC includes listings that shouldn't be there, that probably means selected text in your document has been formatted with a heading style. You'll need to track down that text and change the applied style to one that won't be listed in your TOC.

If you want all the text assigned to a particular style to *not* appear in your TOC, you can omit that heading style from the TOC. Select Insert ➢ Index and Tables to display the Index and Tables dialog box, then select the Table of Contents tab. Click the Options button to display the Table of Contents Options dialog box, then delete the TOC number or style you don't want to appear in the TOC.

An Index Entry Has a Backslash (\) Instead of a Colon (:)

When Word builds an index, every time it encounters a colon (:) or a pair of quotation marks (""), it inserts a backslash (\) before the colon or quotation marks. This tells Word to print the colon or quotation marks as part of the index entry—and *not* as a subentry. (Word otherwise uses colons to indicate subentries and quotation marks to surround entry text.) Don't worry, though—the backslash appears only onscreen and will not print.

Troubleshooting Headers and Footers

Headers and footers are easier to use than some users might think, even though improper use can result in some interesting problems. Read on to discover the most common header- and footer-related problems in Word.

Your Header or Footer Is Missing or Only Partially Printed

If you can't see your headers and footers, make sure you're in Print Layout view; headers and footers won't be displayed in any other view. In addition, if you save your document as a Web page, your headers and footers won't be displayed or print at all. However, if you save your document back into normal Word format, your headers and footers will be retained.

If your header or footer appears on all pages but the first page of your document, you've probably opted to display a different first-page header or footer. You can change this by selecting File ➤ Page Setup to display the Page Setup dialog box, selecting the Layout tab, and then unchecking the Different First Page option.

If your header or footer displays properly onscreen but doesn't print, you've probably placed your header/footer text in the nonprinting area of your page. (In most cases, you should allow at least one-half inch of nonprinting margin around the edges of your page.) To solve this problem, go to the Page Setup dialog box, select the Margins tab, and in the From Edge section, select larger values for the Header and Footer settings.

Codes Are Visible in Your Header or Footer

When you add page numbers, dates, times, and other similar elements to your header or footer, these elements are added via field codes. If you're seeing the codes instead of the results (that is, if you're seeing { PAGE }, { DATE }, or so on), press Alt+F9.

Date, Time, or Other Items Are Incorrect

Since all of these elements are added via fields, you have to update the fields occasionally to ensure that they display the correct information. To update any individual field, right-click the field and select Update Field from the pop-up menu.

You Can't View Page Numbers

If you're having trouble viewing page numbers in your headers and footers, here are a few things to note.

First, page numbers aren't visible in Word's Normal view. You'll have to switch to Print Layout view to see your page numbers. Even in Print Layout view, you'll find your page numbers dimmed; this is because they're in fields that you can't edit unless you display the header or footer.

Second, if you find your page numbers overlapping other text or graphics in your header or footer, that's because you used the Insert ➤ Page Numbers command. This command inserts page numbers in frames, which are not positioned in-line with your header/footer text. Fortunately, frames are easy to move—so if your page number is getting in the way, just use your mouse to move it.

You Can't Remove Page Numbers

If you delete a page number from a header or footer, then switch to another page and find the page number is still there, one of two things has probably happened.

If your document is divided into several sections, when you deleted the page number, it was deleted only from the current section. You'll need to go into each section and remove the page numbers separately.

It's also possible that you've configured your header/footer for different first pages or odd/even pages. If so, you'll have to go into the separate headers/footers and remove the page numbers there.

Your Top or Bottom Margin Changed after Creating the Header or Footer

If you have a lot of text, large text, or graphics in your header or footer, it might be too large to fit within the selected top or bottom margin. If this happens, Word automatically increases the margin to accommodate all of your header or footer.

To prevent Word from adjusting the margins, select File ➤ Page Setup to display the Page Setup dialog box, then select the Margins tab. In the Top or Bottom box, add a hyphen to your margin measurement (-1 for 1, for example). This tells Word to hold the margins, no matter what.

 WARNING If your header or footer doesn't fit within the dedicated margin you set, the document text may overlap the header or footer area.

Changing One Section Header or Footer Changed Them All

When you change the header or footer for a section, Word automatically changes the same header or footer for all sections of the document. To create a different header or footer for a section, you need to break the connection between the sections. See Chapter 10 for detailed instructions.

Troubleshooting Footnotes, Endnotes, Captions, Cross-References, and Bookmarks

All the extra text you add to your document—footnotes, endnotes, captions, cross-references, and bookmarks—can be confusing and somewhat difficult to manage. Read on to discover the problems that others have with these elements and to learn how to prevent them from happening to you.

You Deleted Footnote Text, but the Reference Still Appears in the Document

You probably thought that deleting the footnote text deleted the footnote reference. You were wrong. It's the footnote (or endnote) reference mark that's important. So go back into your document and delete the reference mark; this will also delete any associated footnote or endnote text.

Some Footnotes or Endnotes Have Disappeared

First, make sure you're viewing your document in Print Layout view; this is the only view that displays footnotes and endnotes as they'll appear on your printed page.

The most common cause of missing footnotes or endnotes is deleted text. If you delete a block of text that contains footnote or endnote reference marks, Word also deletes the associated footnote/endnote text. The only way to retrieve this deleted text is to undo your deletion.

 TIP If you want to retain footnote/endnote text before you delete a block of body text, move or copy the footnote/endnote mark to another location before you delete the text block.

Part of a Footnote Was Continued on the Following Page

This isn't a problem, it's a feature. Word automatically makes the end of footnotes flow to a second page if the text is too long to fit comfortably on the original page. About the only way around this is to reduce the size of the footnote.

Some Captions Aren't Numbered Correctly

There are three instances where the automatic numbering of captions might go awry:

You Deleted a Caption Sometimes Word doesn't handle deletions well and numbers your remaining captions out of sequence. If this is the case, you'll need to manually fix each of the misnumbered captions.

You Inserted More Than One Caption in a Text Box Word lets you anchor only one text box to a specific paragraph, and you can include only one caption in that text box. So if you added more than one caption to a text box—or to multiple linked text boxes, which Word treats as a single text box—you'll need to scale back to a single caption to avoid duplicated or out-of-sequence numbering.

You Grouped a Caption with a Floating Object If you attach a caption to any object not positioned in-line with your text, Word may display all your caption numbers as zeros. To fix this, you'll have to ungroup the offending caption and then manually update the other captions.

Cross-References or Captions Aren't Updated Correctly

Since Word inserts cross-references and captions as fields, you'll need to manually update any of these items that aren't displaying the proper information. To update a cross-reference or caption, right-click the item and select Update Field from the pop-up menu.

A Bookmark Error Message Is Displayed

You are typically alerted to bookmark-related problems with the following error message:

```
Error! Bookmark not defined
```

If you see this error message, check to see whether the bookmark referred to still exists. If the bookmark itself—or the text containing the bookmark—has been deleted, any references to the bookmark will obviously be broken.

PART

IX

Tips, Tricks, and
Troubleshooting

It's also possible that the bookmark has simply moved. Right-click the referencing field code and select Update Fields from the pop-up menu to update the bookmark reference.

Troubleshooting Tables and Sorting

Tables are useful tools in your Word documents, and so is the ability to sort text—either within a table or in normal text. Read on to learn about some common table and sorting problems.

Part of the Text within a Cell Is Hidden or Cut Off

If you're having trouble seeing some of the text in your table, there are a couple of things to check.

First, you might need to adjust the paragraph indentation for the text within a cell. To do this, click anywhere within the offending cell, select Format ➢ Paragraph to display the Paragraph dialog box, select the Indents and Spacing tab, and then go to the Indentation section and specify new measurements.

It's also possible the problem is within the table, and not with the table text. If you set an exact row height that's smaller than the text you are trying to display, part of the text will be cut off. To fix this, click anywhere within the cell, select Table ➢ Table Properties to display the Table Properties dialog box, select the Row tab, pull down the Row Height Is list, and select At Least. This will allow the table row to resize if larger elements are inserted within the cell.

Your Table Is Cut Off at the End of a Page

If you've enabled text wrapping for your table and the table extends past the end of a page, the table will be cut off—and will not flow to the following page. To enable your table to span more than a single page, select the table, select Table ➢ Table Properties to display the Table Properties dialog box, select the Table tab, and select None in the Text Wrapping section.

Your Table Extends past the Edge of the Page

If you insert a new column into a table that is already wide, you may push the right edge of the table clear off the edge of your page. When this happens, you need to resize the individual columns to make the table fit again—which can be a problem if you can't even access the right-most column.

If this happens to you, try switching to Word's Normal view. In this view you can typically access elements that have been pushed off the page and are inaccessible in Print Layout view.

If you still can't access columns in your table, select the entire table, then select Table ➢ AutoFit ➢ AutoFit to Window. This will resize your entire table to fit within your page boundaries.

Numbers That Contain Hyphens Are Sorted Incorrectly

If you choose to sort a numeric list, numbers that contain hyphens—such as phone numbers or ZIP+4 postal codes—might be sorted incorrectly. You can sometimes work around this problem by choosing to sort the data by text instead of by number. Just select Table ➢ Sort to display the Sort dialog box, then pull down the Type list and select Text.

If this doesn't provide a proper sort, you'll have to replace the hyphens. Use Word's Replace command to replace all the hyphens with periods, perform your sort, and then use Replace again to replace the periods with hyphens. (When you use Replace in this fashion, select the list or table first to limit the parameters of the Replace command.)

Troubleshooting Graphics

Graphics in Word—pictures, drawings, and other inserted objects—open up a whole new world of potential problems. If you're having problems with any graphic object in a document, look here for a possible solution.

Graphics Aren't Displayed or Don't Print Properly

The general problem of *my graphic doesn't look right* can be caused by any number of specific problems. The following sections present some of the more common graphic display issues.

Graphics Aren't Visible

If you're working in Normal or Outline view, you won't be able to see any of the drawing objects—including text boxes, AutoShapes, WordArt, or clip art—in your document. You need to switch to Print Layout or Web Layout view to see how drawing objects will look in your final document.

You also might have opted to display placeholders instead of graphics. To turn off picture placeholders, select Tools ➢ Options to display the Options dialog box, select the View tab, then uncheck the Picture Placeholders option.

PART

IX

Tips, Tricks, and
Troubleshooting

Similarly, you may have turned off the option to view drawings in your document. To turn on the drawings display, go to the View tab in the Options dialog box and check the Drawings option.

It's also possible that field codes used to display some graphics are displayed instead of the graphics themselves. To turn off the field codes and display your graphic, press Alt+F9.

Only Part of a Graphic Is Displayed

This can happen if you insert a graphic in-line with text that has had an exact line spacing specified—and that line spacing is smaller than the graphic. You'll need to change the line spacing to accommodate the larger graphic; select Format ➤ Paragraph to display the Paragraph dialog box, select the Indents and Spacing tab, then pull down the Line Spacing list and select At Least.

Graphics Don't Print

Several things can cause graphics not to print when you print your document. These include the following:

You May Be Printing in Draft Mode   When you choose to print in Draft mode, Word doesn't print any borders or graphics. To turn off Draft-mode printing, select Tools ➤ Options to display the Options dialog box, select the Print tab, then uncheck the Draft Output option.

Drawing Objects May Not Be Selected   You have the option to print or not print drawing objects in your documents. To enable the printing of drawing objects, go to the Print tab in the Options dialog box and check the Drawing Objects option.

You May Be Printing Field Codes for Linked Objects   If you have a linked graphic object in your document, you could have selected to print field codes rather than the objects themselves. To turn off the printing of field codes, go to the Print tab of the Options dialog box and uncheck the Field Codes option.

Your System May Be Low on Memory   Low system memory will cause graphics and complex documents to either not print or print at lower-than-normal resolutions. If you think this is the problem, try closing any open documents or programs, then print again. If the problem persists, you may need to add more memory to your computer.

Your System May Be Short on Disk Space   Windows uses spare disk space as virtual system memory; if you're short on space, it has the same effect as being low on memory. Try deleting some unused files and printing again.

Lines Are Jagged Onscreen

In drawing objects, any curved line—or any straight line drawn diagonally—will display some degree of jaggedness onscreen. This is normal and does not reflect the way the drawing will print; even if it looks jagged onscreen, a line will print smoothly on paper.

Colors Aren't Smooth Onscreen

Similar to the jagged-line problem, colors—especially color gradients—can look blocky onscreen, even though they appear normal when printed. This problem is exacerbated if you're viewing your document at anything other than 100-percent zoom.

The solution is to change to 100-percent magnification and adjust your monitor—if possible—to display 256 or more colors. The more colors your monitor can display, the less your colors will appear distorted onscreen.

Objects Don't Align, Distribute, or Position Properly

Aligning, distributing, and positioning objects can sometimes be tricky, as the following problems attest to.

Aligned Objects Are Stacked on Top of Each Other

Depending on the alignment option you select, objects will move either straight up, straight down, left, or right—and might cover objects already in those positions. If this happens, undo the alignment and move the unaligned objects out of the way.

Objects Don't Align or Distribute as Commanded

If your objects aren't aligning or distributing as you expect, make sure the Relative to Page option on the Align or Distribute menu isn't checked. When this option is selected, objects are forced to move in relation to the page as well as in relation to other selected objects; you want to turn off this option to have total control over the repositioning process.

Items on the Align or Distribute Menu Are Unavailable

You have to have two objects selected to align them and three objects selected to distribute them. Selecting any fewer objects causes the related menu items to be unavailable.

 NOTE This rule holds unless you've checked the Relative to Page option on the Align or Distribute menu—in which case you can align or distribute a single object relative to the page.

Tips, Tricks, and Troubleshooting

Objects Jump when Realigned

If you've opted to align objects to a grid, any attempt to align an object to a position between grid points will cause the object to jump to the nearest grid position. If you want to position an object between grid points, press Alt when you drag or draw the object; this temporarily overrides the grid.

Object Alignment Changed when the Document Was Opened on Another Computer

If you try to display a Word 2000 document on a computer with Word 97 (or previous version) installed, not all of your object-positioning options are retained. In particular, expect the following changes:

- Objects formatted with middle or bottom alignment are shifted to top alignment.
- Objects positioned relative to a character are shifted to be positioned relative to a column.
- Objects positioned relative to a line are shifted to be positioned relative to a paragraph.
- Objects with right, center, inside, or outside horizontal alignment are shifted slightly.
- Objects with tight or through text wrapping are displayed with square text wrapping.
- Overlapping objects may be obscured.
- Pictures with text wrapping in tables will be moved above the table.

In addition, complex drawings may appear somewhat simplified.

The bottom line is to expect changes when you transfer a graphically complex document to a non-Word 2000 system. Personally, I've spent many long hours at Kinko's reformatting my Word 2000 documents to work on their Word 97 systems—and the only way to avoid the problem is to not use Word 2000's advanced object-positioning features.

You Can't Move a Paragraph without Moving a Graphic

If you want a graphic to remain in place when you move the surrounding text, you have to make sure the graphic isn't locked to the paragraph you want to move. To do this, select the graphic, then select Format ➤ *Object* to display the Format dialog box. Select the Layout tab, then click the Advanced button to display the Advanced Layout dialog box. Select the Picture Position tab and uncheck both the Move Object with Text and Lock Anchor options.

You Encounter Problems while Editing Pictures

The following sections detail some of the issues involved with editing pictures in your documents—either pictures you've imported or pictures you've drawn with Word's drawing tools.

You Can't Change the Picture's Color

You should first try ungrouping the image (if possible—see next problem) and then changing the colors of the various picture parts individually. If this doesn't work and Word won't let you edit the picture in this fashion, open the original picture in a separate picture-editing program (such as Microsoft Photo Editor) and then reimport the edited picture back into your document.

You Can't Ungroup a Picture

Most drawings you create within Word can be ungrouped into their component parts, as can most of Word's clip-art images. However, most pictures that you import into Word—GIFs, JPGs, bitmaps, and the like—cannot be ungrouped and converted into drawing objects. If you want to edit these images, you have to use a separate picture-editing program, such as Microsoft Photo Editor.

You Can't Change an Animated GIF Picture

Animated GIFs are a special type of GIF file that displays multiple images in a type of crude animation. Word will not allow cropping, grouping, or changes to the fill, border, shadow, or transparency of animated GIF files. To edit animated GIF files, you will have to use a separate picture-editing program with animated GIF compatibility.

Your Pictures Look Wrong when Resized

Two things can go wrong when you manually resize a picture. First, you can change the proportions of the picture and distort the image. To return a picture to its original dimensions, select Format ➤ Picture to display the Format Picture dialog box, select the Size tab, then click the Reset button. Now you can resize the picture while maintaining its original dimensions, by using only the *corner* sizing handles, not the ones on the sides, top, or bottom of the picture.

Second, when you print the picture, poor quality or strange banding effects are created. This can happen when you resize a bitmapped graphic; these graphics aren't always designed to be resized and thus print with unpredictable results. The only real solution is to return the bitmapped graphic to its 100-percent size, although sometimes an even multiple of 50 percent or 200 percent will print acceptably.

PART

IX

Tips, Tricks, and
Troubleshooting

A Picture Won't Rotate

Only drawing objects can be flipped or rotated—not imported picture files. If you can convert an object to a drawing object—by ungrouping it and regrouping it—you will be able to flip or rotate the object.

You won't, however, be able to flip or rotate GIF, JPG, or similar files. If you want a rotated version of one of these files, you'll have to use a separate picture-editing program to do this before you import the file into Word.

You Encounter Border, 3-D, and Shadow Problems

You can add borders, shadows, and 3-D effects to almost any object in a Word document. When you add one of these effects, however, you also add a number of potential problems.

A Border Isn't Displayed Properly

An object's border will not be displayed if you've added a 3-D effect to the object, or if you've formatted the object as embossed or engraved. In addition, you won't be able to see the border (even though it's still there) if the border is the same color as the page background. Check all these items if you're having trouble seeing the object's border.

Adding a 3-D Effect Replaces Borders and Shadows

Within Word, you cannot apply both a shadow and a 3-D effect to the same object—the 3-D effect takes precedence. In addition, adding a 3-D effect to an object turns off the object's normal border.

3-D and Shadow Colors Don't Change when You Change the Object's Color

Changing the fill color of an object affects only the face of the object—not the shadow or the 3-D effect (nor, for that matter, does it change the object's border color). You have to change the color of a shadow or 3-D effect separately from the object's fill color.

You Can't Control Freehand Drawing

Drawing in Word isn't easy, even if you have artistic talent and good eye-hand control. To make drawing a little easier, try increasing the magnification in the Zoom control; 200 percent is better for detailed drawing than is 100 percent.

You also might want to try adjusting the tracking speed on your mouse. A slower tracking speed will make your mouse a little easier to control.

Finally, consider using Word's Freeform drawing instead of the Scribble drawing—you might find the results slightly easier to control.

A Drawing Object Disappeared when You Ran the Letter Wizard

This is an extremely odd problem, but one that you may encounter. When you anchor any drawing object to a paragraph in a letter that the Letter Wizard changes, Word may delete the drawing object when you run the Letter Wizard. The only solution to this problem is to undo the Letter Wizard's changes and then move the object to another position in your document—and anchor it to a paragraph that is not a Letter Wizard element, such as the body of the letter.

Troubleshooting Revisions

You'd think that by the time you got to revising a document, all your problems would be over, wouldn't you? Of course, you'd be wrong—there are a few common problems you might encounter when using Word's track changes feature.

Tracked Changes Don't Appear in Your Document

If you don't see revision marks in your document, select Tools ➢ Track Changes ➢ Highlight Changes on Screen. If this doesn't display the tracked changes, it's possible that the changes might be in hidden text or field codes. To view any hidden elements, select Tools ➢ Options to display the Options dialog box, select the View tab, then check both the Field Codes and Hidden Text options.

You Can't Accept or Reject Changes

If Word won't let you use the Accept Change and Reject Change buttons on the Reviewing toolbar, it's likely that the document is protected for tracked changes. You'll need to turn off document protection by selecting Tools ➢ Unprotect Document.

Comparing Documents Doesn't Work

To use Word's compare documents feature, the two documents have to have different filenames or different extensions—you can't compare two files with the exact same name. In addition, if you want to compare multiple *versions* of the same document, you'll have to save one of the versions as a separate file.

Your Document Lost Its Versioning Information

This will happen if you save your document as a Web page. Although Word retains most other aspects of a document when it converts from document to Web page

PART

IX

Tips, Tricks, and Troubleshooting

format, versioning information is one of the few things that get lost in the translation. The only workaround for this problem is to save a separate copy of your file as a document before you save it as a Web page.

Troubleshooting Linking and Embedding

Object linking and embedding (OLE) is a somewhat complex technology that has to work across multiple software programs manufactured by multiple software manufacturers. As you might expect, problems are likely to ensue anytime you try to get a Microsoft document to link to any non-Microsoft document. Read on to learn some workarounds for the more common OLE-related problems.

You Can't Edit a Linked or Embedded Object

If, when you double-click a linked or embedded object, Word can't open the source file or program, you'll see an error message that tells you that you can't edit the object. If you see this *can't edit* error message, try any of the following workarounds:

- Check to see whether the source program is actually installed on your computer. (You may have deleted the program, or you may be opening a document created on another computer that does have the program installed.) If the source program is not installed, you can convert the object to another file format that you can edit on your computer by selecting Edit ➢ Object ➢ Convert to display the Convert dialog box, and then selecting a different file type from the Object Type list.

- Check to see whether you have enough memory on your system to run the source program *and* Word together. You may need to close some open programs or documents, or (as a longer-term solution) install more memory on your PC.

- It's possible that the source program is actually running, but has a dialog box open that is preventing the editing operation from continuing. Press Alt+Tab to cycle through all open Windows programs to find an open source program.

- If you're on a network, it's possible that another user has the source file open, preventing you from editing it. Check to see whether the file is open elsewhere, then wait for the other user to close the file before you make another attempt to access it.

- If the name of the source file has been changed since you created the link to it, the link is effectively broken. Fortunately you can select Edit ➢ Links to display the Links dialog box, then click the Change Source button to specify a new filename for this link.

Large Linked or Embedded Objects Appear Cropped

If you add a large linked or embedded object to your document, it may appear cropped on the right or bottom side—even if there is more than enough room to fit the entire object on your page. This happens because Word converts the object into a Windows metafile (.WMF), which has a maximum height and width; if your object exceeds this maximum size, it appears cropped onscreen.

To prevent a linked or embedded object from being cropped in this fashion, you can reduce the size of the linked or embedded data in the source program, by reducing font or column size. Alternately, you can paste or link the data into your Word document as formatted or unformatted text (use the Edit ➤ Paste Special command), which gives you more control over the look and feel of the imported data within your document.

You Encounter Problems with Excel Objects in Word

Even Microsoft applications don't always work well together. For example, you may have trouble opening an Excel object from within Word. If this happens to you, switch to Excel, select Tools ➤ Options to display Excel's Options dialog box, select the General tab, then uncheck the Ignore Other Applications dialog box. That's right, Excel can be configured to ignore requests from other applications, including Word. Turning off this option makes Excel a tad more communicative.

You may also experience problems when you paste text into Word that was copied from an Excel worksheet—it's not uncommon to see the font size change from 10 point to 12 point. This is because both Excel and Word apply their respective Normal styles to the text. Since Excel's Normal style is 10 point and Word's Normal style is 12 point, the text gets bigger when you paste it into Word. To return the pasted text to its original 10 point size, just reformat it manually after you've pasted it.

Troubleshooting Mail Merges

Mail merges are some of the more difficult tasks you can accomplish with Word. As you might expect, with difficulty come more difficulties, as detailed in the following sections.

Merge Fields Are Printed Instead of Data

If your form letters, labels, or envelopes are printing merge field codes instead of the merged data, you forgot to turn off the display of field codes before you initiated printing. To turn off field codes, select Tools ➤ Options to display the Options dialog box, select the Print tab, then uncheck the Field Codes options.

PART

IX

Tips, Tricks, and
Troubleshooting

It's also possible that you tried to print a merge mailing by using the File ➤ Print command. This doesn't work—unless, of course, you've saved a completed merge to a new document. Instead, you want to use the Merge to Printer command.

Merged Document Contains Blank Lines

Blank lines will appear in a merged document when a field is inserted and that field is empty in a particular record. The solution is to check the Don't Print Blank Lines when Data Fields Are Empty option in the Merge dialog box.

An Error Message States the Data File Is a Main Document

You'll receive this type of error message if your data source was the active document when you selected Tools ➤ Mail Merge—thus accidentally selecting the data source as the main document.

To fix this situation, you need to display the data source document, then select Tools ➤ Mail Merge to display the Mail Merge Helper dialog box. Click the Create button, and then select Restore to Main Document. Now save and store the data source document.

Next, you have to open the document you want to use as the main document, then select Tools ➤ Mail Merge to redisplay the Mail Merge Helper. Click the Create button, and then select the type of main document you want to use. When the Microsoft Word dialog box appears, click the Active Window button.

You're now all set up with the proper main document and data source for your merged mailing.

A Mail Merge Field Changed when the Letter Wizard Was Launched

When you create a mail merge main document and then run Word's Letter Wizard, the Letter Wizard replaces some merge fields with the { AUTOTEXTLIST } field. (When you consider all the little things it changes without any regard for previous work, the Letter Wizard is an annoying little convenience.)

To fix this problem, you need to replace the { AUTOTEXTLIST } fields with the proper merge fields. You do this by deleting the { AUTOTEXTLIST } field, clicking the Insert Merge Field button on the Mail Merge toolbar, and then selecting the appropriate merge field.

Troubleshooting Printing, Faxing, and E-mail

Many Word users encounter problems when they're done editing and ready to print their final documents. Print-related problems can have many causes, from configuration issues in Word and driver issues in Windows to hardware issues with your printer itself. In this section, you will learn about the most common output problems and how to fix them.

Tracking Down Common Printer Problems

Most printer problems will *not* be caused by Microsoft Word. Instead, you should typically look to either your printer hardware or Microsoft Windows when you're having trouble printing.

Checking Your Printer Hardware

The first place to look when you're having printing problems is your printer. Quite often a vexing problem can be solved by pressing the right button or reconnecting a loose cable. Before you proceed to complicated computer troubleshooting, check out all of the following:

- Make sure that your printer's power cable is plugged in (at both ends!) and that it actually has power. Make sure the power switch on the wall is turned on and that your circuit breaker hasn't blown.

- Make sure that your printer is turned on. (Don't laugh!) Then make sure that your printer is activated (online) and not just in a holding mode.

- Make sure that your printer has paper in the proper paper bin and that no paper is jamming the paper path.

- Make sure that your printer has a sufficient supply of ink or toner.

- Make sure that your printer is properly connected to the printer port on the back of your computer's system unit. Check both ends of the cable to make sure they fit snugly and that no pins on the connectors are bent or broken. Make sure the printer cable doesn't have any severe bends or kinks that could break the wires inside.

Once you're sure that your printer is plugged in and ready to go, turn it off—then wait ten seconds and turn it back on. This will reset your printer and clear its internal memory, which will cure some types of printing problems. You should then run the printer's self-diagnostic test to make sure the printer is functioning properly.

If your printer appears to be working properly, you should turn your attention to Windows—and Windows' printer setup.

PART

IX

Tips, Tricks, and Troubleshooting

If, on the other hand, your printer is *not* printing properly at this stage, you should have your printer examined by a qualified computer hardware technician.

 TIP To be extra sure that your printer is working correctly, hook it up to another computer and try printing from that computer. If everything works fine with the other PC, you can be fairly sure the problem does not lie in your printer.

Running the Print Troubleshooter

If your printer is OK, it's time to start troubleshooting your Windows printer setup. Fortunately, both Windows 95 and Windows 98 include a Print Troubleshooter tool that walks you step by step through some of the more common troubleshooting procedures.

If you're running Windows 98, you start the Print Troubleshooter by following these steps:

1. Click the Windows Start button, then select Help to display the Help window.

2. Select the Contents tab.

3. Select Troubleshooting ➢ Windows 98 Troubleshooters ➢ Print to start the Print Troubleshooter.

If you're running Windows 95, you start the Print Troubleshooter by following these steps:

1. Click the Windows Start button, then select Help to display the Help window.

2. Select the Contents tab.

3. Double-click the Troubleshooting topic.

4. Double-click the If You Have Trouble Printing topic to start the Print Troubleshooter.

Answer the questions in the Print Troubleshooter to narrow down the possible causes of your printing problems.

Verifying Printer Properties

The next thing to check is the configuration of your printer within Windows. Incorrect printer property settings can cause garbled or unacceptable output—or cause your printer not to print at all.

You check your printer properties by following these steps:

1. Click the Windows Start button, then select Settings ➢ Printers to display the Printers window.

2. Right-click the icon for your printer and select Properties to display the Properties dialog box.

3. Walk through the Properties dialog box tab by tab, verifying the settings with those settings recommended by your printer manufacturer.

One sure sign of trouble is if your printer doesn't appear in the Printers window. If your printer is missing, you'll need to install it; see the following section for more information.

Removing and Reinstalling Your Printer Driver

One prominent cause of print problems is a missing, damaged, or outdated printer driver. (A driver is a small file Windows uses to "drive" your printer from within the operating system, and it contains important configuration and operation information.) The best way to check your printer driver is to remove it and then reinstall it.

 TIP You should check with your printer's manufacturer to make sure you have the latest version of your printer driver. In many cases, you can download updated drivers from your manufacturer's Web site.

To remove and reinstall your printer driver, follow these steps:

1. Click the Windows Start button, then select Settings ➤ Printers to display the Printers window.

2. Right-click the icon for the printer you want to remove and select Delete.

 WARNING If your printer doesn't appear in the Printers window, proceed to step 4 to install the printer driver.

 NOTE If you are prompted to remove all the files associated with the printer, click Yes.

3. Return to the Printers window.

4. Select the Add Printer icon to launch the Add Printer Wizard.

5. Follow the instructions in the Add Printer Wizard to install the driver for your make and model of printer.

PART

IX

Tips, Tricks, and
Troubleshooting

Checking Your Printer Port

If you still have printing problems after reinstalling your printer driver, your printer port may not be configured and working properly. You can use Windows' Device Manager to check your printer port settings—and to make sure that no conflicts exist between your printer and another device on your computer system.

To run Device Manager, follow these steps:

1. On the Windows Desktop, right-click the My Computer icon and select Properties to display the System Properties dialog box.

2. Select the Device Manager tab.

3. Double-click the Ports (COM & LPT) icon to expand that section.

4. Double-click the icon for your printer port—typically Printer Port (LPT1)—to display the Properties dialog box.

5. Select the Resources tab.

6. Verify that the settings are correct for this printer port and that the Conflicting Devices list displays *No conflicts.*

If the Conflicting Devices list shows a conflict with another device, make note of the other device. You will need to reassign either your printer or the other device to a different port on your system.

 NOTE See your Windows documentation for instructions on how to reassign devices and ports.

Other Windows-Related Printing Issues

A handful of other Windows-related issues can affect the printing of your Word documents (as well as documents from other programs):

Read the `Printers.txt` File Both Windows 98 and Windows 95 include a file called `Printers.txt`, located in the `\Windows\` folder, that contains additional information about known printing issues. Read this file to see whether any of these issues apply to your system setup.

Decrease Your Print Resolution Some print problems occur when your printer is configured to print at its highest resolution. Try selecting a lower resolution setting (from your printer's Properties dialog box) to see whether this fixes your problem. If this *does* fix your problem, you may want to consider adding more memory to your computer system, since a higher-resolution printer consumes more system memory.

Check Your Hard Disk   Some printing problems can occur if your hard disk contains too many temporary files, is fragmented, is damaged, or does not contain enough free space. You should perform routine maintenance on your hard disk using Windows' ScanDisk or a similar utility; defragment your hard disk with Windows' Disk Defragmenter; and periodically delete all the .TMP files from the \Windows\Temp\ folder. Your goal should be to reserve at least 3Mb of hard-disk space to be used by the Windows printing system.

Upgrade to Windows 98   If you're still running Windows 95, you should seriously consider upgrading to the latest version of Windows 98. In Windows 98, many of the bugs present in Windows 95 have been fixed, and Windows 98 just plain runs more smoothly, with fewer errors and crashes. In addition, Windows 98's Plug-and-Play technology is more robust and makes installing new devices—such as new printers—relatively trouble-free.

Word Won't Print

When you can't print in Word, the first thing to check is your printer. Is it plugged in, connected properly, and online? Does it have paper and toner? Does it perform its own self-diagnostic test?

If your printer is OK, turn to Windows' printer setup. As discussed previously, make sure that the driver for your printer is installed and configured properly, and that there are no conflicts between your printer and other devices.

Next, you should check Word's printer settings. Select File ➢ Print to display the Print dialog box. Make sure the correct printer is selected, then click the Properties button to display the Properties dialog box so you can check specific printer properties.

You should also check Word's Print options. From within the Print dialog box, click the Options button to display the Print tab from the Options dialog box. Make sure that the desired options are selected.

Now return to the Print dialog box. Make sure you've selected the correct page range (or to print all pages) and that all other options are selected as appropriate and necessary. Click the Print button to initiate printing.

If your printer still doesn't print, see whether you can print from any other Windows program. If you *can,* you should refocus your efforts on Word's printer settings and options. If you *can't* print from other Windows programs, turn again to Windows' printer settings and to your printer itself.

Graphics Don't Print Right or At All

There are many possible causes of a graphics printing problem, including the following:

You May Be Printing in Draft Mode   When you select Draft mode printing, Word does not print graphics or borders in your document. To disable Draft mode,

PART

IX

Tips, Tricks, and
Troubleshooting

select Tools ➢ Options to display the Options dialog box, select the Print tab, and then uncheck the Draft Output option.

You May Have Disabled Printing of Drawing Objects   You must have the Drawing Objects option enabled to print graphics in your documents. Turn this feature back on by going to the Print tab of the Options dialog box and checking the Drawing Objects option.

You May Be Printing Field Codes for Linked Graphics   If you're printing a linked graphic, make sure you've toggled off the printing of field codes. Go to the Print tab on the Options dialog box and uncheck the Field Codes option.

You May Need to Print at a Lower Resolution or a Higher Resolution   If a large graphic is consuming too much memory to print fully, lowering your print resolution may enable the complete printing of the graphic—albeit at a lower resolution. On the other hand, if a complex graphic doesn't look right at a lower resolution, try increasing the print resolution to improve the detail of the printing.

Your System May Be Low on Memory   A system with too little memory will make graphics either not print, print at a low resolution, or print incompletely. If you have a memory problem, try closing other documents and programs, and consider adding more memory to your PC.

Your System May Be Low on Hard-Disk Space   Windows needs at least 3Mb for most printing operations and more to print complex documents and graphics. If you don't have enough free disk space, delete any unused files before you retry the printing operation.

Your Graphic May Not Be Compatible with Your Printer   This is a specific problem with Encapsulated PostScript (.EPS) files, which are designed to be printed on PostScript printers. Trying to print an .EPS file on a non-PostScript printer may produce unsatisfactory results.

Your Printer May Not Be Configured to Dither Graphics   Some printers have a configuration option (typically set in the Printer Properties dialog box) to dither, or blend, printed images. If dithering is turned off, any gradated graphics will appear blocky. Turn on dithering or blending for more accurate printed reproduction of what you see onscreen.

Complex Documents Don't Print Right or At All

The same issues that apply to printing graphics also apply to printing complex documents. The more elements—graphics, borders, tables, objects, etc.—there are in your document, the more memory is required to print the document. If your system doesn't have enough memory—or enough free disk space—your document will not print correctly. You should examine all the solutions presented in the previous section, with the added workaround of simplifying your document before you try to print it again. Try removing some of the graphics and other objects, page borders, backgrounds, and watermarks. You can also try printing your document in parts, or even one page at a time, to produce a print document with a size small enough for your system to handle.

Your Document Looks Different on Paper than Onscreen

If what you print does not accurately reproduce what you see onscreen, you could have any one of the following problems:

You May Have Fonts in Your Document That Aren't Available on Your Printer This should be a problem only if you're using a non-TrueType font. If this is the case, change all your fonts in your document to TrueType fonts.

You May Have Fonts in Your Document That Aren't Installed on Your System If this is the case, neither your printer nor your screen is truly representing what your document should look like. Use Word's font-substitution feature to substitute available fonts for any missing fonts.

You May Be Printing Draft Fonts To check this, select Tools ➢ Options to display the Options dialog box, select the View tab, and uncheck the Draft Font option.

You May Be Printing a Draft Version of Your Document Drafts print faster, but don't use all the fancy fonts, graphics, and borders contained in your real document. Turn off draft printing by opening the Options dialog box, selecting the Print tab, then unchecking the Draft Output option.

Your Document May Have Been Formatted for a Different Paper Size To resize the document for this printing session, select File ➢ Print to display the Print dialog box, then pull down the Scale to Paper Size list and select the paper size currently loaded in your printer.

Text Is Cut Off at the Edges

If text runs off the sides or bottom of your paper, you probably have a mismatch somewhere in your settings. Make sure that you have the correct printer selected in Word's Print dialog box and that you've selected the correct paper size in the Page Setup dialog box.

Also in the Page Setup dialog box, check your margin settings; most printers require a minimum margin setting, since printers can't print to the edge of the page. Make sure that your margins are set wide enough for your printer. (Typically you want at least a half-inch margin all around.)

PART

IX

Tips, Tricks, and
Troubleshooting

An Extra Page Is Printed with Each Document

If you keep printing a blank page after the end of your documents, there are three items to check.

First, that blank page may not actually be blank—that is, there may be a few stray paragraph marks at the end of your document that spill over onto an extra page. Click the Show/Hide button to display all the paragraph marks in your document, then focus on the very last page. Delete any lingering paragraph marks after the end of your text.

Second, if you're printing to a network printer, look to see whether the printer has a form-feed option. If it does, turn it off—that form-feed command is creating an extra page at the end of your document.

Finally, some Hewlett-Packard printers (or printers that emulate HPs) that connect via a PS/2-style parallel port may generate an extra page *before* each print job. This extra page contains either PJL codes or a single character in the upper-left corner. You can eliminate this page by configuring the port in your computer's CMOS settings to a non-PS/2 mode. You can also install an updated Lpt.vxd file (located on the Windows 95 installation CD), which will fix this problem.

NOTE This problem should not occur if you're running Windows 98, because Windows 98 already contains the updated Lpt.vxd file.

You Receive an Error Message when Printing

Windows is pretty good about letting you know when something goes wrong. If you see an error message onscreen when you try to print, read the following sections for some advice.

"Windows cannot print due to a problem with the current printer setup"

The cause of this error message is typically one of the following:

No Default Printer Driver Is Installed   You need to install a new printer on your system, using the Add Printer Wizard in the Printers window.

There Is a Damaged Entry in the Windows Registry   This is a major problem—because the Windows Registry holds all your important system settings—but one that is easily fixed. You need to add a new printer to your system (just add a generic one via the Add Printer Wizard), make the new printer your default printer, and then make your *old* printer your default printer. This effectively resets the Registry back to its proper state.

There Is a Damaged Printer Driver The printer driver for your current printer is bad and needs to be reinstalled. Use the procedure described earlier in this chapter to uninstall and then reinstall your printer driver.

There Are Damaged Windows Printing Subsystem Files If you're running Windows 98, you can fix any damaged system files with the System File Checker utility. Click the Windows Start button and select Accessories ➤ System Tools ➤ System Information to launch the Microsoft System Information utility. Select Tools ➤ System File Checker to display the System File Checker dialog box; select the Scan for Altered Files option, then click the Start button. When the utility finds a bad file, follow the on-screen instructions to reinstall the file.

NOTE Windows 95 does not include a similar file-checking utility. If you're running Windows 95, you may need to reinstall your entire operating system—or upgrade to Windows 98—to fix this problem.

There Is a Device Conflict on the Printer Port Another device is trying to use the same port being used by your printer. You need to change the port assignment for one of the two devices. Follow the advice earlier in this section and run Device Manager to identify your port conflict.

There Is a Problem with Your Fax Setup If you received this error message when attempting to send a fax, there may be a problem with the configuration of your fax software.

"Word cannot bring up the Properties dialog box because the printer returned an error"

If you see this error message when you click the Properties button in the Print dialog box, it's possible that your printer driver is damaged or missing. If this is the case, try uninstalling and reinstalling your printer driver.

It's also possible that you're trying to use a network printer, but the printer has an invalid network name. If this is the case, contact your network administrator for assistance.

Finally, the regional settings for your printer may be corrupted. To fix this, open the Windows Control Panel, select the Regional Settings icon to display the Regional Settings dialog box, then choose a different setting. Shut down your computer, restart it, open the Regional Settings dialog box again, and rechoose your original regional setting.

PART

IX

Tips, Tricks, and
Troubleshooting

"Too many fonts"

This message is generated when there are so many different fonts used in your document that Windows—and your printer—can't handle them all. The chief solution is to reduce the number of fonts used, and then print again. You can sometimes work around this problem by selecting the Print TrueType as Graphics options in the Properties dialog box for your printer; note, however, that not all printers offer this option.

Troubleshooting Fax Problems

If you're having problems sending faxes from within Word, check all of the following:

- Do you have fax software installed on your PC? (Neither Windows 98 nor Word 2000 come with their own fax software.)
- Is your fax software properly installed and configured—does it appear as a selection in your Printers list?
- Do you have a modem connected to your PC—and is your modem connected to a free phone line?
- Is another device or program trying to use your modem while you're trying to send a fax. (You can't send a fax while you're connected to the Internet.)
- Are you sending the fax to a valid fax number, not a standard voice number?

If all these items check out, consult technical support options for your fax software.

Troubleshooting E-mail Problems

If you're having trouble sending Word documents as either e-mail messages or attachments, check all of the following:

- Do you have a MAPI-compatible e-mail application installed on your system?
- In particular, do you have Outlook 2000 or Outlook Express installed on your system?
- Is your e-mail program running? (In some instances, you may need to have Outlook running before you can send messages from Word.)
- Is your e-mail program configured properly for your ISP's e-mail server?
- Do you have a valid e-mail account at your ISP?
- Do you have a solid connection to the Internet—and is your modem working properly?

In general, if you can send and receive e-mail properly from Outlook 2000 or Outlook Express, you should be able to do the same from Word.

Troubleshooting Web Pages

Working with Web pages is slightly different than working with normal Word documents. You have to deal with hyperlinks, as well as with commands and operations that aren't quite the same as you're used to in the normal Word environment. Read on to discover some of the more common problems you may encounter when creating Web pages with Word.

The Hyperlink Command Doesn't Appear on the Pop-Up Menu

Normally you can add a hyperlink to a piece of text by either clicking the Hyperlink button on Word's Standard toolbar or right-clicking the selection and choosing Hyperlink from the pop-up menu. If the Hyperlink command doesn't appear on the pop-up menu, however, it's because the selected text contains a spelling or grammatical error. When you correct the spelling or grammar mistake, the Hyperlink command reappears.

An Error Message Appears when You Click a Hyperlink

On occasion you may receive the following error message when you click a hyperlink in a Word document:

```
The destination of the hyperlink might have been removed or renamed.
```

This error message may have any number of causes. First, you may have simply entered the wrong URL for the hyperlink. Check the address for mistakes and edit as necessary.

Second, you may have created a link to a fixed file location on your hard disk or network, and the file might have been moved to a new location. If this is the case, you'll need to edit the hyperlink to reflect the new file location.

Finally, this message is generated any time the linked page can't be accessed—if you're not connected to the Internet (and thus can't access the linked page), you'll receive this message any time you click *any* hyperlink in your document. You'll also receive this message if you're connected to the Internet, but the linked site is too busy to accept your request.

Graphics Don't Display on Your Web Page

If you access your Web page and see a big, red X where a graphic should be, that means the link to that graphic has been broken. Broken links can be caused by any number of

PART

IX

Tips, Tricks, and
Troubleshooting

problems, from deleted files and mistyped links to files being moved to another location. A frequent cause is moving your Web page and *not* moving the supporting graphics files—which results in misdirected (and broken) links.

If you access your Web page and see a *blank* image where a graphic should be, it's likely that your Web browser has been configured to *not* display graphics. Reconfigure your browser and take another look.

Text and Graphics Aren't Positioned Properly

You get your page laid out just so, then you publish it to the Web. Now, when you view your page with your Web browser, your page looks different—the text and the graphics aren't positioned in quite the same way you intended. What went wrong?

This, believe it or not, is normal—because Word provides more detailed formatting and positioning options than are supported by most Web browsers.

Because Word provides formatting options that most Web browsers do not support, some text and graphics may look different when you view them on a Web page. In particular, most of Word's text-wrapping options and positioning of floating graphics and text just don't translate to HTML. You can plan for this translation, however, by working in Web Layout view, which uses HTML standards to display your page—and takes into account all that can and can't be done on the Web.

Frames Are Missing or Displayed Incorrectly

Frames pages are a little tricky, in that you're dealing with a page holding the frames and separate pages displayed in each of the frames. If you enter the wrong filename or URL, you'll end up seeing the frame content instead of the frames page—or vice versa.

If it appears that some of the frames are missing when you open a frames page, you've probably opened one of the individual content pages instead of the frames page itself. Go back and check your filenames, and open the page that you saved when you created the frames page.

If the first page you see in a frame is not the correct page, you can easily change it. Just right-click anywhere in the frame to display the pop-up menu, select Frame Properties to display the Frame Properties dialog box, then select the Frame tab. Pull down the Initial Page list and select the document you want to display as the initial page.

If you click a hyperlink to a frames page and the Web page appears in the wrong frame, you have to fix the hyperlink. Right-click the hyperlink to display the pop-up menu, then select Hyperlink ➤ Edit Hyperlink to display the Edit Hyperlink dialog box. Pull down the Click the Frame where You Want the Document to Appear list and select the name of the destination frame.

> ⚠️ **TIP** If you're not sure of a frame's name, hover your mouse over the frame in the frame graphic in the Edit Hyperlink dialog box.

HTML Codes Change after You Save a Web Page

Sometimes Word will change the HTML source code of a Web page after you save the page. This is because you may have entered nonstandard code—inserted things in not quite the right order or used lowercase letters—and Word fixes them before writing the final code. These changes won't affect the way your page is displayed, they just make for cleaner code.

Users Can't Access Your Web Page

If you saved your Web page using a long filename, some Internet surfers won't be able to access your pages. In particular, users of Windows prior to Windows 95 can only read pages using the 8.3 naming convention and simply can't access pages with longer names. For compatibility's sake, consider renaming all your pages with short filenames.

Troubleshooting Forms

Forms and fields are a tad hard to understand and thus can be somewhat problematic for some users. If you're experiencing problems with your forms, consult the following sections for information and advice.

Form Fields Don't Work

The most common reason for a form field *not* accepting input is that you forgot to protect your form document. Until the document is protected, users can't type in your list boxes, select your check boxes, or pull down your drop-down lists.

To make your form work, all you have to do is click the Protect Form button on the Forms toolbar.

Field Codes Are Displayed Instead of Form Fields

If Word displays { FORMTEXT }, { FORMCHECKBOX }, or { FORMDROPDOWN } instead of your designated form fields, it's because Word is displaying field codes. To switch off the field-code display (and display the proper form fields), press Alt+F9.

The Tab Key Doesn't Move the Insertion Point to the Correct Form Field

This is a tricky one, because pressing the Tab key always moves the insertion point to the next form field in your form. The problem is that you may have designed your form in such a way that the next field really isn't the next field—at least visually. If you want the Tab key to move around your form in a different order, you may have to create an on-exit macro to send the insertion point to the field of choice.

Check-Box Size Doesn't Change when Formatted

When you change the formatting of your document—in particular, when you change the font size—you would expect all your form fields to change accordingly. Well, all the form fields do—*except* the check-box field. The check-box field automatically changes size to match the surrounding text, no matter what formatting you apply to the check box itself. If you want the check box to appear at a precise size, you have to double-click the check box to display the Form Fields Options dialog box, check the Exactly option, and then enter a value in the box.

Problems with Form Macros

If you find that users of your form are unable to run any of the macros associated with the form, you probably forgot to send along the macros when you sent them the form file. Make sure that you add all the macros to the form template, so that they travel with the template file.

Likewise, if you try to add an entry or exit macro, but find that the Entry and Exit lists are empty, you need to add the macros to the template. Remember that you can't choose or use any macros until the template contains the macros.

Troubleshooting Macros and VBA

Word macros and Visual Basic for Applications programming are the two most complex components of Microsoft Word. One could write an entire book on either subject, and devote several chapters to potential problems and troubleshooting, so I can't cover all potential problems here in this short space. I will try to present some of the problems more frequently encountered by casual users, along with the appropriate troubleshooting advice.

You Made a Mistake while Recording a Macro

It's quite common to make a mistake while recording a macro. If this happens to you, you have two options:

- Rerecord the macro (without mistakes, this time).

- Keep the recorded macro, but use the VB Editor to edit out your mistake.

Which option you choose depends on your fluency with the VB Editor environment and your comfort level in editing macro code. For most casual users, rerecording the macro is probably the wisest choice—although editing a line or two of macro code might be the most efficient solution.

Running a Macro Produces an Error Message

Since a macro records specific operations, it's likely that those actions might not be appropriate in every situation. If you run a macro when you *shouldn't* run a macro— when the conditions are not the same as when the macro was recorded—the macro is likely to encounter difficulties and generate an error message.

For example, if you create a macro to search for hidden text, that macro won't run properly if hidden text isn't displayed in your current document. If you encounter an error message when running a macro, think through the operation of the macro, compare it to the elements and conditions present in your current document, and then rethink whether that macro is applicable to the conditions at hand.

You Copied a Toolbar, but Your Macros Weren't Copied

You have to remember that copying a toolbar (via the Organizer) from template to template does not copy the macros associated with buttons on the toolbar. You have to use the Organizer to copy the macros separately.

A Macro Won't Run

Word's inability to run a macro can have several causes—typically related to Word 2000's new macro security levels. First, the security level setting in Word may have disabled all macros automatically. When you set the security level to High, all unsigned macros and add-ins are disabled. To run unsigned macros and add-ins, change the security level to Medium (or lower)—and then reload the document containing the macros.

When the security level is set to Medium, you're prompted as to whether you want to run unsigned macros whenever you open a document containing macros. If you

PART

IX

Tips, Tricks, and
Troubleshooting

chose to disable macros at that time, your macros won't run. To run these macros, close and then reopen the document, choosing to enable the macros when prompted.

You can also encounter problems running macros when you open an e-mail message while you're using Word as your e-mail editor. If Word's security level is set to Medium or High, any messages you reply to or forward will have its macros automatically disabled. To run the macros, you'll need to save the message as a Word document, close it, reopen it, and then choose to enable macros.

You Can't Change Word's Security Level

This can happen if you're on a network and your network administrator has applied a specific security level for your entire workgroup or corporation. If this is a problem for you, you'll have to contact your network administrator.

A Macro Virus Warning Appears when There Are No Macros in a File

If Word thinks your document has macros when it really doesn't, it could create problems for you—especially if you have Word's security level set to Medium or High. This situation is caused when a document contained macros that were subsequently deleted—but, unfortunately, some macro storage components were left behind. Word senses these abandoned components and then generates the macro warning message.

To ease this problem, you can try to delete the leftover component(s) of the macros. To do this, you'll need to use the VB Editor. From within the VB Editor environment, open the project for the problematic file, select the module that contained the macro, and then select File ➢ Remove *modulename*. Answer No to the query *Do you want to export* modulename *before removing it?* You may have to repeat this procedure for every module listed for the current project.

If you're uncomfortable working within the VB Editor environment, you can simply create a new blank template and copy all the styles, AutoText entries, toolbars, and so forth from the problem template to the new template—but *don't* copy any macros.

Finally, you can save the problem document as an .RTF (Rich Text Format) document, and then save it back to Word format. When you save to .RTF format, all macros are lost; this operation has the effect of cleaning macros from your document.

A Word Document Is Infected with a Macro Virus

If you don't use the proper security-level protection and you don't have an antivirus program installed on your system, it's possible that your system will become infected with a macro virus. For a macro virus to infect your system, all you have to do is open a document or template that contains an infected macro; opening the document runs the macro, which then infects your system.

After you've been infected, there's not much you can do except assess the damage inflicted by the virus. Some viruses are merely mischievous, displaying harmless messages onscreen. Other viruses are clearly malevolent, destroying system files and rampaging through your system settings and hard disk. Still other viruses replicate themselves and send themselves out over the Internet, attached to self-generated e-mail messages addressed to recipients in your Outlook Address Book. You'll find out what type of damage a virus can do as soon as you open the document containing the offending macro.

To cleanse a virus from your system, you need to install and run an antivirus program. Two of the best are Norton AntiVirus and McAfee VirusScan. You can find these programs wherever computer software is sold, or order or download them directly from the companies' Web sites.

NOTE Norton AntiVirus is available at `www.symantec.com`, and McAfee VirusScan is available at `www.mcafee.com/centers/anti-virus/`.

To protect against future macro-virus infections, you can use either of these major programs, or a program that specializes in detecting macro viruses. Two such programs (Virus ALERT for Macros and ChekMate Lite) are included on the CD accompanying this book; see Chapter 33 for more information on these programs.

You Encounter Problems Starting the Visual Basic Editor

If you try to start the VB Editor and receive an error message, you could have one of several problems:

Insufficient Disk Space or System Memory To free available memory, close any open documents or programs; if you still don't have enough memory, close Word, reboot Windows, and then try again with a clean system. To free up necessary disk space, delete any unnecessary files from your hard disk, including .TMP files in the \Windows\Temp directory.

A Corrupt Normal Template in Word If the Normal.dot file is corrupted, rename or delete it to force Word to create a new Normal.dot file (which it does automatically).

PART

IX

Tips, Tricks, and
Troubleshooting

The Wrong Version of the Vbe6.dll File Installed on Your System   You can reinstall this file from your Office 2000 installation CD; on your hard disk, this file is typically found in the program files\common files\microsoft shared\vba\ vba6\ folder.

A Network Rights (Permissions) Issue, if Your Temp Directory Is Located on a Network Server   Contact your network administrator to sort out any permissions issues regarding this directory.

Master's Reference

Master's Reference

Throughout this book you've learned how to perform hundreds of different tasks within Microsoft Word 2000. Once you've mastered these skills, you want an instant reference to the specific steps necessary to perform these procedures—so you don't have to reread this entire book every time you want to get something done!

This Master's Reference is your handy guide to these essential Word operations—arranged in alphabetical order. Turn here when you have to get something done *fast!*

Access

Access 2000 is the high-powered database application included with many versions of Office 2000. You use Access as a data source for merged mailings or any other Word document that requires controlled insertion of large blocks of data.

Importing Access Data

You use the Insert Database command on Word's Database toolbar to insert data from an Access query or table directly into your Word document. Follow these steps:

1. From within Word, position the insertion point where you want to insert the contents of the database.

2. From the Database toolbar, click the Insert Database button to display the Database dialog box.

3. Click the Get Data button to display the Open Data Source dialog box.

4. Navigate to and select the Access database you want to use.

5. Click the Open button to display the Microsoft Access dialog box.

6. To import a table, select the Tables tab; to import a query, select the Queries tab.

7. Select the table or query you want to import.

8. Click OK to return to the Database dialog box.

9. To filter or sort records and fields from your database, click the Query Options button to display the Query Options dialog box.

10. To filter which records are imported, select the Filter Records tab; to sort the records in the database, select the Sort Records tab; to import only selected fields from the database, select the Select Fields tab.

11. Make the appropriate selections, then click OK to return to the Database dialog box.

12. Click the Insert Data button to display the Insert Data dialog box.

13. To insert all records from your database, check the All option; to insert only selected records, check the From option and enter a range of records.

14. To automatically update your Word document when the data source changes, check the Insert Data as a Field option.

15. Click the OK button.

Publishing Access Data

The preceding section detailed how to import Access data from within Word; you can also export Access data (to Word) from within the Access program. When you do this, the Access data is inserted into a new Word table, which you can then edit and format as you would any Word table.

Follow these steps to send data from Access to Word as a table:

1. From within Access, select or display the item you want to send to Word.

2. Select Tools ➤ Office Links ➤ Publish It with MS Word.

3. Access sends the selected data to a table in a new Word file.

4. You can now save this new document as a Word file, or copy the table into an existing Word file.

AutoCorrect

AutoCorrect is a powerful feature of Word 2000 that can automatically detect and correct all manner of common typing mistakes—misspelled words, bad grammar, incorrect capitalization, and so on. It works automatically *while you type*, so that your mistakes are corrected almost instantaneously. You can also use AutoCorrect to quickly replace selected text with special replacement text—for example, when you type (c) AutoCorrect can instantly replace it with the © character.

Activating AutoCorrect

To activate and configure AutoCorrect, follow these steps:

1. Select Tools ➤ AutoCorrect to display the AutoCorrect dialog box.

2. Select the AutoCorrect tab.

3. Check the AutoCorrect options you wish to activate.

4. Click OK to activate.

Using AutoCorrect on the Fly

Once AutoCorrect is activated, it starts working the very next time you enter text into a document. When you make a mistake, misspell a word, or enter any text found in the AutoCorrect list, AutoCorrect will change or replace the text you just typed, automatically.

Spell Checking with AutoCorrect

You can also use Word 2000's AutoCorrect feature to automatically correct misspellings as you type. To turn on AutoCorrect Spell Checking, follow these steps:

1. Select Tools ➢ AutoCorrect to display the AutoCorrect dialog box.

2. Select the AutoCorrect tab.

3. Check the Automatically Use Suggestions from the Spelling Checker option.

4. Click OK.

When AutoCorrect Spell Checking is enabled, AutoCorrect will automatically correct most—but not all—misspellings as you type.

Adding Entries to the AutoCorrect List

To add a new listing to the AutoCorrect list, follow these steps:

1. Select Tools ➢ AutoCorrect to display the AutoCorrect dialog box.

2. Select the AutoCorrect tab.

3. Enter the word or phrase you want to replace in the Replace box.

4. Enter the correct word or phrase in the With box.

5. Click the Add button.

To delete an entry from the AutoCorrect list, go to the AutoCorrect dialog box, select the entry you want to remove, then click Delete.

Adding an AutoCorrect Entry from Your Text

You can also add an AutoCorrect entry directly from your text. When you use this method, you can include formatting with your replacement text—or select a graphic object to use as your replacement.

1. In your document, select the text or graphic that you want to store as the Auto-Correct entry.

2. Select Tools ➢ AutoCorrect to display the AutoCorrect dialog box; the AutoCorrect tab will already be selected, and the text or graphics you selected in your document will already be pasted into the With box.

3. Enter the text you want to replace in the Replace box.

4. If you want to save the replacement text *without* its original formatting, check the Plain Text option; if you want to save the replacement text *with* its original formatting, check the Formatted Text option.

5. Click the Add button.

Managing AutoCorrect's Exception List

New to Word 2000 is the AutoCorrect *exception list*, which enables you to specify corrections you *don't* want AutoCorrect to make. To add items to AutoCorrect's exception list, follow these steps:

1. Select Tools ➢ AutoCorrect to display the AutoCorrect dialog box.

2. Select the AutoCorrect tab.

3. Click the Exceptions button to display the AutoCorrect Exceptions dialog box.

4. To keep AutoCorrect from capitalizing a word after a specific abbreviation, select the First Letter tab, then enter the abbreviation (including the period) in the Don't Capitalize After box.

5. To keep AutoCorrect from "fixing" a word with mixed uppercase and lowercase letters, select the INitial CAps tab, and then enter the word in the Don't Correct box.

6. To keep AutoCorrect from correcting specific misspellings, select the Other Corrections tab, and then enter the word in the Don't Correct box.

7. Click Add to add your entry to the exceptions list and return to the AutoCorrect dialog box.

You can also configure the AutoCorrect exceptions list to automatically include any AutoCorrect changes that you undo while editing. Just check the Automatically Add Words to List option in the AutoCorrect Exceptions dialog box. With this option enabled, any time you *undo* an AutoCorrect correction, that correction will be added to the exceptions list—so that AutoCorrect won't repeat the same mistake twice.

AutoFormat

AutoFormat is similar to AutoCorrect in that it can automatically replace certain characters with symbols as you type—as well as automatically apply headings, bullets, numbered lists, and borders to your text. You can use AutoFormat either as you type, or in a separate document-wide operation.

Configuring AutoFormat

You configure the two different types of AutoFormat on separate tabs in the AutoCorrect dialog box. Both tabs share many of the same options, although some options are specific to just one of the operations.

To configure either type of AutoFormat, follow these instructions:

1. Select Tools ➤ AutoCorrect to display the AutoCorrect dialog box.

2. To configure the real-time version of AutoFormat, select the AutoFormat as You Type tab; to configure the single-operation "batch" AutoFormat, select the AutoFormat tab.

3. Check those options that you want to apply to your documents.

4. Click OK.

Using AutoFormat as You Type

As soon as you enable options on the AutoFormat as You Type tab, Word will begin automatically formatting any new text you enter into your document. No further actions are necessary on your part.

Running AutoFormat on Your Finished Document

You can also run AutoFormat in a separate operation on your entire document. To execute the AutoFormat operation, follow these steps:

1. Select Format ➤ AutoFormat to display the AutoFormat dialog box.

2. To run AutoFormat completely automatically—with no interaction on your part—check the AutoFormat Now option. To confirm or reject each suggested AutoFormat change, check the AutoFormat and Review Each Change option.

3. Select one of the following document types from the pull-down list: General document, Letter, or Email.

4. Click Go to begin formatting.

If you selected the AutoFormat Now option, all the formatting changes are made automatically. If you selected the AutoFormat and Review Each Change option, you'll see a new AutoFormat dialog box.

If you want to accept all of AutoFormat's changes without reviewing them individually, click the Accept All button. If you want to reject all of AutoFormat's changes without reviewing them, click the Reject All button. If you want to review AutoFormat's changes one at a time, click the Review Changes button; this displays the Review AutoFormat Changes dialog box.

AutoSummarize

Word 2000's AutoSummarize feature analyzes your document and creates an automatic summary of the document's key points. Each sentence in your document is assigned a score; sentences that contain frequently-used words are assigned a higher score. You choose what percent of the highest-scoring sentences to display in the summary, and Word automatically generates text you can use as an executive summary for your document. To create an automatic summary of your document, follow these steps:

1. From within the document you want to summarize, select Tools ➢ AutoSummarize to display the AutoSummarize dialog box.

2. To insert an executive summary at the beginning of your document, select Insert an Executive Summary or Abstract at the Top of the Document. To create a new document containing your summary, select Create a New Document and Put the Summary There. To simply highlight the key points within your document (without creating a separate summary) select Highlight Key Points. To display only those highlighted points (while hiding the rest of the document onscreen), select Hide Everything But the Summary.

3. Select the level of detail you want to display from the Percent of Original Box; the bigger the number, the longer the summary.

4. To have AutoSummarize replace existing keywords and comments in your document's Properties dialog box, check the Update Document Statistics option; to maintain the existing keywords and comments, *uncheck* this option.

5. Click OK to create the summary.

AutoText

AutoText lets you create pre-written snippets of text, and then enter them into your documents with a few clicks of your mouse.

Inserting an AutoText Entry

To insert an AutoText entry into your text, follow these steps:

1. Position the insertion point where you want to insert the AutoText entry.

2. Select Insert ➢ AutoText to display the AutoText submenu.

3. Select a category and specific entry.

Creating a New AutoText Entry

You can quickly and easily create your own AutoText entries for text that you find yourself entering on a frequent basis. Just follow these steps:

1. Enter the text for your AutoText entry somewhere in your current document, then select the text.
2. Select Insert ➤ AutoText ➤ New to display the Create AutoText dialog box.
3. Enter a name for the new entry (or accept the suggested name).
4. Click OK.

To delete an AutoText entry, select Insert ➤ AutoText ➤ to display the AutoCorrect dialog box, select the AutoText tab, select the name of the AutoText entry you want to delete, and then click Delete.

Bookmarks

When you create a bookmark in your document, the bookmarked section can be easily accessed and referenced from elsewhere in your document.

Adding a Bookmark

To add a bookmark to your document, follow these steps:

1. Position the insertion point where you want to add the bookmark, or select the block of text you want to bookmark.
2. Select Insert ➤ Bookmark.
3. When the Bookmark dialog box appears, enter a name in the Bookmark Name box.
4. Click the Add button.

Deleting a Bookmark

To delete a bookmark, follow these steps:

1. Select Insert ➤ Bookmark to open the Bookmark dialog box.
2. Select the bookmark to delete.
3. Click the Delete button.

Viewing Bookmarks

By default, bookmarks are hidden when you're viewing your document. To display all bookmarks, follow these steps:

1. Select Tools ➤ Options to display the Options dialog box.

2. Select the View tab.

3. Check the Bookmarks option.

4. Click OK.

Jumping to a Bookmark

To jump to a specific bookmark, follow these steps:

1. Select Insert ➢ Bookmark to display the Bookmark dialog box.

2. Select a bookmark.

3. Click the Go To button.

You can also jump to a bookmark with the Go To command, or from the Select Browse Object tool.

Borders and Shading

Word 2000 enables you to add a border around any selected paragraph or page, or to add shading behind the paragraph text. You can also apply borders and shading to most objects in your document, and to cells within a table.

Adding a Border

You can add borders to the top, bottom, left, or right of the selected object or text. Word lets you apply several pre-selected border types—or you can choose your own border style, width and color.

To add a border, follow these steps:

1. Select the text or object to format.

2. Select Format ➢ Borders and Shading to display the Borders and Shading dialog box.

3. Select the Borders tab.

4. Select the type of border you want to apply from the Setting section.

5. If you want to change the style of the border, make a selection from the Style list.

6. If you want to change the color of the border, make a selection from the Color list.

7. If you want to change the width of the border, make a selection from the Width list.

8. If you want to turn off (or on) the border for any specific side of your selection, click the Top, Bottom, Left, or Right buttons in the Preview section.

9. Make sure that the correct type of object is selected in the Apply To list.

10. Click OK.

Applying Shading

You can add color shading behind selected text and objects—whether or not the selection is bordered. To apply shading, follow these steps:

1. Select the text or object to format.

2. Select Format ➢ Borders and Shading to display the Borders and Shading dialog box.

3. Select the Shading tab.

4. Select a shading color from the Fill section; click the More Colors button to choose from an expanded palette of colors.

5. Select a shading percent from the Style list.

6. Make sure that the correct type of object is selected in the Apply To list.

7. Click OK.

Breaks

To insert any manual break within Word, position the insertion point where you want the break to occur, then select Insert ➢ Break to display the Break dialog box. From here you can select the type of break you wish to apply, then click OK to insert the break.

Here are the options you find in the Break dialog box:

Page Break   Forces the text after the break to appear at the top of the next page. (Press Ctrl+Enter to insert a page break directly from your keyboard.)

Column Break   Forces the text after the break to appear at the top of the next column. (Press Ctrl+Shift+Enter to insert a column break directly from your keyboard.)

Text Wrapping Break   Forces the text after the break to continue below the next picture, table, or other object.

Section Break: Next Page   Starts a new section at the top of the next page.

Section Break: Continuous   Starts a new section *at the break*, without forcing a page break of any kind.

Section Break: Even Page   Starts a new section at the top of the next even-numbered page.

Section Break: Odd Page   Starts a new section at the top of the next odd-numbered page.

You can eliminate any break by deleting the break marker; all break markers are visible in Word's normal view.

Bulleted Lists

Bulleted lists are used to set off item listings within your documents. You can choose from Word's built-in bullet characters, or you can create your own bullet character from any graphic object.

Creating a Bulleted List

The fastest way to create a bulleted list is to highlight the paragraphs in your list, then click the Bullets button on Word's Formatting toolbar. This indents the selected paragraphs and applies the default button character at the start of each paragraph.

You can also insert a bulleted list from the Bullets and Numbering dialog box, as follows:

1. Select the paragraphs for your list.
2. Select Format ➤ Bullets and Numbering to display the Bullets and Numbering dialog box.
3. Select the Bulleted tab.
4. Select a bullet type.
5. Click OK.

Changing Bullet Characters

If you don't like Word's default bullet character, you can select a new character (and apply additional bullet formatting) from the Bullets and Number dialog box. Follow these steps:

1. Select the bulleted text you want to reformat.
2. Select Format ➤ Bullets and Numbering to display the Bullets and Numbering dialog box.
3. Select the Bulleted tab.
4. Select a new bullet type.
5. Click OK.

If you don't like any of the bullet types presented, you can choose to use any character from any installed font family as your list bullet. Just click the Customize button on the Bulleted tab; this displays the Customize Bulleted List dialog box, from which you can choose a new font and/or character for your bullet.

Creating a Picture Bullet

Word 2000 also enables you to use any graphic as a bullet character. Follow these steps:

1. Select Format ➤ Bullets and Numbering to display the Bullets and Numbering dialog box.
2. Select the Bulleted tab.
3. Click the Picture button to display the Picture Bullet dialog box.
4. Select the Pictures tab.
5. Click on a bullet and select Insert Clip from the pop-up menu.
6. Click OK.

To add your own images to Word's bullet gallery, click the Import Clips button on the Picture Bullet toolbar to display the Add Clip to Clip Gallery dialog box. Navigate to the graphics file you want to include, select the file, then click the Import button.

Captions

To annotate figures, tables, equations, and other similar elements, you use *captions*. Word automatically numbers your captions, and assigns them a label corresponding to their object type (table, equation, or figure).

Adding Captions Manually

To add a caption to an existing element, follow these steps:

1. Select the object you want to caption.
2. Select Insert ➤ Caption to display the Caption dialog box.
3. Pull down the Label list and select the type of label—Figure, Table, or Equation.
4. Pull down the Position list and select where you want to place the caption.
5. In the Caption box, either accept the default text or enter your own text.
6. Click OK to insert the caption.

Word automatically inserts the caption, in the position you specified, in the format "Figure 1," "Table 4," or something similar.

Adding Captions Automatically

You can also configure Word to automatically add captions to every figure, table, or equation you create. Follow these steps:

1. Select the object you want to caption.

2. Select Insert ➤ Caption to display the Caption dialog box.

3. Click the AutoCaption button to display the AutoCaption dialog box.

4. In the Add Caption When Inserting list, check those items you want to automatically caption.

5. Pull down the Label list and select the type of label—Figure, Table, or Equation—you want to apply to the selected items. (If you want to create a new label not on the list, click the New Label button.)

6. Pull down the Position list and select where you want to place the caption.

7. Click OK to enable the automatic captioning.

With automatic captioning enabled, whenever you insert one of the selected objects, Word automatically inserts the appropriate caption.

Changing the Number Format

By default, Word numbers your captions in the 1,2,3 format. If you want to use another number format for your captions, follow these steps:

1. Select Insert ➤ Caption to display the Caption dialog box.

2. Click the Numbering button to display the Caption Numbering dialog box.

3. Pull down the Format list and select a different number format.

4. Click OK.

Click and Type

Word 2000's new Click and Type feature allows you to double-click in any blank space in a document and then start typing, without first inserting a text box. To activate Click and Type, select Tools ➤ Options to display the Options dialog box. Select the Edit tab, check the Enable Click and Type option, and then click OK. (Note that Click and Type is active in only Print Layout and Web Layout views.)

To insert text or other items with Click and Type, follow these steps:

1. From within Print Layout or Web Layout view, position your cursor over a blank area of your document.

2. When the cursor changes shape, double-click.

3. To insert text, start typing. Your text will be automatically aligned according to its position on the page. (For example, Click and Type text inserted on the far right side of a page will be right aligned; text inserted in the middle of the page will be centered.)

4. To insert a table, graphic, or other item, pull down the Insert menu and select the item you want to insert. The item will be automatically inserted at the Click and Type insertion point.

Clip Art

Word 2000 comes with thousands of clip art images, which are stored in the Clip Gallery. Most of the clip art images in the Clip Gallery are stored in the Windows metafile (.WMF) format, and can be edited and "ungrouped" into their separate lines and components.

Inserting Clip Art

To insert clip art images from the Clip Gallery, follow these steps:

1. Anchor the insertion point where you want to insert the image in your document.
2. On the Drawing toolbar, click the Insert Clip Art button (or select Insert ➢ Picture ➢ Clip Art from Word's menu bar) to display the Insert Clip Art window.
3. Select the Pictures tab.
4. To search for a specific image, enter your query in the Search for Clips box and press Enter, *or*

   To display images within a major category, click the category icon.
5. To insert a specific image into your document, click the image to display the pop-up menu, then click the Insert Clip button.

Modifying Clip Art

If a Clip Gallery image is in the Windows metafile format (.WMF), you can convert it to a group of drawing objects—which can then be *ungrouped* and modified using tools on Word's Drawing toolbar. Follow these steps:

1. Select the image in your document.
2. Select Format ➢ Picture to display the Format Picture dialog box.
3. Select the Layout tab.
4. Select any wrapping style *except* In Line With Text.
5. Click OK to close the dialog box.
6. With the image still selected, move to the Drawing toolbar and select Draw ➢ Ungroup.

The single image is now ungrouped into many smaller images. Use the tools on the Drawing toolbar to modify the picture as appropriate, then *regroup* the images back into a single picture by following these steps:

1. On the Drawing toolbar, click the Select Object button.
2. Use your mouse to draw a boundary around all the images you want to regroup.
3. From the Drawing toolbar, select Draw ➢ Group.

Adding Images to the Clip Gallery

Word lets you add your own images to the Clip Gallery. Follow these steps:

1. From the Drawing toolbar, click the Insert Clip Art button to display the Insert Clip Art window.
2. Click the Pictures tab.
3. Select the category where you want to add the new image.
4. Click the Import Clips button to display the Add Clip to Clip Gallery dialog box.
5. Navigate to the image you want to add, then select that file.
6. To place a copy of this file in the Clip Gallery, select the Copy Into Clip Gallery option. To cut this file from its current location and paste it into the Clip Gallery, select the Move Into Clip Gallery option. To keep the file in its current location—and have the Clip Gallery access it there—select the Let Clip Gallery Find This Clip In Its Current Folder or Volume.
7. Click the Import button to display the Clip Properties dialog box.
8. Click the Description tab and enter a description of this image.
9. Click the Categories tab and confirm the category (or categories) you want to add this image to.
10. To assign a keyword to this image, click the Keywords tab, click the New Keyword button, enter a new keyword in the New Keyword dialog box, then click OK.
11. Click OK to add the image to the Clip Gallery.

Columns

Certain types of documents lend themselves to multiple column layouts. Word 2000 lets you quickly and easily apply multiple-column formatting to your entire document, or just to selected sections.

Applying a Multiple Column Layout

To change the layout of the current section of your document (or, if your document isn't divided into sections, your entire document) to a multiple-column layout, follow these steps:

1. Position your cursor where you want the multiple-column layout to begin.
2. Select Format ➢ Columns to display the Columns dialog box.
3. Select one of the preset column styles: One column, Two column, Three column, Left (two columns with smaller left column), or Right (two columns with smaller right column).

4. If you want a line between your columns, check the Line Between option.

5. Pull down the Apply To list and select whether you want to apply this column layout to your Whole Document, or just This Point Forward to the end of your document.

6. Click OK.

If you want to return to a single (or other) column layout later in your document, just repeat these steps and select a different layout at that point.

Adjusting Column Widths and Spacing

If you don't like any of Word's preset column layouts, you can create your own—by specifying custom column widths and spacing. Follow these steps:

1. Position your cursor where you want the new column layout to begin.

2. Select Format ➢ Columns to display the Columns dialog box.

3. Select how many columns you want from the Number of Columns list.

4. If you want your columns to be of equal width, check the Equal Column Width option; if you want columns of different width, *uncheck* this option.

5. If you selected unequal column widths, select the width and spacing for each column in the Width and Spacing area. (Don't worry—Word won't let your total width exceed the total available width.)

6. If you want a line between your columns, check the Line Between option.

7. Pull down the Apply To list and select whether you want to apply this column layout to your Whole Document, or just This Point Forward to the end of your document.

8. Click OK.

Comments

In addition to making changes to the text, a reviewer can also insert non-printing *comments* into the document. When a comment is added, Word assigns it a number and enters it in a separate comment pane beneath the main document. Word then inserts a comment *reference mark* in the document and applies a yellow highlight to the text commented on. As with revision marks, Word tracks each reviewer's comments in a different color.

Inserting a Written Comment

To insert a comment, follow these steps:

1. Select the text you want to comment on.
2. Click the Insert Comment button on the Reviewing toolbar.
3. When the comment pane appears, enter your comment.
4. Click the Close button to close the comment pane.

Inserting a Spoken Comment

You can also record a spoken comment into a document by following these steps:

1. Select the text you want to comment on.
2. Click the Insert Sound Object button (in the comment pane) to display the Sound Object dialog box.
3. Click the Record button and speak into your PC's microphone.
4. When you're done commenting, click the Stop button and close the Sound Object dialog box.

When you insert a spoken comment, Word inserts a sound object icon in your document, following the text commented on. Double-click the icon to play back the spoken comment.

Reading Comments

You can read comments in a document in one of two ways:

- Hover your cursor over the comment in your document to display a ScreenTip containing the text of the comment.
- Double-click the comment to display the comment pane and read the comment there.

You can find the next comment within a document by clicking the Next Comment button on the Reviewing toolbar; click the Previous Comment button to jump back to the last comment. In addition, you can open the comment pane and edit any comment by clicking the Edit Comment button, and delete a comment completely by clicking the Delete Comment button.

Copy, Cut, Paste, and Delete

Word's most common editing operations involve moving, copying, or deleting text and other objects.

Copying

To copy an object or a block of text, follow these steps:

1. Select the object or text you want to copy.

2. Select Edit ➢ Copy. (Alternatively, you can press either Ctrl+C or Ctrl+Ins, or click the Copy button on Word's Standard toolbar.)

3. Reposition the insertion point where you want to paste the object or text.

4. Select Edit ➢ Paste. (Alternatively, you can press either Shift+V or Shift+Ins, or click the Paste button on Word's Standard toolbar.)

Cutting

To use Word's Cut commands to move an object or block of text, follow these steps:

1. Select the object or text you want to move.

2. Select Edit ➢ Cut. (Alternatively, you can press either Ctrl+X or Shift+Del, or click the Cut button on Word's Standard toolbar.)

Pasting

To paste a cut object or block of text into a different location in your document, follow these steps:

1. Position the insertion point where you want to paste the object or text.

2. Select Edit ➢ Paste. (Alternatively, you can press either Shift+V or Shift+Ins, or click the Paste button on Word's Standard toolbar.)

Using Paste Special

When you use the standard Paste command, the text will be inserted in its native format, with its original formatting. While this may be acceptable, you may prefer to paste text into your document in a different format.

To change the way Word pastes text into your document, use the Paste Special command, as follows:

1. Select Edit ➢ Paste Special to display the Paste Special dialog box.

2. Select a specific format from those displayed.

3. Click OK.

Using Collect and Paste

Word 2000 enhances the standard Cut/Copy/Paste function with the new Collect and Paste feature, which stores up to twelve different cut or copied items in the Clipboard. You can then select which of the multiple items you want to paste back into your document.

To best use Collect and Paste, you should have the Clipboard toolbar displayed on your desktop, then follow these steps:

1. Cut or copy the text you want to paste.

2. Reposition the insertion point where you want to paste the text.

3. Go to the Clipboard toolbar and click the button for the item you want to paste. (If you have the Clipboard menu docked, you'll need to pull down the Items menu to display the Clipboard items.)

Deleting

To permanently delete an object or block of text, follow these steps:

1. Select the object or text you want to delete.

2. Select Edit ➢ Clear, or press the Del key.

Cross-References

A cross-reference is a mention of one part of your document in another part of your document.

Inserting a Cross-Reference

While you can insert cross-references via field codes, the easiest way to insert a cross-reference is with Word's Cross-Reference command. Follow these steps:

1. Within your document, type the lead-in text to the reference.

2. Select Insert ➢ Cross-Reference to display the Cross-Reference dialog box.

3. Pull down the Reference Type list and select what kind of element you want to reference—Numbered Item, Heading, Bookmark, Footnote, Endnote, Equation, Figure, or Table.

4. Pull down the Insert Reference To list and select how you want to reference the selected item.

5. If you want your references to include an "above" or "below" pointer, check the Include Above/Below option. (Not available for all options.)

6. Select the specific item you want to reference from the For Which list.

7. Click Insert to insert the automatic cross-reference.

Editing a Cross-Reference

To edit any cross-reference, follow these steps:

1. Select the entire cross-reference text.

2. Select Insert ➤ Cross-Reference to display the Cross-Reference dialog box.

3. Make any appropriate changes to the cross-reference text.

4. Click OK.

Customization Settings

Most of Word 2000's customization settings are located in two dialog boxes—the Customize dialog box and the Options dialog box. The Customize dialog box is where you customize Word 2000's toolbars, menus, and keyboard shortcuts. The Options dialog box is where you configure most of Word 2000's operating and display options.

You access the Customize dialog box by selecting Tools ➤ Customize. You access the Options dialog box by selecting Tools ➤ Options.

Database

When you insert database data into a Word document, you can filter, sort, and select specific fields to extract exactly the information you want from the database. You can also establish a link to the database file, so that whenever the data is changed in the source file, it is automatically updated in your Word document. To import database data to your Word document, follow these steps:

1. Position the insertion point where you want to insert the data.

2. Right-click any toolbar and select Database, to display the Database toolbar.

3. From the Database toolbar, click the Insert Database button.

4. When the Database dialog box appears, click the Get Data button.

5. When the Open Data Source dialog box appears, select the file you want to import, then click the Open button.

6. If you're importing data from a Microsoft Access database, Word displays the Microsoft Access dialog box. Select the Tables tab to select a specific table to import, or select the Queries tab to select a query to import, then click OK to return to the Database dialog box.

7. Click the Query Options button to display the Query Options dialog box.

8. Select the Filter Records tab to select which records you want to import.

9. Select the Sort Records tab to select how you want the imported records sorted.

10. Select the Select Fields tab to select which fields you want to import.

11. Click OK to return to the Database dialog box.

12. Click the Insert Data button to display the Insert Data dialog box.

13. To import all records from the database, check the All option. To import only selected records, check the From option and enter a range.

14. If you want the inserted data to be linked to the original data source—and be automatically updated when the original data source changes—check the Insert Data as Field option.

15. Click OK to insert the data.

When importing database data, it's best to link the data back to the source file, by checking the Insert Data as Field option in the Insert Data dialog box. This actually inserts the data into your document as a DATABASE field, which can be updated either manually or automatically.

Date and Time

To insert the current date and time into your document, follow these steps:

1. Position the insertion point where you want to insert the date or time.

2. Select Insert ➤ Date and Time to display the Date and Time dialog box.

3. Select a date/time format from the list.

4. To automatically update the date/time in your document, check the Update Automatically option.

5. Click OK.

Discussions

Word 2000 includes a new collaboration feature, called *Discussions,* which is available to users on a Windows NT network where a dedicated *discussion server* has been set up and configured with the Microsoft Office Server Extensions. This feature enables you to share and edit workgroup files over your network.

Connecting to a Discussion Server

Before you can participate in a discussion, you first have to connect to a specific discussion server on your network. To do so, follow these steps:

1. Open the document you want to discuss.

2. If the Discussions toolbar is not displayed, select Tools ➤ Online Collaboration ➤ Web Discussions.

3. From the Discussions toolbar, select Discussions ➤ Discussion Options to display the Discussion Options dialog box.

4. Pull down the Select a Discussion Server list and choose your discussion server.

5. If your discussion server is not listed, click the Add button to display the Add or Edit Discussion Servers dialog box; enter the type and name of your discussion server, then click OK to return to the Discussions Options dialog box.

6. Click OK to access the selected server.

Viewing Discussions

Whether you're accessing a Web discussion with Word 2000 or with your Web browser, you view all existing and ongoing discussions from the discussion pane, which is displayed underneath the main document. You also use the discussion pane to reply to, edit, and delete specific discussions.

To display the discussion pane, click the Show/Hide Discussion Pane button the Discussions toolbar. Click the button again to hide the discussion pane (the button is a toggle).

Starting an Inline Discussion

To start an inline discussion, follow these steps:

1. From within the document, select the text or graphic you want to comment on.

2. Click the Insert Discussion in the Document button on the Discussions toolbar.

3. When the Insert Discussion dialog box appears, enter a name for the discussion in the Discussion Subject box.

4. Enter your comments in the Discussion Text box.

5. Click OK to register your remarks.

When the discussion pane appears, a Discussion icon also appears at the end of the section you were discussing.

Starting a General Discussion

Starting a general discussion is similar to starting an inline discussion, except you don't have to select any specific text or graphic. Follow these steps:

1. From within the document, click the Insert Discussion About the Document button on the Discussions toolbar.

2. When the Insert Discussion dialog box appears, enter a name for the discussion in the Discussion Subject box.

3. Enter your comments in the Discussion Text box.

4. Click OK to register your remarks.

Replying to an Inline Discussion

To reply to an existing inline discussion, follow these steps:

1. Open the document containing the discussion to which you want to reply.
2. Click the Discussion icon next to the section you want to reply to.
3. Click the Show a Menu of Actions icon in the Discussions pane.
4. Select Reply to display the Reply dialog box.
5. Enter your reply in the Discussion Text box.
6. Click OK.

Replying to a General Discussion

To reply to a general discussion, follow these steps:

1. Open the document containing the discussion to which you want to reply.
2. Click the Show General Discussions button on the Discussions toolbar.
3. Click the Show a Menu of Actions icon next to the discussion you want to reply to.
4. Select Reply to display the Reply dialog box.
5. Enter your reply in the Discussion Text box.
6. Click OK.

Document Map

The Document Map can be accessed by selecting View ➢ Document Map, or by clicking the Document Map button on Word's Standard toolbar. When the Document Map is displayed, an outline of your document appears in a separate left pane, while the document itself (in whatever standard view you select) is displayed in the right pane. You can't edit the outline in the Document Map pane (as you can the outline in Outline view), but you can click on a heading in the Document Map to jump directly to that part of your document in the right pane.

Documents

You manage your Word documents and templates using commands found on Word's File menu.

Creating a New Document

When you click the New Blank Document button on Word's Standard toolbar, Word loads a blank document, based on the Normal template, into the Word workspace. To create a new Word document based on a specific document template, follow these steps:

1. Select File ➢ New to display the New dialog box.
2. Select the tab that contains the type of document you want to create.
3. Select the document template you wish to use; a sample document is previewed to the right of the template list.
4. Make sure the Document option is checked in the Create New section.
5. Click OK; your new blank document—based on your selected template—is now displayed in the Word workspace.

Opening an Existing Document

To open a previously created document, follow these steps:

1. Select File ➢ Open to display the Open dialog box.
2. Navigate to and select the file to open.
3. Click Open.

Saving a New Document

The first time you save a document, you need to give it a name and select a location for the saved file. You do so by following these steps:

1. Select File ➢ Save As to display the Save As dialog box.
2. Navigate to the folder where you want to save the document.
3. Enter a name for the document in the File Name box.
4. Make sure that Word Document (*.doc) is selected in the Save as Type list.
5. Click the Save button.

Saving an Existing Document

If you've saved a document once, it already has a name and a location so you don't have to use the Save As command when it's time to save your next round of changes. Instead, use the simpler Save command, which saves your changed document without displaying any dialog boxes or prompting you for any input.

There are three ways to save a document with the Save command:

- Select File ➢ Save

- Click the Save button on Word's Standard toolbar
- Press Ctrl+S

Saving a Document in a Different Format

If you want to save your document in a format other than the default Word 2000 format, you have to use the Save As dialog box and select a different file type from the Save as Type list. Follow these steps:

1. Select File ➤ Save As to display the Save As dialog box.
2. Navigate to the folder where you want to save the document.
3. Enter a name for the document in the File Name box.
4. Pull down the Save as Type list and select a different file type.
5. Click the Save button.

Displaying Document Properties

All Word documents can be described via a set of file properties and statistics. You display the file properties for the current document by selecting File ➤ Properties to display the File Properties dialog box.

Drawing

When you want to draw a picture in your document, you use Word's AutoShapes to create a *drawing object*. A drawing object is composed of lines and shapes you add via the AutoShape commands that can then be formatted with different styles and colors.

Inserting an AutoShape

To create a drawing in your document, start with an AutoShape, as follows:

1. From the Drawing toolbar, click the AutoShapes button and select the type of AutoShape you want to draw.
2. Use your mouse to position the cursor where you want to start the AutoShape in your document.
3. Depress and hold the mouse button while you drag the cursor across the area where you want the AutoShape.
4. When you're done drawing the AutoShape, release the mouse button.

Changing AutoShapes

Once you've added an AutoShape to your document, you're not necessarily stuck with it. Word allows you to change from one AutoShape to another, without deleting and redrawing. Follow these steps:

1. Select the AutoShape you want to change.

2. From the Drawing toolbar, select Draw ➢ Change AutoShape, then select a new AutoShape.

Word now changes the original AutoShape to the new shape you selected.

Creating a Freeform Drawing

You can also use Word's AutoShape line tools to draw an object from scratch. Word includes six different AutoShape line tools; three draw straight lines or arrows, and three draw curved lines. You use the curved line tools to make a freehand drawing.

Curve   The Curve tool enables you to draw a curved line. After you click the Curve button, position your cursor where you want the line to start, then click the mouse button to anchor the starting point. Now move the cursor to where you want the midpoint of the curve to appear, and click the mouse button again. Finally, move the cursor to the end of the curve, and *double-click* the mouse button to anchor the end of the curved line.

Freeform   The Freeform tool works just like the Curve tool, except it draws a sharp corner at each click of your mouse, not a smooth curve. You click at each point you want your line to change direction, and double-click to end the line.

Scribble   To draw in a truly freeform fashion, use the Scribble tool. When you click the Scribble button, your cursor changes to a pencil. You click and hold your mouse button to draw with the cursor; when you release the mouse button, you stop drawing. You can draw anything you're capable of—straight lines, curves, scribbles, and so on.

E-mail

In addition to printing and faxing, Word 2000 enables you to output your documents via e-mail—as either an e-mail message or as an *attachment* to another e-mail message.

E-mailing Your Document as a Message

To send a Word document as an e-mail message, follow these steps:

1. Select File ➢ Send To ➢ Mail Recipient (or click the E-mail button on Word's Standard toolbar). Word now adds an e-mail header to your document.

2. Enter the e-mail address of the intended recipient in the To: box. To enter multiple recipients, either press Enter after each recipient or insert a semi-colon between recipients.

3. If you want to send a carbon copy of this message to other recipients, enter their e-mail addresses in the Cc: box.

4. If you want to send a *blind* carbon copy of this message to other recipients, click the Bcc button to display the Bcc: box, then enter the e-mail addresses in the Bcc: box.

5. Enter a title for this message in the Subject: box.

6. If you want to assign a priority level to this message (so that recipients receive the message flagged as High, Medium, or Low priority), click the down arrow on the Priority button and select a priority.

7. To attach another file to this message, click the Attach File button to display the Insert Attachment dialog box. Locate and select the file(s) you want to attach, then click the Attach button.

8. When all the forms are filled in and all the options selected, click Send a Copy to send this message.

When you click the Send a Copy button, Word activates the Outlook (or Outlook Express) engine, connects to the Internet, and sends your message on its way.

E-mailing Your Document as an Attachment

You can also choose to send any Word document as an *attachment* to an e-mail message created with another program. This option is preferred if your recipients are incapable of receiving HTML e-mail—or if you're not using Outlook or Outlook Express as your standard e-mail program.

To send a Word document as an attachment to an e-mail message, follow these steps:

1. Select File ➤ Send To ➤ Mail Recipient (as Attachment).

2. Your e-mail program will now create a new e-mail message, with your Word document loaded as an attachment.

3. Complete the address information and enter the text of your message as is normal for your e-mail program, then send the message.

After the message is sent, your recipients will receive your new message with your Word file (in standard .DOC format) attached. They can then open the document directly, or save the document to their hard disk to open and edit later.

Envelopes

You use the Envelopes and Labels dialog box—displayed when you select Tools ≻ Envelopes and Labels—to print envelopes one at a time from your printer. This tool also lets you "attach" envelopes to Word documents for printing at a later time.

Configuring Word for Envelope Printing

Before you print your first envelope, you need to tell Word what kind of envelope you're using. To do this, follow these steps:

1. Select Tools ≻ Envelopes and Labels to display the Envelopes and Labels dialog box.

2. Select the Envelopes tab.

3. Click the Options button to display the Envelope Options dialog box.

4. Select the Envelope Options tab to set the options detailed in the following sections.

5. Select the Printing tab to configure the envelope feed method and direction for your printer. Select the Feed Method that best represents how envelopes feed into your printer, then select whether your envelopes feed in face up or face down, and what tray you're feeding from.

6. Click OK.

Printing a Single Envelope

To create and print a single envelope, follow these steps:

1. Select Tools ≻ Envelopes and Labels to display the Envelopes and Labels dialog box.

2. Select the Envelopes tab.

3. Enter the name and address of the recipient in the Delivery Address box.

4. If *your* name and address do not appear automatically, enter them in the Return Address blank.

5. If you *don't* want to print your return address on the envelope—if you're using a preprinted envelope that already includes a return address, for example—check the Omit Return Address option.

6. Insert an envelope in your printer as displayed in the Preview section of the dialog box.

7. Click Print to print the envelope.

Attaching an Envelope to a Document

Once you've created an envelope, you don't have to print it right away. Word 2000 provides the option of *attaching* the envelope to your open document, for later printing. When you attach an envelope to your letter, it actually becomes part of your original Word document.

To attach an envelope to your document, follow these steps:

1. Select Tools ➢ Envelopes and Labels to display the Envelopes and Labels dialog box.

2. Select the Envelopes tab, and enter the appropriate information to create the envelope.

3. Click the Add to Document button.

To print an attached envelope, make sure the insertion point is somewhere in the envelope part of your document, then select File ➢ Print.

Equations

To create mathematical and scientific equations in your document, you use the Equation Editor applet, as follows:

1. Anchor the insertion point where you want to add the equation.

2. Select Insert ➢ Object to open the Object dialog box.

3. Select the Create New tab.

4. Select Microsoft Equation 3.0 from the Object Type list and click OK.

5. Word now inserts an equation object in your document and displays the Equation toolbar. The top row of the toolbar contains mathematical symbols, while the bottom row contains templates or frameworks with additional symbols. Click each button to display a menu with additional symbols and options.

6. Build the equation by selecting symbols from the Equation toolbar and by typing variables and numbers from the keyboard.

When you're done editing your equation, click anywhere else in your Word document to close the Equation Editor and return to the Word workspace.

Excel

Excel 2000 is the spreadsheet program included with Microsoft Office 2000. There are two ways to add Excel data to Word documents—you can paste the data, or you can embed the data.

Pasting an Excel Worksheet

When you paste an Excel worksheet into a Word document, you essentially paste the data from the worksheet into a Word table. You can then format the table as necessary or appropriate.

To paste Excel data into Word, follow these steps:

1. From within Excel, select the cells you want to send to Word.

2. Select Edit ➢ Cut or Edit ➢ Copy.

3. Switch to your Word document and position the insertion point where you want to add the new table.

4. Select Edit ➢ Paste.

Word now creates a table, with each cell in the table representing a cell from the Worksheet.

Embedding Individual Cells

To embed selected worksheet data into a Word document, follow these steps:

1. From within Excel, select the cells you want to send to Word.

2. Select Edit ➢ Cut or Edit ➢ Copy.

3. Switch to your Word document and position the insertion point where you want to add the new table.

4. Select Edit ➢ Paste Special to display the Paste Special dialog box.

5. If you want to create a link between the embedded object and the original worksheet, check the Paste Link option. If not, check the Paste option.

6. Select Microsoft Excel Worksheet Object from the As list.

7. Click OK.

Embedding an Entire Worksheet

To embed an entire worksheet into a Word document, follow these steps:

1. From within Word, select Insert ➢ Object to display the Insert Object dialog box.

2. Check the Create From File tab.

3. Enter the location and name of the Excel worksheet file in the File Name box, or click the Browse button to locate the file.

4. Click OK.

Creating a New Worksheet Object

To create a new Excel worksheet object from within Word, follow these steps:

1. From within Word, select Insert ➤ Object to display the Insert Object dialog box.
2. Check the Create New tab.
3. From the Object Type list, select Microsoft Excel Worksheet.
4. Click OK.

Embedding an Excel Chart

To copy an Excel chart into a Word document, follow these steps:

1. From within Excel, select the chart you want to send to Word.
2. Select Edit ➤ Copy.
3. Switch to your Word document and position the insertion point where you want to add the chart.
4. Select Edit ➤ Paste.

To edit or format the chart, double-click it. This switches the Word workspace into Excel editing mode, from which you can use Excel chart editing and formatting commands.

Creating a New Chart Object

You can also create a new Excel chart object from within Word, by following these steps:

1. From within Word, select Insert ➤ Object to display the Insert Object dialog box.
2. Check the Create New tab.
3. From the Object Type list, select Microsoft Excel Chart.
4. Click OK.

To edit the chart's source data, double-click the chart to enter Excel editing mode, then select Chart ➤ Source Data to display and edit the Excel spreadsheet on which the new chart is based.

Fax

To send a Word document as a fax, you must have fax software installed on your system. You can then follow these steps:

1. Select File ➤ Print to display the Print dialog box.

2. Pull down the Printer Name list and select your fax program from the list of printers.

3. Select any other desired options from within the Print dialog box.

4. Click OK to send your document to your fax program.

From here you follow the instructions of your fax program to complete the fax process.

Fields

A field is a placeholder for data that might change within your document. Fields are updated with the actual current value of the data they reference.

Fields are inserted into your text through a field *code*. Each field code represents a certain type of data or action to be inserted in your text. For example, the PAGE code inserts the number of the current page; the DATE code inserts the current date. Field codes are inserted in your text surrounded by curly brackets, like this: { **PAGE** }.

Showing Field Codes and Shading

You can toggle between the code and the result for any specific field by highlighting the field and pressing Shift+F9. You can toggle between showing and hiding the field codes for your entire document by pressing Alt+F9.

You can also configure Word to *always* display field codes instead of results. Follow these steps:

1. Select Tools ➢ Options to display the Options dialog box.

2. Select the View tab.

3. Check the Field Codes option; uncheck this option to display results instead of codes.

4. To shade the fields in your documents, pull down the Field Shading list and select Always. To display shading only when a field is selected, pull down the Field Shading list and select When Selected. To *never* display shading, pull down the Field Shading list and select Never.

5. Click OK.

Inserting Fields with the Field Dialog Box

The easiest way to add a field to your document is via the Field dialog box. When you use this method, you're presented with all the arguments and switches and formatting options for the field you choose. Follow these steps:

1. Position the insertion point where you want to insert the field code.

2. Select Insert ➤ Field to open the Field dialog box.

3. Select a field category from the Categories list.

4. Select a specific field from the Field Names list.

5. To apply switches, formatting, or other options to your code, click the Options button to display the Field Options dialog box. Select the appropriate switches/options/formatting, then click OK.

6. To preserve the field formatting when you update your field codes, check the Preserve Formatting During Upgrades option.

7. Review the code you've constructed in the code box.

8. Click OK to insert the code.

Inserting Fields Manually

To insert a code manually—without the aid of the Field dialog box—follow these steps:

1. Position the insertion point where you want to insert the field code.

2. Press Ctrl+F9.

3. Word inserts a set of field code brackets ({ }) at the insertion point.

4. Type your field code—and all appropriate switches—between the brackets. Make sure you leave a space between the beginning/end of your code and the curly bracket on either side.

To view the results of your newly inserted field code, highlight the code and press F9.

Updating Field Results

By default, the field results displayed in your document display their original values—until you update them. There are several ways to update the field results in your document:

- To update a single field, select the field/results you want to update and then press F9.

- To update all the fields in your document, select your entire document and then press F9.

- To update all the fields in your document before you print the document, select Tools ➤ Options to display the Options menu, then select the Print tab and check the Update Fields option in the Printing Options section.

Locking and Unlocking Fields

If you want to *temporarily* keep a field from updating, you can lock the field by pressing Ctrl+F11. When you want to display updated results, you unlock the field by pressing Shift+Ctrl+F11.

Find and Replace

Find and Replace are versatile commands that let you specify detailed criteria for finding places and things within your documents—and, if you choose, replace what you find with something different. With these commands you can search for—and replace—specific text, formatting (including styles), and special characters.

Finding Text

To use the find command to search for text and other elements in your document, follow these steps:

1. Select Edit ➢ Find (or press Ctrl+F) to display the Find tab of the Find and Replace dialog box.

2. To display all search options, click the More button.

3. Enter the text you're searching for in the Find What box.

4. Select any additional options for your search.

5. If you want to find specific formatting in your document, click the Format button and choose a formatting option from the list.

6. If you want to find special elements in your document, click the Special button and choose an element from the list.

7. Click the Find Next button to jump to the next instance of what you're searching for.

Once you've entered your search criteria, you can press Shift+F4 to find the next instance of the item without displaying the Find and Replace dialog box.

Replacing Text

Word's Replace command works similarly to the Find command, except you have the added option of replacing the item you found with something different. To use the Replace command, follow these steps:

1. Select Edit ➢ Replace (or press Ctrl+H) to display the Replace tab of the Find and Replace dialog box.

2. To display all find and replace options, click the More button.

3. Enter the text you want to replace in the Find What box.

4. Enter the replacement text in the Replace With box.

5. Select any additional options for the operation.

6. If you want to replace specific formatting in your document, click the Format button and choose a new formatting option from the list.

7. If you want to replace special elements in your document, click the Special button and choose an element from the list.

8. Click the Replace button to replace the current instance.

9. Click the Replace All button to find and replace all instances in your document.

10. Click the Find Next button to find the next instance.

You can choose to replace the current instance of the designated text or item (click the Replace button), or automatically search your document and replace all instances that match your search criteria. If you choose to replace one instance at a time (which lets you confirm or cancel each potential replacement), you can either click the Find Next button or press Shift+F4 to find the next instance of the item.

Font and Text Formatting

Text formatting in Word is essentially font formatting. For any given character in your document, you can change its typeface, size (in points), style (bold, italic, etc.), color, spacing, kerning, and other attributes.

To format fonts—fast—use the buttons on Word's Formatting toolbar. This toolbar includes the most common formatting commands you'll use on your text. A larger selection of font formatting options is available from the Fonts dialog box.

Changing Basic Formatting

To change the basic font (typestyle), style, and size of any selected text, follow these steps:

1. Select the text to change.

2. Select Format ➤ Font to display the Font dialog box.

3. Select the Font tab.

4. Select a new font from the Font list.

5. Select a new style (Regular, Italic, Bold, or Bold Italic) from the Font Style list.

6. Select a new font size from the Size list.

7. Click OK to apply the new formatting.

Changing Text Color

To change the color of selected text, follow these steps:

1. Select the text to recolor.

2. Select Format ➤ Font to display the Font dialog box.

3. Select the Font tab.

4. Pull down the Font Color list and select a new color.

5. Click OK to apply the new formatting.

To apply a color not listed in the Font Color list, select the More Colors option at the bottom of the pull-down list. This displays the Colors dialog box. Click the Standard tab to select from palette of 124 colors; to see even *more* colors, select the Custom tab and drag your cursor to a new color, or use the Hue, Saturation, Luminance, Red, Green, and Blue controls to custom "mix" a specific color.

Underlining Your Text

To apply sophisticated underlining to your text, follow these steps:

1. Select the text to underline.

2. Select Format ➢ Font to display the Font dialog box.

3. Select the Font tab.

4. Pull down the Underline Style list and select a specific style.

5. Pull down the Underline Color list and select a color for your underline; the underline can be a different color from your text.

6. Click OK when done.

Animating Your Text

Word 2000 enables you to "animate" text onscreen. (Obviously, you can't animate text on a printed page!) You apply animation effects by following these steps:

1. Select the text to animate.

2. Select Format ➢ Font to display the Font dialog box.

3. Select the Text Effects tab.

4. Select an animation effect from the Animations list; you can check out any animation in the Preview box.

5. Click OK.

Changing Text Case

If you need to change uppercase text to lowercase (or vice versa), follow these steps:

1. Select the text to change.

2. Select Format ➢ Change Case to display the Change Case dialog box.

3. Select one of the following options: Sentence case., lowercase, UPPERCASE, Title Case, or tOGGLE cASE.

4. Click OK to apply the new case.

Highlighting Selected Text

To apply a colored highlight to selected text—much as you would with a colored marker to printed text—follow these steps:

1. Select the text to highlight.
2. Click the Highlight button on Word's Formatting toolbar.

You can change the color of the highlight by clicking the down-arrow on the Highlight button, and selecting a new color from the drop-down menu.

Applying Text Scaling

Text scaling is simply the stretching or narrowing of selected characters, horizontally. To apply text scaling, follow these steps:

1. Select the characters you want to scale.
2. Select Format ➢ Font to display the Font dialog box.
3. Select the Character Spacing tab.
4. Pull down the Scale list and select a value (in terms of percent of the original). Select a value greater than 100% to stretch the text; select a value less than 100% to compress the text.
5. Click OK to apply the scaling.

Adjusting Character Spacing

Character spacing involves the adjustment of the space between characters. To adjust character spacing, follow these steps:

1. Select the text you want to adjust.
2. Select Format ➢ Font to display the Font dialog box.
3. Select the Character Spacing tab.
4. To increase character spacing, pull down the Spacing list and select Expanded; to decrease character spacing, select Condensed.
5. Pull down the By list and select a value for expanding or condensing your text.
6. Click OK.

Kerning Character Pairs

While character spacing changes the spacing between all characters equally, kerning adjusts the spacing only between certain *pairs* of letters. For example, a character with a wide top (such as V) can be spaced closer to a character with a wide bottom (A, for example).

To activate kerning in your documents, follow these steps:

1. Select the text you want to kern.
2. Select Format ➤ Font to display the Font dialog box.
3. Select the Character Spacing tab.
4. Check the Kerning for Fonts option.
5. Select a point size from the Points and Above list; all text this size or larger will be kerned, while smaller text will remain as is.
6. Click OK.

Adding Subscripts and Superscripts

To apply subscript or superscript formatting, follow these steps:

1. Select the text you want to format.
2. Select Format ➤ Font to display the Font dialog box.
3. Select the Character Spacing tab.
4. To create a subscript, select Lowered from the Position list. To create a superscript, select Raised.
5. Select a point value from the By list.
6. Click OK.

Adding a Drop Cap

To create a drop cap at the beginning of a paragraph, follow these steps:

1. Place the insertion point anywhere within the paragraph to contain the drop cap.
2. Select Format ➤ Drop Cap to display the Drop Cap dialog box.
3. Select the type of drop cap you want to apply (None, Dropped, or In Margin) in the Position section.
4. Select a new font for the drop cap from the Font list, or leave as is for the drop cap to be the same font as the rest of the paragraph.
5. Pull down the Lines to Drop list to select how big you want the drop cap to be.
6. Pull down the Distance from Text list to determine the spacing between the drop cap and the rest of the paragraph.
7. Click OK.

To remove a drop cap, repeat steps 1–3, and select None for the Position.

Footnotes and Endnotes

Footnotes and endnotes function similarly, differing only in where they appear in your document; footnotes appear on the bottom of the page they reference, where endnotes appear in a group at the very end of your document.

Viewing Footnotes and Endnotes

Footnotes and endnotes appear in their actual position onscreen when you're using Word's Print Layout view. If you're using Normal or Outline views, however, you don't see the corresponding note text—you only see the note reference marks. To view or edit footnotes in Normal or Outline views, double-click a note mark—or select View ➢ Footnotes—to display Word's Notes pane. Edit your note text appropriately, then click the Close button to close the pane.

Adding a Footnote or Endnote

To insert a footnote or endnote in your text, follow these steps:

1. Position the insertion point at the end of the word or phrase you want to reference.
2. Select Insert ➢ Footnote to display the Footnote and Endnote dialog box.
3. Select whether you want to insert a Footnote or an Endnote.
4. To use standard note numbering, make sure the AutoNumber option is checked.
5. Click OK.
6. Word inserts a note reference mark in your text and the reference number in the note text, and moves the insertion point to the beginning of the note text.
7. Enter the note text, then return to writing/editing the rest of your document.

You can return to edit your note text at any time. If you're in Print Layout view, just navigate to the appropriate footnote or endnote; if you're in Normal or Print Layout view, double-click a specific note reference mark to display the Notes pane for editing.

Copying, Moving, and Deleting Footnotes and Endnotes

When you want to copy or move a footnote or endnote, you don't copy/move the note text itself—all you move is the note reference mark. When you move the mark, the note text automatically moves with it.

Here's how you copy/move a footnote or endnote:

1. Select the note reference mark you want to copy or move.
2. Select Edit ➢ Cut or Edit ➢ Copy, as appropriate.

3. Reposition the insertion mark where you want to insert the footnote or endnote.

4. Select Edit ➢ Paste.

Word now pastes the note reference mark into your text, and repositions the corresponding note text in its proper place in your document.

Deleting a footnote or endnote is as simple as deleting the note reference mark. You don't have to manually delete the note text; it goes away when the note reference mark is deleted.

Changing the Appearance of Footnotes and Endnotes

If you want to use a different note reference mark or change the footnote/endnote font, you can change Word's default footnote/endnote settings—most of which are found in the Note Options dialog box, as follows:

1. Select Insert ➢ Footnote to display the Footnote and Endnote dialog box.

2. Click the Options button to display the Note Options dialog box.

3. Select either the All Footnotes or All Endnotes tab.

4. Change the settings as appropriate, then click OK.

Converting Footnotes to Endnotes

To convert all your footnotes to endnotes—or vice versa—follow these steps:

1. Select Insert ➢ Footnote to display the Footnote and Endnote dialog box.

2. Click the Options button to display the Note Options dialog box.

3. Click the Convert button to display the Convert Notes dialog box.

4. Select one of the following options: Convert All Footnotes to Endnotes, Convert All Endnotes to Footnotes, or Swap Footnotes and Endnotes.

5. Click OK to begin the conversion.

Forms

An automated form is one that the user completes onscreen, from within Word. The user opens Word, creates a new document based on the form template, follows the onscreen instructions and fills out the appropriate information, then saves the document under a designated file name. The form file is then collected and the data within compiled, usually in an Access database or Excel worksheet.

Creating a Form Template

All forms have to be saved in Word template (.DOT) format. To create a new template for your form, follow these steps:

1. Select File ≻ New to open the New dialog box.
2. Select the General tab.
3. Select the Blank Document template.
4. Check the Template option in the Create New section.
5. Click OK to open the template.
6. Select File ≻ Save As to display the Save As dialog box.
7. Enter the name for your new template in the File Name box.
8. Pull down the Save As Type list and select Document Template.
9. Use the Save In list to navigate to and select the folder where you want to save the template.
10. Click the Save button.

Adding a Form Field

To add a form field to your document, follow these instructions:

1. Position the insertion point where you want to add the form field.
2. Click either the Text Form Field, Check Box Form Field, or Drop-Down Form Field buttons on the Forms toolbar.

Changing Form Field Options

Once you've added a form field to your form, you need to configure the field for your particular use. To set a field's properties, follow these steps:

1. Select the field you want to configure.
2. Click the Form Field Options button on the Forms toolbar to display the Options dialog box for that field.
3. Enter the necessary information and select the desired settings.
4. Click OK.

Adding an ActiveX Control

To add an ActiveX control to your form, follow these steps:

1. From within your form, click the Design Mode button on the Control Toolbox toolbar to switch to Design mode.
2. Position the insertion point where you want to add the control.

3. From the Control Toolbox toolbar, click the button for the control you want to add.

4. Use your mouse to position the control on your form.

Setting ActiveX Control Properties

Once you've added an ActiveX control, you need to set its properties. While properties differ by type of control, you typically can set the control's name, appearance, caption, and contents.

To set the properties of an ActiveX control, follow these steps:

1. Click the Design Mode button to switch to Word's Design mode.

2. Select the control you want to configure.

3. Click the Properties button on the Control Toolbox toolbar to display the Properties dialog box.

4. To view the properties alphabetically, select the Alphabetic tab; to view the properties by category, select the Categorized tab.

5. Change the desired properties.

6. Close the Properties dialog box by clicking the X button in the top right corner.

Programming an ActiveX Control

The Properties dialog box sets the look and feel of an ActiveX control; to determine what a control actually *does*, you have to *program* the control, using the Visual Basic for Applications programming language.

All VBA programming is done in the Visual Basic Editor. You display the editor—and write the code for a specific control—by following these steps:

1. Click the Design Mode button to switch to Word's Design mode.

2. Select the control you want to program.

3. Click the View Code button on the Control Toolbox toolbar to open the Visual Basic Editor.

4. Write the appropriate VBA code, then close the Visual Basic Editor and return to your form.

Protecting a Form

Before you distribute a form to others, you must protect it so that other users can't edit the form, only enter data in the designated areas. To protect your form in this fashion, follow these steps:

1. Select Tools ➢ Protect Document to display the Protect Document dialog box.

2. Check the Forms option.

3. To assign a password to the form, enter a password in the Password box.

4. Click OK.

When you are creating or editing a form, you can quickly protect or unprotect the form by clicking Protect Form button on the Forms toolbar.

Frames

Web page *frames* enable you to display multiple pieces of information on a single page. Each frame contains its own separate Web page that can be viewed separately; the page containing the frames is called a *frames page*.

Adding a Frame

To add a frame to your current Web page, make sure you're in Web Layout view, then follow these steps:

1. Position your cursor on the page or in an existing frame adjacent to where you want to add the new frame.

2. To add a frame to the left of your page, click the New Frame Left button on the Frames toolbar. To add a frame to the right of your page, click the New Frame Right button. To add a frame at the top of your page, click the New Frame Above button.

Adding a Navigation Frame

To create a table of contents in a navigational frame, follow these steps:

1. Anchor the insertion point in the main frame on your Web page.

2. Click the Table of Contents in Frame button on the Frames toolbar.

Deleting a Frame

To delete a frame—and its contents—from your Web page, follow these steps:

1. Position the insertion point within the frame you want to delete.

2. Click the Delete Frame button on the Frames toolbar.

Go To

The fastest way to jump to a specific point in your document is by using Word's Go To command. Follow these steps:

1. Select Edit ➢ Go To to display the Go To tab in the Find and Replace dialog box.

2. Select what type of element you want to go to from the Go To What list.

3. Enter the specific element you want to go into the Enter box. (This box varies depending on the type of element selected.)

4. Click the Go To button to go to the selected location.

If you don't enter a specific element to go to, the Go To button changes to a Next button, and a Previous button is enabled. This allows you to go to the next or previous instance of a particular element (for certain types of elements only), instead of to a specific location within your document.

Graphs

Word 2000 uses a separate applet to create graphs in your documents. Microsoft Graph 2000 is an extremely versatile graphing tool, functioning almost identically to the graphing functions in the Microsoft Excel 2000 spreadsheet program. When you choose to insert a graph in a Word document, Word automatically launches the Graph 2000 applet, which you then use until you finish your graph and return to Word.

With Graph 2000 open, you have access to two parts of your graph object—the *datasheet* (a mini-spreadsheet) and the graph itself. The graph is created from data in the datasheet; you can enter data into the datasheet manually, or have Word insert the data automatically when you create a graph from existing Word data. Any time you change the data in the datasheet, the graph is automatically updated to reflect the new data.

Creating a Graph from Existing Data

If you used Word's table commands to create a table full of data, or if you have data separated by tab stops, you can use Graph 2000 to automatically display that data in a graph. Follow these steps:

1. Select the table or data listing that you want to use.

2. Select Insert ➤ Picture ➤ Chart.

Word launches Graph 2000 and creates a bar chart directly underneath the data you selected.

Creating a Linked Graph from Data in Your Document

To create a graph that is linked to the data in your document and is automatically updated when your data changes, follow these steps:

1. Select the table or data listing that you want to use.

2. Select Edit ➤ Copy.

3. Position the insertion point where you want to add the graph to your document.

4. Select Insert ➤ Picture ➤ Chart.

5. When Graph 2000 launches and creates its "dummy" chart, position your cursor within the datasheet and press Ctrl+A to select the entire datasheet.

6. Press Del to delete the "dummy" data from the datasheet.

7. Position the insertion point in cell A1 (top left corner) of the datasheet, then select Edit ➤ Paste Link.

8. When asked if you want to replace existing data, answer Yes.

Graph 2000 now pastes your selected data into the datasheet and creates the corresponding chart.

Creating a Graph from Scratch

You don't need to have data in your Word document in order to create a Graph 2000 graph. You can create graphs from scratch, and enter data directly into the Graph 2000 datasheet. Follow these steps:

1. Position the insertion point where you want to insert the graph.

2. Select Insert ➤ Picture ➤ Chart.

3. When the Graph 2000 workspace appears, delete the "dummy" data from the datasheet and enter your new data.

Headers and Footers

Headers and footers are repeating sections at the top (header) or bottom (footer) of your document. You can use headers and footers to display information about your document, such as title, subject, author, date, chapter number, or page number.

Viewing Headers and Footers

Headers and footers do not appear as part of your normal document text. To work within a header or footer, you have to select View ➤ Header and Footer. This switches Word to Print Layout view, opens the header for editing, and displays the Header and Footer toolbar. You use the commands on this toolbar to edit and format your header and footer.

Editing Header and Footer Text

To add text to a header or footer, follow these steps:

1. Select View ➤ Headers and Footers to open the header editing area.

2. Enter text as usual within the header.

3. Click the Switch Between Header and Footer button on the toolbar to switch to the footer editing area.

4. Enter text as usual within the footer.

5. Click Close to close the header/footer editing areas.

Creating a Unique First Page Header or Footer

If your document has a separate title page, you may want to create a different header or footer for that page than the running header/footer used throughout the rest of your document. Follow these steps:

1. Position your cursor on the first page of your document.

2. Select View ➤ Header and Footer to display the header/footer editing area.

3. Click the Page Setup button on the Header and Footer toolbar to display the Page Setup dialog box.

4. Select the Layout tab.

5. Check the Different First Page option.

6. Click OK.

7. Edit the first page's header and footer as desired; if you don't want a header or footer on the first page, simply delete all text and other elements from the header/footer areas.

8. To edit the header/footer for the following pages, navigate to the next page and begin editing.

9. Click the Close button to return to the body of your document.

Selecting Different Odd and Even Headers and Footers

If you're producing a bound document with opposing pages, you may want to create slightly different headers or footers for the left and right pages. If so, follow these steps:

1. Select View ➤ Header and Footer to display the header/footer editing area.

2. Click the Page Setup button on the Header and Footer toolbar to display the Page Setup dialog box.

3. Select the Layout tab.

4. Check the Different Odd and Even option.

5. Click OK.

6. Move to an even-numbered page (typically a left-hand page) and edit the header/footer.

7. Move to an odd-numbered page (typically a right-hand page) and edit the header/footer.

8. Click the Close button to return to the body of your document.

Inserting a Page Number

To add an automated page number to your header or footer, click the Insert Page Number button on the Header and Footer toolbar.

Calculating the Total Number of Pages

To add an *X* of *Y* Pages line to your header or footer, start by inserting the page number, then typing **of**, then clicking the Insert Number of Pages button on the Header and Footer toolbar. This field contains the calculated total number of pages in your document.

Inserting the Date and Time

To add today's date to your header/footer, click the Insert Date button on the Header and Footer toolbar. To add the current time, click the Insert Time button.

Help

When you press F1 (or select Help ➤ Microsoft Word Help) you open Word's built-in Help system. From here you can browse through the system's table of contents, ask specific questions from the Answer Wizard, and look up key words in the system's index.

When you select Help ➤ What's This (or press Shift+F1), your cursor changes into a question mark. When you click any screen element (toolbar button, menu item, or any element in a dialog box), Word displays a ScreenTip describing that element. If you turn on What's This and click a character in your document, Word displays a pop-up box detailing the paragraph and character formatting of the selection.

When you select Help ➤ About Microsoft Word, you display the About Microsoft Word dialog box. This dialog box contains version and technical information about your Word installation.

Additional support resources are located on the Internet at the Microsoft Office Update Web site. You access this site by selecting Help ➤ Office on the Web.

HTML

HTML (Hypertext MarkUp Language) is the pseudo programming code used to create Web pages. For more precise control of your Web pages, Word enables you to view and edit the HTML code directly, using the Microsoft Script Editor. Follow these steps:

1. While viewing an HTML-format document, select View➤HTML Source to display the Microsoft Script Editor with the current document loaded.

2. Make any changes to the HTML code.

3. Select File ➤ Exit to save the changes and close the Script Editor.

Hyperlinks

A hyperlink is a way to immediately jump to another section within the same document, to another document, or to a page anywhere on the Web. When a user clicks a hyperlink, he or she is taken directly to the linked document or page.

Inserting a Hyperlink

Follow these steps to insert a hyperlink into any Word document:

1. Within your document, select the text to which you want to apply the hyperlink.

2. Click the Insert Hyperlink button on Word's Standard toolbar to display the Insert Hyperlink dialog box.

3. Click the Existing File or Web page button at the left of the dialog box.

4. If no text appears in the Text to Display box, enter the text for the hyperlink.

5. Enter the URL for the hyperlink in the Type the File or Web Page Name box, *or*

   Click the Web Page button to connect to the Internet, launch your Web browser, and navigate to the page you want to link to, *or*

   Select from the list of links displayed in the dialog box; you can choose to list Recent Files, Browsed Pages, or Inserted Links.

6. If you want to display a ScreenTip when a cursor is hovered over the link, click the ScreenTip button to display the Set Hyperlink ScreenTip dialog box; enter the text in the ScreenTip Text box, then click OK.

7. Click OK.

Creating an E-mail Link

Some links in Web pages don't jump to another Web page; instead, these links (called *Mailto links*) open your e-mail program to create and send an e-mail message. To insert a Mailto link into your document, follow these steps:

1. Within your document, select the text to which you want to apply the hyperlink.
2. Click the Insert Hyperlink button on Word's Standard toolbar to display the Insert Hyperlink dialog box.
3. Click the E-Mail Address button.
4. Enter the e-mail address you want messages addressed to into the E-Mail Address box.
5. Enter a subject for these messages into the Subject box.
6. Click OK.

When you click your new Mailto link, your e-mail program will launch and open a new message window; the selected e-mail address will be preloaded into the To: box, and the selected subject will be preloaded into the Subject: box.

Hyphens

By default, none of the words in your document are hyphenated. Without hyphenation, your documents can include huge gaps of white space on individual lines—especially if the text in the host paragraph is justified. Instead, you might want to consider hyphenating words that appear at the end of long lines of text.

Using Automatic Hyphenation

Word 2000 includes the capability to automatically hyphenate your document as you type. With automatic hyphenation enabled, Word will automatically insert hyphens as needed to ensure smooth line breaks throughout your document.

To turn on automatic hyphenation, follow these steps:

1. Select Tools ➤ Language ➤ Hyphenation to display the Hyphenation dialog box.
2. Check the Automatically Hyphenate Document option.
3. Use the Hyphenation Zone control to select the amount of space you want to leave between the end of a line, between the end of the last word in a line, and the right margin.
4. Use the Limit Consecutive Hyphens To control to select the number of consecutive lines that can be hyphenated.

5. If you don't want to hyphenate words in all uppercase, uncheck the Hyphenate Words in Caps option.

6. Click OK to activate the automatic hyphenation.

When you activate automatic hyphenation, any existing text in your document will be automatically hyphenated. To *unhyphenate* a document, follow the above steps and *uncheck* the Automatically Hyphenate Document option.

Hyphenating Words Manually

If you'd rather choose when and where to apply hyphenation in your document, you want to disable automatic hyphenation and use Word's manual hyphenation feature. When you manually hyphenate your document, you'll be asked to confirm all proposed word breaks in your document.

To use manual hyphenation, follow these steps:

1. Select Tools ➤ Language ➤ Hyphenation to display the Hyphenation dialog box.

2. Click the Manual button.

3. Word now proceeds through your document checking for necessary hyphenation. When it finds a long word at the end of a line (or at the beginning of the following line), it displays the Manual Hyphenation dialog box containing the selected word. Dictionary-proper hyphens are inserted between each of the word's syllables, and the recommended breaking hyphen is selected and blinking.

4. To accept the recommended breaking hyphen, click Yes. To choose *not* to hyphenate this word, click No. To select a different breaking hyphen, click a new hyphen and click Yes.

You can end the manual hyphenation process at any time by clicking the Cancel button.

Controlling Hyphenation for Specific Words

To better control potential hyphenation, you can manually insert either *nonbreaking hyphen* or *optional hyphen* characters within specific words in your text.

A non-breaking hyphen tells Word *not* to hyphenate the word at that point. An optional hyphen tells Word that if the word has to be hyphenated, this is where you want to hyphenate it.

You insert a non-breaking hyphen by pressing Ctrl+Shift+-. You insert a breaking hyphen by pressing Ctrl+-. None of these marks appear in your printed documents unless the word is actually hyphenated.

Index

To create an index, you first have to mark all the words or terms you want to appear in the index. Once the index terms are marked, you can then automatically build the index.

Marking Index Entries

To mark a word or phrase as an index entry, follow these steps:

1. Select the word or phrase you want to index.
2. Press Alt+Shift+X to display the Mark Index Entry dialog box.
3. If you want the selected word or phrase to be a main index entry, make sure the selection appears in the Main Entry box. If you want the selection to be a subentry, copy the selection from the Main Entry to the Subentry box and enter the name of the main entry in the Main Entry box. If you want the selection to be a third-level entry, enter a Main Entry and a Subentry, then enter a colon (:) after the Subentry and type the selection after the colon—leaving no space in between.
4. Make any other selections within the dialog box.
5. Click Mark to mark this entry, or click Mark All to mark all occurrences of this word.

The Mark Index Entry doesn't close after you mark the entry; it stays open so you can mark additional entries in your document. You'll need to click the Cancel button to close this dialog box.

Marking a Range of Pages

If a concept is covered over a range of pages in your document, you may want to reference the entire page range in your index. To do this, you first have to bookmark the page range, and then mark the bookmark as an index entry. Follow these steps:

1. Select the entire range of text you want to index.
2. Select Insert ➢ Bookmark to display the Bookmark dialog box.
3. Enter a name for the bookmark in the Bookmark Name box, then click Add.
4. With the insertion point anywhere within the bookmarked text, press Alt+Shift+X to display the Mark Index Entry dialog box.
5. Check the Page Range option, then pull down the Bookmark list and select the bookmark you want to index.
6. Click the Mark button.

Editing and Deleting Index Entries

To edit an index entry, you have to edit the inserted field code. Click the Show/Hide button on Word's Standard toolbar to display all hidden codes, then go to the index entry you want to edit. Position the insertion point within the code, and then edit appropriately.

To delete an index entry, highlight the entire field code (including the curly brackets) and press Del.

Creating an AutoMark File

Some users prefer to make a list of the words they want included in the index separate from the main document itself, and to then build the index from this separate word list. To create an AutoMark file and use it to automatically index your document, follow these steps:

1. Click the New button on Word's Standard toolbar to create a new blank document.
2. Select Table ➤ Insert ➤ Table to display the Insert Table dialog box.
3. Select 2 for number of columns and 1 for number of rows, then click OK to insert the table in the new document.
4. In the first column of the first row of your table, enter the word or phrase you want Word to search for and mark as an index entry.
5. In the second column, enter the text for this index entry you want to appear in the index listing.
6. Press Tab to create a new row in your table for your next entry.
7. Repeat steps 4–6 for each index entry you want to mark.
8. When you're done entering index entries, select File ➤ Save As to save the file with a name of your choosing.
9. Open or switch to the document you want to index.
10. Select Insert ➤ Index and Tables to display the Index and Tables dialog box.
11. Select the Index tab.
12. Click the AutoMark button to display the Open Index AutoMark File dialog box.
13. Find and select your AutoMark file, then click Open.

Word now searches through your main document for each occurrence of the text in the first column of the table in your AutoMark file, and marks each occurrence as an index entry.

Building an Index

To create an index for your document, follow these steps:

1. Anchor your insertion point where you want to insert the index.
2. Make sure that all field codes and hidden text are *not* visible in your document.
3. Select Insert ➢ Index and Tables to display the Index and Tables dialog box.
4. Select the Index tab.
5. If you want subentries to appear indented and below their main entries, check the Indented option; if you want subentries to appear on the same line as the main entry, check the Run-In option.
6. Select the number of columns for your index from the Columns list.
7. If you want page numbers to line up at the right margin, check the Right Align Page Numbers option, then select a tab leader (for the space between the entry and the page number) from the Tab Leader list. If you want page numbers to appear next to the entries, uncheck this option.
8. Select a format for the index from the Formats list, or click Modify to create your own format.
9. When all options are selected, click OK to create the index.

Word now scans your document for all index entries (actually, for XE field codes) and builds the index based on these entries and according to the options you selected.

Updating Your Index

After you make changes to your document, you should always update your index by selecting the entire index and pressing F9.

Keyboard Shortcuts

All of Word's menus can be accessed via the keyboard. To access the menu bar, press F10; this positions the cursor over the menu bar, and lets you navigate through the menus using the left and right arrow keys. Use the down arrow key to open a menu, then use the Enter key to select a specific menu item.

You can also go directly to any main menu by pressing the Alt key plus the underlined letter on that menu. Once a menu is opened, you can press the underlined letter for any menu item to activate that command immediately.

Some of Word's most popular operations have been mapped directly to the function keys at the top of your computer keyboard. Many other Word operations can be accessed directly via a series of key combinations. These *shortcut keys* let you press two or more keys together to initiate a specific operation.

Assigning Shortcut Keys

To assign other commands and operations to new shortcut keys, follow these steps:

1. Select Tools ➤ Customize to display the Customize dialog box.

2. From any tab, click the Keyboard button.

3. When the Customize Keyboard dialog box appears, select a category from the Category list, then select a specific command or operation from the Command list.

4. Move your cursor to the Press New Shortcut Key box, then press the key combination you wish to use for this shortcut.

5. Select a document or template from the Save Changes To list; this will be where the shortcut is stored.

6. Click the Assign key to assign this command/operation to the selected key(s).

To remove shortcut keys from a command/operation, select the command and click the Remove button. To reset all shortcut keys to their original assignments, click the Reset All button.

Viewing Shortcut Keys

To create a list of all Word shortcut keys and menu commands, follow these steps:

1. Select Tools ➤ Macro ➤ Macros to display the Macros dialog box.

2. Pull down the Macros In list and select Word Commands.

3. Pull down the Macro Name list and select ListCommands.

4. Click the Run button.

Labels

Creating a mailing label is similar to addressing an envelope. Word lets you use just about any type of blank labels; you can find labels in all different sizes, typically with several labels per sheet.

Configuring Word for Specific Types of Labels

Before you print your first label, you need to tell Word what specific type of label you'll be using. Follow these steps:

1. Select Tools ➤ Envelopes and Labels to display the Envelopes and Labels dialog box.

2. Select the Labels tab.

3. Click the Options button to display the Label Options dialog box.

4. Select either the Dot Matrix or Laser and Ink Jet option; if you're using a laser or inkjet printer, also select which tray of your printer you'll be using to print your labels.

5. Pull down the Label Products list and select the brand of label you're using.

6. Select the specific label type from the Product Number list.

7. If you want to confirm the information about the label you selected—or if your printer isn't printing a specific label properly—click the Details button to display the Label Information dialog box. Change any measurements, if necessary, then click OK to return to the Label Options dialog box.

8. Click OK.

Creating a New Label Type

If the label you're using isn't listed in the Label Options dialog box, you can create a new label template for your label. Follow these steps:

1. Select Tools ➤ Envelopes and Labels to display the Envelopes and Labels dialog box.

2. Select the Labels tab.

3. Click the Options button to display the Label Options dialog box.

4. Click the New Label button to display the New Custom dialog box.

5. Enter the measurements of your label, and assign it a name.

6. Click OK.

Printing a Label

To print a single label from the Envelopes and Labels dialog box, follow these steps:

1. Select Tools ➤ Envelopes and Labels to display the Envelopes and Labels dialog box.

2. Select the Labels tab.

3. Type the recipient's name and address in the Address box.

4. If you want to print a POSTNET barcode on your label, check the Delivery Point Barcode option.

5. To set the font used on your label, highlight the entire address and then right-click your mouse. When the pop-up menu appears, select Font. When the Font dialog box appears, select a font, style, and font size, then click OK.

6. If you want to print a full page of this label, check the Full Page of the Same Label Option. If you want to print a single label, check the Single Label option, then select which row and column on your label sheet you want to print.

7. Confirm that everything is configured properly, insert the sheet of labels into your printer's feed tray, then click Print to print the label(s).

Macros

A macro is a set of instructions that automates a repeated or repetitive operation. Word 2000 creates macros using the Visual Basic for Applications (VBA) programming language, which is a subset of the more robust Visual Basic language. Each macro consists of multiple lines of programming code, each line containing a specific instruction.

Recording a Macro

To record a macro, follow these steps:

1. Select Tools ≻ Macro ≻ Record New Macro to display the Record Macro dialog box.

2. Enter a name for the macro in the Macro Name box.

3. Pull down the Store Macro In list and select where you want to store the macro—in the current document, in the current template, or in *all* documents.

4. If you want to enter a description for the macro, do so in the Description box.

5. To assign the macro to a toolbar or menu, click the Toolbars button to display the Customize dialog box. Select the Commands tab, select the macro you're recording, then drag it to a toolbar or menu. Click the Close button to proceed to step 7 and start recording.

6. To assign the macro to a shortcut key, click the Keyboard button to display the Customize Keyboard dialog box. Select the macro you're recording, enter the desired key or keys into the Press New Shortcut Key box, then click Assign. Click the Close button to proceed to step 7 and start recording.

7. If you don't want to assign the macro to a menu, toolbar, or shortcut key, click the OK button to start recording.

8. Word now closes the Record Macro dialog box and displays the Macro Recording toolbar with recording activated.

9. Perform the actions you want to include in your macro.

10. When you're done recording your macro, click the Stop Recording button.

Editing a Macro

You edit macros in the Visual Basic Editor, as follows:

1. Select Tools ➤ Macro ➤ Macros to display the Macros dialog box.
2. Select the name of the macro you want to edit from the Macro Name list.
3. Click the Edit button to open the Visual Basic Editor.
4. Make the appropriate changes to your macro code, then close the Visual Basic Editor and return to your Word document.

Running a Macro

To run a macro from the Macros dialog box, follow these steps:

1. Select Tools ➤ Macro ➤ Macros to display the Macros dialog box.
2. Select the macro you want to run from the Macro Name list.
3. Click the Run button.

Copying a Macro to Another Document

To copy a macro project from one document or template to another, follow these steps:

1. Select Tools ➤ Macro ➤ Macros to display the Macros dialog box.
2. Click the Organizer button to display the Organizer.
3. Select the Macro Project Items tab. The macro projects in the active document are displayed in the left list; the macro projects in the Normal template are displayed in the right list.
4. To change *where* you want to copy the macro project to or from, click the appropriate Close File button, then click the Open File button and select a new document or template.
5. From the appropriate list, select the macro project you want to copy.
6. Click the Copy button.

Macro Virus

A computer virus is similar to a biological virus. Just as a biological virus invades your body's system and replicates itself, a computer virus invades your computer's system and also replicates itself—or inflicts damage on your system.

One of the newest types of computer viruses is the *macro virus*. These viruses are stored in the macro code contained in a document, template, or add-in, and thus can be transmitted within a Word document or template file. When you open the document or template, you run the macro and activate the virus.

You protect against macro viruses by activating Word's security settings, and by using anti-virus software programs. These programs scan your files for viruses, and then "clean" any viruses it finds from your files.

Mail Merge

Word's Mail Merge Helper completely automates the process of merging data from a data source into a Word document. When you select Tools ➢ Mail Merge and follow the step-by-step instructions in the Mail Merge Helper, you'll create a perfectly merged mailing with a minimal amount of work. You use the Mail Merge Helper to create form letters, mailing labels, envelopes, and other documents that merge data from external sources. Here are the general steps you'll go through when creating a merged mailing with the Mail Merge Helper:

1. **Create your *main document***, which should contain the generic text you want to repeat in each form letter, envelope, or mailing label.

2. **Open or create a *data source***, which should contain the individual data to be merged into the main document. For example, for a merged envelope, the data source should contain the names and addresses of all the intended recipients. Word can work with various types of data sources, including Excel spreadsheets, Access databases, or tables in other Word documents.

3. **Insert *merge fields* into your main document**. Merge fields are placeholders for the data that will be inserted from your data source.

4. **Merge the data and output the merged documents.** Whether you're merging from a database, spreadsheet, or Word table, each row or record in the data source will produce an individual form letter, envelope, or label—which can then be sent directly to your printer for printing, or distributed via e-mail or fax. You can also collect all the merged documents into a single new document, which can be edited and printed at a later time.

Margins

In Print Layout view only, you can control your document's margins from Word's rulers. The dark areas on either end of the ruler are your document's current margins; use your mouse to drag the *inside* end of a margin and resize it. If both horizontal and vertical rulers are displayed, you can adjust all four margins in your current document.

You can more precisely set the margins for a document from the Page Setup dialog box. Follow these steps:

1. Select File ➢ Page Setup to display the Page Setup dialog box.

2. Select the Margins tab.

3. Select values (in inches) for the Top, Bottom, Left, and Right margins.

4. Click OK.

Master Documents

A master document is a framework that contains multiple smaller documents; each *subdocument* can be edited as a separate document, but then combines with all the other subdocuments into the master document for indexing and printing.

Creating a New Master Document from Scratch

You use Word's Outline view to create the structure of your master document. When you designate major headings in your outline as subdocuments, Word automatically breaks up your document into its component parts, assigning names to each subdocument based on the text in the outline headings.

To create a master document from scratch, follow these steps:

1. Open a new blank document and switch to Outline view.

2. In Outline view, create an outline of your master document. Wherever you want to start a new subdocument (section), use outline level one (Heading 1); use different levels/headings for all headings and text within a section/subdocument.

3. Select all text you wish to turn into subdocuments.

4. From the Outline toolbar, click the Create Subdocument button.

Word now creates multiple subdocuments within your master document. Each subdocument is designated by a border around its section in the outline.

Converting an Existing Document into a Master Document

If you've already created a long document and wish to turn it into a master document (by breaking it into subdocuments), you follow a similar procedure to that of starting from scratch. Follow these steps:

1. Open the document you want to convert into a master document.

2. Switch to Outline view.

3. Select the text or sections you want to turn into subdocuments; make sure that the selection starts with a heading, and that the heading level is consistent for each location where you want to start a new subdocument.

4. From the Outline toolbar, click the Create Subdocument button.

Word now breaks your existing document into subdocuments based on the text and headings selected.

Assembling a Master Document from Existing Documents

Word also lets you combine documents you've already created into a single master document. Word will automatically assign styles from the master document to all subdocuments, although you can choose to print subdocuments separate from the main document—and thus preserve the original document's formatting.

To create a new master document from existing Word files, follow these steps:

1. Create a new blank document and switch to Outline view.

2. Click the Insert Subdocument button to display the Insert Document dialog box.

3. Select a document to insert, then click OK.

4. Repeat steps 2 and 3 for each new document you wish to insert into your master document.

Each document you insert into your new master document becomes a separate subdocument.

Converting a Subdocument into Part of the Master Document

If you want a subdocument to revert back into part of the master document (and thus *not* be available for separate editing), follow these steps:

1. Display your master document in Outline View.

2. Click the Expand Subdocuments button to expand all subdocuments.

3. Select the subdocument you want to convert.

4. Click the Remove Subdocument button.

Word now removes the section breaks for the selected subdocument, making it part of the master document.

Deleting a Subdocument from the Master Document

If you want to completely delete a subdocument from your master document, follow these steps:

1. Display your master document in Outline view.

2. Click the Collapse Subdocuments button to collapse all subdocuments.

3. Select the subdocument you want to delete by clicking the Subdocument icon next to the subdocument hyperlink.

4. Press Delete.

Adding a New Subdocument

To add a new subdocument to your master document, follow these steps:

1. Display your master document in Outline view.

2. Click the Expand Subdocuments button to expand all subdocuments.

3. Position the insertion point where you want to add the new subdocument.

4. Click the Insert Subdocument button to display the Insert Document dialog box.

5. Select a document to insert, then click OK.

Menus

Word's menus are organized by function, so if you know what kind of thing you want to do, pull down that menu and look for the specific command you need. To choose a menu item, move your cursor to the menu you want and click the name of the menu. This pulls down the menu; click a specific menu item to select it.

You can also access the menus with your keyboard. When you press the F10 key, Word's focus changes to the menu bar, and you can use the right and left arrow keys to move through the menus, the down arrow key to pull down any menu, and the Enter key to select any menu item.

Turning Off Personalized Menus

Word 2000 incorporates *personalized* menus that (by default) only show those items that you've recently used. These menus are sometimes called "short" menus, since they don't include all the commands found on the full "long" menus. So if you never use a particular menu item, you won't see it cluttering up things when you pull down that menu.

To display the full range of menus, click the down arrow at the bottom of any "short" menu. This expands the menu to show all items, recently used and otherwise.

To turn off the personalized menu feature and display all the items on all menus, follow these steps:

1. Select Tools ➢ Customize to display the Customize dialog box.

2. Click the Options tab.

3. Uncheck the Menus Show Recently Used Commands First option.

4. Click OK.

Adding Items to the Menu Bar

To add new items to Word's menu bar, follow these steps:

1. Select Tools ➤ Customize to display the Customize dialog box.

2. Select the Commands tab.

3. Select a category from the Category list, select a menu or command from the Command list, then use your mouse to drag the selected item from dialog box onto the Menu bar.

4. Click Close when done.

To remove an item from the Menu bar, open the Customize dialog box and then drag the item off the Menu bar.

Microsoft Script Editor

The Microsoft Script Editor can be used to view and edit HTML code and create scripts using VBScript. You launch Script Editor from within a Word document by selecting Tools ➤ Macro ➤ Microsoft Script Editor, or by clicking the Microsoft Script Editor button on the Web Tools toolbar. When the Script Editor launches, your current document will be displayed.

One way to create a script is to start in the Script Outline window. The Script Outline window shows you all scriptable elements in your page. You select an element form the Script Outline window, and then write the corresponding script in the Document window.

You can also insert a standalone SCRIPT block within the Document window. Anchor your insertion point where you want to add the script, then select either HTML ➤ Script Block ➤ Client or HTML ➤ Script Block ➤ Server. The Editor inserts a SCRIPT block within the HTML code; you can then write the script within the <SCRIPT> and </SCRIPT> codes.

Numbered Lists

Numbered lists function similarly to bulleted lists, but with some unique formatting options.

Creating a Numbered List

The fastest way to create a numbered list is to highlight the paragraphs in your list, then click the Numbering button on Word's Formatting toolbar. This indents the selected paragraphs and applies the default numbering style.

Follow these steps to create a numbered list:

1. Select the paragraphs you want to number.
2. Select Format ➢ Bullets and Numbering to display the Bullets and Numbering dialog box.
3. Select the Numbered tab.
4. Select a number type.
5. Click OK.

You can also insert a bulleted list using the Bulleted tab in the Bullets and Numbering dialog box.

Changing Number Formats

To change the style of your numbered list, follow these steps:

1. Select the numbered text you want to reformat.
2. Select Format ➢ Bullets and Numbering to display the Bullets and Numbering dialog box.
3. Select the Numbered tab.
4. Select a new number type.
5. Click OK.

If you don't like any of the numbered lists presented, you can create a custom list style by clicking the Customize button on the Numbered tab; this displays the Customize Numbered List dialog box, from which you can select a new font and/or style for your list.

Continuing Numbering in Other Lists

To select whether or not to continue numbering from one list to another, follow these steps:

1. Position your cursor in the first numbered item in the second list.
2. Select Format ➢ Bullets and Numbering to display the Bullets and Numbering dialog box.
3. Select the Numbered tab.
4. To start the numbering of this new list at the number 1 (or *A* or *I* or whatever the first item is in your selected list style), check the Restart Numbering option.

5. To continue the numbering from the previous numbered list, check the Continue Previous List option.

6. Click OK.

Using Outline Numbering

If you're working with an outline, you can apply special *outline numbering* to your document. Outline numbering includes numbering for *subsections*—such as 1.1 or A.1—for documents with a hierarchical structure.

To apply outline numbering, follow these steps:

1. Select Format ➢ Bullets and Numbering to display the Bullets and Numbering dialog box.

2. Select the Outline Numbered tab.

3. Select an outline number type.

4. Click OK.

Object Formatting

Within Word, graphics, pictures, tables, text boxes, and most other non-text elements are *objects*. The appearance of most objects can be modified using a series of standardized formatting commands.

Moving an Object

To move an object, simply select it and then—after your cursor changes to a four-pointed arrow—drag it to a new position. To precisely position an object, follow these steps:

1. Select the object.

2. Select Format ➢ Object to display the Format Object dialog box.

3. Select the Layout tab.

4. Click the Advanced button to display the Advanced Layout dialog box.

5. Select the Picture Position tab.

6. In the Horizontal section, check the Absolute Position option. Pull down the To the Left Of list and select next to what element you want to position this graphic; most often you'll select Page or Margin. Now use the Absolute Position list to select how far from this element you want to position your object horizontally.

7. In the Vertical section, check the Absolute Position option. Pull down the Below list and select below which element you want to position this graphic; most

often you'll select Page or Margin. Now use the Absolute Position list to select how far below this element you want to position your object vertically.

8. If you want your object to move as you add or delete text, check the Move Object With Text option; if you want your object to lock into its current position, uncheck this option and check the Lock Anchor option.

9. If you have multiple objects on the same page sharing the same text wrapping style, you can allow them to overlap to checking the Allow Overlap option; unchecking this option forces the objects to reposition themselves to avoid overlap.

10. Click OK when done.

Resizing an Object

To resize an object, grab one of its selection handles and drag it to a new position. If you want the object to retain its original vertical/horizontal ratio, hold down the Shift key while you resize the object.

You can also precisely resize or scale any object by using the Format Object dialog box. Just follow these steps:

1. Select the object.

2. Select Format ➤ Object to display the Format Object dialog box.

3. Select the Size tab.

4. Use the Height and Width controls in the Size and Rotate section to adjust the object's dimensions separately, *or*

   Use the Height and Width controls in the Scale section to select dimensions as a percentage of the picture's original size. (Check the Relative to Original Picture Size option to maintain the percentages as they relate to the original, unedited picture.)

5. Click OK when done.

Aligning Objects Vertically

If you have more than one object on a page, you can precisely align them vertically, by the top, middle, or bottom of the objects. To align multiple objects, follow these steps:

1. Select the objects you want to align, by either selecting each object individually (while holding the Shift key) or using the Select Objects tool to draw a boundary around all the objects.

2. From the Drawing menu, select Draw ➤ Align or Distribute, then select one of the alignment options.

Distributing Objects

You can also choose to equally space multiple objects on the page by *distributing* them horizontally or vertically. To distribute multiple objects, follow these steps:

1. Select the objects you want to space.

2. Select either Draw ➤ Align or Distribute ➤ Distribute Horizontally, or select Draw ➤ Align or Distribute ➤ Distribute Vertically.

Layering Multiple Objects

If you have multiple objects on your page, you can overlap them so that an object in front of another object obscures the object behind. To send an object to the front or the rear of a stack, follow these steps:

1. Select the object to move.

2. From the Drawing toolbar, select Draw ➤ Order, and then select one of the following layering options:

Bring to Front   Sends the selected object to the top of the stack.

Send to Back   Sends the selected object to the bottom of the stack.

Bring Forward   Moves the selected object up or forward one layer.

Send Backward   Moves the selected object down or backward one layer.

Bring in Front of Text   Moves the selected object on top of the text on your page—thus obscuring the text beneath.

Send Behind Text   Moves the selected object below the text on your page—thus making the object a *background image*.

Rotating an Object

Many—but not all—objects can be turned clockwise or counterclockwise on your page. Word includes a Free Rotate tool and the capability to automatically rotate an object in ninety-degree increments.

To freely rotate an object, follow these steps:

1. Select the object.

2. Click the Free Rotate button on the Drawing toolbar; green rotation handles now appear around the object, and your cursor changes shape to match the Free Rotate icon.

3. Grab any one of the rotation handles and drag the object around either clockwise or counter-clockwise.

To rotate an object in ninety-degree increments, simply go to the Drawing toolbar and select either Draw ➢ Rotate or Flip➢ Rotate Left (to rotate counter-clockwise) or Draw ➢ Rotate or Flip ➢ Rotate Right (to rotate clockwise).

Flipping an Object

To create a mirror image of an object left-to-right, follow these steps:

1. Select the object.

2. On the Drawing toolbar, select Draw➢ Rotate or Flip ➢ Flip Horizontal.

To create a mirror image of an object top-to-bottom, select Draw ➢ Rotate or Flip ➢ Flip Vertical from the Drawing toolbar.

Wrapping Text around an Object

Word enables you to wrap text around an object in the following ways:

In Line with Text   The object is treated as a character of text. The object is placed at the insertion point and the text resumes on the other side of the object.

Square   Wraps text around all sides of a square surrounding the object.

Tight   Wraps text tightly around the edges of the actual image—*not* around the object's borders.

Through   Wraps text tightly around the edges of the actual image—and allows text to display inside any parts of the object that are open.

Top and Bottom   Wraps text around the top and bottom of the object only—no text will display around the sides of the object.

Follow these steps to select a text-wrapping option:

1. Select the object.

2. Select Format ➢ Object to display the Format Object dialog box.

3. Select the Layout tab.

4. If the wrapping style you want is on this tab, select it and click OK. To see more text-wrapping options, click the Advanced button to display the Advanced Layout dialog box.

5. Select the Text Wrapping tab.

6. Select a wrapping style.

7. For the Square, Tight, and Through styles, select whether you want to wrap the text on Both Sides, Left Only, Right Only, or the Largest (side) Only.

8. For the Square, Tight, Through, and Top and Bottom styles, move to the Distance From Text section and select how large a buffer you want to place between the object and the surrounding text.

9. Click OK when done.

Applying Borders and Fills

Most objects placed on your page can be assigned a border. Some objects (not pictures, and not all drawing objects) can be "filled" with a color or pattern. Follow these steps:

1. Select the object.

2. From the Drawing toolbar, click the arrow next to the Line Color button and select a new color for the border.

3. Click the Line Style button and select a new width for the border.

4. If you want your border to consist of dashed lines, click the Dash Style button and select a specific type of dash.

5. To fill the object, click the arrow next to the Fill Color button and select a new color. To see additional colors, select More Fill Colors to display the Colors dialog box. To add gradients, textures, patterns, or pictures to the object's background, select Fill Effects to display the Fill Effects dialog box.

Adding a Shadow

To add a shadow to an object, follow these steps:

1. Select the object.

2. Click the Shadow button on the Drawing toolbar.

3. Select a shadow style from the pop-up menu.

If you want to remove a shadow from an object, click the Shadow button and select No Shadow. If you want to change the size or color of the shadow, select Shadow Settings to display the Shadow Settings toolbar. From here you can move a shadow up, down, left, or right, or click the Shadow Color button and choose a different color for the shadow.

Adding a 3-D Effect

Word lets you add a variety of 3-D effects to your objects. Follow these steps:

1. Select the object.

2. Click the 3-D button on the Drawing toolbar.

3. Select a 3-D style from the pop-up menu.

Word's 3-D effects come with numerous formatting options, all available when you click the 3-D button and select 3-D Settings to display the 3-D Settings toolbar.

Object Linking and Embedding

When you use Object Linking and Embedding (OLE), you can create a Word document that uses data created and updated in other programs. For example, you can create an Excel worksheet to store financial data, then link or embed that data in your Word document; whenever you update the spreadsheet, your Word document will automatically reflect the changes.

Linking and embedding both allow you to share data between your document and other programs—although they differ in where the source data is stored and how it is updated after you place it in your Word document. When you link an object to your Word document, the source data is stored in its original program, and updated only when you open the original program and edit the original file. When you embed an object in your Word document, you embed the entire data file. Embedded objects become part of your Word file, and are no longer part of the original source file; you modify embedded data from within Word.

Inserting a Linked Object with the Paste Special Command

The easiest way to insert an OLE object from another application into a Word document is to copy that object and then use the Paste Special command to paste a link into your document. Follow these steps:

1. In the source file, select the text, data, image, or object you want to link.
2. Select Edit ➢ Copy to copy the source object.
3. Move to your Word document, and position the insertion point where you want to insert the linked object.
4. Select Edit ➢ Paste Special to display the Paste Special dialog box.
5. Select the object's native format from the As list.
6. Check the Paste Link option.
7. Click OK.

Inserting a Linked Object with the Object Command

The second way to insert a linked object into your document is with the Object command. Follow these steps:

1. Anchor the insertion point where you want to insert the object in your document.
2. Select Insert ➢ Object to display the Object dialog box.
3. Select the Create From File tab.
4. Enter the name of the source file—or click the Browse button to navigate to the source file.

5. Check the Link to File option.

6. Click OK.

Editing Linked Data

To edit the data in a linked object, you have to open the source file and application, and edit the data there. You *cannot* edit the source data from within Word. To edit the source data, follow these steps:

1. Select the linked object.

2. Select Edit ➤ Linked Object ➤ Edit Link.

You edit the data in the source file, save the edited source file, then close the source application. When you return to your Word document, the linked object will be automatically updated.

Embedding Existing Data

You use the Paste Special command to insert existing data from another application as an embedded object, as follows:

1. In the source file, select the text or data or image or object you want to embed.

2. Select Edit ➤ Copy to copy the source object.

3. Move to your Word document, and position the insertion point where you want to insert the linked object.

4. Select Edit ➤ Paste Special to display the Paste Special dialog box.

5. Select the object's native format from the As list.

6. Check the Paste option—*not* the Paste Link option!

7. Click OK.

Creating a New Embedded Object

When you choose to embed an object, you don't have to start with an existing object—you can launch the object's source application *within Word* to create a brand-new object.

Follow these steps:

1. Anchor the insertion point where you want to insert the object in your document.

2. Select Insert ➤ Object to display the Object dialog box.

3. Select the Create New tab.

4. The Object Type list lists all the different documents you can create from the OLE-compatible applications installed on your hard disk. Select an object from this list.

5. Click OK to open the source application.

6. When the source application window opens, create your new object.

7. Close the source application window to permanently embed the object in your Word document.

Editing Embedded Objects

Since the source file for your object is now embedded in your Word file, you have to open the source file and application from within Word. Follow these steps:

1. Select the embedded object.

2. Select Edit ➢ Object ➢ Edit.

Word now opens the source application—within the Word workspace—with the source data loaded. Make the appropriate changes to the source data, then click within your Word document to close the source application and see your changes.

Organizer

Word's Organizer enables you to copy elements and settings from one template or file to another. The Organizer includes four different tabs—for Style, AutoText, Toolbars, and Macro Project Items. You select the source and the destination templates, then choose whether to copy, rename, or delete selected elements.

To use the Organizer, follow these steps:

1. Select Tools ➢ Templates and Add-Ins to display the Templates and Add-Ins dialog box.

2. Click the Organizer button to display the Organizer.

3. To change the source or destination template or file, click the appropriate Close File button, then click the Open File button and select a different template or file.

4. Select the tab containing the element you want to copy, rename, or edit.

5. To copy an element, select the element from the source template list, then click the Copy button to copy it to the destination template.

6. To rename an element in one of the templates, select the element, then click the Rename button to display the Rename dialog box; enter the new name in the New Name box, then click OK.

7. To delete an element from one of the templates, select the element, then click the Delete button.

8. Click OK when done.

Outlines

You use Word's Outline view to quickly and easily organize your document. You can enable Outline view for *any* document—even if you haven't consciously created an outline—by clicking the Outline View button next to the horizontal scrollbar.

In Outline view, higher-level headings appear to the left of lower-level headings, and all non-heading text appears as a single body text level, regardless of what non-heading style is assigned to the text. The highest-level heading in your outline is designated *outline level one*; the next highest-level is outline level two, and so on.

Displaying Specific Levels

Word can display up to nine levels of headings (plus the body text level) within your outline. If you only want to view the major sections of your document, however, you may not want to see all of the outline levels on screen. To display only selected outline levels, click one of the Show Heading level buttons on the Outline toolbar.

To quickly show *all* levels of your outline—including the body text level—click the Show All Headings button. This button is actually a toggle, so clicking the button a second time will *hide* all levels of your outline.

Expanding and Collapsing a Section

If you want to see all the text and subheadings within a certain section of your document—but *not* within all sections—then you can *expand* that section of your outline.

To expand a section of your outline, double-click the "+" icon next to that heading. You can also collapse the text and headings underneath an expanded heading by double-clicking the "+" again. You can expand or collapse sections at any heading level; you could, for example, expand a level-one heading but then collapse a level-two heading underneath the expanded heading.

Displaying the First Line of Text Only

To condense the display of your outline, you can choose to display only the first line of all headings and body text in your outline. Click the Show First Line Only button to condense your display in this fashion.

Assigning Outline Styles

By default, Word's built-in heading styles (Heading 1, Heading 2, and so on) are assigned corresponding outline levels. Any *non-heading* style—including heading styles you've created from scratch—are assigned to the body text level within your outline.

You can assign a new outline level to any style within your document by editing that style's properties. Follow these steps:

1. Position the insertion point anywhere within a paragraph formatted with the style you want to reassign.

2. Select Format ➢ Style to display the Style dialog box.

3. Click the Modify button to display the Modify Style dialog box.

4. Click the Format button and select Paragraph to display the Paragraph dialog box.

5. Select the Indents and Spacing tab.

6. Pull down the Outline Style list and select a different outline level.

7. Click OK to return to the Modify Style dialog box; click OK to return to the Style dialog box; click Cancel to close the Style dialog box.

Promoting and Demoting Outline Levels

To change the outline level of a specific paragraph, you *promote* or *demote* that paragraph within your outline. Promoting a paragraph assigns the next-highest heading style to that paragraph; demoting a paragraph assigns the next-lowest heading style to that paragraph.

To promote a paragraph within your outline, select the paragraph, then click the Promote button on the Outline toolbar (or press Shift+Tab). To demote a paragraph within your outline, select the paragraph, then click the Demote button on the Outline toolbar (or press the Tab key). If you want to demote a paragraph to the body text level, click the Demote to Body Text button.

Rearranging Sections

The easiest way to move an entire section is to use your mouse to grab the "+" icon next to the section's heading. This will automatically select the entire section (including all subheadings and body text, including all collapsed elements); you can then drag the selected section up or down your outline to a new location.

You can also use the Move Up and Move Down buttons on the Outline toolbar to move a selected section up or down. Note, however, that these buttons will only move *selected* elements; if you only select a heading, the Move Up and Move Down buttons will only move the heading, *not* any uncollapsed subheadings or body text underneath the heading.

Outlook

Outlook 2000 includes a utility called the *Journal*. You use the Journal to track the amount of time you spend working on any Office document. When you activate the Journal, it will record when and how long you've had any Word document open for editing.

Activating the Journal

To have the Outlook Journal track the time you spend working on Word documents, follow these steps:

1. From within Outlook, select Tools ➢ Options to display the Options dialog box.
2. Select the Preferences tab.
3. Click the Journal Options button to display the Journal Options dialog box.
4. In the Also Record Files From list, check the Microsoft Word option.
5. Click OK.

Tracking Your Word Sessions

Once you've activated Word tracking, all your Word editing sessions will appear in Outlook's Journal folder. You display the Journal by clicking the Journal button in the Outlook bar.

When the Journal is displayed, you see a list of all files you've opened, organized by date and time. You can choose to list files by day, week, or month; if you choose to display by day, the duration of each open project is indicated by a horizontal bar above each filename.

Viewing a Journal Entry

To display detailed information about a particular document editing session, right-click the file icon and select Open Journal Entry from the pop-up menu. When the Journal entry appears you can view the precise time the file was opened and the duration of the editing session. You can also assign this file to a contact by clicking the Contacts button and selecting a name from your Outlook contact list. Close the Journal entry by clicking the Save and Close button.

Page Numbering

If you're creating long documents, it's important to display page numbers that help readers keep track of where they are within the document.

Inserting a Page Number in Your Text

To insert a page number in your text, follow these steps:

1. Position the insertion point where you want to add the page number.
2. Press Alt+Shift+P.

This inserts a page number field, which automatically calculates the current page number—even if the page breaks change as you edit your document.

Adding Page Numbers to a Header or Footer

To add automatic page numbering to your document's header or footer, follow these steps:

1. Select Insert ➤ Page Numbers to display the Page Numbers dialog box.
2. Pull down the Position list and select either Top of Page (Header) or Bottom of Page (Footer).
3. Pull down the Alignment list and select a horizontal alignment for the page number: Left, Right, Center, Inside, or Outside.
4. To configure the number format of the page number, click the Format button to display the Page Number Format dialog box. Pull down the Number Format list to select a number format, configure any other appropriate settings, and then click OK.
5. If you don't want to show the page number on the first page of your document (if you have a separate title page, for example), *uncheck* the Show Number on First Page option.
6. Click OK.

Changing Page Numbering in Different Sections of Your Document

The Page Number Format dialog box provides options that allow you to change your page numbering for different sections of your document. Follow these steps:

1. If you haven't yet, insert a section break to start a new section in your document.
2. Click the first page of the new section.
3. Select Insert ➤ Page Numbers to display the Page Numbers dialog box.
4. Click the Format button to display the Page Number Format dialog box.
5. To change the starting page number of this section, check the Start At option and select a page number from the Start At list. To continue page numbering from the previous section, check the Continue from Previous Section option.
6. Click OK.

Page Formatting

There are many ways you can format an entire page in Word—from paper size to orientation to backgrounds and borders.

Setting Paper Size

To set the size of your document, follow these steps:

1. Select File ➤ Page Setup to display the Page Setup dialog box.
2. Select the Paper Size tab.
3. Pull down the Paper Size list and select a preconfigured paper type, *or*

   Adjust the Width and Height controls to create a custom paper size.
4. To apply this new size to your entire document, pull down the Apply To list and select Whole Document; to apply this new size from this point forward in your document, select This Point Forward.
5. Click OK.

Setting Orientation

Normal orientation (taller than wide) is called *portrait* orientation. Turning the paper on its side (wider than tall) creates a *landscape* orientation. To change from portrait to landscape mode (or vice versa), follow these steps:

1. Select File ➤ Page Setup to display the Page Setup dialog box.
2. Select the Paper Size tab.
3. Check the Portrait option if you have a tall document; check the Landscape option if you have a wide document.
4. Click OK.

Setting Vertical Text Alignment

In addition to standard horizontal alignment of your text (left, right, centered, or justified), Word enables you to set the *vertical* alignment of all text on your page. To configure your document's vertical text alignment, follow these steps:

1. Select File ➤ Page Setup to display the Page Setup dialog box.
2. Select the Layout tab.
3. Pull down the Vertical Alignment list and select one of the following options: Top, Center, Justified, Bottom.

4. To apply this alignment to your entire document, pull down the Apply To list and select Whole Document; to apply this new size from this point forward in your document (leaving previous pages at their original size), select This Point Forward.

5. Click OK.

Applying a Page Background

To change from a white page to a color background, follow these steps:

1. Select Format ➤ Background.

2. Select a format from the color submenu, *or*

Select More Colors to display the More Colors dialog box and select from a larger palette of colors, *or*

Select Fill Effects to display the Fill Effects dialog box, then select a new fill effect or texture for your background.

3. Click OK.

Applying a Watermark

While you can't use a picture in the background of your printed documents, Word does let you insert a *watermark* (linked to a header or footer) to appear behind your text. Follow these steps:

1. Select View ➤ Header and Footer.

2. Position the insertion point in either the header or footer, then select Insert ➤ Picture ➤ *item*, where item is the type of object (picture, clip art, Word Art, etc.) you want to insert.

3. Double-click the picture to display the Format Picture dialog box, select the Layout tab, select Behind Text, then click OK.

4. Use your mouse to reposition and resize the object as appropriate.

5. Click the Close button on the Header and Footer toolbar.

To view your watermark, switch to Print Layout view (or activate Word's Print Preview).

Adding a Page Border

To add a border to the pages in your document, follow these steps:

1. Select Format ➤ Borders and Shading to display the Borders and Shading dialog box.

2. Select the Page Border tab.

3. Select the type of border you want to apply from the Setting section: None, Box, Shadow, 3-D, or Custom.

4. If you want to change the style of the border, make a selection from the Style list.

5. If you want to change the color of the border, make a selection from the Color list.

6. If you want to change the width of the border, make a selection from the Width list.

7. If you want to turn off (or on) the border for any specific side of your page, click the Top, Bottom, Left, or Right buttons in the Preview section.

8. Pull down the Apply To list and select what part(s) of your document you want to border: Whole Document, This Section, This Section–First Page Only, This Section–All Except First Page.

9. Click OK.

To set the spacing between the border and the text on your page, click the Options button to display the Border and Shading Options dialog box. From here you can select the margin for your border, as well as whether the border appears in front of or behind your text.

Pagination

To control the way paragraphs break across pages, follow these steps:

1. Position the insertion point anywhere within the paragraph you want to format.

2. Select Format ➢ Paragraph to display the Paragraph dialog box.

3. Select the Line and Page Breaks tab.

4. To prevent the last line of a paragraph from printing by itself at the top of the next page, check the Widow/Orphan Control option.

5. To prevent a paragraph from breaking across pages, check the Keep Lines Together option.

6. To keep the current paragraph and the following paragraph on the same page with no page breaks in between, check the Keep with Next option.

7. To force a page break before the current paragraph, check the Page Break Before option.

8. Click OK.

Paragraph Formatting

Paragraph formatting affects how an entire paragraph looks, and is typically applied via the Paragraph dialog box.

Changing Paragraph Alignment

You can set alignment for the current paragraph by clicking the appropriate alignment button on Word's Formatting toolbar, or by following these steps:

1. Select Format ➢ Paragraph to display the Paragraph dialog box.
2. Select the Indents and Spacing tab.
3. Pull down the Alignment list and make a selection.
4. Click OK.

Indenting an Entire Paragraph

To indent a paragraph using the Paragraph dialog box, follow these steps:

1. Select Format ➢ Paragraph to display the Paragraph dialog box.
2. Select the Indents and Spacing tab.
3. In the Indentation section, choose both Left and Right values in inches.
4. Click OK.

You can also change indentation from Word's horizontal ruler. All you have to do is click and drag the left and right indent markers to new positions.

Indenting the First Line of a Paragraph

Word also lets you indent just the first line of a paragraph. You can choose to have the first line either indented or "outdented" as a hanging indent. To set first-line indenting, follow these steps:

1. Select Format ➢ Paragraph to display the Paragraph dialog box.
2. Select the Indents and Spacing tab.
3. In the Indentation section, pull down the Special list and select First Line, Hanging, or (none).
4. Select a value for the indent from the By: list.
5. Click OK.

Setting Spacing between Paragraphs

To apply specific paragraph spacing, follow these steps:

1. Select Format ➢ Paragraph to display the Paragraph dialog box.
2. Select the Indents and Spacing tab.
3. In the Spacing section, select Before value for the space above the current paragraph, and an After value for the space below the paragraph.
4. Click OK.

Setting Line Spacing within a Paragraph

While the Spacing controls in the Paragraph dialog box affect the space above and below the paragraph, you can also control the *line spacing* within your paragraph. Follow these steps:

1. Select Format ➢ Paragraph to display the Paragraph dialog box.

2. Select the Indents and Spacing tab.

3. In the Spacing section, select a new value from the Line Spacing list.

4. Click OK.

Passwords

Word 2000 lets you restrict access to your documents to those users with a password. You can use passwords to keep unauthorized users from making changes to a document, or from even viewing the document.

To password-protect a document, follow these steps:

1. Open the document you want to protect.

2. Select File ➢ Save As to display the Save As dialog box.

3. Click the Tools button on the toolbar to display the pull-down menu.

4. Select General Options to display the Save dialog box.

5. To keep unauthorized users from opening the file at all, enter a password in the Password to Open box.

6. To keep unauthorized users from editing the file (while still allowing them to view the file), enter a password in the Password to Modify box.

7. When prompted, reenter your password(s).

8. When you're returned to the Save As dialog box, click the Save button to save the file with the selected password protection.

Once a file is password protected, anyone trying to open the file will be prompted for a password. When the correct password is entered, the file opens normally. If an incorrect password (or no password) is entered, Word generates an error message without opening the file.

Pictures

Word can work with pictures in all major graphics formats, including .JPG, .GIF, .BMP, .WMP, and .TIF.

Inserting a Picture File

To insert a graphics file into your document, follow these steps:

1. Position the insertion point where you want to add the picture.

2. Select Insert ➤ Picture ➤ From File to display the Insert Picture dialog box.

3. Navigate to the file you want to insert, select the file, and click the Insert button.

Inserting a Scanned or Digital Photograph

Word 2000 lets you import digital photographs directly from any TWAIN-compatible scanner or digital camera. Follow these steps:

1. Select Insert ➤ Picture ➤ From Scanner or Camera to display the Insert Picture from Scanner or Camera dialog box.

2. Pull down the Device list and select the device (scanner or camera) you're using.

3. If you're using this picture in a Web-based document, check the Web Quality option. If you'll be printing this picture in a normal document, check the Print Quality option.

4. If you're scanning an image and using predefined scanner settings, click Insert. If you're scanning an image and want to change image settings—or if you're uploading the image from a digital camera—click Custom Insert to open the software that came with your scanner or camera; make the appropriate adjustments, then click initiate the scan or upload.

If the Insert button is grayed out, it's probably because your scanner software doesn't support automatic scanning; if this is the case, use the Custom Insert button instead.

Formatting Pictures

To format pictures in your document, follow these steps:

1. Select Format ➤ Picture to display the Format Picture dialog box.

2. Select the Colors and Lines tab to format fill color and line style and color.

3. Select the Size tab to size, scale, and rotate your picture.

4. Select the Layout tab to configure text wrapping and object placement.

5. Select the Pictures tab to crop your picture and adjust brightness and contrast.

6. Select the Web tab to enter alternate text if your picture is to be displayed on the Internet.

7. Click OK when done.

Cropping a Picture

If your picture contains extraneous elements that you'd rather not display—or if you simply want to focus on one element within your picture—you can crop the edges of the picture to focus on an interior element.

You can manually crop your picture with the cropping tool from the Picture toolbar—or more precisely crop your picture with controls in the Format Picture dialog box.

To manually crop a picture, follow these steps:

1. From the Picture toolbar, click the Crop button; the cursor changes to a cropping tool.

2. Grab a selection handle and drag it *in* to trim that edge of the picture.

To *precisely* crop a picture from the Format Picture dialog box, follow these steps:

1. Select the picture you want to crop.

2. Select Format ➤ Picture to display the Format Picture dialog box.

3. Select the Picture tab.

4. In the Crop From section, select how much you want to crop from the Left, Right, Top, and Bottom.

5. Click OK.

You can also use this dialog box to undo any cropping you've done to this picture. Just click the Reset button to return the picture to its uncropped state.

Preparing Pictures for the Web

If the picture you've added is intended for viewing on the Web, you can specify *alternate text* to display either while the picture loads, or if the picture *doesn't* load. Follow these steps:

1. Select Format ➤ Picture to display the Format Picture dialog box.

2. Select the Web tab.

3. Enter the alternate text into the large text box.

4. Click OK.

PowerPoint

PowerPoint 2000 is the presentation graphics program included with some versions of Office 2000. Since PowerPoint and Word work extremely well together, Microsoft has introduced special commands into both programs that makes it easy to transfer information back and forth between the two applications.

Sending a Word Outline to PowerPoint

You send a Word document directly to PowerPoint by selecting File ➤ Send To ➤ Microsoft PowerPoint. When you do this, PowerPoint launches with your Word document imported; every Heading 1 paragraph that PowerPoint encounters is used to start a new slide.

Creating Presentation Handouts

To use Word to create handouts or notes based on your PowerPoint presentation, follow these steps:

1. From within PowerPoint, select File ➤ Send To ➤ Microsoft Word to display the Write-Up dialog box.

2. Select one of the first four options—Notes Next to Slides, Blank Lines Next to Slides, Notes Below Slides, or Blank Lines Below Slides.

3. To paste copies of the PowerPoint slides in your Word document, check the Paste option; to paste the slides as links back to the PowerPoint document, check the Paste Link option.

4. Click OK.

Creating a New Document Based on Your Presentation

To import your PowerPoint presentation into Word as an outline, follow these steps:

1. From within PowerPoint, select File ➤ Send To ➤ Microsoft Word to display the Write-Up dialog box.

2. Check the Outline Only option.

3. Click OK.

Word now creates an outline based on your PowerPoint presentation. Slide titles become Heading 1 headings; first-level bullets on each slide become Heading 2 headings; second-level bullets become Heading 3 headings; and so on.

Printing Meeting Minutes and Action Items

PowerPoint lets users take notes or schedule action items during presentations, using the Meeting Minder feature, which can then be exported to Word for editing, formatting, and printing.

To send Meeting Minder notes and items to Word, follow these steps:

1. From within PowerPoint, select Tools ➤ Meeting Minder to display the Meeting Minder dialog box.

2. To display notes, select the Meeting Minutes tab; to display action items, select the Action Items tab.

3. From either tab, click the Export button to display the Meeting Minder Export dialog box.

4. Check the Send Meeting Minutes and Action Items to Microsoft Word option.

5. Click the Export Now button.

Inserting a PowerPoint Slide

Word lets you insert blank PowerPoint slides into your documents. Once a blank slide has been inserted, you can add text to the slide and format the slide, just as you would from within PowerPoint.

Follow these steps to add a single PowerPoint slide to your document:

1. From within Word, select Insert ➢ Object to display the Insert Object dialog box.

2. Check the Create New tab.

3. From the Object Type list, select Microsoft PowerPoint Slide.

4. Click OK.

Once the slide has been added, you double-click the slide to activate the PowerPoint editing mode.

Embedding an Entire Presentation

For the ultimate in integration, you can embed an entire PowerPoint presentation in your Word document.

To embed a presentation, follow these steps:

1. From within Word, select Insert ➢ Object to display the Insert Object dialog box.

2. Check the Create From File tab.

3. Enter the location and name of the PowerPoint presentation file in the File Name box, or click the Browse button to locate the file.

4. Click OK.

The first slide of the PowerPoint presentation now appears onscreen. To run the presentation, double-click the slide.

Print

The fastest way to print a document is with Word's fast print option, which you activate by clicking the Print button on Word's Standard toolbar. When you initiate a fast print of your document, you send your document directly to your default printer—bypassing the Print dialog box and all other configuration options.

If you need to print more than one copy or configure specific printer settings, you need to use Word's Print dialog box for printing. Follow these steps:

1. Select File ≻ Print (or press Ctrl+P) to display the Print dialog box.

2. Select how many copies you want to print with the Number of Copies control.

3. Select which part of the document you want to print from the Print Range section of the dialog box.

4. Make any other adjustments to the print settings, as necessary.

5. Click the Print button to print your document.

Print Preview

To preview your documents onscreen *before* you print them, select File ≻ Print Preview or click the Print Preview button on Word's Standard toolbar. Exit Print Preview by clicking the Close Preview button.

Publisher

Microsoft Publisher is included with many versions of Microsoft Office 2000, and is used to create simple desktop published documents, such as newsletters, brochures, and so on. You can use Word to write and edit your Publisher stories.

Editing Publisher Stories in Word

To edit Publisher text within Word, follow these steps:

1. From within Publisher, select the story or text frame you want to edit.

2. Right-click your mouse to display the pop-up menu.

3. From the pop-up menu, select Change Text ≻ Edit Story in Microsoft Word.

4. Word now launches with the Publisher story or text loaded. Enter or edit text from within Word, as you would a normal document.

5. When you're done editing the story or text in Word, select File ≻ Close & Return to Publication.

Word now closes, and your edited text is automatically inserted into your Publisher document.

Inserting Word Documents into Publisher Documents

You can also insert Word documents directly into Publisher stories or text frames. Follow these steps:

1. From within Publisher, select the story or text frame where you want to insert the Word document.
2. Select Insert ➢ Text File to display the Insert Text File dialog box.
3. Navigate to and select the Word file you want to import.
4. Click OK.

The Word file is now inserted into the selected frame.

Sections

When you need to make major layout changes to different parts of your documents, you use Word's *sections* feature. Word lets you break documents up into multiple sections, with each section having its own formatting and layout.

Starting a New Section

When you need to start a new section in your document, follow these steps:

1. Position your cursor where you want to start a new section.
2. Select Insert ➢ Break to display the Break dialog box.
3. Select one of the four Section Break Types.
4. Click OK.

Note that the new section maintains all the formatting of the previous section—until you change it. At that point, any layout or page formatting changes you make apply only to the current section, not to other sections (either earlier or later) in your document.

Viewing Section Breaks

If you're working in Word's Normal view, you'll see a section break marker wherever a section break occurs. The section break marker will also indicate which type of section break (Next Page, Continuous, Even Page, or Odd Page) it represents.

If you're using Print Layout or Outline views, section breaks are not automatically displayed—and are thus hard to locate. To toggle on section break visibility in these two modes, click the Show/Hide button on Word's Standard tool bar. When toggled on, this command not only displays paragraph marks, but also section, page, column, and text wrapping breaks.

Deleting Section Breaks

To delete a section break—and thus merge the first section with the second section—simply delete the section break marker. Note that when you merge two sections together, the second section assumes the formatting (including header/footer contents and formatting) of the first section.

Copying Section Formatting

All the formatting information for a given section—page layout, margins, page borders, shading, column layout, and so on—are contained within the section break marker. To copy formatting from one section to another, all you have to do is copy the section break marker and paste it at the start of where you want the new, identically formatted section to begin.

Security

Word 2000 enables you to set three different *security levels* to protect against macro viruses; the higher security levels require that any macros included in documents be accompanied by digitally signed certificates of authentication or okayed by you before they're loaded and run. If Word encounters a macro without the proper authentication, it warns you of a potential security problem.

To change Word's security level, follow these steps:

1. Select Tools ➤ Macro ➤ Security to display the Security dialog box.
2. Select the Security Level tab.
3. Choose either High, Medium, or Low security.
4. Click OK.

Sort

When you use Word's Sort command outside of a table, it sorts any selected text by paragraph, as follows:

1. Select the text you want to sort—typically multiple paragraphs, or multiple list items.
2. Select Table ➤ Sort to display the Sort dialog box.
3. Make sure that Paragraphs is selected in the Sort By list.
4. Pull down the Type list and select either text, number, or date.
5. Check whether you're sorting in Ascending or Descending order.
6. Click OK.

Spelling and Grammar

Word's proofing tools are used to catch spelling and grammatical errors in your documents.

Spell Checking as You Type

By default, Word 2000 is set with Automatic Spell Checking enabled. With Automatic Spell Checking, Word checks the spelling of each word as you type it into your document. Any word not found in the spelling dictionary is assumed to be misspelled and flagged with a wavy red underline.

To correct the spelling of an underlined word, follow these steps:

1. Right-click the underlined word.

2. Select one of the recommended spellings from the pop-up menu.

You can also choose to ignore this and all other instances of this particular word by selecting Ignore All from the pop-up menu.

Spell Checking Your Finished Document

You can also choose to check the spelling of your document as a separate operation. To check the spelling of your document, follow these steps:

1. Select Tools ➢ Spelling and Grammar (or click the Spelling and Grammar button on Word's Standard toolbar).

2. When Word's spell checker finds a potentially misspelled word, it displays the Spelling dialog box.

3. To accept a suggested correction, select the correction from the Suggestions list and click the Change button. Click Change All to change all occurrences of this word throughout your document.

4. To edit the misspelled word manually, position your cursor in the Not in Dictionary box, make your changes, then click either the Change or Change All button.

5. To add the selected word to the spelling dictionary, click the Add button.

6. To ignore the selected word, click the Ignore button; to ignore all appearances of the word throughout your entire document, click Ignore All.

After you change or ignore a misspelling, Word's spell checker moves to the next potentially misspelled word in your document. When the spell checker reaches the end of your document, it displays a dialog box informing you that the spell checking is complete.

Correcting Your Grammar as You Type

When Automatic Grammar Checking is enabled, Word checks your document as it is being typed. Any grammatically questionable phrases are flagged with a wavy green underline.

To examine (and possibly fix) a flagged phrase, follow these steps:

1. Right-click anywhere within the phrase to display a pop-up menu with grammatical advice.

2. To edit the flagged phrase, return to your document and make the appropriate changes.

3. To ignore any possible grammatical errors in the phrase, select Ignore.

Correcting the Grammar in Your Finished Document

To run Word's grammar checker at the same time you run Word's spell checker, go to the Spelling & Grammar tab in the Options dialog box and check the Check Grammar with Spelling option. With this option selected, you run the grammar checker (and the spell checker) when you select Tools ➢ Spelling and Grammar or click the Spelling and Grammar button on Word's Standard toolbar.

Styles

If you have a preferred paragraph formatting that you use over and over, you don't have to format each paragraph individually; you can assign all your formatting to a paragraph *style*, and then apply that style to multiple paragraphs across your entire document. Styles include formatting for fonts, paragraphs, tabs, borders, language, and frames, and numbering.

Viewing Styles

There are a number of ways to view the styles available in a word document:

- The style assigned to the current paragraph is always displayed in the Style box on the Formatting toolbar. The most frequently used styles in your current document are also listed here; just pull down the Style list (or press Ctrl+Shift+S) to view all available styles.

- To view all paragraph/style associations within your document, use Word's Normal view (click the Normal View button) and activate the Style area (select Tools ➢ Options to display the Options dialog box, then select the View tab and select at least a 1" value for Style Area Width).

- To view *all* styles available in the current template, select Format ➢ Style to display the Style dialog box. You can then pull down the List list to select what styles you want to list: just those Styles In Use, All Styles, or User-Defined Styles.
- To view the specific text and paragraph properties of the style assigned to a particular paragraph, press Shift+F1 (or select Help ➢ What's This?). When the cursor changes to a question mark, click any character within the paragraph, and Word displays a pop-up box listing the properties of the assigned paragraph style.

Applying a Style

To apply a style to a specific paragraph, follow these steps:

1. Position the insertion point anywhere in the paragraph.
2. Pull down the Style list on Word's Formatting toolbar (or press Ctrl+Shift+S).
3. Select a style.

Modifying a Style by Example

You can configure Word so that any time you manually change the formatting for a paragraph, the style for that paragraph is automatically updated to reflected the new formatting. This option is enabled separately for each style in your document.

To turn on this option for a specific style, follow these steps:

1. Select Format ➢ Style to open the Style dialog box.
2. Select the style you wish to enable.
3. Click the Modify button to display the Modify Style dialog box.
4. Check the Automatically Update option.
5. Click OK.

With this option enabled, all you have to do to globally modify a style is change any paragraph formatting in any paragraph using the selected style. All other paragraphs using the same style will be updated to reflect your changes.

Modifying a Style Manually

You can manually modify any or all properties of any style from the Modify Style dialog box. Follow these steps:

1. Select Format ➢ Style to display the Style dialog box.
2. Select the style you want to edit.
3. Click the Modify button to display the Modify Style dialog box.
4. Click the Format button to display a list of properties to format.

5. Select the style property you want to edit.

6. When the selected property dialog box appears, make your changes and click OK to return to the Modify dialog box.

7. To change the style that automatically follows this style in your document, select a new style from the Style For the Following Paragraph list.

8. To make your changes apply to *all* documents using this template, check the Add to Template option. To have your changes affect only the current document, leave this option unchecked.

9. Click Apply to apply this style to the current paragraph and close the dialog box, or click Cancel to close the dialog box without applying the style.

This is the preferred method for modifying styles, as you can easily see the current settings and go directly to the property you want to change.

Creating a New Style by Example

The easiest way to create a new style is to format a paragraph as you'd like the style to appear, and then use that paragraph as the basis for the new style. Follow these steps:

1. Format a paragraph exactly as you want your style to appear.

2. Select the entire paragraph.

3. Click inside the Style box on Word's Formatting toolbar, and type over the existing style with a name for your new style.

4. Press Enter.

You have now created a new style, based on the formatting in the selected paragraph.

Creating a New Style in Detail

A more precise method of creating a new style involves selecting an existing style, modifying it, and saving the new style under a new name. This method allows more sophisticated formatting options than does the simpler "by example" method just discussed.

To create a new style using the detailed method, follow these steps:

1. Select Format ➢ Style to display the Style dialog box.

2. Click the New button to display the New Style dialog box.

3. Enter a name for your new style in the Name box.

4. Pull down the Based On list and select the existing style on which you're basing the new style.

5. Pull down the Style for the Following Paragraph list and select which style should follow this style in your document.

6. To change a specific property, click the Format button and select the style property you want to edit; when the selected property dialog box appears, make your changes and click OK to return to the New Style dialog box.

7. To add your new style to all documents based on this template, check the Add to Template option; to add this style only to the current document, leave this option unchecked.

8. To assign your new style to a shortcut key, click the Shortcut Key button to display the Customize Keyboard dialog box; enter the shortcut key in the Press New Shortcut Key box, then click Assign.

9. Click OK.

Your new style will now appear in the Style list on the Formatting toolbar, and is available for use in the current document.

Subscriptions

Available only to users of a network with the Microsoft Office Server Extensions installed, Word 2000's new Subscriptions feature enables you to be notified via e-mail of any selected changes made to a specific document or folder.

To subscribe to a document or folder, follow these steps:

1. Open the document or folder you want to be notified about.

2. Click the Subscribe button on the Discussions toolbar to display the Document Subscription dialog box.

3. If you're subscribing to a specific document, check the File option. If you're subscribing to all the files within a folder, check the Folder option, and select an option from the Modified By list.

4. Pull down the When list and select the specific conditions for when you want to be notified.

5. Enter your e-mail address in the Address box.

6. Pull down the Time list and select when or how often you want to notified of changes.

7. Click OK.

To cancel your subscription to a document or folder, click the Cancel This Subscription hyperlink in any notification e-mail message you receive about that document or folder.

Symbols and Special Characters

To insert symbols and special characters into your text, follow these steps:

1. Position the insertion point where you want to insert the symbol or special character.

2. Select Insert ➤ Symbol to display the Symbol dialog box.

3. Select the Symbol tab to display all symbol characters from all installed font families; select the Special Character tab to display all special characters in the current font family.

4. On the Symbol tab, select the Font family that contains the symbol you want, then either scroll through all characters or jump to a subset of characters by selecting an option from the Subset list.

5. Click the symbol or special character you want to insert.

6. Click the Insert button.

This procedure adds the symbol or special character at the insertion point, and keeps the Symbol dialog box open for additional use. To close the Symbol dialog box, click Cancel.

Tables

A table is a great way to organize information, using a structured series of rows and columns. Looking somewhat like a spreadsheet, a table in Word can span multiple pages and its cells can contain both text and graphics.

Inserting a Table—Precisely

The most precise way to insert a table is to use the Insert Table dialog box. Follow these steps:

1. Select Table ➤ Insert ➤ Table to display the Insert Table dialog box.

2. In the Table Size section, select the Number of Columns and the Number of Rows.

3. In the AutoFit Behavior section, select whether you want your columns to have a Fixed Column Width (and if so, if you want the width to be determined Automatically, or if you want to select a column width manually); whether you want your columns to be automatically size to the width of their contents (AutoFit to Contents); or whether you want your table and its columns to automatically size to the width of a Web browser (AutoFit to Window).

4. If you want to apply a predesigned format to your table, click the AutoFormat button to display the Table AutoFormat dialog box; select a format and click OK.

5. If you want the options you selected to apply to all new tables you create, check the Set As Default for New Tables option.

6. Click OK to create the table at your document's insertion point.

Inserting a Table via a Grid

Another way to insert a table is to visually select the number of rows and columns it should contain. This method is available when you click the Insert Table button on Word's Standard toolbar, as follows:

1. Click the Insert Table button on Word's Standard toolbar to display the pull-down grid.

2. Using your mouse—and starting from the top left corner—drag your cursor over the number of rows and columns you want your table to contain.

3. When you have the correct number of rows and columns selected, click your mouse button; a table drawn to you specifications is added at your document's insertion point.

Drawing a New Table

When you click the Tables and Borders button on Word's Standard toolbar, you display the Tools and Borders toolbar. On this toolbar is the Draw Table command, which lets you draw borders and gridlines on your page to define your column graphically, as follows:

1. Click the Tables and Border button on Word's Standard toolbar to display the Tables and Borders toolbar.

2. From the Tables and Borders toolbar, click the Draw Table button.

3. The cursor changes to a pencil shape. Move the cursor to where you want to place the top left corner of your table, then click and hold your mouse button while dragging the cursor down and to the right; release the mouse button when you've reached the bottom right corner of your table.

4. Use the pencil-shaped cursor to "draw" lines within the table border you just created. Draw a horizontal line to represent a gridline separating two rows; draw a vertical line to represent a gridline separating two columns.

5. If you want to erase a gridline you've drawn, click the Eraser button on the Tables and Borders toolbar and use your mouse to "erase" the line in question.

Use this drawing method when you need to create a table with an unusual row-and-column arrangement.

Converting from Text to Table

You can take any existing text in your document and turn it into a table. This works best if the text you want to convert is table-like, with tabs inserted to separate elements within lines.

To convert text to a table, follow these steps:

1. Select the text you want to convert.

2. Select Table ➢ Convert ➢ Text to Table to display the Convert Text to Table dialog box.

3. Word tries to figure out the best way to create a table from your selected text, and enters what it thinks are the proper settings in this dialog box. Confirm or change the settings as appropriate, then click OK.

Converting from Table to Text

You can also take an existing Word table and turn it into standard text—with no rows or columns. To do this, follow these steps:

1. Select the entire table—or that part of the table you want to convert.

2. Select Table ➢ Convert ➢ Table to Text to display the Convert Table to Text dialog box.

3. Select how you want the column breaks to convert—into paragraphs, tabs, commas, or some other character.

4. Click OK to convert the table.

Word now takes your table and turns it into standard text.

Inserting a Row or Column

To insert a new row or column into your table, follow these steps:

1. Select the row or column next to where you want to add the new row or column.

2. Select Table ➢ Insert, and then choose Rows Above, Rows Below, Columns to the Left, or Columns to the Right.

Deleting a Row or Column

To delete a row or column from your table, follow these steps:

1. Select the row or column you want to delete.

2. Select either Table ➢ Delete Columns or Table ➢ Delete Rows.

Merging Cells

If you want the contents of one cell to spread across several rows or columns, then you can *merge* that cell with other cells to create a single large cell. Follow these steps:

1. Select the cells you want to merge.
2. Select Table ➢ Merge Cells.

Splitting Cells

To split apart any cells you've previously merged, follow these steps:

1. Select the merged cell.
2. Select Table ➢ Split Cells.

Resizing Your Table to Fit Its Contents

Word 2000's new AutoFit command automatically resizes your table's columns to fit the width of their contents. To use AutoFit, follow these steps:

1. Position your insertion point anywhere in your table.
2. Select Table ➢ AutoFit ➢ AutoFit to Contents.

Once you activate AutoFit, your table's columns will resize themselves automatically as you enter new text into each cell. To turn *off* this interactive AutoFit feature, select Table ➢ AutoFit ➢ Fixed Column Width.

Distributing Rows and Columns Evenly

If you'd rather your columns be the identical width, follow these steps:

1. Select the columns you want to resize.
2. Select Table ➢ AutoFit ➢ Distribute Columns Equally.

A similar command exists for equally sizing rows in your table. Select the rows you want to resize, then select Table ➢ AutoFit ➢ Distribute Rows Equally.

Applying Borders and Gridlines

To add or modify the borders and gridlines in your table, follow these steps:

1. With the insertion point anywhere in your table, select Format ➢ Borders and Shading to display the Borders and Shading dialog box.
2. Select the Borders tab.
3. Select the type of border you want to apply from the Setting section: None, Box, All, Grid, or Custom.

4. If you want to change the style of the border, make a selection from the Style list.

5. If you want to change the color of the border, make a selection from the Color list.

6. If you want to change the width of the border, make a selection from the Width list.

7. To apply the border style, color, and width to any side border or inside gridline of your table, click the appropriate line segment in the preview diagram.

8. Make sure that Table is selected in the Apply To list.

9. Click OK.

Remember, you can select different border styles and colors for the outside border and the inside gridlines of your table. Whatever selections are made in the Style/Color/Width section apply when you click a line segment in the preview diagram.

Applying Shading

You can add color shading to your entire table or to selected cells by following these steps:

1. With the insertion point anywhere in your table (or with specific cells selected), select Format ➤ Borders and Shading to display the Borders and Shading dialog box.

2. Select the Shading tab.

3. Select a shading color from the Fill section; click the More Colors button to choose from an expanded palette of colors.

4. Select a shading percent from the Style list.

5. To apply the shading to the entire table, pull down the Apply To list and select Table; to apply the shading to selected cells, select Cell.

6. Click OK.

Formatting the Entire Table Automatically

The easiest way to apply formatting to your entire table is to use Word's AutoFormat command. With this command you can choose from dozens of predesigned table formats (affecting borders, gridlines, shading, and fonts)—and apply them to your table with a click of your mouse.

To apply an AutoFormat to your table, follow these steps:

1. With your insertion point anywhere in your table, select Table ➤ Table Auto-Format to display the Table AutoFormat dialog box.

2. From the Formats to Apply section, select those elements to which you want to apply formatting: Borders, Shading, Font Color, or AutoFit.

3. Select whether you want to apply "special formats" to your table's Heading Rows, First Column, Last Row, or Last Column.

4. Select the table format you want from the Formats list; you can preview each format (with your specific options applied) in the Preview section of the dialog box.

5. Click OK to AutoFormat your table.

Sorting Cells

Once you've entered text or numbers into a table, you might find that you want to re-order the way this data appears. To sort your table, follow these steps:

1. Select all the rows and columns in your table that you want to sort—including the header row.

2. Select Table ➢ Sort to display the Sort dialog box.

3. If your table has a header row, check the Header Row option; if not, check No Header Row.

4. Pull down the Sort By list and select which column you want to sort by.

5. Pull down the Type list and select what type of data is in the selected column (text, number, or date).

6. Check whether you want to sort in Ascending (1,2,3 or a,b,c) or Descending (3,2,1 or c,b,a) order.

7. If you want to subsort by a second column, select a column in the Then By list, select the Type of data, and choose an Ascending or Descending sort.

8. If you want to subsort by a *third* column, fill in the information in the last Then By section.

9. Click OK to sort your table.

Totalling Numbers in Your Table

To quickly total a row or column of numbers within your table, follow these steps:

1. Position the insertion point in a blank cell at the bottom of a column of numbers, or in a blank cell at the end of a row of numbers.

2. Click the AutoSum button on the Tables and Borders toolbar.

AutoSum automatically totals all the numbers in the previous cells, and inserts the total in the current cell.

Using Formulas in Your Table

You can create simple formulas within any Word table cell, using common algebraic operators, such as + and –, to add and subtract. In addition to the algebraic operators, Word formulas can also contain numbers, references to cells within your table, and *functions*.

To insert a formula in your table, follow these steps:

1. Position the insertion point in the cell that will contain the formula.
2. Select Table ➢ Formula to display the Formula dialog box.
3. Enter your formula into the Formula box, starting with an equal sign (=), and then enter the rest of your formula *after* the equal sign.
4. To add a function to your formula, pull down the Paste Function list and select the function you want to insert.
5. Click OK to add the formula to your table.

Tables of Authorities

Citations are used in many legal documents to cite cases, rulings, statutes, and other items of relevance to the current document. You mark citations in your document similar to the way you mark index entries, and then create a master list of citations—called a *table of authorities*—at the end of your document.

Marking Citations

Follow these steps to mark citations in your document:

1. Select the first occurrence of a citation in your document.
2. Press Alt+Shift+I to open the Mark Citation dialog box.
3. The selected citation appears in the Select Text Box. Edit this text as you want it displayed in the table of authorities.
4. Pull down the Category list and select the category for this citation.
5. Edit the text in the Short Citation box as appropriate (typically only the case reference).
6. Click Mark to mark this selection, or Mark All to mark all occurrences of this citation.

Building a Table of Authorities

Once you have all the citations marked in your document, you can build your table of authorities (TOA). Building a TOA is very similar to building an index or a TOC; follow these steps:

1. Anchor the insertion point where you want to insert the table of authorities.
2. Select Insert ➢ Index and Tables to display the Index and Tables dialog box.
3. Select the Table of Authorities tab.

4. Select what type of authority to include in your TOA from the Category list. By default, Word includes all citation types in your TOA; you can choose to create different TOAs for different categories of citations.

5. If you want to replace any instance of five or more references to the same authority with the word *Passim*, check the Use Passim option.

6. To retain the original character formatting for long citations, check the Keep Original Formatting option.

7. Select a tab leader (for the space between the citation and the page number) from the Tab Leader list.

8. Select a predesigned TOA format from the Formats list, or click the Modify button to modify individual TOA styles.

9. When all the options are selected, click OK to build the table of authorities.

You can create one TOA that includes all the different authorities in your document, or different TOAs for each specific type of authority.

Tables of Contents

To build a logical table of contents (TOC), your document needs to be constructed in a logical manner. The most important thing to remember is that you have to assign specific styles to different levels of headings within your document. You also have to be *consistent* when you assign these styles; don't assign Heading 1 to one chapter head and Heading 2 to another.

Word creates a table of contents based on these heading styles—as well as any individual entries you mark separately. When you create a TOC, Word looks for every paragraph formatted with a specific style, and uses those paragraphs as TOC entries. So, if Heading 1 is assigned to the first-level listing in your TOC, all paragraphs formatted as Heading 1 are listed at first-level entries in your TOC.

Marking a TOC Entry

To mark a TOC entry separate from the heading style entries, follow these steps:

1. Select the text you want to appear as the TOC entry.

2. Press Alt+Shift+O to display the Mark Table of Contents Entry dialog box.

3. If necessary, edit the text in the Entry box to reflect how you want the TOC entry to appear.

4. Make sure that *C* is selected in the Table Identifier list.

5. Pull down the Level list and select the TOC level you want to apply to this entry.

6. Click OK.

Building a Table of Contents

Word builds a TOC from selected heading styles in your document and from entries you've marked manually; specific styles are assigned to specific levels in your TOC, and Word does the rest automatically.

Follow these steps to insert a table of contents in your document.

1. Anchor the insertion point where you want to insert the table of contents.
2. Select Insert ➤ Index and Tables to display the Index and Tables dialog box.
3. Select the Table of Contents tab.
4. If you want to show page numbers in your TOC, check the Show Page Numbers option. If you check this option, you can also select to right-align your page numbers by checking the Right Align Page Numbers option.
5. Select a design for your TOC from the Formats list; if you want to customize your TOC design, click the Modify button to modify the styles used in your TOC.
6. Select how many levels you want to display in your TOC from the Show Heads list.
7. To assign different heading styles to specific TOC levels, click the Options button to display the Table of Contents Options dialog box. Check the Styles option, then a number in the TOC Level box next to each Available Style you want to include in your TOC. For example, if you want the Heading 1 style to be the first level in your index, enter **1** in the Heading 1 TOC Level box. Click OK when done to return to the Index and Tables dialog box.
8. When all options are selected, click OK to build the table of contents.

Updating Your Table of Contents

Whenever you modify your document, you'll need to update your TOC. To do this, select the entire TOC, then press F9.

Tables of Figures

If your document includes a lot of figures, tables, or equations, you might want to create a *table of figures* listing all the figures used in your document. You create a table of figures (TOF) similar to the way you create a table of contents, and you can create separate tables for figures, tables, and equations.

To insert a table of figures into your document, follow these steps:

1. Anchor the insertion point where you want to insert the table of figures.
2. Select Insert ➤ Index and Tables to display the Index and Tables dialog box.

3. Select the Table of Figures tab.

4. If you want to show page numbers in your TOC, check the Show Page Numbers option. If you check this option, you can also select to right-align your page numbers by checking the Right Align Page Numbers option, and then select a specific tab leader from the Tab Leader list.

5. Select a design for your TOF from the Formats list; if you want to customize your TOF design, click the Modify button to modify the styles used in your TOF.

6. Pull down the Caption Label list to select what kind of table you want to build: Figure, Table, or Equation.

7. If you want to base your TOF on a style other than Caption, Table, or Equation, click the Options dialog box to display the Table of Figures Options dialog box. Select an alternative style or table identifier, then click OK to return to the Index and Tables dialog box.

8. When all the options are selected, click OK to build your table of figures.

Tabs

You can use tabs in your text to align blocks of text or indent individual lines. Word allows you to use multiple tabs on a line, so you can create multi-column lists without inserting a formal table in your text.

Setting Tabs with the Ruler

The easiest way to insert tab stops is via the horizontal ruler. Follow these steps:

1. Click the Tab button (at the far left of the horizontal ruler) until it changes to the type of tab you want to insert.

2. Click the horizontal ruler where you want to insert a tab stop.

You can move any tab on the ruler by grabbing it with your mouse and dragging it to a new position. To remove a tab, simply drag it off the ruler.

Setting Tabs with the Tabs Dialog Box

If you want to set more precise tab stops, or if you want to use *leader characters* in between tabs, you need to use the Tabs dialog box. Follow these steps:

1. Select Format ➢ Tabs to display the Tabs dialog box.

2. Enter the position for the tab stop (in inches from the left margin) in the Tab Stop Position box.

3. Choose an alignment for the tab stop.

4. Choose a leader character for the tab.

5. Click the Set button to set this tab.

You can set multiple tab stops for any given paragraph. You can also delete all tab stops in the current paragraph by clicking the Clear button.

Templates

Any new Word document you create is based on what Word calls a *template*. A template is a specific combination of styles and settings, including page layout settings, fonts, keyboard shortcuts, menus, AutoText entries, macros, and other special formatting.

When you create a new document, you select (from the New dialog box) the document template on which you wish to base your new document.

Loading a Template

When you manually load a template or add-in, it remains loaded for the current Word session only. If you quit and then restart Word, the template or add-in is not automatically reloaded.

To load a template into your current document, follow these steps:

1. Select Tools ➢ Templates and Add-Ins to display the Templates and Add-Ins dialog box.

2. If the template you want to load is listed in the Global Templates and Add-Ins list, check the box next to that item.

3. If the template you want is *not* displayed, click the Add button to display the Add Template dialog box. Navigate to and select the template you want to use, then click OK to return to the Templates and Add-Ins dialog box. The template should now be listed; return to Step 2 and execute that procedure.

4. Click OK when finished.

Switching Templates

To change the template used by the current document—which is different from simply using the features of a template by temporarily loading it into your document—you have to *attach* a new template to the document. This template then replaces the template previously attached. Follow these steps:

1. Select Tools ➢ Templates and Add-Ins to display the Templates and Add-Ins dialog box.

2. Click the Attach button.

3. When the Attach Template dialog box appears, select the template you want, then click OK.

4. If you want to update all the styles in your document to reflect the styles in the new document template, check the Automatically Update Document Styles option.

5. Click OK when done.

Making Changes to an Existing Template

You can customize any of Word's existing templates by changing any of the template's elements—styles, fonts, page settings, and so on. When you save your modifications to a template, the next document you create based on that template will reflect those changes.

To change an existing template, follow these steps:

1. Select File ➤ Open to display the Open dialog box.

2. Pull down the Files of Type list and select Document Template.

3. Navigate to the folder containing the template you want to modify.

4. Select the folder to modify and then click the Open button.

5. Make whatever changes you want to the template.

6. When you're done modifying the template, select File ➤ Save (or click the Save button on Word's Standard toolbar).

Creating a New Template Based on an Existing Template

The easiest way to create a new template is to base it on an existing template, then make the appropriate modifications. Just follow these steps:

1. Select File ➤ New to open the New dialog box.

2. Select the tab that contains the template on which you want to base your new template.

3. Select the template on which you want to base your new template.

4. Check the Template option in the Create New section.

5. Click OK to open the template.

6. Make whatever changes you want to the template.

7. When you're done creating the template, select File ➤ Save As to display the Save As dialog box.

8. Enter the name for your new template in the File Name box.

9. Pull down the Save As Type list and select Document Template.

10. Use the Save In list to navigate to and select the folder where you want to save the template. By default, Word will save the template in the \Windows\Application Data\Microsoft\Templates folder and place it on the General tab in the New dialog box.

11. Click the Save button.

Creating a New Template Based on an Existing Document

You can turn any *document*—including the document's text and graphics—into a template. This is a great way to create a template for form letters or for documents with a lot of boilerplate text. Just follow these steps:

1. From with the document you want to save as a template, select File ➢ Save As to display the Save As dialog box.

2. Enter the name for your new template in the File Name box.

3. Pull down the Save As Type list and select Document Template.

4. Use the Save In list to navigate to and select the folder where you want to save the template. By default, Word will save the template in the \Windows\Application Data\Microsoft\Templates folder and place it on the General tab in the New dialog box.

5. Click the Save button.

Text Boxes

To add a text box to your document, follow these steps:

1. Select Insert ➢ Text Box (or click the Text Box button on the Drawing toolbar).

2. Your cursor changes to a crosshair shape; position the cursor in your document and draw the text box with your mouse.

To add text to a text box, simply position your cursor inside the text box; this should activate the insertion point. Once the insertion point starts blinking, you can start typing.

Thesaurus

In Word 2000, you can choose to access the full thesaurus, or to display a short list of possible synonyms.

Using the Full Thesaurus

To use Word's thesaurus, follow these steps:

1. Position the insertion point anywhere in the word you wish to look up—or simply highlight the word.

2. Select Tools ➢ Language ➢ Thesaurus (or press Shift+F7) to display the Thesaurus dialog box.

3. If the selected word has more than one definition, select the proper meaning from the Meanings list.

4. Select a word from the Replace With Synonym list.

5. To look up synonyms of the selected synonym, click Look Up; click Previous to return to the original word.

6. To replace the selected word with the selected synonym, click Insert.

Looking Up Synonyms Quickly

Word 2000 also offers the option of displaying a short list of synonyms directly from a pop-up menu. Follow these steps:

1. Just right-click the desired word.

2. Select Synonyms from the pop-up menu.

3. Select any of the synonyms displayed on the submenu, or select Thesaurus to display the more full-featured Thesaurus dialog box.

Toolbars

Word 2000 contains sixteen built-in toolbars, two of which—Standard and Formatting—are displayed by default at the top of the Word workspace. Other toolbars can be displayed as needed, and you can move any toolbar to occupy any part of your screen.

Displaying or Hiding Toolbars

To display or hide a toolbar, follow these steps:

1. Select View ➢ Toolbars to display a submenu listing all available toolbars.

2. Check those toolbars you want to display, and uncheck those you want to hide.

Moving Toolbars

You can move any toolbar to any area of the screen by grabbing the thick handle on the far left of the toolbar with your mouse and dragging the toolbar to a new position. If you drag a toolbar to any side of the screen the toolbar automatically "docks" to the side. If you drop the toolbar in the middle of the screen, it remains there in a floating window.

Adding and Removing Toolbar Buttons

To add and remove toolbar buttons from any toolbar, follow these steps:

1. Select Tools ➤ Customize to display the Customize dialog box.
2. To remove a button from any visible toolbar, use your mouse to drag the button off the toolbar.
3. To add a button to any visible toolbar, select the Commands tab in the Customize dialog box, select a category from the Category list, select a command from the Command list, then use your mouse to drag the command from the dialog box onto the toolbar.
4. Click Close when done.

You can also add and remove toolbar buttons directly from the toolbar, without first opening the Customize dialog box. To edit a toolbar in place, click the More Buttons button at the end any docked toolbar, click the Add or Remove Buttons button to display a list of available buttons, and then check those buttons you want to display.

Creating New Toolbars

To create a new toolbar, follow these steps:

1. Select Tools ➤ Customize to display the Customize dialog box.
2. Select the Toolbars tab.
3. Click the New button.
4. When the New Toolbar dialog box appears, enter the new toolbar's name in the Toolbar Name box.
5. Select which template(s) this toolbar is assigned to from the Make Toolbar Available To pull-down list.
6. Click OK.

Track Changes

Word offers the capability for multiple users to edit a document—and for each user's comments and changes to be tracked individually. The author of the original document can then review the editing changes, and choose to accept or reject any change made to the document.

Enabling Revision Tracking

When revision tracking is enabled, Word inserts revision marks to highlight all changes to the original document. Later, when you review the changes, you can easily see what has been changed, and by whom—since each reviewer's changes are marked with a different color.

To turn on revision tracking, follow these steps:

1. Open the document to be edited.

2. Select Tools ➢ Track Changes ➢ Highlight Changes to display the Highlight Changes dialog box.

3. Check the Track Changes While Editing option.

4. Click OK.

Merging Revisions from Multiple Reviewers

You may have distributed individual copies of your document for review by several reviewers. If so, Word enables you to *merge* all the changes from all the different versions of the document into a single document, which you can then review in a single pass. To merge revised documents, follow these steps:

1. Open the original document.

2. Select Tools ➢ Merge Documents to display the Select File to Merge Into Current Document dialog box.

3. Select one of the files to merge, then click OK.

4. Repeat steps 2 and 3 to merge multiple documents.

Your original document now displays all the changes and comments made by each of the reviewers, with each reviewer tracked in a different color.

Accepting Changes

When you accept a change into your document, you permanently add that change to your text, and remove all revision marks. To accept a change, follow these steps:

1. Position the insertion point somewhere within the changed text.

2. Click the Accept Change button on the Reviewing toolbar.

You can also choose to accept all the changes in the document with a single command. Select Tools ➢ Track Changes ➢ Accept or Reject Changes to display the Accept or Reject Changes dialog box, then click the Accept All button.

Rejecting Changes

When you reject a change to your document, you permanently delete that change from your text, and remove all revision marks. Follow these steps:

1. Position the insertion point somewhere within the changed text.

2. Click the Reject Change button on the Reviewing toolbar.

You can also choose to reject all the changes in your document with a single command. Select Tools ➤ Track Changes ➤ Accept or Reject Changes to display the Accept or Reject Changes dialog box, then click the Reject All button.

Undo/Redo

To reverse your most recent action, click the Undo button on Word's Standard toolbar, or select Edit ➤ Undo. To undo additional actions, continue clicking the Undo button; you can also display a list of all actions available for undoing by clicking the down arrow on the Undo button.

To *redo* any action you've undone, click the Redo button (next to the Undo button on Word's Standard toolbar). Like the Redo button, you can click the button to redo one action at a time, or click the down arrow on the button to display a list of all actions that can be redone.

User Information

When you first install Word 2000 you are prompted to enter a few bits of personal information—your name, initials, and address. This information is used both to identify your documents and as default information for certain templates and wizards. You can change this user information by following these steps:

1. Select Tools ➤ Options to display the Options dialog box.
2. Select the User Information tab.
3. Edit or enter the appropriate information.
4. Click OK.

Versions

Word's *versioning* feature enables you to save a copy of your document in each stage of development. When you enable this feature, Word saves the current version of your document within the current file. You can then, at a later time, choose to view any saved version from within your main document file.

Saving the Current Version

To manually save the current version of the file within the current document, follow these steps:

1. From within your document, select File ➤ Versions to display the Versions dialog box.

2. Click the Save Now button to display the Save Versions dialog box.

3. Enter any comments about this version of your document, then click OK.

Viewing a Previous Version

Each time you save a version, Word records the date and time the version was saved, as well as the name of the person who made the changes. You can then choose to view any of the saved versions, in a separate window, at any time.

To view a saved version, follow these steps:

1. From within your document, select File ➤ Versions to display the Versions dialog box.

2. Select a version from the Existing Versions list.

3. Click the Open button.

Once a previous version is open, you can choose to save that version as a separate file (by using the Save As command), or to print that version. You can also delete a previous version by selecting it from the Existing Versions list and clicking the Delete button.

Visual Basic Editor

Visual Basic for Applications—*VBA*, for short—is a variant of Microsoft's Visual Basic programming language. VBA is used to create *programs* (called *projects*); each Word document or template is a separate project, which consists of multiple elements—objects, modules, forms, and references to other documents or templates. Each element contains multiple lines of programming *code*, in the form of *statements* and *procedures*.

To create a VBA program, you use the *Visual Basic Editor* (VB Editor). The VB Editor is a program separate from Word that includes the menus and toolbars and commands necessary to create a full-featured VBA program.

You launch the VB Editor from within Word by following these steps:

1. Open the document that contains the macros you want to edit.

2. Select Tools ➤ Macro ➤ Visual Basic Editor.

Views

Word allows you to view a document in a fashion that best suits your own particular needs. All four views are "live," in that you can fully edit all text and graphics from any View. You switch views by clicking the appropriate view button next to the horizontal scrollbar, or by selecting the view from Word's View menu.

Word's four Views are:

Normal View Displays your document with a simplified layout. You'll see all your text normally, but certain types of graphic objects, backgrounds, headers and footers, and pictures won't be displayed.

Web Layout View Used to work on documents that will be displayed on the Web. In this view you can see all elements of your document (including graphics and backgrounds) as they would be displayed in a Web browser.

Print Layout View Displays all the elements on your page (including graphics, headers and footers, and backgrounds) as they appear when printed.

Outline View Displays your document as an outline. While headers and footers, graphics, and backgrounds do not appear in this view, you can collapse an outlined document to see only the main headings, or expand a document to show all (or selected) headings and body text.

In addition to the four editing Views, Word 2000 also includes two *preview* views, both accessible from the File menu. Print Preview displays your current document exactly as it will appear on the printed page, while Web Page Preview opens your Web browser and displays your current document as a Web page.

Web Documents

There are three ways to create a Web page with Word 2000. You can simply save an existing document in HTML format; you can walk through the step-by-step instructions of the Web Page Wizard; or you can start a Web page from scratch by using one of Word 2000's built-in Web page templates.

Saving a Document in HTML Format

Any Word document can be saved as a Web page by following these steps:

1. From within the document, select File ➤ Save As Web Page to display the Save As dialog box.
2. Make sure Web Page is selected from the Save As Type list.
3. Assign a name and location for your page.
4. Click the Save button.

When you save a Word document as a Web page, the elements of your document are automatically coded so that they appear in a similar fashion when viewed with a Web browser. You can convert documents from .DOC to .HTML and then *back* to .DOC format, losing virtually nothing in the translation.

Using the Web Page Wizard

The easiest way to create a *new* Web page or site is to use Word 2000's new Web Page Wizard. This wizard automates Web page creation with customized Web templates, and leads you step-by-step through the process; all you have to do is follow the onscreen instructions.

To create a Web page or site with the Web Page Wizard, follow these steps:

1. Select File ➢ New to display the New dialog box.

2. Select the Web Pages tab.

3. Select Web Page Wizard.

4. Click OK to display the Web Page Wizard.

5. Follow the Wizard's step-by-step instructions to create one or more Web pages.

Starting from a Web Page Template

You can also manually create a new Web page based on any of Word 2000's new Web page templates. These templates work similar to traditional Word templates, but are optimized for frame-based Web pages. To create a Web page from a template, follow these steps:

1. Select File ➢ New to display the New dialog box.

2. Select the Web Pages tab.

3. Select the template you want to use.

4. Click OK to create a new page based on the selected template.

Inserting a Horizontal Line

You use horizontal lines to break up various sections of your Web page. You can insert plain lines or fancy lines; Word uses graphics to create the horizontal lines in your Web page.

To insert a horizontal line, follow these steps:

1. Position the insertion point where you want to add the horizontal line.

2. Select Format ➢ Borders and Shading to display the Borders and Shading dialog box.

3. Click the Horizontal Line button to display the Horizontal Line dialog box.

4. Make sure the Pictures tab is selected.

5. Click the line you want to insert; this displays a pop-up menu.

6. Click the Insert Clip button.

Web Folders

A Web folder is essentially a shortcut to a Web server. To use this feature, your host server must support the Web folders feature.

Creating a Web Folder

The easiest way to create a Web folder is with Microsoft's Web Folder Wizard. Follow these steps:

1. Open My Computer.
2. Select the Web Folders icon to open the Web Folders window.
3. Click the Add Web Folder icon to launch the Web Folder Wizard.
4. Enter the location of your Web folder. This is typically the URL of your Web site; you can click the Browse button to launch your Web browser and navigate to the appropriate URL.
5. The wizard now validates the URL you provided, then creates the designated folder.

Saving a Document to a Web Folder

Once you've created a Web folder, you can save your Web documents to the Web folder. Follow these steps:

1. From within your document, select File ➢ Save As Web Page to display the Save As dialog box.
2. Click the Web Folders icon.
3. From the list of Web folder sites, double-click the appropriate folder, then double-click the location where you want to save the page.
4. Enter the name of your page in the File Name box.
5. Click Save.

Word will now connect to the Internet and save your file to the Web server hosting your pages.

Managing the Contents of a Web Folder

When you're using Web folders, you use My Computer or Windows Explorer to manage the contents of your Web site. From within My Computer or Windows Explorer, you can move, copy, rename, and delete files within your Web folder just as you would the contents of a normal folder.

From within My Computer or Windows Explorer, open the Web Folders window, then open the Web folder you want to manage. Windows will now connect to the Internet and access your Web server, where you can manage your Web pages.

Web Forms

A Web form is used to collect data from Web users, and then initiate some kind of action. You use Word 2000's Design mode to create Web forms on your Web pages; your form can be a complete page onto itself (like the "check out" pages at Amazon.com and other e-tailers), or just part of an existing page (like Yahoo!'s Search box). You add interaction to your forms with Web controls, which range from check boxes to list boxes to text boxes.

Switching to Design Mode

To insert most—but not all—controls, you first have to click the Design Mode button on the Web Tools toolbar to switch to Design mode. When you're in Design mode, the Word workspace looks just like normal, except for the Exit Design Mode button floating on top of the workspace. You click the Exit Design Mode button to exit Design mode and return to Word's normal *Run mode*.

Adding a Form to a Web Page

When you create a form, Word inserts a Top of Form boundary to the top of the form and inserts a Bottom of Form boundary below the form. To create a form, you start by inserting a control into your document (while in Design mode). Then you add to your form with other controls. Just follow these steps:

1. From within Design mode, position the insertion point where you want to begin the form and add the first control.

2. Click the control you want to insert from the Web Tools toolbar.

3. The control is now inserted between the Top of Form and Bottom of Form boundaries.

4. If you want to resize the control, use your mouse to grab a selection handle on the control and resize it.

Setting the Properties of a Web Form Control

After you have added a control to your Web page, you have to set the properties for that control. The properties of a form control determine how data is communicated to a Web server and (for some controls) how the control appears on your Web page.

To set a control's properties, follow these steps:

1. From within Design mode, select the control.

2. Click the Properties button on the Web Tools toolbar to display the Properties dialog box for that control.

3. Select the Alphabetic tab to view the properties alphabetically; select the Categorized tab to view the properties by category.

4. Set the appropriate properties.

5. Close the Properties dialog box.

Web Themes

A theme is a combination of fonts, text colors, and background colors applied to a Web page or group of Web pages. You pick a theme, and then Word applies the selected formatting throughout your entire Web document.

To apply a theme, follow these steps:

1. From within your Web document, select Format ➤ Theme to display the Themes dialog box.

2. Select a theme from the Choose a Theme list; the preview window shows how a sample page looks with this theme applied.

3. To display the theme with a brighter color scheme, check the Vivid Colors option.

4. To display the theme with animated elements (such as buttons or bullets that change color or shape when selected), check the Active Graphics option.

5. To display a background graphic instead of a background color, check the Background Image option; to display a background color, leave this option unchecked.

6. Click OK to apply the theme.

You can change themes at any time by repeating the above procedure. Word will automatically reformat your Web page based on any new theme you select.

Wildcards

Wildcards are special characters that let you search for multiple characters in a query. As an example, the * wildcard searches for any combination of characters from its insertion point onward. When you enter **DEAD***, you search for any word that starts with *dead*, including *deadline*, *deadly*, and *deaden*.

Another popular wildcard is the ? character. You use this wildcard to stand in for any individual character. For example, when you enter **DE?D**, you return the results *dead* and *deed*.

Word Art

WordArt is a special tool that enables you to create shadowed, skewed, rotated, and stretched text. WordArt inserts text as a drawing object, which means you can use any of Word's drawing tools to add additional formatting to the WordArt text.

Inserting WordArt

To insert WordArt text, follow these steps:

1. Position the insertion point where you want to place the WordArt text.
2. From the Drawing toolbar, click the Insert WordArt button to display the Word-Art Gallery window.
3. Select a WordArt style, then click OK to display the Edit WordArt Text dialog box.
4. Select a font from the Font list and a font size from the Size list.
5. If you want to boldface or italicize your WordArt text, click the Bold or Italic buttons.
6. Enter the text for your WordArt in the Text box.
7. Click OK to insert the WordArt object into your document.

Editing WordArt

When you select a WordArt object, Word automatically displays the WordArt toolbar. From this toolbar you can perform the following operations on the selected WordArt:

Edit WordArt Text To edit the text in your WordArt object, click the Edit Text button to display the Edit WordArt text dialog box. Enter, edit, and delete text in the Text box, then click OK.

Switch to a Different WordArt Style To switch to a different WordArt style for your object, click the WordArt Gallery button to display the WordArt Gallery and choose from another one of the preselected styles of WordArt.

Change Color and Outline Style To change the color and outline style for your object, click the Format WordArt button to display the Format WordArt dialog box, and then select the Colors and Lines tab. Select a fill color, as well as a line color and weight, and then click OK to apply.

Apply a Different Shape   To change the shape "container" for your WordArt, click the WordArt Shape button and choose from one of the forty different shapes.

Rotate Your Text   To rotate your WordArt object clockwise or counter-clockwise, click the Free Rotate button to display the green rotation handles on the WordArt object. Grab one of the handles with your cursor and drag the object around to a new position.

Determine Text Wrapping   To determine how text wraps around your WordArt object, click the Text Wrapping button and select one of the options from the pull-down menu.

Change the Height of Your Letters   To make all the letters in your WordArt text the same height, click the Same Letter Heights button.

Stack Text Vertically   To flow your WordArt text top-to-bottom instead of left-to-right, click the Vertical Text button.

Align Text Horizontally   To left align, center, right align, or justify your WordArt text, click the Alignment button and select from the pull-down menu.

Stretch the Text   To stretch the letters in your text to fill the full width of the WordArt object, click the Alignment button and select Stretch Justify. To add extra spacing between letters to fill the full width, click the Alignment button and select Letter Justify.

Adjust Letter Spacing   To tighten or loosen the spacing between characters in your WordArt text, click the Character Spacing button and select from the pull-down menu.

Zoom

Word's Standard toolbar includes a Zoom command, in the form of a pull-down list. Pull down the list and select a pre-set zoom level (from 10% to 500%); 100% zoom displays your document at the size it will appear when printed. You can also choose to have your document automatically fill up the entire width of your screen by selecting the Page Width option.

Another way to change the display size of your documents is to select View ➤ Zoom. This displays the Zoom dialog box, where you can select from both preselected and custom zoom levels.

Finally, you can choose to hide all of Word's menus and toolbars and display your document using your entire computer screen. When you select View ➤ Full Screen, your document fills up your entire screen; to return to normal viewing, click the Close Full Screen button in the floating toolbar.

APPENDIX <u>A</u>

Installing and Updating Word

Understanding Word 2000's system requirements   1092

Installing Word 2000   1092

Installing additional Word 2000 components   1095

Repairing a damaged installation   1096

I f you already have Word 2000 installed on your system, you may be able to skip this appendix. However, if you ever need to install a component that wasn't included as part of a typical installation or repair a damaged Word installation, then you will need the information presented here.

Understanding Word 2000's System Requirements

As stated by Microsoft, these are the minimum system requirements to run Word 2000 on your personal computer:

- Microsoft Windows 95, Windows 98, Windows NT Workstation version 4 (with Service Pack 3 or later), or Windows 2000
- Pentium 75MHz computer or better
- 20MB of RAM (under Microsoft Windows 95 or Windows 98) or 36MB of RAM (under Microsoft Windows NT)
- 146MB hard disk space (typical installation)
- CD-ROM drive
- VGA or higher monitor (800 × 600 resolution recommended)
- Microsoft Mouse, Microsoft IntelliMouse, or similar pointing device

To have full use of all of Word 2000's Internet-related features, Microsoft recommends that your system also include a modem (minimum 14.4Kbps, although 56Kbps is preferred), that you have an account with an Internet service provider, that you have either Microsoft Outlook or Microsoft Exchange Client installed on your system, and that you have an additional 8MB of memory (to run Office e-mail).

Installing Word 2000

Installation of Word 2000 is fairly automatic, with only a handful of responses necessary on your part. Ideally, the Word setup program should start automatically when you insert the Word (or Office) installation CD into your CD-ROM drive; the setup program should then correctly sense any installed components on your system and proceed directly to the typical Word installation.

NOTE Given the sheer size of the program, the default installation process for Word 2000 uses an installation CD-ROM. You can install Word from a set of installation diskettes, but you'll have to obtain these optional diskettes direct from Microsoft.

Examining a Typical Installation

Just in case your situation is less than ideal, we'll walk through a typical installation, step-by-step, as follows:

 NOTE For simplicity of presentation, this appendix assumes you've installed Word as part of Microsoft Office 2000, and thus are using the Office installation CD. If you installed Word as a separate installation, the same instructions apply, except you'll be using a Word installation CD.

1. Insert the installation CD in your PC's CD-ROM drive.

2. The first screen of the setup program should now appear. If this screen does not appear automatically, click the Windows Start button and select Run to display the Run dialog box, enter **x:\setup.exe** (where *x* is the letter of your CD drive) in the Open box, then click OK. Click the Next button to proceed.

3. When the Customer Information screen appears, enter your username, initials (Word will insert these automatically, based on your username), organization (optional), and CD Key. Click the Next button to proceed.

 WARNING The setup program will not install Word without the proper CD Key. The CD Key is a 25-character code located on the back of the case for the installation CD. Whatever you do, *don't lose this key!*

4. When the License and Support Information screen appears, read the agreement carefully (or not), then select the I Accept the Terms in the License Agreement option. Click the Next button to proceed.

5. The Installation Location screen now appears. By default, Word and other Office applications are installed into the \Program Files\Microsoft Office\ folder; to change this location, click the Browse button and select a different folder. Click the Next button to proceed.

TIP Because so many other programs look for Office programs in their default directory, I recommend that you accept the default location during the installation process.

6. If the setup program detects a previous version of Word on your system, the Remove Previous Versions screen will now appear. If you want to keep the older version on your system (along with Word 2000), select the Keep These Programs option. In most cases, however, you want to delete the older version, and you'll leave the Keep These Programs option unselected. Click the Next button to proceed.

7. If the setup program detects an older version of Internet Explorer on your system, the Microsoft Internet Explorer 5 Upgrade screen will now appear. Pull down the Update Windows to Include list to select an installation option, then click the Next button.

8. When the next screen of the setup program appears, select the type of installation you want. The options presented vary from system to system, but typically include Upgrade, Full, Typical, Minimal, and Custom. Click the Next button to complete the installation.

 TIP For most users, the Typical installation is the appropriate choice; power users may prefer the flexibility of the Custom installation.

Choosing Custom Installation Options

If you choose a Custom installation, you now are presented with a list of available components you can install for the Word program. Click the + sign to show all components of a specific type; click the icon with the down arrow to display a pop-up menu with installation options for a selected component.

For each component, you can select from the following installation options:

Run From My Computer   Installs a component normally, onto your hard disk.

Run All From My Computer   Installs the selected component and all sub-components onto your hard disk.

Run From CD   Doesn't install the component, but instead instructs Word that the component will be run from the CD.

Run All From CD   Instructs Word that the selected component and all subcomponents will be run from the CD.

WARNING If you select either of the Run From CD options, you'll need to insert your installation CD every time you access the selected program component(s).

Installed on First Use Instructs Word to automatically install the component the first time you access that component during normal program use.

Using the Installation CD—*After* Word Is Installed

After you've installed Word 2000, you'll still have use for the installation CD. As explained later in this appendix, the CD can be used to install uninstalled program components and to repair or reinstall damaged files. While all of these operations can be implemented from within Word or Windows, you can also access these and other functions directly from the installation CD.

When you insert the installation CD *after* you've installed Word, you'll see the Maintenance Mode screen. This screen presents three options:

Repair Office When you click this button, the setup program scans your Office or Word setup for damaged or missing files, then reinstalls those files as necessary.

Add or Remove Features When you click this button, the Update Features screen is displayed. Select new components to install or deselect components you want to remove from your system.

Remove Office When you click this button, Word 2000 (or Office 2000) is deleted from your system.

 NOTE You may need to run x:\setup.exe (where *x* is the letter of your CD drive) to display the Maintenance Mode screen.

Installing Additional Word 2000 Components

The Word 2000 software contains the main program and a variety of additional components. These components are added into the main program to enhance the functionality with task-specific operations. For example, all the converters that let you export and import files to and from other programs are optional components within Word—although when you use the converters, they are fully integrated with the main program.

When you first installed Microsoft Word 2000, you chose between a Typical and a Custom installation. If you chose the Typical installation, the setup program didn't actually install *all* of Microsoft Word. Because Word is comprised of a variety of different components, the Typical installation includes only those components that are frequently used by typical users. Less frequently used components were not installed during the initial installation, but they can be installed as you need them.

Some uninstalled components will be automatically installed the first time you try to use the associated program feature. For example, Asian fonts are not part of the Typical install but will be installed automatically the first time you try to use Asian fonts in one of your documents. When you encounter an "install on first use" component, Word will prompt you to insert your installation CD and then install the necessary component automatically.

Other uninstalled components remain uninstalled until you manually install them. These components are most often used in very special situations, and thus are not necessary for the majority of Word users.

To install a component manually, follow these steps:

1. Close all open programs.

2. Click the Windows Start button, and then select Settings ➢ Control Panel to open the Control Panel.

3. Select the Add/Remove Programs icon to launch the Add/Remove Programs Properties dialog box.

4. Select the Install/Uninstall tab.

5. If you installed Word from the Microsoft Office Setup program, select Microsoft Office from the list of programs; if you installed Word separately, select Microsoft Word.

6. Click the Add/Remove button.

7. Follow the onscreen instructions.

Repairing a Damaged Installation

It is possible, over the course of time, for the files that compose the Word 2000 program to become damaged, corrupted, or deleted. Any of these things can happen because of inadvertent actions on your part, computer viruses, improper program or system shutdowns, or reckless disregard for installed program files by newer programs you install on your system.

Microsoft Windows can detect and repair some problems associated with all installed Office 2000 programs, including Microsoft Word 2000. Typically, the Windows installer can find and fix missing or damaged program files and Registry settings; it does not repair .DOC or .DOT files.

To repair your Word 2000 installation, follow these steps:

1. From within Word, select Help ➢ Detect and Repair to display the Detect and Repair dialog box.

2. To restore Word's program shortcuts on the Windows Start menu, check the Restore My Shortcuts while Repairing option.

3. Click the Start button to begin the repair operation.

If Detect and Repair discovers damaged or missing files, you'll be prompted to insert your Word or Office installation CD so the proper files can be reinstalled.

 WARNING If you run Detect and Repair and your program problems persist, you may need to uninstall and then reinstall the complete Word program from scratch.

INDEX

Note to the Reader: Page numbers in **bold** indicate the principal discussion of a topic or the definition of a term. Page numbers in *italic* indicate illustrations.

Numbers and Symbols

3-D effects
for objects, *489*, 490–491, 1040
troubleshooting, 950
3-D graphs, **451–454**
Auto Scaling option, 454
Elevation option, 451, *452*
Height option, 454, *455*
Perspective option, 453, *454*
Right Angle Axes option, 454
Rotation option, 452, *453*
' (apostrophe) in Visual Basic for Applications, 774
* (asterisk) in Find and Replace dialog box, 175
@ (at sign) in Find and Replace dialog box, 175
\ (backslash)
in field codes, 335–336
in indexes instead of colons (:), 939
: (colon)
in indexes, 939
in VBA statements, 773
… (ellipsis) in menus, 20
(number sign) in index entries, 357
? (question mark) in Find and Replace dialog box, 175
; (semicolon) in index entries, 357

A

About Microsoft Word dialog box, 896–897, *896*, 1019
accented character shortcuts, 811–812
accepting
AutoFormat changes, 208
revision changes, 610–611, 1080
accessing menu commands with Alt key, 8
Acrobat Reader, 866
activating. *See* enabling

Active Server Pages (ASP) scripts, 667, 682
ActiveX controls. *See also* controls; fields; forms; scripts
in automated forms, **716**, **727–734**, **1013–1014**
adding, 727–729, 1013–1014
additional controls in Control Toolbox toolbar, 730–731
check boxes, 729
combo boxes, 730
command buttons, 729
Control Toolbox toolbar and, 728, 730–731
defined, **727**
Design mode and, 728–729
designing, 716
versus form fields, 720
image controls, 730
label controls, 730
list boxes, 730
option buttons, 729
programming, 732–733, *733*, 1014
scroll buttons, 730
setting properties, 731–732, *732*, 1014
spin buttons, 730
text boxes, 714, *714*, 729
toggle buttons, 730
Visual Basic for Applications (VBA) and, 718, 720, 727–728, 729, 732–733
in Web page forms, 670
Add Procedure dialog box in Visual Basic for Applications, 778–779
add-in programs. *See also* templates
Aladdins ~ Word Documents Outlook add-in program, 866, 877–878
defined, **701**
loading, 702–703
loading automatically, 710
unloading, 703–704
adding. *See also* inserting
3-D effects to objects, *489*, 490–491, 1040

AutoCorrect entries, 201–203, 824–825, 976 977
to AutoCorrect Exceptions list, 203–204, 977
bookmarks, 167, 980
borders to frames, 654
buttons to Office Shortcut Bar, 841
captions
    automatically, 325–326, 984–985
    manually, 325, 984
chapter numbers
    to captions, 327–328
    to page numbers, 301
clip art to Clip Gallery, 464–465
controls to forms in Visual Basic for Applications, 772
custom spelling dictionaries, 185–186
dialog boxes to macros, 785–786, 790–793
files to Office binders, 842–843, *842*
fonts, 235
to forms
    ActiveX controls, 727–729, 1013–1014
    field shading, 714, *715*, 727
    fields, 721, 1013
    Help text for fields, 725–727, *726*
forms to Web pages, 668–669, *668*, 1086
FTP site addresses to Word, 693–694
graph elements, **434–441**
    callouts, 440–441
    data labels, 436–437
    graph elements defined, **434**, *435*
    gridlines, 438
    legends, 438–440
    titles, 435–436
    trendlines, 437
graphics to envelopes, 517
headers and footers to documents in Office binders, 843
items to menu bar, 101–102
macro developers to list of trusted sources, 755
menus to toolbars, 96–97
message boxes to macros, 784–785, *784*, *785*
page borders, 295–296, *295*
PresentIt command to toolbars, 854
script commands to Tools menu, 679–680
subdocuments to master documents, 597, 1033
templates, 124–125, *124*
text to headers and footers, 303–304, 1017–1018
toolbar buttons, 94–96, 1079
words to custom spelling dictionaries, 187–188
Address Books
    addressing envelopes from, 515

GPDATA address book utility, 867, 876–877, *876*
    as Mail Merge data sources, 532
addressing envelopes, **514–515**. *See also* envelopes
    adding return address automatically, 514
    automatically adding name and address from a letter, 515
    Delivery Address options, 512
    Return Address options, 512–513
    selecting names from Windows Address Book, 515
Adobe Acrobat Reader, 866
agreeing on rules for group revisions, 606–607
Aladdins ~ Word Documents Outlook add-in program, 866, 877–878
aligning
    and justifying paragraphs, 254–255, *255*, 926–927, 1051
    objects, 481, 947, 948
    tables, 400–402
    text in table cells, 49, 406–407
    vertical alignment
        in columns of text, 309
        of objects, 1037
        in page setup, 291–292, 1048–1049
all caps font style, 241–242, *241*
Alt key. *See also* Ctrl key; keyboard shortcuts; Shift key
    + Ctrl + D (Endnote), 317
    + Ctrl + F (Footnote), 317
    + Shift + D (DATE field), 340
    + Shift + I (Mark Citation), 373
    + Shift + O (Mark Table of Contents Entry), 371
    + Shift + P (PAGE field), 340
    + Shift + T (TIME field), 340
    + Shift + X (Mark Index Entry), 357
    + Tab (switching between documents), 41
    accessing menu commands with, 8
    Ctrl + Alt + + (Keyboard Shortcuts), 800–801
    navigating tables with, 380
    navigating with, 161
alternate text for Web page graphics, 471, 647, 1054
Always Create Backup Copy option, 156
animated cursors, 106
animated GIFs, 949
animated text
    creating, **242**, **1008**
    hiding, 86
annotations. *See* bookmarks; captions; cross-references; footnotes and endnotes
Answer Wizard tab in Help, 891–892, *892*, 1019

anti-virus programs. *See also* viruses in macros
    ChekMate Lite, 38, 866, 882–883
    McAfee VirusScan software, 38
    Norton AntiVirus software, 38
    Virus ALERT for Word 2000, 38, 753, 867, 881–882, *882*
apostrophe (') in Visual Basic for Applications, 774
applying
    borders and fills to objects, 1040
    borders and shading to table cells, 409, *410*
    borders to tables, 403–404, 1068–1069
    gridlines to tables, 403–404, 1068–1069
    outline numbering to lists, 269–270, 1036
    shadows to objects, 1040
    styles, 276, 1062
    table shading, 404–405, 1069
arguments
    in field codes, 335
    in table formulas, 416
arrow keys, navigating with, 161
ASP (Active Server Pages) scripts, 667, 682
assigning
    hyperlinks to toolbar buttons, 99–100
    keyboard shortcuts, 103–104, 1026
    keyboard shortcuts from keyboard, 800–801
    macros
        to keyboard shortcuts, 750, 793, *793*
        to menus, 749
        to toolbars, 749
    outline levels to styles, 564, 1045
assignment statements in Visual Basic for Applications, 773, 775
asterisk (*) in Find and Replace dialog box, 175
at sign (@) in Find and Replace dialog box, 175
attaching
    documents to e-mail messages, 229, 999
    envelopes to documents
        in Mail Merge, 549
        overview of, 515–516, *516*, 1001
        printing attached envelopes, 516
    templates to documents, 125, 704
audio clips in Web pages, 665–666
Auto Scaling option for 3-D graphs, 454
AutoCaption feature, 325–326
AutoCorrect feature, **50**, **110**, **182–183**, **199–204**, **824–825**, **975–977**
    adding entries, 201–203, 824–825, 976–977
    adding to AutoCorrect Exceptions list, 203–204, 977
    AutoCorrect Spell Checking, 182–183, 976
    automatically converting Web and e-mail addresses to hyperlinks, 57, 633

    configuring, 110, 199–201, *200*, 975–976
    creating shortcuts for long words, 824–825
    defined, **199**, **975**
    deleting entries, 203
    enabling, 199–200, 975–976
    how AutoCorrect works, 201
    keyboard shortcuts for special characters, 808–809
    new features, 50, 199
    saving symbol characters as AutoCorrect entries, 199, 202
    troubleshooting, 910
AutoFit feature, 399, 1068
AutoFormat feature, **111–112**, **204–208**, **977–978**
    AutoFormat as You Type options, 207, 812–813, 978
    configuring, 111–112, 204–206, *205*, 978
    creating bulleted lists, 206, 207, 264, 812–813
    creating numbered lists, 206, 207, 264
    creating tables, 383–384
    defined, **204**, **977**
    reviewing and accepting changes, 208
    running, 207–208, 978
    Style Gallery option, 208
    Table AutoFormat feature, 405–406, 1069–1070
    uses for, 207
AutoMark files, 355, 360–361, 1024
automated forms, **718–738**, **1012**. *See also* forms
    creating form templates, 718–719, 1013
    creating with macros, 734
    defined, **718**, **1012**
    designing, 719
    distributing, 735–736
    filling in, 736–737
    printing form data only, 218, 737
    protecting, 735, 1014–1015
    saving form data as text files for sending to databases, 737–738
automatic backups, 156
automatic capitalization problems, 923–924
automatic cross-references, 328–329
Automatic Grammar Checking, 192, 1061
automatic hyperlink creation, 57, 633
automatic hyphenation, 197, 1021–1022
automatic macros, 786–787
automatic repagination, 106
automatic spacing adjustment for cutting and pasting, 105
Automatic Spell Checking, 180–182, *181*, 1060
automatically converting Web and e-mail addresses to hyperlinks, 57, 633

automatically creating hyperlinks to e-mail or Web addresses, 57, 633
automatically saving current version, 615
Automatically Update option for styles, 279
automating
Mail Merge with fields, 535–537
operations with keyboard shortcuts, 24
Word, **823–831**
AutoCorrect shortcuts for long words, 824–825
creating Click Here and Type fields, 825
creating documents from dialog boxes, 826–828, *826, 827, 829*
creating tables of contents from another document, 830
creating Windows Desktop shortcuts to templates and documents, 831
line spacing shortcuts, 824
reusing documents with Letter Wizard, 829
shrinking documents to fit paper size, 52, 115, 214, 217–218, 824
AutoRecover feature, 155–156, 157, 919
AutoScroll macro, 803, *804*
AutoShapes, **475–477, 997–998**. *See also* graphics
creating free-form drawings, 477, *478,* 950, 998
defined, **475–476, 997**
as drawing objects, 475, 997
drawing objects disappear when Letter Wizard is run, 951
Drawing toolbar options, 476, 477
editing, 476, 998
Freeform drawing cannot be controlled, 950
inserting, 476, 997
printing, 116
Word 2000 as a drawing program, 834–835
AutoSum button in Tables and Borders toolbar, 413–414, 799, 1070
AutoSummarize feature, 582–584, *584,* 979
AutoText feature, **112, 144–145, 979–980**
creating entries, **145, 980**
creating headers and footers with, 305
customizing, 112
defined, **144**
inserting AutoText entries, 144, 979
inserting page numbers with, 301
printing entries, 145
troubleshooting, 931
axes of graphs
configuring axis settings, 443–445
Right Angle Axes option in 3-D View dialog box, 454
switching category (x-axis) and value (y-axis) axes, 428–431, *429, 430, 431*

B

Baarns Consulting Web site, 902
background repagination feature, 106
background saves, 154
background sound clips in Web pages, 665–666
backgrounds, **291–295**. *See also* page setup
blends and gradients, 292–293
color backgrounds, 292–293, 1049
do not print, 934
graphics, 293
patterns, 293
shading
field shading, 87, 337, 1004
in forms, 714, *715,* 727
paragraphs, 262–263, 982
table cell shading, 409, *410*
table shading, 404–405, 1069
textures, 293
watermarks, 293–295, *294,* 819–820, *820,* 934–935, 1049
backing up documents, **155–157**. *See also* saving
with AutoRecover feature, 155–156, 157, 919
creating automatic backups, 156
recovering unsaved or damaged documents, 156–157
backslash (\)
in field codes, 335–336
in indexes instead of colons (:), 939
Backspace key, 7
balancing columns of text, 806, 933
bar charts, graphics in, 816–817, *816, 817*
barcodes
on envelopes, 511–512, *512*
FIM-A Courtesy Reply Mail option for envelopes, 512
on labels, 520
on merged envelopes, 546, 547
on merged labels, 544
batch converting file formats with Conversion Wizard, 62–63
Bcc (blind-carbon-copy) e-mail recipients, 227
binders, **841–844**. *See also* Microsoft Office
adding files to, 842–843, *842*
adding headers and footers to documents in, 843
creating, **842–843,** *842*
defined, **841**
editing binder files, 843
hiding sections of, 844
printing, 843–844

saving, 843
starting Microsoft Office Binder, 842
BioSpel spelling dictionary, 186, 866, 886
bitmapped images, 460, 467
blends. *See* gradient fills
blind-carbon-copy (Bcc) e-mail recipients, 227
Blue Background, White Text option, 91, *91*
.BMP files, 460, 467
bold font style, 237–238, 239, 241–242, *241*
bookmarks, **166–168**, **980–981**
  adding, 167, 980
  bookmark error message is displayed, 943–944
  for creating tables of contents, 370
  cross-references to, 330
  defined, **166**
  deleting, 980
  displaying, 86
  displaying hidden bookmarks, 167
  in formulas in tables, 416
  marking index entries with, 359
  marking ranges of pages for index entries, 359, 1023
  moving to, 168, 981
  naming, 167
  viewing, 167, 980–981
  in Word versus Web browsers, 166
books
  on companion CD-ROM, 866, 867
  about VBScript and Visual Basic, 679, 760
borders. *See also* frames; lines; shading; shadows
  form borders, 714, *715*
  frame borders, 654
  graph borders, 427
  in graphics
    borders for objects, 488, 1040
    troubleshooting, 950
  page borders, **295–296**, **1049–1050**
    adding, 295–296, *295*, 1049–1050
    borders do not display properly, 935–936
    creating graphical borders, 296, *297*
  paragraph borders
    borders are cut off, 929
    creating, **261–262**, **981**
    styles for, 273
  in tables
    cell borders, 409, *410*
    defined, **378–379**, *378*
    table borders, 403–404, 1068–1069
    Tables and Borders toolbar, 379, *379*
Borders and Shading dialog box, **261–263**
  border settings, 261–262, 981
  shading paragraphs, 262–263

breaking links to source files, 500–501
breaking tables across pages, 396
breaks. *See* columns of text; page breaks; sections
brochure templates, 123
browsing. *See* moving; navigating
built-in keyboard shortcuts for styles, 275
built-in templates, **123–124**, **701–705**. *See also* templates
  changing template in current document, 704, 1075–1076
  downloading from Microsoft Web site, 702
  installing, 701
  listed, 123–124
  loading, 702–703, 1075
  previewing in Style Gallery, 704–705
  unloading, 703–704
  using templates from earlier versions of Word, 702
bulleted lists, **263–267**, **983–984**. *See also* lists
  bullets do not display properly, 927
  creating with AutoFormat feature, 206, 207, 264, 812–813
  creating with Formatting toolbar, 264–265, 983
  creating graphical bullets, 266–267, 813–814, *814*, 984
  customizing bullet characters, 265–266, 812–813, 983
  fonts for bullets, 266
  tabs and paragraph indents disappear when bullets are added or deleted, 927
business support line and Web site, 904
business Web pages, publishing, 688, 690–691
buttons. *See also* toolbars
  adding to Office Shortcut Bar, 841
  on toolbars
    adding or deleting, 94–96, 1079
    assigning hyperlinks to, 99–100
    changing button display, 97–98
    changing or editing button images with Button Editor, 98, *99*
    grouping, 97
    More Buttons button, 94
    troubleshooting when buttons cannot be found, 915

C

calculating totals
  with AutoSum button in tables, 413–414, 799, 1070

in documents with ToolsCalculate command, 799

total number of pages in headers and footers, 305, 1019

callouts in graphs, 440–441

canceling print jobs, 214

capitalization

automatic capitalization problems, 923–924

case-sensitivity in passwords, 605

Change Case dialog box, 242–243, 1008

drop caps, 247–248, 1010

Match Case option in Find and Replace dialog box, 170

captions, **324–328**, **984–985**

adding automatically, 325–326, 984–985

adding chapter numbers, 327–328

adding manually, 325, 984

captions are not numbered correctly, 943

captions do not update correctly, 943

changing numbering format, 327, 985

creating with tables, 324

defined, **324**, *324*, **984**

selecting caption labels, 326–327

case

automatic capitalization problems, 923–924

case-sensitivity in passwords, 605

Change Case dialog box, 242–243, 1008

Match Case option in Find and Replace dialog box, 170

catalogs, 550–551, *551*

CD Key for installing Word 2000, 1093

.CDR files, 467

CD-ROM (book's), **866–887**

Adobe Acrobat Reader, 866

Aladdins ~ Word Documents Outlook add-in program, 866, 877–878

anti-virus programs

ChekMate Lite, 38, 866, 882–883

Virus ALERT for Word 2000, 38, 753, 867, 881–882, *882*

BioSpel spelling dictionary, 186, 866, 886

ChekOf security utility, 867, 883

Document Converter, 867, 874–875, *875*

EasyHTML/Help development tool, 867, 885, 893

GPDATA address book utility, 867, 876–877, *876*

KazStamp envelope printing software, 514, 867, 878–879, *879*

Mastering Word 2000 Premium Edition, 867

MedSpel spelling dictionary, 186, 867, 886

MightyFax software, 222, 867, 880, *881*

Office 2000 Complete, 866, 867

OfficeExpress 2000 graphics software, 472, 867, 872–873, *873*

PRIME for Word 2000 utilities, 867, 868–871, *869*

programs

installing, **868**

listed, **866–868**

ScreenPro template, 867, 886–887

SOS Office Helpers, 867, 871–872, *871*

Symbol Selector utility, 867, 873–874, *874*

Word Workshops tutorial, 867–868

WordToWeb utility, 629, 868, 884–885

cells in tables, **378–379**, **406–409**

clearing all cells, 393

defined, **378–379**, *378*

deleting, 392–393

entering tab stops, 389

entering text or graphics, 389, *390*

formatting, **406–409**

aligning text, 49, 406–407

applying borders and shading, 409, *410*

changing text orientation, 407–408, *407*

setting margins, 408–409

inserting, 392

merging or splitting, 394–395, *394*, 1068

moving or copying text in cells, 393–394

navigating between, 389

numbering, 413

referencing cells in formulas, 415–416

resizing manually, 398–399

sorting, 410–412, 1070

certificates. *See* digital signatures

CGI (Common Gateway Interface) scripts, 667

.CGM files, 467

Change Case dialog box, 242–243, 1008

changing. *See also* customizing; editing

caption numbering format, 327, 985

default scripting language in Microsoft Script Editor, 684

fonts, styles, and size, 239, 1007

footnote and endnote numbering, 321

form field options, 724–725, 1013

graph type, **432–434**

with Chart Type dialog box, 433–434

from Standard toolbar, 432

how linked and embedded objects are displayed, 501

how links are updated, 500

hyperlinks in documents, 634

macro security levels, 754–755, 970, 1059

number format for lists, 267–269, 1035

Office Assistant characters, 895

page orientation or paper size in columns of text generates error message, 933–934

passwords, 606

revision colors and marks, 611–612

source files for links, 500

template in current document, 704, 1075–1076

text column widths and spacing, 308–309

text orientation in table cells, 407–408, *407*

toolbar button display, 97–98

toolbar button images with Button Editor, 98, *99*

vertical text alignment
  in columns of text, 309
  in page setup, 291–292, 1048–1049

chapter numbers
  in captions, 327–328
  in page numbers, 301

character code shortcuts for special characters, 809–811

character formatting. *See* fonts; text formatting

character spacing options, 243, 244–245, *245*, 1009

character styles versus paragraph styles, 271–272

chart area in graphs, 441–442

Chart Type dialog box, 433–434

charts. *See* graphs

"Check drive" message, 922

checkbox controls
  in automated forms, 729
  check box form fields, 722–723, *723*
  form check box size does not change when formatted, 968
  in Web page forms, 670–671, *670*

checking. *See also* troubleshooting
  Mail Merge for errors before merging, 537–538
  printer hardware, 955–956
  printer ports, 958

ChekMate Lite anti-virus program, 38, 866, 882–883

ChekOf security utility, 867, 883

citations for tables of authorities, 373, 1071

class modules in VBA, 772–773

classes in Visual Basic for Applications, 779

Clear command in Edit menu, 991

clearing table cells, 393

Click and Type feature, **46–47**, **104–105**, **140–141**, **384**, **924**, **985**

clip art, **460–467**, **986–987**. *See also* graphics
  adding images to Clip Gallery, 464–465, 987
  bitmapped images, 460, 467
  creating categories in Clip Gallery, 465
  creating graphical bullets with, 266–267, 813, 984

defined, **460**

in forms, 715, *716*

inserting from Clip Gallery, 461–463, *461*, *462*, 986

line art, 460

ungrouping and editing .WMF file images, 463, *464*, 949, 986

Web sites, 466–467

Clipboard. *See also* copying and pasting; cutting and pasting
  Collect and Paste feature, 48–49, 149–150, 990–991
  copying and pasting text with Paste command and multiple text objects in Clipboard, 150
  displaying contents of, 48, 150

closing Office Shortcut Bar, 839

Code windows in Visual Basic Editor, 762–763, *762*

codes. *See* fields

collaboration features. *See* comments; Track Changes feature; Web-based collaboration

collapsing
  menus, 20–21
  outline sections, 561–562, 1044
  subdocuments, 594, *595*

Collect and Paste feature, **48–49**, **149–150**, **990–991**

collections in Visual Basic for Applications, 779

colon (:)
  in indexes, 939
  in VBA statements, 773

color. *See also* shadows
  changing revision colors, 611–612
  color backgrounds, 292–293, 1049
  color backgrounds in Web pages, 646
  coloring text, 240, 1007–1008
  Line Color button in Drawing toolbar, 488
  shading
    field shading, 87, 337, 1004
    in forms, 714, *715*, 727
    paragraphs, 262–263, 982
    table cell shading, 409, *410*
    table shading, 404–405, 1069
  troubleshooting
    3-D and shadow colors don't change when graphics color is changed, 950
    colors are not smooth onscreen, 947
    graphics colors won't change, 949

columns in tables
  and converting databases to tables, 388
  copying, 393
  defined, **378–379**, *378*
  distributing evenly, 399, 1068

inserting or deleting, 391, 1067
moving, 393
resizing with AutoFit feature, 399, 1068
resizing manually, 397–398
columns of text, **307–310, 806, 932–934, 987–988**
balancing, 806, 933
changing column widths and spacing, 308–309, 988
changing vertical alignment, 309
creating, **307–308, 987–988**
creating column breaks, 309–310, 982
defined, **307**, *307*
troubleshooting, **932–934**
changing page orientation or paper size generates error message, 933–934
columns are not visible, 932
columns don't work in headers, footers, comments, or text boxes, 934
columns of text are narrower than expected, 932
columns won't balance, 933
tables in columns disappear, 933
text above columns turns into multiple columns, 933
vertical lines between columns are not visible, 932
combining subdocuments, 597–598
combo box controls in forms, 730
command buttons in forms, 729
commands. *See* menus
Commands tab in Customize dialog box, 73–74, *73*
comments, **612–614, 988–989**
columns of text in, 934
defined, **612, 988**
finding and replacing, 174–175
inserting spoken comments, 613, 989
inserting written comments, 612, *613*, 989
moving to, 163–164
printing, 116
reading, 614, 989
in Visual Basic for Applications, 774
commercial Web pages, publishing, 688, 690–691
Common Gateway Interface (CGI) scripts, 667
Compare Documents command, 609, 951
compatibility issues, **35, 60–66, 67, 83, 116–118**
compatibility of new features, 35
configuring Word compatibility options for WordPerfect users, 67
converting file formats with Conversion Wizard, 62–63

disabling incompatible features, 61–62, *61*, 66, 116–117
Font Substitution option, 118, 237
listed, 64–65
object placement controls, 35
options for compatibility with specific programs, 61–62, *61*, 117
Options dialog box Compatibility tab, 61–62, 83, 116–118
overview of, 35, 60
saving to previous Word formats, 60–62, *61*
composing e-mail messages, 122
compressed text, 244, *244*
Computertips Web site, 902
condensing text, 244–245, *244, 245*
configuring. *See also* customizing; formatting
AutoCorrect feature, 110, 199–201, *200*, 975–976
AutoFormat feature, 111–112, 204–206, *205*
AutoText feature, 112
editing options, 77–78, *78*, 104–106
e-mail options, 114, 225–227
envelope options, 510–513, 1000
field shading, 87
Grammar Checker, 80–81, *81*, 107–108, 189
grammar rules, 108, 190–192
in graphs
axis settings, 443–445
gridlines, 445
hyphenation rules, 109
label options, 518, 1026–1027
printing options, 114–116
Spelling feature, 80–81, *81*, 107–108, 179–180
user information, 82, *82*, 104, 514, 1081
Web settings, 113
Word compatibility options for WordPerfect users, 67
Word on a corporate scale, 85
connecting to discussion servers, 616, 617, 993–994
constants in Visual Basic for Applications, 774
Contents tab in Help, 890–891, *891*
context-sensitive menus. *See* right-click menus
continuation notices for footnotes, 319
continuing numbering in new lists, 269, 1035–1036
Control Toolbox toolbar, 728, 730–731
controls. *See also* fields; forms; scripts
ActiveX controls in automated forms, **716, 727–734, 1013–1014**
adding, 727–729, 1013–1014
additional controls in Control Toolbox toolbar, 730–731

check boxes, 729
combo boxes, 730
command buttons, 729
Control Toolbox toolbar and, 728, 730–731
defined, **727**
Design mode and, 728–729
designing, 716
versus form fields, 720
image controls, 730
label controls, 730
list boxes, 730
option buttons, 729
programming, 732–733, *733*, 1014
scroll buttons, 730
setting properties, 731–732, *732*, 1014
spin buttons, 730
text boxes, 714, *714*, 729
toggle buttons, 730
Visual Basic for Applications (VBA) and, 718, 720, 727–728, 729, 732–733
in Visual Basic for Applications, 765–767, 772
in Web page forms, **57, 669–678**
ActiveX controls, 670
Checkbox controls, 670–671, *670*
Control Toolbox toolbar, 670
Dropdown Box controls, 671–672, *672*
Hidden controls, 678
List Box controls, 672–673, *673*
Option Button controls, 671, *671*
Password controls, 674, *674*
Reset controls, 677–678, *678*
setting control properties, 669–670, 1086–1087
Submit controls, 675–676, *676*
Submit with Image controls, 676–677, *677*
Text Area controls, 674–675, *675*
Textbox controls, 673–675, *673*
VBScript controls, 57, *58*
converting
cross-references to hyperlinks, 330
documents
Document Converter utility, 867, 874–875, *875*
an existing document to a master document, 590–591
file formats with Conversion Wizard, 62–63
to Web pages, 629
embedded objects to another file format, 504–505
file formats with Conversion Wizard, 62–63
footnotes and endnotes, 322–323, 1012

footnotes and endnotes to hyperlinks in Web pages, 317
subdocuments into part of master document, 596, 1032
tables, **385–388, 1067**
databases to tables, 387–388
tables to text, 386–387, 1067
text to tables, 385–386, 1067
Web and e-mail addresses to hyperlinks, 57, 633
WordBasic macros to VBA, 743
Copy command in Edit menu, 148
copying
elements between templates with Organizer, 706–708, *707*
footnotes and endnotes, 319–320, 1011–1012
formatting
with Format Painter, 238, 805–806
multiple times, 806
section formatting, 299, 1059
text and paragraph formatting, 805
graphs, 424–425, *424*
macro projects to different documents or templates, 751, *751*, 1029
scripts, 681
styles
with Organizer, 277–278, *278*
from Style Gallery, 277, *277*
tables, 400
in tables
columns, 393
rows, 393
text in cells, 393–394
copying and pasting, **574–578, 989–991**. *See also* cutting and pasting
Excel worksheets into Word tables, 849–850, 1002
hyperlinks in documents, 634
with Insert key, 105
from other Windows programs, 150–151
with Paste Special dialog box, 150–151, 497, *497*, 575, 576–577, *577*, 990
text
with Collect and Paste feature, 48–49, 149–150, 990–991
with Copy and Paste commands, 148–149, 575–576, 990
in footnotes and endnotes, 320
as a link, 577–578
with Paste command and multiple text objects in Clipboard, 150
uses for, 574–575
corporate-wide customizing, 85

crashes, 156–157
creating. *See also* generating
    alternate text for Web page graphics, 471, 647,
        1054
    animated text, 242, 1008
    automatic backups, 156
    automatic document summaries, 582–584, *584*,
        979
    AutoShapes, 477, *478*
    AutoText entries, 145, 980
    borders, 261–262, 981
    bulleted lists
        with AutoFormat feature, 206, 207, 264,
            812–813
        with Formatting toolbar, 264–265, 983
        with graphical bullets, 266–267, 813–814,
            814, 984
    categories in Clip Gallery, 465
    Click Here and Type fields, 825
    column breaks, 309–310, 982
    columns of text, 307–308, 987–988
    custom spelling dictionaries, 187
    digital signatures, 755–756
    document summaries, 582–584, *584*, 979
    documents, **6**, **120–127**, **996**
        from dialog boxes, 826–828, *826*, *827*, *829*
        from existing documents, 127
        from Letter Wizard, 125–126, *126*, 829, 951,
            954
        with New Blank Document button, 120
        from Office Shortcut Bar, 122, 840
        from outlines, 569–571, *570*
        from Outlook contacts, 866, 877–878
        overview of, 6, 996
        from Start menu, 122
        from templates, 120–124, *121*
        with Wizards, 125–127, *126*, 829
    e-mail or mailto links in documents, 632–633,
        1021
    e-mail messages, 122
    embedded objects, 502–503, *503*, 1042–1043
    equations, 417–418, *418*
    Excel charts from Word, 853, 1003
    Excel worksheets from Word, 852, 1003
    footnotes and endnotes, 316–318, 1011
    forms
        form templates, 718–719, 1013
        printed forms, 717
        in Visual Basic for Applications, 772, 788–
            789, *788*, *789*, *790*
    frames, 56, 653, 1015
        navigation frames, 653, 1015

free-form drawings with AutoShapes, 477, *478*,
    950, 998
graphical bullets, 266–267, 813–814, *814*, 984
graphical page borders, 296, *297*
graphs, **422–423**, **434**, **1016–1017**
    custom graphs, 434
    Excel charts from Word, 853
    from existing data, 422, 1016
    linked to data in documents, 422–423,
        1016–1017
    from scratch, 423, 1017
headers and footers
    with AutoText feature, 305
    odd and even headers and footers, 306,
        1018–1019
    unique first page headers and footers,
        305–306, 1018
Help files, 893
hidden text, 241
highlighted text, 237–238, 243, 614
hyperlinks, 56–57, *57*
hyperlinks to e-mail or Web addresses, 57, 633
indexes, 361–363, *362*, *363*, 1025
label templates, 518–519, 1027
macros, **740–741**, **742–746**, **1028**
    explained, 740–741, 742
    Macro Recorder and, 742–743
    mouse movements and, 745
    recording macros, 743–745, *744*, 1028
    recording tips, 745–746
    suspending recording, 746
    with VBA, 740, 742
in Mail Merge
    attached merge envelopes, 549
    data sources from Word tables, 527–529, *528*,
        529, *530*
    main documents, 525–526
    merged envelopes or labels with Direct Mail
        Manager, 123, 549–550
master documents, **586–591**, **1031–1032**
    converting an existing document to a master
        document, 590–591, 1031–1032
    from existing documents, 591, 1032
    overview of, 586–587
    from scratch, 588–590, *589*, *590*, 1031
non-breaking and optional hyphens, 198–199,
    1022
numbered lists
    with AutoFormat feature, 206, 207, 264
    with Formatting toolbar, 267, 1035
Office binders, 842–843, *842*
page borders, 295–296, *295*

page breaks, 254, 258–259, 309–310, 982
personal menus, 798
presentations in Word without PowerPoint, 832–833, *832*
projects in Visual Basic for Applications, 771
scripts in Microsoft Script Editor, 685
section breaks, 297–298, 309–310, 982, 1058
signatures for e-mail messages, 225–226, *225*
spreadsheets in Word, 833–834, *833*
styles, **281–283, 1063–1064**
    by example, 281, 1063
    to follow specific styles, 280
    with Style dialog box, 282–283, 1063–1064
tables, **380–384, 417, 1065–1066**
    with AutoFormat feature, 383–384
    with Draw Table button on Tables and Borders toolbar, 382–383, *383*, 395, 821–822, *822*, *823*, 1066
    from Excel worksheets, 417
    with Insert Table button, 382, 1066
    with Insert Table dialog box, 381, 1065–1066
    side-by-side tables with Click and Type feature, 384
tables of authorities, 374, 1071–1072
tables of contents, 366–369, *367*, *368*, 1073
    from another document, 830
    in frames, 653
    manually, 371
tables of figures, 372, 1073–1074
tabs in New dialog box, 709
templates, **176–177, 518–519, 708–710, 718–719**
    creating tabs in New dialog box, 709
    from documents, 710, 1077
    from existing templates, 709–710, 1076
    form templates, 718–719
    label templates, 518–519
    saving to New dialog box tabs, 708–709
text boxes, 141–142, *142*, 1077
toolbars, 100–101, 1079
VBA procedures with Add Procedure dialog box, 778–779
watermarks, 293–295, *294*, 819–820, *820*, 934–935, 1049
Web folders, 691–692, 1085
Web pages, **629, 637–642, 1083–1084**
    converting Word documents to Web pages, 629
    Design mode and, 658–659, *660*, 666
    disabling Word features not supported in Web browsers, 640

saving Word documents in HTML format, 638–640, 1083
    from Web page templates, 124, 641–642, 1084
    with Web Page Wizard, 54–55, *55*, 640–641, 1084
cropping graphic objects, 484–486, *485*, 1054
cross-references, **318–319, 328–331, 358–359, 601, 991–992**
    to bookmarks, 330
    converting to hyperlinks, 330
    cross-references do not update correctly, 943
    defined, **328**
    editing, 991–992
    fields and, 331
    in footnotes and endnotes, 318–319
    in indexes, 358–359
    inserting automatic cross-references, 328–329, 991
    in master documents, 601
Ctrl key. *See also* Alt key; keyboard shortcuts; Shift key
    + Alt + + (Keyboard Shortcuts), 800–801
    + F11 (Lock Field), 342, 1005
    + F (Find), 168
    + H (Replace), 171
    + P (Print), 215
    + Spacebar (Delete Formatting), 806
    Alt + Ctrl + D (Endnote), 317
    Alt + Ctrl + F (Footnote), 317
    line spacing shortcuts, 824
    navigating with, 161
    Shift + Ctrl + F11 (Unlock Field), 342
cursors
    animated cursors, 106
    insertion point cursor, 6–7, 139–140
    moving to previous cursor locations with Shift + F5, 163, 804
custom dictionaries, **178–179, 185–188, 815**. *See also* Spelling feature
    adding, 185–186
    adding words to, 187–188
    BioSpel spelling dictionary, 186, 866, 886
    on book's CD-ROM, 186
    creating, **187**
    defined, **185–186**
    deleting, 186
    editing, 187–188, 815
    error messages, 910
    how spelling dictionaries work, 178–179
    MedSpel spelling dictionary, 186, 867, 886
custom graphs, 434

Custom installation options, 1094–1095
Customize dialog box, **72–75**. *See also* customizing;
Options dialog box
Commands tab, 73–74, *73*
defined, **72**
Keyboard tab, 75, *75*
Options tab
defined, **74**, *74*
Menus Show Recently Used Commands First
option, 42
Reset My Usage Data option, 43, 102
Toolbars tab, 44, 72, *73*, 92, 95, 100
customizing, **42–45**, **84–118**. *See also* configuring;
Options dialog box
bullet characters, 265–266, 812–813, 983
on a corporate scale, 85
keyboard shortcuts, 103–104
Mail Merge documents, 541
menus, **43–44**, **101–102**, **798**, **1033–1034**
adding items to menu bar, 101–102, 1034
creating personal menus, 798
customizing keyboard shortcuts, 103–104
moving the menu bar, 101
new features, 43–44
personalized menus, 20–21, 35, 42–43, 102,
798, 1033–1034
rearranging menu commands, 102
Normal view, 90–91, *90*
number formats for lists, 267–269, 1035
Outline view, 90–91
Print Layout view, 89, *89*
style area, 91, 274, *274*, 799, *800*
templates, **705–708**
copying elements between templates with
Organizer, 706–708, *707*
existing templates, 706, 1076
toolbars, **44–45**, **92–101**, **1079**
adding or deleting buttons, 94–96, 1079
adding menus, 96–97
assigning hyperlinks to buttons, 99–100
changing button display, 97–98
changing or editing button images with Button Editor, 98, *99*
creating toolbars, 100–101, 1079
Customize dialog box Commands tab, 73–74,
73
Customize dialog box Toolbars tab, 44, 72,
73, 92, 95, 100
displaying or hiding toolbars, 16, 22, 92–93
grouping buttons, 97

moving or docking toolbars, 93–94
new features, 44–45
overview of, 92
restoring default settings, 95
Web Layout view, 89, *89*
workspace, **8**, **84–92**, **798–803**
assigning keyboard shortcuts from keyboard,
800–801
AutoScroll feature, 803, *804*
Blue Background, White Text option, 91, *91*
calculating totals in documents, 799
configuring field shading, 87
configuring Normal and Outline views, 90–
91, *90*
creating personal menus, 798
customizing style area, 91, 274, *274*, 799, *800*
disabling Screen Tips, 86
displaying bookmarks, 86
displaying field codes, 87
displaying or hiding objects in Print Layout
and Web Layout views, 89, *89*
displaying or hiding scroll bars, 85–86
displaying highlighted text, 87
displaying measurements in ruler, 801, *802*
displaying placeholders, 86–87
displaying tabs, spaces, paragraphs, hidden
text, and optional hyphens, 87–88, *88*
displaying vertical ruler, 86, 89
hiding animated text, 86
hiding status bar, 86
imitating Word 97 interface, 92
opening dialog boxes with double-click hot
spots, 802
printing lists of keyboard shortcuts and
menu commands, 24, 103, 801, 1026
workspace defined, **8**, *9*
cutting and pasting. *See also* copying and pasting;
moving
automatic spacing adjustment for, 105
with Collect and Paste feature, 48–49, 149–150,
990–991
with Cut and Paste commands, 150, 990
with Insert key, 105
versus linking or embedding, 495
from other Windows programs, 150–151
with Paste Special dialog box, 150–151, 497,
497, 575, 576–577, *577*, 990
Smart Cut and Paste option, 105
text in footnotes and endnotes, 320
c|net Web site, 902

D

damaged document problems, 916–918
data labels in graphs, 436–437
data series and data points in graphs, 446–448
data sources, **527–532**. *See also* Mail Merge
 creating from Word tables, 527–529, *528*, *529*, *530*
 Database toolbar and, 530
 defined, **526**, *527*
 using Address Books, 532
 using databases or spreadsheets, 531–532, 859–860
databases. *See also* Mail Merge; Microsoft Access
 Database dialog box, 388, 580–582, *580*
 Database toolbar, 388, 530, 860, 974–975
 importing data into Word documents, 552–553, 580–582, *580*, 860–861, 974–975, 992–993
 importing data into Word tables, 387–388, 861–862, 974–975
 as Mail Merge data sources, 531–532
 Microsoft Query and, 552–553, 581
 saving form data as text files for exporting to, 737–738
 using Word as a database program, 834
datasheets for graphs
 defined, **420–421**
 editing, 427–428
 formatting numbers, 431–432
 navigating, 428
dates
 Alt + Shift + D (DATE field), 340
 Date-Time Picture field switch, 336
 entering in graphs, 428
 in headers and footers, 304, *304*, 305, 940
 inserting in documents, 993
debugging in Visual Basic for Applications
 defined, **780**
 statements, 773
 stepping through code, 780
 Visual Basic Editor Debug toolbar, 771, *771*
 Visual Basic Editor Immediate window, 768–769
 Visual Basic Editor Watch window, 769
deciphering error messages, 908
decision statements in Visual Basic for Applications, 776
declaration statements in Visual Basic for Applications, 773, 775
default font setting, 236
default page setup, 287

default scripting language in Microsoft Script Editor, 684
defining. *See also* creating
 what styles follow specific styles, 280
Delete key, 7
deleting
 AutoCorrect entries, 203
 bookmarks, 980
 custom spelling dictionaries, 186
 discussions, 617–618
 field shading in forms, 727
 footnotes and endnotes, 320, 1012
 formatting, 806
 frames, 653, 1015
 graphs, 426
 hyperlinks in documents, 635
 index entries, 359
 macro arguments in Visual Basic for Applications, 783
 macro projects, 752
 macro properties in Visual Basic for Applications, 782–783
 macros from macro projects, 752
 manual hyphens, 198
 passwords, 606
 print jobs, 214
 printer drivers, 957
 section breaks, 299, 982, 1059
 styles, 278
 subdocuments, 596–597, 1032–1033
 tables, 393
 in tables
  cells, 392–393
  columns, 391, 1067
  data, 393
  rows, 391, 1067
 text, 7, 148
 toolbar buttons, 94–96, 1079
Delivery Address options for envelopes, 512
Delivery Point Barcode option
 for envelopes, 511–512, *512*
 for labels, 520
 for merged envelopes, 546, 547
 for merged labels, 544
demoting outline levels, 565, 1045
Design mode
 and ActiveX controls in forms, 728–729
 for Web pages, 658–659, *660*, 666, 1086
Design View in Microsoft Script Editor, 684
designing
 forms, **712–716**, **719**
  automated forms, 719

borders and shading, 714, *715*

controls and fields, 716

graphics and clip art, 715, *716*

overview of, 712–713

tables, 713, *713*

text boxes, 714, *714*

laying out documents with tables, 821–822, *822,*
823

margins and page design, 289

Visual Basic for Applications macros, 787–788

Details button for error messages, 908

Details view in Open dialog box, 131

Detect and Repair utility, 36, 1096–1097

device drivers

printer driver problems, 909, 957

video driver problems, 910

dialog boxes

adding to macros, 785–786, 790–793

creating documents from, 826–828, *826, 827,*
829

opening with double-click hot spots, 802

.DIB files, 467

dictionaries. *See* custom dictionaries

digital signatures, **755–758**. *See also* security;
signatures

creating and installing, 755–756

defined, **755**

digitally signing macro projects, 756–758

Direct Mail Manager utility, 123, 549–550, 844

directories. *See also* folders

directory templates, 123

merged directories, 550–551, *551*

disabling. *See also* enabling

automatic hyphenation, 197

Automatic Spell Checking, 180

form fields, 725

incompatible features, 61–62, *61*, 66, 116–117

Office Assistant, 894–895

personalized menus, 21, 42, 1033–1034

Screen Tips, 86

Word features not supported in Web browsers,
640

Discussions feature, **59, 616–620, 993–995**. *See*
also Web-based collaboration features

connecting to discussion servers, 616, 617,
993–994

defined, **59, 616–617, 993**

editing and deleting discussions, 617–618

replying to general discussions, 619–620, 995

replying to inline discussions, 619, 995

starting inline or general discussions, 618–619,
994

viewing discussions, 617–618, *618*, 994

disk drives. *See* hard disk drives

diskettes, installing Word 2000 from, 1093

displaying. *See also* hiding; viewing

bookmarks, 86

changing how linked and embedded objects are
displayed, 501

Clipboard contents, 48, 150

document properties, 997

draft fonts in Normal and Outline views, 90–91,
90

Drawing toolbar, 458

field codes, 87, 336, *337*, 362, 1004

files in Open dialog box, 129–133

frame scroll bars, 654

full versus personalized menus, 20–21, 35, 42–
43, 102, 798, 1033–1034

hidden bookmarks, 167

hidden text, 87–88, *88*, 362

highlighted text, 87

measurements in ruler, 801, *802*

menus in templates, 107

objects in Print Layout and Web Layout views,
89, *89*

Office Shortcut Bar, 838, *839*, 840

Outline and Normal views simultaneously, 562–
563, *563*

outlines, **561–563, 1044**

all levels, 561

expanding or collapsing a section, 561–562,
1044

first line of text only, 562, 1044

or hiding text formatting, 562

Outline and Normal views simultaneously,
562–563, *563*

specific levels only, 561, 1044

placeholders, 86–87

readability statistics, 194

rulers, 290

script anchors, 680, *680*

scroll bars, 85–86

section break markers, 298, *299*

styles in Normal view, 10

table gridlines, 380

tables in Outline view, 568–569

tabs, spaces, paragraphs, hidden text, and
optional hyphens, 87–88, *88*

text formatting in outlines, 562

toolbars
  or hiding, 16, 22, 92–93, 1078
  on Office Shortcut Bar, 840
  in templates, 107
vertical ruler, 86, 89, 290
distributing
  forms, **735–736**
    distributing automated forms, 735–736
    protecting, 735, 1014–1015
  objects, 481, 947, 1038
  table columns and rows evenly, 399, 1068
.DOC files, 6, 7, 61
docking toolbars, 93–94
Document Converter utility, 867, 874–875, *875*
Document Depot Web site, 902
Document Map view, 14, 165–166, *166*, 925, 995
document properties
  defined, **138–139**, *138*
  displaying, 997
  printing, 115, 138
Document Subscription dialog box, 59, 620–621, 1064
document templates, 120–121, 700–701
documents, **120–157**, **995–997**. *See also* files; master documents
  adding to Office binders, 842–843, *842*
  attaching envelopes to
    in Mail Merge, 549
    overview of, 515–516, *516*
    printing attached envelopes, 516
  attaching templates to, 125, 704
  automatic summaries in, 582–584, *584*, 979
  backing up, **155–157**
    with AutoRecover feature, 155–156, 157, 919
    creating automatic backups, 156
    recovering unsaved or damaged documents, 156–157
  calculating totals in, 799
  comparing, 609, 951
  converting
    Document Converter utility, 867, 874–875, *875*
    an existing document to a master document, 590–591
    file formats with Conversion Wizard, 62–63
    to Web pages, 629
  copying macro projects to different documents, 751, *751*
  creating, **6**, **120–127**, **996**
    from dialog boxes, 826–828, *826*, *827*, *829*
    from existing documents, 127

from Letter Wizard, 125–126, *126*, 829, 951, 954
  with New Blank Document button, 120
  from Office Shortcut Bar, 122, 840
  from outlines, 569–571, *570*
  from Outlook contacts, 866, 877–878
  overview of, 6, 996
  from Start menu, 122
  from templates, 120–124, *121*
  with Wizards, 125–127, *126*, 829
creating Click Here and Type fields, 825
creating document summaries, 582–584, *584*, 979
creating templates from, 710, 1077
creating Windows Desktop shortcuts to, 831
defined, **122**
document statistics, 139
editing multiple documents in multiple windows, 18
editing text, 6–7
e-mailing
  as attachments, 229, 999
  as e-mail messages, 52–53, 227–229, *228*, 998–999
entering text, 6–7
File Properties dialog box, 138–139, *138*
finding with Open dialog box, 133–136, *134*
finding specific places in documents, **163–168**
  with bookmarks, 166–168
  in Document Map view, 14, 165–166, *166*, 925, 995
  with Go To tab in Find and Replace dialog box, 164–165, *164*, 1015–1016
  with Select Browse Object tool, 163–164, 323, 338
hyperlinks in documents, **35**, **630–635**, **807–808**, **1020–1021**
  automatically converting Web and e-mail addresses to hyperlinks, 57, 633
  changing links, 634
  copying and pasting links, 634
  creating e-mail or mailto links, 632–633, 1021
  deleting links, 635
  formatting links, 635
  inserting hyperlinks, 35, 630–631, 807–808, 1020
  linking to uncreated documents, 632
  linking within a document, 632, 808
  selecting hyperlinks, 634
importing database data into, 552–553, 580–582, *580*, 860–861, 974–975, 992–993

inserting date and time, 993
inserting files, **578–580**
 linked files, 580
 part of a file, 579
 whole files, 578–579
inserting into Publisher documents, 863, 1058
inserting PowerPoint slides in, 857–859, *858*, 1056
laying out with tables, 821–822, *822*, *823*
Mail Merge main documents, **525–526**, **533–537**
 automating merges with Word fields, 535–537
 creating, **525–526**
 inserting merge fields, 533–534, *534*
 Mail Merge toolbar and, 533
naming, 154
navigating, **160–162**
 with keyboard, 160–161
 with mouse, 161–162, *162*
 with WordPerfect Navigation feature, 67
opening, **6**, **105–106**, **127–139**, **996**
 converting and opening documents, 105–106
 document opens with a different filename, 920
 document won't open, 918
 documents from other programs, 137
 from Office Shortcut Bar, 840
 with Open dialog box, 6, 128–137, *129*
 overview of, 6, 128, 996
 from Windows Desktop shortcuts, 831
printing, **216–220**
 canceling print jobs, 214
 controlling what prints with documents, 115–116, 138, 217
 document information, 217
 document properties, 115, 138, 217
 drafts, 115, 218
 multiple copies, 217
 paper source options, 217
 part of a document, 216–217
 previewing printouts, 13, 212–214, *213*
 with Print button, 214, 1056
 Print Data Only for Forms option, 218, 737
 to print files, 218–220
 ranges of pages, 216–217
 resizing documents to paper size, 52, 115, 214, 217–218, 824
 two pages per sheet of paper, 291
 updating fields and links before printing, 114, 501

Recently Used File List control, 106
resizing to paper size, 52, 115, 214, 217–218, 824
returning to where you left off in a document, 804
reusing with Letter Wizard, 829
saving, **7**, **60–62**, **152–157**, **996–997**
 in background, 154
 and backing up documents, 155–157
 current version of a document, 615, 1081–1082
 document is saved with unexpected filename extension, 922
 existing documents, 154–155, 996–997
 file save error messages, 920–922
 in HTML format, 638–640, 1083
 new documents, 7, 153, *153*, 996
 in non-Word 2000 formats, 155, 997
 and password-protecting documents, 604–606, 1052
 to previous Word formats, 60–62, *61*
 recovering unsaved or damaged documents, 156–157
 to Web folders, 692, 1085
single document interface, 41
splitting
 into Outline and Normal views, 562–563, *563*
 into view panes, 17–18, *17*
switching between, 41
switching template in current document, 704, 1075–1076
versus templates, 122
tracking document editing with Outlook Journal utility, 847, *847*, 1046
troubleshooting, **916–922**
 AutoRecovered document recovery problems, 919
 "Check drive" message, 922
 damaged documents, 916–918
 document cannot be found, 920
 document is saved with unexpected filename extension, 922
 document opens with a different filename, 920
 document won't open, 918
 file save error messages, 920–922
 file was accidentally deleted, 916
 identifying damaged documents, 917
 recovering damaged documents, 917–918
 "The disk is full or too many files are open" message, 921–922

"The disk is full trying to write to *drive…*"
message, 921
"The document is read-only" message, 922
"The file is too large" message, 922
"There has been a network or file permission
error. The network connection may be lost.
Filename.doc" message, 921
updating after changing templates, 706
Versions feature, **614–615**, **1081–1082**
automatically saving current version, 615
defined, **614**
saving current version of a document, 615,
1081–1082
viewing previous versions of a document,
615, 1082
viewing multiple documents in multiple windows, 18
domain names, 690
.DOT files, 122, 708
double-clicking. *See also* mouse
embedded objects, 502, 504
linked objects, 499
opening dialog boxes with double-click hot
spots, 802
downloading templates from Microsoft Web site,
702
draft fonts in Normal and Outline views, 90–91, *90*
drafts, printing, 115, 218
drag-and-drop feature, 105, 148–149
Draw Table button in Tables and Borders toolbar,
382–383, *383*, 395, 821–822, *822*, *823*
drawing objects. *See* AutoShapes
Drawing toolbar. *See also* graphics
3-D options, 490–491
AutoShapes options, 476, 477
defined, **458**, *458*
displaying, 458
Fill Color button, 488
Flip options, 484
Free Rotate button, 484
Grid button, 479
Group and Ungroup options, 483, 949
Line Color and Line Style buttons, 488
Shadow button, 489–490
drivers
printer driver problems, 909, 957
video driver problems, 910
drives. *See* hard disk drives
drop caps, **247–248**, **1010**
drop shadows
in graphs, 427

for objects, 489, *489*
shadow font style, 241–242, *241*
drop-down controls
Dropdown Box controls in Web page forms,
671–672, *672*
drop-down form fields, 723–724, *723*

E

EasyHTML/Help development tool, 867, 885, 893
Edit Categories dialog box, 373
Edit menu
changes to, 43
Clear command, 991
Copy command, 148–149, 575–576
Edit menu Find command versus Tools menu
Find command, 168
Find command, 168–171, *169*
Paste command, 148–149, 150, 575–576
Paste Special command
copying and pasting with, 150–151, 575,
576–577, *577*, 990
defined, **150–151**
linking objects, 497, *497*, 1041
Redo command, 152, 1081
Repeat command, 152
Replace command, 171–172, *171*
Undo command, 152, 924, 1081
Edit toolbar in Visual Basic Editor, 770, *770*
editing, **923–925**. *See also* changing; customizing
AutoShapes, 476, 998
cross-references, 991–992
custom spelling dictionaries, 187–188, 815
customizing editing options, 77–78, *78*, 104–106
discussions, 617–618
embedded objects, 503–504, *504*, 1043
graphics editing software, 471–472, 864, 867,
872–873, *873*
graphs, **427–431**
datasheets, 427–428
orientation of axes, 428–431, *429*, *430*, *431*
HTML code, 655
index entries, 359
linked data, 499, 1042
macros with Visual Basic Editor, 740, 746–748,
747, 781–783, 1029
multiple documents in multiple windows, 18
Office binder files, 843
Options dialog box Edit tab, 77–78, *78*, 104–106
in Print Preview, 805

Publisher text in Word, 862, *863*, 1057
returning to where you left off in a document,
804
scripts, 681
styles, **279–281**, **1062–1063**
by example, 279–280, *279*, 1062
manually, 280–281, 1062–1063
subdocuments, 595–596
tables of authorities citation categories, 373
text
overview of, 6–7
from right-click menus, 148
undoing and redoing changes, 152, 924,
1081
toolbar button images with Button Editor, 98,
99
tracking document editing in Outlook Journal
utility, 847, *847*, 1046
troubleshooting, **923–925**
automatic capitalization problems, 923–924
Click and Type feature does not work, 924
Document Map view does not display document headings, 925
entering text deletes existing text, 923
Find and Replace does not produce expected
results, 925
text accidentally deleted or cut, 923
text is automatically selected on mouse click
or key press, 923
Undo command generates error message, 924
WordArt text, 474–475, 1088–1089
editing tools, **45–49**. *See also* AutoCorrect; Grammar Checker; Spelling; Thesaurus
Click and Type feature, 46–47, 104–105,
140–141, 384, 924, 985
Collect and Paste feature, 48–49, 149–150, 990–
991
object placement controls, 35, 47–48, *47*
table editing and formatting enhancements, 49
Web editing tools, **53–57**
frames, 56
Insert Hyperlink dialog box, 56–57, *57*
themes, 55, *56*, 283, 642–645, *643*, *644*, 1087
VBScript controls, 57, *58*
Web Page Preview, 13, 53, *54*, 636
Web Page Wizard, 54–55, *55*, 640–641, 1084
Elevation option for 3-D graphs, 451, *452*
ellipsis (…) in menus, 20
e-mail, **223–229**, **998–999**
blind-carbon-copy (Bcc) recipients, 227
composing, 122

creating e-mail or mailto links in documents,
632–633, 1021
creating hyperlinks to e-mail addresses, 57, 633
creating signatures, 225–226, *225*
distributing automated forms via, 736
e-mail options, 114, 225–227
e-mailing merged documents, 540–541
enhanced features, 52–53
HTML e-mail messages, 224
Outlook and e-mailing Word documents, 53,
227, 228, 845
saving, 122
selecting stationery and fonts, 226–227
sending documents
as e-mail attachments, 229, 999
as e-mail messages, 52–53, 227–229, *228*,
998–999
system requirements, 223–224
troubleshooting, **964**
embedding, **496**, **501**, **502–505**, **952–953**, **1042–
1043**. *See also* linking
changing how embedded objects are displayed,
501
converting embedded objects to another file format, 504–505
creating embedded objects, 502–503, *503*, 1042–
1043
versus cutting and pasting, 495
defined, **496**, **502**, **1041**
double-clicking embedded objects, 502, 504
editing embedded objects, 503–504, *504*, 1043
Embed TrueType Fonts option, 237
embedding existing data, 502, 1042
Excel cells or worksheets in Word tables, 850–
852, *851*, 1002
Excel charts in Word documents, 852–853, 1003
identifying embedded objects, 496
versus linking, 495–496
PowerPoint presentations in Word documents,
859, 1056
troubleshooting, **952–953**
embossed font style, 241–242, *241*
.EMF files, 467
enabling. *See also* disabling; Options dialog box
AutoCorrect, 199–200, 975–976
AutoCorrect Spell Checking, 183
automatic hyperlink creation, 57, 633
automatic hyphenation, 197
AutoRecover feature, 156
backup copies, 156
Click and Type feature, 46–47, 104–105, 141,
985

drag-and-drop feature, 105
event sounds, 106
Help for WordPerfect Users, 66–67, 106
Insert or Overtype mode, 105
line numbering, 270
Outlook Journal utility, 846, 1046
Track Changes feature, 607, 1079–1080
Word macro security, 38–39, 753–754
WordPerfect Navigation, 67
End key, navigating with, 161
endnotes. *See* footnotes and endnotes
engraved font style, 241–242, *241*
enhancements. *See* new features
entering
  date and time in graphs, 428
  in tables
    tab stops, 389
    text or graphics, 389, *390*
  text
    AutoText entries, 144, 979
    with Click and Type feature, 46–47, 104–105,
    140–141, 384, 924, 985
    overview of, 6–7
enterprise-wide customizing, 85
envelopes, **510–517**, **1000–1001**. *See also* labels;
 Mail Merge
  adding graphics, 517
  addressing, **514–515**
    adding return address automatically, 514
    automatically adding name and address from
    a letter, 515
    Delivery Address options, 512
    Return Address options, 512–513
    selecting names from Windows Address
    Book, 515
  attaching to documents
    in Mail Merge, 549
    overview of, 515–516, *516*, 1001
    printing attached envelopes, 516
  Envelope Options dialog box, **510–513**, **1000**
    Delivery Address options, 512
    Delivery Point Barcode option, 511–512, *512*
    Envelope Size option, 511
    FIM-A Courtesy Reply Mail option, 512
    font options, 512–513
    opening, 510
    Printing Options tab, 511
    Return Address options, 512–513
  Envelope Wizard, 514
  formatting, 517
  KazStamp envelope printing software, 514, 867,
  878–879, *879*

merged envelopes, **545–550**
  barcode options, 546, 547
  creating attached merge envelopes, 549
  creating with Direct Mail Manager, 123,
  549–550
  printing, 545–549, *547*, *548*
printing
  envelopes attached to documents, 516
  postage on envelopes, 821
  single envelopes, 513–514, *513*, 1000
saving as templates, 517
third-party software, 514
Eon Solutions Ltd., 885
.EPS files, 467
equations, 417–418, *418*, 1001. *See also* formulas;
 tables of figures
Eraser button on Tables and Borders toolbar, 395
error messages, **906–912**. *See also* troubleshooting
  AutoCorrect problems, 910
  bookmark error message is displayed, 943–944
  changing page orientation or paper size generates error message, 933–934
  "Check drive" message, 922
  clicking Web page hyperlinks generates an error
  message, 965
  cross-references in master documents are
  replaced by error messages, 938
  custom dictionary problems, 910
  deciphering the message, 908
  determining the scope of problems, 908–909
  examining the timing of errors, 908
  fatal exception errors, 907
  file save error messages, 920–922
  font problems, 910
  illegal operation errors, 907
  in indexes and tables of contents, 939
  kernel errors, 907
  Mail Merge error message says data file is main
  document, 954
  master document tables of contents or indexes
  contain error messages, 938
  printer driver problems, 909
  printing error messages, 962–964
  reinstalling Word, 912
  repairing Word, 911
  running a macro generates an error message,
  969
  "The disk is full or too many files are open"
  message, 921–922
  "The disk is full trying to write to *drive...*"
  message, 921
  "The document is read-only" message, 922

"The file is too large" message, 922
"There has been a network or file permission error. The network connection may be lost. *Filename.doc*" message, 921
"Too many fonts" message, 964
Undo command generates error message, 924
uninstalling Word, 911–912
video driver problems, 910
viewing Details button, 908
"Windows cannot print due to a problem with the current printer setup" message, 962–963
"Word cannot bring up the Properties dialog box because printer returned an error", message, 963
E-Stamp Internet Postage Web site, 821
even and odd headers and footers, 306, 1018–1019
events
    event sounds, 106
    in Visual Basic for Applications, 780
eVirus Corporation, 882
executable statements in Visual Basic for Applications, 773, 775
expanding
    character spacing, 243, 244–245, *245*, 1009
    menus, 20–21
    outline sections, 561–562, 1044
    subdocuments, 595
exporting. *See also* importing
    Access data to documents, 552–553, 580–582, *580*, 860–861, 974–975
    Access data to tables, 387–388, 861–862, 974–975
    form data as text files to databases, 737–738
    Meeting Minder notes to Word, 856–857, 1055–1056
    PowerPoint handouts to Word, 855, *855*, 1055
    PowerPoint Meeting Minder notes to Word, 856–857, 1055
    PowerPoint presentations to documents, 856, 1055
    Word outlines to PowerPoint, 853–854, 1055
expressions in Visual Basic for Applications, 774
Extensions for Microsoft Office, 58, 616, 620, 621

F

F keys
    Ctrl + F11 (Lock Field), 342, 1005
    displaying as a toolbar, 24
    F9 (Update), 370, 374
    listed, 23
    Shift + Ctrl + F11 (Unlock Field), 342, 1005
    Shift + F5 (Return to Last Edit), 804
    Shift + F9 (Field Code/Result toggle), 336
fatal exception errors, **907**
fax-back support, 904
faxes, **123**, **220–223**, **1003–1004**
    fax software, 221–222
    fax software on book's CD-ROM, 222
    fax templates, 123
    Fax Wizard, 222–223
    faxing merged documents, 540–541
    Microsoft Fax software, 221
    MightyFax software, 222, 867, 880, *881*
    Office 2000 Symantec WinFax Starter Edition software, 221–222
    sending, 220–221, 1003–1004
    third-party fax software, 222
    troubleshooting, **964**
    upgrading WinFax Starter Edition to WinFax Pro, 222
fields, **334–352**, **1004–1005**. *See also* ActiveX controls; controls; scripts
    automating Mail Merge with, 535–537
    backslash (\) in, 335–336
    controlling database data with, 860
    creating Click Here and Type fields, 825
    cross-references and, 331
    defined, **334**
    field codes
        arguments in, 335
        displaying or hiding, 87, 336, *337*, 362, 1004
        Instant Reference, **343–352**
        keyboard shortcuts, 340
        printing, 115
        printing codes instead of results, 338
        TOC field code, 369
        XE field code for indexes, 357, 358
    field results, **341–343**, **1005**
        formatting, 342–343
        locking and unlocking fields, 336, 342, 1005
        unlinking fields, 342
        updating, 341–342, 1005
    finding and replacing, 174–175
    form fields, **716**, **720–727**, **1013**
        versus ActiveX controls, 720
        adding, 721, 1013
        adding or deleting shading, 714, *715*, 727
        adding Help text, 725–727, *726*
        changing field options, 724–725, 1013
        check box field, 722–723, *723*
        designing, 716
        disabling, 725

drop-down fields, 723–724, *723*
formatting form field results, 727
Forms toolbar and, 720
overview of, 720
text fields, 721–722, *721*, *722*
=(FORMULA) field, 799, 849
formulas and, 335, 415
in headers and footers, 305
inserting, **338–340**, **1004–1005**
    with Field dialog box, 339–340, *339*, 1004–1005
    with macros, 741
    manually, 340, *341*, 1005
inserting page numbers with page fields, 302
navigating, 163–164, 338
shading, 87, 337, 1004
switches, 335–336, 342–343
types of, 334–335
Update Field command in right-click menus, 371
File menu
changes to, 43
New command, 6
Open command, 6
Recently Used File List control, 106
Save As command, 7, 39, *40*, 153, *153*
Save command, 7, 154–155
sending faxes, 220–221
filename extensions
.BMP, 460, 467
.CDR, 467
.CGM, 467
.DIB, 467
.DOC, 6, 7, 61
.DOT, 122, 708
.EMF, 467
.EPS, 467
.FPX, 467
.GIF, 467
.HTM, 122
.JAH, 468
.JBH, 468
.JPG, 467
.JSH, 468
.OLB, 779
.PCD, 468
.PCT, 468
.PCX, 468
.PNG, 468
.RLE, 467
.RTF, 576
.TIF, 468

.WMF, 463, *464*, 468
.WPG, 468
files. *See also* documents
adding to Office binders, 842–843, *842*
AutoMark files, 355, 360–361, 1024
creating Help files, 893
displaying in Open dialog box, 129–133
File Locations tab in Options dialog box, 83–84, *84*, 116
file operations in Open dialog box, 137
File Properties dialog box, 138–139, *138*
finding text versus finding files, 168
graphics files, **467–472**, **1052–1054**
    animated GIFs, 949
    creating alternate text for Web page graphics, 471, 647, 1054
    editing software, 471–472, 864, 867, 872–873, *873*
    file formats, 467–468, 1052
    formatting options in Picture toolbar, 470, 1053
    inserting, 468, 1053
    linking, 497, 498
    OfficeExpress 2000 graphics software, 472, 867, 872–873, *873*
    scanning and importing digital photographs, 468–470, 1053
Mail Merge data sources, **527–532**
    creating from Word tables, 527–529, *528*, *529*, *530*
    Database toolbar and, 530
    defined, **526**, *527*
    using Address Books, 532
    using databases or spreadsheets, 531–532, 859–860
opening backup files, 157
printing documents to print files, 218–220
Recently Used File List control, 106
RTF files, 576
sound file formats, 665
template files, 40–41
filling in automated forms, 736–737
fills
Fill Color button in Drawing toolbar, 488
Fill Effects dialog box, **448–451**, **818–819**. *See also* graphs
    defined, **448**
    Gradient tab, 449
    Pattern tab, 450
    Picture tab, 450
    Texture tab, 449

using gradient fills in headers and footers, 818–819, *818*

gradient fills
in graphs, 449
in headers and footers, 818–819, *818*
for page backgrounds, 292–293
for objects, 488, 1040

FIM-A Courtesy Reply Mail option for envelopes, 512

Find and Replace dialog box, **20**, **164–165**, **168–176**, **1006–1007**
defined, **168**
Edit menu Find command versus Tools menu Find command, 168
Find All Word Forms option, 170
Find operations, **168–171**, *169*, **1006**
Find Whole Words Only option, 170
finding and replacing formatting, 172–173
finding and replacing special elements, 174–175
Go To tab, 164–165, *164*, 1015–1016
Match Case option, 170
opening from status bar, 20
Replace operations, **171–172**, *171*, **1006–1007**
Sounds Like option, 170
troubleshooting, 925
wildcards in, 170, 175–176

finding
documents with Open dialog box, 133–136, *134*
Edit menu Find command versus Tools menu Find command, 168
with Find Fast feature, 136
fonts, 172
foreign language text, 173
frames, 173
highlighted text, 173
hosts for business Web pages, 688, 690–691
hosts for personal Web pages, 688–690
Microsoft Knowledge Base information, 899–901, *900*
paragraphs, 172
specific places in documents, **163–168**, **323**
with bookmarks, 166–168
in Document Map view, 14, 165–166, *166*, 925, 995
with Go To tab in Find and Replace dialog box, 164–165, *164*, 1015–1016
with Select Browse Object tool, 163–164, 323, 338
tab stops, 172
text versus finding files, 168
Wizards, 125

first page headers and footers, 305–306, 1018

first-line indenting, 256–257, *256*, 1051
fixing macro errors, 781–782

flagging
grammar errors as you type, 192, 1061
spelling errors as you type, 180–182, *181*, 1060

Flesch Reading Ease and Grade Level scores, 194
flipping objects, 483–484, 1039
floppy disks, installing Word 2000 from, 1093
flowing tables across pages, 396

folders
folder views in Open dialog box, 129–133
supporting folders of files for Web pages, 692, 696
template folders, 40–41, 706
Web folders, **691–692**, **1085–1086**
creating Web folders, **691–692**, **1085**
managing Web folder contents, 692, 1085–1086
saving documents to Web folders, 692, 1085
Web Folder Wizard, 692
Web folders defined, **691**

fonts, **90–91**, **118**, **172**, **226–227**, **234–242**. *See also* text formatting
adding, 235
all caps font style, 241–242, *241*
bold font style, 237–238, 239, 241–242, *241*
for bullets, 266
defined, **234**
draft fonts in Normal and Outline views, 90–91, *90*
in e-mail messages, 226–227
embossed and engraved font styles, 241–242, *241*
on envelopes, 512–513
error messages, 910
finding, 172
Font dialog box, **238–242**, **243–247**
animating text, 242, 1008
changing fonts, styles, and size, 239
character spacing options, 243, 244–245, *245*, 1009
coloring text, 240
kerning character pairs, 245–246, *246*, 1009–1010
overview of, 238, *239*
scaling, stretching, or condensing text, 244, *244*
selecting font styles, 239–242, *241*
setting default font, 236
subscript and superscript font styles, 241–242, *241*, 246–247, 1010
Text Effects options, 242

font styles
  defined, **234**
  selecting, 237–238, 239, 240–242, *241*
Font Substitution option, 118, 237
formatting with Formatting toolbar, 237–238, 239, 240, 243
italic font style, 237–238, 239, 241–242, *241*
monospaced fonts, 234
outline font style, 241–242, *241*
points, 234
proportional fonts, 234
serif versus sans serif fonts, 234
shadow font style, 241–242, *241*
small caps font style, 241–242, *241*
strikethrough font style, 241–242, *241*
styles for, 272
subscript and superscript font styles, 241–242, *241*, 246–247, 1010
troubleshooting
  font does not display properly, 926
  font problems, 910
  text point size changed, 927
  "Too many fonts" message, 964
  underlining does not work on blank spaces or lines, 928
TrueType fonts
  defined, **235**
  Embed TrueType Fonts option, 237
typefaces, **234**
underline font style, 237–238, 239, 240–242, *241*, 928, 1008
viewing installed fonts and font styles, 235–236
Windows font settings, 235
footers. *See* headers and footers
footnotes and endnotes, **163–164, 174–175, 314–323, 1011–1012**
  continuation notices, 319
  converting, 322–323, 1012
  converting to hyperlinks in Web pages, 317
  copying, 319–320, 1011–1012
  creating, **316–318, 1011**
  cross-references in, 318–319
  cutting, copying, and pasting text in, 320
  defined, **314–315**, *314*, *315*
  deleting, 320, 1012
  finding and replacing footnote marks, 174–175
  formatting, **320–322, 1012**
    changing note numbering, 321
    Note Options dialog box and, 320
    placement options, 321
    selecting note reference marks, 321
    text and separators, 322

moving, 319–320, 1011–1012
navigating with Select Browse Object tool, 163–164, 323
in Normal view, 315, *316*, 319
note reference marks
  defined, **314**, *314*
  selecting, 321
in Outline view, 315, *316*
Print Layout view and, 315
troubleshooting
  footnote continues on following page, 943
  footnote text is deleted, but reference still appears in document, 942
  footnotes or endnotes disappear, 942
viewing, 315–316, *316*, 318, 1011
foreign language support, **59–60**
  finding foreign language text, 173
  global interface, 60
  international character shortcuts, 811–812
  Language AutoDetect feature, 60
  language setting for styles, 273
  Language Settings window, 60
Format field switch, 336
Format menu changes, 43
Format Object dialog box, 458, 459–460
Format Text Box dialog box, 47–48, *47*, 143
formatting. *See also* page setup; paragraphs; styles; text formatting
  AutoFormat feature, **111–112, 204–208, 977–978**
    AutoFormat as You Type options, 207, 812–813, 978
    configuring, 111–112, 204–206, *205*, 978
    creating bulleted lists, 206, 207, 264, 812–813
    creating numbered lists, 206, 207, 264
    creating tables, 383–384
    customizing, 111–112
    defined, **204, 977**
    reviewing and accepting changes, 208
    running, 207–208, 978
    Style Gallery option, 208
    Table AutoFormat feature, 405–406, 1069–1070
    uses for, 207
  copying
    with Format Painter, 238, 805–806
    multiple times, 806
    section formatting, 299
    text and paragraph formatting, 805
  deleting, 806
  envelopes, 517
  field results, 342–343

finding and replacing, 172–173
footnotes and endnotes, **320–322**, **1012**
  changing note numbering, 321
  Note Options dialog box and, 320
  placement options, 321
  selecting note reference marks, 321
  text and separators, 322
form field results, 727
Format Painter tool, 238, 805–806
frames, 653–654
French formatting, 105
graphs, **441–454**
  chart area, 441–442
  data series and data points, 446–448
  datasheet numbers, 431–432
  plot area, 442–443
  text, 446
hyperlinks in documents, 635
indexes, 356, 364–365
manual formatting versus styles, 272
master documents, 599
objects, **478–491**, **1036–1040**
  3-D effects, *489*, 490–491, 1040
  aligning objects, 481, 947, 948
  aligning objects vertically, 1037
  applying grids for positioning graphics, 479
  borders and fills, 488, 1040
  cropping objects, 484–486, *485*, 1054
  distributing objects, 481, 947, 1038
  flipping objects, 483–484, 1039
  formatting options in Picture toolbar, 470, 1053
  grouping and ungrouping objects, 483, 949
  layering objects, 482–483, *482*, 1038
  moving objects, 479–480, 1036–1037
  resizing objects, 480–481, 1037
  rotating objects, 483–484, 950, 1038–1039
  shadows, 489, *489*, 1040
  wrapping text around objects, 486–488, 1039–1040
paragraphs
  copying with Format Painter, 238, 805–806
  deleting formatting, 806
  with Formatting toolbar, 252–253
  overview of, 252
  with Paragraph dialog box, 253–254
  selected paragraphs, 252
  with themes, 283
subdocuments, 599
table cells, **406–409**
  aligning text, 49, 406–407
  applying borders and shading, 409, *410*

changing text orientation, 407–408, *407*
  setting margins, 408–409
tables, **49**, **400–406**
  aligning tables and wrapping text, 400–402
  applying borders and gridlines, 403–404, 1068–1069
  applying table shading, 404–405, 1069
  copying tables in documents, 400
  moving tables in documents, 49, 378–379, *378*, 400
  new features, 49
  setting cell margins, 402–403
  with Table AutoFormat feature, 405–406, 1069–1070
tables of contents, 370
tables of figures, 372
text boxes, 142–143
troubleshooting, **926–930**
  bullets do not display properly, 927
  font does not display properly, 926
  graphics or text in a line appear cut off, 928–929
  justified text leaves gaps between words, 926–927
  new paragraphs do not have expected formatting, 928
  outline numbering does not number headings, 929
  paragraph borders are cut off, 929
  paragraph formatting changes when text is deleted, 927–928
  tabs and paragraph indents disappear when bullets or numbering are added or deleted, 927
  text point size changed, 927
  text unexpectedly appears as a hyperlink, 929
  underlining does not work on blank spaces or lines, 928
vertical text alignment
  in columns of text, 309
  in page setup, 291–292, 1048–1049
Web pages, **642–651**
  applying Web themes, 55, *56*, 283, 642–645, *643*, *644*, 1087
  color or graphic backgrounds, 646
  formatting horizontal lines, 649
  inserting horizontal lines, 648–649, 1084
  with tables, 650–651, *650*, *651*
  Web page text, 645–646
Formatting toolbar
  aligning text in table cells, 407
  creating bulleted lists, 264–265, 983

creating numbered lists, 267, 1035
formatting paragraphs, 252–253
forms, **218**, **712–738**, **967–968**, **1012–1015**
    ActiveX controls, **716**, **727–734**, **1013–1014**.
    See also automated forms
        adding, 727–729, 1013–1014
        additional controls in Control Toolbox tool-
            bar, 730–731
        check boxes, 729
        combo boxes, 730
        command buttons, 729
        Control Toolbox toolbar and, 728, 730–731
        defined, **727**
        Design mode and, 728–729
        designing, 716
        versus form fields, 720
        image controls, 730
        label controls, 730
        list boxes, 730
        option buttons, 729
        programming, 732–733, *733*, 1014
        scroll buttons, 730
        setting properties, 731–732, *732*, 1014
        spin buttons, 730
        text boxes, 714, *714*, 729
        toggle buttons, 730
        Visual Basic for Applications (VBA) and, 718,
            720, 727–728, 729, 732–733
    automated forms, **718–738**, **1012**. *See also*
        ActiveX controls; fields
        creating form templates, 718–719, 1013
        creating with macros, 734
        defined, **718**, **1012**
        designing, 719
        distributing, 735–736
        filling in, 736–737
        printing form data only, 218, 737
        protecting, 735, 1014
        saving form data as text files for sending to
            databases, 737–738
    creating
        form templates, 718–719
        printed forms, 717
        in Visual Basic for Applications, 772, 788–
            789, *788*, *789*, *790*
    defined, **712**, **718**, **1012**
    designing, **712–716**, **719**
        automated forms, 719
        borders and shading, 714, *715*
        controls and fields, 716
        graphics and clip art, 715, *716*
        overview of, 712–713

tables, 713, *713*
text boxes, 714, *714*
fields, **716**, **720–727**, **1013**. *See also* automated
    forms
    versus ActiveX controls, 720
    adding, 721, 1013
    adding or deleting shading, 714, *715*, 727
    adding Help text, 725–727, *726*
    changing field options, 724–725, 1013
    check box field, 722–723, *723*
    designing, 716
    disabling, 725
    drop-down fields, 723–724, *723*
    formatting form field results, 727
    Forms toolbar and, 720
    overview of, 720
    text fields, 721–722, *721*, *722*
troubleshooting, **967–968**
    check box size does not change when format-
        ted, 968
    field codes are displayed instead of form
        fields, 967
    form fields don't work, 967
    macro problems, 968
    Tab key does not move insertion point to cor-
        rect form field, 968
in Visual Basic for Applications
    adding controls, 772
    creating, **772**
    defined, **771**
    Visual Basic Editor UserForm toolbar, 770,
        771
    Visual Basic Editor UserForm window, 768,
        768
forms in Web pages, **666–678**, **1086–1087**. *See also*
    scripts
    adding to Web pages, 668–669, *668*, 1086
    controls, **57**, **669–678**
        ActiveX controls, 670
        Checkbox controls, 670–671, *670*
        Control Toolbox toolbar, 670
        Dropdown Box controls, 671–672, *672*
        Hidden controls, 678
        List Box controls, 672–673, *673*
        Option Button controls, 671, *671*
        Password controls, 674, *674*
        Reset controls, 677–678, *678*
        setting control properties, 669–670, 1086–
            1087
        Submit controls, 675–676, *676*
        Submit with Image controls, 676–677, *677*
        Text Area controls, 674–675, *675*

Textbox controls, 673–675, *673*
VBScript controls, 57, *58*
Design mode and, 658–659, *660*, 666, 1086
how forms collect data, 667
overview of, 666–667
Run mode and, 659
scripts and, 667
Web Tools toolbar and, 658–659, *659*, 670
=(FORMULA) field, 799, 849
formulas in tables, **335**, **413–418**, **1070–1071**
  arguments of functions, 416
  AutoSum button for quick totals, 413–414, 799,
    1070
  bookmarks in, 416
  creating complex equations, 417–418, *418*
  fields and, 335, 415
  importing Excel worksheets, 417
  limitations of, 417
  operators, 415
  referencing cells, 415–416
  simple formulas, 414–415, 1070–1071
  using functions, 416
.FPX files, 467
frames, **56**, **651–654**, **1015**. *See also* borders; Web
pages
  adding borders, 654
  creating, **56**, **653**, **1015**
  creating navigation frames, 653, 1015
  creating tables of contents in, 653
  defined, **651**, *652*, **1015**
  deleting, 653, 1015
  displaying or hiding scroll bars, 654
  finding, 173
  formatting, 653–654
  frames are missing or displayed incorrectly,
    966–967
  Frames toolbar, 652, *652*
  resizing, 654
  styles for, 273
Free Rotate button in Drawing toolbar, 484
Freeform drawing, 950
freezes, 156–157
French formatting, 105
FTP sites, **693–694**
  adding FTP site addresses to Word, 693–694
  uploading Web pages to FTP sites, 694
full menus, 20–21, 35
Full Screen view, **16**, **1089**
function keys
  Ctrl + F11 (Lock Field), 342, 1005
  displaying as a toolbar, 24

F9 (Update), 370, 374
  listed, 23
  Shift + Ctrl + F11 (Unlock Field), 342, 1005
  Shift + F5 (Return to Last Edit), 804
  Shift + F9 (Field Code/Result toggle), 336
function procedures in VBA, 778
functions in tables, 416

G

general discussions. *See also* Discussions feature
  replying to, 619–620, 995
  starting, 618–619, 994
general field switches, 335–336, 342–343
General tab in Options dialog box
  Blue Background, White Text option, 91, *91*
  defined, **77**, *77*
  E-mail options, 114
  Web options, 113
generating. *See also* creating
  document summaries, 582–584, *584*, 979
  indexes, 361–363, *362*, *363*
  tables of authorities, 374, 1071–1072
  tables of contents, 366–369, *367*, *368*, 1073
  tables of contents from another document, 830
  tables of contents manually, 371
  tables of figures, 372, 1073–1074
.GIF files, 467
global interface, 60
global templates, 120, 700–701
Go To tab in Find and Replace dialog box, 164–165,
  164, 1015–1016. *See also* navigating
GPDATA address book utility, 867, 876–877, *876*
Grade Level score, 194
gradient fills. *See also* fills
  in graphs, 449
  in headers and footers, 818–819, *818*
  for page backgrounds, 292–293
Grammar Checker, **51**, **80–81**, **107–108**, **188–194**,
  1061. *See also* Spelling feature; Thesaurus
  advantages and disadvantages, 188–189
  Automatic Grammar Checking, 192, 1061
  configuring, 80–81, *81*, 107–108, 189
  configuring grammar rules, 108, 190–192
  flagging errors as you type, 192, 1061
  Flesch Reading Ease and Grade Level scores, 194
  new features, 51
  Options dialog box Spelling & Grammar tab,
    80–81, *81*, 107–108, 189
  Readability Statistics feature, 108, 193–194, *194*

running, 192–193, *193*, 1061
selecting Writing Style, 189
Word Count feature, 194
graphics, **458–491**, **945–951**, **1036–1040**, **1052–
1054**. *See also* objects; tables of figures
   AutoShapes, **475–477**, **997–998**
      creating free-form drawings, 477, *478*, 950,
        998
      defined, **475–476**, **997**
      as drawing objects, 475, 997
      drawing objects disappear when Letter Wiz-
        ard is run, 951
      Drawing toolbar options, 476, 477
      editing, 476, 998
      Freeform drawing cannot be controlled, 950
      inserting, 476, 997
      printing, 116
      Word 2000 as a drawing program, 834–835
   in bar charts, 816–817, *816*, *817*
   captions, **324–328**, **984–985**
      adding automatically, 325–326, 984–985
      adding chapter numbers, 327–328
      adding manually, 325, 984
      captions are not numbered correctly, 943
      captions do not update correctly, 943
      changing numbering format, 327, 985
      creating with tables, 324
      defined, **324**, *324*, **984**
      selecting caption labels, 326–327
   clip art, **460–467**, **986–987**
      adding images to Clip Gallery, 464–465, 987
      bitmapped images, 460, 467
      creating categories in Clip Gallery, 465
      creating graphical bullets with, 266–267, 813,
        984
      defined, **460**
      in forms, 715, *716*
      inserting from Clip Gallery, 461–463, *461*,
        462, 986
      line art, 460
      ungrouping and editing .WMF file images,
        463, *464*, 949, 986
      Web sites, 466–467
   drawing objects. *See* AutoShapes
   Drawing toolbar
      3-D options, 490–491
      AutoShapes options, 476, 477
      defined, **458**, *458*
      displaying, 458
      Fill Color button, 488
      Flip options, 484
      Free Rotate button, 484

      Grid button, 479
      Group and Ungroup options, 483, 949
      Line Color and Line Style buttons, 488
      Shadow button, 489–490
   on envelopes, 517
   Format Object dialog box, 458, 459–460
   formatting objects, **478–491**, **1036–1040**
      3-D effects, *489*, 490–491, 1040
      aligning objects, 481, 947, 948
      aligning objects vertically, 1037
      applying grids for positioning graphics, 479
      borders and fills, 488, 1040
      cropping objects, 484–486, *485*, 1054
      distributing objects, 481, 947, 1038
      flipping objects, 483–484, 1039
      formatting options in Picture toolbar, 470,
        1053
      grouping and ungrouping objects, 483, 949
      layering objects, 482–483, *482*, 1038
      moving objects, 479–480, 1036–1037
      resizing objects, 480–481, 1037
      rotating objects, 483–484, 950, 1038–1039
      shadows, 489, *489*, 1040
      wrapping text around objects, 486–488,
        1039–1040
   in forms, 715, *716*
   gradient fills
      in graphs, 449
      in headers and footers, 818–819, *818*
      for page backgrounds, 292–293
   graphical bullets, 266–267, 813–814, *814*, 984
   graphical page borders, 296, *297*
   graphics files, **467–472**, **1052–1054**
      animated GIFs, 949
      creating alternate text for Web page graphics,
        471, 647, 1054
      editing software, 471–472, 864, 867, 872–
        873, *873*
      file formats, 467–468, 1052
      formatting options in Picture toolbar, 470,
        1053
      inserting, 468, 1053
      linking, 497, 498
      OfficeExpress 2000 graphics software, 472,
        867, 872–873, *873*
      scanning and importing digital photo-
        graphs, 468–470, 1053
   in graphs, 450
   marking for index entries, 357
   in master documents separate from subdocu-
      ments, 587, 596
   Picture toolbar

Crop button, 484–485, *485*
defined, **459**, *459*
displaying, 458
graphics formatting options, 470, 1053
in tables, 389, *390*
text boxes, **47–48**, **141–143**, **478**
    columns of text in, 934
    creating, **141–142**, *142*, **1077**
    defined, **141**
    Format Text Box dialog box, 47–48, *47*, 143
    formatting, 142–143, 478
    in forms, 714, *714*, 729
    Textbox controls in Web page forms, 673–675, *673*
troubleshooting, **945–951**
    3-D effects replace borders and shadows, 950
    3-D and shadow colors don't change when object color is changed, 950
    Align or Distribute menu items are unavailable, 947
    aligned objects are stacked on top of each other, 947
    animated GIFs cannot be changed, 949
    borders do not display properly, 950
    colors are not smooth onscreen, 947
    colors won't change, 949
    drawing object disappears when Letter Wizard is run, 951
    Freeform drawing cannot be controlled, 950
    graphics are not visible, 945–946
    graphics in a line appear cut off, 928–929
    graphics in Web pages are not positioned properly, 966
    graphics won't print, 946
    graphics won't resize correctly, 949
    graphics won't rotate, 950
    graphics won't ungroup, 949
    lines are jagged onscreen, 947
    object alignment changed when document was opened on another computer, 948
    objects do not align or distribute as commanded, 947
    objects jump when realigned, 948
    paragraphs won't move without moving graphic, 948
    part of graphic does not display, 946
in Web pages
    background graphics, 293, 646
    creating alternate text for graphics, 471, 647, 1054
    graphics are not positioned properly, 966

graphics do not display, 965–966
inserting, 646–647
Submit with Image controls in Web page forms, 676–677, *677*
WordArt text, **472–475**, **1088–1089**
    defined, **472**
    editing with WordArt toolbar, 474–475, 1088–1089
    inserting, 472–474, *474*, 1088
graphs, **420–455**, **1016–1017**
    3-D graphs, **451–454**
        Auto Scaling option, 454
        Elevation option, 451, *452*
        Height option, 454, *455*
        Perspective option, 453, *454*
        Right Angle Axes option, 454
        Rotation option, 452, *453*
    adding graph elements, **434–441**
        callouts, 440–441
        data labels, 436–437
        graph elements defined, **434**, *435*
        gridlines, 438
        legends, 438–440
        titles, 435–436
        trendlines, 437
    axes
        configuring axis settings, 443–445
        Right Angle Axes option in 3-D View dialog box, 454
        switching category (x-axis) and value (y-axis) axes, 428–431, *429*, *430*, *431*
    borders, 427
    changing graph type, **432–434**
        with Chart Type dialog box, 433–434
        from Standard toolbar, 432
    copying, 424–425, *424*
    creating, **422–423**, **434**, **1016–1017**
        custom graphs, 434
        Excel charts from Word, 853
        from existing data, 422, 1016
        linked to data in documents, 422–423, 1016–1017
        from scratch, 423, 1017
    datasheets
        defined, **420–421**
        editing, 427–428
        formatting numbers, 431–432
        navigating, 428
    deleting, 426
    drop shadows, 427
    editing, **427–431**

datasheets, 427–428
orientation of axes, 428–431, *429*, *430*, *431*
entering date and time, 428
Excel charts, **852–853**, **1003**
creating from Word, 853, 1003
embedding in Word, 852–853, 1003
Fill Effects dialog box, **448–451**, **818–819**
defined, **448**
Gradient tab, 449
Pattern tab, 450
Picture tab, 450
Texture tab, 449
using gradient fills in headers and footers, 818–819, *818*
formatting, **441–454**
chart area, 441–442
data series and data points, 446–448
datasheet numbers, 431–432
plot area, 442–443
text, 446
graphics in bar charts, 816–817, *816*, *817*
gridlines
adding, 438
configuring, 445
keyboard shortcuts, 428
Microsoft Graph 2000 applet, **420–421**, **1016**
defined, **420–421**, **1016**
navigating, 421, *421*
moving, 424–425, *424*
resizing, 426
selecting, 424, *424*
text
formatting, 446
wrapping text, 426–427
gridlines
in graphs
adding, 438
configuring, 445
in tables
applying, 403–404, 1068–1069
defined, **378–379**, *378*
displaying or hiding, 380
grids for positioning graphics, 479
group collaboration features. *See* comments; Track Changes feature; Web-based collaboration
grouping
objects, 483
toolbar buttons, 97
gutter margins, 290–291

H

handouts for PowerPoint presentations, 855, *855*
hanging indents, 256–257, *256*
hard disk drives
"Check drive" message, 922
"The disk is full or too many files are open" message, 921–922
"The disk is full trying to write to *drive...*" message, 921
headers and footers, **303–306**, **940–942**, **1017–1019**. *See also* page setup
adding text, 303–304, 1017–1018
adding to documents in Office binders, 843
creating
with AutoText feature, 305
odd and even headers and footers, 306, 1018–1019
unique first page headers and footers, 305–306, 1018
creating watermarks, 293–295, *294*, 819–820, *820*, 934–935, 1049
field codes in, 305
formatting text, 304
gradient fills in, 818–819, *818*
Header and Footer toolbar, 303, *303*
inserting date and time, 304, *304*, 305, 940, 1019
inserting page numbers, 300–301, 304–305, *304*, 940–941, 1019, 1047
inserting total number of pages, 305, 1019
in sections, 306
troubleshooting, **940–942**
changing header or footer in one section changed all, 942
codes are visible, 940
columns of text don't work in headers and footers, 934
date, time, or other items are incorrect, 940
header or footer is missing or partially printed, 940
page numbers cannot be deleted, 941
page numbers do not show, 940–941
top or bottom margin changed after creating header or footer, 941
viewing, 303, *303*, 1017
headings
moving to, 163–164
tables of contents and heading styles, 366, 368

Height option for 3-D graphs, 454, *455*
Help, **890–904**, **1019**
  About Microsoft Word dialog box, 896–897, *896*, 1019
  Answer Wizard tab, 891–892, *892*, 1019
  business support line and Web site, 904
  changes to Help menu, 44
  Contents tab, 890–891, *891*
  creating Help files, 893
  Detect and Repair command, 36, 1096–1097
  fax-back support, 904
  Help text for form fields, 725–727, *726*
  Index tab, 892–893, *893*
  Microsoft Certified Solution Providers (MCSPs), 904
  new features, 37, *37*
  Office Assistant, **894–895**
    changing characters, 895
    defined, **894**, *894*
    disabling, 894–895
  online Help, **897–903**
    Microsoft Knowledge Base, 899–901, *900*
    Microsoft Office Update Web site, 898–899, *898*, 1019
    Microsoft Word-related newsgroups, 901–902
    non-Microsoft resources on the Web, 902–903
  technical support phone numbers and Web sites, 903–904
  TTY/TDD support, 903
  What's This? feature, 895, *895*, *896*, 1019
  WordPerfect Help, **66–69**
    configuring compatibility options for Word-Perfect users, 67
    enabling, 106
    enabling WordPerfect Navigation, 67
    Help for WordPerfect Users dialog box, 66–67, *66*, 106
    Word keyboard shortcuts for WordPerfect commands, 68–69
Hero Software, 877
hidden bookmarks, displaying, 167
Hidden controls in Web page forms, 678
hidden text
  creating, **241**
  displaying, 87–88, *88*, 362
  printing, 116
hiding. *See also* displaying; viewing
  animated text, 86
  field codes, 87, 336, *337*
  frame scroll bars, 654
  menus, 16

  objects in Print Layout and Web Layout views, 89, *89*
  Office binder files, 844
  Office Shortcut Bar, 839
  scroll bars, 85–86
  spelling error flags, 180
  status bar, 86
  table gridlines, 380
  text formatting in outlines, 562
  toolbars, 16, 22, 92–93, 1078
highlighted text
  creating, **237–238**, **243**, **614**
  displaying, 87
  finding, 173
Home key, navigating with, 161
home-page communities, 689
horizontal lines in Web pages
  formatting, 649
  inserting, 648–649, 1084
hosting. *See* publishing Web pages
hot spots for opening dialog boxes, 802
hotkeys. *See* keyboard shortcuts
HTML (Hypertext Markup Language). *See also* Web pages
  defined, **626–628**, *627*, **1020**
  EasyHTML/Help development tool, 867, 885, 893
  editing HTML code, 655, 1020
  .HTM files, 122
  HTML codes change after saving Web page, 967
  HTML e-mail messages, 224
  saving Word documents in HTML format, 638–640, 1083
  Web sites about, 627
hyperlinks. *See also* linking; Web pages; Web sites
  assigning to toolbar buttons, 99–100
  converting cross-references to, 330
  converting footnotes and endnotes to in Web pages, 317
  creating, **56–57**, *57*
  creating automatically, 57, 633
  troubleshooting
    clicking Web page hyperlinks generates an error message, 965
    Hyperlink command does not appear on right-click menu, 965
    text unexpectedly appears as a hyperlink, 929
  in Word documents, **35**, **630–635**, **807–808**, **1020–1021**
    automatically converting Web and e-mail addresses to hyperlinks, 57, 633
    changing links, 634

    copying and pasting links, 634
    creating e-mail or mailto links, 632–633, 1021
    deleting links, 635
    formatting links, 635
    inserting hyperlinks, 35, 630–631, 807–808, 1020
    linking to uncreated documents, 632
    linking within a document, 632, 808
    selecting hyperlinks, 634
hyphenation, **196–199**, **1021–1022**
    automatic hyphenation, 197, 1021–1022
    configuring hyphenation rules, 109
    Hyphenation dialog box, 109
    manual hyphenation, 198, 1022
    non-breaking and optional hyphens
        creating, **198–199**, **1022**
        displaying optional hyphens, 87–88, *88*
        finding and replacing, 174–175
    overview of, 196–197, 1021

I

identifying linked versus embedded objects, 496
illegal operation errors, **907**
image controls in forms, 730
images. *See* graphics
Immediate window in Visual Basic Editor, 768–769
importing. *See also* exporting
    database data into documents, 552–553, 580–582, *580*, 860–861, 974–975, 992–993
    database data into tables, 387–388, 861–862, 974–975
    digital photographs, 468–470, 1053
    Excel worksheets, 417
improvements. *See* new features
In Margin drop caps, 247–248
indenting paragraphs
    first-line indenting, 256–257, *256*, 1051
    hanging indents, 256–257, *256*
    indents disappear when bullets or numbering are added or deleted, 927
    with keyboard, 105
    overview of, **255–257**, *255*
    Paragraph dialog box options, 253, 256, 1051
    with ruler, 256, 257
Index tab in Help, 892–893, *893*
indexes, **354–365**, **600–601**, **938–939**, **1023–1025**
    creating, **361–363**, *362*, *363*, **1025**
    defined, **354**

    editing or deleting entries, 359, 1024
    formatting, 356, 364–365
    indexing part of a document, 365
    marking entries, **355–361**, **1023–1024**
        after completing documents, 355
        all occurrences of a word, 357
        with AutoMark files, 355, 360–361, 1024
        cross-references, 358–359
        marking ranges of pages with bookmarks, 359, 1023
        overview of, 355–357, 1023
        subentries, 354, 356, 360
        symbols and graphics, 357
        and using different text, 358
        XE field code and, 357, 358
    for master documents, 365, 600–601
    titles for, 363
    troubleshooting, **938–939**
        contain error messages in master documents, 938
        index entries have backslashes (\) instead of colons (:), 939
        page numbers are incorrect, 938–939
        unwanted codes or error messages are displayed, 939
    updating, 365, 1025
inline discussions. *See also* Discussions feature
    replying to, 619, 995
    starting, 618–619, 994
Insert Hyperlink dialog box, 56–57, *57*
Insert key, 105
Insert menu
    changes to, 43
    defined, **7**
    Object command, 498, *498*, 502–503, *503*
Insert mode, 105
Insert Table button on Standard toolbar, 382
Insert Table dialog box, 381
inserting. *See also* adding
    automatic summaries in documents, 582–584, *584*, 979
    AutoShapes, 476, 997
    AutoText entries, 144, 979
    comments
        spoken comments, 613, 989
        written comments, 612, *613*, 989
    cross-references, 328–329, 991
    database data in documents without Mail Merge, 552–553, 580–582, *580*
    date and time in documents, 993
    fields, **338–340**, **1004–1005**

with Field dialog box, 339–340, *339*, 1004–1005
with macros, 741
manually, 340, *341*, 1005
files in documents, **578–580**
linked files, 580
part of a file, 579
whole files, 578–579
footnotes and endnotes, 316–318
graphics
AutoShapes, 476
clip art, 461–463, *461*, *462*
graphics files, 468
WordArt text, 472–474, *474*, 1088
in headers and footers
date and time, 304, *304*, 305, 940, 1019
page numbers, 300–301, 304–305, *304*, 940–941, 1019
total number of pages, 305, 1019
horizontal lines in Web pages, 648–649, 1084
hyperlinks in documents, 35, 630–631, 807–808, 1020
merge fields in main documents, 533–534, *534*
modules in VBA projects, 773
page numbers
anywhere on the page, 301
with AutoText feature, 301
with chapter numbers, 301
in headers and footers, 300–301, 304–305, *304*, 940–941, 1019, 1047
into text, 301–302, 1047
with page fields, 302
total number of pages in headers and footers, 305, 1019
PowerPoint slides in Word documents, 857–859, *858*, 1056
symbols and special characters, 248–249, 1065
in tables
cells, 392
columns, 391, 1067
rows, 391–392, 1067
text fields with macros, 741
Word documents into Publisher documents, 863, 1058
insertion point cursor, 6–7, 139–140
Install on Demand feature, 35–36
installing
digital signatures, 755–756
programs on book's CD-ROM, 868
templates, 701
Word 2000, **35–36**, **911–912**, **1092–1097**
CD Key, 1093
Custom installation options, 1094–1095

from diskettes, 1093
Install on Demand feature, 35–36
installing additional components, 1095–1096
Maintenance Mode screen, 1095
reinstalling, 912
repairing installations with Detect and Repair, 36, 911, 1096–1097
system requirements, 1092
troubleshooting and, 911–912
Typical installations, 1093–1094
uninstalling, 911–912
uses for installation CD after Word is installed, 1095
interfaces
global interface, 60
imitating Word 97 interface, 92
single document interface, 41
international support features, **59–60**
finding foreign language text, 173
global interface, 60
international character shortcuts, 811–812
Language AutoDetect feature, 60
language setting for styles, 273
Language Settings window, 60
Internet. *See* e-mail; hyperlinks; Web sites
Internet Service Application Programming Interface (ISAPI) scripts, 667
Internet service providers (ISPs), 689
italic font style, 237–238, 239, 241–242, *241*

J

.JAH files, 468
Java applets, 682
.JBH files, 468
Journal utility, **846–848**, **1046**. *See also* Microsoft Outlook
defined, **846**, **1046**
enabling, 846, 1046
tracking document editing, 847, *847*, 1046
viewing entries, 848, *848*, 1046
.JPG files, 467
.JSH files, 468
justifying paragraphs, 254–255, *255*, 926–927

K

Kaczynski Software, 879
KazStamp envelope printing software, 514, 867, 878–879, *879*

keeping lines of text together, 258–259, 1050
kernel errors, **907**
kerning, 245–246, *246*, 1009–1010
keyboard
 assigning keyboard shortcuts from, 800–801
 indenting paragraphs from, 105
 inserting symbols and special characters from, 249
 Keyboard tab in Customize dialog box, 75, *75*
 moving insertion point from, 140
 navigating with, 160–161
 selecting text from, 147
keyboard shortcuts, **22–31**, **1025–1026**. *See also* Alt key; Ctrl key; Shift key
 assigning, 103–104, 1026
 assigning from keyboard, 800–801
 assigning macros to, 750, 793, *793*
 automating operations with, 24
 character code shortcuts for special characters, 809–811
 defined, **22–23**, **1025**
 for field codes, 340
 function keys
  displaying as a toolbar, 24
  listed, 23
 for graphs, 428
 international character shortcuts, 811–812
 listed, **24–31**
 for menu commands, 8, 20, 23
 printing lists of, 24, 103, 801, 1026
 for special characters, 808–809
 for styles
  assigning keyboard shortcuts to styles, 281
  predefined shortcuts, 275
 for WordPerfect commands, 68–69
keywords in Visual Basic for Applications, 774
KH Software Development, 875

L

label controls in forms, 730
labels, **517–521**, **1026–1028**. *See also* envelopes; Mail Merge
 barcode options, 520
 for captions, 326–327
 configuring label options, 518, 1026–1027
 creating new label templates, 518–519, 1027
 data labels in graphs, 436–437
 Label Options dialog box, 518, 1026–1027

Mailing Label Wizard, 514
merged labels
 barcode options, 544
 creating with Direct Mail Manager, 123, 549–550
 printing, 542–544, *543*, *545*
 printing, 519–521, *520*, 1027–1028
 printing return address labels, 519
 printing sheets of labels, 521
landscape page orientation settings, 288–289, 1048
language support, **59–60**
 finding foreign language text, 173
 global interface, 60
 international character shortcuts, 811–812
 Language AutoDetect feature, 60
 language setting for styles, 273
 Language Settings window, 60
language tools. *See* Grammar Checker; hyphenation; Spelling feature; Thesaurus
layering objects, 482–483, *482*, 1038
laying out documents with tables, 821–822, *822*, *823*
leader characters for tab stops, 261
legal documents
 legal pleadings, 123
 tables of authorities, 373–374
legends in graphs, 438–440
letter templates, 123
Letter Wizard, 125–126, *126*, 829, 951, 954
line art, 460
Line Color and Line Style buttons in Drawing toolbar, 488
line numbering, 270
line spacing, 253, 257–258, *258*, 824
lines. *See also* borders
 horizontal lines in Web pages
  formatting, 649
  inserting, 648–649, 1084
 vertical lines between columns of text, 932
linking, **495–501**, **952–953**, **1041–1042**. *See also* embedding; hyperlinks
 breaking links to source files, 500–501
 changing how linked objects are displayed, 501
 changing how links are updated, 500
 changing source files for links, 500
 copying and pasting text as a link, 577–578
 creating graphs linked to data in documents, 422–423
 versus cutting and pasting, 495
 defined, **495–497**, **1041**

double-clicking linked objects, 499
editing linked data, 499, 1042
versus embedding, 495–496
graphics files, 497, 498
identifying linked objects, 496
inserting linked files in documents, 580
Links dialog box, 499–501, *499*
with Object dialog box, 498, *498*, 1041–1042
with Paste Special dialog box, 497, *497*, 1041
troubleshooting, **952–953**
unlinking fields, 342
updating links before printing documents, 114, 501

list box controls
in automated forms, 730
in Web page forms, 672–673, *673*

List view in Open dialog box, 130

lists, **263–270**. *See also* paragraphs
bulleted lists, **263–267**, **983–984**
bullets do not display properly, 927
creating with AutoFormat feature, 206, 207, 264, 812–813
creating with Formatting toolbar, 264–265, 983
creating graphical bullets, 266–267, 813–814, *814*, 984
customizing bullet characters, 265–266, 812–813, 983
fonts for bullets, 266
tabs and paragraph indents disappear when bullets are added or deleted, 927
numbered lists, **264**, **267–270**, **1034–1036**
applying outline numbering, 269–270, 1036
continuing numbering in new lists, 269, 1035–1036
creating with AutoFormat feature, 206, 207, 264
creating with Formatting toolbar, 267, 1035
customizing number formats, 267–269, 1035
styles for, 273
tabs and paragraph indents disappear when numbers are added or deleted, 927

loading
templates and add-in programs, 702–703, 1075
templates and add-in programs automatically, 710

Locals window in Visual Basic Editor, 769
locations of templates, 706

locking
fields, 336, 342, 1005
subdocuments, 601–602

lowercase
Change Case dialog box, 242–243, 1008
Match Case option in Find and Replace dialog box, 170

M

McAfee VirusScan software, 38
macros, **38–39**, **734**, **740–758**, **968–972**, **1028–1030**. *See also* scripts; Visual Basic for Applications
assigning
to keyboard shortcuts, 750, 793, *793*
to menus, 749
to toolbars, 749
automating forms with, 734
AutoScroll macro, 803, *804*
converting WordBasic macros to VBA, 743
creating, **740–741**, **742–746**, **1028**
explained, 740–741, 742
Macro Recorder and, 742–743
mouse movements and, 745
recording macros, 743–745, *744*, 1028
recording tips, 745–746
suspending recording, 746
with VBA, 740, 742
creating documents from dialog boxes, 826–828, *826*, *827*, *829*
defined, **740**, **1028**
editing with Visual Basic Editor, 740, 746–748, *747*, 1029
examples, 741–742, 826–828, *826*, *827*, *829*
formatting text with, 741
inserting fields with, 741
macro projects, **741**, **750–752**, **756–758**, **1029**
copying to different documents or templates, 751, *751*, 1029
defined, **741**, **750**
deleting, 752
deleting macros from, 752
digitally signing, 756–758
Organizer and, 750–751, *751*
renaming, 752
macro viruses, **38–39**, **752–758**, **970–971**, **1029–1030**
adding macro developers to list of trusted sources, 755
antivirus software, 38, 753
changing macro security levels, 754–755, 970, 1059
ChekMate Lite program, 38, 866, 882–883

creating and installing digital signatures, 755–756
defined, **752–753**, **1029–1030**
digital signatures defined, **755**
digitally signing macro projects, 756–758
enabling Word macro security, 38–39, 753–754
McAfee VirusScan software, 38
Norton AntiVirus software, 38
troubleshooting, 970–971
Virus ALERT for Word 2000 software, 38, 753, 867, 881–882, *882*
Macros dialog box
AutoScroll feature, 803, *804*
printing lists of keyboard shortcuts and menu command, 24, 103, 801, 1026
naming, 744
running, 748, 780, 1029
troubleshooting, **748**, **931**, **968–972**
copied toolbar does not contain macros, 969
macro virus warning appears for files without macros, 970
macro viruses in documents, 970–971
macro won't run, 969–970
macros are missing from templates, 931
making mistakes when recording macros, 969
running a macro generates an error message, 969
security level cannot be changed, 970
stepping through macros, 748
in Visual Basic for Applications, **781–787**
adding dialog boxes, 785–786
adding message boxes, 784–785, *784*, *785*
automating, **786–787**
converting WordBasic macros to VBA, 743
creating with VBA, 740, 742
deleting arguments, 783
deleting properties, 782–783
editing, **740**, **746–748**, *747*, **781–783**
fixing errors, 781–782
running, 780
running automatic macros, 786
stopping automatic macros, 786–787
troubleshooting, 748
Visual Basic for Applications macro example, **787–793**
assigning to a keyboard shortcut, 793, *793*
creating the form, 788–789, *788*, *789*, *790*
defined, **787**
designing, 787–788

displaying dialog box, 790–791
making the dialog box work, 791–793
writing code, 790–793
Mail Merge, **524–553**, **953–954**, **1030**. *See also* envelopes; labels
creating merged mailings from Outlook contacts, 845
data sources, **527–532**
creating from Word tables, 527–529, *528*, *529*, *530*
Database toolbar and, 530
defined, **526**, *527*
using Address Books, 532
using databases or spreadsheets, 531–532, 859–860
defined, **524–525**, *525*, **1030**
inserting database data in documents without Mail Merge, 552–553, 580–582, *580*
Mail Merge Helper dialog box, 525, *525*
main documents, **525–526**, **533–537**
automating merges with Word fields, 535–537
creating, **525–526**
inserting merge fields, 533–534, *534*
Mail Merge toolbar and, 533
merged catalogs or directories, 550–551, *551*
merged envelopes, **545–550**
barcode options, 546, 547
creating attached merge envelopes, 549
creating with Direct Mail Manager, 123, 549–550
printing, 545–549, *547*, *548*
merged labels
barcode options, 544
creating with Direct Mail Manager, 123, 549–550
printing, 542–544, *543*, *545*
merging, **537–542**
checking for errors before merging, 537–538
customizing individual documents, 541
e-mailing or faxing merged documents, 540–541
merging and printing documents, 538–540
previewing merged documents, 538
troubleshooting, **953–954**
error message says data file is main document, 954
merge field changes when Letter Wizard is run, 954
merge fields print instead of data, 953–954
merged document contains blank lines, 954

mailto links in documents, 632–633, 1021
main documents. *See* Mail Merge
Maintenance Mode screen, 1095
making revisions, 608
Manawatu Software Solutions, 878
manual formatting versus styles, 272
manual hyphenation, 198, 1022
manually adding captions, 325
manually adding fields, 340, *341*
manually editing styles, 280–281
manually marking table of contents entries, 371,
  1072
margins, **247–248, 289–291, 1030–1031**. *See also*
  page setup
    gutter margins, 290–291
    In Margin drop caps, 247–248
    mirror margins, 291
    page design and, 289
    printing 2 Pages Per Sheet option, 291
    printing outside printable area of printer, 289
    setting with Page Setup dialog box, 290, *290*,
      1030–1031
    setting with ruler, 289–290, *289*
    in tables
      setting all cell margins, 402–403
      setting individual cell margins, 408–409
    top or bottom margin changed after creating
      header or footer, 941
marking
    citations for tables of authorities, 373, 1071
    index entries, **355–361, 1023–1024**
      after completing documents, 355
      all occurrences of a word, 357
      with AutoMark files, 355, 360–361, 1024
      cross-references, 358–359
      marking ranges of pages with bookmarks,
        359, 1023
      overview of, 355–357, 1023
      subentries, 354, 356, 360
      symbols and graphics, 357
      and using different text, 358
      XE field code and, 357, 358
    table of contents entries manually, 371, 1072
marquees in Web pages, 660–662, *661*
master documents, **365, 370, 586–602, 936–938,**
  1031–1033
    advantages of, 587–588
    creating, **586–591, 1031–1032**
      converting an existing document to a master
        document, 590–591, 1031–1032

      from existing documents, 591, 1032
      overview of, 586–587
      from scratch, 588–590, *589*, *590*, 1031
    cross-references in, 601
    defined, **586**
    formatting, 599
    indexes for, 365, 600–601
    master document buttons on Outline toolbar,
      586–587, *587*
    in Normal view, 589–590, *590*
    opening, 593
    in Outline view, 588–590, *589*, 593–594
    printing, 593
    saving, 592
    saving as a Web page, 592–593
    subdocuments, **586, 592, 593–599, 601–602,**
      1032–1033
      adding, 597, 1033
      collapsing, 594, *595*
      combining, 597–598
      converting into part of master document,
        596, 1032
      defined, **586**
      deleting, 596–597, 1032–1033
      editing, 595–596
      expanding, 595
      formatting, 599
      locking and unlocking, 601–602
      moving, 597
      opening, 594, 596
      in Outline view, 594–596, *595*
      overview of, 593–594
      printing, 599
      rearranging, 595
      renaming, 598
      saving, 592
      splitting, 597
      text and graphics in master documents sepa-
        rate from, 587, 596
    tables of contents for, 370, 600
    troubleshooting, **936–938**
      cross-references are replaced by error mes-
        sages, 938
      master documents or subdocuments won't
        open, 936–937
      page number, headers, or footers are incor-
        rect or missing, 937
      problems saving master documents or sub-
        documents, 937

styles appear differently in master documents and subdocuments, 931
subdocuments are created incorrectly, 938
tables of contents or indexes contain error messages, 938
when to use, 587–588
Mastering Word 2000 Premium Edition on book's CD-ROM, 867
Match Case option in Find and Replace dialog box, 170
MCSPs (Microsoft Certified Solution Providers), 904
measurement display in ruler, 801, *802*
MedSpel spelling dictionary, 186, 867, 886
Meeting Minder notes, exporting to Word, 856–857, 1055–1056
memo templates, 123
menus, **8**, **20–21**, **1033–1034**. *See also* keyboard shortcuts; toolbars
    accessing commands with Alt key, 8
    adding to toolbars, 96–97
    assigning macros to, 749
    changes to menu commands, 43–44
    customizing, **43–44**, **101–102**, **798**, **1033–1034**
        adding items to menu bar, 101–102, 1034
        creating personal menus, 798
        customizing keyboard shortcuts, 103–104
        moving the menu bar, 101
        new features, 43–44
        personalized menus, 20–21, 35, 42–43, 102, 798, 1033–1034
        rearranging menu commands, 102
    displaying in templates, 107
    ellipsis (...) in, 20
    expanding or collapsing, 20–21
    full versus personalized menus, 20–21, 35, 42–43, 102, 798, 1033–1034
    hiding, 16
    keyboard shortcuts for menu commands, 8, 20, 23
    menu bar
        adding items to, 101–102
        defined, **8**, *9*
        moving, 101
    Menus Show Recently Used Commands First option, 42
    printing lists of menu commands, 24, 103, 801
    resetting, 43, 45, 102
    right-click menus
        adapting to, 34
        Automatic Spell Checking options, 180–182, *181*
    customizing toolbars, 93
    defined, **21**
    drag-and-drop operations, 149
    editing text from, 148
    formatting commands, 237
    Hyperlink command does not appear on right-click menu, 965
    Spell Checking commands, 180–182, *181*
    Synonyms command, 50–51, 196, 815, 1078
    Update Field command, 371
    selecting menu commands, 20
    short menus, 20–21, 35
    submenus, 20
merging. *See also* Mail Merge
    combining subdocuments, 597–598
    revisions from multiple reviewers, 608–609, 1080
    table cells, 394–395, *394*
message boxes, adding to macros, 784–785, *784*, *785*
methods in Visual Basic for Applications, 780
Microsoft Access 2000, **859–862**, **974–975**. *See also* databases
    controlling data with Word Database toolbar and fields, 388, 530, 860
    databases as Mail Merge data sources, 531–532, 859–860
    defined, **859**
    exporting data to Word documents, 552–553, 580–582, *580*, 860–861, 974–975, 992–993
    exporting data to Word tables, 387–388, 861–862, 974–975
    saving form data as text files for exporting to databases, 737–738
Microsoft Business Planner, 844
Microsoft Certified Solution Providers (MCSPs), 904
Microsoft Direct Mail Manager, 123, 549–550, 844
Microsoft Excel 2000, **417**, **531–532**, **848–853**, **1001–1003**
    charts, **852–853**, **1003**
        creating from Word, 853, 1003
        embedding in Word, 852–853, 1003
    defined, **1001**
    worksheets, **848–852**, **1002–1003**
        copying and pasting into Word tables, 849–850, 1002
        creating from Word, 852, 1003
        embedding cells or worksheets in Word tables, 850–852, *851*, 1002
        as Mail Merge data sources, 531–532
        using Word data in, 848–849
        versus Word tables, 417

Microsoft Fax software, 221
Microsoft Graph 2000 applet, **420–421**, **1016**. *See also* graphs
    defined, **420–421**, **1016**
    navigating, 421, *421*
Microsoft IntelliMouse, 162, 803
Microsoft Knowledge Base, 899–901, *900*
Microsoft Office 2000, **838–844**
    binders, **841–844**
        adding files to, 842–843, *842*
        adding headers and footers to documents in, 843
        creating, **842–843**, *842*
        defined, **841**
        editing binder files, 843
        hiding sections of, 844
        printing, 843–844
        saving, 843
        starting Microsoft Office Binder, 842
    defined, **838**
    Find Fast feature, 136
    Language Settings window, 60
    Microsoft Business Planner, 844
    Microsoft Direct Mail Manager, 123, 549–550, 844
    Microsoft Office Server Extensions, 58, 616, 620, 621
    Microsoft Office on the Web feature, 37, *37*
    Microsoft Small Business Customer Manager, 844
    Microsoft Small Business Financial Manager, 844
    Office 2000 Complete on book's CD-ROM, 866, 867
    Shortcut Bar, **122**, **838–841**
        adding buttons to, 841
        closing, 839
        creating documents from, 122, 840
        defined, **838**
        displaying, 838, *839*, 840
        displaying toolbars on, 840
        hiding, 839
        moving, 839
        opening documents from, 840
    small business tools, 844
    SOS Office Helpers, 867, 871–872, *871*
    Symantec WinFax Starter Edition software, 221–222
Microsoft Office Assistant, **894–895**
    changing characters, 895
    defined, **894**, *894*
    disabling, 894–895
Microsoft Office Update Web site, 898–899, *898*

Microsoft Outlook 2000, **845–848**, **1046**
    Aladdins ~ Word Documents add-in program, 866, 877–878
    creating documents from Outlook contacts, 866, 877–878
    creating merged mailings from Outlook contacts, 845
    defined, **845**
    and e-mailing Word documents, 53, 227, 228, 845
    Journal utility, **846–848**, **1046**
        defined, **846**, **1046**
        enabling, 846, 1046
        tracking document editing, 847, *847*, 1046
        viewing entries, 848, *848*, 1046
Microsoft Photo Editor, 472, 864
Microsoft PhotoDraw, 472
Microsoft PowerPoint 2000, **499**, **504**, **853–859**, **1054–1056**
    defined, **1054**
    double-clicking linked or embedded PowerPoint objects in Word, 499, 504
    exporting Meeting Minder notes to Word, 856–857, 1055–1056
    presentations
        adding Word's PresentIt command to toolbars, 854
        creating in Word without PowerPoint, 832–833, *832*
        embedding in Word documents, 859, 1056
        exporting handouts to Word, 855, *855*, 1055
        exporting to Word documents, 856, 1055
        exporting Word outlines to create presentations, 853–854, 1055
        inserting slides in Word documents, 857–859, *858*, 1056
    starting PowerPoint from Word, 499, 504
Microsoft Publisher 2000, **862–863**, **1057–1058**
    defined, **862**, **1057**
    editing text in Word, 862, *863*, 1057
    inserting Word documents into Publisher documents, 863, 1058
Microsoft Query, 552–553, 581
Microsoft Script Editor, **57**, **682–685**, **1034**. *See also* scripts; Visual Basic for Applications
    changing default scripting language, 684
    creating scripts, 685
    defined, **682**, **1034**
    Design View, 684
    opening, 57, *58*, 682
    Quick View, 683–684, *684*
    Source View, 683, *683*

Microsoft Small Business Customer Manager, 844
Microsoft Small Business Financial Manager, 844
Microsoft Windows
    configuring printer options, 211–212
    creating Desktop shortcuts to templates and
        documents, 831
    creating documents from Start menu, 122
    font settings, 235
    printing documents from, 220
    "Windows cannot print due to a problem with
        the current printer setup" message, 962–963
Microsoft Word 2000, **60–69**, **838–864**, **1092–
    1097**. *See also* new features; tips and tricks
    automation tips and tricks, **823–831**
        AutoCorrect shortcuts for long words, 824–
            825
        creating Click Here and Type fields, 825
        creating documents from dialog boxes, 826–
            828, *826, 827, 829*
        creating tables of contents from another doc-
            ument, 830
        creating Windows Desktop shortcuts to tem-
            plates and documents, 831
        line spacing shortcuts, 824
        reusing documents with Letter Wizard, 829
        shrinking documents to fit paper size, 52,
            115, 214, 217–218, 824
    compatibility issues, **35**, **60–66**, **67**, **83**, **116–
        118**
        compatibility of new features, 35
        configuring Word compatibility options for
            WordPerfect users, 67
        converting file formats with Conversion Wiz-
            ard, 62–63
        disabling incompatible features, 61–62, *61,*
            66, 116–117
        Font Substitution option, 118, 237
        listed, 64–65
        object placement controls, 35
        options for compatibility with specific pro-
            grams, 61–62, *61*, 117
        Options dialog box Compatibility tab, 61–62,
            83, 116–118
        overview of, 35, 60
        saving to previous Word formats, 60–62, *61*
    as a database program, 834
    defined, **4**
    as a drawing program, 834–835
    installing, **35–36**, **911–912**, **1092–1097**
        CD Key, 1093
        Custom installation options, 1094–1095
        from diskettes, 1093

    Install on Demand feature, 35–36
    installing additional components, 1095–1096
    Maintenance Mode screen, 1095
    reinstalling, 912
    repairing installations with Detect and
        Repair, 36, 911, 1096–1097
    system requirements, 1092
    troubleshooting and, 911–912
    Typical installations, 1093–1094
    uninstalling, 911–912
    uses for installation CD after Word is
        installed, 1095
    Mastering Word 2000 Premium Edition on book's
        CD-ROM, 867
    running from installation CD, 1094–1095
    starting, **5–6**, **913–914**
    troubleshooting
        Word starts, then freezes or quits, 914
        Word won't start from documents, 913–914
        Word won't start from a shortcut, 913
    as a Web browser, 637
    as a Web page editor, 628–630
    Word Workshops tutorial, 867–868
    WordPerfect Help, **66–69**
        configuring compatibility options for Word-
            Perfect users, 67
        enabling, 106
        enabling WordPerfect Navigation, 67
        Help for WordPerfect Users dialog box, 66–
            67, *66*
        Word keyboard shortcuts for WordPerfect
            commands, 68–69
MightyFax software, 222, 867, 880, *881*
Modify Style dialog box, 279–281, *279*
modules in Visual Basic for Applications
    class modules, 772–773
    defined, **771**
    inserting in projects, 773
    standard modules, 772
    types of, 772–773
    Visual Basic Editor Code windows and, 762
monospaced fonts, **234**
More Buttons button in toolbars, 94
mouse. *See also* right-click menus
    double-clicking
        embedded objects, 502, 504
        linked objects, 499
        opening dialog boxes with double-click hot
            spots, 802
    drag-and-drop feature, 105, 148–149
    Microsoft IntelliMouse, 162, 803
    mouse movements and creating macros, 745

moving outline sections, 566
navigating with, 161–162, *162*
with scroll wheel, 162
selecting text, 146–147
movie clips in Web pages, 663–665, *663*
moving. *See also* cutting and pasting; rearranging
    to bookmarks, 168, 981
    to comments, 163–164
    to fields, 163–164
    to footnotes and endnotes, 163–164
    footnotes and endnotes, 319–320, 1011–1012
    graphs, 424–425, *424*
    to headings, 163–164
    insertion point, 140
    the menu bar, 101
    movie clips in Web pages, 665
    to objects, 163–164
    objects, 479–480, 1036–1037
    Office Shortcut Bar, 839
    outline sections, 565–566, 1045
    to pages, 163–164
    to previous cursor locations with Shift + F5, 163, 804
    scripts, 681
    scrolling text or marquees, 662
    to sections, 163–164
    subdocuments, 597
    in table columns and rows, 393
    tables, 49
    to tables, 163–164
    tables, 378–379, *378*, 400
    text, 149
    text in table cells, 393–394
    toolbars, 22, 93–94, 1078
multimedia in Web pages, **660–666**
    background sound clips, 665–666
    movie clips, 663–665, *663*
    scrolling text or marquees, 660–662, *661*
multiple columns. *See* columns of text
multiple copies of documents, printing, 217
multiple documents, viewing and editing in multiple windows, 18
multiple tables of contents, 369
MyHelpDesk.com Web site, 903

N

naming
    bookmarks, 167
    documents, 154

macros, 744
renaming macro projects, 752
renaming styles, 278
renaming subdocuments, 598
styles, 282
navigating, **160–162**. *See also* moving
    bookmarks, 168, 981
    comments, 163–164
    fields, 163–164, 338
    footnotes and endnotes, 163–164, 323
    graph datasheets, 428
    headings, 163–164
    with keyboard, 160–161
    Microsoft Graph 2000 applet, 421, *421*
    with mouse, 161–162, *162*
    objects, 163–164
    pages, 163–164
    returning to where you left off in a document, 804
    sections, 163–164
    with Shift key, 163
    to specific places in documents, **163–168**, **323**
        with bookmarks, 166–168
        in Document Map view, 14, 165–166, *166*, 925, 995
        with Go To tab in Find and Replace dialog box, 164–165, *164*, 1015–1016
        with Select Browse Object tool, 163–164, 323, 338
    to tables, 163–164
    in tables, 379–380
    with WordPerfect Navigation feature, 67
navigation frames, 653, 1015
nesting tables, 49, 384–385, *385*
networks
    publishing Web pages over, 695–696
    "There has been a network or file permission error. The network connection may be lost. *Filename.doc*" message, 921
New Blank Document button in Standard toolbar, 120
New dialog box
    creating tabs, 709
    defined, **6**
    saving templates to, 708–709
new features, **34–60**. *See also specific entries for new features*
    adapting to, 34–35
    compatibility of, 35
    customization features, **42–45**
        menu command changes, 43–44

personalized menus, 20–21, 35, 42–43, 102, 798, 1033–1034
toolbar customization, 44–45
editing tools, **45–49**
Click and Type feature, 46–47, 104–105, 140–141, 384, 924, 985
Collect and Paste feature, 48–49, 149–150, 990–991
object placement controls, 35, 47–48, *47*
table editing and formatting features, 49
e-mail enhancements, 52–53
file management features, **39–41**
Open and Save As dialog box enhancements, 39, *40*
single document interface, 41
template files and folders, 40–41
international support features, **59–60**
global interface, 60
Language AutoDetect feature, 60
Language Settings window, 60
overview of, 34–35
Print dialog box enhancements, 51–52, *52*
program management features, **35–39**
Detect and Repair utility, 36, 1096–1097
Help system enhancements, 37, *37*
Install on Demand, 35–36
macro virus protection, 38–39
user profile settings, 36–37
proofing tools, **50–51**
AutoCorrect enhancements, 50
Spelling dictionary, Thesaurus, and Grammar Checker enhancements, 50–51
Web editing tools, **53–57**
frames, 56
Insert Hyperlink dialog box, 56–57, *57*
themes, 55, *56*, 283, 642–645, *643*, *644*, 1087
VBScript controls, 57, *58*
Web Page Preview, 13, 53, *54*, 636
Web Page Wizard, 54–55, *55*, 640–641, 1084
Web-based collaboration, **58–59**
defined, **58**
Discussions, 59
Microsoft Office Server Extensions and, 58, 616, 620, 621
Subscriptions and Notifications, 59, 620–621, 1064
New Window command in Window menu, 18
newsgroups about Microsoft Word, 901–902
NewSoft Office Express 2000 graphics program, 873
newspaper columns. *See* columns of text

non-breaking hyphens
creating, **198–199**, **1022**
finding and replacing, 174–175
non-Microsoft resources on the Web, 902–903
Normal style, 273
Normal template, 706
Normal view, **9–10**, **15**, **1083**. *See also* views
customizing, 90–91, *90*
defined, **9–10**, *10*, **1083**
displaying draft fonts in, 90–91, *90*
displaying Outline and Normal views simultaneously, 562–563, *563*
displaying styles in, 10
footnotes and endnotes in, 315, *316*, 319
master documents in, 589–590, *590*
section break markers, 298, *299*
when to use, 15
Norton AntiVirus software, 38
notes. *See* comments; footnotes and endnotes
Notifications feature, 59, 620–621, 1064
number sign (#) in index entries, 357
numbered lists, **264**, **267–270**, **1034–1036**. *See also* lists
applying outline numbering, 269–270, 1036
continuing numbering in new lists, 269, 1035–1036
creating with AutoFormat feature, 206, 207, 264
creating with Formatting toolbar, 267, 1035
customizing number formats, 267–269, 1035
styles for, 273
tabs and paragraph indents disappear when numbers are added or deleted, 927
numbering. *See also* page numbers
captions, 327
chapter numbers
in captions, 327–328
in page numbers, 301
footnotes and endnotes, 321
lines of text, 270
outline numbering
in lists, 269–270, 1036
in outlines, 567–568, *568*
troubleshooting, 929
Numeric Picture field switch, 336

O

Object dialog box, 498, *498*, 502–503, *503*, 1041–1042

Object Linking and Embedding (OLE), **494–505,
1041–1043**
versus cutting and pasting, 495
defined, **494, 1041**
embedding, **496, 501, 502–505, 952–953,
1042–1043**
changing how embedded objects are displayed, 501
converting embedded objects to another file
format, 504–505
creating embedded objects, 502–503, *503*,
1042–1043
versus cutting and pasting, 495
defined, **496, 502, 1041**
double-clicking embedded objects, 502, 504
editing embedded objects, 503–504, *504*,
1043
Embed TrueType Fonts option, 237
embedding existing data, 502, 1042
Excel cells or worksheets in Word tables, 850–
852, *851*, 1002
Excel charts in Word documents, 852–853,
1003
identifying embedded objects, 496
versus linking, 495–496
PowerPoint presentations in Word documents, 859, 1056
troubleshooting, **952–953**
linking, **495–501, 952–953, 1041–1042**
breaking links to source files, 500–501
changing how linked objects are displayed,
501
changing how links are updated, 500
changing source files for links, 500
copying and pasting text as a link, 577–578
creating graphs linked to data in documents,
422–423
versus cutting and pasting, 495
defined, **495–497, 1041**
double-clicking linked objects, 499
editing linked data, 499, 1042
versus embedding, 495–496
graphics files, 497, 498
identifying linked objects, 496
inserting linked files in documents, 580
Links dialog box, 499–501, *499*
with Object dialog box, 498, *498*, 1041–1042
with Paste Special dialog box, 497, *497*, 1041
troubleshooting, **952–953**

unlinking fields, 342
updating links before printing documents,
114, 501
support for, 495
objects, **478–491, 1036–1040**. *See also* graphics
3-D effects, *489*, 490–491, 1040
aligning, 481, 947, 948
aligning vertically, 1037
applying grids for positioning graphics, 479
borders and fills, 488, 1040
cropping, 484–486, *485*, 1054
defined, **1036**
displaying or hiding objects in Print Layout or
Web Layout views, 89, *89*
displaying placeholders, 86–87
distributing, 481, 947, 1038
equations, 417–418, *418*, 1001
finding and replacing, 174–175
flipping, 483–484, 1039
formatting options in Picture toolbar, 470, 1053
grouping and ungrouping, 483, 949
layering, 482–483, *482*, 1038
moving, 479–480, 1036–1037
moving to, 163–164
object placement controls, 35, 47–48, *47*
resizing, 480–481, 1037
rotating, 483–484, 950, 1038–1039
Select Browse Object tool, 163–164, 323, 338
shadows, 489, *489*, 1040
in Visual Basic for Applications, **779–780**
classes, 779
collections, 779
events, 780
methods, 780
object libraries (.OLB), 779
properties, 779
Visual Basic Editor Object Browser, 764–765,
764
Visual Basic Editor Properties window, 767–
768, *767*
wrapping text around, 486–488, 1039–1040
odd and even headers and footers, 306, 1018–1019
Office 2000 Complete on book's CD-ROM, 866, 867
Office Assistant, **894–895**. *See also* Microsoft Office
changing characters, 895
defined, **894**, *894*
disabling, 894–895
Office on the Web feature, 37, *37*
OfficeCert.com Web site, 903

OfficeExpress 2000 graphics software, 472, 867, 872–873, *873*
.OLB files, 779
OLE. *See* Object Linking and Embedding
online Help, **897–903**
    Microsoft Knowledge Base, 899–901, *900*
    Microsoft Office Update Web site, 898–899, *898*, 1019
    Microsoft Word-related newsgroups, 901–902
    non-Microsoft resources on the Web, 902–903
Open dialog box, **6**, **39**, **128–137**
    defined, **128**, *129*
    Details view, 131
    displaying files, 129–133
    file operations, 137
    finding documents, 133–136, *134*
    folder views, 129–133
    List view, 130
    new features, 39, *40*
    opening documents, 6, 133
    opening documents from other programs, 137
    Preview view, 132–133
    Properties view, 132
    wildcards in, 130
opening
    backup files, 157
    dialog boxes with double-click hot spots, 802
    documents, **6**, **105–106**, **127–139**, **996**
        converting and opening documents, 105–106
        document opens with a different filename, 920
        document won't open, 918
        documents from other programs, 137
        from Office Shortcut Bar, 840
        with Open dialog box, 6, 128–137, *129*
        overview of, 6, 128, 996
        from Windows Desktop shortcuts, 831
    Envelope Options dialog box, 510
    Find and Replace dialog box from status bar, 20
    master documents, 593
    Microsoft Script Editor, 57, *58*, 682
    subdocuments, 594, 596
    templates from Windows Desktop shortcuts, 831
operators
    in formulas, 415
    in Visual Basic for Applications, 774
Option Button controls in Web page forms, 671, *671*
option buttons in forms, 729
optional hyphens
    creating, **198–199**, **1022**

displaying, 87–88, *88*
finding and replacing, 174–175
Options dialog box, **75–84**, **104–118**. *See also* Customize dialog box; customizing
    Compatibility tab, **61–62**, **83**, **116–118**
        defined, **83**, *83*
        Font Substitution option, 118, 237
        options for compatibility with specific programs, 61–62, *61*, 117
    defined, **75–76**
    Edit tab, 77–78, *78*, 104–106
    File Locations tab, 83–84, *84*, 116
    General tab
        Blue Background, White Text option, 91, *91*
        defined, **77**, *77*
        E-mail options, 114
        Web options, 113
    Print tab, 78, *79*, 114–116, 210–211
    Save tab, 79, *80*, 156
    Spelling & Grammar tab, 80–81, *81*, 107–108, 179–180, 189
    Track Changes tab, 81, *82*, 106–107
    User Information tab, 82, *82*, 104, 514, 1081
    View tab, 76, *76*, 799
Options tab in Customize dialog box
    defined, **74**, *74*
    Menus Show Recently Used Commands First option, 42
    Reset My Usage Data option, 43, 102
Organizer
    copying elements between templates, 706–708, *707*
    copying macro projects to different documents or templates, 750–751, *751*
    copying styles, 277–278, *278*
    defined, **1043–1044**
orientation
    changing page orientation in columns of text generates error message, 933–934
    page orientation settings, 288–289, 1048
    of text in table cells, 407–408, *407*
orphan controls, 258–259, 1050
outline font style, 241–242, *241*
Outline view. *See also* views
    customizing, 90–91
    defined, **12–13**, *13*, **558**, *559*, **1044**, **1083**
    displaying draft fonts in, 90–91
    displaying Outline and Normal views simultaneously, 562–563, *563*
    displaying and rearranging tables in, 568–569
    displaying section break markers, 298
    footnotes and endnotes in, 315, *316*

master documents in, 588–590, *589*, 593–594
subdocuments in, 594–596, *595*
when to use, 14
outlines, **558–571**, **1044–1045**
    assigning outline levels to styles, 564, 1045
    creating documents from, 569–571, *570*
    displaying, **561–563**, **1044**
        all levels, 561
        expanding or collapsing a section, 561–562,
        1044
        first line of text only, 562, 1044
        or hiding text formatting, 562
        Outline and Normal views simultaneously,
        562–563, *563*
        specific levels only, 561, 1044
    exporting outlines to PowerPoint, 853–854
    moving sections, 565–566, 1045
    outline numbering
        in lists, 269–270, 1036
        in outlines, 567–568, *568*
        troubleshooting, 929
    Outline toolbar
        defined, **559–561**, *560*
        master document buttons, 586–587, *587*
        moving sections, 566
    page breaks, 571
    printing, 571
    promoting or demoting levels, 565, 1045
    sorting sections, 566–567
Overtype mode, 105

P

page breaks
    automatic repagination, 106
    creating, **254**, **258–259**, **309–310**, **982**
    and displaying field codes or hidden text, 362
    finding and replacing, 174–175
    keeping lines of text together, 258–259, 1050
    in outlines, 571
    pages do not break properly, 935
    Paragraph dialog box options, 258–259, 1050
    widow and orphan controls, 258–259, 1050
page numbers, **106**, **300–303**, **1046–1047**. *See also*
    numbering
    adding chapter numbers, 301
    automatic repagination, 106
    inserting
        anywhere on the page, 301
        with AutoText feature, 301
    in headers and footers, 300–301, 304–305,
    304, 940–941, 1019, 1047
    into text, 301–302, 1047
    with page fields, 302
    total number of pages in headers and footers,
    305, 1019
    in sections, 302–303, 1047
    troubleshooting
        in headers and footers, 940–941
        in indexes and tables of contents, 938–939
        in master documents, 937
page setup, **286–310**, **934–936**, **1048–1050**. *See
also* formatting; paper; paragraphs; styles
    backgrounds, **291–295**, **1049**
        blends and gradients, 292–293
        color backgrounds, 292–293, 1049
        do not print, 934
        graphics, 293
        patterns, 293
        textures, 293
        watermarks, 293–295, *294*, 819–820, *820*,
        934–935, 1049
    borders, **295–296**, **1049–1050**
        adding, 295–296, *295*, 1049–1050
        creating graphical borders, 296, *297*
    columns of text, **307–310**, **806**. *See also* trouble-
    shooting
        balancing, 806, 933
        changing column widths and spacing, 308–
        309
        changing vertical alignment, 309
        creating, **307–308**
        creating column breaks, 309–310, 982
        defined, **307**, *307*
    default page setup, 287
    headers and footers, **303–306**, **940–942**, **1017–
    1019**. *See also* troubleshooting
        adding text, 303–304, 1017–1018
        adding to documents in Office binders, 843
        creating with AutoText feature, 305
        creating odd and even headers and footers,
        306, 1018–1019
        creating unique first page headers and foot-
        ers, 305–306, 1018
        creating watermarks, 293–295, *294*, 819–820,
        820, 1049
        field codes in, 305
        formatting text, 304
        gradient fills in, 818–819, *818*
        Header and Footer toolbar, 303, *303*
        inserting date and time, 304, *304*, 305, 940,
        1019

inserting page numbers, 300–301, 304–305, *304*, 1019

inserting total number of pages, 305, 1019

in sections, 306

viewing, 303, *303*, 1017

landscape and portrait orientation settings, 288–289, 1048

margins, **247–248**, **289–291**, **1030–1031**

gutter margins, 290–291

In Margin drop caps, 247–248

mirror margins, 291

page design and, 289

printing 2 Pages Per Sheet option, 291

printing outside printable area of printer, 289

setting all table cell margins, 402–403

setting individual table cell margins, 408–409

setting with Page Setup dialog box, 290, *290*, 1030–1031

setting with ruler, 289–290, *289*

top or bottom margin changed after creating header or footer, 941

overview of, 286

paper size settings, 287–288, *287*, 1048

sections, **163–164**, **174–175**, **297–299**, **309–310**, **934–936**, **1058–1059**. *See also* troubleshooting

copying section formatting, 299, 1059

creating section breaks, **297–298**, **309–310**, **982**, **1058**

defined, **297**

deleting section breaks, 299, 1059

finding and replacing section breaks, 174–175

headers and footers in, 306

moving to, 163–164

numbering pages in, 302–303

types of section breaks, 298

viewing section break markers, 298, *299*, 1058

title pages, 295, *295*

tools for, 286

troubleshooting, **934–936**

backgrounds do not display or print, 934

page borders do not display properly, 935–936

pages do not break properly, 935

watermarks do not display properly, 934–935

troubleshooting columns of text, **932–934**

changing page orientation or paper size generates error message, 933–934

columns are not visible, 932

columns don't work in headers, footers, comments, or text boxes, 934

columns of text are narrower than expected, 932

columns won't balance, 933

tables in columns disappear, 933

text above columns turns into multiple columns, 933

vertical lines between columns are not visible, 932

troubleshooting headers and footers, **940–942**

changing header or footer in one section changed all, 942

codes are visible, 940

columns of text don't work in headers and footers, 934

date, time, or other items are incorrect, 940

header or footer is missing or partially printed, 940

page numbers cannot be deleted, 941

page numbers do not show, 940–941

top or bottom margin changed after creating header or footer, 941

troubleshooting sections and pages, **934–936**

backgrounds do not display or print, 934

changing header or footer in one section changed all, 942

page borders do not display properly, 935–936

pages do not break properly, 935

watermarks do not display properly, 934–935

vertical text alignment

for columns of text, 309

in page setup, 291–292, 1048–1049

pages

Alt + Shift + P (PAGE field), 340

breaking or flowing tables across pages, 396

moving to, 163–164

ranges of pages

marking for index entries, 359, 1023

printing, 216–217

pagination. *See* page breaks

panes for viewing split documents, 17–18, *17*

paper. *See also* page setup

changing paper size in columns of text generates error message, 933–934

paper size settings, 287–288, *287*, 1048

paper source options for printing, 217

printing 2 Pages Per Sheet option, 291

resizing documents to paper size, 52, 115, 214, 217–218, 824

stationery for e-mail messages, 226–227

paragraph marks
  displaying, 87–88, *88*
  finding and replacing, 174–175
paragraph styles versus character styles, 271–272
paragraphs, **105, 172, 252–270, 1050–1052**. *See
  also* page setup; styles
  aligning, 254–255, *255*, 926–927, 1051
  borders
    creating, **261–262, 981**
    styles for, 273
  bulleted lists, **263–267, 983–984**
    bullets do not display properly, 927
    creating with AutoFormat feature, 206, 207,
     264, 812–813
    creating with Formatting toolbar, 264–265,
     983
    creating graphical bullets, 266–267, 813–814,
     814, 984
    customizing bullet characters, 265–266, 812–
     813, 983
    fonts for bullets, 266
    tabs and paragraph indents disappear when
     bullets are added or deleted, 927
  finding, 172
  formatting
    copying with Format Painter, 238, 805–806
    deleting formatting, 806
    with Formatting toolbar, 252–253
    overview of, 252
    with Paragraph dialog box, 253–254
    selected paragraphs, 252
    with themes, 283
  indenting
    first-line indenting, 256–257, *256*, 1051
    hanging indents, 256–257, *256*
    indents disappear when bullets or numbering
     are added or deleted, 927
    with keyboard, 105
    overview of, **255–257**, *255*
    Paragraph dialog box options, 253, 256, 1051
    with ruler, 256, 257
  justifying, 254–255, *255*, 926–927
  keeping lines of text together, 258–259, 1050
  line numbering, 270
  line spacing, 253, 257–258, *258*, 824, 1052
  numbered lists, **264, 267–270, 1034–1036**
    applying outline numbering, 269–270, 1036
    continuing numbering in new lists, 269,
     1035–1036
    creating with AutoFormat feature, 206, 207,
     264
    creating with Formatting toolbar, 267, 1035

    customizing number formats, 267–269, 1035
    styles for, 273
    tabs and paragraph indents disappear when
     numbers are added or deleted, 927
  Paragraph dialog box
    aligning paragraphs, 254–255
    formatting paragraphs, 253–254
    indenting paragraphs, 253, 255–256, 1051
    Indents and Spacing tab, 253
    Line and Page Breaks tab, 254
    line and paragraph spacing options, 257–258,
     258
    opening, 252
    overview of, 253–254
    widow, orphan, and page break options, 258–
     259, 1050
  paragraph spacing, 253, 257–258, 1051
  shading, 262–263, 982
  sorting, 412, 807, 1059
  tab stops, **172, 259–261, 1074–1075**
    entering in tables, 389
    finding, 172
    leader characters for, 261
    setting with ruler, 260, 1074
    setting with Tabs dialog box, 260–261, 1074–
     1075
    styles for, 272
    types of tabs, 259
  troubleshooting
    new paragraphs do not have expected for-
     matting, 928
    paragraph borders are cut off, 929
    paragraph formatting changes when text is
     deleted, 927–928
    paragraphs won't move without moving
     graphic, 948
    tabs and paragraph indents disappear when
     bullets or numbering are added or deleted,
     927
  widow and orphan controls, 258–259, 1050
passwords, **604–606, 1052**. *See also* security
  case-sensitivity in, 605
  deleting or changing, 606
  Password controls in Web page forms, 674, *674*
  password-protecting documents, 604–606, 1052
Paste command in Edit menu, 150
Paste Special dialog box
  copying and pasting with, 150–151, 575, 576–
   577, *577*, 990
  defined, **150–151**
  linking objects, 497, *497*, 1041

pasting. *See* copying and pasting; cutting and pasting
patterns
    in graphs, 450
    for page backgrounds, 293
PC Magazine Web site, 903
.PCD files, 468
.PCT files, 468
.PCX files, 468
permissions, "There has been a network or file permission error. The network connection may be lost. *Filename.doc*" message, 921
personal Web pages, publishing, 688–690
personalized menus, 20–21, 35, 42–43, 102, 798, 1033–1034
Perspective option for 3-D graphs, 453, *454*
PgDn and PgUp keys, navigating with, 161
phone numbers for technical support, 903–904
photographs, scanning and importing, 468–470, 1053
Picture toolbar. *See also* graphics
    Crop button, 484–485, *485*
    defined, **459**, *459*
    displaying, 458
    graphics formatting options, 470, 1053
placeholders, displaying, 86–87
placing footnotes and endnotes, 321
pleading templates, 123
plot area in graphs, 442–443
.PNG files, 467
points, 234
pop-up menus. *See* right-click menus
portrait page orientation settings, 288–289, 1048
ports, printer ports, 958
postage, printing on envelopes, 821
postal barcodes
    on envelopes, 511–512, *512*
    FIM-A Courtesy Reply Mail option for envelopes, 512
    on labels, 520
    on merged envelopes, 546, 547
    on merged labels, 544
PostScript printing option, 115
pound sign (#) in index entries, 357
predefined keyboard shortcuts for styles, 275
predefined templates, **123–124**, **701–705**. *See also* templates
    changing template in current document, 704, 1075–1076
    downloading from Microsoft Web site, 702
    installing, 701
    listed, 123–124

    loading, 702–703, 1075
    previewing in Style Gallery, 704–705
    unloading, 703–704
    using templates from earlier versions of Word, 702
presentations. *See also* Microsoft PowerPoint
    adding Word's PresentIt command to toolbars, 854
    creating in Word without PowerPoint, 832–833, *832*
    embedding in Word documents, 859, 1056
    exporting handouts to Word, 855, *855*, 1055
    exporting to Word documents, 856, 1055
    exporting Word outlines to create presentations, 853–854, 1055
    inserting slides in Word documents, 857–859, *858*, 1056
previews
    Preview view in Open dialog box, 132–133
    previewing merged documents, 538
    previewing templates in Style Gallery, 704–705
    Print Preview, 13, 212–214, *213*, 363, 805, 824, 1057
    Web Page Preview, 13, 53, *54*, 636
PRIME for Word 2000 utilities, 867, 868–871, *869*
Print dialog box, **51–52**, **211**, **214–220**, **1057**
    new features, 51–52, *52*
    overview of, 211, 214–215, *215*
    Print What option, 217
    printing, **216–220**, **1057**
        drafts, 218
        information about documents, 217
        multiple copies, 217
        part of a document, 216–217
        to print files, 218–220
        ranges of pages, 216–217
    resizing or shrinking document pages, 217–218
    selecting printer, 215
Print Layout view. *See also* views
    Click and Type feature, 46–47, 104–105, 140–141, 384, 924, 985
    customizing, 89, *89*
    defined, **11**, *12*, **1083**
    displaying or hiding objects in, 89, *89*
    displaying section break markers, 298
    footnotes and endnotes in, 315
    object placement controls, 35, 47–48, *47*
    when to use, 15
Print Preview, **13**, **212–214**, *213*, **363**, **805**, **824**, **1057**
printed forms, 717

printers
    configuring printer options in Windows, 211–212
    printing outside printable area of printer, 289
    selecting, 215
    troubleshooting
        checking printer hardware, 955–956
        checking printer ports, 958
        deleting and reinstalling printer drivers, 957
        printer driver problems, 909
        verifying printer properties, 956–957
        "Windows cannot print due to a problem with the current printer setup" message, 962–963
        "Word cannot bring up the Properties dialog box because printer returned an error", message, 963
printing, **210–220**, **955–964**, **1056–1057**. *See also* Mail Merge
    AutoShapes, 116
    AutoText entries, 145
    comments, 116
    configuring printer options in Windows, 211–212
    configuring printing options, 114–116, 210–211, 217
    document information, 217
    document properties, 115, 138, 217
    documents, **216–220**
        canceling print jobs, 214
        controlling what prints with documents, 115–116, 138, 217
        drafts, 115, 218
        multiple copies, 217
        paper source options, 217
        part of a document, 216–217
        previewing printouts, 13, 212–214, *213*
        with Print button, 214, 1056
        Print Data Only for Forms option, 218, 737
        to print files, 218–220
        ranges of pages, 216–217
        resizing documents to paper size, 52, 115, 214, 217–218, 824
        two pages per sheet of paper, 291
        updating fields and links before printing, 114, 501
        from Windows, 220
    drawing objects, 116
    envelopes
        envelopes attached to documents, 516
        KazStamp envelope printing software, 514, 867, 878–879, *879*
        postage on envelopes, 821
        single envelopes, 513–514, *513*, 1000
    envelopes attached to documents, 516
    field codes, 115, 338
    form data only, 218, 737
    hidden text, 116
    labels
        overview of, 519–521, *520*, 1027–1028
        return address labels, 519
        sheets of labels, 521
    lists of keyboard shortcuts and menu commands, 24, 103, 801, 1026
    in Mail Merge
        merged documents, 538–540
        merged envelopes, 545–549, *547*, *548*
        merged labels, 542–544, *543*, *545*
    master documents, 593
    Office binders, 843–844
    from Open dialog box, 39
    Options dialog box Print tab, 78, *79*, 114–116, 210–211
    outlines, 571
    outside printable area of printer, 289
    PostScript option, 115
    and resizing documents to paper size, 52, 115, 214, 217–218, 824
    Reverse Print Order option, 115
    from Save As dialog box, 39
    speeding up, 115
    subdocuments, 599
    troubleshooting, **955–964**
        backgrounds do not print, 934
        checking printer hardware, 955–956
        checking printer ports, 958
        complex documents won't print, 960–961
        deleting and reinstalling printer drivers, 957
        documents look different on paper than onscreen, 961
        an extra page is printed with documents, 962
        graphics won't print, 946, 959–960
        header or footer is partially printed, 940
        merge fields print instead of data, 953–954
        printer driver problems, 909
        printing does not work, 959
        printing error messages, 962–964
        running Print Troubleshooter, 956
        text is cut off at the edges, 961
        "Too many fonts" message, 964
        verifying printer properties, 956–957
        "Windows cannot print due to a problem with the current printer setup" message, 962–963

Windows-related printing problems, 958–959
"Word cannot bring up the Properties dialog box because printer returned an error", message, 963
updating fields and links before printing documents, 114, 501
Printing Options tab in Envelope Options dialog box, 511
procedures in Visual Basic for Applications, **771, 777–779**
  coding by hand, 778
  creating with Add Procedure dialog box, 778–779
  defined, **760, 771, 777**
  function procedures, 778
  property procedures, 778
  subprocedures, 778
  types of, 778
  viewing code, 763
profiles, 36–37
program management features, **35–39**
  Detect and Repair utility, 36, 1096–1097
  Help system enhancements, 37, *37*
  Install on Demand, 35–36
  macro virus protection, 38–39
  user profile settings, 36–37
programming ActiveX controls in forms, 732–733, *733*
projects in Visual Basic for Applications
  creating, **771**
  defined, **760, 771**
  inserting modules in, 773
  running, 780
  Visual Basic Editor Project Explorer, 763–764, *763*
promoting outline levels, 565, 1045
proofing tools. *See* AutoCorrect; editing tools; Grammar Checker; Spelling; Thesaurus
properties
  deleting macro properties in Visual Basic for Applications, 782–783
  document properties
    defined, **138–139**, *138*
    displaying, 997
    printing, 115, 138
  Properties view in Open dialog box, 132
  Properties window in Visual Basic Editor, 767–768, *767*
  property procedures in Visual Basic for Applications, 778
  setting ActiveX control properties in forms, 731–732, *732*

Table Properties dialog box, 397–398, 401–402
verifying printer properties, 956–957
in Visual Basic for Applications, 767–768, *767*, 779
"Word cannot bring up the Properties dialog box because printer returned an error" message, 963
proportional fonts, **234**
protecting forms, 735, 1014–1015
Provide Feedback with Sound and Provide Feedback with Animation options, 106
publication templates, 123
publishing Web pages, **628, 676, 688–696**. *See also* exporting
  defined, **628, 688, 691**
  domain names and, 690
  finding hosts for business Web pages, 688, 690–691
  finding hosts for personal Web pages, 688–690
  to FTP sites, **693–694**
    adding FTP site addresses to Word, 693–694
    uploading Web pages to FTP sites, 694
  to home-page communities, 689
  hosting defined, **628**
  managing supporting folders of files, 692, 696
  over networks, 695–696
  Submit with Image controls and, 676
  with Web folders, **691–692, 1085–1086**
    creating Web folders, **691–692, 1085**
    managing Web folder contents, 692, 1085–1086
    saving documents to Web folders, 692, 1085
    Web Folder Wizard, 692
    Web folders defined, **691**
  with Web hosting services, 695
  with Web Publishing Wizard, 694–695

Q

question mark (?) in Find and Replace dialog box, 175
Quick View in Microsoft Script Editor, 683–684, *684*

R

ranges of pages
  marking for index entries, 359, 1023
  printing, 216–217
Readability Statistics feature, 108, 193–194, *194*

reading comments, 614, 989
Reading Ease score, 194
rearranging. *See also* moving
    menu commands, 102
    outline sections, 565–566, 1045
    subdocuments, 595
    tables in Outline view, 568–569
Recently Used File List control, 106
recording macros, 743–746, *744*, 1028
recovering unsaved or damaged documents, 156–157
Redo command in Edit menu, 152, 1081
referencing table cells in formulas, 415–416
reinstalling
    printer drivers, 957
    Word 2000, 912
rejecting revision changes, 611, 1080–1081
renaming. *See also* naming
    macro projects, 752
    styles, 278
    subdocuments, 598
repairing installations with Detect and Repair, 36, 911, 1096–1097
Repeat command in Edit menu, 152
Replace dialog box. *See* Find and Replace dialog box
replying
    to general discussions, 619–620, 995
    to inline discussions, 619, 995
report templates, 124
Reset controls in Web page forms, 677–678, *678*
Reset My Usage Data option, 43, 102
resetting menus, 43, 45, 102
resizing
    documents to paper size, 52, 115, 214, 217–218, 824
    fonts, 239
    frames, 654
    graphs, 426
    movie clips in Web pages, 665
    objects, 480–481, 1037
    scrolling text or marquees, 662
    table cells manually, 398–399
    table columns
        with AutoFit feature, 399, 1068
        manually, 397–398
    table rows, 398
    tables, 49, 378–379, *378*, 396
restoring
    default menus, 45
    default toolbars, 95
return addresses
    printing return address labels, 519
    return address options for envelopes, 512–513

returning to where you left off in a document, 804
reusing documents with Letter Wizard, 829
Reverse Print Order option, 115
reviewing
    AutoFormat changes, 208
    revisions, **609–611**, **1080–1081**. *See also* comments; Track Changes feature
        accepting changes, 610–611, 1080
        overview of, 609, *610*
        rejecting changes, 611
Reviewing toolbar, 608
revisions. *See* comments; Track Changes feature
Right Angle Axes option for 3-D graphs, 454
right-click menus. *See also* menus
    adapting to, 34
    Automatic Spell Checking options, 180–182, *181*
    customizing toolbars, 93
    defined, **21**
    drag-and-drop operations, 149
    editing text from, 148
    formatting commands, 237
    Hyperlink command does not appear on right-click menu, 965
    Spell Checking commands, 180–182, *181*
    Synonyms command, 50–51, 196, 815, 1078
    Update Field command, 371
RKS Software Store, 874, 880
.RLE files, 467
rotating
    3-D graphs, 452, *453*
    objects, 483–484, 950, 1038–1039
rows in tables
    and converting databases to tables, 388
    copying, 393
    defined, **378–379**, *378*
    deleting, 391, 1067
    distributing evenly, 399, 1068
    inserting, 391–392, 1067
    moving, 393
    resizing, 398
RTF files, 576
rulers
    defined, **8**, *9*
    displaying, 290
    displaying measurements in ruler, 801, *802*
    displaying vertical ruler, 86, 89, 290
    hiding, 86
    indenting paragraphs, 256, 257
    setting margins, 289–290, *289*
    setting tab stops, 260
rules
    agreeing on rules for group revisions, 606–607

customizing hyphenation rules, 109
defining grammar rules to apply, 108
Run mode in Web pages, 659
running. *See also* starting
    AutoFormat feature, 207–208, 978
    automatic macros, 786
    Grammar Checker, 192–193, *193*, 1061
    macros, 748, 780, 1029
    Print Troubleshooter, 956
    Spelling Checker, 183–185, *184*, 1060
    Thesaurus, 195–196, *195*, 1077–1078
    Visual Basic for Applications projects, 780
    Word 2000 from installation CD, 1094–1095

S

sans serif fonts, 234
Save As dialog box, 7, 39, *40*, 153, *153*
Save command in File menu, 7, 154–155
saving
    backing up documents, **155–157**
        with AutoRecover feature, 155–156, 157, 919
        creating automatic backups, 156
        recovering unsaved or damaged documents, 156–157
    documents, 7, **60–62**, **152–157**, **996–997**
        in background, 154
        and backing up documents, 155–157
        current version of a document, 615, 1081–1082
        document is saved with unexpected filename extension, 922
        existing documents, 154–155, 996–997
        file save error messages, 920–922
        in HTML format, 638–640, 1083
        new documents, 7, 153, *153*, 996
        in non-Word 2000 formats, 155, 997
        and password-protecting documents, 604–606, 1052
        to previous Word formats, 60–62, *61*
        recovering unsaved or damaged documents, 156–157
        to Web folders, 692, 1085
    e-mail, 122
    envelopes as templates, 517
    form data as text files for sending to databases, 737–738
    master documents, 592
    master documents as a Web page, 592–593
    Office binders, 843

Options dialog box Save tab, 79, *80*, 156
subdocuments, 592
symbol characters as AutoCorrect entries, 199, 202
templates to New dialog box tabs, 708–709
Versions feature, **614–615**, **1081–1082**
    automatically saving current version, 615
    defined, **614**
    saving current version of a document, 615, 1081–1082
    viewing previous versions of a document, 615, 1082
scaling
    Auto Scaling option for 3-D graphs, 454
    documents to paper size, 52, 115, 214, 217–218, 824
    text, 244, *244*
scanning digital photographs, 468–470, 1053
Screen Tips, disabling, 86
ScreenPro template, 867, 886–887
scripts, **667**, **678–685**. *See also* macros; Visual Basic for Applications; Web pages
    adding script commands to Tools menu, 679–680
    adding to Web pages, 681
    ASP (Active Server Pages) scripts, 667, 682
    CGI (Common Gateway Interface) scripts, 667
    creating scripts in Microsoft Script Editor, 685
    defined, **678**
    displaying script anchors, 680, *680*
    editing, 681
    ISAPI (Internet Service Application Programming Interface) scripts, 667
    Java applets, 682
    Microsoft Script Editor, **57**, **682–685**, **1034**
        changing default scripting language, 684
        creating scripts, 685
        defined, **682**, **1034**
        Design View, 684
        opening, 57, *58*, 682
        Quick View, 683–684, *684*
        Source View, 683, *683*
    moving or copying, 681
    types of, 667
    VBScript
        books about, 679
        how VBScript works, 679
        VBScript controls in Web pages, 57, *58*
    Web page forms and, 667
    Web sites about, 667

scroll bars
  AutoScroll feature, 803, *804*
  defined, **8**, *9*
  displaying or hiding, 85–86
  displaying or hiding frame scroll bars, 654
  navigating documents with, 161–162, *162*
scroll buttons in forms, 730
scroll wheel on mouse, 162
scrolling text in Web pages, 660–662, *661*
searching. *See* finding
sections, **163–164**, **174–175**, **297–299**, **309–310**, **934–936**, **1058–1059**. *See also* page setup
  copying section formatting, 299, 1059
  creating section breaks, **297–298**, **309–310**, **982**, **1058**
  defined, **297**
  deleting section breaks, 299, 1059
  finding and replacing section breaks, 174–175
  headers and footers in, 306
  moving to, 163–164
  numbering pages in, 302–303, 1047
  troubleshooting, **934–936**, **942**
    backgrounds do not display or print, 934
    changing header or footer in one section changed all, 942
    page borders do not display properly, 935–936
    pages do not break properly, 935
    watermarks do not display properly, 934–935
  types of section breaks, 298
  viewing section break markers, 298, *299*, 1058
security
  ChekOf security utility, 867, 883
  digital signatures, **755–758**
    creating and installing, 755–756
    defined, **755**
    digitally signing macro projects, 756–758
  macro security, **753–755**
    adding macro developers to list of trusted sources, 755
    changing macro security levels, 754–755, 970, 1059
    enabling Word macro security, 38–39, 753–754
  passwords, **604–606**, **1052**
    case-sensitivity in, 605
    deleting or changing, 606
    Password controls in Web page forms, 674, *674*
    password-protecting documents, 604–606, 1052
Select Browse Object tool, 163–164, 323, 338

selecting
  caption labels, 326–327
  e-mail stationery and fonts, 226–227
  font styles, 237–238, 239–242, *241*
  footnote and endnote reference marks, 321
  formatting selected paragraphs, 252
  graphs, 424, *424*
  hyperlinks in documents, 634
  menu commands, 20
  printers, 215
  with Shift key, 160
  table contents, 390–391
  text, **105**, **146–147**
    with keyboard, 147
    with mouse, 146–147
    overview of, 146, *146*
    words, 105
  Writing Style for Grammar Checker, 189
semicolon (;) in index entries, 357
sending. *See also* exporting
  documents
    as e-mail attachments, 229, 999
    as e-mail messages, 52–53, 227–229, *228*, 998–999
  faxes, 220–221, 1003–1004
separators for footnotes and endnotes, 322
series in graphs, 446–448
serif fonts, 234
Server Extensions for Microsoft Office, 58, 616, 620, 621
setting
  ActiveX control properties in forms, 731–732, *732*
  control properties in Web page forms, 669–670, 1086–1087
  default font, 236
  default page setup, 287
  envelope size, 511
  margins
    with Page Setup dialog box, 290, *290*
    with ruler, 289–290, *289*
  tab stops
    with ruler, 260, 1074
    with Tabs dialog box, 260–261, 1074–1075
shading. *See also* backgrounds; borders; color
  field shading, 87, 337, 1004
  in forms, 714, *715*, 727
  paragraphs, 262–263, 982
  in tables
    cell shading, 409, *410*
    table shading, 404–405, 1069

shadows. *See also* backgrounds; borders; color
  in graphs, 427
  for objects, 489, *489*, 1040
  shadow font style, 241–242, *241*
  troubleshooting, 950
sharing documents. *See* comments; Track Changes
  feature; Web-based collaboration
sharing program settings with user profiles, 36–37
sheets of labels, printing, 521
Shift key. *See also* Alt key; Ctrl key; keyboard shortcuts
    + Ctrl + F11 (Unlock Field), 342, 1005
    + F5 (Return to Last Edit), 163, 804
    + F9 (Field Code/Result toggle), 336
    Alt + Shift + D (DATE field), 340
    Alt + Shift + I (Mark Citation), 373
    Alt + Shift + O (Mark Table of Contents Entry),
    371
    Alt + Shift + P (PAGE field), 340
    Alt + Shift + T (TIME field), 340
    Alt + Shift + X (Mark Index Entry), 357
    moving to previous cursor locations with, 163,
    804
    selecting with, 160
short menus, 20–21, 35
Shortcut Bar, **122, 838–841**. *See also* Microsoft
  Office
    adding buttons to, 841
    closing, 839
    creating documents from, 122, 840
    defined, **838**
    displaying, 838, *839*, 840
    displaying toolbars on, 840
    hiding, 839
    moving, 839
    opening documents from, 840
shortcut keys. *See* keyboard shortcuts
Show/Hide button in Standard toolbar, 298
shrinking documents to paper size, 52, 115, 214,
  217–218, 824
side-by-side tables, 384.
signatures
    digital signatures, **755–758**
      creating and installing, 755–756
      defined, **755**
      digitally signing macro projects, 756–758
    for e-mail messages, 225–226, *225*
single document interface, 41
sizing
    documents to paper size, 52, 115, 214, 217–218,
    824
    fonts, 239

frames, 654
graphs, 426
movie clips in Web pages, 665
objects, 480–481, 1037
scrolling text or marquees, 662
table cells manually, 398–399
table columns
    with AutoFit feature, 399, 1068
    manually, 397–398
table rows, 398
tables, 49, 378–379, *378*, 396
small caps font style, 241–242, *241*
Smart Cut and Paste option, 105
Solutionsoft Web site, 885
sorting
    cells in tables, 410–412, 1070
    numbers with hyphens sort incorrectly, 945
    outline sections, 566–567
    paragraphs, 412, 807, 1059
SOS Office Helpers, 867, 871–872, *871*
sounds
    background sound clips in Web pages, 665–666
    sound files formats, 665
    for Word events, 106
Sounds Like option in Find and Replace dialog box,
  170
source files. *See* linking
Source View in Microsoft Script Editor, 683, *683*
Spacebar, Ctrl + Spacebar (Delete Formatting), 806
spaces
    displaying, 87–88, *88*
    finding and replacing nonbreaking spaces, 174–
    175
    finding and replacing white space, 174–175
    underlining words only, 240, 928
spacing
    automatic spacing adjustment for cutting and
    pasting, 105
    character spacing, 243, 244–245, *245*, 1009
    columns of text, 308–309
    line spacing, 253, 257–258, *258*, 824, 1052
    paragraph spacing, 253, 257–258, 1051
special characters. *See also Symbols section of index*
    AutoCorrect keyboard shortcuts, 808–809
    character code shortcuts, 809–811
    inserting, 248–249, 1065
    international character shortcuts, 811–812
    marking for index entries, 357
    saving symbol characters as AutoCorrect entries,
    199, 202
    Symbol Selector utility, 867, 873–874, *874*

Spelling feature, **50**, **80–81**, **107–108**, **178–188**, **1060**. *See also* Grammar Checker; hyphenation; Thesaurus
    AutoCorrect Spell Checking, 182–183, 976
    Automatic Spell Checking, 180–182, *181*, 1060
    configuring, 80–81, *81*, 107–108, 179–180
    custom dictionaries, **178–179**, **185–188**, **815**
        adding, 185–186
        adding words to, 187–188
        BioSpel spelling dictionary, 186, 866, 886
        on book's CD-ROM, 186
        creating, **187**
        defined, **185–186**
        deleting, 186
        editing, 187–188, 815
        error messages, 910
        how spelling dictionaries work, 178–179
        MedSpel spelling dictionary, 186, 867, 886
    flagging spelling errors as you type, 180–182, *181*, 1060
    hiding spelling error flags, 180
    new features, 50
    Options dialog box Spelling & Grammar tab, 80–81, *81*, 107–108, 179–180
    overview of, 178–179
    running Spelling Checker, 183–185, *184*, 1060
Spike feature. *See* Collect and Paste feature
spin buttons in forms, 730
splitting
    documents
        into Outline and Normal views, 562–563, *563*
        into view panes, 17–18, *17*
    subdocuments, 597
    table cells, 394–395, *394*
    tables, 395–396
spoken comments, 613, 989
spreadsheets. *See also* Microsoft Excel
    creating in Word, 833–834, *833*
    as Mail Merge data sources, 531–532
Standard toolbar. *See also* toolbars
    E-Mail button, 52–53
    Format Painter button, 238, 805–806
    Insert Hyperlink button, 56–57, *57*
    Insert Table button, 382
    New Blank Document button, 120
    Open button, 128
    Print button, 214, 1056
    Redo button, 152, 1081
    Show/Hide button, 298
    Undo button, 152, 924, 1081
    in Visual Basic Editor, 769, *770*
    Zoom button, 15, 1089

standard VBA modules, 772
Start menu, creating documents from, 122
starting. *See also* running
    inline or general discussions, 618–619, 994
    Microsoft Office Binder, 842
    PowerPoint from Word, 499, 504
    source applications from embedded objects, 502, 504
    source applications from linked objects, 499
    Visual Basic Editor, 761, 1082
    Word 2000, **5–6**, **913–914**
statements in Visual Basic for Applications, **771**, **773–777**
    assignment statements, 773, 775
    colon (:) in, 773
    decision statements, 776
    declaration statements, 773, 775
    defined, **760**, **771**, **773**
    error checking, 773
    executable statements, 773, 775
    syntax of, 773, 776–777
stationery for e-mail messages, 226–227
statistics
    document statistics, 139
    Readability Statistics feature, 108
status bar
    defined, **8**, *9*, **18–20**, *18*
    hiding, 86
stepping through
    macros, 748
    Visual Basic for Applications code, 780
stopping automatic macros, 786–787
stretching text, 244, *244*
strikethrough font style, 241–242, *241*
Style Gallery
    AutoFormat feature and, 208
    copying styles, 277, *277*
    previewing templates in, 704–705
styles, **10**, **91**, **271–283**, **930–932**, **1061–1064**. *See also* page setup; paragraphs; templates; text formatting
    applying, 276, 1062
    assigning outline levels to, 564, 1045
    Automatically Update option, 279
    borders and, 273
    copying
        with Organizer, 277–278, *278*
        from Style Gallery, 277, *277*
    creating, **281–283**, **1063–1064**
        by example, 281, 1063
        to follow specific styles, 280
        with Style dialog box, 282–283, 1063–1064

customizing style area, 91, 274, *274*, 799, *800*
defined, **271**
defining what styles follow specific styles, 280
deleting, 278
displaying in Normal view, 10
editing, **279–281**, **1062–1063**
    by example, 279–280, *279*, 1062
    manually, 280–281, 1062–1063
fonts and, 272
formatting options, 272–273
frames and, 273
keyboard shortcuts
    assigning to styles, 281
    predefined style keyboard shortcuts, 275
language setting, 273
versus manual formatting, 272
Modify Style dialog box, 279–281, *279*
naming, 282
Normal style, 273
numbered lists and, 273
paragraph styles versus character styles, 271–272
renaming, 278
tab stops and, 272
tables of contents and heading styles, 366, 368
templates
    applying styles from other templates, 276–
    278, *277*, *278*
    styles and, 272
troubleshooting, **930–932**
    styles appear differently in master documents
    and subdocuments, 931
    styles are missing from Style list, 930
    styles change unexpectedly, 930
uses for, 271, 272–273
viewing, 274–275, *274*, *275*, 1061–1062
viewing in style area, 91, 274, *274*, 799, *800*
subdocuments, **586**, **592**, **593–599**, **601–602**,
1032–1033. *See also* master documents
    adding to master documents, 597, 1033
    collapsing, 594, *595*
    combining, 597–598
    converting into part of master document, 596,
    1032
    defined, **586**
    deleting, 596–597, 1032–1033
    editing, 595–596
    expanding, 595
    formatting, 599
    locking and unlocking, 601–602
    moving, 597
    opening, 594, 596

    in Outline view, 594–596, *595*
    overview of, 593–594
    printing, 599
    rearranging, 595
    renaming, 598
    saving, 592
    splitting, 597
    text and graphics in master documents separate
    from, 587, 596
subentries in indexes, 354, 356, 360
submenus, 20
Submit controls in Web page forms, 675–676, *676*
Submit with Image controls in Web page forms,
    676–677, *677*
subprocedures in Visual Basic for Applications, 778
subscript and superscript font styles, 241–242, *241*,
    246–247, 1010
Subscriptions feature, 59, 620–621, 1064
substitution of fonts, 118, 237
summarizing of documents, 582–584, *584*, 979
supporting folders of files for Web pages, 692, 696
suspending macro recording, 746
switches in field codes, 335–336, 342–343
switching
    category (x-axis) and value (y-axis) axes in
    graphs, 428–431, *429*, *430*, *431*
    to Design mode, 658–659, *660*, 666, 1086
    between documents, 41
    template in current document, 704, 1075–1076
Symantec WinFax Starter Edition software, 221–
    222
symbols. *See also Symbols section of index*
    AutoCorrect keyboard shortcuts, 808–809
    character code shortcuts, 809–811
    inserting, 248–249, 1065
    international character shortcuts, 811–812
    marking for index entries, 357
    saving symbol characters as AutoCorrect entries,
    199, 202
    Symbol Selector utility, 867, 873–874, *874*
Synonyms command, 50–51, 196, 815, 1078
syntax of Visual Basic for Applications statements,
    773, 776–777
system crashes, 156–157
system requirements
    for sending documents as e-mail, 223–224
    for Web-based collaboration features, 616, 617,
    620, 621
    for Word 2000, 1092

T

tab characters
    disappear when bullets or numbering are added
      or deleted, 927
    displaying, 87–88, *88*
    finding and replacing, 174–175
Tab key
    Alt + Tab (switching between documents), 41
    does not move insertion point to correct form
      field, 968
    indenting with, 105
tab sections in New dialog box, creating, 709
tab stops, **172, 259–261, 1074–1075**. *See also* paragraphs
    entering in tables, 389
    finding, 172
    leader characters for, 261
    setting with ruler, 260, 1074
    setting with Tabs dialog box, 260–261, 1074–1075
    styles for, 272
    types of tabs, 259
tables, **378–418, 944–945, 1065–1071**. *See also*
tables of figures
    borders
        cell borders, 409, *410*
        defined, **378–379**, *378*
        table borders, 403–404, 1068–1069
        Tables and Borders toolbar, 379, *379*
    breaking or flowing tables across pages, 396
    cells, **378–379, 406–409**
        aligning text, 49, 406–407
        applying borders and shading, 409, *410*
        changing text orientation, 407–408, *407*
        clearing all cells, 393
        defined, **378–379**, *378*
        deleting, 392–393
        entering tab stops, 389
        entering text or graphics, 389, *390*
        inserting, 392
        merging or splitting, 394–395, *394*, 1068
        moving or copying text in cells, 393–394
        navigating between, 389
        numbering, 413
        referencing cells in formulas, 415–416
        resizing manually, 398–399
        setting margins, 408–409
        sorting, 410–412, 1070
    changes to Table menu, 44
    columns
        and converting databases to tables, 388
        copying, 393

        defined, **378–379**, *378*
        distributing evenly, 399, 1068
        inserting or deleting, 391, 1067
        moving, 393
        resizing with AutoFit feature, 399, 1068
        resizing manually, 397–398
    converting, **385–388, 1067**
        databases to tables, 387–388
        tables to text, 386–387, 1067
        text to tables, 385–386, 1067
    copying and pasting Excel worksheets into, 849–
    850, 1002
    creating, **380–384, 417, 1065–1066**
        with AutoFormat feature, 383–384
        with Draw Table button on Tables and Bor-
          ders toolbar, 382–383, *383*, 395, 821–822,
          822, 823, 1066
        from Excel worksheets, 417
        with Insert Table button, 382, 1066
        with Insert Table dialog box, 381, 1065–1066
        side-by-side tables with Click and Type feature,
          384
    creating captions with, 324
    creating Mail Merge data sources from tables,
    527–529, *528, 529, 530*
    defined, **378–379**, *378*
    deleting
        cells, 392–393
        columns, 391
        data, 393
        rows, 391
        tables, 393
    elements of, 378–379, *378*
    embedding Excel cells or worksheets in, 850–
    852, *851*
    entering text or graphics, 389, *390*
    formatting cells, **406–409**
        aligning text, 49, 406–407
        applying borders and shading, 409, *410*
        changing text orientation, 407–408, *407*
        setting margins, 408–409
    formatting tables, **49, 400–406**
        aligning tables and wrapping text, 400–402
        applying borders and gridlines, 403–404,
          1068–1069
        applying table shading, 404–405, 1069
        copying tables in documents, 400
        moving tables in documents, 49, 378–379,
          378, 400
        new features, 49
        setting cell margins, 402–403
        with Table AutoFormat feature, 405–406,
          1069–1070

formatting Web pages with, 650–651, *650*, *651*
in forms, 713, *713*
formulas and functions, **335**, **413–418**, **1070–1071**
    arguments of functions, 416
    AutoSum button for quick totals, 413–414, 799, 1070
    bookmarks in, 416
    creating complex equations, 417–418, *418*
    fields and, 335, 415
    importing Excel worksheets, 417
    limitations of, 417
    operators, 415
    referencing cells, 415–416
    simple formulas, 414–415, 1070–1071
    using functions, 416
gridlines
    applying, 403–404, 1068–1069
    defined, **378–379**, *378*
    displaying or hiding, 380
importing database data into, 387–388, 861–862, 974–975
laying out documents with, 821–822, *822*, *823*
moving, 49, 378–379, *378*
moving to, 163–164
navigating in, 379–380
nesting, 49, 384–385, *385*
new features, 49
in Outline view, 568–569
resizing, 49, 378–379, *378*, 396
rows
    and converting databases to tables, 388
    copying, 393
    defined, **378–379**, *378*
    deleting, 391, 1067
    distributing evenly, 399, 1068
    inserting, 391–392, 1067
    moving, 393
    resizing, 398
selecting contents, 390–391
shading
    cells, 409, *410*
    tables, 404–405, 1069
splitting
    cells, 394–395, *394*
    tables, 395–396
Table Properties dialog box, 397–398, 401–402
Tables and Borders toolbar
    AutoSum button, 413–414, 799, 1070
    defined, **379**, *379*
    Draw Table button, 382–383, *383*, 395, 821–822, *822*, *823*
    Eraser button, 395

troubleshooting, **944–945**
    numbers with hyphens sort incorrectly, 945
    table extends past edge of page, 944–945
    table is cut off at end of page, 944
    tables in columns of text disappear, 933
    text in cell is hidden or cut off, 944
in Web pages, 650–651, *650*, *651*
tables of authorities, **373–374**, **1071–1072**
    creating, **374**, **1071–1072**
    defined, **373**
    editing citation categories, 373
    marking citations, 373, 1071
    updating, 374
tables of contents, **366–371**, **600**, **938–939**, **1072–1073**
    bookmarks and, 370
    creating, **366–369**, *367*, *368*, **1073**
    creating in frames, **653**
    creating from another document, **830**
    creating manually, **371**
    defined, **366**
    formatting, 370
    guidelines, 369–370
    heading styles and, 366, 368
    marking text manually, 371, 1072
    for master documents, 370, 600
    multiple tables of contents, 369
    for part of a document, 370
    preparing, 366
    titles for, 369
    TOC field code, 369
    troubleshooting, **938–939**
        contain error messages in master documents, 938
        page numbers are incorrect, 938–939
        some headings don't appear, 939
        table of contents contains nonheading text, 939
        unwanted codes or error messages are displayed, 939
    updating, 370–371, 1073
    for Web pages, 370, 653
tables of figures, **371–372**, **1073–1074**
    creating, **372**, **1073–1074**
    defined, **371**
    formatting, 372
    updating, 372
tabs in New dialog box, creating, 709
TDD/TTY support, 903
technical support phone numbers and Web sites, 903–904
templates, **40–41**, **107**, **120–125**, **700–710**, **930–932**, **1075–1077**. *See also* add-in programs; styles
    adding, 124–125, *124*

applying styles from other templates, 276–278, *277*, *278*
attaching to documents, 125, 704
built-in templates, **123–124**, **701–705**
    changing template in current document, 704, 1075–1076
    downloading from Microsoft Web site, 702
    installing, 701
    listed, 123–124
    loading, 702–703, 1075
    previewing in Style Gallery, 704–705
    unloading, 703–704
    using templates from earlier versions of Word, 702
copying macro projects to different templates, 751, *751*
creating, **176–177**, **518–519**, **708–710**, **718–719**
    creating tabs in New dialog box, 709
    from documents, 710, 1077
    from existing templates, 709–710, 1076
    form templates, 718–719
    label templates, 518–519, 1027
    saving to New dialog box tabs, 708–709
creating Click Here and Type fields, 825
creating documents from, **121–122**, *121*
creating Windows Desktop shortcuts to, 831
customizing, **705–708**
    copying elements between templates with Organizer, 706–708, *707*
    existing templates, 706, 1076
defined, **120**, **700–701**
Direct Mail Manager utility and, 123, 549–550
displaying toolbars and menus in, 107
document templates, **120–121**, **700–701**
versus documents, 122
.DOT filename extension, 122, 708
fax templates, 123
global templates, **120**, **700–701**
legal pleading templates, 123
letter templates, 123
loading
    templates, 702–703, 1075
    templates automatically, 702, 710
locations of, 706
memo templates, 123
Normal template, 706
opening from Windows Desktop shortcuts, 831
publication templates, 123
report templates, 124
saving envelopes as, 517
saving to New dialog box tabs, 708–709
ScreenPro template, 867, 886–887

styles and, 272, 276–278, *277*, *278*
template files and folders, 40–41, 706
troubleshooting, **930–932**
    custom toolbars disappear when documents are saved as templates, 931
    document template won't save as a Word document, 931–932
    items won't copy to a template, 931
    macros, AutoText entries, and other settings are missing from templates, 931
updating documents after changing templates, 706
Web page templates, 124, 641–642, 1084
text
    adding to headers and footers, 303–304, 1017–1018
    animated text
        creating, **242**, **1008**
        hiding, 86
    AutoText feature, **112**, **144–145**, **979–980**
        creating entries, **145**, **980**
        creating headers and footers with, 305
        customizing, 112
        defined, **144**
        inserting AutoText entries, 144, 979
        inserting page numbers with, 301
        printing entries, 145
        troubleshooting, 931
    Collect and Paste feature, 48–49, 149–150, 990–991
    columns of text, **307–310**, **806**, **932–934**, **987–988**. *See also* troubleshooting
        balancing, 806, 933
        changing column widths and spacing, 308–309, 988
        changing vertical alignment, 309
        creating, **307–308**, **987–988**
        creating column breaks, 309–310, 982
        defined, **307**, *307*
    copying and pasting
        with Collect and Paste feature, 48–49, 149–150, 990–991
        with Copy and Paste commands, 148–149, 575–576
        in footnotes and endnotes, 320
        as a link, 577–578
        with Paste command and multiple text objects in Clipboard, 150
        with Paste Special dialog box, 150–151, 497, *497*, 575, 576–577, *577*, 990
    deleting, 7, 148
    drag-and-drop feature, 105, 148–149

editing
overview of, 6–7
from right-click menus, 148
undoing and redoing changes, 152, 924, 1081
entering
AutoText entries, 144, 979
with Click and Type feature, 46–47, 104–105, 140–141, 384, 924, 985
overview of, 6–7
finding text versus finding files, 168
in graphs
formatting, 446
wrapping text, 426–427
hidden text
creating, **241**
displaying, 87–88, *88*, 362
printing, 116
highlighted text
creating, **237–238**, **243**, **614**
displaying, 87
finding, 173
inserting page numbers into text, 301–302
keeping lines of text together, 258–259, 1050
in master documents separate from subdocuments, 587, 596
moving, 149
scrolling text or marquees in Web pages, 660–662, *661*
selecting, **105**, **146–147**
with keyboard, 147
with mouse, 146–147
overview of, 146, *146*
words, 105
in tables
aligning in cells, 49, 406–407
changing text orientation in cells, 407–408, *407*
converting tables to text, 386–387
converting text to tables, 385–386
entering in cells, 389, *390*
moving or copying in cells, 393–394
wrapping text, 400–402
tips and tricks, **804–808**
balancing columns of text, 806, 933
copying formatting multiple times, 806
copying text and paragraph formatting, 805
creating links within and between documents, 807–808
deleting formatting, 806
editing in Print Preview, 805
returning to where you left off, 804
sorting paragraphs, 412, 807, 1059

troubleshooting
entering text deletes existing text, 923
justified text leaves gaps between words, 926–927
paragraph formatting changes when text is deleted, 927–928
printed text is cut off at the edges, 961
table of contents contains nonheading text, 939
text accidentally deleted or cut, 923
text appears garbled, 915–916
text is automatically selected on mouse click or key press, 923
text is not visible, 915
text in a line appears cut off, 928–929
text point size changed, 927
text in table cell is hidden or cut off, 944
text unexpectedly appears as a hyperlink, 929
text in Web pages is not positioned properly, 966
troubleshooting columns of text, **932–934**
changing page orientation or paper size generates error message, 933–934
columns are not visible, 932
columns don't work in headers, footers, comments, or text boxes, 934
columns of text are narrower than expected, 932
columns won't balance, 933
tables in columns disappear, 933
text above columns turns into multiple columns, 933
vertical lines between columns are not visible, 932
Unicode text, 576
vertical text alignment
for columns of text, 309
in page setup, 291–292, 1048–1049
in Web pages
creating alternate text for graphics, 471, 647, 1054
formatting text, 645–646
scrolling text or marquees, 660–662, *661*
Text Area controls in forms, 674–675, *675*
Textbox controls in forms, 673–675, *673*
WordArt text, **472–475**, **1088–1089**
defined, **472**
editing with WordArt toolbar, 474–475, 1088–1089
inserting, 472–474, *474*, 1088
wrapping text
around objects, 486–488, 1039–1040

in graphs, 426–427
in tables, 400–402
Text Area controls in Web page forms, 674–675, *675*
text boxes, **47–48**, **141–143**, **478**. *See also* graphics
   columns of text in, 934
   creating, **141–142**, *142*, **1077**
   defined, **141**
   Format Text Box dialog box, 47–48, *47*, 143
   formatting, 142–143, 478
   in forms, 714, *714*, 729
   Textbox controls in Web page forms, 673–675, *673*
Text Effects options, 242
text fields, inserting with macros, 741
text form fields, 721–722, *721*, *722*
text formatting, **234–249**, **1007–1010**. *See also* formatting; styles
   all caps font style, 241–242, *241*
   animated text
      creating, **242**, **1008**
      hiding, 86
   bold font style, 237–238, 239, 241–242, *241*
   Change Case dialog box, 242–243, 1008
   character spacing options, 243, 244–245, *245*, 1009
   coloring text, 240, 1007–1008
   copying with Format Painter tool, 238, 805–806
   deleting, 806
   displaying or hiding in outlines, 562
   drop caps, 247–248, 1010
   embossed and engraved font styles, 241–242, *241*
   finding and replacing, 172–173
   fonts, **90–91**, **118**, **172**, **226–227**, **234–242**
      adding, 235
      changing fonts, styles, and size, 239, 1007
      defined, **234**
      draft fonts in Normal and Outline views, 90–91, *90*
      in e-mail messages, 226–227
      finding, 172
      Font dialog box, 238, *239*
      Font Substitution option, 118, 237
      formatting with Formatting toolbar, 237–238
      monospaced fonts, 234
      outline font style, 241–242, *241*
      proportional fonts, 234
      selecting font styles, 237–238, 239–242, *241*
      serif versus sans serif fonts, 234
      setting default font, 236
      Text Effects options, 242

TrueType fonts, 235, 237
      viewing installed fonts and font styles, 235–236
      Windows font settings, 235
   in footnotes and endnotes, 322
   Format Painter tool, 238, 805–806
   formatting commands in right-click menus, 237
   with Formatting toolbar, 237–238, 239, 240, 243
   French formatting, 105
   in headers and footers, 304
   hidden text
      creating, **241**
      displaying, 87–88, *88*, 362
      printing, 116
   highlighted text
      creating, **237–238**, **243**, **614**
      displaying, 87
      finding, 173
   in indexes, 356, 364–365
   italic font style, 237–238, 239, 241–242, *241*
   kerning character pairs, 245–246, *246*, 1009–1010
   with macros, 741
   outline font style, 241–242, *241*
   overview of, 7
   scaling, stretching, or condensing text, 244, *244*
   for scrolling text or marquees, 662
   shadow font style, 241–242, *241*
   small caps font style, 241–242, *241*
   strikethrough font style, 241–242, *241*
   subscript and superscript font styles, 241–242, *241*, 246–247, 1010
   symbols
      inserting, 248–249
      saving symbol characters as AutoCorrect entries, 199, 202
   in tables of contents, 370
   in tables of figures, 372
   underline font style, 237–238, 239, 240–242, *241*, 928, 1008
   viewing formatting applied to any character, 236
   in Web pages, 645–646
textures
   in graphs, 449
   for page backgrounds, 293
"The disk is full or too many files are open" message, 921–922
"The disk is full trying to write to *drive...*" message, 921
"The document is read-only" message, 922
"The file is too large" message, 922

themes
  formatting paragraphs with, 283
  for Web pages, 55, *56*, 642–645, *643*, *644*, 1087
"There has been a network or file permission error. The network connection may be lost. *File-name.doc*" message, 921
Thesaurus, **50–51**, **195–196**, **1077–1078**. *See also* Grammar Checker; Spelling feature
  new features, 50–51
  running, 195–196, *195*, 1077–1078
  Synonyms command, 50–51, 196, 815, 1078
third-party fax software, 222
3-D effects
  for objects, *489*, 490–491, 1040
  troubleshooting, 950
3-D graphs, **451–454**
  Auto Scaling option, 454
  Elevation option, 451, *452*
  Height option, 454, *455*
  Perspective option, 453, *454*
  Right Angle Axes option, 454
  Rotation option, 452, *453*
.TIF files, 468
time
  Alt + Shift + T (TIME field), 340
  Date-Time Picture field switch, 336
  entering in graphs, 428
  in headers and footers, 304, *304*, 305, 940
  inserting in documents, 993
tips and tricks, **798–835**
  automating Word, **823–831**
    AutoCorrect shortcuts for long words, 824–825
    creating Click Here and Type fields, 825
    creating documents from dialog boxes, 826–828, *826*, *827*, *829*
    creating tables of contents from another document, 830
    creating Windows Desktop shortcuts to templates and documents, 831
    line spacing shortcuts, 824
    reusing documents with Letter Wizard, 829
    shrinking documents to fit paper size, 52, 115, 214, 217–218, 824
  bullets and special characters, **808–814**
    AutoCorrect keyboard shortcuts for special characters, 808–809
    AutoFormat characters for bullet types, 812–813
    character code shortcuts for special characters, 809–811
    creating graphical bullets, 266–267, 813–814, *814*, 984
    keyboard shortcuts for international characters, 811–812

  customizing the workspace, **798–803**
    assigning keyboard shortcuts from keyboard, 800–801
    AutoScroll macro, 803, *804*
    calculating totals in documents, 799
    creating personal menus, 798
    displaying measurements in ruler, 801, *802*
    opening dialog boxes with double-click hot spots, 802
    printing lists of keyboard shortcuts and menu commands, 24, 103, 801, 1026
    viewing styles in style area, 91, 274, *274*, 799, *800*
  document formatting, **816–822**
    creating watermarks, 293–295, *294*, 819–820, *820*, 934–935, 1049
    laying out documents with tables, 821–822, *822*, *823*
    printing postage on envelopes, 821
    using gradient fills in headers and footers, 818–819, *818*
    using graphics in bar charts, 816–817, *816*, *817*
  editing and formatting text, **804–808**
    balancing columns of text, 806, 933
    copying formatting with Format Painter, 238, 805–806
    creating links within and between documents, 807–808
    deleting formatting, 806
    editing in Print Preview, 805
    returning to where you left off in a document, 804
    sorting paragraphs, 412, 807, 1059
  extending Word functionality, **831–835**
    using Word as a database program, 834
    using Word as a drawing program, 834–835
    using Word for presentations, 832–833, *832*
    using Word as a spreadsheet program, 833–834, *833*
  proofing documents, **814–815**
    editing custom spelling dictionaries, 187–188, 815
    finding synonyms from right-click menu, 50–51, 196, 815, 1078
title bars, **8**, *9*
title pages, 295, *295*
titles
  for graphs, 435–436
  for indexes, 363
  for tables of contents, 369
TOA. *See* tables of authorities
TOC. *See* tables of contents

TOF. *See* tables of figures
toggle buttons in forms, 730
toolbars, **8**, **22**, **44–45**, **92–101**, **1078–1079**. *See also* keyboard shortcuts; menus
  adding PresentIt command to, 854
  assigning macros to, 749
  Control Toolbox toolbar, 670, 728, 730–731
  creating, **100–101**, **1079**
  customizing, **44–45**, **92–101**, **1079**
    adding or deleting buttons, 94–96, 1079
    adding menus, 96–97
    assigning hyperlinks to buttons, 99–100
    changing button display, 97–98
    changing or editing button images with Button Editor, 98, *99*
    creating toolbars, 100–101, 1079
    Customize dialog box Commands tab, 73–74, *73*
    Customize dialog box Toolbars tab, 44, 72, *73*, 92, 95, 100
    displaying or hiding toolbars, 16, 22, 92–93
    grouping buttons, 97
    moving or docking toolbars, 22, 93–94
    new features, 44–45
    overview of, 92
    restoring default settings, 95
  Database toolbar, 388, 530, 860
  defined, **8**, *9*, **22**
  displaying
    or hiding, 16, 22, 92–93, 1078
    on Office Shortcut Bar, 840
    in templates, 107
  displaying function keys as a toolbar, 24
  Equation toolbar, 417–418, *418*
  Formatting toolbar
    aligning text in table cells, 407
    creating bulleted lists, 264–265, 983
    creating numbered lists, 267, 1035
    formatting paragraphs, 252–253
  Forms toolbar, 720
  Frames toolbar, 652, *652*
  Header and Footer toolbar, 303, *303*
  hiding, 16, 22, 92–93, 1078
  More Buttons button, 94
  moving, 22, 93–94, 1078
  Outline toolbar
    defined, **559–561**, *560*
    master document buttons, 586–587, *587*
    moving sections, 566
  Picture toolbar
    Crop button, 484–485, *485*

    defined, **459**, *459*
    displaying, 458
    graphics formatting options, 470, 1053
  Reviewing toolbar, 608
  Shortcut Bar, **122**, **838–841**
    adding buttons to, 841
    closing, 839
    creating documents from, 122, 840
    defined, **838**
    displaying, 838, *839*, 840
    displaying toolbars on, 840
    hiding, 839
    moving, 839
    opening documents from, 840
  Standard toolbar
    E-Mail button, 52–53
    Format Painter button, 238, 805–806
    Insert Hyperlink button, 56–57, *57*
    Insert Table button, 382
    New Blank Document button, 120
    Open button, 128
    Print button, 214, 1056
    Redo button, 152, 1081
    Show/Hide button, 298
    Undo button, 152, 924, 1081
    in Visual Basic Editor, 769, *770*
    Zoom button, 15, 1089
  Tables and Borders toolbar
    AutoSum button, 413–414, 799, 1070
    defined, **379**, *379*
    Draw Table button, 382–383, *383*, 395, 821–822, *822*, *823*
    Eraser button, 395
  ToolsCalculate command, 799
  troubleshooting
    copied toolbar does not contain macros, 969
    custom toolbars disappear when documents are saved as templates, 931
    toolbar buttons cannot be found, 915
  in Visual Basic Editor, 769–771
  Web toolbar, 637
  Web Tools toolbar, **658–659**
    defined, **658–659**, *659*
    Design Mode, 658–659, *660*, 666
Toolbox in Visual Basic Editor, 765–767, *765*
tools. *See* CD-ROM (book's); utilities
Tools menu. *See also* Grammar Checker; hyphenation; macros; Options dialog box; Spelling feature; Thesaurus; Track Changes feature
  adding script commands to, 679–680
  changes to, 44

Edit menu Find command versus Tools menu Find command, 168
Word Count command, 194
ToolsCalculate command, 799
totals
 AutoSum button in tables, 413–414, 799, 1070
 ToolsCalculate command in documents, 799
Track Changes feature, 81, **106–107**, **606–612**, **951–952**, **1079–1081**. *See also* comments; Web-based collaboration
 agreeing on rules for group revisions, 606–607
 changing revision colors and marks, 611–612
 Compare Documents command, 609, 951
 defined, **606**, **1079**
 enabling, 607, 1079–1080
 making revisions, 608
 merging revisions from multiple reviewers, 608–609, 1080
 reviewing revisions, **609–611**
  accepting changes, 610–611, 1080
  overview of, 609, *610*
  rejecting changes, 611, 1080–1081
 Reviewing toolbar, 608
 Track Changes tab in Options dialog box, 81, *82*, 106–107
 troubleshooting, **951–952**
tracking document editing with Outlook Journal utility, 847, *847*, 1046
trendlines in graphs, 437
troubleshooting, **748**, **906–972**
 columns of text, **932–934**
  changing page orientation or paper size generates error message, 933–934
  columns are not visible, 932
  columns don't work in headers, footers, comments, or text boxes, 934
  columns of text are narrower than expected, 932
  columns won't balance, 933
  tables in columns disappear, 933
  text above columns turns into multiple columns, 933
  vertical lines between columns are not visible, 932
 editing, **923–925**
  automatic capitalization problems, 923–924
  Click and Type feature does not work, 924
  Document Map view does not display document headings, 925
  entering text deletes existing text, 923
  Find and Replace does not produce expected results, 925
  text accidentally deleted or cut, 923
  text is automatically selected on mouse click or key press, 923
  Undo command generates error message, 924
 e-mail, **964**
 error messages, **906–912**
  AutoCorrect problems, 910
  bookmark error message is displayed, 943–944
  changing page orientation or paper size generates error message, 933–934
  "Check drive" message, 922
  clicking Web page hyperlinks generates an error message, 965
  cross-references in master documents are replaced by error messages, 938
  custom dictionary problems, 910
  deciphering the message, 908
  determining the scope of problems, 908–909
  examining the timing of errors, 908
  fatal exception errors, 907
  file save error messages, 920–922
  font problems, 910
  illegal operation errors, 907
  in indexes and tables of contents, 939
  kernel errors, 907
  Mail Merge error message says data file is main document, 954
  master document tables of contents or indexes contain error messages, 938
  printer driver problems, 909
  printing error messages, 962–964
  reinstalling Word, 912
  repairing Word, 911
  running a macro generates an error message, 969
  "The disk is full or too many files are open" message, 921–922
  "The disk is full trying to write to *drive...*" message, 921
  "The document is read-only" message, 922
  "The file is too large" message, 922
  "There has been a network or file permission error. The network connection may be lost. *Filename.doc*" message, 921
  "Too many fonts" message, 964
  Undo command generates error message, 924
  uninstalling Word, 911–912
  video driver problems, 910
  viewing Details button, 908

"Windows cannot print due to a problem with the current printer setup" message, 962–963

"Word cannot bring up the Properties dialog box because printer returned an error", message, 963

faxes, **964**

files and damaged documents, **916–922**

    AutoRecovered document recovery problems, 919

    "Check drive" message, 922

    damaged documents, 916–918

    document cannot be found, 920

    document is saved with unexpected filename extension, 922

    document opens with a different filename, 920

    document won't open, 918

    file save error messages, 920–922

    file was accidentally deleted, 916

    identifying damaged documents, 917

    recovering damaged documents, 917–918

    "The disk is full or too many files are open" message, 921–922

    "The disk is full trying to write to *drive…*" message, 921

    "The document is read-only" message, 922

    "The file is too large" message, 922

    "There has been a network or file permission error. The network connection may be lost. *Filename.doc*" message, 921

footnotes, endnotes, captions, cross-references, and bookmarks, **942–944**

    bookmark error message is displayed, 943–944

    captions are not numbered correctly, 943

    cross-references or captions do not update correctly, 943

    footnote continues on following page, 943

    footnote text is deleted, but reference still appears in document, 942

    footnotes or endnotes disappear, 942

formatting, **926–930**

    bullets do not display properly, 927

    font does not display properly, 926

    graphics or text in a line appear cut off, 928–929

    justified text leaves gaps between words, 926–927

    new paragraphs do not have expected formatting, 928

    outline numbering does not number headings, 929

    paragraph borders are cut off, 929

    paragraph formatting changes when text is deleted, 927–928

    tabs and paragraph indents disappear when bullets or numbering are added or deleted, 927

    text point size changed, 927

    text unexpectedly appears as a hyperlink, 929

    underlining does not work on blank spaces or lines, 928

forms, **967–968**

    check box size does not change when formatted, 968

    field codes are displayed instead of form fields, 967

    form fields don't work, 967

    macro problems, 968

    Tab key does not move insertion point to correct form field, 968

general problems, **913–916**

    menu commands or toolbar buttons cannot be found, 915

    text appears garbled, 915–916

    text is not visible, 915

    Word starts, then freezes or quits, 914

    Word won't start from documents, 913–914

    Word won't start from a shortcut, 913

graphics, **945–951**

    3-D effects replace borders and shadows, 950

    3-D and shadow colors don't change when object color is changed, 950

    Align or Distribute menu items are unavailable, 947

    aligned objects are stacked on top of each other, 947

    animated GIFs cannot be changed, 949

    borders do not display properly, 950

    colors are not smooth onscreen, 947

    colors won't change, 949

    drawing object disappears when Letter Wizard is run, 951

    Freeform drawing cannot be controlled, 950

    graphics are not visible, 945–946

    graphics in a line appear cut off, 928–929

    graphics won't print, 946

    graphics won't resize correctly, 949

    graphics won't rotate, 950

    graphics won't ungroup, 949

    lines are jagged onscreen, 947

    object alignment changed when document was opened on another computer, 948

    objects do not align or distribute as commanded, 947

objects jump when realigned, 948
paragraphs won't move without moving
  graphic, 948
part of graphic does not display, 946
headers and footers, **940–942**
  changing header or footer in one section
    changed all, 942
  codes are visible, 940
  columns of text don't work in headers and
    footers, 934
  date, time, or other items are incorrect, 940
  header or footer is missing or partially
    printed, 940
  page numbers cannot be deleted, 941
  page numbers do not show, 940–941
  top or bottom margin changed after creating
    header or footer, 941
indexes and tables of contents, **938–939**
  contain error messages in master documents,
    938
  index entries have backslashes (\) instead of
    colons (:), 939
  page numbers are incorrect, 938–939
  some headings don't appear in table of con-
    tents, 939
  table of contents contains nonheading text,
    939
  unwanted codes or error messages are dis-
    played, 939
linking and embedding, **952–953**
macros, **748**, **931**, **968–972**
  copied toolbar does not contain macros, 969
  macro virus warning appears for files without
    macros, 970
  macro viruses in documents, 970–971
  macro won't run, 969–970
  macros are missing from templates, 931
  making mistakes when recording macros,
    969
  running a macro generates an error message,
    969
  security level cannot be changed, 970
  stepping through macros, 748
  Visual Basic Editor problems, 971–972
Mail Merge, **953–954**
  error message says data file is main docu-
    ment, 954
  merge field changes when Letter Wizard is
    run, 954
  merge fields print instead of data, 953–954
  merged document contains blank lines, 954
master documents, **936–938**

cross-references are replaced by error messages, 938
master documents or subdocuments won't
  open, 936–937
page number, headers, or footers are incorrect or missing, 937
problems saving master documents or subdocuments, 937
styles appear differently in master documents
  and subdocuments, 931
subdocuments are created incorrectly, 938
tables of contents or indexes contain error
  messages, 938
printing, **955–964**
  backgrounds do not print, 934
  checking printer hardware, 955–956
  checking printer ports, 958
  complex documents won't print, 960–961
  deleting and reinstalling printer drivers, 957
  documents look different on paper than
    onscreen, 961
  an extra page is printed with documents, 962
  graphics won't print, 946, 959–960
  header or footer is partially printed, 940
  merge fields print instead of data, 953–954
  printer driver problems, 909
  printing does not work, 959
  printing error messages, 962–964
  running Print Troubleshooter, 956
  text is cut off at the edges, 961
  "Too many fonts" message, 964
  verifying printer properties, 956–957
  "Windows cannot print due to a problem
    with the current printer setup" message,
    962–963
  Windows-related printing problems, 958–959
  "Word cannot bring up the Properties dialog
    box because printer returned an error", mes-
    sage, 963
sections and pages, **934–936**
  backgrounds do not display or print, 934
  changing header or footer in one section
    changed all, 942
  page borders do not display properly, 935–
    936
  pages do not break properly, 935
  watermarks do not display properly, 934–935
styles and templates, **930–932**
  custom toolbars disappear when documents
    are saved as templates, 931
  document template won't save as a Word
    document, 931–932
  items won't copy to a template, 931

macros, AutoText entries, and other settings are missing from templates, 931

styles appear differently in master documents and subdocuments, 931

styles are missing from Style list, 930

styles change unexpectedly, 930

tables, **944–945**

numbers with hyphens sort incorrectly, 945

table extends past edge of page, 944–945

table is cut off at end of page, 944

tables in columns of text disappear, 933

text in cell is hidden or cut off, 944

Track Changes feature, **951–952**

Web pages, **965–967**

clicking hyperlinks generates an error message, 965

frames are missing or displayed incorrectly, 966–967

graphics do not display, 965–966

HTML codes change after saving Web page, 967

Hyperlink command does not appear on right-click menu, 965

text and graphics are not positioned properly, 966

users cannot access Web page, 967

TrueType fonts. *See also* fonts

defined, **235**

Embed TrueType Fonts option, 237

trusted sources, adding macro developers to list of, 755

TTY/TDD support, 903

turning off. *See* disabling

turning on. *See* enabling

typefaces, 234

Typical installation process, 1093–1094

typos. *See* AutoCorrect feature; Spelling feature

unlocking

fields, 336, 342, 1005

subdocuments, 601–602

updating

Automatically Update option for styles, 279

changing how links are updated, 500

documents after changing templates, 706

field results, 341–342, 1005

fields and links before printing documents, 114, 501

indexes, 365, 1025

tables of authorities, 374

tables of contents, 370–371, 1073

tables of figures, 372

Update Field command in right-click menus, 371

upgrading WinFax Starter Edition to WinFax Pro, 222

uploading Web pages to FTP sites, 694

uppercase

automatic capitalization problems, 923–924

Change Case dialog box, 242–243, 1008

drop caps, 247–248, 1010

Match Case option in Find and Replace dialog box, 170

User Information tab in Options dialog box, 82, *82*, 104, 514, 1081

user interface. *See also* workspace

global interface, 60

imitating Word 97 interface, 92

single document interface, 41

user profiles, 36–37

UserForm toolbar in Visual Basic Editor, 770, *771*

UserForm window in Visual Basic Editor, 768, *768*

utilities. *See also* CD-ROM (book's)

for customizing Word on a corporate scale, 85

Detect and Repair, 36, 1096–1097

graphics editing software, 471–472, 864, 867, 872–873, *873*

U

underline font style, 237–238, 239, 240–242, *241*, 928, 1008

Undo command, 152, 924, 1081

ungrouping

objects, 483, 949

.WMF file images, 463, *464*

Unicode text, 576

uninstalling Word, 911–912

unlinking fields, 342

unloading templates and add-in programs, 703–704

V

variables in Visual Basic for Applications, 774

VBScript. *See also* scripts; Visual Basic for Applications

books about, 679

how VBScript works, 679

VBScript controls, 57, *58*

VBScript controls in Web pages, 57, *58*

Versions feature, **614–615**, **1081–1082**
  automatically saving current version, 615
  defined, **614**
  saving current version of a document, 615,
    1081–1082
  viewing previous versions of a document, 615,
    1082
versions of Word, compatibility of, **35**
vertical alignment
  in columns of text, 309
  of objects, 1037
  in page setup, 291–292, 1048–1049
vertical lines between columns of text, 932
vertical ruler, 86, 89, 290
video clips in Web pages, 663–665, *663*
video driver problems, 910
View buttons, 8, *9*
View menu
  changes to, 43
  Full Screen command, 16, 1089
  Zoom command, 15–16, *16*, 1089
View tab in Options dialog box, 76, *76*, 799
viewing. *See also* displaying; hiding
  bookmarks, 167, 980–981
  Details button for error messages, 908
  discussions, 617–618, *618*, 994
  footnotes and endnotes, 315–316, *316*, 318, 1011
  headers and footers, 303, *303*, 1017
  installed fonts and font styles, 235–236
  multiple documents in multiple windows, 18
  Outlook Journal entries, 848, *848*, 1046
  previous versions of a document, 615, 1082
  procedure code in Visual Basic for Applications,
    763
  section break markers, 298, *299*, 1058
  styles, 274–275, *274*, *275*, 1061–1062
  styles in style area, 91, 274, *274*, 799, *800*
  Web pages in Word, **635–637**
    using Word as a Web browser, 637
    in Web Layout view, 635–636, *636*
    in Web Page Preview, 13, 53, *54*, 636
    Web toolbar, 637
views, **9–18**, **1082–1083**
  defined, **1082–1083**
  Document Map view, 14, 165–166, *166*, 925,
    995
  editing multiple documents in multiple win-
    dows, 18
  folder views in Open dialog box, 129–133
  Full Screen view, 16, 1089
  Normal view, **9–10**, **15**, **1083**
    customizing, 90–91, *90*

  defined, **9–10**, *10*, **1083**
    displaying draft fonts in, 90–91, *90*
    displaying Outline and Normal views simul-
      taneously, 562–563, *563*
    displaying styles in, 10
    footnotes and endnotes in, 315, *316*, 319
    master documents in, 589–590, *590*
    section break markers, 298, *299*
    when to use, 15
  Outline view
    customizing, 90–91
    defined, **12–13**, *13*, **558**, *559*, **1044**, **1083**
    displaying draft fonts in, 90–91
    displaying Outline and Normal views simul-
      taneously, 562–563, *563*
    displaying and rearranging tables in, 568–569
    displaying section break markers, 298
    footnotes and endnotes in, 315, *316*
    master documents in, 588–590, *589*, 593–594
    subdocuments in, 594–596, *595*
    when to use, 14
  Print Layout view
    Click and Type feature, 46–47, 104–105, 140–
      141, 384, 924, 985
    customizing, 89, *89*
    defined, **11**, *12*, **1083**
    displaying or hiding objects in, 89, *89*
    displaying section break markers, 298
    footnotes and endnotes in, 315
    object placement controls, 35, 47–48, *47*
    when to use, 15
  Print Preview, 13, 212–214, *213*, 363, 805, 824,
    1057
  splitting documents into view panes, 17–18, *17*
  Web Layout view
    Click and Type feature, 46–47, 104–105, 140–
      141, 384, 924, 985
    customizing, 89, *89*
    defined, **10**, *11*, **1083**
    displaying or hiding objects in, 89, *89*
    object placement controls, 35, 47–48, *47*
    viewing Web pages, 635–636, *636*
    when to use, 15
  Web Page Preview, 13, 53, *54*, 636
  when to use each view type, 14–15
  Zoom features
    defined, **13–16**, *16*, **1089**
    in Print dialog box, 51, *52*
    in Print Preview, 214
    Zoom button on Standard toolbar, 15, 1089
    Zoom dialog box, 15–16, *16*, 1089

viruses in macros, **38–39**, **752–758**, **970–971**, **1029–1030**
   anti-virus programs
      ChekMate Lite, 38, 866, 882–883
      McAfee VirusScan software, 38
      Norton AntiVirus software, 38
      Virus ALERT for Word 2000, 38, 753, 867, 881–882, *882*
   defined, **752–753**, **1029–1030**
   digital signatures, **755–758**
      creating and installing, 755–756
      defined, **755**
      digitally signing macro projects, 756–758
   macro security, **753–755**
      adding macro developers to list of trusted sources, 755
      changing security levels, 754–755, 970, 1059
      enabling, 38–39, 753–754
   troubleshooting, 970–971
Visual Basic for Applications (VBA), **760–793**. *See also* macros; scripts
   and ActiveX controls in forms, 718, 720, 727–728, 729, 732–733
   apostrophe ('), 774
   books about, 679, 760
   comments, 774
   constants, 774
   creating documents from dialog boxes, 826–828, *826, 827, 829*
   debugging
      defined, **780**
      statements, 773
      stepping through code, 780
      Visual Basic Editor Debug toolbar, 771, *771*
      Visual Basic Editor Immediate window, 768–769
      Visual Basic Editor Watch window, 769
   defined, **760**
   expressions, 774
   forms
      adding controls, 772
      creating, 772, 788–789, *788, 789, 790*
      defined, **771**
      Visual Basic Editor UserForm toolbar, 770, *771*
      Visual Basic Editor UserForm window, 768, *768*
   keywords, 774
   macro example, **787–793**
      assigning to a keyboard shortcut, 793, *793*
      creating the form, 788–789, *788, 789, 790*
      defined, **787**
      designing, 787–788

      displaying dialog box, 790–791
      making the dialog box work, 791–793
      writing code, 790–793
   macros, **781–787**
      adding dialog boxes, 785–786
      adding message boxes, 784–785, *784, 785*
      automating, **786–787**
      converting WordBasic macros to VBA, 743
      creating with VBA, 740, 742
      deleting arguments, 783
      deleting properties, 782–783
      editing, **740**, **746–748**, *747*, **781–783**
      fixing errors, 781–782
      running, 780
      running automatic macros, 786
      stopping automatic macros, 786–787
      troubleshooting, 748
   modules
      class modules, 772–773
      defined, **771**
      inserting in projects, 773
      standard modules, 772
      types of, 772–773
      Visual Basic Editor Code windows and, 762
   objects, **779–780**
      classes, 779
      collections, 779
      events, 780
      methods, 780
      object libraries (.OLB), 779
      properties, 779
      Visual Basic Editor Object Browser, 764–765, *764*
      Visual Basic Editor Properties window, 767–768, *767*
   operators, 774
   procedures, **771**, **777–779**
      coding by hand, 778
      creating with Add Procedure dialog box, 778–779
      defined, **760**, **771**, **777**
      function procedures, 778
      property procedures, 778
      subprocedures, 778
      types of, 778
      viewing code, 763
   projects
      creating, **771**
      defined, **760**, **771**
      inserting modules in, 773
      running, 780
      Visual Basic Editor Project Explorer, 763–764, *763*

statements, **771**, **773–777**
    assignment statements, 773, 775
    colon (:) in, 773
    decision statements, 776
    declaration statements, 773, 775
    defined, **760**, **771**, **773**
    error checking, 773
    executable statements, 773, 775
    syntax of, 773, 776–777
variables, 774
Visual Basic Editor, **740**, **746–748**, **760–771**, **971–972**, **1082**
    Code windows, 762–763, *762*
    controls, 765–767
    Debug toolbar, 771, *771*
    defined, **760–761**, *761*, **1082**
    Edit toolbar, 770, *770*
    editing macros, 740, 746–748, *747*, 1029
    Immediate window, 768–769
    Locals window, 769
    Object Browser, 764–765, *764*
    Project Explorer, 763–764, *763*
    Properties window, 767–768, *767*
    Standard toolbar, 769, *770*
    starting, 761, 1082
    Toolbox, 765–767, *765*
    troubleshooting, 971–972
    troubleshooting macros, 748
    UserForm toolbar, 770, *771*
    UserForm window, 768, *768*
    Watch window, 769

W

Watch window in Visual Basic Editor, 769
watermarks, 293–295, *294*, 819–820, *820*, 934–935, 1049
Web Developer's Virtual Library, 667
Web editing tools, **53–57**. *See also* editing tools; frames
    Insert Hyperlink dialog box, 56–57, *57*
    themes, 55, *56*, 283, 642–645, *643*, *644*, 1087
    VBScript controls, 57, *58*
    Web Page Preview, 13, 53, *54*, 636
    Web Page Wizard, 54–55, *55*, 640–641, 1084
Web folders, **691–692**, **1085–1086**
    creating Web folders, **691–692**, **1085**
    defined, **691**
    managing Web folder contents, 692, 1085–1086
    saving documents to Web folders, 692, 1085
    Web Folder Wizard, 692

Web hosting services, 695
Web Layout view. *See also* views
    Click and Type feature, 46–47, 104–105, 140–141, 384, 924, 985
    customizing, 89, *89*
    defined, **10**, *11*, **1083**
    displaying or hiding objects in, 89, *89*
    object placement controls, 35, 47–48, *47*
    viewing Web pages, 635–636, *636*
    when to use, 15
Web Learning Center site, 667
Web pages, **122**, **626–696**, **965–967**, **1083–1084**. *See also* hyperlinks
    creating, **629**, **637–642**, **1083–1084**
        converting Word documents to Web pages, 629
        Design mode and, 658–659, *660*, 666
        disabling Word features not supported in Web browsers, 640
        saving Word documents in HTML format, 638–640, 1083
        from Web page templates, 124, 641–642, 1084
        with Web Page Wizard, 54–55, *55*, 640–641, 1084
    defined, **122**, **626**
    formatting, **642–651**
        applying Web themes, 55, *56*, 642–645, *643*, *644*, 1087
        color or graphic backgrounds, 646
        formatting horizontal lines, 649
        inserting horizontal lines, 648–649, 1084
        with tables, 650–651, *650*, *651*
        Web page text, 645–646
    forms, **666–678**, **1086–1087**
        ActiveX controls, 670
        adding to Web pages, 668–669, *668*, 1086
        Checkbox controls, 670–671, *670*
        Control Toolbox toolbar, 670
        Design mode and, 658–659, *660*, 666, 1086
        Dropdown Box controls, 671–672, *672*
        Hidden controls, 678
        how forms collect data, 667
        List Box controls, 672–673, *673*
        Option Button controls, 671, *671*
        overview of, 666–667
        Password controls, 674, *674*
        Reset controls, 677–678, *678*
        Run mode and, 659
        scripts and, 667
        setting control properties, 669–670, 1086–1087

Submit controls, 675–676, *676*
Submit with Image controls, 676–677, *677*
Text Area controls, 674–675, *675*
Textbox controls, 673–675, *673*
Web Tools toolbar and, 658–659, *659*, 670
frames, **56**, **651–654**, **1015**
    adding borders, 654
    creating, **56**, **653**, **1015**
    creating navigation frames, 653, 1015
    creating tables of contents in, 653
    defined, **651**, *652*
    deleting, 653, 1015
    displaying or hiding scroll bars, 654
    finding, 173
    formatting, 653–654
    frames are missing or displayed incorrectly,
      966–967
    Frames toolbar, 652, *652*
    resizing, 654
    styles for, 273
graphics
    background graphics, 293, 646
    creating alternate text for graphics, 471, 647,
      1054
    graphics are not positioned properly, 966
    graphics do not display, 965–966
    inserting, 646–647
    Submit with Image controls in Web page
      forms, 676–677, *677*
HTML (Hypertext Markup Language)
    defined, **626–628**, *627*, **1020**
    EasyHTML/Help development tool, 867, 885,
      893
    editing HTML code, 655, 1020
    .HTM files, 122
    HTML codes change after saving Web page,
      967
    HTML e-mail messages, 224
    saving Word documents in HTML format,
      638–640, 1083
    Web sites about, 627
multimedia components, **660–666**
    background sound clips, 665–666
    movie clips, 663–665, *663*
    scrolling text or marquees, 660–662, *661*
publishing, **628**, **676**, **688–696**
    defined, **628**, **688**, **691**
    domain names and, 690
    finding hosts for business Web pages, 688,
      690–691
    finding hosts for personal Web pages, 688–
      690

to home-page communities, 689
    hosting defined, **628**
    managing supporting folders of files, 692,
      696
    over networks, 695–696
    Submit with Image controls and, 676
    with Web hosting services, 695
    with Web Publishing Wizard, 694–695
publishing to FTP sites, **693–694**
    adding FTP site addresses to Word, 693–694
    uploading Web pages to FTP sites, 694
publishing with Web folders, **691–692**, **1085–
  1086**
    creating Web folders, **691–692**, **1085**
    managing Web folder contents, 692, 1085–
      1086
    saving documents to Web folders, 692, 1085
    Web Folder Wizard, 692
    Web folders defined, **691**
saving master documents as, 592–593
scripts, **667**, **678–685**
    adding script commands to Tools menu,
      679–680
    adding to Web pages, 681
    ASP (Active Server Pages) scripts, 667, 682
    books about VBScript and Visual Basic, 679
    CGI (Common Gateway Interface) scripts,
      667
    changing default scripting language, 684
    creating scripts in Microsoft Script Editor,
      685
    defined, **678**
    displaying script anchors, 680, *680*
    editing, 681
    forms and, 667
    how VBScript works, 679
    ISAPI (Internet Service Application Program-
      ming Interface) scripts, 667
    Java applets, 682
    moving or copying, 681
    switching between views in Microsoft Script
      Editor, 683–684, *683*, *684*
    types of, 667
    using Microsoft Script Editor, 682–685
    Web page forms and, 667
    Web sites about, 667
tables of contents in, 370, 653
themes, 55, *56*, 283, 642–645, *643*, *644*, 1087
troubleshooting, **965–967**
    clicking hyperlinks generates an error mes-
      sage, 965

frames are missing or displayed incorrectly, 966–967

graphics do not display, 965–966

HTML codes change after saving Web page, 967

Hyperlink command does not appear on right-click menu, 965

text and graphics are not positioned properly, 966

users cannot access Web page, 967

viewing in Word, **635–637**

    using Word as a Web browser, 637

    in Web Layout view, 635–636, *636*

    in Web Page Preview, 13, 53, *54*, 636

    Web toolbar, 637

Web Page Preview, 13, 53, *54*, 636

Web page templates, 124, 641–642, 1084

Web Page Wizard, 54–55, *55*, 640–641, 1084

Web Tools toolbar, **658–659**

    defined, **658–659**, *659*

    Design Mode, 658–659, *660*, 666

Word 2000 as a Web browser, 637

Word 2000 as a Web page editor, 628–630

WordToWeb utility, 629, 868, 884–885

Web Publishing Wizard, 694–695

Web sites. *See also* hyperlinks

    Aladdins ~ Word Documents Outlook add-in program, 878

    Baarns Consulting, 902

    business support site, 904

    ChekWARE, 883

    for clip art, 466–467

    Computertips, 902

    creating hyperlinks to Web addresses, 57, 633

    customizing Web options, 113

    c|net Help, 902

    defined, **628**

    distributing automated forms via, 736

    Document Converter utility, 875

    Document Depot, 902

    EasyHTML/Help software, 885

    E-Stamp Internet Postage, 821

    eVirus Corporation, 882

    GPDATA utility, 877

    Hero Software, 877

    for hosting business sites, 690

    for hosting personal Web pages, 689

    about HTML, 627

    Kaczynski Software, 879

    KazStamp software, 879

    KH Software Development, 875

    Manawatu Software Solutions, 878

Microsoft Knowledge Base, 899–901, *900*

Microsoft Office Update, 898–899, *898*, 1019

Mighty Fax software, 880

MyHelpDesk.com, 903

NewSoft Office Express 2000 graphics program, 873

non-Microsoft resources, 902–903

Office on the Web feature, 37, *37*

OfficeCert.com, 903

PC Magazine, 903

PRIME Consulting, 871

RKS Software Store, 874, 880

about scripts, 667

Solutionsoft, 885

SOS Office Helpers, 872

Symbol Selector utility, 874

technical support sites, 903–904

templates in Microsoft Web site, 702

Virus ALERT for Word 2000 program, 882

Web Developer's Virtual Library, 667

Web Learning Center, 667

WordInfo, 903

WordToWeb software, 885

ZDNet Help & How-To, 903

Web Tools toolbar, **658–659**

    defined, **658–659**, *659*

    Design Mode, 658–659, *660*, 666

Web-based collaboration features, **58–59, 616–621**. *See also* comments; Track Changes feature

    defined, **58, 616**

    Discussions feature, **59, 616–620, 993–995**

        connecting to discussion servers, 616, 617, 993–994

        defined, **59, 616–617, 993**

        editing and deleting discussions, 617–618

        replying to general discussions, 619–620, 995

        replying to inline discussions, 619, 995

        starting inline or general discussions, 618–619, 994

        viewing discussions, 617–618, *618*, 994

    Microsoft Office Server Extensions and, 58, 616, 620, 621

    Subscriptions and Notifications feature, 59, 620–621, 1064

    system requirements, 616, 617, 620, 621

What's This? feature, 895, *895*, *896*, 1019

White Text, Blue Background option, 91, *91*

widow controls, 258–259

wildcards

    defined, **1087–1088**

    in Find and Replace dialog box, 170, 175–176

    in Open dialog box, 130

Window menu, New Window command, 18

windows, editing multiple documents in multiple windows, 18

"Windows cannot print due to a problem with the current printer setup" message, 962–963

WinFax Starter Edition software, 221–222

Wizards
    Answer Wizard tab in Help, 891–892, *892*, 1019
    creating documents with, 125–127, *126*, 829
    Envelope Wizard, 514
    Fax Wizard, 222–223
    finding, 125
    Letter Wizard, 125–126, *126*, 829, 951, 954
    Mailing Label Wizard, 514
    Web Folder Wizard, 692
    Web Page Wizard, 54–55, *55*, 640–641, 1084
    Web Publishing Wizard, 694–695

.WMF files, 463, *464*, 468

Word Count feature, 194

word selection option, 105

Word Workshops tutorial, 867–868

WordArt text, **472–475**, **1088–1089**. *See also* graphics
    defined, **472**
    editing with WordArt toolbar, 474–475, 1088–1089
    inserting, 472–474, *474*, 1088

WordBasic macros, 743

WordInfo Web site, 903

WordPerfect Help, **66–69**
    configuring compatibility options for WordPerfect users, 67
    enabling, 106
    enabling WordPerfect Navigation, 67
    Help for WordPerfect Users dialog box, 66–67, *66*, 106
    Word keyboard shortcuts for WordPerfect commands, 68–69

WordToWeb utility, 629, 868, 884–885

workgroup features. *See* comments; Track Changes feature; Web-based collaboration

worksheets. *See* Microsoft Excel

workspace, **8**, **84–92**, **798–803**. *See also* user interface
    assigning keyboard shortcuts from keyboard, 800–801
    AutoScroll feature, 803, *804*
    Blue Background, White Text option, 91, *91*
    calculating totals in documents, 799
    configuring field shading, 87
    configuring Normal and Outline views, 90–91, *90*
    creating personal menus, 798
    customizing Normal and Outline views, 90–91, *90*
    customizing style area, 91, 274, *274*, 799, *800*
    defined, **8**, *9*
    disabling Screen Tips, 86
    displaying bookmarks, 86
    displaying field codes, 87
    displaying or hiding objects in Print Layout and Web Layout views, 89, *89*
    displaying or hiding scroll bars, 85–86
    displaying highlighted text, 87
    displaying measurements in ruler, 801, *802*
    displaying placeholders, 86–87
    displaying tabs, spaces, paragraphs, hidden text, and optional hyphens, 87–88, *88*
    displaying vertical ruler, 86, 89
    hiding animated text, 86
    hiding status bar, 86
    imitating Word 97 interface, 92
    opening dialog boxes with double-click hot spots, 802
    printing lists of keyboard shortcuts and menu commands, 24, 103, 801, 1026
    workspace defined, **8**, *9*

.WPG files, 468

wrapping text
    around objects, 486–488, 1039–1040
    in graphs, 426–427
    in tables, 400–402

X

XE field code for indexes, 357, 3

Z

ZDNet Help & How-To Web site, 903

Zoom features. *See also* views
    defined, **13–16**, *16*, **1089**
    in Print dialog box, 51, *52*
    in Print Preview, 214
    Zoom button on Standard toolbar, 15, 1089
    Zoom dialog box, 15–16, *16*, 1089

"The family is one of nature's masterpieces."

— George Santayana

Share your masterpiece from
generation to generation.

Generations® Grande Suite 6.0

You have a unique family heritage. And to share that story is to create a family gift that will be treasured forever. Now researching your history and creating beautiful charts has never been easier. Search for relatives and ancestors all over the world with access to over 300 million names and resources. Organize and record family history and information. You can even repair and preserve treasured photos and save cherished family recipes. Simply put, Generations® Grande Suite is the easiest, most complete software for preserving a masterpiece: your family history.

For more information, visit us at www.sierrahome.com or call 1-800-757-7707

SIERRAHome™
WE'VE GOT YOUR HOME COVERED.™

·GENERATIONS·
Your Partner In Genealogy

You can install any or all of the programs on the accompanying CD directly from the CD's main menu. All you have to do is click the name of the software program on the CD's menu, and then follow the onscreen instructions to install the software to your computer's hard drive.

PRODUCTS ON THE CD

Adobe Acrobat Reader Lets you read books and other documents onscreen.

Aladdins ~ Word Documents Enables you to quickly compose Word documents using Outlook contact data.

BioSpel Custom dictionary of 15,000 biological terms.

ChekMate Lite Anti-virus utility.

ChekOf Monitors Word's security level settings.

Document Converter Converts documents between a number of popular formats.

EasyHTML/Help Enables you to create Windows Help files from Microsoft Word documents.

GPDATA Address book for Word documents.

KazStamp Creates great-looking, custom envelopes.

MedSpel Custom medical dictionary.

Mastering Word 2000 Premium Edition Complete text of this book, in Adobe Acrobat format.

Mighty Fax Enables you to fax directly from Word.

Office 2000 Complete Comprehensive guide to Microsoft Office 2000, in Adobe Acrobat format.

OfficeExpress 2000 Full-featured image scanning and editing.

PRIME for Word 2000 Collection of Word tools and utilities that provides enhanced functionality.

ScreenPro A Word template for screenwriters.

SOS Office Helpers Tools and utilities that provide enhanced program functionality.

Symbol Selector Select and insert symbols and special characters into your documents.

Virus ALERT for Word 2000 Detects macro viruses in Word templates and documents.

Word Workshops Learn how to create eight different types of documents, step-by-step.

WordToWeb Converts existing Word documents to HTML format.